WICK OF THE NORTH
The Story of a Scottish Royal Burgh

Supported by
Caithness
District
Council
1975 - 1996

Aerial view of Wick 1995 – George Robb.

WICK OF THE NORTH

The Story of a Scottish Royal Burgh

By

Dr Frank Foden, MBE

Commissioned and Published by
North of Scotland Newspapers,
42 Union Street, Wick, Caithness
to mark the 160th Anniversary of the
John O'Groat Journal
1836 - 1996

COVER

Wick Harbour during the herring fishing, drawn by Samuel Read, which first appeared as an extra supplement to the Illustrated London News on the 28th August, 1875.

Typeset in 10pt Palatino

A Catalogue Record
for this book is available from
The British Library.

Copyright © 1996 North of Scotland Newspapers
ALL RIGHTS RESERVED

No part of this publication may be reproduced, stored in a retrieval system, or transmitted in any form or by any means, electronic, electrostatic, magnetic tape, mechanical photocopying, recording or otherwise, without permission in writing from the publishers.

ISBN 1 871704 17 0

Typeset by North of Scotland Newpapers, 42 Union Street, Wick, Caithness, Scotland.
Printed by Scottish Provincial Press Ltd, Henderson Road, Inverness, Scotland.

FOREWORD

Frank Foden is a historian of some repute. His credentials are impeccable and his experience in his field is considerable. Now retired and living in Orkney, he was formerly a Head of Department at Loughborough College in Leicestershire and has written books and papers on a variety of subjects including education, science, technology and social history. He has also written two biographies. He was awarded the MBE in 1978 for his educational and conservation work.

This volume represents the first serious work of its kind to be written about Wick in modern times. It was commissioned by North of Scotland Newspapers to add to the growing list of publications about Caithness undertaken in recent years by that organisation.

Dr Foden has carried out his task with the impartiality and objectivity which only an outsider can really achieve. He has written his history in a style that is both readable and authoritative. His research has been meticulous, a fact evidenced by the vast number and variety of sources he has cited. This attention to detail has paid off handsomely as contained in the text are many episodes from Wick's history which have not seen the light of day for a considerable number of years.

Dr Foden's book traces the history of the town from its earliest days when it was little more than a handful of sod-covered shanties (only 500 people lived there in 1660 almost a century after it was made a Royal Burgh), right up to the present day. He describes graphically its turbulent past where, in early days murder, treachery and betrayal were the norm against those families who sought to dominate the area. Families with names like Mackay, Sinclair, Sutherland and Gunn, names still familiar in Caithness today, all fought in and around Wick Parish. Along the way he even manages to shed some light on the origins and reasons for the rivalry between Wick and Thurso which began centuries ago but continues, albeit on a friendly basis, to this day. His graphic account of the rise and fall of Wick as the premier herring port of Europe are both fascinating and enlightening as are his descriptions of life there during those times.

Local politics, a topic close to my heart, also feature and combining of the burghs of Wick and Pulteneytown with all the attendant controversy is a clear sign that some things have not changed that much.

In writing his history Dr Foden has carried out a painstaking examination of a vast array of sources. He has managed to untangle them and to make sense of them and in so doing has produced a work which does justice to Wick and does its author much credit. He is clearly a fine historian and I for one am indebted to him for his efforts to tell Wick's story.

Councillor John M. Young, OBE.
4th August, 1995.

A Tribute from Margaret, Viscountess Thurso, to her late husband, Robin, Viscount Thurso, who himself and whose remarkable ancestors, contributed so much to the fortunes of Wick.

In the long happy years of our marriage my late husband and I often teased each other about our respective towns of Wick and Thurso. When he told me, therefore, about the proposed visit of Dr. Foden who was researching for the book he was writing on the Royal Burgh of Wick, he suggested to me that perhaps it was I, being the "Wicker" who should know more of the recent history of the town than he. But on our meeting with Dr Foden for the first time my husband very quickly established a happy and enthusiastic relationship with the Doctor, and it was manifestly clear to me, to my delight I may say, that it was my husband who had the better claim through his ancestry (from Sir John Sinclair of Ulbster to my late father-in-law Sir Archibald Sinclair, first Lord Thurso) to be associated with Wick. After all, my great grandfather Alexander Robertson came from Mount Eagle Farm in Ross-shire to Caithness only in the 1820s.

From the first meeting with Dr Foden, Lord Thurso became deeply interested in the idea of producing a new book to be a comprehensive and updated history of Wick. It is very sad that my husband's untimely death meant that he never saw the finished copy. My husband was deeply interested in his Sinclair heritage and in particular in Sir John Sinclair of Ulbster whom he called his "three-greats" grandfather.

Dr Foden writes in his book of the similarities of outlook between Sir John and (his great great great grandson) Robin, and of the enterprise shown by both men, albeit two centuries apart, and in very different ways of fostering the well being of Wick and Caithness. I am certain that Robin would have been proud and pleased to be likened to Sir John, for whom he had a profound admiration, for his original thinking and inventive mind.

Since my husband's death, many people have spoken of his utter dedication to the county of Caithness which he loved. He was totally committed to the task of finding ways and means of bringing employment to the area and I remember clearly the day in the late 1950s when I found him reading the Encyclopedia Britannica to find out what the composition of glass was. When I asked him the reason for his research he said quite simply, "to make glass in Caithness".

The establishing of Caithness Glass in Wick was quite deliberate, simply to try to counteract the flow of young men going to work at

Dounreay. I think I know, better than anyone else, the uphill struggle it was before the factory was able to be built, with much to-ing and fro-ing between the Scottish Office, the Department of Trade & Industry and the Treasury. It was entirely due to Robin's imagination, enthusiasm, original thinking, and perhaps above all, his optimism that Caithness Glass ever came into being at all.

It pleases me greatly to have been asked to write a tribute to my late husband in Dr Foden's book. I would also pay tribute to Dr. Foden for his zeal and energy in undertaking an update of the history of Wick and at the same time I would like to mention Clive Richards, and North of Scotland Newspapers, for their part in the co-operation and production of "Wick of the North – The Story of a Scottish Royal Burgh". My maternal great grandfather, Peter Reid, who started and owned the John O'Groat Journal would surely be giving his approval for this timely and excellent history.

AUTHOR'S PREFACE

When first invited to consider writing a 'comprehensive' history of Wick, I agreed, with two reservations: would there be enough to go at in a small community of northern Scotland, separated by geography and much tradition from the mainstream of Scottish history? and, as an 'outsider' (and not even a Scot!), would I be able to get the feel of things?

For the purposes of *Wick of the North*, I was little hampered on either score. There is certainly not much direct information to be had on the early and founding days of Wick, and like J T Calder, author of *The Civil and Traditional History of Caithness*, I was obliged to rely on the, Saga, Torfaeus and other antiquarian and anecdotal material. It is forever unlikely that the original settling of Wick, either in Viking or Pictish times – if there was a Pictish 'Wick' – can be discovered, though the work of researchers such as Anna Ritchie and Barbara Crawford have perhaps enabled us to see back a little more perceptively through the mediaeval murk.

I noted that Thomas Sinclair, editor of the second edition of Calder's history, believed that record material on Wick was 'unusually plentiful'. He could only be referring to the known existence of the complete collection of burgh record books from the Restoration in 1660. Some later historians were unable to find those records, but fossicking round the cupboards and stores of the Caithness District Council, I was fortunate in locating them all, except for the book covering the period between 1710 and 1740, as it happens, one of crucial significance. I have little doubt that sooner or later it will turn up. In the meantime I was able to make good and original use of the official record for the whole of the eighteenth century and the early years of the nineteenth, apart from the thirty-year gap caused by the missing book.

Neither Calder nor Sinclair seemed to be unduly interested in the incomparably rich vein of historical matter that began in their own day, the accumulating pages of the *John O'Groat Journal*, started in 1836 and the *Northern Ensign*, recording in great detail what was then being revealed as the most significant ingredient of the whole history of Wick, its phenomenal rise and growth as a major 'herring town'. This development proved to be a vastly more important factor in the forming of modern Wick than all earlier events, the subject of the antiquarian, traditional and anecdotal material amassed by Calder, including his fascinating accounts of such events as the 'feud of the earls,' and the curiously improbable event of Wick's becoming in 1589 the most northerly royal burgh in mainland Scotland, the Battle of Altimarlach two miles from Wick. Calder was not, in any case, writing specifically about Wick.

Until the herring fishing began in earnest at the turn of the eighteenth century, Wick had little importance as a port of any kind, and until it got going as 'the herring port of Europe' was even unable to assert its full jurisdictional rights as royal burgh and county town in Caithness as against the claims of Thurso. Accordingly, two thirds of my book coheres around the catching of *Clupea harengus*, gutting, packing and selling it to the world. Wick and Thurso were too far north and too cut off by high mountains from central Scotland to share in its conversion into one of Europe's major industrial areas. Wick's transformation into a modest industrial centre is a consequence, ironically, of the collapse of the herring trade in the middle years of this century.

Even before this calamity struck, Wick had been long outdistanced by other and younger Scottish herring centres, Peterhead, Fraserburgh, Aberdeen, and in later days, Shetland. Two special factors determined the herring ascendancy of Wick from 1800 onwards, both closely related to one another: one was the entrepreneurial and seigneurial connection of Sir John Sinclair of Ulbster with the town; and the other the promotional and investment activities in this area of the British Fisheries Society, itself partly an outcome of Sir John's urgings. A curious and infrequently noted element of this development was the creation here of one of the most successful 'new towns' ever started in Scotland, a venture at least as significant as New Lanark and much less lauded. Pulteneytown on the south bank of the river of Wick, for nearly a century municipally independent of Wick, was wholly built from scratch on land of the Hempriggs estate, eventually to house thousands of fishers and their families. It came greatly to exceed the area and population of the ancient royal burgh of Wick itself, a near but not very friendly neighbour of the new town. Formal union between the two did not come until 1902. Wickers rather dismissively regarded Pulteneytown as quite another place, and to some extent still do. Pulteneytowners returned the compliment. Pulteneytown was the biggest single thing that ever happened to Wick, but for a hundred years the two communities tried to 'keep themselves to themselves'. They have been together now for nearly another hundred, but still do not quite see themselves as the same sort of people.

For all its eccentricities, Scottish historians have not noticed Wick much. It hardly rates a mention in most indexes. Smout achieves a slight single reference, on the decline of the fishing industry in the 1920s, without a word about its remarkable rise. Before coming to this part of the world and taking on this assignment I have to confess that I was quite unaware of Pulteneytown and Thurso as model new towns, planned a century before Bournville and Welwyn Garden City. There is scanty mention too of the quite incredible exercise, overseen by scores of eminent engineers, from John Rennie to Thomas Stevenson, Robert Louis' father, which resulted in the creation in the wild Wick Bay of a major artificial harbour, and nothing at all of the disasters associated with it. The most celebrated comment on Wick is that of the disaffected Robert Louis Stevenson, who in consequence did not endear himself to Wickers. Historians of the 'Empire' often wrote about the 'Cape to Cairo Railway', which was never completed. Who ever heard of the 'London to Wick and Thurso,' which was? Wick has long wanted to be wanted, as witness the great stone plaque on a wall in Station Road listing the names of nearly forty eminences that have from time to time paid the town a fleeting visit.

Local historians, indeed, make much of Wick's status as 'herring capital' but usually say little about what that means in comparative terms, how it was achieved and how it was lost. Such a stricture cannot be applied to the work of Iain Sutherland who, if anything, awards Wick with the star role in the making of the Scottish fishing industry.

I have sought in this study to place Wick firmly in the wider contexts, regional, national and European, in which, during the nineteenth and first half of the present century the town became a place of some note. Using Wick as the example, I have tried in some sense to represent the workings over several centuries of that peculiar entity, the Scottish royal burgh, its 'sett' or constitution, powers, privileges, and procedures, parliamentary representation.

I wish to emphasise the special importance in the story of Wick of the celebrated *Statistical Surveys of Scotland*, those of the 1790s and the 1840s and to a lesser extent that of the 1980s. These represent a benefit to the social historian of Scotland during the last two hundred years of a kind not matched by any similar compilation in England, three amazing 'dipstick' assessments of the state of things in the parishes of the country at three clearly indicated periods. I have given considerable prominence to the portraits of the parish of Wick, that of 1794 by the Rev William Sutherland and that of 1840 by the Rev Charles Thomson, not only on account of their 'statistical' content, but also because of their general and detailed informativeness, objectivity and readability. The account of Wick in 1794 is of very special interest, for at this time Sir John Sinclair was its provost; it was his own burgh. William Sutherland's contribution thus stood as a sort of model for the other contributors. Both compositions, that of Sutherland and that of Thomson, incidentally illustrate something of the immense authority wielded by ministers of religion in the life of Scottish communities in the eighteenth and nineteenth centuries, and of their considerable secular involvements and scholarship. The *Statistical Account* would never have been possible without the services of the parish ministers so shrewdly recruited by Sir John.

It may seem to some of those thoroughly familiar with the turbulent history of reformed religion in Scotland, that I have paid a great deal too much attention to this aspect of life in Wick. There are cogent reasons for doing so. Religion in its various forms, reformed and reforming doctrines and secular commitments of ministers, played a part in the life of most Scottish communities that it is now rather difficult to appreciate. It may seem odd that the strange going-ons in St Andrew's Church, George Street, Edinburgh, on 18 May, 1843 should prompt a great 'walkout' of virtually the entire 1,500 strong congregation of Wick parish church a short while later, more than three hundred miles away. The reasons for this 'copycat' religious event so far away from the capital are complex and thoroughly symptomatic of community problems in Wick, not at all understandable without some explanation of the national background against which the episode was played out. Religion tended to serve the community's needs for spiritual consolation, recreation, social discipline and it also provided in many parts of Scotland, an outlet for discontent.

It may surprise some to learn that Wick had its part in the political and social unrest of the years 1845 to 1848, the 'Year of Revolutions'. The burghers of Wick share with those of Glasgow the distinction of having in these troublous times called out the military. The working out of Wick's own special communal tensions, those between the 'natives' and the masses of immigrant workers from the Highlands and west coast annually during the fishing season culminated some years later in 'The War of the Orange', an event, too, of quite special interest.

Thus it may be seen, I have not in any way been handicapped by poverty of resources, rather by an *embarras de richesses*. My second reservation, that concerning my fitness to write a history of Wick because I was an outsider, also soon dissolved when I set to work. To begin with I experienced a severe discouragement. For many years a local heritage society has flourished in Wick, building up in the course of its existence a collection of materials including documents, photographs and an astonishing variety of artefacts, many permanently exhibited in an impressive Heritage Centre. My approach to the Society about the possibility of consultation with members, collaboration when and if appropriate and perhaps associate membership of the group, was flatly turned down.

However, I started and persisted with the attempt, discovering as I went on an immense fund of curiosity about, interest in and goodwill towards the project among ordinary folk, many with specialist knowledge and insights. I also consulted and have been helped by several local historians and others far away from the town, some quite far afield. Though dour in aspect, I found Wick to be a lively, friendly place, full of variety and surprises. In a community so self-contained, closely knit and distant from metropolitan Scotland, I expected to find much parochialism and neighbourly groupings. I found that it was indeed so, but nearly always combined with this inward-lookingness a robust citizenly pride, widespread awareness of major issues in the history and life of the town, and familiarity with its mythology.

I have, I believe, made many friends in Wick, and living in a similar sort of community in Orkney, where a vigorous parochialism also prevails, I have come to appreciate and admire the tough, tenacious virtues of the people of Wick, and especially their ability to survive, with fortitude and sardonic good-humour their constantly changing conditions, especially in recent times.

My last chapter, 'Wick Today' was much the most difficult to write. It is bound to strike some readers as patchy and incomplete. There are so many facets to the topic that it could indeed fill a book all on its own. My object was to put a term to a long and varied account of the adaptations, triumphs and vicissitudes that have enabled this royal, fishy burgh of the north to become what it is and to continue on its way. Through the recent centuries its people have bravely vindicated their earthy, unpretentious and stolidly Scottish town motto: *Wick Works Weil*. It does indeed.

Kirkwall,
September, 1995.

ACKNOWLEDGEMENTS

Many people have contributed in different ways to the completion of this book. They include authors and publishers who have kindly allowed the publication of (sometimes at considerable length) passages from books and articles, diagrams, maps and other illustrations still under copyright. These are generally identified in context and most illustrations in particular are expressly acknowledged where they appear in the book.

The author and publishers of *Wick of the North* wish here to record their grateful appreciation and thanks for the permission granted to all those listed below. Letters and other attempts at communication have in a few cases failed to elicit response. Assumption has accordingly been made that the authors (and/or publishers) concerned have no objection to quotation of their material. Though considerable endeavours have been made to include in this list sources of all copyright material quoted or otherwise used, it is possible that inadvertently some references may have been missed. For any such omissions author and publishers apologise, and the author undertakes to write to anyone who draws his attention to his shortcomings in this matter.

Jean Munro (neé Dunlop) and John Donald (publisher): excerpts from *The British Fisheries Society* (1978) and excerpts and diagrams from *Pulteneytown and Planned Villages of Caithness* (from A Cultural Crossroads, Scottish Society for Northern Studies, Ed. John Baldwin, Edina Press, 1982). Additionally permission from the Scottish Record Office for the sketch-maps.

David M. Ferguson: *Shipwrecks of North East Scotland, 1444-1999*, Mercat Press (1991).

Kenneth Gelder and Edinburgh University Press: excerpts from *Stevenson's Scottish Stories* (1989).

I F Grant: two quotations from *The Social and Economic Development of Scotland Before 1603*, Oliver and Boyd (1930).

Malcolm Gray: quotations and diagrams from *The Fisheries of Scotland, 1790-1914*, University of Aberdeen Press (1978).

Neil Gunn and Souvenir Press: a quotation from *Whisky and Scotland* (1967).

F R Hart and J B Pick and John Murray Ltd, publishers: quotations from *Neil M. Gunn: A Highland Life* (1981).

Professor Michael Lynch: quotations from his *History of Scotland*, (Pimlico, 1992).

R J S McDowell and John Murray, Publishers Ltd: a quotation from *The Whiskies of Scotland* (1975).

Sir Fitzroy Maclean, Kt CBE: a quotation from *A Concise History of Scotland*, (Thames and Hudson, 1983).

Rosalind Mitchison: quotations from *Agricultural Sir John: the Life of Sir John Sinclair of Ulbster* (Bles – 1962).

Jeff Morris for excerpts from *Wick and Ackergill Lifeboats* (the Lifeboats Enthusiasts' Society, 1993).

Professor Herman Pálsson and the wife of Paul Edwards, for numerous quotations from *The Orkneyinga Saga* (Hogarth Press – 1978).

Donald Omand: quotations and maps from *The Caithness Book* (Highland Printers Ltd - 1972).

John Prebble and Penguin Books for brief excerpts from *The Highland Clearances* (1960).

John Thomas and David Turnock (XL Publishing Services and subsequently Transport Atlantic, publishers) for a quotation from *North of Scotland: Vol 15 of A Regional History of the Railways of Great Britain* (1989).

David Rendell for an excerpt from *The Memoirs of E E Fresson*, (1967).

Iain Sutherland for numerous quotations from *Wick Harbour and the Herring Fishing* (1984), *From Herring to Seine Net Fishing on the East Coast of Scotland* (1985), *The Wick and Lybster Railway* (1987 – and a sketch-map), *Dounreay: An Experimental Reactor* (1990). Also excerpts from Mr Sutherland's pamphlets: *The War of the Orange* and *Vote No Licence* (no dates).

H A Vallance, (publishers David and Charles) for a quotation from *The Highland Railway* (1985).

In addition to the authors and publishers of regular books, I am grateful for permission to use other material, usually made available to me as a result of direct contact:

The authors of *The Church in the Square* for a quotation and drawings (Wick, 1992).

The Rev R Frizzell for notes and information on the subject of Wick Parish Church, and in addition the permission of Mr Ian Mackenzie to use his drawings of the Wick Parish Church (front cover of the Church Magazine) and notes contributed by John Cormack, an elder of the church.

David Conner of the Highland Regional Police for extensive notes and verbal information on the history of policing in Wick and Caithness.

Mrs N Simpson of the Wick Harbour Board and Mr J Simpson of Arch Henderson Partners, Thurso, for permission to make extensive use of a Memorandum on Wick Harbour prepared for Sir Archibald Sinclair. Bart, MP (1929).

Roy N Pedersen of 6 Drumdevan Road, Inverness, for permission to use a portion of the map, *Orknejar Og Katanes* published by Mr Pedersen.

The British Library and The Keeper of the Scottish Records for permission to reproduce various maps and sketch-plans, including a portion of the Caithness Map of Timothy Pont and drawings from Thomas Telford's notebooks.

David and Charles who have allowed the reproduction of drawings of Thomas Telford and John Rennie from their re-issue (1969) of Vol. II of Samuel Smiles' *Lives of the Engineers, Vol. II*; also sketches of the 'Cas Chrom' and Sinclair's ploughs from the same volume.

W Gibson for permission to reproduce a drawing of a Dutch Herring Buss from his *Stronsay: The Herring Fishing*, Vol I.

Richard and Rebecca Hallewell of Perth for their permission to reproduce drawings of various fishing vessels from *Scotland's Sailing Fishermen: A History of the Scottish Herring Boom*, written, illustrated and published by them.

The Ulysses S Grant Society of the University of South Illinois, USA, for published material on the visit of President Grant to Wick and Thurso in 1877.

Of crucial value in researching this work has been the availability of a continuous run of the *John O'Groat Journal* from the first issue in February 1836 to the present time. This priceless resource is housed in the premises of the *Groat* and since much of the work was done on these premises the volumes have been readily accessible to the author – though some are badly in need of repair and re-covering. It was immeasurably more convenient to handle, quote from, to check and re-check data by direct reference to the original issues than would have been the case had the author been obliged for all purposes to use the excellent micro-film sequence of the *Journal* kept in the Wick Public Library. This sequence was, nevertheless, useful on occasions, as was the micro-film sequence of the *Northern Ensign*, sadly not complete. I was also supplied weekly with current issues of the *Journal* and the *Caithness Courier* during the whole period of my research work and the writing of the book. These were very useful in writing the last chapter, 'Wick Today' as were the numerous special issues of the *Journal* miscellanies and new publications of North of Scotland Newspapers.

Most encouraging and heart-warming of the Groat's contributions has been the unfailing helpfulness and cheeriness of the paper's staff, especially Clive Richards, Commercial Manager, whose enthusiasm for the project has never wavered. His lively and good-humoured office staff have tolerated my frequent presence, have run off hundreds of xeroxed sheets and supplied me liberally with coffee during the whole exercise; and have patiently taken and dealt with many calls from me when I was not in Wick. The conditions under which this book has been produced may, for the record, be characterised as co-operatively ideal.

My work in the actual business of research has been greatly assisted by the people and organisations listed below, who have provided written and oral information, have read, checked and re-checked text, copied and duplicated material and read proofs. In addition, I wish to thank very heartily the many people who have in one way or another contributed to my comfort and well-being during the entire long exercise of researching, writing and personal reading and checking of text. Some have helped in several of these ways. The list is a long one and includes:

Andy Anderson for information, notes and advice on the Wick lifeboats; Arlette Bannister for information, hospitality and a guided tour of Ackergill Tower; Rob Bayliss for textual reading and checking; Alistair Beattie, Chief Executive of the Caithness District Council administration, for copious information and advice; John E Bogle, Finance Administrator to Caithness General Hospital for information and advice; Ally Budge for comments and advice on the topic of the world wars; David Conner of the Highland Police Department for information and extensive notes on the history of policing in Wick; Angela Donaldson, Manager of Wick Airport for information and advice on that topic; Mrs Dunnet, Housekeeper of Keiss Castle for information, hospitality and a conducted tour of the house; Mr J Edgar, Caithness Divisional Education Officer, for information on contemporary education in Caithness; HM Queen Elizabeth, the Queen Mother and her staff for permission to visit the Castle of Mey and especially to Mrs Webster, the Housekeeper for her instructive guidance on that tour; Dot Ferguson for information and documents on the subject of 'The Wick Project'; the Rev Ronald Ferguson,

Minister at Kirkwall Cathedral, for information, advice and reading of text on the religious picture; Ronnie Fraser for information and loan of books; J Hunter, Manager, for information about Grampian Records; David Richard-Jones, Development Officer of the Highland Regional Development Board for information on the Wick Industrial Estate and other related topics; Donald and Murray Lamont of Mackay's Hotel, for information, hospitality and general affability and for the excellent service provided to me by their cheerful and good-natured staff; John Livitt of the Coastguard Service, Kirkwall for information on present arrangements in the service; Lorraine Macdonald, Librarian, Wick Public Library, and Library staff, including Trudi Mann and Sheila Mather for their help and advice in many matters; Jim Miller for patient reading and constructive advice; Donald Omand for a similar service; Morris Pottinger for information, and helpful advice; Ray Richard for information on Caithness Glass and the Wick Chamber of Commerce; Leslie Rowe, Secretary of the Caithness and Sutherland Liberal Party, for information and advice; the Rev Alistair Roy for information and advice; Mr H R Holmes, Director, Leisure and Recreation Services, Fiona Smith and Mr N C Scott, Treasurer of the Caithness District Sports Council for information about the scope and work of the Caithness District Sports Council; Colin Salsbury for technical information on wave enhancement theory; Donald Sutherland for information and advice on a great variety of subjects; Alistair Taylor, manager until recently of the Wick Creamery for information about this and the Wick to Lybster Railway; Sandy Taylor of the Coastguard Service for information about the service in Wick; Robin, Lord Thurso and Lady Thurso for information, help and the loan of a rare book (Lord Thurso was to have written the Foreword in this book, but, sad to say, died before this could be accomplished); Andrew Thin for information about CASE (Caithness and Sutherland Enterprise); William Watt, Construction Site Manager of Rockwater, for information about this, and helpful comment on the piece I wrote on this topic; Fiona Watson, Archivist to the Highland Regional Health Board; Brian Whitelaw, Chief Executive Depute, for much information, advice and detailed comment on the work as a whole; Councillor John M Young, for helpful information and advice and for the Foreword to this book; Captain C J Young, Restoration Director of the *Great Britain* project, Bristol, for special information and advice on the work of James Bremner.

Special thanks are due also to members of my family: my wife, Peggy, for patient reading and correction of proofs, Kim, my daughter-in-law for helpful information, especially on the subject of early flight routes in the north and final proof-reading; to my son, Robert, Manager of Herald Print Shop, Kirkwall, for much advice on matters of design, illustration and arrangement of text and for endless quantities of duplicated sheets for test and interim purposes and, not least, to my young grandson, Alistair, for keeping everyone cheerful and for wise comment beyond his six years.

Frank Foden,
September, 1995

CONTENTS

Prefatory: Foreword – John M. Young   v - vi
Tribute to Viscount Thurso (Lady Thurso)   vii-viii
Author's Preface   ix - xiii
Acknowledgements   xiv - xix

PART I   WICK EMERGENT   1
Chapter 1   That Was Wick – This Is   3
2   Early Days   19
3   Sinclairs   39
4   Bishops, Sutherlands and Others   64
5   Royal Burgh   85

PART II   WICK ARISING   117
Chapter 6   Wick 1700 - 1800   118
7   The Sett of Wick: A Scottish Royal Burgh I   144
8   The Sett of Wick: II   175
9   Improvement   195
10   Religion   227

PART III   WICK ASCENDANT   271
Chapter 11   Clupea harengus harengus   272
12   'Our Northern Athens'   305
13   Sodom of the North   354
14   Voice of the People   401
15   Those in Peril   442

PART IV   WICK ON HOLD   493
Chapter 16   Wick Over The Hill   494
17   Wick On The Line   538
18   A Tale of Two Cities   562
19   Wars and Rumours of War: I   599
20   Wars and Rumours of War: II   650
21   Some People and Places   692
22   Wick Today   735

Post Scriptum – Post Mortem?   794
Bibliography   798
Index   803

LIST OF MAPS AND ILLUSTRATIONS

Page

Fig	1	Simplified geology of Caithness	6
	2	The parishes of Caithness	18
	3	Lambaborg (Buchollie Castle)	31
	4	Caithness (Katanes) in Viking Times	38
	5	Sinclair and Girnigoe Castles	57
	6	Caithness (showing Wick as small settlement c1706)	86
	7	Wick houses of the eighteenth century	89
	8a	Altimarlach Cross	106
	8b	The Battle of Altimarlach	116
	9	The Parish of Wick, 1822	137
	10	John Rennie	197
	11	Thomas Telford	197
	12	Telford's roads in Scotland	199
	13	The Cas-Chrom plough	200
	14	Sir John Sinclair's plough	201
	15	Sir John Sinclair by Benjamin West	203
	16	Wick Bay – from Telford's Notebook	212
	17	Wick Water – c1803	216
	18	Roads of north Caithness	222
	19	Wick Old Parish Church	257
	20	Clupea harengus	273
	21	Dutch Herring Buss (16th and 17th Century)	275
	22	Keiss Bay – Telford 1790	282
	23	Staxigoe Bay – Telford 1790	282
	24	Telford's Plan of Pulteneytown, 1807	295
	25	Wick, 1847	306
	26	Export of cured herring, 1812-1885	312
	27	Price of cured herring, 1837-1880	312
	28	Map of fishing villages of Caithness	315
	29	The Bremner Memorial	321
	30	Pulteney Distillery	356

		Page
31	Disruption in Edinburgh	370
32	Pulteneytown Parish Church	381
33	The Pulteneytown Academy	385
34	Peter Reid – founder of the *John O'Groat Journal*	408
35	Benjamin Kennedy – first editor of the *John O'Groat Journal*	408
36	First page of an early issue of the *John O'Groat Journal*	412
37	*John O'Groat Journal* Office Building	435
38	The *Great Britain* beginning to rise	447
39	Herring lugger and nets	451
40	Scaffie	454
41	Fifie	454
42	Zulu	455
43	Wick fishing boat	468
44	Map of the Highland Railway	542
45	The Caithness Line 1870-1874	547
46	The Wick and Lybster Railway	556
47	The combined burgh (1906)	598
48	Wick Carnegie Free Library	599
49	The new steam liners	609
50	Map of Central Europe 1914	612/613
51	Captain G. A. Sutherland	628
52	Wick's War Memorial	691

LIST OF PHOTOGRAPHIC PLATES

Aerial view of Wick 1995 – *George Robb* Frontispiece

between pages 278 and 279

Women sorting and gutting fish in J More's Yard, Shaltigoe – c 1935.

Herring packers in D Water's Yard – c 1935.

Herring boats and other vessels in Pulteneytown Harbour c 1865.

Herring drifters near entrance of Pulteneytown Harbour c 1913.

Rough seas at Pulteneytown Harbour Bay – c 1935 (and many other years!)

The Barque *Hans* stranded on rocks at Broadhaven – 1905.

Wick River and Bridge – west of the bridge the ice accumulates – Winter 1937.

Wick under water – Alexandra Place during the Flood of 1933.

between pages 502 and 503

A town centre scene – Northern Ensign office in High Street, 1912.

Bank Row and Saltoun Street, Lower Pulteneytown, c 1946.

A Relic of the Old Days – a demonstration of coach travel staged in Market Square in 1934.

The Newer Mode – The Highland Railway Locomotive *Glenbruar* at Wick Shed – c 1906.

Locomotive stuck in a snowdrift beyond Halkirk – 1905.

Wick and District Territorials leaving – August, 1914.

Bank Row – houses demolished in an Air Raid, 1 July, 1940.

Members of the Wick Division of County Police, about 1910 (some years after Wick and Pulteneytown combined).

All above photographs, with the exception of frontispiece, from the Johnston Collection, courtesy of the Wick Society

The Storm – an imaginative reconstruction of the Great Storm of 19 October, 1848 by R. Anderson, 1880, *Courtesy Wick District Council.*

PART I:

WICK EMERGENT

Chapter 1: That Was Wick – This Is.

Chapter 2: Early Days.

Chapter 3: Sinclairs

Chapter 4: Bishops, Sutherlands, and others.

Chapter 5: Royal Burgh.

CHAPTER 1

THAT WAS WICK – THIS IS

WICK. Where's that?

Don't you know? That's the place we went through on the way to John O'Groat's.

We went through a lot of funny places.

Yes, I know. But you must have noticed Wick. It's where we were held up at the traffic lights on the A9.

Oh. I remember. A bit of a river and huddle of grey houses. So that's Wick, is it?

This or similar lamentable conversations must have occurred often enough among folk who have ventured so far north, especially those from south of the Border. Wick, if remembered at all, a stopping place on the way to that less than charismatic but geographically memorable spot, John O'Groats. Memorable to the seekers of car and ruck-sack badges showing that they have been 'somewhere different', and television watchers of countless charity walkers – Jimmy Savile, Ian Botham, followed by their trains of camera-men, microphone carriers, first-aid and refreshment vans. Wick, if noticed at all, was a place 'on the way'.

As few Wickers will need telling, their town is a great deal more than that. They are also philosophically aware that their place is a 'long way north', 58° 27' North to be exact, nearly on the same latitude as the tip of Greenland and on a line that crosses the broad middle of Hudson's Bay and the north 'panhandle' of Alaska and well north of Moscow. Though Wick has its winter tribulations, it shares none of the hard, snowy, icy blanketing that covers these places from November to March – some of them much longer. In some winter seasons Wick gets no snow at all. (Wick is, incidentally, just over three degrees *west* of Greenwich.)

'North' and 'South' represent to most people not so much compass bearings as mysterious 'lands beyond', like the 'Northland' of Noggin the Nog and, indeed, 'Norway' itself, the 'land on the way north' – 'Nord-vei'. There are those in the south of England who think of anything beyond Reading – on the Thames – as 'North', a notion that

WICK OF THE NORTH

is fostered by frequent direction signs on the motorways which say just that. Wick is less than twenty miles from as far north as you can go on the British mainland, and certainly the last town north on the A9, the main road from Edinburgh to the 'North'. At its end is John O'Groats, no sort of place at all except that it marks the opposite end of the proverbial 878-mile run from Land's End all through England and Scotland to the 'furthest north' (and, of course, John's octagonal tower).

But Wick is not the most northerly mainland 'town' (whatever that means), for Thurso has that distinction. Thurso is Wick's civic rival and has been through the centuries, a town of similar size and aspect, like Wick commanding the entrance to its own river, the one flowing north and the other east. It lies twenty-three miles west by north-west of Wick, connected along the Wick and Thurso valleys by the A882 and by the northern arms of the Highland Railway by the same route. Its latitude is 58° 36' N. And even at that – to settle at once arguments often raised by mapless travellers – Thurso lies south of John O'Groats. And to get things absolutely straight, John O'Groats is *not* the most northerly place on mainland Britain; that honour belongs to Easter Head, the north point of Dunnet Head at 58° 41'N. Dunnet Head is a mighty bleak hump of sandstone standing out beyond the latitudes of either Duncansby Head in the east and Cape Wrath in the west, but only just.

While explaining the basic geography of the area, we may as well mention that Caithness in the north-east corner, formerly Britain's 'most northerly county' (and perhaps soon to resume that description), is flanked by Sutherland on the west. Wick, accordingly is – or was – the county town. It is still the administrative centre of the 'District' of Caithness, now in terms of population one of the smallest in Britain, with a total of 26,733 at the 1991 census. Wick itself, according the same census, has 8,754, while Thurso is slightly larger with 9,233.

As we shall see, in earlier times Thurso usually had the edge on Wick in matters of population, civic and trading importance, an issue of some controversy and sometimes ill-feeling between the two 'burghs'. Both Wick and Thurso have Norse or Orcadian Viking origins, both being small settlements on river estuaries accessible to Viking war vessels and 'knorrs', perhaps the two only safe places along the deeply indented rocky coasts of Caithness. Safe, that is, for the Viking mariners from the fierce storms that raged and still rage in this part of the world. This may seem strange, since in later times fishers in particular made good use of the many 'goes' or cliff-edged rocky inlets all along the coast. Vikings, it must be remembered, sailed in wide, shallow-draught ships, immensely sea-worthy, but very vulnerable to battering and break-up on wild rocky coasts. In the Wick and Thurso estuaries, shallow enough in places to paddle through at low tide, the rowers were able to take in their ships at high tide and beach them on the sand and mud flats round the bends behind the river estuaries.

UNCONFORMITY

A very useful concept in geology is that of the 'unconformity', a break in the sequence of deposition that is out of place, in the conventional order of the stratigraphy. Geological sequences, like those of conventional history, are indeed history in a vastly different set of time scales. Attempting to grapple with this idea, the old hymnarist wrote:

> Time like an ever rolling stream
> Bears all its sons away.
> They fly forgotten as a dream
> Dies at the opening day.

As indeed they do. 'History' is perhaps a vain attempt to recall to mind a few of the incidents and episodes that coloured and conditioned the experience of earlier 'sons of time'. The scale here is, of course, based on the classic 'three-score years and ten' of a man's life. In an attempt to cope with the more imponderable aspects of the relentless flow of time, Watts tried with:

> Before the hills in order stood,
>   And earth received her frame;
> From everlasting thou art God,
>   Through endless years the same.

That was in 1719 before the revelations of geologists, who added dimensions to the issue no less wondrous to contemplate. For the very conditions of human existence are geologically determined, and nowhere more dramatically and demonstrably than in Caithness where, in a sense, the two concepts, those of geological and historical time, come together. Caithness is as it is because a great slab of Old

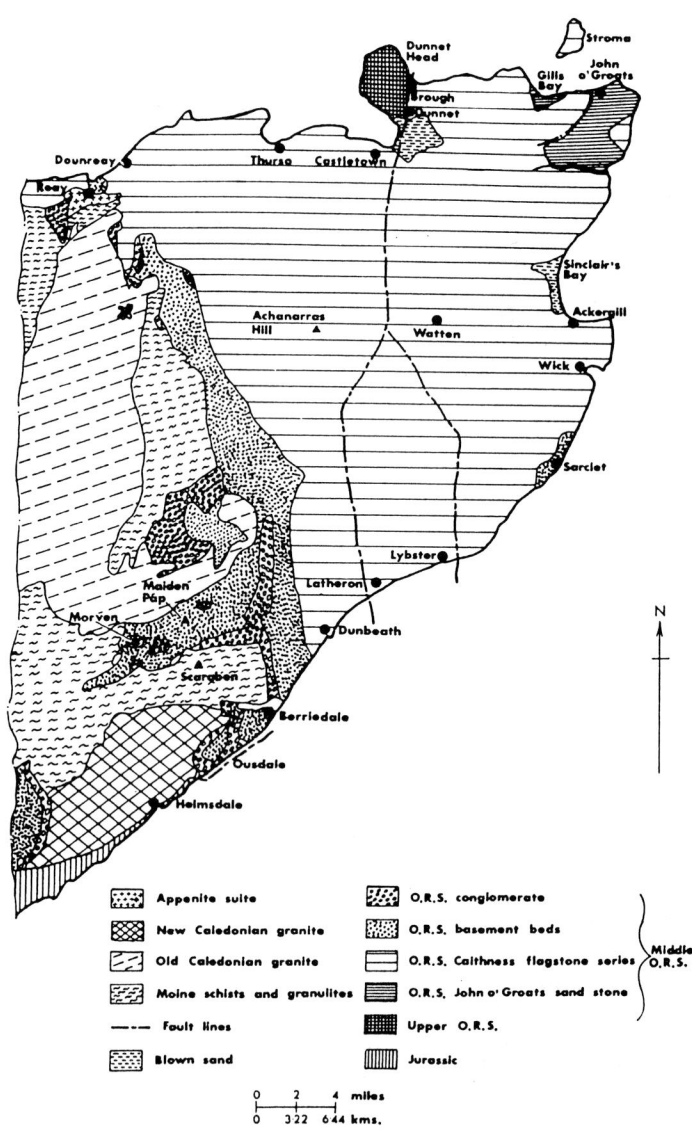

Fig. 1 The simplified geology of Caithness.
(Courtesy D. Omand, The Caithness Book).

Red Sandstone, some three hundred and sixty five to three hundred and ninety-five million years old, lies at the north-eastern tip of Scotland, and that is the province of Caithness. Off the coast lie other fragments of the mass, and they are the islands of Orkney, with whose fortunes Caithness is so closely connected in historical time.

It was Archibald Geikie, another notable Scottish geologist, who identified the processes in the Devonian period, 408-369 million years ago (my), which produced the immense 'Red Sandstone' deposits of northern Scotland. These occurred, he believed, in the conditions existing in and around a great, brackish 'lake', named by him 'Lake Orcadie' (now thought to have been located in a desert area about 30° south of the Equator, a terrain that drifted as a result of tectonic forces to 10°S during the Devonian and since to these northern latitudes). Without going into detail, silt and sand deposited in and on the shores of this lake, produced the 'flagstones' that are the characteristic rock forms of Caithness, and of which the so-called Wick Beds, are just one sequence of the Middle Devonian. Throughout Caithness there are other main beds – and 'sub-groups' of beds – that constitute the whole Upper Caithness Flagstone succession of this area and some of the Lower.

A complicated system of 'faults' – downward/upward movements of whole blocks of rock from the levels at which they were originally deposited (usually a long time later), has displaced rocks all over Caithness, so that unrelated sequences lie alongside one another, often in quite limited areas. Thus, in the area of the present Wick parish, no less than six 'sub-groups' of rocks belonging to the Upper Caithness Group, and three to the Lower are blocked in, providing a considerable variety of rock forms underlying the surface soil of the parish and exposed along the coast line – though not differing fundamentally in their lithology, as they were all formed in roughly the same conditions.

All of these formations are subject to a special kind of coastal erosion. Flagstones and sandstones form deep vertical 'joints', that is

---

1 Hugh Miller, a native geologist of north-east Scotland, born in Cromarty, defined and described this rock. Miller first published his influential *Old Red Sandstone*, in 1841, but it was greatly revised for the 1873 edition in the light of the considerable researches of Robert Dick of Thurso. The first edition of the book was dedicated to Roderick Impey Murchison, (later Sir Roderick) notable President of the Royal Geological Society, later a significant visitor himself to this area. His connection is celebrated in the naming of one of the streets of Pulteneytown after him, and on the plaque of 'eminent visitors' in the wall along Station Road, Archibald Geikie (later Sir Archibald) was Scotland's most eminent nineteenth century geologist.

splits or contraction cracks downward through the beds (this has to do with the chemical and crystalline nature of the sandstone), digging deeper into the rocks, sometimes for as far as half-a-mile-inland. Sometimes these 'geos' or 'goes' (as spelt in Caithness – derived from the Old Norse, 'gja', a cleft or narrow bay) remain narrow, but where the rock is softer they may broaden into quite deep and wide steep-sided inlets, especially where the original joints have intersected.

The Wick coast has some of the most spectacular goes in Scotland, including the complex of the 'Old Man' of Wick, the formation on one of whose narrow ribs stands the Old Wick or 'Auldwick' castle, just south of the estuary, the Gote o' Tram, half-a-mile further down, and in the Papigoe, Staxigoe and Girnigoe areas north of Wick. Among the features produced by this kind of wave-action are caves, bridges and borings through rock masses, examples of which are all to be seen at the Gote o' Tram where the Brig o' Tram is a favourite tourist feature. Also there are small islands such as the Brough in the same locality, and pyramids of rock upstanding in the sea, cut off from their parent rock. 'Staxigoe' derives its name from a handsome stack standing inside the goe. The most famous stacks of the Caithness coast are the remarkable pyramids standing off the cliffs at Duncansby[1].

It may be mentioned here that some of these formations have a direct relationship to the human occupation and development of the Caithness coast, especially its eastern face. Here the goes are aligned mostly east-west, with the easterly winds blowing straight into them. Some, however, have twists and turns in them, and even pebbly or sandy beaches at their inland extremity. Possibly it was familiarity with such inlets, seeking protection while the storm below itself out, that the Viking rovers of the eighth and ninth centuries, persuaded them to investigate further and in due course to take up occupation. Also, they and their successors – notably the Sinclairs, used some of the less accessible headlands, cut out by the waves, as locations on

---

[1] Writing of one of the 'coves of the coast', the Rev. William Sutherland, author of *Wick, 1794*, of the *First Statistical Account of Scotland (Q.V.)*, refers to one specially interesting feature:

> On the estate of Hempriggs (just south of Wick) in the mouth of a creek, one very remarkable rock forms a small island, about a gun shot in length and 24 feet in width, covered with green, and open at the top, where sea-fowl nestle; it is supported by two long pillars, completely intersected, so widely, that a boat can easily pass through, and so regularly, that it appears more like a work of art than of nature.

This is, in fact, the Stack of Brough (Scotties Island), on the seaward side of which over 200 pairs of kittiwakes meet, along with razorbills, shags and cormorants.

which to build their virtually impregnable castles. Such castles were the 'Lambaborg' of Svein Asleifarson (later Buchollie), and the keep of Old Wick. Girnigoe and Sinclair are built on an astonishing complex of headlands lying between goes just to the west of Noss Head.

One system of goes that was almost certainly thus exploited would have been the Haven, just inside Sarclet Head, six miles south of Wick. This is another remarkable complex lying in the Sarclet Formation, a very small coastal block of rock, cut off from the rocks of the surrounding Clyth Sub-Group by a fault system, the inland end of which bends round deeply southward from the east-west inlet itself. At this end in addition to a pebble beach are a series of slab-like pavement rocks, forming a natural landing stage which would not only have been of interest to the Vikings, but also came to be used by later herring fishers. Still to be seen are the additional masonry, put in by nineteenth century herring men (together with a rotting iron capstan) and a stone fish-curing shed. Sarclet was one of the very earliest herring-fishing havens of the eighteenth century.

Cut off on west, north and south by a series of faults, downthrown outwards, Wick town and estuary lie on the 'Wick Beds' (nowadays spoken of as a portion of the Lybster Sub-Group, of the Lower Caithness Flagstone Group). These beds consist largely of very dark coloured thin laminations ('laminites'), hard and firm in texture, extensive exposures of which may be seen on the walls of the quarries opened up in the early nineteenth century when the great Wick harbour works had begun. It is these flags from which much of Wick town is built; they weather even more drably than the fresh-cut stone, contributing to the impressions of glum greyness that first views of the town tend to convey.

Yet one other geological feature remains to mention as contributing to the configuration and surface character of the Wick area. This is the 'till' or glacial drift material (often called 'boulder clay') left behind by the glaciation of Caithness during the Ice Age, the last period of which (the Devensian) ended with retreat about 10,000 years ago. There was coverage of till over the 'lowland' area of the province, the ice movement being generally northwards from the Moray Firth.

The presence of till has affected the nature of the soil in Caithness and, as in Orkney, it underlines much the pasture land of the district. Without positive drainage, such lands are apt to be damp and boggy. Peaty 'uplands' rise westwards and become increasingly boggy. Boggy land is not uncommon in the lowland areas, as for instance (at one time) the Skitten Mire, near Killimster, where a battle – perhaps two battles were fought during Norse times. In the burn valleys and the flats of the Wick river valley there are stretches of alluvium, also liable to bogginess unless deliberately drained. Stock farming has been the main agricultural activity along the Wick coast and down the Wick valley since – and probably before – the coming of the Vikings.[1]

So much of the basic geology of Caithness is necessary for an understanding of the peculiar configuration of the coast, its general lack of safe natural harbourage, significant both to the Vikings and to the later herring fishers. The estuary of the Wick River was the only entry along this coast for relatively safe sailing in of Viking vessels (according to weather), on high tides. The Devonian flags have, of course, served during the centuries as a main source of building materials.

BACK TO HISTORY

Or, for the moment, to 'pre-history'. Here pre-history is much nearer to our time than in, say, Egypt or Greece; but so far as the area of Wick parish is concerned, not much of it is discernible. For pre-historians must rely mostly on artefacts and archaeological site evidence. While Caithness as a whole is fairly rich in such items as chambered tombs, cairns and standing stones, not overmuch is known about their significance. The articles in *The Caithness Book* of 1972 and *The New Caithness Book* of 1992 (by a different selection of authors), provide interesting summaries of recent and present knowledge of the Caithness cairns, artefacts etc of the earlier peoples, neolithic, bronze and iron-age, and catalogues of the brochs and other relics of the Picts; but it is evident that most of the important locations are not in Wick parish. This probably does not signify that these coasts and the Wick valley were not much favoured by pre-Viking settlers; it is more likely that with greater subsequent development and more intensive farming in the area, less of the material has survived than on the moors.

1 A useful background to this discussion is that of Donald Omand: *The Making of the Caithness Landscape*; in *Caithness: A Cultural Cross Roads*; Ed. John R. Baldwin, Edina Press, Edinburgh (1982). Omand argues that it would be a mistake to assume that glaciation played a significant part in shaping the Caithness landscape. Its extent was limited. 'It seems,' he says, 'that the passage of the ice has left little imprint on the higher plateaux of Caithness'; that 'ice would have played its part in emphasising the existing relief features of Caithness'; and that 'the low-lying nature of the District might give the casual observer the impression that Caithness is thickly plastered with glacial drift. This is not so.'

One sketch-map shows something like a dozen brochs and perhaps 'potential brochs' in the locality. The one 'most easily reached' is that of Keiss, where in addition there are 'post-broch extra-mural settlements . . . . . and much evidence of later re-use of the courtyard' of the broch itself. Interestingly, near the same place is a 'pill-box' defence post of the 1940-45 period, already much deteriorated and unlikely to last even as well as the footings and rubble of the broch and settlement (unless, of course, some measures are undertaken to preserve it for later generations of archaeologists); while a mile up the coast are the unsafe remains of the splendid L-shaped Keiss tower of the sixteenth century.

But now, to get back to a more parochial time-sequence. Neither Thurso nor Wick became settlements of any great importance until fairly recent times. Both were built up – though not in any spectacular way – in the later middle ages during the rule of the Caithness and Sutherland Scottish earls, Sinclair and Sutherland. Such importance as they achieved had much in early days to do with their use as ferry points for Orkney, to the earls of which, Caithness and Sutherland were subject from the ninth to the thirteenth centuries. And it is likely that in this matter, Thurso did more business than Wick; both places were, in fact, colonial settlements of Orkney Vikings, and there is evidence of strong Norse influence all along the north coast of Scotland, and down the east coast as far as Dornoch. In fact, the Vikings established on the north coast of Moray the stronghold of Burghead which remained in Norse hands until quite late in the day.

The eventual ascendancy of Wick over Thurso had more to do with rivalries between the earls than geography or economics. The politics involved were complicated, as we shall see later in the text. As Scottish influence superseded the Norse in the area, it may be true that Thurso became relatively the less accessible to armies and administrators from the south. Thurso, like Wick, was more accessible by sea than by land, provided that conditions were right; but Thurso lies at the west end of of the Pentland Firth, where flow some of the most dangerous seas of the world. Vessels from Edinburgh, Aberdeen and Inverness could reach Wick rather more easily than Thurso, as navigation westward beyond Duncansby Head was very hazardous in most weathers. Which is not to suggest that entrance to Wick was all that easy; but provided that the easterlies were not blowing, anchorage in Wick Bay would allow access to the town and the valley behind by traders, travellers and even troops. There was not much in it, and until the later sixteenth century, Thurso remained the more advanced and prosperous settlement.

Ecclesiastical influence and power, which in the early days came like the political from Orkney and Norway, also had a base in Thurso. St Peter's Church, Thurso, was, in the fourteenth century, a much finer building than anything known to have existed in Wick. The early bishops of Caithness operated from here and from Halkirk, seven miles inland along the Thurso valley.

THE PARISH OF WICK

Caithness District is divided into ten parishes, some of them, such as the parishes of Latheron and Halkirk, very extensive in area. This, of course, is because they take in large expanses of the very lightly populated stretches of moorland and bog stretching westward from the coast. Wick parish lies centrally along the east coast for a distance of about fifteen miles along the A9 highway from south to north and, at its widest about six miles along the A882 to Watten and Thurso. Even in terms of the entire parishes, the population of Thurso exceeds that of Wick, but not by a very considerable margin. Keiss, a moderately populous village on the coast at the north end of Wick parish, has 639 people, while Thrumster, a less concentrated settlement, has 425. The parish as a whole has lost some 159 people since the 1981 census, a fall of 1.6 per cent. This would be higher had not Keiss increased its population by a factor of 7.8 per cent; Thrumster fell by 16.5 per cent and Wick itself by 1.4 per cent, a loss of 121 souls. These figures are part of an overall fall of 908 people in Caithness over the ten years, a decline of 3.3 per cent. The fall in Thurso parish was 6.7 per cent, some 593 people. Almost all this decline may be attributed to fall-off in employment at the Dounreay, United Kingdom Atomic Energy Authority plant; Dounreay is a considerable employer of folk from all over the county, though the concentration is obviously higher in the Thurso area. The decline represents a resumption of the downward trend that was in progress before the setting up of the plant in the mid 1960s, and it seems likely to continue.

Along the Wick coast, at varying distances inland lies much of the best cultivable land of Caithness, seldom more than three miles in width except along the Wick valley itself; and most of this is cattle and sheep – grazing land, no doubt first developed as such by Viking

THAT WAS WICK – THIS IS

farmers, for their chief interest and means of livelihood was cattle farming – supplemented when enterprise and occasion permitted, by loot from raids on other people's land and wealth, often far away.

Neither Wick parish nor Caithness as a whole shows a general pattern of nuclear settlement, except for the two 'big' towns and one or two other moderate sized communities, such as Lybster, Castletown and Halkirk. The parish, nevertheless, contains a number of fairly well-known small settlements, reference to which will occur in this history, since the 'Wick' of the title is taken to include its surrounding parochial area. Among these, going from south to north, are Ulbster, Sarclet, Hempriggs, and north of Wick, Papigoe and Staxigoe, virtually parts of the town of Wick itself, Ackergill, Reiss, Killimster and Auckengill. Just south-west of Wick is Newton and further west the old community of Stirkoke. Events and personalities associated with these places, as often as not involve Sinclairs of one style or another, for in this area above all others were the Sinclairs. Sinclairs from the fourteenth century onwards came to dominate affairs in Caithness.

In the story which follows, no less than five, possibly six pitched battles were fought in the territory of what is now Wick parish, and there have been as many sieges of the numerous castles of this coast line. There cannot be any comparable length of coast anywhere in Britain more embattled than the east coast of Caithness. On the coast of Wick parish alone there are Auldwick, the ancient keep of Wick itself, Girnigoe and Sinclair (which may be counted as one, since Sinclair was the 'improved' lodging accommodation of Earl George Sinclair III alongside the earlier Girnigoe), Ackergill Tower and Keiss tower. Just beyond the parish to the north were Buchollie and Freswick tower, and just south were Halberry and Clyth, Latheron, Dunbeath and Berriedale, most of which were either built or occupied at some time by Sinclairs. Whether or not Wick and district are rich in people and wealth, they are certainly rich in 'history'.

As for the religious life of the parish, very little is known about the church before the arrival of the Reformed rite in this part of Scotland. There are known to have been 'chapels' in several localities, but little is left of any of them. The reformers made a fairly clean job of extirpating 'popery' and all its symbols and appurtenances, including documents, publications and usually the very stones among which the mediaeval 'idolaters' worshipped. Some remains of at least one mediaeval church are still to be found in the parish, the so-called

'Sinclair Aisle' in the kirkyard of the present Parish Church, once St Fergus Church, in Wick itself. The memory of St Fergus is an anomaly preserved, it is believed, as the tale will show, by the drastic will of the people themselves in spite of the reformers; for Fergus was a papistical Irish monk from the days of darkness of the eighth century, who first brought Christianity to the north of Scotland and is thought to have built a church at Wick.

WICK TOWN

In later times numerous churches have been built in Wick, ranging from an Ebenezer Chapel through all the variants of 'Secession' to the Episcopal Church of Scotland. In fullness of time, the Catholics returned, to worship now in an even more exotically dedicated chapel, that of St Joachim, a first century saint reputed to be the husband of Anne and father of the Blessed Virgin. His connections with Wick must be tenuous indeed. The nucleus of the modern Catholic community was the Irish who in one way or another came to build up the new Wick, quarrymen and construction workers, railway navvies and fisher folk. Quite a few of the churches of Wick, especially those of Pulteneytown, are no longer in use – at least for religious purposes.

The town of Wick stands astride the estuary of the Wick river. Its oldest parts are on the north side, reaching eastward to the sea through Louisburgh and into Broadhaven where are most of Wick's 'council' estates. On the south side is Pulteneytown, the nineteenth century planned fishers' city so named in honour of the then Chairman of the British Fisheries' Society, largely responsible for the financing and development of Wick's great fishing trade. Until 1902 it was administered as a separate burgh, with its own town council and officers, and still to be a 'Pulteneytowner' is be something rather different from a 'Wicker'. To be a 'Backsider' from Upper Pulteneytown, the area of Nicolson, Wellington, Vansittart and Huddart Streets etc is something even more special. South of Pulteneytown the housing peters out towards the Cemetery, the rifle butts and, on the deeply fissured coast, Old Wick or Auldwick Castle, an ancient keep with no provenance but probably dating back to Viking times.

Out of the town beyond North Head is the rocky Broad Haven, Papigoe and beyond that Staxigoe, one of the earliest of the fishing havens of this coast. The real story of Wick is the rise of the herring fishery of the late eighteenth and early nineteenth centuries. It is to this development that Wick owes its harbours, none of which existed before John Rennie appeared on the scene. He was followed by Thomas Telford, then James Bremner and latterly Thomas Stevenson (father of Robert Louis) who, between them, equipped Wick with a suite of modern stone and concrete basins and sea-walls, providing accommodation (albeit inadequate) for over a thousand fishing boats at any one time.

Stone was quarried on a large scale from immense quarries opened on the shores of the South Head of Wick Bay, which not only supplied the engineers and builders with the durable material from which they constructed the harbour walls (at minimal transport costs), but also provided expanses of open space in which to undertake the vast exercise of fish gutting, curing and packing on which the town's phenomenal prosperity was built in a matter of three decades.

As our story will show, there could have been few indications in mediaeval and even later times, that Wick Bay could be the locus for a major maritime industry. Such sea-borne trade as there was here had to be brought in and taken out in fairly hazardous conditions. Eastern gales, especially at the equinoxes, funnel up the Wick estuary making it a dangerous place for sail-boats to be unless protected behind high strong walls, as boats are now. Nor was there deep anchorage in the narrows of the estuary; the River Wick is short and shallow by the standards of almost all other Scottish sea-port rivers. Fortunately there is a high tidal rise, so that deeper draught vessels can approach at high tide and, with the help of dredging, reasonably deep harbourage can be provided. This was sufficient for some development of the fishing industry when steam trawling and seine-netting came in; though the port has never been a place for deep-draught shipping, coastal or ocean-going.

Wick has never been much of a packet or ferry port. Of course, there were never enough travellers here seeking transit to sustain commercially viable passenger lines. The essential ferry-trade of this area, from and to Orkney, inevitably gravitated to Thurso – rather, to Scrabster Bay, more directly in line with the islands and with reasonably safe deep-water harbourage. John O'Groats, in fact, achieved its fame, such as it is, and gained its name from the enterprise and ingenuity of a certain Dutchman, Jan de Groet or Groat (a not uncommon name in Orkney) who, during the reign of James IV

WICK OF THE NORTH

(1473-1513), settled with his brothers on the bleak flats of north Caithness. He is said to have built an eight-sided house with a door in each face so that, sitting round the table, no brother could claim precedence at meals. Whether this tale is true or not, it is fairly certain that John gained a concession from the earls to run a ferry from Caithness to South Ronaldsay in Orkney, the ancestor of the present (summer) ferry across the Pentland Firth from John O'Groats to Burwick.[1]

Access to Wick from the south was, nevertheless, mostly by sea in older times. The town's connections by road and rail, excellent as they are, are an outcome of the fishing trade. Thomas Telford, under government contract at the instigation of the British Fisheries Society, constructed roads and bridges (and churches) all the way up to Wick, in fact the route of the present A9. The greatest feat in making this road was the crossing of the Ord, the 400 foot granite cliff that blocks off coastal south Caithness from the Helmsdale valley, in a series of hairpins that still require careful navigation and good brakes. Among Telford's fine bridges was one across the Helmsdale river, and the Bridge across the Wick river leading into Bridge Street, at the end of which the A9 turns sharply left. This was, like most of Telford's bridges, a humped affair; it was replaced in 1877 by the present three-arch level bridge. There is another bridge at the narrows of the estuary. Telford had much to do with the designing of the 'new town' of Pulteney.

The railway came to Wick in 1874, the end (or one of the two ends, the other at Thurso) of the system built in stages from Inverness northwards. This was the Caithness and Sutherland Railway, which arrived too late in the day to make much impression on the fish trade. The whole system was one of the great enthusiasms of the Duke of Sutherland, who played trains up and down the Sutherland coasts for some years. Another railway was brought into Wick in 1903, the Wick and Lybster Light Railway, a standard-gauge track but constructed under the provisions of the Light Railways Act of 1896. This not very successful line was closed in 1944, and is now chiefly represented by indications on the 1:50,000 OS Map, 'Disused Railway'.[2]

---

1 The historians of Canisbay (in the church of which there is a great stone plaque in memory of John) claim that his fourpenny fare to the islands was the origin of the fourpenny coin called the 'groat'.

2 In fact, the closure of 1944 was a war-time economy measure as it was so under used. The question of re-opening remained under consideration until 1947 when the final decision on closure was reached.

THAT WAS WICK – THIS IS

Throughout its history, wars have been fought around Wick, mostly contests of neither national nor international significance, but encounters between northern war lords. Inevitably the town was drawn into the first and second world wars of this century, as was the whole of Caithness to an extent, on account of the British Grand Fleet in Scapa Flow of Orkney. Wick had little to offer in terms of strategic or defence locations, but there was certainly some expectation in 1940 that the Germans might seek to land an expeditionary force on these northern shores. Remnants of beach defences are to be found on lower shores near Wick, notably at Keiss and along the dunes of Sinclair Bay. Tank landings anywhere along the rocky coasts elsewhere in the parish were wildly unthinkable.

The Wick area, like the rest of northern Scotland, was for the duration a restricted area, entrance to which required a special pass. Wick's most considerable war effort was the creation and manning in the parish of two of the four airfields constructed in Caithness. One of these was the now disused (and largely obliterated) airfield of Skitten (Killimster), and the other just north of Wick town itself, the present Wick Airport. Wick and parish were bombed several times during 1940 and 1941. There were two damaging raids in 1941 on a decoy 'drome, well dotted with dummy planes (and protected by anything but dummy anti-aircraft batteries), at Thrumster just south of the town. Servicemen were almost as numerous in the area as visiting fisher-folk had once been in building up the town's wealth, and they too contributed quite a lot to Wick's well-being.

Wick, then, is something of an urban oasis (like Thurso) in the sparsely populated north. It has a vigorous and enterprising contemporary life, and a long and variegated history behind it. The aim of this book is to recount Wick's unique story, more or less in chronological sequence, but dilly-dallying on the way whenever there is something interesting or specially entertaining to engage attention.

The town has been written about in dozens of different ways, by dozens and dozens of local antiquarians, historians and commentators. As one local historian put it – rather mistakenly – the tale has been 'hashed and re-hashed' with 'nothing new to be said'. Even if it were true, there are always new ways of looking at old things. Thomas Sinclair in 1887, adding notes to a revised edition of J T Calder's wonderfully garrulous and urbane *Civil and Traditional History of Caithness,* said of Wick: 'It would take a volume to do justice to the history of the burgh, the materials being unusually plentiful'.

That volume has not yet been written, and it would be egregiously immodest for this author to claim that the present book does the trick. Nevertheless, he has made an attempt to fill in the outlines limned in this introductory chapter, and so provide amusement and perhaps edification for those who wish to know a little more about Wick, Britain's most northerly mainland county town.

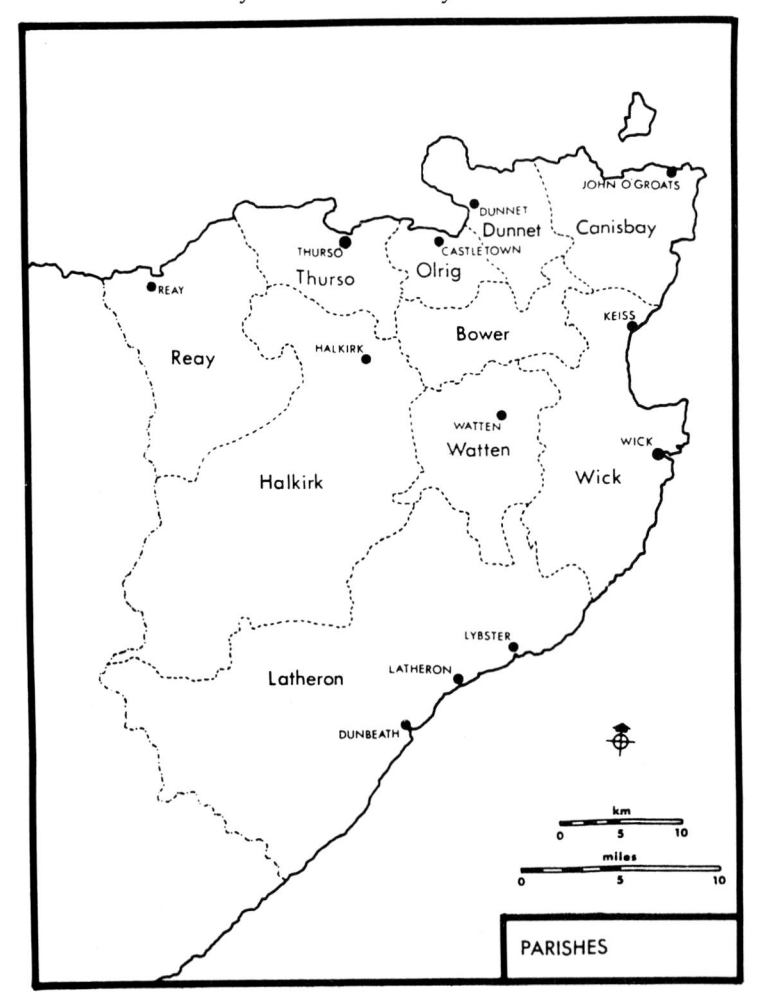

Fig. 2 The parishes of Caithness.

(Courtesy D. Omand, The Caithness Book).

CHAPTER 2

EARLY DAYS

FROM all available indications, it would be vain to look for the beginnings of Wick in the misty past when the Land of Cat was inhabited by Picts. Even the Viking connections are limited to the fairly certain derivation of the town's one syllable name, 'Vik', a bay, and several intriguing references to the place in *The Orkneyinga Saga*. As late as 1503, Wick was, to quote *The Caithness Book*, a 'tiny settlement . . . a small village of thatched houses', granted nevertheless the status of Royal Burgh in 1589 by King James VI. How it came to such an honour we shall shortly mention. Such importance it ever had until the nineteenth century was entirely the result of its geography, a settlement on the banks of a small river in the north-eastern corner of Britain's most northerly 'county', accessible by sea and moderately safe from the North Sea's ravages. Its closest neighbour was Sutherland, the Søderland – the South Land.

Both Caithness and Sutherland were named by the Norsemen, many of whom came from much further north. Caithness was for them 'Katanes', the 'headland of the Cat people'. Sutherland lies west and south. The ancient first king of the Picts is said – somewhat improbably – to have divided his kingdom into seven provinces, each governed by one of his seven sons, one of whom was 'Caitt', his province named, of course, as the 'Land of Caitt'. The Norsemen most interested in this land were the colonists of the new Norse territory of Orkney, with whose fortunes the people of Cat became closely connected for the best part of three centuries. While the influence and power of the Picts, such as it was, had driven north, the thrust of the Northmen had been south. The early days of Wick belong to that early southward drive of vigorous tribes of Teutonic origin who virtually obliterated the Pictish regimes of Orkney and the northern provinces of 'Alba'.

There are few enough authenticated sources of reliable information about the arrival of the Norsemen in Orkney and fewer still about the occupation of Katanes. Doubtless the creeks or 'goes' of the coasts of both were used as refuge by Norse raiders well before settlement, but it is fairly certain that Norse control of areas of mainland Scotland came some time after the establishment of the Orkney earldom, perhaps in the later eighth century when King Harald the 'Fairhaired'[1] decided to clean things up in the northern seas.

> Wheresoever the vikings heard of him they all took to flight, and most of them out into the open ocean. At last the king grew weary of this work, and therefore one summer he sailed with his fleet right out into the West sea. First he came to Shetland, and he slew all the vikings who could not save themselves by flight. Then King Harald sailed southwards, to the Orkney Islands, and cleared them of all vikings . . . .

Harald carried his cleansing operations across to the Hebrides, and into Scotland itself, and this, according to Snorri, is how the Norsemen came to Caithness. He plundered in the Hebrides,

> and slew many vikings who formerly had men-at-arms under them. Many a battle was fought, and King Harald was usually victorious. He then plundered far and wide in Scotland itself, and had battles there. When he was come westward as far as the Isle of Man, the report of his exploits on the land had gone before him; for all the inhabitants had fled over to Scotland, and the island was left entirely bare of people and goods, so that King Harald and his men made no booty when they landed . . .
>
> In this war fell Ivar, a son of Rognvald, Earl of More; and King Harald gave Rognvald, as a compensation for the loss, the Orkney and Shetland Isles; but Rognvald immediately gave both these countries to Sigurd the earldom of them. Thorstein the Red, son of Olaf the White and Aud the Deep-minded, entered into partnership with him; and plundering in Scotland, they subdued Caithness and Sutherland, as far as Ekksjalsbakke.[2]

How authentic is this account of the Viking occupation of northern Scotland is still a matter for discussion and conjecture. Various versions of the sagas add little to our understanding of how and exactly when the Vikings took over in Shetland, Orkney and the north of Scotland. And little is known about the earlier inhabitants and what happened to them. The issues, including the very nature of the

---

1 There is much doubt as to whether or not Harald was 'king' in the accepted mediaeval sense; rather an ambitious lord seeking to extend his power throughout Norway and the northern isles.
2 Ekkjal was the Norse name for Oykel, the main river flowing into Dornoch Firth; 'these countries' were Sutherland, Caithness, Ross and Cromarty.

'conquest' – infiltration or forceful entry – are still debated in periodic Viking Congresses. Nothing can be added here to the many controversies about how the Vikings took over and virtually obliterated the 'Catti' or other Gaelic peoples who had probably long inhabited the north-eastern tip of Scotland. We are, in any case concerned only with the emergence of Wick, which gains a number of references in the *Orkneyinga Saga* and a few less definite in other sagas.[1]

In the sagas there is much telling of intrigue, disputing, fighting, treachery and murder between members of the families with claim – or seeking claim – on the islands of north and west Scotland. Various stories are told of the 'process' as Barbara Crawford puts it 'by which land was wrested from the Celts,' and by which this territory was acquired by early earls of Orkney. Sigurd the Mighty (thought to have been the first Earl of Orkney, a province granted to him by King Harald Finehair in the later years of the ninth century) is said to have conquered, 'in a heroic way', Caithness, Sutherland, Moray and Ross, thus extending Norse influence 'across the northern half of the mainland of Scotland'.[2] He was assisted in this by another formidable warrior, Thorstein the Red, whose father was Olaf, King of Dublin and whose mother was Aud (or Unn) the Deep-minded, who is believed to have had a hand in arranging a dynastic claim to Caithness for Thorstein's successors by getting her grand-daughter, Thorstein's daughter, married to a native Caithness chief, Dungadr. This chief's name is thought to be commemorated in the famous headland and territory of Duncansby.[3]

Even if more and more accurate information were available, it would not profit us here greatly to follow through the inter-

---

[1] Among the 'sources' specially considered in this connection have been: *Orkneyinga Saga: The History of the Earls of Orkney*; translated by Hermann Palsson and Paul Edwards, London, The Hogarth Press (1978). Another standard translation is that of Magnus Magnusson, published by Penguin. Torfaeus Thermodus: *Ancient History of Orkney, Caithness and the North*; William P.L. Thomson: *History of Orkney*, Edinburgh, the Mercat Press (1987); J.T. Calder: *History of Caithness*; Barbara E. Crawford: *Scandinavian Scotland* (Scotland in the Early Middles Ages 2); Leicester University Press (1987); Iain Crawford: *War or Peace – Viking Colonisation in the Northern and Western Isles of Scotland*; Report of the Eighth Viking Congress, Arhus, August 1977. (This paper discusses the controversial issue of whether or not the Vikings 'conquered' by peaceful infiltration or attack and extermination. Crawford leans to the attack and exterminate theory, which does perhaps explain why in the northern isles and Caithness, Norse place names almost completely dominate.)

[2] B. Crawford, op cit p.57

[3] Ibid, p. 64

relationships and encounters between these early Scottish Vikings. They are explored in more detail (though not necessarily with greater accuracy) by Torfaeus, Calder and Crawford, and there is much entertaining reading about the events and colourful personalities involved in the sagas, especially the *Orkneyinga Saga*. Wick and localities in the Wick area appear from time to time in this saga, usually in connection with some warlike event or act of violence. Thorfinn Skull-splitter, Earl of Orkney (and Caithness), died in his bed in 963 AD – a most unusual end for a Viking earl. There was dispute as to who should succeed in the earldom. The issue was settled by a battle near to Wick.

Two of Thorfinn's sons, Ljot and Skuli, who had taken over the earldom of Orkney, each in his turn, had been disposed of as a result mainly of the machinations of Ragnhild (daughter of King Eric Bloodyaxe), who married first Arnfinn and then Havard Happy-Harvest and arranged for their deaths. She next got her hooks into Ljot, Thorfinn's third son. The story continues in the words of the saga writer:

> Skuli, Ljot's brother, travelled to Scotland (from Orkney), where he was given the title of earl by the King of Scots. Then he went north to Caithness to gather an army, and from there he sailed back to Orkney to claim the earldom from his brother. When they met, Skuli insisted on making a fight of it, but after a fierce battle Ljot won the victory and Skuli fled, first over to Caithness and then to the south of Scotland. Ljot went after him and spent some time in Caithness adding to his army.
>
> Later, Skuli rode back north with a large following supplied by the King of Scots and Earl Macbeth, and the brothers met in the Dales of Caithness (in the Thurso valley). The battle was hard-fought, with the Scots attacking fiercely in the early stages, but when Ljot urged his men to fight and stand firm the Scots failed to gain ground. Ljot kept shouting encouragement to his men and he himself fought like a hero. After a while the Scottish ranks began to crumble and soon they were on the run. Skuli battled on but in the end he was killed.
>
> Earl Ljot took over in Caithness and this led to trouble with the Scots, who were angry over their defeat. When Earl Ljot was in Caithness, Earl Macbeth came north from Scotland with a large army and they met at Skitten in Caithness. Ljot was outnumbered but fought so well that the Scots had to fall back.

EARLY DAYS

The battle was a short one: all the Scots who survived took to flight, most of them wounded. After this victory, Ljot went back to the islands. Many of his men were suffering from wounds and Ljot himself had one that led to his death. People thought it was a great loss.[1]

Yet another battle is reported as having been fought in the same place when Sigurd the Stout, son of Ljot, took over the earldom. According to the saga he was challenged by 'a Scottish earl called Finnleik' to fight him on a particular day at Skitten. The tale goes on:

Sigurd's mother was a sorceress so he went to consult her, telling her that the odds against him were heavy, at least seven to one.

'Had I thought you might live for ever,' she said, 'I'd have reared you in my wool-basket. But lifetimes are shaped by what will be, not by where you are. Now, take this banner. I've made it for you with all the skill I have, and my belief is this: that it will bring victory to the man it's carried before, but death to the one who carries it.

It was a finely made banner, very cleverly embroidered with the figure of a raven, and when the banner fluttered in the breeze, the raven seemed to be flying ahead.

Earl Sigurd lost his temper at his mother's words. He got the support of the Orkney farmers by giving them back their land rights [Sigurd, like several of the earls, sought from time to time to deprive of and sometimes restore to the farmers, what, in due course, came to be known as their 'udall rights' on the land they worked], then set out for Skitten to confront Earl Finnleik. The two sides formed up, but the moment they clashed Sigurd's standard bearer was struck dead. The Earl told another man to pick up the banner but before long he'd been killed too. The Earl lost three standard bearers, but he won the battle and the farmers of Orkney got back their land rights.[2]

---

1 There are various elements of this story that are doubtful. Since this battle of Skitten must have been fought about 950, there could certainly have been no 'Earl Macbeth' (at least, not the Macbeth of the play) in the fight. Macbeth, Mormaer (local ruler of Moray) from 1032 to 1042, and King of Scotland from 1042 to 1057, could not have been at war more than fifty years earlier. This, by the way, is the same Macbeth whose story is violently traduced in 'the Scottish play'. It is, nevertheless, very possible that a local chieftain – even perhaps the then Mormaer of Moray, was making use of an opportunity to advance his own cause by joining in a dispute that was dividing the Norse lords of the north of Scotland.

2 *Orkneyinga Saga,* Palsson and Edwards; op cit. Section 10 pp 37-38.

SVEIN THE PIRATE

So far there is no mention of Wick itself in the saga. Skitten is a locality near to Killimster, about four miles along the Castletown road (B876), where one of Caithness's four wartime airfields was constructed during the Second World War. Wick earns most of its references in the *Orkneyinga Saga* in connection with a series of episodes involving Svein Asleifarson, one of the great rogues of the Viking world. They occurred during the earlships of Hakon Paulsson, the slayer of his cousin, Magnus Erlendsson, Orkney's tutelary saint, Rognvald Kali Kolsson, from 1103 to 1158, and Harald Maddadarson, earl until 1206.

Svein Asleifarson (he took his patronymic – strictly, matronymic – from his mother, Asleif), 'the celebrated Norse pirate who fills many pages of the *Orkneyinga Saga*, did not aspire to become earl himself,' but became much involved in the making and breaking of earls. He had much to do with the discomfiture and death of Paul Hakonsson, and the rise to power of his brother, Rognvald, and later was a chief agent in setting up Rognvald's co-earl from 1138 to 1158, Harald Maddadarson, who took over when Rognvald died, and remained Earl of Orkney until 1206.

But before we can make much sense of these manoeuvres, and in particular Asleif's connection with Caithness and the Wick coast, it is necessary to say a word more about the background of Scottish politics in general during the twelfth and thirteenth centuries. To all intents and purposes the whole of the northern provinces, Caithness, Sutherland and quite a lot of Ross, the Hebrides and the Isle of Man were under Norse rule for some 300 years. On the coast of Moray, the Norsemen had a stronghold at Burghead, the Scottish headquarters of Thorfinn 'Raven Feeder' (Earl of Orkney, 1014 to 1065). Thorfinn is generally believed to have been Macbeth's half-brother, sharing as mother Doada, daughter of Malcolm II (1005-1034), King of Scotland of the dynasty of Kenneth Macalpin, the semi-legendary first King of Scotland.

Macbeth was killed in 1057. A year later the Canmore ('Bighead') kings of Scotland took over. During the long reign of David I, 1085-1153, the Scottish claims to the Norse provinces became more assertive. From 1103 to 1158, when Earl Rognvald died (was murdered), the Orkney earldom, which included Caithness and Sutherland, was in constant dispute and division. The Scottish kings were always ready to listen to and sometimes take part in intrigues to displace the Orkney earls, and David was particularly disposed this way. So it comes as no surprise to find Svein Asleifarson from time to time at the Scottish court and especially conspiring with King David about affairs in Orkney, for Svein was no great loyalist. In fact, he had much to do with the ultimate return of Caithness and Sutherland to *de facto* Scottish rule.

Over the same period the kings of Norway were striving to assert *their* authority in Orkney and Shetland, for the earls of Orkney had got into the habit of behaving as independent sovereigns, referring to the king when they wanted his help or a favour rather than when he ordered obedience. Rule in Orkney by the kings of Norway became more or less consolidated during the reign of Hakon IV (Hakonsson), 1217-1263, who died in Orkney in 1263 on his return from the battle of Largs. It was in this battle that the Norse kings lost control of the Hebrides, an area that remained in some confusion as to who really ruled there, the King of Scotland or the various 'Lords of the Isles' until the time of Bruce.

Significant turnaround began with the long earlships of Harald Maddadarson, 1138-1206, and of his son John, 1206-1203. Harald began his rule as junior earl in a twenty-year partnership with Rognvald (1138-1158). He was part Scots, his father being Maddad, Earl of Atholl and his mother, Margaret, daughter of Hakon Paulsson. Though there had been various nominal grants to Norse chiefs of the 'earldom' of Caithness, it was via the Maddadarson connection that the Scots became claimants to the Orkney earlship and, by the same token, gained a legitimate 'reclaim' on Caithness. During the transition to wholly Scottish rule, the Norse blood line got thinner and weaker. It was this transition, as we shall see, that made it possible for the Sinclairs to take over in Caithness (and Orkney) in 1336.[1]

Undivided Scottish rule in Caithness came about gradually, but was more or less effectively established some years before the battle of Largs (1263), which 'historians customarily mark as the end of Scandinavian rule in the north'. Maddadarson and his son John, partially Scottish, provided the link between Norse and Scottish (Sinclair) earldom in Caithness.

We return to the topic of Svein Asleifarson and his part in the affairs of Caithness during the critical years of the earlships of Paul II, Earl of

---

1 An excellent account of the transition is to be found in Thomson's *History of Orkney*, op cit.

Orkney and Caithness, Rognvald and Erlend III and Harald Maddadarson, from 1123 to 1206, and in particular Svein's activities in the locality of Wick. Svein's home territory was the island of Gairsay in Wide Firth, Orkney, a small island consisting of a 'low brown cone', used by him mainly as a base for his frequent journeyings. On the strength of various concessions and commissions from the earls, he had a couple of bases too on the Caithness coast, one at 'Dungesbi' (Duncansby), the other at Lambaborg, some ten miles south. In notes to the *Orkneyinga Saga* Lambaborg is identified as Buchollie, a castle of some notoriety in the days of the Sinclairs.[1]

Lambaborg was his own castle. A ruin still stands on the site, a narrow neck of land sticking well out to sea, cut off from easy access by a deep trench cut across the peninsula. It is a gloomy place, fierce and forbidding. The original 'keep' which must have been Svein's fortress, disappeared a long time ago. Svein used it as a safe and almost impregnable pirate's lair, from which he sailed on profitable raids and in which he stored loot. Duncansby, on the other hand, does not appear to have been a stronghold. Svein inherited it from his father, Olaf Hroaldsson, who had a farm there and was appointed by Rognvald as the Earl's 'governor' of Caithness, a duty that for a time after Olaf's death Svein seems to have exercised himself. Death came to Olaf in one of the most common ways of destroying their enemies practised by the Vikings, burning them in their own homes. The deed was done by a brutal character called Olvir Brawl (or Breastrope), who had recently been worsted by Svein in an Orkney battle. The raid on Duncansby was, however, probably instigated by Frakokk, a scheming unpleasant lady who had sought in 1123 to alter succession to the earldom by poisoning one of the brothers Harald and Paul. Unfortunately for him, Harald put on the poisoned shirt intended for his brother. For this Frakokk was banished to Caithness.

Frakokk had a grudge against Svein on another count. They probably intended the victim to be Svein himself, for he had gone over to Duncansby to spend Christmas with his mother and father, Asleif and Olaf, but Svein had gone fishing three days before. When Olvir and his five men arrived, Asleif and his brother Gunnar went to visit friends, so that only the old man and some servants were left in the house. The raiders 'surrounded the house, set fire to it, and burned to death Olaf and five other men, though they allowed the rest to go

---

1 Robert P Gunn *Swein Asleifson: A Northern Pirate*; Latheronwheel, Caithness; Whittle Publishing (1990).

outside. Then Olvir went off with all the property they could lay hands on.'

At this time Svein was hesitating between allegiances. He had provided help to Paul, who was contesting the earlship with Rognvald. Svein bided his time on the matter of revenge, undertaking several expeditions and enterprises during the next year or two. On one of these occasions he found himself at Atholl, staying with Maddad and Margaret his wife, Paul's sister. It seemed evident to Svein that Paul's days as a co-earl were numbered, and in a consummate act of treachery, he kidnapped Paul while he was staying at Westness, Rousay on the Eynhallow Sound, and abducted him by force to Atholl. He had probably been put up to it by Margaret, who wanted Paul out of the way so that her young son, Harald, might be accepted in his place as co-earl. She asked Svein 'to go to see Earl Rognvald in Orkney and ask which he would prefer as co-ruler, Earl Paul or Harald, the son of herself and Maddad, three years old at the time'. There can be little doubt which of the two Rognvald would have preferred, since during the last year or two Paul had given him a very rough time. In fact Paul is said to have overheard the announcement, and knowing what it portended, offered to relinquish his claims anyway, and never go back to Orkney. This made no difference to his fate. The chronicler writes:

> After that Svein Asleifarson set off for Orkney, but Earl Paul stayed behind in Scotland. This is Svein's account of what happened, but according to some people, the story was a lot uglier: Margaret hired Svein Asleifarson to blind her brother, Earl Paul, then put him in prison, and later on hired someone else to kill him. We can't say which comes near the truth, but this much is known, that he never came back to Orkney and never gained power in Scotland.

Whether or not Rognvald knew anything about all this – and in spite of his later rise to sainthood, he was during his life neither a very holy man nor an over scrupulous one. In 1138 he became sole Earl of Orkney and Caithness. Two years later he cheerfully accepted the arrangement by which the now five-year old Harald Maddadarson became his co-earl. Needless to say, this young man's admission to earldom did not cramp Rognvald's style at all. The fix was clearly Svein Asleifarson's doing, and it is not surprising to learn that Svein was by this time back in Rognvald's good books. Then, so far as Svein was concerned, came the *quid pro quo:*

WICK OF THE NORTH

One day Svein Asleifarson had a word with Earl Rognvald, asking for men and ships so that he might take his revenge on Olvir and Frakokk for the burning of his father Olaf.

'Don't you think, Svein,' said the Earl, 'that we've little to fear now from Olvir and old Frakokk, who's hardly capable of much?'

'As long as they're alive they'll always cause trouble,' said Svein, 'and after all I've done for you I wouldn't have expected you to refuse me this small favour.'

'How much do I have to give you to satisfy you?' asked the Earl.

'Two ships,' answered Svein, 'both well-fitted out.'

The Earl said that Svein would get what he asked for, and after that Svein prepared for the voyage, sailing south as soon as he was ready to the Moray Firth with a north-easterly wind as far as Banff, a market town in north-coast Scotland. From there he made his way beyond Moray to the Oykel, then on to Atholl where Maddad provided him with guides who knew the mountain and forest route he might choose. From Atholl he travelled by forest and mountain above the settlements till he reached Helmsdale in the centre of Sutherland.[1]

Olvir and Frakokk had posted spies in every direction from which they might expect trouble from Orkney, but they didn't bargain for an attack from this one and had no idea the men were there until Svein led them down the hillside behind Frakokk's farmstead. There Olvir Brawl faced them with sixty men, but though it didn't take long for the fighting to begin there was little resistance. Olvir and his men were unable to get away into the forest so they retreated to the farmhouse, where there was fearful slaughter. Olvir managed to run to Helmsdale River and from there up the mountain, over to the west coast and across to the Hebrides. Now he is out of the story [the 'now' is the saga-writer's].

After Olvir had escaped, Svein and his men went to the farmstead and looted everything they could lay their hands on, then set fire to the house and burned everyone inside to death. That is how Frakokk died.[2]

Svein plundered all over Sutherland before he and his men

---

1 If this location was Helmsdale, the saga-writer is a little out in his geography.
2 *Orkneyinga Saga*, op cit. Section 78 pp 129-130.

went back to their ships. Throughout the summer they lay out at sea, making raids on Scotland, and in the autumn got back to Orkney. Svein came to see Earl Rognvald who gave him a great welcome. Then Svein went across to Duncansby in Caithness where he spent the winter.

WICK COMES INTO THE PICTURE

As we have seen, Wick is mentioned several times in the saga, usually in the context of some dubious or nefarious activities of Svein Asleifarson, who had a considerable foothold in Caithness. The only Norseman named as actually living in Wick was a farmer called Hroald. He seems to have been a man of some importance, and was once visited by Earl Rognvald while Svein Asleifarson was on the rampage in the Hebrides.[1] Hroald had invited Rognvald to a feast. The visit gave rise to another bloody transaction. A warrior called Thorbjorn Clerk (he could evidently read and write), grandson of Frakokk, met Rognvald in Wick to talk about mutual problems. Whatever they talked about, the two of them went back to Orkney in company, The Earl took Hroald's son, Svein, with him as cup-bearer, an honour quite valued in those times – this Svein is not to be confused with the pirate. He is known in the record as Svein Hroaldsson. Thorbjorn appears to have left Rognvald as soon as they arrived in Orkney, went secretly to Gairsay, and in Asleifarson's absence slaughtered two of the men who had been with Svein at the burning of Frakokk.

Svein returned from the Hebrides, and went straight home to Gairsay 'without visiting Earl Rognvald as he usually did at the end of viking expeditions'. The earl found this odd, and shrewdly questioned Thorbjorn Clerk, back with him, as to why he thought it might be. A laconic conversation followed:

> 'It's my guess,' said Thorbjorn, 'that Svein is angry with me for having killed the men who were with him at Frakokk's burning.'
>
> 'I don't want you two at loggerheads,' said the Earl.

After that the Earl went over to Gairsay to arrange a settlement between them, an easy enough task since they both wanted the Earl himself to fix the terms. So he reconciled them

---

[1] The date of this visit is given as 1140 (J. Horne *The County of Caithness;* Wick (1907) p.450)

and the settlement lasted for a long time.

The reconciliation did not really last for long. Svein set off, together with his friend Thorbjorn, on a grudge trip to the Hebrides, having once more persuaded Rognvald to let him have some ships. The enemy he sought had fled from the Hebrides, when he heard that Svein was after him, so 'Svein and his men killed a lot of people there, plundering and burning in a number of places. They picked up plenty of loot.'

When they got back to Duncansby, from where they had set out, a new quarrel arose between Svein and Thorbjorn since they could not agree on how all these winnings should be shared out; everyone should have fair shares, announced Svein, except himself. He was commander-in-chief and, anyway, since 'he was the one for whom the Earl had sent along support', he was entitled to more. All the captains, including Thorbjorn, had to accept Svein's idea of fair shares for, as the saga puts it, 'he had much the greater support there in Caithness'.

Thorbjorn and the others went straight off to Orkney to complain to the earl, who agreed with them that Svein had shown himself, not for the first time, as unjust and a bully. Rognvald recommended to Thorbjorn, however, not to make a fuss, backing up his suggestion with a promise, 'I'll give you as much from my own pocket as you're losing to him'. Thorbjorn accepted the advice and the offer, promising 'not to argue with Svein about this, but,' he continued, 'I'll never be his friend again and I'll find some other way to humiliate him.'

The sequel centres again on Wick. While he was away in the Hebrides, Svein, as Rognvald's 'governor general' in Caithness, put in charge at Duncansby a 'vicious trouble-maker' named Margad Grimsson, who took the opportunity to work out one of his own grudges. This was against Hroald of Wick, who was in the habit of giving refuge to some of the victims of Margad's bullying. Margad 'went south to Wick on business with twenty others and before he came back he set upon the farmer Hroald and killed him at his own home along with a number of his men'. Svein knew that this misbehaviour of one of his ruffians would not go down well with the earl, so, as a precaution,

> Svein gathered his forces and went over to Lambaborg ready to take a stand. The fortress stood on a sea-cliff with a stoutly built stone wall to landward. The cliff stretched quite a distance along the coast. They committed many a robbery in Caithness, taking the loot into their stronghold and soon became

thoroughly unpopular.

Svein's misdeeds, of course, soon came to the ears of the earl. Together with a group of chieftains, one of whom was Thorbjorn, Rognvald set off for Duncansby, and learning there that the bird had flown to Lambaborg, they sailed on to Svein's rock fortress, about ten miles down the coast. Conditions must have been reasonably good, for the earl and Svein set up an exercise in megaphone diplomacy. If Svein would hand over Margad, the earl promised there would be no repercussions, but Svein, with a little more compunction and loyalty than usual said, 'I don't much feel like surrendering Margad to Svein Hroaldsson, or to any other enemies of mine with you now.' Svein Hroaldsson was, of course, the son of the 'farmer' of Wick whom Margad had killed, and revenge or suitable compensation to the family was a cardinal principle of Viking law, so Margad could expect little mercy. 'But,' added Svein Asleifarson, 'as for you, my lord, I'll gladly be reconciled.'

This rejoinder called from Thorbjorn Clerk a furious and contemptuous response: 'Listen to the way the traitor talks'. Rognvald cut short the slanging match that set in between the two old enemies, and in which Svein Hroaldsson also had joined. The earl and his party decided that the best thing would be to lay seige to the Lambaborg

Fig 3 Lambaborg – The site of Svein's Castle, later the castle of the Mowats, known as Buchollie.

(From T. Pennant's Tour of Scotland, 1769).

fortress; it was impossible to storm it, so the besiegers settled down to starve out the defenders. Inevitably, supplies in the castle began to run low, so Svein called together his men:

> 'As I see it,' he said, 'the least respectable thing we could do would be to starve here, then surrender to our enemies. It's all turned out as might have been expected. Compared with Earl Rognvald, we're short on luck and wisdom. We've tried for peace and a settlement for my comrade Margad and we've got neither. On the other hand, I know that there are others here who have a chance of coming to terms, but personally, I don't care to put my head under the axe. I know it's unfair that so many should have to suffer because of his problems, but I can't bring myself to abandon him, not just yet.'

> After that, Svein tied together all the rope they could find and during the night they lowered Svein and Margad from the wall of the stronghold down into the sea. They started swimming and managed to get ashore beyond the end of the cliff, then travelled through Sutherland to Moray and from there to Banff.

On their way south Svein and Margad fell in with an Orkney cargo-boat, and true to form, Svein led his new companions on a spree which took them to the monastery on the Isle of May in the entrance to the Firth of Forth, where they enjoyed the hospitality of the monks and then looted the monastery. He then visited King David (1124-1153) in Edinburgh who seems to have given 'Svein a friendly welcome', and learned from Svein a good deal about affairs in Orkney and Caithness and arranged for Margad to stay with him out of harm's way. The King sent messengers to Rognvald to 'make things up with Svein'; the old pirate then returned to his estates in Gairsay and Duncansby. This was not the end of Svein's career of engineering betrayals and alliances in connection with the Orkney earldom.

The full story behind the last mention of Wick in the *Orkneyinga Saga* is too long and complicated to be repeated here except in the barest details. As usual, Svein Asleifarson is at the centre of the trouble. In the later years of the rule of Rognvald as Earl of Orkney (1136-1158), a nephew of his, Erlend, son of Harald of the poisoned shirt, put in a claim 'for the title of earl, and authority over Caithness', for which purpose he visited his 'kinsman Malcolm, King of Scots' (this was Malcolm IV, and the year must have been about 1153. Malcolm ruled from May 1153 to December 1165). The claim was based on the reputed grant of the same earldom to Harald, Erlend's

EARLY DAYS

father, by David I, a grant which, if ever made, had never been consummated since Harald died in 1123.

Rognvald was away at the time on a visit to the Holy Land, a pilgrimage of the kind often made by kings and princes of these times with ill-doings on their conscience. In his absence, his co-earl, Harald Maddadarson, took up Erlend's challenge. Moves were made to reach a settlement, but at that point Erlend extended his claim to include half of Orkney as well as Caithness. A truce in the dispute was arranged while Erlend went to Norway to get support from the King of Norway for his claim on Orkney, leaving behind one of his chieftains with sufficient forces to ensure that the claim would not lapse in his absence.

Needless to say, Svein Asleifarson was there helping to keep the waters muddied. In fact, his brother Gunni, had 'fathered a child on Margaret, Earl Harald's mother' (we have met this lady before, when she, together with Svein's assistance, got Earl Paul out of the way thus enabling Harald Maddadarson to become co-earl), so Harald made him an outlaw, and this 'created bad feeling between Harald and Svein Asleifarson'. Svein was accordingly rather disposed towards helping out Erlend, away in Norway, and is reported in the sagas as being 'at Freswick in Caithness at the time, looking after the estate of his stepsons'. Evidently, to counter any move that the Erlend faction, assisted perhaps by Svein, might make, 'Earl Harald travelled over Caithness and spent the winter in residence at Wick'.

Keeping up the pressure, Svein lost no opportunity short of outright war, of harassing Harald, and the story continues that,

> on the Wednesday of Holy Week [this would probably be the spring of 1154], Svein Asleifarson happened to go up to Lambaborg with a few men and they saw a cargo-boat travelling south across the Pentland Firth. They guessed this must be Earl Harald's men sent to collect the tributes in Shetland. Svein told his companions to come down to the ships with him and sail out to the cargo-boat, which is what they did, capturing it along with everything on board and ferrying Earl Harald's men ashore. The men travelled on foot to Wick and told the Earl about it, but he had little to say apart from remarking that he and Svein were taking turns at making money. He billeted them out over Easter, and the men of Caithness said that the Earl was on well-trodden ground.

That is the entire sum of Wick's reported involvement in the affairs of Norse Caithness. The saga goes on to describe the savage unravelling of the tangle in these affairs, a tale of chicanery, temporary alliances, abductions and robbery, appeals to both the Scottish and Norwegian kings, which ended with the mysterious murder of Erlend at Christmas, 1154, when his body was found under a pile of seaweed on the little island of Damsay in the Wide Firth of Orkney near what is now Finstown, with a spear-shaft sticking out of the pile.

Rognvald had come back from Palestine and played his part in concluding the action by which he and Harald returned to amicable co-earlship. Rognvald met his own end in a nasty encounter with the treacherous and unpredictable Thorbjorn Clerk in 1158, which occurred as the two earls, Rognvald and Harald, closed in on the rebel at a farm in Forsie, on the Forss Water some miles west of Thurso. Both Rognvald and Thorbjorn were fatally wounded in the engagement. The event is actually dated as 'the fifth day after the Feast of Assumption', which would therefore have been 2 August, 1158. Harald took the body 'in great style' to Kirkwall, where it was buried in St Magnus' Cathedral, Rognvald's greatest work and still the glory of Orkney, a magnificent Romanesque church on latitude 59°N. He was made a saint like his uncle, Magnus, in whose honour the building was raised. His remains are inhumed in a north-aisle pillar of the chancel of the church, while those of Magnus lie in the stonework of the matching south-aisle pillar, uncle and nephew, the most famous of all the earls of Orkney.

Earl Harald Maddadarson became sole Earl of Orkney and Caithness, his long rule lasting until 1206. From the time of Maddadarson onwards the Scottish rather than the Norse political influence came to prevail in Caithness and in due course in Orkney itself. Svein Asleifarson continued his adventurous career, mainly on good terms with Harald, and is believed to have taken a leading part in the last attempt of the Orkney Vikings to interfere in the affairs of Ireland, probably in the year 1171. He was leading an attack on Dublin, which he thought he had captured, but was out-manoeuvred on the day after the supposed capture, by the citizens of that city who had dug pits around the town into which Svein and his men fell as they approached to receive tribute. 'The story goes,' says the chronicler, 'that Svein was the last to die, and these were his last words: "Whether or not I'm to fall today, I want everyone to know that I'm the retainer of the holy Earl Rognvald, and now he's with

God, it's in him I'll put my trust"......'

The tale concludes:

> The survivors amongst Svein's men went straight back to their ships, and there's nothing worth recording of their journey except that they got back to Orkney. That, then is the end of Svein's story, but people say that apart from those of higher rank than himself, he was the greatest man the western world has ever seen in ancient and modern times.

A high claim for a very tough rogue. He certainly left his mark on the minds of his contemporaries, and by this token, had a considerable effect on the lives of the people of Caithness in the twelfth century. There is one other explicit reference in the *Orkneyinga Saga* to the doings of Svein Asleifarson in the Wick area, in fact, to Freswick. Svein became involved in the complicated intrigues by which Harald Maddadarson and another pretender to the earldom, Erlend Haraldsson (nominated a joint earl by the king of Norway 1157), sought to displace or kill Earl Rognvald (1136-1138). It is, as usual, too complicated a tale to repeat here, telling of an attempt by some of Svein's men, sent over by him in a small ship from Orkney, to rescue one of Erlend's men imprisoned by Earl Harald in what is described in the saga as 'a fortress' near to 'the farmstead at Freswick.' The raid was evidently successful, the prisoner, Arnfinn, being released and one of Harald's men captured and carried away (See section 93 of *Orkneyinga Saga*). Freswick, of course, has been the scene of recent excavations, where considerable evidence of Norse occupation has been revealed. In the light of these revelations, Barbara Crawford[1] suggests for Freswick some significance both as a defensive site (very probable in view of the saga reference to 'fortress') and as some sort of centre of trading activity, and perhaps fishing[2]. It seems possible that Freswick, approachable via a sandy bay and possessing a creek (or 'cove' as referred to in the saga), became a place of greater importance in Viking times than Wick or Thurso.

Nothing in the tale gives much idea of the ways of life of the folk of Caithness in these turbulent times. Farming was clearly the chief means of livelihood, with the work being done by the various chiefs' 'hirdmen', liable to be called out from time to time to fight intruders along the straths and to man the ships in which Caithnessmen, as readily as Orkneymen, defended their coasts and went a-viking. There

---

1 B. Crawford, op cit p. 138
2 Ibid, p. 134

is no reference anywhere to fishing as a means of supplementing diet, thought doubtless common folk, mostly Gaelic in origin and perhaps even in speech, went out from the geos in their cobbles or small curraghs for inshore herrings, lythe and haddock.

As for Wick itself, it could not have been much of a centre, a farm or two ('garth' or 'bolstadr' along the Wick River, with some 'kvis' – quoys – along the rough hillsides). It would have had no 'port facilities'. The Bay was then much too open to North Sea storms for the maintenance and survival of such structures, and in any case, the Vikings would enter the river on the tide and sail up far enough to be safe and to beach their war vessels and knorrs where there was firm enough ground beyond the muddy reaches for disembarkation, boarding, lading and unlading. There was probably no bridge, but the Wick river even then must have been easily fordable at low tide.

That the place is named Wick at all is sufficient indication that this is where the Vikings came.[1] The *Orkneyinga Saga* confirms that the locality was fairly well known, and that at least one substantial farm – perhaps a 'bu', that of Hroald, was here, a good enough place in which to entertain Earl Rognvald. It is rather unlikely that this was Auldwick (Old Wick) Castle, the ancient structure on a tongue of land between two deep geos to the south of Wick town, consisting now of little more than the spectacular remnants of a twelfth or thirteenth century 'keep', but like Buchollie, cut off from easy access on the mainland side by a deep ditch. It would clearly have suited the needs of Svein Asleifarsson, probably quite as well as his Lambaborg, and may, for all we know, have had some connection with him. There is no documentary provenance to connect Auldwick with the Vikings at all, but the mode of construction, using the native flagstones in a manifestly dry-walling technique, suggests strongly the same sort of thinking that governed the construction of 'Cubbie Roo's' castle on Wyre, Orkney.[2] Back home in Norway the Vikings were little familiar with stone building of any kind, but there is ample evidence that when they came to Orkney and Caithness, where easily worked

---

[1] This at least is the accepted view. At one time there was a notion among scholars, over familiar as many doubtless were with the classic as against more modern studies – that the name was derived from *vicus*, the Latin for 'village'. There are no classical references to warrant the view. (Mentioned in *Statistical Account of Scotland, 1794*. See also A T Simpson and S Stevenson: *Historic Wick* (A83); also Nicolaisen, 1970, p 192).

[2] 'Cubbie Roo' is the popular nickname for Kolbein Hruga, a semi-legendary chief who built a castle on Wyre. Its ruins are still there. Historic Scotland claims it as the oldest stone castle in Scotland. Hruga's son is said to have been the influential Bishop Bjarni of Orkney during Harald's rule. *(continued at foot of next page)*.

building blocks from the Devonian beds were readily available, they made good use of such material, both for their homes and for defence purposes.

We shall come to Auldwick again, when in the fourteenth century it has a recorded occupation and defensive role in the area. But for the present, we must leave it as 'very probably Viking'.

(continued from foot of previous page). Additional Note: Another thirteenth century reference to Wick (see *Historic Wick*, op cit) relates that 'in 1290, when a party of Englishmen were about to take ship from there to the Orkneys to receive into their custody Margaret, Maid of Norway, her death in October, 1290 made further travel unnecessary.' (K. Nicholson: *Scotland: the Later Middle Ages;* Edinburgh (1974).

There is also a fourteenth century mention: 'In 1304 two burgesses were sent from Inverness to Wick to arrest a vessel freighted with wool and hides, but which was refusing to pay the king's customs. By the time they arrived the erring merchants had fled leaving one on shore who was captured and "put under good bail by the custom of the country".' (CDS (ii) 441 – see *Historic Wick*, op cit).

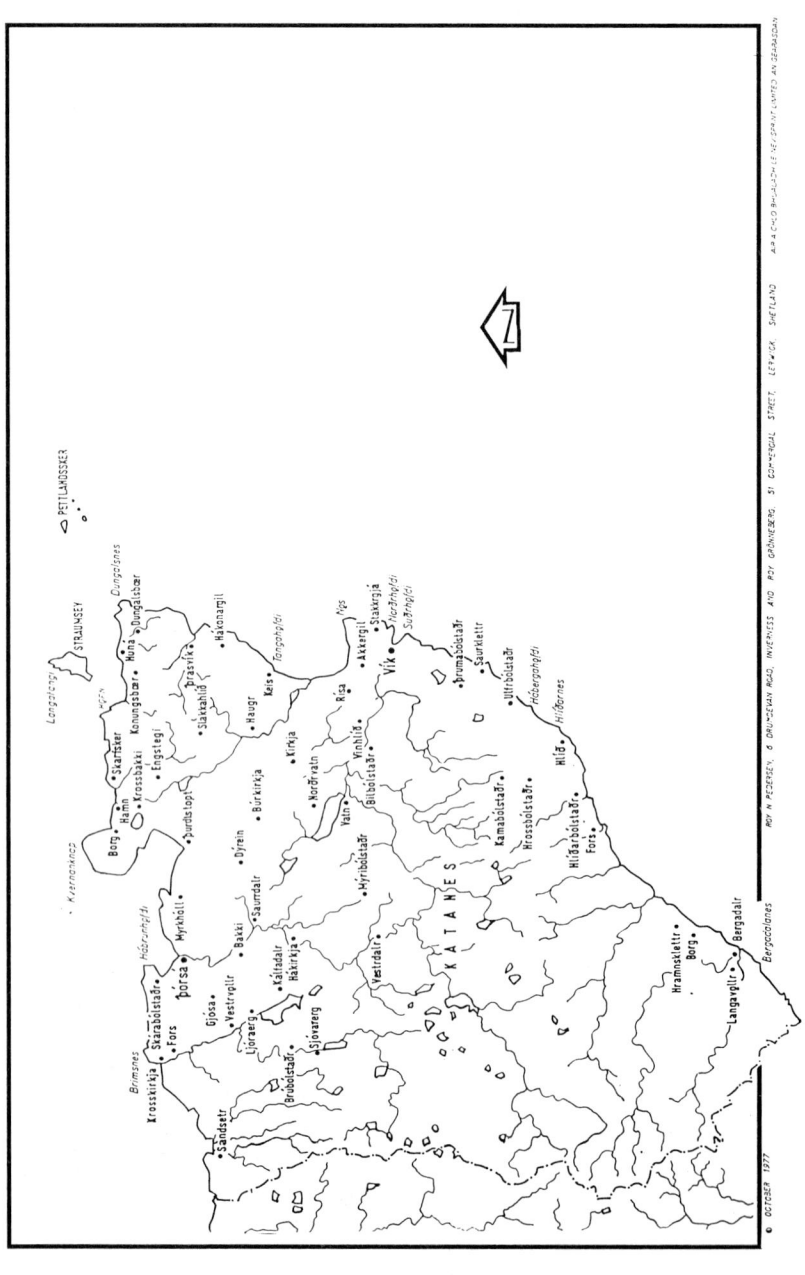

Fig 4 Katanes in Viking Times.

(Adapted from Orkneyjar ok Katanes). (Courtesy of Roy N. Pedersen, Inverness).

CHAPTER 3

SINCLAIRS

GETTING to grips with early Wick is a bit like flying in the wind – there isn't much to hold on to. As capital of the northern mainland province, it lacks mediaeval provenance entirely, as compared with Kirkwall, the remarkably advanced chief city of Orkney from which the Norsemen governed their territories. It appears as the only settlement in Caithness on a map dated about 1250 kept in the Bodleian Library; and since it had to be somewhere, a sheriff court was established here in 1503. In 1589 Wick gained the status of royal burgh during the reign of King James VI – later James I of England. Neither event says much for the size and state of the place except that it was relatively easy to get to from Edinburgh, such as it was. Its importance was determined by the needs and conditions of life in what must have been one of the poorest earldoms of Scotland. It remained the patrimony of Sinclairs, a prestigious family which arrived in 1379 and is still influential in the area.

Of all the identifiable influences shaping the affairs of Caithness after the departure of the Norsemen, and hence Wick, that of the ubiquitous Sinclairs was the longest continuing and most significant, until the late eighteenth century at least. Accordingly, we must take a brief look at the lives and doings of various members of this remarkable family, beginning with a glance at the peculiar circumstances which brought these 'foreigners' to the north of Scotland.

Though not a very common name in Scotland as a whole (it is 64th in the list), Sinclair is common in Caithness and the most common name of all in Orkney. On the face of it this is strange, since it is neither Gaelic nor Norse. By contrast many Caithness place-names are distinctively Norse in origin and those of Orkney even more so. Not so strange when we recognise that Sinclair lords of varying degrees from earl downwards were, from the later fourteenth century onwards, the combative masters of the land in both communities, Orkney and Caithness, fiercely combative with one another as well as with other clan groups.[1]

1 The fact that so many common folk bear the name *(continued at foot of next page)*

Like so many other notable family names in the Scottish Clan books, Sinclair is manifestly not 'Scots' or Gaelic in origin. Most of these names hark back to the Norman Conquest of England, the ancestors having come over with the Conqueror, some of them, like the Bruce, holding feudal rank and property in England long before they gained a Scottish connection. Debrett explains that the 'Sinclair' title is the accepted pronunciation of 'St Clair', a name which is held to originate from the village of St Clare near Pont l'Evêque in Normandy. The fact is that once the Scottish monarchy became more or less hereditary, it took up the forms and aspirations – if not all the characteristics of feudal overlordship of land and vassals, on the lines of the regimes of England and France. Kings of the Macmalcolm (or Canmore) dynasty (1058 to 1290 – it ended with a Queen). The Scottish kings got into the habit of inviting experienced English warlords, especially some, like Bruce, who gained territorial footing in Scotland, to take up the feudal rulership of territories they found it difficult themselves to keep in order.

The complicated politics of Caithness from the eleventh to the fourteenth centuries, and to an extent those of Orkney itself, were largely determined by the alternating and sometimes coincident pressures of the kings of Scotland from the south and the kings of Norway, upon Earl Harald Maddadarson (1138-1206), and his sons and their immediate successors (1206-1256). The partially Scottish lineage of these earls (including cousinship with several of the Canmore kings), provided the Scottish kings with increasingly plausible excuses and opportunities for intervention in Caithness, and to some extent also in Orkney.

To attempt here an analysis of the alliances, deals, betrayals and breaches of trust between the earls of the northerly provinces and the kings, interesting though it might be, would be a sidetrack exercise throwing little light on the origins of Wick.[1] The early years of

(continued from foot of previous page) Sinclair in both Orkney and Caithness was nothing to do with possible or imputed noble connection. It was usual here as in other parts of Scotland in the sixteenth and seventeenth centuries when names began to be written down, for people who had no 'surname' and for whom the patronymic was not sufficient, to give as their identity the name of the Lord who employed them or to whom they paid their rents or other dues. Sinclairs were the dominant lords in these localities, so that it is nor surprising to find the name cropping up so frequently. It should be added, too, that the Sinclairs were never organised as a true clan and not accustomed to Gaelic usages; though they have in more recent and romantic times acquired both the tartan and a Gaelic name: *Mac na Ceardadh*.

1 An excellent short account of all these episodes is to be found in Thomson, op cit, pp 68-91.

Harald's earlship provide an interesting example of these complications when, in 1138 he was manoeuvred into the role of co-earl of Orkney with Earl Rognvald. It is believed that Rognvald's acceptance of the arrangement, favoured by David I, the then King of Scotland, was the essential condition of his being recognised as earl in Caithness too. An earnest of Rognvald's good faith with the Scottish king was the presence at the Battle of the Standards in North Yorkshire in 1138 of a contingent from Orkney fighting on the Scottish side.[1]

Harald became sole Earl of Orkney and Caithness in 1158 on the murder in Caithness of Rognvald. He was not an over astute ruler, and found himself from time to time at serious odds with both the kings to whom he nominally owed fealty, with one king or the other upsetting things by recognising – or threatening to recognise – other candidates for the earldom. Unwisely Harald took part in a Norwegian civil war (between the two contending successors of King Magnus Erlingsson – who had succeeded Eyestein – Sigurd, Erlingsson's son and Sverre), sending an invading force to Florvåg near to Bergen (where his force was defeated), thus earning the Norwegian King Sverre's stern hostility and, in the upshot, the permanent and abject submission of himself and future Orkney earls to the Norwegian crown, at least so far as Orkney itself was concerned. King William the Lion of Scotland (1165-1214) on the other hand, invaded the north of Scotland twice partly on account of Harald Maddadarson's reputed treasonable dealings.

The first invasion followed the campaign of 1196 in which Harald's son, Thorfinn, inflicted a defeat on the king's men near to Inverness. Harald had been attempting to regain territory taken from him in Ross and Moray at the time when William was seeking to put Harald Unge (the Younger – a grandson of Earl Rognvald) into the Caithness earldom. William himself is said to have marched north and, perhaps quailing at the danger of going too far in his opposition to the Scottish king, Harald withdrew from encounter and went to meet King William on his own and ask for clemency. William made no bones about it but put Harald in chains, took him to Edinburgh and imprisoned him, at the same time formally depriving him of all the lands he held from the Scottish crown. He was released and allowed

---

1 This fairly pointless battle was fought near to Northallerton in Yorkshire, when David I intervened in the wars between Stephen and Matilda. It gained its name from the banners of St Peter of York, St John of Beverley and St Wilfred of Ripon, mounted on a carriage which preceded the English army. Neither Scots nor English gained a 'victory', but the Scots retreated back to Scotland.

back into his earldom when his son, Thorfinn, had been brought from Orkney to take his place as a hostage.

The King's second invasion of Caithness occurred in 1201, following a sequence of violently unseemly episodes. William had Thorfinn castrated and blinded after Harald Maddadarson had taken the field against his rival, Harald Unge, and killed him in battle. A description of this battle forms the last scenario of the *Orkneyinga Saga*, though its location is not given; it must have been near the coast since Earl Harald is depicted as having 'come ashore' from his ships and deploying 'very much larger forces' than his opponent, Harald the Younger. The banks of the Wick river might well have been the battlefield. The episode is worth repeating:

> Sigurd Mite [he is described in another version as 'Sigurd Minnow', a valiant little man] and Lifolf led the troops of the younger Earl, commanding one wing each. Sigurd Mite was wearing a scarlet tunic and had the front hem tucked under his belt. Some of his men suggested he should do the same with the back, but he told them not to touch it.
>
> 'They won't be seeking my back today,' he said.
>
> When they had formed up, the battle got under way, and the fighting was fierce, there were plenty of hard fighting men in the army of Harald the Old, very tough and well-equipped, the bishop's kinsmen, for instance, as well as many of the other captains. After a while Sigurd Mite was killed, fighting bravely like a true champion. Among the others, Lifolf fought best and the Caithness people say that he cut his way three times through the enemy ranks before he was killed and died a hero's death. Once both Lifolf and Sigurd were dead, the rest of the army scattered.
>
> Earl Harald the Younger was killed near some peat-diggings, and that same night a great light could be seen where his blood had been spilt. People in Caithness think of him as a true saint and a church stands where he was killed. He was buried there on the headland, and as a result of his virtues, great miracles have been performed by God as a reminder that Harald wished to go to Orkney and join his kinsmen, Earl Magnus and Earl Rognvald.
>
> After the battle, Earl Harald the Old laid the whole of Caithness under his rule, then went straight back to Orkney, boasting of his great victory.

This time the Scottish king sold the Caithness province to King

Rognvald Gudrodsson of the Kingdom of Man (a cousin of Harald); and this Rognvald raised an army and marched to Caithness to make good his claim to the earldom. The invading army melted at the first sign of opposition, and Harald was riding high, even hoping for the help of King John of England in his opposition to William. Then came the unfortunate business of the maiming of Adam, Bishop of Caithness, who spoke out against Harald's 'treachery', upon which William came north again, meeting Harald's possibly superior force at 'Eysteindalr' (Ousdale) on the border of Caithness. Again there was no stand up fight, for neither side was disposed to push matters too far and the episode concluded with 'diplomatic activity'. On this occasion (1201), Harald was forced to pay to the King of Scotland a hefty fine of 'every fourth penny in Caithness' (of tax). But, concludes Thomson, Harald 'now received undisputed control over all of Caithness and so he may have considered himself fortunate to have come out of the Scottish wars as well as he did.'[1]

CAITHNESS COMES TO SCOTLAND

The earlship of Harald's two sons, John and David (1206-1230 – David was co-earl until he died in 1214), carried Caithness further away from Norway and closer to undivided Scottish rule. Their rule was troubled by further tensions between the earls and their kings. It ended with the murder of John in Thurso by the King of Norway's 'sysselman' (representative of the king's interests and estates in Orkney),[2] possibly as the result of hot heads at a 'bout of heavy drinking'. Hanef, the sysselman, holed up in 'Cubbie Roo's castle' (he may have been Kolbein Hruga's son) on Wyre, which the dead earl's followers beseiged. They failed to take the castle, but the king of

---

[1] This potted account of events is taken from Thomson, op cit. However, various critical details are questioned by Barbara Crawford, in her study, *The Earls of Orkney-Caithness and their Relations with Norway and Scotland, 1158-1470*. She suggests, for instance, that William himself did not come north on either occasion; that Harald did not sue for terms with William quite so abjectly as the conventional view indicates, that in fact he had no need to do so, since William was less anxious to enforce his authority in Caithness than is sometimes supposed – it was far away from Edinburgh, and as the Norse drive southwards weakened the province's strategic importance was lessened; that the 'sale' of Caithness to Rognvald Gudrodsson of Man was less a genuine transaction than a continuation of the game of fostering in the province rivalry between claimants and so weaken the earl's rule. Crawford calls the battle of 1198 in which Harald Unge was killed 'the battle of Wick', but does not identify the battleground. Neither does anyone else.

[2] The *sysselman* was a king's officer, first appointed in Orkney by King Sverre Florvåg following Harald Maddadarson's attack at Florvag (1194), with the duty of looking after the king's interests and estates in earldom lands.

Norway was invited to settle the matter. On the return journey from a voyage in 1232 over to Norway to settle the terms of the agreement between the earl's men and the king, the entire delegation, consisting it seems of the earl's kinsmen, was drowned in a storm.

The incident came to be known as the loss of the 'Godings Ship', 'Goding' signifying 'important leader owing his position to kinship'. It served to mark a break in the record of the earls of Orkney and Caithness, described by Thomson as a 'period of almost impenetrable obscurity'. The next seven earls, about whom very little is known, are usually described as the 'Angus' earls, on account of a connection with the Angus family, itself a shadowy line. It seems likely that the Angus claim to Caithness resulted from a marriage between an Angus son and a daughter of Earl John, who had no sons; it was taken up in 1231 by Magnus, second son of Gilbride, Earl of Angus, who is listed as Malcolm II, Earl of Orkney and Caithness, who ruled in Orkney until 1239 and was followed by his brother Gilbert. From then on Angus son succeeded father for nearly a hundred years until 1321, when again direct heirs seem to have run out.

From 1331 another line of earls took over, this time by an even more bizarre succession, through a great-grandmother. By this, Malise IV, 7th Earl of Strathearn, gained the Orkney-Caithness earldom, in addition to his own earldom, to be succeeded by his son, Malise V; and after him came the most puzzling of all earls of Orkney, Erengisle, a Swede who arrived by the curious route of marriage to Agnetta, second daughter of Malise V. It was by no means an uncontested succession, and what the family historian of the Sinclairs calls the 'Disputed Succession', fills the gap between the Strathearns and the Sinclairs, from 1357, when Erengisle was ousted from the job, to 1379 when Henry St Clair took over as Earl of Orkney.

It would neither be profitable nor very interesting in the context of the present account, an outline of the history of Wick, for us to divert effort and to enter too deeply here into the complexities, turns and twists of these interim dynastic sequences which, however, provided the route by which the Sinclairs came on to the scene in the most northerly province of Scotland. Those who wish to delve will find elsewhere a thesis and publications that have gone quite thoroughly into these rather arcane issues.[1]

1 These include Crawford: *The Earls of Orkney*, op cit. Rev Angus Mackay: *History of the Province of Cat (Caithness and Sutherland) from the Earliest Times to 1615*; Wick, Peter Reid (1914); and extremely informative, R. Saint-Clair: *The Saint-Clairs of the Isles*; Aukland, NZ (1898).

THE SINCLAIRS COME TO CAITHNESS

The 'Disputed Succession' brought on to the scene three claimants who had on the face of it little right or chance of succession to the dignities of Earl of Orkney and Earl of Caithness. From now on the two became separated, except for a short period in the fifteenth century when they were brought together again by the third Sinclair (we should still speak of St Clair) Earl of Orkney, Lord William, in 1455, only a few years before the Earldom of Orkney itself was detached entirely from its allegiance to the crown of Norway.[1]

A certain Thomas Sinclair is reputed to have held the post of 'ballivus' or 'baillie' in Orkney for the king of Norway in the year 1364. If, as sometimes supposed, a genuine contender for the earlship, he disappears almost immediately. Henry, Lord of Roslin, was the first authentic Sinclair Earl of Orkney, awarded the dignity by King Robert II, grandson of The Bruce. Sinclairs had been among the specially favoured retainers and friends of the kings of Scotland. Henry's father had been one of the five knights who carried King Robert I's heart in a casket to the Holy Land in 1329 for it to be buried in the Church of the Holy Sepulchre. His great-grandfather, William de St Clair, had been made Lord of Roslin (or Rosslyn) by King Alexander III in 1280 for services rendered. Another Sinclair had been Bishop of Dunkeld, premier bishop of Scotland. So that the Sinclairs were not unknown adventurers from nowhere. There was even a connection with Orkney-Caithness, for Sir Henry St Clair, son of the first Lord of Roslin is described in one genealogy as 'ballivus' of Orkney.[2]

Henry, first Sinclair Earl of Orkney, was formally granted his earlship of Orkney by King Hakon VI of Norway, reluctantly perhaps,

---

[1] As a historical event this does not much concern us here, but it is worth mentioning that in 1468 the Danish King (now King of all Scandinavia, including Norway), short of cash to provide a dowry for his daughter, Margaret, who was to marry King James III of Scotland, pawned the Orkney earldom, Orkney and Shetland, to Scotland. This is usually referred to in Orcadian history as the 'impignoration', a somewhat grander word than 'pawning'. By it Orkney became Scottish, and has remained so, since the pawn-ticket has never been redeemed. Caithness, no longer in any sense Norwegian, was not involved in the deal. In any case, the earlship itself was now firmly in Sinclair, that is, Scottish hands.

[2] The rise of the Sinclairs in Scottish politics is a complex and not well understood phenomenon. Not only were Sir William, first Lord of Roslin, and his sons and grandsons, well thought of by the Scottish kings; they and their successors also became much involved in the affairs of the Scottish Freemasons, having it is believed, inherited mysterious duties connected with the Knights Templars, brutally suppressed by the French kings in the early fourteenth century. The Chapel of Roslin became the virtual ritual headquarers of the Masonic movement in Scotland.

but there was no other acceptable claimant. His claim, such as it was, came through his mother, Isabella, eldest of the five daughters of Malise (V), the Earl of Strathearn, Caithness and Orkney. There was little Norwegian relationship left in the line. The kings of Norway had no acceptable candidates, but in any case had been losing their grip not only in Caithness but also on Orkney. After the departure of Erengisle it becomes quite unclear as to who exactly was the Earl of Caithness for some years after the death of Malise V in 1345.

Ironically, the more Scottish of the two provinces, Caithness did not come to this Henry at all. One of the claimants during the period of disputed succession was Alexander de l'Ard, who reckoned to have a claim through his mother, Matilda, another daughter of Malise, and he was appointed in 1375 for a year by the King of Norway as 'Governor' of Orkney, presumably to see how he shaped up. He failed to impress and was relieved of his post in Orkney and was forced under pressure from Robert II, the Stewart King of Scotland at that time – no doubt on petition from Isabella, mother of Henry Sinclair – to resign any claims he may have had to the 'Castle of Brathwell' (Braal, near to Halkirk) 'and all lands in Caithness, or any part of Scotland' which he had inherited in right of his mother, Matilda de Strathearn'. David, for whatever reason, however, returned the dignity to the crown, leaving Caithness ostensibly without an earl as chief of its fortunes.

'Earl' was at this time the highest dignity used in Scotland, and it is fairly evident that for the next sixty or so years no-one was especially willing to accept the status of Earl of Caithness, perhaps because of its poor revenues and high responsibilities. In fact, Isabella, widow of William Sinclair of Roslin, and mother of Henry, the new Earl of Orkney, maintained a *de facto* hold on the Caithness earldom until she died in 1424, at least, she held on to the revenues of its estates. On her death the king, now James I, the third of the Stewart kings, formally bestowed the earldom on a kinsman, Walter Stewart, Earl of Athol, who forthwith assigned it to his son Alan, who died a few years later, leaving Walter with the unvalued earldom. In 1437 Walter became involved in the plot which resulted in the assassination of King James, and was himself executed by the new king, James II.[1] Thus Caithness yo-yoed back to the crown. It was awarded in 1450 to George, Lord

---

1 The actual murder took place in the Dominican Friary of Perth, and was led by Athol's grandson, Sir Robert Stewart. James, seeking to escape, was caught and stabbed to death in a sewer. All the conspirators were tried and executed with unusual 'ritual ferocity' early in the reign of the seven-year old James II.

Crichton, Chancellor and Lord High Admiral of Scotland, an eminent member of an up-and-coming family in Scottish affairs. This arrangement did not last either. In 1455 James was persuaded to restore the Caithness earldom to the Sinclairs, and the two earldoms, Caithness and Orkney were briefly reunited in the person of Lord William Sinclair, Earl of Orkney.

Orkney came firmly and unambiguously under Scottish rule on the marriage of James III to Margaret of Denmark in 1468. William, the earl, formally surrendered the title and jurisidiction of Orkney in 1471 to the crown. Sinclair 'earldom' as such thus disappeared at a stroke, though the Sinclairs remained as a power in the land until 1560. William, earl at the time of the impignoration, was a shrewd man. Knowing the way the wind was blowing on both sides of the North Sea, he began building up his private holdings of land in Orkney and Caithness, and these, known to the lawyers as 'conquest lands', remained in the possession of the Sinclair family. Thus, though no longer earls, the successive heads of the Orkney branch of the family survived not only as substantial landlords, modern fashion, in their own right; they also became 'tacksmen' of the entire jurisdiction, that is, administrators with full powers in the islands responsible to the king for their good government and the collection of rents and taxes, especially the 'scat', the tax payable by occupiers of land. The 'tack' was a straightforward financial transaction, the person to whom it was awarded paying to the crown an agreed annual fee. First 'tacksman' of Orkney was William's grandson, Lord Henry, who gained the tack in 1489. Henry, in a flush of patriotism, went off in 1513 to fight for King James IV and was killed on Flodden field.[1] His widow, Margaret Hepburn, continued the tack until 1540, when it was taken up by another Sinclair, James Sinclair of Brecks, a rather distant relative of the main Orkney line, whose chief representative at that time was Lord William, son of Lord Henry. Though the fortunes of the Orkney Sinclairs are of no further concern to us here, we shall

---

1 However little impact the affairs of Caithness may have been making during these years on the affairs of Scotland – and *vice versa*, the fifteenth and sixteenth centuries were exciting times in Scotland and in England. In 1485 the Tudors ousted the Yorkist kings, notably in the person of Richard III who was killed at the Battle of Bosworth in 1485. Henry VII, the victor of Bosworth, was succeeded in 1509 by Henry VIII, who inaugurated the glories of the Tudor reigns. Among his objectives Henry sought to keep France and Scotland from making effective their alliance. King James, however, sent an army into England in August with the idea of hampering Henry's operations in France; he was met by a superior English army at Flodden in Northumberland in 1513. The Scottish defeat was devastating. James was killed, twelve earls, fourteen lords and 10,000 soldiers were lost.

encounter both of these characters again.

As already mentioned, the arrival of Sinclair lords as earls of Orkney did not automatically signify their arrival in Caithness too, however closely the two provinces had been joined in the past. The de L'Ard pretender was compelled to surrender all claims and properties in Caithness to the crown and, as we have seen, the various kings of Scotland from 1375 onwards experimented with several ways of disposing of the jurisdiction, none successful until in 1455 Lord William, third Sinclair Earl of Orkney succeeded in attaching Caithness once more to Orkney, only to lose both fifteen years later.

In fact, after his abdication in 1471, Earl William formally passed over his claims on Caithness to a second son of his named William, in 1476, and this William thus became the first Earl of Caithness solely, and the first of a long line of Sinclair lords of the northern province who, for better or worse, ruled quite despotically and sometimes cruelly and capriciously until the eighteenth century. The line with numerous breaks, contortions and slithers, continues to the present day. Just as important in the affairs of Caithness have been the numerous 'cadet' (and 6 'illegitimate') branches of the family which have proliferated in the province, notably round the coast but also at various strategic locations inland. Several of these have had more impact on Wick than the earls, who never based themselves on the place that became royal burgh and county town.

GOOD EARLS, NOT SO GOOD AND WICKED EARLS

The story of the Sinclairs of Caithness (we will give them a last nod of traditional recognition as the Saint-Clairs as their family chronicler insists) from the time of William, Earl of Caithness, onwards, is a tale of enterprise, ebullience, villainy, tyranny, conquest and violence. The temptation after reading the middle chapters of *The Saint-Clairs of the Ises*, the romantically cast prose of J T Calder and, not least, the highly fluorescent language of the anonymous author who contributed long *Anecdotes Relative to the Earl History of Caithness* to the earliest issues of the *John O'Groat Journal* from 1836 onwards, is to divert wildly from our elusive theme of Wick, for they must be among the most outrageous and entertaining in all the annals of Scotland – and this is saying something.[1] We shall, nevertheless, mention a number of the episodes involving the Sinclair Earls and some of their relatives, off-

1 The series, which ran to about fifteen pieces, began in an early issue of the *John O'Groat Journal*, (1836) began as *Reminiscences of the (continued on foot of next page)*

shoots and connections, which touch on, however lightly the affairs of Wick.

While not a great deal is known about Wick itself during the fifteenth, sixteenth and seventeenth centuries, nor much about associations of Sinclairs with the town, we shall make the most of what there is. A fairly recent summary of the best known facts about Wick puts the matter with stark brevity. Leaping from a reference to the Bodleian map of 1250, the account continues:

> In the year 1503 Wick was made a seat of the sheriff court; in 1589 it was raised to the status of royal burgh by King James VI. The town must have looked a sorry sight when the accolade of royal burgh (giving it important trading rights) was bestowed upon it, as, it had been burned and looted the previous year by the Earl of Sutherland as part of a feud with the Earl of Caithness, who virtually owned the town and the land around it. Wick in the late sixteenth and seventeenth centuries was still apparently a very small town, as judging from a map of 1608 by Timothy Pont[1] . . . . it was divided into four straggling groups of buildings scarcely 1.6km (1 mile) in length.

We shall return to the details of this sparing sketch. The new Earl of Caithness made his home not at Wick – or Old Wick ('Auldwick'), a mile down the coast from the estuary of the Wick river, to which, presumably, the town was attached – but some three miles north, where he built a castle on a rocky promontory facing north just west of Noss Head, now known as Girnigoe castle. It says much for the conditions of the times that one of the first tasks of the new ruler of Caithness was to build for himself a near impregnable fortress on the coast, accessible from land only by one approach. Impressive ruins still stand there. It is a grim, forbidding place and could hardly have been very cosy and comfortable as a family home. A charter dealing with affairs of the earl was executed at Girnigoe Castle in 1496, so that it must have been built or being built then.

Just how dangerous life could be for earls and their ilk is illustrated

---

(continued from foot of previous page) County of Caithness by 'a gentleman whose knowledge of the early history of Caithness has rendered him particularly well qualified for the task'. The gentleman in question is now known to have been Captain Robert Kennedy of Wester, a considerable antiquarian, whose manuscript, often referred to in the series, was written originally about 1814. He was father of the first editor of the *Journal*.

1 A minister of Dunnet church from 1601, 'an accomplished mathematician and cartographer' who, on the basis of his own surveys – two counties each summer, compiled the first atlas of Scotland.

by a tale told in the *Anecdotes* printed in early issues of the *John O'Groat Journal* and again in Calder's *History*. Earl William was married to Mary, daughter of Sir William Keith of Inverugie in Moray. Like many other lairds of the time, the Keiths were busy acquiring landed property – by purchase, exchange, marriage etc, becoming landowners in the modern sense rather than feudal or more ancient forms of tenure. Among their acquisitions were the lands of Ackergill in Caithness, lying to the west of Girnigoe at the foot of Sinclair Bay. He was now staying in the Tower of Ackergill, the Keith's stronghold on this embattled coast. Keith had quarrelled with Earl William, a not unusual state of relationship between noble neighbours and kin in this part of the world. The story continues:

> Having quarelled with his son-in-law, the Earl of Caithness, he (Keith) took an opportunity, on a New Year's morn, when the former (Earl William) and some of his attendants had been out early coursing with greyhounds, and were returning on horseback, within bow-shoot of the battlements of Ackergill Tower, to wound him with an arrow, which struck in the back of his neck. The Earl finding himself struck, did not attempt to withdraw the arrow, but having clapped spurs to his horse, soon arrived at his own home at Castle Girnigoe. On his Lady enquiring what sport he had met with, he replied – Not much; only that, in passing Ackergill Tower her father had sent home a New Year's gift for her, which she might find fixed in the back of his neck.

However prone might be the local chiefs to fall out and war with one another, the arrival in Caithness of a resident earl marked a change, not indeed in the actual behaviour of the chiefs, but in the attitude of the government in Edinburgh towards this lawlessness. There was now, it was considered, a possibility of bringing to the north some measure of order and peace. Accordingly, in 1503, Parliament passed an Act which stated:

> Because there has been great lack and fault of justice in the north parts, as Caithness and Ross, as fault of want of division of the sheriffdom of Inverness, to our regret, and these parts are so far distance from the burgh of Inverness, through which people cannot come speedily there by reason of the great expense, labour and travel, and therefore great enormities and trespasses have grown in default of officers within these parts who have power to put good rule among the people . . . . . (there shall be here a sheriff of Ross and one of Caithness) the

latter sitting at Dornoch or Wick as convenient.

1503 is the date usually given for the bringing of Wick into the picture as the centre of civil government of Caithness. It must be added that Sinclair, author of *The Saint-Clairs of the Isles*, follows this piece of information with the more sobering one that the Act, through passed, was 'not operative till ratified for Caithness in 1641 and Ross in 1649'. So that if Wick did glow slightly in 1503 through the murk of time, it was a very still, small light. And it must be supposed, though there is nothing to say so, that Wick was thus nominated because of the presence in the area of Earl William Sinclair, thought well of by King James (IV). In any case, Thurso was a larger and rather more important town at the time, and it was here that the courts, such as they were, actually sat.

Without doubt the government meant business and there was evidently some confidence that William Sinclair, Lord of Caithness had the will and the power to civilise the place. It is believed, too, that William had good intentions in these matters and the ability to improve things. However, it was slow work, and in 1513 William, like his cousin Henry from Orkney, went to the fatal field of Flodden and never returned. He was another of the twelve earls of Scotland lost on that day.

For all this, Wick must have been a location of some consequence, however slight, for King Robert III (1390-1406) had granted it status as 'ane burgh of barony' to Nicholas Sutherland. The Sutherlands were another rising family in the new Scottish aristocracy. Its origins are obscure, but an ancestor of Nicholas was Freskin of Duffus (Duffus is in Moray), himself a descendant of yet another Norman, knight named de Moravia, who gravitated to the north of Scotland. He is thought to have married Joanna, daughter of Earl John, son of Harald Maddadarson, after whom the line of Scottish-Norse earls of Orkney and Caithness drifted into the Angus line. The lands she inherited, consisted of the southern parts of the Caithness earldom; part she gave to the church in Moray, and the other part to one of her daughters, Mary, married to Reginald de Cheyne who, it is reported, 'gathered to himself all the lands of Caithness' in the mid-fourteenth century.

Hugo's branch of the Freskin family inherited the Sutherland territories which became the new Earldom of Sutherland. De Cheyne (sometimes called 'Chen' and sometimes 'Cheney'), whose family 'came north with the Sinclairs', gained through his marriage, possession of a large part of Caithness including Auldwick, in effect the parish of Wick, living in the area and hunting, it is said, around Halkirk. He was a swashbuckling character who went as a loyal supporter of his king, David II, to fight against the English in the campaign that ended in the disaster of Halidon Hill, 1333, when once again – Bannockburn notwithstanding – the English king, Edward II, re-established for a time, hegemony over the south of Scotland. His companion, the Earl of Sutherland, was killed and De Cheyne was taken prisoner by the English, though not for long and he was enabled to return to Auldwick.

The story is told that De Cheyne's wife, 'a lady of considerable talent and beauty', gave birth in succession to two daughters, much to the laird's chagrin, for he wanted a son to succeed to his possessions. He gave orders for each of them to be drowned, but they were hidden by a lady of Mary's entourage until they were young women. On an occasion they were invited to a ball where De Cheyne was captivated by the two young beauties. On being told they were his daughters, he was consumed with remorse. On his death he ordered his estate to be divided between them. One of them, Marjorie, married Nicholas Sutherland who thus became owner of Auldwick. In this manner Auldwick – and thus Wick – became a possession of the Sutherland family.

Dates are uncertain, but during the next two centuries Auldwick was occupied by the Oliphants, another family of rising fortune, and then by the Earl of Caithness. As already mentioned, the town gained the nominal status of seat of the sheriff's court, a dignity which it did not in fact enjoy until much later. Its next appearance, if not in the limelight yet, in brighter illuminance than at any time previously, was when the Earl of Sutherland put it to the torch in 1588 (a time, indeed of bonfires, for this was the year of the Spanish Armada).

How this came about requires us to go back over two generations of Sinclair earls in Caithness. Good Earl William died at Flodden in 1513. He was succeeded by his son, John, not so good and not too wise a chief. He carried on the work of his father in converting earldom territories into 'feus', that is, holdings for which the tenants paid rents rather than service, abandoning if they possessed them – doubtless under pressure – 'udall' (or 'odall') rights of 'owner-occupation' that had been characteristic of land-holding in Viking times.[1] John began

---

[1] This was a process going on in various parts of Scotland, by which earls and lairds were consolidating their power and establishing themselves firmly as territorial landowners rather than feudal or semi-feudal lords. Among other things it meant, in the long run, cropping for the market rather than for *(continued on foot of next page)*

getting ideas too of territorial aggrandisement, and evidently with some encouragement from the crown during the weak reign of James V (1513-1542), William, Lord of Orkney, was expelled in 1528 from his castle and lands in a rebellion led by relatives dissatisfied with his rule and disposition of earldom lands. With the support of his cousin, John, Earl of Caithness, William invaded Orkney in an attempt to recapture his patrimony at the head of an army of Caithnessmen. They were heavily defeated by the Orkneymen at the Battle of Summerdale in 1529,[1] near to Stenness, and Earl John of Caithness was killed. Thus the second Sinclair Earl of Caithness came to a violent end like the first.

The new Earl of Caithness was George, a rumbustious character who got himself deeply involved in the intrigues and nefarious doings associated with the marriages, and ultimate abdication of Mary, Queen of Scots, daughter of James V, who succeeded James in 1542. Entertaining though they be, these episodes, recounted in *The Saint-Clairs of the Isles* and in Calder's *History*, must be left aside here, for they have little to do directly with affairs in Caithness – except that George's collusions with Bothwell tended to persuade Mary to 'pardon' George for some of his more outrageous acts in his own province. And these were considerable, though as often as not they were acts of retaliation against the Sutherlands with whom, for all of his reign, George maintained a ferocious feud. The first was an episode in which the Sutherlands of Berriedale, 'countenanced by the Earl of Sutherland, committed some gross outrages in Caithness and killed several inhabitants of the county, against whom they had a grudge.' George marched down, punished the miscreants and confiscated the Castle of Berriedale, a few miles north of the present southern border of Caithness at the Ord. According to Roland St-Clair, it is 'to this incident we trace the foundation of that hatred which the two rival Houses of Caithness and Sutherland bore each other for such a long period.'

(continued from foot of previous page) subsistence, though, subsistence crofting remained for a long time in most places. It had happened or was happening at a much greater rate in the eastern earldoms than in the west, still under the rule of traditional clan chiefs, to whom their people owed service, virtually family loyalty in all causes. Caithness and Sutherland had, in some sense, been 'liberated' from clan relationships by the Norse occupation. To an extent, what was happening in Caithness was about to happen in Orkney, for the Orkney earls were very assiduously extending their 'conquests' (personal land acquisitions), and during the next two centuries, the islands became almost wholly organised into personal estates, owned by 'lairds' as they came to be called – mostly Scotsmen, and some, the progency of Edinburgh lawyers.

1 The story is told in the (not very exciting) novel of James Gunn, *The Battle of Summerdale*; London, Nelson.

WICK OF THE NORTH

There were other lurid episodes including the capture and imprisonment of a young Earl of Sutherland in Girnigoe, a raid on the Sutherland's castle at Dunrobin, and a quarrel between George and his son, John, master of Caithness, which resulted in John's being immured for some years in his father's dungeons at Girnigoe. This, as it happens, had to do with a raid conducted by John on Dornoch where he pillaged the town and burned the cathedral. His father considered he had gone too far in beheading all his hostages. Another and more probable version suggests that the earl considered he had not gone far enough.

This earl came to be known as 'Cock o' the North'[1] on account of the Gallic cock on his family crest. Queen Mary's favour procured for this earl of dubious morality the appointment in 1566 as 'Justiciary of the North of Scotland', which included the power to 'banish and kill and pardon any crime except treason'. This doubtless served as licence for some of his crueler subsequent acts. He died in September, 1582, while on a visit to Edinburgh, and his remains were interred in the chapel at Roslin castle, the Sinclairs' family base. The inscriptions on his tomb read:

>Hic jacet nobilis et potens Dominus Sinclair,
>Justiciarius hereditarius, Diocesis Cathanensis,
>qui obit Edinburgi, 9 die mensis Septembris, Anno Domini 1582.

George left instructions that his heart be extracted, encased in a leaden casket and then deposited in the church at Wick. His greatest achievement during his 52 years as earl was, as St-Clair puts it, that he 'greatly enlarged the hereditary property' of the family.

One other earl of this period must engage our brief attention, George II's grandson, George III, the 'Wicked Earl', who reigned from 1582 to 1643, 61 years, through some of the most turbulent times of all, both in Caithness and in the British nation itself – for such a 'nation' was born in 1603 when James VI of Scotland since 1567 became King James I of England too.

St-Clair devotes fifteen pages to the exploits of George III, the most colourful and outrageous of all the Sinclair earls. 'This Earl,' he begins, 'is remembered in Caithness as the "Wicked Earl George", though perhaps the soubriquet might be more fairly awarded to the 42nd Earl' (that is George II), a very debatable proposition. He goes on immediately to tell of George's first murder:

---

1 The soubriquet is also applied to the nineteenth century Duke of Gordon.

He signalled his accession to the Earldom by deliberately killing, in broad day, Ingram and David Sinclair, the two principal keepers of his late father. David lived at Keiss and Ingram at Wester. Ingram was laird of Blingery, and a large landed proprietor of over 3,000 acres. Ingram's daughter was to be married, and a large party, including his lordship, invited to the wedding. On the forenoon of the appointed day, as the Earl was taking an airing on horseback, he met David on the links of Keiss, on his way to Wester, and ran him through with his sword. Immediately on doing so he galloped over to Wester, and calling aside Ingram, who was at the time amusing himself with some friends at football, he drew out a pistol and shot him dead on the spot. He then coolly turned his head towards Girnigoe, and rode off with as little concern as if he had just killed a moor fowl. Being a nobleman, possessed of ample power of 'pit and gallows', he escaped with impunity. Tradition adds that during the alarm and confusion caused by this shocking affair, the wedding guests dispersed, and the ring was lost. Not many years since a finger ring of a curious construction – supposed to be of the identical wedding ring – was found at Wester.[1] It was of pure gold, twisted so as to represent a serpent coiled with tail in mouth as emblematic of eternity.

THE BURNING OF WICK

With just as much ease as James's mother, Queen Mary, had excused the excesses of Earl George II, King James himself in 1585 gave 'letters of remission' to George III and several other gentlemen for their bad deeds. Time after time the earl was involved in violent encounters with neighbours, especially the Sutherlands, sometimes the Gunns and sometimes the Mackays of Strathnaver. It is difficult from the accounts of St-Clair and Calder to decide whose behaviour was the worse, that of the Wicked Earl of Caithness or that of the Wicked Earl of Sutherland. Tit-for-tat seems to have been the rule, with intermissions of 'friendship' which usually did not last for long. One series of encounters early during George's reign were the *'Creach larn'* and *'La na creachmore'*, the harrying of Latheron and 'the great spoil' of 1588. This ended in disaster for Wick. It began in the autumn

1 Probably about 1895-1896. St-Clair's book was published 1898.

of 1586 with a piece of 'malicious mischief', as St-Clair calls it (Calder tells the same story):

> George Gordon, bastard of Gartay, waylaid the servants of the Earl (of Caithness), cutting off their horses' tails, bade them tell their master he had done so. Resenting the indignity, the Earl, knowing the futility of seeking redress from the Earl of Sutherland, whose follower Gordon was, resolved to himself punish the offender. For this purpose he set out with a picked body of men to Helmsdale, hard by and tried to make his escape by swimming across, but a shower of arrows was discharged upon him, and he was slain in the water. The Earl of Sutherland, although he disliked the conduct of George Gordon, who was also guilty of improper intimacy with Sutherland's sister, resolved to request satisfaction from the Earl of Caithness. The latter replied by assembling his forces, and being joined by Mackay and the Strathnaver men, together with John, Master of Orkney, and the Earl of Carrick, brother of Patrick, with a contingent of Orcadians, marched to Helmsdale to meet the Earl of Sutherland. Neither party cared to risk an engagement, and by the mediation of mutual friends the two Earls agreed to a temporary truce on the 9th of March, 1587, from the benefits of which Mackay of Strathnaver was carefully excluded. The latter, however, came to an amicable understanding with the Earl of Sutherland at Elgin, in the month of November, 1588 [this should be 1587]. On the expiration of the truce, Lord Sutherland, supported by his allies Mackay, Macintosh, Assynt, Foulis and Rasay, entered Caithness with all his forces in the beginning of 1588, having obtained a commission from the Privy Council against Earl George for killing the Bastard of Gartay. His great object was to secure the person of the earl of Caithness, but that nobleman prudently withdrew within the iron walls of Castle Girnigoe, a fortress strongly fortified, and prepared to withstand a siege. Foiled in his attempt, Sutherland ravaged Latheron, returning home with a large booty of cattle, which was divided among his followers . . . . The town of Wick was pillaged and burnt, but the church was preserved. In it was found the heart of the late Earl of Caithness encased in a leaden casket, which was opened by John Mac-Gille-Calum of Rasay, and the ashes were scattered to the winds. Such was the singular fate that befell the

heart of that proud and cruel nobleman. After twelve days the Earl of Sutherland raised the siege of Girnigoe, and ravaged the county as far as Duncansby, killing several of the peasantry and returning with great spoil.

Calder (who is St-Clair's main source) includes a few details about the events in Wick, presenting them in a different order, though clearly informed by imagination rather than reliable original sources – which are few:

> Sutherland's first exploit was the burning of the town of Wick, an achievement of no great difficulty, as the place at that time merely consisted of a few mean straggling houses thatched in straw. The only building that was spared was the church, when his eye lighted on the leaden case containing the heart of the late Earl of Caithness. He broke it open, but finding that it contained no treasure, he flung it away in disgust, and thus scattered the ashes to the winds. Such was the singular fate which befell the heart of that proud nobleman.

St-Clair repeats some of Calder's comments word for word. Another writer who tells the same story is Mackay in his *History of the Province of Cat*.[1]

Fig 5 Sinclair & Guernigo (From Pennant's *Tour of Scotland* 1769).

1 Rev Angus Mackay: *History of the Province of Cat (Caithness and Sutherland from Earliest Times to the Year 1615:* Reid, Wick 1914.

These encounters were by no means the last in which Lord George Sinclair III, Earl of Caithness, was involved. Many people lost their lives and property during the rule of this unscrupulous baron of antique habits, and it cannot be supposed that keeping of the King's Law was greatly improved in this, the most northerly province of Scotland, while George was Earl. Though himself the law's chief representative, he often acted as though completely above it, not only disturbing the King's Peace himself, but also, as in the Arthur Smith affair, aiding and promoting one of the most serious offences on the statute book, that of coining. This is the story:

The Earl of Caithness at this time (last years of the sixteenth century) possessed an extensive and valuable landed property in the county, including the whole of the parish of Wick. By his recklessness and extravagent habits, however, he had become deeply invoved in debt, and was obliged to mortgage several portions of his estate to satisfy his creditors. To recruit his exhausted finances he fell, it is alleged, on a desperate expedient, and employed an ingenious vagabond of the name of Arthur Smith to coin money for him. Smith was originally a blacksmith in Banff, but being detected counterfeiting the coin of the realm, he and his assistant were apprehended in 1599 by the Countess of Sutherland and were forwarded to Edinburgh for trial. They were duly tried and condemned. Smith's assistant was executed, being guilty of crimes of a deeper dye, but he himself was reserved for further trial, during which period he devised a lock of rare and curious workmanship, which took the fancy of the king and resulted in his procuring a release. He then went North and offered his services to the Earl of Caithness, who accommodated him with a workshop in a retired apartment of castle Sinclair, which the Earl had lately built close by the Castle of Girnigoe.[1] The workshop was under the rock of Castle Sinclair, in a quiet retired place called the 'Gote', to which there was a secret passage from the Earl's bedchamber. There Smith diligently plied his vocation for seven or eight years, at length removing to Thurso, where he ostensibly prosecuted his calling as a blacksmith. In the meantime Orkney, Caithness, Sutherland and Ross were

1 This stands alongside Castle Girnigoe on its own promontory, connected with Girnigoe at one time by a drawbridge. It was built by Earl George in 1606 as a residential block, with comforts that could not be afforded in Girnigoe.

inundated with counterfeit coin, which was first detected by Sir Robert Gordon in 1611, and he on returning to England made the King acquainted therewith. A commission was thereon granted to Sir Robert, John Gordon, younger of Embo, and Donald Mackay to arrest Smith – whom all suspected of the offence – and bring him once more to Edinburgh for trial. Mackay and Gordon proceeded to Thurso where they secured Smith and found in his house a quantity of base money. The citizens, although satisfied of Smith's guilt, were yet, from recollections of the past, distrustful of the Sutherland authorities and regarded the commission very much in the light of a hostile invasion. So the alarm-bell was rung to assemble the inhabitants, who accordingly rushed to the street, and presently John Sinclair, younger of Stirkoke, James Sinclair of Durran, James Sinclair brother of Dunn, and other relatives of Lord Caithness who happened to be in the town on a visit to Lady Berriedale, made their appearance. The commissioners produced the royal authority for the arrest, but Sinclair of Stirkoke transported with rage, swore he would not allow any man whatever his commission to carry away his uncle's servant in his uncle's absence. Swords were drawn, but the Thursoese, who were not so well armed as their opponents, finally gave way and retreated to their houses. Sinclair of Stirkoke was slain, James Sinclair of Dunn severely wounded, and James Sinclair of Durran saved himself by flight. None of the men of Sutherland were killed, but many were badly wounded. Sir John Sinclair of Greenland, who then lived at Ormlie Castle, and Sinclair, Laird of Dunn, arrived when the fray was ended. Dunn proposed to renew the attack, but Sir John, considering what had already happened, would not agree to any such hazardous undertaking. The men of Strathnaver slew Smith to prevent his rescue, and they and the Sutherland friends returned home with their wounded.

This, needless to say, did not end the affair so far as Earl George was concerned. King James had a soft spot for rogues and on several occasions eased Lord George of his burden of guilt, on this occasion by recommending 'arbitration' between the Earls of Caithness and of Sutherland. Caithness gained no satisfaction from this but in 1614, an opportunity arose for him to get himself right in the king's eyes. This was an offer on his part to liberate the Castle of Kirkwall in Orkney from its illegal occupation by Robert the son of the discredited Earl Patrick Stewart of Orkney[1], in prison in Edinburgh on charges of suspected treason. He was provided with sixty men and two cannon from Edinburgh Castle; when his vessel reached Sinclair Bay, he embarked some of his own Caithness men and sailed for Orkney with a 'natural' brother of his, Henry. They disembarked at Carness two miles east of Kirkwall and opened an attack on the rebels. St-Clair continues the story of the events of the campaign (various records of which exist in Orkney itself);

> He (Earl George) besieged and took in succession the different points occupied by the insurgents. The last was the Castle of Kirkwall, which Robert Stewart, with only sixteen men, bravely defended for the space of three weeks. The King's cannon made little impression on the iron walls of the citadel and it was taken at last through the treachery of Patrick Halcro, one of the besieged. The prisoners, with the exception of Halcro, were all brought south and executed; and very soon after Earl Patrick himself was beheaded for high treason at the Market Cross of Edinburgh. Before leaving Orkney the Earl of Caithness delivered up the castle of Kirkwall to Sir James Stewart of Kilsyth, afterwards Lord Ochiltree, on whom in the capacity of farmer-general of [actually 'tacksman'] the King had conferred a new grant of the county; and a few months after the siege the government ordered the Castle of Kirkwall to be demolished [not a stone of it now stands].

Though by this action George improved his standing with the king, this did not last, and at one stage in later years he was forced to flee the country on account of debt and misdemeanour. Various Sinclairs, all of them relatives of the earl, including the Sinclairs of Murkle (Sheriff of Caithness), Mey, and Rattar, among the lairds, were called in to assist in the disciplining of George – following his slaughter of a 'brother-uterine' (bastard brother), Thomas Lyndsay and arraignment for debt. 'The Earl of Caithness, seeing now no longer any chance of

---

[1] Patrick Stewart, Earl of Orkney, was son of Robert Stewart, a bastard brother of Mary, Queen of Scots, made Earl of Orkney by the King at a time of considerable confusion in Orkney affairs. Neither Earl Robert nor Earl Patrick was a very savoury character, Patrick having many of the qualities of George III, Earl of Caithness. King James kept him under arrest for several years on account of his fears that Patrick ('Black Pate') had ambitions of 'independence' for Orkney. Patrick's son Robert's rebellion put paid to both of them. Early in 1615 Patrick was beheaded as a traitor, and Robert hanged as a rebel. The earldom of Orkney was once more resumed to the Crown.

evading the authority of the laws, prepared to face the storm by fortifying his castles and strongholds.' But it was not to be. All the Sinclair castles of the Wick coast, Keiss, Ackergill and Sinclair itself, were for some years surrendered to the crown on the orders of the Privy Council, and Castle Sinclair was occupied by the earl's son, Lord Berriedale, 'until the further pleasure of his Majesty should be known. The commissioners drew up a set of instructions at Wick, leaving Lord Berriedale in charge, and an annuity was allowed the Earl during good behaviour', a not ungenerous but also not especially dignified way for a powerful and wayward war lord to end his career.

Lord George lasted another twenty years, dying in 1643 at the age of 79. St-Clair concludes:

> By his tyrannical conduct he procured himself many enemies and probably his faults may have been thereby much exaggerated. Some of the many crimes at least, with which he was charged were never fully proved against him; and it is clear, from the whole course of his history that he had a very bitter enemy in Sir Robert Gordon, almost the only authority for the events of that period. 'The quietness and moderation,' says Mackay, 'with which he appears to have conducted himself during the last twenty years of his life plead strongly in his favour'.[1]

As we have seen, by the time of Lord George III, there were many other Sinclairs in the county of Caithness, some of them near neighbours of the earl and most of them related. Henderson lists no less than twenty-five Sinclair families of importance in the area. There were also close marriage connections with other Caithness families. Many of them were intensely loyal to the earl, as were their tenants. This was one of the difficulties of dealing with George III. Lord Berriedale reported in 1623 when the Privy Council was seeking to prosecute or outlaw his father, 'that many of the inhabitants stood well affected to the Earl'.

Most of the castles of the area have at one time or another been occupied – some were built – by Sinclairs.[1] The earls themselves were inveterate castle builders. Auldwick, Ackergill and Keiss, all in the

---

1 John Henderson: *Caithness Families*; Edinburgh, David Douglas (1884). Henderson was a lawyer trained in Aberdeen who set up practice in Wick where he became Procurator-Fiscal in 1828. He was factor at various times to several important estates, including Hempriggs, Freswick, Thrumster, Forse, Lochen, Forss and Rattar.

parish of Wick, were – again at one time or another – inhabited by members of the earl's family, as were castles at Mey, Brims, Thurso, Braal, Dunbeath and Berriedale. The sixteenth and seventeenth century Sinclairs, earls and the rest, were territorial magnates, quarrelsome among themselves, often embattled with other neighbours and frequently during the reigns of Earls George II and George III, standing alongside and in support of the earl. Some were experienced cattle reivers, as were many of the Scotttish lords of these and earlier centuries. Cattle, of course, were the main form of wealth in these times and in these parts, hence the many reports in their encounters with one another of 'a good booty in cattle'. Arable farming and trade were not main interests of the Sinclair chiefs, at least until the 'improvement' of the eighteenth century and in particular the activities and example of Sir John Sinclair of Ulbster who, in his lifetime (1754-1835), probably did more for the well-being of the citizens of Caithness than all the generations of Sinclairs before him.

As for the impact on Wick town (at least in the beneficial sense), of all these Sinclairs, this was not very considerable until later times. Wick was never the 'seat' of any of the earls nor of any of the lesser Sinclairs, but as it rose somewhat in importance, notably in 1503 (or whenever the actual administration of justice came to be located here), the place became of more interest to them. George II (1529-1582) is thought to have built the church of which the 'Sinclair Aisle' in the graveyard of the parish church is a remnant, exhibiting here perhaps a concern for souls not wholly apparent in many of his other doings. This, sad to say, is where his own heart was interred, to be rudely and irreverently disinterred and cast away by the Earl of Sutherland in 1588 when, in full measure of his exasperation with Earl George III, he destroyed the town.

It may be added that, for better or worse – if the wording of the Charter issued to Wick in 1589 is anything to go by, King James clearly connected his 'trusty cousin', Earl George III, with the town of Wick. Whether or not the association was of any great benefit to the

1 The castles of Wick parish, from north to south, are Keiss: (a 'Z Plan' tower), built on the coast probably by Earl George III at the end of the sixteenth century (the white-towered modern Keiss castle, inland from the tower, has no ancient connection); Ackergill, a tower orginally part of the de Cheyne estate, passed to the Keiths, then passing to the Earl of Sinclair in the early seventeenth century; Girnigoe and Sinclair, traditional stronghold of the earls of Caithness; Auldwick, the old castle of Wick, with origins perhaps in thirteenth century, but provenance unknown.

citizens of Wick is an issue of some uncertainty.[1]

---

[1] A full translation of the Charter is given in *Addendum* at the end of Chapter V, 'Royal Burgh'.

CHAPTER 4

BISHOPS, SUTHERLANDS AND OTHERS

NO family, or rather group of same name families, in all Britain can have enjoyed more power and influence in a distinctive territory than the Sinclairs of Caithness. From the time of their arrival in the fifteenth century until the end of the eighteenth, earls and lesser lairds of this remarkable lordly dynasty ruled, dictated, managed and exploited this land and people in imperial style. But they were never on their own, in undisputed possession of all. Hampering their progress to greater power and influence from time to time were other notable families, not only affecting the lives and fortunes of the Sinclairs but also those of all other Caithnessians: the Sutherlands, Keiths, Gunns and Mackays, and for full measure, other groups who came and disappeared or moved on to bigger and better things. These include the Cheynes, Oliphants and, in later days, the Dunbars.

In addition, the Sutherlands in particular, and to a lesser extent the Keiths, Gunns and Mackays, held on their own account land or had dealings with north-east Caithness and had their effects on Wick and parish. We have already encountered them all in some of their escapades, but to get the feel of life among the nobles, lairds and men of the clans then in Caithness, perhaps the least disposed of all Scottish counties to typical clan relationships, we shall take a look at the backgrounds of these families, whose names at least are well known.

Their stories are, however, so interesting that there is a temptation, as always when Scottish clan histories are in discussion, to follow them through wherever they lead, since the doings of the clans are seldom less than exciting and often preposterous. If, however, we follow the Caithness clans too closely the trek will take us far from our topic, the story of Wick. All clans take themselves rather seriously. Mighty partisan volumes have been written about some clans by chroniclers who usually show undisguised animosity towards the others. Each of our Caithness families figure in the clan books, each with the whole paraphernalia of clan crest, badge, motto, Gaelic name, pipe tunes, march and war cry. Mackay, Gunn and Sutherland clans include septs of different name; they have all at one stage or another intermarried with one another and many other clans, and all cherish royal connections at various times down the centuries.

The Sinclairs and Sutherlands had been from their earliest days aggressive competitors and acquisitors of land. The actual nature of land holding itself changed greatly in Scotland between the thirteenth and present centuries, nowhere more so than in the northern provinces. Here the ancient Gaelic modes of common tribal ownership, gave place to the Norse system in which local chieftains, presided over holders of land lots graded downwards from the 'boer', the chief's lot, thought 'bolstadr' and 'garth' to 'kvi', reflected in Caithness place names such as 'Duncansby', and especially in the many '. . .sters', Bilbster, Lybster, Stemster, etc.[1] These were generally 'udall' or 'odal' lands, 'owned' by their occupying families mostly on unwritten terms. In due course, as in Orkney, udallers were replaced by tenants of 'feus', paying rents and 'scat' (taxes) to the big landowner, who may or may not have acquired his holding by grant from the king or from the bishop, for in the middle ages, the church became a substantial landowner. At no stage did the classic 'feudal system' prevail in the north, though it was doubtless among the intentions of the monarchs that it should. The kings of Scotland gained few of the benefits of feudal tenure, armies and the sinews of war from their northern vassals. The land regime that succeeded the Norse occupation may perhaps be described as 'quasi-feudal'.

Among the reasons for the failure to implant traditional feudal tenures and relationships in Caithness were its vast distance from the centre of government, and doubtless the persistence here among the folk of ingrained attitudes of Norse individualism, through not to the extent that these persisted in Orkney until the impignoration. Such attitudes, in any case, did not penetrate very deeply inland, so that traditional clan relationships tended to apply among Gunn and Mackay communities as distinct from those under Sinclair, Sutherland and Keith control. Indeed, the Gaelic and many of the kinds of tribal connection characteristic of the clans persisted in some parts of central and eastern Caithness and much of Sutherland until the nineteenth century.[2]

1 For a fuller discussion of the 'toponymy' of north-east Scotland see various papers by WFH Nicolaisen. A list of these is included in the bibliography of Barbara Crawford's *Scandinavian Scotland* (q.v.). Crawford herself has an interesting chapter on place-names and settlements (see *Scandinavian Scotland,* op. cit pp 92-115).

2 Neither the Sinclairs nor the Sutherlands ever constituted true clans. Their chiefs were alien, non-Gaelic – at least in their early generations, *(continued on foot of next page)*

BISHOPS IN CAITHNESS

Before briefly describing the clan rivals of the Sinclairs, we must mention the land-owning and jurisdictional roles of the mediaeval church in Caithness. It is customary to think of bishops as holy men concerned chiefly with the moral and religious well-being of the flock. The bishops of Caithness – some of them at least – were doubtless holy enough, but they were also important custodians of the king's interest – and their own. During the earlship of Harald Hakonsson (1123-1154), King David I, an innovator in the whole art of kingship in Scotland, appointed his own Bishop of Caithness in about 1128. This was another breakaway move, for up to this time, the Bishop of Orkney, subject to the Archbishop of Trondheim, or Nidaros, as the cathedral area was called, had been ecclesiastical chief in Caithness too. This, as J. Miller sees it, was a method by which David 'advanced his power north under the guise of the church' while Omand comments on the fact that the 'church (in Caithness, which then included Sutherland) held a vast amount of real estate throughout the diocese'. We have already mentioned two episodes in which earl and bishop quarrelled, much to the king's displeasure, when one bishop had his tongue cut out, and another was burned in his palace.

Bishops themselves were often political appointees, expressly put there to keep an eye on the king's affairs, to exercise church discipline on the earls and to mediate in quarrels. Their relations with earls and other chiefs were not always over cordial. Adam, the bishop burned to death at Halkirk in 1222, was almost certainly appointed at the wish of the king, and his fate at the hands of a group of Earl John's tenants, if not ordered by John, was inspired by his hatred of the idea that Bishop Adam should exercise a jurisdiction not under the earl's control. Bishop Gilbert Moray (sometimes given as 'de Moravia'),

(from foot of previous page) put in place by express royal patent or grant, their role in principle being to establish crown control in areas remote from the centre of royal government. They and their like were quasi-feudal lords, introduced from the reign of David I (1124-1153) onwards, the model being the feudal lords of England. The fact that they spent much of their energy in internicine strife was not part of the plan. The authority of earldom was not always necessarily accompanied by land grant. Sinclairs, Sutherlands and Keiths acquired family possession of land in the form of 'real-estate' by grant, purchase, outright annexation and by 'conquest', that is, acquisition of estates through marriage. One of the peculiarities of the land regime that came to apply in Caithness, as Miller hints, was the persistence of Norse attitudes to duty and worship:

> The Sinclair earls in Caithness and the Sutherland earls obviously gained their tenantry along with their estates and claims of kinship reflect political imperatives rather than genetic realities. Unfortunately, we can only speculate how the relict Norse culture in Caithness mingled with incoming Scots influences and affected how tenants saw themselves in relation to their lairds.

BISHOPS, SUTHERLANDS AND OTHERS

who followed Adam probably sought to bring more order into Caithness affairs and is believed to have built a substantial church at Thurso, a symbol of ecclesiastical if not royal authority; but conceivably coming to the conclusion that even Thurso was none too safe a place, he shifted the seat of the Caithness bishopric to Dornoch, where eventually the cathedral was built.[1] Gilbert may have thought this a safer place from which to administer the Caithness diocese, but this did not prevent a Sinclair force, during one of their many feuds from sacking the town in 1570 and burning the cathedral.

As for church property, according to Omand:

> The church held a vast amount of real estate throughout the dioceses in the form of lands and fishing – both salt and fresh water. These lands were at Scrabster, Lythmore, Stemster, Dorrery (which was used as a shieling) and Scotscalder. On Braehouse Burn the Bishops had built a mill for their tenants. Moreover, in each parish of the diocese the Church exacted a tenth part or tiend [in England this imposition was 'tithe'] of all oats, bere, hay etc, raised by tenants of church lands.

Omand refers also to the parishes listed in Caithness in connection with the assessment for papal taxes ('Peter's Pence' as they are sometimes called, a subject often of high controversy) in 1274 and 1275 by Baiamundus de Vitia, the then collector-general for such taxes in Scotland. The parishes of Olric (Olrig), Dinnosc (Dunnet), Cranesby (Canisbay), Ascend (Skinnet), Haukyrk (Halkirk), Turishau (Thurso), Haludal, Lagheryn (Latheron) and Durness contributed to the cost of a Crusade.[2] Wick is not mentioned in this connection. However, Wick was one of the parishes marked out by Bishop Gilbert; six of the Caithness parishes were assigned by him to the upkeep of the cathedral establishment at Dornoch, together with others in what was now the separate earldom territory of Sutherland, while the teind revenues of Reay, Thurso, Wick and Latheron were allocated to the

---

1 This removal of the seat of the Caithness see to Dornoch gives rise to the speculation that, had not this happened, Thurso might itself have become established as the cathedral city of the north. Scrabster castle, of which there are fragmentary remains, is believed to have been built (1328) and maintained by the bishops of Thurso; it housed a small garrison 'to look after the considerable property and interests of the Church in the area' (Falconer Waters: *Thurso Then and Now*). The last bishop recorded as having lived there was Robert Stewart in 1566. The ancient and ruined St Peter's Church of Thurso (a date of 1222 is posted on the wall plaque), has the aspect of a very noble building. Bishop Gilbert, incidentally, was canonised and is thus regarded as the saint of Caithness.
2 This would be the disastrous Eighth Crusade of 1270-1272 led by Louis IX, King of France – the Christian forces were finally driven out of Syria in 1291.

upkeep of the bishop's establishment. Omand suggests that the various kirks 'must have been serviced by monks or priests with lay assistance, but no records remain of these people'. Religious orders, however, do not seem to have penetrated at any stage into Caithness, although there are records of hospitals such as the one at Spittal, the maintenance of which became at one stage the responsibility of the Earl of Caithness.

After many complex evolutions of monarchy and religion, Scotland became Protestant, by Acts of Parliament that abolished the authority of the Pope in Scotland and forbade the celebration of the Mass. Bishops remained for the time being, though their role changed. The Stewart Bishop of Caithness spent some time in exile during the crucial years, on account of his brother's involvement with a dissident movement led by James Hamilton, Earl of Arran; but in 1563 he came back, took up Protestantism, and was re-installed (though not consecrated) in the county, appointed ministers and constituted the Caithness Presbytery, which included the present ten parishes of the county, one of which, Halkirk, was then divided into two parishes, Halkirk and Skinnet. There were two other parishes outside the present county, Farr and Arduress.

Little is known about the enthusiasm or otherwise of Caithnessians for the reformed religion, though it is known that, whether they approved or not, numerous 'popish' chapels in the area were closed or dismantled. Their records, like their stones, disappeared in the radical process of clearing out the relics of Catholicism, so that the stories of present Caithness parish churches tend to begin in the sixteenth and seventeenth centuries. Catholic practices did not disappear overnight. For quite a time the gospel was preached by protestant 'readers or exhorters', most of the established clergy having been dismissed. Some of the new 'ministers' were the converted former priests, as for instance at Wick, where the Reverend Andrew Graham, vicar of the parish, embraced the new religion and held on to the benefice until 1574. This sort of thing, says Miller, 'should not be put down to nifty theological footwork; the idea of reformation had been in the air for decades and Graham, like some other clerics, may have been genuinely glad of the chance to practise openly what he had long felt to be true'.

In fact, there is ample evidence that 'debased' Catholic practice persisted for well into the eighteenth century in some places, and the story of Richard Merchiston, suggests that Wick was one of these places. This story is one of the 'Tales and Legends' gleaned by Donald Omand and repeated in *The New Caithness Book*. Dr Merchiston of Bower, 'a member of the Reformed church and zealously anti-Catholic', in the year 1613

> was pursuing his religious crusade through the parish of Wick and entered the Royal Burgh, where he discovered a stone statue of the town's patron saint, St Fergus.[1] To the astonishment and deep shock on many people the crusading cleric smashed the image. A number of Wickers threatened vengeance and pursued him as he returned to Bower (west of Keiss). They caught hold of him and drowned him in Wick river; legend says that St Fergus was seen sitting astride the person, holding his head under the water.

That the lords of Caithness were not keen on the reformed faith may be guessed. Unlike the Lords of Congregation (later styled the 'Confederate Lords') who pushed through both the formal terms of the Reformation in 1560, and the abdication of Mary, Queen of the Scots (1567), the earls in Caithness and Sutherland lacked zeal for the Reformation, probably seeing it as 'stemming from the lower orders of society' and 'dangerously subversive'. The Earl of Caithness (George III, the 'Wicked Earl') and the Earl of Sutherland were both regarded by the General Assembly in 1587-1588 as acknowledged Catholics, while in 1639 there was a complaint from the minister of Canisbay that Sir William Sinclair of Mey was 'influencing his parishioners to disobey him'. The case of Earl George IV (1643-1676), was considered by the General Assembly in 1649 (the year of Charles's execution, when feeling was high). He was believed to be still 'popishly inclined' and not ensuring that his children were being brought up in the new faith.

To return to the issue of the 'other clans', with their rivalries, feuds, alliances and treacheries towards one another, a strong tradition grew up that virtually by nature they could never agree. A popular jingle ran:

> Sinclair, Sutherland, Keith and Clan Gunn,
> Never was peace where these four were in.

---

[1] St Fergus was an Irish saint of the eighth century who preached in Scotland, including Caithness. He is reputed to have founded churches in Halkirk and Wick. He was adopted as the patron saint of Wick and the old parish church was dedicated to him.

SUTHERLANDS

In the eleventh and most of the twelfth centuries Sutherland was technically part of the Caithness Norse earldom, drifting as we have seen towards firmer allegiance under the Scottish crown, especially during the rule of Harald Maddadarson (1138-1206), until, during the fourteenth century, the Norwegian connection failed entirely. The Caithness Sinclair earls as such date their accession from 1455 when William became first designated Earl of Caithness, and they 'so stand on the books of Parliament at the Union' (1707). The Sutherlands claim to have been the earliest designated Scottish earls, and thus regard themselves as the 'Premier Earls'; they have borne the 'comitial title' since 1228, granted by Alexander II following forfeiture of the Sutherland portion of his earldom (the area north and west of the Helmsdale valley or Strath Donan) by the then Earl John of Orkney and Caithness.

The story of the Sutherlands is at least as varied and entertaining as that of the Sinclairs, and the temptation to follow it through is strong. Nevertheless, we must be content here with reference to those occasions when the affairs of the three distinct dynasties of Sutherland have expressly affected those of Wick. The original Sutherland earls were Freskins from Moray, the first, William Freskin being another of the 'Norman' knights who came north to put things right for the king. Unlike the Sinclairs, the Freskins dropped their early family name for that of 'Sutherland'.

The first of the several main periods of impact of Sutherlands on Caithness, and Wick in particular, was the occasion when Nicholas, brother of the second Earl of Sutherland, married one of the beautiful daughters of Reginald de Cheyne, thus bringing possession of Auldwick into the Sutherland family, whose main home was established at Dunrobin near to Golspie.

In the early sixteenth century the Freskin line ran out and the 'Seton-Gordon Sutherlands' took over. This line stemmed from the marriage of Adam Gordon to the Sutherland heiress, Elizabeth, in 1508. This family remained in possession until 1766, and it was Adam, Alexander, John and William of this line who maintained a fearful feud with the Sinclair Earls George II and III. The most violent of their encounters was that between Alexander, Earl of Sutherland and Earl George III Sinclair between 1586 and 1589, which resulted in the burning of Wick in 1588 and the siege of Girnigoe castle. A curious outcome of this, as we have seen, was the raising of Wick to the status of Royal Burgh.

BISHOPS, SUTHERLANDS AND OTHERS

In the eighteenth century occurred another main switch in the Sutherland line. The eighteenth earl – sometimes counted the twenty-third – died in 1766, leaving only a baby daughter, Elizabeth, who was adjudicated by the House of Lords in the face of other claims, to be Countess of Sutherland. She was married at the age of twenty to George Granville Leveson-Gower, later Marquis of Stafford; and though he did not thus become Earl of Sutherland (though his wife was Countess), in 1833 he achieved 'the highest honour of the Peerage of the United Kingdom', being made Duke of Sutherland, a few months before his death.[1] The Stafford family had made their money – and were to make a lot more – in mine owning in the rich Staffordshire coalfields and South Wales, from vast land-holdings in north Staffordshire and in Shropshire, and, from his marriage, the virtual ownership of most of Sutherland.

Helmsdale as a settlement was 'improved'. Several of its streets are named reminiscently after the southern localities which the Marquis of Stafford inhabited and ruled, 'Stafford Street', 'Trentham Street' etc (there is even a 'Stafford Place' in Wick). Later Dukes of Sutherland, true to their Sassenach predilections, had built a 'palace' on the site of the ancient monastery of Trentham, near to Stoke-on-Trent, later abandoned and early this century pulled down. The gardens alongside the River Trent, which flows through, now form a popular pleasure park. It is said that the Duke and Duchess left the place on account of the stench from the polluted river, carrying down, as it did, much of the filth of the highly industrialised 'Five Towns'.[2]

During the years 1810 to 1830 the Marquis and Marchioness of Stafford, in the role of 'Great Improvers', were pioneers in the savage business of clearing out the thousands of poor 'tenants-at-will', crofting in their lands of Kildonan and Strathnaver, burning their houses and bringing in their place vast herds of Cheviot sheep. They,

---

1 John Prebble in his book *The Highland Clearances* describes Lord Stafford's honours and appointments thus:
> He was coal and wool joined by a stately hyphen and ennobled by five coronets. He was a Knight of the Garter, a Privy Councillor, Recorder of Stafford, a Trustee of the British Museum, a Vice-President of the Society of Arts, and an Hereditary Governor of the British Institution. He was the Most Noble George Granville Leveson-Gower, second Marquess of Stafford, third Earl Gower and Viscount Trentham, fourth Lord Gower of Stittenham in Yorkshire, eighth baronet of the same place, and ultimately and pre-eminently from the last six months of his life he was the first Duke of Sutherland.

2 A quaint, even comic portrait of Trentham (and of a later Duchess), is to be found in Arnold Bennett's *The Card*.

or more strictly, their ruthless agents, factors and 'commissioners', notably Patrick Sellar, William Young and James Loch, fully armed with the authority of their chiefs, undertook a programme of clearance in the northern valleys that left the ancient 'townships' free to become sheep pastures. Some of the families were sent to the coasts near Bettyhill (at the northern sea-end of Strathnaver), and to the Helmsdale area itself, to eke out a pitiful existence on thin, bad soil; others found the passage-money to emigrate to Canada under the scheme of Lord Selkirk, who took a poor view of the Staffords' activities. Yet others went to localities such as Helmsdale town, Latheron, Berriedale and above all Wick, to take part in the rapidly growing herring industry.

Lord and Lady Stafford took credit in later years for contributing to this growth, especially in the construction of a large serviceable harbour for the fishing boats at Helmsdale, for the building of roads and bridges in this area and throughout Caithness. A togaed effigy of Stafford – from 1833, Duke of Sutherland – stands on a high plinth on the great hill of Ben Bhraggie behind Golspie, a tribute to his good works and benificence. It is rather a monument to shame than to goodness. All the Staffords' (we must now call them Sutherlands again) good works were undertaken in pursuance of the then popular doctrine of *laisser-faire*, expressed in social terms as 'Utilarianism' or 'Benthamism' – the greatest good of the greatest number.[1]

In an ironic comment on the Sutherland achievement, John Prebble writes:

> He (Sutherland) was the Great Improver. Where there had been nothing in his opinion but wildness and savagery, he built, or had built for him by the Government, thirty-four bridges and four hundred and fifty miles of road. The glens, emptied by his commissioners, factors, law-agents and ground-officers (with the prompt assistance of police and soldiers when necessary), were let or leased to Lowlanders who grazed 200,000 True Mountain Sheep upon them and sheared 415,000 pounds of wool every year. He pulled the shire of Sutherland out of the past for the trifling cost of two-thirds of one year's

---

[1] The taint on the memory of the Duke survives. Early in 1994 a councillor of the Sutherland District Council sought to have the statue dismantled, for it was an insult to the memory of the people who were ruthlessly burnt out of their homes during the Highland Clearances! Although the stones were to be used to shore up the crumbling sea wall at Dunrobin, the council considered that the 'logistics of the plan would make it a non-starter.' *Caithness Courier*, 23 March, 1994.

income. And because he was an Englishman and spoke no Gaelic, he did not hear the bitter protests from the poets among his people.

Such was the most influential and famous of the Sutherlands in more recent times. Their behaviour in Sutherland was as rapacious, aggressive and inconsiderate as that of the Sutherland forebears, but *mutatis mutandis*, they were never in arms against their people or the other clans. Nonetheless, they called the military in whenever they had need. And it may be added, the *Ban mhorair Chataibh*, Elizabeth, their hereditary chieftain, thought nothing of conscripting five hundred of the young sons of her people to serve, willy-nilly, in the war against Napoleon.

Lord Gower, the first duke's son and later second duke became intimately connected with Wick as its provost, in succession to Sir John Sinclair of Ulbster, as the result of the purchase by the Sutherlands of the 'superiority' of Wick. The third and fourth Dukes of Sutherland were much involved in improvement and development, especially in the promotion of the Highland Railway, and later the Lybster to Wick line. We shall come to these events in later chapters.

KEITHS

One of the deliberate acts of the early Stuart kings was to strengthen the baronage of Scotland, with a particular flurry of creations during the reign of James II (1437-1460). One of these was the elevation to 'Earl Marischal' of the then 'Great Marischal', William Keith, who lived at Inverugie near the present town of Peterhead. The Keiths were a warrior family which had become established in the Aberdeen area as early as the twelfth century. Herveius de Keith was made 'King's Marshal' by Malcolm IV (1153-1165). A later Keith was made 'Great Marischal' by Robert Bruce in 1320. It was a hereditary office concerned ostensibly with ceremonial functions, especially coronations. The enoblement of William in 1457 confirmed the family in a new access of power and influence.

It was by marriage that the Keiths gained foothold in the Wick area, John Keith, second son of Edward Keith, married Margery Cheyne, the other of Reginald de Cheyne's beautiful daughters, at about the same time (1337) that Nicholas Sutherland married Mary. Calder explains how Andrew, son of John and Mary Keith, in right of his mother became possessed of the lands of Ackergill. By the same right he obtained the castle of Inverugie and the estate connected with it. The family of the Keiths were among the most powerful in Scotland. They had extensive property in the south; and their residence when in this county [Caithness], was the Tower of Ackergill.[1] It is not known when this formidable stronghold was erected, but it cannot be less than from four to five hundred years old [Calder was writing in the mid-nineteenth century]. In the *Origines Parochiales Scotiae* it is mentioned that in 1538 the castle was granted by James V, with half the lands of Ackergill to William, Earl Marischal, and Lady Margaret Keith . . . . .

> The tower – the only part of the old building which remains – stands on a level plain, close by the sea, and is of rectangular form, measuring about eighty-two feet in height; and in breadth, at each of the angles, forty-five feet. It consists of four storeys, two of which are arched; and the massive walls are from ten to eleven feet in thickness. In the centre of these are arched passages, from three to four feet wide, with slits in the walls for the discharge of arrows and other warlike missiles. On the land side, the castle was defended by a deep and broad moat. The winding stair in the middle is so narrow, that even should an enemy have forced the external defences, a resolute retainer or two could have kept a whole host at bay, and prevent them from getting to the upper storeys. The ground, too, in the vicinity of the castle is low, and before the invention of artillery, it might well be considered impregnable. There was, moreover, a draw-well within the tower, twenty-four feet deep, which afforded the inmates a constant supply of water, and nothing but sheer famine could have forced the garrison to surrender. I may here notice a tradition connected with the well. One of the domestics, a black man, is said to have fallen into it, and was drowned. After this accident, the water was

---

[1] Calder adds a note: 'Sir George Dunbar, the proprietor (in the 1850s), has lately added a splendid new mansion, with which the old tower is finely incorporated. He has made many other admirable improvements about the place; and Ackergill Tower, which name it still retains, is now one of the finest gentlemen's seats in the north.' One of the boasts of the Keith chief was that when journeying from Dunnottar to Ackergill, he was able each night to stay in one of his own houses. Dunnottar, the virtually impregnable castle built on a mighty 'pudding-stone' rock on the coast near Stonehaven by Sir William Keith, about 1390, remained the Keith's main home. Ackergill was never a main seat of the Keiths, and during the time in Caithness, the Tower was occupied by a junior or cadet members of the family – usually called a 'Captain'. The *Clan Heritage* book does not mention Ackergill.

never used again, and the well was shut up.[1]

Today the Tower looks as impressive as ever. It stands on a low rock shore at the south end of Sinclair Bay, commanding a view in every direction, including Sinclair and Girnigoe, about two miles away, from which once the menace would come. Its present owners have converted the place into a conference and residential centre, available for hiring in its entirety for periods of as much as a month at a time, and is used by industrial, trade and official organisations as a sort of retreat. Ackergill is about three miles north-west of Wick in which parish it belongs.

George, Fifth Earl Marischal, founded Marischal College of Aberdeen University in 1593. Other Keiths since the days of James II have achieved fame, notably James, a younger son of the Ninth Earl Marischal, who turned out in 1715 in favour of the Old Pretender;[1] then wisely went to the continent, where he joined the Russian army in 1728, and became a General in that army in 1738. Ten years later he was fighting in the army of Frederick the Great of Prussia who made him Field-Marshal. The Keiths, again, are not strictly a 'clan', though they have crest, motto *(Veritas vincit,* a rather pretentious one in the light of their past history) and tartan. They are said to derive their name from the little town of Keith in Strath Isla in Banffshire. Their Gaelic name is *Ceiteach.*

Several stories of the Keiths of Ackergill have already been mentioned (see 'Sinclairs'). Several more remain to be told, but they may better be reserved for the following sections in which we meet the Gunns and the Mackays, with whom the Keiths were mostly on bad terms.

GUNNS

One of the smaller clans of Scotland, the Gunns nevertheless have a formidable reputation. They were, according to the entry in *The Clans and Tartans of Scotland,* 'noted for their war-like and ferocious character, and continued to extend their possessions until the fifteenth century, but their continual feuds with other clans led to their settling, at a later date, chiefly in Sutherland.' It might have been added that it

---

1 John, the Earl Marischal himself, was one of the earls who favoured the Prince (that, is James, the 'Pretender'), and it was at his castle, Fetteresso of the Mearns, that the Prince met his supporters, the Earls Marischal and Mar, Cameron of Lochiel and others, in December, 1715, just after he had disembarked at Peterhead. The story of this subversive gathering is told in Donald Sage's *Memorabilia Domestica.*

was very probably this ferociousness, and the clansmen's readiness to ally themselves, according to interest and opportunity, with Sinclairs, Sutherlands, Keiths and Mackays, that led to their ultimate poverty and poor placing.

How the Gunns came to be located in the border valleys between Caithness and Sutherland, is largely a matter for speculation.[1] Whatever the reason, the Gunns became the implacable enemies of the Keiths. Calder retails the traditional story of how this enmity arose:

> Lachlan Gunn, a small proprietor in Braemore, had an only daughter, named Helen, who was particularly distinguished for her good looks and was called the 'Beauty of Braemore'. The fame of her personal charms had spread through the whole of Sutherland and Caithness. A long and ardent attachment, commencing, it may be said, from childhood, had subsisted between her and her cousin, Alexander Gunn; and the day of their marriage was fixed. About this time, Dugald Keith, a retainer of Keith of Ackergill, and who acted as factor on his property in Caithness, having seen Helen Gunn, was greatly struck with her beauty, and made a dishonourable proposal, which she indignantly rejected. Mortified with this repulse, the proud unprincipled villain resolved to gratify his passion at all hazards. Accordingly, having mustered a strong party of Keiths, he set out for Braemore, and on the wedding eve surrounded the house of Lachlan, where a few of the relations had met to partake of the festivity usual on such an occasion. The Gunns, who were quite unprepared for such an attack, were after a brave resistance, mostly all killed; and the young bride was forcibly seized and carried away to Ackergill Tower, where she was kept a prisoner, and became the victim of the brutal and licentious Keith. The unfortunate young woman could not endure the disgrace and misery of her situation. Like another Lucretia, she resolved on self-destruction; and, having found an opportunity one evening when the keepers were off their guard, she ascended to the top of the tower, and threw herself headlong from the battlements. This tragical affair inspired the whole clan with implacable resentment against the Keiths, and was the cause of much future strife and bloodshed.

[1] Thoughts on the subject may be suggested by a visit to the Clan Gunn Museum, recently established in the old Latheron kirk, just off A9.

Then followed a tale about warfare between the Keiths and the Mackays, to which we shall return shortly when the Mackay clan itself has been presented. In the meantime, there is yet one more encounter between Gunns and Keiths to be retailed. This concerned 'Crowner' George Gunn and the then chief of the Keiths. George is usually referred to in accounts of the Gunns as perhaps their most eminent chief.[1]

The Gunns at this time occupied an area in the south of Caithness and had established as their headquarters 'Castle Gunn' at Clyth, another almost inaccessible stronghold on the rocky Caithness coast, about ten miles south of Wick – it has now virtually disappeared. Legends are associated with this castle about a Gunn chief and his Danish princess bride.[2] For some reason, this castle was abandoned in favour of Halberry, a little further down the coast, where George ruled 'in great feudal splendour'. The tale continues (as quoted in the *Clan Gunn Heritage* book):

> George or 'Crowner' Gunn, or as he was called by the Highlanders, *N'm Braistach More* (the 'Great Brooch'), from a great brooch which he wore as the badge or cognizance of his office of crowner. He had a deadly feud with the chief of the Keiths; and having met at St Tyre's chapel for the purpose of effecting a reconciliation, but without success, they were solemnly agreed to decide their quarrel, if they could not do so amicably on a future day, by equal combat between twelve sons or relatives of each chieftain. The crowner and the leader of the Keiths approached each other in full armour; but it was soon

---

[1] 'Crowner' (or *chruner*) Gunn, the chief of the clan in the mid fifteenth-century, so called because of his appointment as the local 'officer to whom it belonged to attach all persons against whom there was an accusation in matters pertaining to the Crown. He had also the charge of the troops raised in the county.' There was such an office in various localities, and the need for it was considerable, especially in such lawless places as Caithness and Sutherland. To find a Gunn holding such office is curious; in an area dominated by Sinclairs, Sutherlands and Keiths, who regarded themselves as 'the law', is odd indeed. It may be that this was precisely why George Gunn was chosen, though his clan could hardly be regarded as exemplary abiders by the law.

[2] A reference to this event occurs in a footnote in the *First Statistical Account*, op cit: 'There is a rock near Ulbster called Lechan Ore, a name which, according to tradition, is obtained from the following circumstance: Gunn of Clyth, a gentleman of Caithness, going over to Denmark, prevailed upon a Danish princess to marry him. In returning home, to make preparations for the reception of the lady and her attendants, the vessel, with the expected guests, was wrecked upon this rock, and every soul perished. A pot full of gold, the remains of the wreck, having been found upon this rock, it hence obtained the name of Lechan Ore, or golden flags. The body of the Princess was thrown ashore, and interred in the neighbouring burying-ground at Ulbster, where Sir John Sinclair's family tomb is situated. The stone, which is said to cover her grave, is still extant; and has some heiroglyphick characters inscribed, though not much obliterated by time.'

discovered by the Gunns that there were two riders on every horse in the party of Keiths, and consequently the latter party had twenty-four men opposed to the twelve followers of the Gunns that their destruction, by unfair means, was determined upon.[1] They scorned, notwithstanding the great odds against them, to retreat before their enemies, the Keiths; and fought most desperately, but could not withstand the great odds opposed to them. After a long struggle, the survivors of both sides were so much exhausted, that the combat was mutually dropped – the Keiths being so far the victors as to leave the field with their banner displayed, and to be able to carry with them their slain companions; while in the ranks of the Gunns, the crowner and seven of his party were killed, and the remaining five were all severely wounded.

The event is dated by Calder as 1464 (during the reign of James III), and the location as the Chapel of St Tears, 'or, as it was vulgarly called, St Tayre', The chapel stood, evidently, 'half-way between Castle Sinclair and Girnigoe and the Tower of Ackergill', though there is nothing of it left. According to the *Statistical Account* of 1840: 'Within the memory of persons yet living, it was customary for people to visit the Chapel of St Tears on Innocents' Day, and leave in it bread and cheese, as an offering to the souls of the children slain by Herod: but which the dog-keeper of a neighbouring gentleman used to take out and give to the hounds.' This is mentioned as evidence that until recent times, 'hagiolatry still lurked in the parish of Wick'. There is no monument to the episode of 1464.

As might be expected, the Gunns were not likely to leave such a defeat unavenged. The chronicler continues:

> The Keiths proceeded to Dilred castle, in Strathmore (Dirlot, a keep downstream from Loch More, 'yet another of the castles of de Cheyne and afterwards in turn held by the Gunns, Sutherlands and Mackays), then occupied by the Sutherland of Dilred, where they were hospitably entertained. The five surviving Gunns, who were all sons of the crowner, also retired, but tarried at another stream, since then called Alt-

---

1 This kind of 'stratagem', carried through with comparable treachery, is similar to that by which, according to the *Orkneyinga Saga*, Earl Magnus was 'martyred' by his cousin, Earl Hakon, with whom he had agreed a meeting on Egilsay to settle differences. Each was to bring an equal number of men. Hakon brought twice the agreed number, with the inevitable result. Another version of the story is to be found in Sage's *Memorabilia*, op cit, pp 83-86, but in this account the battle is located in Strathmore.

Torquil, after Torquil Gunn, one of the survivors, who there dressed the wounds of the brothers. Towards evening, Henrybeg, the youngest of the surviving brothers of the Gunns, proposed that they should follow the Keiths, and endeavour to obtain revenge, even by strategem such as the Keiths had recourse to. They arrived at Dilred Castle soon after nightfall.

On approaching the castle, its wooden windows or shutters were found open, and around a large fire in the lowest apartment the survivors of the Keiths were quaffing bumpers of ale; and Henry, who went close to one of the windows, heard them narrate, with boisterous delight, the losses sustained by the Gunns. The chief of the Keiths, not apprehensive of any danger, accidentally approached the window where Henry stood, and the later then bent his bow, and in another instant his arrow pierced the chieftain's heart; Henry at this time boldly accompanying the deadly flight of his arrow with the exclamation (afterwards used in the Highlands as a proverb) of 'the Gunn's compliment to Keith' (in Gaelic, *Iomach gar n' Guinach gu Kaigh*). The old chief dropped down dead; a panic seized the other Keiths; and the three Gunns, having darted forward to the door of the castle, slew some of the first persons who ventured out by it; but finding they could not retain their position long, Henry and his brothers retired silently under cover of darkness of the night, and hurried back to the assistance of the other brothers who had been unable to accompany them.[1]

The Gunns never commanded great tracts of territory like the Sinclairs, Sutherlands and Keiths, and for most of the following centuries they made their home in Kildonan, the upper valley of the Helmsdale river in Sutherland country. It was in consequence of this that the Gunns found themselves at the mercy of the factors of the Marquis of Stafford when the clearances began in this area in 1813. By this time the majority of Gunns were poor crofters with no powerful chieftains or allies to help them in their need. Even so, serious rumours spread that the once fearsome Clan Gunn was on the march down to Golspie, 'threatening to hang Sellar and Young, expel all sheepfarmers and burn Dunrobin Castle'. They neither had the means

---

1 If the rock in the bend of the Thurso river shown today as Dirlot castle is the authentic site, the Gunns' stratagem on this occasion would have been very difficult to accomplish. The 'Castle' today consists of a great tower of rock rising almost vertically out of the stream bed on the north side.

nor the intention, but soldiers from the 21st Foot (mostly Irishmen) were brought in to make sure they were cleared from the valley. Prebble comments:

> At Whitsun (1813) large areas of Strath Kildonan were cleared and left to grass which, even after a century and a half, still grows greenest where the people had their tiny potato-patches. They were offered meagre lots of land on the cliffs of Helmsdale, the choice of becoming herring-fishers or leaving the country altogether.

Some joined other victims of clearance and emigrated to Canada, especially to the Red River valley in Manitoba, where there are today numerous Gunns cherishing mixed feelings towards their ancient homeland. Some certainly became herring-fishers, not only in Helmsdale and upwards along the coast in Dunbeath, Latheronwheel and Lybster, but also in Wick, then beginning its rise to the status of 'the herring capital of Europe.' Gunns are very numerous in modern Wick. One Gunn, who does not seem to have qualified for inclusion in the Clan Gunn Heritage Book as a 'Clan Notable', is Neil M Gunn, a native son of Dunbeath, whose novels of Gunn country are among the most moving and revealing of all writings in this strange, tortured land.[1]

Yet other Gunns are to be found in Orkney. Gunn is a common name especially in Stromness. The most famous Gunn of them all for many years inhabited 'Treasure Island'.

MACKAYS

When not quarrelling with Sinclairs, Sutherlands or Keiths, the Gunns were likely to be at odds with the Mackays. The main group of this ubiquitous family established their home, possibly in the fifteenth century, in Strathnaver, the long valley of the Naver river in north Sutherland. They are the only 'Macs' among the northern clans and their history has more in common with the clans of the west than the others we have discussed. Their original clan name is said to have been Morgan, which was also known as Clan Iye, or *Aoidh*, and their present Gaelic name is *MacAoidh*.

---

[1] Curiously he does not appear either in the *Oxford Companion to English Literature,* where many far less notable contributors to the canon of English literature (it may be safer to say 'Scottish literature') find a place. Gunn's *Silver Darlings* is essential reading for anyone who wishes to know about the herring-men of clearance times.

BISHOPS, SUTHERLANDS AND OTHERS

They gained over the centuries a reputation for ferocious quarrelsomeness and fighting qualities, often as allies of other groups. In 1438 they became involved in a fierce encounter between the Keiths and Gunns. The story goes:

> Having heard that the Gunns had got a number of the other inhabitants of Caithness to join them, and were preparing for an immediate attack, Keith of Ackergill, mistrustful of his own strength, applied for aid to Angus Mackay, son of the famous Neil Bass Mackay, who readily complied with the request, and having assembled all the able-bodied of his followers, made a hurried march of about thirty miles through Caithness to assist his friend. The hostile armies met on the moor of Tannach, about three miles from Wick (south-west), where a furious conflict ensued, attended with great slaughter on both sides. In the end the Keiths obtained the victory, chiefly through the extraordinary prowess of a herculean Highlander, who rejoiced in the euphonious appellation of John More-Macean-Reawich-Mackay. The battle, however, did not terminate hostilities between the two contending parties. The feud continued for a long time after, during which they strove to harass and inflict as much injury on each other as possible.

In due course, the Mackays began to put their fighting abilities to uses other than that of clan warfare. For all the lawlessness and rebellion of the sixteenth and seventeenth centuries, central government gradually established closer control of affairs in the northern provinces and, in the words of a clan writer, 'the Mackays' war-like spirit did not find sufficient outlet at home, and in 1626 Sir Donald Mackay of Farr (near Bettyhill) raised an army of 3000 men for service in Bohemia, and afterwards in Denmark. Finally, with a large force from the North of Scotland, he served under Gustavus Adolphus with great distinction. He was raised to the peerage with the title Lord Reay by Charles 1, in 1628, and died in Denmark in 1649. His grandson, Aeneas, was colonel of the Mackay Dutch regiment and settled in Holland, where the family were enobled with the title of Baron, and when the Scottish succession ceased Baron Eric Mackay van Omphert, Holland, became 12th Baron Reay.'

Like the Gunns of Kildonan, many Mackays of Strathnaver in the later years had became 'tenants-at-will' of the Sutherlands, that is, after 1803 the Marquis of Stafford and his Lady – Countess of Sutherland in her own right. They were the main victims of the evictions and burnings of 1814 when Patrick Sellar, himself now owner of large tracts of sheep-pasture on the banks of the Naver at Skaill, supervised the operation.[1] At the same time most of the remaining inhabitants of Upper Kildonan – where the railway now runs from Kinbrace to Forsinard – were evacuated. Summing up the effects of this drastic clearance of Kildonan Strath in 1815, John Prebble writes:

> Now it was time for Loch [Stafford's Commissioner, an enthusiastic Utilitarian[2]] to clear away the rest, to drive them down to Helmsdale, where his workmen were building herring-stores, curing-sheds and harbour offices, all bearing Stafford arms and the date of the year in grey Highland stone [some of these buildings are still there]. And if the people were too lazy (in Loch's opinion) to leave the plough for the trawl [this is a bit previous – the 'trawl' came later], they might walk to the emigrants' ships at Wick and Thurso, and the country would be well rid of them.

Unlike Gunns who are numerous in Wick, Mackays do not seem to have come to rest in the county capital or in east Caithness generally in any great numbers, as reference to today's telephone book will confirm – though the town's premier hotel bears the Mackay label. They became, however, like the Children of Israel in the Diaspora, spread widely about the world, especially the north of Scotland. Quoting the contemporary Presbyterian minister, Donald Sage – one of the very few of his kind who took the part, verbally, at least – of the Gunns and Mackays being 'cleared', Prebble's account continues:

> The whole inhabitants of Kildonan parish, with the exception of three families, nearly 2,000 souls, were utterly rooted and burned out. Many, especially the young and robust, left the country, but the aged, the females and children, were obliged to stay and accept the wretched allotments allowed them on the

---

1 In 1816 Sellar was arraigned before the Lord Commissioner of Justiciary at Inverness, on charges of 'culpable homicide', 'oppression' and 'real injury', and with many witnesses against him was completely exonerated. In fact, only a few of the witnesses were called.

2 Adherence to this philosophy was a characteristic of most 'improvers'. Many administrators of relief programmes to the distressed and displaced of these times were of the same cast of mind, notoriously Charles Trevelyan, concerned with relief in Ireland in 1846-1847. The 'greatest good' notion often led them into indifference to cases of individual suffering. James Loch outlived his reputation as a ruthless supervisor of the clearance policies of the Sutherlands to become in later years the repeatedly re-elected Liberal MP of the Northern Burghs from 1830 to 1850, gaining much favourable coverage in the *John O'Groat Journal* as a keen promoter of the interests of Wick.

sea-shore and endeavour to learn fishing.

Perhaps the most poignant irony of this whole episode of the removal of Gunns and Mackays from the lands of their fathers is provided by the story of the 93rd Regiment, the Sutherland Highlanders. 'Frequently described as "the most Highland of Highland regiments"', says Prebble in *Mutiny*, 'it was also the last to be raised in the old way as a clan levy and thus, perhaps, the last real Highland regiment.' Whether or not the Sutherlanders constituted a true clan (the clan was certainly of an unusual kind), this famous regiment was raised directly by the *Ben mhorair Chataibh*, the 'Great Lady of Sutherland', in response to the appeal in 1793 of Henry Dundas, Home Secretary (1791-1794) and a short time later Secretary at War (1794-1801) in Pitt's government, to the Highland lairds to muster their tenants, ostensibly for the defence of the realm in the war now being waged against the French Revolutionary government.[1]

The first regiment of 'Fencible Men'[2] raised after this call was the Strathspey Regiment of the Grants; the second was the Sutherland Fencibles, re-mustered in 1799 as the 93rd Sutherland Regiment. There had been earlier Sutherland Fencibles, the first raised in 1759 by the then Earl of Sutherland during the Seven Years' War. This had been 'reduced' or stood-down some time later. A second local Fencible Regiment was recruited in 1779 under the command of Colonel William Wemyss, a relative of the Countess, who as an MP had offered to 'call upon the young men of Strath Fleet (behind Golspie), Strath Naver and Strath Helmsdale'. Men from this and the Fencibles of 1793 were absorbed into the Sutherland Regiment, officially dating from 1800.

The circumstances of the recruitment of this famous regiment are well put by Prebble (whose partisanship must be admitted):

1 'Ostensibly', since this appeal was by the Home Secretary, less concerned in 1793 with the war than with the unrest developing in the Highlands as the result of 'over-population' resulting largely from the 'improvements', already advancing in the area under the influence of the British Wool Society, and marked by the arrival in the north of 'the Great Cheviot'. These were, indeed, times of considerable public disquiet, quite apart from the war. Britain was going through a drastic social revolution precipitated by industrial and agricultural changes usually described as the 'Industrial Revolution'.

2 A shortened form of *defensible*, first used in the sixteenth century to describe men fit and able for military service. In the eighteenth century the term 'Fencible men' was used to describe those who could be mustered for training, perhaps 'home guard' activities but most important, men who could be re-mustered or re-enlisted in marching regiments. Most fencibles were promised, in the first instance, that they would not be sent on foreign service, a promise often broken and a cause of the 'mutinies' with which the army was plagued in these times. See John Prebble, *Mutiny: Highland Regiments in Revolt, 1743-1804*; Penguin (1977).

For all their exasperating sloth, their winter dreaming about their peat-fires, their scandalous habit of living cheek by jowl with their livestock, the Highlanders of Sutherland had one virtue on which the nation greedily fastened. This was their courage and their belief that nowhere in the world was there a fighting-man to equal the Gael with a broadsword in his hand. The Countess Elizabeth was the last among the Scottish chiefs who raised their people for service in the Napoleonic Wars, but she surpassed them for volunteers. She did not go among her clan with six pipers, like the Duchess of Gordon, giving a kiss and a guinea to every recruit. She imposed a form of conscription that would have won Bonaparte's approval. She called for a census of her tenants and sub-tenants, and when this was done five hundred able-bodied young men among them were told that service in the Sutherland Highlanders would be a test of their duty to the *Ban mhorair Chataibh* and their loyalty to King George III. Though parents may have grumbled bitterly about the choice they were forced to make between the loss of a son and the loss of their tenancy the young men went willingly enough.

They made an incredible regiment. 'They are all brave,' said David Stewart of Garth. In nineteen years not one man of the light company, for example, was punished for misconduct. And many of those who survived the heat of South Africa, the fevers of the West Indies, or American Musketry at New Orleans came home at last to find their glens empty, their homes pulled down stone from stone, and their families dispersed.

For Mr Sellar and Mr Young and Mr Loch had been busy, improving Lord Stafford's estates.[1]

Though not expressly much to do with Wick, this was a key element of the Sutherland and Caithness background against which the herring industry grew, putting Wick on the map. Among the fishers, packers, carters and coopers working on the Wick, Lybster and Dunbeath fish-quays must have been quite a number of the demobbed and dispossessed Sutherland Highlanders; and among the gutters would have been their wives and daughters.

---

1 Prebble, *The Highland Clearances,* op cit pp 57-58. An alternative view of the Duke, as being 'lavish with capital to ameliorate social dislocation' is suggested by TC Smouth, p 92, writing about Helmsdale in *The Landowner and the Planned Village.*

CHAPTER 5

ROYAL BURGH

TO become a 'burgh' was less an honour for a town than a signal of arrival at a useful and sometimes more prosperous status. Towns of any size and importance during feudal times were few and far between, and the folk of those that existed were usually subject to and often mistreated and overtaxed by their lords. Towns were even fewer in Scotland than in England and their status even more menial. As one Scottish historian puts it, they 'were an almost new feature of twelfth-century Scotland'.

It was King David I, (1124-1153) - former Earl of Huntingdon, and thoroughly familiar with English ways of managing things – who began promoting settlements in Scotland to the dignity of 'burgh', under his Leges Burgorum, which he had copied from the statutes of the borough of Newcastle upon Tyne – a town well known to the Scots, who had overrun it more than once. Among the new 'burghs' were no less than fifteen towns, not all of which have survived, for instance Roxburgh, but including Edinburgh, Dunfermline, Perth and Stirling. A town's status as burgh signified various advantages such as freedom from impositions other than those of the king, certain rights as to customs affecting trade, especially exports, freedoms of town government and rights of association for craftsmen and tradesmen in guilds, with defined powers as to the regulation of manufacturing and trade activities. Also a number of burghs were allowed to set up royal mints. By 1250, during the reign of Alexander III, there were no less than sixteen towns with a mint, including Berwick, Ayr, Roxburgh and Inverness. Trading outside the jurisdiction of the king's burghs came under severe restriction.

Two kinds of burgh came into existence, those established and governed under a royal charter, specifically granted to that town, and known as 'royal burghs', and 'burghs of barony', usually smaller towns granted similiar but less extensive privileges by the lord of the county under sanction of the king. As might be supposed, neither burghs of barony nor royal burghs were numerous in the north of Scotland. In Caithness two towns eventually qualified for burgh status, Wick and Thurso. Wick became a burgh of barony some time

Fig. 6 A portion of Timothy Pont's Map of Caithness. (Note the four lines of cottages denoting Wick). *(Courtesy of the Scottish National Library).*

during the earlship of Nicholas of Sutherland, probably in the time of King Robert III (1390-1406), the first Stewart king. Nicholas, as we have seen, came into possession of Auldwick in about the year 1350 when Reginald de Cheyne, its previous 'owner' died. This was before Sinclairs came to Caithness and long before the classic rivalry between the two families, Sutherland and Sinclair, set in.

However deserving or undeserving Wick might have been for the honour, it was 'erected a royal burgh in 1589, by James VI'1 when George Sinclair III was owner and chief power in Caithness. 'This municipal honour, with its accompanying privileges, was conferred on it at the request of the Earl of Caithness,' says Calder, with whatever authority. If this was so, it would explain how so undistinguished and isolated a community as Wick was at this time came to be chosen. 'It would only have been,' continues Calder, 'a mean looking village, consisting of a few thatched houses.' Calder enters the caveat, that 'it would have been a place of some little trade, for in an inroad of the Sutherland men in 1588, it is said that among other acts of spoliation, they plundered the ship and carried away the goods of one Andrew Wardlaw, a merchant of the town.' George Sinclair, as we have noticed before, was usually in King James's good books, and although this was some years before his signal services on behalf of the king in Orkney, this was probably one of the times when he was in favour. That it was a move against Sutherland can hardly be doubted. Even if the Sutherlands had relinquished their privileges in Wick when the property was sold to the Oliphants, George was at that time seeking in every way he could, to revenge himself on Sutherland; and the designation in his earldom of a royal burgh, especially one that had recently been ravaged by Sutherland, would be one up to the Earl of Caithness. This is certainly how some historians have seen it.2 Thurso at this time was under Sutherland's control, and Thurso, by all indications, was a larger town and trading centre than Wick; but it still had no burgh status until 1633, when it became under Charles I a

---

1 An elaborate Quater Centenary was celebrated in Wick in 1989. A translation of the Burgh Charter of Wick, awarded in 1589, the original in Latin, is given at the end of this chapter. The evidence for the creation of Wick as a 'burgh of barony' is based somewhat shakily on a reference to a lost charter, quoted in Historic Wick (q.v.), p1, of about 1393-1394, quoting in its turn G S Pryde: The Burghs of Scotland; London, (1965), p 47. Pryde also comments that the creation of Wick as a royal burgh encountered the hostility of other northern royal burghs and, as Historic Wick puts it, 'thus Wick was not admitted to Parliament or the Convention of Royal Burghs until 1661 (the year after the Stewart Restoration)'; see Pryde, op cit, p 28.

2 See notes of Thomas Sinclair to Calder's History, reproduced in Addendum at the end of the chapter, p 114.

'free burgh of barony'.1

That George Sinclair, Earl of Caithness, cared anything about the royal burgh in his domain does not appear in his actions. No sooner had Sutherland gone home after abandoning the siege of Girnigoe, on the way out committing a spate of damage in Caithness, than the Earl 'retaliated by a succession of inroads into Sutherland', and later in 1589 was fought the 'Battle of Clyne'. George was doubtless too concerned with the feud to give much attention to such a trivial matter as the well-being of Wick, though after the Clyne blood-letting there came a period of several years' peace between the two earls.

Few clues exist as to the size and shape of Wick in these times. Thomas Sinclair who wrote some notes to the second edition of Calder's History comments:

> In 1608, judging from Pont's map, Wick was divided into four rather straggling groups of buildings, the smallest near Proudfoot Point, and the two largest opposite an island in the river. The church stood in the fourth group, which was also somewhat larger. On the east side of the church the road went, which crossed by a bridge to Newton. The whole town was less than a mile in length.

The description of the town in the John O'Groat Journal Anecdotes, probably owes as much to the writer's imagination as to established knowledge. Nevertheless the picture presented by Captain Kennedy is doubtless realistic enough:

> It was not until the reign of the Sixth James . . . . . that this town was constituted a burgh by royal charter, and its importance, appearance, and commerce, at the epoch we speak of, were by no means of such a nature as to distinguish it in any particular way from the other villages or townships in its vicinity. From one to one hundred and fifty houses then formed the village, all of them of the meanest description, built in complete defiance of architectural rule, and scattered in every direction with the most thorough contempt for order and regularity. The houses, if such they could be termed, were constructed of turf, with a steeth or basement of stone, and

---

1 King James, it may be added, was a notorious seller of honours and dignities, for his treasuries, both in Edinburgh and London, were always empty. It was James who, on the advice of his Chancellor, invented the dignity of 'Baronet', conferring it willy-nilly on a large number of candidates whose chief merit was possession of wealth, a decent portion of which James coveted and required them to pay for the honour.

Fig. 7 Wick houses of the eighteenth century

covered in with turf or a divot roof, which, sometimes laid over with straw, and sometimes not, were, in either case, peculiarly well adapted for offering a retreat to the various insects and vermin by which they were infested. Nor were the interior arrangements, from which the air was totally excluded, and through which the smoke found its way by an aperture, gave the greater part of such houses the appearance of bandits' caves, while the many holes and crevices with which the walls were indented, left for seemingly no other purpose than to gather filth, and the various recesses reserved for the accommodation of the cows, pigs, hens etc of the establishment, left no favourable impression of the habits of the biped inhabitants. Indeed, the familiar and friendly footing on which these animals appeared to be with the family, would naturally have led a stranger to infer that in the construction of their houses the inhabitants were more swayed by the desire of rendering the apartments agreeable to the brute creatures than to themselves. Such, too, was the poverty of the people, and the abject state of servitude to which they were subjected by their too often despotic masters, the Earls of Caithness, that not until many years after did they dare to represent to the Superior the necessity of having certain civic privileges granted to the town, or of taking such steps as might be conducive to improvement and the advancement of its trade.[1]

---

[1] The John O'Groat Journal would be by no means far from the truth. Even in the traditional Orkney and Caithness 'long-house', examples of which survive, the animal accommodation was designed to ensure ease of access to (contined on foot of next page)

It is unlikely that the inhabitants of this tiny, poor, windy city soon gained much benefit from its enhanced status as a royal burgh. The town was awarded a 'set', a town government consisting of a provost, two bailies, a dean of guild, a treasurer and seven councillors, elected by the burgesses.1 For all its new constitution the town, nevertheless, remained subject to the domination of the earl who possessed the 'superiority' of the town, that is, a status in some respects not unlike that of the English 'lord of the manor'. His rights as to revenue due from the town and his powers of interference in town government were written into the Charter (given in full English translation at the end of this chapter). These rights remained until extinguished in the nineteenth century. As a royal burgh Wick was entitled to parliamentary representation, but the creation 'encountered the hostility of other northern burghs, and thus Wick was not admitted to Parliament or the Convention of Royal Burghs until 1661.'2

THE CASTLE OF WICK

We shall return shortly to the civic history of Wick between its arrival at royal burgh status and the days of its take-off as a town of some economic importance in the late eighteenth century. In the meantime there is more to be said about the castle, the gloomy square pile that stands on a forbidding rocky peninsula along the coast south of the town, in an area marked on the map as 'Old Wick'. As already mentioned, little is known about the keep's early history. Rather more is reported of it later.

Calder's picture of the ruin is lurid:

> About two miles to the south of Wick, on a tongue of land having a steep goe on each side, stand the remains of the Castle of Auldwick. This huge unshapely ruin forms an excellent landmark to vessels approaching the coast, and is by seamen called the 'Auld Man of Wick'. It consists of a grim looking tower or keep of rudest masonry, perforated here and there

---

(Continued from foot of previous page) byres and pens during winter and making maximum use of for mutual advantage as between men and animals of natural warmth. The implications of this for stench hardly bear thinking about.

1 The model for this type of town government, quite unlike that of English towns, was French, first instituted in France by Phillip II (1180-1223) in the royal demesne. The bailli was a senior officer over existing officials (a sort of 'chief executive'), and the prévot was directly responsible to the crown.

2 The peculiarities of 'Superiority' are discussed in Chapter 6, pp 125-134 and N3 pp 126-127), and those of parliamentary representation of royal burghs in Chapter 6, pp 164-168).

with small arrow-slits, and rising to the height of three storeys. It is entirely roofless, and open within from top to bottom. A deep and broad moat defended it on the land side. Behind, or rather in front of the tower – for the only door looked towards the sea in the direction of north-east – there were two ranges of lower buildings for domestic purposes, and a small space, near the extremity of the peninsula, would seem to have been used as a garden. Traces of a wall that surrounded it are still discernible. At this point the rocks shelve down in the form of rugged terraces; and, in front of the entrance, a dangerous position, lie large black isolated lumps of rock, waiting, as it were, to destroy any boat that, without a proper knowledge of the place, might venture to enter either of the goes. The whole aspect of the scene is peculiarly wild and repulsive, without a single redeeming feature of beauty. With a gale from the east or north-east, the sea-branch is horrible, reminding one of the poet's epithet of a 'hell of waters'. The maddened breakers roar, and foam, and dash in fiend-like fury against the iron cliffs, while the old keep, dry and weather-beaten, scowls amid the storm, like an angry demon.1

The castle's origins are unknown, though according to Calder 'it is one of the oldest buildings of the kind in Caithness'. The first known occupants of the castle were the de Cheynes, one of the numerous Norman families who, through various services, worked their way into Scottish affairs and became possessors of considerable property. They first appear as owners of land in Aberdeenshire. In the thirteenth century a de Cheyne became Lord Chamberlain of Scotland during the reign of Alexander III (1249-1286). Another became Bishop of Aberdeen, and another one, Ronald or Reginald, gained a legendary reputation for furious fighting qualities as the result of his part in the Battle of Harlaw in 1411, a battle fought in Aberdeenshire between the Lord of the Isles and a royal army, led by the Earl of Mar.

A little of the story of Auldwick castle has already been told. From

---

1 Calder, like many of his contemporaries, was given to the excesses of expression sometimes described as the 'Pathetic Fallacy', in which writers tended to ascribe to features and events of nature human attributes and emotions. His reading would have included pre-Romantics such as Horace Walpole (The Castle of Otranto), possibly Mrs Ratcliffe (The Mysteries of Udolpho), and certainly Romantics such as Scott, Wordsworth and Coleridge. Coleridge in particular would often present nature as though it were a malevolent force. Words such as 'horrid', 'dreadful', 'menacing', 'fearsome', were favourites for describing scenes of rugged nature in nature in mountains and on the sea; breezes were 'zephyrs' and the rain was usually 'gentle'.

the de Cheynes the castle passed to the Sutherlands in 1337, from whom it went to the Oliphants, another family of Norman origins. James IV (1488-1513) awarded the 'superiority' of Auldwick and Berriedale to George, Lord Oliphant of Wick, the first George who, for whatever reason, fell foul of the Earl of Caithness, William the first Sinclair earl. This was generally not a difficult thing to do, even though William is usually thought of as a 'good' earl.

As always there are different versions, but the Anecdotal account is doubtless as satisfactory as any:

> A deadly feud, originating in a dispute about property, is said to have arisen between this George, styled Lord Oliphant, and the Earl of Caithness (who in those days would have been John, third independent Earl of Caithness); and he, as he happened to be out one day hunting, in the vicinity of the hill of Yarrows (which overlooks Ulbster), was attacked by the Earl and some of his retainers. Oliphant was without any attendants; but, fortunately for him, he had a fleet horse. He immediately set spurs to the animal, and galloped home towards Auldwick, hotly pursued by the Earl and his dependants. On approaching the castle he found that the drawbridge was not lowered. His pursuers were close behind him, and he had not even time to wind his hunting-horn, and warn the inmates of his return. It was a critical moment, and the noble animal on which he rode seemed fully to understand the danger. No application of spur or whip was needed. Exerting his full power, the horse leaped across the terrific chasm – clearing at one bound twenty-five feet – and landed his rider safe on the other side. Lord Oliphant's leap was long talked of in Caithness, and was a familiar saying among the people.1

According to another account Oliphant had two attendants (though there is no mention of what happened to them), and Oliphant's horse was killed in the leap. Yet another tradition, repeated in the Statistical Account of 1794, and quite unsubstantiated, is that 'one of the Lords

---

1 Imagination has been at work here too. Unless there has been a lot of infill since Oliphant's leap, the 'terrific chasm' – presumably the man-made ditch across the peninsula on which the castle stands (no watered moat was possible here), for it is over this that the drawbridge would have swung – could without any great exertion of strength, have been leapt by a fit man. Great chasms, indeed, separate the castle rock from its surroundings on either side, but neither of these could conceivably have been leapt by man or beast. Stories of great leaps occur elsewhere in Caithness, notably the feat of Ian McCormack Gunn who, chased by his enemies, once leapt the gorge in Dunbeath Strath.

Oliphant . . . . . is said in ancient times, to have been murdered, at a place not far distant from the castle.' It is a poor castle that has no tales of daring, deadly deeds and ghosts.

This episode of the leap is followed by another lurid story. According to this, Earl John was anxious to gain possession of Auldwick, and made a compact with the Seneschal of the castle, a certain Patrick Dow. The plan was for Dow to deliver up the castle when Oliphant was away on a visit to Berriedale down the coast. Dow was seen near to Girnigoe the night before the action, presumably making the final arrangements with the earl. The earl and his men slept in Wick that night, and in the morning waited for Dow's signal, a white flag to fly above the castle wall. The flag was duly raised, the earl and his men arrived before the garrison of Auldwick was properly awake, and after a short encounter overpowered the men-at-arms within. For whatever reason, distrust, failure of Dow to fulfil all the articles of the treacherous agreement, or just simply cruel whim, the earl ordered Dow to be hanged over the very place where the flag had flown. The 'traitor's gibbet . . . for many years projected from the wall of Castle Oldwick; but the tower (adds the chronicler) having some years ago fallen in at the top, the one which Dow suffered fell with it and was buried in its ruins.'1

Dow had a daughter, Margaret Dow ('Dow' is thought to be a version of 'Dhu', 'black', one of the names of Angus, 'presumed founder of the clan name' of Mackay, who is said to have been eighteen at the time of the siege of Auldwick. She escaped to a relative in Strathhalladale, to the home of a Mackay, consumed with a burning determination to be revenged on the Earl of Caithness. Courting her was Ronald Mackay, a young man from the north of Strathnaver, the Mackay country; but she would have nothing of him unless he would commit himself to becoming her 'instrument of revenge'. This he consented to, and set off across the bogs. He lost his way and his horse, but somewhere near the Loch of Stemster (now no longer marked on the map; it was somewhere along the valley of the Acharn Burn a few miles from Wick), laid up for the night in a bothie where he had a macabre dream which included visions of an altar, a funeral service, Margaret, and the 'pale phantom of her murdered father', hanging from his gibbet on the walls of Auldwick. All very Gothic.

Mackay fell in with a party of 'two Highland musketeers', returning from a raid in Sutherland, servants of the Earl of Caithness.

2 This is one of the tales told by the antiquarian writer of Anecdotes in the early issue of the John O'Groat Journal (no VIII).

They accepted his offer to join them for the rest of their journey to Girnigoe, where, under a false name, he obtained service on the castle kitchen staff. His intention was to make an entrance to the earl's bedroom by impersonating a domestic, whom he had waylaid and murdered, but somehow alarmed a sentry on duty and had to make hurried escape from Girnigoe by diving into the sea in the deep geo below the castle. 'Long before the cause of alarm was discovered he had climbed the rock, and was half way on his journey to the neighbouring town of Wick.'

With numerous embellishments (including the description of Wick town already quoted), the chronicler tells how Ronald escaped from Wick where 'he was by no means desirous of prolonging his stay in a place which offered him so insecure an asylum, and aware that Earl John would, after the bloody deed which had been committed at Castle Girnigoe, cause a strict enquiry to be made as to the arrival of strangers in that part of the county, he determined on leaving Wick with as little delay as possible.' The story continues (though no source is given, and it could just as well have written by a Walter Scott):

> The only tavern or hostelrie then in the place was 'The Sinclair Arms', a one-story, mean-looking building situated in the well-known area of the 'Kirk Stile', then the residence of the better or higher class of citizens. To this house of entertainment, kept by Patrick or Peter Swanson (history saith not which) did our hero find his way, and while employed in discussing a coarse but plentiful meal provided for him by 'mine-hostess', was joined by a square-built, portly, fair-haired, red-faced individual, dressed in a seaman's jacket and trowsers, who, after unceremoniously taking a deep draught from a quaigh of Mrs Swanson's best ale, which she had placed before our hero, asked him without further circumlocution, and in broken English, if he 'wanted a passage to Orkney'. Under other circumstances Ronald M'Kay was not the man to pass over in silence any infringement on the rules of good breeding, still less an insult to himself; but reflecting on the critical situation in which he was placed, and perceiving that the new guest was a character, he resolved to humour him, and keep a 'calm sough'. The question put to him also, though unlooked for, was by no means a disagreeable one, and having unhesitatingly answered in the affirmative, he learned to his infinite satisfaction that the Kokosnoedder of Bergen, Hans Jarlsen, schipper, de parson voo

has de pleasars to drunk hims helz (a second dip in the quaigh) would staart from vaater of Vick dat saam naght for Kirevaal. Accordingly, about two o'clock the same day, our hero, having no arrangements to make, was transported on board the Norwegian schooner, then lying at anchor off Cairn Doona on the south side of the Bay of Wick. Captain Jansen, who had business to attend to, did not make his appearance until one o'clock next morning. Our manuscript does not explain the nature of the transactions engaged in. A lurking suspicion exists as to its having been nothing else but indulging in Peter Swanson's favourite mixture of warm, home-brewed and real Nantz, a beverage designated by the aforesaid Peter as 'Kirkstile Punch'. Immediately on the Captain's appearance, which plainly indicated that his business had been exciting, the anchor was weighed, and a smart south-wester having declared itself, away went the Kokosnoedder under a press of canvas for the Orkney Isles.1

How much credence can be put in this tale and in the description of Wick in the early sixteenth century must be a matter for judgement, since our anonymous author does not identify his 'Original Manuscript'. Though cast in elaborately romantic style, the story is not all improbable, and since there are several significant references to Wick, it is too good to leave out. That Wick was a place of little importance or charm at the time can hardly be doubted. That it was a port of any standing may be doubted too. The fact that the Kokosnoeder had to stand out in the roads off the south side of Wick Bay illustrates perhaps how little anchorage there was in the area, though if she was a smuggler she would probably lie off anyway.

According to records of 1660 there were some 500 people in Wick, with ten merchants, six tailors, five weavers, four smiths, four coopers, four shoemakers, and 'an unknown number of glovers, who along with the shoemakers, were reprimanded in 1665 for causing damage to the bridge over the river, probably by beating their skins upon it.'2 Wick is said to have had no vessels of her own but trade is

---

1 Kokosnoeder means 'Coconuts' – the correct name would probably have been Kokosnoeden, 'The Coconut'. The Captain's 'business' would almost certainly, as the author supposes in his coy language, have been smuggling, though this is rather early for what in the seventeenth and eighteenth centuries became a major industry in Orkney and Caithness.
2 D Omand: The Caithness Book, p 135. His information is derived from W Macfarlane: Geographical Collections; Edinburgh, (1906-1908). See also A T Simpson & S. Stevenson: Historic Wick; Scottish Burgh Survey, Glasgow (1983).

reported as including items such as timber, tallow, hides, wool, millstones, beef mutton, port, butter, cheese and whisky. Even as late as 1760 there were less than a thousand inhabitants, and it was described as 'pleasantly situated in a little bay which has no harbour'. It was this lack of harbour facilities until much later that accounts for Wick's modest showing as a royal burgh for more than two centuries after it achieved the honour. We shall turn later to its rapid rise in all aspects in the later eighteenth and early nineteenth centuries.

SINCLAIRS COME TO GRIEF

The death of the 'Wicked' Earl in 1643 by no means ended Wick's close association with and dependence on the earls of Caithness. Two Sinclair earls, George IV and George V, occupied the earldom between 1643 and 1698, and the doings of both affected the fortunes of Caithness and in particular those of Wick fairly drastically. For the most part Earl George IV sought to isolate himself from the calamities that afflicted Britain from 1641 to 1646, the Civil War between King and Parliament, though was unable to stand completely aside in the 1650-1651 episode when James Graham, Marquis of Montrose, brought the fight to Caithness itself.

There could have been earlier involvement had not John Sinclair, the then Master of Berriedale, who was the heir of Earl George IV, died four years before George himself. John subscribed to the famous National Covenant, 'the true religion'. By the General Assembly of Glasgow, agreed to by King Charles who, like his father before him, was insisting on the rule of bishops as the proper mode of governing the church, bishops were abolished. Existing bishops were forthwith deposed or excommunicated, and the King's Prayer Book was condemned as 'heathenish, Popish, Jewish and Arminian'. Berriedale was one of the five commissioners appointed by the Assembly to get the 'Band' asserting the principles of the reformers 'subscribed throughout the entire kingdom'.

So far as Charles was concerned this meant war, and so followed the two, so-called 'Bishops' Wars' in which Charles marched armies to the Scottish border in an attempt to bring the rebels to order, but was each time defeated by a well organised army led by Alexander Leslie, a veteran of the Protestant army in the campaigns of Gustavus Adolphus in what came to be called the Thirty Years' War, and by James Graham, Earl of Montrose, at this stage strong for the Covenant. It was these short wars that really set in train the whole series of events resulting in British Civil War of 1642 to 1646 which brought the setting up of the Commonwealth under the rule of Lord Protector Cromwell, and the execution of the King.

This much of the background of national politics is necessary for understanding the troubles which afflicted Caithness in 1650 and 1651, and how it was that in the main the earldom avoided becoming involved in these politics. It could have been otherwise. John, Master of Berriedale, as a subscriber to the National Covenant, might well have brought the earldom into the thick of it. John married Jean, daughter of the Earl of Seaforth, a strong supporter of the Covenant, and is said to have accepted service in this earl's army which mustered in the Spey valley. John, however, caught a fever and died in 1639. His son, George, great-grandson of George III, thus inherited the earldom when the old rogue died in 1643.

Earl Sinclair, George IV (1643-1676) had no desire for commitment in the national struggle. He spent much of his time at Thurso, where in 1660 – troubles over – he built a new castle on the east shore of the Thurso estuary (or, more probably, refurbished an existing site), and died there in 1676. Calder describes this George as 'not distinguished by any remarkable qualities'; his great achievement was to build up a great debt (on top of the one bequeathed to him by his great-grandfather), which eventually persuaded him to sign away the Sinclair patrimony to a Campbell. George put down his indebtedness to 'the effect of the civil wars on his mansions; "I can give account of £200,000 Scots of loss I sustained by Generals Middleton and Morgan, besides the burning of my houses which put me in such a condition that I had not a place to settle myself in till I laid out a thousand pounds to repair the house I live in"'. This was Thurso Castle.[1]

George's neutrality was seriously compromised when the Marquis of Montrose landed on the beach of the Bay of Sannick near to Duncansby on 9 April, 1650. Early in the Civil War Montrose had fought the King as a Covenanter, but dismayed at the political excesses of the revolutionaries, changed sides and became Charles's most successful general. On the total collapse of the royal cause with Charles's execution in January, 1649, Montrose escaped to the

[1] This castle was deliberately destroyed by this George's Sinclair successor to prevent its occupation by the Campbell claimant. The Sinclairs of Ulbster, who acquired the estate in 1710 built a new castle on the site, and in the nineteenth century this was destroyed and yet another built. Even this is now a ruin, though its towers stand impressively enough by the side of the estuary, well in sight of the town, approachable on the outside along the coast path, and on the inside (only with permission) through Lord Thurso's estate.

Continent where he sought to raise an army in support of Charles II. It was this army, supplemented by a thousand Orkneymen, which landed in Caithness. Although advised to go immediately south, which would have taken him through Wick, he chose instead to go first to Thurso, staying only long enough to 'compel the heritors and ministers to swear obedience to him as the King's lieutenant-governor'.

'The unusual sight of so many troops at first greatly alarmed the inhabitants of the district, many of whom fled from their houses, and hid themselves among the rocks,' says Calder. A report reached Dunbeath about the landings, and Sir John Sinclair 'took horse and posted off to Edinburgh to communicate the alarming intelligence to the Convention of Estates [the 'provisional government' during these times in Scotland], leaving the castle to be defended by his lady and servants.' Montrose marched south to Dunbeath via Latheron, and besieged and captured the castle, feebly defended by its weak garrison. Then he crossed the Ord and went down to the borders of Sutherland and Ross. Here he was met by General Strachan, ahead of the main army sent to deal with the invasion, and was defeated at Carbisdale in May, 1650. Though he escaped, he was unfortunate enough to seek refuge in Ardvreck castle, where McLeod of Assynt, a 'sordid wretch' as Calder calls him, 'sold' him for twenty thousand pounds Scots to General Leslie. He was taken to Edinburgh where he was tried and hanged as a traitor (to which cause?) on a gibbet thirty feet high above the Grassmarket.

Cromwell marched against a Scottish army raised in support of the new king, Charles II,[1] defeating the Scots at Dunbar in September, 1650. After this Cromwell overran Scotland, and by a Treaty of Union, formally forced Scotland into the Commonwealth. Caithness had a part in all this. 'A Colonel Overton,' says Miller, 'marched through Caithness and crossed to Orkney in February 1652.' A contingent of Cromwellian troops was quartered at Ackergill Tower, since 1612 a possession of the Earls of Caithness and doubtless one of the castles of which Earl George IV complained of being deprived. Other troops were stationed at Canisbay. Calder supposes, rightly, that these men were on their way to Orkney where, indeed, the trouble for Cromwell had started. Two hundred 'Englishes' certainly occupied Kirkwall and built themselves – or had built for them – a fort to the east of the town

---

[1] Charles 1 was executed 30 January, 1649. His son, Charles II, was crowned at Scone on 1 January, 1650, but not restored to the throne until 29 May, 1660.

which was demolished only a hundred years ago. A recent researcher has discovered what he considers to be the probable location of a fort, if not a Cromwellian encampment on the Ness of Quoys, behind Canisbay Church.1 The 'Camps' on the north bank of the river of Wick is said to have been so named because a group of religious 'independents' (probably soldiers) camped up here.

There was, and in any case, more activity in Caithness itself, some of it rebellious though not promoted or participated in by the Earl of Caithness, who regarded it all as a regrettable inconvenience. Caithness was represented in the deliberations that led to the setting of the Union Parliament by John Sinclair of Tannach (not mentioned by St-Clair or Henderson) and George Munro of Newton, both near to Wick. The county was combined with Orkney and Shetland as a single parliamentary constituency, not represented by an MP until the second parliament in 1656, when the Cromwellian Colonel Robert Stewart was elected.

Though it was not generated in Caithness, the county was the scene of the break-up of rebellion organised by 'Cavalier' Middleton (later first earl of Middleton), whose army, though defeated in a battle at Dalnaspidal in Glengarry by General George Monck, retreated to Caithness, where Colonel Morgan boxed-in the rebel army and received their surrender. Middleton escaped and Lord Reay (chief of the Mackays) surrendered 'on honourable terms'. Caithness was, nevertheless, occupied, and Castle Sinclair was garrisoned with fifty soldiers and fifteen cavalrymen. This, of course, was the origin of the inconvenience suffered by Earl George of Caithness at the hands of 'Generals Middleton and Morgan'.2

That the English were at Canisbay is amply attested by references to them in Old Canisbay Presbytery records. One of the entries refers

---

1 Notes supplied by M Pottinger. In a recent article in The Orkney View, No 60, October/November, 1993, Mr Pottinger suggests that the presence of Cromwell's men had less to do with keeping the north in order, than guarding against foreign incursions, especially Dutch, of the kind that had arrived in Orkney in 1650. The location of the Cromwell fort in Kirkwall, on a promontory in Kirkwall, and the cannon placed there, would support such a view. Mr Pottinger describes the Canisbay site as a 'Cromwellian Battery and Powder Magazine'. The Kirkwall battery remained armed with cannon for many years.

2 See J. Miller, From Reformation to Improvement, 1560-1880 in The New Caithness Book, p 95. Thomas Sinclair, in his notes to Calder's History of Caithness refers to the moralistic comments of a visitor to Sinclair and Girnigoe in 1698. 'Both castles had been then, by a 'righteous God turned to a ruinous heap on account of "much sin" that was alleged to have been committed within their walls'. There had, indeed, been plenty of that. He also mentions Thurso East, likewise in a state of ruination for the same reason, 'haunted by a fox' until 'about nine or ten years ago, when a part of the house was repaired'.

to the disciplining of a parishioner for entertaining 'Inglishe men' to 'drinking' and 'masking plays' on the Sabbath. Calder comments wryly: 'Cromwell's soldiers are represented in history as rigid sectaries of the most austere cast, to whom everything in the shape of amusement, and especially on the Lords-day, was a heinous sin, but it would seem that such of them at least as came to John O'Groat's were not so strict.'[1] Wick was probably a bit far out for these exiles to reach, but we know of at least one pub then in the county capital, the 'Sinclair Arms'. Included in his comments on the state of affairs in Canisbay (seventeen miles from Wick) at these critical times is the following:

> One crying evil, the parent of many others, was intemperance. Whisky was then a rare beverage in the county, but there was a capital substitute for it in strong ale. Ale-houses as they were called were plentifully scattered over the parish. There old and young congregated, got drunk, and quarrelled and fought; and as these breaches of the peace were all brought before the kirk-session, the minister and elders had always plenty of business in hand.

Calder adds a note drawn from 'Burgh Records' of Wick:

> Much attention has been paid throughout the county to the quality of the popular drink. In the burgh of Wick 'tasters, as they were called, were appointed to try the strength of the ale which was to be sold in the public-houses, and if it did not come up to the proper test, the brewers of the same had to pay a certain fine.

The ambivalence of the attitudes of Wickers, on the one hand as members of an abstemious flock and on the other as merry pot-men, was borne out again in the present century when, by popular vote, Wick went 'dry' for twenty-five years, during which the really thirsty drank in shebeens and speak-easies. We shall come to that episode later. Not long after the Canisbay presbytery reports of 1650, the undoubted liking of the Caithnessmen for the potent useque bagh a few years later led a whole army of them to disaster.

Whether or not heavy drinking was among his failings, George IV (44th earl, as the record goes), to avoid bankruptcy, sold his 'property, title and all, to Lord Glenorchy, who was one of his principal creditors'. How a Campbell comes into the story is curious. In 1657

---

[1] See D Beaton (Ed): Parish Registers of Canisbay (Caithness), 1652-1666, Edinburgh (1914).

George IV had married a Campbell wife, Mary, daughter of the Marquis of Argyll, one of the Scottish lords who made peace with Cromwell, even though in 1649 he was a keen supporter of Charles II. At the Restoration in 1660, he paid for his 'treason' with his head, which was set on the same spike of the Edinburgh Tollbooth lately occupied by the head of that other 'traitor', the Marquis of Montrose. Whether or not Earl George's association with Argyll in 1657 had anything to do with his anxiety to keep out of political trouble, after the Restoration he became, according to Saint-Clair, 'a decided royalist, and manifested great zeal in suppressing conventicles', the gatherings of convenanting dissidents made unlawful under the new regime.

As a signal mark of favour the King had George made a Privy Councillor in 1674, and he served for the remaining two years of his life as the King's Lord-Lieutenant of the county. As a mark on his part of his loyalty, the Presbytery records that the 'noble lord, presented ane bond from the council qlk should be subscribed by in name of his majesties honable privie councill, desired that the 29 of May should be keeped a preached day in commemoration of his majesties hapie restauration to ye exercise of his royal dignitie.'

George became an elder of the church of Thurso. His service to the cause earned him solemn consideration at the time of his death in May, 1676. 'Mr Andrew Munro,' it was minuted in the Caithness Presbytery records, 'minister of Thurso, did represent that the Earl of Caithness, being visited with heavie sickness, did earnestlie desire that all the Brethren of the Presbie, should remember him in their publick and private prayers to God, which desire was cordially entertained.' His wife forthwith married 'her kinsman Glenorchy, who was created Earl of Caithness by patent.'

The story is more complicated than that. John Campbell of Glenorchy, whose own castle was that of Kilchurn (a spectacular ruin today on the north shores of Loch Awe), claimed Caithness quite simply as a creditor, to whom its Lord owed perhaps as much as a million pounds. In two 'dispositions' of 1661 and 1662 the Earl made over 'all and sundry, the lands etc' to Glenorchy; in the second was a clause signifying that in 'case of non-redemption, Glenorchy and his heirs shall be holden and obliged to assume, wear, and use the name of Sinclair and the arms of the House of Caithness'. It is believed that Glenorchy insisted on this inclusion, in the confidence – as he thought – that no genuine Sinclair claimant would appear, since George had 'no issue' and no close relatives left.

On the Earl's death in 1676, Glenorchy went to London to get his claims confirmed by patent and royal charter. A hearing of the Privy Council approved the claims and King Charles was persuaded to issue a proclamation forbidding George Sinclair of Keiss, a relative of the former earl from persisting in a claim he had advanced and from calling himself 'Earl of Caithness'. Sinclair ignored both injunctions, held on to land which, under the disposition should have gone to Glenorchy, and ignored yet another pronouncement by the Privy Council, an 'Act' requiring 'haill kin, friends, and followers of John, Earl of Caithness (meaning Glenorchy) to concur and assist' in recovering for Glenorchy the disputed land. Glenorchy decided to back up this injunction by force of arms, invading Caithness in the summer of 1680.

This was not the first time that John Campbell had been fishing in these troubled waters. The 'rebel' Sinclairs, William of Dunbeath and Sir James of Murkle, were ordered to attend the Court of Justiciary in connection with a series of raids and cattle reivings in which Mackays were also involved. They failed to appear and were in consequence outlawed. Campbell decided it was his duty to discipline the outlawed Sinclairs. He marched north with a troop and besieged Dunbeath castle without success and returned home. William Dunbar of Hempriggs, just south of Wick, was imprisoned in Castle Sinclair for 'intercommuning' with the outlaw, Sinclair of Dunbeath. Dunbeath gained his release 'on finding caution to the amount of 5000 merks Scots', while the two Sinclairs, 'by the mediation of friends,' soon afterwards had their sentences of outlawry reversed.

BATTLE ON THE RIVER OF WICK, 1680

Glenorchy's invasion of 1680 was a more systematic affair. There were perhaps 1000 or more men. They crossed into Caithness over the rough country near to Braemore. George Sinclair of Keiss, who enjoyed considerable support in the county, collected a force of 1,500 men, mostly, however, old and not well trained, and with only one experienced senior officer, Major Sinclair of Thura, a veteran of war in Germany. Keiss and his men advanced toward the enemy and met them near Stirkoke, a few miles south-west of Wick. Glenorchy declined battle and took his tired men up on to the hills of Yarrows, where he encamped on the 'Torran na Gael', the Highlander's Hill.

Accounts of the battle vary. As told in Calder, the story lacks nothing in excitement, and perhaps nothing much in accuracy:

The Sinclairs marched into Wick and celebrated their supposed advantage in a deep carousal, being liberally supplied with drink by a secret agent of the Campbells. Pennant says: – 'Glenorchy thought proper to add stratagem to force. He knew that in those days whisky was the nectar of Caithness, and in consequence ordered a ship laden with that precious liquor to pass round, and wilfully strand itself on the shore. The Caithnessians made a prize of the vessel, and in indulging themselves too freely, became an easy prey to the Earl.' Such seems to have been the current tradition in the county at the time of Pennant's visit; and it is most likely to be founded in truth. Be that as it may, the Sinclairs spent the night in riot; but the Campbells acted prudently. Glenorchy appointed a strict watch, and took every precaution against a sudden surprisal. The men that were not on guard wrapped themselves in their plaids, and laid down to sleep on the bare heath. About eight o'clock next morning (July 13), Glenorchy quitted his bivouac, and crossed the river of Wick below Sibster, nearly opposite Stirkoke Mains. His men are said to have leaped across; and from the narrowness of the stream at one particular spot in this quarter, the feat would not seem impracticable to an agile, long-legged Highlander. The news rapidly reached Wick, where it excited the utmost consternation and alarm. The Sinclairs, from the state in which they were found, were mustered with great difficulty, and then hastily led up the river to meet the enemy. Glenorchy's intention was to proceed to Keiss, but as soon as he saw the Sinclairs advancing, he prepared for battle by drawing up 500 of his men on the haugh, some 200 yards further up the river than the point where it is joined by the burn of Altimarlach. This burn, or rather water-course, which in the summer is quite dry, has steep banks on each side, and may be described as a huge gully. It lies about two miles to the west of Wick. Nothing could be better adapted for an ambuscade, of which Glenorchy with great tact availed himself. He accordingly ordered the remainder of his men to lie down and conceal themselves in the deep gorge, and not to stir from the spot until the officers should give them the word to rise. As the Sinclairs advanced, they made a detour to the right at some distance from the head of the ravine, and of course did not see the ambuscade that was laid for them. Their object in this movement was to have the advantage of the higher ground, and thus to place the enemy between them and the river. In the meantime Glenorchy animated his men with the following short address, originally delivered in Gaelic:– 'We are this day in an enemy's country. He that stands this day by me, I'll stand by him, my son by his son, and my grandson by his grandson; but if this day goes against us, he will be a lucky man that ever gets home, for long is the cry to Lochawe, and far is the help from Cruachan.'[1] When the two hostile forces were within a few yards of each other, Glenorchy gave the signal to attack, and the deadly strife commenced. The onset of the Campbells was so furious, that the Sinclairs, enfeebled as they were with the debauch of the previous evening, instantly gave way, and fled with precipitation in the direction of the burn of Altimarlach. At this moment, the reserve corps of the Highlanders starting up from their ambush with a savage shout, met the fugitives in the face, and being pressed in front and rear, and at the same time outflanked on the left, the Sinclairs made a rush for the river. The Campbells chased them into the water as they attempted to escape to the other side, and committed such dreadful havoc that it is said they passed dry shod over their dead bodies. Not a few of the Sinclairs who endeavoured to save their lives by running for the open plain were cut down by the murderous battle-axe and broadsword of the infuriated victors. Sinclair of Keiss himself, Sinclair of Thura, and the other leaders of the party, who were all on horseback, owed their safety to the fleetness of their chargers. The engagement did not last above a few minutes, and it was as bloody as it was brief. There is another account of this affair which says that Glenorchy's men were advantageously posted on the west side of the burn of Altimarlach, and that the Sinclairs in their impatience to attack them, instead of going round the head of the ravine, plunged recklessly down into it, and attempted to scramble up the opposite bank. In this exposed and defenceless condition a great many of them were slain at length, daunted by the difficulties of the place, and the slaughter of their comrades,

[1] This is very reminiscent of Henry V's Crispin Crispian speech, which, of course, Glenorchy very probably did not know. Gaelic commanders, like the ancient Greeks, were given to such pre-battle histrionics, if the story-tellers are to be believed. 'Cruachan' is the great mountain overlooking Kilchurn, and the Campbell battle-cry.

they fled in disorder through the gully towards the river, whither the Campbells pursued them, and massacred a great number of them without mercy. Of the two accounts, that of the former appears to us the most entitled to credit. We can hardly believe that any body of men would be so foolhardy as to attempt climbing up a steep and rugged bank in the face of a formidable enemy ranged along the top. Such was the issue of the famous battle of Altimarlach, so disastrous to the county, and so humiliating to the pride of the Sinclairs. It was the last great fight of the kind originating in a family quarrel – in Scotland, and in this respect it possesses a general as well as local interest.[1]

It is possible even today to follow the course of the battle on the site, for the ground has been little altered since 1680. If the reconstruction is correct, it may easily be seen just how the ambush was accomplished. The little gorge of the burn is still as it was, except guarded on the rim by that universal system of fencing, lines of barbed wire, a protection against penetration of the enemy trench not available in those times. If the gorge was as cluttered with rough growth as it is now, this too would favour the first version of Campbell tactics, for to both scramble down and scramble up for the Sinclairs would have been extremely difficult. The name 'Altimarlach', incidentally, is said to signify in the Gaelic, 'Thieves burn', a perfectly appropriate name so far as appearances go; though an alternative interpretation is that the word is a corruption of 'Altnmarbh', meaning 'the stones of the dead' or 'the burn of the dead'. From the top of the hill above the gorge is a fine view of the

---

[1] Among the sources used by Calder were Thomas Pennant's Tour of Scotland in 1769, written nearly a hundred years after the battle but while numerous folk tales about it were still in currency. He uses too History of the Highland Regiments. A recent version is to be found in Robert P. Gunn: Tales from Braemore, Whittles Publishing, Latheron, Caithness (1991), with the titles 'The Battle of Altimarlach'. Miller quotes from W Macfarlane: Geographical Collections relating to Scotland; Edinburgh (1960-1908), a version that 'rings more true than some other versions':

> Upon which the Earle [Glenorchy] obtained a party of the Kings forces and what friends he could make to assist the Sheriff of Innerness to repone him to the possession, but he having gathered together about 300 men did enter the countrey without the Sherif, earle George knowing of his Motion, had gathered two or three hundred Commons together, who, having gone to Week, were followed at a distance by E. John. But E George's men, being far inferior in numbers and arms, resolved to return to their Houses quietly, and going without care or order, as from a fair, E John, who waited this opportunity, set upon them about a mile from week and killed and drowned in the Water of Week above 80, beside many wounded, most part after they had thrown away their Arms and sought Quarter, for which and other crimes there is process of Treason against the said E John.

River Wick winding through the peaceful valley below, and on an eastern rise across the valley beyond is the entire town of Wick. Beyond the south rim of the valley can be seen the Stirkoke Mains still, as it probably was then, deeply surrounded by plantation. Among the damp pastures on either side the river wander herds of fat cows, and on the slopes of the drier hills flock the white Cheviots, the 'White Farm' glistening behind in the sunlight. Over a low span across the Wick river rattles the occasional 'Sprinter' on its way to or from Georgemas Junction. Few on the hill that fateful day would have been admiring the views.

On the centre of the hill is a granite Celtic cross, carrying the inscription:

> The Battle of Atlimarlach
> was fought around this spot,
> 13th July 1680.
> The last feudal battle in Scotland.[1]
> Erected 1901.

Fig. 8a Altimarlach Cross.

---

[1] This attribution is not correct. The last recorded clan battle in Scotland was fought at Mulroy in Inverness-shire when the MacDonalds of Keppoch met the MacIntosh on 4 August, 1688. John Horne of Ye Towne of Wick in Ye Oldene Tymes was a prime instigator of the move to have the monument erected in 1901. In a memoir, Janey Horne Robertson, Horne's daughter, tells of the day when, as 'a small girl in a poke bonnet' she accompanied an 'armada' up the Wick river because as she says, 'I was to unveil the cross.' (George Cameron: John Horne: His Life and Works; Wick, North of Scotland Newspapers (1993), p.27). One other posthumous item of interest probably associated with the battle of Altimarlach was the discovery during the excavation of 1797 for foundations when the parish was rebuilding the church on Kirkhill, Wick, of a collection of remains of 'people slain in a battle'. This, fairly evidently, was the mass grave in which the dead of Altimarlach (most of them from the Sinclair side) were buried after the battle.

Though virtually forgotten – if ever heard of – everywhere except in Caithness, the Battle of Altimarlach, or at least the way to it, is said to have generated one durable popular memory. This was the tune 'The Campbells are Coming,' believed to have been composed and played by Glenorchy's piper, Finlay McIver, on the march north, together with the less well-known 'The Hills of Glenorchy'. At the battle itself, Finlay struck up a tune which later came to be named in the Gaelic as the 'Bodach na briogais', in English, 'The Bodies in the Breeks', composed as a contemptuous comment on the trousers worn by the Sinclairs. The Campbells, of course, being genuine Highlanders, wore the kilt (but not in 1680). The tune is still played, and is titled 'The Carles with the Breeks'.

McIver, in addition to being a talented piper was, according to a chronicler, 'afflicted with a disease very common among pipers, namely, an unquenchable thirst'. He stayed behind with a few companions after the main party left for home, and on his own way south, holed up at the inn at Dunbeath drinking the landlady's fine ale. This story is thus rendered in the recent version:

> He had spent his money, and in order to settle his debt, the landlady had taken possession of his bagpipes. He pleaded with her to let him have his pipes returned, but out of sympathy with the defeated Sinclair, she turned a deaf ear to all his pleas. Finlay was in a sore plight and felt much worse than if Glenorchy had been defeated by the Bodies with the Breeks; and the disgrace would have been nothing compared to the loss of his pipes in such circumstances.
>
> However, William Roy McIver, one of Glenorchy's factors who lived near Dunbeath, heard of Finlay's predicament. He came to the inn, paid all Finlay's debt, and asked that the pipes should be restored to their rightful owner. 'Now my good fellow,' said the factor, clapping Finlay on the shoulder and handing him enough money to pay for his expenses on the way home, 'I hope that you will be a little more moderate in your drinking in future and will not get in such a fix before you reach the braes of Glenorchy, for, mind you, I will not always be at hand to redeem the pipes.'
>
> Finlay was too overjoyed to express his gratitude in words to the factor, so he composed a beautiful Gaelic song in his honour and named it 'Failt Clan Ibhair'. The factor was very pleased with the song, which recorded his good qualities, and it is said

that it was never sung in his company without him treating the company to half an anker of brandy. The song survived as long as Gaelic was spoken in the Highlands of Caithness.

It is true that the battle was 'disastrous to the county' and 'humiliating to the Sinclairs'. The number killed that day was reckoned at two hundred or more Caithnessmen; and it is a bitter thought that they owed their evil fortune to the after-effects of whisky fumes. Glenorchy went on to make himself very unwelcome in Caithness by quartering some of his troops in Wick and elsewhere. Calder tells that he 'levied rents and taxes as in a conquered country, ... subjecting the people to the most grievous oppression'.

The Sinclair lords, of course, being mounted escaped unhurt from the battlefield. Sinclair of Keiss persisted in his oppostion to Glenorchy, who now carried the title and arms of the earldom of Caithness. At one stage Keiss laid seige to Sinclair castle where Glenorchy had stationed some of his troops, taking it after a rather feeble resistance. It is believed that firearms and perhaps cannon were used in this attack.[1] Keiss was assisted in this venture by two other Sinclair lairds and Mackay of Strathnaver, all of whom had been declared rebels by the government.

In the end, as the result of support from James, Duke of York, later King James II, Keiss finally secured his claim to be Earl of Caithness, and also full repossession of his own property of Keiss, Northfield and Tister. As Calder reports:

> The sale of the earldom [by George IV] was manifestly an illegal transaction, and the decision of the Scotch lawyers in favour of Glenorchy is not a little strange [there is a strong suggestion that they were bribed by the Campbells, in those years very influential in the affairs of the state]. 'The earldom of Caithness,' as observed by Mackay, 'was a male fee by the original grant, which would seem a bar in the way of its being gifted or disposed of to a stranger, and even of the King's altering its tenure, where there was no previous forfeiture.'

Glenorchy had to relinquish his claim on the Caithness earldom after six years in the title, but retained much of the property he had acquired under the dispositions of George IV in 1661 and 1672. In

---

[1] Though built or altered in the sixteenth century, when siege cannon were now in common use, the Caithness castles and towers for the most part do not seem to have been built to withstand cannon fire. Rather they were designed, as various incidents mentioned in this history suggest, as strongholds of local warlords whose chief enemies were likely to be other warlords using traditional and familiar weaponry.

compensation for the loss of the title he was created Earl of Breadalbane and Baron of Wick.1 He was an extremely unpopular figure during his time in the area. Not only was he a harsh landlord; he was also unable to live down his reputation as a military butcher, the slaughterer at Altimarlach of many of the friends and relations of his tenants. According to Calder, local people:

> took every method of annoying him. They waylaid and thrashed his factors; they burned the corn, and houghed [hamstrung] the cattle of his tenants; and, even after his death, they vexed his successor so much that, despairing of bettering his affairs in the north, he divided the lands into separate portions, and sold the whole in 1719.

In this manner Wick came into the possession of the Ulbster Sinclairs, since it was they who bought most of the Glenorchy properties. George, the Sinclair of Keiss who wrested the earldom from Glenorchy, died at Keiss in 1698, and was succeeded as earl by his second cousin, Sir John Sinclair of Murkle.

As a postscript to these tales, Glenorchy, successively Earl of Caithness, Earl of Breadalbane and Baron Wick, was deeply implicated in the dreadful affair of Glencoe in 1692, as the result of which a charge of high treason was raised against him. He was committed to prison in Edinburgh, but was released without being brought to trial. This was not the end of Breadalbane's career of political intrigue and moral turpitude, both on behalf of and against the Revolution of 1688. He died in 1715, and one of the last acts of his life was to despatch a troop of 500 men to join the Earl of Mar when he raised the standard of rebellion in 1715 at Braemar in favour of James, the 'Old Pretender'. A contemporary comment on Breadalbane, by General Hugh Mackay, sums up the character of this noble villain, who reigned for a time in Caithness: 'He was grave as a Spaniard, wise as a serpent, cunning as a fox, and slippery as an eel.' He was certainly the last of the robber Earls of Caithness.

It may or may not be wholly advisable to add what must be the veritable last word on the subject of Altimarlach, a 'Ballad' quoted in a 'Postscript' contributed by Colonel George Sinclair (probably

---

1 The full title is: Lord Glenorchy, Beneraloch, Ormlie and Wieck, Viscount of Tay and Paintland, Earl of Breadalbane and Holland. It still exists. Nevertheless, the 'Superiority' of Wick was retained for some years by the Breadalbanes. A later Earl Breadalbane became associated with the British Fisheries Society's development of Pulteneytown, and the road connecting Sinclair and Smith Terraces running along the riverside crest of Upper Pulteneytown, is Breadalbane Terrace.

composed by himself) to Calder's History. It is placed at the end of this chapter so that those who have no stomach for nineteenth century balladeering may skip it:

'Twas morn; from rustic cot and grange
   The cock's shrill clarion rung;
And fresh on every sweet wild flower
   The pearly dew-drop hung.

Given up to thoughtless revelry,
   In Wick lay Sinclair's band,
When suddenly the cry arose,
   'Glenorchy's near at hand.'

For now the Campbell's haughty chief
   The river Wick has crossed,
With twice seven hundred Highlanders –
   A fierce and lawless host.

'To arms, to arms.' from street to lane
   The summons did fast go;
And forth the gathered Sinclairs marched
   To meet the coming foe.

Where Altimarlach opens up
   Its narrow, deep ravine,
Glenorchy's force, in order ranged
   Were strongly posted seen.

They meet, they close in deadly strife,
   But brief the bloody fray;
Before the Campbell's furious charge
   The Caithness ranks give way.

Flushed with success, Glenorchy's men
   Set up a savage cheer,
And drove the Sinclairs panic-struck
   Into the river near.

There, 'neath the Campbell's ruthless blade
   Fell more than on the plain,
Until the blood-dyed stream across
   Was choked up with the slain.

ROYAL BURGH

But who might paint the flood of grief
    That burst from young and old,
When to the slaughtered Sinclair's friends
    The direful tale was told.

The shrieking mother wrung her hands,
    The maiden tore her hair.
And all was lamentation loud,
    And terror and despair.

Short time Glenorchy Caithness ruled,
    By every rank abhorred;
He lost the title he usurped,
    Then fled across the Ord.

While Keiss, who firm upheld his claim
    Against tyrannic might,
Obtained the Sinclair coronet,
    Which was his own by right.

The coronet which William wore,
    Who loved his Prince so well,
And with his brave devoted band
    At fatal Flodden fell.

Addendum

COPY OF THE CHARTER
OF THE
ERECTION OF THE BURGH OF WICK INTO A FREE
ROYAL BURGH, 1589

JAMES, by the grace of God, King of Scots, to all true men of his whole land, clergy and laity, greeting: Know yet that we, understanding that not only are the annual revenues or income of our crown increased by the industry and increase of free burghs within our kingdom, but also that the lieges of the same are very greatly enriched by the foreign commerce and trade of the burgesses and free inhabitants of the said burghs; and, also, considering that there is no free burgh within the limits or bounds of Caithness, and that the town of Wick, lying within our sheriffdom of Inverness, is situated on the seacoast in a place very suitable and fit for navigation: so that, if the said town of Wick were erected into a free royal burgh, and the ordinary magistrates of the same were elected, with the advice of our trusty cousin, George Earl of Caithness, his heirs, and successors, not only would our said annual revenues be increased by the customs and taxes of the said burgh, and those living within the said bounds of Caithness be enriched by the frequent access of merchants and foreign traders and rendered more civilized, but also thefts, rapines, murders, and other oppressions committed among the said inhabitants, would be repressed through fear of punishment. Therefore, and for various reasons and considerations us moving, from certain knowledge and of our own accord, after our perfect and legitimate age of twenty-one years completed, declared in our Parliament and our general revocation made in the same, we have made, constituted, created, erected, and incorporate the whole and entire aforesaid town of Wick with all and sundry houses, buildings, tenements, waste places, yards, orchards, tofts and crofts lying within the territory of the same into one royal free burgh, with a free harbour, to be called the burgh of Wick in all time coming: with special and plenary power to the free inhabitants and burgesses of the said burgh and their successors in the future, with the express advice and consent of our said cousin, George Earl of Caithness, his heirs and successors, and not otherwise or in other manner of making, electing, constituting, and creating a provost, and four bailies, indwellers or inhabitants of the said burgh, together with a treasurer, dean of guild, councillors, burgesses, serjeants, and other officers necessary within the said burgh for the government of the same, and those as often as shall be deemed expedient for reasonable causes, or depositing one-half of the monies paid by the said burgesses in respect of their freedom in our said burgh for our said cousin and his successors in future, and the other moiety of the same monies be applied for the public good of the said burgh. With free, also and special, power to the said burgesses and free inhabitants duly elected, received and admitted to the freedom of the said burgh, through the present and future councillors and dean of guild of the same, of buying and selling within the said burgh and freedom of the same (lie) papkeil and wine, ale, cloth, as well linen and woollen, narrow, long, and broad, and other kinds of commerce and goods (lie) those called stapill guidis (lie), taip. And also with power to the said provost, bailies and councillors of the aforesaid burgh and their successors of admitting and receiving within the same burgh bakers, tinsmiths, butchers, fishers, dealers in fish and flesh, tailors, blacksmiths, weavers, fullers, carpenters, and all other necessary artificers and operatives pertaining and relating to the freedom of a free burgh, with power also to the said craftsmen of using and exercising their aforesaid trade as they are used and exercised in any royal burgh within our said kingdom. And likewise with power to the said provost, bailies, councillors, burgesses, and their successors of building one public prison or more within the said burgh, and a market cross; and of holding a market every week on Friday, together with three free fairs thrice in the year, viz., on the Feast of All Saints, on the Lord's Day for the Palm Branches, and on the Nativity of John the Baptist, which are popularly called Allhallowmas, Palm Sunday, the Midsummer, and these for the space of four days each; and of charging, levying, receiving, and collecting the customs and dues of the same, and of applying them to the public good of the said burgh; also of charging, levying, receiving, and collecting all and sundry petty customs of the aforesaid harbour of the aforesaid burgh, as well as by land as by sea, and of applying them to the aforewritten use. And also with the power to the said bailies, and their successors of receiving resignations of all sundry lands, tenements, annual rents, yards, tofts, crofts, and others lying within the said burgh and freedom of the same, and of handing over and disposing of the same to any person or persons, with infeftments, charters, sasines, and other necessary evidents; of appointing, fixing, beginning, confirming, holding, and, as often as need be, of adjourning burgh courts within the said burgh and freedom of the same twice in the week, viz., on Tuesday and Saturday; of making, creating, and appointing clerks, sergeants, bailiffs, and all other officers and necessary members of the court; of punishing transgressors according to the form of law; of levying and applying to their peculiar uses the forfeitures and fines of the said courts, and, if necessary, of seizing and distraining for the same; of making or ordaining acts, laws and statutes within the said burgh and freedom of the same, for the keeping of good order; of apprehending, arresting, imprisoning, punishing, and, according to the laws of our kingdom, beheading and hanging all transgressors and delinquents with pit, gallows, in fang thief out fang thief and generally of using and exercising, all, any and sundry, with all privileges, and liberties whatsoever, as freely in all respects, as in any other royal burgh within our said kingdom. To hold and have the whole and entire burgh of Wick, with all and sundry houses, tenements, waste places, yards, tofts, crofts, and others whatsoever lying within the territory of the same, together with the harbour aforesaid, anchorages and customs of the same; and with all and sundry liberties and immunities and privileges aforewritten of the said burgh to the provost, bailies, councillors, and free inhabitants of the same, and their successors, of us and our successors, in free burgage in perpetuity, by all their righteous ancient meathes and divisions, according as they lie in length and breadth, in houses, buildings, bounds, grazings, fields, tofts, moors, marshes, ways, paths, waters, pools, streams, meadows, pasturages, mills, multures, and their sequels, fowlings, huntings, fishings, peats, divots, coals, coal-pits, rabbits, rabbit-warrens, pigeon-cots, forges, malt-kilns, and breweries, woods, forests, thickets, beams and timber, quarries of stone and lime, with courts and their ishes, bloodwits, and with all the sundry liberties, commodities, profits, assythments, and their proper pertinents whatsoever, as well those not named as those named, as well those under the earth as those above the earth, far and near, belonging or seeming in any manner whatsoever justly to belong to the said burgh, harbour and others particularly mentioned before, with their pertinents, in all time coming, freely, quietly, fully, entirely, honourably, well, and in peace, and without revocation, contradiction, hindrance, or obstacle in any way. The said provost, bailies, councillors, burgesses and free inhabitants and their successors, to render therefor annually to us and our successors the sum of ten merks of the money of this our realm, on the Feast of Pentecost, in name of alba firma only, together with the due and accustomed burghal service only.

In testimony of which we have commanded our seal to be put to this our present charter in presence of our much-loved cousins and advisers, John Lord Hamilton, commendator of our monastery of Aberbrothock, Archbald Earl Angus, Lords Douglas, Dalkeith, and Abernethy, our very reverend and venerable fathers in Christ Patrick Archbishop of St Andrews, Walter Prior of Blantyre, keeper of our Privy Seal; our chosen privy councillors, Alexander Hay of Easter Kennet, clerk of the register and council of our rolls; Lewis Bellenden of Achnoul, knight, clerk of our justiciary; and Robert Scott, director of our chancery. At Edinburgh, the twenty-fifth day of the month of September, in the year of our Lord, one thousand five hundred and eighty-nine, and twenty-third of our region.

Extracted from the registers in the archives, kept under the Parliament House on this and the two preceding pages, by Mr Thomas Gibsone, one of the principal clerks of Council and seesion, having power to the effect from the Lord Clerk of the Register.

(Signed)   Tho.   Gibsone.

There seems little doubt, both from the timing and the wording of this Charter, that its granting was expressly the result of a direct approach by George, Earl of Caithness, to King James. In it he is the King's 'trusty cousin', who provided 'express advice and consent' to the grant.1 It would be interesting to see his 'advice' on the trading and revenue potential of Wick at this time.

The burning occurred in late 1588; the grant was made less than a year later, and in the interval George spent time in Edinburgh. There was further provocation. According to Thomas Sinclair, who supplied the additional notes to the 1887 edition of the History:

A 'second marauding exploit took place in the following year but a few months (Whitsunday 1589) prior to the date of the charter, when Earl Alexander sent Alexander Gordon of Kilkalmekill, with three hundred chosen men, into Caithness, who struck terror into the inhabitants, ranged the country at large, spoiled and wasted freely all over the country before them, filled many places with ruin and desolation, and pursued their enemies with a bloody execution as long as their fury lasted, and slew a number of their inhabitants.

Earl George and the victims of the Earl of Sutherland's cruelty resident in the town, doubtless considered that having the town erected into a free burgh, under the King's seal, would prevent the recurrence of such like depredations in future, ensure the protection of the lives and property of the inhabitants from fierce and furious freebooters, and, in the words of the charter, 'thefts, rapines, murders, and other oppoessions committed among the inhabitants would be repressed through fear of punishment'.

All this, of course, was written by a Sinclair. It is doubtful if, given the temperament revealed in these clan exchanges, if Earl Alexander would be unduly intimidated by the 'fear of punishment' mentioned, but offending the King would have been another matter.

One other point worth observing is that the charter indicates just what financial benefit Earl George and the King are to gain from the 'erection' of Wick to royal burgh status. The earl is to receive 'one half of the monies paid by the said burgesses in respect of their freedom in our said burgh for our said cousin and his successors in future.' The King is to receive every Pentecost 'the sum of ten merks of the money of this our realm'. It was never James's habit to give something for nothing. Omne compretio.

---

1 D Bremner: Caithness Incorporating Wick and Thurso; Glasgow (no date). Bremner comments: 'this together with other deeds of rapine seems to have been the reason why James VI extended [to Wick] his royal protection' (see Historic Wick, op cit).

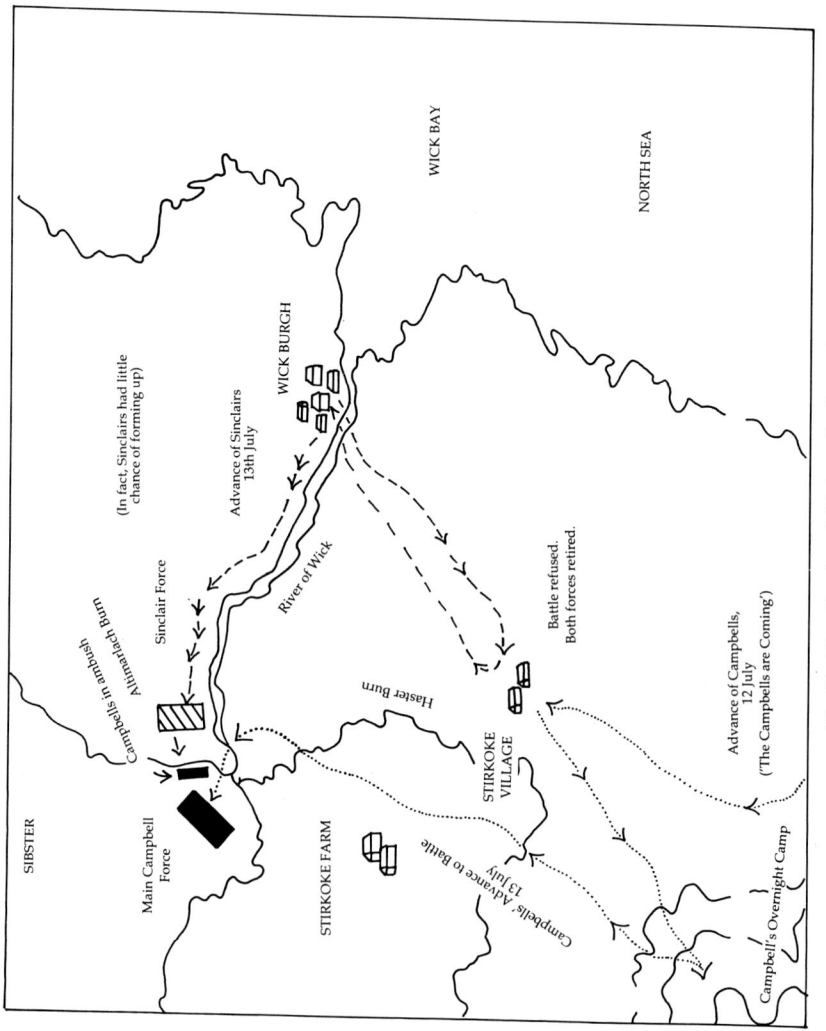

Fig 8b The Battle of Altimarlach, 12/13 July, 1680.

PART II:

WICK ARISING

Chapter   6: Wick 1700-1800

Chapter   7: The Sett of Wick: I

Chapter   8: The Sett of Wick: II

Chapter   9: Improvement

Chapter 10: Religion

CHAPTER 6

WICK 1700-1800

ROYAL burgh or no, in 1700 Wick was a place of little account and standing. Several glimpses of the town are afforded in contemporary writings, though in none does it appear very exciting or inviting. In 1670 it was recommended as a subject for discussion at a future meeting of the Convention of Royal Burghs.[1] As we have seen (p94), the town's population was said to have been about 500 in 1660, the year of the Restoration. Nevertheless, its taxable rate rose between 1670 and the beginning of the next century from 3 shillings in the pound to 4 shillings, while Dingwall, a royal burgh of similar size and status which was assessed at 2 shillings in 1670, went down to 1s 4d in 1692 and recovered to 2 shillings only in 1700. The higher stent almost certainly meant that from however modest a base, the trading prosperity of Wick was improving. As we shall see, the burgh records bear this out.

One early description is that of Mr Oliphant, Minister of Wick, dated 1726, and included in Macfarlane's *Geographical Collections:*

> The parish of Wick in the shire of Caithness hath to the N.E. the parish of Canisbay, to the N.W. the parish of Bowar to the W. the parish of Wattine, to the S.W. the parish of Latheron and on the S. & S.E. it is washen by the German Ocean.
>
> The church of Wick stands at the W. end of the town of Wick the head Burgh of the shire and has the church of Canisbay at 12 miles distance to the N.E. and the church of Bowar 6 miles to the N.W. It stands upon the N. side of the Water or Burn of Wick, which runs into the sea, at the East end of the town. It is called St. Fergus church and there is in the E. end of it on the N. side under a little pend, a hewen stone with a man at full length on it, which is said to be his effigies engraven on this stone.[2] The

---

[1] The Convention of Royal Burghs had been formed by the burghs on an initiative of their own in the 1550s, mainly as a means of collective protection of their interests as against government and the nobles, constituting in the early days that Lynch describes as the 'most coherent voice in national politics' until, in later days regular parliamentary representation became available to the burghs.

[2] This could hardly have been the 'statue' of St Fergus about which the Wickers became so emotional when Dr Merchiston is said to have smashed it up in his crusading zeal, for this event occurred more than a hundred years earlier, in 1613.

steeple on the W. end of it seems to be a very ancient work: but there are no letters nor figures on it to know of its antiquity.

On the N. side of the church stands the Sinclairs Isle the ancient buryal place of the Earles of Caithness, where many of them ly interred in a vault. To the E. of that on the same side as the church stands the Dunbars Isle, the burying place of the family of Hemprigs and in it a handsome monument of hewen stone.[1]

The description continues with comments on 'the houses of Castle Sinclair and Girnigoe, both now in ruins,' the rugged coast round Noss Head, the 'Castle of Airigill [Ackergill], the chapel of St. Tears. Oliphant then tells of the 'Castle of Keisse another house built by the Earls of Caithnesse and at the side of it, a convenient house largely built, both in repair, belonging to Sir James Sinclair of Dunbeath', not there today – though some distance inland stands the present Castle of Keiss, a nineteenth century confection' all white and shining. Of interest too are Oliphant's reference to some ancient ecclesiastical locations, no longer marked on maps.

From the town of Wick to the N.W. stands Killimster at two miles distant, where of old stood the mansion house of the Bishops of Caithness. There is one remarkable story taken notice of by some historians that the last bishop who resided there was boil'd to death in a cauldron by the orders of the then Earle of Caithness, it stands upon the East side of a great flow moss two miles large in breadth and in the middle ot it, there is a chappel called St. Dudoch's Kirk by the commons, of very difficult access at any time of the year, by reason of the flow.

Oliphant mentions also 'ane old chapple called Marykirk' about a mile west of the town 'which the commons did superstitiously frequent on the first Sabbath after the new moon'. Also there was the 'chappel of Haulster called St. Cuthbert's Church,' where 'the common people bury their dead about it,' and yet another called 'St Martines Chappel, now erected into a tomb' near to Ulbster, which had become 'the burial place of the family of Ulbster', the Sinclairs of Ulbster who, some years later became closely associated with the affairs of Wick town. Though all that he reports has to do with a now largely forgotten past, it is evident that around Wick the old faith and its trappings lingered long. As for the town itself:

1 This 'Aisle' or mausoleum still stands alongside the Sinclair Aisle, a smaller, gloomier and later construction, like the Sinclair Aisle, roofless, derelict and not much cared for. Such tomb markings as there were are now obliterated.

The Burgh of Wick a small town of little trade lyes on the E. end of the church and N. side of the water, where it runs into the sea, and before it, is a bay formed more than a mile in breadth between the head of Week on the N, and the head of Old Wick on the S. with a harbour at the end of the toun, to which ships of between 20 and 30 last burden can come in safely. At the head of Wick is the Chappell of St Ninian; to the N.E. of Wick about a mile is the harbour of Staxigoe, where ships of good burthen come in the summer time and ly safely. Near by which are two large granaries for victual belonging to the family of Hempriggs....

There is salmon fishing at the toun and many trouts and small fish in the water. There is a bridge at the toun of Wick for the conveniency of the Parish of eleven pillars built with loose stones and only timber laid over them, they are maintained by the southside of the parish for carrying them to the church. The water being broad there by swelling of the tide.

Manifestly a town of no great note. Aeneas Bayne, AM, also probably a minister, 'judged by the length of his references to matters religious, though not on any list of Caithness ministers', provides another picture of Wick in 1735. Bayne's account, ten years later than that of Oliphant, is somewhat fuller and gives a different emphasis:

OF WICK PAROCH

It is bounded in the S. by Latron Parish, on the E. by the Murray Firth, on the N. by Canesbay and on the W. and S.W. by Bowar and Wattin Parishes.

Its Dimensions from N. to S. are 13 miles, as to its inhabitants it is by far the most populous parish in the Shyre, containing at least 4,000 Examinable persons. Yet such is the fertility of their soil, the commodiousness of their situation for fishing and their good improvement of these advantages, that they generally live very happy.

WICK

The Town of Wick, a free Burgh, which gives its name to the Parish, stands hard by the sea. Its inhabitants maintain themselves by trade and Fishing, in it is the Parish Church, a very good large Edifice of an oblong forme as most of the Churches of the County area are, like one of the old Roman

Basilica[s]. the Minister has a living of £80 Sterling.

The Principal Heritors are Sir James Sinclair of Mey, Sir James Sinclair of Dunbeath, Sir William Dunbar of Hempriggs, John Sinclair of Ulbster, Donald Sinclair of Oldrig, John Sinclair of Stircock, John Sinclair of Barrack, Charles Sinclair of Bilbster. [We comment later on this rich supply of Sinclairs].

Heretors Seats here are from Wick about 2 miles North, Ackergill, 2 miles South, Hempriggs, which are conveniently and well adorned Lodgings belonging to Sir William Dunbar. Ackergill stands close to the sea, as does the house itself, an exceding strong Tower of a square forme about 6 stories high with a pleasant Balesan on the tope, with a strong wall about 8 foot thick, the Hall wherof is an arch 24 feet high, comprehending the whole breadth of the Tower, with severall rooms in the upper stories designed more for strength than beauty. It has an outer wall of 16 feet high with a ditch around it wherin the sea flows and ebbs. This belonged to the family of Marshall [Bayne here is referring to the Earls Marischal, the Keiths], as did the Castle of Oldwick (which lies a mile South East from the Burgh of Wick) belongs to Lord Oliphant [here he is quite confusing. The Keiths never owned Old Wick, while the Oliphants disappeared from the scene a long time before. Old Wick was at this time owned by Sinclair of Ulbster, who purchased it from Lord Breadalbane]. This latter is built upon a rock stretching out in the sea with several commodious offices, houses and a pleasant situation upon the German Ocean, but it is now quite demolished. 2 miles West of Wick lyes Thurster, the seat of Donald Sinclair of Oldrig. 5 miles North, Kees belonging to the above designed Sir James Sinclair of Dunbeath, but presently possessed by William Sinclair his son, with severall other Gentlemen's Seats which for brevity I omitt.

The Water of Wick furnishes good salmond fishing, the property of which belongs to Sir William Dunbar. The Parish is most plentifully furnished with all supports of life the Countrey affords, and the yearly rent of it is very considerable.

Visitors to Wick.

This impression of prosperity and good living in the parish is not that conveyed by some visitors to the county, notably Thomas

Pennant, one of the great travellers of the age.[1] He came to Caithness in 1769. This was admittedly some thirty-four years later, but there is no evidence to suggest that either Wick burgh or parish were on the decline. For all that, Pennant, writing of his journey, made some disparaging observations on what he saw. He begins with impressions of the castles:

> Went along a fine hard sand on the edge of *Sinclair* bay. On the south part, near Noss head, on the same rock are *Sinclair* and *Girnigo* castles; but, as if the joint tenants, like beasts of prey, had been in fear of each other, there was between them a draw bridge; the first too had an iron door, which dropped from above through grooves still visible.

He was evidently not aware that these two castles represented two different stages and moods in the life of the same family of Sinclair earls. He, nevertheless, regarded them as symbols of the degradation and low state of the people. 'The common people,' he said, 'are kept here in great servitude, and most of their time is given to the Lairds, an impediment to the prosperity of the country.' His picture of the landscape in the vicinity of Wick is a rather gloomy one:

> *Caithness* may be called an immense morass, mixed with some fruitful spots of oats and barley, much coarse grass, and here and there some fine, almost all natural, there being very little artificial. At this time was the hay harvest both here and about *Dunrobin*: the hay on this rough land is cut with very short scythes, and with a brisk and strong stroke. The country produces great quantities of *oatmeal*, and much *whisky* is distilled from the barley: the great thinnes of inhabitants throughout enables them to send abroad much of its productions. No wheat has been raised this year in the county; and I was informed that the grain is sown here in the spring, by reason of the wet and fury of the winters; the country is supposed to send out, in some years, 2,200 head of cattle; but in bad seasons, the farmer kills and salts numbers for sale.

---

1 Thomas Pennant: *Tour of Scotland, 1769;* B White, London (1772). This was a time of great travelling. Roads were becoming better, and numerous 'enlightened' gentlemen (and some ladies) exploring the land (and other lands) especially those like Arthur Young, were imbued with the idea that great 'improvement' was possible in the sluggish British countryside. One of the great improvers was Sir John Sinclair of Ulbster. To someone familiar with improved farming in some parts of the lowlands of Scotland in the eighteenth century, Caithness must have seemed a poor, backward place. This came to be a received view – of Scotland as a whole – among 'improvers'. See Samuel Smiles: *Lives of the Engineers;* Vol II, David and Charles (1968).

Great numbers of swine are reared here; they have long erect ears and most savage looks, and are seen tethered in almost every field. The rest of the commodities of *Caithness* are butter, cheese, tallow, hides, the oil and skins of seals, and the feathers of geese.

'Here are neither barns nor granaries,' says Pennant; 'the corn is thrashed out and preserved in the chaff in *bykes,* which are stacks in the shape of beehives thatched quite round, where it will keep good for two years.' One thing specially noticed by Pennant on the farms and small plots of this area was the way in which the women were obliged to do much of the heavy dirty work of the land:

> The tender sex (I blush for the *Caithnessians*) are the only animals of burden; they turn their patient backs to the dunghills, and receive in their *keizes,* or baskets, as much as their lords and masters think fit to fling in with their pitchforks, and then trudge of the fields in droves of sixty or seventy.

'Passed through *Wick,*' Pennant continues, 'a small burrough town with some good houses, seated on a river within reach of the tide.' He speaks of the fish, oil and other trading that goes on in the area: He makes one of the earliest references to the herring industry, which during the years after Pennant became Wick's main business, hardly established in 1769:

> Much salmon is taken at *Castle-hill, Dunnet, Wick* and *Thurso.* The miraculous draught at the last place is still talked of. At a small distance from *Sinclair* castle, near *Staxigo* creek, is a small herring fishing, the only one on the coast: Cod and other white fish abound here; but the want of ports on this stormy coast is an obstacle to the establishment of fisheries on this side of the country.

Pennant notices a special maritime industry of this coast at the time but one which faded into insignificance during the herring boom of the following century. This was seal-catching:

> In the month of November numbers of Seals are taken in the vast caverns that open into the sea, and run some hundred of yards underground. The Seal-hunters enter these in small boats with torches, which they light as soon as they land, and then with loud shots alarm the animals, which they kill with clubs as they attempt to pass. This is a hazardous employ; for should the wind blow hard from sea, these adventurers are inevitably lost.

WICK OF THE NORTH

Seal-oil was of considerable importance to the locality, as a main source of lighting in the houses (where *crusies* were still much in use), and for such export trade as Wick enjoyed. One specially interesting fact about Wick is recorded by Pennant, the practice in the county and even in Orkney of 'innoculation' by 'an ingenious physician', Dr Mackenzie of Wick. The result was a reduction of the numbers suffering from small-pox, which was 'very fatal in the natural way'. Pennant also notes that 'colds, coughs and very frequent palsies' are prevalent – not surprisingly – in the area.

Another visitor who passed through a few years before Pennant was Bishop Forbes of the Episcopal Church of Scotland. This was a sign of the times. The blind anti-popery of the seventeenth century was giving way to a spirit of toleration that, even though it did not yet run to allowing open Roman Catholic worship again, nevertheless permitted a kindlier view of English episcopalianism, and in 1792 the Episcopal Church officially became a tolerated religion in Scotland. The purpose of Bishop Forbes's excursion to the north of Scotland was to see how things were and to confirm the sons and daughters of such local folk who desired it according to the Church of England rite. His candidates belonged exclusively to the gentry. He confirmed altogether twenty-seven people in and around Thurso and Wick. The confirmation and first communion in Wick of three daughters of Mr Hugh Campbell, brother to Campbell of Lochend, was conducted at Mr Campbell's house since no episcopalian consecrated building now existed in the area.

The Bishop's progress from John O'Groat's to Wick included overnight stays at Sinclair of Freshwick's 'fine new House, close upon ye Shore, and founded on Rock', Keiss, 'the seat of Sir William Sinclair, the preaching knight'[1] and the 'grand lofty tower' of Ackergill, the home of Sir William Dunbar of Hempriggs. The Bishop speaks highly of the hospitality he enjoyed, especially at 'Freshwick', where 'we dined on many good things, particularly a large Dish of Muir-Fowl, as Freshwick's servant thinks nothing of going out a Morning or Evening with a pointer and Fowling-piece, and bringing

---

1 See J B Craven: *A History of the Episcopal Church in the Dioceses of Caithness;* Kirkwall, Peace (1908), pp 269-277. Sir William Sinclair of Dunbeath and Keiss was a religious eccentric, a campaigning Baptist convert. His father, the first baronet was 'violent and unscrupulous' who, among other outrageous acts, in 1734 held criminal court on his own recognizance and condemned a certain William Sinclair to death for theft; the proceedings were quashed and Sinclair raised an action against Sir James, and obtained heavy damages. Keiss was bought from the Earl of Breadalbane. Sir William found himself heavily in debt and sold Keiss to Sinclair of Freswick in 1752.

home wt. him a dozen and a half, or perhaps two Dozens, of Muir-Fowl at once.'

Forbes makes interesting observations on the shore of Keiss, where he saw 'evident testimonies that the Clat [stack] has been detached from the Shore by the violence of the Tides and Storms.' He is mightily impressed by several of the creeks and stacks 'as one of the grandest pieces of Nature's Ruin I had ever beheld.' Ackergill impressed him for its size and ingenuity of construction, while the 'august Ruin' of Girnigoe and Sinclair castles, whither he walked from Ackergill, struck him as 'one of the grandest I ever looked upon'.

Forbes's comment on Wick itself is short. He left Ackergill at 4 o'clock in the evening 'and travelled along one of the finest natural Roads in the world, a long mile to the town of Wick, where he put up at the said Mr Campbell's House.' He 'drank Tea with Lord and Lady Duffus, who importuned [him] much to be all Night under their Roof,' but he politely declined because of the early hour at which he intended to leave. He had time, however, to observe that 'Wick is pleasantly situated at the Mouth of the Water of Wick, where a ship of 50 or 60 tons only can enter and lie safely, and where there is a small Salmon-Fishing, let by Hempriggs at 100 merks Scots a year.' A brief comment on Old Wick castle and the ancient antagonisms of Keiths, Sinclairs and Oliphants and he was on his way to the Ord.

SINCLAIRS AND OTHER 'SUPERIORS'

The lairds most concerned with Wick, burgh and parish, during the eighteenth century were, inevitably Sinclairs. Practically all the 'seats' of importance in the area were occupied by Sinclairs, mostly offshoots of the earls' families, at some stage in the history of Caithness. Henderson (writing in the late nineteenth century) as already mentioned, lists no fewer than twenty-five Sinclair 'cadet' families in Caithness (of course, he says nothing about the common Sinclairs, very numerous then and now) and of these, five had estates in the Wick parish. There were another half-dozen Sinclair lairds who had affairs in Wick, several of them at one time or another – or for long periods – 'merchants' and burgesses of the burgh, notably the Sinclairs of Ulbster, John, who negotiated the famous purchase in 1719 of the Breadalbane estate, and was (according to Calder) invited to become 'heritable provost' of Wick, George, who died in 1770, and the later John (Sir John from 1788), sometimes called 'Agricultural Sir John',[1] with whom we are concerned in Chapter 9.

Even so, the actual connection between the Ulbster lairds and both Wick and Thurso was a complicated and constantly changing one, complicated because of the persistence into the eighteenth century and beyond of some elements of the ancient feudal (or quasi-feudal) conditions of land tenure in Scotland, a long time after they were phased out in England. As a result of the reversion to Lord Glenorchy in 1676 of former earldom properties, future earls were deprived of the extensive estates formerly belonging to the Caithness earldom. For although the Sinclairs, in the person of George Sinclair of Keiss, a distant cousin of Earl George IV, successfully reclaimed the Caithness title, Lord Glenorchy – now Earl Breadalbane and Baron Wick – retained much of the landed property for which, in fact, he had paid good money. Glenorchy had even intended to take the name Sinclair, but his claim was invalidated by the same Privy Council (leaned on by James, Duke of York) in 1681 that a year before had urged Caithness men to 'concurr and assist' Glenorchy to gain possession. George of Keiss died in 1698, leaving no direct heir. He was succeeded by a second cousin of his, Sir James Sinclair of Murkle.[2]

Wick was one of the territories involved in the transfers of property, and even though sold to Sinclairs, Glenorchy (now Breadalbane), Wick remained under the 'Superiority' of Breadalbane. Until 1719 Breadalbane was named as 'Superior', when the superiority was formally transferred to John of Ulbster (see pp 156 below). The feudal connotation of 'superiority' implied the payment of a rent, feu or other land-duty to the superior, reduced in its latter days to a sort of long-term lease or 'ground-rent'; whether or not it signified a monetary obligation, a family or institution subject to a 'superiority' was never enabled to feel itself entirely independent.[3]

---

1 See Rosalind Mitchison: *Agricultural Sir John: the Life of Sir John Sinclair of Ulbster:* London, Bles (1962) p14. Although from 1723 an Ulbster Sinclair (or close relative) remained for the rest of the century as Provost of Wick, there was no viable legal concept of 'hereditary' provostship, nor warrant for it in the Burgh Charter.
2 Several of the Caithness Sinclair lairds gained either knighthoods or baronetcies, notably Sir James of Canisbay/Mey, created baronet in 1631; Sir James of Latheron/Dunbeath, 1704, and Sir John of Ulbster, 1788. Roland Sinclair describes their families quaintly as the 'baronetical branches'.
3 See Mitchison, op cit, pp 14-15. This mysterious concept of 'superiority' persisted in Scottish land law until recent times. Vestiges still persist. Until the Parliamentary Reform Act of 1832, the county franchise in Scotland was possessed by those who commanded a £400 (Scots – about £30 sterling) 'superiority'. In many cases these parliamentary superiorities were virtual fiction; genuine owners of superiority often awarded portions of it to relatives, sometimes even friends *(continued on foot of next page)*

The impact on Wick of the claims of the Earls of Breadalbane and of Caithness was not considerable during the eighteenth century, except in the case of the Earl of Caithness on one critical occasion which we discuss below (pp 155-164). They were involved from 1855 as lords lieutenant. That of the Ulbsters, however, was a different matter. The town benefited greatly from the Ulbster connection, but the price in terms of subservience was not negligible.

The succession of the earldom progressively took the earls and their family establishment further and further from Wick. Sinclair and Girnigoe ceased to be inhabited, becoming in course of time the gloomy ruins they are today, seldom visited, derelict, uncared for and inaccessible. Earl John (1698-1705), was succeeded by his son, Alexander, who attended, as a peer of Scotland, the last Scots Parliament of March, 1707. Sir William Dunbar of Hempriggs, as Commissioner for Wick to the Convention of Royal Burghs, voted also for Union. Earl Alexander lasted until 1765, over a time of changing conditions and fortunes in the county, and in the whole of Scotland. The most severe disturbances of the relative peace overtaking Caithness in this century were those associated with the '15 and the '45. Strong feeling in favour of the Stewarts manifested itself among the Caithness lairds, less among the rising trading community, the merchants and burgesses of Wick. In 1715, Robert Dunbar, the rich and powerful laird of Northfield, just south of Wick, appeared with a party at the cross of Wick, and drank the health of the Chevalier; while David Sinclair of Brabster-dorran joined the Earl of Mar, and was present at the battle of Sheriffmuir.'[1]

The Caithness involvement in 1745 was rather more serious. Earl Alexander and George Sinclair of Ulbster, Sheriff of the county, 'were staunch friends to Government, and gave no countenance to rebellion.' Wick Burgh Council, at this time dominated by George, was vociferous in its repeated expressions of loyalty and abjuration of the Stewarts, but early in 1746, Lord Macleod, son of the Earl of Cromarty (a Sinclair relative), came to Caithness to recruit for the Prince. He made Thurso his headquarters – probably aware of the more Hanoverian spirit of Wick. His recruiting was none too successful; about forty-five men joined and these marched into

---

(continued from foot of previous page) to establish on the roll sufficient votes to capture the seat. The system became fearfully corrupt. Sinclair of Ulbster, a relatively honest laird for the times, was not, as we shall see, above such manipulation.

1 Calder, op cit, footnote, p 198.

Sutherland where they met up with Lord Cromarty's force marching north. Cromarty and Macleod were trapped and arrested in Dunrobin and their entire force, '350 in number were marched under the command of subaltern officers, and with little precaution, on to the ferry, where they were to embark [to cross the Dornoch and Moray Firths]. Thither they were chased by comparatively a mere handful of the Sutherland militia, and the greater part of them were destroyed.' Macleod and Cromarty were sent to London, tried for high treason, and condemned to death, but reprieved. John Sutherland, on the other hand, laird of Forse, raised a formidable troop of 1250 men, the 'Loudon Highlanders' (after their colonel, John Campbell of Loudon). Some of these fought at Culloden. Thus was the country divided in its loyalties, with a preponderance in favour of the government. Apart from a fright, the county suffered little as a result; and Wick's almost uniform support for the Hanoverian government doubtless benefited it in the developing trade rivalry with Thurso.[1]

Earl Alexander left no heir and was succeeded by William Sinclair of Rattar, another distant cousin. This was a disputed succession. There is a touching story of how the sins of the fathers were visited by long process on the 'illegitimate' offspring of David Sinclair of Broynach, brother of John Sinclair of Murkle who, in 1698 became Earl of Caithness. The illicit liaison between David and his housekeeper, Janet Ewing, resulting in the birth of their child (which died), brought on them both the condemnation of the kirk. A 'court' of the Caithness Presbytery, unable to deal with Broynach because he refused their jurisdiction, condemned the unfortunate Janet Ewing to 'to be drummed through the streets of Thurso bearing a paper crown inscribed with the assigned reason, and an official was appointed to finish her punishment by so many lashes on her uncovered shoulders.' Broynach rescued her from the mob witnessing the punishment, egged on by two ministers, by brandishing a pistol and drawing his sword. Subsequently he persuaded a proscribed episcopal clergyman to marry him to Janet, for which offence the 'disestablished performer' was ordered 'henceforth not to perform any ministerial function within the kingdom, under the highest

---

1 Donaldson in the Introduction to *The Mey Letters* quotes evidence to suggest that 'four or five of the lower gentry (among whom was George Sinclair of Geese) had raised 400-500 men in readiness to join Sir James Steuart from the Orkneys [Steuart was certainly a rebel, and was sent for trial to London, where, however he died from gaol fever in Southwark Gaol].' The whole enterprise was, however, aborted, though Geese and four of his tenants were arrested later for 'complicity'. Among those who deponed evidence against them were merchants of Thurso and Wick.

penalty of the church.' The ultimate significance of the episode is that when, in 1766 Earl Alexander died, Sinclair of Broynach's grandson, was disqualified from claiming the succession, although he was a considerably closer relative than William of Rattar whose claim was upheld by the Court of Session and the House of Lords in 1772.[1]

Earl Alexander was not at all enthusiastic about the Rattar succession. He and Rattar disliked one another, as Alexander reported in some correspondence to one of the Lords of Session:

> Rattar is next, tho' very remote. Though he lives within four miles of me he never comes to see me, from which it seems he is disobliged because I did not give him all I had, and depend for subsistence on his generosity. He cannot be very wise, for he could not have taken a more effectual way to disappoint his expectactions.

William, in fact, died in 1782, and was succeeded by his son, John, Lord Berriedale, a major in the army, who did not last long either. He served in the American War of Independence and was involved in the siege of Charleston, where he was severely wounded and died soon after his return to London. The line was switched once more, this time to the Sir James Sinclair of Mey. 'in whose family' says Calder in 1887, 'it still remains'.[2]

Even though the earls no longer played a significant part in the affairs of Wick, for that matter, in Caithness generally, lesser Sinclairs of all shapes, sizes and styles were now much in evidence. Some two thirds of 'Caithness families' listed by Henderson are either Sinclairs or in some way closely related to them. This was the age of the 'lairds' rather than the 'lords', but not lairds in the sense usually applied in Scottish clan relationships. They were, as compared with the mighty landowners of the past, owner-occupiers of greater or less pretention, some of them enjoying a considerable acreage (and often farming for themselves on the 'Mains'), feuing land to smaller farmers but increasingly relying on money rents for their income rather than services and rents in kind, in fact, closely resembling the English landed squirearchy. There were of course many small 'crofters' and

---

[1] The grounds of disqualification were the supposed invalidity of the marriage to Janet, even though Broynach's son was by a later wife. Roland St Clair disputes the decision; that the marriage was celebrated is, he says, not in question but, he suggests, that is irrelevant since 'Scottish law .. recognises that a public declaration on the part of the man to be sufficient to constitute a marriage.'

[2] Calder was writing in 1863. The Earl at that time, Lord Lieutenant and Vice-Admiral of Caithness, was created Baron Barrogill. There have been two switches of line since.

'cottars', increasingly apprehensive for their traditional and usually unwritten contracts of tenure.

Nevertheless, although there was some ejection of crofters and cottars in Caithness at the time of the clearances, the county was spared much of the misery of wholesale removal of poor families from their land, so scandalously prevalent during the early nineteenth century in the neighbouring county of Sutherland. In any case, Caithness was, and remains, a cattle rather than sheep-farming area, the broad inland moors being largely suitable for neither sheep nor cattle. Also, as several writers mention, Caithness produced and 'exported' considerable quantities of grain, especially bere. Much of this was grown in Wick parish.

The Caithness Sinclair and other lairds mostly lived on their own lands, usually constructing for themselves comfortable houses. Among such houses built in the neighbourhood of Wick in the eighteenth century were those of Sinclair of Freswick (1760), Dunbar of Northfield and Bowermadden, and Dunbar of Hempriggs, both in the earlier years of the century, built fine houses.

In the following century much grander lairdly homes were established, often on the site of the older house, as at Stirkoke (1855-1859). Fine houses were built at Latheronwheel (1851), and Keiss, where a structure of 'solid baronial' was erected inland from the old castle. The popular architect of that age of 'conspicuous consumption' was the Edinburgh specialist in 'baronial' and 'Scots Jacobean', David Bryce. It was the rising prosperity of Wick that gave rise to much of the wealth on show in the country homes of Caithness.

An interesting picture of the life style of the eighteenth century Sinclair lairds emerges from *The Mey Letters,* a compilation of letters to and from various members, relatives, friends of and others to do with the Mey family. The compiler, John Donaldson, comments on their frequently 'extravagant style of living', requiring for instance regular supplies (from Wick and Thurso merchants) of luxury food commodities such as sugar, prunes, raisins, candy, currants, spices and pepper, oranges, lemons and 'confected carvie', high class tailoring for themselves, high fashion clothes for their wives, private tutors for their children, books, and of course, ample quantities of Lisbon wine, brandy by the 'anker', sherry, claret and rum – rendering them, by the way, generous customers of the smugglers and doubtless dabblers themselves from time to time in the trade itself. 'One gets the impression,' says Donaldson, 'that these gentlemen lived very much *en grand seigneur.'* The expensive styles and taste were based, Donaldson believes, very much on 'an extensive system of credit', which certainly landed Sir James Sinclair of Mey (1692-1732), for instance, in fatally serious trouble.

The story of his profligacy and ultimate fate is told with relish by the sardonic old tale teller of Kirkwall, Buckham Hossak, in his *Kirkwall of the Orkneys*. Hossack discovered in Kirkwall burgh records an extraordinary entry dated 2 March, 1732, referring to the acknowledgement, by Sir James Sinclair of Mey, Bart. then a virtually permanent resident in the Kirkwall gaol, of a debt owing to the Kirkwall magistrates of £1095 Scots and £456 5s Scots for gaol fees, 24 August, 1729 to date. Sinclair undertook either to pay this debt himself or remit it to his heirs. A considerable portion of this debt was due to expenditures on 'conviviality', enjoyed by the prisoner in the gaol itself, where friends were invited, or in a 'private dwelling', when James was on parole. The occasion of Sir James's promise to pay in 1732 persuaded the Kirkwall bailies to celebrate. Another entry refers to: '8 bottles Rum punch, to the Magistrates and Council, when they got Sir James Sinclair's obligation for the Tolbooth mealls [maintenance] – £280.' The magistrates were wise to celebrate while they could, for they had to wait until 1738 for their money until after Sir James died, still in the Kirkwall Tolbooth; and the bill was settled in 1738 by his son, the new Sir James, who 'took on himself the obligation granted by the deceased prisoner.'[1]

How Sir James became a prisoner at all across the water from Mey

---

1 See B H Hossack: *Kirkwall in the Orkneys;* re-issued edition, published by Kirkwall Press in 1986 (p. 154). See also John Horne: *Ye Towne of Wick in ye Olden Tyme,* Wick (1895), and Donaldson, op cit. Donaldson has Sir James dying in Kirkwall prison in March of 1732, Hossack has him lasting until 1738. It is Hossack who is out of this matter. The story is even more complicated than he understood. Sir James, had in fact fallen into the hands of Sir Patrick Dunbar, laird of Northfield, Wick, via a certain Patrick Smith of Orkney who had advanced money against a bond to Sir James's father, Sir William Sinclair, the author of the original debt. According to Donaldson, Dunbar (known as Dunbar of Northfield and Bowermadden), who had taken up the bond (for 6000 marks Scots), had his son force the impecunious Sir James in 1718 'to grant him the whole estate [that of Mey] in tack for ten years. Then, presumably in order to get rid of Mey, Sir Patrick Dunbar of Bowermadden allowed him to be arrested in 1720 for a debt of £40 sterling and incarcerated at Kirkwall. Mey did not allow his imprisonment to cramp his sartorial style, 'ordering hats, cravats and other finery, for which he had no earthly hope of paying, from a merchant in Sutherland who was unaware of his customer's bankruptcy'. During his incarceration for some time his children were boarded out with a family in Wick, under instruction by a schoolmaster of Bower, their unkeep contributed to by Dunbar of Bowermadden. The estate was eventually prized out of the hands of Bowermadden 'after much litigation' by the young Sir James, He, characteristically, was soon deep in debt himself.

in Orkney is told in *Ye Town of Wick in ye Oldene Tymes* of John Horne (qv) – quoted by Hossack:

> In 1721, the sister of the Laird of Stirkoke [then Francis Sinclair], was pregnant to the Laird of Mey, a married man; and the minister, fearing designs upon the child, called a special meeting of the Session in order to take her judicial confession. It came out that the Laird had provided a nurse to attend her, and also a manservant to carry off the child as soon as it was born. The nurse was ordered out of the parish; and when search was made for the man, it was found that he had taken flight for Orkney. The Laird was also discovered in another county in close custody for debt.

The 'other county' was also Orkney. It looks as though Sir James was already being pursued for his enormous debts, many of which he had inherited, though his own life-style was evidently not one of prudent frugality. Evidently he found Kirkwall Tolbooth a very tolerable alternative to the responsibilities of regaining and running a bankrupt estate and satisfying his many creditors. He remained in gaol for ten years and never went again to Mey (then Barrogill).

The most influential of the Sinclairs in the eighteenth century came to be those of Ulbster, not close to the earls, and unlike most of the noble earls, men of business. This branch of the Sinclair clan grew from the same stem as the Mey Sinclairs. William, second son of George (II), Earl of Caithness (1529-1582), one of the 'Wicked' Earls, was the brother of the unhappy John who 'was imprisoned by his father in Castle Girnigo', allegedly with William's connivance and, according to another story, cruelly done to death in 1572 or 1573. According to this story, William was prevented from 'legitimising by subsequent marriage either of his two natural sons Patrick and John', though in fact they were, nevertheless, legitimised by official letters of legitimation which 'passed the Great Seal on 20 June, 1567 for *"Patricio et Magistro Joanni Sinclair Filiis Quondam Wilhelmini de Mey"*.[1]

There seems to be a confusion of dates here. Patrick, got a 'disposition' of the lands of Ulbster in 1596 from his cousin, George (III), Earl of Caithness. Patrick was succeeded by his brother John, and from 1601 onwards the line became known as 'Sinclair of Ulbster', most of the heads being named John. The exception was Patrick, the third Sinclair of Ulbster, whose family acquired Brims (by the marriage of Patrick's son, John) in 1660, and 'various lands by purchase from the Earl of Caithness, and other from Lord Glenorchy in 1676.' The fourth generation John left no direct heirs, the first substitute being John of Brims, eldest son of John of Tannach and Brims; the next heir thus became known as Sinclair of Brims and Ulbster.

John Sinclair of Ulbster (VI), who died in 1736 was the first of the Ulbsters to become closely identified with Wick. He was persuaded in 1723 to become 'heritable provost of the burgh', a 'curious and lengthy' process (according to Thomas Sinclair) which was not, to say the least, strictly in accordance with the terms of the Charter. Nevertheless, for most of the rest of the century, a Sinclair of Ulbster (including James of Harpsdale, son of this John) held the provostship. The town with perpetually empty coffers hoped that Ulbster would recover for them the 'Hill of Wick' from the Dunbars of Hempriggs (see Chapter 8 pp 190-193), 'pay the town's debts, set burghers up in trade etc'. In fact, the Ulbsters did Wick proud over the years, but never succeeded in getting them fully out of debt.

The memory and reputations of George Sinclair of Ulbster, merchant and Provost of Wick during the mid-eighteenth century, and James of Harpsdale, brother, to James, were greatly overshadowed by those of his son, John, who succeeded to the Ulbster property in 1776, and was created baronet in 1786. He was also merchant, provost and 'Superior' of Wick, but ultimately became much more widely known as an 'improver', pioneer of the new agriculture, founder of the British Wool Society (and as such one of the authors of the later miseries of the folk of Sutherland), statistician, virtual creator of the national Board of Agriculture and a voluminous writer on many matters of public policy. We shall return to the work of this remarkable man after taking a close look at the internal affairs and development of the Royal Burgh of Wick during the eighteenth century.

Ulbster, which gave its name to the dynasty, is today a rather inconsiderable settlement strung along the A9 about eight miles south of Wick. From the time that John Sinclair, the baronet's grandfather, acquired the properties of Wydal, Ormlie and Thurso West, probably in the 1719 purchase, the Sinclairs of Ulbster lived in the 'fortalice' of Thurso. It was here that John was born in May, 1754. The family's connections with Thurso, still a 'burgh of barony', were as close as those with Wick, perhaps closer, but it is Wick with which we are concerned and which, for good and sufficient reasons, Sir John Sinclair of Ulbster, is now usually associated.

One other family important in the affairs of Wick deserves mention at this stage, the Dunbars of Hempriggs who lived not at Hempriggs just south of the town but at Ackergill just to the North. They were descended from the Earls of Moray, appearing in the area early in the seventeenth century. Their two families, Hempriggs and Northfield and Bowermadden are said by Rosalind Mitchison to have represented before the ascendancy of the Sinclairs of Ulbster 'the main political power of the county'; besides having accumulated considerable wealth and acreage of land, they produced the last three members of parliament. The first baronet was Sir James Dunbar, created in 1706; his son, Sir William, with property in Wick and possession of Old Wick, a freeman of the burgh, made several moves to capture superiority in Wick. In this he was outmanoeuvred by the Sinclairs of Ulbster.

WICK 1794

Much the fullest picture of Wick in the eighteenth century is that presented in *The Statistical Account of Scotland*. This *Account* is the most memorable and enduring of the achievements of Sir John Sinclair of Ulbster, containing as it does a picture of almost every parish in Scotland about the end of the century. Each was contributed by the minister of the parish, in many cases as a result of direct approach by Sir John himself. He supervised personally the entire account of the Caithness parishes, that of Wick being written by the then minister of the parish, William Sutherland, of whom Sinclair regarded himself as a personal friend.

It is a thorough, excursive study of Wick, town and parish, in terms of contemporary knowledge of its geography, geology and minerals, agriculture, fisheries and other industries, landowning, settlement and population, occupations, education and religion. There is little need here to repeat all the detail of this eminently readable description, since much of it would be to repeat what has already be said. Since, however, Sutherland's study presents the most authoritative picture of the locality before the great expansion of Wick in the early nineteenth century, attention must be drawn to several critical elements of the scene. There are a few intimations in the account that hopes were arising about a new and more prosperous Wick; the main focus of attention was, of course, the harbour.

Accordingly, we shall direct attention to those features which are of special evolutionary interest. Mr Sutherland derives the name of the place from *vicus*, a village; this, and lack of reference anywhere to Viking origins, reveals that the kind of scholarship popularised by Samuel Laing in Orkney some decades later had as yet made no impact. Nor, understandably, has Mr Sutherland anything new to say about the historical background generally.

Objects Worthy of Attention

Sutherland comments on the small fishery developed on the Hempriggs estate in the 'Salmon Craig' loch which, he thinks, 'might be carried on more extensively in the bay and river of Wick'. He even suggests a diversion in the course of the river where 'this fishery would be more productive', feasible in view of the projected construction of a new harbour. Such a harbour would, he considers be 'not only an object of the highest importance to the town itself and its immediate neighbourhood, but to the kingdom at large.' While there were several 'creeks, or *goes*' along the coast where small fishing boats were resorting during the season (he mentions in particular the development going on at Staxigoe, 'a kind of port'), there was urgent need for a 'harbour commodious for a number of vessels, and safe in all weathers' in the Wick Water. A survey was produced in 1793 by John Rennie for just such a harbour on commission from the British Fisheries Society, though Sutherland does not mention Rennie, nor for that matter the visitation of Thomas Telford in 1790 – though it is doubtful if he would have known of this, anyway. On the other hand, he refers to the correspondence he knew to be going on at the time between Sir Benjamin Dunbar of Hempriggs, the proprietor of that property, with the British Fisheries Society 'for feuing out', on the south side of the water, opposite the town of Wick, several hundred acres of land, for building a fishing village.

The great hope, Mr Sutherland strongly suggests, lies in the sea. He mentions salt-panning at Keiss, and *sea-ware* (sea-weed)[1] among the resources capable of development, but it is the fisheries that are of most interest. The coast, he explains, 'abounds with a great variety of

---

1 'Sea-ware' at this time was a major export from Orkney to Glasgow and other areas of chemical manufacture, where it was a main source of soda and potash for glass and soap making. It was also used as manure, its main use in Caithness. John Donaldson considered that 'the kelp industry .. must have given employment to quite a number of people' in Caithness, and he speaks of the leasing of 'kelp shores' by Wick merchants, especially in Mey; but the industry nowhere reached the proportions that it came to do in Orkney. (See John E. Donaldson: *Caithness in the Eighteenth Century*, op cit pp 149-153.)

fish, which, besides what is annually exported, furnishes the inhabitants with a liberal supply during every season of the year. 'Salmon, trout, herring, cod, ling, haddock, whiting, mackerel, halibut, which the fishers here call turbot, skate, flounder, dog-fish' are listed with other species, shell fish, crabs and lobsters which could, he believed, sell well on the London market if they could be got there. He speaks too of an icehouse, recently built here, 'to supply ice for carrying fish to London'.

But the main issue is the herring fishery. Great shoals have always 'visited this coast', says Sutherland, but 'till late years, however, they were very much neglected, the people contenting themselves, year after year, with catching a few on hooks; and proceeding with that excellent bait to the cod-fishing'. He tells the story (to which we shall return) of how John Sutherland of Wester, Messrs John Anderson of Wick, and Alexander Miller of Staxigoe, despite much discouragement, set a new example of how to fish successfully on a larger scale. The result was that 'the herring fishery yearly increased; a spirit of emulation arose between the natives of the town and several adventurers, who, on account of the fishery, resorted to Wick from other places. Curing of red, as well as white herrings became an object of attention; and both the red and white herrings of Wick have met with the highest approbation in the London and other markets.'

Sutherland tells of the striking rise in activity, the number and size of vessels engaged and quantities of barrelled herring shipped out; from 363 barrels of white herring in 1782, the trade rose to 'no less than 10,514 barrels of white, and above 2000 barrels of red herrings' in 1790. This was a vast increase but further development was 'greatly hampered for want of a good harbour'. On this topic Sutherland becomes more explicit.

> A good harbour is much wanted, as nothing of the kind can be found on all the coast of Caithness; a circumstance that has occasioned much damage, as well as loss of lives, even during the herring fishing season, which at this place is in summer and the beginning of autumn. The coast being very open and dangerous, fishermen will not venture out in small boats but in very promising weather. The abolition of the duty on coal would be of great use by encouraging the resort of settlers to carry on both fisheries and manufactures; and lastly it would be of importance to have a large supply of salt and casks laid up in storehouses.

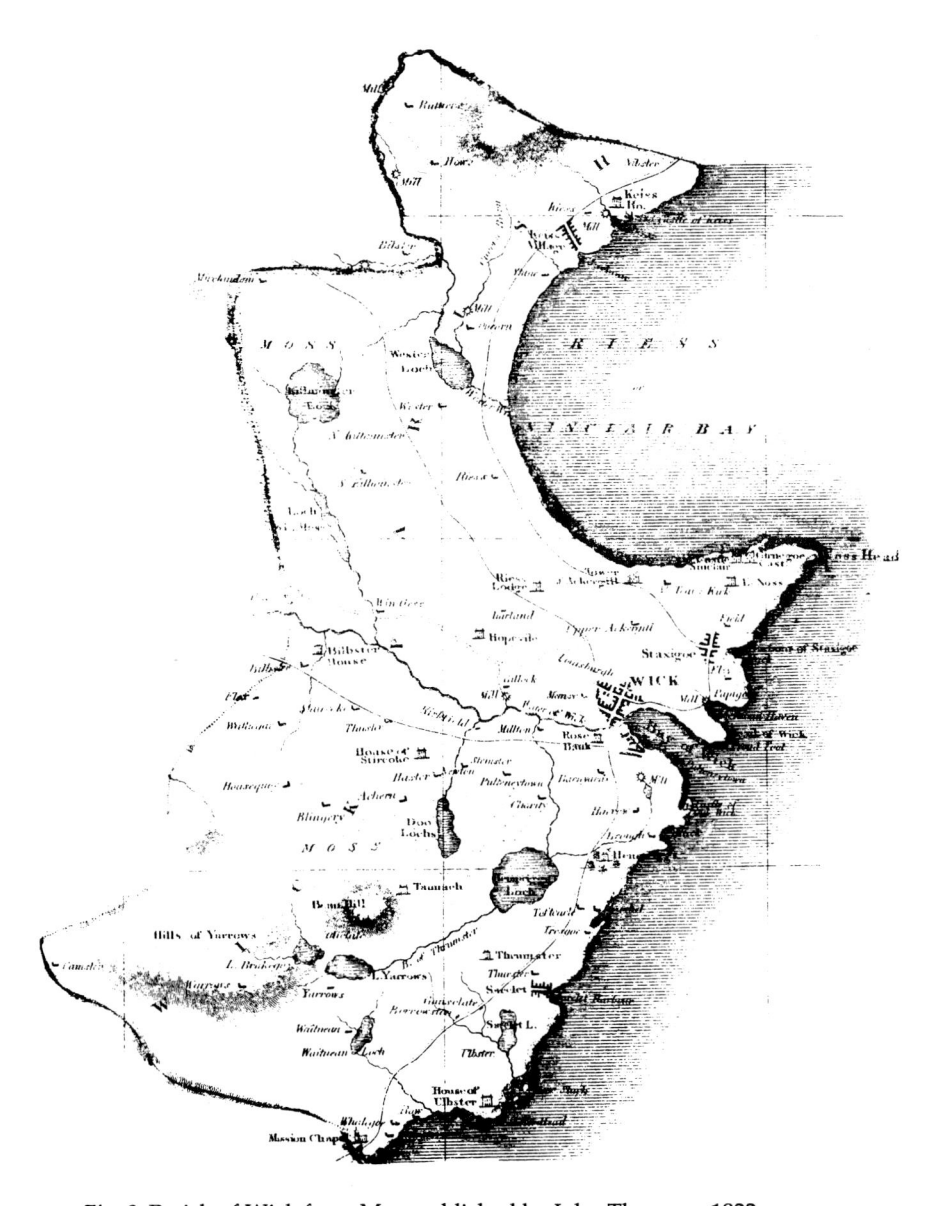

Fig. 9 Parish of Wick from Map published by John Thomson 1822.

There were many other factors restricting development of the herring trade. Salt was heavily taxed at this time. Sutherland recommended that the duty on salt be entirely taken off.[1] Conditions were such that 'although this parish affords as good a fishing coast and as good stations as could be wished, yet it is to be regretted that there are hardly any real fishermen belonging to it, those alone excepted who resort to Wick from any parts of the kingdom, during the fishing season only'. As things were at present, 'weavers, taylors, shoemakers, house and boat carpenters, blacksmiths, masons, etc. in this and the neighbouring parishes, having made a little previous preparation, repair to the fishing boats, go to sea at night, the only time for catching herrings, and spend all day in sleep, by which their customers are sure to be ill served.' There was a severe shortage of hemp for cordage and netting. The growing of hemp ought to be encouraged. 'There is not a doubt, 'adds the minister, 'that hemp would thrive here, there being plenty of excellent manure, and abundance of fine rich black loamy soil.'

Farming in Wick Parish

As in the rest of Caithness, farm-work was the chief means of livelihood in Wick parish. Wick town, indeed, though a royal burgh, was really very rural, having, as Donaldson puts it, like Thurso, 'the sole monopoly of a large agricultural hinterland, thus relieving them of the endless disputes about encroachments which vexed most Scottish burghs.'[2]

Agriculture in general could be much improved. There were 'immense tracts of uncultivated green ground, with a good depth of soil, and ready for the plough,' that could 'be converted into good arable land,' while improved cropping rotations could greatly increase yields. Dunbar of Hempriggs is mentioned several times as an enterprising innovator. He is, for instance, growing 12 to 14 acres of clover and rye-grass, 'though winter herding has not yet been fully established'. Deplorably persistent in the area is the 'pernicious custom' called *'rig and rennal,* or run-rig, that is to say, each tenant, in a particular farm or district, has a ridge alternately with his neighbours. This is necessarily attended with confusion and disputes,

---

[1] The salt excise was a most unpopular tax, abolished in 1730 but reimposed in 1732 by Walpole's government. It was retained until 1825, when a whole list of commodities were removed from the excise schedules.
[2] Donaldson, *Caithness* op cit, p 196.

and is a practice requiring to be abolished.' Abolishing this and many other instances of backwardness, came to be a main preoccupation of the chief landlord of Caithness, Sir John Sinclair of Ulbster, the 'great improver'. The 'most considerable estate' in the Wick parish was Hempriggs, letting 'many well cultivated fields to tenants, which about a century ago were no better than common pasture.' The chief arable crops were black and grey oats and 'bear' (sometimes spelled 'bere'), which, as already mentioned, formed a staple element in the diet of local people, quantities also being exported.

Black cattle abound in the parish and county, 'considerable numbers of which young and old are purchased by drovers at from 40s. to 50s. *per* head, and are driven to Falkirk, Edinburgh and England'. Sheep are not numerous although 'different attempts have been made to rear sheep in this parish, but not with success.' The best place in the parish for sheep 'is no doubt the hills of Yarrow, a part of Sir John Sinclair's estate.' But at present a 'preposterous method is practised by the tenants in that region ... of penning up their sheep in summer (to keep them from their corn), whilst in the winter season, they are allowed to stray to the shore, where they live partly on sea ware. Many of these neglected but valuable animals are killed by foxes, and many are found lying dead on the shore drowned by the sea.' All this was to change, for one of Sir John's interests was the improvement in breeds of sheep and the exploitation of hill pastures.

Industry and Occupations.

As for industrial activity, some fresh water lochs in the area were providing a water supply to turn mills: for example, on the Hempriggs loch were already 'a waulk-mill, a distillery, a snuff-mill, a lint-mill and three corn mills.' The district's mineral resources were meagre. Lime was burned at Hempriggs. 'The county abounds with stones,' says Sutherland, 'very fit for building, which might be much more employed than they are at present for drains and inclosures, the want of which greatly retards the progress of improvement.' Sutherland comments on the plentifulness of flags 'useful for paving', and in a footnote he notices, prophetically enough, that 'in an angular cavity in the face of a flat rock near old Wick, covered by the sea at high water, there is a small mineral well which fills and empties with the tide every 24 hours,' – prophetic, that is, if he meant mineral oil, for such phenomena are known in the Caithness rocks. Today oil platforms exploiting lower level concentrations are often visible from the coast of Wick.

The population was said to be increasing, particularly on the coast and in the burgh of Wick 'as the fisheries have become more extended and successful'. There being no reliable official enumerations, Sutherland's estimates are in very round figures: 'at least 5000 young and old' in the parish, as compared with Dr Webster's count of 1755 of 3938; and in Wick burgh itself about 1000 in 200 families. 'In consequence of the villages projected on the north and south of the town,' Mr Sutherland expects that the population 'will be considerably augmented'. In addition to the development south of the river under discussion with the British Fisheries Society, he alludes to the creation of the 'village' of Louisburgh, a planned rural settlement just north of the town, consisting of 'houses worth at least 10 pounds' each on an acre of 'excellent land fit for garden ground', 33 acres altogether, a project of Mr Dunbar of Hempriggs. This village, named 'in compliment to Mrs Dunbar, whose Christian name is Louisa . . . can scarcely fail to prosper from the many advantages it possesses.'

There is not much variety of occupation in the 'county part' of Wick parish, 'which is principally inhabited by farmers, 'mostly on short leases from the nine proprietors or 'heritors' in the parish, and the 'seven principal tacksmen'. Tenants have a hard life, many of them still having 'to perform heavy and almost unlimited services to the landlord'. In addition to the general run of farming work on the *Mains* besides his own, 'tenants have to take their master's victual, kiln-dry, mill and sift it, and deliver in meal at a proof; and when it is sold to a merchant, they are obliged to carry it, as well as their own victual rent [tenants paid rent partly in kind] to the neighbouring port and put it on shipboard, their horses often standing all the time, for many hours, starving with cold and hunger.' This kind of 'abject servitude', sometimes called *master-work* was on the way out, some landlords already having converted tenants' services to money rent and 'given them leases for nineteen years'. There were also 'cotters . . . . an inferior kind of farmers, who possess small cot-houses with a little land, for which they pay a trifling rent in money or in kind, but they are likewise bound to pay personal services for a certain number of days of the week.'

In the country there were few craftsmen but in Wick town 'there are about 12 shop-keepers, 9 or 10 shipmasters, 50 coopers, including apprentices, a few house, ship and boat carpenters, together with masons, smiths, weavers, shoemakers, taylors, etc. sufficient for the size of the place. The greater part of these tradesmen are occasionally employed as fishermen.'

The Rev. Sutherland gives some figures for wage-rates which he evidently regarded as a considerable improvement on the past: a ploughman, for instance, once earning from 13s. 4d to 18s. for a half year, now earns 20s. to 28s., while women improved from 6s. to 8s. and 'must now have from 20s. to 24s. half yearly . . . . A grieve or overseer has at present from £3 to even £10.'

The Trade of Wick in the Eighteenth Century

Apart from his fairly lengthy comments on Wick and the herring trade, Mr Sutherland has little to say about Wick as a trading port. Its disadvantages for the purposes of herring fishery applied also to the town's development as a general trading centre, the want of safe berthing facilities in deep water. As John Donaldson establishes in his *Caithness in the Eighteenth Century*, there was no lack of commodities for export; surplus grain and meal was available for shipment to other parts of Scotland and overseas, and he quotes a writer of 1783 who refers to the '"salting and exporting beef" as being a thriving business' in the town.[1] John Horne (who also quotes the same writer) in *Ye Town of Wick* (q.v.) comments that 'beef-curing was a branch of industry in the old town for over a century', and that the beef 'was mainly cured for the navy victualling contractors at Inverness.'[2] There is mention in the *Mey Letters* of a cargo of salt being sent to the Lord of Mey from Dysart to Wick in 1697, probably for salting fish, which seems to have been carried on as a 'side-line' on the Mey estate even at this early date; and it is clear from another and later reference in the letters that Wick merchants were accustomed to importing salt, doubtless for the beef trade as well.[3] Hides, too, were an export from Wick. An early record tells of a Dutch ship loaded with 'fish, tallow, hides and beef', captured as she left Staxigoe by a Commonwealth frigate in 1651, all contraband at the time since it was meant to benefit the royal cause; and Horne tells of a cargo of similar processed beef products shipped to Holland by the Wick merchant, Bailie Robert Calder and others, to the value of £8678 19s 4s, Scots (£723 3s sterling).

1 Donaldson: *Caithness*, op cit, P192.
2 Horne, op cit. pp 14-15.
3 John E Donaldson (Ed): *The Mey Letters*; Sydney, Australia; Donaldson (1984), various letters, p38 and pp 88-92; and Donaldson: *Caithness* op cit. p 190.

As an indication of the variety of goods in transit at Wick in the eighteenth century, in 1740 tolls were paid to the Wick burgh on a list of goods including 'bear, double trees, single trees, birks, large couple legs, small couple legs, bark, dealls, beef, mutton, pork, butter, cheese;, oil, cloth-woollen and linen, wool, meal, tallow, ale, "acquavity" (whisky), cart wheels, mill stones, grave stones and free stone.' Most of the foodstuffs listed were 'home products', the timber coming from Norway and the cloth from Morayshire. The reference to cartwheels, as Donaldson believes, 'gives the lie to Sir John Sinclair, John Henderson and other writers who assert that carts were unknown in Caithness until the end of the eighteenth century,' though Mr Sutherland records that 'the use of carts has been only of late years introduced into this country; and they are as yet far from being so generally used, as every good farmer would wish,'[1] – and the minister would surely know.

For its size and location, Wick, as Donaldson says, had been a 'busy little town long before the eighteenth century had dawned.' It had ten merchants as early as 1660, and during the years after 1700 the still more numerous Wick traders had considerable business to keep them going. In addition to the bulk goods already mentioned, they handled lucrative orders for the luxury goods required by the lairds, wines from Portugal and France, tea, coffee, silks, satins and high-class woollens such as 'shalloons' and serges.[2]

None of this ought to leave the impression that Wick was a major port in any sense. Few, if any ships, belonged to Wick. In the *The Mey Letters* there are slight hints of 'shipes' of Wick, but it seems likely that most ships used in the trade of Wick and Thurso were chartered by merchants of the two towns from Leith, Montrose, Banff or Inverness, though there were not many ships owned in Inverness even though, according to Donaldson, 'from at least 1700, Inverness had been the great entrepot of trade in the North of Scotland.'[3] Although classed by Donaldson as one of the 'four ports' of Caithness, Wick shared with Thurso the handicap of being in the 'situation at the mouth of a river where the ships were left high and dry at low tide, and even at high water it was apparently difficult for vessels to land cargoes there.'[4]

In the circumstances, Scrabster on the west side of Thurso Bay had to do duty for Thurso in the berthing of deeper draught vessels, while

1 Donaldson, *Caithness* op cit, p190.
2 Ibid, p190.
3 Ibid, p181.
4 Ibid, p188.

Staxigoe did the same for Wick. Though its harbour was very limited in space, and not too easy of access from the town (most of the transport between Wick and Staxigoe was by pack-horse), Staxigoe had become, by the end of the century virtually the 'port of Wick'. Evidence of this is still to be seen in the village in the form of the two 'girnals', (storehouses for grain, meal and other goods brought in as rents in kind), still standing, empty and dilapidated, facing the harbour front of Staxigoe.

Character of the People

Of the religious disposition of the people, Mr Sutherland does not say much except to suggest that they are mostly run-of-the-mill members of the 'established church of Scotland'. There are, he says 'the remains of some popish chapels' still extant, and a little evidence that a few people still cherish 'popish' supersititions. (We return to this topic in Chapter 10). As for the people's general character, Sutherland praises them for their 'martial spirit'. Wick has proved, says Sutherland:

> an excellent nursery for soldiers and sailors. Nowhere have recruiting officers been more successful. Want of manufactures and other means of employment, make young men, who are averse to labour in husbandry, and have no good way of livelihood, readily betake themselves to the army and navy, more especially when a Highland corps is to be raised.[1] On the late alarm of a Spanish war, the town of Wick cheerfully furnished its quota of seamen, and of course procured protections for those employed in the fisheries.

Thus the picture of Wick in 1794 provided by Mr Sutherland (supplemented by a few observations from others), is that of a locality where most people were poor but, by the standards of the time, not ill fed, poorly housed, dependent for their employment and well-being on gentry who, apart from notable exceptions, were neither generous in the terms of service offered nor in their benefactions. There were burgeoning signs of improvement, but no lively expectations that a better life was soon to come. It was well that Wickers had a 'martial spirit' for, although Mr Sutherland does not mention it, what was to be Britain's longest and most arduous war with France had just broken out. Who was to know that this was to be the making of Wick?

1 A view borne out by the ease with which Sir John Sinclair recruited his two 'Fencible' battalions in 1794 and 1795.

CHAPTER 7

THE SETT OF WICK; A SCOTTISH 'POCKET' BOROUGH: 1[1]

THE royal burgh created by King James in 1589, 'to be called the burgh of Wick in all time coming', was to have 'special and plenary power to the free inhabitants and burgesses of the said burgh and their successors in the future, with the express advice and consent of our said cousin, George, Earl of Caithness, his heirs and successors, and not otherwise or in any other manner of making, electing, constituting, and creating a provost and four bailies, indwellers or inhabitants of the said burgh, together with a treasurer, dean of guild, councillors, burgesses, serjeants, and other officers necessary within the said burgh for the government of the same.'

This was, and remained until the local government reforms of the 1830s, the governing body, 'set' or 'sett' of Wick, similar to that of sixty or so other royal burghs that had come into existence before the Union in 1707. Most Scottish burghs were small indeed, but bigger or smaller, their government followed a similar pattern. A burgh such as Wick, with an estimated early seventeenth century population of perhaps 500, naturally lacked the resources, experience and scope for self-government that large towns like Edinburgh, Aberdeen or Perth commanded, but enjoyed the same sort of official establishment, titles and duties as the great. The provost, bailies and burgesses thrived on self-esteem; there was seldom any lack of candidates for office. In any case, being a burgess, that is, a 'free' citizen, carried with it important privileges, including the right to vote in such 'elections' as were conducted by the council. The number on the annually prepared list of burgesses of Wick usually ran to between thirty and seventy. The rest of the citizens, the 'un-freemen', the 'hewers of wood and drawers of water' had far fewer privileges.

In a country where feudal – or quasi-feudal – conditions prevailed, it may be thought surprising that burgh status, royal and baronial,

---

[1] The term is not strictly applicable. Borough representation in England before the Reform Act of 1832 was thoroughly unbalanced and mostly corrupt and often in the 'pocket' of a substantial landowner. Scottish burghs were on a somewhat different footing, but the franchise was equally restricted and thoroughly corrupt. John Robinson (one of Lord North's ministers) called them 'a parcel of very compound boroughs'.

was so frequently awarded by the king. The creation of Wick as a royal burgh in this respect illustrates typically the two main reasons for the king's liberality: firstly, self-regulating communities of merchants and craftsmen were *producers* of wealth, and hence likely to be more reliable taxpayers – especially when their status depended upon such payment – than the lords and lairds who, until habits began to change in the eighteenth century, were apt to be inordinate *consumers*, even wasters of the king's wealth. Secondly, ordered communities of self-respecting citizens were also more likely to be dependable maintainers and administrators of the law than wayward and self-seeking nobles. In the affairs of Caithness the burgesses of Wick, and to a lesser extent those of Thurso, became in effect, custodians of the king's peace. It is notable, for instance, that the merchants of Wick had far less enthusiasm for the Pretenders of the eighteenth century than some country gentlemen.

The full apparatus of the law, courts, prison and ultimately the police came to be located in the 'county town'.[1]

None of this must be taken to suggest that the burghs, and Wick in particular, were hives of democracy. The franchise was extremely restricted until later in the nineteenth century. The 'burgesses' or 'burghers' were the big men of the place, and in due course numbers of the local gentry, who did not necessarily live – or at least have their main homes – in the burgh joined in the merchant activities of the town. A constitutional historian explains in lucid terms the main constitutional features of the royal burghs, determined largely under an act of 1469 in the reign of James III (1460-1488):

> The burghal authorities were elected yearly at Michaelmas. The old council chose the new council, and, together, they prepared leets of names of new officials, provost, bailies etc. Then acting together, but with the addition of the deacons, the actual officials were chosen. The practice of choosing new officials and the town council by the old was, indeed, the universal method of conducting burghal elections in the royal burghs of Scotland until the electoral reforms of the nineteenth century.[2]

---

1 On the other hand, the most important law officer in the county was the sheriff, appointed often from among the lesser gentry by the king. The Sheriff's Court in Caithness was located at Thurso.

2 I F Grant: *Social and Economic Development of Scotland before 1603*; Edinburgh, Oliver and Boyd (1930). See especially the section dealing with royal burghs and the Convention of Royal Burghs, pp 440-471. There is also a useful discussion on some of these matters in Michael Lynch: *Scotland: a New History; (continued at foot of next page)*

To what extent 'Superiority' hampered or enhanced the efficacy of town government is impossible to estimate. Early in the century the 'Superior of Wick' was the Earl of Breadalbane, until the superiority was formally transferred in 1719 to John of Ulbster whose family had, in any case, been the dominant landowners in the area for some years. The impression left by the records themselves is that concern for the superiority had little effect on the deliberations of the burghers – except the advisability of keeping on the right side of the superior. Provostship was another matter: there was undoubtedly interference from the outside at least twice, when it was claimed that legitimate process in the election of provost and bailies had not been followed, and it is fairly certain these challenges were connected with the running contest between the Sinclairs of Ulbster and the Dunbars of Hempriggs as to who should have the upper hand in Wick.

What value to either was the 'possession' of the town in terms of parliamentary interest is not easy to assess. As one of five widely separated royal burghs in a group constituency, all with different superiors, it was not easily possible to manipulate the necessary three votes to command the seat, though such alliances were attempted. Gerrymandering was a much easier proposition in the county, and the two chief families of Caithness kept up the rivalry here too, though they had in this constituency to cope with the problem of 'alternation' of county representation with Bute.

Of great importance in the management of all external – and some internal affairs of Wick and other royal burghs, was the role of the Convention of Royal Burghs, of which Wick was an assiduous member. To quote our constitutional historian again:

> A rather common enterprise undertaken by the Convention of Royal Burghs [formed as we have seen in the 1550s] was the levying of the customs in 1582. When James VI had assumed control of affairs it will be remembered that the state of the national finances was deplorable. A much stricter administration of the customs was instituted, and, owing to friction and complaints, both by the King's comptroller and by

(continued from foot of previous page) London, Pimlico Press (1992). Two other comments: *Deacons* were officers appointed by individual town guilds, represented in the town council by the *Dean of Guild*. The most powerful guilds were those of the merchants. We may note that the Scottish parliament, before its dissolution in 1707, more closely resembled the French system than the English, a convention of the 'estates' – lords, bishops and commons. The bishops as ecclesiastical functionaries were abolished; their parliamentary place was taken by the lairds (as distinct from the nobles), the local landowners.

THE SETT OF WICK: 1

the merchants, the Convention of Royal Burghs resolved to take a tack of the customs and administer them itself. A sum of £4,000 was to be paid and also 30 tuns of wine, and the lease was to last for four years. The burghs appointed customars to collect the customs of all ports, and Edinburgh, Perth, Dundee and Aberdeen became sureties for payment of the rent. The undertaking was not at all successful. It was not lucrative to the burghs, and, although an Act of Parliament had been passed to safeguard the lieges from undue exactions, there was discontent with the way that the customs were collected, and in 1587 a dearth was attributed to this cause.[1]

In his *Wick 1794* of the *First Statistical Account of Scotland*, William Sutherland gives a summary of the 'set or government of the borough of Wick' in 1716, as he understands it. Sutherland states that the set was determined 'on a general order from the convention of the Royal Burghs'.[2] According to this the set was 'ultimately fixed' in 1716, two years (three if the 1719 date of transfer is correct) before the 'lands and tenements of Wick' were sold by the Earl of Breadalbane to 'the family of Sinclair of Ulbster'. The 'set' was thus fixed

> by which in all time coming, the consent of the original founders of the borough, and their successors, was declared to be necessary to the election of magistrates. By this set, the old magistrates make out a leet, consisting of two out of which a Provost, four out of which two bailies are to be chosen, by the burgesses on the roll, and the leet must be presented 30 days before Michaelmass, to be approved of by the superior. The Provost and the two bailies elected have the right of chusing seven councillors, a treasurer, and dean of guild. In consequence of these regulations, Sir John Sinclair of Ulbster and his predecessors, have annually been in the practice, of approving a leet, presented to them, of the magistrates to be chosen. Wick is one of the five burghs each of whom chuses a delegate for returning a member of Parliament for the northern district. The income or common good of the town is very trifling, but it is on the increase, and arises from the Customs payable on different articles sold at market, shore dues on ships

---

[1] I F Grant, op cit. p 451.
[2] In the action described below (pp 155-164) there is no mention of this 'order'. The whole action relates to explicit interpretation of the terms of the Charter. It is not at present possible to check Calder's notes, since the relevant burgh record book is missing. The validity of 'heritable' office is doubtful.

etc. The borough pays no stipend, nor schoolmaster's salary, nor has it any real property in the church. Its tolbooth is seldom occupied by prisoners, except for petty riots; and a very few civil debts.

In fact, matters as to the 'sett' were not perhaps quite as straightforward as the Rev Sutherland – or J T Calder later believed. The Convention certainly had no power to issue orders. What had happened, according to a later commentator who had consulted the records of the Convention itself, was that the Convention, 'finding by experience that nothing doth create more trouble to them than irregularitys and abuses committed by particular Burghs in electing their Magistrates, it was resolved to send [for?] the sett of each particular burgh.' The statement of the magistrates of Wick referred to the occasion in September, 1589 when

> The Town of Wick was erected into a Royal Burgh . . . . by George (sixth) Earl of Caithness, who by the Charter of Erection granted to the town, obliged them to choose their magistrates by his advice, *so that the constant sett of the town was to allow the Earls of Caithness to be Provosts, and him to choose one of the bailies and the town only choosing the other, and thereafter the Provost and the two Bailies to nominate seven Councillors of Burgesses and heritors within the said town. But now, since the Earl of Caithness does not concern about the Provostrie, the town has been, and are in use to chuse their own Provost and Bailies by the plurality of the Roll* . . . . . This is the true sett of this Burgh as verified by Alexr. Doull, Baillie, (and five Councillors).[1]

Efficient or inefficient, the system continued and, as we shall see, the running of affairs in Wick generally followed the lines laid down in the statement – with certain latitude. In the late 1740s however, the council found itself involved in a legal action bringing into question the propriety of the actual procedure adopted at the annual leet. The period from 1741 onwards also affords some interesting episodes in the context of Wick's parliamentary representation. It is also evident from the record that the expenditures and income of the council were indeed 'trifling', and that they often had difficulty in collecting the small sums accruing from customs and harbour dues. The prison, too, was 'seldom occupied'.

---

1 *John O'Groat Journal*, 15 May, 1862. The actual wording of the opening of this statement must be questioned. The 'erection' was the prerogative of King James, not George, Earl of Caithness. The italics are the author's.

WICK BURGH RECORDS

A detailed record of the routines of the set of Wick, the doings and problems of provost, bailies, other officers and magistrates of this diminutive royal burgh is contained in one seventeenth and three eighteenth century town record books. Thomas Sinclair in his Notes to Calder's *History of Caithness* comments that record material in Wick is 'unusually plentiful' from as far back as 1660. When writing her *Agricultural Sir John* Rosalind Mitchison was evidently unable to locate any such records, for she says, 'Wick claims to have lost its eighteenth-century records'. This seems to have been the conclusion reached by most of the local historians. There is certainly nothing now known about the crucial second record book, dating from 1710 to 1741, but the others exist. Two wrinkled calf-skin covered early volumes are extant, the first running from 1660 to 1710, the other from 1741 to 1755. From here on the volumes are hard-backed and cloth-covered, in remarkably good condition, two covering between them the remainder of the eighteenth century and beyond, 1755 to 1794 and 1794 to 1815.

The two antique record books are difficult to read, the first especially so on account of the very different kind of script used in the sixteenth century, though beautifully penned; the second less on account of difficult script than the perfunctory penmanship of the clerks. Some eighteenth century writers appear not to have taken their duties too seriously even though these were governed by statutory requirement. The order of entry in the first volume has more to do with the availability of the odd space than dated sequence.

Much coverage is given to ritual and repetitive routines, composition especially of the oaths and abjurations of the 1740s being cast in rotund and idiomatic Scots of the time. There are few records of actual discussion and often not much about decisions reached. Doubtless then, as almost certainly now, more is said and decided informally in the council chamber than it might have been discreet to write down. Some of the occasions recorded indubitably lent themselves to such discretion. On the other hand, in at least one episode, a challenge to the dominance in the council of the Ulbster Sinclairs in 1772-1773, every word of abuse, insult and impropriety uttered by the contestants about their opponents, is meticulously written down. On this occasion the clerk had a field day, taking up twenty pages of closely written text to record for posterity the details of a ferocious quarrel in the chamber. Most of the time the record is much less entertaining.

The town's records open in 1660 with the quaint introductory, 'In the name of the Father, Son, and Holy Ghost.' Thomas Sinclair whose notes conclude the 1887 edition of Calder's *History of Caithness* comments that the town's records from 1660, 'are now being published and give much insight into the town's past.'[1] He may have been referring to an extended series of articles that appeared in the *John O'Groat Journal* from 1 May to 4 December, 1862, (perhaps written by himself), for no other publication dealing with these matters is known. The articles in question are richly informative and will be referred to fairly often in the coming pages.

Thomas Sinclair continues:

> The relations of the Ulbster family to the Provostship are in the yet unpublished portion, and especially Harpsdale's doings, James Sinclair, Thrumster House. The proposal of the inhabitants to John of Ulbster to become hereditary provost, in 1723, accepted by him, is a curious and lengthy document. He was to recover the Hill of Wick for them from the Dunbars of Hempriggs, pay the town's debts, set burghers up in trade, etc. In the 'Acta Parliamentorium', the burghs' rights are printed, but it seems to have been for long periods unaware or deprived of them.

We examine below (pp 155-ff) the problematic issue of the 'hereditary provostship' of the Ulbster Sinclairs mentioned by Thomas Sinclair, though under some handicap, since the volume of burgh records referring is still not available. Its contents would doubtless reveal a number of cogent facts about the state of affairs in Wick in the years before the '45, though there is throughout the eighteenth century burgh records little overt reference to 'the political condition of the country', probably a shrewd matter of policy. No records exist before 1660 which the writer of the *John O'Groat* articles suggests may be the result of earlier records being cannily destroyed on the Restoration 'by the Royalists, in order to prevent unpleasant consequences.'[2] There would certainly be no wish among the burgesses of Wick during and after the '15 and '45 to attract

---

1 Calder, op cit. Notes by T Sinclair MA, Note 30 pp 317-318.
2 *JOGJ*, 15 May, 1862. Since this date much work has been done on ancient Scottish handwriting, so that transliteration is not usually so difficult as it once was. However, the present author must confess to a certain quailing before the difficulties, and has made use, wherever possible of other transliterators' efforts. As to the speculation about earlier records, burghs were officially required to keep records from 1660 onwards.

unfavourable attention as a result of indiscretions in the town's official records.

THE SETT OF WICK: 1660-1710.

Fascinating as it is to read – or attempt to read – the minutes in this first volume, the difficulties are considerable. The writer of the *Groat* articles of 1862 (collectively they are titled 'The Burgh of Wick in the Olden Time', and they run to thirty pieces), puts it fairly:

> The first volume, an insignificant looking book, roughly bound in sheepskin [or is it calfskin?], contains the minutes from 1660 to 1710. The minutes of the first 9 years are all written in one hand, in the old black-lettering writing, and so minute as to be almost microscopic. The ink is much faded, and the exceeding smallness of the writing makes it very difficult to decipher. It could be only read intelligently by one who, from long habit, has been accustomed to divine the meaning of such ancient documents by a sort of antiquarian instinct. After much poring and spelling, and guessing, we were compelled to give it up, having made out only a few lines here and there, with sufficient certainty to get at the general import of the minutes of those nine years.

As revealed in the first minute book the Wick magistracy in 1660 consisted as required by the charter of provost, two bailies, seven councillors, a Dean of Guild and Treasurer. There does not appear to have been a 'town clerk', the record being kept by one of the bailies – Alexander Doull. No entries (except declarations) are signed and there are no indications of procedure. The very first item of business recorded, has to do with the trying of an 'unfreeman' on 26 May, 1660, 'The quhilk day on ane Borrows (Burgh) Court . . . . the noble and potent Earle George of Caithness, provost of he said Burgh, James Doull and Alexander Cormack, Bailies . . . within the tolbooth of the said burgh, 'for trading within the burgh without being a 'freeman' of the burgh, 'contrair to the liberties of the said Burgh, wherein loss and damage to their resident burgesses and inhabitants,' had acrrued.[1]

This entry provides a keynote for the whole record of the burgh's business. The powers and duties of the burgh as defined in the charter had to be interpreted as best the burgesses might. As the writer of the 'Wick in the Olden Time' articles puts it:

1 *JOGJ*, 15 May, 1862.

The Bailies and Council of the Burghs in old times took cognizance of everything that concerned the welfare of the community, moral and physical. They did not exercise their jurisdiction, according to Acts of Parliament, for there were few Acts of Parliament in those days, but they made laws on their own minute-books, and scored them off when it became convenient. In cases of extremity or perplexity they 'convenit the haill nybours,' or, as we would have it, called a public meeting, and not only discussed the subject, but legislated upon it in a full parliament of burgesses.[1]

On an assumption that the burgesses were democratically elected representatives, this would not have been too unsatisfactory a form of local government; but the burgesses had no such warrant for their status as burgesses was arbitrary, determined mainly by their wealth, influence and connection in the community. They were recruited to the body of burgesses by the existing burgesses. In 1660 there were 30 burgesses of Wick, ten listed as 'merchantes', six as 'tailyours', five 'schomakers', five 'weaures' (weavers), four 'smiths' and 'coupers'.[2] They enjoyed privileges not open to the 'unfree', who were subject to the legislative and juridical authority of the burgesses in council. Unequal treatment as between burgesses and 'unfreemen' before the law was the rule, as illustrated by a statute quoted by our writer from another royal burgh's rules of 1563:

> It is statute be the bailyes and counsell gyf ony man mispersone ane of the town's flesh-prissers [officers appointed to determine the price of meat] and ony uder officers in the execution of the office thairoff, thay, be, thay burges or his wyf, and say oft as they mak falt to be dowblit; and gyf they be onfree, they man sall be put in the stockis, and the woman in the gowis for the first tym, and gyf thay commit sik lyk thay sall be banist the town for yeir and day.[2]

The early burgh record books do not reveal much about the day-to-day life of the town. This is partly the result of the scrappiness and disorder of entries, and partly no doubt the judicious reticence of the magistrates as to what should be revealed. In any case, it must not be assumed that the records were 'open book', and that anyone seeking information about the doings of the burgesses in council was entitled to read the record.

1 *JOGJ*, 8 May, 1862.
2 *JOGJ*, 1 May, 1862.

THE SETT OF WICK: 1

One early example of official reticence is that of the entry of 16 January, 1685: which reads:

> Qras [whereas] upon several complaints given in upon the several unfreeman within the Burgh of Wick, that they will not work for payment to any person within the said Burgh, Ordains ilk ane of ym [them] to work for payment to any person sall happen to call ym, and yt [that] under ye paine of 20 sh. qho refuses, toties quoties, and impressionment, and to find surtie for yr good deportment in tyme coming betwixt an ye 19th inst.[1]

No sequel is recorded. Whether or not the truculent workmen knuckled under to this 'stringent proclamation' is not revealed. It cannot be assumed – as does the writer of 'Wick in the Olden Time' – that no further allusion signifies that the 'ordinance' must 'have had a very salutary effect upon the recusants.' What the entry does signify is that the under-class of Wick were not lacking in truculence in the seventeenth any more than in the nineteenth when, as we shall, the army was called out to discipline them.

Among the less unintelligible entries in the 1660-1710 book are the occasional declarations of loyalty to the crown. One of the earliest entries is that of 4 June, 1660, which begins: 'Ths Court assize in King Charles ye second his Royal Name, God Save the King. At Wick, the 4th Junii, 1660.'[1]

There were in 1660 some thirty burgesses. A hundred years later there were still only 44. The roll, frequently numerated from the mid-eighteenth century onwards, steadily rose after that to something like 70 burgesses, but never beyond. The lists are difficult to interpret since there are always so many crossings out. In 1741 at least four of the burgesses were landowners or heritors from outside the burgh, a subject of some contention later in the decade, especially as these included the provost. Three of the outsiders were merchants in Thurso. In 1771 only 37 of the listed burgesses lived in Wick itself. In 1772, at a time of the renewal of the argument about entitlement through residence, the non-residents were struck off, but shortly another 19 residents nominated, bringing the roll up to 52.

The commonest names on the roll of 1755 were, predictably, Sinclair and Sutherland, five of each. Eight burgesses at this time are labelled

---

1 As illustrative of the kinds of entry in this earliest of the Wick record books (and of the difficulties of reading them – these are by no means the most obscure), these two are reproduced at the end of this chapter (See p. 174).

as merchants, though probably most of the others were involved in trading of one kind or another. There is one shop trader mentioned, John Coghill, ironmonger; eight craftsmen are listed of whom four are weavers, one each of mason, joiner, shoemaker and tailor. John Calder is shown as a barber. Others too may have been craftsmen as later lists suggest; names are often entered without reference to their trades. None of the trades mentioned was large enough to constitute an independent guild. The Dean of Guild was the spokesman in council for the trades and merchants. (A complete roll of burgesses for 1795 is given in an Addendum at the end of Chapter 8).

The nominal fee for burgess-ship was said to be seven guineas (sterling), but it was not always paid promptly and sometimes not at all. The burgh was constantly in financial difficulty. Its revenue, in addition to burgess fees, included fines and 'customs' dues, all of them uncertain both as to rates and return. There was for the whole of the eighteenth century no such thing as property rates, and certainly no central government funding.

In one thing the burgesses of Wick were assiduous, and that was in their affirmations of loyalty to the crown. The declaration of 1660 was modest and brief, but those of the eighteenth century were more effusive. In 1711 there is a lengthy declaration, dated 29 September, acknowledging and professing on the part of the burgesses and on behalf of the citizens of Wick, their trust and loyalty to 'Our Sovereign Lady Queen Ann,' as the true and rightful 'queen to this realm and all territories Dominions and Countries belong thereto'. They reject entirely the claims of the son of the 'late King James' and his pretending to be taking upon himself the title royal of King of England in the name of James III. Such declarations of loyalty, not only for Anne but also for the Hanoverians, following as they did formal rejection of the pretenders of '15 and '45, fill much space in the Wick Burgh record books. We return to this topic.

THE SETT: 1741-1800

Though resident in Thurso during much of the period covered by the Wick minute books, Ulbster Sinclairs ruled Wick, 'heritable' provosts or not. John, first of the 'hereditary' provosts, died in 1736 and was followed by his son George. In due form, the Ulbster Sinclair was listed annually at the top of the leet and was duly 'elected' against a nominated opponent, it being understood that the opponent was not for election. As purchaser of the 'superiority' of Wick, Sinclair had the ritual duty of approving his own nomination.[1] As provost he enjoyed the prestige of office, the frequent opportunity of nominating his own 'set', attending the Convention of Royal Burghs, of being chosen as Commissioner for Wick at the five-burgh Conventions when a parliamentary candidate had to be elected, and he often went as 'Commissioner' to the Convention of Royal Burghs. Since influence in at least three of the burghs was necessary in order to swing a burgh parliamentary election, the provostship had only limited value in controlling parliamentary representation for the Northern Burghs, and it seems doubtful that the Ulbsters' interest in the office had as much to do with that side of things as Rosalind Mitchison alleges. As we shall see (pp 164-ff), control of county superiorities had more value in this sort of connection.[2] One thing the Ulbsters sometimes found themselves doing, was to contribute handsomely to the shaky finances of a very impecunious burgh, a sufficient reason for the burgesses' continuing loyalty to the family.

'The War of Independence'.

This Ulbster dominance in Wick affairs did not go unchallenged. A long report in the minutes for 1 October, 1750, tells of an action brought before the Court of Session in Edinburgh (nominally) by the Earl of Caithness (then Alexander) 'with respect to presenting the Leet in terms of the Charter'. The charge was that the annual leet of the Wick burgh was not being conducted in the terms of the Charter; firstly, the 'Leet for the provost and Two Bailleys' was not being submitted for consideration and approval by the Earl of Caithness, his 'express advice and consent' being required by the Charter; secondly, the requirement that provost and bailies must be 'Residenter' was not being properly observed. If upheld, this would mean that Sinclair of Ulbster was not eligible to be provost, since he was not a resident of Wick.

1 According to Mitchison, there is some doubt as to what property if any was 'purchased' in 1719, since much of it was already mortgaged to Ulbster. What was transacted, she argues, was 'the feudal superiorities of lands, the teynds and patronage of the parishes and the hereditary sheriffdom and other offices of the county' (op cit, p12).
2 Ibid: 'As the eighteenth century progressed, the great landowners of the county discovered that they could increase their voting strength by dividing the larger parcels of superiority into several smaller fictitious units to be held by their friends, relatives or hangers-on. These "faggot votes" or "parchment baronies" could be created at moderate cost, so long as the titles were properly conveyed and at the right time.' (p 15).

Their lordships heard submissions and issued interlocutories over a period of months from November, 1747 and January, 1749, a typical action of the kind that rendered the Scottish law system of the time the country's greatest growth industry. In the end the Court came down with the view that the earl's rights were 'inalienable' and had indeed been flouted.[1]

According to the writer of 'Wick in the Olden Time' the process was begun by a petition raised by three burgesses of Wick, John Anderson, George Sutherland, merchants, and William Anderson, dyer, all burgesses, 'in the name of themselves and the inhabitants of the burgh. The respondents were George Sinclair of Ulbster, the provost, Robert Winchester and John Sinclair of Assery, bailies, William Calder, Dean of Guild, and the whole of the councillors. The object of the action was 'to have it declared':

> 1st. That the election of the Magistrates ought to be made conformably to the original charter of 1589.
>
> 2nd. That none be eligible for office or capable of voting at the election but actual indwellers in the burgh.
>
> 3rd. That George Sinclair of Ulbster, or his successors, as pretending right from the Earl of Caithness or Breadalbane, had no right to demand a leet from which to choose the Magistrates, subject to their approval, far less to choose them.
>
> 4th. That the Act of Convention, dated 3rd July, 1716, and the 'sett' of the burgh given therein be not effective except so far as agreeable with the terms of the charter.[1]

The *John O'Groat Journal* writer characterises the action and its sequels as a sort of rebellion of the burgesses (if not the citizens) of Wick against lairdly dominance in the affairs of Wick, though strangely he nowhere refers to the principle of 'superiority', on the strength of which Ulbster and his supporters defended their position. The respondents argued in effect that the Ulbsters, having purchased the estates of Breadalbane had also thus purchased the 'superiority' (in 1719). They also made great play of the 'Act of Convention' of 1716 which, as we have seen, probably had no legal validity other than representing the 'registration' of the set of Wick with the Convention of Royal Burghs. Curiously also, there is no mention in this action of the 'heritable provostship' which is said to have been agreed between John of Ulbster and Wick Burgh in 1723.

1 *JOGJ*, 17 July, 1862.

In her biography of (the later) John of Ulbster, Rosalind Mitchison invests the incident with a different significance. According to her reading of the affair, action was begun in 1746 on the instigation of Sir William Dunbar of Hempriggs, 'probably in alliance with gentlemen outside the county who would have found the Wick vote useful in an election'. Intimation that such action might be brought was indeed contained in a minute of 29 September, 1746 (date of the Michaelmas election): 'John Anderson' she says, 'complained that James Sinclair of Harpsdale, John Sinclair of Assery, and George Sinclair of Ulbster are neither of them inhabitants of the burgh, so no leet can be made including them'. There is further reference here to the 'Custome of Ellictione' and an 'Act of Leet' of 1716 (whatever that signified) which conferred no right of election to such outsiders. The petition was, claims Mitchison (a fact not mentioned in the Wick minutes), signed by 'an opposition of twenty-four, containing two burgesses who could not sign their names and another two only marginally literate', who between them sought to 'assert that the neighbouring gentry could not take part in burgh affairs'. This, she suggests was 'a claim which could not be allowed for it would have overturned the social and political structure of much of Scotland', a dire thought.[1]

'Ulbster therefore won,' she blandly concludes, though the precise significance of the 'therefore' is not clear, nor does Mitchison say how Ulbster 'won'. There is nothing in the minutes to show either how the 'inalienable' obligation to present the leet to the Earl of Caithness was disposed of (for Caithness does not appear again in the submissions) nor how Ulbster qualified as a burgess. He continued to live in Thurso Castle, and in the later challenge of 1773, Ulbster's lack of qualification is raised again.

It is true, however, that the Court of Session's judgement went against Wick, which was obliged ostensibly to conform to the town's charter. The case had lasted with its various 'submissions' and 'interlocutories' from 1747 to 1749, and is profusely documented with these statements. The Court came down with the view that the earl's 'rights' were 'inalienable', except, presumably, that they could pass legitimately to a purchaser of the superiority. The Lords of the Court of Session too seem to have tacitly allowed that the owning of property in the burgh was tantamount to 'residence'. It is probably true, as Mitchison asserts, that Sir William Dunbar of Hempriggs was at this time vying with Ulbster for paramount interest in local affairs

1 Wick Record Book, Minutes of 14 January, and 3 February, 1749.

and he may well have started off the business.¹ This was not the only clash to have occurred between the two families. Though what benefit Wick might have been in a county election, which is where the Dunbar interest mostly lay, is problematical, since Wick was a constituent of the Northern Burghs and thus was not involved in county representation. This interpretation turns the action into something, *mutatis mutandis,* rather more like an old-fashioned territorial squabble between local lairds than a bold attempt on the part of the citizens of Wick to claim back the rights of the people.

After George died in 1770 while his son, John, was still in his minority and thus not eligible for public office of any kind, there was another fracas. This seems to have been a rougher affair altogether, but still centred on the issue of the eligibility of the Ulbsters to hold the provostship. The council minutes of July and August fill twenty pages, but without some external clues are not easy to interpret. The business starts with the announcement in March, 1773, that the MP for the Northern Burghs, the Hon Alexander Mackay, has 'taken the Chiltern Hundreds', that is, he has resigned his seat in parliament, thus precipitating a by-election in the burghs. The provost of Wick, for the moment, is John Sutherland of Wester, a merchant of the town, with the death of George Sinclair in 1770, the provostship becomes vacant, his son John being too young to occupy the chair. Sutherland duly attended the Northern Burghs convention at Dingwall, where the election occurred on 13 April, 1773.

Sutherland's election as provost was the first move in the rumpus, James Sinclair of Harpsdale (who lived in Thrumster House), brother of the deceased laird of Ulbster, had taken it upon himself to occupy the chair as provost, claiming this as his 'right' during his nephew's minority. Two bailies, James Miller and Hugh Brock, raised objection in the meeting of 11 August, 1772, called to discuss the leet to go forward for the coming year, to the inclusion of Sinclair on the list as not being eligible. James was offended and 'demitted and went out of Court'.

However irregular the proceedings from now on, the council went ahead and elected John Sutherland, who acts and signs the minutes as provost for the following year, though here in the book are several

---

1 Mitchison, op cit, pp 18-19. Mitchison quotes: HM Register House, Unextracted Decreets, Innes Durie, A1/98, Anderson v the Magistrates of Wick; and for Dunbar's complicity, Signet Library, Law papers 158;4, Sutherland and others v Sinclair and others, 1773.

blank pages, suggesting in the light of what came next that the clerk, John Russell, a supporter of Harpsdale, was unwilling to record all that he heard. At the meeting of 13 July, 1773 – leet time coming round again, Russell is sacked because he 'has malvers'd in his office, and has acted in contradiction to the oath *de fidele* and of the Trust reposed in him .... by Several Times refusing to write and Subscribe what was dictated to him by the Baillies and particularly by his pretending to act as Clerk for James Sinclair of Harpsdale in contradiction to the Baillies'.

John Russell is forthwith 'degraded from office for various misdemeanours, going out of town [and] refusal to make copies of documents for James Sinclair of Harpsdale', that is, copies for the bailies of his record of the business that had evidently been transacted by Harpsdale and his rump of followers at a meeting called by Harpsdale and from which his opponents were excluded. This meeting is, of course, not recorded.

Along with Russell at this meeting of 13 July, 1773, Thomas Doull, the council 'doorkeeper' is 'called upon and examined by the Bailies' for not being 'properly on his guard'. This is an odd charge for the bailies to bring, since it was they who had, on the face of it, been excluded from the 'fenced' (that is, *in camera*) meeting. Doull's defence was that at the time he was confused. From the chamber he could hear 'Harpsdale and some of his friends' calling out to him to 'fence the Court' while Miller and Brock were shouting to him not to fence the court. In any case, Robert Manson Sinclair of Bridgend, a cousin of Harpsdale, 'addressed him in a menacing manner, having a Cudgell Bent in his hand to repeat the word he had heard Harpsdale or John [?] utter, he Declared through fear of being worse treated by Bridgend. He repeated the words, notwithstanding that the Bailies were threatening him with Imprisonment and degrading from office'. Degraded from office he was, and Kenneth Bain put in his place.

The wrangling went on for some weeks more. The minutes now give a copious but bewildering account of what had happened, charge and counter-charge meetings 'Illegal and Unconstitutionall and Arbitrary Proceedings' by one side or the other. To retail all this here would be tedious and unedifying, but a quotation from James Harpsdale's explanation and defence of his alleged high-handed actions, recorded in the minutes for 20 July, which he attended, at least gives the flavour of the acrimonious exchanges in the Wick Council Chamber during that summer of 1773. He claimed that the 'leit' which he and his friends had prepared at his house a few days before was 'valid' and the Council should accept it. The minutes of a meeting of his opponents on 16 July 'in order to render the Leit already made up Ineffectual' were, he claimed 'void of Foundation and truth, so frivolous and Impertinent' that they 'Scarce deserve any Notice and much less ought they to Influence the Conduct of this Meeting, as an member of it must be Con[s]cious'. If they were accepted, warned Harpsdale, 'the Provost [himself] from regard to the Good of the Burgh, and for the sake of his Character as Chief Magistrates Thereof will take care, that he will take no part in such Proceedings'. He is sorry to have to say all these things, and 'if the Pill should be ill to digest, the Constituent Members of the 16th have only themselves to blame'. The lofty tone of Harpsdale's expression (or perhaps the clerk's) does not disguise the fact that he was very cross.

He ends his disquisition with a justification of his probity in all that has happened. He totally denies that he

> or the Gentlemen who accompanied him to Wick on the thirteenth had any designs whatsoever against the freedom of this Burgh or that they meant to Violate the rights of the People in Generall, or that of any Individual. His Intentions were in fact the very reverse of this for he wisht to preserve the rights of the Burgh Inviolate and if possible to give a check of that Spirit of discord and Conflict which of late seemed to Operate so Violently upon the minds of the People through the Influence of Someself Interested Persons.

Wordy as they are, the minutes coyly throw little real light on the events of the 'thirteenth' when James and his 'gentlemen' came to Wick. Rosalind Mitchison's account of the episode, based on other documents, makes things clearer. She sees these events yet again in terms of rivalry between those groups of lairds and townsmen who wished to get rid of Ulbster's control of Wick. She has young John of Ulbster, eighteen, 'illegally' enrolled as a 'freeholder' of the county, taking steps to ensure that Ulbster control remained intact in both Wick and Thurso. Whether or not John's Uncle James of Harpsdale was put up to his part in the affair by the ambitious young laird of Ulbster seems rather doubtful, for James Sinclair was a cunning enough operator to determine his own programme. In fact, at the September election of 1773, James was confirmed provost of Wick and remained so until 1780 when John took over. Mrs Mitchison's story is worth quoting; the incident was, she suggests, 'probably instigated

THE SETT OF WICK: 1

from outside, as that of 1746 had been:

> The disaffected [burgesses] who claimed the right to a free election of officers [Treasurer, Dean of Guild, Clerk etc], tried to get control over the town's equipment. The town seal was neatly confiscated by them; one asked to have a look at it at the meeting when it was in use, and then simply put it in his pocket. A midnight attempt to seize the town books was less successful; the official was away, but his wife had hidden them safely. Ulbster's forces were equally high-handed, for strategic violence could save a lot of lawsuits. Harpsdale, his uncle, whom he had made Provost of Wick [this is a fairly 'high-handed' statement], held an impromptu meeting of the council while the baillies were away in a pub, and called upon the clerk to declare the meeting 'fenced' or sealed off. Robert Manson Sinclair of Bridgend stood over the clerk with a raised cudgel to encourage compliance, but the baillies arrived and forced their way in. Harpsdale hoped to persuade them to leave by ostentatiously doing no business at the meeting, but they stuck it out and he had to keep his 'leet', the list from which Ulbster would choose the next office holders, for later. At the election of this leet Ulbster was prepared to use more force. He rode over from Thurso followed by friends and tenantry and a selection of the 'more substantial' inhabitants of Thurso. Their opponents had swivel guns which they let off ineffectually, and there was a good deal of rioting through the narrow streets, but Ulbster held the town and won the two years' series of lawsuits that followed. This enabled him to own the Wick vote for the general election of 1774, when he entered into an alliance with David Ross of Tain, the later Lord Ankerville, to put in Sinclair's trustee Adam Fergusson of Kilkerran. Fergusson was standing for two other constituencies, and may have been put up only to hold the seat for a year until Sinclair came of age. No trace of such a bargain exists but since it would have been illegal this is not surprising. In any case, they lost to the candidate of the Sutherland family. It was Sinclair who petitioned unsuccessfully. He was left with a grudge against the Sutherland interest.[1]

Mitchison is almost certainly correct in attributing 'instigation' to

---

1 See Mitchison, op cit, p 19. The sources quoted are those already referred to in the affair of 1746. A grudge between Sinclair and Sutherland was no new thing.

Sir William Dunbar. Dunbar, though a considerable landowner in the area (and in fact in Wick), has not been listed until now as a burgess. The council meeting of 20 July voted against Harpsdale, so that for the time being he is still 'out'. At another quarrelsome meeting on 30 July, James Sinclair is allowed to give his version of events on the 20th:

> Although the Burgesses did declare me as their Provost and made me welcome to the chair as President of this Council, these unwarrantable measures were the Operations of Sir William Dunbar of Hempriggs who took upon himself tho' no Constituent Member of the Meeting to Dictate all the Minutes and resolutions . . . . [he] usurped and not only my authority defied But also that of the Supreme Court by whose decree I was appointed to my office.

At this meeting of the 20th a Dunbar partisan stated 'that it is well known that Sir William Dunbar is a Heritor in the Town' and that he had 'probably been thrown off' the burgher roll, 'to serve some purpose and he did not Incline till now to Trouble himself about it. But now,' it was claimed, 'he Craves to be Enroll'd *de novo* which desire the Burgesses Though[t] reasonable and ordered his name to be Enroll'd accordingly'. Clearly it was a put up job.

A specially interesting version of events so far is that supplied by John Sinclair himself. Though still a minor, he was allowed to make a submission to the Court of Session in 1772 while the action was proceeding. He attributes the action to 'factious spirits in Wick as in greater burghs, and the same extravagance of politiks, which has produced so much confusion and tumult in the metropolis at the other end of the island, has actuated this little burgh in Caithness.'[1]

Sinclair is in little doubt that there are 'greater men behind the curtain; 'the *'visible agents* as ringleaders of the disturbance are John Sutherland of Wester, factor to Sir William Dunbar of Hempriggs, Baronet; James Miller, one of the late bailies, an inn-keeper in the place; and his son, Alexander, a forward youth who affects much to be thought a man of consequence.' He tells how

---

1 This and the following details are quoted in *JOGJ*, 17 July, 1862. The 'confusion and tumult in the metropolis' to which the young, and well-informed politician, John Sinclair, referred, was without doubt the disturbances associated with the demagogue John Wilkes, whose expulsion from parliament in 1769, occasioned demonstration and riot in the capital. The rioters' slogan was 'Wilkes and Liberty!' The young John Sinclair was, incidentally, very resentful of what he regarded as the evident ungratefulness of Wick towards the 'heretable provosts' who had shown the town 'such attention and kindness'.

On the Thursday preceding the election [of provost], Wester came into the town, and from that day to the hour of election, he and his associates continued to drink, dance and riot every manner of way with the burgesses; cajoling them as men entrusted with mighty concerns; impressing them with a notion of their being in a state of slavery to Ulbster, inconsistent with the constitutional liberty of the citizens of a royal burgh, and representing a thousand supposed advantages that would acrue to them from shaking off the yoke.

We need not concern ourselves with the petty detail of manoeuvres and misdoings in the council as understood by John Sinclair, but his description of the 'riot' in the town on the day of election lacks nothing in dramatic effect:

On the day of election, those pretended champions for liberty had swivel-guns mounted, and pointed to the town house, which continued firing incessantly during the election; and were so near to the place of election that the pressure of the air broke one of the windows, to the no small harm of the electors who sat near to it, and at the same time scarce a word could be heard with the noise or martial music of bagpipes. And to make the scene still more warlike and as complete as possible, colours taken from the ships in the harbour flew on the tops of the most conspicuous houses. In short, a train of proceedings more adverse to good order, decency, and true freedom of election can hardly be conceived. The legislature has provided that the King's troops must remove from the burghs at the time of elections; but surely so military a mob as paraded in the town of Wick on this occasion might intimidate and overawe as much as any regular forces.

Mitchison perhaps over-stresses the gerrymandering aspect of the Ulbster manipulations; such activities were the rule rather than the exception in the days before the Reform Act and, in any case, a sort of paternal benevolence was among the motives behind the Ulbster dominance in the management of Thurso and Wick. There is no evidence of comparable benefactions to Wick by Sir William Dunbar. In the event, the Court of Session decided once more in favour of Ulbster, and James Sinclair of Harpsdale was confirmed as provost of Wick. He maintained the Ulbster authority until James's nephew, John, took over in 1780. The Ulbster Sinclair remained in control until the end of the century much, as we shall see, to the advantage of the town.

Both Thurso and Wick benefited considerably from the Ulbster connection. Referring to the *Baron Baillie Book* of Thurso, still in the keeping of the Ulbster family, Mrs Mitchison describes how George Sinclair (John's father), a resident burgher of Thurso, practised 'domination' in that town:

> The Baillies and Councillors . . . would appeal to him on all types of business: for authority to make regulation about the moral character and efficiency of the ferrymen for the town's Coble, even for getting rid of dogs and swine in the town. Even when he was away in Edinburgh his written permission was needed for the normal functioning of the town's court.[1]

The same kind of paternal intimacy probably governed the relationship between the town council and the Ulbsters in Wick, though George, and later his son John, must often have found it difficult to attend meetings. They were, nevertheless, surprisingly often in the chair, and from this and other indications, it is evident that the Ulbsters were, on the whole, a 'good thing' for both towns, and much less cynically self-interested in their handling of local affairs than Mitchison seems to suggest; they were models of rectitude as compared with some of their contemporaries.

Parliamentary Representation

Having said all this, there is no doubt that the Ulbsters and others of the local gentry of Caithness were much concerned with parliamentary representation, freely manipulating and adapting the existing and manifestly corrupt system to benefit their own interests. As a royal burgh, Wick was not part of the county system. Such burghs had enjoyed the privilege of parliamentary representation since the time of Bruce when, for the first time on record, in 1326, the three 'estates', nobles, clergy and commons (representatives of the burghs), met together in a parliament at Cambuskenneth (near to Stirling). The Convention of Royal Burghs though not itself represented, monitored and advised the burghs on many of the matters coming before parliament. The Convention itself consisted of 'Commissioners' from each of the burghs, and in due course, the five 'church burghs', awarded their status by the bishops and recognised

---

1 Mitchison, op cit, p 19.

THE SETT OF WICK: 1

by the king. The election of the Commissioner for regular and extraordinary meetings of the Convention was one of the customary items of business on the agenda of the Wick Council. It was usually the provost who was drafted, enabling him to meet and rub shoulders with other provosts and great men such as those from Edinburgh, Glasgow and Aberdeen. The journey from Wick was long and arduous, doubtless usually accomplished by sea.

The Union of 1707, of which in principle the burghs were in favour, though objecting to the actual terms, radically reduced the numbers being sent to parliament, now in far-away Westminster. The old system of representation of 'estates' disappeared altogether in favour of the English mode of election of MPs from shire and borough. The total complement of Scottish MPs was now to be 45 (in a parliament of some 300), 30 to the shires and 15 only for the burghs. To conform with this arrangement the burghs had to operate collectively in groups, while lesser counties had alternate representation. For this purpose Caithness was 'paired' with Bute. Wick was combined for its purposes of parliamentary representation with four other small royal burghs, Kirkwall of the Orkneys, Tain, Dornoch and Dingwall. From 1707 onwards a regular commitment of each burgh was to appoint a 'Commissioner' to meet his colleagues from the other burghs of the group in order to 'elect' the MP who would represent the 'Northern Burghs'. As a franchise it was ludicrous; although mandated by their own councils, the choice fell to just five representatives, meeting in the chambers of one of the burghs – each of the five burghs took it in turn to host the parliamentary convention. As we shall see, this arrangement sometimes led to considerable fun and games. References to these matters in the Wick Burgh minutes are, however, frustratingly brief and uninformative.

Just how difficult it was to manipulate the burgh elections so as to produce the desired result is illustrated by the election of 1784 when John Sinclair of Ulbster himself became the defeated candidate. The circumstances were bizarre. Ulbster's opponent in the April election of that year was the illustrious Charles James Fox. Fox was without doubt the most brilliant parliamentarian of the day. A Whig radical and a chief member of the 'Administration that could no longer possess the Confidence' of King George's people, as a peculiar Loyal Address sent up by the Wick Burgh Council to London only a year before quaintly put it. He was, nevertheless, nominated as a candidate for the Northern Burghs seat in the 1784 election, not, it must be said, by Wick Council.

WICK OF THE NORTH

By what must have been dubious means, Fox had become a registered burgess of the burgh of Kirkwall in Orkney. Only three votes would be required at the convention of the burghs to get him elected, since there were only five all told. His opponent was to be none other than John Sinclair of Ulbster, nominated by Wick. Kirkwall politics at the time was passing through a period of intense corruption and the provost of Kirkwall had himself elected as Commissioner, that is, the burgh's representative at the convention of the five burghs, to be held at Tain. (In one of the episodes leading up to the choice of Provost Riddoch as Kirkwall's 'Commissioner', the provost's men had an opposition lawyer thrown down the stairs of Kirkwall's new Tolbooth!)

By another stratagem, Riddoch got himself elected as Chairman of the Convention. His fellow commissioners were Major-General Charles Ross of Tain, Duncan Munro from Dingwall, John Sutherland from Wick and John Gordon from Dornoch. The meeting actually began with an objection from John Gordon as to the legitimacy of Riddoch's occupation of the Chair, indeed, his status as a delegate at all, his election having been 'brought about by open force'. Nevertheless, the voting went ahead. The delegates divided three to two, Riddoch, Ross and Munro for Fox, with Sutherland and Gordon for Ulbster. 'The victory, looking at the way it was brought about was not one to be proud of,' wrote Mackintosh, the Orkney journalist who wrote up the story many years later.[1]

The story did not quite end there. Fox, as Mackintosh records, 'seemed to take a different view of the matter'. To mark his gratitude he handed over a portrait of himself to Kirkwall as 'a present to the community'. Whether or not the Kirkwall Council valued this very personal gift, it did not long adorn the walls of the Council Chamber. By some means it came into the possession of Robert Laing, a rich merchant of Kirkwall, laird of Papdale, from 1788, bailie then provost, after a spell during which it was 'owned' by Sir Thomas Dundas, the inheritor of the former earldom properties of Orkney (and MP for the Northern Isles). Laing reported to the Council that he had acquired the portrait and that is the last that was ever heard of it.[2]

---

[1] Charles Mackintosh: *Curious Incidents from the Ancient Records of Kirkwall*, Kirkwall, Orcadian Press (1897) pp 244 - 248.

[2] This still was not the end of the story. What the burgesses of the Northern Burghs did not know at the time was that C J Fox had, with dubious legality, double-banked his chances of getting back to parliament by having himself nominated also in the constituency of Westminster. The other candidates in this two-member constituency were Lord Hood (a famous naval commander under *(continued at foot of next page)*

THE SETT OF WICK: 1

There is no mention in the burgh records. Apart from the election of a Commissioner to attend the convention of the five burghs on the occasion of a general election, there is usually no indication of what actually happened, nothing about the actual choices of MP made by the Commissioners in execution of their awesome duties, no comment on actual representations of any kind ever made by MPs on behalf of their constituents, satisfaction or dissatisfaction with the serving MP, until, that is, John Sinclair took the Caithness seat in 1780. The impression conveyed is that the real external politics of the burgh were raised mostly in the Convention of Royal Burghs; another, that once elected, the MP made few visits to his constituent burghs, that it did not matter greatly what his political complexion might be, Whig or Tory. At the time of the '45, the representation was probably mainly Whig, for the burghs as a whole had a very canny attitude to Jacobite aspirations.

However the election of September 1780 gained slightly more lavish and prideful mention. On this occasion Wick was the 'Presiding Burgh'. There is in the minute of 9 September, a brief account of the solemn procedure. John Sinclair of Ulbster had been elected Provost, and also Commissioner to the Convention. In turn the members of the

(continued from foot of previous page) Rodney) and Sir Cecil Wray (a 'Pittite'). Supporting Fox was 'a beauty chorus of aristocratic ladies: Georgina, Duchess of Devonshire, Viscountess Duncannan, the Countess of Carlisle, the countess of Derby, Viscountess Beauchamp [who] all bought votes with smiles.' Lady Buckinghamshire, a rather large lady, ungallantly dubbed 'Lady Blubber' by the opposite side, took the field for Hood and Wray. The beautiful bevy of canvassers was carried round Westminster in sedan chairs, by an army of chairmen, mostly Irish. Lord Hood, on his own account, 'brought in a party of sailors to protect his voters, which they did by knocking down those of the other side.' In the event no return was made. Wray contested the apparent result which gave Fox and Hood victory, but, as the *Oxford History* puts it, this 'did not keep him [Fox] out of the house as he had been returned for the Orkney and Shetland islands.' (see Watson, op cit, p 275). This, of course, is a mistake – his constituency was that of the Northern Burghs. Orkney and Shetland had their own county member, Thomas Dundas. 'naturally preferred to sit for the constituency which had fought so hard for him [meaning Westminster]'. Fox took his seat for the Northern Burghs since he had been kept out of the Westminster seat. A scrutiny was set up, supported by Pitt, leaving Westminster unrepresented for five months. Then in spring 1785 there was a government defeat; 'the scrutiny was ended and Fox and Hood took their seats', leaving, in effect, the Northern Burghs unrepresented. They remained unrepresented until the following year when a by-election put in Captain Ross of Balnagowan as MP for the Northern Burghs. The *Oxford History* attributes to this rather squalid event other consequences. The scrutiny which had kept out Fox and Hood for Westminster was ended because Pitt as Prime Minister had kept it going. 'In effect the house of commons had found Pitt guilty of ungenerous and personal intrigue against an opponent, a charge, considering the circumstances of his coming to power, particularly dangerous to him.' It did, in fact, produce serious difficulties for him, including a defeat in the Commons in 1785 on a matter of defence estimates. (See Watson, op cit. pp 275-276). The burgesses of Wick had thus become caught up in affairs beyond their ken.

'Court of Delegates', Donald Macleod of Geanies for Tain, David Ross or Arkewill for Dingwall, Alexander Baillie of Little Farral for Dornoch, Thomas Traill of Frotoft for Kirkwall and John Ulbster himself were 'compeired' before the 'officers' of Wick to declare their votes. Colonel Charles Ross of Moray was elected.

In the 1784 election the Wick choice was for John of Ulbster, dubiously Whig in outlook – though his party connections were, to say the least, opportunist. As the *DNB* comments, his 'attitude as a party politician was never very decisive'. John had, in fact, been returned as MP for the county of Caithness itself in the 1780 election, and made various attempts at bridging the gap between Whigs and Tories. He was, nevertheless, 'an ardent advocate of parliamentary reform'. The posture of Wick Burgh at the time of the collapse of North's government was certainly not one that could have pleased him.[1]

Loyalty

Though really out of their depth in most matters to do with their parliamentary privileges, the councillors and magistrates of Wick took very seriously their duty to the Crown. During the 1740s and '50s, allegiance in these parts was an issue much to the fore. The Oath of Abjuration administered in March 1742, required them to reject entirely any notion of support for the Stewart Pretenders. As a condition of office they had to state ambiguously that

> I do Solemnly and sincerely declare that I doe believe in my Conscience that the persone pretended to be Prince of Wales during the life of the late King James and since his decease pretending to be and take up himself the Style and title of King of England by the Name of James the third hath not any right or title whatsoever to the Crown of the realm or any other Dominiones thereto belonging. And I doe swear that I will bear faith and true allegiance to his ma-tty, and him will I defend to the outmost of my powers agt. all traitorous Conspiracy and attempts whatsoever which shall be made against his persone, Crowne or dignity And I will doe my Outmost Endeavour to disclose and make knowen to his magestie and his Successors

---

1 Ulbster lost his Caithness seat in the 1784 dissolution, and was unable to stand here again, as this time it was Bute's turn. Ulbster succeeded, however, in gaining the seat for Lostwithiel in Cornwall; his new seat cost him £3,000 (see Mitchison, op cit, pp 47-48).

all traitorous Conspiracies I shall know [to] be against him or against any of them: And I doe faithfully promise to the outmost of my power To support the Crown agt. him the said James and all persones whatsoever.[1]

Abjurations continued as long as the Jacobite cause continued to attract support, however limited – and even beyond. The cause ended conclusively with the bloody defeat of the Jacobite army at Culloden, on 16 April, 1746. Oaths of loyalty continued as routine, but in February 2, 1784 appeared a very different sort of declaration of loyalty than the one regularly required from magistrates and councillors. This was 'An Address of Loyalty to His Majesty [King George III] on the overturning of the government in that year'. This was something quite out of the ordinary, and impossible to understand without some reminder of the background of national politics at the time. As it turned out, Wick found itself involved in the subsequent general election of spring 1784 in the peculiar way described.

George III had become King in 1760 during the Seven Years' War (1756-1763), in which Britain defeated the French on a grand scale at sea, in India and Canada, thus establishing the main outlines of the later immensely powerful and widespread British Empire. What might have remained an impressive 'jewel in the crown', the thirteen British colonies on the eastern sea-board of North America, was lost in the subsequent War of American Independence (1775-1782), in which France had in some measure 'got her own back' by assisting the American colonists to rebel. This loss, together with other factors, produced a period of great turmoil in British domestic politics.

Among these factors were moves by the King during the 1770s to gain greater powers of constitutional intervention in government than had been permitted to the two earlier Georges. There grew up in Parliament an informal group who came to be known as the 'King's Friends', regarded by others, especially some of the Whigs, as a threat to the constitution. The sharpest expression of this fear was the famous resolution of John Dunning (MP for Calne, Wilts) 'that the

---

1 The James here referred to is, of course, James the 'Old Pretender', sometimes called James VII (or III), on whose behalf his son, Prince Charles Edward, the 'Bonny Prince' invaded in 1745, creating great perturbation in Scotland, if nothing else. This kind of oath was not, of course, peculiar to Wick, and the willingness of burgesses to take oath or refuse it became associated with notions of movement generated in mid-century by 'dissenters' from developments in the Established Scottish Church. See below, Chapter 10, pp 243-244. This came to be known as the 'Anti-burgher' movement.

influence of the Crown has increased, is increasing and ought to be diminished'. Other factors included growing popular demands for radical reform of government, and for free trade, stimulated by the publication in 1776 of Adam Smith's *The Wealth of Nations*. Crowding the agenda at the same time was the need for better government in Ireland, and in India, where the East India Company still ran affairs.

The actual events that led up to this, the fall in 1782 of Lord North's government (North's policies were blamed by many for the loss of the American colonies), and the ill fortunes of the succeeding short-lived administrations of Rockingham and the coalition between Lord North and Charles James Fox, are too complicated for explanation and analysis here. A young new politician came on to the scene in 1783, William Pitt, son of Lord Chatham, the 'Elder Pitt' (the Churchill of his day), who had brought the country through the Seven Years' War. Pitt could not resolve the conflicts that were preventing effective government, and persuaded the less than reluctant King George to order a dissolution of parliament in January, 1784.[1]

The Wick 'Address' was cast in richly obsequious terms:

> We your Majesty's most dutiful and Loyal Subjects the Magistrates, Councill And freemen of the Burgh of Wick, begg leave at this Important Crisis to Assure your Majesty of Our unshaken Loyalty to your Sacred person and Government.
>
> We have long beheld with deep regret the efforts of a ffaction Struggling for power to Distract your Majesty's And Retard the Measures of Government. We Saw with no less concern and Abhorence the late Attempt made by these Men when in power to create a New System of Government in this Countrey, Dangerous to the Constitution as it was Calculated to increase their Influence and perpetual Authority.
>
> We Rejoiced therefore at your Majesty's Overturning the Administration that could no longer possess the Confidence of your people And Setting in their Place Men deserving of your Majesty's Approbation and of the Popular Esteem And we trust that Neither Clamours of that disappointed faction nor the Support they appear to have received from a Sett of Representatives who speak not with the Language nor the

---

[1] For a full account of these matters see J Steven Watson: *The Reign of George III, 1760-1815*; The Oxford History of England, Oxford, Clarendon Press, Chapter X, 'The Conflict of Groups', pp 243-272. Intermittently John Sinclair regarded himself as a 'King's Friend'.

Sentiments of their Constituents will influence your Majesty to dispence with the Exercise of that part of your Royal prerogative which forms so essential a part of our Happy Constitution.
Signed In the presence And by Appointment of this Council
in the Absence of the Provost by
Will. Mackay
James Macphaull.

It is evident that the honest burghers of Wick, for all their distance from the centre, knew something about what was happening in London. The 'ffaction' alluded to were doubtless the dissident Whigs and 'independents' (of whom Sinclair of Ulbster, MP for Caithness at this time was one), Charles James Fox, Edmund Burke, Lord Shelbourne and the ertswhile Tory, Lord North, whose ramshackle administration had been thrown out. What, almost certainly they objected to, was the prospect of a reformed sett for the burgh, loss of various burghal privileges. There were dire rumours of a wider franchise, perhaps measures of municipal reform and consequent loss of the benefits they enjoyed in monopoly control of trading, customs collection and other benefits, were the radicals in Westminster to obtain power. By the 'Sett of Representatives who speak not with the Language of their Constituents' the Wick councillors probably meant that the Convention of Royal Burghs had indicated support for reform, to which the Wick folk objected.

That this was the case is fairly confirmed by a reference, dated 11 April, 1785, authorising a response to a 'letter from the Lord Provost of Edinburgh about a proposal for alteration of representation of the Royal Burghs of Scotland, strongly opposing such moves and urging retention of the present 'Excellent Constitution, as alteration would be 'productive of many hurtful and mischievous consequences As it would unhinge a Constitution that has stood the test of Ages, And are Sensible the Constitution of this Burgh would be Materially affected by it.'

The absence of the provost, then John Sinclair of Ulbster, is not without significance. He was at this time often away in London, but it is unlikely that he would have been wholly sympathetic to this excessively conservative point of view. He was already on record as a reformer in economic matters, and as an agricultural 'improver'. He was probably one of the few on the Wick Council – perhaps the only one – who had read and understood *The Wealth of Nations*. From a critic, Sinclair soon became an admirer of Pitt who turned out to be a considerable reformer himself, and Sinclair was rewarded on his attachment in February, 1786, by the award of baronetcy. It was also, perhaps, some recognition of Sinclair's part in gaining for Scotland a grant of £15,000 as a measure of relief at a time of serious crop failure in 1782.

In any case, the Wick Council could hardly do without an Ulbster at the helm, and Sir John continued to be elected provost at the annual leet. Sir John slipped one across his colleagues in council when, on 2 January, 1791, he got them to approve an expression of support for the setting up of the British Wool Society, and agree 'to contribute out of the narrow funds an annual sum of Two Guineas' for the next ten years, to encourage and promote 'the Patriotic and Beneficial measures adopted by the Society'.

Roup of the Customs

The most repetitive series of entries in the burgh records from 1741 to 1790, is that of the 'roup' of the customs, an 'auction' of the right to farm the burgh customs. Such a system was allowed for in the rules created by the Convention of Royal Burghs. The formula was exactly the same for each year throughout the century, though the clerk laboriously wrote this out each time on one or two pages. The roup was held on 2 February in the Council Chamber, 'In which Roup,' the formula ran, 'none are privileged to offer Excepting those who are Burgesses and Inhabitants.' The bidding must start at £3 sterling, proceed in overbids of 5 shillings; the 'farmer' (that is 'tax farmer') who succeeded should 'give a Crown for a treat, to be allowed out of the proceeds of the Roup', that the roup should run for a quarter of an hour, 'determined by a Magistrat by a Watch', that 'whoever carrys the Custom shall have his Cautioner [guarantor] ready at the bar Who is to be a Burgess and Inhabitant of the Burgh And in case of failzie [sometimes written 'ffailzie', 'feuilzie' or even 'spulzie', meaning default] it shall be [not decipherable] in the penalty contained in a former Enactment and minute made there anent'. Especially interesting was the proviso that 'all oyll that shall come to the Town for public Sale [that is, presumably, seal or whale oil] shall according to use and wont, be exempted from payment of Customs'.

The successful bidder in February 1747 was 'George Sutherland, merchant in Wick ffor Seven pounds, ffifteen shillings sterling', while

THE SETT OF WICK: 1

his cautioner was James Sutherland, a man of some eminence in the affairs of Wick. Between them they undertook to pay half the sum 'at terme of Lammas next [1 August] and the other half at Candlemas thereafter, 1748 [Feast of the Virgin Mary, 2 February, the regular day of the roup]. 'The roup for 1791 brought in £14 15s. Even so, it was down to £10 again by the end of the century, evidence that the war was hitting trade quite badly. It is evident too that in Wick at least, the customs revenue was not very great; but the readiness with which bidders came up each year for the role of *customar*, suggests it was lucrative enough for the customar himself (one of the reasons, perhaps why the public revenue was not great) – for, once the privilege was paid for, there were no other charges and no income tax!

The policy of recent governments of this country of 'contracting out' public services clearly has plenty of precedents; whether or not present practice will become just as open to corruption as was undoubtedly the case in the eighteenth century remains to be seen. It looks, incidentally, as if George Sutherland did not retain his duties as customar for the whole year, for in December, his cautioner was permitted (without a roup) to take over, 'to be Collector of the Customs and Stent', on payment on 'yearly quartering for the sum of 26s and 4d', that is, a last quarterly payment due on the 1747 roup. No explanation is given as to why George Sutherland did not continue to the end of his term.

A table for the Customs of the Burgh of Wick is available for the year 1749-1750:

Value of the Chalder of bear [bere] to ane Freeman	10s. 6d (Scots)	
Double trees each dozen	2	0
Single trees each dozen	3	0
Birks each dozen	3	0
Dealls each dozen	3	0
Large Couple Leags	2	0
Small do	3	0
Bark per boll,	3	0
Each beef that comes to the Cross [Wick Market Cross]	3	0
Each mutton	3	0
Each pork	0	6
Each doublestone butter and cheese	3	0
Each pynt of oyll of export [seal oil]	0	4
Ships in Staxigo or Wick each tun is	0	8
Each boat for ankerage	3	4

Each yard of cloath, woollen or linning	0	4
Each pound of wool	0	4
Each boll of meal that comes to the meall house for seall or shipt on shore by ane unfreeman	3	0
Each hyde to ane Freeman	0	6
Each stone of tallow to an unfreeman	1	0
Each brower that brows, for each browst	1	0
Each anker of Aquvity sold in the burth	3	4
Each pair of cart wheels landd in Wick or Staxigo	1	0
Each mill stone landed at either places	2	0
Each grave stone landed	1	0
Each boat load of freestone left to the shoar master's discretion in proportion to the lastage or fraught to be paid.[1]		

The list prompts a number of observations: it is scrappy and haphazard, suggesting that the council's policy was to tax what, from experience, it could; the disabilities of 'unfreemen' were considerable and addressed pointedly to the farmers of the parish, to whom the freedom was not available; that (whatever travellers said about Caithness) there must at this stage have been carts in use, mostly perhaps in the town – but there were no wheelwrights and cart builders in the area; the tax on liquor, if not swingeing, was high. This would almost certainly mean that in and around the Wick area there was a smuggling trade in liquors. Little direct evidence of this is available, but it would be surprising if the merchants of Wick were immune from the temptation to smuggle in liquor, tobacco, spices etc, while the merchants of Stromness and Kirkwall were building a good part of their fortunes on such trade. Smuggling in Orkney during the eighteenth century is well attested.

---

1 *JOGJ*, 29 May, 1862. (The list is not actually dated).

CHAPTER 8

THE SETT OF WICK: II

JUST how much trade there was in the town in uncertain. We do know that until the onset of the herring business in the later years of the century (an export trade in any case, subsidised and not paying dues), the volume of trade entering the Wick harbour was not very great. There were, however, an appreciable number of 'merchants' among the burgesses, not necessarily concerned with imports and not necessarily paying all the customs due, for this was a time when smuggling flourished in these northern waters, especially in the kinds of goods sought by the high-living lairds, brandy, port, canary and other fine wines, tobacco and snuff, fine cloths and leathers. *The Mey Letters* provide ample evidence that merchants in Wick and Thurso catered handsomely for trade in luxury goods.

The Port of Wick

There are various indications that the burgesses were less than satisfied with the town's port facilities. Improvement and development was quite beyond the scope and resources of the public authority itself, but as an entry for 2 April, 1756 shows, the council very much approved of the idea of private development. John Sutherland, Merchant, applied for permission to extend wharfage facilities of his own on the north side of the river. The council considered that the whole stretch of 'that part of the shore is like Enough for the loading and Unloading of Bulkie goods and Containing Such numbers of Horses and people as doe frequent the Ships and boats loading and unloading as it might be useful to John Sutherland.' Permission was given for the new wharf and also for the building of a stone house as 'Near to the Weather Side as can be That is to say the North Wall of the said house and the East side Wall shall . . . . . be different from the Scholl [school] house.'

That there was developing pressure for the improvement of harbour facilities is suggested by the emphasis placed on exports from Caithness at this time by John Donaldson. Apart from a rising interest in fishery, 'the total amount of bear and meal sent from Caithness in the 18th Century ran to a considerable figure,' says Donaldson. He quotes figures from Bayne, Pennant and the *Statistical Account* of 1794 (he gives 1793), to show that such exports (mainly for the Firth, Clyde and other entrepôt areas) ran at times as high as 40,000 bolls. By 1812 he reckons the figure might have run as high as 80,000 bolls of meal and 27,000 bolls of bear.[1] This, of course was war time, when demand was very high. How much of this trade went through Wick can only be guessed at, but it is unlikely to have been outdone by Thurso. Staxigoe, with all its disadvantages as to size and access is believed to have been a prime area of activity. Several writers, too, mention the extent of 'the salting and exporting of beef' towards the end of the century. 'The beef,' according to Horne, 'was mainly cured for the navy victualling contractors at Inverness.'[2] Since the development near to Inverness of the great Fort George on the head at Ardersier, the army too could well have been a consumer of salted beef from Wick.[3]

To return to the management of port affairs in Wick, Mr Sutherland's enterprise sometimes evidently extended to the disadvantage of other users of the sea if, of course, the entry of 29 June, 1765 refers to the same gentleman. This was to say that 'John Sutherland, Shipper and Seaman in Wick', is warned by the magistrates through his cautioner, David Sinclair, against 'Cutting Lines at Sea and of Taking off Hook, and Fish from any one whatsoever That does not belong to himself.' Sutherland is put under notice that if during the next eleven months he infringes this ban he – or rather his cautioner on his behalf – is due to pay a fine of £20 Scots.

In 1771 there is a reference to the frequency with which ships are damaged when entering or leaving the harbour 'guided by local boatmen acting as pilots'. In future 'none is to act except those appointed by the magistrates or shoremaster of the Burgh.' In the meantime, William Mowat, James Bremner and David Sinclair are authorised to 'act as pilots and no-one else', with a fine of 40 shillings sterling for each offence and incarceration in the town gaol for a month. The magistrates added the warning too that: 'Any pilot convicted of drunkeness while employed in bringing ships in and out of the harbour to be fined 20 shillings and imprisoned at the discretion

---

1 John E Donaldson: *Caithness in the Eighteenth Century*: Edinburgh, the Moray Press (1938), pp 187-191.
2 John Horne: *Ye Towne of Wick in ye Olden Tyme*; Wick, Rae (1895), pp 14-15.
3 Fort George, the largest in Britain, was built as part of the plan to control the Highlands after the '45.

of the magistrates.'

Some idea of how the port of Wick, severely lacking in sea defences walls and basins, coped with shipping at the time, is conveyed by an entry on roup day (2 February, 1781, when, sadly, the former customar died owing money to the council), as well as something of the frustration of the council as port authority when it claimed dues:

> Shipmasters and Owners of Ships and Vessels belonging to this Town have for years [been] liable and refused to pay anchorage under pretence that they have disbursed large sums of money in fixing Poles in the Water of Wick, and as they have never given in to the Magistrates and Council a rate of the outlays on that account, it is presumed that they are long ago refunded by the Detention of anchorage and Shore dues. Therefore the Magistrates and Town Council ordain each of them to lay their respective Accounts before them between now and 1st April that they may see which have been completely paid or not with certification to them that if they fail in so doing their vessel shall be distrained for anchorage and shore dues as often as they come into the said Water and into the harbour of Staxigo, in regard that their Placing such Poles was entirely a gratuitous Deed of their own without any authority or sanction of the magistrates of the Town in so doing. The Magistrates think it is merely a piece of Indulgence to allow them any Detention at all on that score.

These seem to have been private mooring poles, driven into the mud of the estuary – presumably at low tide, the shippers' argument being that since the port itself provided few mooring facilities, there was no good reason why they should pay dues. Whether or not the magistrates and town council succeeded in their attempts to get the shippers to pay proper dues is not revealed. The impetus for improvement in the harbour came from a quite different direction. A minute of 9 September, 1794, reports a suggestion from the provost, Sir John Sinclair, that 'an application to the Board of Trade might be of Service in procuring for the *Adventurer* in the Herring Fishing the Bounties still due to them.' The council forthwith unanimously resolved to make such an application, 'stating the circumstances of the case, the hardship upon the *Adventurer*, and the loss which is likely to follow to the Fishing upon this Coast, which has already been experienced.'

Sinclair was already a man of great account in the affairs of government, having the year before this urged on the government the setting up of a national board of agriculture; it was formed in August, 1793 and Sinclair was appointed president. He was also enthusiastic for the activities of the British Fisheries Society, the popular name of the government-backed British Society for Extending the Fisheries and Improving the Sea Coasts of the Kingdom, formed in 1786. Its chief business in early days was the disbursement of 'bounty' payments to fishermen on their catches, and fostering the building of harbours and fishing villages in suitable places.

We have already referred to the initiatives of Sir John Sinclair, Provost of Wick, in seeking to get support for improvement of the port. Almost certainly the first direct move was that reported in the burgh records of 2 July, 1790, when Councillor James Horne was drafted as Commissioner for that year's meeting of the Convention of Royal Burghs. The council decided at the same time on a petition to the Convention, 'to be conveyed by Sir John Sinclair of Ulbster' (almost certainly proposed by Sir John himself):

> to be drawn up in the name of the magistrates Town Council and Burgesses of Wick praying for the assistance of the said Convention for Improving the Harbour belonging to the Borough which is highly necessary . . . . . . Thereafter, the Provost stated to the Meeting that Mr Brown had been appointed under the Authority of the Commissioner in Chief for Scotland, to make a survey of the Roads to the North of Scotland, and that he had actually begun his survey through the roads of the Shire of Ross.

There was doubt, however, as to whether Mr Brown had received orders about Sutherland and Caithness, but Sir John had 'applied to Lord Adam Gordon for having the survey extended to the North in the course of the season'.

In any case, among the places attracting the Society's attention was Wick. Two eminent Scottish engineers, Thomas Telford and John Rennie, paid visits to Wick on the invitation of the Fisheries Society to 'report as to the best means of improving the harbour of Wick'. Though Rennie's plan was never accepted, this was the starting point of a massive development of harbourage in the 'Water of Wick', and the launching of Wick as a great herring port. In one vast sweep, Wick was transformed in a few decades from a drab, tiny feudally managed seaport town on a rocky northern coast, barely able to cope with its frail dignity as a royal burgh, into the herring capital of Europe.

THE SETT OF WICK: II

Keeping the People in Order

The burgh records give a few insights into the tedious business of keeping the town reasonably decent and in good order. Much of the responsibility of persuading folk in the ways, if not of exemplary righteousness, at least of neighbourly behaviour to one another, was regarded as a duty of the kirk. In fact, in these times, the minister sometimes found himself acting as a virtual magistrate himself (sometimes was one), and the elders quite often sat in judgement of their fellows in a manner that would be utterly unacceptable today. We shall, in a later chapter, take a look at the role of the kirk in the affairs of the burgh, but this must wait until more has been said about the ecclesiastical background itself. There were, however, occasions when kirk and council went hand in hand. On 27 November, 1776, the council considered a petition from William Sutherland, Minister of Wick, asking for the enforcement of regulations on the 'keeping of disorderly houses for dancing, drinking etc.' (It was probably the 'etcetera' that was the real issue). The magistrates responded by announcing a 'penalty' of £10 for any householder keeping such house not closing at 10 pm, *'toties quoties'*.

The full law-keeping responsibilities remitted to the good burgesses by the king are referred to in the Charter rather grimly as

> the keeping and observing of good order; of apprehending, arresting, imprisoning, punishing, and, according to the laws of the kingdom, beheading and hanging all transgressors and delinquents with pit and gallows, in fang thief, out fang thief, and generally of using and exercising all, any, and sundry, with all privileges, immunities, and liberties whatsoever, as freely, in all respects, as any other free royal burgh within our said kingdom.

In addition they were to make and ordain 'acts, laws, and statutes for the observance of good order', 'hold courts as often as need be', hold and regulate markets and fairs. For the purpose of enforcing the law they should appoint 'clerks, sergeants, bailiff', and other necessary officers – all within a burgh that for most of the seventeenth and much of the eighteenth century numbered less than 1000 'examinable' persons. It was a tall order. By whom, and by what means, were often the problem.

One intractable issue was how to deal with vagrants and 'indigent persons'. James Andersone, Merchant, is 'compeired' in September,

1741, 'for himself and some of the inhabitants of the said burgh', so that he make his complaint that 'Several Indigent persons from the Country flock into the burgh who being Destitute of Means to Subsist themselves' and also that they are 'not only a burden upon the burgh but also do Pilfer and Steal peats, Kaill and other things from the Inhabitants', and 'trouble and molest them.' Andersone requests the magistrates that they 'would make such regulation as would prevent the like for the future.' The magistrates oblige by enacting that 'when any landlord is approached by such persons for accommodation they shall make enquiries and shall be liable for any damage caused.'

At the next session of the magistrates (2 October, 1741 – no distinction seems to be made at this time between reporting judicial sessions of the magistrates and business meetings of the council), the case was heard of William Callum who confessed to stealing a sheep belonging to Robert Gregg of the 'head of Wick and slaughtered same'. His misdeed had readily come to light since at his house were found the sheep's heart, 'fresh still and four leages'. William's punishment was not at all unusual for the time. Sheep, cattle and horse stealing were capital offences in eighteenth century Britain. William avoided the attentions of the hangman by taking on the appointment as town executioner himself. The entry (commented on by Calder), continues:

> William Callum, fisherman in Wick, guilty of sheep-stealing, is liberated from prison, etc., on agreeing to become common hangman and executioner for the burgh, etc., and he binds and obliges himself to execute and perform everything proper and incumbent on him in that office, as he shall be ordered and authorised by warrant of the magistrates or of the sheriff of Caithness and his depute. And as he cannot write, he empowers William Calder, notary public and clerk of the said burgh, to subscribe the enactment and obligation for him.

There is no subsequent mention of the worthy new public hangman being called on to perform his grisly duty in Wick, and since public executions were in those days also a very popular form of public entertainment, such an event could hardly fail to have been recorded.

John Horne makes quite a story of this event, adding that the hangman had 'certain perquisites pertaining to his office'

> such as a fish out of every dozen caught, etc; and he occupied, free of rent, a plot of ground above the shore of Wick, at the extreme east of the old royal burgh. The plot was long known

as The Hangman's Rig.

Horne tells also of how Callum came to be offered the job:

> Tradition has affirmed that when another unfortunate had committed a capital crime, his friends bribed the sureties of the previously-appointed hangman to get him to 'bolt', with a consideration to himself for his kindness in doing so. Thus the office became vacant, and the last criminal saved his neck by accepting the appointment.[1]

Equally concerned were the magistrates of Wick with trading misdemeanours in the burgh. The case is brought (4 April, 1768) of David Sinclair, 'who lacks a licence from Alexander Bain, "Customar" in Wick for retailing snuff [a dutiable commodity] according to use and wont.' He has refused to pay the necessary 15 shillings sterling. The magistrates rule that Sinclair must 'take a licence and pay yearly the sum agreed with the Customar.' They take the opportunity to warn that 'anybody selling snuff without a licence to forfeit £5 sterling, one half to be applyed to the public good and the other half to the poor of the parish.' In order to ensure that this rule is well understood, the 'Act of the Council is to be read in the Tolbooth' publicly.

On another occasion (4 November, 1778), the magistrates consider the 'inconvenience of the town markets 'not being properly regulated, particularly as to the sale of Fish.' As from 1 December next:

> anyone who goes to sea and kills fish for sale shall be obliged to bring same to [the] ordinary Market Place before the Town House and expose for sale at least two hours under penalty of £2 Scots.... Anyone buying fish after this enactment except on the Market [is] liable to a fine of £1 Scots.

This, of course, has nothing to do with customs. Here the magistrates are acting in conformity with their own powers as regulators of market and trading conditions within the burgh. Since most of the representation on the council consisted of merchants and tradesmen, it is not surprising that they looked with great suspicion on anyone setting up among them who was not a freeman of the burgh. A case came before them on 4 April, 1793, of two men, John Innes and John Miller who 'have Set up Trade in the Burgh as Merchants in Direct Violation of an Act of Council passed on 9th day of February, 1789, and that they continue to Carry on trade and keep

---

1 Horne, op cit. p 49.

open Shop without taking out their Freedom to the Great hurt and prejudice of the Freeman Burghers of the Burgh who are in actual Trade.' Accordingly, the magistrates ordered that the interlopers be required immediately to pay 'Seven Guineas each for the freedom or other wise to desist from carrying further Trade in the Town.' At the same time they ordered that a previous offender, George Worse, who had not paid his 'Demission Dues' be now compelled to do so.

On three occasions, the gaolkeeper himself is up before the justices for 'allowing' prisoners to escape. On the first of these (17 September, 1755) the gaoler, Robert Craigie is fined £100 Scots, payable to the Town Treasurer for 'allowing David Campbell to escape from the town prison.' On another occasion (30 January, 1786), the gaoler, William Geddes, is arraigned for having allowed William Bain, 'imprisoned as a deserter to escape . . . and for several other acts of malversation.' His cautioner on his appointment, James Miller, 'by a plurality of voices', becomes liable in the penalty of £300. Nevertheless, on the strength of Bailie Miller's willingness to continue his support for Geddes, the delinquent gaoler is reappointed 'during pleasure and his good behaviour for the future.' Yet another gaol-break is reported in 1775 (9 September). This time James Charleston, accused of shoplifting and theft, escaped by 'the negligence or connivance of William Coghill, jailer', who himself is to be 'confined' or otherwise punished. It was decided that in future there were to be two gaolers, to be paid between them a 'salary' of twenty shillings. Condition of the tolbooth itself was none too robust. At the beginning of the new century the councillors are looking out for funds for 'repairing the town house and gaol' (minute of 29 September, 1800).

The town gaol, of course, was not intended for the incarceration of long-term, serious offenders. Wick Council did not consider it appropriate that those they did commit should lie in luxury at the town's expense. An enactment of the magistrates of 20 September, 1741, ordered that prisoners in the town's tolbooth should be obliged to pay for their 'mealls' (upkeep). The enforceable sanction was that they should pay six shillings before they could be set at liberty. The site of the tolbooth is now occupied by Woolworth's at the bottom end of Tolbooth Lane (the bars on the windows along the Lane were those of the vaults of a bank that stood there before Woolworths came).

There are occasional references to other modes of punishment. Fines, cautions and sometimes public floggings were ordered. An entry for 26 October, 1772, records that

THE SETT OF WICK: II

I William Bremner in Bankhead of Wick do hereby of my own free will Bind and Oblige me to Give to William Elder and Alexander McDonald at present prisoners in the Tolbooth of Wick the Number of Twenty-Five Stripes to each of them upon their Naked backs, in the Mercate Place of Wick upon Friday the Sixth Day of November next, and In case I am Employed by the Sheriff Depute of Caithness or his Substitute to Wheep the saids William Elder and Alexander McDonald in the Town of Thurso I Oblige myself to do same upon the paying me handsomely in ready money before performing the Same. In Testimoney Whereof I have subscribed these presents a Place Date and Year forsaid before these Witnesses Baillie George Paterson Merchant in Thurso and John Anderson Merchant in Wick

W B Bremner (his initials WB)

Of this appointment, John Horne comments:

Wull Bremner, 'Whippie', was a tall, half-witted 'swack chiel,' whose dress in summer was a harn shirt, kilt or pettie, or short jacket. He resided at Bank[h]ead with his sister, who was an imbecile. The boys of the town tormented him much, throwing stones at him. He did not always heed them, but when he made up his mind to punish them his appearance was followed by an instant stampede. In physical strength 'Wull' could hold his own with any on whom he inflicted the lash.[1]

The 'Mercat Place' or Market Place was immediately in front of the Town House. The site of the Mercat Cross, where public announcements were made, and where flogging and public humiliations took place, is marked today in the middle of the road by a cross of granite blocks let into the road surface. Again there are no references to such humiliations occurring, but that is no guarantee that they did not.

Keeping Wick Clean, Decent and Accessible

Like most Scottish towns and cities, Wick was none too savoury a place in the eighteenth century. As one recent commentator on the scene puts it:

The towns . . . . .were small, dirty places; thatched houses

---

1 Horne, op cit. pp 50-51.

with no water or sanitation, peat stacks and a byre attached, for the townsfolk had their cattle and their pigs too. In both Wick and Thurso townspeople had livestock within the burgh boundaries until well on in this century [the twentieth]. Donald Grant, in *Old Thurso*, records, the efforts, usually unavailing, of the authorities in Thurso to keep livestock under control and to keep the town a bit cleaner. The files of the *John O'Groat Journal* show that the sale of dung was at one time a source of revenue to Wick which sorely needed it.[1]

An entry in the records (4 November, 1778), reveals the town fathers trying to do something about the muck. They are considering the 'Neauseances that lie up the publick streets of this Town, such as Dunghills, Peatstacks and other Incumbrances which ought to be removed.' Their solution to the problem is to 'Enact to remove all .... which do in the least incroach upon the publick streets and Avenues leading into the Town.' The streets are henceforth to be kept clear. The Dean of Guild is 'to send Requisition to owners of Dunghills etc. to remove them.' If they do not, the Dean of Guild is to employ labourers to do the work at the Expence of the Proprietors.' For this purpose the magistrates will issue summary warrants and fines of £4 Scots will be levied for future offences.

The measure does not seem to have been too successful. As always the question was not one of inadequate bye-laws but the problem of enforcing them. On 30 September, 1799, the burgesses are again complaining that 'the Streets and Kennels of the Burgh aree shamefully choaked up with Dung and Fulzie'. They decree that

> from this day foreward the Inhabitants shall be obliged to clear the streets and kennels opposite to their respective Houses and Properties and to keep the same always Clean and free from Dung Fulzie or other Impediments and that under the Penalty of Ten Shillings to be paid for each offence, such Penalty to be used for and at the instance of the Town's Fiscal to be recovered by Poinding or Imprisonment and disposed of as the magistrates and Council may direct.

At the 4 November meeting of 1778, the councillors considered the matter of putting through a new road to serve as 'the most public

---

1 Donald Omand (Ed): *The Caithness Book*, op cit; M Gunn: 'After the "Forty-Five"', p140.

entry of the town'. The Dean of Guild is to fix upon a route and mark out 'the most fitt direction', from the Hink Burn to the entry of the High Street at the back of the Minister's House and to remove all obstructions.

The 'Avenues leading to the Town from the North side particularly William Millikin's and Mount heeleys Kennels [today's Shore Lane, the site probably of the original parish church. 'Heeley' is probably a corruption of 'Holy'] were,' reminded the magistrates, 'rendered almost impassable by Quarrys and other Obstructions.' The magistrates ordered that 'inhabitants of the town be called out and employed in Filling up the said Quarrys and removing said Obstructions and to make a road through the Kennel or entry called Mount heeley's.'[1]

Also at this same meeting the magistrates go on to consider what they regard as misuse of 'the Bridge which has been built at so much Expence' just recently. This is part of a story all of its own. The town, built on the north banks of Wick Water, was approached from the south across a shaky bridge of stone and wood (probably the bridge referred to by Alexander Bayne), little more than a footbridge of dubious stability; heavier traffic and stock would pass through the ford at low tide. John Horne, and writer of 'Wick in the Olden Time' speculates on the nature and use of the ancient bridge, and mentions 'the braking doune of the Brige of Weick be the schomakers and gloueres (glovers).' How they accomplished this is not explained, but it is probable that the bridge, not being in much use for its appointed purpose, these leather workers used it as a rack for drying their skins.

Horne, as usual, has a tale to tell, of

> A certain mid-wife who attempted to cross the 'auld-brig' under peculiar circumstances. It appears that this important personage, who lived in all haste on the south side. It also happened that the mid-wife's weaver lived on the south side, and, knowing that Saunders would be in want of a waft for the web he was weaving for her distressed patient at the same

---

[1] Roads into and out of the burgh were really little more than tracks. Access into the town from the north was evidently down Mount Heeley Kennel (today Shore Lane), steep and fairly hazardous. The present main route via High Street and George Street, the A9, is part of the main road system pioneered but not completed by Thomas Telford. The north-western section of Telford's turnpike road went westward out of the town along the Wick valley, the present A882. We may remember, however, that Bishop Forbes travelling from Ackergill to Wick in 1760, considered that 'one of the finest natural roads in the world'. Calling out the citizens to work on the roads was a perfectly legal right of the burgesses under the terms of the statute labour laws.

time. Accordingly, she filled her pockets and apron with the requisite clews, and fastened another round her waist. Burdened thus, and having also a sack of sidds for the dressing, our heroine set forth, accompanied by her trusty dog 'Help'. After sundry frantic efforts to steady herself, she fairly flopped in the river (which was then in spate), clews, sidds and all. In falling she grasped despairingly at the tail of her unwitting companion, but to no purpose. Her clews, however, saved her. Acting like buoys, they floated her on the stream until she was dragged ashore. A spectator remarked that the 'howdie's appearance, with all her clews about her, closely resembled that of a *yoll* (yawl) setting her nets during a herring fishing night.'[1]

It was revealed to the councillors on 9 March, 1776, that there had been a wreck in Sarclet Bay from which timber was lying in the bay. This timber was 'exceedingly fit' for the purpose of building a 'sufficient bridge' across the water; it could be procured cheaply 'at an Easier Rate than such materials could be imported'. The councillors were urged to 'exert themselves to the outmost of their powers to accomplish so necessary a work'. As always, the council coffers were empty, so that it would be necessary to call on the aid of the 'country gentlemen'. On the strength of the hope that the country gentlemen would provide the money, the council voted a sum of £80 to put the job in hand. The bridge would be supported by stone pillars erected on the bases of the existing pillars. The books were opened; on 25 March it was announced that £8 18s 3d had been collected.

Nothing more is said of the business until five years later (22 March, 1781). On this occasion James Sinclair of Harpsdale (John of Ulbster's uncle), 'former Provost of Wick', was compeired before the Council. In a lengthy rigmarole it was decided to 'discharge' James Sinclair from the sum of £84 18s 9½d sterling, 'expended by him upon said Bridge . . . now completely finished and well executed.' £15 was, however, to be withheld (representing perhaps the amount of his own 'voluntary' contribution to the project as one of the 'country gentlemen' appealed to for help). What apparently had happened was that James had advanced the entire capital necessary for the building of the bridge, engaged the contractors and seen the work through.

It seems probable that James was never reimbursed, at least, not fully, for his generous outlay. He gave in his account for the sum of

---

1 Horne, op cit, pp 59-60. For an alternative account of developments from 1776 see 'the Bridge of Wick', *JOGJ*, 12 June, 1862.

£84 18s 9d 'for the work and balance of £15 due to him.' The confused minute of 22 March, 1781 is worth quoting for its circumlocutions and lavish use of capitals; it reads as though the councillors wish young John to pay the balance for them, and seeing that the creditor was his uncle, that is probably what he did:

> The Partys Did and hereby Do Discharge One Another Accordingly . . . And they and Do Hereby Declare their Obligation to Harpsdale for this Laudable Undertaking For which they Return him the Most Hearty Thanks, And in Regard to That the Towns funds be Very low and that they Cannot afford to pay up the Ballance, That is justly due to Harpsdale for years to come, and they think it would be Very hard for him to be Out of it any longer considering his Advances. They Did and hereby Do Recommend it, to John Sinclair of Ulbster Esq. their Superior And Provost To Pay the Ballance to James Sinclair of Harpsdale with all Convenient speed. And as the Town was not Able themselves to Execute this work without the Assistance of Neighbours and Friends, And as Many of the county Gentlemen were Very Liberal in their Subsciptions, they Ordain the Clerk to write a list of Subscribers in this Book. The Account now provided by Harpsdale the Undertaker is now subscribed by him and Magistrates and Council as relative hereto.

Confusion arises over the world 'Ballance'. When he submitted his account James spoke of a 'balance of £15' due. It seems rather unlikely that, seeing the low state of their finances, the burgesses would pay the £84 and leave the £15 in abeyance. The interpretation of the *John O'Groat* writer that by not paying at all the burgesses of Wick had hit upon a 'convenient way of getting clear of their liabilities', is all too probable. He concludes with the cynical comment:

> This convenient way of getting clear of their liabilities, together with the masterly manoeuvre of minuting Mr Sinclair as Provost and undertaker of the bridge, shows that our municipal forefathers were not destitute of what, in learned parlance, is sometimes termed *nous*.

It was Harpsdale's bridge, brought into use before it was completed, that was concerning the councillors at their March meeting in 1778. They considered that the bridge,

> now so beneficial to the publick is now in danger of being damaged by driving Horses, Cattle and Carriages upon it, even

when the Ford is safe and passable and that such Practice may be dangerous to Foot Passengers of which an Instance has already occurred by a child being thrown over the Bridge into the water and in danger of being drowned by a cow that was being driven along the Bridge.

Accordingly, it was decided to fine anyone driving a horse, cow, other cattle or wheel carriage on the bridge, except when the ford was impassable, one shilling for each offence, on pain or imprisonment or the impounding of the offender's property. A notice to this effect was to be published in the parish kirk.

This bridge must have been quite ramshackle. Twenty-two years later, at the 29 September meeting, 1800, the burgesses are considering – among their other problems – the 'insufficiency' of their bridge 'which has occasioned the loss of lives, and is dangerous to all Passengers'. They 'Resolved to make Application to the Road Trustees for authority to pull down the Timber on said Bridge and to erect a coble for the conveniency of the Publick.'

This, of course, was the method of river crossing at that time still employed in Thurso. The provost and bailies were authorised 'to open up a subscription for a new bridge'. Eventually the town gained a drastic and spectacular solution to its river crossing problem, a new stone bridge by the greatest of all then existing bridge builders, Thomas Telford.

Miscellany

Several other entertaining items of burghers' business may be mentioned before we leave the eighteenth century affairs of the Wick Town Council. Some are quite trivial; others involve quite important issues. In March 1781 the council considered the matter of who should supply the handbell which it was customary to have rung at funerals, the burgh or the kirk. Further, there was some doubt as to whom the fees for this solemnity should be paid after they had been collected by the Customar. They were, decided, the council, to be 'allocated to the poor of the parish'.

A not unimportant decision of the councillors was that of 1 April, 1751 to appoint a 'deforming Man to teach the children' and to build a school 20 feet in length and 16 in breadth with a 'fireroom 14 feet in length adjoining.' The five walls of the school and school house were to be 10 feet high and the building was to be lofted and be provided with a chimney. This year's 'Town Publick' (evidently an annual allocation or collection for charitable purposes) was to be dedicated to the project. Voluntary contributions were to be sought and James Bainbridge of Toftingall was to 'go amongst the heritors to get their respective contributions'. There is nothing further on this subject but presumably this is the 'Wick School' referred to by the Rev William Sutherland in his 1794 report, supported by two gospel societies. According to this, Sir John Sinclair, the 'heritable provost' was the provider of school, schoolhouse and schoolmaster, which suggests that the direct cost to the burghers of this admirable public endeavour was negligible.

The burgesses' concern for education was engaged once again when on 27 November, 1776, they were asked (probably via the Convention of Royal Burghs) for their views on the unification of King's and Marischal Colleges, Aberdeen, a scheme which they forthwith fully endorsed. Also from the Convention came a request for their views on a proposal for the altering of the corn laws; they approved of that too, but not that specific proposal, which did not, it must be assumed, sufficiently benefit the farmers. In the same package of civic measures, the burgesses approved a plan recommended by the Convention for better 'regulation of Hawkers and Pedlars in Scotland'.

Repeatedly, in these later years of the century, tighter connections between burgh and kirk were signalled by election of one of the burgesses as Commissioner to attend the annual General Assembly of the Church of Scotland. On 4 April, 1794 James Horne Esq., Writer to the Signet and Ruling Elder of the Wick parish kirk, is selected for this honour, to go to Edinburgh where the Assembly is 'indicated' to meet on 15th May, next. To ensure that Mr Horne is properly empowered to represent them, the burgesses 'Ordain the Clerk to make out a Commission for him and authorize him to subscribe the same'. What exactly were the purposes and what the benefits of the Commissioner's long journey are not mentioned, nor is there any evidence of reporting back.

On 11 April, 1785, the council consider a letter from the Lord Provost of Edinburgh about a proposal that was under discussion at the Convention of Royal Burghs for some alteration of burgh representation in parliament. The burghers of Wick responded in the vein of their sentiments of the year before when they had expressed their 'Abhorence' of the intentions of the 'Men in power' who had proposed a dangerous 'New System of Government'. The existing constitution of their burgh suited them very well.

The councillors were doubtless well aware that such expressions of political feeling were not quite in tune with those of John Sinclair of Ulbster. They were, however, especially 'sensible' of the benefits to Wick and themselves of the benevolence and bounty of the Ulbsters, and in April, 1794, they determined (as usual) that the 'Leet of Magistrates of the Borough of Wick to be chosen at Michaelmas next in the present year' was to be 'presented to Sir John Sinclair of Ulbster, Baronet, to be approven by him as Successor to the Earl of Breadalbane in Superiority of the said Borough [the English word was actually used in this statement] conform to the Sett established by the Act of the Convention of the Royal Burghs.' This doubtless is a reference to the mysterious *Acta Parliamentorium* of Thomas Sinclair's Notes of which no copy now seems extant in Wick.

The Hill of Wick Case

Almost at the end of the century (29 September, 1799) is a reference to the 'Hill of Wick', an area of land to the north of the town, now largely occupied by the airport and the industrial estate, over which the burgesses exercised 'right of common property which they have exercised from time immemorial', and where 'Encroachment and Intrusion' at the hands of Sir Benjamin Dunbar of Hempriggs was occurring. A certain Benjamin Wares and some other tenants of the Hempriggs estate had set about constructing a dyke across the land, as part of what the burgesses believed to be a plan of wholesale enclosure.

That such an encroachment was not unexpected is indicated by Thomas Sinclair's reference to the matter in his account in his Notes to Calder's *History* (p 318). According to these notes, recovery of the Hill of Hempriggs was of the conditions subscribed by John Sinclair of Ulbster in 1723 when he was installed as 'heritable provost'. These conditions, it may be remembered, also included paying the town's debts, setting the burghers up in trade etc! Obviously these moves of 1799 were not the first in a process that had become exceedingly common in England during the eighteenth century, when vast areas of common land were enclosed, mostly to the benefit of the greater landowners.

Sir Benjamin's encroachments in fact continued, and resistance on the part of the burgesses of Wick became a frequent topic of comment in the early nineteenth century records. Thomas Sinclair gives a full 'Sketch of the Hill of Wick Case' in his Notes. This four-page summary is dense and detailed, but by comparison with the vast volume of papers generated by the action brought by the magistrates and feuars in February, 1813, against Sir Benjamin Dunbar, it is a model of brevity. The Court's first judgement on the matter was delivered fairly quickly in five years, but the magistrates and feuars objected and the whole process began again.

It would be supererogatory here to do more than attempt to illustrate the content and style of such a classic case of Scottish territorial litigation. The printed record of the summons, 'proofs' of the litigants, verbatim reports of the interrogations at the many hearings, reports of surveyors and land valuers and the Commissioner's own reports, covering a period of eighteen years, from 1 February, 1813, to 30 May, 1831, runs to 200 pages. The crucial issue for the feuars and other witnesses called before the Commissioner, James Gregg, Sheriff-Substitute of Caithness county, is stated very early in the reports: had they, or had they not 'rights and titles' to the share of the what they regarded as the 'commonty' (the 'common land') of Wick on which they were in the habit of pasturing their sheep and cattle. Many of the early witnesses, consisting of old inhabitants (some as old as 80) of Wick, Louisburgh, Staxigoe and Papigoe, were able to assure the commissioner that cattle and sheep had been driven on to the Hill for as long as anyone could remember, and probably long before that. The question was, had they any right to do so, meaning by 'right,' documentation to prove it so. Typical of the dozens of depositions was that of

> DAVID BAIN, residing at Staxigo, married man, aged 50 years or thereby, who being solemnly sworn, purged of malice and partial counsel, examined and interrogate, Does the witness know the commonty called the hill of Wick? depones affirmative. Interrogate, How long has the witness been acquainted with that commonty? depones, That it is about 39 years; and continued herding thereon for about eight years. Interrogate, was the witness acquaint with the said commonty before he began to herd? depones, 'That he lived in the near neighbourhood of the said commonty from his infancy, to the period when he began to herd as aforesaid, but has no recollection of any thing previous to his becoming a herd theron. Interrogate, where has the witness resided since the

periods before mentioned? That he has resided in Staxigo all the time since he ceased to herd upon the said common. Interrogate, does the witness know whether the feuars of Wick have been in the practice of pasturing their cattle in the said commonty, during his remembrance? depones affirmative. Interrogate, Can the witness say how near the town lands of the field of Noss, Quoystain, Mossedge, Blackbridge, and west Noss were the cattle of Wick in use to pasture? depones, That he knows the sheep of Wick were in use to pasture along with the sheep of the said other places of the said common. . . . . . .

. . . . . And so on, endlessly. 'JOHN MALCOLM, residing at Bankhead of Wick, married man, aged 70 years, or thereby &c, &c', is quizzed as to whether his father was 'moss-man', or 'moss-grieve of the moss of Hayland.' He 'depones that from the first of his remembrance, as may of the feuars of Wick as had pieces of the said moss, which they claimed as their property, cast peats there without paying any consideration for liberty to do so.'

The action officially ceased when 'The Lord Ordinary' on 11 July, 1833 came in with the judgement:

> Having heard parties' procurators, and considered the cases together with the proofs, finds that the parties now appearing as pursuers have not a title to insist in the present action; therefore refuses the representation given against Lord Alloway's interlocutor of the 3rd July, 1818 years; sustains the defences for Lord Duffus, and assoilzies him from the conclusions of the libel, but finds no expenses due, and decerns.

Twenty feuars of the burgh had made claims in connection with the action; ten were upheld but the main case went against the burgh. Though costs of the interminable action were not awarded against the magistrates, 'yet', says Sinclair, 'the expenses amounted to £580, being paid by them out of the burgh funds. The council proposed to bear the one-half thereof, and to apportion the other among the feuars. But few of those for whom the magistrates "fought and bled" paid their share of the expense allocated upon them.' As late as 1877 the affairs remained on the burgh books, where the Hill of Wick was listed as an 'asset'. The final cost to the burgh was £500. Sinclair concludes his account:

> Had the ten feuars whose claims were sustained continued to send their cattle to the common, it is not in the least degree probable that they would have been prevented, but failing to do

THE SETT OF WICK: II

so for the past fifty years, their right has doubtless lapsed.

The Hill of Wick at the beginning of the century [that is, the nineteenth century] was a large tract of uncultivated land, but has for the last thirty years been all under cultivation, and yields excellent crops. The road formed in 1847 to Nosshead Lighthouse runs through it, having about a fourth of its extent to the east of the road.[1]

Such of this land that is today not under the concrete and tarmac, of Wick Airport and the Industrial Estate, still produces 'excellent crops'.

---

1 See Calder, op cit, pp 340-343. The main documentation consulted is the printed PROOF, *Led in 1831 and also in 1830, 1831, in Process of the Division of Commonty of the Hill of Wick.*

WICK OF THE NORTH

ADDENDUM

Roll of Burgesses of Wick, 1795

Sir John Sinclair of Ulbster. Bart.
James Sinclair of Harpsdale
Sir Benjamin Dunbar of Hempriggs
John Sutherland of Wester
Baillie William Macleay of Wick
John Rose, Town Clerk of Wick
James Miller of Tidewater in Wick
Alexander Bain, Merchant in Wick
Thomas Henderson, Weaver in Wick
William Swanson, Writer in Wick
George Palinson, Merchant in Wick
John Harper, Wright in Wick
Alexander Miller, Merchant in Wick
James Asherson, Joiner in Wick
Elexander Miller, Merchant in Staxigo
Alexander Horne, Cooper in Wick

James Sanderson, Merchant in Wick
George Banks, Merchant in Wick
James Macphaull, Merchant in Wick
John Rhind, Mason in Wick
William Taylor, Mason in Wick
John Darrant, Merchant in Wick
Donald Clark, Flaxdresser in Wick
Baillie Robert Corner
Benjamin Calder Esq. of Mount Pleasant
James Farquhar, Merchant in Wick
Harry Bain, Merchant in Wick
James Horne, Writer to the Signet
George Sinclair, Merchant in Wick

Lieutenant Robert Kennedy
Captain Patrick Campbell of Barcaldine
John Davidson of Buckies
George Sutherland of Brabster
Captain John Sinclair of Barrock
Captain Kenneth Steward.

CHAPTER 9

IMPROVEMENT

DURING the later years of the eighteenth century, 'improvement' was the order of the day in Britain. The word had become the cliché of the 'enlightened' middle-classes, who were beginning to see marvellous opportunities for development and profit all around. From profitable investment in overseas ventures they were now turning their attention to investment in two home-based activities: on the one hand 'manufacture', the exploitation of the country's vast coal and iron resources, and the mass production of woollen and cotton goods to sell at home and in the 'colonies'; on the other, in 'agricultural reform', the enclosure of land, drainage, manuring and new cropping cycles, improvement in pasturage and the breeding of stock. While investment in industry increasingly took the form of 'joint-stock' enterprise, that on the land was largely in the hands of the great landowners, some commanding recently accrued resources gained from participation in colonial development, especially at the hands of cadet members of aristocratic and other substantial landowning families, some quite new to landowning.

The whole process is usually described as the 'industrial revolution', a historian's rather than a vernacular term, of which a significant element was the 'agricultural revolution'. Key words in the mighty movement of which the industrial and agricultural revolutions were practical and pragmatic expressions, were 'reform', 'enterprise', 'progress', all implying both the possibility of and the opportunity for more efficient use of material resources, higher productivity and maximisation of 'wealth'. With all this went higher and nobler ideas about how society might be improved, become more just and be better governed, wealth perhaps a little more fairly distributed. The old order must go. It was a time of new ideals and much money-getting. The prophets of this kind of change included the 'Physiocrats' of France and in Britain Glasgow's Professor of Moral Philosophy, Adam Smith, whose *Wealth of Nations*, was one of the most influential books ever published.

Other philosophers were more concerned with the condition of the people: in France, Voltaire and Jean Jacques Rousseau, and in England

Tom Paine. In France the forces for change and improvement ran into fearful and frustrating obstructions, resulting in the great social and political upheaval we call the French Revolution, usually taken to have begun with the storming of the Bastille in 1789. This is not the place in which to explore and moralise on the reasons why the tensions and pressures which exploded into violent revolution in France, while similar forces in Britain did not issue in similarly violent political excesses. It may suffice to say that revolutionary energies released in Britain were largely diverted in other and generally more materially profitable directions.

This is not to say that Britain did not have its revolutionary moments. Alarms and excursions there were, not least in the north of Scotland where 'clearances' gave rise to rumours and threats of violence, much exaggerated, and capitalised on by the forces of law and order as an excuse for sending in the troops. Much of the energy that might have turned in against governments of the day, however, was channelled into supporting and fighting a long and strenuous war with revolutionary France. And a special factor in Britain's survival without radical political and social change throughout the years of revolution, was the country's mounting success in that conflict. After 1802 when the war against France became an all out campaign against Napoleon's regime, British triumphs, especially at sea, ensured an outward turning of native aggression – the 'martial spirit' as the Rev William Sutherland called it, against the external enemy. Mastery of the seas and an almost complete lack of French and Spanish interference in the management and exploitation of Britain's now vast overseas colonies, enabled the country, war across the Channel notwithstanding, to get on with the hard-headed business of improvement. Napoleon's alleged contemptuous remark, *L'Angleterre est une nation de boutiquiers,* was something wide of the mark; while he was making himself Emperor of France and Master of Europe, Britain was turning itself into 'the workshop of the world'.

Improvement took some fairly hideous forms as it established itself. Industrial spoil tips began littering the landscape, and the skies began to foul and blacken with the soot and sulphur of factory chimneys. Folk flocked into the new, ugly, grimy and uncouth towns thrown up to house them, as they learned to serve the merciless steam-driven machinery in the factory sheds. Some had been driven off the land by the very forces of agricultural improvement that were dramatically changing the configuration of the countryside. Improvers had brought

IMPROVEMENT

into existence a monster that neither they nor governments knew how to regulate and control. Tom Paine, Britain's own prophet of revolution, author of *The Rights of Man*, was devoted to the idea of 'improvement' and an enthusiast for iron bridges, a classic symbol of that process.

IMPROVERS IN CAITHNESS

Though delayed by some twenty or thirty years behind the English agrarian revolution, significant change began to affect Scotland just as radically as it did England. The manner and consequences of change were different, not least because the initial circumstances of rural Scotland were very different. We cannot give much attention here to these differences. Some notion of the nature and extent of Scotland's 'backwardness' is conveyed by Samuel Smiles, writing years later in his *Lives of the Engineers,* two of whom, John Rennie and Thomas Telford, both lowland Scots, became improvers *par excellence* of the

Fig. 10 John Rennie

Fig. 11 Thomas Telford

From *Lives of the Engineers* (David and Charles, 1969).
These pictures, together with Figs 12, 13 and 14, are reproduced by kind permission of the publishers.

Scottish scene.[1] Like Macaulay in his celebrated Chapter 3, Smiles made the most of the positivist contrast between 'then' and 'now', especially in his treatment of Scotland. Nevertheless, his picture of Scottish agriculture at the time when Rennie was born in East Lothian in 1761 came to be an accepted view of how things were.

This picture shows Scotland as incredibly backward, as compared with England and even Ireland. According to this, even in the Lothians, the country near Edinburgh, the fields were 'not much removed from the state in which nature had left them'. North and west of Edinburgh were 'in no better state or worse'. Modern cropping had appeared nowhere, and 'no cattle were fattened'. Communication everywhere was difficult: 'the country was as yet almost without roads', even south of the capital. 'All loads were as yet carried on horseback; but where the farm was too small, or the crofter too poor, to keep a horse, his own or his wife's back bore the load'. The Highlands were still wild and the people lawless, many 'regarding the Lowlands as their lawful prey. General Wade's roads had opened up the Highlands for the benefit of marching soldiers, but did nothing for local transport and communication.' Across Scotland few bridges had been built since the Reformation; indeed, according to Smiles, 'the art of bridge-building in Scotland, as in England, seems for a long time to have been lost, and until Smeaton was employed to erect the bridges of Coldstream, Perth and Banff, next to nothing was done to improve this essential part of the communications of the country.'[2]

Smiles returns to the topic of 'then' and 'now' when introducing his account of Thomas Telford's survey of Highland roads and bridges. He quotes Samuel Romilly, another great reformer and improver, writing from Stirling in 1793:

> I have been perfectly astonished at the richness and high cultivation of all that calumniated country through which I have passed, and which extends quite from Edinburgh to the mountains where I now am. It is true, however, that almost

---

1 Allowance must be made for the euphoric enthusiasm of Smiles for the 'spirit of enterprise' which he believed had governed the 'progress' of Britain since the mid-eighteenth century, expounded not only in his compendious *Lives* (most of his engineers were 'self-made men'), but also in his astonishing *Self-Help*, published in 1859 (same year as *The Origin of Species*), a mighty catalogue of the self-helpers who had improved Britain. The book ran into some forty editions before 1900. Smiles tended to over emphasise the pioneering spirit as the prime force in improvement, giving less attention than is perhaps warranted to the benefits of shrewd investment.
2 Samuel Smiles: *Lives of the Engineers*, Vol 2; David and Charles Reprints, (1969 - first issued in 1862); pp 93-104.

IMPROVEMENT

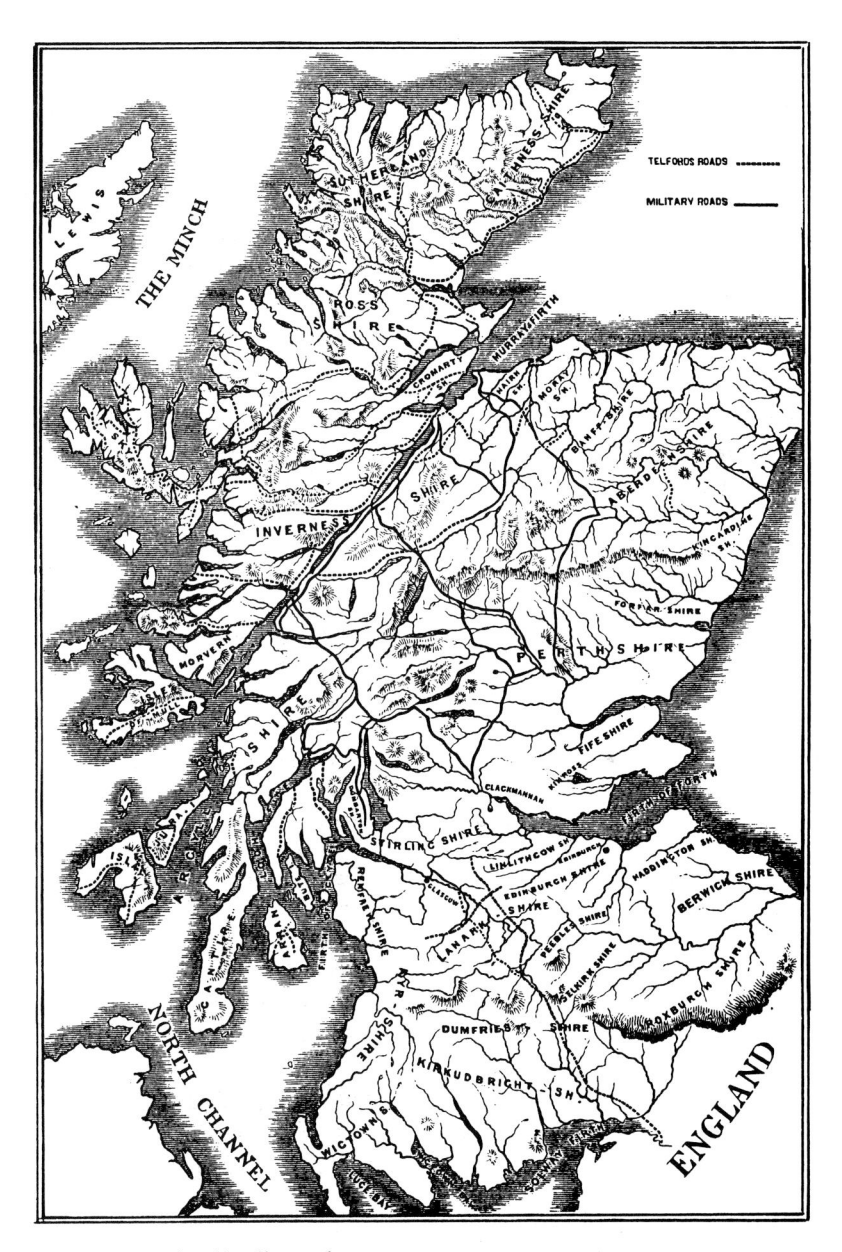

Fig. 12 Map of Telford's roads.

everything which one sees to admire in the way of cultivation is due to modern improvements; and now and then one observes a few acres of brown moss, contrasting admirably with the cornfields to which they are contiguous, and affording a specimen of the dreariness and desolation which, only half a century ago, overspread a country now highly cultivated and become a copious source of human happiness.[1]

Improvement in the Highlands and the counties beyond, necessarily lagged further behind that of the lowland south. In the same chapter which we have just quoted, Smiles describes the *cas-chrom*, the 'crooked foot', the instrument of cultivation used in the Highland, symbolic of the primitive state of agriculture in these parts. This was a sort of hand-plough, a 'rude combination of a lever for the removal of rocks, a spade to cut the earth, and a foot-plough to turn it'. It was clumsy, heavy and not very efficient. This *cas-chrom* was 'almost the only tool employed in tillage in those parts of the Highlands which were separated from the rest of the United Kingdom.' Though its use in Caithness is not mentioned, it was almost certainly here the main instrument of agriculture, where draught animals, carts, and roads along which they could go, hardly existed. It is thus entirely appropriate that Caithness county's native and most vigorous improver, Sir John Sinclair of

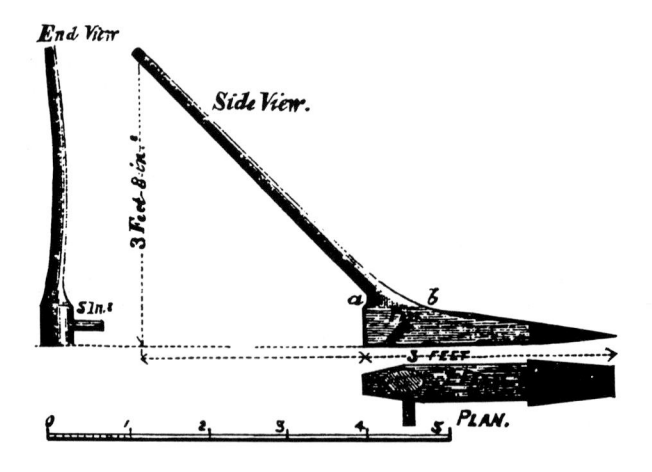

Fig. 13 The Cas-Chrom Plough.

1 Ibid pp 374-376.

IMPROVEMENT

Fig. 14 Sir John's visiting card.

Ulbster, chose as the adornment of his visiting card, an illustration of a (then) modern horse plough, with iron share and coulter.

Sir John Sinclair of Ulbster.

The laird of Ulbster has already been frequently mentioned as the Sinclair with the closest association of all with the Royal Burgh of Wick. John Sinclair inherited the extensive Ulbster estates in 1770 when his father, George Sinclair died. Unlike many of the estates of the area, that of Ulbster was unencumbered with large debts. Its worth per annum has been estimated at £3,240 in 1795. In the *Book of Valuation of the Shire of Caithness*,[1] the value of Sir John's property in the parish of Wick is given as £1,503 17s (Scots) – only a small portion of the entire estate, as compared with £2,892 4s 8d (Scots) for the estate of Sir Benjamin Dunbar of Hempriggs at the same date, Dunbar's being the larger of the two in the Wick parish. Dunbar, in fact, owned most of the real estate of Wick burgh itself. Both of these large landholders were establishing reputations as improvers; they were enclosing fields within stone-slab fences (a feature of the parish even today), beginning to cultivate root crops including turnips for the feeding of sheep, putting in drainage and introducing new breeds of

1 Rosalind Mitchison: *Agricultural Sir John: The Life of Sir Sinclair of Ulbster, 1754-1835*; London, Geoffrey Bles (1962); p 24. See also Addendum to this chapter. Other references to Sir John in this chapter are derived mostly from Mitchison and from the article on Sir John Sinclair in the *Dictionary of National Biography*.

sheep and cattle.

There are indications that improvements began on the Hempriggs estate quite some time before they began to happen on the Ulbster lands. The Dunbar salmon fishery is commented on by each of the visitors to Wick mentioned in chapter 6, while the report of the Rev William Sutherland of 1794 shows considerable development as having already occurred there. It was, nevertheless, Sir John Sinclair who became by far the better known of the local improvers; his biographer designates the 'promotion of improvement' as his 'real occupation' during the later years of the eighteenth and early years of the nineteenth centuries.

Ulbster also established a similar name for himself regionally and nationally. By means of letters and personal contact, he became a confidant, if not friend of some of the most important land improvers of the day, including Sir Joseph Banks, President of the Royal Society, explorer, botanist and experimental sheep breeder, Arthur Young, journalist, commentator and critic on all matters agricultural, Britain and European-wide traveller, John Baker Holroyd (who became Lord Sheffield), Sir William Pulteney MP, and George Dempster of Dunnichen. He was a key member at the time of the St Alban's Club, an influential discussion and lobby group, of about eighty members who were mostly less than loyal and reliable Whigs or Tories, their main theme being 'improvement'. It included quite a number of MPs, among whom was Sir William Pulteney, then MP for Shrewsbury.[1]

As MP for Lostwithiel from 1785 and later for Caithness, Sinclair was in touch with parliamentary activists of various kinds, often a thorn in the side of Pitt, supporter of Warren Hastings at the time of his impeachment, troubler of Henry Dundas, Home Secretary from 1791. In 1793, perhaps partly to keep him quiet and busy and partly as a reward for his contributions to a scheme for stabilising the currency at a time of great financial turmoil, he was allowed by Pitt to form a national 'Board of Agriculture', an innovatory quasi-government body (today it would be known as a 'quango') with a semi-promotional task of investigating, disseminating information and encouraging development in British agriculture, passing at the time through a crisis, following the outbreak in 1793 of war with France. Of particular importance to Caithness were three enterprises in which Sinclair played a leading part: the founding by Sinclair on his own initiative as an active member of the Highland Society of the British

1 Ibid pp 38-42, 45-47.

Fig. 15 Sir John Sinclair of Ulbster by Benjamin West.
(Courtesy Caithness District Council).

Wool Society; promotional help in the development of the British Society for Extending the Fisheries and Improving the Sea Coasts of Britain, founded in 1786, better known later as the British Fisheries Society; and the creation in 1790 of the *Statistical Account of Scotland*.

The direct impact on Wick of the first of these was probably negligible. Enthusiasm for new breeds of sheep was not a monopoly of Sinclair's. Robert Bakewell in Leicestershire, Lord Sheffield in Sussex and Joseph Banks in Lincolnshire, all in their different ways, were seeking to improve the wool producing characteristics of sheep. Sinclair's special interest was in Shetland sheep, which, he believed, by selective breeding along with Merinos and Southdowns, might become producers of fine soft wool, and at the same time be hardy enough to thrive on highland pastures. Sinclair's communications with Banks, Sheffield the Duke of Argyll and Lord Oxford, conceivably had some influence at least in persuading Highland landlords to try out unfamiliar breeds on their hillsides. The 'Roman-nosed' Cheviots proved rather successful, and they are still numerous on Scottish hill patures to this day. Mitchison concludes that the 'British Wool Society fizzled out as Sinclair turned his attention to his Board of Agriculture. It had never attained to any life of its own without him.'

One effect of Sinclair's propaganda in favour of Scottish hill sheep farming, however, he did not fully foresee. This was the encouragement it gave to his neighbours, the Sutherlands, to clear the land. The Countess of Sutherland and Marquis of Stafford, later Duke and Duchess of Sutherland, and their factors, Young, Sellar and Loch, were all dedicated improvers, who between them almost totally depopulated the Helmsdale and Strathnaver valleys. 'Clearance' was never part of Sir John Sinclair's plan.[1]

The British Fisheries Society was another offshoot of the Edinburgh Highland Society, not especially a project of Sinclair himself, promoted in the first instance rather by George Dempster of Dunnichen and John Mackenzie of Arcan. It was Sinclair, however, who especially urged on the Society – and the government – the advisability of developing Wick as a main east coast harbour for the herring fishers. This was as early as 1789 and 1790. According to

---

[1] It should be mentioned, however, that his son George is lumped in with other rapacious sheep-grazing landlords by Andrew Matheson in his *The British Looking-Glass*, originally published in 1870 and suppressed as the result of nefarious activities by northern landlords but recently re-issued by Laidhay Preservation Trust and published by Whittles Publishing Services, Latheronwheel, Caithness (1993). This curious and bitter pamphlet was a belated but fierce animadversion against the clearances. See p 10.

Mitchison, Sinclair backed 'his opinion by reports from Telford and Rennie,' though, as we shall see, these reports were directly commissioned by the Fisheries Society itself, that of Rennie 1793 and that of Telford in 1803. We return to this topic.

The *Statistical Account of Scotland*, launched in 1790, and completed in about 1797, was expressly and almost entirely a project of Sinclair's own, largely paid for by himself. A full description of this innovatory and, for its time, unique project for Scotland, Britain and indeed Europe, is given by Rosalind Mitchison in her biography of Sir John. Though by modern standards this survey of the whole of Scotland, parish by parish, lacks system and coherence, it provides a detailed picture of social, agricultural and industrial life unmatched by any comparable survey elsewhere. Sinclair's informants (some of whom he had to badger quite sternly to send in their reports) were the country's parish ministers, authorised and urged to undertake the work by the General Assembly of the Scottish Kirk in May 1790. When completed the entire *Account* ran to some twenty-one volumes. The habit caught on and there have been two *Accounts* since, those of 1834-1845 and of the 1980s. The account of Wick, dated 1794, we have already considered in some detail. Reference to the *Accounts of Wick* of 1845 and of 1983 will appear in their proper place.

The Developer

John Sinclair of Ulbster was a fixer *nonpareil*. As chief landlord in Caithness, Superior in Thurso and Wick (and various other localities in the county), an enthusiastic and well informed improver and propagandist for improvement, he left his permanent mark on the two towns and on the county generally. He was MP for Caithness from 1780 to 1784, and from 1790 onwards for a longer period, and though 'independent' was often able to influence the decisions of North's and later Pitt's governments. He had a hand in several important initiatives, persuading the government in 1782-1783 to spend £15,000 on family relief when the harvest failed, promotion of the 'Loyalty Loan' of 1796, and especially important, the setting up of the Board of Agriculture in 1793, of which he remained the imperious chairman – except for a break about 1800 – until the Board was dissolved in 1806. His voice was strong for improvement of the Highlands.

The Board's achievements never measured up to Ulbster's intentions for it. Again his Board was innovatory, conceded by Pitt on account of concern at the time about the ability of British agriculture to respond to the needs of war, but against the rising tide of *laisser-faire*, the doctrine advanced by Adam Smith and now becoming accepted, that government 'intervention' in the market did more harm than good. Starved of funds Sinclair's Board had little opportunity for intervening very purposefully and was never, during its years of existence, able to accomplish the general Act of Parliament which Sinclair hoped would save the vast amount of time, trouble and expense of promoting the individual Acts still necessary for each local measure of land enclosure. The lawyers saw that as too severe a restriction on their opportunities for lucrative litigation.

Sinclair's increasing preoccupation with national affairs took him more and more away from Caithness, though he and his family made a point of spending at least a month of the summer at Thurso Castle. His concern with Caithness affairs did not suffer. On the contrary, his awareness of what was going on, the need to raise men for the army, the need for more and better housing in Thurso and Wick, the need to do something about Wick harbour, his anxieties about emigration from the north and in particular, the clearances, caused him to undertake several enterprises of considerable and ultimate benefit to the area. In August 1804 he wrote to Lord Melville (the former Henry Dundas, Pitt's Home Secretary), to tell of his experience when driving north to Caithness:

> I was quite distressed in the road from Perth to Inverness to meet with several bodies of Emigrants, men, women and children, travelling with carts of baggage and hastening to Greenock to obtain a passage to America. At a time when France is getting such immense accessions of population [these were the years of Napoleon's dramatic advances across Europe] and we cannot raise enough for the army, nor for the militia itself, it is shocking to see the martial part of the kingdom thus rapidly depopulating . . . I find that nothing will satisfy the greater part of these people but allotments of land. I have brought to great perfection, the system of what may be called *Cottage farms*, or amassing small lots of land from five acres to cottages, which enables the poor to keep from one or two cows of the small Highland breed, and to raise potatoes and other articles for their families. They have it in their power to live very comfortably in the neighbourhood of fishing and manufacturing towns and villages. I have already erected above

fifty such farms in different parts of Caithness: and though the experiment has answered hitherto in point of view of comfort to the cottager than profit to the landlord, yet I should have no objection, having land enough to provide for a number of such cottages, notwithstanding the want of immediate profit, to carry on the plan on a very extensive scale, provided His Majesty's Government think it an object meriting their attention. I do not intend to apply for any grant of public money, but there are various modes, as establishing volunteers corps, making roads and harbours etc., by which the countenance and assistance of Government might be of the most essential service in promoting such a measure . . . [1]

Sinclair was unable to get the Board of Agriculture, much less the government, to back such a scheme, but good as his word, he undertook on his own initiative several ambitious projects of the kind in Caithness. Among them were the planned villages of Sarclet, about eight miles south of Wick, and Halkirk, several miles south of Thurso on the Thurso river. For the Sarclet project Sinclair cooperated with his tenant, Captain David Brodie. Sarclet is one of the 'five fishing stations' in the parish of Wick mentioned in *Wick 1794*, that rarity on the coast of Caithness, a natural harbour, protected from the weather by a fortuitous southward bend inside the geo, with remarkable flagstone shelving near the shore, providing an effective though diminutive natural landing stage. During the years following, additional quayside accommodation was built, a curing house and mooring equipment; but the bay was much too restricted to accommodate more than a few of the larger fishing boats then coming into use as the herring fishery expanded. Nor was landward access very good. Cottages were provided for the fishers but Sarclet was not a success. Again, as Mitchison comments:

Brodie and Sinclair planned for their generation and it would be unfair to criticise them for failing to foresee the trend of industrial concentration produced by the railways and by the enlarging scale of and capacity of the fishing industry. But Sarclet, a depressing picture of a long line of houses, on a windswept cliff, too small and too low for comfort, too far apart for shelter, with its trailing debris of croft land, should be remembered in comparison to Wick for an appreciation of long term development. Its haven was good enough for 1800 to

1 Mitchison, op cit, pp 194-195.

merit development; it is not good enough today.[1]

Halkirk was hardly a success. On the site of the ancient village where the Earls and Bishops of Caithness once lived, two-roomed workers' cottages were built, each with about an acre of land around it. The result was a settlement of houses 'scattered down a network of long roads which failed ultimately to satisfy changes in the daily pattern of work'. Crofting, even with the assistance and blessing of the landlord, was not destined to become the essential mode of farming in Caithness, for which in any case an acre of land was too small an amount for making a living. Over the two centuries since its inception, the planned village of Halkirk has adapted itself to something like satellite status to Thurso, from which is has remained easily accessible.

Sinclair's most determined effort of planned development was his almost single-handed creation of the 'New Town' of Thurso. New town design was much in vogue at this time among the improvers. Edinburgh 'New Town' on the north side of Princes Street was the classic model, but it is a matter of considerable surprise to find that the next important ventures of this kind in Scotland occurred in the most northerly town of mainland Britain. John Sinclair had the idea that his native town on the banks of the Thurso river was well placed to become a model new town, especially as there was a great need for improved housing, not as in Edinburgh for wealthy city-dwellers, but for ill-housed but deserving common folk. To quote Mitchison again:

> Sinclair had great hopes for Thurso. If the harbour could be enlarged it could become a fisheries' base; it was already the social centre of Caithness and the market town for half the county. It could become a port for shipping to the South. He had the inspiration to use its other advantages, a building stone of good working quality . . . In the flat landscape of Caithness, neatly edged by the sea, the rectangular tidiness and low formal elevations that Sinclair prescribed for his streets have fitted with complete appropriateness. He overbuilt for the needs of his day, and much of the economic growth he foresaw did not happen . . . . As it was, Thurso had enough to do to keep going, to fill its houses slowly; so it has remained one of the few early planned towns of Britain [Mitchison was writing in the early

---

1 Early this century the Wick and Lybster Light Railway was constructed, mostly alongside the line of Telford's road, with a station at Thrumster, at the end of the Sarclet lane, but this was much too late to do anything for Sarclet.

IMPROVEMENT

1960s before the great spate of new towns in the south of England] and one of the very few pretty towns north of the Highland line, a group of low roofs behind the curve of the bridge, with church spire for contrast. The bridge the landowners of Caithness built by subscription is a long way from the older passage, ferried in the town by two coblemen whose good behaviour had been certified by the minister. Thurso counts as one of Sir John's successes, though not on the terms he intended. His plans for an academy, and infirmary and a public wash house did not get beyond paper . . . The proposed harbour, which Telford planned to cost £7,000, got its Act of Parliament and its incorporation, with a loan of £1,200 from the British Fisheries Society, but subscriptions were lacking. Money was tight at the crucial period; undertakings had failed and even the Act of 1806 which allowed for six roads in the county, half the cost to come from the government, was beyond the means of the landowner. Only one road was built before 1830, and the harbour was dropped. But the town is there, and is Sinclair's.

Mitchison does not mention what must have been the critical element in the relative failure of Thurso, the undoubted fact that the development of Wick, nearly twenty miles away, and for all the town's seeming inadequacies, was proceeding apace. Not only was Telford's harbour plan for Wick adopted and the harbour constructed, the Fisheries Society backed development at Wick up to the hilt. Wick Water, in any case, was a better place than the Thurso estuary for a herring fishery harbour. Although it faced directly the foul weather that so frequently blows from the east, and although up to the end of the eighteenth century its harbour facilities were inferior to those of Thurso, Wick was nevertheless on the North Sea coast, much more immediately accessible to the rich herring fishing grounds. The Thurso river flows into Thurso Bay, opening to the Atlantic at the western end of the Pentland Firth, notorious for its fierce fast-changing currents. Until the construction later in the nineteenth century of the harbour at Scrabster in Thurso Bay, Thurso lost out as against Wick. John Sinclair's interest in Wick, somewhat less personal and paternal perhaps than his concern for Thurso, was nevertheless considerable, and it is no small measure due to Sir John, and his father before him, both long-term provosts of the town, that Wick gained the attention and resources to develop more rapidly and extensively than its county rival. The south side of the Wick river, too, became the location for an even more adventurous experiment in new town development, for here, up and beyond the south Wick river bank, was built Pulteneytown, named after that other great improver, Sir William Pulteney, patron of Telford and chairman of the British Fisheries Society. Though its conjunct neighbour, in fact, Pulteneytown did not merge its identity with Wick for another century. (See Addendum at p 224).

The Engineers

Two other improvers of note who crucially affected the fortunes of Wick at the turn of the eighteenth century have already been mentioned a number of times. They are John Rennie, born in East Lothian 1761, and Thomas Telford, born in Westerkirk, Eskdale, Dumfries, in 1757. Rennie learned the basics of what became his trade as apprentice to a clever mill-wright of Saltoun, Andrew Meikle, spent three years studying at Edinburgh and gained his first major appointment from the famous Scottish engineer, James Watt, then building steam-engines in partnership with Matthew Boulton at their Soho works in Birmingham. Rennie was engaged in 1784 to design and build mills and machinery in fulfilment of contracts now frequently coming in to the Birmingham firm. His first major work was the fitting out of the newly built Albion corn mill on the Thames, and it was not long before Rennie was designing and building bridges, constructing canals, draining fens. He was on call all over the country for his bridges, his most famous being the Waterloo and Southwark bridges over the Thames. Rennie strongly favoured the new material, cast-iron, in much of his bridge work. He became involved in the modernisation of London Docks, and undertook extensive harbour work in Glasgow, Holyhead and Hull.

His contribution to the development of Wick came quite early in his career when, in 1793 at the age of 32 he was invited by the British Fisheries Society 'to report as to the best means of improving the harbour of Wick, – the only haven capable of affording shelter for ships, in certain states of the wind, which was to be found along an extent of 120 miles of rock-bound coast.' In his 'masterly report', Rennie

> boldly proposed to abandon the old system of jetties, and to make an entirely new harbour beyond the bar; thus at once getting rid of the great and dangerous obstacle to improvement,

securing at the same time greater depth of water, better shelter, and the means of easier access and departure for vessels of all burdens. In order to accommodate the trade of Wick, he recommended that a canal should be made from the new harbour, having a basin at its termination in the town, where vessels would have been enabled to float, and to load and unload at all times. He also proposed an effective plan of sluicing, with the view of scouring the outer harbour when necessary. It is much to be regretted that this plan was not carried out, and that so important a national work has been postponed almost until our own day; nor does the plan since adopted, though exceedingly costly, seem calculated to secure the objects which would have been obtained by executing Mr Rennie's more comprehensive yet much more economical design.[1]

The money at this stage was not forthcoming and Wick failed to get its improvement. However, the pressures did not cease, and some years after Rennie's visit, Thomas Telford was called in. A mason by training, Telford obtained work in Edinburgh and then in London, where he worked on the new Somerset House. From here, where he was already becoming known as a man of some originality, with literary pretensions and useful connections, he went as foreman of masons to work in Portsmouth Dockyard, his influential connection here being Sir William Pulteney, MP. As MP for Shrewsbury it was mainly Pulteney who secured for Telford the appointment as county engineer in Shropshire, where Telford undertook many significant road, bridge and canal projects. Like Rennie, Telford greatly favoured the use of cast-iron in his bridge building. His most remarkable construction in the area was the cast-iron Pont-cysylltau aqueduct across the Dee valley, carrying his Ellesmere canal in a cast-iron trough, high above the valley, still in use.

It was through his connections with Shropshire that Telford became involved in the modernisation of the 'Watling Street', the ancient Roman road from London to Chester and on to Holyhead. His most famous bridge was that over the Menai Strait, a magnificent suspension bridge that still carries heavy traffic from the mainland on to Anglesey.

In 1801 Telford, in the company of Colonel Dixon of Dumfries,

---

1 Samuel Smiles: *Lives of the Engineers*, op cit, p. 204. The *Lives* was published in 1862.

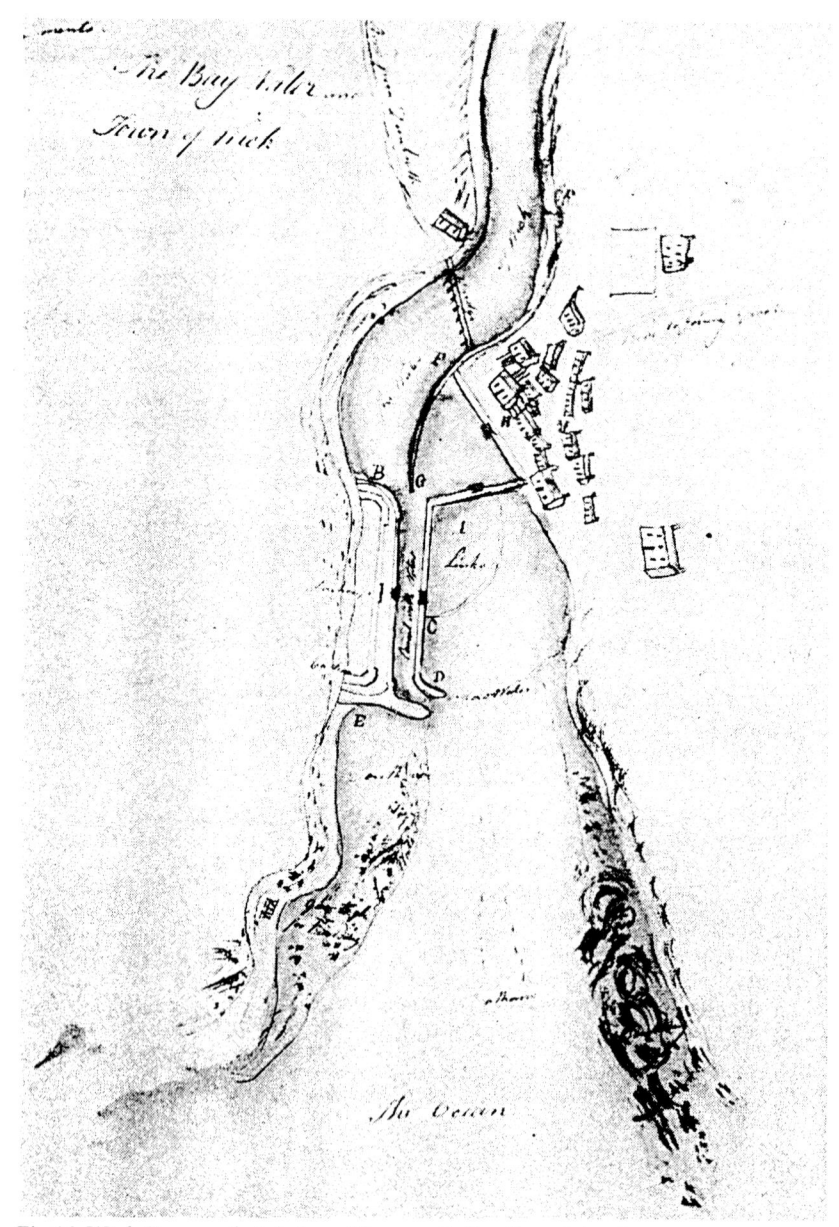

Fig 16 Wick Bay – a sketch from Thomas Telford's notebook.
(Reproduced by kind permission of the Keeper of the Records of Scotland.)

made a tour and survey of the north of Scotland on the invitation of the government; he was 'to report as to the measures which were necessary for the improvement of the roads and bridges of that part of the kingdom, and also on the means of promoting the fisheries on the east and west coasts, with the object of better opening up the county preventing further extensive emigration.' He had, it seems, even earlier been commissioned by the British Fisheries Society – through his friend Sir William Pulteney 'to inspect the harbours at their several stations, and to devise a plan for the establishment of a fishery on the coast of Caithness.' Telford included Annan, Aberdeen, Wick and Thurso in his tour before returning to Shrewsbury, accumulating on his way a 'large mass of data for his report, which was sent to the Fisheries Society, with charts and plans, in the course of the following year.'

Now appears an interesting gap in the story as told by Smiles, who gives no date for Telford's earlier tour nor does he award the resulting report much significance. According to the records of the British Fisheries Society, Telford's first journey was in fact made in 1790, three years before Rennie was invited on the scene. Telford's brief from the Society was 'to inspect the harbours at their several stations, and to devise a plan for the establishment of a fishery on the coast of Caithness.' On his way he visited Ullapool where the Fisheries Society had started a project to create a fishing port at the entrance to Loch Broom. His tour of the coast of Caithness was detailed and thorough.

Among the places visited by Telford were most of the inlets where development of any kind was conceivable, including Keiss in Sinclair Bay, Staxigoe and Broadhaven just above Wick. He also explored several localities south of Wick Water, including Sarclet, Whaligoe, Clyth, Lybster and Latheron. Some kind of development was going on in most of these places, mostly on the initiative of local landowners. He assessed all these places as possible locations for further development: all, he determined, had very limited possibilities. Staxigoe and Broadhaven were already partially opened up owing to the activities of Sir Benjamin Dunbar, who had also started the village of Louisburgh where, conceivably, new fishers could live. He found enterprising activity going on at Sarclet, on the estate of Sir John Sinclair of Ulbster, which he described, expressively enough as a 'harbourlet', and reported that it was 'used by the country people for fishing from in boats and there is a curing house there belonging to Creswell and Company'.

Whaligoe, two miles south, he found 'a dreadful place', though he was astonished at what was going on there. He was impressed by the enterprise he found in evidence at this strange place, where the landowner, James Henderson, had 'already been at 4 guineas expence and a good deal of trouble' in blasting and clearing away rocks. He speaks also approvingly of Henderson's 'spirited and perservering conduct'. He inspected and provided sketches of Clyth and Lybster, observing of Lybster that 'it is seldom where there is a place whose shore is so clear of Rocks'.

Telford was in no doubt that for all its disadvantages, Wick was the best place to undertake a fishing port development project. As Jean Dunlop puts it:

> In 1790 Telford had come down heavily in favour of the improvement of the natural harbour of Wick. He thought that when cleared it would hold 150 vessels of 80 to 100 tons, the total expense of such improvement being estimated at £3500. He was followed by many others including the writer of the *Old Statistical Account* [the Rev William Sutherland]. It was obviously a large undertaking for a private individual or company, and all eyes were turned and hands held out to the British Fisheries Society.[1]

This report of Telford's thus pre-dated the Rennie recommendations of 1793, and must have influenced the composition of Rennie's own report. Why indeed Rennie was called in at all is a bit of a mystery. Neither plan was sufficient at this stage to persuade the parties involved, particularly the government to authorise the development and the expenditure. After Rennie there followed several more years of havering. Then in 1801 Telford came in again, this time on a commission from the Lords of Treasury, to visit the Highlands and 'to report as to the measures which were necessary for the improvement of the roads, and bridges of that part of the kingdom, and also on the means of promoting the fisheries on the east and west coasts, with the object of better opening up the county and preventing further extensive emigration.' Telford travelled on this occasion with Colonel Dixon of Dumfries; his report was presented in April, 1803.

One of Telford's recommendations was that in addition to new

---

1 Jean Dunlop: *Pulteneytown and the Planned Villages of Caithness;* in *Caithness: A Cultural Cross Roads;* published by the Scottish Society for Northern Studies, with Edina Press; Editor, John Baldwin (1982), pp 148. Most of the detail of this summary of Telford's journey of 1790 is drawn from Miss Dunlop's (now Mrs Munro) study, pp 136-148.

roads, bridges should be constructed at a number of places, including Dunkeld, across the Tay, the Spey at Fochabers, and the Findhorn at Forres. North of Inverness

> matters were still worse. There was no bridge over the Beuley or the Conan. There being no roads, there was little use of carts. In the whole county of Caithness there was scarcely a farmer who owned a wheel-cart. Burdens were conveyed usually on the backs of ponies, but quite as often on the backs of women.

These Telford reports 'excited much interest in the north. The Highland Society voted him their thanks by acclamation; the counties of Inverness and Ross followed; and he had letters of thanks from many of the Highland chiefs.' Telford was highly gratified, and in a letter to Andrew Little of Langholm he wrote:

> If they will persevere with anything like their present zeal, they will have the satisfaction of greatly improving their country that has been too long neglected. Things are greatly changed in the Highlands. Even were the chiefs to quarrel, de'il a Highlandman would stir for them. The lairds have transferred their affections from their people to flocks of sheep, and the people have lost their veneration for the lairds. It seems to be the natural progress of society; but it is not an altogether satisfactory change. There were some fine features of the old patriarchal state of society; but now clanship is gone, and the chiefs and people are hastening into the opposite extreme.[1]

'This seems to me quite wrong,' he adds rather ruefully, and not very logically, since Telford was one of the main agents of the changes about which he was writing. He was elected a member of the Royal Society of Edinburgh. Later in 1803 a Parliamentary Commission was set up to supervise the actual execution of Telford's plan, 920 miles of roads and bridges throughout the Highlands. Half the cost was to be met by the government and the other half by local assessment; in addition many county roads were constructed by other means, nearly 300 miles of new roads in Sutherland alone at the landowners' own cost.

---

1 Smiles: *Lives of the Engineers;* op cit. pp 381-383. Among the immediate consequences of Telford's reports was the setting up two official commissions, one for Highland Road and Bridges and the other for the Caledonian Canal. Telford was appointed engineer to both. In passing, it is an indication of the social value systems of the time, that while 'gentlemen' developers could readily qualify for honours such as baronetcies, commoners such as Rennie and Telford, for all the compliments, plaudits and civic honours, were not in the running for knighthoods and the like. Nor later did James Bremner qualify.

WICK OF THE NORTH

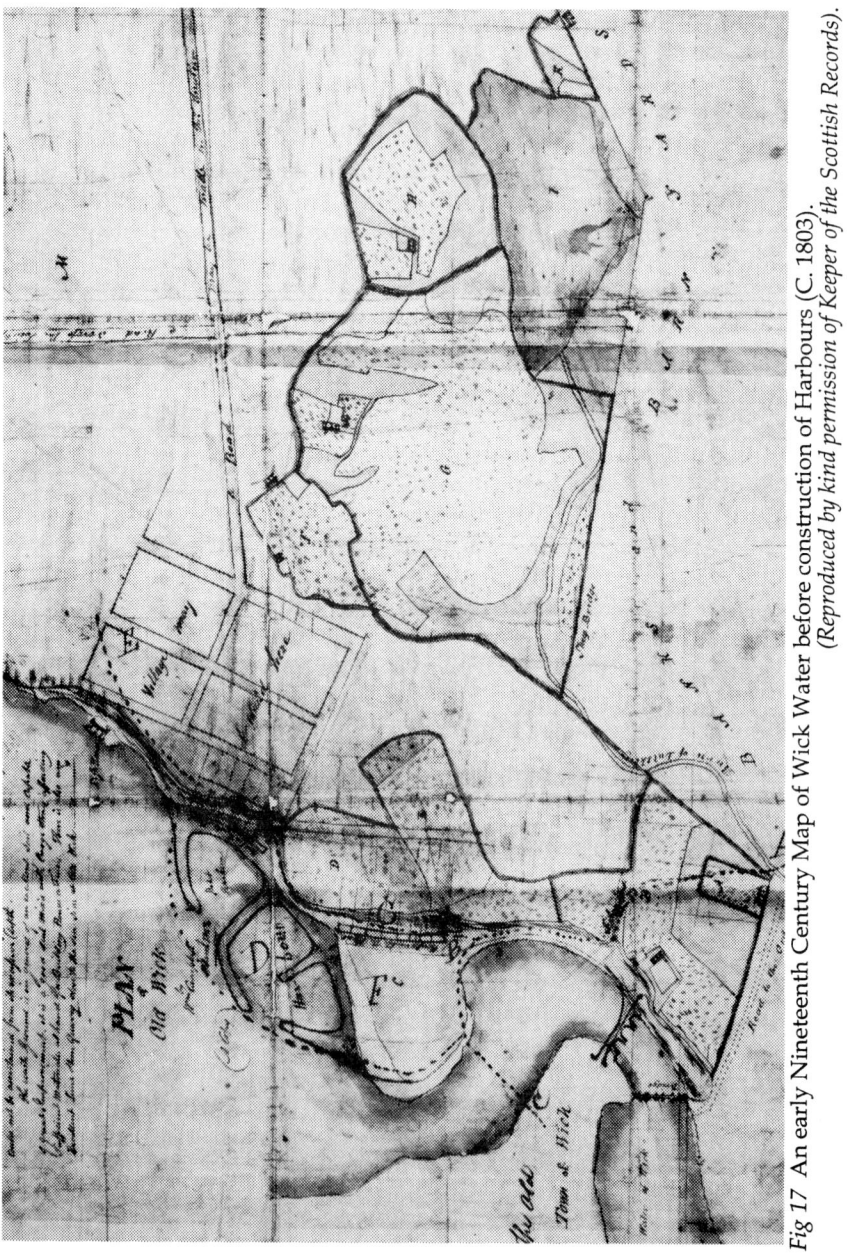

Fig 17 An early Nineteenth Century Map of Wick Water before construction of Harbours (C. 1803).
(Reproduced by kind permission of Keeper of the Scottish Records).

WHY DEVELOP CAITHNESS?

It is not immediately obvious why at a time of national crisis, so much decision, effort and expense were directed at the north of Scotland, ostensibly one of the least inhabited and productive of all parts of Britain. Britain was now fiercely at war with France and there were great strains on the public funds. *Laisser-faire* doctrine in any case ran counter to lavish government interference in the workings of the economic system, though at this stage it was not in full spate; nevertheless, Telford's road, bridge and port programme went ahead. It seems very probable that among the government's motives was alarm at the kind of depopulation against which John Sinclair was warning, and there was concern at the possible effects of the country's isolation from the continent. The British navy had set up a blockade of west European ports. This and what after Trafalgar (October, 1805) came to be called Napoleon's 'Continental System', aimed at cutting off all European trade with Britain, were already biting. The blockade and Napoleon's ban, though a boon to British farmers, was depriving the country of supplies formerly brought in from Europe.

There was, moreover, some well backed-up explicit concern growing for the herring trade. Among other commodities, there was a virtual cessation of herring imports from Holland. Until the later years of the eighteenth century the British herring fishery had been much less assisted and developed than the Dutch; except for the relatively small quantities fished just off Scottish shores, there was no herring 'industry'.[1] With more foresight and considerable investment, the Dutch had come to dominate the herring trade. Their 'busses' collected the catch of their fisher vessels off the coast of Scotland, and took the fish back to Rotterdam for curing and packing; Holland was thus the main source of supply for the London market, which was growing; the herring, it was being discovered, could be a nutritious and cheap addition to the diet of the workers now teeming into London and other towns. The Dutch were also supplying herring to Ireland and to the British West Indies, especially Jamaica, where it had become the food of slaves.

---

1 The full extent of the British herring fisheries in the eighteenth century is discussed in Jean Dunlop's *The British Fisheries Society, 1786-1893;* Edinburgh, John Donald (1978); see especially Chapter 2, pp 7-16. There was, in fact, a considerable fishery based on the Shetlands, dominated by the Dutch busses. British government aid to the fisheries began in the form of bounties for the construction of busses, and though numbers were launched – especially in western Scotland – there was never serious competition with the Dutch.

Discussion of the need to boost the British fishing industry had been going on for quite a long time. As we shall see in Chapter 11, various moves in this direction were made during the eighteenth century including the creating of the fishing bounty system and the setting up of the British Fisheries Society. That there was considerable parliamentary concern is evidenced by the reports of two Select Committees, the first appointed in 1785 to *inquire into the State of British Fisheries,* and the other appointed in 1798 to *inquire into the State of British Herring Fisheries.*

The war created more urgent conditions. Chairman of the Society was Sir William Pulteney, and a keen promoter of north Scottish fishing was Sir John Sinclair of Ulbster, a friend of Pulteney who, as we have seen, was friend and patron of Thomas Telford. The minute book of the Burgh Council of Wick covering the years 1794 to 1815 (Volume OA) affords convincing evidence that significant moves, involving Sir John, Sir William and the Fisheries Society, and the Burgh Council itself, were afoot at the turn of the century.

At this time Sir John Sinclair put in only irregular attendances at the Burgh Council meetings. He was faithfully re-elected provost each year at the Michaelmas meeting to act on the 'leet', and he was usually there for the meeting, which fell during his annual visit to his home and his Caithness constituency. Dull and routine as were most of the council's meetings, Sinclair always livened things up by items of business that were not on the regular agenda. Among several such items on 29 September, 1800 he stated,

> that by a Letter from Alexander Macleay Esq. of the Transport Office it appeared that nine Dutch Fishermen who were in the Prisons of the country [almost certainly interned], were willing to be sent to Caithness to prosecute the Fisheries if met with encouragement.

Manifestly on Sir John's urging, the Meeting required

> the Provost and Baillies to make application to the Lords Commissioners of His Majesty's Treasury, to any Committee of the House of Commons that may be appointed on the subject of the Fisheries; for the Board of Trustees to the British Fisheries Society and the Highland Societies of Edinburgh and London, for any assistance that can be procured for Settling the said Fishermen up the Coast.

What exactly happened as a result of these representations is not revealed, but the episode clearly shows which way the wind was blowing. Another resolution of the same meeting was to the effect that an attempt would be made to establish in Wick some 'useful manufacture in the Town and neighbourhood', possibly in the form of a factory for making sailcloth or sacking, 'well calculated for this part of the country', and communications were to be made to various people for advice and assistance, in Sunderland and Montrose and to the Cromarty Sacking Company. What the name of this was also is not reported.

However, at the next September meeting (19 September, 1801)

> the Provost [still Sir John], stated to the Magistrates and Council that he entertained the most flattering expectations that something effectual will soon be done towards constructing a Harbour at Wick and begged to propose that the Thanks of Magistrates and Council together with the Freedom of the Burgh should be presented to that respectable Senator and Statesman Sir William Pulteney, Bart, MP and to Nicholas Vansittart Esq. MP, Secretary to the Treasury who had given the assistance in procuring the survey to be made of the said Harbour by Mr Telford and whose attention to the Improvement and prosperity of the British Fisheries in general as well as to that of Wick in particular was entitled to every possible acknowledgement and mark of Respect.

The clerk was instructed to

> affix the seal of the Burgh, and Burgesses Tickets in favour of the above Gentlemen and to deliver the same and two Extracts of these Resolutions to the Provost of whom they request to transmit the same to the said Sir William Pulteney Bart, and to Nicholas Vansittart Esq.[1]

Work having been put in hand, at the meeting of (30 September, 1805 – three weeks before Trafalgar), another resolution was passed for

> the Freedom of the Royal Burgh to be granted to the Honble. Charles Abbott, Speaker of the House of Commons as a mark of respect entertained by magistrates and other inhabitants of the Royal Burgh of Wick for the great attention he has shown to the improvement of the Northern District of Scotland and the

---

1 Nicholas Vansittart (1766-1851) later became Irish Secretary and in 1812, Chancellor of the Exchequer. He became first Baron Bexley. He is honoured in both names by streets in Pulteneytown.

Ability which he Displayed on so many occasions as a Senator and Statesman and they request that he will wear the said Burgess Ticket is his Hatt on the day he receives it.

It is evident from these extracts that not the least of the causes of activity beyond Inverness was the lobbying and badgering of the government by Sir John Sinclair and Sir William Pulteney. However, as the Wick Burgh Council recognised, its own harbour development was only a part of vast improvements that were set going at this time in the north of Scotland. These included the construction of modern fishing harbours on both the west and east coasts, a wholesale network of new roads and bridges, and most spectacular of all, completion of a ship canal through the Great Glen, the Caledonian Canal. This was largely prompted by strategic considerations and proved the least beneficial and profitable of all these major engineering ventures. They all, however, involved unprecedented expenditures of state funds on public works, and among the beneficiaries (which included Dundee, Peterhead, Tobermory and Aberdeen and several minor ports); none was more improved and thus transformed than Wick.

The Wick project commands two pages in *The Lives of the Engineers*, and Smiles's account is worth quoting in full:

> The harbour of Wick was one of the first to which Mr Telford's attention was directed. It will be remembered that Mr Rennie had reported on the subject of this improvement as early as 1793, and his plans were not adopted only because their execution was beyond the means of the locality at that time. The place had now, however, become of increased importance. It was largely frequented by Dutch fishermen during the herring season; and it was hoped that, if they could be induced to form a settlement there by improving the accommodation of the harbour, their example might exercise a beneficial influence upon the population generally. Mr Telford reported that, by the expenditure of about 2890 *l.*, a capacious and well-protected tide-basin might be formed, capable of containing about two hundred herring-busses. The Commission adopted his plan, and voted the requisite funds for carrying out the works, which were begun in 1808. The new station was named Pulteney Town, in complement to Sir William Pulteney, the Governor of the British Fisheries Society; and the harbour was built at a cost of about 12,000*l.*, of which 8000*l* was granted

from the balance of forfeited estates.[1] A handsome stone bridge erected over the river Wick 1805, after the design of our engineer, connects these two improvements with the older town: it is formed of three arches, having a clear waterway of 156 feet. The money was well expended, as the result proved; and Wick is now, we believe, the greatest fishing station in the world. The place has increased from the dimensions of a little poverty-stricken village to those of a large and thriving town, which swarms during the fishing season with lowland Scotchmen, fair Northmen, broad-built Dutchmen, and kilted Highlanders. The bay is then frequented by upwards of a thousand fishing boats, and the take of herring in some years amounts to more than a hundred thousand barrels. The harbour has of late years been considerably improved to meet the growing requirements of the herring trade, the principal additions having been carried out, in 1823, by Mr Bremner, a native engineer of great ability.

NEW ROADS IN CAITHNESS

In the Appendix of his *History of Caithness,* Calder includes some 'Memoranda Connected with Public Roads in the County of Caithness' which add a little more to our knowledge of the background to all these events, and at least one other facet of Sir John Sinclair's determination to get something done:

> The first attempt at road-making on a large scale in Caithness was by the late Sir John Sinclair, who called out the statute labour of the district to form a road or tract from the hill of Ben Cheilt. Across the moss or bog called Causeway Myre,[2] towards Thurso. The calling out of the inhabitants to perform the

---

1 These were monies accumulated from the confiscation, mainly in the Highlands, of estates of landowners who took the field for the Young Pretender in 1745-6. In fact, the great landowners who had greatly benefited (often to the great distress of the former small farmers and crofters) from the clearances, were not usually unduly unwilling to spend some of their profits on road-making, for this eased the marketing of their wool. R H Campbell: *Scotland Since 1707;* Oxford, Basil Blackwell (1965), gives the following figures for all expenditures involved: 'The Commissioners for Highland Roads and Bridges constructed a total of 920 miles of new roads and 1,117 bridges, notably those over the Dee, Tay, Beauly Conon and Spey, at a cost of over £500,000, £367,000 of which was contributed by the government. Piers and harbours were also improved by the Commissioners, who contributed about half the total cost of approximately £110,000 from funds which arose from the return of the Forfeited Estates.'
2 The Causeway Myre (Mire) or *Causeymire* (a slight corruption of Causeway and Mire – a stretch of bog in the area of Spittal crossed by a causeway) was at one time an area associated with witches, ghosts and dire doings *(continued on foot of next page)*

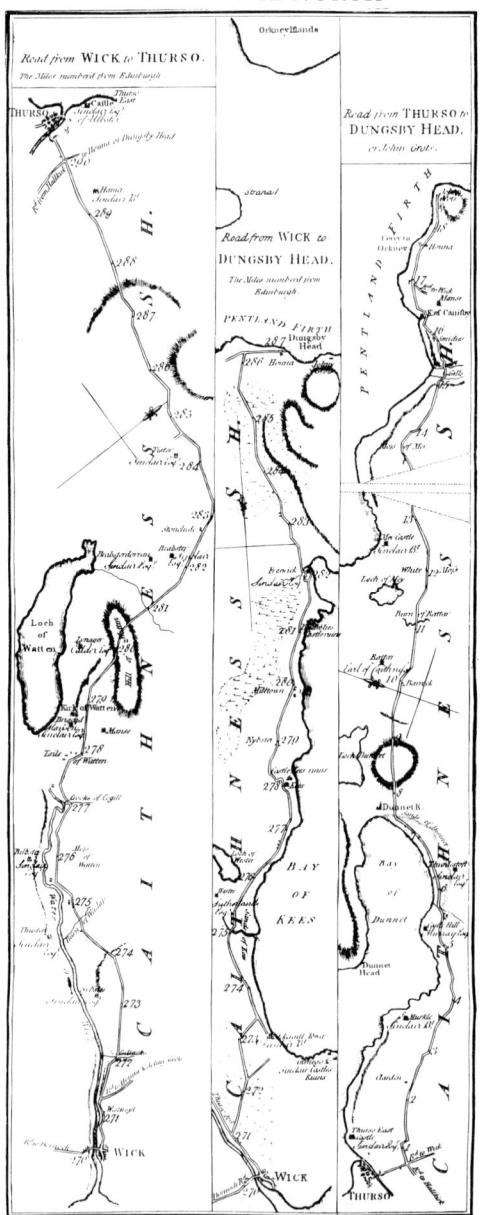

Fig 18 An early map of roads in the north of Scotland, Wick to Thurso, Wick to Duncansby, Thurso to Duncansby from Taylor-Skinner's Road Book, 1776.
(Courtesy Margaret Brown).

IMPROVEMENT

statutory service of six days' work at roads was found so unprofitable and oppressive, that an Act *(33 Geo. III., cap. 120)* was obtained in 1793 to commute the statute labour into a money payment by occupants of land, at the rate of 30s sterling for every £100 Scots of valuation held by them, by cottagers and the inhabitants of towns at the current rate of wages for the six days work. This would produce about £500.

In 1803 an Act *(46 Geo. III., cap. 80)* was passed, appropriating £20,000 for that year towards making roads and bridges in the North of Scotland, 'whereby its fisheries may be encouraged, and the industry of the inhabitants greatly promoted.' It being provided that one-half the cost of the roads and bridges shall be paid by the county or district .

In 1806 an Act *(46 Geo. III., cap. 138)* was passed, authorising making six roads in the county of Caithness, of which one-half was to be paid by the Parliamentary Commissioners under the previous Act of 1803, and the other half by the county. Of these six roads, one only, that from the Ord to Wick, and thence to Thurso, and known as the Parliamentary Road, was made under this Act – half the cost amounting to £16,437 9s 9d, having been paid by the owners of lands throughout the county.[1]

Thus was accomplished the seeming miracle by which a potty little burgh, located in the very far north of Britain, rouping its customs for as little as £10 per annum in 1800, was transformed over three decades into a 'large and thriving town', the 'greatest fishing station in the world', about whch Sam Smiles was enthusing in 1862. Wick had found itself at the centre of a quite extraordinary programme of improvement, thrust forward by the drive and determination of such high-powered improvers as Sir John Sinclair, Sir William Pulteney and Thomas Telford and financed from unprecedented expenditures by government and the rich landowners of the area.

(continued from foot of previous page) (as bogs often are). It is the subject of the little collection of *Strange Tales of Causeymire* by Archie Sinclair, Wick (1988). The road now forms part of the A895 from Georgemas to Latheron.
1 Calder, op cit, pp 276-277

ADDENDUM

Sir John set out his whole programme of ideas for improvement in 'The Northern Parts of Scotland' in a remarkable set of twelve *Essays on Miscellaneous Subjects,* published by 'T Cadell Jun, and W Davies in the Strand' in 1802, referring to some measures already accomplished or launched, and others still to be put in hand. It is not possible here to examine the detailed contents of these well written and technically very varied issues, but a list of the topics covered provides some idea of the scope and generous intentions of the owner of an extensive estate in northern Scotland, himself. The topic headings of the twelve essays are:

I   Observations on the Nature and Advantages of Statistical Inquiries; with the Sketch of an Introduction to the proposed Analysis of the Statistical Account of Scotland [The first Statistical Account, of course, had already been published.]

II   Observations on the Means of enabling a Cottager to keep a cow, by the Produce of a small Portion of Arable Land.

III   Hints as to the Advantages of old Pastures, and on the Conversion of Grass Lands into Tillage.

IV   Hints regarding Cattle.

V   On the improvement of British Wool; containing the Substance of an Address to a Society constituted in Edinburgh for that purpose, on Monday, January 31, 1791. [This refers to his British Wool Society].

VI   Address to the Board of Agriculture, on the Cultivation and Improvement of the Waste Lands of the Kingdom, presented to the Board by Sir John Sinclair (then President) on the 17th November, 1795.

VII   Substance of a Speech in a Committee of the Whole House [of Commons] on improving the System of Private Bills of Inclosure, and the Resolutions of the Select Committee upon that Subject. [Sir John failed completely to get this measure going.].

VIII   Hints regarding certain Measures calculated to improve an extensive Property, more especially applicable to an Estate in the Northern Parts of Scotland. [This was his own estate of 100,000 acres, for at this time, Sinclair of Ulbster had the largest estate in north Scotland, and was intent upon wholesale improvement. Among the measures discussed were:

IMPROVEMENT

1 Agricultural improvements – new ploughs, seeded grass-land, drainage of boggy land, cattle farming, sheep farming, farm buildings, leases, tree planting.

2 Miscellaneous improvements – commerce, manufacturers [Sir John's favourite project in this connection was flax growing and linen manufacture], fisheries – *'There is probably, no district in Europe better calculated for carrying on the fisheries, either in point of profit, variety or extent, than Caithness'.*

– mining for copper, lead and marble, roads and bridges, harbours, new villages.

For our purposes, the most interesting of his radical proposals was contained in an Appendix to this Essay No. VIII: *1, On the means of establishing the Dutch Mode of catching and of curing Herring; 2 On the Variety of Fish caught in the Northern Ports of Scotland; and, 3, On the Means of Promoting the Fisheries in the North.* This Appendix is referred on p 284-286 below, Chapter 11, *Clupea harengus harengus.*

IX   Account of the Origin of the Board of Agriculture, and its progress for three years after its establishment, originally drawn up, on 1796.

X   Proposals for Establishing by Subscription a new Insitution, to be called the Plough; or Joint Stock Farming and [an] Experimental Society for Ascertaining the Principles of Agricultural Improvement.

XI   Letter to the Proprietor of an Extensive Property, on the Means of promoting the Comfort, and improving the Situation, of the People in his Neighbourhood. [This study of the Ulbster estates and its opportunities for improvement takes the form of a letter to Sir John himself].

XII On Longevity. Sir John's conclusions as to the benefits that the kind of improvement he advocates is that those involved could live longer and happier lives: *such is the substance of the observations which have occurred to me on this interesting subject. I shall conclude with remarking, that on the whole, it is more than probable, by proper attention and good management, persons in general, might not only live longer, but might enjoy life with more relish, than is commonly the case at present; and it is to be hoped that, in respect of this, as well as other particulars, that human nature is still on the threshold of acquirement, that it will obtain yet greater and more important acquisition of knowledge, and may reach further improvement, both with regard to the extent of personal and mental gratifications, which our species may be found capable of enjoying, and also the means of possessing them, with more satisfaction and comfort, and for a much longer period of time.*

CHAPTER 10

RELIGION

LIFE for ordinary folk in eighteenth century Caithness was hardly idyllic. Its routines were simple, repetitious and people seldom moved far from home. Much time was spent in hard daily toil in the fields, from which men, women and children retired at the day's end to dingy, smoky, task-ridden homes in which to feed, rest and love. The seasons here were wayward and less propitious for outdoor sport and merry-making of the kind than is sometimes represented as the way of village life in the south. Southern commentators on the northern scene were apt to characterise Highlanders, among whom they included Caithnessians and Sutherlanders, as slothful, backward and resistant to 'improvement'.

Conditions of life in the north of Scotland were undeniably harder, offering perhaps less colour and variety than in places south. Excitements that had once enlivened the scene, such as cattle raids and lairdly feuds, the march of volunteers for the '15 and '45, had now been abolished. Pennant drew attention to the 'great servitude of the people', and it is true that there was a vast difference between the material standards of the common folk and the lairds. Pennant notices, however, that the people feed well, and William Sutherland in his *Wick 1794* survey comments that 'this parish is abundantly able to supply itself with provisions of all kinds'. He adds a mouth-watering list of home-grown provender cheaply available in the parish, including 'enough of malt, and too much whiskey, which is prejudicial to the morals and constitutions of many'.

Variety was provided by the customary celebrations of births, marriages and funerals. Weddings in particular usually lasted several days, with fun and food for all in the locality, with whisky and ale flowing freely. These were occasions for wearing finery. The Rev Sutherland comments on the fondness of the young men and women for dress; whereas at one time folk had to do with the 'common stuff' of the 'housewife's own manufacture', they 'are not now satisfied without good English cloth, muslin gowns, white stockings, silk ribbands etc. particularly at fairs, weddings, and other public appearances.' Servants now insist on a decent allowance for hats and shoes. 'This turn for dress,' continues Mr Sutherland,

> and the many fairs or markets held in the county, (which being called after some saint, as the Marymass, Fergusmass, Magnusmass, Petermass, etc. seem to be the remains of holy days observed in Roman Catholic times), draw servants away from a proper attention to their own business, and make them very unprofitable assistants to the farmer. In regard to amusements, they are extravagantly fond of dancing in Caithness, especially about the time of Christmas and the new year, when almost every town, or village, keeps a day in honour of the tutelar saint of the place, and devotes it to mirth and jollity.

When Utilitarian benefactors spoke of raising the 'happiness' of the people by 'improvement', they had less in mind the quips, cranks, wanton wilies and tripping of the light fantastic toe on which Mr Sutherland was reporting (in a somewhat deprecating tone), than the solid material benefits of devoted industriousness. Life in old Wick parish was not entirely an endless round of gloom and discomfort.

PARISH LIFE IN THE NORTH OF SCOTLAND

One ingredient in the life of Wick and of Caithness generally not unduly emphasised by contemporary commentators is that of religion. Sutherland writes of the 'good moderate, and peaceable dispositions' of the parishioners of Wick, 'not ignorant of the principles, nor inattentive to the practice, of religion'. Donald Sage, who wrote *Memorabilia Domestica, or Parish Life in the North of Scotland* in 1840,[1] reveals a rather similar picture of religion in the whole of the north of Scotland during the years towards the end of the eighteenth century and beginning years of the nineteenth. Sage portrays religion as a present, useful, but not passionate, concern of the people. His account gives few indications throughout the territory of intense religious feeling or commitment, among the people, the gentry or the ministers themselves. Little here in the far north was to be found of the dead embers, let alone the furies of past religious controversies between Scots, covenanting, 'succession' or 'anti-burgherism'; a touching acceptance by the folk of such service and comforts as could be administered by a conscientious parish minister – where there was

1 Rev Donald Sage: *Memorabilia Domestica, or Parish Life ijn the North of Scotland*, Edited by his son; Wick, W Rae (1889).

RELIGION

one; occasional outbursts of hostility towards ministers who exhibited too much 'Whiggish' zeal in trying to convert them from their old ways; appreciation of such ministers – few and far between – capable of preaching a good, enjoyable, hell-fire sermon.

Episode after episode testifying to the difficulties and uncertainties of ministry in the northern counties is recounted by Mr Sage during the incumbencies of his paternal grandfather, Eneas, minister of Lochcarron from 1726 to 1774, who died 'in the 88th year of his age and 48th of his ministry', and of his father, Alexander, minister successively in Dirlot, Caithness, Dornoch and then Kildonan in Sutherland, from 1784 to 1824. His maternal grandfather was a minister in these parts, so were the fathers of Donald's own two wives. None of these gentlemen had an easy time, nor does Mr Sage convey the impression that their ministries were wholly successful in improving significantly the moral standards of members of their flocks. One reason could well have been the manifest, consciously cultivated class distinction between shepherd and sheep. The ministers' houses, stipends and living standards, though not lavish, were handsomely better than those of most villagers. During the clearances in Sutherland in the first decade of the nineteenth century, sympathy, more support and help for the ejected families from their ministers might not have come amiss. With honourable exceptions, most ministers went along with the merciless landlords. Alexander Sage was himself a tacksman, disposing of several small rentals in Kildonan village, occasionally earning hostility on this account, especially as his tack included the mill.

As for the gentry, most were fairly indifferent – again with honourable exceptions – to the religious state of the people. Their chief concern as often as not was to ensure that their contributions should be kept to a minimum. Sardonically, Sage tells how even his grandfather, an earnest labourer in the vineyard, took part in the extinction of a parish by combining the two parishes of Suddie and Kilmuir, Wester (Ross) so that 'the heritors might not be burdened with the payment of a stipend to each minister'. The plan, says Sage, 'was readily countenanced by the Presbytery [of Chanonry], and by none of the members more so than by my grandfather who was clerk.'

Although from time to time concerned about religion in the nation, the government was not especially generous in helping to sustain the church, either in the way of funds for the building and maintenance of churches, or for the payment of stipends. The Scottish Reformation settlements of 1560 and 1567 ostensibly handed over the control and management of the church to the 'people', but they deprived it of most of the revenues that the former Catholic church had traditionally enjoyed.[1] Main church funds now had to come from people's pence and it was expected that the nobility and local gentry would assist the presbyteries to financial solvency. Whatever happened elsewhere in Scotland, the gentry of the north were less than generous in their support. In central parts of Ross, Sutherland and Caithness, distances, inhospitable terrain, lack of candidates for ministry and sheer lack of money forced the presbyteries to combine parishes and where, for whatever reason, no minister could be put in, 'missions' were set up, usually attached to a regular parish but often a long way from it. Alexander Sage's service at Dirlot in the 1780s was such an appointment, and Donald himself did a stint as missionary in Achness of Strathnaver. He writes about the system:

> Missions, particularly in the Highlands and Islands of Scotland, were of very long standing, for I was the seventh and last in succession of the missionaries appointed to officiate at Achness . . . . The object of the Church in establishing these missions was to supply the almost total lack of ministerial service in the extensive parishes of the north. Parishes of forty, fifty, and even sixty miles in length are there of frequent occurrence, and both the larger and smaller parishes are absurdly divided. The principle adopted in settling the bounds was not, evidently, to take into account the distance from, or proximity of, the population to any place of worship erected for them, but solely as to include the landed property of the heritors of the district. This was called a parish, and in many cases it exceeded in extent many whole counties in the south. Missions were established for whom it was a physical impossibility to attend the parish church.

As for official financial support for 'missionary-ministers', there were two recognised external sources: the General Assembly's Committee for Managing the Royal Bounty, set up earlier in the eighteenth century, its disbursements maintained by an annual grant of £2000 from 'the last Sovereigns of the House of Hanover'; and the Christian Knowledge Society, established in 1701 to send forth

---

1 Much to the disgruntlement of Knox the Reformed church was 'forced to make do with a compromise settlement reached early in 1562; only a third of the income from benefices of the Catholic clergy was released and the Protestant ministers had to share even that with the crown.' See Michael Lynch, op cit. p 200.

ministers, catechists and schoolmasters, each in their respective departments of moral and religious usefulness in the Highlands and Islands of Scotland.' As a missionary Donald Sage drew a salary of £50. Just before he came to Achness occurred the first Sutherland clearance of 1814. He preached his last sermon at Achness just before the greatest and most ruthless clearance of all, when over a thousand people were expelled from Strathnaver, their homes burned in some cases virtually over their heads. Sage tells in graphic detail some of the horrors and infamies perpetrated by Patrick Sellar and his men on that final day in April, 1819, all in the name and with the authority of *Ban-mhorair-Chatta*, the heartless and grasping Countess of Sutherland.

It does not appear that the Rev Sage was able to do much, or sought to do much, to aid his 'poor and defenceless flock' when the 'dark hour of trial came'. Pious resignation and acknowledgment of the 'mighty hand of God in the matter' seems to have been his chief advice to the victims. There were, he says, some 'who were strangers to such exalted and ennobling impressions of the gospel', and who 'breathed deep and muttered curses on the heads of the persons who subjected them to such treatment. The more reckless portion of them,' he goes on to deplore, 'realised the character of the impenitent in all ages, and indulged in the most culpable excesses, even while this divine punishment was still suspended over them.'

Now on his way to Aberdeen, well away from all this, to take up an appointment as minister to the Gaelic Chapel there, he concludes:

> The Strathnaver Clearance of 1819 dissolved my connection with my first congregration, and extinguished a ministerial charge in that part of the Highlands. The Assembly's committee for the Royal Bounty, on being certified of the removal not only of their missionary but of his whole congregation along with him, withdrew the stipend and dissolved the mission.

It is doubtful if the ministers of these northern parishes, including some dedicated but also, if Sage is to be believed, quite a number of less than fully committed pastors, were able greatly to improve the moral tone of the people. If the meekness which Sage commends to those expelled from their lands by the Sutherlands is an indication, it may be argued that one effect of more earnest ministry was to tame the pugnacious spirit of the natives just at a time when greater militancy was called for. Some ministers themselves, including the Sages, had experienced such pugnacity, as when great-grandfather

Sage, as minister of Lairg was invested by the county sheriff 'with power to inflict corporal punishment' on his parishioners. Grandfather Eneas on one occasion avoided assassination by a fugitive from Cumberland's butcheries with cunning and kindness, as he rode his horse on the road to Dingwall. Father Alexander quelled a mutiny on the part of pupils in school, some as big as himself (for ministers often took school), who conspired to flog him as mercilessly as he had flogged them. 'The onset was so sudden,' says the chronicler,

> so unexpected, that for a moment, he offered no resistance. But his apparent passiveness was but as the calm which is the prelude to the storm. With his ponderous arm he dealt heavy blows on his assailants, and, in a few minutes, cleared the schoolroom. The lesson of subordination which he so impressively taught was not forgotten so long as he filled the office, and he received from his pupils ever afterwards an implicit obedience.

That the flock were capable of resistance to what they might regard as high-handedness on the part of priests and patrons is illustrated by the story Donald Sage tells of the men of Assynt, who objected strongly to the appointment as their minister, of a certain Duncan MacGillivray on the say-so of the patrons, Lord and Lady Stafford (the Sutherlands), who did not bother at all to consult the parishioners. They requested as their minister John Kennedy, assistant to the former minister who had died, to whom 'they had formed a strong attachment'. The story continues:

> Their request, was, however, peremptorily refused, and Mr MacGillivray was appointed. The Presbytery of Dornoch, therefore, met on the appointed day to settle the presentee. They reckoned, however, without their host. As they were assembled in the manse parlour, with the exception of my father and Mr Keith, and were about to proceed with the settlement, their attention was directed to a strong body of Assynt Highlanders, each armed with a cudgel, who presented themselves to the manse window. As if significantly to express the purpose of the assemblage, each pulled off his neckcloth with one hand, and wielded his cudgel with the other, and loudly demanded the compearance of the Presbytery. The members resolved to go out and remonstrate with the rioters, but it would not do. The mob which now assembled told them

through their leaders that the only way by which they could escape broken bones was that each should get to his nag with all convenient speed, nor slack bridle till they had crossed the boundaries of the parish, for they were determined that the presentee on that day, nor on any other day, be settled minister of Assynt. To this peremptory condition the Presbytery members were compelled to submit, and each and all of them, together with the presentee, his wife, family and furniture, were sent back the way they came, closely followed by the men of Assynt.

Laconically, Sage ends the tale, showing just how ineffectual in the long run was people power when faced with that of the Sutherlands. The Sutherlands' nominee came back and was confirmed, but, Sage adds drily:

> This affray was productive of consequences obstructive to the subsequent usefulness of Mr MacGillivray in the parish. The ringleaders were discovered, tried before a Justiciary Court at Inverness, and, in spite of the earnest entreaties of their pastor, sentenced to nine months' imprisonment.

Though not immediately relevant to affairs in Wick, the memoirs of Donald Sage provide the best picture we have of the ecclesiastical regime prevailing in the north in these critical times. Sage does in fact refer several times to William Sutherland, minister in Wick, whom he encounters on occasion during his peregrinations. His Achness assignment rendered him fairly peripatetic. He tells how in 1818, a year before his expulsion from Achness, while on a visit to Thurso,

> late on Saturday evening, an express arrived from Mr. Phin, minister at Wick, who administered the sacrament on the same day, very earnestly craving assistance, as those whom he had engaged to officiate had taken ill. I rode to Wick on Sabbath morning and arrived there to breakfast. After Mr. Phin had, very ably indeed preached the action sermon I served the tables alternately with him, when he concluded with an exhortation. I preached also on Monday both in the forenoon and afternoon. The services of the Sabbath and weekday on that occasion at Wick were conducted in the open air, as the parish church was then in a ruinous state, the foundation having some years before given way, and rents having appeared in the back wall. The church itself was comparatively new, having been erected, after a long litigation with the heritors, during the incumbency

of Mr. Phin's immediate predecessor, Mr Sutherland.

Sage provides a few more facts about the state of affairs in Wick at this time. 'The foundation' of the church, he says

> was unsound, and the building soon gave way. The consequence of this was, that the heritors were under the necessity, very soon thereafter, of erecting a new church at an enormous expense. Mr. Phin was then married and had two of a family, a son and a daughter. His wife was a daughter of Bailie Macleay of Wick, a native of Invergordon, and in his younger years ferryman there. From this humble sphere he rose rapidly to wealth and distinction, after having emigrated to Caithness. Mr. Phin, his son-in-law, was a popular preacher, and popularity he very much affected. His sermons were very excellent, but the best of them were said to be borrowed; the people of Wick said, 'He's a guid man, oor minister, an' a' the things we hear frae him on the Sawbath we can read in godly authors when we come hame.'

The Editor of Sage's memoirs, his son, Donald Fraser Sage, adds two informative footnotes to his father's account of the Wick visit:

> 1 Mr W Sutherland, AM (whose father and grandfather were eminent ministers in Ross-shire), was ordained minister of Wick on 1st May, 1765. He got the parish church rebuilt in 1799. He was a man of great tact and unbounded hospitality, but had considerable trouble with obdurate heritors. In public prayer he used to intercede 'for the magistrates of Wick, *such as they are.*' He died 23rd June, 1816 in the 79th year of his age and 52nd of his ministry. His son, the Hon. Jas. Sutherland, became judge, and member of the Council, Bombay, where he lived in princely style. His daughter Elizabeth was married to James Miller, Esqre., merchant in Leith and St. Petersburg; their son, the late Sir William Miller, Bart. of Manderston; his daughter Christian was married to Mr. Mackintosh, minister of Thurso. His wife, Catherine Anderson, by whom he had a large family, died 3rd October, 1813.

> 2 Mr. Robert Phin was ordained assistant and successor to Mr. Sutherland, 13th March, 1813. He was a man of energy, and had a new parish church erected in 1830; he died 22nd March, 1840, aged 63 years. Dr Kenneth Macleay Phin, minister of Galashiels, who became, latterly, a conspicuous ecclesiastic in the present Established Church of Scotland, was his son.

William Macleay was one of the two senior bailies who chaired Wick Burgh Council meetings during the absences of Sir John Sinclair, Provost, and signed the minutes. Here again is borne out the impression, left by Donald Sage, that the north of Scotland ministry of these times was a virtual 'closed shop', ministers' sons following as ministers, ministers marrying other ministers' daughters or, if stepping outside ministerial relationship, marrying into the local merchant or heritors' families the *petit* or *haut bourgeoisie,* as Lynch calls them. Working men's sons seldom gained entry to the profession, doubtless one of the reasons why so often minister and flock were out of tune with one another.

Another was undoubtedly the huge disparity between the educational standards of shepherd and sheep. Uniformly the many ministers whose lives, incumbencies and characters Donald Sage so meticulously – and critically – records, attended and graduated from one of the two Aberdeen colleges, while several, including himself, had a spell at Edinburgh. Sage's account of his life as a student in Marischal College from 1805 to 1809 is not the least interesting element of his memoirs; his salty comments on the professors are usually less than complimentary, and they reveal something of the spirit of diffidence on their part towards revealed religious 'truth' that was clearly running through the theological, as well as other departments, of Scottish universities in the late eighteenth century. This was the generation succeeding the days of such great Scottish sceptics and empiricists as David Hume, Adam Smith and Joseph Black. Though in his book Sage frequently protests the purity and depth of his own faith, it is evident in much of his writing that he was not untouched himself by the half-belief of his age.

Popish Practices and Places

Two other main aspects of the general religious scene in north Scotland need to be mentioned before we leave it. Both are essential to understanding the history of the church in Wick, or in any locality in this area. The first has to do with the lingering, well into the eighteenth century, of old 'popish' sentiments, if not belief. The second must be some reference to the strange movements of dissent that caused division and conflict within the Scottish church, especially those of the eighteenth and nineteenth centuries.

Acceptance here of Presbyterian principles in place of the old faith was a more sluggish and protracted business than in the south. Looking back to the later years of the previous century, Mr Sage tells of Angus McBean, minister of Inverness (of whom it was 'refreshing' to Sage to claim as his great-great grandfather), the 'subject of a popish sovereign' [James VII and II], and an eye-witness of James's 'insidious efforts to restore popery' who 'bore an undaunted testimony against it; and finding that even within the limits of his own charge at Inverness were to be found the abettors of popery, he considered it his duty to resign his charge.' McBean continued to preach reformed principles, and was hauled before the Privy Council which had him imprisoned for 'insubordination and treason'. His imprisonment ruined his health and shortly after being released McBean died at the age of 33.

Mr Sutherland reported in *Wick 1794* remnants of popish practices in the Wick area, mentioning in particular the chapel of St Tears where 'some old people, even within these few years, were so superstitious, that they thought it their duty to retire for their devotions . . . . and there leave small gifts of bread and cheese etc.'

In his *Ecclesiastical History* the Rev Donald Beaton comments on what he considers the reason for the late turning of Caithnessians to the new faith. 'The work of Knox,' he says,

> while accepted with genuine enthusiasm by multitudes of the Scottish people, was by others accepted simply as a new order of things which had gained the day. This Laodicean spirit manifested itself particularly in the outlying districts of the kingdom. There is abundant evidence to show that Caithness fell into line with the party of progress and liberty, but this evidence does not allow us to conclude that the Reformation doctrines were received with enthusiasm in these northern parts. Bishop Stewart [the reigning Bishop of Caithness at the time of the Reformation] . . . accepted the new doctrines; and in 1563 a commission was given him 'to plant kirks'.[1]

A similar commission was given to Robert Pont (father of the mapmaker) to 'plant kirks in the shiredom of Innerness and the

---

1 Rev Donald Beaton: *Ecclesiastical History of Caithness and Annals of Caithness Parishes;* Free Presbyterian Church, Wick; Wm Rae, Wick (1909), p 107. The vandalism of the Knox reformers in this respect is a prime cause of the paucity of documentation on some aspects of mediaeval history, making the writing of some periods of Scottish history very difficult. Church histories in Scotland tend to begin in the mid sixteenth century, as does Mr Beaton's work, except for the assiduously collected but scrappy material of the first chapters.

countreis adjacent'. Donald Monro was required 'to doe the like within the bounds of Rosse', and the Bishop of Orkney, like Stewart of Caithness, was given a 'yeere, to plant kirks etc'. The necessity for this programme was dictated by the compulsive urge of the reformers to destroy everything, rituals, buildings, works of art, books and monastic records that had anything to do with 'popery', so that many churches and chapels left standing were taken out of use. The old churches were, in any case, not in the least suitable for the new rite from which ceremonial before the altar was abolished and the pulpit became the focus of the congregation's attention. Sermons, instruction, exhortation and prayer, especially of the extempore kind, took the place of chanting, incantation and the mass.

In the place of the mediaeval churches were erected the characterless little barn-like kirks, so common in the Scottish countryside, usually topped by a bell turret for a single bell (for bell-ringing – where it existed – went out too) to call the faithful to prayer. Sage gives a touching picture of the building of a new parish kirk in his childhood home village:

> When my father was settled at Kildonan, the church used was a small popish building, thatched with heather. At its west end was the burial place of the chiefs of the clan Gunn, *MicSheumais Chattaich*, as they were styled, and who, under the Earls of Sutherland, ever since the middle of the thirteenth century, had held lands in the parish, where they also had their principal residence. Their mortuary chapel was a small window with a Gothic window, attached to the church, and entered by a low arched door. About a year after my father came to Kildonan, this venerable fabric was taken down, and a new church erected on the same site according to a plan by James Boag, a church architect of repute. The building may be described thus. The front wall contained two large windows, reaching from half a foot from the eaves to within three feet of the foundation. On each side of these windows were doors leading into the floor of the church, and, within two feet of each of these southern doors, were two small windows. In the gables half-way up the walls were gallery doors, each surmounted with a window nearly its own size, and separated from it by a lintel common to both. In the back wall was another door entering on the gallery, merely to obviate inner passages. These gallery doors were furnished with flights of outside stone stairs,

which had no parapet, and, instead of being built close to the side of the wall, projected at right angles from it, in the manner of a ladder. As to the inner furnishing of the building, it was regularly seated, and the pulpit stood against the south wall, between the two large windows. It was in the form of a pentagon and panelled. Below it, one on each side, were the only two square seats, the rest, both in the area and in the galleries were pews. The fronts of the galleries were also panelled; the front gallery was three, and the east and west galleries six or seven seats deep. Directly in front of the pulpit below stood the elders' seat, or *lateron,* an area of considerable breadth, which ran nearly from one end of the church to the other, and was accommodated with a seat all along its north side, intended for the poor. The elders sat at the south side of it, and when the communion was dispensed, it was fitted up for the table services, the walls of the church within, as well as the roof, were unplastered, and there was neither bell nor belfry.

'In the parish of Wick,' says Beaton, 'the sites and ruins of early ecclesiastical buildings are . . numerous.' He identifies not less than six going back to pre-Reformation times. The first of which he speaks is that of Kirk Stanes in the Moss of Killimster where was once there was a chapel 'with a foundation of Duthac'. Some stones of the building were (and still are) to be seen with evidences of a burying-ground. He mentions James Oliphant's reference of 1726 to the chapel called 'St Dudock's Church by the Commons', saying that 'it was very difficult of access at any time' on account of its location in boggy ground. Beaton recommends would-be visitors to take the train to Bilbster Station on the Wick Line, now long closed. He goes on to describe it as a former 'centre of superstition', quoting the account of it by the Rev Charles Thomson, minister of Wick, in the *New Statistical Account* of 1840[1], who says that

> Till within a few years, it was customary for all the inhabitants of Mirelandhorn [a richly expressive name for one of the small settlements outside Wick] to visit the Kirk of Moss every Christmas before sunrise, placing on a stone, bread and cheese and a silver coin, which, as they alleged, disappeared in some mysterious way.

'This stone', adds Beaton, 'used to stand in the centre of the burn,

---

1 The *New Statistical Account of Scotland;* Vol XV, Sutherland-Caithness-Orkney-Shetland; Edinburgh, Wm Blackwood (1845), p 161.

and part of it was removed by Mr Thomson [presumably in an effort to discourage the continuance of such a *Popish* practice – Thomson still uses this opprobrious term]'. He mentions, too, the tradition 'that there was once a monastery at Killimster, but its site cannot now be located unless it be the case that the buildings around Duthac's Kirk were monastic.' These had been recently identified by a local antiquarian as two earth houses of uncertain provenance.

Thomson actually goes on to give further evidence of popish superstition in Caithness:

> There are still several holy lochs, especially one at Dunnet, to which the people go from Wick, and, indeed, from all parts of Caithness, to be cured of their diseases. They cast a penny into the water, walk or are carried widdershins around the loch, and return home. If they recover, their cure is ascribed to the mystic virtues of the *Halie Loch*; and if they do not, their want of faith gets all the blame.

Beaton next describes the chapel of St Tears, which has already been mentioned (pp 76-77), demolished but still identifiable by lines of the foundation. He believes that 'the chapel was evidently of the larger type of such buildings found in Caithness. It appears,' he says, 'to mark the foundation of a chapel by one of the early Celtic missionaries, Drostan by name, whose missionary labours in Caithness are commemorated in a number of chapels'. The story of this chapel with the feud between the Gunns and Keiths has also been told (pp 72-78). Bishop Forbes found the place on his walk along the shore during his brief stay at Ackergill as guest of Sir William Dunbar of Hempriggs and wrote of it:

> the Ruines of a very singular littel Chapel of stone and mortar, without any Lime, and without Windows either in the east or west gable, all the windows being in the South Wall. It is called the Chapel of St Tear, and the country people to this very day, assemble here in the morning of the Feast of the Holy Innocents and say their Prayers, bringing their Offerings along with them, some Bread, others Bread and Cheese, others Money etc., and putting these into Holes in the Walls. In the afternoon they get Music – a Piper and Fiddler – and dance on the Green where the Chapel stands. The roof is off, but the walls are almost all entire. One of the late presbyterian preachers of Wick thought to have abolished this old practice; and for that end appointed a Diet of catechising in that corner of the Parish upon

the day of the Holy Innocents, but no-one attended him; all went as usual to St Tear's Chapel. I saw the Font-Stone for Baptism lying on the Green at the East End of the Chapel. Mr Sutherland, of Wester, observed that no doubt it had been called the Chapel of St Tear from the Tears of the Parents and other Relations of the murdered Innocents.[1]

Beaton writes too of the Chapel of St Ninian. The location of this mediaeval chapel, 'probably the first building in Caithness used for Christian worship', is uncertain. He speculates as to whether or not the building, which 'at least takes us back to the missionary labours of Ninian in the beginning of the fifth century', was near the Wick river bridge or on the North Head above Wick. The 'Service Bridge' site is favoured by Beaton, but there is not much evidence of the chapel's locations or, for that matter, its existence.[2]

The next earliest church building in Wick is identified as the chapel of St. Fergus, whose existence is certain, but again is doubtful as to site. It is usually 'assigned to Mount Hooly', mainly on the strength of the name of 'Hooly (Hellie or Halie)' which 'seems to indicate the existence of a church or chapel'. Beaton mentions too the discovery of foundations of a building in the Temperance Hall Park which was in the vicinity of Mount Heely, together with what was said to be a baptismal font.[3] It was, however, just as probable, thought Beaton that

---

1 See J B Craven, op cit p 272.

2 The 'Service Bridge' referred to by Beaton was the bridge, since replaced, immediately above the new dock area of Wick as part of the construction work undertaken during the years from 1806 onwards. The evidence quoted by Beaton is flimsy but interesting in its own right:
> The earliest references which have as yet been discovered, that seem to point to the lcoation of the Chapel and what is meant by the Head of Wick Bay, are found in the Wick Burgh records. For 9th September, 1663, the Records have an entry referring to a proposed combat between 'Alexander Pruntoch, merchant, and William Beib, junior, tailor, who both being drunk in the house of John Nactie, merchant, the said persons undertook a party combat, to have met with their seconds at St Ninian's Head, *below the said burgh*'. From the statement that St Ninian's Head was *below* the burgh of Wick, it would seem to favour the interpretation that locates the Head of Wick Bay at the Service Bridge; for the North Head could scarcely be described as *below* the burgh of Wick. The next entry does not help us much, but it has the advantage that it does not run counter to the clearer evidence in the foregoing extract. On 21st April, certain persons were appointed as watchmen in the burgh, as may be seen in the following record:– 'The day which anent the keeping of a watch within the town, and always until St Ninian's Head, for the Dutch shipping, ordained to be kept by the Earl of Caithness.'

3 Quoting Beaton again:
> A writer in the *Northern Ensign* gives the *(continued on foot of next* page)

it was on or near the site of the present parish church.

Yet other ancient chapels near to Wick are mentioned. The first is that of the chapel of St Mary or Marykirk, as some writers call it, 'directly opposite the spot where the Burn of Haster joins the Wick River'. It was thus on the north bank of the river near where the railway now crosses on a short viaduct. There was evidence of the foundations, and a burying ground; what was believed to be the font, 'lay long at Haster Smithy, [and] is now at Stirkoke House'.

Especially interesting is the extract that Beaton culls from the Kirk-Session of Wick, dated 21 January, 1722, attesting to the difficulty experienced by the Wick minister, then James Oliphant, 'in stamping out superstition' in connection with this chapel:

> This day W-C-, J-F, M-C-, and C-T, being all summoned & compearing were charged wt frequenting Mary Chappell the first Sabbath after the new moon & particularly of being there this day fortnight and superstitiously bowing and kneeling about the Chappell thereby profaning the Lord's Day. W-C- positively denied his being there or frequenting that place on the Lord's Day. The other Three Confest their being there that day that they walked about the Chappel & bowed and kneeled & confest Yr Sorrow for it. The Session considering that they were poor old Ignorant people & that it would be as much if not more for Edification to rebuke you here wt Certification than to bring before ye Congregation they desired the minr might reprove the greatness of yr Sin & ye Evil tendency of it & rebuke you for it with Certification. They being called in were accordingly instructed & rebukt and in order to mair others following their Example, they appointed intimate and told from ye pulput next Lord's Day on any account whatsoever on pain of Church Censure. And appoint the Elders living thereabout by turns to particularly observe yt noe person come to the Chappell on the Sabbath after the new moon and Inform if they

(Continued from previous page)
following interesting piece of information in connection with the above:- 'Before the Reformation, this park or tenement was doubtless in possession of the Bishop of Caithness, as in the titles it is designated the Bishop's land – the north east being specially styled Mount Holy, which includes a portion of the ground immediately opposite to the east side of Shire Lane. After the spulzie of the clergy and division of the spoil, this 'land' was divided, and a strip on the east was called "Brisbane's Tenement" and the larger portion, that on the west "Vicar's Tenement".' See Beaton op cit, pp 53-54.

doe.[1]

The other chapels mentioned were those of St Cuthbert on the Burn of Haster near to the farm of Haster, and one at Thrumster, which Muir also visited in 1861. The stones had recently been removed, but there was evidence of several buildings. The traveller Muir (who wrote *Ecclesiastical Notes*) saw it and gave some description of the chapel's shape and dimensions. The Thrumster chapel had, like the others, been surrounded by a burial ground, visible in Beaton's day to travellers on the Wick to Lybster Railway. It is now encompassed by the Thrumster cemetery, known as the 'Chapel Burying-ground'.

Muir, a visitor of 1861, writes of a 'low circular barrow surrounded by a cairn, and a small burying ground containing traces of a chapel at Thrumster'. Beaton's catalogue continues:

> To the eastwards near the sea at Ulbster, stood the old chapel dedicated to St Martin, which may have had some connection with Ninian, owing to his great admiration for Martin of Tours. The burial-ground around the chapel is very ancient, and it was from this place that the famous Ulbster Stone, already described, was taken to the grounds at Thurso Castle. The chapel was used as far back as 1726 for a tomb for the Sinclairs of Ulbster. It is now closed, but the building is still standing.

Dissent and Secession

In most movements, religious and political, dissent thrives on dissent. The habits of mind engendered by radical break-away do not usually forthwith give way to a new permanent spirit of conformity; a storm as vigorous as the Protestant Reformation in Scotland, which disturbed at their roots the conformities of many centuries, did not subside into seas of doctrinal tranquility. And since the Reformation put into the hands of its congregations the Scriptures, though the veritable source of all truth, it could hardly be expected that there would be no further argument. Scriptures – the writings of the servants of God, nay, as many aver, the very words of God Himself – are notoriously susceptible to varying interpretations and thus disagreement. The Reformation itself was the work of many of the best – and most controversial – minds of the time. It is too much to

---

1 Beaton, op cit pp 55-56.

imagine that later generations of fine and controversial minds could have been be perennially satisfied with the lucubrations of their forefathers; and in any case, the 'authority' of a book is a different commodity from that of an embodied ruler with court and sanctions.

No Moderator of the Church of Scotland could ever expect to command the sort of obedience, *mutatis mutandis*, that the Pope commanded, nor would reasonably aspire to such authority. It can be argued that Knox did thus aspire, but without the decisive backing of the sovereign (which he specially abjured), he was doomed to failure. It may be suggested that the English Church (which generally has taken its religion less seriously), has survived with less dissent than the Scottish (though by no means immune to it), precisely because there was kingly authority behind it, and management exercised by a bench of bishops. Episcopal rule was indeed, the very bane of Scottish ecclesiastical politics.

Be that as it may, the Scottish Presbyterian Church has, until recent times been the subject of many splits. The first major 'dissent' was that of the Covenanters, dissent of course not from the main tenets of Presbyterianism but in *defence of them*. As we have seen, Covenanting as such made little impact in the north of Scotland, though it may be mentioned in passing that the wreck of the *Crown*[1] in Deerness Sound in Orkney in 1679 brought into this area some victims of the persecutors of Covenanters, if not much knowledge of their cause. There is no evidence that the seventeenth century Covenanters or their ideas became a matter of much interest or concern to the presbyteries of Caithness. In Orkney they were regarded as an embarrassment.

Nor did any other kind of dissent shake religion here to its foundations. There is, however, a remark in Sutherland's *Wick, 1794* that may cause some modern readers a little puzzlement. Under his heading, *Religious Persuasions,* Sutherland says: 'Of late, some seceders (antiburghers) have made their appearance, but they are much on the decline, and have at present no settled minister.'

This is a reference back to the 1747 'Anti-Burgher' movement, by

---

1 This was the sinking in Deerness Sound of the ship *Crown*, chartered by the government to deport to Barbados, quite illegally and with considerable brutality, the remnant of two hundred and fifty intransigent Covenanters, taken prisoner at the battle of Bothwell Brig (from a total of 1200), when the Duke of Monmouth destroyed the rebel Covenanting army. They were kept below hatches as the ship broke up, though some escaped but were treated as unwelcome visitors by the authorities in Orkney.

which the 'Seceders' of 1743 themselves split into 'Burghers' and 'Antis', a highly complicated, obscure but bitter dispute that destabilised the Presbyterian Church of Scotland in the middle of the eighteenth century. Many of the Church's problems stemmed from the Union of 1707, by which the affairs of Scotland as a whole became mixed up with those of England. The Presbyterians had been suspicious of the Union from the start, with good reason, for it signified for them the probability of clashes between themselves and the crown, whose wearer (Queen Anne), although a Stewart, was by law, head of the powerful episcopal Church of England – *Defender of the Faith,* no less, a title earned by Henry VIII defending the Catholic Church.

Remembering the various efforts of James VI (and I), both Charleses and the seventh (second) James to put the bishops back into Scotland, the Scots had many apprehensions that it might all begin again. Specific guarantees were included in the Union Act of 1706 that this would not be so, but fears remained. During the next few years there were several developments affecting the integrity of the Presbyterian Church in Scotland. The first was the Greenshields case of 1711, by which the House of Lords was invited to interfere in the case of an episcopalian Scottish minister who had been prosecuted by the Presbyterian Church for using an Anglican prayer book; the immediate upshot of this was the passing in 1712 of the Toleration Act which, among other relaxations, allowed freedom of worship 'to episcopalians willing to pray for the reigning monarch'. This was regarded by many Scots as an unwelcome policy of indulgence forced on them by the 'English' parliament, an impression reinforced by the Patronage Act of the same year. By this the system of preferment to church benefices by 'patrons', that is, local landowners or gentry ('heritors' in Scotland) rather than by kirk sessions and presbyteries, was made permissible (though not compulsory) in Scotland. This struck directly at a central principle of the Presbyterian Church, selection of ministers by church elders representing the congregation.

Reluctantly perhaps, the General Assembly of the Church of Scotland accommodated itself to the changing law, earning for themselves increasing resentment and contempt for what was regarded by various radical and evangelical groups, betrayal of the principles of presbyterianism. Controversy hotted up when in 1722, twelve ministers of one such group, the 'Marrow Brethren', were investigated by the General Assembly, and became even hotter when

RELIGION

in 1732 an evangelically disposed minister of Stirling, Ebenezer Erskine, raised a protest about patronage. Lynch describes the establishment's behaviour as 'the unscrupulous tactics used by the court interest, largely exercised through the royal commissioner to the General Assembly and a team of influential *moderate* churchmen'. Just as the Covenanters before them, champions originally of the rights of the people's church, were marginalised, and eventually suppressed by the conforming majority, the dissenters were pushed to the side, their majority opponents coming to be known, curiously, as the 'Moderates', more or less in favour of toleration, more or less in favour of patronage. The Moderates now represented not the rights of the congregation, but those of heritors and elders. Though a protester in some things, Donald Sage like most of his colleagues, was imbued with 'Moderate' principles, and wrote without disapproving passion of patronage, of which he gives several examples, especially that exercised by the Countess of Sutherland. Patronage had come to be just part of the system in the affairs of the church as was 'superiority' in politics.

The 'Seceders', as they came to be called, were originally a small group of ministers led by Ebenezer Erskine, breaking away from the main congregation of the Presbyterian Church on the sorts of issues already mentioned. To begin with they called themselves the 'Associate Presbytery' and started to attract other dissidents, including the remnants of Covenanting groups who were meeting in 1743, to celebrate the centenary of the Solemn League and Convenant. As Lynch puts it:

> Seceders were the most important of the dissenters of the eighteenth century, not least because their position seemed to point towards a new, fragmented world of dissenting congregations, but they actually belonged firmly in the Convenanting past. They were, as a result, both a haven for more refugees from patronage disputes and a disruptive force within the increasingly complex diaspora of presbyterian dissent.

In no time dissenters started dissenting from dissent. As a result of the alarms of the '45, as we have seen in Wick, burgh burgesses began taking oaths of loyalty, probably following the example of the large burghs of Edinburgh, Glasgow and Perth. In 1747 an 'Anti-Burgher' group split off from the parent group of seceders, reckoning that the taking of such oaths constituted recognition, not just of the

Hanoverian monarchy, but also of the 'Moderates' and government's fell intentions to suppress genuine presbyterianism.

During the rest of the century dissent continued. Evangelism grew, following the example set in England by George Whitefield and the Wesleys, and exacerbating the patronage controversy. In 1761 was formed the Relief Church, offering 'relief of Christians oppressed in their Christian privileges'. At no time, however, did the movement of dissent seriously threaten the hegemony of the General Assembly of the established Presbyterian Church, which drew strength from its admitted close connection with government. Not only was the government represented in the councils of the Assembly in the person of royal commissioners; as we have seen in the case of Wick, the burghs also began sending 'commissioners' to the annual Assembly, usually a senior elder of the kirk in that burgh. From Wick was sent repeatedly to Glasgow, Councillor James Horne, Writer to the Signet, senior elder of St Fergus parish kirk. The term 'anti-burgher' came to be accepted as a generic name for presbyterians not accepting the rule of the General Assembly, growing in numbers, but not at this stage, offering a dangerous threat to the authority of the established church.

Such a threat, however, did develop in the new century. The evangelicals began to gain more and more support in the rapidly growing industrial towns, just as Wesleyanism thrived in Lancashire and South Wales; the dissenters were, in fact, more in touch with the lives of the people, and more sympathetic to their sufferings and needs than most ministers of the established church. In the early 1830s the evangelicals gained a majority in the General Assembly, which began to take steps to remedy some of the disabilities under which they considered established religion was now labouring in Scotland, in particular, the matter of patronage. An Act of Veto was passed in the Assembly which would have given a local congregation the right to veto the appointment by a patron of an 'intruder', that is, an incumbent of whom congregation and elders had not approved. The politics and manoeuvres that followed are too complicated for consideration here. They involved, to begin with, a particular case of appointment by patronage, vetoed by elders, then taken to the Court of Session in Edinburgh and from there to the House of Lords.

The 'compromise' arrangements resulting from all this drawn out action was accepted by the Assembly, but led by an earnest and fiery dissenter, Thomas Chalmers, a large number of ministers withdrew from membership of the Assembly in 1843, to set up a new Free

Church. This event has come to be known as the 'Disruption'. These seceders, ministers and laity, thus excluded themselves from the established church and during its early years the ministers held their services 'anywhere they could, including barns, gravel pits, makeshift boats and at least one disused public house.'

Thus came into existence an alternative national church, one that later gained considerable support in Wick, or rather, Pulteneytown, for it was here that the new congregations were to be found. We return to this topic in a later chapter, and to the story of the Wick parish church later; but two shrewd comments on these events by the historian Michael Lynch are worth quoting before we leave matters at this juncture. The first refers to the general background to dissent in the north of Scotland:

> There was little dissent on the surface of the Established Church in the late eighteenth-century Highlands, but it had already within it the seeds of separation. Paradoxically, a greater social division already existed within the Highland Church than in the Lowlands, which had seen a series of splits and secessions from the 1740s onwards. Moderate ministers represented the landowners, their factors and the wealthier single tenants; increasingly evangelicals spoke for the crofters and cottars. A disruption had already taken place, in all but name, long before 1843.[1]

The story told by Donald Sage amply bears out this thesis. Free Church sentiment burgeoned in the western isles, and gained a considerable following too in Caithness and Orkney, where several parishes went over, minister, laity and all, to the Free Church. As for the broader and later picture, Lynch's summary is also very revealing:

> The Free Church, according to Chalmers, was intended as a national establishment, committed to the goal of a Christian commonwealth. But it was a child of the age of religious revivals .... Its Evangelicals drew inspiration alike from events like the 'awakening' at Kilsyth [one of the centres of revival both in 1743 and the 1830s]. It had the inspiration of a local, gathered church and the ambition to be a national and highly centralised organisation. After 1847 the Free Church moved away from Chalmers's vision of a Christian Commonwealth. Inevitably, the drive to establish itself began to wane. Its

---

1 See Michael Lynch, op cit. p 365.

working-class members grew tired of its incessant demands for contribution, however small. The sneer of the Established Church – 'Money! money! money! with the Free Church is everything' – had some substance to it. By the 1860s, the Free Church was as thoroughly middle-class, in both its eldership and ethos, as the Established Church, although there is room for wondering, on the basis of an analysis of elders in Aberdeen, whether it was *petit* or *haut bourgeois*. Only in the Highlands, where Clearances in the years after 1846 and the Crofters' Wars in the 1880s provided a vehicle for religion with a more sympathic face, did the Free Church break out of the embrace of respectable middle-class morality.[1]

Episcopals

In their origins, Wick church and parish, were as 'episcopal' as any other in Scotland. Until 1560, Roman Catholicism was the religion of the state, and Protestants were unwelcome and persecuted; only seven Scottish Protestants were executed for their faith, but when it came in by Act of Parliament in 1560, the regime of the reformed faith was absolute. The authority of the Pope in Scotland was abolished; the Latin mass was forbidden; and Knox's *Confession of Faith, First Book of Discipline,* and *The Book of Common Order* provided the basis for an entirely new and austere religious regime, very much more radical and severe than the 'botched-up compromises and equivocal half measures' that prevailed in England.

As another historian so succinctly puts it

> Henceforth the Church of Scotland was governed not by a hierarchy of Bishops and Archibishops but by Kirk Sessions of lay elders and later by district Presbyteries, possessing the power to ordain the Ministers. The General Assembly of the Kirk, meeting once or twice a year to settle questions affecting the Church as a whole, soon become a forum for Scottish opinion on secular as well as on ecclesiastical matters. Every parish, in theory at any rate, was to have its school, an ideal that in practice long remained unfulfilled.[2]

---

1 See Michael Lynch, op cit, pp 399-402. For earlier background see, also, pp 198-200; and 320-322. It should not be supposed, however, that the Disruption was a 'working-class' movement. In Wick, as elsewhere, the majority of the seceders on this occasion were 'business folk, shopkeepers, doctors etc.'.
2 Fitzroy Maclean: *A Concise History of Scotland;* London, Thames and Hudson (1983) p94.

RELIGION

Soon the regime became more austere still:

> Christmas and Easter were no longer observed and Knox's liturgy was abandoned in favour of spontaneous prayer. Singing was unaccompanied. The churches were unadorned. Holy Communion, which Knox had intended should be central to the life of the Church, was celebrated less and less frequently. Through Scotland the influence of parish ministers became paramount in lay as well as church matters and Kirk Sessions exercised widespread influence.

The history of the parish of Wick so far as it is known came, as we shall see, to exemplify in all details the new practices. It is unlikely that there were many Protestants in Caithness before these measures came in, but it is said that such as there were would assemble at Kirk Stanes on the Kirk Burn, and 'that religious services were held at the spot is a tradition still handed down by the older people of Keiss'; thus wrote Beaton in 1898.[1]

That there was hankering here after the livelier solemnities and 'supersitions' of the old religion, evidenced by survival in this part of Caithness of the kinds of 'popish practices' already described, is not really surprising. Life here was austere enough without the severities of a harsh religion. Nevertheless, it seems probable that the official change-over was accomplished here without much fuss. The incumbent of 1567 (the year of Mary's abdication which virtually ensured survival of the new church system), was Andrew Philp (or Philip), who, as like as not, was one of the considerable number of priests who accepted the changes. Part of his charge from 1574 was the parish of Latheron. As his 'reidare' (reader), doubtless one of the new unqualified assistant ministers put in to fill gaps left by the expulsion or defection of priests unwilling to accept reform and to strengthen the movement's evangel, was Alexander Mernys. Philp is recorded as 'presented to the Vicarage of Wick [a very English term] by James VI'; he was 'translated to Thurso prior to 1576'.

He was followed in Wick by Thomas Keir, who went to Olrig in 1580. To Wick then came 'John Prunto or Prontoch. He had been

---

1 Beaton, op cit, p 50. The evidence is very flimsy. Beaton is purporting to quote from MacFarlane's *Geographical Collections*, Vol 1, p 156. The actual reference reads: 'The Kirk of Strubster or rather ane hermitage being a small spot of green in the midst of a remote wide desert . . . There being no apparent vestiges of a building at this place called the Kirk of Strubster I'm apt to think it has been a place where Protestants have used to assemble for worship about the beginning of the Reformation, when they could not do it safely in places more publick and acessible.'

minister of the joint charge of Wick and Lateron in 1574'. Two other ministers of Wick, John Innes (1607-1611) and Thomas Annand (1614-1636), then officiated in Wick; but in 1638, Annand's successor, John Smart, ran into difficulties. He was 'deposed for his compliance with Montrose' and was not re-admitted to ministry until 1661, when he became minister of Dunnet, and 'received a grant from Parliament . . . on account of his sufferings'.

The Caithness Presbytery records are reticent about this succession and these curious details. Developments here in Wick were, in fact, governed during the early years of the seventeenth century by significant switches in national ecclesiastical policy. King James VI, though still a minor of seventeen, escaped from Ruthven castle where he had been held by some of his nobles, and declared himself de facto king in 1583. Though Protestant in outlook, he had no liking for Knox's virtual ecclesiastical state, less on account of objections to its doctrinal principles, than to the unashamed threat to his regal authority posed by Knox, who on one occasion characterised James as 'God's silie vassal'.

James's method of re-establishing his sway was to put back the bishops. His policy did not gain much momentum until after his accession to the English throne in 1603, when he began governing Scotland from London under the provisions of an Act of Union passed in 1607 by the Scottish Parliament. From this time on the bishops were in once more.

However, the presbyterian revolution had gone too far for the new bishops to gain the sort of hold on the church enjoyed by English bishops; their role as managers of church affairs was spatchcocked into the presbyterian system. Kirk ministers were obliged to acknowledge their authority, but change was minimal. Mr Innes and Mr Annand seem to have adapted in Wick without any bother. In 1638 came a much more severe disturbance. King James had been succeeded in 1625 by his son, Charles I (of both countries), much more adamantly determined to have his way with the churchmen of Scotland. His attempts to impose on the Scots a new prayer book, English fashion, led inevitably to the forming of the National Covenant movement in 1638, one of whose chief leaders was James Graham, Earl of Montrose, (later in the Civil War Montrose changed sides). The chief principle of the Covenant was that forthwith its supporters would have nothing to do with bishops and in November of that year, the General Assembly in Glasgow deposed or

RELIGION

excommunicated Scottish bishops and abolished the Laudian prayer book.

Charles's response to Scottish intransigence was to assemble an army and march against the 'Covenanters'. Led by Montrose, the Scottish army efficiently defeated Charles's troops in what came to be called 'the First Bishops' War', and again under Montrose and Leslie in the Second Bishops' War. These short wars were the prelude to what became the English (and Scottish) Civil Wars of 1642 to 1646, quite drastic in their effects in both countries. The Scottish bishops were thus out again and remained so until after the Restoration of 1660, when Charles I's son, Charles II, badly advised by his Scottish ministers, brought them back once more. Their third removal in 1688 was accomplished without much ordinance and violence at all; the accession of William and Mary of Holland in the year that had seen the ignominious departure of James VII (and II), not quite the last of the Stewart monarchs (since Mary and her sister Anne, who followed, were Stewarts) before the accession to both Scottish and English thrones of the Hanoverians.[1]

It is evident from the scanty references that John Smart, minister of Wick, and probably his predecessors, went along with the return to episcopacy of James VI and Charles I, and that his deposition was one of those ordered by the once more ascendant General Assembly of the Presbyterian Church in 1638. What were his 'sufferings' are not revealed, nor the nature and amount of his 'grant' at the time of the Restoration. Ministry in Wick seems to have been a bit of a mess from the beginning of the civil wars until 1659. A certain 'Harry Forbes, AM, officiated for three or four years, and in the Presbytery Records (5th December, 1654), he is described as "preacher at Wick".' Mr Forbes seems to have been less than happy with Wick, for Beaton continues: 'The following year the Presbytery appointed Mr Harry Smyth to admit Rev. Harry Forbes as minister of Wick but, as Mr Smyth had received a letter from Mr Forbes saying that he would on no account accept of the appointment, no further steps were taken.'

Mr William Geddes, AM, graduate from King's College, Aberdeen, was called to Wick in November. He seems to have quickly earned the special confidence of the burgesses of Wick, who asked him in to a meeting of the Council for a curious purpose:

---

[1] See Fitzroy Maclean, op cit, Chapters IV and V, pp 101-156, for a neat summary of these events.

> William Geddes, minister of the said burgh, being present and hearing the said bailies admitted and sworn for lawful administration of Justice, William Ruthven, notary public there, continued clerk, being present also; and thereupon the said bailies and clerk gave their oath of fidelity upon the lawful execution of their offices. In like manner it is agreed and concluded upon by the said bailies, council and remanent townsmen, and burgesses, that the charter, rights and evidents of the said burgh be put in the custody and keeping of Mr William Geddes, minister, until the same upon good and sufficient reasons be requested from him, tending to the weal of the said burgh, which evidents the said Mr William Geddes has accepted.[1]

What exactly this signifies has to do with the critical events of 1659 and 1660, set in motion by the departure of General Monck, until this time the chief Commonwealth General in occupied Scotland, 'to reconcile the Westminster parliament to a restoration of Charles II'. The restoration itself was accomplished in Scotland on 14 May, 1660, when Charles was proclaimed King of all three of his kingdoms, Scotland, England and Ireland at Edinburgh Castle. Cromwell had died in 1658, and it became clear during the confusions of the following months that the only possible conclusion to the Interregnum was Charles's restoration. Wick as one of the burghs of Scotland had done its best to keep well in with the Cromwellian regime, not least doubtless on account of the presence in Caithness of Cromwellian soldiers. The prospect of a royalist return was perhaps not especially welcome to some of the burghers, who were taking precautions against the day when the king's commissioners might be coming along to impose penalties on the burgh for its acquiescence in the Cromwellian establishment.[2] When the bailies and burgesses took back the documents and other 'evidents' is not recorded. It did not take the burgesses long to return to loyalty to their Stewart king.

Mr Geddes had his own adjustment to make. King Charles insisted on the restoration of bishops, and the measure was ratified in May 1662. Geddes was one of the local ministers to be called before the Synod where 'no fair means [were] unassayed to bring them to a

---

[1] Minutes of the Royal Burgh of Wick, 18 October, 1660.
[2] There is in Wick a curious tradition (not well supported by documented evidence), that a group of English 'independents' or evangelical non-conformists established themselves in Wick at the 'Camps', a river-bank settlement on the north shore. They were probably soldiers.

submission to the present [Episcopal] regime'. The presbytery was happy to record that 'The said day Mr William Geddes, minister at Wick, compeered and declared himselfe in order to the present Episcopal government.' He was, however, 'sharply rebuked by the Synod' in 1664, 'as he had been married by the Rev. James Dunbar of Watten, without the usual proclamation.' He left Wick in 1677 to become minister in Urquhart in Moray, but in 1682 he resigned from his Urquhart appointment following his refusal to 'take the Test Oath' and was invited to return to Wick, where his successor, appointed to Wick in 1681, had died the year before. Geddes was a man of considerable scholarship and wrote a number of historical, Latin and Hebrew studies, all of which were approved for publication by the Scottish Privy Council in 1683 (which exercised a censorship), but only one, *The Saints' Recreation*' (mainly devotional songs and poems) was ever printed. He died in 1692, by which time the bishops had gone for good.[1]

These details have been included under the heading of *Episcopals* since episcopacy of a sort prevailed during much of the seventeenth century in Scotland. On its demise bishops of any kind disappeared from the Scottish scene. The Church of England was devotedly episcopal, and following the Restoration the establishment acted almost as intolerantly towards 'dissenters' – of which there were now large numbers – as did the General Assembly of Scotland to dissenters in its territory. Animosity towards Roman Catholics was stronger still, a sentiment shared by the dissenters. A Toleration Act was passed in the English parliament in 1689, the year after the arrival of William, allowing the right of religious worship to Protestant non-conformists, though not to Catholics.

The manifest partiality of James II (VII) for Catholicism was one of the main causes of his deposition, and England, like Scotland, maintained throughout the eighteenth century a ban against the entry of Catholics into public life. Commenting on the state of post-Restoration public feeling in England, G M Trevelyan writes:

> The Roman Catholics, being the backbone of the Jacobite party, obtained no legal relief for its adherents, and from time to time fresh laws were passed against them. But in practice the policy of William and the spirit of the times secured for them a considerable degree of free religious worship in England; the

1 Beaton, op cit, pp 297-299.

infamous penal laws were usually inoperative, and were only brought into partial vigour in times of Jacobite insurrection. Worship in private houses was hardly ever interfered with, and public chapels were erected and priests often went about openly in spite of the laws.[1]

Neither Anglicans nor Catholics had, for the time being, much comfort in Scotland. A Scottish Toleration Act was passed in 1712 (in the Union parliament), but toleration gained little credibility in the country for many years to come. Among the reasons for continuing hostility towards episcopals and Catholics was the fact that both Pretenders made little secret of their adherence to the old religion. According to Craven, a genuinely tolerated Episcopal Church did not begin ministration in Scotland until 1792. By this time, however, the spirit of toleration was working even in the north. Bishop Forbes's visitation to Caithness we have already described (pp 124-125). It is evident from this account that the few adherents to the Anglican communion in the Wick area were mainly gentry. It is worth noting too that by this date toleration of more outlandish confessions was extended, at least to the gentry, as instanced by the case of the eccentric Sir William Sinclair of Keiss, a born-again Baptist.

Craven avers that in the area of Wick 'we hear no more of attempts at restoration of episcopal service till 1839, "when several families in the neighbourhood of Wick made a proposal to Bishop Low, who then had charge of all the district north of the Spey, for the erection of a church in that town. The matter lay in abeyance till December 1854."'[2]

THE PARISH OF WICK

Much of the little that is known about the early days of the parish of Wick has already been recounted. The connection of the church with the fortunes of the earls of Caithness is symbolised by the 'Sinclair Aisle', the reputed mausoleum of the earls and their families, still standing rather forlornly and not well kept in the Wick parish churchyard, one of the few examples of 'Gothic' architecture in the north of Scotland. Alongside is the also poorly cleansed and maintained 'Dunbar Tomb', thought to have 'been built before 1576. It was repaired in 1728 and again in 1752.' This was the time when the

---

1 George Macaulay Trevelyan: *History of England;* London, Longmans, Green & Co (1945) p 474.
2 J B Craven: *History of the Church in Caithness;* op cit, pp 282-283.

Dunbars of Hempriggs were the main heritors of the parish and determined to keep up a style to match that of the Sinclairs. Beaton quotes James Oliphant's observations in 1726 that 'There is at the E. end of it on the N. side under a little pend, a hewn stone with a man at full length on it, which is said to be his (Fergus's) effigies engraven in stone'.[1]

The church building standing in Oliphant's time was demolished at the end of the century and another erected on much the same site, and that also had to be demolished before the present church was completed in 1830. 'The steeple' of this building, says the church's quater-centenary handbook of 1957, 'is seen from all parts of the town from the sea. To many people coming by train to Wick the first glimpse of the town is the tall steeple standing across the river.'[2]

The 'Old' Kirk

An earlier celebratory publication from 1906 commends the same view from the railway and tells of 'the "Big" Kirk, or the "Muckle" Kirk, as it is familiarly called by the inhabitants'. The unromantic writer of this piece speaks of 'a commodious building seated for some fifteen hundred people but only biassed [sic] tongues would call it handsome.' He goes on to describe it as 'the oldest church building in Wick still used as a place of worship,' but as 'compared with other parish churches, it is still an ecclesiastical infant.' He complains that although it was then less than eighty years old, little of its provenance was known; 'Heritors records do not exist,' he says, 'the Town Council minute books of the period have been lost [most of them still exist],' and, 'although the Kirk Session met frequently there, and there are ample minutes, curiously enough there is not a single mention in them either of the building of the new church or of the moving from one church to another.' It was, thought the writer strange, 'since the previous church was for some years condemned as dangerous, owing to the giving way of its foundations, and the congregation met either in the open air or in some temporary place of worship.'[3]

Yet this building whose provenance puzzled the writer was itself less than thirty years old. In his *Wick 1794* the then minister of Wick,

1 D Beaton, op cit, p 54.
2 *Wick Old Parish Church: Quater-Centenary 1567-1967*; issued 1967.
3 *The Bazaar: A Local Literary Magazine and Official Programme of the Wick Parish Church Bazaar*; 6 & 7th September, 1906.

William Sutherland, wrote of the existing church as 'very old, a long dark and ill-constructed building, perhaps the worst in Caithness: a new fabric will soon be necessary.' Just such a new building was decided on by the Presbytery of Caithness, and the principal heritor, Sir Benjamin Dunbar 'consented to become undertaker for the erection of the building'. The new building was estimated to cost £1250 15s 11d, sterling, and the heritors were assessed to provide this money. As principal heritor Sir Benjamin could be expected to provide the lion's share of this sum.

The reason for lack of mention in records, or burgh, kirk and presbytery probably lies in the story of what happened next. Sir Benjamin was 'obliged very soon thereafter to leave the county on military duty', and he resigned as undertaker of the project. There was, of course, a war on, and some of the local gentry were involved in running the militia and 'fencibles'. The Rev Sutherland offered to take over. His appointment was approved by the presbytery, and he, with Robert Corner, merchant in Wick, and Captain Harry Bain, both burgesses, as his cautioners entered into a contract under penalty of £250 sterling to get the job done by January 1798.

The work was not completed until June, 1799, when Sutherland 'applied to the Presbytery of Caithness to have the church inspected and taken off his hands. There followed a bitter wrangle as to who should do the inspection, and whether or not some of the workmen who had done the work should be allowed to give evidence, as the heritors, led by Sir Benjamin, believed that 'the foundations were bad, and that there was a great quantity of improper or bad materials'.

The quarrel between heritors and the minister, as undertaker of the work, went on for several years, and was carried in 1808 to the Court of Session by Sir Benjamin Dunbar of Hempriggs, Sir John Sinclair of Ulbster, and other heritors. Great masses of 'information', submissions, interlocutors, passed to and fro with no ultimate resolution of the dispute, mainly for the sufficient reason that Mr Sutherland died on the 23 June, 1816. As already mentioned, Mr Sutherland was believed by Donald Sage to have had 'considerable trouble with obdurate heritors' which is clearly no less than the truth. His prayers for the magistrates of Wick 'such as they are' have also been noticed; knowing Sutherland's problems, no doubt the Lord accepted the petition in good part.

Whatever may be said about the merits of the case on either side of the dispute, it seems that the Caithness Presbytery, mindful as always of the need to keep on the right side of heritors, gave Mr Sutherland only qualified support. The bill for the new building came to £1350 17s 2d in 1798. It is also evident that the building was never safe, that the foundations began giving way almost as soon as it was completed. The onus was obviously on Sutherland as undertaker to accept responsibility for the defects, but he seems to have had bad technical advice from the professionals. The church had been built on the north slope of Wick river bank, and the foundations were not taken down to sufficient depth in the subsoil to ensure stability. 'Despite its substructural weakness,' says the writer of the 1906 article, 'it never collapsed, and it stood for a time after the present building was in use.' The presbytery condemned the building in 1816, the year of Sutherland's death. The lack of information in the public record about all this may stem from an inclination on the part of the council, presbytery and elders to say as little as possible about affairs that some members may have found embarrassing; it is a tendency we have noticed before in the public records of Wick.[1]

WICK OLD PARISH CHURCH

Fig 19 (Courtesy Mr Ian Mackenzie and Rev R Frizzell).

1 Most details are drawn from the *INFORMATION*, dated 21 June, 1808 for 'Sir Benjamin Dunbar, Sir John Sinclair of Ulbster. James Sinclair, Esq. of Forse, Mrs Henrietta Wemyss of Southdun, and David Brodie of Hopeville, Esq., all Heritors in the Parish of Wick' etc. against the Reverend William Sutherland, and his Cautioners.

The 'New' Kirk

As for the present church, minister and elders must have thought that there was a hoodoo on that too. Again the story is told by the contributor of the article to *The Bazaar*, who quotes as his authority a workman who was involved in the building and who only died in 1905. Work on this church began in 1822. The article continues:

> The walls were hardly more than above ground when operations ceased. The contractor found the undertaking too heavy for him. Digging for the foundation of the western gable he had come upon running sand, and in order to avoid the mistake of the previous church he had to bore through the sand, it is said, to the fabulous depth of 30 feet. This proved too much for him and he failed. For several years the walls stood just appearing above ground till a contractor from Watten, a Mr Davidson, undertook the work, and carried it to a successful completion about 1830. The cross beams are solid logs, 66 feet long, 10 inches broad and 15 inches deep, supported by upright and cross ties of proportionate strength.

The main pine roof timbers for the new church – still in good condition today – were brought by ship from Russia, but were so large that they had to be floated from the harbour on the river to the site since they could not pass through the narrow streets of the town. The building has been refurbished a number of times since its erection. One of the problems experienced by some of the ministers has been its huge interior which, with a small congregation, has made it seem distressingly barren. Very recently the church has undergone a major interior reconstruction. The 1830 building cost considerably more than the earlier church to build. As early as 1808 the estimate was running at £2107, 15s 7½d.

The writer of the *Bazaar* Magazine article refers interestingly to the old kirk which, 'despite its substructural weakness . . . never collapsed', standing for some time after the new kirk was built alongside and at right angles to it. 'Those who have sufficient curiosity,' says this writer of 1906, 'may see in the Carnegie Library an old picture of Wick from the river side, in which the two Parish churches stand, if not side by side, at least end to side.'[1]

We return to the topic of the parish church later, since it played a

---

1 The picture is still to be seen in the Wick Public Library. It is dark and in oils and seems to have been painted about 1835. Though unsigned, it is known to have been the work of a 'Mr Munro, an artist who practised his vocation some years in this town; and was kindly lent for the purpose [of public exhibition?] by *(Continued on foot of next page)*

considerable part in the life of the town during the nineteenth century. Though it could perhaps physically accommodate, it could not cater for the needs of the polyglot population that was already crowding into the town at the time it was built. One church, that of the Wick Baptist Union, was built in 1806 before the new Wick parish church was completed, and after, no less than eight other churches (and a Salvation Army citadel), mainly for different denominations, were erected in Wick and Pulteneytown before the end of the century. As may be imagined, the religious history of Wick during these turbulent years is a very different business from that of the parish's earlier years.

Some Ministers of Wick.

Not the least of the difficulties encountered by some of the ministers of Wick was that of getting on amicably with the heritors and burgesses of the burgh, on account of which there were some periods when the town had no minister at all. In 1698, the Caithness Presbytery recommended 'earnestly to, and seriously exhorted the said heretors and magistrates to call a minister'. The General Assembly's Commission sent to Wick in 1698 a certain Rev Alexander Steadman, with whom the burgesses agreed so ill 'that there was no prospect of Mr Steadman being settled at Wick'. The burgesses promised so 'to doe when the Lord trysted them with occasion of hearing any minr. sent from the south in mission that would be satisfying to them in life and doctrine.'

They were little better off with the next minister who came along in 1701, Charles Keith, who 'seems to have had little support from his kirk-session'. A year after arriving he was complaining to the presbytery 'that he had several insuperable difficulties and crushing grievances in the said parish (Wick), having none to strengthen his hands there in the exercise of church discipline against scandalous

(Continued from foot of previous page) Provost Bruce, to whom it belongs.' This information is given in the *John O'Groat Journal* of 19 March, 1847, when the paper printed an engraving of the picture (its first illustration of this kind), amended by means of pencil sketching by an artist signing himself 'J Bishop', to bring it up to date. The skyline now shows the addition of four smoking 'chimney-stalks', indicating the arrival in Wick by 1847 of such modern improvements as a gas-works, and steam meal and saw-mills. The foreground is also altered; in the original two boys are preparing to fly a kite; now appears a woman and child. This picture appears at page 306 in this book. In detail each gives an informative commentary on the appearance and activities of the town in 1835 and 1847. The title given is *WICK & PULTENEY TOWN*, and below is printed an extensive description of the skyline as illustrated.

delinquents, but on the contrary his hands were much weakened by heritors and elders.' The presbytery sent in a 'deputation' to Wick which met the elders and heritors on 12 February, 1702, 'and asked the elders to be more faithful and to have "more of the fear of God in them and less of humane (human) slavish fear."' The elders were evidently not very moved and were again 'sharply rebuked' for what the presbytery terms their 'neglect of duty'. Rev Beaton who is quoting from the Caithness Presbytery records, continues with the comment that 'the conduct of the elders is in keeping with what is recorded of many who were nominated to that office in Wick in 1700. According to the Rev. William Innes, he 'found many of them ignorant of God'. He was ordered by the presbytery 'to ordain "such elders as are most knowing and best affected to the Presbyterian government."'

To rescue the heritors, elders and congregation from their parlous sinful state, came James Oliphant, a conscientious young minister from Linlithgow, 'called unanimously 14th September, and ordained 25th September, 1707'. We have met Mr Oliphant several times already, and chiefly as author of the account of the parish in *Macfarlane's Collections* of 1727. Oliphant died in 1726. He was followed by James Ferme, invited by the presbytery 'to come north to reside in the bounds, as they had "savoury accounts of this young man from several hands" . . . . He is credited,' says Beaton, 'with being the first among Caithness Presbyterian ministers to have preached Arminian doctrine.' This is a doctrine not wholly favoured by the Presbyterian establishment, based on the teaching of Jacob Harmensen (Latinised to Jacobus Arminius), a Dutch theologian who asserted that, contrary to Calvin's severe doctrine of predestination, 'forgiveness and eternal life are bestowed on all those who repent of their sins and unfeignedly believe in Jesus Christ'. The teaching came to be part of the Wesleyan Methodist theology in England, and its adoption by some Scottish ministers represents a significant stage in the development of evangelical sentiment in the Scottish church.

A young Dunbar of Olrig (a member of the now proliferating Dunbar family) was presented in Wick on the death of Mr Ferme, but he died before he could take up the ministry. He was followed by James Scobie, a graduate from Marischal College, Aberdeen, and he died very young, at the age of thirty and in only the third year of his ministry. He is chiefly interesting as being the first minister in Wick to be 'presented' by a patron, Lieutenant Colonel John Scott, a heritor connected with the Dunbar family. He was succeeded by William Sutherland, a graduate of Aberdeen from King's College. We have already had much dealing with the Rev Sutherland, under whose direction the new but ill-constructed parish church was built.

Kirk Records

Much of the story already told is drawn from the kirk parish records, mostly intact for the nineteenth century, like that for the burgh of Wick, reveals, nevertheless, some very interesting aspects of the life of the parish in those times. The church was governed by the kirk session of elders and ministers. Its responsibilities were very varied and extended well beyond what would be required of a modern kirk session. They usually met weekly to consider all kinds of issues, the appointment and stipend of the minister (though they had no independent powers in these respects), the provision and supervision of such schools as there were in the parish, the appointment of school-masters and, above all, the consideration of 'discipline' cases.

Elders were recruited from among the eminent men of the town and church heritors (the chief landowners of the parish). Like the burgh council new elders were nominated by the existing body, and were subject to approval by the Caithness presbytery, on which they were represented. In 1718 there were sixteen of them 'to cover the whole parish of Wick from Keiss to Ulbster and from Staxigoe to Bilbster.' In 1761 they numbered 24, though the body was down to 8 in 1835. Individual elders undertook particular duties. Two elders, for instance, were charged in 1701 with the duty of going round the town during the church services and reporting back to the kirk session on who was not attending kirk and otherwise not observing the Sabbath. The elder for Killimster in 1761 had to supervise the building of a new school in his district. In 1832 an elder was expelled from kirk session 'for frequenting Public Houses'. To them reported the 'church officers', one for each side the river. 'Their work varied, ranging from normal church building duties, attending the Kirk Session and going out to summons people to appear before the Session for discipline.' In 1770 one church officer was dismissed, 'as he had been unfit to carry out his duties due to drink.'

Session clerks kept the records and there is a long list of the clerks from 1701 right through the century. The clerk was usually the local schoolmaster. Alexander Gibson, session clerk in 1701, was paid a salary of £3 (Scots) a quarter.

The session was represented on the Caithness presbytery and in some years, either minister or a senior elder attended the national General Assembly in Glasgow. This was a long and arduous journey and much too expensive for most elders. In 1718 the Rev. James Oliphant was away from Wick from April until July to attend the Assembly. Sometimes a representative attended on Wick's behalf from a parish much nearer to Glasgow; for instance, in 1774 a merchant from Edinburgh was asked to speak for Wick, while in 1778 a representative from a parish in Fife was nominated, but since he owned no property in Wick parish, and was 'a stranger to this place', the session resolved that he had 'no right to represent them'. At the turn of the century – as we have seen from the burgh records, Bailie James Horne, Writer to the Signet and a senior elder of the kirk, was sent to Glasgow several times to represent the burgh as well as the parish.

Money was a perennial problem for the Wick parish. For this reason the parish failed to fulfil most of its formal obligations on public education, and when schools were opened in Wick town and other localities in the parish, the main issues seems to have been the getting of money from heritors or from the SSPCK and the SSPG. The schoolmasters had a thin time of it. For example, there is an entry for 1768 which shows funds to be so low that 'schoolmaster could not be paid'. Yet it was possible when the pressure was on to raise the very considerable sums that were needed when the new church had to be built; two churches, in fact, within thirty years.

The heritors paid up when they had to. The upkeep of church property was indeed the responsibility of the heritors; collections taken up each Sunday were allocated to the benefit of the poor. Total collections for the year 1779 amounted to £10,19s 4d, so that the beneficiaries mostly did not receive great amounts. Allocations were made twice a year from a list of those eligible and the list of intended recipients was read out from the pulpit. A few allocations are mentioned in the records: in 1701 a dumb person received three shillings, and a cripple got seven shillings. Sometimes the amounts available were much bigger; in 1742 £57 was distributed among a hundred and twenty people, and in 1759 £100 was divided among one hundred and eight.

In his catalogue of affairs *Anent the Kirk* and *The Doings of the Kirk*

RELIGION

Session, John Horne (*Ye Town of Wick in Ye Oldene Tymes*), comments too on other benefactions of the elders to the poor:

> Sometimes, consideration of the poor gave pleasing variety to the proceedings; and occasionally a foster mother had to be found for some 'orphant'. We find it solemly recorded on a certain day (surely New-Year's Day!) that 'Ye Session appoints saxpence to be given to Robert Robertson, a poor man;' on another occasion, a collection of over 'three pounds' is 'allowed for ye payment of ye physician qt. cutt a certain poor man, in ye country, for ye gravel.'

The session also ran the churchyard. In 1766 the elders wrote to the magistrates to have the churchyard cleared of swine that were overrunning it, 'as they have already caused damage to it'. They were, of course, in charge of burials and memorials, and a visit to the old churchyard today gives vivid impression of the keen use of this terraced ground by the quality of the town. Many of the burgesses and other notables of nineteenth century Wick are here buried, their memorials and grave plaques still well kept and polished, Indeed, it might be said of this touching page of the town's history, as of Housman's Hughley:

> To south the headstones cluster
> The sunny mounds lie thick;
> The dead are more in muster
> At Kirkhill than the quick.

The burial of David Bain's wife 'including the King's duty plus the officers' fees for use of mortcloth and bells' cost seven shillings and sixpence. In 1711 the minister had been authorised 'to take sufficient money out of the box to buy "green cloathe and fringe" for the pulpit, and also for a mort-cloth for the poor of the parish.' However, it was reported in 1791 that 'fewer of the people being buried made use of the bell and mortcloth so the income from this was reduced', though the number of poor was increasing. Burials were from now on to cost the same, the money going to the Poor Fund; but subject to investigation, poor folk were to be buried free. One interesting consequence, it may be said, of the excavations of 1797 for foundations connected with the building of the new church, was the discovery of 'people slain in a battle and which had been buried with the "usual attention"'. Nothing more is said about this curious find. Fairly certainly these were corpses brought in 1680 from the battlefield of Altimarlach, two miles up river. Where and how solemnly they were re-buried is not mentioned.

A curious entry in 1774 records that 'the elders wanted to be entitled to the benefit of the bell and best mortcloth when they were buried, without charge to their heirs.' The mortcloth was a black pall for covering the coffin, and the bell referred to was a hand-bell rung on the occasion of the burial of common folk. Gentry did not usually have the bell. The matter of who should provide the bell, the burgh or the kirk, came as we have seen before the council in 1781 and it was decided, that as it was a 'public service' the burgh was quite willing to provide the bell (and ringer) if the fees for the ringing should go to the Customar who would allocate them to the 'poor of the parish'.

Kirk Session Jurisdictions

The most curious and probably strenuous of the Kirk Session's responsibility was its judicial work, much of it to do with the kirk, but also extending into areas of secular justice. The role of the kirk in the maintenance of what they usually refer to as 'discipline' by the end of the eighteenth century was giving way to more explicitly secular arrangements, but it is interesting to see from the session records just how much responsibility for public order, as we should call it, fell to the church authorities. Although, say the notes drawn from the session records, a main source used here:

> the Kirk Session was responsible for most of the discipline in the parish . . . it is not clear how it was informed of misdeeds or how it decided when to take action. Wrongdoers received a summons delivered by hand by one of the church officers and were duty bound to appear before the Kirk Session. If they were summoned three times and did not appear they then had to appear before the Caithness Presbytery whose meetings alternated between Wick and Thurso.

The sorts of offences that came before the session ranged from those simply to do with sabbath breaking and other breaches of church discipline, to secular criminal offences. Ordinary disciplinary misdemeanours included, for example, 'not attending church', 'not completing business on a Saturday night', 'drinking during the hours of divine service', recreations of the young such as 'playing marbles at the church door (and then throwing stones at the church officer)', and doing any kind of work that could be postponed to a weekday. Examples quoted include cases of 'gathering seaweed', 'cutting cabbage', 'digging potatoes' 'washing yarn' and 'drying malt'.

John Horne, writing of the Session's 'almost unlimited' jurisdiction, lists 'fornication' as 'very common', drunkenness as 'the cause of continual trouble'; 'fighting, lying and slander furnished its victims almost every week, while cases of "swearing horriblie" were scarcely less frequent.' 'Scolding', a common misdemeanour of the 'feminine disposition' was 'a favourite indulgence', while 'obstinacie' was a common crime of 'the man o' independent mind'.

Needless to say, 'breach of the seventh commandment' was quite common, visited by penalties prescribed by Act of Parliament, according to the social position of the offender. 'It is recorded of one individual,' says Horne, 'who had been fined the amount leviable on a "gentleman", that he appealed to the Court of Session against the decision of the Kirk. Their lordships quashed the decision on the ground that the appellant "had not the face or air of a gentleman".'

'Fornication', which doubtless included rape, attracted serious 'chastisement'. One account is 'chronicled':

> The sinner concerned hap [hath?] indulged in certain 'enormities,' which shall be nameless, and had wickedly added to his crime by using what was majestically declared to be 'vilipending language' about the minister. For these highhanded affronts the following sentence was pronounced upon him:– He is to be 'carried down from the Kirk of Wick to the Cross, with ane paper hood bearing the inscription of his crime, and to sit there two hours in the stocks wt. the hood on his head. It is also ordered that he must appear before the congregation and 'give satisfaction' for his misdeeds.

It is almost as bad for the innocent as for the guilty; 'if,' says Horne, 'it fell out that a charge – say of fornication – that was made against a man, and he declared himself innocent, he was allowed an opportunity of "purging himself by oath" before the Session and "in the face of ye congregation".' The oath was administered to him on his knees and (modernised) ran thus: –

> I, – – – , do solemnly declare, before the Almighty and Heartsearching God, the righteous Judge of all the earth, that I am innocent and altogether free of fornication; and for the more verification of this, and satisfaction of all, I imprecate upon myself these following plagues, if I be guilty: That I may be a vagabond like Cain on the earth; that some signal judgement from God may be inflicted upon my body, even here on earth:

that I may be deprived of the presence of God hereafter for evermore; and that all the curses that are denounced against Sin in the Scriptures may fall upon me: and I solemnly declare that I take this oath upon me in the literal meaning of the words, without equivocation or mental reservation.

After such a declaration before his fellows of the congregation, it would be a hardy man who could hold up his head again in public for a long time. The punishments visited on female partners in such crime, especially those who carried with them the evidence, would be no less severe.

One special sacerdotal offence was that of 'visiting St Mary's RC Chapel' a case of which we have already discussed (pp 238). Others were 'forging a paper to enable a child to be baptised', 'sorcery', and 'swearing'. Some offences had both a church and civil connotation, for example, 'fighting', 'drunkenness', 'wife beating' and 'adultery'. It fell to the kirk session to handle cases of incomers to the parish, under vague provisions of the Scottish Poor Law Act of 1575 (a pale copy of the Elizabethan Poor Law of 1572), as we noticed, to deal with incomers. The chief concern was whether or not they had means of support; if they had not they would probably become a charge on the very inadequate funds maintained by the kirk for poor relief. Thus, cases are mentioned of persons 'living in Wick parish without a reference from their home area'. If they could not produce one in a given time they had 'to go back home or be handed over to the magistrates and be classed as a vagrant'. As we have seen, the magistrates still did not know what to do with them – except turn them out of the burgh.

Outright criminal offences such as theft and murder could come before the session and be dealt with in terms of their significance as breaches of the church's jurisdiction. Thus, in 1709, two men came before the elders on a charge of murdering a man from Thurso. They were excommunicated. After that they were, of course, handed over to the magistrates. It may be doubted that by this date 'excommunication' had the penal effect that it might have had in the time of the middle ages. The impression remains that in the eighteenth century the integrity of one's 'immortal soul' was a matter of less personal worry to folk than it might once have been.

Other punishments that could be awarded by the session included fines or the 'mulct', a form of fine 'regarded somewhat favourably by the people, who looked on it in the light of an equivalent for their wrongdoing.' Personal humiliation was a very common sort of sentence. This, as we have seen, could take the form of standing in disgrace before the congregation (probably with a card marked with the offence round the delinquent's neck), standing outside the kirk ringing a bell to draw attention to onesself as a wicked person, or receiving a reprimand or rebuke from the minister. In 1771, a man 'trying to hide the facts in a case of discipline' was required to appear before the congregation for six months, not missing a single Sunday. In 1791, it was noted that more cases of drunkenness, including women, were coming before the session. As late as 1841 a man found guilty of drunkenness was sentenced to 'lesser excommunication', that is, denial of the sacraments until he repented.

Sometimes, as in the administration of civil justice, the church law officer broke the traces. One of Horne's best stories is of a certain William Abernethie, who

> to wit – appears, in our modern phrase, to have been a 'rare youth'. In November, 1711, Willie, though occupying the distinguished position of parish beadle, resolved on a 'burst'. In the full flood of his enjoyment and greatness, he visited on the minister, opening his mind to that favoured individual with overpowering frankness, and abusing him in choice and select language [the minister at that time was the Rev. James Oliphant]. Thereafter, he opened the church without a key (one of his private tricks, and now exhibited as an off-show to his genius) and entered the church. Here he wrathfully seized the chair of Helen Henderson – maybe an 'old lass' – and brought it to triumphant desolation. Willie's exploit was not appreciated by an ungrateful public, and 'the Session, after mature deliberation did discharge him from his office forever.' The appointment was offered to the second officer, who was asked 'either to provide one who would assist him in his office for the whole parish, and yrby he should have the right to all the emoluments yrfrom belonging to both offices; or to chuse one side of the parish and the emoluments yrfrom according, and the Sess. would dispnse of the oyr. side of ye parish and ye emoluments yrof. to anoyr., and he was appointed to give his answer the next day yr. would be a Sess.

Horne made great use of eleven articles in the 'Wick in the Olden Time' series, all devoted to the absorbing issue of the kirk and its jurisdictions. The *Journal* writer moralises on the 'power of the keys' exercised by the kirk during earlier centuries, from the point of view of the mid-nineteenth century when invasions of civil by 'spiritual power' had all ceased. He gives dozens of examples from the kirk records of the seventeenth and eighteenth centuries of the policies and practice of the session in maintaining public order and religious conformity, even to the extent of appointing two members of the session to walk through the streets on a Sunday morning to bring in those not attending morning service; while on fast days 'elders who took charge of the collections, had to go round the town and see that there were none in the change-houses who should have been at church.' Breach of Sunday regulations observance in all its rigour seems at times to have been little short of criminal offence. Carrying water in a large vessel on a Sunday was put to a stop to by ordering that on Sundays water might not be carried in anything larger than a 'pint stoup'.

Perhaps the most serious case listed in this detailed record is that of 29 January, 1720, when the kirk session tried a publican in connection with a report that may or may not have been false:

> The minister informed the Session yt yr [that there] was a report going, yt ye three soldiers who had murdered ye two tinkers on ye street of Wick Sabbath was eight days, at night, had all be entertained at Wm. Murray's house till it was late, and that the quarrel among them had begun there. He also told that, having examined one of ye tinkers before his death anent ye affair, who had declared to him that they had drunk none but five chopins of ale in that house, and that there were seven persons about it, and that they had removed to another house, where they quarrelled, and that this declaration of his had made him decline troubling the Session with it, seeing nothing could be charged against that or any other family in Wick, the villainy having been committed in the street; but that ye report spreading far and wide, now he had ordered Wm. Murray and his yf [wife] to be summoned to try what could be made of it, all of which the Session approved, and ordered them to be called in. Wm. Murray and Jean Groat, his yf, lawfully summoned, called, compeared, and being charged with entertaining these soldiers with drink till it was late on Sabbath night, the foresaid William Murray answered, 'that for his part he knew nothing of the matter, for he went to bed that night a little after day-set, and sawn none of these men.' His wife

declared that the two tinkers came into their houses a while after sermon, and that they drank none but only five chopins of ale at most, and sent out ye house a little after day set, and that the soldiers was not with them. The Session thought fit to call witnesses.

A number of witnesses were called, who naturally revealed nothing that reflected discredit on William Murray and his wife, and, of course, nothing at all about the murder itself:

> The Session taking these depositions into serious consideration found nothing proven in ye terms of ye lybell, not one word in their depositions of a quarrel, nor of their having drunk more than what might have been necessary, and ye soldiers who committed ye murder were not in company with ye tinkers in that house; upon all which the Session thought that Wm. Murray should be admonished for ye future, that they should take care not to entertain any company with drink on ye Lord's day, and further, appoints ye substance of ye depositions may be declared from ye pulpit next Lord's day, that a stop may be put to false reports.[1]

It is difficult from the whole record to judge just how seriously the kirk's judicial role was taken. Apart from the sabbath offences and the like, it seems that the elders were seldom able to bring in a 'guilty' verdict and that they made ample use of the 'not proven' formula. In any case, really serious criminal matter had to be passed on to the civil authorities – though it is evident that among the church elders were several of the town magistrates.

The kirk session continued in its juridical role throughout the nineteenth century though mainly now concerning itself with church offences. It was, of course, increasingly difficult for the session both to police and to assert its judicial role in the vastly larger community that Wick had now become, especially among the large numbers of folk who did not recognise the validity of the presbyterian rite. In 1868, the Rev D R Jack of the recently built Presbyterian Church in Pulteney, had himself made an elder of the Wick Parish Church so that he could have some say in 'the discipline of the people' in his own area, since the Wick Church 'still had power over the whole of Wick. Normally wrongdoers from his area were referred to Mr Jack for a reprimand.' The last recorded disciplinary case dealt with by the

1 *JOGJ*, 23 October, 1862. The articles 'Wick in the Olden Time' run from 1 May to 4 December, 1862, numbering 1 to XXX.

Wick kirk session was in 1903.

We return in Chapter 12 to the story of the much enlarged parish church of the nineteenth century during a time when it experienced rapid growth of its congregation, and when it became for a time probably the largest Gaelic speaking congregation in the north of Scotland. The character of the parish church, however, changed markedly in the conditions of religious 'competition' that were set up in the ferment of the new Wick, of which, perhaps, the most potent symbol was the setting of of St Joachim's Catholic Church in 1833.

Note. The comprehensive notes used in this brief account were compiled quite recently from the kirk session records by church officers preparing material for a history of the Wick Parish Kirk, mainly in connection with the Burgh Quater-Centenary of 1989. The actual records are now deposited with the National Register in Edinburgh. Where indicated some pieces have been taken from John Horne's *Ye Towne of Wick in Ye Olden Tymes,* op cit.

PART III:

WICK ASCENDANT

Chapter 11: *Clupea harengus harengus.*

Chapter 12: 'Our Northern Athens.'

Chapter 13: Sodom of the North.

Chapter 14: Voice of the People.

Chapter 15: Those in Peril.

CHAPTER 11

CLUPEA HARENGUS HARENGUS

A mere column of three inches is all that *Encyclopaedia Britannica (Micropaedia)*, can afford to tell about *Clupea harengus,* the common Atlantic Herring, the most 'fished' pelagic fish in the world – and in *Macropaedia* it makes no appearance at all. Various other sources tell of a fish about 40cms long, very similar to its cousin (*Sprattus sprattus*). It has a bony dorsal and pelvic fins which have much to do with the ease with which it is caught.[1] Herring live in shoals; at one time the North and Baltic Seas were noted for the vastness of the shoals that, during the year, tended to migrate southwards with considerable regularity. They prefer the relatively shallow waters of the west-European continental shelf.

Their diet consists chiefly of small crustacea and other planktonic species that abound in these northern waters; they themselves provide food for larger predators such as cod, salmon and tuna. On this account, until the rise of the great Scottish fisheries, herring were largely caught for use as bait in white fish line-fishing. Provided that conditions are right, herring spawn on a prolific scale, mainly the earlier months of the year. Individual females can produce as many as 40,000 sticky eggs which sink and adhere to seaweed and rocks etc. The eggs hatch quite rapidly, the spawn itself providing food for many other species. If allowed to, the fish grow to maturity in about four years. Their spawning and feeding habits are conditioned quite sensitively by climatic and geographical variations, and this partly explains the great fluctuations in yearly catches that were such a feature of the 'herring industry' of last century.

The herring deserves at least this much of a *curriculum vitae* in a history of Wick, since it has contributed vastly more to the wellbeing of that place than the earls of Caithness, Sinclair of Ulbster, the burghers of the burgh, Telford, Bremner, Stevenson and the rest. Practically all the features of *Clupea* mentioned have a bearing on the

---

1 Nets are so designed that the mesh allows the fish to swim forwards (as they try to escape) into a mesh – graded to suit the size and age of fish sought. The backward pointed fins engage with the mesh when the fish tries to 'get out'. An interesting though scrappy account of the migrations of *Clupea harengus* appears in the very first issue of the *John O'Groat Journal,* 2 February, 1836.

story of relations between this ubiquitous sea creature and Wick. Its habits, inshore and off-shore, its prolific breeding and shoaling, have determined the very techniques and routines by which it is caught; its torpedo shape, its opercula (gill covers) and bony fins ensuring ease of capture. As a nutritious food for the largest and most efficient predator of all, capable of hauling in at one go enormous numbers of the prey, the herring has completely dictated the shapes, size and numbers of ships sailing in and out of Wick harbour during the high days of the burgh's fishing industry, the extent and security of those harbours, the astonishing and rapid increase of its population and the very dimensions, style and prosperity of Wick town itself. The fish's nineteenth century preference for the North Sea redounded to its destruction and the benefit of Wick. The cliché oft repeated that Wick became the 'herring capital of Europe' – is quoted in this book. *Britannica* says nothing about this! If that ever was a justifiable description, then no 'capital' ever earned its status in a more single-minded monocultural style.

Wick and its herrings have indeed been much written about. One tendency about some of this writing has been to create the impression that the nineteenth century herring industry of Scotland was *centred* on Wick. This is hardly the case. Wick certainly came rapidly to dominate the Scottish herring fishery during the first forty or so years of the century, and remained important throughout. But then with larger vessels, better harbourage and nearer domestic markets,

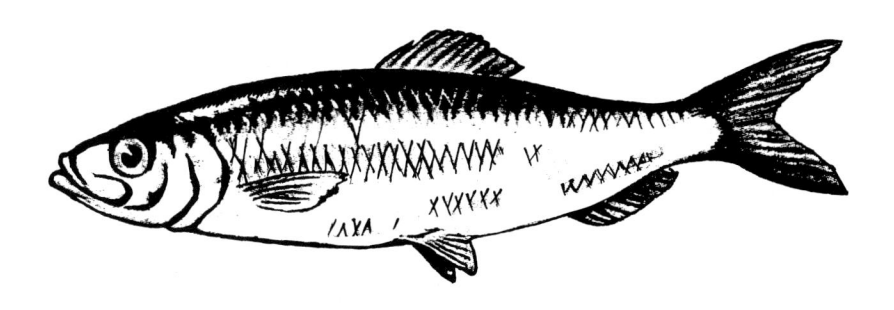

Fig 20 Clupea harengus.

Fraserburgh, Peterhead, Aberdeen and the Fifeshire coast began to take up a larger and larger portion of the trade; and it should be said, too, that Wick and the villages of the north-east coast of Scotland had no exclusive role in the early exploitation of the herring shoals of this part of the North Sea. Profitable herring fisheries were begun in Stronsay, Burray and South Ronaldsay of the Orkneys in the early years of the nineteenth century, while several smaller stations began operating on Mainland Orkney.

BEFORE 1790.

The rise of the fishing industry of north-east Scotland was an episodic and belated business, that is, belated as compared with the flourishing Dutch herring trade of the sixteenth and seventeenth centuries. Reasons for this are explored by Malcolm Gray in his account of *The Fishing Industries of Scotland, 1790-1914.*[1] Except in so far as it is necessary to set the background against which the herring fishery of Caithness and Wick in particular grew up, there is little need here to repeat much of Gray's lucid explanations in his opening chapter of the conditions prevailing in the trade at the end of the eighteenth century. By that time fishing was a significant and integral part of the life of the east coast of Scotland, but not a developed or major contributor to the Scottish economy. There were along that coast from Berwick northwards numerous 'fishing settlements', mostly small individual communities of fishers and their families, separated off from their agricultural neighbours, and from one another, concentrated in three main stretches, the Firth of Forth, with special emphasis on the Fifeshire coast along the East Neuk, the coasts of Angus, Kincardine, Aberdeen and Moray, from Dundee to Buckie, and Sutherland-Caithness from Helmsdale to Keiss. This third area operated under the most severe handicaps, lack of suitable harbourage and distance from markets.

Dutch Fishers in the North Sea.

The Dutch had fished the North Sea for herring from as early as the fourteenth century. Their problem, as for the Scots in later times was that of preserving their herring catch long and efficiently enough to bring it to market. In 1397 a Dutchman, William Buekel, is said to

---

[1] Malcolm Gray: *The Fishing of Scotland, 1790-1914:* Published for the University of Aberdeen by Oxford University Press (1978), pp 9-26.

have discovered methods to 'grill, salt, and pack herrings in casks'. The historian of the herring fishery of Stronsay, Orkney, describes their vessels and techniques:

> Several types of boats were used by the Dutch. Firstly, there were the 'busses' – sturdy, slow moving but roomy boats of from 60 - 100 tons. These had large holds with compartments for salt, nets, fish barrels and provision. To facilitate net handling they sailed low in the water with side rollers and leeboards. They carried two sets of nets, had two masters and a crew of about 14 including two coopers; and as expected the busses were said to be like the other Dutch boats immaculate and spotless.

The other main type of boat used was the 'dogger', a very seaworthy smaller boat, carrying nevertheless a crew of 10 men and 2 boys. Busses collected catches from the smaller vessels, and their crews processed and barrelled the fish while still at sea. 'And so,' says the author of the Stronsay book 'the Dutch prospered. By the end of the 17th century it was estimated that the [fishing] industry supported directly and indirectly about 1 million of her population and the

Fig 21 Dutch Herring Buss 16th and 17th Century. From *Scotland's Sailing Fishermen*, Rebecca Hallewell, published by Hallewell Publications. *By kind permission of the publishers.*

valuation of the herring side of the business was about £3,000,000 a year.'[1] By the end of the eighteenth century the Scottish fishing industry did not begin to compare with this, even though, as Iain Sutherland explains, 'the industry was given a boost in 1702 when the French attacked and sank 400 Dutch fishing boats of Bressay [Shetland]'.[2]

In the earlier part of the century nothing so sophisticated as busses operated in the Scottish fish trade. Most fish were caught from small open boats with keels of sixteen or even less feet. The most common type used in Caithness was the 'Scaffie', with a raked stern and bows also raked but at a steeper angle. It was very manoeuvrable in good conditions especially near to the shore but liable to 'sucking down' in certain conditions, and not at all suitable for the more distant cod fishing grounds.

In 1750, however, 'it was felt that since the Dutch were so successful with busses, an effort should be made to build and equip a British fleet of them for trial at the Shetland fishery.' Such busses were expensive to build; a buss of 50 tons cost £700 or more. An Act of Parliament (23 Geo. II Cap 24) provided for a bounty of £1 10s per ton to be paid to 'the Owner or Owners of all Decked Vessels from 20 to 80 tons burden' built for and employed in the fisheries. In order to qualify for bounty vessels had to make a rendezvous in Bressay Sound, Shetland on or before 11 June. There could be no fishing before 13 June. A rendezvous point was set up for fishers on the west side of Scotland at Campbeltown, in time for the autumn fishing. Thus originated the bounty and rendezvous system, not at this stage of much value or interest to inshore fishers.[3]

So far herring was less important than haddock, cod and ling. Herrings were mostly taken inshore and often used simply as bait for cod fishing lines further out to sea for which rather larger but still open boats were used. Nevertheless, the herring was coming to be recognised as a palatable culinary fish in its own right, and it

---

1 W M Gibson: *Stronsay (Vol I), The Herring Fishing;* Kirkwall, Herald Printshop – Reprint (1989), pp 4-5.
2 Iain Sutherland: *Wick Harbour and the Herring Fishery;* Wick, Camps Bookshop and the Wick Society, p20. It may be added that much of the detail contained in this chapter is derived from this well researched and informative text which, regrettably, contains no references and no bibliography, and unhelpfully there is no index. Nor is the book dated.
3 Jean Dunlop: *The British Fisheries Society, 1786-1893* Edinburgh, John Donald (1978), p9. By the early 1770s there are reckoned to have been 261 busses in service in Scotland (as compared with 22 in England (Dunlop, p 11) Bounty was not payable on smaller boats, and 'it appears that the buss bounty had reacted very unfavourably on the boat fishery'.

was above all very plentiful. Once caught, however, the herring was very perishable. There was little chance of getting it in the fresh state to the markets of Edinburgh, Glasgow and London. For this the fish had to be 'cured' as soon as it was landed.

The Dutch had not only devised means of getting pickled or smoked herring to markets in England, but also took considerable quantities to the West Indies where the fish came to be valued as a cheap foodstuff for slaves. The coasts of Scotland were not at all efficiently geared for the curing of herrings even if they could be got ashore in decent condition. And the shores nearest to the teeming shoals of herring, those of north-east Scotland, had very few harbours capable of taking in more than a few boats at a time; so that the problems of building up a Scottish herring fishery were formidable: small open boats, which, however seaworthy, were not adequate to bring in large catches, lack of suitable beaches and harbours, few facilities for processing and packaging the fish and no easy means of conveying them to market.

Early Developments in the Wick Area

We have suggested that among the reasons for the improvement of Caithness that set in towards the end of the eighteenth century was almost certainly consideration of these issues by government, and doubtless of trade problems created by the war between Britain and France that began in 1793. Development in the Wick area had begun well before 1790, as the Rev William Sutherland recorded in his *Wick 1794*. Mr Sutherland comments on the 'vast variety of fish' along the shores of the parish, not exploited however to anything like the extent possible. There was, for instance, a London market now 'in agitation' for the abundant shell-fish that could be caught in the waters of Caithness and, he avers:

> Many years ago, the cod fishing was carried on to a considerable extent on this coast: but, from the inattention or unskilfulness of the fishermen, had for some time been given up, except merely for the supply of the inhabitants, until of late it was resumed by the Messrs Falls of Dunbar, who entered into contracts with the fishermen, not only of this place, but all along the coast of Caithness, for what fish they could take. – The fishermen receive quarterly the price of the fish they deliver, at the rate of 2d. for every cod, not below 12 inches in

length. Small as the price is, yet, as it ensures a market, it enables the fishermen, who are mostly farmers, to pay their rents much better than before.

The Rev Sutherland also comments on some quite successful entries into the fish trade with London:

> A boil-house for the pickling of salmon caught in the River Thurso, from which they are carried overland to save the trouble and risk of crossing the Pentland Firth. Several hundreds of kits, each containing about 40lb of salmon, are annually sent to London. They fetch in general about a guinea *per* kit, but sometimes more, and are reckoned among the very best that come to the London market.

Also, he adds: 'An ice house has been built here, to supply ice for carrying fish to London, but the last two winters being mild, little or no ice could be got; the plan, however, is by no means given up.' However, he is in no doubt that the great development ought to be that of the herring trade. 'From time immemorial', he says,

> great shoals of herrings have visited this coast; till of late years, they were much neglected, the people contenting themselves, year after year, with catching a few on hooks; and proceeding with that excellent bait to the cod-fishing. But in 1767 and 1768, a more enterprising spirit arose. John Sutherland of Wester, Messrs John Anderson of Wick, and Alexander Miller of Staxigoe, fitted out two sloops on the bounty. They proceeded to Shetland, then the nearest place of rendezvous, where they were entered on the Custom-house books; returning to the coast of Caithness. They fished successfully, but, owing to some informality, were deprived of the bounty, then amounting to 50s. *per* ton. This disappointment, however, did not deter them from making another trial next year, though on a lesser scale. They fitted out only one sloop, and had the same success, but it was with some difficulty that the bounty was recovered. The adventure, on the whole, not being very encouraging, their ardour was abated for some years, but the place of rendezvous being at last altered, the herring fishery yearly increased; a spirit of emulation arose between the natives of the town and several adventurers, who, on account of the fishery resorted to Wick from other places. Curing of red, as well as white, herrings became an object of attention; and both the red and white herrings of Wick have met with the highest

Women sorting and gutting fish in J More's Yard, Shaltigoe – c 1935.
From the Johnston Collection. Reproduced by kind permission of the Wick Society.

Herring packers in D Water's Yard – c 1935.
From the Johnston Collection. Reproduced by kind permission of the Wick Society.

Herring boats and other vessels in Pulteneytown Harbour – c 1865.
From the Johnston Collection. Reproduced by kind permission of the Wick Society.

Herring drifters near entrance of Pulteneytown Harbour – c 1913.
From the Johnston Collection. Reproduced by kind permission of the Wick Society.

Rough seas at Pulteneytown Harbour Bay – c 1935 (and many other years!)
From the Johnston Collection. Reproduced by kind permission of the Wick Society.

The Barque *Hans* stranded on rocks at Broadhaven – 1905.
From the Johnston Collection. Reproduced by kind permission of the Wick Society.

Wick River and Bridge – west of the bridge the ice accumulates – Winter 1937.
From the Johnston Collection. Reproduced by kind permission of the Wick Society.

Wick under water – Alexandra Place during the Flood of 1933.
From the Johnston Collection. Reproduced by kind permission of the Wick Society.

approbation in the London and other markets.

The success of the herring fishing has been various, but, on the whole, increasing in proportion to the number of adventurers, and the skill they acquire. In 1790, 32 vessels on the bounty, measuring 1,610 tons, lay at Wick, but were greatly hampered for want of a good harbour.[1] In 1791, the number amounted to 44, crammed close to one another, in a worse condition than ever. They were much damaged by the storm at the height of the fishing season, notwithstanding which, the quantity caught was reckoned not inferior to that of 1790; and was sufficient to load all the bounty vessels. Many more might have been caught, had there been a good harbour for the vessels; and it is an agreeable sight, in a fine evening, to see upwards of 200 of them at once under sail, the crews in high spirits, setting out for the fishing; it would, however, be still more pleasing to see as many large vessels busied in the same occupation, which might be the case were the harbour made more commodious. Notwithstanding the success of late years, the fisheries of Wick are yet in their infancy. Before they can flourish, so as to become a national object, different encouragements would be necessary.

Rev Sutherland continues to complain of the severe disadvantages which restrict development of the herring fishery in Wick and district. One is the fact that few of those fishing near Wick are experienced 'real fishermen belonging to it, those alone except who resort to Wick, from different parts of the kingdom, during the season of herring fishery only.' Wick fishermen are mostly part-timers, causing shortage of service in their other trades when they take to the sea. The duties on salt, and coal ought to be abolished, and the town should have 'a large supply of salt and casks laid up in storehouses'. Wick had a poor harbour; its curing and storage facilities were very sparse. 'The last,' says Mr Sutherland, 'is an object worthy of the attention of the British Fishing Society' in an appended note:

> as many thousand barrels might often be caught in one night here; but, from its uncertainty, private adventurers cannot afford to have by them so great a stock of salt and casks, as would be necessary on such occasions; the consequence is that

1 The bounty laws were changed in 1786, busses receiving 20s per ton, and boat fishers 1 shilling per barrel landed (Dunlop: *British Fisheries Society*, op cit, p 23; Gray and Sutherland give 2s).

when the herrings run beyond expectation, the private stocks are exhausted, the industry of the poor fisherman cramped, and the fish allowed to lie on their hands, though perhaps the merchants were bound by paction to receive them. The best remedy would be to take off entirely the duty upon salt, an impost in many respects impolitic and injudicious.[1]

It would be easy to exaggerate the extent of development that was going on in Wick parish during the last years of the eighteenth century. It was impressive enough but very modest as compared with what happened later. The number of boats fishing in the area, the number of men involved and the striking increase in the number of barrels of herrings exported all indicated rising activity. According to custom-house books, William Sutherland was able to show a spectacular 300 per cent increase in the quantity of barrelled white herring sent out from Wick between 1782 and 1790, to say nothing of 2000 barrels of 'red herrings' exported in 1790 as compared with none at the earlier date.[2] Iain Sutherland believes that by 1790 'over 150 boats, both local and from the south side of the Moray Firth, were fishing off the [Caithness] coast during the summer season, which lasted from June to nearly October.'[3]

While all this development was centred on Wick, it must be mentioned that there was considerable activity on several 'goes' (geos) north and south of Wick. The most important of these, as mentioend by the Rev William, was Staxigoe, a village two miles north-east of Wick, a relatively safe natural harbour which was, at this time, serving not only as a base for fishing 'adventurers' such as Miller of the Field, Anderson and John Sutherland, but also as a valuable ancillary to Wick as a port; though very limited, its harbourage was much safer, and all kinds of goods were now coming in and going out through Staxigoe. The story of Staxigoe's substantial development as a port for the herring fishery, though much smaller in scale, is as interesting in

---

1 The salt tax – intended to discourage the import of salt – was abolished in 1825. In fact, fish curers were entitled to import salt duty free, but under such onerously bureaucratic restrictions (and they need to keep the imported salt 'under lock and key') that 'only determined curers, men with money and time, were likely to take it up'. (Gray, op cit p 6).

2 The actual figures quoted are: 1782, 363 barrels of white herrings; 1783, 700 barrels; 1,774, 1,800 barrels; 1,785, 9,613 of red and white; 1,790, 10,514 barrels of white and 'above 2,000 barrels of red herrings, besides about 700 barrels estimated to be consumed in the county'. 'Red-herrings' were, in fact, those preserved by salting and smoking; they commanded a higher price on the market.

3 Iain Sutherland: *Wick Harbour;* op cit, p 21.

its own way as that of Wick itself. Though owing much to the enterprise of Alexander Miller, the development was financed and encouraged by the landowner, Sir Benjamin Dunbar.[1]

Other creeks that underwent a measure of development, mostly after 1790, were Broadhaven and Papigoe between Staxigoe and Wick, Keiss in Sinclair Bay and Sarclet and Whaligoe also in the parish of Wick. Clyth, Lybster, Swiney, Forse, Latheronwheel, Dunbeath and Berriedale in the Caithness parish of Latheron, with or without much in the way of development, all became involved in the herring trade. Sarclet has already been mentioned as the scene of enterprise initiated by Sir John Sinclair and David Brodie; Brodie invested here £61, and the new settlement was called 'Brodiestown'; at Whaligoe near Ulbster, he invested £53 on 'clearing the harbour by blasting and removing large stones and building a platform for boats to secure them from being carried away'. The famous 'Steps of Whaligoe' cost him £8.[2] One of the problems of these fishing settlements south of Wick was the depth of the goe below the cliff top, so that access to and from the boat harbour had to be up and down a steep slope, a seriously discouraging factor for growth of the trade. There is a long flight of steps down to the harbour at Latheronwheel; and there is quite a descent to the harbour of Keiss, constructed in the 1818 by the engineer James Bremner, a native of Keiss (see pp 318 ff below).

In passing, though not directly involved with Wick, what happened at Helmsdale, just beyond the southern boundary of Caithness, deserves mention. Here was also developed a sizeable herring fishery partly connected with the 're-settlement' policies of the Sutherland

---

1 The fully story of Staxigoe is told in two remarkable wall exhibits executed by Iain Sutherland in the village hall of Staxigoe. The detailed text is illustrated by accompanying maps and sketches of various features of the scene. See also Dunlop: *British Fisheries Society*, op cit. p 154. There is also a short but informative account of it in Jean Dunlop: *Pulteney Town and the Planned Villages of Caithness*; in *Caithness: A Cultural Crossroads*; (Ed John Baldwin), Scottish Society for Northern Studies, Edina Press (1982).

2 Dunlop: *Pulteney Town*, op cit. pp 137-144. The *Statistical Account of Caithness, 1794*, tells how at Whaligoe 'fishermen, on this part of the coast, to get to their boats descend a huge precipice by winding steps in the face of the rock, by which some lives have been lost, and yet, from frequent practice, it is often done without assistance by a blind fisherman in Ulbster. To secure their boats from being dashed against the rocks, particularly in storms and stream tides, the fishers hang up their yauls ['yoles' or boats] by ropes, on hooks fixed in the face of the rock, above the level of the water, where they are safely suspended till the weather is fit for going to sea'. Dunlop adds that in 1808 some seven boats were using Whaligoe, and in 1814 there were 14. Another description of Whaligoe, quoted by Dunlop and dated 1841, tells how 'vessels entering there, anchor outside, and letting out their cable, they are hauled in stern foremost, and then moored on each side'. The popular tradition is that there are 365 steps, one for each day of the year.

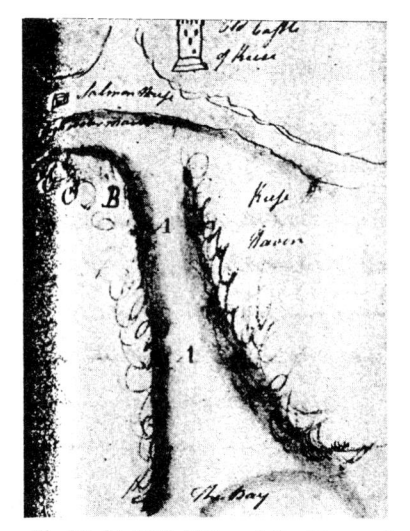

Fig 22 (P. 137) (PT and the Planned Villages of C.)
KEISS – 'A fine bay with plenty of water and may be useful for ships to pass a tide in previous to their passing the Pentland firth'.
Telford 1790

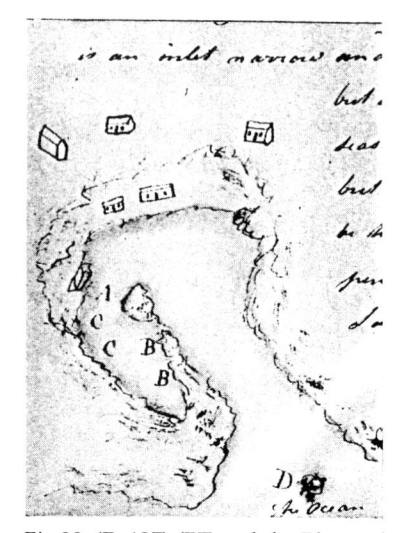

Fig 23 (P. 137) (PT and the Planned Villages of C.)
STAXIGOE – Staxigoe showing the prominent rock at 'A' and Miller's herring houses.
Telford 1790

By kind permission of the Keeper of the Scottish Records.

estates. The then Marquis of Stafford recruited the services of John Rennie in creating at Helmsdale a good harbour, completed in 1818, so that a herring 'cure' of 5,000 barrels in 1815, rose by 1839 to 46,571 barrels, with 200 boats operating from the village in 1839.[1] Refugees from the clearances supplied labour in Helmsdale and Dunbeath and also fishing settlements just north of Dunbeath. This experience of involuntary re-settlement and development is touchingly described in Neil Gunn's richly expressive novel, *The Silver Darlings*, to which we shall return.

But all this is to anticipate. Perceptively and prophetically, the Rev William Sutherland in 1794 declared: 'the fisheries of Wick are as yet in their infancy'. However, it seems unlikely that later development could have amounted to much had it not been, as Iain Sutherland

1 James Miller: *Portrait of Caithness and Sutherland*; London, Robert Hale (1985), pp 61-68.

expresses it, 'for two events which finally opened the door wide to the opportunities which lay beyond.' The two events are connected: the decision in 1786 that the government bounty on catches could be paid 'either on the boat or the herring caught'[1]; the other was the later decision to enlarge, deepen and protect Wick harbour. The British government made a desultory decision in 1750 to pay a bounty to fishermen in an attempt to encourage the growth of the fishing industry, 'as a reaction to the success of the Dutch fishing industry. Indeed,' says Gray, 'the shadow of the Dutch – with a herring fishing that spread along the coast of Europe – lay across the aspirations of other nations to successful fishing.' The bounty system was a moderate success, but much disappointment and frustration was caused to fishermen by the method of payment and delays in payment when it was due. (We have noted several examples of this). The scale related to the size of the vessel; but 'no payment was made relating to the size of the catch [at that time]'.

Also in 1786 was formed The British Society for Extending the Fisheries and Improving the Sea Coasts of the Kingdom, better known as the British Fisheries Society. This curious enterprise had government backing though its status was that of a joint-stock company, its main object being to assist in providing necessary centres for developing commercial fishing activities. Among its promotions on the west side of Scotland were Torridon, Gairloch, Lochinver, Plockton, Lochbay (Skye), Tobermory (Mull) and Ullapool. The last three were started in 1788, but abandoned respectively in 1838, 1844 and 1848 as failures. R H Campbell explains the Society's relative failure on the west as having been caused by enemy interference with shipping during the Napoleonic wars and rising prices of raw materials. He also suggests that the new western fishing ports failed 'through the centre of the herring industry moving from the Minch to the Moray Firth, especially after 1797, and through European demand beginning to displace the older West Indian demand for herring.'[2] The Society also had effect in getting some amelioration of the salt laws and 'by providing a pattern for official action under the Fishery Act of 1808'. This Act brought into existence the Commission for the Herring

1 Iain Sutherland, *Wick Harbour*, op cit. p 29 and ff. Sutherland gives the date 1785, but the Act authorising the change was passed in 1786. Gray, op cit (p 6) comments: 'The Act of that year promised bounties at the rate of 2s per barrel, on herring caught from small boats and cured to conform with regulations. This, added to 2s 4d, due on each barrel of herring exported, gave a substantial subsidy to all forms of herring fishing.'
2 R H Campbell: *Scotland Since 1707: The Rise of an Industrial Society*, Donald (1985) p.171.

Fishery which placed resident Fishery officers in suitable localities.[1] This body was re-constituted in 1842, and in 1882 was replaced by the Fishery Board for Scotland.

The Society's great success was the creation of Pulteneytown, the new fishery town on the south bank of the Wick river, and administered until this century as a separate community from Wick. It was this remarkable foundation, harbour and village, on land 'offered to the Society by Sir Benjamin Dunbar, proprietor of the estate of Hempriggs' that provided the essential impetus for the huge growth of the herring fishing at the entrance to the Wick river. Telford began work on the harbour in 1803, and although work was slow to begin with, progress accelerated as masons, blacksmiths and other tradesmen, necessary for the vast programme of construction now embarked on, were attracted to a locality which, whatever its other disadvantages, was soon able to offer the craftsmen and professional fishers a decent home and place to live in. 'The first of the yards were being let,' says Iain Sutherland, and 'in 1807 the first teashop, originally for meeting the demands of the construction force, was opened. By 1813 there were over 300 inhabitants in an area where 14 years before there had been about 15, and the population passed 1000 in 1816,'[2]

Sir John Sinclair's Proposals

In his *Miscellaneous Essays,* Sir John includes a knowledgeable eight-page comment on the 1, *Means of Establishing the Dutch mode of catching and curing herring; 2, On the variety of fish caught in the Northern Part of Scotland; and, 3, on the Means of promoting the Fisheries of the North.* This clearly indicates his state of mind on the subject before serious development began, and the nature of his motives in putting such matters before Wick Burgh Council (in which he was provost), the British Fisheries Society and his many government and political friends. He comments on the extent to which a 'herring fishery has been carried on along the coast of Caithness, particularly in the

1 R H Campbell, op cit, pp 171-172.
2 Iain Sutherland, op cit, p 23. It must be assumed that Mr Sutherland is referring to the 'cookshop' which, according to Jean Dunlop's reading of the Fisheries Society records, had 'early been established to cater for workmen on the harbour and the bridge'. This seems a more likely sort of establishment than a 'teashop' at that stage of affairs. The cookshop was in fact opened by a Mr David Bremner. Of this Jean Dunlop comments that Bremner 'showed considerable enterprise in erecting a cookshop which must have been very popular among the workers on the bridge and the harbour.' (Dunlop: *British Fisheries Society,* op cit p 161.).

neighbourhood of Wick.' Seven to ten thousands of barrels were now being caught in the area, but this catch could be 'considerably improved', bearing in mind the recommendations of that 'intelligent engineer (Mr Telford)' and 'some Dutch fishermen' whom he, Sir John, had consulted. As large a quantity as 'a million barrels could be got' if the improvements suggested were put in hand, and even half a million without undue additional effort, producing, perhaps, fish to a market value per year of £625,000. To achieve such an object the following measures should be undertaken:
1 'It is essential that some harbours should be made along the coast,' so that fishermen could fish further out and come in safely. 'It will appear' he said 'what harbours ought to be formed' from Telford's survey. Telford had not yet reported.
2 'It is absolutely necessary that it [the herring fishery] should be carried on by busses,' so that larger and deeper nets could be used, so that fishery could carried on more safely in poor weather and at greater distance from the shore, and with less damage to the catch than was usual with small boats. As we have seen, the busses were much more expensive to build than the small craft that local folk could build or have built for themselves, costing perhaps £20 or £30. Sinclair calculated that a buss might cost as much as 13,000 guelders in Holland or £1,550 sterling. Though the Fisheries Society favoured them, the funds never became available for a Wick-based fleet of busses.
3 Dutch type nets could be used with the bigger vessels – 'seventeen fathoms long and four nets deep' as compared with Caithness nets only 22ft deep and much shorter.
4 Attention might be given to the salt used in the curing. For this the Dutch used Lisbon salt; 'perhaps the Liverpool salt might answer just as well, if properly prepared.'
5 There were some problems as to the kind of provender on which the Dutch seamen lived, longer at sea than the Caithness men. Whatever may be the case,' says Sinclair 'with English fishermen, it is certain that the Scotch do not fare so well.' The Dutch every morning 'got a glass of gin, and two tumblers of white wine on Sundays and Thursdays.' Sinclair says nothing about the Scots and their whisky; perhaps in his time the habit of taking a firkin or two of local brew on their voyages had not yet been established. The Dutch vessels worked cooperatively in high season. The Caithnessmen went out singly at sunset and returned the following morning, 'seldom delivering their cargo till ten or twelve o'clock, when, at that season of the year [July],

the fish must be greatly injured by the influence of the sun, and this renders more staff necessary to prevent putrefaction.'

6 The Dutch method of curing ought to be studied. It was greatly superior to that of the Scots:

> As soon as the Dutch fishermen get the herring on board, they are immediately put in vats in the hold [of their busses], and gutted as soon as possible, with a small knife, and not with the fingers, as practised in Caithness. When gutted, they are *rouzed* or sprinkled in a kind of VAT, and immediately afterwards salted in a barrel. The Dutch use much less stuff than the Caithness fishermen, one barrel of salt being sufficient to *rouze* eleven barrels of herring, and another barrel will cure from six to seven barrels of fish for home consumption, whereas in Caithness, they generally use one barrel of salt to two barrels of herring, more especially cured for a foreign market. The method of packing the fish also varies a little. The fish thus cured are not repacked, but when the buss arrives in Holland, the barrels are opened, and another row of herring put in with a little salt, in which state they are sold.

7 Sinclair notes that the Dutch method of eating herring raw puts the commodity in a quite different category of comestible to the usage in Britain. The Dutch says: 'When the herring comes in, the doctor goes out.' The market offered by Germany to the Scots is one that should be systematically and effectively exploited.

8 There should be changes in British law to encourage a more efficient and profitable mode of paying bounty; taxes on barrel staves and salt should be abolished.

9 (10 in Sinclair's list):

> It would appear from the preceding observations, what an important source of national wealth, of food, and naval strength, might be secured to Great Britain, were wise and vigorous measures pursued for that purpose; and this, it may be proper to add, is the fit time to bring that object to bear, when, from the convulsions on the Continent, and particularly in Holland, so many industrious persons, conversant with the herring themselves from revolutionary storms in their kingdoms, and if settled here, will be happy to furnish this county with all the benefit of their skill and experience.[1]

1 Sir John Sinclair, Bart: *Essays on Miscellaneous Subjects:* T Cadell, Jun, and W. Davis in the Strand (1802): Appendix to Essay No 8, pp 253-258.

THE YEARS 1790-1815

As suggested in Chap 9 (pp 218-219), there cannot be much doubt that the boost given to the north Scottish economy by the government during the later years of the eighteenth century was motivated by a combination of circumstances, anxieties about depopulation, strategic considerations and worries about food. There was too a developing awareness of the benefits to be gained from more efficient exploitation of the fisheries. Not least of the immediate causes was the lobbying of Sir John Sinclair of Ulbster and his friends.

There had, in fact, been in existence since 1718 a Commission and Board of Trustees for Improving Fisheries and Manufactures in Scotland, which made interventions in such areas of concern as roads, canals and especially the development of Scottish linen manufacture. This body was partly instrumental in persuading the government to adopt a fishing bounties scheme.[1] In 1786 came the British Fisheries Society ('promoted by men of the landlord and merchant classes with an over-riding interest in social development'), and about the same time a relaxation of the formerly tight rules governing the payment of bounty. As an indication of the heightening interest of parliament and government was the appointment respectively in 1785 and 1789 of House of Commons Committees, the one to *inquire into the State of British Fisheries* and the other *into the State of British Herring Fisheries*.

We have also seen how things began to move quite rapidly in Wick at the turn of the century. It could have been otherwise. The first great surge in herring fishing off the east coast of Scotland occurred not in the north but in the Firth of Forth, where great shoals of herring moved close inshore in 1794 and for several subsequent years. This was fortuitously very convenient for marketing in Edinburgh and Glasgow the great quantities of fish netted: some 800 to 900 boats became rapidly engaged and about 100 curing yards were set up near to Burntisland in Fife. Then suddenly the fish disappeared, and the sudden boom in herring business collapsed.

No such sudden influx or departure of herring occurred in Caithness. Instead fishers continued taking decent catches in less varying conditions. Merchants from the Firth of Forth area were already becoming accustomed to buying in quantities of fish from

---

1 This was one of a number of government-based 'quasi-managerial' bodies set up in Scotland after the Union of 1707 'to take over some of the functions of the defunct privy council'. See Lynch op cit, p 324. Government 'intervention' of this kind in Scottish affairs became commoner and more acceptable than in England.

Caithness fishers, 'either "by contract or by daily bargain" on the beach when the fish were landed', and were sending these quite highly prized 'white' herrings back to Edinburgh. This trade too, fluctuated, especially in the matter of price paid by the merchants. In 1789 'occurred the greatest fishing ever known on the Wick coast. Four nights of it completely exhausted all salt and casks and the price fell from 8s. to about 2s. per cran.'[1]

Getting in the Herrings

Conditions of war and a seemingly assured market, boosted for the Caithness fishermen by the sudden decline after a few years of boom for the fishers of the Firth of Forth, brought into being a thriving and expanding herring trade here in the north, where before there had never been any such expectations. Gray explains it:

> The high prospective profit drew many small men – for example, local Caithness tradesmen – into curing, along with the big southern firms which had been the first to engage boats for herring fishing. By 1800 there were sixteen firms engaged in curing in Wick alone. About two thirds of the catch was pickled and one third 'reddened'. The average firm, then, would be turning out less than 500 barrels a year and would give seasonal employment to twenty or thirty workers. The curers were mainly local men, of varied original trades, who saw the chance of a good profit on modest capital in enterprise that need not occupy their full time (for herring fishing was so definitely a seasonal effort that it needed to occupy curers or fishermen for only three months in the year).[2]

The resources needed for expansion were not exorbitant and did not require the intervention of the 'capitalist'. Many farmers in the area had boats, costing little more than £30; and for those that had not, in view of the profits now to be made, groups of farmers and even cottagers would pool their resources to buy a boat, certain that they could sell what they could land. Nets must also be bought and were usually hand-made by women from linen or hemp. The nets in use

---

1 This state of affairs was commented on by William Sutherland in *Wick 1794*. The 'cran' (was) is a quayside measure of fresh herrings, now fixed at 37½ gallons, about 750 fish.
2 M Gray, op cit, p 30.

consisted of an extended chain or 'drift', which would be 'shot' or 'cast into the sea and hang as a curtain with the upper edge a short distance below the surface of the water. The length of the drift was governed by the size of the maximum haul that could be safely brought home by the little boat.' Boats were crewed by no more than four, often consisting of perhaps three who had contributed to the outlay, and a boy or youth. All apart from the boy took more or less equal shares in the profit.

The life of a community of Caithness cottar-fisher folk and the actual dangerous and exciting business of fishing for herring during these actual years of the century is evoked in Neil Gunn's *The Silver Darlings*. Gunn himself was born in 1891, and so only learned of the fishing from his father and grandfather, both fishers, the family having originally migrated from Kildonan to Dunbeath during the first wave of clearance by the Countess of Sutherland. The harbour of Dunbeath ('Dunster' in the story), still had boats and there was some fishing when Neil was a boy. He had ample opportunity during the early life to get to know the sea along this coast. In the early years of the century Dunbeath was one of the 'rivals' of Wick; but by 1840 Dunbeath had built up a fleet of 76 boats.

The story opens with an account of Tormad and his mates, out fishing just away from the coast near Berriedale; when the boat was run down by a government cutter whose skipper, quite brutally and legally took Tormad and his companions aboard the cutter together with their catch, leaving the fishing smack adrift. They were the press-gang afloat. These were the days when the British Navy was championing freedom against the tyrant; the 'jolly tars' of Britain's 'hearts of oak' were made up largely of pressed men and convicts, men who had less knowledge of freedom than the writer of the popular sea-song. The press was yet one other of the many hazards of fishing off the Scottish coast; the fishers were ideal recruits, brave experienced seamen. 'Pay no attention,' called Tormad to his mates as the cutter bore down on them. 'The sea at least is free.' Though one of his companions came back, Tormad was never seen again in Sutherland.

The main story of the novel is that of the fortunes of Roddie Sinclair and Catrine, newly married to Tormad at the beginning of the book. Catrine's young son, Finn – who never sees his father, discovers the sea and the fishing as a boy in the boat, and crews with Roddie as he and two other comrades take up the fishing in a boat initially paid for by Hendry, the inn-keeper, a thoroughly typical arrangement; Roddie himself eventually becomes a locally celebrated skipper of his own boat and Finn's step-father when he finally persuades the widowed Catrine to marry him, (Roddie is generally regarded as something of a portrait of Neil Gunn's own father, James, though James came on the scene quite a bit later than Roddie). The tale is told as through the eyes of young Finn, who himself grows up to be a formidable Caithness fisherman.

A chief value – and joy – of the book is its vivid and accurate representation of the terrors, excitements and satisfactions of the kind of fishing that dominated the Caithness coast for forty or more years, the shifts between depression and elation as the fishing fails or succeeds, the ups and downs of the market, and the tight community relations of the fisher-folk of the village. Not the least interesting episode of the book is the voyage of Roddie's boat, the *Seafoam*, through the fearsome Pentland Firth and the Minch to Stornoway, a reminder that it was not only Caithness at this time that was involved in the explosion of the herring trade. It also demonstrates how it was that Thurso was not preferred to Wick as the great herring port.[1]

Gunn provides other pictures of the fishing scene. His biographers quote from an occasional piece by the novelist:

> A fisherman, who has hardly reached the alloted span (this was 1938), once gave me a remarkable picture of the herring fleet sailing out of a creek on the Caithness coast [Dunbeath] when he was a boy. Though the curing stations and cooperages are now a ruinous decay, about one hundred and fifty boats fished out of the creek during summer seasons of his boyhood and indeed until he was a grown man. How lovely a sight from that river-mouth, from the small horse-shoe bay in the gaunt cliff-wall of Caithness, then all under sail, left for the fishing grounds in the afternoon or early evening.[2]

The Caithness herring fishery in these early days was a very economically capitalised industry. Most of the boats and their equipment were owned or part owned by skippers and crew. If an inn-keeper or other local capitalist put up the money originally, there were usually arrangements, as in the case of Roddie's first boat, the *Morning Star*, for buying out the capitalist by instalments.

Gutting and curing also required only modest capital outlay,

---

1 Neil Gunn: *The Silver Darlings*; London, Faber and Faber, (1969).
2 F R Hart and J B Pick: *Neil M Gunn: A Highland Life*; London, John Murray (1981).

mainly for white herring, a stock of barrels and salt, a quayside large enough to accommodate enough gutters and packers to cope with the catch coming ashore, for the work had to be done immediately the fish were landed and in the open air, all weathers. Gray graphically describes this process too:

> This would be performed by women grouped in teams (crews) of three, with two to gut and one to pack. Several crews would stand around the large rectangular container into which the fish were thrown on first arrival in the yard. The gutters prepared for the next stage by gutting the fish – which was done in a single deft movement – and by dropping the gutted fish into containers which were differentiated according to grade. From there packers would take the herring to complete barrels of designated grade. Whatever the overall size of the curing yard, the crew of three was the basic work unit. The division into crews also gave a standard to determine the size of the labour force needed to serve the fleet; one crew of women would be hired for each boat engaged by the curer. The women were engaged for the whole season but, apart from the earnest money (arles), paid upon agreement, remuneration was mainly by the piece. A crew would perform the whole curing process for the barrels on which it operated and was paid at a rate per barrel. The women's earning depended upon their speed and skill, and, in fact, they acquired great speed of hand in the continually repeated operation in which a fish was lifted from farlin, was split, the gut removed and the carcass passed to the packer.[1]

Yet another vignette from Neil Gunn brings life to the scene. He recalls from his own early life the 'last of the exuberance' on the quayside:

> I can remember as a very small boy watching a woman gutter to see if I could follow how she did it and being baffled. There they were, row after row of them, in stiff rustling oilskins, well-booted and shawled, silver-scaled and blood-flecked, with faces all alive, quick-voiced in retort of laughter, working, as we said, 'like lightning'. And all of them local women or girls, making their little bit while the going was good. Any visitor got a fry of herring from the generous skipper, whether a black-hooded

---

1 Gray, op cit. pp 53-54.

widow from the hills or the friendly policeman from beside the church.[1]

Fish were packed in standard sized barrels in layers with at least a specific quantity of salt; the barrel then stood open for at least fourteen days, was topped up and closed. Fishery Officers ensured maintenance of quality by sampling. When closed the cask was branded, and the 'rising reputation of the Scotch cured herring was undoubtedly furthered by the use of the "brand".'

Wick was not only deficient in harbour room; there was also, until 1811, far too little space for curing operations. The Telford harbour works construction on the south side of Wick Water, included yards but not sufficient for the growth that occurred. So far the local labour force proved adequate to cope with Wick's herring trade, but with the spurt of greater activity that began in 1808, more and more incomers, from as far away as the Fife and Berwickshire coasts came in during the high season, the two months of July and August, as many as a third of all those engaged. Many of these, unlike the Caithness fishermen, were full-time fishers and hired men, moving into and away from different districts as opportunity allowed. Work in the yards would be carried out by local women, wives and daughters of the men in the boats, outsiders coming in for the season and the women-folk too of the visiting fishermen. During the season the population of Wick was liable to double, and 'from this seasonal influx the little town acquired some more permanent residents, as a few of the hired men chose to stay and become permanent fishermen. In its growth Wick became a melting-pot for the migrant people of the north and north-west', pulling in during the second decade of the century and onwards considerable numbers of Gaelic-speaking folk from the west, including people displaced by the clearances.

By 1814 the number of boats engaged in the Wick area had risen fourfold from 214 in 1808 to 822, and Telford's harbour was already proving inadequate. 'Apart from the difficulties experienced with the press of vessels trying to use it, the harbour entrance was continually silting up very badly,' says Iain Sutherland. Although most of the boats were still 15 to 20-foot 'scaffies', the press now included the larger boats of some of the visitors. 'Even with the highest tides,' continues Iain Sutherland:

> there was only 13ft of water at best and at low water it was

1 F R Hart and J B Pick, op cit, p 28.

impossible for any but the smallest boats to use the harbour. Shipmasters reverted to loading and unloading their vessels in the bay, using barges with oar power only, to ferry the cargoes ashore rather than risk being trapped for what could be weeks in the harbour. The process was very expensive, as the barges had to be hired and much injury was done to life and limb when the cargoes were being handled under difficult sea conditions. Eventually, concluding that they were no worse off using ports which had no harbours, such as Broadhaven and Greenigoe, the shipowners threatened to take their trade there unless something was done about it.[1]

Accordingly, pressure built up for an extension to the harbour, but this did not come until several years later. Most development so far had occurred during wartime. 1815 marked the end of the war, with the effect of opening up to the Caithness fishing industry a prospect of lucrative outlets for its products on the continent and especially the Baltic, and hence accelerated growth. But, as summed up by Gray:

> Even by 1815 Caithness fishermen and curers had achieved much. For twenty-five years they had been operating a fishery of no little scale and at the end they were swiftly expanding it yet further. But perhaps just as important was the example it gave of how the herring stocks of the east coast of Scotland could be cheaply and reliably exploited. It provided a model that was capable of being moved to other parts of the Scottish coastline. In fact, the means had been discovered by which the whole of a rapidly growing body of fishermen up and down the east coast could find profitable employment in at least a seasonal herring fishing. And once they turned to herring fishing, much of their traditional way of life had to change.[2]

And this was certainly true of Wick, whose traditional way of life changed out of all recognition. The most drastic of the changes was the creation in the wayward Water of Wick of a substantial new harbour, completed between 1803 and 1807, and the rise beyond the south bank of the Wick river, of a new town, soon to rival in size Wick itself, and incomparably cleaner, richer (though not necessarily much grander) than the old royal burgh.

1 Iain Sutherland, *Wick Harbour*, op cit, p 28.
2 M Gray, op cit, p 38.

THE RISE OF PULTENEYTOWN

Thomas Telford's report of 1790 had set going a ferment of discussion, most importantly in Wick parish itself, and not least in the mind of Sir Benjamin Dunbar, who owned both banks of the Wick river. At first Telford had favoured the idea of a new harbour works on the north side of the estuary, but was later persuaded that the south bank would be more suitable. Not only was there less cultivation on this side; there was also a possibility of developing 'mills and manufactures' powered by water led in from the Loch of Hempriggs, from which there was a fall of some 175 feet down to the riverside. After long discussion between the Fisheries Society and Sir Benjamin – during which a proposition to undertake the development at Clyth was considered and rejected, Sir Benjamin agreed to lease 390 acres, including the South Head, the hill of Old Wick (including the castle) and the area known as Harrow. On the property, especially towards the Head, were ample supplies of building stone, later exploited for constructing the extensive harbour works and the houses, churches and factories of what came to be called Pulteneytown.

Telford explained his reasons for choosing this location for his harbour:

> On the west coast of Scotland, every loch is a Harbour, and no vessels can ever be at a loss to find protection but the case is very different on the N.E. coast, at present there is no place where a vessel can run into or even lye with safety; from the bay of Cromarty in Murray Firth to the Roadstead of Scrabster on the Western side of the Pentland Firth. Vessels frequenting the Herring Fishery in this Quarter lye in the River of Wick, but they are confined within a shallow Bar in a Narrow Channel, and so exposed to the N.E. that they dare not wait the equinoctial Gales, and instead of Fishing for the whole season they push off as soon as they can get anything like a Cargo. They have no place but the Beach on which to land and stack their Fish, and they frequently cannot get over the Bar, even to reach their Beach, but lye with their Fish in their open boats exposed to the Sun until they are spoiled. It is generally allowed that the deep sea fishing might be carried on this Quarter, but no person will risk his vessel and Capital while there is no place of security for them to run into in case of Stormy Weather nor any convenience whatever to enable them to carry on their

business with advantage.[1]

Much the most imaginative – and enduring – element of this whole radical project was the idea of Pulteneytown. A prime purpose set by the British Fisheries Society for itself was, as Gray puts is, 'to create villages – or to set the conditions for the growth of villages – in which fishermen would congregate.' Whether or not Rennie was asked by the Fisheries Society to bear in mind the need for improved accommodation for fishers, his report of 1793 was shelved on account of cost. It is, however, difficult to imagine that there could have been any rapid expansion of the fishing at Wick without attention to this necessity. Not only was Wick and the Caithness coast generally lacking an efficient harbour of any kind; it also had few full-time professional fishermen, dedicated to the trade, fully experienced and knowledgeable in its ways; and without somewhere to live in reasonable comfort it was unlikely that many such workers would come to settle on what was in so many respects such a remote, inhospitable place.

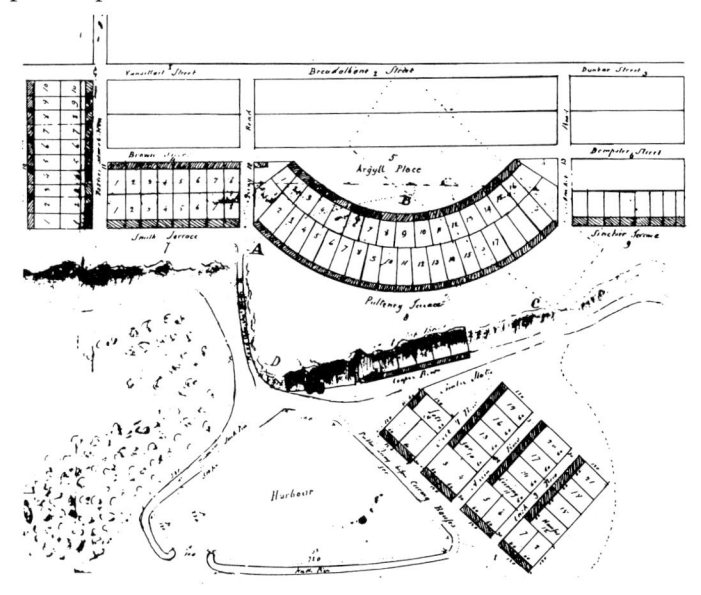

Fig 24 Telford's plan of Pulteneytown village and harbour area, dated August 1807. *(By kind permission of the Keeper of the Scottish Records).*

1 Jean Dunlop: *Pulteney Town and the Planned Villages of Caithness;* from *Caithness: A Cultural Crossroads;* Scottish Society for Northern Studies, and Edina Press; Editor: John R Baldwin (1982), p 150. Much of what follows is derived from the same source.

Both Dunbar of Hempriggs and Sinclair of Ulbster were enthusiasts for new settlements for workers and their families, and both had launched schemes of their own in the area, Dunbar at Louisburgh and Sinclair at Sarclet (in conjunction with David Brodie), Halkirk and Thurso, but none of these had been efficiently related to the industrial or commercial prospects of the place. Telford's commission of 1801, backed this time by the Treasury Commissioners, to whom it had doubtless become evident that harbour development must be accompanied by housing development, expressly referred to the issue, and a new town became a significant part of the whole project.

Pulteneytown, named after Sir William Pulteney who had, sad to say, died while the project was hatching, was designed by Telford himself, the only one of the Society's villages to come from his drawing board. It was eventually fulfilled in much the same form as Telford envisaged it. Though engaged elsewhere, he kept the new town in the north under constant review.[1]

The harbour work was authorised by Act of Parliament (46 Geo III, cap. 155) in 1806. Telford's 'clerk of works', George Burn, a local architect, saw the bridge and harbour project through to completion in December, 1811. Fishermen continued as best as they might to land their fish on the Wick foreshore while the work was continuing, with an increasing number of boats coming from further south. 17 boats arrived from the Firth of Forth in 1807 as compared with 3 the previous year.

Work on Pulteneytown began at about the same time and the main section of the town was completed in 20 years, 'almost completely according to the plan' Telford made. The first sector of 72 lots, to which the earliest inhabitants were to be confined, consisted of Breadalbane Terrace and a group of streets on the north and east side of Argyle Square. These and later streets were

> named for directors of the Society and this practice continued and included some of the officials as well. Each lot was 50ft (15.2m) on the street frontage and 100ft (30.5m) deep. Almost the whole frontage had to be filled and the building had to be right on the street. It seems to us rather strange that front gardens should not be allowed – there was plenty of room

---

[1] Perhaps the finest tribute to this astonishing road, bridge and church builder and town-planner, paid by our century, has been that of giving the name 'Telford' to one of the most ambitious of all new town projects ever undertaken in Britain, in an English county where Telford's own work was almost as prolific as that in Scotland.

behind of course – but the regulation was an attempt to keep the usual midden off the main street. Indeed the settler was required to lay flag paving stones, 6ft (1.8m) wide with a kerb 2ft (0.6m) deep, the flags to be 4ins (10.2cm) thick. The pavement had to be 4ins (10.2cm) below the level of the ground floor of the house. Each house was to have a narrow access to its garden from the street without going through the house – modern flat and terrace dwellers will appreciate the convenience of that bit of planning. The streets were to be 30ft (9.1m) wide and covered with a coat of sea gravel 10in (12.5cm) thick. Telford supplied suggested plans for houses – two storeys for the better streets to be not less than 17ft (5.2m) at the gable, door 67ft x 3ft (18m x 0.9m) and windows 5ft x 3ft (1.5m x 0.9m) 6 total cost about £300. He had hoped for 'uniformity of Building in point of Elevation of the Houses and Dimensions of the Doors and Windows' but as he feared he never really got that from individual builders. The lesser streets could have single storey houses at least 8ft (2.4m) high at the gable, doors also 6ft x 3ft (1.8m x 0.9m) but windows only 4ft x 3ft (1.2m x 0.9m) – the cost reckoned to be about half, or £150. All houses were to be stone-built and roofed with slate, though tiles were permitted. In June 1815 Telford admitted that houses were not built to specifications and hardly two were alike but he agreed that to challenge them would lead to endless disputes.[1]

Telford's anxiety about uniformity was characteristic of town-planning ideas of the time. Classical elegance, grace and uniformity were styles cultivated by urban designers such as the Woods who had created the terraces of Bath that figures centrally in Jane Austen's work, and James Craig, designer of New Edinburgh. Though not aiming at the standards appropriate to the affluent middle-classes, Robert Owen's New Lanark and the designers of working-class villages in other parts of Scotland, nevertheless thought in terms of moderate comfort, light and air for the inhabitants of the new communities, very different from the higgeldy-piggeldy traditions of the past. Uniformity was an aspect too of economy in building costs. It was no accident that Telford had as patron, Sir William Pulteney, whose original name was Johnstone and adopted the Pulteney name when he married a daughter of William Pulteney, Earl of Bath, on whose property so much new town building was occurring. Sir

---

1 Jean Dunlop, *Pulteneytown*, op cit, pp 151-152.

WICK OF THE NORTH

William's connection with Bath became even closer than that required by family ties; he was for some years MP for the town.

In Edinburgh and Bath architects had no need to associate the new housing with people's work; the inhabitants of the Bath terraces had neither any use for work nor any desire to be close to the mines and factories where the wealth of some of them was generated. The working-class village planners, on the other hand, had directly 'to face the problem of drawing together and keeping sufficiently large numbers of women and children', for most of the new villages were associated with work in textile mills, where the labour of women and children was at a premium.[1]

Pulteneytown, Wick, was very much intended as a working-class community; the aim here was to attract a population whose men would work the boats and serve as boatbuilders, masons, coopers and the like, and whose women (though not perhaps the children) would process the fish on landing. Lower Pulteneytown, the sandy flats below the high river bank marked by Breadalbane Terrace was allocated by Telford to quayside services and some residence associated with them. This was divided into 21 lots of 60ft by 120ft (18.3m x 36.6m) for curing houses. The curing houses

> had to be at least 60ft x 22ft and 18ft high (18.3m x 36.6m x 5.5m) with proper sheds and cellars at the rear or under the building. The frontage, which had to be filled, could be used for a dwelling house (provided it was 18ft (5.5m high) and the sheds built at the side of the lot, but in any case the buildings had to be used by fish curers, fishermen or people employed by them. It was estimated that it would cost a settler £500 to fit up one of these curing lots.

The remains of some of the old curing houses are still to be seen. The area is (and was) one of lower tone than Upper Pulteneytown. It was here that Telford himself and George Burn were honoured by a street name, reflecting no doubt their lower caste status as compared with that of Sinclair, Dempster, Breadalbane, Argyle and the other lords and gentry connected with the project and honoured in the Upper Town. Later, inhabitants of the newer parts of Pulteneytown were to call themselves 'Backsiders' – and proud of it. Williamson Street running north-south through Lower Pulteneytown and crossing

---

1 T C Smout: *A History of the Scottish People, 1560-1830*; London, Collins Fontana Press (1985), p 381. See also comment on Smout's *The Landowner and the Planned Village in Scotland* in *Additional Note* on p. 304, infra.

Telford and Burn streets is named after James Williamson, the Fishery Society's Agent in Wick, 'soldier turned farmer, and though considered excellent in dealing with people' was no great penman nor much of an accountant.

Far from seeking to rehouse local peasant folk as in some sense Sinclair and Dunbar had sought to do in Halkirk, Thurso and Louisburgh, the British Fisheries Society expressly wished to attract to Wick a new and quite different sort of tenantry for its model houses. Advertisements were placed in newspapers further south. One such appeared in the *Aberdeen Journal*, 6 April, 1808:

> TO FISHERMEN, FISH-CURERS,
> MANUFACTURERS, &c
> PULTENEY TOWN, N.E. Coast of SCOTLAND
>
> NOTICE is hereby given, that the British Society for Extending the Fisheries and improving the Sea Coasts, are now constructing and have considerably proceeded with a secure and commodious Harbour on the south side of the Bay of Wick, which will be capable of containing above 100 Fishing vessels, and with such a depth of water as will enable vessels drawing nine feet of water, to enter and depart at high water in neap tides and at half tides in spring tides; and immediately adjoining the harbour the scite *(sic)* has been laid out by MR TELFORD, with proper situations for Curing-Houses, an extensive Grass-plat for the repairing and backing of Nets, a sufficient space for the erection of frames to dry them, and a healthy walk for the inhabitants, commanding a full view of the Bay and Offing.
>
> The Town and Harbour are within little more than half a mile of the populous town of Wick, and communicate with it by a newly erected Stone Bridge. The ground belonging to the Society is all flat and capable of cultivation. There is a regular and plentiful supply of Water, with a sufficient fall adjacent to the Village and Harbour for several water wheels; and there is an excellent Spring within a short distance of the Town and Harbour. The Herrings have set in, on this part of the coast, for the last 30 years, without a single failure, about the 1st August; in the last season no fewer than 30,000 barrels were taken, and, in the opinion of the fishermen upon the spot, the quantity might have been doubled, had the Harbour been then sufficiently advanced to afford shelter to the boats.
>
> The Town is divided into Building Lots of 50 feet in front by 1000 in depth, which may be feued in perpetuity at an easy rate of 25 and 20 shillings, according to the position of the Lots. The choice will be regulated by the priority of the application, the first year's rent remitted to those who shall have completed their Houses within the year; and the first 12 real fishermen who become settlers, will receive other advantages. The Curing House Lots will be disposed by auction in July next, and future notice will be given of the day and place.
>
> Further particulars may be learned from the Society's Agent, James Williamson Esq. Upper Ackergill, Wick; from Lewis Gordon, Esq. W.S. Edinburgh; and their Secretary, Gilbert Salton, Esq. Furnival's Inn, London.

Growth of the new settlement from now on was fast and vigorous. 'Settlers came and they prospered,' says Jean Dunlop. There was, to begin with, doubt as to whether or not sufficient numbers of 'declared professionals' would come, willing to put sufficient effort into the fishing to make enough 'to pay for any food they did not grow in their back gardens or pull out of the sea.' This could have happened if the harvest of the sea had not continued to be good; the hauls of herring, though variable, continued on average to rise, and soon after its opening the Telford harbour was proving inadequate for the boats now coming.

By 1810 sixty of the Pulteneytown lots were taken 'and building was going on both above and below the bank', that is, both in Lower and Upper Pulteneytown.[1] In Lower Pulteneytown some problems arose from its nearness to the sea. A feuar, George Wares, wrote that 'he had built sunk vaulted cellars for salt and had begun a red-herring house, but as the harbour had not yet been finished his property was not properly defended from the sea,' and during bad weather his cellar was drowned and filled with sand. Wares and some other feuars who had suffered were let off rent payments for three years in compensation. The Agent, James Williamson, wrote that same year:

> Tho' at all times sanguine, the rapid increase of settlers far exceeded my expectations . . . In my early operations as the Society's Agent I had to bear the scoffs of many who from malice or selfish motives ridiculed the idea of such settlement on such a scale; I may now be permitted without arrogating too much to myself to claim some merit in having at so early a period feued off one third of the village.[2]

The curing lots were rouped in August, 1808, five being taken by local Wick men, another by James Henderson of Clyth (one of the developing landlords), two by James Miller, a merchant of Leith, two by a merchant from Dundee, Peter Davidson, and one by a cooper, David Kid, also from Leith. A millwright from Wick, John Sinclair, set up his mill in Lower Pulteneytown, and is reported by Williamson as already working in February, 1809. It is, he says, 'this day grinding a grist of corn for me'.

---

1 For those not familiar with Wick, Lower and Higher Pulteneytown are separated by a high steep bank, negotiable to traffic only at either end. Along the upper edge of the bank runs Sinclair Terrace into Breadalbane, and on the flat immediately below Union Street and Bank Row.

2 Dunlop, *Pulteneytown*, op cit. p 155.

The Deputy Governors of the Society, Sir William Smith MP (grandfather of Florence Nightingale) visited in 1809 during the fishing season, and told of his difficulties in finding lodgings at a reasonable price. A guinea or a guinea and a half per month was being asked, and 'even at that unexampled price a lodging was difficult to be procured'. He spoke of 400 to 500 boats being employed in the fishing at one time in the season, and as many as 6,000 barrels of herring being taken in one night.

Telford continued to give 'minute attention' to the building of Pulteneytown, though fully occupied at the time building the Caledonian Canal. He was particularly concerned about the location of privies for the new houses, determined to establish high standards of cleanliness and hygiene in his new town despite the inclination of some local builders to be careless about such matters. On his visit in October, 1813 he inspected the pier, checking with iron rods to ensure that the foundations were correctly laid. The harbour remained 'one of the permanent problems for the Society – it was no sooner finished than it was found to be too small for the increased number of boats (and their larger size) and it was continually filling up with sand.'[1]

By 1812 the population of Pulteneytown was 211, with more coming and the population 'likely to be doubled after another good season. February, 1813 saw carts employed daily carrying stones, and masons were said to be full at work.' Dram shops had opened all over the place and a vintner from Wick, Mr Oal, took a corner site for an inn (on which he proposed to spend £1000). Was this what became the Mackay's Hotel in later years? In January 1812 Telford recommended a site on the riverside for a boat-building yard and 'in May 1813 the first ship was reported to have been built – a sloop called *Brothers*. The owner was George Burn the architect, but the builder was almost certainly James Bremner,' who had recently returned from Greenock to set up his own yard. In 1815 Bremner was building a brig to be named *Duke of Wellington* for which he himself cut a fine figure-head of the Duke in uniform. The brig was of 94 tons and designed to ferry herring to the Baltic, now free, the war having ended.

Pulteneytown, 1815

An unusually detailed picture of the new town is provided in the diary kept by Gilbert Salton (the spelling Saltoun is sometimes

---

1 Dunlop, *Pulteneytown* op. cit. p 155.

mentioned), Secretary of the Fisheries Society in London, who came on a visit in 1815 to survey at first hand developments in the Society's great venture. He came too as plenipotentiary for the Society, to negotiate with the Wick Burgh Council a number of issues in discussion between the two bodies. Salton stayed during his two months visit, between 17 January and 9 March, with the Provost of the Burgh, William Macleay, who had succeeded the Sinclairs in that office. Mr Salton's arrival was reported to the Burgh Council as 'Commissioner appointed by the British Fisheries Society with full power to settle all matters connected with the Society's Settlement at Pulteneytown,' the main issue between burgh and Society being an agreement on the collection and division of harbour dues in the Water of Wick.[1]

Salton's main business was with the affairs of Pulteneytown itself, wholly administered at this stage by the Society with little reference to the burghers of Wick. 'He spent days,' says Jean Dunlop, 'meeting the settlers and preparing the first detailed rent roll.' There were still matters to settle with Sir Benjamin Dunbar, on whose former territory the new town was being built. 'He had some new feuars including Major Innes of Keiss [a member, in fact, of the Burgh Council] who proposed to take two lots in Breadalbane Terrace and two in Argyle Square and to build good houses, one almost certainly for himself. Other local notables with whom he had business were David Brodie of Hopeville, who as we know was himself a fishery developer at Sarclet and Whaligoe,' and with Joseph Rhind, 'accountant of the Caithness bank who later acted as agent for the Society.'

It was not all business. Mr Salton 'was present at the wedding of his host's daughter [Miss Macleay], with a mixture of dancing, prayers and supper. He attended Sunday service and heard Mr Gunn, minister of Watten, preach for 1 hour and 37 minutes [Gilbert evidently had his watch out]' . . . 'He is a man of talents,' says Mr Salton, sardonically, 'but his sermon was tiresome and repetitious and without repetition it is difficult to conceive how 1 hour and 37 minutes could be expended.' His next visit to church was followed with a dowsing by the wild waves of Wick. 'On 29 January he'

> went to the Parish Church and dismissed about 12 minutes from 3. High water was about 3 and as the Spring Tides continued and there was a heavy sea, I wished to visit the Harbour and Mr J Macleay accompanied me . . . At the Bend of

1 Minutes of Wick Burgh Council, 18 January, 1815.

the Pier I was foolishly curious to see the effect of a heavy wave upon the back of it. Having got my toes rested on a small projection I fixed my right hand by way of security across the Buttress, my Curiosity was in a few seconds not only gratified, but infeftment was given me as the Society's Representative by delivery not of Earth and Stone but of a body of water in which my head and back were completely enveloped; and my poor friend did not escape much better . . . Luckily we were Great Coated and buttoned up to the Throat, so that by casting loose and shaking our Coats and Hats we got off tolerably well.[1]

'The first ten years,' says Jean Dunlop,' can best be summed up in the Agent's report dated early in 1818'. Her summary continues:

By now 102 building lots had been feued on which had already been built 7 red herring houses, at least 12 cooperages and many salt cellars, and 108 dwelling houses – 8 more houses being under construction – but privies were still almost nonexistent [so much for Telford's anxieties about hygiene]. Part of the quay had recently been allocated as curing lots for letting to strangers, more streets were to be laid out as soon as Telford and John Mitchell, his deputy in the north, came to do it, while the start of a much needed extra boat harbour was being delayed by yet another dispute with Sir Benjamin Dunbar. 50,043 barrels of herring had been shipped the previous year – $5\frac{1}{4}$ thousand to the Baltic, $8\frac{1}{2}$ to Ireland and the rest coastwise much probably for re-export. The total resident population had risen to 832 in Pulteneytown itself and the establishment of a school was being pressed for. The total number of male residents over the age of 12 was 247 and their professions were listed so that we can have a picture of the community as it existed 10 years after the first feu was allocated. There were 1 architect (Burn), 6 fish curers, 5 merchants and shop keepers, 42 carpenters, 8 blacksmiths, 11 carters, 6 weavers, 1 bookbinder, 2 customs-house tidewaiters, 2 plasterers, 8 shoemakers, 5 tailors, 5 ship and boat carpenters (this increased greatly the following year when the work swung from houses to boats), 2 millwrights, 4 innkeepers, 1 miller and 37 labourers and others, including 1 excise officer.[1]

Dunlop attributes the 'great increase in prosperity at Pulteneytown and Wick' that followed 1818, very justly to 'the efforts of the Society –

1 Jean Dunlop, *Pulteneytown*, op cit p 157.

indeed the directors seem to be dragged along by the momentum. But it was a momentum that they had created – their foundations had been good even if luck played a large part in the success of this most important planned town.' The 'luck' of course, was the continued abundance in the waters off the Wick coast of *Clupea harengus,* a factor over which the Society, Thomas Telford and the happy burghers of Wick had not the slightest control. And this was only the beginning. The continued presence of the silver darlings on the scene of their ruthless removal and ultimate extinction ensured the continuing rise of material prosperity of Pulteneytown and Wick for another fifty years.

Additional Note

An interesting view of 'planned' villages in Scotland is provided by T C Smout in *The Landowner and the Planned Village in Scotland,* in *Scotland in the Age of Improvement,* Ed. N Philipson and Rosalind Mitchison, Edinburgh University Press (1970). Smout writes of as many as 150 planned villages of the eighteenth and nineteenth centuries, illustrative of a tendency of some Scottish landowners in those times to seek to 'improve' land and settlement to render their property more productive. Most of these ventures were, of course, associated with land improvement projects. Smout identifies Pulteneytown as one of the 'four villages' set up by the British Fisheries Society'. Pulteneytown was, in the upshot (and was originally envisaged) as something more than a 'village'. Smout is, in any case mistaken in his description of Pulteneytown as a 'town suburb of the old Royal Burgh of Wick'. As we show later in this book, Pulteneytown was, and remained for a century, an entirely separate and independent community from Wick, joining the ancient burgh only in 1902.

CHAPTER 12

'OUR NORTHERN ATHENS'

ON the front page of its issue for 19 March, 1847, the now well established *John O'Groat Journal* broke new ground by printing an engraving entitled 'Wick and Pulteny Town', showing the river, bridge and church from the west under a skyline of the whole town from George Street to Breadalbane Terrace. The picture is specially interesting, since the engraver adapted for his purposes the picture painted by Munro, an artist of Wick in 1835, thus illustrating the kind and extent of alteration to the town that had occurred between the two dates. It was considerable as comparison between the two pictures demonstrates.

The *Groat* thought that its readers might find the picture 'at least gratifying to that portion of them who belong to, but have been long absent from, the place,' and for their benefit, said the *Journal*, 'we will attempt a short description of the more prominent buildings, more especially as most of them have sprung up within the last twenty years.' The description proceeds:

> The first house to the left (as the penny showman would say) is the residence of Mr Louttit, ropemaker; next is the Established Church, a huge square building, capable of holding about 2000 persons. It is a substantial edifice, but not very elegant as to its architecture, especially the spire, which was described some years ago by a stranger visiting the place as having the resemblance of 'a bayonet screwed on to a musket.' This church was finished in 1828. The church-yard or burial ground, as the grave stones indicate, lies contiguous, betwixt the church and the river. The next prominent house on the high ground is that of Mr Alexander Oag, fishcurer. The next is Montpelier House, the property of Mr Kirk, merchant, and occupied by Dr Sinclair. Further down, with the shrubbery in front, is the residence of Miss Macleay; formerly that of Provost Macleay, and, about fifty years ago, the Manse of Wick. The the right of the shrubbery, is the Wellington Hotel, an old four-storey building; and above that is seen the chimneys of 'Kirk's Buildings,' a modern structure in High Street, also four storeys high, towering above its fellows out of all proportion. Still farther to the right, is seen the range of buildings, once the property of Bailie Miller, and still occupied by his descendants. Lower down, with the windows fronting the south, is the house of Mr Tait, Blacksmith. To the south of

Fig 25 Sketch of Wick from *John O'Groat Journal* (19 March, 1847).

that, on the low ground, is the back view of the Free Church of Wick, built about two years ago; a commodious building on one floor; seated to hold about 1500 persons; the intended spire of the building is not yet erected. The first chimney stalk seen in the distance to the left, is that of the Gasworks, erected on the links of Pulteneytown. These works are the property of a joint-stock company, and have cost nearly £4000. They have hitherto been more useful than profitable, but are expected, in the course of time, to pay the interest on the money invested. The next tall chimney stalk seen in the distance to the left, is that of Gunn's saw-mill. The shipping in Pulteneytown Harbour is seen to the right, over the top of the Caledonian Hotel. The Town's County Hall and buildings, with jails, come next, mostly finished about the same time with the Established Church, viz., 1828 and 1829. A little to the right, exactly at the end of the Bridge, is the branch office of the Commercial Bank, built a few years later than the Courthouses, and is a handsome freestone building. The chimney-stalk seen off the end of the Bank is attached to Bremner's saw and meal mills, the property of Mr Bremner, shipbuilder and civil engineer, Harbour Place, Pulteneytown. The houses seen to the right of the Bank, in the low ground, are in Lower Pulteneytown; and that farthest in the distance, on the height, belongs to, and is occupied by, Mr David Bremner, fishcurer. Still higher up, is the house occupied in 1832 as an hospital, and known by the name of 'Cholera Hospital.' The place chosen for taking this view is not favourable to Pulteneytown; whole streets are only seen as a few houses. This brings us to the Academy, situated on the high ground, with the north front in view. This commodious and neat structure has been built by the British Fishery Society, at a cost of nearly £2000, and is endowed to a certain extent by that corporation. The Roman Catholic Chapel is in the immediate vicinity, and is distinguished by the cross at the end. In front of this is seen the tall and handsome chimney of the Pulteneytown saw-mills, the property of Mr Stephen Davidson. Sinclair's Terrace forms the range of houses running west from the Catholic Chapel, and over the north end of it the belfry (which the artist has converted into a spire) of the Free Church, Pulteneytown. The next large building is Rosebank House, formerly occupied by Mr Macleay of Newtonmore, and now the property of, and occupied by, James Henderson. Esq. Farther to the right is the house presently tenanted by Mr Davidson of Strath, belonging to Provost Rhind. The farthest house of all is the property of James Smith, Esq. of Olrig, and is tenanted by Mr Reid, book-seller. Low down, at the south end of the Bridge is the Exchange Reading Room, and the 'John O'Groat Journal' attached. In the middle of the river are islands on which the inhabitants bleach their clothes. The small pic-nic party on the banks is the production of the artist; our lawns require the benefit of the drainage act, before they be exactly suited for ladies and gentlemen squating [sic] themselves on to drink lemonade and eat pastry.

The artist, signing himself 'J Bishop' explains that 'the more recent erections were sketched by pencil bringing the view down to July last [July 1846].' Since that time, says the *Groat*, 'we cannot boast of any great addition to our Northern *Athens*.' It can hardly be said that Wick was ever fully qualified for such a brave title; none of the new buildings of the town boasted much that was, even in the way of ornament, reminiscent of the 'glory that was Greece'. On the other hand, to some of the Wickers who had lived through the transforming years from 1800 to the 1840s, the change to the face of the ancient burgh and the attachment to it of a southern suburb already twice the size of the old town, must have seemed little short of miraculous. A somewhat exaggerated sense of pride in it all was not out of place. And, as we shall see, the *John O'Groat Journal* itself, was a fluent purveyor of hyperbole.

Not the least interesting aspect of the *Groat's* description is the detailed identification of the houses and establishments of the transformers themselves. Most of the people named appear again, some of them frequently, in our story, for in addition to their entrepreneurial activities, several of them – or members of their families – had roles in the civic development of the town.

There is, indeed, something unique about the rise of Wick, as compared with most of the other Scottish towns that grew in size and importance during the days of the industrial revolution. Wick did not share with towns such as Greenock, Paisley, Kilmarnock and Falkirk, which rose from small beginnings to much larger populations, the commoner reasons for that growth. These included the expansion of mass-production industries, especially the manufacture of textiles, dependent for their development and prosperity on overseas markets, commanded from Glasgow.

Wick, so to speak, developed and commanded its own markets for a product that, in principle at least, required equipment and techniques little altered from those of the middle-ages. The markets which Wick cultivated were not specially those of the rising industrial towns of the south and, in fact, they only became fully available as the Napoleonic Wars ended. A 'herring industry' as such hardly existed until the countrymen fishers of Wick and other localities on the coast of Caithness began catching and pickling herring in large quantities. The contribution of Wick to the industrial expansion of Scotland is hardly noticed by economic historians; Smout, for instance, has no reference to Wick at all in his first history. *A History of the Scottish People, 1560-1830,* and only one in the later *A Century of the Scottish People, 1830-1950,* and that has to do with the 'end of the vast East European export trade in herring . . . rusting trawlers and rotting nets [which] littered the ports from Stornoway to Lerwick, and from Wick to Anstruther,' in the years after the First World War. Virtually nothing in either volume about the origins and development of this 'vast trade in herring'.

'Till 1815 the growing herring industry had been virtually confined to Caithness, but then came a sudden widening to envelop a string of new bases,' says Malcolm Gray at the beginning of his chapter on 'The Widening Sphere of the Herring Industry, 1815-1835'. It had been fortunate for the Caithness fishermen that the movement of the herring shoals in their part of the North Sea were not so erratic as those in the Firth of Forth where, after 1808, catches declined sharply. However,

> within two years the harbours of the south shore of the Moray Firth were astir with the activities of herring fishing, pursued over the same period of the year as had been

established for the herring fishing of Caithness; and when, by 1820, Peterhead had opened as a herring station, a fleet of over 2,000 boats would gather every year in the stations dotting the coast all the way from the north tip of Caithness to the eastern coast of Buchan.[1]

Wick had already lost its virtual monopoly status, but it continued to grow even more rapidly than before. Total production of Scottish barrelled herring per year by 1840 had risen to something like 550,000 barrels, of which, nearly 65,000 were sent from Wick, about 12 per cent of the total, a formidable figure. According to the Rev. Charles Thomson, who wrote the 1840 *Statistical Account* for Wick, the actual 'average annual quantity of fish for the last twenty years' (1820 to 1840) was 88,500 barrels, and on that showing 1840 was a rather 'bad' year. In fact, catches varied considerably according to season, and income passed through several troughs owing to price falls. But a combination of good fortune at sea, improvements in fishing technique and expansion of markets on the Continent, especially in Germany, ensured that Wick continued to thrive and grow as a fishing port and as a community.

HERRINGS GALORE

With the end of the war in 1815 came considerable change in the herring trade. The pattern of fishery itself changed. There was no longer danger of enemy vessels coming down on the fishers, and 'nearly every fishing community lying anywhere on the eastern Scottish coastline was sending some boats and crews to the summer herring fishing of the more northerly stretches.' As yet there was not much change in the type of vessel used; the open 'scaffie' was still the rule, with capacity perhaps for ten to twelve crans, but keels were lengthening to 20 or 22 feet. In the Wick area itself, greater numbers of professional fishermen were mixing among the local 'amateurs', including those coming to live in the super new 'village' of Pulteneytown.

The crucial issue was the extension of markets. Supply for the present seemed assured. The fishers could take more fish provided that they could sell more. Up to the present the main overseas markets had been Ireland and the West Indies. Neither of these expanded

---

1 Gray, op cit. p 39.

much; in fact, the Irish trade began to decline, and with the abolition of slavery, smaller and smaller amounts were shipped to the West Indies where at one time 30,000 barrels a year had been sent. The domestic market both in the industrial areas of Scotland and in England was considerable, but the most significant opening up of new trade was with the Continent.

The capture and exploitation of continental markets was a steady and consciously pursued policy. It was the Dutch with their very high class product that had so far made the most penetration into Germany, where the people ate herring 'as a relish rather than as a bulk foodstuff'. The Scottish policy was not to seek direct competition with this relatively limited quality trade, but to put on the market a somewhat lower grade of product that could maintain a consistent quality and be increasingly adopted as a regular article of diet by ordinary folk. This is exactly what happened. Standards were set and quality maintained by the inspection system instituted from 1809 onwards by the Commission for the Herring Fishery (later the Fishery Board for Scotland). Approved consignments of 'Fulls' were burned on the lid of the barrel with the 'Crown Brand', and so reliable did the system become that increasingly the Scottish merchants met with little serious competition; the Dutch confined themselves to the high-class trade and the Scandinavians, Norwegians and Swedes, generally penetrated the lower grade markets. To an extent, the Scottish herring trade with central Germany, assisted by the arrangements built up by the Zollverein (Customs Union)[1] became for many years a virtual monopoly.

The Scots sought patiently to penetrate other markets, though this was difficult in France, Spain and Belgium, where the duty levied on imported herrings was prohibitively high. Matters eased in Holland itself after the break-up of the Union of Belgium and Holland in 1830.[2] Various moves were made to get the Russians in particular to lower their tariff, especially discriminatory against Scottish herrings on which a duty of 4s 6d per barrel was levied, as compared with 1s 6d on Norwegian herring.[3] In the *John O'Groat Journal* of 2 July, 1836, James Loch MP is reported as raising the issue of 'the depressed state

---

1 The Zollverein, inaugurated in 1818, was one of the first moves towards the creation of a united Germany, completed in 1870.

2 The Congress of Vienna combined Holland and Belgium into what became an unhappy single state; the union was dissolved in 1830.

3 Gray, op cit, p 60.

of the herring industry' in the House of Commons, and presenting a 'petition from the fishermen of Wick and Cromarty' asking the government to assist them in getting 'a better share of the Russian and Prussian markets'.

By 1850 'the bulk of Scottish exports of herring were going to the Continent and progressively thereafter the proportion increased till only tiny amounts were elsewhere.' Since the cured herring was, however, a semi-perishable foodstuff, it had to be got to its destination quickly. As far as central Germany was concerned, a market dominated in the 1850s by Scotland and Norway, the main ports to which the herrings were sent were Hamburg, Stettin and Danzig, and the main supply centres, such as Wick and Fraserburgh developed a whole network of connections, export and credit agencies doing business direct with German importers. Much of the trade, agreement on prices, size of consignment and shipping arrangements, was done on the quayside, and among the boats now docking in Wick were fast schooners that could make the journey into the Baltic in a couple of days. On the quays the languages of foreign traders was often to be heard.

'Depression', was, as always, a relative term. Both catch and markets fluctuated from year to year, sometimes by as much as some thousands of barrels. The price per barrel paid on the market also fluctuated, but generally not drastically. *John O'Groat Journal* weekly herring reports for Wick, started in 1837, show a rise from 20s in 1837 to nearly 25s in 1840, a fall to about 15s in 1843, a rise again to 20s in 1845 with another fall to 1850; then apart from blips in 1865 and 1870 (both war-scare years) the price rise is steady to 40s or more in 1875 and 1887.[1]

Both price and supply could be affected by 'chance influences'. Among these could be the scares of cholera, typhus and diptheria, which swept through the town on occasion; 'between 1833 and 1834,' says Iain Sutherland, 'cholera was so prevalent along the coast that many visitors stayed away and the fishings were put in check for three years.'[2] The effect of a sudden cholera attack on Dunster (Dunbeath – the smaller fishing villages were no more immune than Wick) is vividly and pathetically told by Neil Gunn in *The Silver Darlings*. Another adventitious factor in price fluctuation was

1 Gray, op cit, p 59. For a full discussion of these issues, see Chapters III and IV, pp 39-79.
2 Iain Sutherland, op cit, p 28.

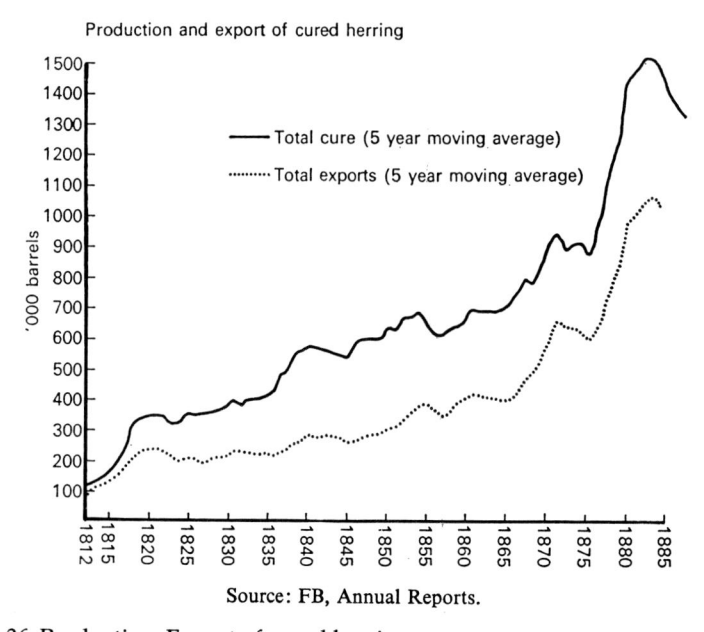

Fig 26 Production. Export of cured herring.
(Courtesy University of Aberdeen Press).

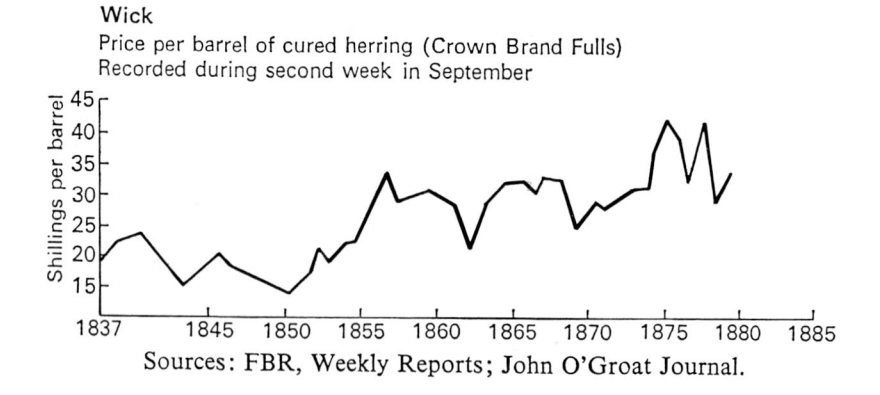

Fig 27 Price per barrel of cured herring.
(Courtesy University of Aberdeen Press).

mentioned in the *John O'Groat Journal,* 24 June, 1847. The reporter noted 'how much the consumption of herrings depends upon a large supply of potatoes has been fully borne out by the recent occurences'. Herrings and potatoes were becoming recognised as a very satisfactory working-class meal of the day. The 'occurences' were the failure of the potato crop that caused so much devastation in Ireland. 'On the other hand, a high price or a scarcity of meat and grain tended to increase the demand for herrings.'[1]

WICK HARBOUR EXTENSIONS

Wick's perennial problem was less the difficulties of handling the market than that of coping with the annual influx of boats to its permanently inadequate harbours. No sooner was Telford's harbour completed in 1811 than it became overcrowded. As early as 1809 the Deputy Governor of the Society 'saw twenty to thirty busses in the harbour'.[2] While Pulteneytown filled up with people, so the south-bank harbour became filled to overflowing with boats. At end of the war the pressure became intense and 'shipowners threatened to take their trade to such lesser harbours such as Staxigoe, Broadhaven and Greenigoe, despite their inadequacies.'

And here, a curious matter comes to light. During the whole of the furious activity on the south side of the Wick river between 1807 and 1811, there is hardly any mention in the minutes of the Wick Burgh Council of the work, nor of the transactions that led up to it. These were, of course, mainly between Sir Benjamin Dunbar of Hempriggs, who owned all the land on which the development was projected, harbour and village, and the British Fisheries Society and, as such, strictly none of the business of the burgh council. Nevertheless, it must have been clear to the city fathers that something drastic was going on. Indeed, several of them as individuals were involved. The burgh was expressly concerned with the new bridge, but since the burghers were not providing the funds, there is little mention of that either.

Up to this time the burgh was the only agency, authorised under its charter, to impose and have collected harbour dues in the Water of

1 Gray, op cit, p 63. These are virtually classical examples of the phenomena of 'complementary' and 'competitive' demand and supply, at one time much emphasised by the political economists.
2 Dunlop, *British Fisheries Society,* op cit. p 159.

Wick. We have already seen the burgesses' attempts to rationalise the collection of dues to which they considered they were entitled. In 1804 Burgess Alexander Miller complained about the 'sleeping sloops' in Wick Water, and the 'collecting of large stones to keep them under in the Harbour and Ship Pool of Wick which is often attended with very great inconveniency to the Shipping and Boats which occasionally be lying there and sometimes forced from their moorings by the Stress of Weather.' What this evidently referred to was the practice of some skippers of sinking their vessels in the shallows of Wick Water at low tide by laying stones along the bilge, and leaving them there for their own convenience.

By 1810 things had become serious. Without discussion or any legal pronouncement the Society had arrogated to itself the collection of harbour dues in Wick Water. Most shippers now evidently preferred the relative safety and convenience of the new harbour to the hazards of tying up in the old roads. On a suggestion of Sir John Sinclair an agreement was to be sought with the British Fisheries Society on the matter of dues by 'shipping frequenting the new harbour of Pulteneytown'. Under its charter, the burgh of Wick was the only authority entitled to 'exact such dues' in the Water of Wick. Though convinced of its right, they would find it preferable to come to an agreement as 'the exaction of those dues might be considerable'. The suggestion was that the Society 'should pay a specific sum in full [recognition] of all those Dues exigible by the Town in the Bay of Wick, exclusive of the creeks of Staxigo and Broadhaven,' over which Wick was now exercising authority. Sir John was authorised to 'undertake decision with the Society'. £40 was the sum suggested.

In the delayed event, the transaction was not completed for several years. The British Fisheries Society, it eventually became evident, was promoting on its own a Bill in Parliament that would confer on it all the rights in the Water of Wick assumed by the burgh under its charter. After much toing and froing, suggestions and counter suggestions, and with the imminent prospect of the Bill becoming an Act, the Rt Hon Sir John Sinclair recommended to Provost Macleay that it would be wise for the burgh to agree to the terms originally proposed in discussion with the Society. Gilbert Salton, the London Secretary of the Society, came to Wick in January 1815, with full powers to 'settle all matters connected with the Society's Settlement at Pulteneytown', a statement clearly implying that the Society regarded it as a matter of grace and favour that they were willing to do business

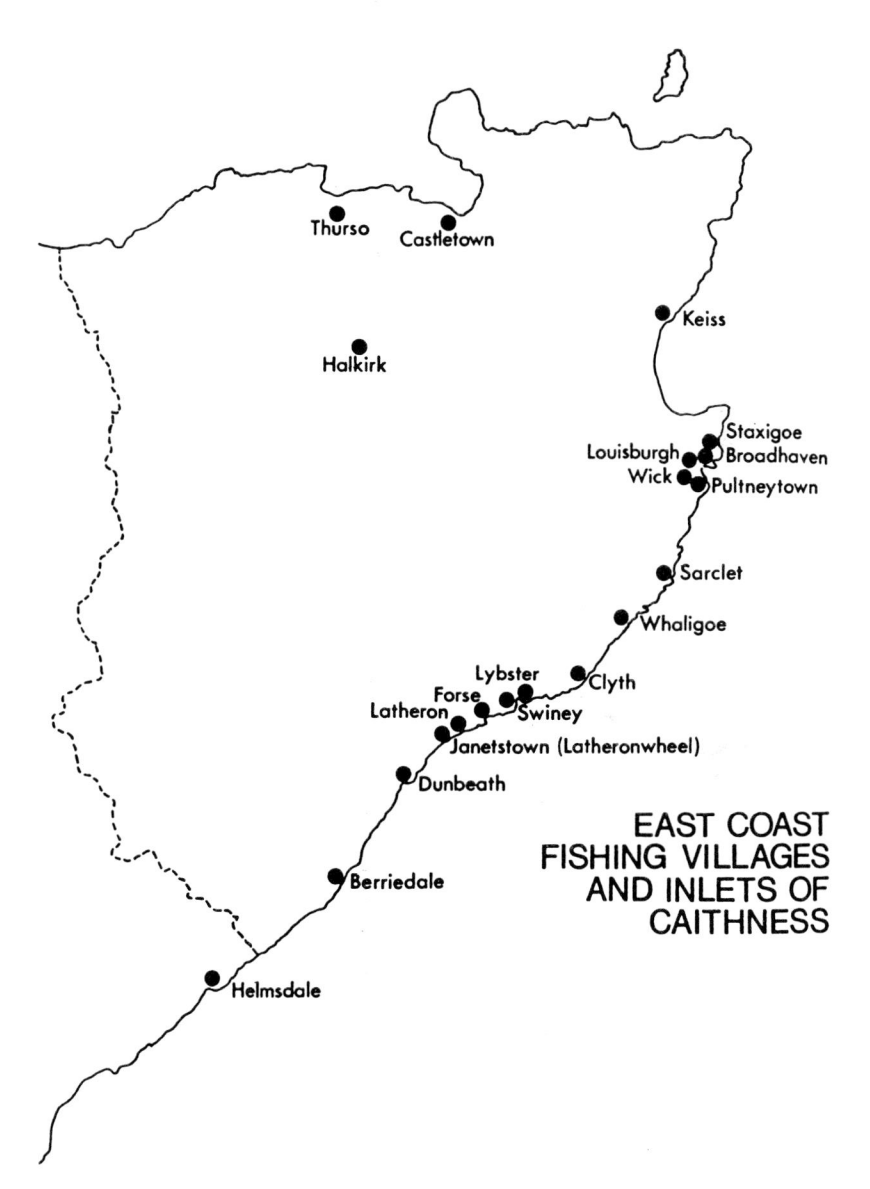

Fig 28 Map of fishing villages of Caithness.
By kind permission of J. Baldwin and Edina Press.

with Wick burgh at all.

The Society held all the winning cards. Sir John was instructed to tell Mr William Smith, Deputy Governor of the Society that the burgesses did not in any way 'wish to start any obstruction to the patriotic exertions of the Society'. After a brave flourish of declarations on the part of the burgh council that it formally waived no rights to which it had been accustomed, it agreed with the Society that (1) the burgh's men should collect dues on the north side as formerly, the return to be made up to £40 by the Society if it fell short; (2) all dues on the south-side should be payable to the Society; (3) 'the Burgh shall surrender for ever all Right and Claim of Right whatever vested or understood to be vested in them under any pretext whatever to the South side'; (4) 'Pauls on either side of the said River shall be supported,' by the burgh, south by the Society, 'all vessels indiscriminately being at Liberty to use of the said Pauls in warping up and down the said River or Water.' ('pauls' were what today we should perhaps call 'bollards'). By this treaty, the Burgh of Wick excluded itself from all ancient jurisdiction over the south side of Wick Water, and by that token any claim to interference in the affairs of Pulteneytown. The Society had, in fact, already secured its rights by obtaining a private Act of Parliament.

Until 1844 Pulteneytown was administered by a 'Commission' appointed by the Society. In that year the citizens of Pulteneytown gained, in effect, the right to elect their own 'town council' on which the Society continued to be represented, but the new civic administration was strictly excluded from any involvement in the affairs of the harbour. The combined municipality today known as Wick, was until 1902 two towns, one on the north the other on the south bank of the River Wick. Most references to fishing and shipping business nevertheless went under the heading 'Wick', a practice we shall continue in this book; though when we are discussing civic affairs at this stage, the name 'Wick' must be taken to signify the ancient royal burgh, exclusive of Pulteneytown unless otherwise stated.

No further serious harbour development occurred on the north bank of the river, but the Pulteneytown Commissioners soon found themselves under great pressure to extend their harbour on the south side, especially after the end of the war. To quote Iain Sutherland:

> The fishing fleet had grown in proportion [to the population of Pulteneytown, though strictly speaking the equation is the

other way round] and the harbour was overcrowded to the extent that it frequently became paralysed. Apart from the difficulties experienced with the press of vessels trying to use it, with fishing and cargo boats, the harbour was continually silting up very badly. Even with the highest tides there was only 13ft of water at best and at low water it was impossible for any but the smallest boats to use the harbour. Shipmasters reverted to loading and unloading their vessels in the bay, using barges with oar power only, to ferry the cargoes ashore rather than risk being trapped for what could be weeks in the harbour. The process was very expensive, as the barges had to be hired and much injury was done to life and limb when the cargoes were being handled under difficult sea conditions . . .

The Society, which administered the village of Pulteneytown quite independently of Wick Town Council, responded, although they were probably planning an extension to the harbour anyway. By 1820 plans were being studied and in 1824 an extension, by way of the construction of a new harbour basin, was authorised. The work began in 1826, under the charge of James Bremner and, as events proved, the extension was sorely needed.

About 600 boats were coming to the summer fishings and the resident population of 1500 was being augmented by an influx of 4000 visitors during the season. Many of these, and their numbers were to increase in the next 30 years, were the victims of the Highland Clearances which were beginning to gather momentum in the counties of Sutherland, Ross and Inverness. Pulteneytown offered the prospect of work and consequently some kind of relief from the deprivation which they suffered. Many of these people, whose only language was Gaelic, walked across the hills to the town, a journey of well over 100 miles which could take a week or more to complete. The extension to the harbour, involving as it did the closure of the original entrance and the opening of another in deeper water, took 4 years and cost £20,000. Of this £5000 had been incurred in repairing the damage to the works by a storm on 20th September, 1827 which demolished most of the work done to that date. However, the completion of the harbour extension signalled the beginning of the most successful era in the history of Pulteneytown and as a result of its construction trade expanded unchecked for the next 40 years.[1]

James Bremner, Harbour Builder

The engineer in charge of the new works, James Bremner, was a native of Wick parish. He was born on 25 September, 1784 at Stain, just north of Keiss, the youngest of a family of nine. His father was a soldier who spent much of his life abroad until his discharge in 1798. James the elder seems, however, to have got home to Janet often enough to father a large family before he went to the West Indies where he spent ten years and was one of only 27 who returned from a regiment of 850 men. James was three times wounded, but survived. He was sent to Ireland at the time of the Irish Rebellion in 1798, and 'served there some time, when, through the influence of a superior officer who had known him in the West Indies, he was appointed to conduct a party of leading rebels, who had been taken prisoners, to Fort-George [the regimental base near to Inverness]'.[2]

Young James was quite a scamp. He was sent to the village school in Keiss 'but all that he learned there was simply to read and write, and that imperfectly. Education in Caithness, 'adds Calder laconically, 'was then at a low stand.' On one of his boyhood adventures he tried paddling across Sinclair's Bay in a large tub. 'Fortunately for him there was not a breath of wind; and one of his brothers having raised the alarm, he was picked up and safely brought ashore.'

The sea and ships were his life. 'Having expressed a strong desire to learn the art of ship-building, interest was obtained to get him into the building-yard of the Messrs Steele of Greenock.' There he went when he was sixteen and remained for six years, then returned to Caithness, 'to prosecute his trade in Pulteneytown . . . He obtained a life lease, near the harbour, and during the time he occupied it, he built upwards of fifty-six vessels, ranging from forty-five to six hundred tons.' This was the yard bought in 1815 by George Burn, the Pulteneytown architect. In 1818 Bremner launched his first ship, a brig

---

[1] Iain Sutherland, op cit. pp 28-29. It should be added that although there were undoubtedly large numbers of refugees who came to Wick as a result of clearances (in 1840 the Wick parish church is claimed to have had the largest Gaelic speaking congregation in Scotland), the fishing was done less by hired men than partners to a boat. Mr Sutherland himself adds that Pulteneytown 'grew in all directions, both physically and industrially. And as it grew so that influence of the British Fisheries Society declined over its affairs.'

[2] Calder op cit, pp 245-260. Bremner also appears in the *DNB*. See also John Mowat: *James Bremner: Wreck Raiser*; Wick, JS Duncan, MBE (no date), a 24-page pamphlet, dealing largely with Bremner's work as wreck-raiser and harbour-builder.

of 94 tons, *The Duke of Wellington,* for which he himself carved the figurehead of the Duke, then Britain's great hero.

As an extension of his expertise with ships, Bremner became nationally well-known for his skills in raising sunken or refloating stranded vessels; during his career he rescued no fewer than 236 such vessels. Among his triumphs was the raising of the *Orion,* a Prussian ship carrying a cargo of 40,000 feet of timber, which sank in Water Sound, on 2 December, 1825. Bremner constructed a huge raft from her cargo of wood on to which the ship was loaded. The raft was provided with hand paddles and sails rigged on masts taken out of the ship and the whole contraption was safely sailed and rowed to Wick Bay, where the *Orion,* was off-loaded and repaired.

'Bremner's use of this type of massive salvage pontoon anticipated by almost 150 years a similar system developed by the British firm of Risdon Beazley and was by a interesting coincidence used to transport the hulk of the *Great Britain* back from the Falkland Islands to Bristol for restoration.' She is now one of Bristol's showpieces. A yet earlier remarkable achievement was the dismantling on the Ness of Quoys, Canisbay, of the *Lord Suffield,* a ship totally wrecked there. Bremner had the pieces carried back to his yard in Wick where he completely rebuilt the vessel.[1]

Quite as remarkable was his work on fishing harbours along the Scottish coast. The first was the harbour of his own village of Keiss, a structure still standing, though Keiss was never a very successful fishing centre. He also remodelled Sarclet harbour in 1825-1826. Altogether he worked on some nineteen harbours in Scotland, including Lossiemouth, Pittulie and Trawleigh. His most influential single harbour work was that of his home town, Wick. The *Northern Ensign* wrote (later) of the set-back of September, 1827:

> In one night, at Pulteneytown harbour, during a terrific gale, works which cost £5000 were thrown down and rendered useless. Any ordinary man would have sunk beneath the disaster. Not so did James Bremner. Eight times during that disastrous night he was prevailed on to go home and get his clothes shifted, and as often was he seen at the head of his men,

---

[1] For each of these episodes see David M Ferguson: *Shipwrecks of Orkney, Shetland and Pentland Firth;* Newton Abbot, David and Charles (1988). The 'coincidence' refers to Bremner's encounter with the *Great Britain* himself. In 1847 he warped this vessel, constructed by I K Brunel, then the largest ship in the world (3,500 tons) when she became stranded on the Dundrum sands on the coast of Ireland. This episode is described infra, Chapter 15, pp 446-449.

cheering them on to their efforts to save as much as possible.[1]

One of the very first advertisements carried in the newly born *John O'Groat Journal*, is of James Bremner's 'NEW FLOATING DOCK' capable of receiving a 500-600 ton vessel.[2]

Over the century and a half since Bremner's death in 1856 tributes have been paid to this most accomplished and versatile son of Wick, but as we have already observed, Bremner, like Telford and Rennie never qualified for the honour of knighthood, so often and so readily bestowed on many of the less worthy. James Calder was moved in 1863 to comment on the posthumous differential treatment awarded on the one hand to 'aristocrats' such as James, Earl of Caithness, Sir John Sinclair of Ulbster, James Traill of Rattar (Sheriff Depute of Caithness), all of whom were honoured by the hanging of portraits in the County Hall of Wick, but not James Bremner, who belonged, in Calder's flowery but appreciative language to the 'aristocracy of nature'.[3] Bremner was, nevertheless, made a Member of the Institution of Civil Engineers in 1833, and was awarded the Telford Medal for several of his significant papers on engineering.

Another comment by Calder on James Bremner may be quoted:

> Mr Bremner was, for the space of twelve years, agent at Wick for the Aberdeen, Clyde and Leith Steam Shipping Company. In conveying goods and passengers to and from the steamboat he was, from the exposed nature of the bay, often placed in situations of great danger; but such was his presence of mind and knowledge of boatmanship, that during the entire period of his management, no accident involving loss of life or property occurred.
>
> The celebrated Hugh Miller, in a geological visit to Caithness, was introduced to Mr Bremner at Wick, and in one of his publications he says of him:– 'I was conscious of a feeling of sadness as, in parting with Mr Bremner, I reflected that a man so singularly gifted should have been suffered to reach a period of his life very considerably advanced in employments little suited to exert his extraordinary faculties, and which persons of the ordinary type could have performed as well. Napoleon – himself possessed of great genius – could have estimated more adequately than our British rules the value of such a man. Had

---

1 Calder, op cit, p 258.
2 *JOGJ*, 1 April, 1836.
3 A portrait of Bremner, nevertheless, now hangs on the staircase of the Town Hall of Wick.

'OUR NORTHERN ATHENS'

Mr Bremner been born a Frenchman, he would not now be a mere agent of a steam company in a third-rate seaport town.

For all this, Wick's most prominent monument is an elegant obelisk dedicated to James Bremner, standing high on the south cliff. It overlooks the entire great harbour which was Bremner's enduring contribution to the well-being of Wick. In any case, to any thoughtful citizen of the town it could be said, *Si monumentum requiris, circumspice.*

The monument bears three plaques:

North facing towards the harbour:

Fellow Caithness men and kinsfolk at home and abroad raised this memorial in 1903 to the resourceful, fearless and benificent genius of
JAMES BREMNER
C.E.
Naval Architect and Harbour Builder.

East facing towards the sea:

Wick Harbour is sheltered by one of 18 yet efficient Breakwaters on this coast by his skill.

He saved scores of wrecked mariners' lives at the risk of his own. He refloated 236 stranded or sunken vessels including the Great Britain.

Fig 29 The Bremner Memorial at the South Head.

West Facing:

> Born at Keiss on Sinclairs Bay in 1784.
> His still active and benevolent life closed very suddenly, three months after the death of his dearly beloved wife in 1856
> At his home in Pulteneytown.
> DUET XXXI 6.

Bremner's harbour failed to suffice. It was reckoned by the Rev Charles Thomson that in 1840 a total of 765 boats were using Wick, 428 'native' boats, and 337 'strange' boats.[1] Bremner himself was one of the growing band of critics who saw great problems looming ahead for Wick. As Iain Sutherland explains, the Society, on whose support Pulteneytown depended, was 'having great financial difficulties because of the heavy drain placed on their funds by the maintenance of Pulteneytown harbour'. Jean Dunlop tells how the Society's unfavourable predicament was building up:

> The herring failed to appear in 1834, but by 1836 the agent was confident that the settlement would soon recover, although commercial confidence had been badly shaken. To add to the Society's difficulties, the new harbour which had been completed in 1834 began to fill with sand and within four years an engineer was sent to report on the situation. The low rent of curing lots, which had fallen from £1,157 annually before 1832 to about £200, and the similar diminishing of harbour dues did not encourage the Directors to spend further large sums on the works. On the other hand there were rumours of a rival harbour being planned at Ackergill to the north of Wick. The difficulty with Pulteneytown was that sand was always liable to be washed up on the shore and so some new feature to prevent this was necessary. In 1842 James Bremner pointed out that a 'considerable portion of the coastal trade is now carried on by steamboats; and ultimately, I have no doubt, the whole of that trade with the exception of coal and lime, will be carried on by steam; and in order to accomplish this in as cheap a manner as possible, the steamboats will be built as large as the extent of the trade they are engaged in will admit of'. Thus, to keep the coastal traffic Pulteneytown harbour must be enlarged.[2]

---

1 *Statistical Survey of Scotland, 1840.*
2 Dunlop, *British Fisheries Society*, op cit, p 185. Curiously, in her detailed study of affairs at Pulteneytown, Jean Dunlop says little else about James Bremner, apparently confusing him with David Bremner, another *(continued on foot of next page)*

The problems did not go away, and as we shall see in Chapter 15, things reached crisis point during 1848 when a severe storm struck Pulteneytown. Much damage was done, and many lives were lost.

WICK, 1840

We turn to the survey of Wick conducted by the Rev Charles Thomson, the newly arrived minister of Wick following the death of the well-loved Robert Phin in March 1840. Mr Thomson was inducted on Kirk-hill on 27th September, 1840, but he must have sweated bountifully during his early months as he worked on his sixty-page excursus on Wick and parish, 'to which he was previously an utter stranger,' having become resident 'only on the 24th October'. The request to compile a report for the *New Statistical Account* did not arrive until December, 1840 and he submitted it in March 1841. Mr Thomson apologises indeed, for its 'manifold imperfections', which he excuses with the explanation that it was done 'in the midst of the numerous vocations and avocations of a most burdensome charge.' He would, he claims, not have attempted it 'could another person have been found to undertake it.'

If the Rev William Sutherland's report of 1794 came to be regarded as one of the best contributions in the whole survey of that time, this of Charles Thomson can be bracketed as similarly meritorious in its own idiosyncratic way. It is thorough, comprehensive, detailed, and well written as certainly few others in his town could have written it, for in those days there were few scholars in Wick. Mr Thomson was, however, a man 'born unto trouble, as the sparks fly upward'. The fishing of Wick occupies his assiduous attention, as do other elements of the Wick scene, but it is his avocation as a 'fisher of men' that Mr Thomson reveals himself most strongly and to which some of his later troubles must be attributed. We shall return to this topic.

The Growth of Wick.

As a community, Thomson's Wick has grown prodigiously. The figures he gives are all derived from presbytery and kirk session records, for until 1841 there was no national census. His table records

(Continued from foot of previous page) local entrepreneur. She attributes to this Bremner completion of the sloop *Brothers*, and other shipbuilding at Wick, and the eventual floating dock. All this was the remarkable James's work.

what he describes as 'catechisable persons':[1]

Year	Families	Males	Females	Total
1695			about	2,000
1707				3,200
1719			about	4,000
1726				3,600
1755				3,938
1792				5,000
1801				3,986
1811	1,044	2,394	2,686	5,080
1821	1,399	3,263	4,450	6,713
1831	1,976	4,830	5,020	9,850

For 1792 and 1811, Thomson gives the figures for the burgh and the new settlements:

1792	200 families and 1000 individuals			
1811	232 families	489 males	505 females	994
In Louisburgh, Pulteneytown & Bankhead		401 males	354 females	755
	Total	890 males	859 females	1,749
1826				7,520
1840		4,325 males	5,021 females	9,346

These are in several ways rather remarkable figures. Assuming the parish totals to be mostly correct (those for 1719 and 1792 must be regarded as dubious; they are both estimates from William Sutherland's survey of 1794, q.v.) – for there are none better available, the increases in population shown are quite startling, viz.

Period	Increase	Percentage Increase		
1726-1755	338	9.4%		
1755-1801	48	0.01%		
1801-1811	1,094	27.4%	} 68.4%	} 147.1%
1811-1821	1,633	32.1%		
1821-1831	3,137	46.7%		

[1] This expression 'catechisable persons' (or alternatively 'examinable persons'), is used regularly by ministers to signify all those people in his 'hold' or parish area who are either subject or likely to become so to the minister's duties as 'catechist' or 'examiner' of a candidate's knowledge of the church catechism before being admitted to communion. In effect it meant all the people.

'OUR NORTHERN ATHENS'

During most of the eighteenth century the population of the parish was fairly static. From 1801 the rate of increase became exponential, rising by two-thirds between 1801 and 1821, and by one-and-a-half times between 1801 and 1831. This, of course, could only have been achieved by massive immigration, partly from the west of the county, the western counties and islands and, very probably, from fishing villages further south along the east coast. For it was particularly the east coast 'professionals' who were aimed at by the Pulteneytown publicity. If we consider the increase only of Wick burgh and its new 'suburbs',[1] 'the increase goes over the top at 331 per cent between 1811 and 1821, a quite startling migration into a 'new town' in a remote corner of northern Scotland.

Rapid population increase was, of course, a characteristic feature of the industrial lowlands of Scotland at this time. Between 1801 and 1821 Edinburgh increased from 81,600 to 138,000, a rise of 54.6 per cent; and Glasgow by 75 per cent from 83,700 to 147,000. The nearest 'large town' to Wick, Inverness achieved a modest 40 per cent, from 8,700 to 12,200.[2] Had Wick burgh continued to grow at the rate prevailing between 1811 and 1821 (331%) it would assuredly have overtaken Inverness, as the greatest town of the north. But that thought takes us into the realms of fantasy.

Having given a lot of information about the population in 'Part III, Population', of his report, Mr Thomson muddles things up in this section by declaring, 'In 1840 the population of Wick was, Males, 561, Females, 693; Total, 1254. The number of families was 300.' This may, of course, be one of the 'imperfections' to which he confesses, for these figures manifestly do not square with his earlier tables, and are almost certainly incorrect.

Under this head his topics include brief comments on town government, the parliamentary burgh, the neighbouring villages and communications. Of the villages nothing needs to be added to what we have already said about Broadhaven, Staxigoe, Thrumster and Sarclet; while he says nothing under this heading about Keiss and the other fishing villages south of Wick. On the subject of communications his summary presents a very different picture of the economic geography of Wick from that of Mr Sutherland in 1794:

> Wick is a post town. In 1829 the revenue of the post-office amounted to L.1200 a-year. A daily mail-coach from Thurso

---

1 But bear in mind reservations mentioned on *Additional Note*, p. 304.
2 Smout, op cit: Table II, p 243. The percentage rates given (on Smout's and Thomson's figures) are the present author's.

passes through the town to the south in the morning, and another from the south through the town to Thurso at night. The mail-coach commenced to run on the 15th of July, 1818. A daily post-gig runs between Wick and Huna [John O'Groats], from which latter place the letters for Orkney are despatched twice a week. A steam-boat of 200 horse-power plies once-a-week from March till November, between Lerwick, Kirkwall, Wick, Aberdeen and Leith.

Another interesting contrast between the surveys of 1794 and this of 1840, is that now there are in the parish nearly fifty miles of road, 'of which the Parliamentary line measures fourteen', whereas in 1794 there were virtually none. The 'Parliamentary' is the stretch south to north between Ulbster and Wick, and west from Wick to Watten, the great north-Scottish highway engineered by Thomas Telford. Mr Thomson speaks appreciatively too of the road to Huna, today's A9 from Wick to John O'Groats, and of the roads that connect Wick up with Castleton (Castletown) and Bower.

Reform in the Royal Burgh of Wick

Since 1794, too, the status and government of the burgh had changed quite a bit. The ostensible domination of the town by the Sinclairs and Dunbars had gone. 'The superiority of it has been bought and sold by the Sinclairs of Caithness, the Glenorchies, the Sinclairs of Ulbster, and the Sutherlands; but the Reform Bill,' says Mr Thomson, 'had reduced this once potential privilege to feebleness. It is, therefore, now little valued.'

Whether or not it was 'valued', the Superiority of Wick had been the subject of a transaction over the heads of the burghers twenty years before, when Sir John Sinclair sold this and a considerable acreage of his property to the Right Honourable George Granville Leveson-Gower, Lord Gower. Times were changing. When they heard of it, several of the burgesses drew up a 'Schedule of Protest' which claimed that the Sinclair title of 'heritable superior' of Wick was not valid. Superiority, indeed, was of feudal origin, an institution that the petitioners argued had been abrogated by the Act of Parliament during the reign of George II, a fact which would have been news to most members of the council of Wick, who had made much of the town's 'heritable' superior and former provost, Sir John. The burden of the complaint was that the present Sinclair of Ulbster, George, was not 'competent' so to dispose of the superiority, especially to 'another

'OUR NORTHERN ATHENS'

family with whom this Royal Burgh has no concern.'[1]

The family in question was that of the Sutherlands, or rather at this stage the Sutherland-Staffords, for the Marquis of Stafford, husband of the Countess of Sutherland, had not yet attained the dignity of Duke of Sutherland. Lord Gower (the Gower property was in South Wales) was his son, and a future Duke of Sutherland. When the ordinance of transfer was issued in 1821 the magistrates noted with regret that Sir John ceases to be Superior of the Burgh,' and they thanked him – as well they might, for his 'liberal attention to its Interest during the many years that he held the Superiority of the Burgh and for his obliging conduct on all occasions to every Individual connected with the Town.' In particular, the address continued, 'the Thanks of this Town and neighbourhood are particularly due to Sir John Sinclair for first turning the attention of the British Fisheries Society to this Place and for his zeal in promoting the establishment of the Harbour of Pulteneytown which has so greatly tended to the prosperity of the Town of Wick and its vicinity.'[2]

Four years after the transfer, the magistrates put Lord Francis Leveson-Gower on the leet, and elected him as Provost of Wick.[3] Gower's reign however, did not last for very long, since like other burghs in Scotland, the Scottish Reform Act of 1832 (in the wake of the English Reform Act of that year), resulted in some important differences both in how the town of Wick itself was now to be

---

1 Minutes of Wick Burgh Council, 5 September, 1820. Almost certainly the 'protest' was referring to the measure of 1747, by which 'most heritable jurisdictions' in Scotland were formally abolished. The landlords much resented this erosion of their paternal rights, 'which', says Smout, 'they so much enjoyed. They were able to nominate the minister of the established church and to assist in the nomination of the schoolmaster, the two ideological teachers of the parish who could henceforth be relied upon to say the safe thing. With the kirk-session they had enough control over the distribution of parochial relief to ensure that the disrespectful would not find themselves among the blessed objects of Christian charity. As landlords they had the reputation of being the most absolute in Britain. In 1700 most of their tenants held at will, with no rights of compensation for any improvements they might have undertaken on their holdings. Their lord sat in judgement over them in the baron court even after the middle of the eighteenth century; in 1747 the Lord President had advised against outright abolition of this heritable jurisdiction on the grounds that without it rent enforcement would be impossible. The baron courts gradually fell into disuse, but only when the landlord discovered he could be sure of collecting his rents by invoking the estate's legal authority. It was a landowners' world, and the possibilities of oppression were enormous.' Smout, op cit, pp 261-262. Quite a number of these 'heritable' rights continued, as we have seen, in the north of Scotland. The citizens of Wick were, indeed, very fortunate to have had the attentions of a genuinely benevolent and intelligent Superior; their fellows in Sutherland, enjoyed less gracious treatment from their Superiors.
2 Mins, Wick Burgh Council, 18 June, 1821.
3 Mins, Burgh Council, (BCW), 1 September, 1824.

governed and in its representation at Westminster. The Scottish electorate was widened to include householders with a £10 or more rental, which still left most people unenfranchised: one in eight of the population instead of one in 125 before the Act, a total electorate of 65,000 as compared with 4,239 in 1820.[1] Thomson gives a figure of 181 'proprietors of houses worth L.10 and upwards in the Parliamentary burgh', and hence eligible to vote.

This meant in Wick a considerable addition to the list of voters, prepared in a more systematic way than the old 'burgher roll'. The *John O'Groat Journal* for 2 July, 1836, carried a notification from the Sheriff's Office that a Register of Voters for Wick, as for the whole of the County of Caithness, would be drawn up on 3 September. Other changes introduced by the Act resulted in a total change of electoral practice in the town, as elsewhere in Scotland. The number of Scottish MPs was increased from 45 to 53; county representation was somewhat reduced and that of the burghs increased by the creation of eight new burghs, and making Glasgow and Edinburgh two-member constituencies. To make room for new representation in the industrial lowlands, there was some squeezing together of the ancient burghs; to the group of five that had formed the northern Convention of Royal Burghs, Kirkwall, Tain, Dornoch and Wick, Cromarty was, in the words of Mr Thomson, 'added to this batch'. To the area of the Parliamentary Burgh of Wick was added most of the parish outside the town and some areas outside the parish.

Municipal government underwent quite drastic change. The old mediaeval huddle of magistrates to prepare a 'Leet' was abolished; and it was enacted that from now on a strict residence requirement would be enforced, which at a stroke removed from eligibility for office a number of the local gentry, including Lord Gower, up to that time Provost. 'Superiority', except as a permanently irritating element in Scottish land law in the form of the superior's entitlement in effect to a sort of 'ground rent', disappeared from local politics. The system of one third of the burgesses retiring and a new third standing at each annual election came in. The first new type election was ordered for the Tuesday, 4th November, 1834, between 12 and 4 of the afternoon, the electors assembling for the election in the Town Hall.[2] It is a pity that the *John O'Groat Journal* had not yet been established, as no report of this unusual event exists, other than slight reference in the Council

1 M Lynch, op cit, pp 391-392.
2 Mins. Burgh Council, (BCW) 4 October, 1834. & BCW, 4 March, 1833.

Minutes. The burghers of Wick objected to the new arrangements so far as the new residence requirements were concerned for, as they complained, many of their fellows, now to be excluded, had 'paid heavy sums for the Freedom'. On the other hand, they thought it a pity that the House of Commons had not opted for a £5 instead of a £10 rental for the admission of electors.[1] Subsequently, the members of the council saw fit to send their thanks to the House of Commons for the reform, but registered their objection to 'what the House of Lords had done to the Bill'.[2]

Raising the Levels of Civic Dignity

Briefly Mr Thomson mentions that 'the church and parish-school, the town and county buildings, and the jail, are within the royal burgh.' So they were, but the placing there of county buildings and the building of a new gaol were recent events accompanied by much circumstance.

'Wick is the county town,' says Mr Thomson. 'The sheriff has held his ordinary court here since 1828, when the Court of Session decided in favour of Wick, in the process of removal of the court from Thurso, where they [sic] had been held from time immemorial.' Getting this highly symbolic jurisdiction to Wick, county town since the days of the 'wicked' earls, was a rather fraught affair. Wick had long resented the fact that a mere 'burgh of barony' should have this privilege and the question of its transfer had been informally raised more than once. Now that Wick was becoming a 'big place' the anomaly was being felt all the more keenly. In March 1820 the Wick Burgh Council submitted to James Traill of Rattar, Sheriff Depute of the County of Caithness, a petition which spoke of 'the long felt want of a proper resident Civil Jurisdiction in the Burgh', now being felt, indeed, 'with peculiar severity'. The town had increased in population and received 'an immense crowd of strangers who frequent the Burgh during the fishing season . . . Why should Wick,' asked its burghers, 'be deprived of an honour and advantage which every other County Town enjoys?'[3]

Little more of this contention is recorded for some years, but it is evident that Thurso, darling of the earls, had no intention of giving way to upstart Wick. The matter was submitted by Wick to the Court of Session in Edinburgh and the usual flurry of statements,

1 BCW, 1 September, 1824.
2 BCW, 4 October, 1834.
3 BCW, 28 March, 1820.

counter-statements and 'informations' occupied the attention of their lordships until 1828.

The members of the Wick Burgh Council were delighted in March of that year to hear from their Agents in Edinburgh of the 'favourable decision of the Court of Session in the Action of Declaration so long in dependence before the court at the instance of the Magistrates of Wick against the Sheriff Clerk and Magistrates of Thurso, for having the Seat of the Sheriff Court removed from Thurso to Wick.'[1]

The judgement read:

> The Lords being advised [of] the Informations of the Parties, together with the Report as to the practice of Holding Courts and the exercise of the Judicial Arts at the Royal Burgh of Wick and Burgh of Barony of Thurso respectively in the County of Caithness and having heard parties . . . thereon: Find that Wick is the Head Burgh of the Shire of Caithness, and that the stated Sheriff Court must be held there without prejudice to the Sheriff's holding courts at other places in the said shire as authorised by Statute 20, Geo. II, cap.43, commonly called the Judicature Act: Therefore Repel the Defences to the Action of Declaration at the instance of the Magistrates of Wick and to the above effect decern and so far declare in terms of the Conclusion of the Sessions.

The burghers decided forthwith to convey the good news to Lord Gower. Removal was not to take place until public buildings at Wick were ready for reception, but although the actual removal is not reported, it was not long before the Sheriff Depute was issuing his notices from Bridge Street, Wick. The burghers of Thurso accepted the judgement with as good grace as possible, but never quite forgave Wick for depriving their town of its county status.

Crime and Punishment.

That other potent symbol of civic dignity, the location in Wick of a decent county gaol had been even longer in negotiation. The inadequacy of Wick's gaol in the Tolbooth building in High Street had been for years a perennial topic on the lips of the burghers but, the war over, they became quite vociferous about the matter, not least, the injustice of having to maintain a county gaol on their own slender

1 BCW, 4 March, 1828.

resources. There was, for instance, a discussion at the council meeting of 30 September, 1816, William Macleay (banker) in the chair as provost, on 'the burden of erecting and upholding jails, and for defining as well as limiting the liability of Burghs in consequence of the escape of prisoners whether confined for crimes of civil debt'. Wick, considered the members of the council, was in no condition to solve on its own the problem of maintaining a county gaol within the burgh; 'fluctuating and variable circumstances', especially those on the sea coasts where, 'so much depends upon the precarious state of the fisheries', the ever fluctating nature of commerce and manufactures, 'depending on the State of Foreign relations', all rendered it too big an issue to be handled successfully by the burgh on its own. Nothing short of a Royal Commission was required to investigate the whole complex subject.[1]

In May 1817, insult was added to injury when the provost and town council of Wick were ordered by the county's Court of Exchequer in the cause of the council's apparent unwillingness to pay bills of £200 and £700 'on account of the escape of certain Persons at the Jail of Wick and who had been imprisoned there for having defrauded the Revenue.' These malignants had, it was admitted, broken prison; 'nay some of them escaped through the Roof after breaking Doors and Locks, and everything in their way.' The burghers went into the attack, drawing the Sheriff Depute's attention to the actual circumstances in which the 'Poor miserable creatures were starving in Prison', since no 'aliment' was allowed them under regulations, the burgh having no funds for such a purpose.

'For the many weeks they remained in Jail,' said the burghers, 'their endeavouring to make their escape is not to be wondered at however vigilant the Magistrates and the Jail-keeper might have been.' If such a charge be accepted, 'no person will be got to Act as Magistrate of a Burgh', warned the Wick magistrates, 'at least in Wick, where so few persons reside who are fit for office, especially while the Wick jail is in such bad report.'[2] Only a week later, Donald Sinclair, jailer in Wick, was 'discharged for malversation', like so many of his predecessors. Donald Mackay of Thurso was appointed on an enhanced salary of £4 'besides all perquisites pertaining to the office'.[3]

In the following year, the burgh agreed to settle a debt of £200 due

1 BCW, 2 May, 1817.
2 BCW, 2 May, 1817.
3 BCW, 10 May, 1817.

to William Bruce on account of Donald Finlayson, a 'late Prisoner in this Tolbooth . . . being allowed to come out of prison by the jailer'.[1] Later that year a Committee of the House of Commons made a point of investigating the 'State of the Town Jail' of Wick. The burgh records give a question by question account of the interrogation of the representatives who spoke for the burgh, too detailed to be repeated at any length. Several of the answers to the searching questions are, however, very revealing, not only in the state of affairs in Wick but, by implication, gaol conditions in many other areas of Scotland (and doubtless, of England).[1]

In summary the record tells that the Wick gaol was built 'in connection with the Court House' in 1750 'at the sole and private expense of George Sinclair of Ulbster [father of Sir John], and consisted of four small rooms, two of them very small, no more than 12ft by 12ft 3ins, far too small for the 'number of persons often confined'. Life in the gaol was very miserable, 'so much so that persons frequently escape from it by breaking out of it through the walls and sometimes the roof.' On average there were 7 or 8 people in the gaol, but lately that number had doubled. Two out of every three prisoners were there for smuggling and defrauding the revenue. Only about 1 in 40 was from Wick itself.

John Horne, in his *Ye Towne of Wick in Ye Oldene Tymes*, retrospectively retails gleefully some tales about what he had been told of goings on in the 'original Tolbooth – not a vestige of which now remains'. He continues:

> Near by, in the market-place, were the stocks. Almost in front of it, close to the Cross of Wick, stood the town pump – a square stone erection – the centre of interest on special days when bonfires were lit. On the weekly market day, mutton was hung around it for sale, and thither buyers and sellers foregathered. The prisoners were said to play pranks on the worthy people assembling round the pump by throwing out, through the prison window, strings with hooks attached, which said hooks gripped the hats and wigs, and sometimes the mutton, of the douce gentlemen attending the market.
>
> Thereupon a hat or some other article might be seen bounding towards the gaol and disappearing through the window. Tricks of this kind were easily accomplished after

1 BCW, 29 June, 1818.

flesh-hooks and nails had been fixed in the jail wall on account of the pump becoming overcrowded with mutton, pork, &c., brought in by the country people.

Yet other yarns of jolly times past (these were not told to the MPs investigating Wick gaol in 1820):

> Imprisonment in the old days was no more than a name. The prisoners were allowed uncommon liberties. They were sometimes committed during the day and released at night. Their friends, too, could visit them and bring such comforts as might tend to cheer them – though their need of such brightening was not dire in those glorious days. Occasionally visits of this nature turned out comically, as the following testifieth: – Bell Dow, a female prisoner, had been consigned to the keeping of Willie Coghill, the jailor. It was Sabbath morning, and all was quiet in the old town. Two cousins of the worthy Bell called to see her, and were admitted by Willie. They carried a good supply of spirits – being in high spirits themselves and bringing another kind of spirits in a bottle. They soon fell to warming up their friend. Willie was not forgotten; and ere long he lay sound asleep on the floor. The prisoner and her friends now secured the keys and treated themselves to a walk in the fresh air. In bidding good-bye to the premises, they locked the door and threw the keys over the stair which led to the hall above. Willie awoke in course of time – to find himself the prisoner! Making for the window with what despatch he was master of, he bawled out for help. As it happened, the people were returning from church as Willie's head was thrust out of the window. Everybody gazed with astonishment at the jailer jailed. Some thought he had lost his reason, while others (too correctly) guessed that he had been indulging. Willie bellowed, danced, and swore; and ultimately losing patience, he roundly abused the crowd. He was at length relieved by order of Provost Macleay. The door was forced open. Willie afterwards found the keys behind the stair. Most likely the prisoner and her friends were allowed the freedom they had so ingeniously purchased.[1]

Another of Horne's tales, too good to leave out, tells of

> four prisoners who requested special attention from the jailer

---

1 John Horne: *Ye Towne of Wick in Ye Oldene Tymes;* Wick, W Rae (1895) pp 23-24.

on a certain Sabbath. That dignitary (who, if we mistake not, succeeded Willie Coghill) was a regular church-goer, and, like a good Christian, he said he would see them all at the Devil before he would give up the church services for them. This was precisely what they wanted – to be sure that he was out of the way. When he had left, they struck up the 23rd Psalm (was it to the tune of *Martyrdom*, we wonder!) While they lustily sang the familiar verses, they worked steadily with an auger, boring holes around the lock of the door. In course of time, the lock fell out, and the four captives were once more free men.[1]

Escapes cost the Wick magistrates substantial sums of money, chiefly as compensation to the county Court of Exchequer. Details were given of the recent cases in which such sums became due, notably that of Donald Finlayson, whose exit from the gaol as a messenger claiming the right to call on the prisoner. 'In this belief, the poor ignorant jailor not only gave Manson admittance at that unreasonable hour but also allowed the Prisoner to accompany Manson to a Public House where they had some drink.' The two actually returned to the gaol but Finlayson was released on a so-called 'letter of liberation' supposed to be from the Court of Session. The gaoler was badly paid (as we have seen) though he made money on the 'perquisites', perhaps as much as £10. It was practically impossible in Wick, they said, to find 'caution' for those committed for debt. Repairs after a break could cost £20 for repairs, but the recent one had cost £50. 'A suitably commodious jail would cost £1000, which Wick could not possibly find, in view of the tiny annual income of the burgh of not much more than £40.'[2]

In 1823 the Comptroller of Taxes law officer confirmed that the 'burgh is bound to aliment all Crown debtors confined in jail', a 'grievous hardship on the Burgh', thought the burghers. Later that year it was confirmed also that no extra funds were likely to be available for building at Wick a county gaol, which might cost as much as £3000, apart from a grant of £800 towards the project from the county, 'hence the need', agreed the councillors, 'to undertake an assessment of all feuars and householders'. Any refusing to accept responsibility on the part of the burgh could well be 'taken to parliament'. A public meeting was arranged to be held in the Town Hall on 10 November to discuss all this, and requests were sent to the British Fisheries Society

1 John Horne: *Ye Towne of Wick in Ye Oldene Tymes*; Wick, W Rae (1895) pp 23-24.
2 BCW, 13 October, 1818.

and Lord Gower to seek their aid.[1]

When exactly the decision was taken to make the best of a bad job and build a new gaol is not clear, but such a plan was adopted, no doubt made more urgent by yet another gaolbreak, which resulted, as always, in the dismissal of the gaoler and appointment of a new one.[2]

At a cost of £1,200, according to Charles Thomson, the new gaol was built behind a new tolbooth (now 'Town Hall') in Bridge Street, and declared to be a 'Legal Jail' by 'Decreet and Act' at a ceremony attended by the Provost Lord Gower and a deputation from the burgh council. A valedictory comment on the old gaol described it as 'incommodiously Situated, extremely insecure and neither sufficiently large nor in other respects well adapted for the confinement of prisoners', thus rendering necessary the building of a new gaol. It was designed by HM Architect for Scotland. Originally three separate gaols were intended, one for debtors and two for criminals, but funds were not adequate, so that only two compartments were built. Dr Joseph Henderson inspected the building and declared it suitable upon which an 'Act and Warrant' was issued, legalising the new gaol of Wick. Again, it is a pity that the *John O'Groat Journal* was not there to celebrate this solemn occasion.

This may have been the end of easy gaol escapes, but not of escapes from custody. A story in the *John O'Groat Journal* for 30 September, 1837, tells how a certain William Gunn, arraigned for stealing sheep from local farmers was condemned in the Sheriff Court to 14 years' transportation, made his escape on the way to gaol and was not recaptured. Another escape reported at the same time, was that of a forger named Gunn from Wester, sentenced to transportation for life. He was 'a perfect madman when in drink'. On his way down the main road at Swiney (it is not said what exactly that journey was for) in the company of an officer from Sutherland, he asked 'on some pretence' (presumably to relieve his bladder) to be released. No sooner released that he 'bounded over the hills like a deer'. The reporter had 'no knowledge of his recapture'.

As a conclusion to all these transactions, the Council decided in May, 1828, to sell the premises of the Old Tolbooth by roup.[1] 'When the new Town Hall and Prison were completed,' says John Horne, 'this tenement was sold by the magistrates to John Kirk, merchant'.

1 BCW, 18 November, 1823.
2 BCW, 8 November, 1826.

The proceeds were applied to the funds for erecting new buildings. The property was conveyed to Mr Kirk by the Right Honble. Lord Francis Leveson-Gower (who was then Provost of Wick) and the other magistrates of the Burgh, by a feu contract, dated 15th May and 12th June, 1830.'

From here on Mr Horne does not make it absolutely clear which of the premises, the old or the new, he is commenting on, as he continues:

> In the hall above were held cock-fights, balls, dancing schools and the public functions of the town. Thither the frizzle-haired, blue-bonneted worthies foregathered, marching in stately form, and congratulating themselves on their fine Town Hall; while the burgh officer did his best to sustain the high dignity of his calling among the boys who giggled on the stair-head.

It is evidently the proud new building on Bridge Street, for he next identifies the site of the 'original Tolbooth – not a vestige of which now remains [1895] – was prior to this building, on the site now occupied by ex-Provost Reiach's shop and the Bank of Scotland,' manifestly the present site of Woolworth's. In a footnote Horne also gives another useful titbit of information about where the old tolbooth and gaol stood: 'The site occupied by this jail was originally the kail–yard of the minister's manse, temporary'; while on another page he explains that 'the Manse at this time [1710] was that small tile roofed house in Tolbooth Lane known as the "Hole in the Wall".'[1]

Thomson gives quite a sketch of crime and prison in Wick shortly after the opening of the new gaol. Taking the year 1 September, 1827 to 1 September 1828, 'there were confined within the jail of Wick, 36 male and 8 female culprits'. During the following year to 1 September, 1829, there were 21 males and 4 females. An analysis of crime figures for the next four years shows that of the 62 people brought to trial, 55 came to trial before the Sheriff and 7 before the circuit-court in Inverness. 'This was little more than 15 for each year, or in the proportion of 1 for every 2,297 of the population; while for the whole of the population of Scotland the proportion was 1 to 1130.' This bears out the general impression left by most commentators, that the general behaviour of Caithnessians and even the new citizens of Wick, if not exemplary, was hardly crime-ridden. The levels of actual crime were low, even though the burgh had no police. These figures, of

---

1 All these stories from Horne, op cit, pp 6 and 19.

course, refer to the whole county, and, understandably, since its population was much higher than elsewhere, Wick parish topped the list of arraignments, 30 as compared with 11 from Thurso and 21 in the other Caithness parishes. The great majority of the crimes were theft (16) and assault and breach of the peace (31). 5 were tried for 'malicious mischief', 4 for 'deforcement' of officers of the law, 2 of concealment of pregnancy, and 1 each of child-exposure, forgery, defaming of judges and reckless riding and injury.

There is also an interesting list of the people in prison in 1840, 29 men and 2 women. As might be imagined nearly half of these are fishermen and seamen, their crimes being mostly assault, breach of he peace and 'rioting'. Most of the commitals occurred between June and October, 23 out of the 31, with no less than 14 in August alone; the age range is considerable, from 17 to 71, but 21 out of the 31 of those in gaol were aged 30 or under, 5 of them teenagers. As Mr Thomson declares, 'the season of the herring-fishery is most productive of crime', and there is a manifest connection between the sorts of crime for which the young seamen and fishermen are doing time and drinking in the 54 inns and public houses of which Mr Thomson so strong disapproves. 4 were sentenced for poaching, still regarded as a serious offence (at least by the landlords and magistrates). These apart, the only two possibly serious offences mentioned are those of 'exposing a child', the offender being 60 years of age (it does not say man or woman) and a case of 'uttering base coin', a carter of 28. 'Attention is paid to the health of the prisoners,' says Mr Thomson, and 'the Rev. David Mitchell, Missionary in Pulteneytown, has been appointed chaplain with a salary of L.20 a-year.'

Other Progress

During these years just before the Reform Act, several other measures were put in motion for improving the administration of the Royal Burgh. These included a determination to put the burgh finances on a better footing. Long pages of detailed accounting begin to appear in the record book. The first moves in this direction were prompted by the receiving in 1817 of a 'peremptory demand' from the estate of Sir John Sinclair (still Superior), presumably for superiority dues. The burghers in an access of conscience agreed that they were legally bound to pay, since 'the Burgh cannot now plead poverty'.

They thought it 'reasonable and just that the Burgh ought to be stented and assessed for the Public Burthen in the same manner as every other Burgh in Scotland.' Accordingly, the Council decided that: 'as a Preliminary Step a Judicial Rental of all Feuars within the Burghs shall be immediately taken, and that the Feuars or the Tenants may be convened for that purpose upon an Early Day. That a Jury of the Burghs inhabitants may be summoned and soon to stent and assess the Burgh' and thus conform 'to the practice of other Burghs.'

Democracy in Wick was breaking out all over, even before the Reform Act. This was, of course, one of the manifestations of Wick's new-found prosperity and some evident pleasure in shedding some of its mediaeval dependency on the goodwill (and cash) of superior and heritors. Quite soon after these resolutions, as mentioned, the pages of the record book begin to fill with accountancy details, among which is the first 'Stent Master's' assessments, which in total showed that the burgh was not quite so poverty stricken as used to be believed, viz:

Feuars		Householders	
Rents	Assessment	Profits on Trade	Assessment
£1,466	£1,244	£2,750	£6 17 6d [1]

Before leaving the topic of the endless problems of improving the quality of life in Wick, it may be mentioned that the place was being improved by the burgh council in other ways. For this money was needed. In January, 1813, the councillors are deciding on a more systematic collection of 'road money', and a list is ordered to be prepared of 'of those due to pay, none to be exempted but apprentices and aged People on account of their Poverty'. These monies are to be collected by the 'Burgh Officer', who is to pay them into the Treasurer 'as often as he has 20s. in his hands, and for which extra trouble he will be allowed a reasonable Gratuity'.[2]

The collection was evidently successful, for in April, the councillors are considering estimates for paving the streets of the town. Those received ranged from £450, 3000 yards a 3s at yard, from William Leask, who asked for decision to be postponed until he could get his bid in, to £275 at 1s 10d a yard, from James Falconer, mason of Pulteneytown. Falconer's bid was accepted; thus was put in hand the first big move

1 BCW, 5 March, 1817.
2 BCW, 21 January, 1813.

to provide Wick with paved streets.[1] But bad habits died hard. Yet again, in 1821, there is complaint about the deplorable habit of Wick citizens collecting and 'laying down dung and all other kinds of filth' in the streets. These were to be removed on pain of forfeiture. James Bain, a 'tacksman of Milton' was appointed to be town 'Scavenger' and a committee was appointed to superintend his work.[2]

Perhaps the nostrils of the citizens were becoming a little more sensitive – and perhaps the merchant burghers were getting aware that more and more visitors were coming to the place; but in 1824 a councillor raised the matter of the 'noisome state' of a sewer outside a tenement of Mr George Wares, 'a receptacle for all kinds of filth and nastiness and highly prejudicial to the health of the inhabitants.' Mr Wares was instructed forthwith to remedy this; but also there was a decision that Bailie Kirk should receive estimates for 'paving and putting in order this lane [where Ware's tenement was] down to the river'.[3] Even so, it was some years before Wick gained a public sewer and a piped water supply.

The Wealth of Wick

That Wick was becoming a richer place is evident, but in assessing this Mr Thomson makes rather more of the farming of Wick parish than of the spectacular rise of the fishing industry, on which Wick's increasing prosperity was based. He takes the 'then and now' approach to agriculture, what it was like before improvement began around 1790 and the extraordinary changes since:

> There was not a cart in the whole county. Not a potato, nor a turnip, nor sown grass was known. No rotation of cropping was observed, except that of arable land alternately in oats and bear, the manure being invariably put on the bear crop. Not a drain was dug; not a fence was to be seen except a field or two around the proprietor's houses.

'In the corrected rental of last century,' he says, 'it stood thus':

Of the landward part of the parish	£6,370 0 2
Of the burgh	166 13 4

In 1830 the values had changed considerably:

---

1 BCW 1,6 and 10 April, 1813.
2 BCW, 28 February, 1821 and 8 May, 1821.
3 BCW, 29 May, 1924.

The real rent of the landward part
of the parish was £12.000 0 0
Of the burgh £3,544 9 0

The rentals of three other significant areas are given for 1830, none of which had much of a value in 1790:

Louisburgh and Blackrock £1,250 0 0
Staxigoe, Broadhaven and Papigoe £1,834 2 0
Pulteneytown, an astonishing £7,333 13 0

In the four most important estates in the Wick parish, Thomson shows similar escalation:

In 1753 Hempriggs had a rental of £642 2 3
In 1830 " (exclusive of
 Pulteneytown) £5,607 18 6

In 1804 Thrumster had a rental of £180 0 0
In 1830 " " " £947 0 0

In 1814 Stirkoke had a rental of £611 0 0
In 1830 " " " £1,834 0 0

In 1753 Ulbster had a rental of £94 0 0
In 1814 " " " £214 3 0
In 1830 " " " £493 0 0

Rent values per acre about doubled over the period from 1792 to 1840. In 1792, 'rent of the best land ranged from 10s to 15s per acre'; in 1840 the average rent was from £1.5s to £1.10s per acre. Prices of most farm produce had risen over the period, but not spectacularly nor had farm wages. Ploughmen, for instance, who got from 13s 4d to 18s the half year in 1792, now got £1 to £1.8s. Women servants, pro-rata, did slightly better, from 6s 8d to £1 to £1 4s, reflecting no doubt the increasing demand for women workers on the quayside, even though that work was only seasonal. Unfortunately, Mr Thomson gives no figures for such workers; it is evident, however, that female labour, though in demand, was very ill paid.

Sheep and cattle, he says, are 'in such a forward state of improvement [whatever that means], as to be capable of being brought into competition with those of southern districts,' though Thomson gives no figures of any kind. However, farmers exhibiting 'of late years have carried off several premiums at the Highland Society's shows.' The amount of land going under the plough is increasing, he says, from its 1833 figure of 12,375 acres.

From all the evidence it is clear that the landowners and richer feuars were doing pretty well; some, like the Dunbars of Hempriggs were doing very well indeed from the sale of land for development. The standards of living of country folk were, by contrast, very modest. Small tenants, too, were being turned off the land, not usually here for making sheep runs, but for enlarging and cosolidating holdings. Not much 'tenderness' was shown to such people.

It may be remembered that Caithness landlords were included in the strictures of Andrew Matheson. Sir George Sinclair of Ulbster (Sir John's son), for instance, is charged by Matheson of practising 'Preference 4th' with some of tenants, viz:

> The landlord lets land 20 per cent less yearly to the grazier than the agriculturer. For instance, sixteen families of agriculturists paid £135 yearly rent for Campster. To Campster was added of Roster land the worth of £40 yearly rent, making Campster in all £175 of yearly rent. Thus, the whole of Campster, the property of Sir George Sinclair of Ulbster, Caithness, was let to D Horne on nineteen years' lease for sheep grazing, at £84 yearly rent, being less than half the rent paid by the preceding tillers.[1]

Wick parish generally was not greatly affected by clearance for sheep. Nevertheless, there is little doubt that even here small tenants were not much favoured, and there was enough unjust removal of them to warrant Mr Thomson's comment:

> violent and extensive ejection of small tenants not having the means of supporting themselves and families till other sources of support are discovered and made available, always occasion an amount of suffering, that can never be compensated nor atoned for by any consequent agricultural improvement.

He might have been echoing Goldsmith's,

But a bold peasantry, their country's pride,
When once destroy'd may never be supplied

It would, indeed, be a mistake to assume that everyone in the 1840s shared in the rising prosperity of the area. According to Thomson the number of registered paupers was substantially down from 1830, when there were 165 on the 'permanent roll of paupers.' In 1840,

---

1 Andrew Matheson, op cit: p 11. Matheson rehearses five different 'Preferences' of large landlords, each adapted to the particular circumstances of the district, for expelling small tenants.

there were 21 males and 76 females on the roll, a decline of nearly 1830. Among them was distributed £53. 0s 3¾d.

But, says Mr Thomson,

> these statements by no means give the correct view of the extent of pauperism in this parish. Many are extremely poor. Public begging is common both in town and county . . . There is no legal assessment for the poor in this parish. By far the largest portion of the funds available for their relief arise from collections at the church-door. The interest of L.300, which has been mortified for the poor, is applied to their relief; for which purpose, also, small donations are occasionally received.

Mr Thomson was not satisfied with the official information and made enquiries. William Bruce, the provost, supplied him with a list of 8 males and 53 females, who were in the habit of going 'round the shops and houses every Saturday, "seeking their piece".' Thomson set up his own investigating committee and found that in the entire parish area there were no fewer than 229 'utterly destitute' persons (52 males and 177 females), besides children. There were no less than 51 such people in the new settlement of Pulteneytown. Wick burgh had 28, Louisburgh 50. The largest single group were those in the 'landward part of Wick', as many as 72.

The women outnumbered the men as might have been expected, in a community where male labour was at something of a premium, many of them widows. Thomson, a minister of concern and compassion, observes:

> The poor are by no means clamant in seeking parochial relief. It is still considered degrading; and there are numerous instances of persons suffering great destitution, rather than make application for relief; and of individuals in but indigent circumstances themselves, taking destitute persons, who have no claim upon them, into their houses, and supporting them without asking or receiving sessional assistance. But it must appear evident that, on consideration of the preceding particulars, that, unless the funds of the session are more plentifully supplied, this state of things will not continue much longer. These means of relief are, at present, altogether inadequate to meet even with the veriest pittance the demands made upon them; and symptoms are appearing that necessity is more and more overcoming the laudable reluctance of the destitute to make application for parochial relief. To bring on a

legal assessment, it needs but the refusal of the benevolent shopkeepers of Wick to give any longer the weekly penny they have spontaneously bestowed on each of the numerous poor who go round on the Saturdays to collect it. Let this be done, and they are threatening to do it, and a compulsory poor-rate, with its innumerable train of economic and moral evils, will come to the parish in half a year. All parties will then find out, but when too late, that it would have been their wisdom to have supported them with greater attention and liberality, the good old system of the Church of Scotland. Nothing can arrest the progress of a country such as this to pauperism, but evangelical churches, pastoral superintendence, and scriptural schools. But these in sufficient abundance would, under the blessing of God, which is to be conferred on the preaching and teaching of the Truth as it is in Jesus, accomplish this.

This is not the place in which to launch into a history of poor relief in Scotland. Suffice to say that as a system it was exceedingly meagre, both before and after passage of the Scottish Poor Law Act in 1845. Before that date, as Smout puts it, 'poor relief depended on the charity of the minister and kirk session: from 1845 it was the prime duty of an elected Poor Law Board,' for each locality.[1] He speaks of the 'exceptional meanness of the Scottish Poor Law, even after 1845, in refusing relief to the unemployed,' and attributes Scottish working-class habits of thrift to an awareness, born of experience, that 'his [the working man's] savings were all that stood between his family and destitution during the repeated downturns in the trade cycle.' How much more must this have been the case in a place like Wick, where much employment was not only cyclical but markedly seasonal? The Rev Thomson's prognostications were quite on the mark. The Royal Commission on the Poor Law, which reported in 1844, was in preparation at the very time Mr Thomson was writing.

Thomson adds little to the picture already presented of the generally flourishing fishing industry (though passing through bad years) which we have already presented, but he includes an interesting table which 'shows the state of the herring-fishery at Wick in 1840'. It requires no additional comment:

---

1 Smout: *Century of the Scottish People;* op cit. p 203 and pp 241-2.

Native boats		428
Strange boats		337
Total of boats	765	
Crews of said boats		3,828
Coopers		265
Women employed as gutters, &c		2,175
Labourers		46
Carters		127
Other labourers employed about the fishing		150
Seamen in coasting vessels (supposed)		1,200
Fish-curers entered		91
Total of persons employed	7,882	
Total of barrels cured	63,495	
Barrels bung-packed, branded		10,333
Barrels exported to Ireland		51,250*
To other places in Europe		4,461
Total of barrels exported	55,711	

*This figure is perhaps open to question. According to Malcolm Gray *(The Fishing Industries of Scotland)*, the steady rise of exports to Ireland continued till the 1830s, then declined.

Thomson has a few things to say about other industries in Wick and Pulteneytown, most of them ancillary to the fishing, including

> four rope-works which employ, besides the masters, 75 men, with occasional hands. The first of these was commenced in 1820. All the rope which they produce is consumed in this port. There are one distiller and brewery, which employs 12 men; one meal and barley-mill, which employs 5; four saw-mills, three of which are driven by steam and one by water, employ 26 hands. A manufactory of pavement for exportation employs from 60 to 80 workmen.[1]

1 The quarry from which the flagstones were obtained was probably that spoken of by William Sutherland in *Wick 1794*, on the Hempriggs estate near the Old Wick Castle where, says Mr Sutherland, there are 'inexhaustible stores of limestone', burnt for lime in a kiln on site. 'The quarry there', he says, 'is interlarded with flags useful for paving.' This may be the quarry from which the flags were obtained for the paving of Wick in 1813. For a further note on the geology of the area see the end of this chapter.'

'OUR NORTHERN ATHENS'

There is a ship-building yard, commenced in 1815, with always one or two vessels on the stocks, employing about 50 ship-wrights [this was, of course, James Bremner's now flourishing ship-yard]. Twelve boat-building yards employ from 70 to 80, who launch from 80 to 100 boats annually. There has lately been established in Pulteneytown a foundery, which gives employment from 6 to 8 men, and promises to be prosperous. A Gas Company was formed in 1840, whose works are in the course of being erected; and it is to be hoped, that, by another winter, both Wick and Pulteneytown will be lighted with gas. There are 265 coopers in the parish. The principal, almost, indeed, the sole occupation for females in and about the town, is the spinning of yarn and making it into nets for the herring-fishing. At this they can earn the miserable pittance of only 2½d. or 3d. a day.

That Mr Thomson was a man of some feeling for the common folk is evident from his report, though, as we shall see, it was conditioned by a stern evangelical austerity of outlook. The strongest chord struck in his composition is that of a pietistic concern for the well being of the souls of the bleating flocks now crowding into the pens of Wick and Pulteneytown. He is also overwhelmed by the apparent hopelessness of the task ahead. His comments on poverty end: 'The kirk-session is composed of the minister and six elders, of whom one is above eighty years of age, and another is in bad health. The elders do what they can for the spiritual and economic good of the people; but what can they do among so many?' It does not take much imagination to see why, three years after this report, the Rev Charles Thomson decamped together with the entire parish church congregation into the wilderness of 'Disruption'.

Light in the Darkness

The Rev Charles Thomson sought to lead Wickers, poor and rich out of spiritual darkness. At least, he was able to report, they were at this time being led out of physical darkness. His dates for the operation were not quite right. In fact, there had been discussion about lighting the town with gas for some time. 'It gives us much pleasure,' said the *John O'Groat Journal* in September, 1838, 'to hear that some public spirited individuals have in contemplation to establish Gas Works in Wick and Pulteneytown.' The prospective 'gas consumers' of Wick were treated in another issue to a long and enthusiastic eulogy on the supreme merits of gas as compared with the alternatives, tallow candles and sperm oil, based on a recently published trade manual from London. A Wick and Pulteneytown Gas-Light Company was formed in February, 1839, with James Henderson, the distiller of Pulteneytown in the chair, and several meetings were reported during the next three years. There were expressions of impatience from time to time about the slowness with which the project was coming along.

Expectations had been aroused by the enterprise of Mr Henderson himself, for he had installed, in August, 1838, at the distillery in Huddart Street, a private gas works which produced marvels of 'brilliancy, convenience and comfort', along with 'no inconsiderable saving of expense . . . We sincerely hope that the great advantages which must follow the introduction of gas into this place will not be overlooked, and that measures may be promptly adopted for setting on foot the desired works.'[1]

Bridge Street, Wick finally broke into a blaze of gas-lit glory on Tuesday, 9 March, 1841; at least, this is the import of the paean of delight printed in the *Journal* on the following Friday. As an account of a unique event in the life of Wick if not as a piece of deathless prose, this deserves repeating in full:

GAS LIGHT IN WICK

> We rejoice to have to announce that the long-looked-for gas-light has at length been introduced into the ancient burgh, and that the greater part of the shops and a good many of the private houses were illumined on Tuesday evening, 9th instant. Although the alteration in the appearance of our streets and warehouses on Tuesday evening, compared with that which they presented in the previous evening, was *glaringly* marked, and might justify us saying that there was light instead of darkness, the brilliancy was by no means equal to that we very soon expect to experience when the gas becomes purer, now we trust on the way, and the

---

1 *JOGJ*, 7 September, 1838. There are numerous other short references to the topic between August 1838 and the opening of the gas-works in 1841. Gas lighting had, by this date, been introduced to most sizeable British towns. The system had developed from experiments in France, Belgium, Germany and England during the later eighteenth century, the main contribution having been that of William Murdock (1754-1839), Scottish inventor and colleague of James Watt, who illuminated the rooms of a house in Redruth, Cornwall with gas in 1792, and the Soho works of Boulton and Watt in Birmingham in 1798.

'OUR NORTHERN ATHENS'

suitable (not *sootable*) coals, now we trust on the way, have arrived. The exhibition on Tuesday evening, however, was, on the whole, very cheering; and we congratulate our townsmen on an event, while it will prove remarkable in the annals of our town, and *shade a lustre* over the many proofs which rise around us to the enterprise of the inhabitants, will, we feel convinced, prove conducive to the comfort of the citizens, and the prosperity of the place. The scene which our streets presented on Tuesday, more particularly Bridge Street, was an exceedingly animated one. Members of both sexes perambulated the town, in order to gaze at the 'new wonder'; and the blythe and cheerful faces met with in all directions, afforded sufficient evidence of the gas having not only lit up that part of the town, but having brightened up the countenance of the lieges also. Assuredly, many a woebegone phiz, stretched out the combined influence of dullness in trade, and low prices of herrings in the Irish markets, to a length which might justify barbers charging for shaving by the yard, gave indication of a vast satisfaction on Tuesday. A brilliant star, which had a particularly pleasing effect, figured over the shop door of Provost Bruce, High Street; and in the window of that of Messrs Waters and Mowat, Bridge Street, the initials 'V.A.' beautifully executed attracted considerable attention. A very remarkable improvement was observed in the appearance of that part of Bridge Street, in which Leith's Caledonian Hotel is situated, by the handsome lamp over the Hotel door being lighted by gas. Nothing indeed could have marked the difference which exists between gas and oil than the appearance of this lamp, the effect of the rays of which extended to the Bridge on one side, and to the extent of Bridge Street on the other. A lengthened detail of the numerous other shops, as also of private houses which were lighted up, we have not space for. In justice to John Kirk, Esq., High Street, we have to add that an excellent lamp is placed in front of his shop door, the entire expense of which that gentleman has with his wonted generosity, and with that regard for the comfort of his fellow-townsmen which have at all times marked his actions, defrayed out of his own pocket. The lamp cannot fail to prove particularly useful during the winter evenings, as High Street, all the way from Mr Kirk's to the Church, was formerly in a state of Cimmerian darkness. A few of the shops of Pulteneytown were lit up, but the exhibitions in this way were no means so numerous as in Wick. The shop of Mr A. Auld, druggist, Pulteneytown, was brilliantly and tastefully lit up, and the stained-glass lamp over the shop door had a very fine effect.

As even the euphoric reporter more less admitted with his 'on the whole', the occasion was not one of quite unalloyed joy. Alongside the article in the next column of the *Journal* was a letter to the Editor from a 'Shareholder' (correspondents seldom signed their letters) in quite different vein. Complimenting the *Journal* on its continuing interest in the 'comfort and convenience of the community'; the writer believed that the newspaper, 'in common with the entire population, must feel exceedingly indignant at the scurvy manner in which the shareholders of the Gas Company, and the public in general, have been treated by the Committee of Management.' Far from being satisfied with the brilliance of the occasion, 'on Tuesday evening we had,' wrote *Shareholder*, 'a display of some murky coloured gas, which, however, was naturally looked for on the first night of lighting up.' The show was poor and, 'as report has it. . . that no more gas is to be issued until the arrival of the *Don* on board of which vessel, it is said, the coals are, from which the new gas is to be produced.' According to this gentlemen the Committee were responsible for 'unrelieved blunders, and repeated vexations and numerous delays, and what the shareholders and the public at large ought not to put up with.' The failure to have decent coals in stock for the grand opening was but the latest example of the Committee's incompetence. *Shareholder* called for an urgent meeting of the Company at which a full explanation of the Committee's failures should be given.

An explanation was forthcoming at the meeting held three months later on Tuesday, 15th June, with Robert McLachlan, Bank-agent, in the chair. The contractor for the 'gas-making apparatus', Robert Guthrie of Berwick, was to blame; his work ran eight months beyond schedule. Guthrie had offered the lowest tender, £707 lower than the highest received, and £313 than the next lowest, an offer which, needless to say, the frugal gentlemen of Wick were unable to refuse. Guthrie's work had netted him £1130, and there could be no question of 'compensation' for delays. Pipes and laying work were done by the Shotts Iron Company at a cost of £1045 16s 9½d. Additional work, building etc had cost £484 16s 6d. Overall the cost of the enterprise had been £2660 14s 3½d, as against an early estimate of £2000.[1]

Thus did the ancient burgh of Wick come into the light. In a world suffused with floods of bright artificial light, it is difficult nowadays to envisage just how traumatic must have been the laying on of gas light

---

1 *JOGJ*, 18 June, 1841. Wick was not alone in its dissatisfaction with gas lighting in the early days. A great deal more development was required in the design of retorts, and much more experiment with coals suitable for gas-making. Not only was the light poor; the stench of gas burning, especially in enclosed spaces, was often overpowering. Nevertheless, it was all an improvement on what went before and, as the writers of *A Short History of Technology* (T K Derry and Trevor I Williams – OUP, 1960) explain, after the introduction of gas lighting to the parish of St Margaret's, Westminster in 1814: 'The growth of the practice of reducing fire-insurance premiums for public buildings and factories lit by gas made it certain that the system would spread.'

in this and every other gloomy northern town, even allowing for the fact that mid-nineteenth century jet gas-light was a pale, flickering illumination as compared with the white glare of the later Welsbach incandescent gas-mantle. Also, it may be remembered that Wick, like everywhere else, had still a long time to wait for municipally supplied gas street lighting. The effusive comments of the *Journal* on the generosity of Mr Kirk, and the very 'remarkableness' of the illumination cast up and down Bridge Street by the light from the lamp over the door of the Caledonian Hotel, was that it abolished the 'Cimmerian' gloom (why did the writer prefer 'Cimmerian' to the rather more familiar 'Stygian'?) that had reigned till 1841 in Wick's main thoroughfares.[1]

CHOLERA

No account of Wick in the middle of the nineteenth century would be complete without reference to the dreaded 'plague', as it was often called. In common with other towns in Britain, Wick suffered from the periodic visitation of cholera, a disease that originated in the far east. Though in no sense comparable with bubonic, the true 'plague', far more deadly in its effect, it scourged workers and their families severely. It thrived in the conditions of desperate overcrowding, dirt and lack of adequate water supplies and sewerage in the new industrial towns. Bad water, flies and infected food were the common carriers, but it could also be carried by people, sometimes those in apparent good health.

At the onset the infected person usually had bouts of diarrhoea, lasting for a day or two followed by the so-called 'rice-water' period, during which the victim passed liquid stools when there was 'generally a state of prostration, accompanied by severe cramps in the legs and abdomen. Vomiting of watery fluid and intense thirst' would add to the victim's misery, and there would follow, either death in a few days or a state of sheer debilitation, lassitude and weakness. It was not uniformly fatal; in fact, most patients recovered,

---

1 A report in the *Journal* on 22 October, 1841, commented that 'all in the south' were astonished that Wick and Pulteneytown 'could boast an extensive gas works and produce gas equal to any in the kingdom', yet was destitute of a single street lamp in the town. A dozen to twenty lamps would be a great improvement, and would help in the business of the shopkeeper. 'Many have not taken the gas' in their homes, complained, the commentator, even though it was not clear, that, unit for unit of light, gas was by far the cheapest illuminant. *Landlords should own the fittings* and so save the fiddle and expense of removal and refitting on change of tenancy.

but usually remained for some time in very poor condition.[1]

Three main waves of the disease struck Britain, 1832, 1848 and 1852, after which the cholera abated as towns installed clean water supplies under the various sanitary acts that were passed. The most influential of these in Scotland was the Poor Law Act of 1845, which, resulted in the setting up of parochial boards with various duties, including sanitary supervision. The disease could linger into a following year or strike in localised epidemics; it was doubtless such an outbreak that afflicted 'Dunster' (Dunbeath), in Neil Gunn's *Silver Darlings*. Wick underwent several epidemics of varying intensity, a not surprising state of affairs considering the large influxes of people during the herring season and their September departure, with the likelihood of bringing in the infection and taking it out.

Few statistics are available to illustrate the impact of the disease on Wick and Caithness; Mr Thomson hardly mentions it, and the *John O'Groat Journal* seldom gives anything more than a brief reference to it. It so happens, however, that a doctor's record book (evidently required under the 1845 Act) has survived from the autumn of the year 1849, when the town suffered a relatively mild epidemic of cholera.

The book records 49 cases between 5 September and 12 December, the majority of the cases occurring in October and November. Only two of the doctor's patients died, two women in middle age, one from Wick and the other from Bank Row, Pulteneytown. The disease was impartial as to whom it struck down, the victims including craftsmen, fishermen, labourers and their wives, servants. One was a druggist, another an excise officer and another still the post-master of Wick Post Office. Three people of 65 and over recovered; one was an old lady of 86 and the eldest of all, a man of 88, neither living in very good conditions. A child of $2\frac{1}{2}$ came through and several children of four to six. Altogether there were 20 men, 18 women and 11 children listed in this record book of the short-lived epidemic.

The doctor was expected to indicate in his records for each patient, in addition to occupation, his or her 'condition and habits' and to give a description of 'locality and houses.' It is fairly true to say that the great number and more severe cases came from 'poor' conditions,

---

1 Though it must be recognised that when the disease struck in large, squalid industrial towns the number of deaths could be quite enormous. In Britain as a whole, no fewer than 32,000 people died in Britain as a result of the 1832 epidemic. It is also true that by 1849, health authorities were getting some measure of the disease.

whatever that might mean, and many from 'damp', 'badly ventilated' and 'dirty' houses. The doctor writes of one Wick house as 'low, damp and filthy' and one in Bank Row, Pulteneytown, as 'situated at the mouth of a river, dirty, badly ventilated and collections of filth in the rear.' The description 'filth in rear' is applied to several of the dwellings, especially in Lower Pulteneytown – these were days when the town governors had still not succeeded in having all middens cleared away; while in two houses in Smith Terrace (in one of which Elizabeth Taylor of eighty-six lived) a sewer from a higher street passed under the house. Smith Terrace seems to have been particularly foul, for near one of the houses there was a 'gully hole of a sewer at the door.' Two children of a fisherman, one of four and the other five, were 'surrounded by every species of filth.' Many houses and general conditions were described as 'comfortable,' 'clean' or 'healthful', but even the wife of a pilot in Huddart Street was said to be living in a house that was 'elevated' yet having a 'collection of filth in the rear.'

The really astonishing thing is that in the face of such a record so few people died. A few patients were diagnosed as having the 'Asiatic' or more virulent form of the disease; the others, if diagnosed at all, had the 'British' or indigenous form. Treatment consisted of doses of acetate of lead, opium, calomel and 'chalk mixture' and sometimes bicarbonate of soda – or combinations of these; or the application of 'sinapisms' (mustard plasters), infusions of mint and in one case, that of Elizabeth Leith of Bank Row, who died, leeches were applied to her temples. In one family of eight, the doctor reported that, one (a child) has cholera, six others diarrhoea, but that the one free from disease in this 'dirty and badly ventilated' house (in Grant Street) was an 'infant at the breast.'

One thing that was plentiful in most parts of Wick was fresh air, especially during windy weather, and this very probably explains why the incidence of cholera in the town, though frequent, was never too serious. Improvements to the sewerage system and water supply in the 1850s and onwards virtually eliminated cholera from the records here and elsewhere.[1]

1 There is a long history of controversy as to what were the causes of the disease and what were the best methods of treatment. There were those who believed it was transmitted by contact, the 'contagionists'; others favoured the 'miasma' theory that is, the process by which the disease was induced by fogs, low-lying conditions, 'miasmas'. There was as yet no germ theory available, but clean water, clearance of muck and rubbish, improved sewerage, and fresh air did wonders.

ADDENDUM

I Thomson's Sources.

At the end of his study, Mr Thomson tenders his

> grateful acknowledgements, and more especially to the Right Honourable Lord Duffus, and to John Henderson, Esq., Pulteneytown, W.S. From the former he received a great deal of curious and important information respecting the mineralogy, sea-coasts, antiquities and progressive agricultural changes of the parish; and to the latter he stands indebted for the free use of extensive and most accurate collections may be his learned and godly brother, the late Patrick Brodie Henderson, illustrative of the history and statistics of Caithness.[1]

Now available to Thomson, mainly through Henderson, was a great deal of geological and botanical information about the Wick area, quite unknown to William Sutherland forty-six years before. Much of this had been collected by Robert Dick of Thurso, and the researches of Hugh Miller were becoming known. It was Miller who identified and defined the geological sequences of the Old Red Sandstone of the Devonian period, and in this area investigated the Caithness beds. 'The North of Scotland,' he said, was 'girdled by an immense Belt of Old Red Sandstone'. His authoritative *The Old Red Sandstone* was published in 1841, but many papers and lectures of his before this were familiar.

II A Note of Thomson's Geological References

Thomson's description of the geology of the Wick area is a world away from the sketchy descriptions of William Sullivan, who tells, for instance of 'stones of a flinty nature . . . which when broken contained the shape of serpents coiled round in the heart of the stone'. The veriest amateur now knows those as 'ammonites'. Through the work of Dick, Agassiz and Miller, Thomson is enabled to write knowingly about 'ichthyolites . . . universally spread over this extensive deposit', the sequence now known as the Wick Beds.

As for the limestone worked on the Hempriggs estate, it should be explained that, unlike that of the Durness area of Sutherland,

---

1 Henderson was the lawyer who for several years was factor of the Hempriggs estate, and from 1828 Procurator-Fiscal in Wick. He was author of *Caithness Families*.

limestone is not a main feature of the Caithness lithology. This area, as Thomson explains, consists of (quoted not for its contemporary accuracy, but to illustrate Thomson's geological vocabulary):

> an immense formation of alternating beds of silicious and calcareo-silicious flagstone or slate-clay; dark, foliated, bituminous limestone; pyritous shale, sandstone etc. The silicious beds predominate in the lowest position of this formation and the calcareo-bituminous bed gives the type to the intermediate part, becoming more silicious; the aggregate thickness of these deposits is very great.

In fact, a distinctive lithological feature of the Caithness beds in this area is the Achanaharras Limestone, not exposed in the immediate area but forming the horizon between the Upper and Lower Caithness Flagstone Groups, thus appearing from time to time and being exploited for lime burning when accessible. The Wick Beds themselves, at the top of the Lower Caithness, when weathered appear grey, greyish brown and dark grey, often finely laminated. Thick exposures are readily visible in the vertical quarried walls of the south bank of Wick Water. Vast masses of rock were taken out from here for the building of the harbour installations, an extremely handy source of the sturdy material needed for the construction work of each of the engineers, Telford, Bremner and Stevenson. It is doubtful if either the harbour or Pulteneytown could have been built so quickly or so economically had it not been for the immediately available supplies of very workable building stone.

Much of the characteristic drabness of housing and other buildings in Wick is the result of weathering of the masses of local rock used in creating the town. Utility and convenience of materials rather than aesthetic choice dictated the building of nineteenth century Wick. What the town's buildings have lacked in charm and elegance they have gained in stability and durability.

Of the Swiss Professor Louis Agazziz, Thomson remarks: 'the celebrated naturalist who has devoted so much of his time to the study of fossil fishes, has determined, and for the first time, with accuracy, the characteristics of the Caithness species.'

CHAPTER 13

SODOM OF THE NORTH

THOUGH disapproving of their inordinate taste for whisky, the Rev William Sutherland spoke kindly in his *Wick 1794* of the Wick folk as 'of good, moderate dispositions, not ignorant of his principles, nor inattentive to the practice of religion'. In his contribution to the *New Statistical Account of Scotland* of 1840, this newly appointed minister of Wick, the Rev Charles Thomson, wrote in less charitable vein. The people had, he believed, been corrupted by plenty; wealth had 'increased the wickedness of the district; and anyone acquainted with the sources of happiness well knows that "a man's life consisteth not in the abundance of things which he possesseth"' *(Luke, 12:15)*. To reinforce his point, a few paragraphs down he quotes from the prophet, *(Haggai 1:6)*:

> 'The ungodly who earneth wages, earneth wages to put them [The Authorized Version gives 'it'] in a bag of holes.' A people cannot be exalted without righteousness, and with righteousness they cannot be degraded; but morality cannot be consummated or upheld without the full and abundant administration of the Gospel. When will legislators, heritors and merchants be convinced of this?

Among the evils of the parish Mr Thomson lists the shortage of places in all of the temples of the different denominations now to be found in the town. Successful mission work could not be accomplished among the poor people of Wick if they could not all be found a place in church. Nor did the poverty of schooling in the parish help.

Whisky Galore

However, for Mr Thomson much of the wickedness of Wick was down to its forest of public houses. Of these, he reported, there were in Wick and Louisburgh, 22, and in Pulteneytown 23; in the 'landward part of the parish' were another 9, a dreadful total of 54. This, in a total population in 1840 of 9,346; of these 4,592 were in Wick burgh and Pulteneytown, that is, one public house to every 173 parishioners, and one to 100 Wickers and Pulteneytowners.

This number of inns and public-houses, Mr Thomson considered, was 'appalling'. Every person 'acquainted with the circumstances of the parish' must admit

> that a dozen were more than enough for all the necessities of the district. An excess of public-houses is one of the most frightful curses which can befall a community. Their effect upon the morals of the people is most disastrous. Multitudes can trace their ruin in body, soul and outward estate, to such seminaries of Satan and Belial, as the lower public-houses generally are. Those to whom it belongs to license such places in the parish of Wick have incurred an awful responsibility.

Thomson allowed that in summer the population more than doubled, and there could be little doubt that the greatest amount of roistering and drunkenness occurred during the fishing season. On the matter of heavy drinking, Mr Thomson comments:

> At all seasons of the year, whisky is drunk in considerable quantities, but during the fishing season enormous potations are indulged in. It may seen incredible, but it has been ascertained, that, during the six weeks of a successful fishing, not less than 500 gallons a day were consumed.[1] Let it be remembered, however, that at that period 10,000 strangers, as boatmen, gutters &c. were crowded into the town of Wick. Of late years the people have been more temperate. Snuffing is almost universal among the men, and both it and smoking are very common among the women. About L.3,500 a year are spent in the parish of Wick on tobacco.

To cope with the demand for these indulgencies, several manufactories were set up. The Rev William Sutherland had spoken of a snuff factory and distillery on the Hempriggs estate as early as 1794. A brewery and maltings were also set going; and in 1837 Mr Burn opened a tobacco factory in Pulteneytown. In pursuit of the ideal of self-sufficiency, a new distillery was founded in Pulteneytown in 1827.

It may be doubted that the Huddart Street distillery of

---

[1] Iain Sutherland gives an alternative of 'over 800 gallons of whisky a week', though mentions no source (see Iain Sutherland, op cit, pp 30-31). This is, perhaps, a more realistic figure. 500 gallons a day would mean that in a week Pulteneytown would consume 3,500 gallons. The place would have been awash with the stuff, and even allowing for the Scots' well-known capacity, it seems doubtful if anyone would daily have been fit for work.

Pulteneytown would have been able to provide in the early days all the drams needed to slake the thirsts of the fishermen, coopers, packers and draymen crowding into the town's many inns, but as many commentators on the Caithness scene have averred, however it came, whisky was never in short supply. It is, indeed, more than likely that well before 'Old Pulteney' began to flow, Wick's needs were ministered to by the distillers of Brora in Sutherland; for the Marquis of Stafford, with his keen concern for the well-being of his workers and tenants, built that distillery in 1819, 'to provide a use for the barley grown by the tenants of his farms', as Professor McDowall explains.

In passing, it may be added that the same celebrated connoisseur says of 'Old Pulteney':

> This whisky comes from the farthest north, from Wick, the county town of Caithness, and is only available locally. It is a whisky of considerable distinction having a succession of flavours and not noticeably peaty; indeed, one is tempted to think that a good whisky could be made without peat at all.
>
> It is to me quite surprising that such a good whisky could be made in this grim, windswept fishing town on the North Sea.

Fig 30 Pulteneytown Distillery.

SODOM OF THE NORTH

Caithness is indeed a bare county and needs a good whisky to warm it up.

The good Professor acknowledges his debt to Neil Gunn, 'a native of these parts', who writes glowingly of his native tipple. In his lyrical *Whisky and Scotland,* Neil pays his tribute to Pulteney whisky as generously as to the silver darlings and the folk of Wick and Caithness:

> I must say something of Pulteney – the whisky of my native county – Old Pulteney, as it was always called, though I have childhood memories of seeing it in bottle perfectly white and certainly new. In those days it was potent stuff, consumed, I should say, on the quays of Wick more for its effect than its flavour! A very individual whisky, it was naturally disliked by some as ardently as it was praised by others. Whisky has its human parallel. It is not a machine-made article and has to be come upon as one comes upon a friend, and then treated with proper respect. When I got of an age to understand Old Pulteney, I could admire its quality when well matured, recognising in it some of the strong characteristics of the northern temperament.[1]

Total Abstinence

The men of Wick were not the only imbibers of Caithness. In January, 1840, the *John O'Groat Journal* published what it called the 'Tippling Statistics' of Latheron, whose inhabitants like those of Wick were into the herring trade. Between Thrumster and Berriedale there were 'no less than 28 public houses.' Having reported this fact, the journalist then speculated that if each of these establishments consumed, say 30 ankers of whisky of 9 gallons each,

> this will at £3.12s, a very moderate calculation, be £72 per annum by each of these thriving establishments, making in all the handsome sum of £2016 laid out for deleterious alcohol [this is very curious arithmetic]. And this is not all. This we must

---

[1] Neil Gunn: *Whisky and Scotland;* London, Souvenir Press (1977), first published 1935 by George Routledge and Sons. R J S McDowall, was Professor of Physiology, University College, London, and a knowledgeable enthusiast for malt whiskies. His book, *The Whiskies of Scotland,* is a standard compendium on the subject. Two Professors of English, David Daiches (educated George Watson's College and Edinburgh University) of Sussex University, and George Saintsbury, of Edinburgh University, were also notable authorities on the subject of whisky. Saintsbury was particularly devoted to Clynellish.

consider as the cost price and if we add to it one third more at for the price at which the whisky is disposed of, it will make upwards of Three Thousand Pounds paid to the parish of Latheron publicans, as a remuneration to them for allowing the said public, for a consideration given and received, the right to pour liquid fire down their throats!!! But this is not all; how much we should like to know is thrown away every year – and it is thrown away – on other spirits, and in ale and porter in the drouthy parish of Latheron. It would startle the consumers were they to make the calculation. The end of these things is misery, ruin, poverty and death.[1]

The publicans were not to have it all their own way. From the beginning of January, 1840, frequent reports began to appear of the temperance movement. At a meeting of a group of people belonging to the 'independent Congregation' on 1 January, it was decided to form in Wick a Temperance Society, 'founded on the principle of total abstinence from all intoxicating liquor.' The meeting was addressed by a Methodist Minister, Mr Hooley. The meeting was 'very crowded'. Following the example of Thurso, it was decided forthwith to form the 'Wick and Pulteneytown Total Abstinence Society'.

The *Journal* moralised sternly on the development. 'Were,' they said,

> the various parish ministers, and others throughout the county, whose powerful influence has told so effectually on other occasions, but to put their shoulders to the wheel, and join a Society which only seeks the good of the community – a marked, beneficial and extensive moral reformation in the habits and morals of the people would soon be perceptible. We, therefore, cannot entertain a doubt that the Ministers of the Gospel of Christ will at once perceive what their duty in the matter ought to be.[2]

This was by no means the last of the *Journal's* strictures on the subject. In fact, the first editor of the *Journal*, Benjamin Miller Kennedy, was himself a prime mover in the founding of the Temperance Society of Wick. He and the founder of the paper, Peter Reid, were strongly Liberal – as was the general tone of the paper.[3] This exemplifies, among other things, the common connections

1 *JOGJ*, 17 January, 1840.
2 *JOGJ*, 3 January, 1840.
3 *JOGJ 150th Anniversary Supplement, 1836-1986*. Kennedy edited too and published the *Northern Abstinence Advocate*.

between liberal political leanings, non-conformist religion and temperance. Similar trends existed in England at the time, with Methodists leading the temperance movement and increasingly supporting Liberal politics. While it would be an exaggeration to suggest that the temperance movement was essentially working-class in its membership and drive, it undoubtedly became in the 1840s and '50s a popular and powerful cause in Scotland, its greatest success being the Forbes-Mackenzie Act of 1853, by which pubs were closed on Sundays in Scotland and a closing-time was fixed for weekdays (of 11 o'clock!). The Act had no parallel in England. It was followed in 1855 with the 'Methylated Spirits Act', 'which hampered the manufacture and sale of meths for consumption.[1] The very necessity of these Acts, however, demonstrates to an extent the greater evils of drink and drunkenness in Scotland and a consequent greater need for legislative control as compared with England, where whisky was still virtually unknown – though gin was popular enough. None of which may be taken to suggest that similar evils did not exist in London, Liverpool and the like.

These were not the only developments. Police in Scotland were given greater powers of entering unlicensed premises 'suspected of being shebeens and working-class drinking clubs' following the report of the Royal Commission on Exciseable Liquors of 1859. 'All this,' says Smout, 'laid the temperance reformers open to the charge of promoting "odious class legislation" which affected the pleasures of the poor on their one day off work but did nothing to stop the rich imbibing claret in their own homes and clubs.'[2]

The pleasures of drink being so basic, however, the leaders of the temperance movement realised from the start that all efforts must fail 'unless an attempt were made to create an alternative to the world of drink'. Though the main drive for temperance came through religion, the enthusiasms of religion would on their own not be sufficient to keep the temperance band-wagon rolling. In England this conviction led eventually to the founding of the Working-men's Clubs and Institute movement, no doubt reflected in Scotland, as were the creation of the Rechabite Friendly Society and the Band of Hope for young people. 'There were evening concerts, soirées, and lectures

---

1 T C Smout: *A Century of the Scottish People, 1830-1950*, London, Collins (1986). p 144.
2 T C Smout: *Scottish People*, op cit, p 144. Smout has an excellent chapter on 'Drink, Temperance and Recreation', pp 133-158.

where the evils of alcohol were demonstrated, often in a highly entertaining way by demonstrations of popular science: if alcohol poured on gunpowder caused an explosion what might it do to the guts of a man? There were temperance hotels and temperance tea rooms . . . The idea was to demonstrate that life without drink could be as full and cheery as life focussed on the bottle.'[1]

Though far away as it was from the excesses of Edinburgh and Glasgow, Wick was as rife a centre of heavy drinking as any in the kingdom. The Abstinence Society recruited and organised furiously. At a soirée held in the Town Hall a few days after the founding, 250 people attended. The Chairman, Bailie William Waters, presided, and, according to the euphoric reporter (probably Kennedy himself), all of those attending, 'were we to judge from the contentment and pleasure that beamed on every countenance, greatly delighted with the intellectual as well as other entertainments of the evening. Beauty shone forth resplendent on this occasion, as it usually does in our good ancient burgh.'[2] The party fed well and took coffee.

At a meeting in March, it was reported that the Society had 720 members[3], and in October 900, when it was decided to build a Temperance Hall.[4] By the time of the first Annual General Meeting in January, 1842, there were reported to have been 922 members in 1841 and now there were 1502 enrolled, exclusive of 342 juniors. Building on a piece of land in Muckle Park between High Street and Louisburgh began briskly and in early in August, 1842, it was 'now about being roofed in and ready for the windows, doors &c. which are in a state of forwardness.'[5] The Hall was opened – though not finished but 'fitted up for the occasion', on Thursday evening, 18 November, 1841, when the Rev Brown, sent to Wick by the Northern Union, delivered a lecture on the evils of drink in a 'pleasing and forcible manner' to an audience of 800. Among the items of information communicated by Mr Brown was the news that 371 public houses had recently been closed in Aberdeen (dismay in the Aberdeen topers' world must have been terrible), resulting in 'great stagnation in the whisky trade', rendering 'many distilleries, both south and north, at present silent.'[5] Wick had its quota of temperance lectures from March,

1 Ibid, p 142.
2 *JOGJ*, 7 January, 1841.
3 *JOGJ*, 6 March, 1841.
4 *JOGJ*, 30 October, 1841.
5 *JOGJ*, 19 November, 1841.

1841, onwards, the first being those of the Rev R G Mason, who was sent on a tour of the north including Orkney and the other parishes of Caithness.[1] In November, 1841, came Captain James Johnson of the sloop *Alexander and Jenny*, who gave two lectures on 'Teetotalism' in the Wick Methodist Chapel; the lecturer's 'strong and well-applied remarks on the dreadful effects of intemperance were given in the Captain's happiest manner.' It is evident from here and elsewhere in Scotland, that one of the appeals of the movement was the entertainment value of its lecture programmes, a factor not ignored by the *John O'Groat Journal*. We should quail a little today, no doubt, at Benjamin Kennedy's jejune sentimentality, but he frequently took the humorous side. Two of his funny tales have a flavour. Both were printed in December, 1840, the first in the issue of 4th and the second the following week. The first plays on the emphasis on water-drinking (still then a rather unsavoury commodity in Wick) forced into the abstentionists' menu by their exclusion of liquor – tea and coffee were still rather expensive, and also on the middle-class affectation of the time that the common speech of Caithness was comic; of course, it was and is rich in folk humour.

A WATER DRINKER

An unsophisticated wench from a country parish, doing service in a family in this town, was lately ordered by her mistress to empty a large tub of river water which had been drawn for some household purpose, but which was afterwards found not required. On receiving her instruction she stared, as the saying is, 'like a stuck pig', and, quite aghast, expressed, in trembling accents, her inability to carry the tub downstairs, adding an enquiry as to the best means to be adopted in order to empty the water previous to such an undertaking. 'Drink it, to be sure,' said her mistress as she left the room, smiling at the imperturable [sic] gravity with which the girl put the question. In about twenty minutes after, she had occasion to return to the kitchen, and there, to her astonishment and amusement, found Peggy on her knees, with her head in the tub as 'if ducking for apples', endeavouring to drink up the contents of her acquatic labours for an instant, and arranging her moistened ringlets, with a dolerous [sic] look at the tub, and an imploring

---

1 *JOGJ*, 19 March, 1841. Rechab was the father of Jonadab who enjoined his family to abstain from wine and live in tents. (*Jeremiah*, 35, 6-7).

one at the lady, 'Losh, in nees, mistress, am no able till doe't; I've been wurkan at it for a quarter a' 'oor, till am just leek a coo swalled an doun, an I have na half doon yet, am sure 'cleeve 'efore hids teem.'

Water, in any case, has always been a comic subject to whisky drinkers. The other tale has an express reference to the temperance movement:

An old woman in this county, whose son, a mechanic, is at present employed in a manufacturing town in the south, complained bitterly to a neighbour, that Johnnie had joined the Reprobate Society. 'Reprobate Society,' said the other, 'ye maun a'thegither vrang, hid'll be the Rechabit Society y'r meanan.' 'I ken naething about nane of 'em,' rejoined the distressed mother. 'I dare say e' tane is as bad as e' tither. I'll thrift upo' at picter; fat wis his business till join her; surely societies wis na made for puir folk, bairns leck him.'

In the same issue of the *Journal* is a story purporting to illustrate the effectiveness of the cause. A deceased Mr Mowat of Watten is buried without the customary drinking. 'The odious whisky was entirely banished. Coffee, 'says the reporter, was the only beverage presented, and we understand that all the company, with the exception of one individual, seemed quite delighted at the innovation thus made on an old but a shameful and pernicious custom.' He was fain to add – 'tell it not in Gath and publish it not in the streets of Askelon' – that the delinquent was 'an elder of the church'. The gentlemen is said to have wisely remarked: 'they micht hae had ae roun' just til tak awa the scandal o' haean nae at a burian.'

There had been a brief discussion in an earlier issue suggesting that middle-class folk themselves were becoming rather self-conscious about their own behaviour during these times of professed teetotalism. This is illustrated by a piece culled from *Chambers' Magazine,* by the *Journal* to the effect that 'in high life' the practice of 'asking another to drink with you' at dinners and functions was now 'quite out.' Such habits were confined now to the *inferior orders.* 'The use of intoxicating liquors at table is obviously declining in the *best circles,*' was the conclusion of this observer of etiquette.

There is little evidence that the drinking habits of those in the *best circles* changed one whit at this time or even through the century, but it is clear that the temperance movement made a deep impression on Wickers. The Total Abstinence Society continued to thrive in Wick and Pulteneytown, its Temperance Hall becoming one of the main venues for interesting activites in Wick. Other bodies began to pull their weight in the movement, including the Freemasons and the Free Templars, the SPCK and the Fishermen's Association. The Hammermen and Carpenters had started campaigning against drink as early as 1825.

The final triumph of the movement was the creation of a dry Wick during the years just after the First World War through and beyond the Second. Wick was one of the few towns of Britain that went the whole way to 'prohibition' at that time, a delayed effect almost certainly of the powerful propaganda of the Wick Temperance Society and its allies in the nineteenth century. To this day, Mackay's Hotel, a salubrious and superior pub, bears on the upper wall of its north face, the scars of these times, for still showing through various layers of paint is the legend 'Temperance Hotel'.

KINGDOM OF THE GLORIOUS GOSPEL

There can be little doubt that strong drink, its plentifulness or its lack, had a considerable influence on the life of Wick. There was, however, mainfestly no shortage in the days of wickedness of more godly influences in Wick and Pulteneytown, to counter the teaching of the 'seminaries of Satan and Belial'.

Mr Thomson had no great trust in the innate goodness of the Wick folk. His estimate of their character was not indeed uniformly ungenerous, but whenever he speaks of their good points there is a stone in the sock: 'The parishioners of Wick are shrewd and attentive to their own interest. Their shrewdness, however, sometimes degenerates into cunning.' While 'they are remarkable for natural affection, and show much kindness to their poorer neighbours', he observes that 'unchastity, both in man and woman, is lamentably frequent, which appears from the records of the kirk session to have been always the case.' Nevertheless, 'no small respect is evinced by the commonalty for the ordinance of religion; family worship is prevalent among them; the Sabbath is much regarded; and their attendance on the preaching of the Gospel is most laudable.' Certainly the majority did not fail to attend kirk. Congregations of a thousand or more were not uncommon.

But there was not enough seating in the parish kirk for its own congregation, much less the new masses of Wick. On Mr Thomson's reckoning, 'taking the number of those who ought to have church accommodation at the proportion of 55 to the 100 [of population], there ought to be church-accommodation for 4132; but the parish church can accommodate only 1835; thus leaving unaccommodated 2297.' Assiduous missionary work in Pulteneytown by the Rev David Mitchell is bringing the gospel of the Church of Scotland to the benighted community that has grown up on the south bank of the Wick river. But, says the minister, 'the great deficiency lies in pastoral superintendence'. Even making allowance for Dissenters, there was, on Thomson's calculation, an unled flock of 5,414 souls in the parish of Wick. The great 'influx of strangers, amounting to near 10,000, during the fishing season' made things very much worse.

The earnest Mr Thomson went on to complain:

> There is not in all broad Scotland, whence issues a more urgent call for help. We are numerous and we are poor; and, from the fisheries and other causes, are exposed to many and great temptations, which nothing but the full, unfettered, and frequent ministrations of the glorious Gospel of the grace of God, carried home by the power of the Holy Spirit, can effectively counteract.

Mr Thomson had only just come to Wick. He apologised for the 'manifold imperfections' of his report, having become a 'resident of the parish, to which he was previously an utter stranger, only on the 24th of October last'. He was asked as late as December to draw up the report, which he submitted in March, 1841. His recent arrival and consequent unfamiliarity with Wick did not inhibit him in any way from expressing opinions about the town and its people nor, by implication, the inadequacy of his predecessors in the parish ministry. The Rev Robert Phin died on 22 March, 1840, to the great sorrow of the community. The *John O'Groat Journal* (27 March, 1840) solemnly black-lined the columns in which Mr Phin's departure is reported. The funeral, says the *Journal*, 'crowded the Kirkhill and other places in the vicinity of the manse and churchyard. Every demonstration of respect was evinced on this occasion by all ranks and denominations to the memory of the kind-hearted minister; and the various shops and warehouses in and about the town were shut during the ceremony.' Clearly Mr Phin had left much to be accomplished.

Phin's successor, Charles Thomson, was a different sort of pastor. He came to Wick with a strong sense of mission. He was born in the parish of Dalserf in Lanarkshire, a Lowlander, ordained in North

Shields, Northumberland. He 'took a great interest in public questions, and among other controversies in which he took a very active part may be mentioned the Apochryphas and Romish controversies during his North Shields ministry . . . He was a powerful advocate on the side of the Non-Intrusionists in Caithness when he came to Wick, and at the time of the Disruption he took the part of the secession, which became the Free Church in 1843. His background before coming to Wick had been strongly 'Evangelical'.

The parish ministry which Thomson took over satisfied the needs of less than half of church-going Wickers. According to his catalogue, there were now in Wick no less than eight other congregations besides that of the Established Church which the rest might choose to join. First in the list were the *United Associate Seceders*, who began in 1770, and now, 'according to their minister, the Rev. William Stewart' numbered 1000, 'of whom 810 were resident in the parish of Wick'; they had a chapel in Pulteneytown built in 1815, a manse built in 1825, and a debt of £130. Mr Stewart's stipend of £100 ('derived from scat-rents and collection') was a few pounds more than that of Mr Thomson himself.

Independents, not mentioned as such by the Rev Sutherland in 1794 had, according to Mr Thomson, a chapel near to Wick as early as 1790; by 1836 they had a reputed congregation of 1000 under their minister, the Rev John Wiseman. Their exact status and location in the religious spectrum is rather difficult to determine, since Scottish sectarians dissatisfied with their own secession group tend to gravitate to another. Seventeenth century English non-conformists were generally known as *Independents,* and also as *Brownists* after Robert Browne who defined the congregational principle, a church in which each congregation manages its own affairs, a step on from Presbyterianism where the minister and presbytery have most to say. Cromwell was an *Independent*. Later the term *Congregationalism* came into common use, and in the eighteenth century was formed the Congregational Union of Scotland.

Other separate groups indentified by Mr Thomson, some without churches or chapels of their own, were the *Anabaptists* (Baptists), 90 of them in 1836; *Separatists*, a congregation formed in 1824, numbering 28 in 1836, but with neither chapel nor minister; *Original Seceders*, established in 1835 with 60 to 80 people 'in the habit of attending worship', also without chapel or minister; the *Reformed Presbyterians*, about 200 of them, a congregation formed in 1836, with a chapel newly built at Pulteneytown in 1839, its galleries not yet erected. They had no minister. Then there was a small group of Wesleyan Methodists, formed in 1837.

Of special interest is the fact that the *Papists* (orthodox ministers could still seldom bring themselves to speak of 'Roman Catholics') now appeared again in Wick. This congregation was formed in 1832, and in 1836, a 'chapel capable of holding, at eighteen inches a sitting, 306 sitters' was built on the corner of Breadalbane Terrace and Malcolm Street in Pulteneytown. It was mostly closed during the winter. 'There is,' says Mr Thomson, 'no priest, except during the fishing season, – when a priest comes, the chapel is opened and service is performed for those of Romish persuasion, who, during that period, come to Wick from Ireland and the Highlands.'

The building of St Joachim's – the name given to the new Roman Catholic chapel[1] – could not have been quite completed by 1836, for on 16 September, 1837, the *John O'Groat Journal* carries the story that a few days before, the scaffolding in the front of the chapel collapsed, the three masons working on the fabric falling 20 feet. Quite quickly 'two recovered from the effects of the accident, but one is still ill but out of danger.' We may be sure that some of the fiercer non-conformists of the burgh would have seen in this accident the Lord's disapproval of the return of popery to Wick.

The 1840s were a time of as great turmoil in the ecclesiastical affairs of Wick as in Edinburgh and Glasgow. The Rev Thomson makes no secret in his report of his own evangelical leanings. Even before coming to Wick he was much exercised by the furious controversies now raging in the General Assembly, and is described by Donald Beaton as 'a powerful advocate on the side of the Non-Intrusionists in Caithness'.

However, before recounting the critical events of the years, 1840 to 1843 and the impact on Wick of the great 'Disruption' of 1843, as it is now universally known, it would be well to conclude reference to Charles Thomson's survey of religion in 1840. In the years after writing this, Thomson himself became deeply involved in the

---

1 The choice of this saint seems somewhat whimsical. Joachim has no demonstrable connection with Wick. He was, according to the apochryphal *Gospel of James* of the second century, the husband of Anne, father and mother of the Blessed Virgin Mary. Neither is mentioned in Holy Scripture. This seasonal rise in the Catholic population of Wick somewhat anticipated a similiar phenomenon in Scotland generally, boosted in the late 1840s by the great influx of Irish into Scotland as a result of the famine. Catholic emancipation in 1829 had, moreover, rendered it legal for Catholic Church services to be held in Scotland.

Disruption which greatly affected the fortunes of the parish and other churches of Wick, Pulteneytown and the rest of the parish. As a participant in hot controversy, he spoke and wrote passionately about the issues. His survey report, dealing with affairs up to 1840, composed for and included in the *Statistical Account*, is by comparison with later utterances, sober and unprejudiced, as befitted such a document. Accordingly, we should mention here the other groups to which Mr Thomson refers in his report, even though they too were affected by the Disruption.

There had been, as Thomson shows, religious ferment in the outer areas of the parish, during earlier years of the century, associated inevitably with the population changes caused by the growth of the fishing villages south of Wick. In Bruan (just south of Ulbster) was established first a 'mission' and 'mission house', and then in 1826 the erection of a 'parliamentary church',[1] intended to serve the needs chiefly of fisher families in Bruan, Clyth, Lybster and over the parish boundary into Latheron parish. Here Thomson listed also 58 'Seceders' and 24 'Independents' as against 946 'adherents of the Church'. In Keiss was a new *quoad sacra* parish where a 'church and manse were built by Government in 1827 at a cost of L.1500'; there were in the Wick civil parish part of Keiss (the rest was in Canisbay parish) about 800 people, of whom '2 are Original Seceders, 12 Anabaptists, 1 is a Reformed Presbyterian, and 1 a Methodist'.

One other group, less easily definable than some of the others, should be mentioned. These are the 'Evangelicals' to which adhered, as it suited them, radicals from other groups. Evangelicals are described by Donald Beaton in some detail. The Evangelical movement as such 'had its source in Rev. James Morison', a United Secession minister of Kilmarnock, whose beliefs harked back to the 'Westminster Confession' of 1643, drawn up in England where it was

---

[1] The curious idea of a 'parliamentary church' probably owes its origins to the urgings of the British Fisheries Society upon the government to assist in its efforts to consolidate new fishing communities in the north, especially Ullapool, where it was difficult to get ministers or school masters, or even 'missionaries' to stay and serve. In 1823 an Act was passed by Parliament (4 Geo. IV cap. 79) which provided a measure of assistance in the building of churches and payment of stipends to ministers. 'The Commissioners for Highland Roads and Bridges were re-appointed as Commissioners for Highland Churches and Telford provided basic plans for these "parliamentary" churches and manses.' (Dunlop, *British Fisheries Society*, op cit, p 178). Altogether some fifteen such Telford churches were built in the north of Scotland, the most curious and remote being the tiny village church on Ulva's Isle off the west coast of Mull. When during the 'Ten Years Conflict' before the Disruption of 1843, the General Assembly sought to persuade the government to support the church generally in this way, such support was adamantly refused.

never imposed but formed the basis of the Covenanters' doctrine, though it was less severe in tone than the Calvinistic statement of belief. Dr Morrison 'held the doctrines of universal atonement, human ability to believe the Gospel along with the doctrine of eternal and unconditional election and irresistible grace.' Whatever exactly that meant Dr Morrison attempted to explain in 1841 to a Synod of the United Secession Church in a harangue that lasted for eight hours. Either mystified or wearied, the Synod expelled Dr Morrison and his doctrine was declared 'a very serious departure from the truth and the people were faithfully warned against its leading tenets'. Understood or not, these tenets became a focus for an extreme type of evangelistic fervour, attracting, at least for a time, dissidents and well-doers from all quarters. 'Wick,' says Dr Beaton, 'joined in the protest.' He explains how it spread in this hotbed of controversy:

> Though the Morisonianism of Wick had not its origins in the United Secession Church, and owed its inception to quite other causes than dissatisfaction with Confessional doctrine, yet because of its association with the Evangelical Union movement it was regarded as with aversion and strongly condemned. The Wick congregation was an offshoot from the Congregational Church. It first met in September, 1844, in the Mason's Hall, and received an occasional supply from the Congregational Union for a time, but at last the supply was stopped. At this stage the Rev. Archibald Duff of the Evangelical Union Church, Fraserburgh, visited the place, and the congregation from this date onwards was dependent on the Evangelical Union for its preachers. It continued worshipping in the Masons' Hall until 1848, when the hall was found to be too small. In 1850, Zion Chapel was built, and opened in January 1851. It was used as a place of worship by the Evangelical Union Congregation until 1902, when the congregation was broken up. Zion Chapel passed into the possession of Wick United Free Church.[1]

Evangelicals never constituted a proper 'church' and recruits were drawn from some of the formal denominations. They represented a cast of mind rather than a faith, – as they do today. They tended towards literal interpretation of the Bible. They emerged strongly in England in the 1830s with demands for church reform, but were also associated with political causes such as the abolition of slavery,

---

1 Beaton, op cit: pp 308-309.

factory legislation and social reform. They became a strong force in the Presbyterian Church of Scotland and it was their alliance, across the formal divisions that captured power in the General Assembly in 1834, a move which led directly to the Disruption in 1843.[1]

The Evangelicals of Wick, as in many other places, were particularly instrumental in creating the ferment of anti-alcoholism that led to the forming in 1840 of the Wick and Pulteneytown Total Abstinence Society, and spreading the sentiments that many years later, converted Wick into a 'prohibition' area. How Wick went 'dry', however, belongs later in our story.

The one sect that gets no mention at all by either Beaton or Thomson, is that of the Episcopal Church of Scotland, for the very good reason that episcopalianism had no footing in the Wick area at all until much later in the century. A Scottish Episcopal Church did not appear in Wick until 1870. 'Episcopalians,' says Smout, were widely scattered and [the faith was] fashionable among the well-to-do but nowhere enjoyed a broad popular following.' This was as true in Caithness as elsewhere.

THE GREAT DISRUPTION

It is difficult today, even among clerics, to recapture much of the feeling, indeed, ferocity of the great emotional storm that swept through Scottish religious life in the mid years of the nineteenth century. As fundamental background to the secession controversies of the eighteenth century and the 'Ten Years' Conflict' that led up to 1843 was the difference in status and outlook of the established churches of the two nations, Scotland and England, the one Calvinistic and presbyterian, and the other episcopalian and much too 'catholic' for most Scottish stomachs. The quarrel did not lie between the two churches as such, but between the two main wings of the Scottish church. The Union between the two countries of 1707 and the complicated relations between Scotland and England during the eighteenth century had placed in ascendance north of the border those who favoured a degree of state involvement in the management of the church, symbolised as we have seen by the hated Patronage Act of

---

1 Like the Evangelists themselves, their story spreads widely. Aspects of the movement in England are described by Elie Halevy: *The Triumph of Reform, 1830-1841*; (Vol III of Halevy's *History of the English People in the Nineteenth Century*); London, Ernest Benn (1961); pp 51652, 84-85, 112-122, 136-168. And for Scotland, ibid, pp 164-165. For Scotland see Smout: *A Century of the Scottish People*, op cit. 184-186.

Fig 31 Disruption in Edinburgh. *Reproduced by kind permission of Martin Gostwick from* The Legend of Hugh Miller.

1712. The majority 'Moderates', as they came to be called, while not caring much for patronage, generally went along with the idea of good relations with the government and, in the process, hoped to get government aid for building more churches and raising the stipends of parish ministers. Most of this was anathema to those ranged against the Moderate majority in the General Assembly, the 'Non-Instrusionists', as the 'liberal', evangelical (yet often *étatiste*[1]) opposition groups were now becoming known.

Little of this might seem to have much bearing on affairs in Caithness and Wick, or for that matter, most of the other out-of-the-way places such as the western isles, Orkney and Shetland, but in fact the Non-Intrusionist cause came to be strongly reflected here in discussion and exchange. Contributory to rebellious sentiments in the minds of local elders of the kirk and like was the customary animosity between parishioners in general and the gentry. 'Patronage' – in Wick itself exercised by Lord Duffus, the former Sir Benjamin Dunbar – rankled, and Lord Duffus, was not very popular among the burghers of Wick on account of his high-handedness in the matter of the Hill of Wick.

Moreover, Charles Thomson, the new minister of Wick parish, now appeared on the scene. Though himself the subject of patronage in his appointment, he was a committed opponent of the system. He had himself spent time and energy before coming here on arguing the 'Non-Instrusionist' cause. Also before arrival he had identified himself as one of those ministers who considered that the religious condition of the people was so dire that the state should assist the church in reaching to the multitudes of the 'unchurched' by a programme of church building. His first big job in Wick was the compiling of a detailed report on the state of the parish. On his own showing, many citizens of Wick and Pulteneytown were among those deprived of godly influence. New churches were needed and new pastors to reach the unchurched who were flocking into the place. Although a newcomer, Thomson if anyone, knew something of the mind of the townsfolk of Wick.

Intimations of the row appeared in 1840 in the *John O'Groat Journal*.

---

1 As Michael Lynch puts it: 'the stance of the Evangelicals was at once anti-Erastian and *étatiste*,' See Lynch, op cit, pp 400-401. 'Erastian' signifies the domination of church by the state, following the doctrines of Erastus, a sixteenth century Swiss divine. The more 'nationalist' minded of the Non-Intrusionists, saw in all this the determination of 'English' government, supposedly Erastian in spirit, to overwhelm Scottish church freedoms.

was about a quite amicable meeting held in the parish church at which several local notables, including the Rev Thomas Gun of Keiss, Rev John Sinclair of Bruan, 'Collector' Waters, John Kirk (Merchant) and Alexander Hislop, parish schoolmaster, aired the varying points of view thrown up by the controversy, essentially as to whether parishioners had the right to choose their own minister, and in particular what validity there might be in their right to 'Veto' an appointment of which they disapproved. All at this stage professed to believe in the possibility of settlement with the government. In a 'powerful, eloquent and convincing speech', Hislop probably expressed the feelings of all. 'No authority on earth . . . was warranted to cram a minister down the throats of a Christian people,' but

> if the countenance and cooperation of the nobility of Scotland, and the patrons of the Church were to be attained by any compromise of its inviolable rights, its friends would scout the idea of receiving either on such terms; but that if these gentlemen continued the support of the Church without any sacrifice of her principles, then aid was incalculable.[1]

Several motions were raised, but the concensus was that things would probably work out all right. They did not. It would hardly be profitable to pursue in this context the intricacies, complexities, and with hindsight, the fatuities of the Scottish Disruption of 1843, but the bare details may be mentioned. In 1834 the Evangelicals, led by Dr Thomas Chalmers (1780-1847), a complex-minded 'Tory Reformer', minister of the Tron Church, Glasgow, and from 1823 Professor of Moral Philosophy at St Andrews, then from 1828 of Theology at Edinburgh, captured a majority in the General Assembly of the Scottish Church. They forthwith passed a 'Veto Act' which gave congregations the right to reject a patron's nominee. The Act was, of course, 'unlawful' in parliamentary terms and in due course declared so by the Edinburgh Court of Session. On appeal, the House of Lords in London upheld the decision, bringing the Assembly into direct conflict with the government. Successive Whig and Tory administrations 'declined to alter the statute', having little understanding of the nature of Scottish ecclesiastical traditions and feelings. They refused to consider providing government funds to aid a penurious Church of Scotland to build new churches and so assist in bringing the gospel – and some social amelioration to the industrial masses in the now crowded industrial cities of Scotland.

1 *JOGJ*, 1 January, 1840.

The years following the Veto Act were filled with argument, expostulation, counter-argument and recrimination, both in and out of the General Assembly, between Intrusionists and Non-Intrusionists. The crucial meeting of the embattled General Assembly was held in St Andrews Church, Edinburgh, on 18 May, 1843. Having failed completely to move either the Scottish authorities or the government, represented at the Assembly by the Marquis of Bute, Lord High Commissioner for Scotland, the embittered delegates staged a spectacular demonstration. By the time the Marquis arrived, the public galleries of the church

> were filled to capacity and by then the street outside was filled with a crowd which numbered thousands. Inside, the retiring Moderator, David Welsh, suddenly departed from procedure after the opening prayer to read out 'amid the breathless stillness' a long statement of protest. After laying it before the Commissioner, he walked out into the street, followed by Thomas Chalmers, the undisputed leader of the Evangelical party within the Church since 1831. According to Henry Cockburn [Solicitor-General in Peel's government], 123 ministers and seventy elders filed out behind them. Outside they were joined by tens of other ministers from recently erected chapels of ease who had not the right, as *quoad sacra* rather than parish clergy, to attend the General Assembly. The press of the crowd forced them to walk in procession, three or four abreast and strung out over a quarter of a mile, the short distance down Hanover Street to Canonmills, where 3000 spectators crowded into Tanfield Hall, a recently converted gas works. There 470 ministers signed a 'Deed of Demission', separating themselves from the 'ecclesiastical establishment of Scotland'. The Disruption, the most momentous event in nineteenth-century Scottish history, had split the established Church of Scotland in two.[1]

Thus was accomplished the Disruption which brought into existence the Free Church of Scotland, accounting for a third of the entire clergy and laity of the Presbyterian Church of Scotland, entirely cut off from the establishment. 'The impetus of the new Church in the mid-1840s was truly astonishing,' says Lynch.

Within a year, 470 new churches were said to have been built

---

1 M Lynch, op cit, p 397. Lynch quotes from A L Drummond and J Bulloch: *The Scottish Church, 1688-1843;* (1973), 246-248.

They were financed by a huge drive of private subscriptions, which raised about £1 million over that period, enough to pay the stipends of the ministers who had abandoned salary and manse as well as their established charges in 1842. By 1847 it was claimed that over 44,000 children were being taught in Free Church schools, with 513 teachers being paid direct from a central Educational Fund.[1]

Not all the Non-Intrusionists attending the famous meeting in Ednburgh, it appears, came out with the Free Church secessionists. The *John O'Groat Journal* reports in May that this group, had a meeting of their own to decide what they were going to do. They were referred to disparagingly by two pro-secession journals of 'Auld Reekie', the *Scottish Guardian* and the *Witness* as the 'forty thieves' who had not the 'determination to vote'. The partisan Editor of the *Scottish Guardian*, was the former headmaster of the Wick Parish School, Alexander Hislop, whose views had sharpened since 1840.[2]

The editor of the *Witness* was an even more interesting contributor to the debate. He was none other than Hugh Miller, the geologist from Cromarty and pioneer of the Old Red Standstone, part of whose work had been done in Caithness. Miller had become a passionate supporter of Non-Intrusionism, and in 1840 he was recruited by Chalmers to take the editoral chair of the *Witness*, a twice-weekly independent newspaper. Miller soon built it up into a hard-hitting 'quality' journal with a circulation of more than 2000, second only to the *Scotsman*. He remained editor for most of the rest of his life, a staunch supporter and apologist of the Free Church and also versatile commentator on political and literary issues.

He continued his writings on geology with *Footprints of the Creator*, (1849), *The Testimony of the Rocks* and *A Sketchbook of Popular Geology*, published after his death in 1856. But these had a different message from *The Old Red Sandstone*. Remaining faithful to his religious commitment, Miller was now seeking to reconcile his understanding of geological phenomena with his sincere but somewhat naive acceptance of holy scripture. Familiar with the work of Lamarck he argued against evidence for the evolution of species: 'all geological history is full of the beginnings and ends of species,' he wrote, 'but it exhibits no genealogies of development.' This was just three years before the publication of *The Origin of Species*.

1 Ibid.
2 *JOGJ*, 26 May, 1845.

It seems probable that Miller was uncomfortably aware that he was kicking against the intellectual pricks of his time, and that conflict between his geology and his religious faith troubled him greatly. He was in his later years a sick man, having contracted silicosis during his years as a quarry worker; he also had a perennial 'morbid, depressive streak' in his personality. He was terrified of going insane before he died. Whether or not these factors or his religious dilemma drove him to his sudden and dreadful suicide by shooting himself in the heart on Christmas Eve, 1856, has been a matter of speculation ever since. It may indeed have been a combination of them all.[1]

The Disruption of Wick.

The minister and congregation of Wick Parish Church were among those thus affected. Mr Thomson took with him most of his elders and congregation. 'On 12 June, 1843,' writes Donald Beaton, 'the Wick kirk-session passed an Act of Demission by which they bade farewell to the Church of Scotland. It is signed by Wm. Craig, eld; John Reiach elder; Donald Harrold, elder; Charles Thomson, moderator'.[2]

Curiously the *John O'Groat Journal* does not make much of the event itself in Wick (Beaton, in fact, derives his information mainly from the *Northern Ensign* account written nearly forty years later – 14 April, 1881); nor does the *Journal* commit itself to a preference between the parties. During the crucial weeks, the *Journal's* columns contain interesting letters and comments on the broad issues. 'What a strange amalgamation of parties this said Non-Intrusion controversy has led to;' philosophises the Editor on 21 April, 1843, in a spirit of bantering detachment, a month before the events in St Andrews Kirk and nearly two before the Act of Demission in Wick. The eloquence continues; there is:

> an equally strange separation of [those] who fought side by side for the passing of the Reform Bill, for Catholic Emancipation, for the abolition of the Corn Laws, and many other liberal measures, are at cut and thrust on the knotty

---

1 See Martin Gostwick: *The Legend of Hugh Miller;* Cromarty Courthouse, Cromarty (1993). The crisis of belief that affected the mind of Hugh Miller, was experienced too by clerical intellectuals in England. In fact, the first professor of Geology in Oxford, William Buckland, was like several others of his eminent colleagues in geology, an ordained priest of the Church of England. But the English Church was ever much more latitudinarian in its outlook than the Scottish, and more easily accommodated to the challenge of science.

2 Beaton, op cit., p 303.

question of Non-Intrusion. We find liberal law-agents in Wick and Thurso ranked on the side of the Evangelical party; and those, who, along with Sir George Sinclair, joined in the cry of 'Church in Danger', a short time ago, have joined hands with the Moderates. In another part of the paper we have the Rev. Mr M Phin [son of the recently deceased minister of Wick] in the Presbytery of Selkirk, moving an overture for the repeal of the Veto, and passing a vote of censure on his countryman, the Rev. Mr Jolly, for intruding into parishes within the bounds of that Presbytery. We have Mr Hislop, again, who fought so hard, along with Mr Phin, in the Conservative ranks for the return of Sir George Sinclair to parliament in 1837, labouring in his vocation on the *Scottish Guardian*, denouncing those who speak of renouncing the Veto, not even sparing Sir George himself, and applying the lash with a merciless hand .... We find wives and daughters (who are all Non-Intrusionists) pitted against fathers and sons; and the controversy rising so high, that not infrequently they or the other lose their breakfast or dinner by reason of the schism. On the other hand, when the wives and daughters happen to live in the manse, we find them chiefly Moderates, and the war of words reversed. Betwixt the 'pressure from without' and the 'pressure from within', the guardian of the house is sadly non-plussed. We have said above, that the ladies are all Non-Intrusionists. We beg their pardon. There are a few who consider the term vulgar; and after weighing the question maturely, have resolved on 'coming out' as Moderates, which they look upon as fashionable. The *canaille* are to be found on the other side. How true it is that times are changed and we are changing with them. If a man were to turn from a distant land, after the absence of even a few years, and compare the state of the parties now with what it was when he left, he would be lost in amazement, and be led to imagine that he had landed in the moon or some other outlandish place.[1]

Sir George Sinclair may have felt a little piqued at the *Journal* send-up. He sent in and authorised for publication in the issue for 5 May, a few days before the General Assembly meeting, a long letter which he, presuming on acquaintance, had sent to Lord Aberdeen, one of the Scottish members of the Cabinet, pleading for Aberdeen to seek to persuade his cabinet colleagues to take a Scottish view of the crisis,

1 *JOGJ*, 21 April, 1843.

and to 'carry their forbearance towards the Church as far as principle and conscience will allow'. They should not assume too readily that (1) the inevitable secession would be 'inconsiderable', and (2), that the 'smallness of the secession' was the thing that mattered. Rather the government should bend itself to the necessity of satisfying Scottish susceptibilities. 'Endowment', the need for state cash was the big issue which, Sir George considered, might be paid for by 'submission to patronage' (he was certainly wrong about this). On the other hand, it would not be satisfactory for parishioners simply to have the status, in the matter of appointments, of merely *objectors* and no other. The government, too, he thought, should not allow its distaste for Thomas Chalmers – author of the illegal Veto Act – to colour its judgement too much; whether they like it or not, Chalmers was, in the eyes of many members and elders of the Church, the man of the moment: 'Whatever Thomas Chalmers is, there is the Church of Scotland'. Sir George pleaded for a 'generous and enlightened' settlement.[1]

To a degree, Aberdeen seems to have accepted these arguments, and early in June, 1843, introduced a Bill which granted certain – carefully hedged – rights of objection to parishioners who, on hearing a ministerial candidate's trial sermon, might take exception. The *John O'Groat Journal* like most others concerned with the patronage issue, regarded his Lordship's initiative as too little too late, and professed to have 'no real regard for his Bill'. It would not, in any case, have persuaded any of the seceders back into the fold. Lord Aberdeen himself led a Tory government as Prime Minister from 1852 to 1855. Could the crisis have been delayed to that time, would a settlement have been reached that would have saved a disastrous schism in the Scottish church? For the great Disruption was nothing less.[2]

To begin with the Wick seceders met in the open air. During the winter months that followed the Demission in Wick, they met in the Temperance Hall 'which was frequently crowded to overflowing. When the warmer weather came, the congregation worshipped in the open-air in the park behind the hall.'[3] A new Free Church was opened in November, 1844; it was, apparently, built on the land now occupied by Wick's Presto Store. This served the needs of the Wick Free Church congregation for the next twenty years, by which time the congregation had found resources to build a new and more elaborate

1 *JOGJ*, 5 May, 1843.
2 *JOGJ*, 7 and 21 July, 1843.
3 Beaton, op cit., pp 303-304.

church on Bridge Street, the present site of the Free Church, opposite the Town Hall.[1] The proceeds of the sale of the building of 1844 went towards the building of the Bridge Street church. Mr Thomson remained minister of the Wick Free Church until his death in 1871, when he was succeeded by the Rev. George Renny, who had seen much of his earliest service in Port Elizabeth, Natal.

Although the *Journal* took a quite pedestrian view of the Disruption in Wick, several notices in June and July issues cast an interesting light on the immediate consequences of what came to be called the 'Walk Out'. That of 16 June, 1843, deserves quoting in full, illustrating as it does in graphic detail, the predicament of hundreds of break-away congregations in Scotland and the quite incredible fortitude with which they maintained, at least for the early years, their determination and integrity. It also demonstrates quite starkly the extent of the break-away in mainland Scotland's most northerly province, remote from the intensity and furore of the immediate scene of the Demission in Edinburgh:

> A meeting of the Presbytery, we understand, was held at Dunnet on Tuesday last, consisting of the ministers of the parishes of Dunnet, Bower and Canisbay, the only three clergymen in this county who remain in the Church, when steps were taken to declare the parishes of the nine clergymen who adhere to the Free Church vacant, and to intimate same to the several patrons, with a view to their being filled up. We may therefore soon expect to see each parish having a double ministry, as the Free Church has also taken steps to supply preachers for the three parishes alluded to – In most parishes throughout the county, divine service was performed in the open air on Sabbath last, and will continue in this way for some time, so long as the weather proves favourable, or until suitable buildings are erected, which are to be gone on with immediately. In the course of next week, it is said, several will have the foundation laid. The Rev. Mr Thomson preached last Sunday in the glebe in the front of the manse, the use of both being kindly granted by Sir George Dunbar. The day, which at first threatened to be wet, turned out rather fine; and the congregation, amounting to upwards of two thousand listened with great patience to an able discourse, notwithstanding the

---

1 It still stands. Its congregation now reconciled to the establishment, is known as Bridge Street Church of Scotland.

greater number had to stand all the while. In some country parishes the people have recourse to novel kind of seats, which they make of bundles of heather. The popular movement is with the Free Church; and in those parishes where the clergymen remain in, the attendance has in general been very small. The Church of Dunnet, we believe, had only about 40 or 50 hearers on Sunday last; and one Church in Sutherland had the minister, one hearer, and the bellman or officer! – Yesterday was held by the Free Church as a fast-day, which in this town was pretty well observed; the attendance at public worship was large, and nearly all shops were shut, and business suspended until the afternoon. The present week is to be one of special collections throughout Scotland for the Free Church, to be applied locally in building a church in each district. Where the local funds are not adequate, application is to be made to the general fund; and in rich and populous parishes where surplus funds may be obtained, it is to be sent to the general fund – It is reported that the Rev. Mr Taylor is coming down from Edinburgh and that he will preach in the Pulteneytown Church next Sunday.[1]

Whatever its religious implications and the depth of religious feeling involved, this represented a genuine folk movement. It is doubtful if many of these thousands had much idea of what had happened at the Edinburgh Assembly, or of the organisational (to say nothing of theological) issues raised. Protest was what mattered.

Steadfast in his purpose, a few weeks later, Mr Thomson presented the 'Sacrament of the Lord's Supper on the same Glebe in front of the manse. It was a fine day.' A crowd of 5000 assembled; 650 took communion. 'The spectacle of so large a congregation, worshipping in the open air, was a solemn and inspiring one, and the utmost decorum prevailed throughout the entire services.' They lasted for some hours, the Revs Thomson and Mackenzie officiating until 4 o'clock and Revs Olrig and Taylor from then on. Doubtless there were plentiful references to the feeding of the five thousand and, in more general terms, Moses leading the Israelites into the wilderness.[2] By this time Mr Thomson had been presented with a 'comfortable' portable pulpit.[3] A Free Church Committee was set up, having been allowed to meet in the new Pulteneytown church, whose congregation

1 *JOGJ*, 16 June, 1843.
2 *JOGJ*, 7 July, 1843.
3 *JOGJ*, 23 June, 1843.

had gone over to the Free Church with those of Wick. Mr D Louttit, a Wick business-man was appointed Treasurer, and he was able to report that already £550 had been subscribed for the building fund, £130 of which was already paid up.[1]

After an interval of a year, Charles Thomson was followed as minister on Kirk-hill by William Lillie from Aberdeenshire. Mr Lillie was a vigorous controversialist himself, but on the 'Moderate' side and even while taking 'a very prominent part in the public life of the town' he took his Doctor's degree at Aberdeen University in 1857. There was, he found, plenty to occupy his mind at Wick. 'Though owing to the hostile feeling between the Established and the Free Churches all was not harmonious, yet he lived to see a good deal of that opposition died down.'[2]

Some time before leaving the parish church, Mr Thomson had played a part in creating what was to become the *quoad sacra* parish of Pulteneytown. His predecessor, Mr Phin (he is sometimes given 'nn'), had formed a committee to draw up a constitution for such a new church; this went up to the General Assembly, and the new building was opened in November, 1842. The inaugural sermon was preached by Mr Thomson on a text from *Exodus. XX v 24*: *An altar of earth thou shalt make unto me, and shalt sacrifice thereon thy burnt offerings, and thy peace offerings, thy sheep, and thine oxen: in all places where I record my name I will come unto thee, and I will bless thee.* 'The church was full but not crowded – perhaps because the opening was not sufficiently advertised.'[3] There is a queer irony in this choice of text. Within months Mr Thomson would be leading an exodus of his own, while the emphasis on 'altar' hardly fits well in a rite where altars were abjured. And the Lord would shortly be asked to shift his presence once again.

The Pulteneytown Parish Church had a rather short life before its congregation 'demitted' at the same time as that of the Wick Parish Church. The need for a regular church in Pulteneytown had been recognised for some time when, in 1837, the British Fisheries Society put up £100 to set the project going. The Chairman of the Society at that time was the Duke of Sutherland, and the deputy chairman James Loch, MP, 'well known for the liberality of their political views,' as the

---

1 *JOGJ*, 30 June, 1843.
2 Beaton, op cit. p 302.
3 *The Church in the Square: Pulteneytown Parish Church, 1842-1992.*, 150th Anniversary publication, Wick, (1992). p 15. *Quoad sacra* signifies parish status without the older jurisdictions.

Fig 32 Pulteneytown Parish Church.

Journal comments, making a highly partisan political point: 'This fact, together with that of the great majority of its members holding similar sentiments, presents us with another instance of the many which can be adduced of liberality of political views, being by no means incompatible (as the Tories would fain make us believe) with a deep regard for the Established Church, and the extension of religion.'[1]

It took three years to build the new 'Chapel', and during this time a 'missionary', the Rev David Mitchell managed the congregation, which met for the time being in the Pulteneytown Academy Assembly Hall, a project also fostered by the Society. Hardly had the new 'chapel of ease' – its status so far – opened, than the Disruption struck, and the congregation departed. So did David Mitchell, being presented by them on his way out with a gold watch, at the end of his valedictory sermon on 20 April.[2]

The Anniversary publication of the Pulteneytown Church 'in the Square' (Argyle Square) is rather reticent on the subject of the 'Disruption' of 1843 as are most references nowadays after

1 *JOGJ*, 22 December, 1837.
2 *Church in the Square*, op cit, p 21.

reconcilation has occurred. It nevertheless puts the event into the national context:

> In 1834 the General Assembly of the Church of Scotland passed the Veto Act which 'gave a majority to the male heads of families' in a parish the right to reject the patrons's nominee. Thereafter Church and State were at 'loggerheads' and disaster was inevitable. Only one year after the congregation had settled into their new Chapel, the Disruption came on the scene. The minister [David Mitchell] 'walked out', It was almost a 100% 'walkout'. So few were 'left in' that they could not afford to support a missionary for some time. There was no efficient Kirk Session left to administer business. Visiting preachers and missionaries helped to fill the gap and keep the Church open. Gradually a new congregation was built up and by the 1860s, it was ready to play its full part again. The people of Pulteneytown had longed for a church of their own and were willing to stand up to the Heritors so that they might have their independence, and be recognised as a Parish in its own right. This was granted in 1878[1].

A new Free Church was also built in Pulteneytown, and opened in November, 1844. It was much modified in 1862-1883 when a spire was added, now 'a Gothic five bay rectangular church with a tall single stage tower at the South. These were tall louvred belfrey openings and tall Y-traceried windows in side walls. The Session House was built to the East. A gabled porch was added and finally a low coped wall was built, with cast-iron railings.'[2]

A final comment on the Disruption in Wick seems warranted. As we have seen, Wick and Pulteneytown shared with some of the bigger cities the problems of population movement and growth. The extent of the 'walkouts' (as the Pulteneytown church historian calls them), minister and congregation at both the parish church and, less than a year after its opening, the Pulteneytown church, give some idea of the intensity of feeling that lay behind disruption. It is difficult not to see in the sequence of events in Wick and Pulteneytown, and in the size of the defection, a climax of the stresses, ill-feeling and antagonisms between the 'lower classes', whose opinion was always the last to be taken into account, and the 'upper' or gentry class, among whom were too often ministers, elders, heritors and merchants, whose wills

1 *Church in the Square*, op cit p 21.
2 Ibid, p9.

and interests dominated local community life. Pulteneytown, above all, was a seething polyglot community among the members of which were residual resentments from 'clearance', refugees from the wayward oppressions of lairds and landlords elsewhere, and Caithness natives who had anything but love for their own landlords and masters. Religious rebellion was very probably as much an expression of political as of religious feeling. The fact that the Disruption was engendered and led by clerics and middle-class elders does not detract from its significance as an outburst of mass liberal sentiment, in tune to some extent even with Chartism, which certainly had no identifiable impact on Wick. What is more, the sudden and enormous proliferation of differing religious groups, represented for many ordinary folk a bursting out into 'freedom' from irksome conformities of generations.

Fun and Games

In a sense, the hankering of Wickers for the perverse delights of popery before 1800, so deplored by Charles Thomson, were an expression of their need for some colour and variety in their lives. The very re-creation in the Wick area, quite early in the history of the new community, of a Roman Catholic congregation, where 'popery' 'papistry' or 'Romish practice', was symbolic both of reaction and revolt. Not that the people of Wick in general had much to do with St Joachim's.

Though manifestly, participation in church activities provided satisfactions for many people in these times, the solemnities and consolations of religion could, *pace* Mr Thomson, hardly have sufficed to provide for all the recreation needs of the masses of the boisterous folk now crowding into Wick. This was doubtless especially true for the young, of whom there must have been a fair proportion. As testified by the Rev William Sutherland in *Wick 1794*, the parishioners of Wick were not indifferent to the callow pleasures of dancing and other forms of gaiety.[1]

Little information of this sort seems to have been sought and gleaned by the Rev Charles Thomson in his survey. He does, however, comment on the year's round of fairs, always in any age jolly occasions, though clearly not greatly favoured by Charles Thomson if only because of their imputed popish overtones. There are

---

1 Comment on references in literature to Scottish religious dissidence (Covenanting, and the Disruption) is to be found at the end of this chapter.

also frequent though brief references in the *John O'Groat Journal* to the various fairs held during the year. Among those listed by William Sutherland in 1794 were the Skitten Market, held at Killimster on the first Tuesday of March; Wick Market, on the first Tuesday after Palm Sunday, and Wick Fair in June. The serious business on these occasions was the selling of cattle. Margaretmas on Tuesday after 20 July was also for cattle, but this was also the local 'hiring fair'; Fergusmas was held at Wick at the end of November, and was also for cattle.

One of the first acts of the burgh council in 1816, after the end of the war, was a decision to revive two fairs, that of April, and St John's Fair in July, both of which had been allowed to 'go into desuetude'. The councillors considered that revival was necessary in view of the 'increase in population now developing'. Rules and regulations for the revived fairs were to be published, and advertisements were to be read to congregations in Caithness, inviting people to 'bring their commodities forward for sale'. The revival was obviously successful.[1]

Mr Thomson adds an interesting footnote, for he finds it necessary to explain why the termination *mas* was so frequently used 'in the names of fairs and term days in Caithness'. It

> shews the deep hold which Popery had taken of the district. Besides Margaretmas and Fergusmas, mentioned above, there are in the county Colmsmas, the term on the 20th of June; Petermas, 29th June, O.S; Georgemas, 15th July; O.S., Marymas, 15th August, O.S; Lukemas, first Tuesday of October, O.S.; Mansmas, or Magnusmas, first Tuesday of December, O.S.; Tustimas, fourth Tuesday of November, O.S.; and a number more masses.

EDUCATION

'It was a favourite maxim with the Scottish Reformation, that there should be throughout the land a kirk and a minister for every 1000 inhabitants, and a school beside every kirk. The nobles and gentry, however,' says Mr Thomson, witheringly, 'voted this a pious imagination, pillaged the church, expended the plunder of their own pleasures, and left the poor to perish for lack of knowledge.' Whatever ministers in other localities may have done to repair the lack, in the matter of education Caithness 'was long behind the rest of the country'. For a long time there were few, and in some periods no

1 *BCW*, 2 February, 1816.

Fig 33 The Pulteneytown Academy (now the Assembly Rooms).

ministers in some of the Caithness parishes, including Wick.

Until the arrival in the parish of Charles Keith ('the second minister of this parish after the Persecution') in 1701, little was done 'to remedy this enormous evil.' Keith found that there was a great number, even among his heritors and elders, 'who could not write their names. In the session records, frequent instances occur where (upon giving evidence) the witness declares that "he cannot write, touches the pen, and allows the clerk to subscribe his name." As late as the beginning of the eighteenth century, only one in every fifty persons within the parish could write.'[1]

The Presbytery, urged on by Keith and his fellow ministers in Thurso, Canisbay, Dunnet, Watten and Bower, began badgering heritors into 'the fulfilment of their duty', and 'did not rest satisfied with shuffling and idle excuses, but did what in them lay to secure for their people the blessings of education, by inviting into their parishes qualified teachers, and affording them every encouragement, by bestowing on them the office and emoluments of session-clerk,

1 John Horne, op cit, 63-64.

and by constantly urging on people the necessity of contributing to their support.' Schools were set up in Wick and Thurso in 1706, and in the other parishes mentioned during the next twenty years . 'In 1759,' says Mr Thomson, 'the parish school of Wick had an income of 20 bolls of meal.'[1] This, presumably was the school built in 1751 and described in the burgh records, where a 'deforming Man [not named]' was appointed 'to teach the children'. 'The heritable provost' (then George Sinclair) is said by William Sutherland to have provided school and dwelling house. The teacher appointed was James Sutherland of Tannach, on a salary of 25s per annum. 'What the fees were worth,' says John Horne, 'we cannot say; but Mr Sutherland's successor in office reminded Alexander Dunbar that his were due, whereupon that worthy up with his fist and "took" the schoolmaster across the mouth "to the lowsen of his teeth" and the covering of his beard with blood.'[2]

Charity schools established in various places by various people made up some of the deficiency, and in the Wick kirk-session records of 1763 there is a list of these schools and their heads. In 1792 there were five charity schools in the parish, 'but they have long ago been altogether discontinued,' says Mr Thomson. The Society for the Propagation of Christian Knowledge became very active in promoting schools in the area in the later eighteenth century, mainly in the person of the Rev. William Hallawell, 'latterly chaplain of the Charity Workhouse of Edinburgh, and overseer of the children's education for more than twenty years, having "a peculiar regard for the inhabitants of that large and populous parish of Wick, where I spent," says he, "a good part of my younger years, with great satisfaction."' Mr Hallawell mortified (left by will) to the SPCK a 'certain property, from which L.21 were annually to be paid for endowing, with L.7 a-year, a school at Keiss; another at Noss; and a third at Ulbster'. These were to be known as 'Hallawall's Schools'. The 'female teacher at Ulbster is allowed L.6 a-year by this society. She teaches the girls to read and sew.'

In 1840 Thomson writes of 18 unendowed schools in the parish, 14 of which were in Wick, Louisburgh and Pulteneytown. One of the seven in Wick was kept by a schoolmaster, the others by

---

1 A Scottish 'boll' was a measure of grain or meal of about 13½ bushels. The livings of ministers, schoolmasters, and the maintenance of kirk and school were, like the income of landlords, often calculated (or part calculated) in terms of the physical amount of produce which could be due in lieu of a money rent or other exaction. Most common folk had no cash and could only pay in kind.
2 John Horne, op cit, p 71.

schoolmistresses; in Pulteneytown four were kept by schoolmasters and three by schoolmistresses. A 'Female School of Industry' was supported at Stirkoke by Mrs Horne of Scouthel. Of the five unendowed schools (Mr Thomson's arithmetic here is a bit shaky, for his total of such schools is 18), two were run by school-mistresses within the *quoad sacra* parish of Keiss, while a school at Reiss, and another at Janetstown were kept by schoolmasters. 'Between the school at Reiss, and the Society's school at Keiss, the Kirk-session divides, in equal sums. L.3 a year, arising from a small mortification.' It is clear that heritors, kirk-session and the burgh were still not accustomed to spending lavishly on education.

Thomson believed that the school at Reiss ought to be endowed, 'and a school should be planted in the populous district of Hempriggs'. This was on the estate of Dunbar of Hempriggs (Lord Duffus) who, whatever his other benefactions, did not think much of the need to educate the children of the poor. The unendowed schools survived chiefly on fees; in the Society's schools quarterly fees for reading were 1s 6d, for reading and writing, 3s, for the full three R's, 4s; with the addition of geography the fee became 4s 6d and with classics, 6s. Of a total parochial school population of 1229 (no age range is indicated), 442 attended in Wick and Pulteneytown, 221 in each.

A substantial increase of the school accommodation in Pulteneytown had recently been supplied by the British Fisheries Society. The *John O'Groat Journal* tells in 1836 of the building of a new school in Pulteneytown opposite the new Catholic church (now the Assembly Rooms), to be 'completed in an elegant and commodious style. We know,' pontificated the *Journal*, 'of no measure which could have possibly been undertaken more meritorious than this, or any one so likely to render the British Fisheries Society popular with us than the establishment of such an Institution.'[1] This was an early reference to the building in Sinclair Terrace of the Pulteneytown Academy, for many years the 'senior' school of this part of the parish. The Society contributed a handsome £1,700 towards the project. The opening of the Academy was advertised in the spring of 1839, and the actual opening was reported in May of that year. 'A niggard economy, in educating the rising generation, is the worst description of parsimony,' declared the *John O'Groat Journal*.[2]

The *Journal* continued:

1 *JOGJ*, 2 September, 1836.
2 *JOGJ*, 10 May, 1839.

and a saving which would be quite justifiable in other matters, inexcusable in this. We have no hesitation in saying, that a few pounds or shillings, as the case may be, now spent on the instruction of their children, will some day or other repay the parents a hundred-fold. It is the best of all investment of capital, as it lays up a *fortune* for their children which, in whatever circumstances they may be placed in after life, can never fail them.

Girls were to be admitted as well as boys. 'The establishment is to be devoted to the instruction of children of both sexes, and of all classes.' The Academy's first pupils numbered a mere 67 but, continued the *Journal*,

four to five hundred ought to be the number at the new Academy. Our streets teem at present with idle and mischievous boys and girls. Let every one of those be put to school, and not only will we have the consciousness of having acted the generous part, but insure ourselves the gratitude of many, who, had they been left to run on in their present idle and evil courses, would have proved an eyesore to their parents, and a curse to society. Let those who can afford to send their children, send them to the Academy, and let those who are willing, but unable to do so, be assisted. We have reason to believe, that a fund collected here, for an educational purpose, will be devoted to the purchase of books and slates for the use of the pupils in the two first classes. This would be a great boon, and be most thankfully accepted by those persons whose means do not admit to their purchasing these indispensable items themselves.[1]

'A number of bachelors, and others, have determined on aiding the poorer classes of society, in their laudable endeavours to procure instruction for their children, by paying the fees of such pupils,' wrote the *Journal* proudly, clearly missing their own quaint *faux pas*. Whatever may have been the shortcomings of earlier educational ventures in this area, there was something quite brave and generous in this one; while not going so far as to advocate an education tax, the founders were anxious to do the best they could for the poorer as well as the children of the better-off. There was to be no segregation as to class or sex. The English press at these times, as well as the Scottish, was advertising and reporting the founding and funding of schools,

1 *JOGJ*, 10 May, 1839.

but usually much more on class and single-sex lines – certainly for middle-class pupils.

The Great Mackay

For some reason the Academy had to close for a time in 1841, following the resignation of the head teacher, Mr Christison. A grand reopening was arranged for September of that year. As consultant for the new venture was called in Benjamin Mackay, a noted headmaster of the Edinburgh High School, a Caithnessian who had not been back to his native county for nearly forty years, as he regularly told audiences during his fêted peregrinations in the county during September, 1841. Mackay was a great man in the affairs of the Edinburgh-Caithness Society, which he had helped to form, and it was through the Society that he had been invited north.

He provided the school with impressive advice on how it should be run and the kind of curriculum it should follow. The advice came in the form of a letter accompanying the advertisement. This included observations on the nature and benefits of the education to be offered, testimonials of the teachers he had recommended for appointment, and a detailed list of subjects to be taught and the charges to be made for admission to courses.

The curriculum to be offered provides interesting insight into the notions of 'comprehensive' education circulating in Scotland at this time. Religion went without saying and is not listed.

THE PULTENEYTOWN ACADEMY COURSE OF STUDY AND TABLES OF FEES

	Per Quarter
English, Reading and Spelling with Recitation and Music, Three halfpence per week.	0 1 6
Ditto, with Mental Arithmetic, Slate Writing Printing and Ciphering, Twopence per week.	0 2 0
Ditto, with English Grammar and the Arithmetic Table, Twopence-halfpenny per week.	0 2 6
Ditto, with an outline of Geography and History, Three pence per week.	0 3 0
Ditto with Practical Arithmetic, Penmanship and Drawing, Twopence per week.	0 4 0

Ditto, with the Elements of French, Latin, Greek, Map-drawing, and a Course of Geography – Ancient and Modern – Five pence per week.	0	5	0
Ditto, with Book-keeping, Business Terms, and Short-hand Writing, Sixpence per week.	0	6	0
Ditto, with the Latin, Greek, and French Classics, Logarithms, Geography, Algebra, Trigonometry and Navigation, Gunnery Land-Surveying, and in short, any Branch of Mathematics – Theoretical and Practical – Sevenpence-halfpenny per week.	0	7	6

In the above, the higher fee, in every instance includes all or any of the previously mentioned Branches. Fees payable quarterly, in advance. Quarter-days, 8th May, 8th August, 8th November, and 8th February. Classes for beginners opened half-yearly on the 8th of May and the 8th of February. House of attendance from 9 to 3, with proper intervals for air and exercise. Private classes in the mornings and evenings.[1]

'In expressing my best wishes for the prosperity of the new Academy at Pulteneytown,'[1] concluded Mr Mackay, adding the gratuitous comment, 'I hope I may be permitted to express equal anxiety for the success and permanence of the Burgh School. It is in the interest of the community to maintain both seminaries in an efficient and flourishing condition, as incitement, and honourable rivals to each other.' Recalling his own days as a pupil of the Wick Parish School, he expresses himself as not too hopeful about the Wick School. 'In my time the accommodation of the Burgh School was very indifferent, and if not improved [and it was not], must now be very inadequate. One or two good rooms might be added at a trifling expense.' Magnanimously he said, 'If the undertaking is set a-going, I shall cheerfully contribute my mite, for the recollections of the days of *auld lang syne.*' Mackay's sentiments were not calculated to endear himself to Mr Hislop, head of the Wick Parish School.

During his visit to Caithness in September, 1841, Mr Mackay went to schools in various villages and in Thurso and Wick, conducting 'examinations' which, it was believed – by himself and some others – did quite a lot of good in the place. He was entertained to civic

---

1 *JOGJ*, 25 June, 1841.

dinners in Thurso and Wick and he made numerous speeches on the subject of the benefits of education. His bravest effort was the after-dinner speech he made at Wick on 9th September when he 'sat down with thirty-eight gentlemen' at the Caledonian Hotel. Mr Mackay had that day, too, been made a Freeman of the Burgh. He spoke modestly of his own role as a promoter of educational development: 'I fear that the partiality of my countrymen has led them to ascribe more merit to my services connected with the scheme than I am entitled to.'[1]

The 'scheme' in question was Mr Mackay's 'competitive examination' system. It wasn't very original. In fact, at this time, the idea of examining school pupils and other students was gaining a certain currency in England as a means of measuring the effectiveness of teaching, and since government, church and community were not unduly anxious to spend 'public' money on education, whatever the manifest benefits that might accrue, certified evidence of achievement gained by examination of candidates, might well persuade parents, especially those of the middle-class, to pay more willingly for such benefits. In fact, the government had already begun paying small grants for educational purposes in 1833 through a specially set up department of the Privy Council. A pioneer of utility instruction was Henry Brougham, a keen promoter of popular education and founder of the Society for the Diffusion of Useful Knowledge in 1825.[2]

Mackay seems to have been among those who took up the idea of systematic examining of pupils, but his scheme had nothing in common with the system that came into being in the 1850s and 1860s by which English secondary schools and part-time 'artisan' education curricula were increasingly regulated by 'external' examination boards. No such apparatus existed in Mackay's day. His plan rather was to organise 'competitions' by which pupils could rival one another in achievement in a range of subjects, measured by visiting 'examinators', as Calder calls them, 'the clergy of the different denominations', who would verbally test the candidates. The successful ones would carry away prizes. Just such an examination

1 *JOGJ*, 17 September, 1841.
2 Henry Brougham (1778-1868) was born in Edinburgh. He was a student of Professor Dugald Stewart, himself an apostle of Adam Smith. Brougham was one of the founders of the *Edinburgh Review* His 'Useful Knowledge' programme included the founding of the *Penny Cyclopadia*. He became Lord Chancellor in the government of 1830, and had much to do with promoting the reform Bill of 1832. For him, as for his followers, the idea of education was the accumulation of knowledge, a notion which easily lent itself to the idea of testing for knowledge gained. Brougham was one of the founders of the 'University of London' in 1828 which eventually developed the idea of 'external degree' examinations. Wick Burgh made him a Freeman on one of his visits north.

was held in Wick Town Hall on 9th September, 1841, Mr Mackay presiding, when pupils from schools in the area, Wick, Pulteneytown, Latheron, Stirkoke and Bower competed. There were, for instance, examinations in 'English Reading, Recitation and Spelling' (25 candidates), 'Mental Arithmetic' (14 candidates), 'Elements of Grammar' (19 candidates), and in a dozen other 'branches'. The largest single group of 24 took Writing, Printing and Ciphering'. Mr Mackay professed himself to have 'come with the anticipation that the examination would have been a failure, but he was agreeably disappointed.'[1]

Mr Mackay expounded his enthusiastic ideas of 'competitive examining' to the assembled burghers at the dinner of 9 September. All who spoke registered high approval. The *Journal* in a special leader likewise gave Mr Mackay an appreciative vote of confidence, wishing him *bon voyage* on 'his return south, carrying with him the respect and affectionate regard of every class of his countrymen.' It was to be hoped, said the paper, 'that the liberality of the county will ultimately so increase the funds of the Association [ie. the Edinburgh-Caithness Association] to enable Mr Mackay to arrange a course of study for a public exhibition or bursary, to be competed for by all the youthful talent of the county.'

There was one dissent from all these tributes. No sooner had the great man departed, Mr Hislop wrote a trenchant letter fundamentally critical of the Mackay system. It was printed (in small type) alongside the columns of the grandiose after-dinner speeches. Hislop made three points: (1), that competition constituted in effect a bribe to teachers to 'bestow superior pains upon a *few* of the cleverest boys'; (2), the system cannot in any case measure or demonstrate intellectual development; it merely puts a premium on memory work, and promotes 'cramming'; (3) while unfavourable to the cultivation of true intellect, it has minimal influence on the religious and moral development of the individual. In case anyone was interested especially in this point, Mr Hislop recommended that they read David Stow's *Moral Training*.

All this was red rag to the bull. The following week Mr Mackay riposted with an enormous two-column letter, full of windy rhetoric, to which Mr Hislop replied, after which Benjamin Mackay, now

---

1 For further background to the rise of the British examination system, see Frank Foden: *The Examiner*; University of Leeds Press (1989). David Stow, a follower of Rousseau and Robert Owen, was an educational pioneer in Glasgow, of nursery education.

exasperated, sought to put down the presumptuous Hislop with a metrical *coup de grace*. 'After writing so much dull prose [Mr Mackay spake truly],' said Mr Mackay, 'I shall try to end this controversy in a single verse,

> GREAT HISLOP, on the old Kirk Hill
> Though vanquished quite, can argue still:
> But now his name strikes not great awe;
> MACKAY has slain his *men of straw*.

The examinations did not survive for long. J T Calder, the historian of Caithness, and an acquaintance of Benjamin Mackay, puts a very benevolent construction of the educational events of 1841 and then describes the sequel:

> The scheme was warmly approved of, and most of the gentlemen and clergy in Caithness, and a good many residing out of it, but connected with the county by property or otherwise joined the [Edinburgh-Caithness] Association, and remitted donations and contributions in order to raise a fund for defraying the necessary expenses. A handsome legacy of over £100 was bequeathed to it by Mr Francis Sutherland, an old Caithnessman who had long resided in the United States. The Earl of Caithness was made honorary president.

The first examinations, attended by Mackay, went well, and the Association was thus inaugurated with great *éclat*. 'Everything promised to go on flourishingly.' But then came the 'unfortunate Disruption' which 'converted the whole of Scotland into an arena of bitter strife.'

> An evil spirit got into the competitions, and, although outward decency was preserved, there was little brotherly kindness among the examinators, and matters did not get on harmoniously. In awarding the prizes cries of partiality were raised, and broad insinuations thrown out of collusion between some of the examiners and the teachers. A system of cramming for the express purpose of carrying off the prizes was carried on; and many parents exclaimed against the practice of certain teachers, who, for several months every year, confined their attention to a few of their more advanced scholars, while the general business of the school was handed over to one or two of the bigger boys.

Thus, in very little time at all, was Mr Hislop vindicated. Such developments were, as considerable experience in later years in England proved, whenever competitive schemes were set afoot, more than likely. The evil lay in the system rather than in the lack of 'brotherly kindness among examinators'; such schemes tend to rely for their effectiveness on the worse rather than the better motives of teachers and pupils. 'Cramming', examiners found, was inevitable.

Mr Calder sees the system out:

> In 1845, The Free Church ministers and their teachers withdrew from the competitions, on the grounds that the Committee of the Association at Edinburgh had arbitrarily appointed as chairman two gentlemen connected with the Established Church, whereas they ought to have left each meeting to choose its own chairman. The seceders set on foot a rival Association, and competitions under its auspices were held at Wick and Thurso for the first time in 1846, and continued a year or two afterwards. The parent Association, however, by certain concessions, brought about a reunion, which continued until 1853, when a second *disruption* took place, and the rival Association was reorganised. In 1857 the committee at Edinburgh obtained the assistance of Dr Cumming, Government Inspector of Free Church schools, as examiner-in-chief at Wick and Thurso – an arrangement they hoped would unite all parties. But in this expectation they were disappointed; for the clergymen of both churches, generally speaking, kept away from the meetings and but few schools sent pupils to them. The rival association, which betrayed symptoms of unhealthiness from the beginning, has ceased to exist [Calder was writing in 1861]; and the original competitions are still carried on, but they are not supported as they ought to be, and they have lost a good deal of the public interest which at first attached to them. Such is the brief history of the Edinburgh-Caithness Association, or rather of the competitions at Wick and Thurso, which shows how extremely difficult it is to work out the most benevolent scheme when it has to contend with the jealousies and prejudices of human nature. It cannot be denied, however, that in spite of these unfortunate jarrings and divisions, the competitions have done good. They have given a stimulus to education in the county; and they might have been productive of still greater benefits if the mischievous spirit of party could have been excluded from the proceedings.
>
> To the honour of the Association it deserves to be mentioned, that since the competitions commenced, not fewer than 1500

volumes of literary prizes, exceeding in value £200, besides £100 expended in bursaries to students in Caithness attending the University of Edinburgh.[1]

Actually the educators of Wick had already been conducting 'examinations' for some time. In July, 1836, the *Journal* reporter wrote glowingly about an 'Examination' of the Wick Parish School, taught by Alexander Hislop, recently conducted by a burghal party, headed by the Rev Phin and his son, K M Phin 'Student of Divinity' and the Provost, John Kirk. The ten members of the party felt it to be

> a very pleasing duty to bear our testimony to the highly satisfactory state of progress in which we found the youth under Mr Hislop's charge. The appearance of the children in all of the different branches of learning in which they were concerned, must have satisfied every one first who was capable of forming an opinion on the subject, that Mr Hislop was a man of excellent talents, and a teacher of great assiduity and success. We were particularly pleased with the Scriptural knowledge displayed by the scholars, and with the intimate acquaintance with doctrines and duties of the Word of God. The extent of the information on the interesting subject of Natural Science was also highly creditable. The whole of the Examination convinced us that Mr Hislop was a proficient in the intellectual system of education practised by Mr Wood of the Edinburgh Sessional School. We have never seen children of the same age evince a more thorough comprehension of every meaning of every word that they read than those taught by Mr Hislop. The result of the Examination has greatly strengthened our conviction that the Parochial School of Wick is eminently suited to the confidence and support of the public.[2]

Frequent accounts of such examination sessions are now reported in the *Journal*, and it does not seem to have mattered greatly who took part, so long as they were important men of the town, ministers, elders, bailies of the burgh. Though there is no information as to the method of 'examination' this was not the kind of thing being advocated by Mr Mackay. It was rather an *ad hoc* kind of inspection by burghers and citizens, to check on how the money coming out of their pockets was being spent. To the 'examiners' of 1836, Mr Hislop was no 'man of straw'. He was indeed taking his cue from a rival of Mr Mackay in Edinburgh.

1 J T Calder, op cit, pp 223-224.
2 *JOGJ*, 2 September, 1836.

Nevertheless, the Rev Charles Thomson's final judgement on schooling in Wick is that 'a great number of the children are very imperfectly educated. Many do not get to school above a quarter or two. Poverty is partly the cause of this; but it must be confessed, that there is not so deep a conviction of the benefits of education as every Christian must desire to see.'

Further substantial improvement in the schooling of Wick, as in many other parts of Scotland, had to await the passage of the Young Act of 1872, which made provision for non-sectarian parish education in Scotland – comparable to the English Act of 1870, which the Scots were accused of aping – and the setting up of the Scotch (later Scottish) Education Department. Nevertheless, with all its considerable faults and furious controversies, Scottish education until this had considerably higher achievements to its credit than the English. The Argyll Commission of 1876 found that in Scotland there was a university place for 1 in a 1,000, compared with 1 to 5,800 in England; 'secondary' schooling was provided in Scotland for 1 in every 140 pupils as compared with the English ratio of 1:1,300, while illiteracy (measured by inability to sign the marriage register), deplorably high though it was only half the figure for England.[1] As we have seen, Wick was making its contribution, thwarted though it was by 'disruption'.

Thomson mentions the 'Sabbath Schools' connected with the Church of Scotland, one each in Wick and Pulteneytown, attended respectively by 250 and 320 scholars, and also in Keiss, Staxigoe, Reiss, Stirkoke, Thrumster and Ulbster. He does not say what was taught and to what levels of success, but it was unlikely to have been much more than a little reading in the scriptures to those children of the poor who were wanted at home for work during the week.

As for adult education, there was not much of this so far. The celebrated endeavours of Dr John Anderson in Glasgow were hardly reflected here; as yet there were few signs of the Mechanics Institute movement having made much penetration into Wick, for the very good reason no doubt, that until recently there had been few mechanics in Wick anyway.[3] The idea of a 'Mechanics Reading Room'

---

1 T C Smout: *Scottish People*, op cit. p 216.
2 *JOGJ*, 2 September, 1836.
3 John Anderson, Professor of Natural Philopony in Glasgow University, began delivering evening science lectures for working men as early as 1760. The 'Andersonian' Institute which he endowed – a sort of prototype Mechanics Institute in Glasgow, Kilmarnock, Greenock, Liverpool and Sheffield. In the 1840s Mechanics Institutes sprang up in most larger towns.

was raised by 'A Working Man' in 1839.[1]

It would be an exaggeration to suggest that the vigorous lectures mounted by the Temperance Society amounted to an Adult Education programme, though they were evidently much enjoyed and doubtless there was, from time to time, some genuine instruction to be gained from them. Intimations of such a programme began to appear however, in 1838, with a sequence of three lectures by the Rev John Wiseman on Astronomy, using as his text part of an intriguing verse from Job, *'God hangeth the earth upon nothing'*, (Job 26:7). There were lectures too from a Mr Mackintosh on Geology, so popular that they were several times repeated, and earned from the Rev Wiseman a warm appreciation in May, 1841.[2] Interestingly, both of these series of lectures were by reverend gentlemen. Although charged with threatening implications for the validity of the scriptures, these topics seemed to fascinate clerics in the mid nineteenth century, both in Scotland and England, and as we have before noticed, much original work, especially in the field of geology, was done by ministers and priests. At this stage it was still generally felt that 'The Heavens declare the glory of God: and the firmament sheweth his handiwork.' Trouble set in when evangelical literalism came into vogue.

There were two reading rooms, one in each of the main settlements, that in Pulteneytown opened in 1829 and that of Wick in 1840. 'Each receives about four daily London, and about the same number of provincial papers', doubtless a day or two old. There was a subscribers' library in Wick 'containing about 1620 volumes', started in March, 1826.[3]

As for newspapers in the town itself, there were in 1840 two, the *John O'Groat Journal*, founded 1836, with a weekly circulation of 800 copies, about one half 'throughout the four northern counties, the other throughout Britain and abroad.' The *Journal* 'advocates what are usually called Liberal principles', while the *Northern Star* a fortnightly newspaper, began publishing in November, 1836, and 'was discontinued in May 1839. It advocated what are usually called Conservative principles'.

So that, for all its apparent educational poverty, Wick was looking

1 *JOGJ*, 18 January, 1839.
2 *JOGJ*, 14 May, 1841.
3 One of these, presumably that of Pulteneytown, is referred to as the 'Exchange Reading Room' in the description of Wick accompanying Bishop's engraving, printed in the *Journal* of 19 March, 1847 (see p. 307).

up intellectually, and if the language of the first issues of the *John O'Groat Journal* is anything to go by, quite a few Wickers and Pulteneytownians were anything but illiterate. There were now in the town two booksellers, 'both of whom have a considerable business'. One of the booksellers was Peter Reid, founder of the *John O'Groat Journal*.

Valediction

The Rev Charles Thomson, energetic, earnest, intense and probably quite humourless, but a man of high integrity, appears as one of the less lovable, and certainly one of the less fortunate of the ministers who ever served in Wick. In 1842, at the height of his worries about the coming disruption, two of his children died, probably as the result of fever then raging in Wick. He was an accomplished preacher, and faithfully kept his congregation going during its tribulations after they had walked away from the comforts of Kirkhill. For better or worse, few men of Wick left a more distinctive mark on the place.

He above all, carried Wick through the Disruption. A local minister of the present Church of Scotland, comments on the Disruption and its effect on Wick:

> Wick Parish suffered a mighty blow from which the disrupters were sure it would never recover – they believing themselves (the disrupters) to be the true church in Scotland. It was the business people and the middle classes that went over to the disrupters . . . things are not dissimilar today. Wick Parish has very few professional or business people and that will continue till the eventual church readjustment in Wick within the next few years. Pulteneytown now has only one Church of Scotland and Wick will eventually be the same as the pattern some four years ago.

. . . .

Note: most unattributed quotations in this chapter (and those in the previous chapter) are from Charles Thomson's contribution to the 1840 *Statistical Account*. In the text it has been consistently dated as 1840. Strictly, Thomson's report was submitted in March, 1841, and the actual publication came later. The entire Second *Statistical Account* was published over a period of seven years, between 1839 and 1846. That of Wick refers mainly to the state of affairs in 1840, hence the labelling.

SODOM OF THE NORTH

References in Literature to Religious Dissidence

Though a significant element in Scottish folk life, religion and religious dissidence get only modest mention in literature. It was, perhaps, regarded by some as too serious an issue for humour and irony – and perhaps too dangerous. Scott deals with aspects of the Reformation and the conflicts of outlook and feeling between adherents of the old religion and the new in *The Monastery*. 'The general plan of the story,' says Scott in his introduction, 'was, to conjoin two characters in that bustling and contentious age, who, thrown into situations which gave some different views on the subject of the Reformation, should, with the same sincerity and purity of intention, dedicate themselves, the one to the support of the Catholic Church, the other to the establishment of the Reformed doctrines.'

In *Old Mortality* he concerns himself with aspects of the tensions and conflicts endured in the late years of the reign of Charles, as a result of the intransigence of the later generation of Covenanters towards the Scottish government, then led by the Earl of Lauderdale. Inevitably in both novels, characters and situations are treated with some irony. Not accidentally the author presents himself in each of these novels as informed in his subject by the solemn and not overtly humorous lucubrations of local antiquarians, in *The Monastery*, by Captain Cuthbert Clutterbuck, and in *Old Mortality* by Jedediah Cleishbottom, two very Dickensian inventions. In each novel the political and military implications of the conflict are explored.

Two novels which attempt to get to the heart of the controversy between establishment and dissidence, in terms of the differences between the attitudes and reactions of common folk, are *Witch Wood*, by John Buchan, which is concerned with the relationships in his parish of a newly appointed minister, sympathetic to the Covenant and *Johnny Gibb of Gushetneuk*, by William Alexander, which deals almost exclusively with the reactions of the parishioners of an Aberdeenshire parish to the Disruption in 1843. Most of the dialogue in *Johnny Gibb* is in the dialect of the Mearns area south of Aberdeen, and the controversy is expressed in terms of astonishing popular knowledgeability about the issues involved. The writer, William Alexander, was a journalist on an Aberdeen newspaper. It is not difficult to imagine the same kind of argument and, indeed, ranting that occurs in Gushetneuk, going on at the same time in Wick and other places in the north where the whole congregation of a parish church, led by an elder or minister of strong conviction, 'marched out'. Smout describes this remarkable (and despite the difficulties of the dialect), very readable novel as 'the finest of the kailyard novels'.

Not the least interesting element of *Witch Wood* is Buchan's attempt to evoke the circumstances and mystery of 'popish' and pagan ritual (more pagan than popish) surviving into the seventeenth century and beyond, and the frustrations of an earnest covenanting minister seeking to extirpate such survivals. That such practices prevailed in out of the way places we have seen from the Wick record; how authentic are the scenes of Buchan's Beltane and Lammas celebrations at midnight in the dense woodland of Melanudrigill (in Border country) can only be surmised. Buchan's presenter, Christopher Harvie, in the Canongate Classics edition, suggests that his description owes as much to his interest in J G Fraser's *Golden Bough* (and other writers on anthropology and mythology contemporary with Buchan) as to genuine evidence of a ritual. Such evidence would, of course, have been very difficult to find. By its very nature, ancient pagan ritual was secretive, but still very pervasive, Congregations or 'covens', as Buchan calls them, too were more likely than not to consist of the illiterates of a parish.

Burns, of course, often turns his banter on to religion, and in fact, some of his poems, satirising the pretensions and solemnities of the kirk-session, especially those referring to the public humiliation of his friend, Gavin Hamilton in 1787, had an effect in the erosion of the intense puritanism that had governed the attitudes of many kirk reformers. 'Holy Willie's Prayer' could not have been greatly admired by many of Burns's ecclesiastical contemporaries.

James Hogg, too, should be mentioned as a Scottish writer who wrestles with the issues, mainly in personal terms, in his *Private Memoirs and Confessions of a Justified Sinner*.

CHAPTER 14

VOICE OF THE PEOPLE

SIN and wickedness were not absent from Wick before 1836, but from that year the citizens could no longer avoid knowing about it, for in that year the tree of knowledge of good and evil came into fruit in the name of the imaginatively named *John O'Groat Journal*, additionally titled *Caithness Monthly Miscellany*. The Journal sported two classical mottoes: *Animi cultus quasi quidam humanitatis cibus* (cultivation of the mind is the very essence of being human – Cicero); and, Othello's valediction, *Nothing extenuate, nor set down aught in malice*. The early issues of this north regional newspaper sought earnestly to vindicate this rhetoric, and few would dispute the *Journal's* claim to have remained faithful to its original declarations of principle.

These were rather pompously set forth – such was the style of much nineteenth century journalism – in a full, densely printed front page 'Prospectus'. A prime purpose of the *Journal* was, as it said in its first sentence, to abolish the utter dearth of 'useful information' and 'expression of public opinion', the 'entire absence' of which were, 'at this moment more seriously felt and more deeply to be regretted in Caithness than in any other County in Scotland'. It nearly satisfied the whole bill in its next Johnsonian sentence, of three column inches and two hundred words, sandwiched between a splendid opening locution which began: 'Amongst an increasing and intelligent community, ever eager for the acquirement of knowledge, and fully alive to the many and important advantages it confers . . . .,' and ended with a fervent expression of determination to 'do away with the reproach which, in the age we live in, must necessarily attach to us, from the circumstance of the non-existence of any periodical whatever in this County.' Though 'tabloid' in form, these first issues were anything but tabloid in language.

Politics of conventional kind do not seem to have flourished in Wick – or Caithness for that matter – up to this time. The state of public opinion could not, perhaps, be quite accurately expressed in terms of the old English tag: 'God bless the squire and his relations, and keep us in our proper stations,' but that represents, without much doubt, the level of public participation in affairs. What the poor folk said to one another in the public houses, and perhaps even whispered on the benches of the kirk – when the minister was not preaching, about the decisions and determinations of the landlords, kirk-session and burgh council, may have relieved feelings, but certainly this must have also applied to some folk of the middle sort. Democratic gathering was almost unknown.

The *John O'Groat Journal*, founded in the wake of the Reform Act, was determined to stir things up and

> Fully persuaded that truth is ever best elucidated by free discussion, and that just conclusions and lasting convictions are almost uniformly the result of solid argument and close investigation, the Proprietors of the Miscellany have determined on throwing open its columns to the communications of ALL PARTIES, as, in their opinion, the best mode they could adopt for the furtherance of the object they have at heart – the diffusion of useful knowledge; and as their own religious views and political predelictions will be found to be strictly in unison with tolerant and liberal principles, they would be acting in complete contradiction to their avowed professions, were they to exclude from their pages the opinions of those, who, although differing from them on minor points, must, doubtless entertain as conscientious and earnest a desire for the public as they themselves do. The unwarrantable length and bitter tone which, unhappily, have too often characterized Political and Religious controversy, must in some degree justify the Proprietors in exluding polemics altogether from their pages; but trusting to the judgement and discretion of such as may feel inclined to treat of either, they confidently hope that both the spirit and length of communications of this description will not exclude the necessity of their non-insertion.

The Proprietors announced that the *Journal* would render itself 'eminently useful in the various matters on which it may treat', giving 'immediate consideration' to 'The Outlet Market, and Prices for our staple Commodity', the Herring Fisheries in all their aspects, 'the facilities which this county affords for the introduction of some other means of industry upon it', the 'extension and improvement of public works', the agricultural interest of the county: 'In short, the advancement and prosperity of our commerce, both internal and foreign being the objects which the Proprietors aim, no efforts shall be wanting on their part to attain such desirable results.'

The proprietors promised 'instructive and interesting extracts from standard works and periodicals of the day', and that they would seek to prevail upon their *Fair Readers* to 'overcome their natural timidity in so far as to occasionally condescend to enrich the Periodical with their literary effusions.' While they would 'support and countenance the higher ranks' they were 'equally if not more desirous of the patronage and aid of the humbler, though not less intelligent part of the community,' and in this respect 'earnestly entreat the working and industrious classes, of all descriptions and denominations, to supply them with their useful communications and beneficial discoveries.'

While the proprietors regarded the exposure of 'dereliction of duty in public men in their official capacities', as 'at all times open to animadversion', and would make 'observations on public grievances', they were 'resolutely determined on banishing from their pages all observations and remarks that may verge on personality, detraction of private character or slanderous insinuation.' A 'department of the Journal will be set apart for the productions of those who may feel inclined to indulge the poetic vein; and poems, sonnets, enigmas, charades &c, be thankfully received.'

The 'Prospectus' ends with the classic reference to brevity as the soul of wit, one of the many wise saws of old Polonius, that great exponent of the 'sergeant-major' principle, 'do as I say, not as I do'. In this connection, it must be said, this first issue of the *Journal* was somewhat delinquent in observing the rule it enjoined on its contributors as an 'absolute necessity'. Not the least of the enjoyable qualities of early *Journals* is their quaint verbosity.

Brave Father of the 'Groat'.

The *John O'Groat Journal* has already celebrated centennial and century-and-half birthdays, in 1936 and 1986 respectively, on each of which occasions *Special Anniversary* Supplements were published, in which founder and first editor were featured. Both belonged to the locality. Peter Reid, creator of the *Journal*, was the son of a Pulteneytown fish-curer, one of the first eight who took up such work in Pulteneytown. Though expected by his father to learn and take over the business on the old man's retirement, Peter chose instead to walk the two hundred and seventy miles to Dundee where he spent three years learning the printing trade. He returned to Wick in 1829 and set up as a bookseller in a building at the Bridgend, Union Street, which had formerly been the offices of the British Fisheries Society. It was from here that seven years later Reid launched the *John O'Groat Journal*, where it still lives. 'To describe Peter Reid as a bookseller is to describe Woolworths as a hardware store,' says the hundred-and-fiftieth anniversary *Special Supplement:*

> His motley stock incorporated nets and fishing gear, rosewood desks, quill pens, stationery, wallpaper, floor coverings, walking sticks, flutes, anything that would turn a penny. Later he dealt in coal, lime and herring, and made frequent trips to Edinburgh, Glasgow and even London buying stock for his ubiquitous [not quite the right word] shop.
>
> On one of these early trips he brought home the second-hand type from Chambers Edinburgh Journal, which was introducing new founts. Indeed, the first issues of the Groat were almost facsimiles of the famous magazine, for not only did they use the identical type but their format was similar – an eight-pages large quarto with three columns to the page and the title engraved in the same semicircular form.

Reid had already begun a printing business before starting the *Journal*, turning out 'many of the run-of-the-mill orders' and a variety of pamphlets. The earliest of these was a religious tract entitled:

The peculiar obligations to devotedness to God arising from the preservation of life in the midst of His terrible judgements: a discourse in reference to the recent visitation of cholera.

The author was the Rev A Ewing, a Minister of the Gospel with connections in Thurso and Wick. Ewing originally had his pamphlets printed by William Todd, another printer who had opened a shop on Bridge Street but whose business 'melted away' in the face of competition from Reid. Reid had evangelical religious leanings himself.

His first venture into local journalism occurred in 1832, when he started running off a regular news sheet during the cholera epidemic of 1832. 'Alarm was running high and rumours were seething in the town, greatly exaggerating the death rate.' There was believed to be a danger that the herring fishing would be 'completely' suspended as the result of 'many of the hired men, most from the west coast' deserting their boats and going home. 'Peter Reid's reaction was to print a daily bulletin on the number of cases of cholera, the number of deaths and recoveries. When people saw that the deaths were few and the recoveries many, they took heart.'

Once it got going, Reid regularly advertised in his own newspaper his book and other sales in the advertisement columns that filled the front pages, along with the weekly collection of public notices. A typical advertisement appears in the issue for 10 January, 1841:

PETER REID
Bookseller and Stationer
Has lately received a Select STOCK of ANNUALS and CHRISTMAS PRESENTS for
1840.
As the Supply is limited to a few copies, early application is respectfully requested. The subjoined is a list:–

The Drawing Room Scrap Book – – –	£1 1 0
Heath's Book of Beauty – – – – – – –	1 1 0
———— Picturesque Annual – – – –	1 1 0
Forget-Me-Not – – – – – – – – – –	0 12 0
Friendship's Offering – – – – – – – –	0 12 0
The Juvenile Scrap Book – – – – – – –	0 8 0
The Juvenile Forget-Me-Not – – – – – –	0 8 0

At present on hand, a Stock of Juvenile and other works, suitable for presents and school prizes, in various bindings.

A great variety of Ladies' and Gentlemen's Pocket Books and Diaries, also Almanacs of every description, from 1d to 4s each.

THIS DAY IS PUBLISHED
REID'S SUPPLEMENT to the Almanacs for 1840
Containing the Official Lists &c., of SUTHERLAND, CAITHNESS, ORKNEY & SHETLAND, carefully collected by different persons in each county, and will be found to contain much useful information, with considerable addition to that of last year.

The SUPPLEMENT is stitched with Oliver and Boyd's THREEPENNY ALMANAC, or *DAILY REMEMBRANCER.*

The rest of the column listed Charts, Sheffield Goods, Perfumery and Patent Medicines, which included well known preparations and remedies such as Rowlands Macassar Oil (and its variants) and Holloway's Universal Ointment, Allison's Cure for Toothache, Floorcloths.

Completing the list was the offer of Bookbinding and Printing Services.

Rowlands and Holloways often had their own adverts in the paper. There was much speculation in later years as to 'where Reid found the capital to springboard his newspaper venture'. A popular notion was that James Traill of Rattar, 'a considerable land-owner and the originator of the pavement trade in Caithness', had lent him the money. That is unlikely; Traill, in fact, was consulted and thoroughly disapproved of the idea. 'His opinion,' says Calder

> was, that such a publication would be a vehicle only for political squabbling and personal abuse, and it would set the whole county by the ears. Caithness would not support a paper and did not need one . . . The evil predicted by Mr Traill and others has not happened. On the contrary, the publication has, in various respects been of immense benefit to Caithness; and by his enterprising spirit as projector of the press in the 'far north', Mr Reid's name will have an honourable place in any future literary record of the county.'[1]

Peter Reid was a lifelong Liberal and

> plunged himself into Wick town life with characteristic energy. He was Justice of the Peace, one of the first members of the Wick Chamber of Commerce, president of the Fish Exchange and the News Room, and an elder of the Wick Free Church. Any project which he reckoned was for the benefit of the town had his backing.

Peter was married to Maria Caldwell, the daughter of the Rev Robert Caldwell, minister of the Independent Chapel of Wick. They had a family of five. One of his sons, James T Reid, became proprietor of the paper when the old man died in 1886, at the age of 75, and remained at the head of the firm until he emigrated to New Zealand in 1893. His elder brother, Alexander, became a journalist, but was drowned at sea, in the Cook Strait, New Zealand. A grandson, Earnest Buik, son of Peter's daughter took over both as proprietor and editor

1 J T Calder, op cit., p 254.

between 1900 and 1910, after which the *John O'Groat Journal*, passed at last out of the ownership of the Reid family.

Peter Reid, founder of the *'Groat'*, as those in the trade usually call it, was never content with one set of irons in the fire. His ventures and investments were not always prudent. In 1850 he put a lot of money into the setting up in Wick of a flax mill, which failed because of difficulties of growing flax in Caithness; and in 1875 'he lost more than half his savings when Glasgow City Bank collapsed.'

'The man who set the presses rolling,' in the words undersetting the portrait of the solemn, burly, *Father of the Early Groat*, in the Anniversary Supplement, 'was a mixture of the bold and the shrewd. A great Liberal, in his lifetime he witnessed and made the *Groat* a platform for social reform.'

First Fearless Editor

As editor of his new paper, Peter Reid appointed Benjamin Miller Kennedy, a native of Wick and son of Captain Robert Kennedy of Wester, author of the 'curious and interesting manuscript' about old Caithness, much of which was published in instalments in early issues of the *Journal*, which we have already sampled. Calder, who greatly admired him, wrote:

> Possessed of excellent abilities, a great fund of original humour [which we have also sampled], with a lively fancy, and much command of language, Mr Kennedy rendered the paper, as long as it was under his management, extremely popular. It is a remark of Dr Johnson, that 'the mass of every people must be barbarous when there is no printing.'

The *Journal*, during Kennedy's command, which lasted until 1842, has a distinctive flavour of the Puckish, but sometimes ponderous humour which clearly marks Kennedy's style. He combines it, as we have seen, with strong liberal sentiment, a wide ranging interest in affairs generally, from contents of the dense 'Local Intelligence' which he made a feature of the paper, to Westminster politics, and often beyond, for in many issues he included a 'Foreign Intelligence' column that instructed his readers in matters probably well outside their ken. Benjamin Kennedy's curiosity was insatiable and his knowledge of the world omnivorous; his patriotism verged on the jingoistic.

In the issue of 18 December he writes in humorous vein about

Fig 34 Peter Reid.

Fig 35 Benjamin Kennedy.

'Waterfordism in Wick' [a reference which today might read, 'The IRA in Wick', were we inclined at all to joke about 'terrorism' – Waterford was in Kennedy's day the classic symbol of Irish 'terrorism']. He reports a 'terrific explosion' when 'quiet, orderly, steady-going inhabitants of this town were roused from their slumbers.' There were broken windows in houses near the gaol, and some 'thought it was a French privateer' while others believed it might be the opening shots of 'hostilities by the Egyptian fleet, the commander of which had resolved on making a second Jean d'Acre of the ancient Royalty.' The actual cause of the blast was the explosion of a can of gunpowder which someone in a waggish mood had placed 'in the passage leading to Bridge Street separating the home of Mr Phister the Town-Officer from that occupied by Mr Leith of the Caledonian Hotel and the lower part by Mr McGregor, Watchmaker.'[1]

Had they not read the 'Foreign Intelligence' column of the previous issue but one, the mention of Jean d'Acre would have passed most of his readers by, as it would today. In that issue the *Journal* had reported the fall of Acre, a town on the coast of Palestine, to British and Egyptian forces. Kennedy gave the event leader treatment too:

>Important intelligence has been received since our last of the fall of St Jean D'Acre, the last of the strongholds possessed by Mehemet Ali, in a country in which that infatuated old man dared to raise the standard of rebellion against his rightful Sovereign. The news arrived *via* Marseilles on the 25th ultimo, and since then, the details, which will be found in another part of our paper, given us fully as space admits of. The particulars of this important and glorious event, afford incontestible proof of British valour being of the same sterling stuff of which it was composed in the times of Rodney, a Jarvis, a Duncan and a Nelson, and of
>>The flag which braves a thousand years
>>The battle and the breeze,
>
>being destined to float in proud victory in days of yore.

The 'Foreign Intelligence' report had the headline:
BOMBARDMENT AND FALL OF ST JEAN D'ACRE
(From the *Malta Times*) Malta, Nov. 15th 1840

Among the details was the information that on this day, 14 British troops had been killed and 42 wounded; 1500 to 1700 Egyptians had been destroyed in the action. The event was, in fact, the outcome of

---

1 *JOGJ*, 18 December, 1840.

an alliance between Britain and Turkey, arranged by the cynical British Foreign Secretary of the day, Lord Palmerston, seeking to bolster up the 'Sick Man of Europe', Turkey, against its former Viceroy of Egypt, Mehemet Ali.[1]

This was long before the days of Reuters or International news agencies. In such a manner, Benjamin Kennedy opened up the whole world to Wick, until this time totally cocooned away from it in the northern seas. 'There can be no doubt,' wrote Calder, 'that they [the citizens of Wick] since then [the starting of the paper] have risen vastly in intelligence and public spirit. The press has in one sense acted the part of schoolmaster, and made the people to read and think, and it has been the means of bringing forth native talent which but for it would have lain in obscurity.'[2]

The first editor's attitude to religion and religious affairs was rather ambiguous. Unlike the proprietor, he took no part in the affairs of any particular congregation. His reporting of religious matters was cool, and his editorial treatment of the Disruption was, as we saw, ironic. Kennedy, nevertheless, had strong feelings on the matter of abstinence, and was much involved in the founding of the Wick and Pulteneytown Total Abstinence Society.

In 1842 Kennedy took his own talents to Arbroath where he became editor of the *Arbroath Journal* and later founded the *Arbroath Guide* and 'a literary magazine of some merit, *The Pennyworth*'. He retired in 1856 and died in 1861.

Kennedy was followed at the *John O'Groat Journal* by a long line of eighteen editors to the present time; portraits of ten (including Kennedy) are printed in the *Supplement* – a bit like the 'show of kings' that passed before the eyes of Macbeth at his last encounter with the witches. Of these the most distinguished and perhaps eccentric, was Joseph Anderson, who came to the chair in 1860 after years teaching in Constantinople, at a time when the British – still in alliance with Turkey – were constructing a naval dockyard in the city. He wrote some articles on this project which were published in Kennedy's *Arbroath Guide*, probably 'Anderson's "leg" into the *Groat* chair'. Anderson became very interested while in Caithness in the excavation of the Camster cairns; he left for even higher things when 'his learned scientific papers earned him the prestigious appointment of Secretary of the Society of Antiquaries of Scotland, a post he held for 50 years.'

1 *JOGJ*, 4 December, 1840
2 J T Calder, op cit. p 254.

The longest serving editor was R J G Millar, who held the chair during two stints, the first from 1889 to 1900, when he moved to the *Dundee Advertiser*; the second for a long reign of 36 years from 1910 to 1946. 'He is remembered as a man who ran a tight ship – a stickler for accuracy and high standards. His leaders trumpeted down the columns of the paper,' which he carried though both world wars. He it was who marked one of the *Groat's* first ventures into popular book publishing with the *John O'Groat's Christmas Number* – 'a glossy magazine full of local pictures and articles. It was a very readable and popular publication, and a bound volume of Christmas numbers can still be seen in Wick Library.' More recently North of Scotland Newspapers has published two *Christmas Numbers* called *Times Gone By*, compilations of best *John O'Groat Journal* Christmas Numbers since 1923, all best-sellers.

Bette McArdle, the *Journal's* only woman editor so far, was in the chair from 1982 to 1985. 'Her talents ranged wide, and somehow besides bringing up six children, she found time to make her mark as an artist, poetess and knitwear designer.' She was promoted in 1985 as group editor of the parent Highland Printing and Publishing Group in Inverness. There has never been a lack of talent and variety on the editorial floor of the *John O'Groat Journal*.

EMINENTLY USEFUL ON VARIOUS MATTERS

Not every newspaper of the time lived up to its own pretentions, but the *John O'Groat Journal* came creditably near to doing so. Files of the *Journal* over the years, reveal a firm integrity of purpose, including in its pages, news, local and national, articles on aspects of the life and history of the area, ample columns of correspondence, verse and titbits of every variety. The *Journal's* readership never wavered in its loyalty, even when an alternative Wick newspaper appeared on the scene in 1851, the *Northern Ensign*.

The *Journal's* early 'Conservative' rival, the *Northern Star* seems to have sunk without trace within two years of its founding. According to the *Supplement*, the *Star* 'launched scurrilous attacks on its rival'. Touched on a 'raw nerve' over a quibble on circulation figures in November, 1847, Kennedy wrote: 'Although a fortnightly Tory paper entitled the Northern Star does us the honour of noticing us on all occasions, it will be observed that we rarely or never deigned to return the compliment.' Bad relations between the two papers persisted. The *Star* limped on from one crisis to another for a full two

Fig 36 Front page of an early issue of the *John O'Groat Journal*.

years before going under. In that time it was accused of using dirty tactics in the build-up to the 1837 elections, of a type that would make editors' hair curl today.

Faint memory of the *Star* lives only in the rather hostile archive of the *John O'Groat Journal*. Two other tales of the *'Journal's* unhappy competitor are too good to miss out of this record.'

The *Star*, run on a shoe-string, often ended up stealing ink from its rival. When the *Groat* editor, Benjamin Kennedy learned of this he was furious, 'It is bad enough to be libelled by the *Star*,' he said. 'But to be libelled in our own ink is taking things too far!' Once the *Star* was so stretched that its editor had to ride back to Thurso on a Sunday to bring back the necessary printers ink in a teapot. Needless to say, the *Groat* made great capital out of this act of 'Sabbath breaking'.

Liberal Politics

The *Journal's* political stance, though not strictly definable in terms of the politics of the time, was cautiously 'liberal', a term coming into popular use in the mid-nineteenth century, gradually replacing 'Whig', the old designation of the political 'left' of the time.[1] The flavour of the *Journal's* contents was distinctly progressive, its proprietors favouring improvement, advancing trade, better conditions of life for the people, information for all.[2] Its range was remarkably wide.

Though not typical of the issues to follow, which were filled with generous helpings of all the fare promised in the prospectus, the contents of the first issue, which the Editor clearly intended to be 'memorable', deserve a brief review. If nothing else, they reveal on the part of the editorial team assembled to launch Wick's first newspaper, a quite astonishing display of literary bravura, if not yet tried and tested journalistic competence, that augured well for Wickers' entertainment and instruction. Not exactly cheap at the price

---

1 The word 'liberal' had come into use as a description of the kind of break from the past represented by the politics of the Reform and various other Acts of the Melbourne government. 'Liberals', however, were regarded with some suspicion by the traditional Tories, who tended to associate the word with the slogan of the French Revolution, *Liberté, Egalité, Fraternité*, and all the horrors that these words connoted to them. The term 'Conservative' was put into circulation by Robert Peel's *Tamworth Manifesto* of 1836. 'Liberal' and 'Conservative' gradually ousted 'Whig' and 'Tory'.

2 The 'Useful Information' movement, inaugurated by Henry Brougham (see Note 2, p 391), became quite a vogue among journalists.

for six pages (6d, stamp duty paid), the readers of the first issue were regaled, less with news than entertainment, in addition to the prospectus, the main topic being the *Journal* itself. There was a piece on 'The Birth of a Periodical', a semi-humorous piece entitled 'Royal Speeches', anticipating the fun readers would later be having with reports on government affairs, the first of a series of 'Anecdotes – partly authenticated and partly traditional, relative to the early history of the County of Caithness' (derived as we now know from the manuscript of Robert Kennedy of Wester), a set of verses addressed 'To the Poetical Contributors to the John O'Groat Journal', an excellent account on the 'Migration of the Herring' and, sad to say, a two column obituary to Sir John Sinclair of Ulbster, who had died a few weeks before.

One of the *Groat's* earliest causes was the campaign to have removed the 'iniquitous restriction on the progress of knowledge,' the newspaper Stamp Act. When the *Journal* started, newsprint, advertisements and the newspaper itself were all subject to duty. A red stamp had to be displayed on every copy of the paper sold; papers issued more frequently than monthly had to pay fourpence. Feargus O'Connor, the Chartist orator and editor of the *Northern Star* (not the feeble Wick paper of that name, but a much more fiery affair), addressing his readers, characterised the 'little red spot in the corner of my newspaper' as 'the Whig beauty spot; your plague spot'. Peter Reid and Benjamin Kennedy were 'passionate gladiators', calling in their second issue for a meeting in Wick to petition Parliament. It took some years to whittle away these taxes; the government was adamantly opposed to the lifting of the taxes, which they considered would lead to anarchy. Newspapers were believed to propagate sedition. Nevertheless, progressively the taxes were first reduced and then removed. First the stamp duty was reduced to 1d from 4d, announced by Kennedy in the third issue of the *Groat*, but not with any enthusiasm, since he argued that the whole tax should go. Some newspapers approved. 'We can view,' said Kennedy, 'with nothing but disgust and loathing the fulsome adulation and nauseous flattery which newspapers have lavished on the Chancellor of the Exchequer.' In 1853 the tax on advertisements was dropped, and in 1855 the penny stamp duty was made optional; those papers on which the duty had been paid could now go through the post free, a considerable benefit to the *John O'Groat Journal*, since many of its copies went out by post all over the north of Scotland. The newsprint tax was reduced in 1836, the year the *Groat* came out, but was not abolished entirely until 1861.

Tory meetings were reported regularly, but in general, the *Groat* treated Toryism as a bit of a joke. A facetious piece in the first issue, 'reflecting on the important responsibility attendant on our Editorial duties,' set the tone.

> Full of this idea, we one morning sallied forth, and soon found ourselves in the snug, comfortable parlour of a Conservative elderly lady of our acquaintance, under whose hospitable roof we are sometimes in the habit of discussing Tea, Politics, Buttered Toast, and the Church question, occasionally interlarded with a little Town's Gossip to please our friend. We have said that our respected acquaintance was of Conservative principles, an amiable failing common, as we find, to all our ladies, and for which, we will admit, we by no means dislike them. The state of mind in which our venerable friend has been ever since the return of the Melbourne Ministry to power, is truly afflicting; and should his Majesty soon change his present Cabinet, we dread the consequences to our respected acquaintance. Popes and Priests, Bulls and Burnings, Fire and Faggots, are unceasingly floating before her disordered fancy. The soothing sound of the Church bell is in her disturbed imagination, a tocsin of revolution, the hurras of the urchins at play, the yells of a blood-thirsty mob, and it is impossible to conceive with what horror she regards the progress of the Catholic Chapel in Pulteneytown, magnified, as that insignificant structure is, in her eyes, to the dimension of St. Peter's in Rome.

On most major issues of the day the *Journal* took the ostensible, and sometimes the explicit liberal line. Lest there were any readers – other than nice old ladies – who saw merit in the Tory line, the *Journal* printed in October a demolishing quote from *The Times* of 29 March, 1832, rich in mixed metaphors:

> We pity a man for being a Tory in these times: he is a poor creature that the march of events has left behind, – a duck-legged drummer boy, who cannot keep up with his regiment. He is a being of a byegone age, singing an old song, telling a forgotten tale; he is the preterpluperfect tense of politics – an extract from the lumber room where we have long since thrown our ghosts, witches and alchymists.[1]

In November, 1840, Kennedy was still at it:

---

1 *JOGJ*, 14 October, 1836.

> The meetings of the Tories in the good town of Wick are like angel visits, few and far between, though it would appear that snug parties of that now reduced section of the political world, ycleped 'Conservatives', are not of such very rare occurence within this Liberal Royalty. Much to our surprise, and not a little to our amusement, we have this moment heard that a hole-and-corner meeting of Tories was actually held, on the evening of Friday the 30th ultimo called, as we understand, for no other purpose, *credat Judaeus,* than that of influencing the Municipal election which took place on the Tuesday thereafter!! The thing was got up with a degree of secrecy worthy of a Chartist conspiracy; and to such a height was silence observed in the proceedings as to the whereabouts of this little knot of *Skiboites,* that a gentleman who had iron heels to his boots was rendered *bootless* ere he was allowed to enter the room which contained this doughty band of *patriots* . . . . . .[1]

At the actual election, held on 3 November, there was a poor 'turn-out'. Victory was certain for the Liberals, but 'little animation was manifested in the Liberals coming forward'. Each of the four Liberal candidates for office on the burgh council collected sufficient votes to get them elected (none higher than 44), but 'the Tory party not having made a show of resistance. No more than 10 to 12 Tories polled.'[2]

Such being the tone and quality of the *Journal's* impartiality when it came to Tories, perhaps it was not all that surprising if the Wick *Northern Star* was tempted into a little 'scurrilous comment'.

The 'Royal Speeches' column of the first issues was, in fact, an earnest that the *Journal* intended faithfully, but critically, to report the business of parliament forthwith. Two days on from publication, Parliament would meet to hear a 'speech from the Throne which, according to the good old custom observed on such occasions, will doubtless occupy, at least a column of the Daily Newspapers, and leave the public as much in the dark (as regards the real measures to be pursued by Ministers) as if they had gazed on blank paper.' The final resolve of the Editors was different, as they indicated in their final paragraph:

> The Speech from the Throne, as we have thus endeavoured to prove, being no land-mark to guide us at to the course which parliament may think fit to pursue; and the nature of their intense interest, the career of both Houses, but also, to examine

1 *JOGJ*, 13 November, 1840
2 Ibid.

VOICE OF THE PEOPLE

measures expected to be brought forward cannot fail to be of the most momentous description, it becomes the duty of the entire body of the people, not only to watch with the most intense interest, the career of both Houses, but also to examine with scrupulous exactness, the votes of every member of which they are composed, and to scrutinize, with a jealous eye, the Parliamentary conduct of their Representatives, on whose honour, firmness, and patriotism the welfare and prosperity of the nation so essentially depend.[1]

From a newly established newspaper in the most northerly mainland constituency in Britain, furthest removed from the deliberations of parliament, this was indeed a brave declaration, and there is little doubt that, to the best of their ability, the Editors fulfilled it. There was no exaggeration in the *John O'Groat Journal's* estimate of contemporary developments as 'momentous'. These involved measures of municipal reform (in England), commutation of tithes, the abolition of slavery, the penny post and, above all the issue of 'Free Trade' culminating in the Abolition of the Corn Laws by Peel in 1846. The Chartist Movement was becoming quite aggressive, and the Anti-Corn Law League was disputing with it the main claim on public attention.

All these issues were reported on by the *Journal* in due course. Some had a particular impact on Wick, notably the abolition of slavery in the British Empire in 1835, resulting among other things in a decline of herring exports to Jamaica, the penny post and free trade. Interestingly, the great apostle of the abolition movement was William Wilberforce; the slave trade was abolished in 1806, and the slaves on British territory finally freed in 1833. Wilberforce was a fellow MP with George Sinclair, who took his father's place in parliament. On Wilberforce's retirement from parliament in 1812, George, as Provost of Wick, persuaded the magistrates to honour Wilberforce with freedom of the burgh. On receipt of his 'Burgess Ticket' Wilberforce sent a fulsome letter of thanks.[2]

The penny post made quite a difference to Wick. More than once the burghers had protested at the postal rates 'augmented in late years in a Ratio much exceeding the increase of any other Tax with which the County is burdened.' Already in 1813, had argued the burghers,

1 The government in power was the 'Liberal' regime of Lord Melbourne, 1836-1841, to be succeeded by that of Peel. Peel's government turned out to be the more progressive of the two. It was the Conservative Peel who abolished the Corn Laws in 1846
2 BCW, 23 November, 1812.

these rates had 'reached a height which it would be unreasonable to go beyond'. Toll charges already levied against mail coaches were high enough, 'without the necessity of imposing any additional Postage upon Letters in Scotland'. The Public Revenue was surely 'productive' enough to bear the additional costs.[1] At a stroke, penny post relieved Wick and places north from the burdensome mileage charge on much mail. Reduction of the newspaper tax to one penny virtually signified free mail despatch.

Free trade was one of the key issues of liberalism, and remained so for the rest of the century. Wick, along with other fishing towns, sought constantly to get continental import duties against their product reduced. The *Journal* was pleased to be able to report an important concession in this direction when, in February, 1837, Russia halved its duty on Scottish herring from 9s 4d a barrel to 4s 6d.

Repeal of the Corn Laws, until finally accomplished in 1846, was a constant topic of reference in the columns of the paper. While Chartist agitation made little impact on Wick, the issue of 'cheap bread' had some appeal in a northern community where the farming interest no longer prevailed. Repeal of the Corn Laws was popular with industrial and commercial employers, now dominating affairs in Wick. A large Anti-Corn Law meeting was held in the Town Hall on the 19 February, 1839, the Hall 'crowded to suffocation', the largest 'assemblage' in the Town Hall since it was opened. More than eighty 'respectable inhabitants' had signed the requisition for the meeting to be held. Provost Rhind took the chair.

Four resolutions were raised and passed, and a Petition to Parliament was agreed too. One of the resolutions was moved by David Bremner, who 'pointed out the mischievous effects of the present corn laws, and their hurtful and baneful effects on the commercial and trading interests of the county.' Wick, of course, as a very active centre of the export trade, had a vital direct interest in the removal of these laws, maintained during and since the Napoleonic War as a means, supposedly, of ensuring that farmers got a good price for their corn by restricting foreign imports until the price reached a certain level, since higher prices for bread had a bearing on wages that had to be paid to fish and factory workers.[2]

1 *JOGJ*, 3 February, 1837.
2 Though strongly supported by the working classes, especially in Lancashire, the Anti-Corn agitation was led mainly by middle-class industrialists and business-men, the most charismatic and dedicated to whose interest were John Bright and Richard Cobden. Bright and Cobden were passionate Liberals and in favour of much amelioration of the lot of working people, but it has to be said that in the *(continued on foot of next page)*

Benjamin Kennedy, moving the fourth resolution, in a flood of typical wordy eloquence, full of concern, compassion and condemnation,

> observed that the practice of shrouding the question of the corn laws in mystery, and thereby rendering it inexplicable to those who suffered most from its effects, though successful for a time, had at length been seen through. The industrious poor man had a right to purchase the staff of life from where and from whom he pleased – yet, here were laws on the Statute Book of a free country, which denied him this privilege. Mr Kennedy afterwards argued at some length on their ruinous effects on our commerce, and adverted to the fearful falling off for some years experienced in our exports of manufactured goods to foreign countries. He maintained their continuance of the system would ultimately drive the British manufacturer from the field, cripple the resources of the Empire and bring ruin and starvation among the most useful members of the community, the working classes.

The corn laws benefited nobody but the landowners. In the indignant words of Benjamin Kennedy,

> even the farmers, instead of reaping any profit from the corn laws, were deprived by them of those comforts, necessities and benefits which they had a right to enjoy from their own industry. The great body of the small farmers wished them wholly done away with. Rackrented and distressed as they were, they derived no benefit from such laws. They could not enjoy the fruits of their own earnings; and save meal and a few potatoes, the poor tenants never tasted any of the produce of their own farms.

The fourth resolution, seconded by James Bremner, along with all the other resolutions, *was* 'carried enthusiastically, and amid thunders of applause.' A hundred names 'were affixed to both Petitions [not one but two!] and we understand that no less than 750 signatures are now attached to it.'[1]

(continued from foot of previous page) minds of many employers supporting the movement was the belief that cheaper bread for their workers might enable them to pay lower wages, often pitifully low anyway. The Anti-Corn Law Leaguers and the Chartists clashed on this issue, the Chartists believing that with abolition the capitalists intended to 'cheat the working class'.

1 *JOGJ*, 22 February, 1839. The Corn Law of 1815 prohibited the import of foreign corn until the home price reached 80s (£4) the quarter; corn *(continued on foot of next page)*

Obituary

In a sense it was a happy circumstance that the *Journal* arrived on the scene at the fortuitous moment for printing a dignified obituary of Sir John Sinclair of Ulbster, who died on 23 December, 1835, at the age of 82, for there was no other organ in Wick before this time either available or competent to present such a public tribute. The two well researched columns recited Sir John's achievements and identified him, rightly, as an 'individual whose highest pride' the County might call its own, a man to whose 'unremitting and strenuous exertions, it may be said, Caithness principally owes its present importance'.

The paper comments on his academic prowess, 'the taste he acquired for the study of Political Economy, under the celebrated Adam Smith', his varied and numerous publications in particular the *Statistical Account of Scotland,* the stimulus which his 'unceasing exertions have given to the now marked improvement in our farming system', but, above all,

> it is not as an Agriculturist alone that Sir John Sinclair has conferred lasting benefit on Caithness. With him originated the British Fisheries Society's Establishment in Pulteneytown, and the rapid rise of that flourishing and important place; and to his unwearied efforts do we principally owe the construction of a harbour at that port, which, by the facilities it afforded, and the encouragement it offered to all individuals at that time embarked in the prosecution of the Herring Fisheries, has raised that increasing department of British commerce to a height, in this County, far surpassing our most sanguine anticipations, and unequalled in extent by any other place in the kingdom.

As a footnote the *Journal* revealed that lately Sir John had 'been occupied in attempting to procure a grant for the erection of a Breakwater in the Bay of Wick.' It is, perhaps, just as well that Sir John did not live to see the ultimate and disastrous collapse of that project.

(*continued from foot of previous page*) from the British colonies could enter when the price was 67s the quarter. Though a modifying sliding scale was introduced during the 1820s, the landed interest was adamantly opposed to abolition. The Anti-Corn Law League was formed in 1838. In 1841 Cobden got into Parliament 'where he kept the subject to the fore'. The Melbourne Whig government had attempted abolition, and fell on that account in 1841. Robert Peel came in as Prime Minister, pledged to maintain the Corn Laws. He it was, however, who led the government that in 1846 abolished them, unable any longer to resist public pressure. James Loch, MP for the Northern Burghs was, of course, an opponent of the Corn Laws.

Our Staple Commodity.

Fittingly, alongside the columns of the obituary to the man, who more than anyone else had brought the herring fishery to Wick, lay a column and a half on *Clupea harengus* itself. No informed technical published comment on the creature that was making Wick's fortune had been possible before this first issue of the *John O'Groat Journal*, since no suitable vehicle had before existed. This told of how the herring army (the very name 'herring' it attributes to the German *heer*, 'a host') swarms down from the northern seas, seeking suitably warmer waters in which to spawn, very conveniently for Britain arriving in British waters just at the time when they can be most readily caught in masses. All the causes of this massive migration, says the article, are not fully understood. Though they are caught mostly in the summer season, 'a fact known to many in this place', is 'that herrings of an excellent quality have been caught in considerable numbers at the mouth of the Bay of Wick, with nets, in the middle of winter.' The piece ends with an informative titbit of explanation, probably not known before to many Wickers, that

> Flanders had the honour of inventing the art of pickling herrings. One William Beauklen, or Peaulken, of Beverlet near Sluys, hit on this useful expedient. Beauklen died in 1397. The Emperor Charles V. held his memory in such an estimation, for the service he has done to mankind, as to do his tomb the honour of a visit.

Faithful to its self-imposed brief, the *John O'Groat Journal* reported regularly and copiously on the herring trade, becoming a virtual national organ on the subject. During the season the *Journal* published detailed weekly records of the state of the trade, number of boats fishing from Wick and neighbouring centres, weather conditions, prices on the market, sizes of catch and averages per boat. In the late August and early September issues, as the season ended, there were often comparative statistics, showing for instance, average catches per boat over a run of years. For example the issue of 27 August, 1841 gives such a run over six years:

1836	Average catch per boat (during season)	48 crans
1837	" " Ditto " "	75 crans
1838	" " Ditto " "	110 crans
1839	" " Ditto " "	105 crans
1840	" " Ditto " "	85 crans
1841	" " Ditto " "	105 crans

Conditions at sea and variations of the size and location of shoals were the chief reasons for variations, rather than state of the market. Though there was some forward dealing, prices in general were determined after rather than in anticipation of the catch, but the conditions of the harvest could not easily be forecast. The low level of catch in 1840 was regarded as something of a disaster. 'Boats have been much hindered in getting to sea', it was reported on 4 September; the catch for the whole of the current week was 7½ crans per boat. No boats were going out some days, 'owing to boisterous weather. Fishermen have become restless and anxious for their homes; and the term of the engagement of hired men expires this week.' A 'stop-press' little notice reads:

> Special Notice: Wick, Friday morning, 7 o'clock.
> The few boats which put out to sea last night, have, we understand, all returned, but without fish, none of them measuring the cran.

In the same issue the price of staves for barrels is given, and curers are said to be laying in stocks since these prices are low. Also, there is information about catches, number of boats etc. from many of the other east coast fishing centres, Lybster, Helmsdale, Hopeman, Findhorn, Fraserburgh, Peterhead, Anstruther, Orkney. This kind of reporting was continued through the century and beyond, and was used by Malcolm Gray as a prime source of information in writing his *Scottish Fishing Industry*. About 1873 the publishers of the *Journal* set up a specialist paper, the *Herring Journal* which dealt with trade details, and this was published until the 1930s when the trade began significantly to decline.

Anecdotes Relative to the Early History of Caithness.

The first article in a series that continued in many subsequent issues of the *Journal*, appeared in the first issue, in pursuance of the editorial promise of interesting *Miscellany*. It dealt with origins in Caithness, the *Catti*, the Cheynes and the 'Harrolds and their successors, of Danish and Norwegian descent' who came to rule in Caithness. Its unrevealed author was the father of the editor, Captain Robert Kennedy. This piece ends with the first account of blood and violence that appeared in this notably peace-minded Journal, the story of the Bishop of Caithness, who, in 1198, came to a bad end after 'repeated acts of great oppression and tyranny'; how the bishop on his way home from Wick to his episcopal palace in Scrabster, and riding through Sibster, attended only by his servants, observed the disorderly troop of [the 'ferocious and infuriated populace', egged on by the Earl] coming forward to meet him; and, suspecting some design against himself, rode off full speed to the right, towards a place since called *Killmster*, or *Kill-minster*, thinking by changing his course, to have avoided this band of desperadoes. Having, however, been observed and pursued, he alighted from his horse at a farm-house, and, to save his life, which he had some apprehension was aimed at, took shelter in a kind of hiding-hole, with which most houses in those days were provided, and which is still, or was very lately to be seen, communicating from the house to the corn-yard, under which it extended for a considerable distance. Here, however, his savage pursuers detected him and having put him to death, they instantly proceeded to cutting his body in pieces and *boiling it* – thus carrying out the hint dropt by the Earl into execution *ad literam.*

Fortunately for the many squabbling divines of later times, this drastic method of dealing with recalcitrant priests passed out of use. In any case, it is a rather dubious tale.

This first issue of the *Journal* is graced by a sample of the kind of verse that is found in many later issues; the quoting of one verse of which will suffice to give the flavour:

>Ye who invoke the tuneful 'nine,'
>Whose tastes to Poesy incline,
>Whose minds imbibe the 'art devine,'
>   Deign aid to give;
>Shine brightly – in our pages shine,
>   And make them live.

The invocation was not in vain. The Muses did not desert the poets who appeared most weeks in the *John O'Groat Journal*. Its interest in *poesie* attracted to the paper in 1841 a correspondent who claimed a certain Aeneas Mackintosh as the authentic author of the 'Burial of Sir John Moore'.[1] The claim was not disputed, at least, not in the columns of the *Journal.*

Later issues of the *Journal* will supply us with snippets, indeed, tracts of information for future reference, though we shall not always follow the example of the *Journal* as to length of treatment of topics.

1 *JOGJ*, 30 April, 1841.

Faithful to its own rule on 28 April, the *Journal* fulfilled its promise to represent the interests of the 'humbler' ranks in society. This took the form of a letter from 'An Operative' and the column was entitled 'Remarks and Observations by One of the Working Class'. Whether or not this composition came from a genuine workman, it was eloquent on priorities (some of which appeared next year among the six points of the 'Charter'), cheap bread, lower taxation, reform of the army, the law, the introduction of state education, annual parliaments, vote by ballot, extension of the franchise, in fact a proper share for working men in the rising prosperity of the nation.[1]

Royal Occasions.

Radical though their general posture was, the *John O'Groat Journal's* proprietor and editor were at all times anxious to prove their loyalty to constitution and crown, and in their pages expressed themselves effusively on all royal occasions. The first such opportunity was the 'Demise of William the Fourth – our beloved, our venerated Sovereign', who died on 20 June (in fact, one of the more harmless but least venerated of all British sovereigns). Mourning was indicated in many columns of the issue by the printing of long black stripes down the length of the paper (now full sheet).

Under the heading 'Local Intelligence' was reported the 'Proclamation of Her Majesty Queen Victoria', on 26th June, when 'a little before one o'clock, the Magistrates, Town Council, Merchants, and a considerable number of the respectable inhabitants of Wick and Pulteneytown, assembled by order of the Sheriff-Substitute of the County in the Town Hall of this place.' From here the 'whole body proceeded in procession, three abreast, to the Cross of the Royal Burgh, all dressed in deep mourning,' when the Proclamation was read and 'was responded to by the hearty and simultaneous cheers of the numerous persons present.'[2]

The gentlemen 'then returned to the Town Hall where an excellent collation had, in the meantime been prepared. The young queen's health was drunk in a 'full, a flowing, and loyal bumper'. Mr Gregg took the chair, and the Rev Mr Phin followed with 'an impressive

---

1 *JOGJ*, 28 April, 1837. The six points of the Charter, formally proposed in Birmingham in 1838 were (1) manhood suffrage, (2) abolition of the property qualification, (3) equal electoral districts (4) vote by ballot, (5) payment of members of parliament, (6) annual parliaments.
2 *JOGJ*, 30 June, 1837.

prayer suitable to the occasion'. Mr Gregg proposed the toast, asking that 'her most gracious Majesty, our Sovereign Liege Lady Victoria, Queen of the United Kingdom of Great Britain and Ireland' be 'blessed with many days to reign over the great United Kingdom, pre-eminent among the nations in power and grandeur, and long may she enjoy the exalted happiness of governing a people whom Providence has committed to her charge, as did her royal ancestors, in a spirit of justice and mercy, in righteousness and peace, and receive her reward in the gratitude and affection of a free and loyal people.' After this the 'memory of William IV was proposed', and another bumper was drunk 'in solemn silence'. From this time on, Queen Victoria, blessed with more than sixty glorious years, appeared often in the columns of the loyal *John O'Groat Journal*.

The first of these appearances was the much trumpeted marriage of the Queen to Albert, Prince of Saxe-Coburg-Gotha. This was announced early in 1840 in a complimentary piece on the young, but at this stage, completely unknown prince, from a minor German state. The forthcoming marriage was referred to the following week, in the young monarch's Speech to Parliament; soon after that Wick's preparations to celebrate the occasion were discussed. William Waters, President of the newly formed Total Abstinence Society, made his mark in the issue for 7 February with an elaborately worded Loyal Address to the Queen, and the next issue carried full accounts of the Royal Wedding itself, held on 10 February, 1840, and of the 'Demonstrations at Wick'.[1]

Wick could never before have had a day quite like this. There was a public holiday and the town was festively decorated and illuminated, the illuminations so numerous and so brilliant, and on such an extensive scale, that modestly the *Journal* writers found it 'right out of their power to enter into any detail'. They would add, however, that 'in the midst of the universal blaze, so remarkable on this occasion, the public offices, the houses of the authorities, and those of the various official gentlemen were particularly conspicuous.' Many ordinary citizens also 'appeared anxious, according to their respective means, to evince that feeling of joy which a union so auspicious as that of our beloved Queen has awakened in their breasts.' Some houses and hotels had illuminated transparencies in their windows; the *Journal* writer was, however, unable to suppress his dreadful propensity for punning in reporting that some citizens had

1 *JOGJ*, 3 December, 1841.

gone to great *panes* to make their loyalty *shine* through.

Writing of the scene at Pulteneytown harbour, the *Journal* man excelled himself in highly coloured verbal confusion. All the vessels were 'gorgeously decorated',

> with flags, and this, together with the salvoes of cannon coming from the *Alderman Thomson,* which continued from morning until dusk, as also the merry peal from the church bell, as well as that of the town, added not a little to the enlivening appearance of the scene. As is his wont, no one was more active on this occasion than our respected townsman, James Bremner, shipbuilder, to whose exertions we are indebted for the continual roar of artillery that saluted our ears the greater part of the day. Mr Bremner had ingeniously contrived to hoist and fire a small cannon at the fore-top of his vessel, the *Alderman Thomson,* and from its commanding position this piece of artillery did its duty most effectively, and as we say of orators, actors and singers, to the admiration of all who heard it.[1]

There was a bonfire 'in which a boat, tar barrels and other combustible materials were consumed,' adding to the 'enjoyment of the evening.' At Leith's Hotel there was a great public dinner, and at the Town Hall the day concluded with a Ball. The Total Abstainers of Thurso held a Soirée though there is no mention of what they did in Wick.

The next royal event to call forth demonstrations of enthusiastic loyalty was, as might have been expected, the birth of the Prince of Wales, on 19 November, 1841. 'Along with millions of our fellow subjects,' declared the *Journal,* 'heartily do we sympathise in the important event which has spread much joy over all the country.'[2] The next after that was not in the schedule; this was rejoicing at the failure of a foiled assassination attempt on the Queen by a sixteen-year-old boy who was arrested carrying a pistol loaded with 'coarse powder, some pieces of tobacco pipe and gravel . . . . . The would-be assassin was tried, condemned to death,' and the *Journal* was pleased to report his sentence was commuted to transportation for life.[3] Kennedy, it may be added, had several times in his paper advocated abolition of the death penalty as a quite useless and vicious form of punishment. He would have been interested but not surprised to know that it

1 *JOGJ,* 14 February, 1840.
2 *JOGJ,* 3 December, 1841.
3 *JOGJ,* 28 April, 1843.

would take over a hundred years for that reform to come in.

The black lining appeared round entire pages again in 1843, when the death of the Duke of Sussex was reported.[1] It is doubtful if many Wickers had the least idea of who this gentlemen was, but he earned obsequies and an obituary in Britain's most northerly newspaper. He was, in fact, the brother of the Duke of Kent, father of the Queen, who had died some time before and to whom, William, Duke of Kent, committed the care of the young queen, still a minor on her accession.

One less than royal death report (of a very few lines) was framed with (thin) black lines at about this time, that of Lord Duffus, the former Sir Benjamin Dunbar, a landlord gentleman whose relations with the royal burgh of Wick had not always been the most cordial. He was, however, a 'decided Liberal'. He went to lie with his forefathers in the Dunbar mausoleum in Wick.[2]

AN OUTRAGEOUS AND RECKLESS PLACE

It was not very often that the *John O'Groat Journal* had the opportunity of describing crowd gatherings of a more sinister kind that those of joyful royalists. Nevertheless, eleven years after the *Journal* was founded such an occasion arose. It was well enough to assemble to send petitions to parliament on the Corn Laws; it was quite another thing to gather in crowds to flout the law, even though the issue was the people's bread.

There was a crisis of government late in 1845, in which Sir Robert Peel found himself under intense pressure to open the ports to let in grain, at least temporarily, as a means of relieving the mass starvation now afflicting the Irish and western islanders of Scotland as the result of failure, two years running, of the potato crop. In June 1846 the Corn Laws were abolished. It was, of course, impossible to relieve the distress of these years by such a single stroke, and in any case the benefit in lower bread prices was only marginal in communities so poor and depressed and considerable hardship was being experienced in most of the Scottish fishing towns and villages.

The people of such places were especially resentful of the shipment of grain away from their own localities. Caithness and other places on the east coast of Scotland had been accustomed to such exports, and the merchants saw no good reason for stopping their customary trade

1 *JOGJ*, 28 April, 1843.
2 *JOGJ*, 3 February, 1843.

whatever the extent of food shortages in their areas, imagined or real. In the winter of 1846 'food disturbances' broke out in a number of places along the east coast of Scotland. On 5 February, 1847, the *John O'Groat Journal* carried the startling news that in Wick a 'turbulent spirit' had driven crowds of people into the streets to demonstrate against the decision of local corn merchants to export locally grown grain. The procession down to the harbour had been led by a piper and a drummer, and some windows had been broken on the way. There was news, too, that similar demonstrations had occurred in Evanton, Lossiemouth, Findhorn, Garmouth, Elgin and Burghead. A contingent of the 76th Regiment had been sent from Aberdeen to keep the peace in Fraserburgh.

A week later things got worse in Wick. On Monday, 8 February, a crowd had assembled and marched to Pulteneytown where 'a small vessel was laid on for the purpose of taking on board a cargo of grain for the south.' The crowd blocked up the quay and prevented the loading. Attempts were to be made the following day to ship the grain. This was a 'stormy day', with the result that 'all outside labour was suspended' thus making the crowd larger. At 12 o'clock a cart was taken to the store, two sacks of grain were loaded; when it reached High Street, 'a long loud cheer burst from the crowd, who accompanied it to the south end of the bridge, where such a complete blockade was made by the mob, that the parties in charge of the cart had to turn the horse's head and retrace their steps.' There were more loud cheers. The matter had been reported to Mr Gregg, Sheriff-Substitute, who forthwith had sworn in a number of men as special constables, of whom, however, only six emerged from the court-house 'when their services were required'.

Sheriff Gregg came out and attempted to tell the crowd that there was plenty of food for the district, and warned them of the danger they were running in making an assembly; but the crowd continued to grow and Gregg ordered the Town Clerk, Mr Mackenzie to read the Riot Act, which had little effect.

The attempt to take the cart to the harbour was repeated, but although the Sheriff was joined by the Provost, the Procurator Fiscal and other officials, together with the special constables who had ventured to come out, the official procession was obliged to return; they were followed back 'by an immense assemblage, cheering, yelling, hissing and hooting. Finding it quite impossible to carry shipment into effect, no further attempt was made, and accordingly the mob took to pelting several of the officials with snowballs.' Fortunately, 'not the slightest injury was done to anyone. We believe,' wrote the reporter, 'that precognition has been gone into since this occurrence, but nothing definite has transpired as to what the authorities have resolved on doing.' For the moment this was how things remained. There were reports of 'meal riots' in Invergordon and Cromarty, and of a riot also in Thurso where an effigy was burned – it does not say whose effigy. The *Journal* added that there was a destitution in villages along the east coast, in fact, 'a state of alarming want'.[1]

A fortnight later matters became much more serious. Popular feeling rose high when it was learned that a shipment of grain was intended, and on Friday evening, 19 February, a great crowd formed again in Bridge Street, headed by a piper. They marched through to Pulteneytown and down to North Quay where they threw half a dozen boats across the fairway to the quay, 'forming a barricade still more formidable than those they had erected on previous occasions.' The mob then went along alongside the vessel; and, 'in an astonishingly short space of time' piled on board a heap of stones which they had brought from quite a distance. They had, apparently intended then to take the vessel out to sea, and presumably to sink her, 'but this was not carried out'.

At midnight, 'ballasting completed,' Sheriffs Thomson and Gregg, along with Mr Henderson, the Procurator Fiscal, 'went to the scene of operations, but most of the mob by this time had made their way up the Quay.' Things remained quiet for the rest of the night, and as the next day was Sunday, nothing more happened. On Monday there was 'not a little excitement' as a rumour circulated that the 'military were hourly expected by a government steamer.' In fact, the Sheriff had made contact with the commander of the 76th Regiment in Aberdeen, and it was true that a contingent of soldiers was in the offing. The soldiers were aboard the lighthouse steamer *Pharos*. She arrived in Wick Bay about midday, 'but as a considerable surf was rolling, no landing could be affected nearer than Ackergill, where the steamer immediately went.'

Here the officer commanding the contingent, Captain Evans Gordon, was met by the Procurator Fiscal. There were two companies of infantry from the 76th Regiment aboard, 104 men in all.

1 *JOGJ*, 12 February, 1847.

Arrangements were made for them to disembark but 'the fishermen refused to aid and to lend the use of boats for the purpose.' A few small boats were found, and the ship's crew and a coastguard with them manned the boats, getting the men ashore in an operation that took two hours. They were 'soon arranged in a military order on Ackergill beach. A sight so unusual in this county, created an immense sensation, and accordingly the road from Wick to Ackergill was literally thronged throughout the day.'

The soldiers entered the town in military order, bayonets fixed, the 'whole streets and every window being crowded with anxious spectators,' as they were drawn up, two deep before the Court House. Then they were marched to the Temperance Hall which had been commandeered as a temporary barracks. Nothing further happened this day, for the soldiers were just off the sea and had a 'worn out and jaded appearance;' but a day or two's rest tended 'to resuscitate their vigour. There was no noise anywhere in the evenings; except for 'a few drunken Buckiemen all was peace and order.'

On the Wednesday, on the order of the Sheriff a 'large number of inhabitants assembled in the Town Hall.' They were sworn in as special constables, told their duties, and at 1 o'clock a procession, headed by the Sheriff and Magistrates set off for the grain store in Pulteneytown; 'after tedious delay for want of men, a cart of grain was carried to the vessel. This was done in the most peaceable manner.' A large crowd gathered, 'attracted by the novel sight of some 200 special constables, most of them with batons.' No attempt was made to obstruct the loading of the grain. The job was not finished. The story from here on is best told by the reporter himself:

> Finding that the parties who had the grain to ship had not made the proper arrangements, the constables began to grumble; . . most had business to attend to. They promised to be on call when the shippers were ready; Sheriff Thomson seeing the justice of these remarks dismissed the constables. A signal was to be given when they were required.
>
> A party of musketeers marched down the Quay to watch the vessel during the night, and here commenced the most alarming part of the whole proceedings. How a mob was created, there are various statements; one thing is certain, previous to the arrival of the military at the Quay, the street presented the usual features of ordinary days. About seven o'clock, the whole remaining body of the soldiery quickly

marched to join their comrades, on a shot being fired from the party on the Quay. At this time there was great excitement among the great crowd, men, women and children . . Deep anxiety was depicted on every countenance.

Rather pusillanimously, seeing that this was the very first time that the *Journal* people had ever found themselves near enough to a really exciting event, they kept away:

Judging those safest who kept in doors, or, at all events, at a safe distance, we did not personally visit the spot, but from the numerous eye-witnesses we learn that great excitement prevailed.

The Sheriff and Provost were present among the mob who surrounded the military on all hands. The Riot Act was read by the Sheriff, but it had no effect. The feeling of the inhabitants was raised to the highest possible pitch, for a direct collision was expected every hour . . . The soldiers divided into several parties and were ordered to disperse the mob, at the point of the bayonet. In this attempt several were wounded, but only slightly . . . The soldiers continued parading in different directions, with the effect of scattering the crowd. Three persons were taken and lodged in jail.

As the party was walking back from Pulteneytown to quarters, when immediately under the brae where the Academy is erected, a volley of stones were thrown by individuals on the top of the brae, and the Sheriff and Provost were both struck. The soldiers were immediately ordered by the Sheriff to fire, and we deeply regret to say that two individuals, a man and a girl, were wounded. The man, William Hougston, former cooper of Mr David Davidson, did not form part of the crowd, nor was he with them at the time. According to his own statement, which seems highly probable, he was proceeding quietly home. A ball went through his right hand, which was so shockingly mutilated that the fingers had to be cut off, and it is even doubtful if a farther amputation will have to be made. The other, a girl named Macgregor, was wounded in the left arm, the ball passing through the fleshy part, but we believe that the damage done was not dangerous. About the time, it is impossible to depict the state of excitement which was visible in every direction. Men, women and children fled, on hearing the report of musketry, and on learning that damage had been done. Parents were anxiously running in search of their children, while the crowd were giving expression to the most vociferous shouts and yells. Soon after, with the exception of the guard at the vessel, all the military were ordered to their quarters, but throughout the greater part of the night groups of inhabitants were assembled at every corner, when the unpleasant events of the evening were canvassed. Nothing, however, occurred to produce a breach of the peace.

Continuing his researches afterwards, the *Journal* man established that 'the soldiers suffered a continuous and most aggravating series of assaults from the crowd, and not a few of them were wounded. Some of them were seized with staves, with which they struck the soldiers; one in particular struck an officer twice, when she received a pretty severe sword cut. Stones were thrown from various directions.' A great many were wounded but not seriously by the bayonets. The girl and the man who were shot were 200 yards away from one another when the shots occurred. The girl soon recovered but Mr Hougston's wrist joint 'was entirely destroyed.' Another man had the sole of his shoe shot off and another had his boot split with a ball while 'sitting on the brae, and watching the proceedings'.[1]

A meeting was held in the Town Hall the following evening, 'crowded to suffocation'; but there were few speeches. The meeting is reported to have approved the action of the authorities, requesting, however, the immediate removal of the military.

A later meeting in the Town Hall, chaired by Josiah Rhind, the Provost, heard and approved of a motion deprecating the conduct of the Sheriff in ordering the military to fire, indeed, of a calling in the military at all.[2] The whole episode was raised in the House of Commons on 4 March, when Sir A L Hay asked the Lord Advocate for Scotland for a report on what had happened at Wick on the occasion of a riot when the populace had been dispersed 'by means of the bayonet', after which the military had 'fired on them, by which several people were severely wounded.' The Lord Advocate replied at some length, giving in effect the details more or less as reported by the *John O'Groat Journal*, but adding some drawn from the officers' reports of the incident, to the effect that:

1 *JOGJ*, 26 February, 1847.
2 *JOGJ*, 5 March, 1847.

> The people assembled in very great numbers, and obstructed all access to the quay. They assaulted one of the officers in command of the party, and many of the soldiers, and rendered it necessary to send down the whole military force to the assistance and protection of their comrades. In the passage of the force through the town they were most violently assaulted by the mob, and several persons were with great difficulty seized . . . While a detachment of military were under a piece of high ground or eminence, the mob, armed with large stones, assaulted them from above. The report of the military officers stated, that the party was attacked by a tremendous volley of stones, by which many of them were struck and severely injured. It was in these circumstances that orders were given to fire; and a few shots were discharged, more, he believed, for the purpose of frightening the mob than inflicting any injury, though, unfortunately, injury had, he was sorry to say, been received.

The Lord Advocate added that he believed that the Sheriff had acted correctly, and that he was 'a man of not only of humanity, but of great firmness of purpose. 'There was, however, one thing that the Lord Advocate could not understand,' and that was

> the conduct of the Provost of Wick [Josiah Rhind], who appeared to have presided at a public meeting, in which imputations that he must have known were unfounded, were cast on the conduct of the Sheriff of the county. With reference to the preceedings in which the Sheriff had acted, not only with the concurrence of the Provost but the other magistrates of the burgh on grounds that he must have known to be untrue.[1]

There were no further repercussions, but the *Journal* editor and some of the city fathers were highly indignant about a report carried on 25 March in the *Daily News* which, according to the *Journal*, had the 'malicious intention of representing Wick as one of the most outrageous and reckless of places.' According to the report 'the spirit and state of the people' was as 'unsatisfactory as possible:' it had been led, said the *News*, by a 'Chartist enthusiast, a carpenter, utterly uninstructed, but gifted with a great memory and flow of words.' With a peculiar contradiction in the next sentences, it was revealed that this 'uninstructed Chartist' had been *instructed* by a writer 'in the pay of Tories'. The bulk of landowners were Tories, and they had a

---

1 *JOGJ*, 12 March, 1847.

vested interest in throwing the lower classes into the 'hands of these men by the short-sighted selfishness of the fishcurers, who, after encouraging the unthrifty habits of the fishermen for years, to serve their own ends, tried to throw the burden of supporting them off our shoulders on the failures of fishing and then potato crop.' The logic of this argument was tortuous, as no doubt the readers of the *Journal* were intended to think. The editor shrieked: *There was no riot!*[1]

And, it may be added, there is no evidence of Chartist involvement in the Wick 'Disturbances'. Most of the unwelcome visitors embarked in Wick Bay on Monday, 1 March, to take care of things in Thurso, whose citizens, not to be outdone by those of Wick, had also taken to the streets in similar cause. There followed in Thurso an episode matching that of Wick, with yellings and hootings, throwing stones and attempts to stop grain being loaded. There was no shooting. Wick was not, however, to be without its military guardians for the time being; a few of the original detachment were left, and having decamped to the Parochial Schools, their place was taken in the Temperance Hall by a detachment of Enniskillens from Fort George, a troop of 145. They brought with them the body of Private Robert Aitchison, who had died on the way. Wick was thus treated to the spectacle of a military funeral, which the *Journal* duly reported:

> The body of Aitchison was consigned to its narrow tomb with the usual military honours. A funeral procession was accomplished into the Church-yard, by an immense concourse of spectators, both young and old, to whom a soldier's funeral was a novel sight. There was no funeral service performed, but we believe that devotional exercises were privately engaged in, by the Rev. Charles Thomson, previously to removal of the body from the Town House. After the usual salute the party returned to Temperance Hall.[2]

One thing soon made clear to the inhabitants of Wick in the coming weeks, was that they were not on their own; similar disturbances – not, however, usually involving the military – were going on up and down the Scottish fishing coasts. In most places the issue was that of 'exporting' grain. At Dingwall there was a 'disgraceful outrage' when the magistrates tried to enrol special constables 'but few chose to come forward'. Here the mob did not quite succeed in nefarious plans to mix the oats, barley and wheat that they found in a warehouse, 'so

1 *JOGJ*, 26 March, 1847.
2 *JOGJ*, 27 February, 1847.

Fig 37 Headquarters of the *John O'Groat Journal*.

that they could not be taken away.' The naughty ones were seen to be mainly 'females and boys'.[1]

What later editions still of the *John O'Groat Journal* also made evident to those interested in affairs (and especially in the issues of the early months of the following year, 1848), was that Scotland, and to a small extent Wick itself, was taking part in a major process of social and political upheaval in Europe as a whole. Historians have dubbed 1848 'the Year of Revolutions'. Hardly any country of Europe was not disturbed by revolutionary fervour and revolt. Paris, Vienna, Rome, Mannheim and Heidelberg, Munich and Budapest were all affected, and for several months a number of countries, including France, Italy and Hungary had revolutionary governments. Ireland was a scene of sometimes violent agitation. Britain was not exempt. There were riots in Glasgow, where the military were called out, and in London was staged in April, 1848, the great Chartist demonstration on Kennington Common, from where the 'Monster Petition' to Parliament in favour of the Six Points set out on its journey to Westminster. Unlike most of the other European capitals, London shrugged off revolution without

1 *JOGJ*, 12 March, 1847.

much violence and with no bloodshed. At Wick, the previous year, just a little blood was shed, and not for Chartism or revolution.

POETS CORNER

In its opening pages the *John O'Groat Journal* invoked the attention of the Muses. Week by week from then on there was one – sometimes two – pieces of verse, some of it dripping in maudlin sentimentality, some touchingly sincere; veins of bitterness and irony ran through much of the verse, often cast in the form of parody. The verse frequently had direct reference to current themes of the *Journal* and, among other things, illustrated the variety of poetic tastes and skills of contemporary Caithnessian versifiers for topical rhyming comment.

One from 1840, takes up the Anti-Corn Law theme:

To our Masters:

> Ye squires, who think that sea and land
>   Are made alone for you,
> 'Tis time that you should understand
>   They are for poor folk too.
>
> Earth was not made that you might squeeze
>   Rent out of every rood, -
> Nor man's great highway of the seas
>   To close against men's food.
>
> Nor man with ill requited toil
>   To wear out strength and health,
> That greedy usurers of the soil
>   Might roll in ill-got wealth.
>
> Earth, our kind mother's feast is spread
>   For us poor sons of clay,
> But from our lips the proffered bread
>   By you is dashed away.
>
> Earth brings forth plenty, and the sea
>   Would waft it to our shores;
> But the rich freight, by your decree,
>   Must rot in foreign shores.

VOICE OF THE PEOPLE

For plenty is a hateful thing
  To landlord parliaments, -
It makes the poor man's heart to sing,
  But lowers the rich man's rents.
Oh, landed law-makers! are these
  The fruits of what ye do?
For us toil, hunger, want, disease -
  Gold and its gifts for you.
Must we, then, hear our little ones
  Cry all in vain for bread?
That your fine daughters and your sons
  On dainties may be fed?
Our wives once were neat and nice,
  Must they go dressed in rags,
That you with bread's extorted price,
  May fill your bursting bags?
The price of bread, the price of blood!
  The tax is on the lives,
Which stints the necessary food
  Whereby the body thrives.
Down then, with the starvation laws!
  Away with this life tax!
Off with the muzzle from our jaws!
  This burden from our backs!
Hear! for we swear by our dear lives
  Of each man's family! -
Yea, by our children and our wives,
  Our bread untaxed shall be.

None of the contributing poets was of laureate calibre, though in one issue the *Journal* printed the actual Laureate's 'Ode' on the occasion of the Prince Consort's election as Chancellor of Cambridge University (not one his best effusions).

Caller Herring is from 1847.

  All is bustle, hurry-hurry
  When the July suns appear, -
  Curers, gutters, crews and coopers,
  All to stations now repair.

Chorus: O, for the herring, call'r herring,
  Caught and gutted ere they spawn, -
  Caller herring, plump and bonnie,
  Roasted in the frying pan.

  Farlens now are rear'd and rigged, -
  Boats in lunners float the sea -
  Barrel-hoops like timmer mountains,
  Here and there now meet the e'e.*
Chor.

  *Salt and tubs are now at freedom -
  Cellar doors wide open flee;
  All in expectation revel, -
  All is hope, and life, and glee.*
Chor.

  *Canvas gunmouths, oilskin jackets,
  Boots, and hats wi' snouts akin, -
  Snugly stowed away in these are,
  Living, breathing, fishermen.*
Chor.

  *Gentlefolks may think they're happy,
  And clodhopper dream of joy:
  Reaper of our herring harvest,
  Only drink without alloy.*
Chor.

  *Wha like fishermen, sae fearless?
  None more useful, all agree:
  Like to him who o'er the wavetop,
  Brings the riches of the sea.*

Chorus: O, for the herring, call'r herring,
  Caught and gutted ere they spawn, -
  Caller herring, plump and bonnie,
  Roasted in the frying pan.

* An Aberdeen colloquialism for the curing trough.

An unsavoury topic mentioned from time to time in the *Journal* was that of public hygiene in the two towns. A social poet of 1847 is scathing about the streets of Pulteneytown, and in case they felt left out, folk of Wick are also castigated, in

VOICE OF THE PEOPLE

Rally Round Your Dunghills

Come rally round your dunghills, for fever is begun,
And many victims shall it slay before its work is done.
It loves to roam midst dingy cells, on dunghills and cesspools,
And dirt, and filth, of every kind, it makes its ready tools.
Come Pulteneytown, sit in the dust, let midden-heap arise –
Let smoke and filth and stagnant pools, ascend up to the skies –
Show dunghills in a legion, and dirty streets galore,
'Tis all that fever needs of you – it cannot ask for more.
Ho! householders of Dempster Street, ho! tenants of Bankhead,
See that your 'strans' be well choked up, your streets a hidden bed:-
Ye sojouners of South Toll Bar, look well to your good name,
Of having been in days gone bye, our gude 'Town's greatest shame!'
Breadalbane, Bexley, and other streets of B's,
Come multiply your dirtiness, and let filth sit at ease;
Vansittart, Wellington, Argyll Square and Dunbar,
Come rival in your bravery, in this your filth war.
. . . .
Wick, join in the cleanly train, and Louisbro' fall in -
Kick all your brooms and besoms out – to use them were a pin.
Coach Road of filthy memory, with myriad stinking seas,
That have for years and years defied the purifying breeze
. . . .
Come rally round your dunghills, and let the work proceed -
Disease shall spread its conquering reign, with fever at its head;
Men, women, children, all, shall fall before its power,
While it sits enthroned in majesty, before each dirty door.

An indication of the poem's popularity perhaps, the *Journal* shot off two long parodies during 1847 of Hood's 'Song of the Shirt'. One verse of the more pathetic of the two runs:

With body weary and worn,
  With visage seedy and sad,
A ditcher wrought from early morn,
  With shovel, and pick, and spade.
And still as he delved midst water and clay
He sung to himself from day to day
  The sorrowful 'Song of the Drain'.

> *'Ditch! ditch! ditch!*
> *For twopence an hour I'm here,*
> *Ditch! ditch! ditch!*
> *For twopence an hour each year.*

The Wick poets were sometimes hard to put to for a decent rhyme. Perhaps the *Journal's* most ingenious poetic conceit (of a kind perhaps invented by Lewis Carroll) was its 'Song of the Decanter', with type set in the form of a decanter itself. The *Journal* constantly returned to the temperance theme:

VOICE OF THE PEOPLE

There was an old decanter, and its mouth was gaping wide; the rosy wine had ebbed away and left its crystal side; and the wind went humming - humming, up and down the wind it blew, and through the reed like hollow neck, the wildest notes it blew. I placed it in the window, where the blast was blowing free, and fancied that its pale mouth song the queerest strains to me, 'They tell me – puny conquerors! the Plague has slain his ten, and War his hundred thousand of the very best of men; but I' - 'twas thus the Bottle spake – 'but I have conquered more than all your famous conquerors, so feared and famed of yore! Then come ye youths and maidens all, come drink from out my cup, the beverage that dulls the brain and burns the spirits up; that puts to shame your conquerors that slay their scores below; for this has deluged millions with its lava tide of woe. Tho' in the path of battle darkness streams of blood may roll: yet while I killed the body, I have damned the very soul. The cholera, the plague, the sword, such ruin never wrought, as I, in mirth or malice, on the innocent have brought. And still I breathe upon them, and they shrink before my breath, and year by year my thousands tread the dusty way to death.

---

1 Carroll used the device in the form of a mouse's tail (tale), 'Fury and the Mouse' in *Alice in Wonderland*, but experimented with the tale much earlier in one of his contributions to *Comic Times*.

CHAPTER 15

THOSE IN PERIL

THEY that go down to the sea in ships, that do business in great waters; these see the works of the LORD, and his wonders in the deep. For he commandeth, and raiseth the stormy wind, which lifteth up the waves thereof. They mount up to the heavens, they go down again to the depths; their soul is melted because of their trouble. They reel to and fro, and stagger like a drunken man, and are at their wits' end. Then they cry unto the LORD in their trouble, and he bringeth them out of their distresses. He maketh the storm a calm, so that the waves thereof are still.

Men of Wick during the great days of the herring fishing, had more cause than most to savour these words of the Psalmist – and doubtless heard them often enough in kirk and chapel. For Wick lived by and on the sea, perhaps more immediately and more dangerously than any other town in Britain. When the elements chose to rage, even those not on the sea had a front row view of the terrors of the deep.

Few issues of the *John O'Groat Journal* went without comment on the seas around, and the weather that governed the town's livelihood. One of the earliest of the many graphic storm reports of the *Journal* was that of 9 January, 1839,

> This town and district was visited on Monday evening and Tuesday morning last, by one of the most tremendous gales of wind ever experienced. With the exception of the memorable 'windy Christmas,' about 32 years ago, nothing approaching it in violence had been felt in this county. The wind was from the N.W., and in consequence of the snow which accompanied it being drifted by its fury, numerous large snow wreaths were formed in this place and its neighbourhood, rendering the footpaths in some quarters impassable. On Sunday we had a slight fall of snow, but a thaw having taken place on the evening of that day, it had entirely disappeared on the morning of Monday, which gave indication of fine weather. As the day advanced, however, and night fell, appearances changed, and from 4 o'clock on Monday evening until about 6 on Tuesday morning, the gale continued to blow with a violence which threatened the most serious consequences. The mercury was

unprecedentedly low previous to the change of the weather, and everything denoted a northern hurricane. From the direction in which the wind was, harbours and shipping did not suffer in the smallest, but the injury sustained by many of the buildings in and about the town was considerable. No less than 40 panes of glass were broken, and blown in, in the Parish Church windows, and about 12 in the Town and County Hall. The above mentioned buildings, were, together with the Commercial Bank, particularly exposed to the fury of the wind, and we learn that in the last named, numerous panes were also blown in, lead torn from the roof and other damage sustained. Chimney-cans, slates and tiles were, in many instances, carried off from the houses, and, in some cases, entire chimney stalks were destroyed. The tall stalk on the saw-mill, near Harbour Place, Pulteneytown, was thrown down. The lead on the roof of Rose-Bank House was completely torn off, and canvas has been substituted in the mean time. The violence of the wind on the bridge, but particularly the east end of it, was of such a description as to render crossing it a matter of no small difficulty and danger, and many persons were, in consequence, obliged to postpone their business both in Wick and Pulteneytown, from the impossibility of venturing out. Many of the shop-doors were obliged to be kept shut on the evening of Monday, and, as may be supposed, the business done was of the smallest. From Monday to Wednesday, the mail coach was unable to proceed northward, and in consequence, those which had gone south were detained at Ausdale. The north mail was conveyed by a gig from Thurso to this place on Tuesday morning, and the south was forwarded here by a horseman. It is with much regret that we have been informed that the beautiful house belonging to John Sinclair Esq. of Barrock, also sustained some damage from this storm. One of its stalks of chimnies was thrown down and fell upon the roof, which was in consequence somewhat slightly damaged. A good many panes of glass were also broken and forced in. It gives us pleasure to find that among the numerous disasters we have recorded, there was no loss of life or personal injuries experienced.

 The following notice relative to the state of the Mercury, has been very kindly handed to us by Mr Wm. Bell, watchmaker, Wick: Lowest range of Barometer on Monday morning, half past seven o'clock, 27in. 56. Thermometer in same room, 36. This is the lowest fall on record, since Barometers were first introduced into this county.[1]

Another brief weather report in the same issue told how

> The snow-storm of Tuesday last has been of but short continuance, a gentle thaw having set in on Wednesday evening. It has since continued to do it work, and the ground is now almost clear of its white garb. The weather is by no means settled, however, and it is not improbable that we may be soon visited with a new storm. On Tuesday last the mail coach, on its way north, was fairly upset, near Helmsdale, by the violence of the storm, and broken to pieces. It gives us great pleasure to add, that the passengers, guard and driver, as well as the horses, escaped uninjured.

There are several interesting features in this account. First the language somewhat stilted, pointed up with numerous cliches of the day (the 'fury' of the storm/weather/wind, 'damage sustained', 'stalks' and chimneys 'thrown down') and the tendency (which we have noticed before) to ascribe to the forces of nature a certain malignancy. It is interesting, too, in that the actual report, written out in copper-plate handwriting, was interleaved with the pages of the archive copy of the *Journal*, a museum-piece reminder of the laboriousness of newspaper-making in those days. Copy had to be written out in legible hand-writing so that the typesetters could make a good job of the tedious task of setting type by hand, using 9-point and even smaller fonts. Running a modest weekly local newspaper required the services of several dozen skilled and semi-skilled workers.

A special feature of this storm was that it came across land from the north-west, leaving the harbour and its boats unscathed. Most storms that made later headlines came from the opposite quarters, and the havoc they created made the calamities of 5 January, 1839, seem quite trivial. For the weather that Wickers learned most to fear was that driving westward from the 'German Ocean'.

Yet one other example of the *Journal* writer's penchant for the 'poetic' style may be mentioned before we leave the topic. This was what today we might find an embarrassingly embroidered exercise in weather reporting, about the 'good' weather of January a year earlier:

1 *JOGJ*, 9 January, 1839.

The Weather: Old Father Winter, with his hoary head and gruff voice, has, for the last few days, been a visitor in this quarter. From the fixed and determined face with which he arrived, he seems resolved to make good his lodgement amongst us for some time. Previous to the change in the weather, ploughing had been pursued to a considerable extent; a circumstance which, in the event of our now having a continuance of snow and frost, must make the grub, and other destructive insects, feel very uncomfortable in their earthy domiciles. The earlier winter spreads his white mantle o'er our hills and fields the better; as any encroachment, which he has lately shown an inclination to make, not only on the privileges of spring, but also on those of summer, is always attended by bad effect – through the labouring season behind, and generally leading to a late harvest.[1]

SEA AND SHIPS

For its size and location, there was probably more sea-going from Wick than from any other port in Britain, but then, Wick never attained to the character of a port in the usual sense of the word. Ships of many shapes, sizes and purposes called at Wick, schooners, sloops, smacks and the occasional brig; ships as large as five hundred tons burthen were built at Wick. But none of the larger vessels was ever able to tie up at Wick (or Pulteneytown) quays. The steamer *Sovereign*, plying between Leith and Lerwick from about 1834, usually included a call at Wick in its schedule, on its way north and on the return, but its intending passengers had to be conveyed by lighter or whaleboat from quay to ship as she stood out in the bay, whenever the weather allowed. At one stage there was high protest at the imposition of a fare of sixpence for the transit, payment for which passengers considered ought to be in with the fare for the *Sovereign* itself. Such ferry services from Wick to Holland, Denmark and the northern islands as were ever attempted, failed through difficulties of harbourage and lack of passengers. With the development of Scrabster, especially after the arrival of the railway at Thurso, Wick had little chance of establishing itself as a packet station for Orkney and Shetland.

Wick offered, too, no advantages for coaling and servicing to

1 *JOGJ*, 12 January, 1838.

shipping lines even after the opening of the railway to Wick in 1874, on the same date as at Thurso. Nor did Wick ever have any serious chance of becoming a naval base of any kind. Wick's perennial problems as a seaport were its frequently atrocious weather, blowing directly into the mouth of the Wick river from the North Sea (still usually called the 'German Ocean' in those days), and the tidal shoaling that made both the construction and use of its harbours hazardous.

The Great Britain

In passing, however, we may well note yet again the remarkable career of shipping expert, designer and builder, James Bremner who, through all his many adventures and activities in these connections, remained a highly respected resident of Wick, burgh councillor and no mean contributor to the prosperity of the peculiar twin towns at the mouth of the Wick river. His work has already been described in outline, but he comes back into our picture in connection with two major episodes, the refloating of the *Great Britain* in 1847, and in the following year his involvement in the aftermath of the 'Great Storm' during which Wick suffered its worst disaster.

Bremner's connection with the *Great Britain* had no direct bearing on affairs in Wick, though his reputation as a salvager of wrecks, and in particular his rescue and reconstruction of the *Lord Suffield* in 1836, had brought him to the attention of I K Brunel, who was at his wits' end what to do about his great iron ship, on its first voyage, driven ashore on the sands of Dundrum Bay, Ireland, in November, 1846. The ship was actually intact, and there were some hopes that she might be refloated. Brunel invited Bremner over to Ireland to inspect the wreck, and in January, 1847, his letter on the subject to the shareholders in Bristol was published in the *John O'Groat Journal*. There were, considered Brunel, only two alternatives: break up the ship where she lay on the sands, a proposal to 'be discarded at once'; or, using the expertise of James Bremner, and an expenditure of £40,000 to £60,000, and perhaps three months work, get the *Great Britain* afloat again.

The two engineers met aboard the ship as she lay on her side in the bay, and although they had a difference of opinion as to how to deal with her, without first undertaking repairs on site, Brunel wrote frankly:

Fig 38 *Great Britain* beginning to rise. (from *Illustrated London News, August 21st, 1847*).

I firmly believe that if a man could take her off (and if it would be prudent to let him do so), that Mr Bremner's great experience and sound practical knowledge and good sense in devising any plan, and his energy and skill in carrying it out, would ensure every chance of success which the circumstances admit of.[1]

The company's directors had sufficient trust in Brunel's judgement that they agreed to the expenditure, and Bremner and his workforce spent much of the summer of 1847 in Dundrum Bay, getting ready for the great effort. The *Great Britain* was a ship of 3000 tons, much the biggest ever yet sent to sea, and made of iron, both facts running against almost every traditional notion of sea-worthiness. To have her built and launched at all, was a tremendous act of faith; to invest many more thousands in her rescue, against the instincts of most maritime pundits, was an act of either magnificently greater faith or monumental folly.

The *John O'Groat Journal* made quite a feature of Bremner's success at the end of August, 1847, with the headline, GREAT BRITAIN AFLOAT AGAIN, below which it was reported that 'the gratifying intelligence' had been received on the previous Tuesday, (31 August) that a 'mighty engineering feat' had been accomplished by 'our eminent townsman, Mr Bremner.' The news had excited the 'liveliest satisfaction' and in no time 'all the vessels in the harbour hoisted their colours, and on many places on land the same signals of rejoicing were manifested.' A triumphal arch was raised over Bank Row, on the way to Bremner's yard, and 'the roaring of cannon and musketry, from both sides of the bay, was ever and anon heard. As night advanced, a profusion of fireworks was thrown off, and a large bonfire was kindled. Up to midnight this exhibition of joy continued.'

The *Journal* congratulated Bremner effusively on 'this crowning act of his life,' and trusted that 'he may be long spared to wear the laurels he has now gained.' Mr Brunel was called in evidence to assert 'that if any man in Great Britain could accomplish that which we now record that man was James Bremner.' Then was quoted Bremner's own report of the event prepared for the *North British Mail*.

Formidable preparations had been made for the actual rescue effort, begun on Wednesday, 26 August, with no guarantee of success. However, the team were favoured by a fine day; out in the bay was the *Birkenhead* with steam up; further out still was the *Scourge* at

1 *JOGJ*, 22 January, 1847.

anchor. This was the first day of the spring tides, ensuring sufficient high water for the vessel to float when she was kedged off. Two bower anchors were attached over the stern of the ship at two cables' length, and the vessel was 'warped sixteen feet seaward' across the sand by strenuous hauling on deck. The ship had not been deeply bedded in and she moved with reasonable ease across the sand. This took the whole of the first day. She was left in the position she had reached for the next stage of the operation.

On the Thursday the *Birkenhead*, whose engines rated 650hp, was used as a tow ship while the *Scourge*, 'a powerful bomb steamer' was anchored 3 cables' length away from the *Great Britain*, taking strain as the *Great Britain* pulled. There was no result, although the *Birkenhead* had 'full steam on,' and it was decided to leave matters until Friday, when a final strenuous effort was made. On the *Britain* herself, fifty pumps were put to work to keep her afloat as she edged off the shore. Bremner had installed a powerful 'draining pump' which delivered three tons of water a minute. More bower anchors were 'laid out'. When the tide race began the hands aboard the ship, assisted by the greater part of the *Scourge's* crew began successfully 'to warp the vessel off the shore by means of the bower anchor.' She was then towed into 80 fathoms of deep water in the bay, where, pumps working, the *Great Britain*, the world's largest ship and the subject of the world's first rescue of its kind, was left, anchored 'where she now lies in position which will allow the *Birkenhead* to remove her.' An inspection of her plates for damage resulted in the assurance that 'she will freely float in any ordinary tide.' There were three 'deafening' cheers for Captain Claxton, 'one of the best natured and jolly old mariners we ever met with, for the Queen, Prince Albert, Ireland and the people who had done it all.' They must have been three exciting days for the hundreds of spectators who had turned up to watch the operation.[1]

WICK – PREMIER HERRING PORT

Wick's association with the sea, intense and pervasive, was monocultural. Unlike most other ports of Britain, its trade, import and export, was related almost exclusively to one trade, the Wick fisheries, and unlike most other sizeable fishery centres, Wick handled few other fish than herrings. As a herring port, Wick – or rather

---

1 *JOGJ*, 3 September, 1847. It should be added that the *Great Britain*, much reconstructed, now lies in the Avon River docks at Bristol, having been brought here from the Falkland Isles.

Pulteneytown – was a triumphant vindication of the British Fisheries Society's policy for developing herring fishery; and in fact the Society pulled back from its involvement in all its other major ventures, which were by comparison failures, concentrating from 1847 onwards all its capital input on Pulteneytown after it had sold Ullapool, and shortly before this, Tobermory. The proceeds of the sale of Tobermory were deposited in the Society's bank at Wick.[1]

Still in 1847, Wick topped the list of herring producers, a total of 114,582½ barrels, by a considerable margin of over 30,000 barrels a year; next in the list was Peterhead, with 81,330, and another 25,000 barrels down was Fraserburgh at 56,562½. Of the rest of the sixteen stations record in the Fisheries Board report of that year only Lybster, Helmsdale and Anstruther, two of them neighbours of Wick, produced more than 30,000 barrels.[2] Wick had been built up on the confident assumption, supported by little marine research, that the herrings would keep on shoaling in the waters off Caithness, which, amazingly, they did for another nearly seventy years, though catches eventually began falling below the levels of the 1850s and '60s.

This concentration on herring meant that by comparison with ports taking in white fish as well, Wick required quite modest installations and depth of harbour. Although the Wick (or Pulteneytown) harbour facilities proved grossly inadequate even for its herring fleets and visiting boats during the season, the British Fisheries Society was for many years able to get away with minimal improvement beyond the enlargements of 1828, despite increasing complaint about the harbour's small acreage, depth and difficulties of entrance.

The herring boats were small, few with keels as long as thirty feet. They were open, undecked, their gear and the catch when drawn in being stored in the well of the boat. Larger boats could have a crew of eight, but most had four and six at most. Most boats were still owned by single owners or small groups; there was no pressure on the harbour authorities from fleet owners, and no fishermen's association inclined to make their collective influence felt. It was every boat and its crew for themselves. In any case, they would only be together for six or seven weeks, and then they would depart for their own places or their customary work ashore – if any.

1 J Dunlop: *British Fisheries Society*, op cit. p 184.
2 *JOGJ*, 22 September, 1847. The largest number of barrels cured was that of Wick; the smallest that of Tongue on the north coast, a mere 460¼ barrels. Stations on the Caithness and the Buchan coasts remained the most productive, most of them with harbourage difficulties. Wick and Pulteneytown's pre-eminence was, as Dunlop suggests, 'partly due to the harbour being the first on the coast.' Dunlop op cit, p 184.

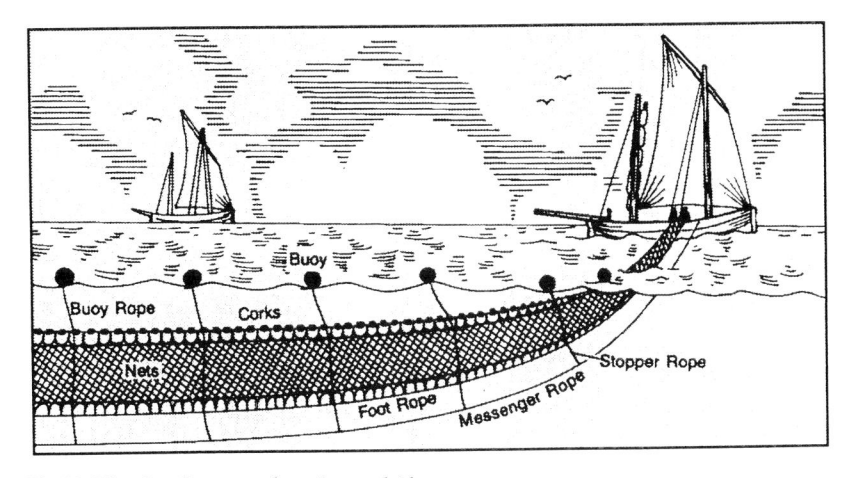

Fig 39 Herring Lugger shooting a drift-net.
(Reproduced by kind permission of Hallewell Publications, as also Figs 40, 41 and 42).

At the fishing there were hundreds of them, putting to sea in the evening, not only from Wick and Pulteneytown, but also from all the creeks along the coast, Sarclet, Broadhaven, Papigoe, Staxigoe, out across the wide area of the ocean, working for an overnight catch then making for harbour the next day, laden if they had been lucky to the gunnels. If the weather became bad they made as fast as they could back to harbour, all flocking in towards the same points, so that the sea could be thick with craft all making for refuge.

In normal times and even in regular bad weather, the boats somehow found space to lie off or berth when not at sea. On a good day the priority was to discharge the catch at quayside, which increasingly at Pulteneytown meant queuing, sometimes for several hours, not good for fish or tempers. Every season the number of boats congregating increased, local fishermen often being quite outnumbered by the visitors, just as anxious to get ashore as the natives.

Accommodation and access to quayside facilities were, accordingly, under great pressure during the season, but all decisions about improvements were the prerogative of the Fisheries Society, which still in 1847 mainly ruled in the civic affairs of Pulteneytown, although there was now some local representation on the town management commission. Even though there had been demand for extension and development of the harbour since the early 1830s, the Society for a variety of reasons, was reluctant to authorise such development. Curers, coopers and other quayside concerns were also, on the whole, content with things as they were.

To begin with, catches fluctuated considerably in the early '30s. In 1832 the town suffered a bad epidemic of cholera: 'The alarm was very great; many crews broke their engagements with the curers and fled, many curers broke up their establishments and withdrew.' There were consequent difficulties in 'completing the complements of the Fishing vessels for the season 1833, and a considerable reduction both in rents of the Curing Stations and the Harbour Dues' was anticipated by the Society.[1]

The Society was thus – at least according to its own reports – constantly short of the money necessary for improvements, even the essentially simple task of clearing the accumulations of sand and silt in the harbours, constantly building up. There were social expenditures too; the Society was committed to improvements in Pulteneytown itself and, as we have seen, was constantly subject to requests for help from the churches and for education. We have also seen that 1846 and 1847 were years of widespread destitution on the west and east coasts of Scotland; among its other outgoings was a scheme for employing destitute labourers on public works, which cost the Society £1000. None of these expenditures was very pleasing to shareholders. By the Act of Parliament which the Society obtained in 1844, it was allowed to borrow only up to £10,000, now quite insufficient for new harbour works. Dunlop sums up:

> The Directors called for six different reports from four engineers between 1838 and 1847, but none of them could recommend a course of improvement within the scope of the Society's funds and few of the solutions could be guaranteed to be successful. Thus, with the risk, the expense, and the prospects of the existing harbour being out of action for many months during reconstruction, the Directors decided to postpone any improvement.[2]

---

1 Dunlop: *British Fisheries Society*, op cit, pp 184-185. Though not referred to by Dunlop, the riot reports of 1847 could not have cheered the Society's directors or shareholders greatly.
2 Dunlop, *British Fisheries Society*, op cit, p 185.

Herring Fishers in Peril.

Sooner or later major calamity was bound to strike. From its earliest days the *Journal* repeatedly reported accidents and death at sea. Sometimes it was of wrecks and loss of life elsewhere, ships from Liverpool or Bristol, emigrant ships in the Atlantic and coastal vessels from nearer places, but usually the casualty report referred to men and boats from Wick and the other vulnerable harbours along the dangerous Caithness coast. Sometimes it was the boat and catch, sometimes the men, sometimes both. A report of August 1838 told how a herring boat, returning to Sarclet with 'an unusually large haul of herrings' was sunk in deep water in a rough sea with nets and gear. The crew were saved,

> most fortunately picked up by a boat belonging to George Gunn of Pulteneytown which happened to be passing at the time and which landed them in safely. It is supposed that about eighty crans of herrings might have been in the boat at the time she went down, all of which were taken at one haul. Two little boys, sons of the skipper were on board at the time of the accident, but although much frightened having been in the water some time clinging to their father, they were happily rescued.

No trace of boat or nets was found, but a new boat and nets were provided for the skipper, Alexander Davidson, and 'equipped with the necessary materials he was,' said the *Journal*, 'to try his luck' again the following evening.[1]

A somewhat less sympathetically cast report was that of August, 1841:

> A decrepit person, belonging to Wick known by the name of *Donley Dunnet*, died in a fishing boat at sea on the night of Thursday week. It appears that he had been addicted to drinking, and often neglectful of food or any regular diet. The night in question was cold and boisterous. Dunnet went with a crew belonging to this place. They tried to rouse him at the time of the hauling, and found him covered up by a sail. His death is supposed to have arisen from cold and the effects of ardent spirits.[2]

On 13 August, 1838, the son of a fisherman from Dunbeath, 'by a

---

1 *JOGJ*, 10 August, 1838.
2 *JOGJ*, 6 August, 1841.

WICK OF THE NORTH

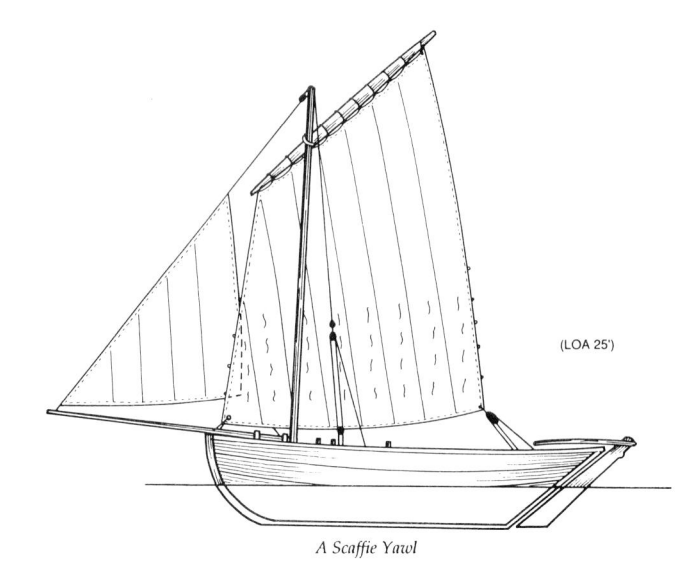

(LOA 25')

A Scaffie Yawl

Fig 40 **Scaffie.**

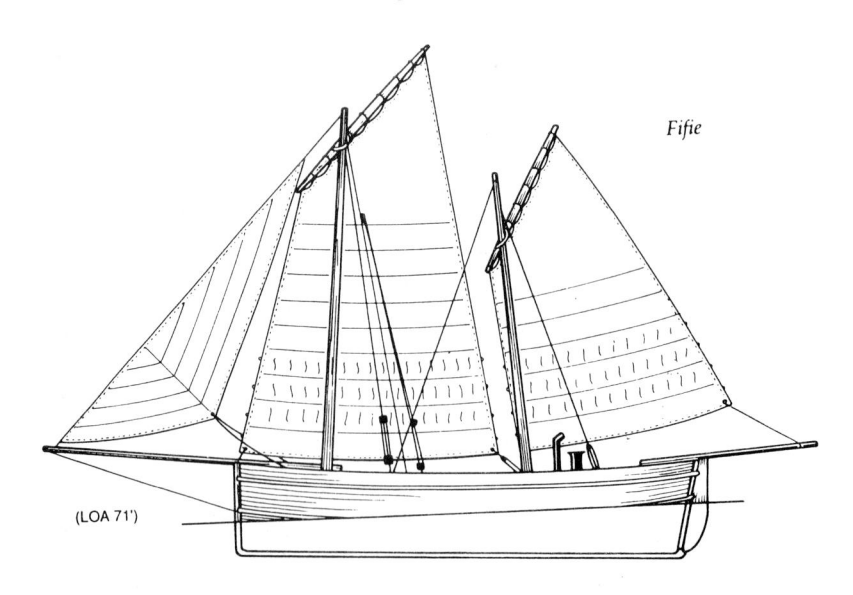

Fifie

(LOA 71')

Fig 41 **Fifie.**

454

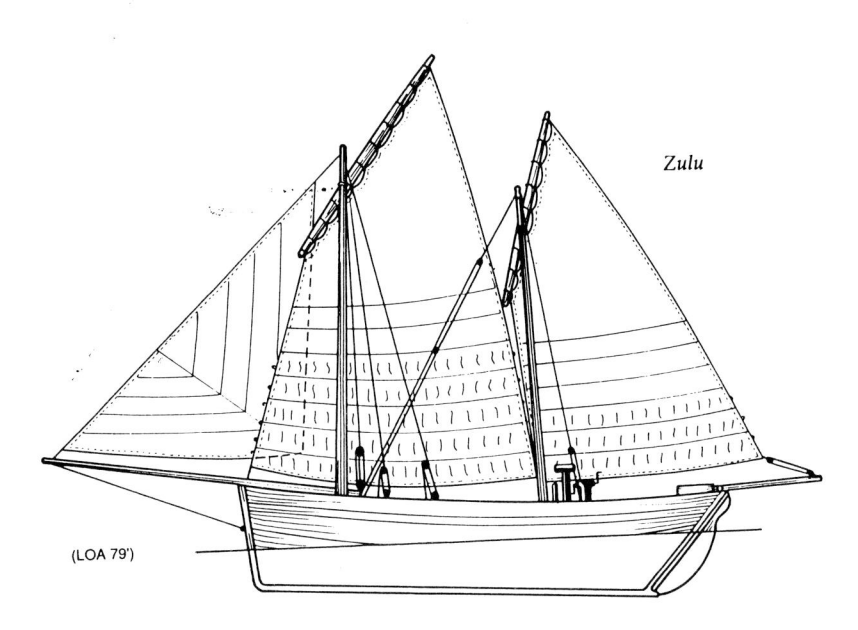

Fig 42 Zulu.

sudden jerk of the sail was swept over the gunwale, and before assistance could be rendered, sunk to rise no more.' No trace of the body was found.[1]

1847 was a bad year. There were food shortages, disturbances and many accidents at sea. Most of these occurred in the later part of the year. A sudden shift of weather in August from 'most pleasant' to 'severe gale' drove boats and vessels scampering for refuge. The *Journal* writer became lyrical: 'At the height of the storm, the scene, towards the sea, was terrific. The white-crested waves, broken as it were, by the violence of the gale, drove across our shores with fearful noise, impelling the vessels before them.' A sloop, loaded with herrings making for the Pentland Firth, was forced on to the sands of Sinclair's Bay near Keiss, the captain having mistaken Noss Head for Duncansby.[2]

Some weeks later came still more spectacular incidents, the wreck of a brig on the coast near to Keiss, and a calamitous drowning at

1 *JOGJ*, 17 August, 1838.
2 *JOGJ*, 27 August, 1847.

Lybster. The brig *Warrior* of Montrose was on her way back home with a cargo of timber for railway sleepers from Riga. A strong gale from east-south-east drove her on to the rocks near to the old Castle of Keiss. She immediately began to break up and men were seen to be clinging to remnants of the rigging, 'the sea was dashing against her with forceful violence'. A crowd gathered while people ran furiously to Wick to seek assistance for the 'poor fellows placed in such imminent danger'. A rescue party arrived together with James Bremner, whose ingenuity was immediately put to the test. He rigged up a 'sliding apparatus'), evidently a primitive sort of breeches buoy, having got a line attached to the wreck (apparently by using the Pulteneytown 'rocket apparatus'). The entire crew of nine was rescued 'in the most efficient manner'; the first ashore was an old man named Lowson from Dundee, carried to the house of Mr Iverach of Keiss. He was, however, so exhausted, that he shortly died, though the other eight soon recovered.[1]

The 'Distressing Accident' at Lybster involved fishermen from the port. On the evening of 21 November, 1847, these fishers went out in mild weather; they were 'some time at their lines when a gale came on' putting the 'unhappy fishermen' in a 'predicament of great peril'. They were evidently cod fishing. The boats set off immediately for the shore. One ran for Whaligoe and the crew was miraculously saved by being hauled ashore with a rope, the boat being driven to pieces, and the lines and materials being totally lost. Those making for Lybster all landed safely except for one boat with a crew of eight 'active fellows'. All 'perished beneath the waves as' they tried to get ashore, and their bodies were not found. Five of the men left widows and twenty-one children. In the same issue of the *Journal* was reported the recovery of pieces of the wreck of the *Maggie Lauder* sloop which loaded herrings in Wick and sailed for Lorne on the west coast. Captain Kennedy and his mate, the 'only efficient hands in the boat' and all the others, including a boy ill with fever 'must have perished'. 260 barrels of herring were lost.[2]

BLACK SATURDAY, THE FEARFUL CALAMITY OF 1848.

Most of the fishing-boat accidents reported at this time did not happen on the high seas. They occurred when boats approached

1 *JOGJ*, 1 October, 1847.
2 *JOGJ*, 26 November, 1847.

refuge in the harbours of the coast, Keiss, Staxigoe, Broadhaven, Wick and Lybster. All the east-coast harbours were recognised to be inadequate, even for normal good-weather traffic, and none offered satisfactory refuge for the fishing and other vessels when strong winds blew in across the German Ocean. A Commission had been appointed in 1846 to enquire into tidal harbours, chaired by Captain John Washington RN, and Washington had taken evidence in the localities affected. He visited Wick on 21 September, 1846, where he was told of the piecemeal development of Pulteneytown Harbour, the nature of the sea-walls erected and the constant filling up of the basins with sand. Among those from whom Washington took evidence were James Bremner, and Lieutenant Medley RN, since 1840 Commander of the Coastguard service in Caithness. Medley had come to identify himself with the urgent need for a 'harbour of refuge' on this beleaguered coast. He favoured development of facilities at Ackergill, considering that Wick was doomed for such a purpose because of the constant sanding up of the basins there. It was on Medley's suggestion that it was decided to erect a lighthouse on Noss Head.[1]

A light of sorts, in fact, had been set up on the pier end at Pulteneytown in 1838, a 'plain, but brilliant and vivid light', a 'cause of much satisfaction to the numerous fishermen belonging to the place, as well as the various stranger crews not here.' According to the *Journal*, this light could be 'observed at a considerable distance', a statement hardly borne out at the time of the great storm of August, 1848.[2]

On the morning of 19 August, 1848, occurred the worst catastrophe ever recorded on this coast. The *Journal* wrote copiously on the scene which broke as dawn rose. 'The morning of 19th of August, 1848 will long and vividly sustain a melancholy freshness in the memories of those who sojourned in the towns and villages of this coast,' he wrote solemnly; 'and will produce a pang of sorrow in bosoms now bleeding around desolate hearths. Often, indeed, have we as public journalists, had to record the occurrence of melancholy disasters amongst the hardy sons of the sea who prosecute their precarious calling on the eastern shores of Scotland; but never were we called upon to narrate as heart-rending a calamity as that which we now proceed to recall':

Fishermen went out as usual on Friday afternoon. They

1 *JOGJ*, 11 February, 1848. See also Obituary to Edwin Medley, who died in May, 1849, *JOGJ*, 18 May, 1849.
2 *JOGJ*, 24 August, 1838.

were obliged to leave early; there was promise of a beautiful night. But before 8 o'clock the sky grew suddenly red; that in the east became dark and portentous, while the barometer rapidly declined. The wind shifted two or three points to eastward, and increased in violence till it blew a stiff gale, raising rather a disagreeable swell. From the ominous appearance of the sky, personal safety overcame the desire of gain in the minds of many, who, judiciously admitted, made their respective harbours. But many remained.

Such a sudden worsening of weather, common enough in the German Ocean, was the subject of the classic *Ballad of Sir Patrick Spens*:

> *They hadna sailed a league, a league,*
> *A league but barely three,*
> *When the lift grew dark, and the wind blew loud,*
> *And gurly grew the sea.*

And as on that occasion, 'sic a deadly storm' blew up late on 18th August, 1848. By midnight the gale abated somewhat, and the wind had turned 'more to a landward direction.' By one o'clock the wind blew fearfully again, 'and the sea rose to such a pitch as to create the great alarm in the minds of all.' At dawn the sea was 'studded with boats all running before the wind, the crews evidently careless of where they landed, provided they were only on shore.' By 4 o'clock boat was following boat towards the land, dashing 'against each other, with fearful violence'. Up to now, so far as the harbour was concerned, there was no loss of life, and watchers were thrilled to see friends and relatives come in; 'but soon after, and ere 5 o'clock struck, the body of a hapless seaman was under the briny wave.' The bar was now almost impassable because of surf rolling over it.

The reporter, doing his best, but hampered by the clichés of his trade, hardly succeeds in conveying the full horror and drama of the scene, later more eloquently evoked by some of the witnesses – who had actually taken part in rescue attempts – at the subsequent enquiry:

> Still, as the poor fellows had nowhere to go, they had to dare its dangers and attempt a landing. Several fishermen have informed us that, there being no light on the Pulteneytown quay-head, they mistook Wick Bay for that of Reiss, to the latter of which they thought they were escaping, not being aware of their mistake till they found themselves among the breakers in the vicinity of Pulteneytown Harbour.

Just before 4 o'clock a boat 'rushing for the bay', broke among the

Proudfoot Rocks on the north side of the bay. 'By one tremendous sea the boat was driven almost dry upon the reef.' Two of the crew perished; when rescuers came some time later, from under the gunwale of the overturned boat, they saw a human hand, and underneath lay the two bodies. 'It appears from the statement of one of the survivors that, running for the land, the rudder gave way,' and the crew tried to steer the boat with two oars. They likewise had mistaken their position since they could see no light in the main harbour, thinking themselves much further south when their boat struck the rocks.

Another survivor, Robert Weir, told how his boat had been run down by the schooner, *Ann and Elizabeth*, from South Shields, the 'crew of which, who paid not the least attention to the poor fellows thus perilled.' Their boat was driven 'almost to shivers, upon Noss Head. The boat and materials were utterly lost.' The crew of the boat of Donald Farquhar had better luck; they were driven on rocks at Helman Head; 'in this perilous state the crew remained a few minutes when one of their number leaped into the waves, and having taken a rope ashore with him, the whole crew got safely landed, and travelled barefooted into town, the boat having gone to pieces a few minutes after they got ashore.'

At about 4.30 boats 'came in as a cluster'. The 'state of the weather was fearful. The bay was almost one entire sheet of wave.' A 'tremendous wave' struck the boat farthest out; it sank and the entire crew were lost. Another sank and 'shared the same dreadful fate.' A third made 'a more than hairbreadth escape, and reached the harbour,' while the boat of William Doull struck against the end of the South Quay. All the crew except Doull climbed up the back of the quay; Doull, 'seeking to save his son, lost the opportunity and was swept back into the sea,' and both he and his son were drowned. Yet another crew came in at the back of the North Quay, and with the help of ropes all got ashore.

'At this juncture,' continues the reporter, witnessing a bold attempt to save another crew, 'Mr John Sutherland, Emigration Agent, at that time almost the only person on the parapet wall, boldly ventured down the solitary ladder affixed to the back of the quay,' and holding one of its steps with one hand, he reached forth the other to the drowning seamen, two of whom he brought ashore; but ere his generous help could be made available, the boat was driven off by the surge,' and the remainder perished.

It was here, at the Pulteneytown Harbour entrance and along the harbour walls that the worst casualties occurred. People were 'deprived of self-possession' as they watched boats approach; and admitted the reporter, 'any account must fall short of the real picture of this terrible scene.' At one time, four entire crews were at the back of the quay, all exposed at the same time 'to the most appalling danger.' The reporter tells of yet another heroic rescue:

> In one case, one poor fellow clung to the mast for considerably more than half-an-hour. He had seen his fellows one by one safely hauled up the quay, and now he alone remained. It was a conflict for life. Gradually the mast floated towards the shore; ropes were thrown, but his stiffened arms could not be raised to take advantage of the aid. At last two brave fellows, Mr George Sinclair, boat carpenter, and Mr William Young, mason, determined to make an effort to save him. They got ropes fastened round their bodies, and swinging themselves over the quay, they dashed into the breakers, and brought him to land.

The whole bay was by this time 'one scene of desolation.' The wrecked boats were floating in every direction, while, 'in the offing, crowds of boats were flying for shelter, wherever the crews thought there was chance of shelter.' In Broadhaven harbour the 'wreck of boats was terrible;' five or six boats were run into by others, sunk or entirely destroyed. Some crews ran for Ackergill, braving the seas around Noss Head, and 30 boats 'found friendly refuge' there. Two boats foundered off Noss Head itself. Watchers at North Head 'observed three poor fellows clinging to spars for some time. One by one they sank;' one remained. 'At this juncture, the *Queen* steamer made her appearance when an affecting scene occurred, as described by a passenger in another part of the paper.'

The *Queen* had arrived with passengers for Wick, but landing them was quite out of the question. The ship was standing off Noss Head at about 5 o'clock, the storm at its worst, when the call 'Man at Sea' went up. They saw a seaman hanging on to a plank. A lifebuoy was thrown to him from the deck of the *Queen* but the man had not strength to seize it. A boat was lowered 'notwithstanding the tempestuous sea which roared and raged, and struck so hard against the side of the vessel, that the attempt to launch at such a time was perilous in the extreme; three hands volunteered and the boat was lowered, but before they had got rightly under way, the object of their pursuit had sunk beneath the raging tide.' The three men were praised for their bravery and a subscription was raised on board for them.

Several of the passengers were landed at Ackergill, giving rise to the reflection, yet again, that Ackergill was 'better suited for a harbour than any other in the district.' The landing was accomplished in comparative safety, 'and this circumstance,' observed the *Journal* (in very twisted language), 'together with the number of fishing boats that had taken shelter in it, led many to remark that if one third of the money had been expended on Ackergill, in building a harbour that would be required in extending that of Pulteneytown, it might be made the safest place and easiest taken on the whole North-east coast of Scotland.'

A Belgian boat 'rode out the gale nobly'. Finding themselves too much to leeward, the crew threw out anchors, 'just among the breakers at the north side of the bay not far from the mouth of the river.' Although the anchors were not expected to hold, they did, and the boat got into Pulteneytown Harbour at 2 o'clock in the afternoon, followed by two other boats, the last of the refugees, except for the boat of Donald Angus, which had 'borne off for Orkney'. She was not expected back in Wick for several days.

Altogether thirty-seven fishers were drowned. Of these two were from Wick and six from Pulteneytown. One was from Staxigoe, and one from Thurso. Six came from Orkney. The largest number from any one place was thirteen from Lewis. The others, mostly crewmen were from various places in Caithness and Sutherland, including Bower, Tongue, Assynt and Lybster. Some boats were lost or severely damaged, and dozens more injured but repairable.

Though Wick was much the worst hit of the east Scotland fishing ports in the disaster of August, 1848, it was not alone. As the *Journal* itself said on 1 September, 'there are other points of the compass.' Eleven lives were lost at Peterhead, seven at Stonehaven, and five at Johnshaven. Nor was Wick alone in the north-east: there was no loss of life at Forse and Latheronwheel, but boats and other property were destroyed; at Dunbeath fifteen boats were damaged. At Lybster a boy was drowned and at Helmsdale three fishers were drowned.[1]

---

1 All these accounts were printed in the *John O'Groat Journal* for 25 August, 1848. The list of dead given on 25 August showed only the numbers lost from the various boats. An amended list showing place of origin of all was printed in *JOGJ*, 15 September, 1848.

Aftermath.

The disaster remained the main topic of interest in the *Journal* for several months, with reminiscences, reports and letters filling the middle pages consistently. The issue for 15 September, 1848, moralised on how Wick had become 'a scene of sobriety', with a hint that the event might have been, perhaps, a visitation of the Lord, for 'on the evening of Saturday week [the day before the disaster] was one in which the demon of intemperance was rampant. We now saw so many Highlandmen in a state of intoxication. The broken windows of public houses, on the Sabbath forenoon, showed the nature of the unholy proceedings of the previous night.'

Fishing finished, the journalist paints a picture of the tranquility now reigning:

> The din is now over. The harbours are thinned of boats – the evening tramp of thick boots has ceased – the noble sight of many hundreds of tiny barks gliding over the surface of the deep, their copper-coloured sails gleaming in the light of the setting sun, is no more seen – the laughable medley of Gaelic, Scotch and other languages, amongst the crowd of brawny fellows that paraded our streets on a Saturday evening, is no more heard – the Highland or Orkney lassie, having made a successful 'git' has gone to her harvest, or, perchance, to mix moggans with Donald or Magnus – the shops lately crowded with the most ridiculous mixture of hard-to-drive-a-bargain customs, are deserted – the boats are drawn – the nets, sails, masts and oars are shelved for a year – the game is up – the sporting season is over, and the sportsmen have gone to their winter quarters – may it be ours never again to see a fishing terminate, at once so favourably to many and so sorrowfully to not a few.

The issue contained an interesting assessment of the costs and benefits of the recent fishing when set against the heavy loss of life. The successful fisher might have made as much as £28, but not much of that would be left 'when the stormy winds of December howl across the fisherman's "cot"'.

The season had been a good one. Until 19 August, it was reckoned, 'not a single accident accompanied by loss of life' had occurred. Weather had been generally favourable; on only two nights had boats been prevented from going out. Frequently upwards of 1200 boats 'over the surface of a few miles, manned by more than 6000 men, in the dead of night [had] been afloat together, having 1200 drift of nets floating under the surface.' All these had 'returned without accident'. The *Journal* could not 'but wonder, and see in it the care of Him who "holds the wind in His fists, and the waters in the hollow of His hand."'

The average catch for the season had been 114 crans for each of 813 boats, making a total of 96,862 crans 'captured'. Supposing each cran to number 70 dozen fish, 'we have,' continued the calculation, '6,487,940 dozen, or 77,852,880 herrings!.' If the fishermen received the 'average of 11 shillings per cran, we have £50,795 1s paid to that industrious class.' Supposing that two-thirds of the crews were 'hired men', paid at an average of £5 each, and allowing 4000 to be employed in the Wick district, 'we find that they have received £13,500.' Following this queer calculation, the *Journal* estimates that £35,600 is left to the 'fishermen' (the boat owners and skippers) as their 'share of the spoil'. Each boat is worth about £110, and assuming 9,883 boats 'here this season', their total value is something of the order of of £80,430. Boats mostly belong to the fishermen themselves, so that from their 'profits' they have to keep their boats in repair, and buy all the materials they need for the maintenance of the fishing, taking supplies from a wide range of providers of such materials: '– forester, hewer, sawyer, carpenter, ironmaster, blacksmith, founder, joiner, tar dealer, rope-maker, sailmaker, and many other trades.' Other contributors to the trade (and hence to the activity and prosperity of Wick) are people making nets, curers, carters, coopers, gutters, packers, labourers, shipping agents, ship owners, sailors, harbour trustees, pilots, fishmongers, all receiving their share from the profits of the whole fishery business.[1] There is little doubt that in good years, Wickers as a whole did not do so badly.

The whisky bill (whisky was a topic which still obsessed the temperance-minded *John O'Groat Journal*) must have been one of the heaviest of the season. Not only did the fishers drink deeply on shore, but most boats would have taken to sea with them not less that 6 gallons each ('a moderate allowance'). Reckoning that some 812 boats put to sea, 4,978 gallons, 'in addition to occasional drams, whose name is legion,' must have been paid for and consumed. The fishermen's direct whisky bill must have amounted to 'a grand aggregate of ONLY £1990!'. Fishermen 'on the English shores' – from

1 *JOGJ*, 15 September, 1848.

Norfolk in particular – the *Journal* believed, 'use no intoxicating drink'. They, like the Scottish fishermen leave their shores in the evening, take along with them the facilities for making a fire, and cooking materials, and are thus able to prepare for themselves hot coffee during the vigil of the night. 'Why should not our abstainers set the example and do it here?'

A week after these discussions appeared the Scottish Fishery Board's annual report for 1847, which accounted for 894,940½ barrels of herrings produced, a decrease of 33,901¼ barrels on the previous year. Wick headed the list of producers with 114, 582½ barrels, their nearest competitors being Peterhead and Fraserburgh. Lybster and Helmsdale were well up the list. Wick at 114 crans per boat was not high among the averages; Peterhead stood at 184, Fraserburgh at 130, while the highest average was that of Boddam, at 220 crans, a little place just south of Peterhead with only a few boats.[1]

Bodies not recovered at the time of the storm came in from time to time during the weeks after. Between Sarclet and Clyth that of one of the men from the *Colin Finlayson* was found during the third week of September, unrecognisable, but identified by means of his knife, and another body, that of John Bain, was found on the Wick north shore.[2]

The British Fisheries Society became a prime target – was indeed already such a target – of criticism in the aftermath of the disaster. It was accused, not without justification, of holding back on investment in harbour improvements at Pulteneytown. As we have seen, several proposals had been considered during the years before 1848 for clearing sand from the harbour, and no less than six engineers' reports had been commissioned. In 1844 the Society had obtained a new Act of Parliament, confirming and strengthening some of its powers in Pulteneytown, but no improvement measures were adopted, partly on account of pure procrastination and partly because of inadequate funds. Now, surely, something had to be done. This was the conclusion of an *ad hoc* meeting of fishermen, held in the Temperance Hall on 23 September, a gathering as the *Journal* described it of 'bone and sinew and respectability of society,' for the purposes of 'taking into consideration of efficient measures that have been hitherto, or are about to be adopted, in the harbour and on the Quays of Pulteneytown, for the preservation of life and property, as well as to impress upon the public the conviction that no effectual means, to

1 *JOGJ*, 22 September, 1848.
2 *Ibid.*

prevent sacrifice of human life, have hitherto been attended to.'[1]

Among such measures now in common discussion were improvement of the harbour's landward facilities, cleaning sand out of the basins, the greater use of decked boats, and extension of the harbour. The actual management of the harbour, shown up as faulty in many respects at Captain Washington's hearing of October, 1848, was the subject of early attention by the Society when, during that month, 'they discussed the appointment of a naval officer with complete control of all works connected with the harbour,' and four months later, in February, Captain Eden was chosen.[2]

The issue of decked boats was not really a matter for the Society, and was in fact never effectively settled. It became the matter of intense controversy in the correspondence columns of the *Journal* during the winter months of 1848-1849. The customary 'Scaffies' and 'Fifies' which had done most of the herring fishing so far, had no decks, all nets, gear, catch and crew amenities, such as they were, being stowed in the open well of the boat. Official opinion was shifting in favour of forward half-decking some time before the 1848 disaster, but proposals for change were strongly resisted by the fishermen themselves and by experienced practitioners such as James Bremner. Letters from Messrs Loch and Hume, MPs, were among those putting the case for decking. Their arguments were rebutted at some length and with force in the issue for 13 October, 1848: 70,000 fishermen were against them; the proposed innovation implied a complete 'overturn of the present system', larger boats carrying curing materials – barrels, salt, a cooper on board; much greater expense of building boats – a Yarmouth buss (half the size of a Dutch buss) would cost £1000, as compared with the £100 to £150 of a Scaffie; such trials as had been made in Scotland had failed – bounty would be needed as in Holland; where were the larger vessels to land? Larger and deeper harbours would be necessary; bigger, decked vessels did not necessarily ride out bad seas better – the losses of August in Wick had not been at sea, but during attempts at landing; the nature of the herring trade required deep-welled vessels and were much easier for hauling in the catch; above all, present boats do not have a high casualty record: 'deducting the number of lives lost, we [the writers] are satisfied that not more than 10 men were drowned off these coasts on the 19th of August. This, be it remembered, is out of

1 *JOGJ*, 29 September, 1848.
2 Dunlop, *British Fisheries Society*. op cit, p 187.

some 1300 at sea on the previous night.' (This must be counted a very ambiguous statement).[1]

One melancholy sequel of the disaster was the activity of the Wick Shipwrecked Fishermen and Marines Benevolent Society. This had been formed years before the 1848 event, and the *Journal* often reported its usually rather dull meetings, and gave details of its hand-outs to the families and dependants of seamen either lost or handicapped by accidents at sea. A public meeting of the Society was held in the Temperance Hall to report on how it had dealt with the recent disaster, its biggest challenge yet.

1847-1848 had already been a busy year for the Society's officers. They had provided relief during the year to no less than 142 widows, 316 orphans and 49 'aged persons'. In the immediate wake of the August calamity the Society had distributed £50 to some thirteen widows and aged persons, and 24 orphaned children. Other and usually more substantial assistance had been provided by the Highland Destitution Board (the Poor Law). Recipients of relief lived mainly in the Wick parish, but there were hand-outs to folk as far away as Castletown and Thurso.[2]

Captain Washington's Enquiry

Far and away the most thorough examination of the events of August, 1848, and the contingent issues, was that conducted by Captain Washington RN, who came back to Wick in October, 1848, on the instructions of the Admiralty 'to enquire into the causes of disaster on 19 August,' and opened his enquiry on 18 October at the Town Hall. The sessions were chaired by Provost Joshua Rhind. It is not possible here to repeat in any detail the patient and often discomforting depositions and questioning that fill some eight closely packed columns of the *John O'Groat Journal*, during which many of the participants in the drama of the 19th and several expert witnesses recalled their experiences and gave their opinions. The picture they present of what actually happened is more vivid and direct than that of the *Journal* reporter after the event itself. Two people who gave evidence of what they saw from the quays were James Crawford, a fish-curer, who spoke at length, and John Sutherland, the Wick Emigration Agent. A few excerpts will give the flavour of their

1 *JOGJ*, 15 September, 1848.
2 Ibid.

evidence. First James Crawford:

> I went down to the North Quay about 4 o'clock on the morning of the storm. The tide was ebbing, high water being about half-past one. As I was going down I was told that two boats had been upset on the bar. I met some individuals that had been rescued; a John Henderson was among them. As I proceeded down I heard a cry; a man was seen clinging to the end of a spar. An attempt was then made by putting a small boat over the back of the North Quay, opposite the old entrance. I should think half-an-hour had elapsed ere the boat was got over the wall, before which time the man was drowned. Three boats then appeared running for the harbour. I went to the end of the quay, but, ere I reached it, the three had foundered. Parts drifted up the back of the quay.
>
> I saw ropes being handed down to save the crews. I tried to get up on to the wall, but it was a great risk to stand upon it, being so much crowded with people. Some of the men were on the ropes ere I came down, and I saw some of them taken from the vessels. Two men jumped out of a boat at the end of the South Quay, and were just saved; the others were drowned. I saw other men saved by ropes, and taken up the back of the North Quay. This was between four and five o'clock. Several boats ran up the river of Wick, and got all safe. I believe that the river saved boats that the harbour could not. It was easier to take the river. If that river had been deepened, I believe there would have been more lives saved. The entrance to the harbour is dangerous as boats and vessels have to round to before they can enter the harbour. I have been 10 years acquainted with the place. The river generally fills up, so that the fisheries every now and then have to deepen it. The British Fisheries Society pay no part of the expense. I believe the expenses in one year was £90.

Crawford, who came from Glasgow and knew the Clyde well, believed that the erection of 'guiding walls' in the river would have been useful in the river of Wick. The trouble with the river, of course, was that it rapidly filled up with silt, and at low tide was extremely shallow.

Mr Crawford had looked up the South Quay (on the end of which the light was supposed to be burning), but could not tell whether the light was showing since it was nearly daylight, though he had been

WICK OF THE NORTH

WICK FISHING BOAT (about 1848) (OPEN)

PRINCIPAL DIMENSIONS

	ft	in
Length overall	36	6
Length of Keel for tonnage	26	8½
Breadth extreme	13	0
Breadth Moulded	12	8
Depth of Hold	4	9
Burthen in Tons O.M.	24	

Draft of Water light afore 2ft 2ins aft 2ft 2ins
            load afore 4ft 0ins aft 4ft 6ins

Displacement to tight draft or weight of hull .. 4 tons
Displacement to load draft 17.74
Weight of Ballast 1¼
Cost of Hull with Spars, Sails &c. £64
No. of Crew .... 5 men
Rig of Boat two, lug Sails
Clench built

SHEER PLAN

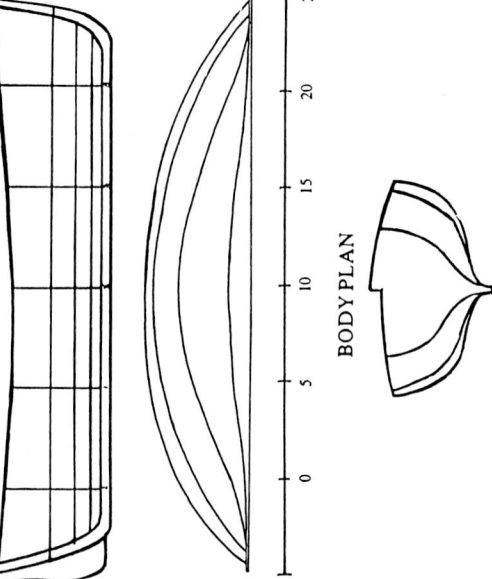

BODY PLAN

Fig 43 Wick fishing boat. Source: Naval Historical Library (Washington Report, 1848).

told the light was out. He heard from others that 'it was there but very imperfect.' He had himself on occasion seen the light from the sea when conditions were calm. 'I believe it has a single burner, and red coloured glass.' He saw no lifebuoys or life ropes on the quays, was not even aware of ropes kept for the purpose. 'There are no rope ladders at the back of the quays. They might be easily fitted.'

The evidence of John Sutherland told a similar story to that of Mr Crawford. Modestly too, Sutherland told how he had himself rescued two men, an incident referred to by the *Journal* reporter:

> I was at this time standing at the end of the South Quay, and saw that had there been a rope ladder at the place where the accidents occurred, few would have perished. I then ascended the iron ladder leading to the top of the parapet on the South Quay, and stood within a foot or two of the top. I saw a boat making for the harbour; the sea carried against the end of the South Quay. I got up and lay on my face on the top of the parapet. By the force of the waves the boat came round the back of the quay. I started up, and called to the men, for God's sake, to save themselves. I descended the ladder at the back of the Quay. On going down, two men jumped out of the boat, the receding sea taking it back, and the rest of the crew perishing. I called out to the men to climb up the ladder. I laid hold of one of them and helped him up; the other I seized hold of by the collar, and aided him in escaping.

Among the questions that kept cropping up were those about the light on the quay, the lack of ropes, and other rescue gear anywhere to hand, rope ladders on the back or seaward sides of the quays; there were also some strange references to 'lifeboats'. Some said the light was there, others that it was out or could not be seen. One of the eleven harbour pilots, 'such as they are,' in the words of pilot William Williamson, asserted that the light was on half the time only. The assistant harbour-master, Francis Luther, said that the lamp was not lighted at midnight on the 18th, but was lighted sometime afterwards; it was, in any case, simply an oil lantern on a pole, usually hoisted when a fast tide was running. Although gas was now available at the harbour, it had not been installed, either for the navigation light or for illuminating the quays.

Peter Taylor, the harbour-master, complained that there were boats lying in the harbour that should not have been there, a point disputed by Captain Washington, who argued that all boats had the 'right' to be there; the question was, were they being charged for the berthing. There was a lifeboat of sorts, kept in harbour. The harbour-master did not know to whom it belonged or who had authority to order it out, though he believed Mr Bremner had told him that it was the property of the Fisheries Society. He had never known it to be taken out for such a purpose as rescue, but even if taken out then, 'no lifeboat could have saved anyone that morning.'

This was a topic on which James Bremner himself commented. He, it seems, had a special interest and role in connection with the lifeboat. He had, he told the enquiry, 'studied the matter' ever since in 1816 he had been involved in an accident in Burlington Bay when a lifeboat, 'as then constructed' had 'failed'. Though he gave no details to the enquiry, he had evidently been conducting experiments at Wick, and had devised a lifeboat driven by side paddles, which were operated by the crew. It had never been property tested. This episode, as it happens, is effectively the first item in the story of the Wick Lifeboat service, to which we return, later in this chapter. So far as the storm of August, 1848, is concerned, clearly the Bremner lifeboat had no part to play, and it is difficult to imagine it surviving in the boiling seas outside the harbour, could it have got out. Bremner's evidence continued:

> The gale was so severe, and the sea so high, that no life-boat could have been of the least service. The boats were running in at the time, so that it would have been impossible to get down through the entrance . . . . . There would have been difficulty in getting her out of the harbour, but she would have been of no use in saving life or property, as she would have been dashed to pieces amongst the boulders. With a crew on board she will draw perhaps 18 inches of water. She was fit to go to sea at the time; she has not been repaired since.

Embarrassing calls from the back of the room – 'I saw a blacksmith repairing her,' and 'She was full of water at the time.' Bremner 'emphatically denied these statements.' There was, he said,

> no crew to man her; either six or eight can row her, according to distance. The barometer did not indicate a storm the night previous. There was plenty of time to get the boat ready; in my absence there is one appointed to take charge of her; she has never been taken out to the rescue of anyone, nor has she ever been required except once, and I was from home at the time.

The reference to the barometer is interesting. Whether or not anyone had been into the harbour office to look at the barometer on the evening of 18 August, according to the harbour-master, 'the fishermen never come in to consult the barometer which we have in the harbour office.' He himself could not say how it stood that evening. Taylor seemed to doubt whether some fishers could read it. A few months later a large barometer was erected on the corner of Begg's Inn (on the corner of Harbour Terrace where the barometer is on view today). This, said the *Journal,* is 'the most central and proper place of the harbour' for the barometer. 'It is very simple, and is quite intelligible to the meanest capacity,' concluded the paper.[1]

This was just one of the measures almost immediately adopted. Another was the formal appointment of Captain Henry Eden RN, as principal harbour-master, who was reported as having put in train the deepening of the existing harbour, 'with a considerable degree of spirit.' During the last two months men with lighters had been clearing 'a very large quantity of sand', night and day. 'Already,' said the *Journal,* 'there is a marked difference to the depth of water where the operations have been going on, and we have no doubt that ere the fishing season arrives, the advantages of the change will be beneficially felt by the shipping trade.'[2] At the enquiry itself, Provost Rhind reported that lifebuoys had been ordered for distribution round the harbour, though he added, rather ruefully that, in view of the many witnesses who had advocated more lifebuoys, nobody had gone to boats lying in the harbour on the 19th and taken up their lifebuoys or thrown any of their bladders to the drowning fishermen. A new 'lighthouse' was to be erected on the quay and it was to be lighted with gas. He promised, too, that 'a new lifeboat would be on the spot soon.'

Another significant contributor to the enquiry was David Davidson, a fish-curer who was also an experienced fisherman himself. The British Fisheries Society, he considered, had had a 'most beneficial influence on a large portion of the Highlands and Islands of Scotland.' The Wick fishing especially benefited a 'large number of hired men from these districts', providing them with 'ample remuneration for their labours, enabling them to pay their rents, habits of industry are taught them, besides their being made acquainted with the best modes of fishing.' However, he was convinced that seven out of ten of 'South country fishermen *object to coming here, in consequence of the*

---

1 *JOGJ*, 9 March, 1849.
2 *JOGJ*, 27 April, 1849.

want of harbour accommodation and deficiency of safety in bad weather [author's italics].' Straight to the point, he believed that the British Fisheries Society, 'are in possession of funds fully equivalent to the expense of erecting a pier from Salmon Rock, as was proposed [at recent meetings between the Pulteneytown Commissioners and the directors of the Society, led by the Duke of Sutherland]'. He added: 'After a political contest we all thought the harbour was immediately to be built.' He was dismayed that the Society had, a few weeks ago, now decided that 'there was no intention of proceeding with the new harbour, that Mr Stevenson had changed his mind, and that the expense and risk of silting had induced the directors to come to this decision. Now,' he continued, 'Mr Stevenson and Mr Bremner had no dread of silting up, and even although they were, why not apply part of the revenue to remove the sand as it accumulates, as is done in other cases?' Stevenson, said Mr Davidson had not changed his mind, and he had a letter in his hand from Mr Stevenson to say just that. He had been assured that the Society had £20,000 in hand that could be used for the necessary harbour extension.

Bremner's own comments on this matter were very positive:

> Having 43 years' experience, I can speak freely on the subject. There is a great want of harbour space accommodation; the present harbour is immensely crowded; sometimes the fishermen had to carry their herrings over five or six boats or three tiers of vessels. There is no remedy that I know of, except another harbour at the Salmon Rock [this rock juts out into the estuary on the south side, but owing to the extensive quarrying that has gone on along this shore, is not longer the landmark it once was]. There is no fear of it silting up. The sand comes from the back of the North Quay. In 1813, I sounded the bay for a breakwater, and again I sounded it ten years ago, and found no difference in the depth of the water. It cannot sand up, as there is no sand at sea till more than two miles off the land, the rest being all hard ground.

Bremner had little use for the idea of harbours elsewhere. He outlined his objections to alternatives, and adumbrated to the Washington tribunal ideas, that continued to run through discussion in the coming years, for all the indecision and procrastination that continued to hamper further development of Pulteneytown Harbour. Broadhaven (on the north side),

> would not afford a small space of shelter at an enormous

expense; beside, I am doubtful of a building there standing in the sea. I remember a storm in 1808, which no building there could stand. As to Ackergill, it would be best for a roadstead and harbour, but the tide off Noss Head would entirely prevent boats from running for it. A breakwater in Wick bay would do admirably, if funds could be obtained for the purpose . . . . It could be executed for L130,000. I would run it from the south side, with no entrance at the centre, but at the north side. Were an entrance made at the middle, the expense would be considerably greater, as it would require another end to be secured, which would be the great expense. If this could be done it would be the best remedy of all, without doubt. With regard to the deepening of the river of Wick, if it were thought to be to the public advantage, it might be done very well; but I fear, after a certain depth down, an obstacle would present itself in shape of rock. Sheet piling would not answer the purpose and the expense of excavating the rock would be immense. There would be a considerable advantage in building a puddle wall at the upper part of the West Quay, but it would be very expensive.

On the subject of the decking of fishing boats, Bremner was equally definite: 'I consider the present boats sufficient. I was the first that cleared out a deep sea fishing decked boat, in 1809, of 28 tons, under the bounty system, but it would not do. *I feel that no improvement can be made on the present boats* [author's italics].' Thus were canvassed at the Washington Enquiry most of the issues that continued afterwards to exercise the British Fisheries Society, the Pulteneytown Commissioners and the government on the matter of the improvement of the fishing harbour on the river of Wick. One thing at least that the storm of 19 August, 1848 accomplished was the dispelling of the kind of complacency that had set in before the event in the affairs of Pulteneytown Harbour. And in case any reminder were needed, another severe storm was experienced in January, 1849. On this occasion no fishermen were lost, since the boats were in harbour, but 'many of the herring boats, drawn up high on the beach, were threatened with destruction, and in several instances they were injured. Some of those lying in the yard at the back of the Commercial Bank were actually floated a considerable distance up, and one or two were taken violently from their moorings and driven up the river.' Considerable damage was done at Broadhaven and Staxigoe. The schooner *Janet* of Putgarden, lying in ballast, was driven ashore and one man was drowned.[1]

THE BRITISH FISHERIES SOCIETY IN THE DOCK

By the time Captain Washington's report came out in January, 1850, virtually all that could be known about the great disaster of 1848 had been hauled into public discussion, and had been argued back and forth in the *John O'Groat Journal*. It was now pretty well generally agreed among Wickers, fairly or unfairly, that the chief culprit in the matter of weaknesses and inadequacies revealed by the disaster and the subsequent enquiry was the British Fisheries Society. An elaborate statement of dissatisfactions was set out in an editorial of the *Journal* on 28 December, 1849, referring to a memorial of the citizens of Wick that had been sent during the year to the Treasury and to the Admiralty, in which:

> praying for enquiry into this lamentable occurrence, the memorialists say they are persuaded that the above disasters might have been to a great degree prevented, had the British Fisheries Society carried out the provisions of the Acts of Parliament. They further stated that 'the harbour is inaccessible at low water'; that it has not been managed in an efficient manner; that the important clauses, which render it imperative to have a lifeboat, with a sufficient crew, and a lighthouse and light at the pier end, have been disregarded, that on the night in question there were neither life-boats, life buoys, beacons, lights or ropes, provided at the Pulteneytown harbour, notwithstanding the similar disaster of 1845.

It was the claim of the 'memorialists' that during the years before the disaster the Fisheries Society had failed to carry out many of its responsibilities and undertakings under both its Acts of Parliament, that of 1814 and that of 1844. Users of the harbour had continued throughout to pay considerable harbour dues, thus fulfilling their part of the contract, so that it was 'difficult to understand on what ground the British Fisheries Society are to be absolved from completing their share of the engagement.' Recently some steps had been taken to obviate grounds of complaint. 'An active, intelligent officer of the navy' had been appointed as superintendent of the harbour, under whose management things had already begun to 'assume a different aspect.' An 'efficient life-boat with carriage to transport it was now on

1 *JOGJ*, 12 January 1849.

the spot;' life-buoys and life-lines had been installed; deepening of the harbour and removal of stones (especially those accumulated round the entrance, including stones 'thrown down' during construction in 1827, and also stones cast out from ballast by thoughtless skippers) had 'been carried out to some extent.'. But the big and critical issue, the enlargement of the harbour to accommodate all its users, remained for urgent action. Figures were quoted to show estimated incomes and expenditures, leaving something like £600 available each year for repairs, which, it was sternly implied, the Society was not spending for this purpose. Captain Washington was quoted as saying in October, 1848:

> How such a sum has been expended those living on the spot are best able to judge. I am aware that the accounts are audited and I have not the least doubt but that they have been correctly rendered; but seeing that when the harbour was inspected in 1846, the stones then down in its construction in 1827 were still lying there, that the harbour was much sanded up, that there were no cranes erected on the quays, nor any gas or other lamps to light them, and that the roadings to the quays were ankle deep in mud and offal of fish, I can only suppose that the funds have been frittered away on temporary or useless measures, instead of having been laid out systematically, under proper management, on the real requirements of the harbour.[1]

Washington's Report.

Though eagerly awaited, when it was published during the first week of January, 1850, Washington's report contained no surprises. It recommended a variety of structural remedies for the now well known difficulties of Pulteneytown Harbour:

1 The construction of a 'harbour' at Salmon Rock, as advocated by Mr Bremner and Mr Gibb (another of the engineers consulted) and approved by Mr Stevenson. Such work might cost £25,700, though Stevenson said £40,000. A portion of the scheme, carrying out to a depth of 10 feet might be done for £20,000.

2 Removal by dredging all of the sand and loose stones at present lodged in the upper part of the bay; and deepening of the present harbours by 4 feet, to render existing quays accessible to fishing boats at all states of the tide. Washington favoured Professor Gordon's

1 *JOGJ*, 20 October, 1848.

recommendations to the Fisheries Society; they would need a 16hp. dredging machine. The North Pier, too, needed prolonging somewhat in a direction different from its present alignment.

3 A breakwater of 18 feet at low water, and 28 feet at high water should be constructed across a portion of the Wick bay, to convert the bay into a harbour of refuge for shipping, at a cost perhaps of £52,000. This could only be done at public expense. It was unnecessary to provide anything more for the fishing boats, 'and it does not appear that the shipping that pass along this coast require much shelter.' Cromarty and Longhope provided good examples of extended harbours of refuge.

4 Extension of the southern breakwater by about 90 feet in its present direction. This plan had been advocated by Mr Mitchell, CE, as the most practicable.

5 The confining and deepening of the Water of Wick itself; in fact, the most obvious remedy of all was to extend the 'natural harbour' of Wick, which had been consistently neglected, but which even in its neglected state afforded 'that shelter in the gale of 19 August which Pulteneytown harbour denied.'

There was considerable discussion in the report of the advice of Joseph Mitchell, CE, a Scottish engineer who had worked often with the British Fisheries Society on other projects, and who at this time had 'been instructed by the Lords of the Admiralty to take part in an investigation and report on the fate of fishing boats on the east coast of Scotland.' On the subject of the confining and deepening of the Wick estuary, Mitchell had argued that it was a question, essentially, of removing the three feet of sand and shingle from the river bed that lay on the rock floor at least 3 feet below low water. The report continued:

> If the river were confined to proper width along the east side of the estuary, by rubble stone dykes, there is little doubt that the winter freshes, assisted by some excavation, would soon cut a channel through the upper soil out to sea. Spring tides it would appear, flow from one to three miles above the bridge; so that by levelling the bed, and removing all obstructions, a fair amount of tidal breakwater might be obtained in addition to the fresh water of the river, which drains a basin of about 30 square miles of extent.

The job might be done, Mitchell thought, for £8,500, but, said the report, 'as it is desirable to cut as deep a channel as can be obtained, say £10,000. With skilful enquiry, suggested Washington, improving the Water of Wick would be one of the best ways of expending money for the benefit of fishermen who resort to this neighbourhood.' He drew attention, however, to the 'impediment to enlarging the basin opposite to the town', imposed by the bad habit of the British Fisheries Society of throwing the soil 'excavated from the harbours within high-water mark in the bight below the bridge, and thus have encroached upon about two and half acres of water space.' This practice, Washington concluded, 'should no longer be permitted'.

Joseph Mitchell considered that such measures, combined with the construction of a pier of 1000 feet long across the bay, to provide a depth of water of 12 feet at low water and 22 feet at spring tides, would render harbourage at Wick and Pulteneytown much more beneficial to the fishermen. The fisherman would be able to come in at all states of the tide and land his cargo immediately, 'and rest quietly at his home until the moment of next sailing arrives (instead of the anxious hours now often spent at a harbour's mouth waiting for the rise of tide).' Such a harbour would, Mitchell considered have wider advantages, too. It would

> probably lead to a larger and safer class of fishing boat (those now being adapted to a shallow, dry harbour), and induce the fishermen to follow the deep sea fishing all the year round, instead of merely during the herring fishing season, and thus cultivate habits of steady industry and occupation which could not but be beneficial to himself, his family and his community.

Captain Washington addressed himself to the issue of the development of Ackergill which, he recognised, had certain advantages over Wick as a location for a safe harbour. He recognised too, however, that it had its disadvantages, not only those discussed during the enquiry, but also the reality that Wick and Pulteneytown had already been developed at great public expense. 'Vast public interest', he continued

> has been created on this coast within the last half century. A fishing village has been raised into a comparatively opulent town. Wealth has been diffused and civilization has followed in its wake. The example here has been a most beneficial influence in a large portion of the Highlands and Islands of Scotland, and habits of industry and the best modes of fishing have been taught to the Highlanders. The large amount of 126,000 barrels of herrings, or one fifth of the whole produce of Scottish fisheries, was cured at Wick during the past year, in addition to

12,000 barrels otherwise covered. The total value of the boats, nets, and lines employed, exceed £61,000, while the catching and curing of the fish occupied 5000 persons; and the carrying of salt, and the export to Ireland and the European markets gave occupation to 16,700 tons of shipping.

AND WHAT IS WANTED? shrilled the *John O'Groat Journal*. The reporter [Captain Washington]

>estimates the cost of improving the river of Wick, (the proposal he most approves of) at L10,000. Only that! Just as much as was voted last year for cleaning drains at Windsor Castle; L3,500 less than that required in 1849 for new furniture in public offices; only 1/14 part of the sums voted for Harwich, Dover, Channel Islands, and Portland harbours; only two year's salary of the Secretary of State; about L1000 less than is annually given out of the public purse to the North American clergy; about L1000 more than was voted last season for supporting Polish refugees and destitute Spaniards. Surely, if L9000 can be spared in one year on behalf of a few Spaniards and Poles, the Government will not, cannot, refuse an equal sum towards preserving the lives and property of thousands of its own people.
>
>It now remains for the people of Wick to take advantage of the tide of circumstances, so much set in their favour.[1]

But the tide soon ebbed. Had the main recommendations of Washington's report been acted on, Wick would have become a quite different place both from what it had been and from what it has since become. Two factors pretty well ensured that such development as that outlined by Mitchell would not occur: one was that Wick was not Pulteneytown and vice versa; the other that neither Lord John Russell's nor the Tory governments that followed, had any inclination to provide the state funds that were necessary.

Wick was still formally the modest royal burgh on the north bank of the Wick river that enjoyed the status of county town but had no other jurisdiction in the community of Pulteneytown on the south bank, even though Joshua Rhind, Provost of Wick, was for a time the Society's agent (and *ex officio* chairman from 1844 of the Pulteneytown Improvement Commission, its *de facto* 'town council') and later cashier, whose main official duty was the collection of rents for the

1 *JOGJ*, 4 January, 1850.

Society. According to Jean Dunlop, 'between 1810 and 1848 . . . the Directors [of the Society] had concerned themselves not at all with the general fishing industry', seeking rather to manage their now considerable estates profitably. They sold most of their other estates during the 1840s, investing their main interest and resources from then on in Pulteneytown, their most successful venture. After the Act of Parliament of 1844, which among other things allowed the Society to borrow money (but only to a limit of £10,000), government of Pulteneytown passed to the so-called Improvement Commission, a mainly elected body which had powers to impose rates and in turn provided for Pulteneytown 'amenities such as street lighting and cleaning, drains and a police force.' The locally elected members of the Commission were 'by no means subservient to the Directors, standing up for what they considered to be their rights equally against the encroachments of Wick Town Council and against the Society.' A result of the delegation of powers of self-government to local people had the effect of greatly increasing, 'the already apparent independence of Pulteneytown.'[1] Little love was lost between the two communities.

Neither the Improvement Commission nor the Wick Burgh Council had much say in the matter of harbour development. Such resources as the Fisheries Society had to invest in such development had been directed exclusively to facilities on the south bank, with one result, that the Wick portion of the river and bay had been under-developed, with the consequences that drew so much comment and criticism after 1848. It had clearly never been much in the minds of the Directors of the Society that investment on the north bank was in any way their concern; and in any case, they had no intention of sharing benefits of any such investment with the burgh. That something had to be done was evident in the light of the Washington enquiry and report, and the Society authorised such relatively inexpensive improvements as have already been mentioned. One change, the appointment of Captain Eden as harbour master, did not work out too well. 'Discretion was not one of Captain Eden's many qualities,' says Jean Dunlop, and despite his 'very efficient work in the improvement of the harbour, his relations with the resident population and especially his behaviour on the Pulteneytown Improvements Commission forced the Directors to demand his resignation.' His style was said to have been that of the 'Quarter Deck'. A 'more diplomatic harbour master

1 Dunlop, *British Fisheries Society*, op cit, p 192.

and agent, Captain Tudor, was appointed in 1854.'

The big issue of major investment continued to be kicked around within the Fisheries Society, and between the Society and government. As Jean Dunlop argues, 'there is no doubt that politics played a considerable part in the controversy.' She tells the story, most of the details of which need not concern us here, of how during the years after the Washington Report, the affairs of the Society wavered to and fro as it sought to cope with its confused concerns. Its Chairman in 1846 was the Duke of Sutherland, and one of the directors, later Deputy Chairman, was James Loch, MP for the Northern Burghs. Already substantial representation on the Board of the Society was of northern interests, which nevertheless did not result in a shift of control from London to Wick. Loch was defeated in the general election of 1855 as MP for the Northern Burghs, his place being taken by Samuel Laing of Kirkwall who also took his place as a director of the Society. Laing was the son of Samuel Laing, the great Orcadian scholar and traveller, but unlike his father, was a Tory.

Unsuccessful attempts were made by local merchants to buy shares in the Society as another move to wrest a measure of control from London, and deputations, including Samuel Laing MP, attended the Annual General Meeting two years running, 1855 and 1856. They found it difficult to get things moving; Laing described the Society as 'a relic of the middle ages'. It was, in fact, seventy years old, and much had happened since its foundation at a time when a number of corporate bodies, state funded and private, were being created. 'If we had the thing to begin a-new,' said Laing in terms that earned him no friends, 'no man in his senses would think of constituting a Society of this kind of noblemen and gentlemen of high standing sitting in London [a quaint way of putting things].' They were neither a 'commercial company, looking to dividends nor yet a body of elected public Commissioners.' Laing went on to suggest that a new Act of Parliament should dissolve the Society and transfer its responsibilities to local commissioners. Though the Earl of Rosebery, an influential member of the Board, supported this proposal, it did not gain the approval of other directors, and 'does not seem to have been backed by more than a small minority in Pulteneytown.'[1]

The problems remained. The story of the next few years is told succinctly by Jean Dunlop, relying for much of her information on the

1 Dunlop, *British Fisheries Society*, op cit. p 193.

Society's own letter file and the *John O'Groat Journal*.

By 1857 it had become clear that the Society, antediluvian though it might be, could still be of greater service to the settlement [of Pulteneytown] than local commissioners. Although their capital was not large enough by modern standards, the Directors had by now a fair sum of money at their command. Immediately after the sale of the western settlements [Ullapool, Tobermory, Lochbay etc] the total stock was in the region of £20,000 and while no dividend was paid this increased annually at the rate of £800 to £1000 from rents and about £600 from interest every year.[1] When in 1856 yet another plan for the harbour was drawn up by Messrs D & T Stevenson of Edinburgh, the Directors offered to pay £25,000 out of a total cost of £46,500. It was proposed to ask parliament to lend the balance. When the Stevenson report was submitted to the Admiralty and then to the Board of Trade, this loan was refused because the Admiralty did not wish the whole of the bay of Wick to be in private hands. At a special meeting of the proprietors of the British Fisheries Society, it was agreed to undertake a limited form of the Stevenson's plan without a loan.

Although the Pulteneytown Harbour Act of 1857 gave the Society authority to do this work and to levy increased harbour dues in return for the expenditure, nothing was done for several years. This was because a nation-wide scheme for building harbours of refuge was under consideration, and in 1858 a Royal Commission inspected Wick bay. The result was deadlock, for the Commissioners saw the advantages of the bay and recommended the building of the breakwater at a cost of £125,000. In spite of this, the Government refused to provide the money, while the Admiralty would not sanction the Society's plans for construction on a smaller scale as they feared this would spoil the bay for future improvement.

Thus, for some years nothing happened. The Society inevitably was blamed. Dunlop continues:

> It was reckoned that between 1845 and 1863 150 fishermen were drowned and over 400 boats wrecked in the

---

1 One of the oft repeated charges against the Society (not well justified) was that they were saving money that should have been spent on development to pay interest to London shareholders.

neighbourhood of Wick. By 1862 the accumulated funds of the Society had reached £42,000 and the Directors suggested that if they could obtain a loan of £60,000 from the Public Works Loans Commission under a new Harbour and Passing Tolls Act of 1861, they themselves would contribute £40,000 towards a more extensive scheme. At last in 1863 it was announced that these plans had been approved by the Admiralty and the Board of Trade and an Act of Parliament had authorised the Society's undertaking. The loan was arranged in three instalments to begin after the Society had spent their £40,000, and was repayable at three per cent interest.

The work on the new harbour, which consisted mainly of building a new outer breakwater [though designed by Stevenson, this was in essence the plan originally advised by Bremner – who was now dead] was begun in 1864 but proceeded slowly with continual damage by storms. The first instalment of the loan was not received until the late summer of 1867, by which time the Society's capital had been reduced to £6,000. On 6th February 1870, after £82,000 had been spent on the work, a storm caused what was estimated at £8,000 worth of damage. Engineers reported that the original plan was not strong enough and although it was recommended to shorten the breakwater, the additional strength needed would cost another £10,000 at least. The Directors applied for an increase in the loan, but although they were exonerated from the charges of inefficiency and haste in their undertaking, the money was refused. The Society had therefore little choice but to meet the cost by a deeper plunge into capital and by a loan from the bank for which the Directors became responsible.

The final blow was administered when in a report on 14th February 1873 the engineers pronounced the now completed works to have failed in their object and that after so much money had been laid out, the harbour was still not a safe refuge. The Directors reported that 'It had always been the view of the Directors that the construction of a breakwater in Wick bay was partly a national undertaking, and was too large for private individuals.' On this ground they regarded the assumption of so great a responsibility with hesitation and reluctance and undertook against their better judgement. Experience has shown that they were justified.[1]

1 Dunlop, *British Fisheries Society*, op cit. pp 193-194.

The end was neither peremptory nor so undramatic as Jean Dunlop's account would suggest. We shall return to the last phase of harbour building, in fact to the last *two* phases of harbour building in Wick in the next chapter. Suffice to say here that the construction programme, after so many delays, begun in 1864, is a quite distinctive episode that left its mark on Wick itself, on the British Fisheries Society and not least on the fortunes of the firm of Stevenson Brothers. Off and on Thomas Stevenson had been involved in the Wick business even before the 1848 disaster; more than twenty years of his and his firm's life became tied up with Wick affairs. Thomas's son, Robert Louis Stevenson, who came at the age of eighteen to Wick with his father in 1868, commented years later on the melancholy end to the endeavours of Stevenson Bros to protect the Bay of Wick from its most formidable friend and enemy, the sea:

> Many harbours were successfully carried out (by Thomas and his brother David): one, the harbour of Wick, the chief disaster of my father's life was a failure; the sea proved too strong for man's arts, and after expeditions hitherto unthought of, and on a scale hypercyclopean, the work must be deserted and now [1887] stands a ruin in that God-forsaken bay, ten miles from John O'Groats.

The story, however, fits more conveniently into the account of the circumstances that accompanied Wick's toppling from the role of chief herring port than to that of its ascendancy. It was, indeed, one of the factors of that decline. It is adorned, too, with vivid recollections by Robert Louis of experiences during his short stay in Wick, and the repetition of these may be left until we reach the fateful years of 1868, 1870 and 1874.

One item of the record of the 1848 disaster may be properly picked up here. That is the beginning of the story of the Wick life-boat service. This, in any case, would seem to be the appropriate topic with which to conclude a chapter dealing with the peril of the seas.

THE WICK AND ACKERGILL LIFEBOATS

A detail revealed during the enquiry must have interested, but puzzled, Captain Washington quite a lot. That was the confused references to the lifeboat that did not leave the harbour that dreadful night of 18-19 August, and evidently did not often leave it at other times either. The actual circumstances of this peculiar business have been the subject of some patient research by a present day lifeboat enthusiast and former lifeboat man, Andy Anderson, whose account of James Bremner's ingenious contribution to this aspect of the conquest of the sea around Wick deserves to be quoted in full. As usual, the detail comes from the *John O'Groat Journal*, dated 29 August, 1846:

> Mr Bremner has just finished a new lifeboat for the use of Wick. It is built entirely on a new construction, the invention of Mr Bremner's ingenious and fertile mind. It was launched in the morning and at 3 pm on the Saturday afternoon it left the harbour and sailed quickly across the bay. The boat was propelled by two paddle wheels, placed in the centre and driven by eight men. The speed with which it sailed was very rapid, having gone a distance of a mile in minutes. Nor is the least important part of her, the great ease with which, and the narrowness of compass in which she turns. The number of individuals on board (thirty) made the boat much heavier than otherwise. Notwithstanding, on a trial of strength it took all that the six men in pilot boat could do to reach the harbour before her.
>
> As the day was fine it was impossible to judge how the boat would stand in a heavy sea, but general opinion appears to be that the strength of power which can be applied to the paddles, and the peculiar construction of the boat render her fit for the important purpose for which she has been made.
>
> There was also a trial made of Dennett's Rockets. They were fired near the Salmon Rock and the distance sent by the line was very great. Combined with the new lifeboat, there has been a considerable increase in the potential for saving life from wrecks in the area.[1]

As already described, an opportunity for using the rocket apparatus soon presented itself when Bremner, arriving at Keiss Castle overland, was able to effect the rescue of nine men from the *Warrior* in October, 1847. There is no record of the Bremner lifeboat being brought into similar beneficial use. A further trial of the unusual craft had been made in March of that year when it was 'well tried in all types of situations,' on an afternoon when 'a considerable surf was running in

---

1 Taken directly from the handwritten notes of Andy Anderson, who uses as his source *JOGJ*, 29 August, 1846. Most quotes in this section are from Jeff Morris, *The History of the Wick and Ackergill Lifeboats;* Lifeboat Enthusiasts Society, Coventry (1993).

the Bay.' The report was that the boat was considered to be 'virtually impossible to capsize,' though it was found 'to be difficult to propel into the face of the breaking surf,' but it was felt that 'this problem could be remedied by the addition of a further paddle wheel.' Whether or not the additional paddle wheel was ever added was not told, nor is there any further record of Bremner's peculiar lifeboat in use or of its mechanism. The historian of the Wick Lifeboat Service speculates that the paddle-wheels 'were turned by a system of cranks and levers.' No picture of it survives, and in view of the boat's apparent uselessness at the time of the 1848 disaster, it seems to have been discarded and replaced by a conventional lifeboat shortly after the disaster.

It is sometimes supposed that lifeboats in Britain are uniformly under the direction of the Royal National Lifeboat Institution, founded in 1824 by Sir William Hillary. In fact, the Wick lifeboat service was not taken over by the RNLI until 1895. Lifeboats were, however, operating in the Wick area long before that. To begin with the kinds of rescue that later became the responsibility and operated according the expertise of the lifeboat service, ordinary boats with *ad hoc* crews would sometimes make brave attempts at rescue. The first such recorded event of this kind was the rescue of three men from the *Thomas Dougall*, a 270 ton brig which was driven on to the rocks at Occumster, 10 miles south of Wick on 12 March, 1839, by a scratch crew of eight men led by Robert McAlister who took out 'a small fishing boat and made their way through a very heavy surf' to the wreck where, already, five of the crew had been drowned and another four had escaped by leaping on to the rocks 'from where they were hauled to safety by some local people.' Other events of a similar kind occurred both before and after 'Black Saturday', 19 August, 1848, when no sea-going rescue attempts were attempted.

The disaster and the following enquiry directed specific attention to Wick's shortcomings in the matter of a lifeboat service. One of the first moves of the Wick and Pulteneytown Harbour Trust to put things to rights was the installing in November, 1848 of a '28ft x 10'3", 12 oared self-righter .... which was almost certainly built on the lines of the famous *Greathead* lifeboats ... by Edward Oliver of South Shields, at a cost of £169.' It was brought to Wick 'on board a steamer, on November 11th, 1848. During trials in the breakers at the back of the North Quay, this lifeboat was repeatedly struck by very heavy waves, but came through the task satisfactorily and the crew expressed themselves very pleased with the boat.'

The new boat's first call out to sea came in July, 1849 when 17 fishing boats were caught at sea 'by a sudden north-easterly gale, which caused a heavy swell in the bay. One of the boats attempted to enter the harbour, but was driven up the back of the North Quay, her crew being rescued by means of ropes. With 16 other fishing boats still out in the bay, the new lifeboat was launched and the crew went to each vessel in turn, checking that their anchors were secure. Later, when the weather eased and the tide rose, all 16 fishing boats entered the harbour safely, escorted by the lifeboat.'

This was, compared with some of the later events, an easy assignment. Most the lifeboat calls were for the bigger vessels that got into difficulties in the waters off Wick, and the challenge was often more dangerous. Such an occasion was the appearance in Wick Bay of the *Vronia Santina* on 8 September, 1857. The Dutch galliot

> missed the dangerous reef off Proudfoot [the expanse of skerries off the North Head, just below Broadhaven Bay] and shortly afterwards, her Captain having decided to try to ride out the storm. But the boat was in such a dangerous position, that Capt. John Tudor, the Agent for the British Fisheries Society [Tudor was in fact also harbourmaster, who in addition had taken on the duty of coxing the lifeboat], decided to launch the lifeboat from the Salmon Rock.

The *John O'Groat Journal* was, as usual on the scene, and named the lifeboat crew of fifteen men:

> Captain Tudor, Allan McLeod (pilot), Alex Cormack, Alex Campbell, George Mackay, James Budge, David Brock, Donald McBeath, Elex Bremner, James Sinclair, Robert Geddes, Donald Campbell, Alex Forbes, – Hossack and Alexander Bain. Away pulled these noble fellows to the scene of peril, to rescue these foreign seamen from impending doom. It may well be imagined with what intensity of eager interest the thousands of spectators that thronged the quays and braes watched the progress of the boat, through the troubled sea, now rising on top of a mountain billow and then hidden in a yawning gulf. Gradually she neared the galliot until almost within hail when a succession of heavy seas broke over both vessels and swept them apart. In spite of many attempts they were unable to make contact.
>
> At this time, the agony of the spectators, particularly those

who had relatives aboard, was truly indescribable. Few expected, but that every wave would cover both boats and crew under their frowning waters. The last, one terrific wave, surging with terrific violence struck the lifeboat with fearful power, that those on land thought it would be destroyed. Although it was flung over and filled with water it reappeared. Three men were seen in the water struggling for survival, and the boat was disabled with the oars broken and washed away. Two men were rescued by means of buoys and lifelines but the other (Alexander Bain) disappeared beneath the waves. The lifeboat was now at the mercy of the waves, a floating oar was recovered and due to the skill of the helmsman was thrown ashore at the harbour entrance. With great difficulty a rope was secured and the boat and crew were hauled ashore. Alexander Bain left a widow and seven children.

Shortly afterwards Captain Tudor intended to relaunch the lifeboat to attempt a rescue. As the volunteers assembled, the seas started to moderate and the attempt was not made.[1]

The galliot survived and sailed away, but was wrecked a month later in the Baltic off Frederikshaven, all her crew being saved. A fund for the family of Alexander Bain collected £150, to which the RNLI contributed £20. Captain John Tudor RN, was awarded a Silver Medal by the RNLI, which also sent to his widow a posthumously awarded medal to Alexander Bain. Tudor also received the Silver Medal of the Board of Trade.

The following year, Tudor was put in charge of another new lifeboat, a self-righting 34ft, 12-oared vessel that cost £500. This lifeboat underwent several adventures during the next two years, including the rescue of the entire crew of a salt-laden schooner in Wick Bay, the *Eva* of Aberdeen in September, 1858, and similarly the crew of another schooner, the *Huntress* in September the following year. On this occasion the lifeboat with its complement of fifteen crew and seven rescued mariners was swamped by a 'huge wave' so that 'she nearly broached to'. However, 'with great skill Captain Tudor brought her under control again, and amidst loud cheers from the crowds lining the quays, the lifeboat entered the harbour safely.' Tudor was awarded a Vellum of Thanks for this service by the RNLI.

He was decorated yet again the following year, after

1 *JOGJ*, 8 September, 1857.

the local sloop *Maria* tried to enter Wick Harbour on Wednesday, November 20th, 1860. A very heavy swell prevented her from doing so and she was forced to seek shelter in Sinclair Bay, where her crew dropped anchor. The weather grew steadily worse until, by next morning, conditions were appalling. Capt. John Tudor set out for Ackergill in a horse-drawn gig, taking with him lines and life-belts, while arrangements were made to get horses to haul the Wick Lifeboat, on her launching carriage, overland to Ackergill, the harbour at Wick having been closed because of the dreadful conditions. However, as soon as Capt. Tudor reached the shore, he realised the need for immediate action and so, a boat belonging to the Caithness Steam Shipping Company was pressed into service, being transported to Shorelands Beach, directly opposite where the *Maria* lay at anchor, being pounded by huge seas. With a crew of 9 men, under Capt. Tudor, the boat – which had been built on the lines of the old Wick Lifeboat and which was used for landing passengers at Ackergill when the steamers were prevented from entering Wick Harbour – reached the *Maria* and, as huge waves swept over both boats, the crew of 2 were rescued and landed safely, just as the Wick Lifeboat arrived on the beach. For his gallantry on that occasion, Capt. John Tudor, RN, was awarded his second Silver Medal by the RNLI. He also received the Silver Medal from the Board of Trade, while each member of his brave crew received the Board of Trade Bronze Medal.

It is neither necessary nor possible to retail here the full tally of episodes involving the Wick lifeboats, providing service from these early days to the present time, though broken in the case of the Wick boat from 1913 to 1921. This record has been fully rendered in the recent closely packed narrative, *The History of the Wick and Ackergill Lifeboats* by Jeff Morris, and for which much of the local research was done by Andy Anderson.

The Ackergill Lifeboat.

The provision of an additional lifeboat for the area at Ackergill came about immediately as a sequel to a serious disaster near to Ackergill Tower in December, 1876, though there had already been moves to establish a lifeboat here. The trouble with relying on the

Wick lifeboat for the waters in Sinclair's Bay, was that passage round Noss Head was often turbulent and dangerous. Even when the Wick boat was called to the area, it was usually safer to trundle the lifeboat on its carriage along the road from Wick to Ackergill and to launch her there. This was time consuming and the launching was not easy. The story of the December night of 1876 was told, as usual, by the *John O'Groat Journal* and repeated in the *History:*

> During a violent storm on December 23rd, 1876, the 120 ton schooner, *Emilie,* of Wolgast, laden with coal from Sunderland, was driven north past Wick, coming ashore 2 miles from Ackergill, near Ackergill Tower. The Rocket Apparatus Team were called out, but in rapidly worsening conditions, it took some considerable time before a line could be fired out to the 6 men aboard the schooner, who had taken refuge in the rigging, huge seas repeatedly sweeping over the stranded ship. Because it was taking so long to get a line fired out to the wreck, a salmon coble was taken overland from Ackergill, to a position directly opposite the wreck. Capt. John Cormack took charge of this boat and called for volunteers to get out with him. There was no shortage of willing men, in fact, when the boat was launched, there were 9 men aboard and some experienced onlookers said that she was already overloaded, with very little room left to take any survivors on board. But, by hard work at the oars and also by pulling on a rocket line which had been then fired aboard the wreck, the small boat reached the *Emilie*. Three men were taken on board – and Capt. Cormack then realised that the small boat was grossly overloaded and so he turned back towards the shore. But as the small boat left the *Emilie*, the rocket line got under her keel and she capsized. The three men from the schooner had been totally exhausted and they quickly disappeared, only 5 of the salmon boat surviving. Of the *Emilie's* crew of 6, only one, a 17 year old youth, survived. A total of 9 men lost their lives that day.

This rather bald account leaves out quite a lot of the drama and frustrations of the episode. The Admiralty ordered an enquiry 'into the loss of life at and near Wick during the year 1876, and more especially on the wreck of the German vessel the *Emilie*, on 23rd December, 1876.' The enquiry, held in Wick Town Hall in January, 1877, was headed by Commander James Prowse RN, who commented on an incident of August last, when a fisherman lost his life coming into Wick Harbour and another in which a boat being towed into harbour capsized. The Ackergill affair lasted for a whole long day and involved frantic attempts to get equipment and men to Ackergill in very difficult circumstances, during which much time was lost. In addition to calls for help from Wick, Mr Duff Dunbar of Ackergill Castle sent off a horseman to Scarfskerry (near Dunnet, a distance of 18 miles) for some 'Board of Trade life-saving apparatus'. The team came as fast as they could: 'They deserved great praise,' said the Inspector, 'for the prompt manner in which they turned out, considering they had to travel in the depth of a winter's night with blinding storms of sleet and snow, the women assisting the men for the first two miles, in dragging the apparatus until horses were procured, but unfortunately they arrived too late.'

Commander Prowse had some critical remarks about failure to send the Wick lifeboat by land – the distance was only two miles. The lifeboat, he revealed had 'never been out for exercise since she was built in 1869, and only twice used for service; the last time was about four or five years since.' Even more surprising, 'there is no regular crew.' The difficulty could be that fishermen 'might be at sea when required,' but at least, there ought to be an exercise once a quarter, 'or at least twice a year.' In any case, when the Commander inspected the lifeboat itself, he found her leaky, 'which is not surprising considering the length of time since she had been in the water.' All this might be thought surprising in a herring port that had suffered such a lesson as 'Black Saturday', but that was twenty-eight years before. Further, Commander Prowse considered that the lifeboat house was not in a good position, being on the landward side of the River Wick service bridge, constructed he admitted, since 'that was built. I think that the best place would now be inside the breakwater.'[1]

An important consequence then of the Ackergill disaster was the setting up there of a lifeboat, for which £400 had already been collected. A handsome donation of £800 was received from Mrs A Bower, of Lessneath Heath, Kent. A site and a boathouse costing £320 were provided by Mr Duff Dunbar, near to Ackergill Tower. Since there were few fishermen at Ackergill to form a regular crew, one of the smaller classes of boat was chosen for this station. 'The new boat and the carriage were taken by rail from London to Wick and then, on March 14th, 1878, they were paraded through the streets of Wick and

---

1 *JOGJ*, 1 March, 1877. The 'breakwater' in question was that constructed by Stevensons, and now abandoned.

on to the sands at Reiss, where after due ceremony Mrs Duff Dunbar stepped forward and christened the boat *George and Isabella*, the names of Mr and Mrs Duff Dunbar. The *George and Isabella* was called out only once during its ten-year life, when in 1887 it rescued 30 fishermen from two boats, in two trips. 'The Wick Lifeboat, which was brought overland, arrived just as the last of the fishermen were being rescued.'

A new lifeboat was placed at Ackergill in January 1888, provided from a legacy of Colonel E A D Brooshoft, a rich Yorkshireman. She took the name *Jonathan Marshall, Sheffield*. She lasted in service until 1907, being called out eleven times during her life, sometimes in difficult conditions. She was replaced by *Co-operator No 3*, so named because she was donated by the Co-operative Union. The *Co-operator* had a rather uneventful career, being called out only 3 times before she was discarded in 1932, at which time the RNLI's Committee of Management decided to close down the Ackergill Station. Still standing on the Ackergill shore – some distance from the original station near the Tower – is the rusting and rotting slipway, constructed in 1907, the first one ever to be built by the RNLI of ferro-concrete.[1]

The story of the Wick lifeboat does not end here, but the later phases of the service may be best reserved until our round-up of Wick today.

---

1 A characteristic tendency in the lifeboat world has been for particular and generous inland benefactors, including private individuals, municipalities and corporate organisations, to donate lifeboats, especially after one has been lost.

The Storm – an imaginative reconstruction of the Great Storm of 19 October, 1848 by R. Anderson, 1880.
Courtesy Wick District Council.

PART IV:

WICK ON HOLD

Chapter 16: Wick Over the Hill.

Chapter 17: Wick on the Line.

Chapter 18: A Tale of two Cities.

Chapter 19: Wars and Rumours of War: I

Chapter 20: Wars and Rumours of War: II

Chapter 21: Some People and Places.

Chapter 22: Wick Today.

CHAPTER 16

WICK OVER THE HILL

AT the census of 1991 Wick had a population of 8,794. This is considerably less than the figure for 1891, which was 13,105, near to the highest population ever reached (13,291 in 1871). As the Rev Douglas Briggs writes in his contribution to the *Third Statistical Account of Scotland* of 1988:

> The figures relating to the population of Wick tell their own story. In 1801 the population of the parish was, 3,986; in 1851 it was 11,851; in 1871 the population reached its peak, 13,291; in 1901 it had fallen to 12,250; in 1911 it had risen slightly to 12,587; in 1921 the decline had really set in, 11,322; in 1931 the decline continued, 10,383; and in 1951 the population was 9,531 (Burgh, 7,161).[1]

Several other points relate. Rise and decline in population over the last two hundred years is characteristic of the whole county of Caithness, which is reckoned to have had a population of 22,609 in 1801; it reached its peak in 1871 with 39,992. By the beginning of this century it was down to 33,870 (1901), and in 1981, it had fallen to 27,380. Rise, fluctuation and decline over the period have affected all the parishes of the county (or 'district' as it now is). Thurso as the only other town in the county has shared in this growth, fluctuation and decline, rising from 3,628 in 1801, to 6,217 in 1881, significantly down to as low as 4,095 in 1931 and then a spectacular rise to nearly 10,000 in 1961, now once again going down. If we look at the figures for Wick Royal Burgh (as distinct from parish), these get an apparently dramatic boost in 1911, from 2,774 in 1901 to 9,086; actually the result of the union of the two 'burghs', Wick and Pulteneytown to form the present Royal Burgh. All of this leaves out of account the annual temporary swelling of the population of the two towns when the fishing season began.

Different factors influenced population concentration in each of the Caithness localities, but there is little doubt the prime cause of growth in the population of Caithness, from the beginning to the end of the

---

1 John E Smith (Ed): *The Third Statistical Account of Scotland: The County of Caithness;* Edinburgh, Scottish Academic Press (1988), p 209. See also statistical table p xi.

nineteenth century was the phenomenal development of the herring fisheries, especially in the parishes of Wick, Latheron[1] and to a lesser extent Canisbay, which includes part of the Keiss area. Thurso and Dunnet, shared though less abundantly, in the fishing, while Thurso was also affected by port development of a more general commercial kind than that characteristic of Wick. The Thurso area's sudden leap in 1961 obviously reflects the establishment, at that time, of the Dounreay fast breeder atomic reactor, a factor which also arrested decline in Wick. Inland parishes such as Halkirk and Watten had only a modest share in growth; both underwent decline from about 1881, though Halkirk has also benefited by residence there of workers from Dounreay.

Of all the Caithness localities, Wick and Latheron had the most spectacular rise in population during the nineteenth century. On the official figures, Wick had a population rise between 1801 and 1851 of nearly 300 per cent, and Latheron of 228 per cent, as compared with Thurso's 40 per cent and Halkirk's 15 per cent. As mentioned elsewhere, the growth of Wick at this time considerably exceeded the rate of most of the towns in Scotland's industrial belt.

The town's rapid rise to importance as a base for the herring fishing and for the export of pickled herrings has been traced in some detail in earlier chapters. As late as 1855 Wick's production topped that of all other centres; the Wick district (excluding Lybster) produced a total of 134,232 crans as compared with the combined total of 43,048 of Fraserburgh and Peterhead.[2] By 1874, the year when the railway arrived in Wick the score was quite completely reversed: Wick produced 66,740 crans (76,601 in 1873), while Fraserburgh alone produced 160,000 crans, and Peterhead 150,000 crans (157,415 and 168,000 respectively in 1873).[3] There continued to be considerable fluctuations in the Wick catch, for instance, after a run of low catches (less than 50,000 crans in 1868), the catch of 1871 topped again the 100,000 cran level (103,056).[4]

Wick slipped quite markedly down the table of main centres of the herring industry from first to about fourth or fifth in some years though, as we shall see, the decline was only marginally absolute; in

---

1 The Latheron parish, the largest parish of Caithness, contains the sizeable fishing communities of Dunbeath and Lybster, both of which received refugees from the Sutherland clearances. Between 1801 and 1851, Latheron increased from 3,612 to 8,224. (Smith, op cit).
2 *JOGJ*, 5 September, 1856.
3 *JOGJ*, 9 September, 1874.
4 Ibid.

the early years of the twentieth century Wick reached some of its highest production figures ever. Above all, the total Scottish catch – to say nothing of the English, continued to climb dramatically. The reasons for the relative decline of Wick up to 1900 are still disputed, though there is little fundamental research evidence on what actually happened. There was yet no serious indication that overall depletion of stocks was occurring in the North Sea as the result of 'overfishing', but there was apprehension that too little was known about such matters, and that it would not do to continue operating in the belief that herring would go on for ever. A rather windy note in the *Journal* in September, 1874, complained that fishers no longer began fishing in the season 'with the proper spirit at the proper time'. This might have signified that the fishers of Wick, relying on nature's continuing bounty, were taking it easy. A very doubtful notion; though in fact, the number of boats now operating from the Wick harbour was 710, as compared with the 1122 of 1862.

It was argued in the same article that it was time for taking stock: 'the whole history of the herring fishing, the classification of known facts, and the relation of these facts bear to a great national industry have got to be be garnered.'[1]

The Dangers of Over Fishing

Actually the writer of this article was a bit behind the times. In 1864 John M Mitchell wrote his classic *The Herring, its Natural History and National Importance* in which, as Iain Sutherland puts it, 'Mitchell wrote not only a history of the fishing up to his time , but an analysis of the life cycle of the herring, how it was caught and processed in various countries, and some opinions on the future of the industry.' Of particular significance was Mitchell's concern about the possible effects of trawling on the industry because of the damage it did to herring spawn. The danger was not only to herring stocks but also to others, notably the cod which fed on numerous herrings a day as did many seabirds. However, Sutherland makes an interesting comment on the relationship between cod and herring:

> Mitchell confined himself to the observation that in 1856, there were 39,000 fishermen in Scotland and if this number were increased by 6000, they would then catch the same amount of herring as the cod were estimated to do; in other words about

1 *JOGJ*, 9 September, 1874.

800 million a year. What Mitchell did not say, possibly because research had not established the fact by that time, is that herring in their turn lived on the spawn of their predators. The cycle was therefore to a greater or lesser degree self-perpetuating but for one key fact that no-one observed. Man alone was the only predator who injected nothing into the cycle but only took from it. Dead whales, seals or seabirds are consumed by one organism or another and thence recycled to the sea for the benefit of its inhabitants. The early writers such as Mitchell, while they did not say in so many words, implied as much and were at some pains to make it clear.[1]

Certainly fears about pollution and exhaustion of fish stocks in northern waters had hardly surfaced by the 1860s. Sutherland draws attention, nevertheless, to at least one other writer of those times whose comments are remarkably prophetic. This was James G. Bartram, who wrote a book called *Harvest of the Sea.* He wrote:

> I have always been slow to believe in the inexhaustibility of the shoals, and can easily imagine the overfishing, which some people pooh-pooh so glibly, to be quite possible, especially when supplemented by the cod and other cannibals so constantly at work, and so well described by the Lochfyne Commission; not that I believe it possible to pick up or kill every fish of a shoal; but, as I have already hinted, so many are taken, and the economy of the shoal so disturbed, that in all probability it may change its ground or amalgamate with some other herring colony. I shall be met here by the old argument, that the 'fecundity of the fish is so enormous as to prevent their extinction,' etc. etc. But the certainty of the fish yielding twenty thousand eggs is no surety for these being hatched, or if hatched, of escaping the dangers of their infancy, and reaching the market as table food. I watch the great shoals at Wick with much interest, and could wish to have been longer acquainted with them. How long time have the Wick shoals taken to grow to their present size? – what size were the shoals when the fish had leave to grow without molestation? – and how long have they been fished? are questions which I should like to have answered. As it is, I fear the great Wick fishery must come some day to an end. When the Wick fishery first began the fisherman

---

1 Iain Sutherland: *From Herring to Seine Net Fishing on the East Coast of Scotland:* Wick, Camps Bookshop (1990), p 48.

could carry in a creel on his back the nets he required; now he requires a cart and a good strong horse.[1]

Such ecological thinking in the mid-nineteenth century was unusual, and such warnings were not much heeded. The positivist mood of the day, reinforced often by profound religious conviction that 'the Lord would provide' bountifully for human needs, ran counter to such notions. Sutherland adds: 'Bartram was to be proven all too accurate in his prophecy and if Wick's demise was not entirely for the reasons he gave, he was not all that far off the mark as far as the fishing generally was concerned.'

It is a fact that little was known of the true nature, habits and numbers of *Clupea harengus*, or for that matter, of any of the fish now being scooped up in increasing quantities in the North Sea and elsewhere round Britain. Virtually no fundamental research had been undertaken by scientific agency into the highly profitable resource of fisheries, although there had been several Select Committee reports, and a variety of other Commission studies on Scottish fisheries and the herring fisheries in particular, two of which had called on the expertise of Professor Thomas Henry Huxley, at that time perhaps the best known biologist – strictly paleologist – in the country. Though no believer in the goodness of providence, even Huxley cherished the notion that herring stocks were virtually limitless, and poured scorn on those who suggested that 'it stands to reason' that over-fishing might ultimately seriously deplete these stocks.

In addition to his work as a commissioner, he had in 1857 conducted some experiments off the island of Arran on the spawning of herring. From 1881 for several years he served as Inspector of Fisheries, and was associated with an exhibition mounted at Edinburgh on herrings. Speaking at a lecture on the subject, he commented on the general lack of knowledge of the fish, its life and 'the singularities of its organisation,' which perplex biologists, let alone ordinary folk. He insisted, however, on the *impossibility* ('borne out by his service with the Fishing Commission') of 'men's fisheries affecting the numbers of herring to any appreciable extent, a year's catch amounting to the estimated number of a single shoal; while the flatfish and cod fisheries remove many of the distinctive enemies of the herring.'[2]

---

1 Iain Sutherland, *Herring to Seine Net*, op cit. p 49.
2 Leonard Huxley: *Letters of Thomas Henry Huxley*; London, Macmillan (1900); Vol. 1 p 155.

Time proved Huxley very wrong. He had, of course, no means of knowing just how efficient and ruthless men's methods of scavenging the seas were to become. Even as late as 1881, the business had hardly begun.

Wick's changing status as a main fishing port began long before any kind of environmental awareness set in; conviction in this matter came very slowly. In its earlier stages it was prompted rather by shifts in the economy of fishing rather than its ecology. And in the first instance it was problems on the supply rather than the demand side that caused, not a decline in the herring industry, but the considerable geographical realignment that left Wick lower down the scale. According to Malcolm Gray, the market for barrelled herring remained buoyant for the whole century, the price being paid especially by German consumers doubling from its levels before 1840 instead of falling. What he calls the 'impulse to expand' was a continual driving force between 1835 and 1884 in the Scottish herring industry, and in fishing in general. Although there were considerable difficulties in finding the capital in some places, money continued to be invested in the fishing and curing of herrings, even in some of the smaller centres such as Helmsdale and Buckie, where in 1877 John Gordon of Cluny built a splendid new harbour at a cost of £60,000. But the most substantial development was that of Fraserburgh, Peterhead and Aberdeen. Improvement schemes for Fraserburgh and Peterhead costing £50,000 and £100,000 respectively had been undertaken by 1860, and by 1873 the bill for improvement at Fraserburgh had run to £100,000. By 1879 the three eastern towns were accommodating between them 1,917 boats, much larger boats, of course, than those of the earlier part of the century. The fishermen were also increasingly concerned with extension of their activities into the white fish and line fishing trades.

Boats were now larger. By the 1870s forty-foot keels were becoming common and even longer in the 1880s. In addition to this, during the 1860s nets had become much lighter and more efficient; cotton was now being used instead of hemp and nets were being made on net machines instead of by hand. Instead of thirty nets, by 1880 many Fraserburgh boats could carry up to sixty, which enabled the fishers to bring home larger catches. These factors also meant that boats could now fish in waters further out from home, and the habit grew of boats sailing round Scotland to fish in the Minch and off Lewis. Stornoway became an increasingly prosperous port of landing, while kit-built or temporary curing stations were set up in many coves and landing places in the west, where harbourage was much less of a problem than on the east coast. There was also no shortage of women to do the gutting.

The other major factor that altered the whole complexion of fishing, herring and all other kinds, was the coming of steam. Steam trawlers began to operate in south-east England in the 1880s and desultorily in Scotland towards the end of the century, a subject of investigation by the Dalhousie Royal Commission on Trawling (of which Professor Huxley was a key member), which reported in 1885. One effect of this was the Herring Fisheries Act of 1889 which, among other things closed off considerable areas of the Scottish coast to trawling. Steam drifters came later still, the first of which began appearing in the 1890s. Wick's first drifter arrived in 1899. Steam, came too late to have much bearing on the status of Wick as a herring port.

'In the early eighties,' says Gray, 'a new area of prolific yield opened up to the east coast fishermen – Shetland,' whose 'high potential for fishing conducted at any time between May and September [encouraged] a rush to develop new stations, and a build-up of fishing stations' strength quicker than any previously known.' Shetland soon outstripped all other herring fishing centres. Thus originated the routine that by the turn of the century was beginning to govern the herring fishing down the east coasts of Scotland and England, by which boats and gutters started their summer labours in May, finishing sometimes as late as October.[1]

These considerations though relevant take us away from the problems of Wick, which continued throughout in business, but where, apart from bumper years, such as 1880, 1883, 1884 and 1898[2] (total catch in each of these years over 100,000 crans), the trend was

1 M. Gray, op cit: pp 58-100.
2 A selection of production figures for Wick, 1837-1885:

Year	No of Boats	Average Catch	Total Catch for season.
1837	600	99 crans	59,000 crans
1847	765	106 crans	80,190 crans
1849	800	140 crans	112,000 crans
1857	1100	72½ crans	79,750 crans
1862	1122	65 crans	72,930 crans
1867	970	83 crans	80,510 crans
1877	702	68¾ crans	48,248 crans
1880	655	173 crans	113,186 crans
1882	600	116½ crans	69,926 crans
1884	520	194 crans	101,180 crans

Figures derived from *JOGJ* issue at end of first week of September.

generally slowly downwards, smaller total catches, fewer boats and higher catches per boat. At best Wick was holding its own, but with fewer fishers, fewer curers (whose capacity was rising) and, by the same token fewer ancillary activities, especially the provision of lodging for visiting workers and hired hands. The use of larger boats almost certainly meant the use of more hired hands, and it is doubtless a matter of no surprise that in 1885 Wick's first trade union, the Workers' Union, was formed at a meeting in the Old Free Church at the end of the fishing season.[1]

THE SEASON 1905 IN WICK

The *John O'Groat Journal*, whose devotion to the herring trade was undeviating and whose journalistic expertise in the subject was unrivalled, was in the habit of giving an assessment of the season each year early in September. The review of 1 September, 1905, occupying two whole columns of editorial comment and analysis of Wick's essential mode of livelihood, the herring fishing, contains much information and shrewd comment on the state of this major Scottish industry and of Wick's contribution to it.[2] The figures quoted are, in fact, a week earlier than usual and the *Journal* compensates for the fact by 'adding a few thousands of crans' to the figures for total catch. The season is estimated as having lasted from the 1 June to the present date, 1 September.

The SEASON'S TOTAL IS 1,112,000 CRANS for the whole east coast of Scotland. This, says the *Journal*,

> is a very large total, and the season must be considered an exceptionally good one. Seldom in the history of the trade has the total turned a million, and this year's total is second of 1,220,000 crans with which last season closed. It is, roughly speaking, about 100,000 crans short of last season's catch. It is considerably ahead of 1903 when the season closed with 925,000 crans, and also ahead of 1902, when the total ran to about, 1,010,000 crans. And there is a material difference too in the value of the catch as the prices this season have run much higher than they have done since 1902. Another very important

---

1 *JOGJ*, 2 September, 1885.
2 About 1873 the *Journal* began publishing its *Herring Circular* which, for the next sixty years or so provided for the benefit of the trade a weekly run of statistics and other information during the six weeks or so of the season.

aspect of the season has been an immunity from any serious loss of life or material. It may thus be said that a very successful season is closing.

'Wick, has, comparatively speaking, done well,' was the *Journal's* opinion, listing the town as 'next to Peterhead and Fraserburgh,' a position in the table that was now well established. Making the small allowance mentioned for the week's catch, the table (in crans) read:

	1905	1904
Shetland	570,000	533,000
Orkney	30,000	25,000
Wick	106,000	120,000*
Fraserburgh	145,000	220,000
Peterhead	120,000	153,000
Aberdeen	57,000	68,000

*A *Circular* statistical summary of 1911, gives figures of 102,954 and 130,591 respectively for 1904 and 1905.

The most striking feature of this listing is the spectacular pre-eminence of Shetland, a record. Only six years before, in 1899, the Shetland catch had been 214,000, less than half the present total. The explanation, according to the *Journal* was that 'during the whole season the boats which went to Lerwick and Baltasound stations prosecuted the fishing there regularly, and remained there longer than usual.'

As for Wick itself,

> At the close of last week the local fishermen in general expected to continue the fishing for this week before finishing up for the season. But as the weather at the beginning of the week turned out rather unsuitable, many abandoned this intention, and prepared for the 'settling up' business earlier than they would have done had Monday night proved a possible sea-night. Still a good number were content to let the foul weather blow past. But unfortunately they have met with little compensation for their pains and patience, the total landings for the week up to last night not exceeding 1600 crans.

Nevertheless, 'assuredly the fishermen have no reason to grumble this year.' They have again topped the 100,000 cran level, an achievement reached only six times since 1855; 'and for an average per boat there is only one year in all that period which can boast a better. That is the year 1902 when 285 boats averaged 437 crans.' The average for this year, 1905 'is nightly 404 crans for 260 boats, as compared with last year's 401 crans for 300 boats.' The average price

A town centre scene – Northern Ensign office in High Street, 1912.
From the Johnston Collection. Reproduced by kind permission of the Wick Society.

Bank Row and Saltoun Street, Lower Pulteneytown – c 1946.
From the Johnston Collection. Reproduced by kind permission of the Wick Society.

A Relic of the Old Days – a demonstration of coach travel staged in Market Square in 1934.
From the Johnston Collection. Reproduced by kind permission of the Wick Society.

The Newer Mode – The Highland Railway Locomotive *Glenbruar* at Wick Shed – c 1906.
From the Johnston Collection. Reproduced by kind permission of the Wick Society.

Locomotive stuck in a snowdrift beyond Halkirk – 1905.
From the Johnston Collection. Reproduced by kind permission of the Wick Society.

Wick and District Territorials leaving – August, 1914.
From the Johnston Collection. Reproduced by kind permission of the Wick Society.

Bank Row – houses demolished in an Air Raid, 1 July, 1940.
From the Johnston Collection. Reproduced by kind permission of the Wick Society.

Members of the Wick Division of County Police, about 1910
(some years after Wick and Pulteneytown combined).
From the Johnston Collection. Reproduced by kind permission of the Wick Society.

received for herrings landed this year is 'the handsome figure of 18s 6d per cran,' a total of £97,125, a gross earning per boat of £370.'[1]

The general view is that 1905 has not been a bad year, though clearly this is no great advance on most years of the mid-nineteenth century, so that at best, Wick is holding its own while Shetland, Peterhead and Fraserburgh surge ahead. Steam drifters 'disturb the balance a bit'. There is 'bound to be a big difference in the monetary result obtained by the drifter in comparison with the boats, for very often were the latter handicapped, owing to light winds as a rule, and occasionally – very seldom mayhap – by head or strong winds.' Fewer drifters came to Wick this year than last, 'the maximum number on any day not exceeding 50 at most.' Shetland, it is noted, proved 'a greater attraction for the many big English boats which last year were so often conspicuous in the harbour,' – of Wick.

This account of the fishing in 1905 differs in one respect quite remarkably from any account that might have been written in the old days – the 'inconveniently long distance away' of 'yielding grounds' from Wick. 'It's a far cry from Wick,' says the *Journal*, 'to the Fair Isle, yet many a good shot was taken from there this year. The most extensively exploited grounds, however, were from 30 to 60 miles east of Wick.' Like other herring centres Wick is clearly gaining its benefits from much further afield than was the case when the town and its harbour grew up. Such fishing and long distance hauling of the catch would not have been physically possible in, say, the 1850s.

However, things have changed, the *Journal* considers that there is cause for satisfaction all round:

> The fishermen should be cheerful over what they have managed to reap. The cooper should be in a pleasant frame of mind, by reason of the fact that all home-made barrels, as well as many others have been filled, and a winter's continuous work at a good wage likely to result. The women workers have filled up many barrels, and that means money. Carters have had little leisure and plenty [of] labour, a condition of things they expect in summer, and appreciate when it comes. The only man who may be in doubt as to how he is to regard the season is the fishcurer [who claims to have had more 'torn-bellies' this year – damaged fish – than usual]. And as yet one can only hope that he will soon join in the joyfully thankful throng.

1 *JOGJ*, 1 September, 1905. In fact, in all the years to 1911 except 1906 and 100,000 crans was passed, reaching 164,507 in 1910.

> Prospects of this are indeed good at present. Every day almost, brings tidings of a slightly increased price in the Continental market. Prices locally have advanced 1s to 2s per barrel. The present rates are – crown-large-fulls and crown-fulls [top quality]; crown-mat-fulls, 25s; crown-matties, 20s 6d to 21s; crown-spent, 14s 6d to 15s; and torn-bellies, 10.6d to 11s.

A familiar topic, perhaps the most familiar of all in discussion about fishing in Wick, from early in the last century onwards, comes in for comment:

> Though the fleet was not so large as last year, and consequently the congestion never so great, there was not wanting examples pointing to the necessity of harbour improvement. The lack of water was often responsible for keeping boats in the harbour, after discharging, the boat frequently being found aground, and all hopes of proceeding to sea thereby frustrated. *Obviously the deepening of the outer harbour at least is one of the most beneficial works that can be executed as far as the present harbour is concerned.* (author's italics).

THE WICK HARBOUR STORY CONTINUED

Generally speaking Wick and the British Fisheries Society continued throughout to take for granted the fundamental factors on which the Scottish fishing industry was based; their pre-occupation was the need to improve the harbour so that Wick could once more take a big share in the bonanza of lucrative fish marketing. The prime and pre-occupying necessity was to get the harbour extended, to allow more and bigger fishing boats in.

There were three main later phases in the development of the harbour: the Stevenson programme, begun in 1863 and ignominiously ended in 1873; an intermittent programme running from the late 1880s to the First World War; and another intermittent programme post-war was finally put paid to by the disappearance of the herring. Until this happened, not only Wick itself but various agencies concerned with the Scottish fisheries industry believed that Wick had a future, even if not so high in the league as it once was, and large sums of money were obtained and spent on Wick Harbour.

The Stevenson Experience

Though much money and effort were expended in later years, in retrospect it is evident that the critical event was the ten years of work and ultimate failure of the Stevenson project between 1863 and 1873. What was intended when the British Fisheries Society was pushing for its Pulteney Harbour Amendment Bill in 1862 was the wholesale improvement of not only the Pulteney harbour itself, but also the development of the Wick river and the north shore, so much talked about by Washington and others. The Act when passed contained clauses giving the Society root and branch powers to

> cause the harbour to be cleared, deepened, altered, and improved, in such manner and to such extent as may be expedient, and to make and maintain all such additional wharfs, warehouses, sheds and other buildings and conveniences connected therewith, as may be necessary for carrying on the fisheries, and for the reception and accommodation of vessels resorting to the harbour, and of passengers and goods shipped or landed therein and to make wide and maintain all necessary roads and accesses to the harbour and its works.

So that there should be no misunderstanding or argy-bargy between the Pulteneytown and Wick burgh authorities, Clause 16 declared that 'the harbour shall include the Bay of Wick or such part thereof' as lay broadly speaking, between North Head and South Head, the line being defined in quite express terms.[1]

Thus, when the Society launched its project in 1863, with D & T Stevenson, Engineers of Edinburgh, in charge, it had ample powers at its command. The real problem was, of course, a sufficient flow of money to ensure the confident forward movement of the project. As Jean Dunlop explains, this assurance was always lacking; the first instalment on the loan of £60,000 officially granted by the Exchequer Loan Commissioners to the Society was not paid until 1867, by which time the Society was almost broke.[2]

In the following year a serious set-back occurred when 200 feet of the breakwater now under construction from Salmon Rock across the bay was 'thrown down' by bad-weather. The £5000 or so for repairs and the modifications to design of the pier and its parapet was found,

1 *JOGJ*, 2 January, 1862.
2 Dunlop, op cit. p 194. The main work programe did not actually begin until 1864.

and work continued. In February 1870, however, came a much more serious collapse, caused by the 'succession of strong gales from the south-east', which 'increased in fury until it blew a hurricane. The account of this calamity is given in the *Groat* in almost as much graphic detail as the famous disaster of 1848, though fortunately there was no loss of life to record. The reporter, as usual, presented a lively series of word pictures:

> The Bay was a mass of foaming billows, and the waves broke with tremendous force over the new breakwater, which every now and then was hidden from view by the dense volume of water which continued to rush over it. In the afternoon the appearance of the bay was awfully grand. The huge rollers striking against the parapet, were shivered into spray which would rise perpendicularly, it was calculated, to a height of 100 feet, and then being driven up the bay by the force of the wind, it had the appearance of driven snow. Such a severe storm had not been experienced here for many years.

The account seeks to explain exactly what happened to the breakwater, and much of this is worth quoting if only to show that many of the popular explanations of the disaster, which proliferated in later years, were beside the point. The engineers 'profiting as they thought by the dearly bought experience of 1868,' when 200 feet of the breakwater had been lost, spent the next year widening the parapet and 'giving the pier a further elevation of five feet.' It would, considered the *Journal*, 'be difficult to find a finer and more substantial piece of masonry anywhere. The seaward-end of the building, was finished up in the most secure manner possible, the large stones being firmly bolted together, and the whole fastened with immense bars of iron, which it was believed, nothing could move.'

The description of the storm continues:

> Throughout Sunday anxious crowds gathered on the heights commanding a view of the bay, eagerly watching the effects of each successive wave on the building and earnestly canvassing the possibilities of its being able to withstand the very severe test to which it was being subjected; and it was very generally believed that if it outlived the storm of that day, there was every likelihood that a breakwater would be erected which could sustain the shock of a storm even in the bay of Wick – a feat the accomplishment of which many believed to be impracticable on the plans adopted by the engineers of the

present structure. Unfortunately, so far as the work has been proceeded the worst fears of the latter have been fully realised.

Then follows a blow by blow description of the ruthless demolition work of the waves:

> The first indication on Sunday that a catastrophe was impending was the snapping of a portion of the staging on the inner side of the works, which took place early in the afternoon, and which was immediately followed by the displacement of a few stones in the roading of the pier. It was then considered all but certain that a breach, however slight having once been affected in the masonry, the immense body of water which was continually pouring over the parapet was sure to enlarge the fracture, and that the catastrophe of 1868 was to be repeated in 1870. Up till darkness hid the breakwater from view, the building appeared to be intact, with the trifling exception just alluded to. The storm, however, increased and about midnight raged with great fury. It is believed that between that hour and four o'clock am, a very large part of the building had been thrown down; but the extent of the disaster could not be ascertained owing to the darkness of the morning. When the day dawned, however, the spectacle which met the gaze of the anxious watchers was a sufficiently melancholy one. The whole work of the past year, which consisted of the reconstruction of that part of the building destroyed in the year previous – about 240 feet of the masonry – had been hurled to the bottom of the bay, and the beach was strewn with broken timber, the wreck of the staging. Although the wind moderated in the morning, the sea was as heavy as ever, and the waves continued to dash against the portion of the building still standing with as great violence as ever, so that in the course of the day increased destruction continued to overtake the doomed works, until evening closed, when about 350 feet of the breakwater above the water mark had altogether disappeared from view.

The gale revived on Monday and more destruction followed so that by Tuesday 'another large portion of the breakwater' had 'succumbed to the fury of the elements.' The pounding continued throughout Tuesday, 'everywhere now and again giving fresh evidence of the power of the sea by the gradual but unmistakeable dissolution of the masonry, so that as evening closed at least 400 feet of the breakwater was destroyed.'

The gale abated on Wednesday 'so that fears of further damage' were 'in the meantime removed.' Some 1050 feet of the breakwater seaward had been completed, but of that not much more than 600 feet were left standing. 'It is generally believed that the rubble foundation under low water remains intact; but this cannot be sufficiently ascertained until the sea calms down as to admit of a survey being made.'

Stevensons were sent for, but already theories abounded as to why the breakwater had not held. Speculation continues to this day, one common belief being that the Stevensons made a mistake in setting the base under-water masonry blocks so that they lay horizontally on the sea bed, and were thus liable to an upward prizing movement from the base of the advancing waves. 'Not a few,' said the *Journal*, 'who pretend to be authorities on the subject attribute the catastrophe to want of knowledge on the part of the engineers of the waves in Wick Bay and the erection of what was called "a straight dyke" was not at all likely to withstand the fury of a winter tempest. Be that as it may, there can be no doubt that the first part of the work which gave way, as on the occasion of the storm of 1868, was the causeway road on the inside of the building, which was forced out by the tremendous body of water which continued to pour over the parapet; and the seaward wall thus losing its principal support became a prey to the force of the waves.'[1]

In the immediate aftermath of the disaster there was speculation that the whole project would have to be abandoned. The *Journal* painted a grim picture of what the effects might be on the economy of Wick and Pulteneytown, and gloomily listed some of these:

> The quantity of stone thrown into the bay cannot fail to injure the anchorage, and must at the same time render the approaches to the old harbours more dangerous than ever. Coming as it does at the back of a series of unsuccessful fishings, the throwing idle of 250 men, who have been engaged throughout the winter months, is a state of matters for which the community is by no means prepared. It is, we need hardly say in present circumstances, difficult to assess the amount of the loss entailed by this deplorable catastrophe; but when we mention that this work is no further advanced than it was three years ago, and that something like an annual expenditure of at least £15,000 has been made upon it, we think we have said

1 *JOGJ*, 10 February, 1870.

enough to indicate the magnitude of the disaster.[1]

In retrospect, whatever the precise sequence of destruction, it seems fairly evident that, as the *Journal* writer speculated, 'want of knowledge of the strength of waves in the Wick Bay' on the part of the engineers was fundamentally to blame for the whole catastrophe. In the same issue carrying the report was printed a letter from 'Delta' referring to the work of John Scott Russell, an eminent naval architect of the day and authority on marine hydraulics, which discussed the nature of the repeated assaults of the waves on a structure such as the Stevenson breakwater. As the report showed, the impact of some waves sent columns of water many feet vertically into the air above the parapet wall. A column of 90 feet would descend, it was calculated, with a pressure of about 45 pounds per square inch, which repeated and repeated would be likely to dislodge masonry on the top surface of the breakwater and so weaken the structure that pounding on the vertical seaward face of the breakwater would cause it to give way. If there was to be any return to building the breakwater, different ideas must be applied to the methods of construction:

> If an upright, or nearly an upright will be the mode of deflecting so great an impact (which is a point admitting of diversity of opinion) there must be a very different arrangement for the reception of so great a mass of falling water; and under existing circumstances the only thing that can be done is to abandon the idea (which ought never to have been entertained) of a 'landing' wharf on a breakwater combined, and at least on all future occasions to carry a sloping heavy pavement from the inside edge of the wall to the top of the parapet, at an angle of about 45 degrees.

In any case, the 'strengthening of the outer wall was absolutely essential.' There followed in the coming months much expert examination of the structure, analysis of the building programme since it started and especially from 1868 onwards. Stevensons sought the opinions of numerous independent engineers, (the names Hawkshaw, Leslie, Coode and Rendel are mentioned). In their detailed report to the British Fisheries Society, it was suggested that even more expert advice must be obtained before, and if, work was to continue. There was general agreement that however satisfactory development might have seemed to the resident engineer and

---

1 Ibid. Fishings in the years 1866 to 1869 had, indeed, been poor, 1868 very poor, viz: 1866, 62,848 crans; 1867, 80,510; 1868 40,973; 1869, 74,480.

contractors at various stages, there had been no anticipation of the sort of ferocious onslaught of waves, lasting for three days and three nights, and of the kind which had done the damage. Waves of more than forty feet from hollow to crest had pounded the structure every seven to ten minutes during the worst of the storm. This 'excessive trial of strength' (between man and nature) had revealed the necessity of more fundamental thinking about the nature of the structure and especially the design of the parapet and top surface of the breakwater, if work was to continue. So far as they were concerned, Stevensons thought that the problems encountered could be solved and recommended that work continue.[1]

So much money had already been spent that the Society deemed it advisable for the project to be completed, the money to be found somehow; and a few months after cessation, work was resumed. But triumph was not to be. In the *Journal* issue for the day after Christmas, 1872, appeared yet again the headline: *Disaster to the Breakwater*. During the previous week there had been a particularly bad storm, which started on the Wednesday by shifting a 'huge concrete block on the seaward end' of the breakwater. The block weighed 1000 tons, and had been placed as a sort of anchor base to maintain the integrity of the vulnerable seaward end of the breakwater. The sea had slewed it round. Even worse, the several blocks of about ninety tons each on which the thousand-ton block was erected, the whole mass, weighing perhaps as much as 1500 tons, pinned with 4ft 'maleable iron bars,' had been 'wheeled round and shifted to a considerable distance during the height of the storm.'

Solemnly the *Journal* commented:

> As is usual in such cases, very exaggerated estimates were formed of the extent to which the work of destruction had gone. The general opinion was that at least 200 feet of the pier had been washed away, but others were certain that the demolition extended to over 300 feet. All along the seaward side of the wall it was quite manifest to the onlookers that stones had been removed, that great holes had been excavated, and that the entire fabric was tottering to overthrow.[2]

When it came in February, Stevenson's report to the Society made no bones about the seriousness, perhaps hopelessness, of the enterprise. It was a long, detailed and thoroughly technical report,

1 *JOGJ*, 24 March, 1871.
2 *JOGJ*, 26 December, 1872.

reviewing every stage of the *Progress of the Work* from 1863 onwards, year by year. It dealt with the criticisms of the engineers' methods that had been put forward, and in view of later criticism (sometimes even heard today), the report commented:

> Another objection we believe applied to the form of the structure we adopted, which it has been suggested ought to have presented a *sloping* and not a *nearly vertical* face to the sea. We fear that those who have suggested this objection have not had before them the whole of the facts, nor have had the necessary experience to enable them to judge of the engineering difficulty of carrying this plausible theory of a sloping face into actual practice in founding a Breakwater in 6 fathoms at low water in Wick Bay. The best form of Breakwater had our most careful consideration when we designed the works: the opinion at which we arrived was what was borne out by what had been proposed by the Royal Commission under the advice of the eminent Engineers and nautical men who were members of that body. It was again most carefully considered in conference with Mr Hawkshaw, which he reported in 1870, and if the joint opinion at which Mr Hawkshaw and ourselves after much careful consultation, is not sufficient to justify the construction that has been adopted, we cannot hope to offer more fully considered advice.[1]

Stevensons could not assure the Directors of the Society that continued work would ensure the survival and stability of the breakwater. The Directors considered matters in solemn conclave at the Annual General Meeting of 1873. They passed no resolution in favour of discontinuing the work, but manifestly there was no way in which they could continue financing so shaky a project without vastly greater help. Concerned for its own welfare, the Society backed away from further involvement in so expensive a commitment. Work was discontinued on the Bay of Wick breakwater, and the sea was left over the coming years to smash up most of the breakwater remaining.

A hundred yards or so of the Stevenson construction still stretch away from the Salmon Rock, an archaeological relic which suggests something of the ambitiousness of the project which was begun so hopefully in 1863. This inconclusive end to the Stevenson scheme for improving the fishing anchorage of Wick, and the statements of the Directors of the British Fisheries Society, left lingeringly alive the

---

1 *JOGJ*, 13 March, 1873.

notion that, perhaps, in due course, the government would see the wisdom of financing a major and more soundly based harbour improvement programme for Wick and, indeed, the hope proved not entirely without foundation.

Robert Louis on the Scene.

The Stevensons came to regard this as their great failure. To the British Fisheries Society they declared: 'It has proved a work of excessive anxiety, inasmuch as it has been carried on under difficulties of exposure which, in Harbour Works, have hitherto been altogether unprecedented.' Robert Louis, who came to stay in Wick in 1868, has left in addition to the requiem on the project already quoted, several vivid impressions of the scene during the actual construction that are less than complimentary to Wick. Of 'subarctic Wick' itself he wrote:

> You can never have dwelt in a country more unsightly than that part of Caithness, the land faintly swelling, faintly falling, not a tree, not a hedgerow, the fields divided by single slates, stones set upon their edge, the wind always singing in your ears and (down the long road that led to nowhere) thrumming in the telegraph wires. Only as you approached the coast was there anything to stir the heart. The plateau broke down to the North Sea in formidable cliffs, their tall out-stacks rose like pillars ringed about with surf, the coves were over-brimmed with clamorous froth, the sea-birds screamed, the wind sang in the thyme on the cliff's edge; here and there, small ancient castles toppled on the brim; here and there it was possible to dip into a dell of shelter, where you might lie and tell yourself you were a little warm, and hear (near at hand) the whin pods bursting in the afternoon sun, and (farther off) the rumour of the turbulent sea. As for Wick itself, it is one of the meanest of man's towns, and situated certainly on the baldest of God's bays. It lives for herring, and a strange sight it is to see (of an afternoon) the heights of Pulteney blackened by seaward-looking fishers, as when a city crowds to a review – or, as when bees have swarmed, the ground is horrible with lumps and clusters; and a strange sight, and a beautiful, to see the fleet put silently out against a rising moon, the sea-line rough as a wood with sails, and even and again and one after another, a boat flitting swiftly by the silver disk.

This mass of fishers, this great fleet of boats, is out of all proportion to the town itself; and the oars are manned and the nets hauled by immigrants from the Long Island (as we call the outer Hebrides), who come for the season only, and depart again if 'the take' be poor, leaving debts behind them. In a bad year, the end of the herring fishery is an exciting time; fights are common, riots often possible; an apple knocked from a child's hand was once the signal for something like a war, and even when I was there, a gunboat lay in the bay to assist the authorities. To contrary interests, it should be observed, the curse of Babel is here added: the Lews men are Gaelic speakers, those of Caithness have adopted English; an odd circumstance if you reflect that both must be largely Norseman by descent. I remember seeing one of the strongest instances of this division: a thing like a Punch-and-Judy box erected on the flat gravestones of the church-yard; from the hutch or proscenium – I know not what to call it – an eldrich-looking preacher laying down the law in Gaelic about some one of the name of *Powl*, whom I at last divined to be the apostle to the gentiles; a large congregation of the Lews men very devoutly listening; and on the outskirts of the crews, some of the town's children (to whom the whole affair was Greek or Hebrew) profanely playing tigg. The same descent, the same country, the same narrow sect of the same religion, and all these bonds made very largely nugatory by an accidental difference of dialect!

Then follows a vivid account of Robert Louis' education as an engineer, a descent to the sea-floor in a diving suit to see the men at work under-sea at the base of his father's breakwater. He was taken down by a 'scamp of a diver' named Bob Bain who got five shillings for guiding a boss's son through a unique experience. Helmet screwed on and lead on his feet, the 'hurdy-gurdy' turning and the air whistling thought the tube, he climbed down the ladder twenty feet under the water into a wonderland where each man, 'in his little world of air, stood incommunicably separate.' Bob, Robert Louis's guide, was

> down with another, settling a stone of the sea-wall. They had it well adjusted, Bob gave the signal, the scissors were slipped, the stone set home; and it was time to turn to something else. But still his companion remained bowed over the block like a mourner on a tomb, or only raised himself to make absurd

contortions and mysterious signs unknown to the vocabulary of the diver. There, then, these two stood for a while, like the dead and living; till there flashed a fortunate thought into Bob's mind, and he stopped, peered through the window of that other world, and behold the face of that inhabitant wet with streaming tears. Ah! the man was in pain! and Bob, glancing downward, saw what was the trouble: the block had been lowered on the foot of that unfortunate – he was caught alive at the bottom of the sea under fifteen tons of rock.[1]

Post Mortem.

One other engineer edges into the picture during the years immediately after 1848, Joseph Mitchell CE, some time engineer to the British Fisheries Board, consultant to the British Fisheries Society, personal friend of James Bremner and companion and consultant at his enquiry of Captain Washington (later Admiral Washington). The chief evidence of Mitchell's involvement comes from his own compendious *Reminiscences.* Commenting on the Washington enquiry Mitchell says:

> The British Fisheries Society, to whom the harbour belonged, was anxious particularly after this disaster, to secure the erection of a safe harbour; but the situation was very difficult, and the schemes were very perplexing. I believe every engineer of eminence in harbour works was consulted; but in this case in the multitude of counsellors there was not safety. Unfortunately the visits of the engineers were generally in fine weather, and they did not seem to have appreciated or believed in the peculiar storms to which this bay is exposed at certain periods of the year.
>
> The width of the bay is about 1600 yards at the entrance, with high cliffs on each side [this is not quite true; it can hardly be said that the 'cliffs' on the north side are high, though the shore is very rocky]. It runs inward about a mile to the harbour and mouth of the river. It is trumpet-mouthed in form, and exposed

---

1 Kenneth Gelder (Ed): *Robert Louis Stevenson's Scottish Stories and Essays*; Edinburgh University Press (1989); pp 269-274. John Horne, in a short piece, *R L Stevenson in Wick*, comments: 'When his lodging-house keeper heard of his after-fame as a writer, he was astonished – and sorry. "Puir chiel," he exclaimed, "did he come to that?"' Further comments on 'Stevenson and Wick' are to be found in Louis Stott: *Robert Louis Stevenson and the Highlands and Islands of Scotland*; Stirling, Creag Darach Publications (1992).

to fourteen points of the compass to the storms of the North Sea; and the waves during a storm rush in towards the harbour with increased and accumulated violence.

Mitchell claims to have been behind the plan to excavate the bed of the river some four feet below low water, so that 'a most secure and efficient fishers' harbour could be made to any extent, amply protected from storms. 'Unfortunately,' he adds:

> the engineers consulted (1862) conceived other designs, and projected a breakwater across the bay 1050 feet. Their plan has proved a failure. Repeated storms destroyed the works, and the whole expenditure amounting to about £82,000, has been literally sunk in the sea. The bay has been rendered more insecure than ever from the accumulation of debris which cannot well be removed.[1]

Mitchell had the great advantage of hindsight and may have been piqued not to have been called in as chief consulting engineer. It is true, however, that he did submit plans to Captain John Washington in 1849 that outlined his ideas of a mainstream river development, and he was an experienced harbour builder. There is little doubt, as Mitchell suggested, that there was less understanding on the part of the engineers actually involved of what may be called the 'wave energy amplification effect', than was the case in later years.[2]

Equally retrospective, it so happens that we have a more recent expert appraisal of what was wrong about the 1862 project. This was written at the request of the Wick Harbour Board in 1915 (not the most auspicious of years in which to consider such a matter and to make proposals for the future), by R Gordon Nicol CE, Consulting Engineer of the Fishery Board for Scotland.[3] It is evident that Mr Nicol

---

1 Joseph Mitchell: *Reminiscences of My Life in the Highlands, containing Notices of the Changes in the County During the Present Century*; Printed privately for the Author at the Graham press, Unwin Brothers, Chilworth and London (1833), Vol. 1, pp 304-305. We meet Mitchell again as a consultant engineer in the building of the Highland Railway.

2 The term is that of a former engineering colleague of the author's, Colin Salsbury, a retired lecturer from the Loughborough College with an intimate knowledge of fluid mechanics. For those who may be interested, details of his theoretical appraisal of conditions in Wick Water, described to him by the author, are given in an *Addendum* at the end of this chapter.

3 The Report was included as Appendix XI in a remarkable compilation entitled: *Wick Harbour: MEMORANDUM for Sir Archibald Sinclair, Bart., MP. etc.*, with an alternative title pencilled in: *Wick Harbour; Chronicle of the Harbour and its Finance, February, 1929*. Sir Archibald was Liberal Member of Parliament of Caithness from 1922 to 1945. He became Secretary of State for Scotland from 1931 in the National Government, and was Minister of Air from 1940 to 1945. He evidently solicited *(continued on foot of next page)*

was much better versed than some of his predecessors in fluid mechanics, which is not surprising since much work was being done on this subject during the later years of the nineteenth century. Nicol's Report is fairly detailed, but so informative that the whole commentary on the Stevenson project is worth quoting.

The full story of Stevenson's engineering failure as understood by Gordon Nicol runs for five pages, most of which is here reproduced since uniquely it reveals so much of the fundamental technical problems of making a great harbour in Wick Bay. The story continues:

> Tenders were invited for the work, and the offer of Messrs McDonald, Glasgow, amounting to £105,000 was accepted.
>
> A loan of £62,000 was obtained from the Public Works Loan Commissioners on the security of the harbour revenue, the money to be advanced after the Society had expended £40,000 on the works. The plans were approved by Mr (now Sir) A M Rendell CE, on behalf of the Loan Board and the works were commenced in 1863.
>
> The rubble mound on which the south breakwater was erected consisted of large stones from the adjoining quarry, which were deposited from a timber staging running out into the bay on the line of the pier. These stones were spread and levelled down by the sea until they assumed natural slopes over a width at parts of about 200 feet. On account of the shelving bottom, the depth of water on the site of the mound gradually increased from low water mark to about 5 fathoms below low water of ordinary spring tides. The top of the mound was made up with fresh stones as it subsided under wave action, and the masonry pier was founded on top of the rubble at a depth of 12 feet below low water level, in conformity with the general practice at that time. As the work advanced, the depth at which the masonry pier was founded was increased to 18 feet below low water. This proved a wise precaution, as in 1868 the rubble was washed down to 15 feet below low water, and serious damage occurred to part of the superstructure; large portions of the contractors' staging were also carried away

---

(continued from foot of previous page) this Memorandum in 1929 to provide background reading for making decisions on continuing requests from the Wick Harbour Board for state aid for improvement and development. Nicol's Report deals with various matters of contemporary significance but the engineer treats the Stevenson project as though it were a cautionary event. From all points of view, the Stevenson experience was a disaster, personal, engineering, financial and, not least, scenic.

by the waves. The pier or superstructure was 32 feet high, and was founded in a trench on the top of the rubble mound. It was 43 feet wide on the top and 52 feet wide at the base, and was formed of blocks of stone from 5 to 10 tons in weight, set on edge, first built above high water of neap tides with hydraulic lime, then with Roman and latterly with Portland cement. In 1868 the superstructure had reached a length of about 1,100 feet without serious interruption. In February, 1870, a severe storm broke out and continued without intermission for three days, with the result that a length of 380 feet – about one-third of the whole was destroyed. An attempt was made to secure the end of the pier by large blocks of concrete of from 80 to 100 tons each, but even this protection failed during the succeeding gales. In February 1872, after the superstructure had been rebuilt solid, with Portland cement, serious damage arose from another cause, the face stones being in many places shattered by the sea, a phenomenon unparalleled in the history of sea works. Lastly, in December, 1872, the great evidence of destructive force was manifested, and is thus recorded in the words of a report by Messrs Stevenson:

> The seaward end of the work, as has been explained, was protected by a mass of cement rubble work. It was composed of three courses of large blocks of 80 to 100 tons, which were deposited as a foundation (in a trench made) in the rubble. Above this foundation there were three courses of large stones set in cement, and the whole was surmounted by a large monolith of cement rubble measure about 26 feet by 45 feet, and 11 feet in thickness, weighing upwards of 800 tons. This block was built *in situ* [deleted]. As a further protection, iron rods, $3\frac{1}{2}$ inches in diameter, were fixed in the uppermost of the foundation courses of cement rubble. These rods were carried through the courses of stonework by holes cut in the stone, and were finally embedded in the monolithic mass which formed the upper portion of the pier. Incredible as it may seem, the huge mass succumbed to the force of the waves, and Mr McDonald, the resident engineer, actually saw it from the adjacent cliff being gradually 'slewed' round by successive strokes until it was finally removed and deposited inside the pier. It was not for some days after that my examination could be made of this singular phenomenon, but the result of the examination only gave rise to increased amazement at the feat which the waves had achieved. It was found on examination by diving that the 800-ton monolith forming the upper portion of the pier, which the resident engineer had seen in the act of being washed away, had carried with it the whole of the lower courses

which were attached to it by the iron bolts, and that this enormous mass, weighing not less than 1,350 tons, had been removed *en masse,* and was resting entire on the rubble at the side of the pier, having sustained no damage but a slight fracture at the edges. A further examination also disclosed the fact that the lower or foundation course of 80 ton blocks, which were laid on the rubble, retained their positions unmoved. The second course of cement blocks, on which the 1,350 tons rested had been swept off after being relieved from the superincumbent weight, and some of them were found entire near the head of the breakwater. The removal of this protection left the end of the work open, and the storm, which continued to rage for some days after the destruction of the cement rubble defence, carried away about 150 feet of the masonry (1/17th of the whole), which had been built solid and set in cement.

The pier was again restored in a similar manner, with the additional precaution that the two upper tiers of concrete blocks were united to the upper work, forming a solid mass of 2,600 tons. The work remained in this state until 1877, when the whole end of the breakwater was carried away and was not restored, the breakwater being abandoned to its fate. Since 1877 the works have been gradually demolished by the sea, and nothing now remains but the debris of the pier which has been deposited over a portion of the bay. The outer blocks of the superstructure are indicated by a beacon showing above high water level for the guidance of shipping.

I consider that the superstructure of this breakwater was a fine piece of work, and it embodied some of the best practices even of the present day. I have examined the root of the structure as it exists today, and better masonry I have never seen anywhere. *Had the breakwater been founded on the bottom of the bay instead of on a rubble mound, I am confident it would have been standing intact today.* [author's italics]. The weakness of the design lay in having a rubble mound in this situation, and the destruction of the breakwater was in my view due entirely to the movement of rubble underneath the masonry pier by the scouring action of the waves. At the period when this structure was erected it was the usual practice to found piers on rubble mounds at depths which are now considered to be dangerous. Recent experience shows that rubble material may be shifted at depths approaching 40 feet below low water. If built now, the pier would be founded on the bottom of the bay.

Breakwaters and Convicts

The disasters of 1868, 1870 and 1872, thoroughly disheartened the Directors of the British Fisheries Society. There were between 1873 and 1879 unhappy meetings of the Board seeking to decide what to do next. They were substantially in debt and a serious question remained as to what could be done about the £60,000 loan made by the Public Works Loan Board and spent vainly. There were approaches to the Society from the Wick Chamber of Commerce 'demanding the transference of harbour policy to local representatives.'

In 1878, Sir Tollemache Sinclair, the MP for Caithness county, proposed that 'the Society confer with representatives of Wick, Pulteneytown and Caithness county organisations for the transference of the Society's property into local hands.' A joint committee of representatives of the Wick Chamber of Commerce, the Pulteneytown Improvement Commission and the Society was appointed. Most of their discussions were about the complex financial implications of the proposed transfer. In the end the Society agreed to abandon all claims to the £40,000 expended on its own behalf since 1863 on the harbour; there was a further £14,092 which it had spent before 1863, which claim to refund the Society eventually agreed to abandon; it also accepted responsibility for the £60,000 loan, which it hoped that the government might agree to waive. The way was clear for pushing through an Act of Parliament confirming all these arrangements. All Society assets in Wick and Pulteneytown were to be transferred to a body of trustees, on which the Society was to have a single representative. The new trustees first met on 29 January, 1890 'and on that day local management [of harbour and Pulteneytown] became an accomplished fact.'

To all intents and purposes the British Fisheries Society thus relinquished its prime interests in the fishing settlement on the Wick river which it had built up during the century. The Society continued desultorily in business for some more years, and in 1890 it put up its estate of Pulteneytown for sale (together with the remnant of its property in Mull, the Tobermory pier), the whole property being eventually disposed of to Mr (later Sir) John Usher of Norton, who paid £20,000 to the Society for the two estates.

Jean Dunlop brings the story of the British Fisheries Society to a close:

> On 20th March, 1893 the shareholders attended their last Annual General Meeting, and on 10th June of that year, the

remaining capital, which must have amounted to less than £15,000 when all debts were settled, was divided among the holders of the 478 shares.[1]

The British Fisheries Society existed no longer.

There was no bang; hardly a whimper. Wick and Pulteneytown, now at less than their prosperous best, were on their own.

The Pulteneytown Harbour Act of 1879 somewhat revived hope and discussion of harbour improvement, and this rumbled on for the next year or two. There were many differing interests to be settled. By 1883 a new scheme of improvement, costing up to £10,000 was under discussion by the Harbour Trustees. Elections for the Trust were held in January, 1883, and an *ad hoc* meeting of fishcurers, fishermen and 'all interested in harbour matters' was held. A memorial was prepared against the terms of the proposed Provisional Order bringing various clauses of the Act into effect, especially the introduction of payment of harbour dues on the north side before a breakwater was completed.[2]

Many points were again raised at a long mass meeting called to consider the whole issue, with emphasis on the urgency of starting works on the north side, and the building of a proper harbour bridge. There were questions about what was to be done in connection with property belonging to the estate of Dunbar of Hempriggs on the north side, and yet more meetings were promised. The *John O'Groat Journal*, faithfully reporting all this talk, complained that they had hoped the many meetings 'so common of late would lead to some practical result.'[3] But things dragged on. It was reported in March, however, that there had been some 'final adjustment of the Provisional Order, which the Board of Trade had at last submitted to parliament.'[4]

The terms of this Provisional Order, promoted by the Pulteneytown Trustees, contained some seven main provisions: 1, extension of the south pier northwards for 600 feet; 2, construction of a pier on the breakwater connected with Port Dunbar on the north shore southwards for 700 feet (Port Dunbar was one of the thoroughly inadequate private wharves on the north shore); 3, removal of about 40 feet of the existing north pier and the widening of the remainder; thus creating a tidal basin set something to the north-west of about 650ft by 250; 4, embankment of the river wall commencing with the

1 Jean Dunlop, *British Fisheries Society*, op cit, pp 194-197.
2 *JOGJ*, 18 January, 1883.
3 *JOGJ*, 15 and 22 February, 1883.
4 *JOGJ*, 8 March, 1883.

north-west side of the basin and a portion on the south bank near to the sawmill in Lower Pulteneytown; 5, a bridge across the river from a point opposite Williamson Street to a point at or near the 'Town's Wharf'; 6, to levy charges on the north side; 7 (and very critically) to borrow £70,000 (from the Public Works Board). A delegation of Trustees was to visit London.

Three months later terms of the Provisional Order were agreed and confirmed.[1] However, just at this time a new and radical complication supervened. As in 1866 a Select Committee on Harbour Accommodation had investigated the whole issue of 'harbours of refuge' along the Scottish coast, its recommendations among other things resulting in more spending by the Fishery Board (recently reconstituted under an Act of Parliament) and encouraging private investment in such development. Wick's scheme was its contribution to the activity thus prompted – though there was little expectation in Wick of substantial private investment.[2]

According to the *Journal* 'the Royal Commission was strongly in favour of Wick' as a major harbour of refuge.[3] The discussion continued. In June, 1883 it was reported that a Select Committee of the House of Commons was investigating 'The Harbours of Refuge Question,' and it was noted that Peterhead and Wick were likely to benefit.[4] Thomas Stevenson was called to give evidence and, as perhaps might have been expected, 'he had not much to say in favour of Wick . . . . . His own work there failed, and of course he would be the last to admit that it was due to the defects of his engineering scheme.' A Mr Abernethy CE, however, 'looked on the issue from an unbiased standpoint,' and in his opinion there was a good case for Wick. The Stevenson breakwater had failed on account of the 'enormous range of the sea, and that to resist the force of the waves, works similar to those of Aberdeen and Fraserburgh would have to be constructed.' Sir John Coode recommended that a breakwater be constructed 'right across the bay entrance.'[5] The matter should be taken up, considered the *Journal*, by the Harbour Trustees, though when the Harbour Trustees had their invitation to attend the Select Committee, the *Journal* congratulated them as having 'acted wisely in

1 *JOGJ*, 14 June, 1883.
2 Malcolm Gray, op cit, p 75.
3 *JOGJ*, 29 March, 1883.
4 *JOGJ*, 5 July, 1883.
5 *JOGJ*, 29 March, 1883.

declining to pay an expensive deputation to London to give evidence.' The advantages of Wick 'as a shipping and fishing port have long been established,' commented the editors, that 'we are sure these will be given due weight to by any Parliamentary Committee that has to do with the question of harbour accommodation.'[1]

At this juncture, however, the issue became entangled with another one, earlier noticed by the *Journal*, a proposition that had 'caused considerable animation at numerous places along the coast.' This was the possibility that convict labour might become available for the construction work.[1] A sub-committee of the Convict Labour Committee, led by Sir Frederick Evans RN, was sent out to investigate 'the most suitable site for the construction of a harbour of refuge by convict labour.' Sir Frederick paid visits to Thurso, Wick and several other places down the coast, examining local representatives and then departing for places further south.[2]

It is not revealed what the representatives of Wick said to Sir Frederick, though James Traill of Rattar, William Mackay and others are mentioned in connection with Thurso. The folklore of Wick maintains a tradition that the citizens greatly objected to the prospect of masses of convicts coming into their midst, even for the benefit of the town and 'turned down' the notion. An implication – not raised in the discussions reported, was that Wick would have to become the site for a large gaol, for Scotland was at this time desperately short of such accommodation. There may have been some such resentment, perhaps on the part of churches and their friends, but the bare fact is that Wick was never seriously in the running. The sub-committee's report finally appeared in June, 1884, announcing the unambiguous decision that Peterhead had been chosen for the construction of a harbour of refuge by convict labour. The *Journal* moralised on the issue:

> More than a year ago this spot had been fixed upon by the authorities, but owing to other ports putting in competing claims a full investigation of the whole question had to be made, with no other result than loss of time and money. It was readily admitted that a suitable harbour at Wick would be of great advantage to the fishing fleet; but the claim of the port was set aside on the ground that its situation was too far north for the general trade, and the natural harbour of the Cromarty

1 *JOGJ*, 19 July, 1883.
2 *JOGJ*, 29 March, 1883.
3 *JOGJ*, 9 August, 1883.

Firth was not far distant.[1] [Cromarty had not been of much use to Wick in 1848!].

In retrospect it may be said that the status, composition and remit of the Committee on Employment of Convicts and of its sub-committee under Sir Frederick Evans, seem rather confused. Besides parliament, there must have been involvement of the Board of Trade and the Scottish Office and the Prison Commissioners. The choice of Peterhead for the site of the Harbour of Refuge and for the prison was evidently unambiguous. As revealed by a contributor to the *Transactions* of the Buchan Field Club, in 1886, came an Act of Parliament,

> entitled the 'Peterhead Harbour of Refuge', Section 23 of which authorised the Prison Commissioners to build a prison. This power enables them legally to detain in Scotland on conviction all male prisoners sentenced by Scottish Courts to penal servitude. Previously these convicts had to be transferred to an English prison after they had completed their probationary period of nine months' solitary confinement in Perth General Prison. The *Peterhead Sentinel and Buchan Journal* of 10 August 1888 described this result as 'part and parcel of a just and unanswerable claim on behalf of Scotland to the services of their own criminals.'[2]

The prison was in fact opened in August, 1888. It reached its full complement in 1891. Convicts began working on the Peterhead breakwater and in the Stirling quarry which was to supply the stone in 1889, the construction being under the direction of an engineer appointed by the Admiralty. The account continues:

> The first intake of prisoners numbered twenty. Their arrival caused considerable excitement in the town and for some days previously the railway station had been besieged day and night by crowds eager to see the prisoners. They travelled in a Prison Van – the only one of its kind in use in Scotland for railway purposes – the warders being accommodated in the middle of the van with ten convicts on each side. They were dressed in the convict garb of the day – rough white sacking marked here and there with the broad arrow and wore smart caps and shoes.[1]

---

1 *JOGJ*, 12 June, 1884.
2 William Macmillan: *H M Prison at Peterhead;* Transactions of the Buchan Field Club, Vol 18, Part 4. Other details are taken from *Bygone Buchan* by Jim Buchan, p 42.
1 Ibid.

Such were the excitements and pleasures denied to Wick. Though Wick had many distinguished visitors arriving at the Station during the later years of the nineteenth century (as witnessed by the tablet in the wall in Station Road), including a former President of the United States, none, so far as is known, came wearing the broad arrow suit and smart hats and shoes from the Prison Commissioners' stores.

For practical purposes, the Peterhead development was really the end of thoughts of the big time for Wick Harbour; although the cry for a larger and better harbour continued – and in view of the improved catches of the early years of the twentieth century, there was justification for its being voiced. In fact, the harbour was improved to something like its present configuration as a result of the Harbour Board's own programme, put into operation as soon as the Board's Provisional Order was approved by the passage of the Bill through parliament in July, 1884. This had been the subject of detailed scrutiny by a small Commons Committee, which was convened in Edinburgh in March, 1884, and attended by Provost Rae who made the most of Wick's needs and opportunities. Inspection on site was conducted at the request of the Committee by Sir A M Rendell, CE. Such a report was necessary to convince the Public Works Loans Board that an outlay by them of the size demanded would be justifiable. As to the amount, this was to be as much as the Harbour's Board could squeeze out of them. Various figures were bandied about. Rendell discussed the whole project with another engineer, James Barron, and between them they came to the conclusion that the job, as set out in the existing proposal, could not be done for less than £120,000: 'and even after that outlay had been incurred there would be a less acreage of harbour than at present,' a puzzling statement. A modified plan, including a 'new pier outside the existing north quay' could be done for £97,000.[1]

In the end it was settled that the Provisional Order should be approved 'to the extent of the largest sum that could be obtained for the purpose.' The £120,000 estimate was trimmed down to £115,000, but with 'the curtailment of some details' the cost could be cut to £90,000, and at this lower level, the project was to go forward. The 'curtailment' included cutting the extension of the south quay from 600 feet to 300 feet, which precluded the development of a new basin on the outside of the north pier; but the building of a new pier from the north side towards the approved extension of what, in effect, was

1 *JOGJ*, 24 April, 1884.

a northward facing spur from the existing 'north pier' (which walled off the two existing basins, the Inner and the Outer Harbours). The curtailed programme was approved and was to consist of:

Extension of the south quay and construction of a lighthouse	£20,000
Walling of new north quay and rewalling of basin	£34,000
Excavation and deepening of existing basins	£19,000
Purchase of a dredger	£7,000
Total	£90,000[1]

Rendell's report had concluded:

> So long as herring continued to pay their annual visit to the East Coast of Scotland, so long is it reasonable to suppose that if provided with a proper harbour, *but not otherwise* (author's italics), Wick will be one of the principal resorts of the herring fishing; and it seems more than probable that the white and trawling fisheries will be established there as well ... These are particularly valuable because of their longer duration during the year.[2]

Rendell added, as a sort of forlorn after-thought: Wick would be 'useful as a Harbour of Refuge, .. if required on this coast.' This was the role that Wick Harbour was never enabled to fulfil. The harbour, as it stands today, with the two main basins, inner and outer, the 'River Basin' behind the pier extensions authorised in 1883, and Wick Harbour Bridge to the west end of the system, to begin with the 'service bridge' but now, wholly rebuilt in recent years, part of the main road system of the town. In 1885 a new bucket dredger was put on order from Fleming and Ferguson of Paisley, to cost £7,900. She was named *Gladstone* in honour of the 'Grand Old Man'.[3]

Wick remained a major producer of herring until the First World War, though now well outdistanced by Fraserburgh, Peterhead and eventually by Aberdeen along the east coast of Scotland in terms of size of annual catch, and left far below Shetland, which, during Wick's heyday had come up from behind to dominate them all. The herring had remained faithful to the waters of the North Sea, but were now congregating most enthusiastically in its very north and more

1 *JOGJ*, 29 May, 1884.
2 *JOGJ*, 29 May, 1884.
3 *JOGJ*, 2 September, 1885.

southern waters, for the English herring ports of Yarmouth and Lowestoft were now each producing annually twice and three times as great a quantity of herring as Wick. The last memories of the herring fisheries in Wick, as we shall notice, are those of the 1930s when the boats and the 'herring girls' made their annual migration southwards from Shetland in May, down the Scottish east coast and to Lowestoft in October.[1]

Wick continued, as it had done since the 1850s, sending much of its output to Germany, especially to such ports as Stettin, Königsberg, Danzig and Hamburg, a total of 94,344½ barrels; another 63,076 went to Russian ports (in those days including Libau and Riga in Estonia, Viborg and Kotka in Finland – none are now 'Russian'). 19,585 barrels were sent to Leith for transhipment. Wick's total of some 157,422 barrels shipped directly to Germany and Russia in 1911, represented about 11 per cent of the entire British export to Germany and Russia of 1,450,033 barrels of herrings.

A note to the tables of statistics for 1911 adds that 'of those [herrings] sent into Germany about fifty per cent are sent across the frontier into Russia,' which suggests that directly and indirectly Russia (or more correctly, the Baltic states) had become the British herring industry's main customer, and by implication that also of Wick. This represents an interesting turn around. Germany in the early days of its ascendancy, when standards of living were low but rising, became a considerable consumer of Scottish herring; in the years after 1870, when Germany became a country of high productivity and improved living standards, it, together with its prime suppliers, the Scottish herring exporters, began to find it

[1] Selected figures for total catches (in crans) in the years from 1907 to 1911 (*JOGJ Herring Circular*, 1911):

	1907	1908	1909	1910	1911
Orkney (about 7/8ths of total from Stronsay)	38,908	42,926	44,606	92,109	14,754
Wick	97,630	129,490	101,509	164,507	153,714
Lybster	907	1,701	832	653	520
Fraserburgh	325,328	251,467	179,777	227,466	193,000
Aberdeen	180,664	208,992	201,685	230,258	192,150
Shetland	438,792	503,647	362,059	463,060*	385,200

*From 1 May to end of season

| Yarmouth | 517,320 | 443,640 | 439,560 | 347,610* | 505,168 |

*Includes 14,479 crans of 'spring' herrings to September.

| Lowestoft | 391,980 | 352,500 | 344,365 | 261,800 | 339,440 |

profitable to export (or rather re-export) herring to territories such as Latvia, Lithuania, Estonia and Finland, where industrial development was beginning (though not on the scale of Germany) to people wishing, like themselves in earlier days, to supplement their monotonous peasant diets with the cheap but tasty Scottish herring.

1870 was, of course, a fateful year for Europe and its trade, for that was the year of the Franco-Prussian War (as it is usually called), triumph in which set Germany on the road to military hegemony in northern Europe, the progress which ended in the monumental disasters of the First and Second 'World' Wars. As we have seen, the 1870s were fateful years, too, for Wick, since it was during those years that the town's position of dominance in the Scottish herring industry was most seriously eroded. In 1884 was published a significant Prize Essay on *Harbour Accommodation for Fishing Boats on the East and West Coasts of Scotland*, by an Edinburgh advocate, Archibald Young, the prize being £25 put up by the Merchant Company of Edinburgh on the occasion of the International Fisheries Exhibition held in the city in 1882. Young wrote about all the main harbours at that time in significant production, commenting too on prospects for some localities not yet much developed – if at all, including remote places such as Melvich Bay and the Kyle of Tongue, where, with proper investment 'there would speedily follow a vast development, not only of the herring fishery, but also the cod, ling, haddock and other hook and line fisheries.'

Of Wick, Young wrote:
> Wick, once the queen of the Scotch herring-fishing, has now fallen from her high estate, owing to the decay of her harbour, and ranks below Fraserburgh, where fishermen are equally industrious and enterprising. The late Captain Macdonald of the *Vigilant* fishing cruiser, than whom no man was better acquainted with the Scotch herring industry and everything connected with it, gave the following evidence at Wick in 1877 with regard to the harbour: 'Bad weather has been exceptionally severe, and the boats are larger than formerly. The fishermen won't go out, because they must return to the harbour at a certain state of the tide, or not at all, and they run great risks in doing so. Wick harbour is the property of the British Fisheries Society.' They have spent a very large sum of money in endeavouring to improve the present harbour. The plan has utterly failed. More than half of the breakwater which

has been constructed has been washed down, and the bay is filled up with the *débris*. It seems hopeless now to improve the present harbour, but a good harbour might be made by excavating the bed of the river and building piers and other work. There are no local funds to accomplish this. But Government might undertake the work of this important industry. Herring harbours of easy access, where the boats could float at all times, would do more than anything else to develop the fisheries. Scotch fishermen furnished four-fifths of the Naval Coast Volunteers when they were originally established in 1857.

Young was in favour of the government advancing money on easy terms to local authorities and of supplementing loans with grants. Though grants were not forthcoming, it was a loan from the Public Works Loans Board that enabled Wick a few years later to undertake its own modest improvement programme, too late and too little to rescue Wick from its predicament. Young also referred to Joseph Mitchell's opinion that the channel of the river was the proper place on which to direct attention if Wick was to be improved, and he quoted the comments of an ex-provost and councillor of the burgh, James Louttit, as being of the same opinion. The harbour was, Young concluded,

> silting up with rubbish from the destroyed breakwater. The material which should have kept out the sea is filling up the bay. This condition of things partly accounts for the failure of Wick. The fishermen are afraid to go to sea because there is no safe landing place in heavy weather. The harbour cannot be taken until half-tide. Unless the harbour is improved, Wick will cease to be the herring capital of Scotland. It is not possible to improve the harbour in Wick Bay. It would be possible to convert the river into a harbour. The general feeling among the local people is that the river should be improved.[1]

The Last Big Effort

This still does not quite bring us up to date. The configuration of Wick Harbour today does not correspond to the picture as we have so far brought it. Though there had been bold and brave attemps to

1 *JOGJ*, 5 June, 1884.

extend, enlarge, deepen and make safer the wholly artificial harbourage of the Wick river, still essentially the Pulteney Harbour consisted of the two basins constructed by Telford and Bremner on the Pulteney shore early in the nineteenth century. Wick Harbour today, manifestly has three basins, the 'Inner' and 'Outer' old Harbours and a third, marked on some maps 'River Basin,' lying between a line of piers running north-south across the Bay and the 'Bridge' running across from Martha Terrace on the south side to the 'Camps' on the north. Few boats are ever to be seen at anchor in the River Basin and, indeed, all too few in the old Inner and Outer Harbours. The fact is that this third basin was the present century's contribution to the scheme only ever half envisaged and only very partially accomplished for converting the whole of Wick Bay into a harbour.

As we have seen, several engineers, including Joseph Mitchell, had a vision of enclosure of the whole Bay, and the plan drawn up for the Harbour Trustees in 1883 by (now on the Harbour Office wall) shows the entire Bay hemmed in by breakwaters stretching from South Head to North Head, apart from a fortified gap on the mid-line of the Bay to allow shipping in and out. Commenting on this issue in 1915, Gordon Nicol wrote:

> There is no doubt that the most complete solution of the problem [of full protection of Wick Harbour] would be attained by the erection of breakwaters projecting outwards from the Heads of Wick at the mouth of the bay, leaving an entrance of convenient width in a suitable position. This arrangement would convert the bay into a harbour of refuge, to which vessels of almost any size could run at all states of the tide and weather. Such a harbour has been contemplated before, and in the report of the sub-committee appointed, to investigate their question of the most suitable place for a harbour of refuge on the East Coast of Scotland of date 28th March, 1884, the following paragraph appears:
>
>> The value of a harbour of refuge at Wick Bay on the grounds set forth in the Royal Commission of 1859 appears to us indisputable; we do not see that the changes in the character of the shipping since the date of their Report have materially altered the question, and the claims of the fishing interests are perhaps less than they then were.
>
> The construction of a harbour of refuge in this place would supply a distinct facility much required by all classes of

shipping. At present the Firth of Cromarty, in the south, and Scapa Flow in the north are the nearest points at which a safe anchorage is to be found during easterly gales. The depth of water at the mouth of Wick Bay, in which the breakwaters would terminate, is about 11 fathom at low water. This is a great depth for the erection of maritime structures, and the cost would, I expect, be prohibitive.

There can be little doubt that, engineering difficulties apart, this is a prime reason why the government opted for Peterhead when the choice had to be made. Nicol's description of the wave enhancement effect in Wick Bay is quite vivid:

> The Bay of Wick is situated on one of the most exposed parts of the East Coast of Scotland. Facing almost due south-east, with a long fetch over deep water, it is open to the full force of the heaviest seas in easterly storms. It is a deep funnel-shaped bay, the width of the mouth on a line between the North and South Heads being about three-fourths of a mile, and the bay gradually narrows until, at a distance of about half a mile from the mouth, the harbour entrance is reached, where the width of the bay is reduced to about one-third of a mile. The immediate approach to the bay, particularly from a south-easterly direction, is over deep water, and in consequence the waves during easterly storms drive into the bay with undiminished force. As they roll inward along the narrowing bay they are piled up and increased in height until they break with extreme violence and hurl themselves upon the harbour works. Not only so, but the form of the bay is such that in south-easterly gales the seas run most heavily towards the north shore, and being partially deflected from this shore they are heaped up on the south pier. Prolonged south-east gales have the greatest effect on the works at Wick Harbour, but all gales from an easterly direction are to be dreaded.

The vast amounts of time, resources and above all public funds expended over the years on Wick Harbour, much having gone to waste, left in the minds of all concerned two conflicting prejudices: the first was against throwing any more money and expertise away, experience having show how easily they could be lost; the second was to the effect that so much having already been expended, there was no sense in giving up now when perhaps one more great heave would render this great northern harbour safe, efficient and prosperous after all. If the second of these urges was to be obeyed, a fundamental condition was that the herring would continue to shoal in their multitudes in northern waters. Up to this time there was little abatement of the naive belief that the herring shoals were imperishable. The scavenging of the waters by seine-netters and trawlers now in progress, had not yet produced any convincing evidence of critical down-turn. Conservation of the resources of the sea was still a rather indecent topic of discussion; the second prejudice still prevailed. Other things being equal, there was a disposition to put the money in and get the work done, especially as now there was so much better understanding of what was technically needful.

Other things were not equal, for from October 1914, virtually the entire Scottish fishing fleet in the North Sea was immobilised by the war with Germany. This did no harm to the fish, in fact, might have enhanced stocks. Obviously construction work would be held up but there was great hope that the war would not last for ever. So there was much sense in setting out plans for improving the Wick Harbour installations, when serious work could begin after the hostilities had ceased.

The essential purpose of Nicol's representation in 1915 was to persuade the powers that be that a new radical programme was not only feasible, but absolutely necessary if existing installations were to survive. What had been perennially lacking in Wick Bay was the kind of outer breakwaters that would break the force of driving seas before this had built up to irresistible intensity; in fact, something like the Stevenson project was required, property grouted in the sea-bed. The Head to Head project was out of the question as being far too difficult a job of marine engineering and far too expensive; a mere repeat of the Stevenson plan would not serve either, and in any case was probably unnecessary. Nicol's belief, as we have seen, was that the most dangerous weather came from the south-east, thrusting the waves towards the north shore where their force tended to be broken as they were reflected up river and on to the existing works, which therefore were always vulnerable and constantly in need of repair and refurbishment. A breakwater running out from the north shore, correctly sited, would break still further the still forceful onrush of the waves although being deflected from the north shore.

Under the terms of the Provisional Order, obtained by the Harbour Trustees in 1903, various works had been going on right up to the outbreak of war. These had included the completion of the river piers, north and south, strengthening of the old North Quay from which the South River quay sprang, and which walled in the Inner Harbour, underpinning of existing walls of the Inner Harbour, construction of a graving dock on the inner wall of the North Quay. The old Service Bridge from Martha Terrace had been interrupted by a swing bridge which allowed smaller vessels to enter the shallower parts of Wick Water without having to ship their masts. It may be added that the swing bridge had no other use, for the water between this bridge and the Bridge of Wick is notoriously shallow, even at high tide; but 1936 boats were no longer using the inner water anyway, since sails had almost disappeared, and the swing-bridge was dismantled to give way to the present concrete three-arch bridge.

A significant element of the 1903 plan was for the construction of a 'groyne' or breakwater running south from a point on the north shore about 400 feet east of the North River Pier and at something of an extended angle to it. This was presumably to serve the purpose of deflecting waves reflected back from the east north shore away from the main works. Nicol had no time for this at all. It is shown in the *Plan of Wick Harbour with Proposed Improvements* for 1921 as work not 'executed or completed' and crossed out in pencil as not required, clearly Nicol's work. In its place Nicol recommends two new breakwaters:

> 1 A NEW NORTH BREAKWATER which 'commences at a point on the north shore above high water mark, and about 1,900 feet eastward of the north river pier. From this point it extends southward in curved outline for a length of 1,640 feet and terminates in a depth of about 6 fathoms at low water. It is a solid structure of concrete, founded on the bottom of the bay, the lower part being constructed in reinforced concrete.'
>
> 2 A NEW SOUTH BREAKWATER which 'runs out from the root of the former structure [the remains of the Stevenson breakwater] in a north-easterly direction. It begins at high-water mark and extends for a distance of 850 lineal feet. It occupies approximately the site of the demolished structure, although the line has been slightly modified, and is constructed of large concrete blocks, dropped irregularly on the mound of debris. The breakwater terminates in a round concrete tower, founded on the bottom of the bay, and situated at a point 90 feet north of the existing beacon and 190 feet to the eastward of it. From this point the head of the new south breakwater bears

east-north-east, the clear distance between the two heads being 620 feet. The centre of the entrance bears south-east-by-east from the head of the existing south pier, and is at a distance of 1,500 feet from it.'

The construction of the north breakwater is to be quite sophisticated. Since it will do the heavier work by breaking the force of the waves during storm conditions (on account of the reflection of waves coming from the east and south-east by the north shore rocks), it is to be built in such a way as to withstand all levels of imaginable buffeting. The substructure up to a level of five feet above low water will consist for much of its length of concrete caissons built on shore and floated out to their positions and sunk on to sea-bed bases prepared for them. On top will lie 'a continuous concrete superstructure, the total length being 1,640 feet.' This mode of construction is intended to facilitate rapid work during periods of fine weather and a final structure that will not be subject to the movements that destroyed the Stevenson breakwater.

Various repairs to and strengthening of existing works already approved or partially completed are to be undertaken. The entire programme will take perhaps six years to complete, taking harbour building work well into the future, for even if approved, work can hardly begin in present conditions. The total cost of the scheme as envisaged will be little short of half a million pounds; the new north breakwater will cost £286,000 and the new south breakwater, £94,000. This is at 1915 prices.

Imaginative and probably sound, the main project was never attempted. Improvements to the existing north and south piers went ahead, as the strengthening of the North Quay. Slipway and dock were completed and more efficient dredging became the rule. But Nicol's North and South Breakwaters were never started. The short-lived post-war boom gave place to industrial unrest and mass unemployment; between December 1920 and March 1921 it more than doubled and in June 1921 passed the two million mark. Economy and retrenchment became the order of the day; and in 1922 'Geddes Axe', brought in ruthless pruning of most major plans for spending elaborated during the euphoric later months of the war, social and constructional. A massive and expensive project such as the Nicol plan for Wick Harbour stood no chance of survival.

Some thoughts of its revival seem to have been in mind during the even more dire years of 1930 and 1931, when unemployment passed three millions, and it is almost certainly in this connection that the Sinclair Memorandum was compiled, especially as Sir Archibald became Secretary of State for Scotland in the 'National Government' of 1931. It was under this sort of impetus that the building of the monster *Queen Mary* on Clydebank was put in hand, a project mainly financed by government money.

It has to be said that while the figures for herring held up reasonably well in the 1930s, as we have seen, there were no indications of a surge upwards. Retrospectively, caution about heavy investment in harbourage in Wick was justified. The trade never really recovered after the Second World War. Figures for the early years of the 1950s demonstrate dramatic collapse in catches, not only in Wick but also along the whole East Coast.

The figures for these years read:

    1951 – 5,424 barrels sent from Wick;
    1952 – 6,977 barrels sent from Wick;
    1953 – 6,605 barrels sent from Wick.

The total barrelage for the East of Scotland 134,110, a very modest total as compared with the old days.[1]

Wick was indeed well over the top.

ADDENDUM

Wave Energy Amplification.

This effect is complicated in its action. During a gale three motions are involved: waves, tidal flow and wind. A wave as such does not move; its energy is conveyed from one level to another. A large wave can deliver its energy to a fixed object if the oscillation is interrupted. This, in fact, is what happens when a big wave strikes a 'breakwater'. The energy delivered may be quite considerable, resulting often in damage to the surface or to the structure as a whole if it is not built to withstand or absorb such shocks.

The energy of a wave is constant (if friction and shore line losses are ignored) so, as the wavefront travels up the estuary and it necessarily becomes shorter, the energy is concentrated into a smaller area. This will tend to concentrate the energy by making the wave taller. When it

---

1 *JOGJ*, 5 September, 1952 and 28 August, 1953.

strikes the breakwater the water of the wave will tend to take the line of least resistance and tower upwards, an effect especially noticed by observers during the storms that attacked the Stevenson works. The wind, of course, contributes to the forward movement of the column of water and since this contains a large volume of water, it crashes down on the inner side of the barrier, creating damage where it is less expected. Spectacular damage to the work inside the parapet was a feature regularly noticed during these Stevenson episodes.

There is another effect that may become exaggerated where the river bed shelves or shoals (a feature of these flagstone coastlines where 'wave-cutting' action is often very pronounced; 'skerries' along the Caithness and Orkney coasts and in the channels between rock masses, are very common). When the depth of a wave is between 0.75 and 1.25 of the wave height the crest overrides the base to form a 'breaker,' which, once again, consists of water in motion at some speed. The bed of Wick Bay or estuary shelves inwards from a depth of about 11 fathoms in the centre between the Heads, to a mere two or three fathoms near the old South Pier. It was recognised early on that shoaling waves could do considerable damage on the outside of the North Quay, even though it is aligned more or less east-west along the river bed; hence the constant attention of harbour repairers to this weather face.

Tidal flow represents an *additive* to the speed of impact of the wave itself; but a tidal current may accelerate as it proceeds up the mouth of the bay. At a breakwater, however, this speed would be small unless disintegration were in progress.

Wind effect is also *additive* if blowing in the same direction as the water – which is usually the case with storms in Wick Bay, where wind speeds can be ferocious. The energy contributed is absorbed into the waves as the wind blows above the water. Stronger winds make bigger waves. The effect also depends on the length of the path of exposure to the wind (the 'fetch'), which in this part of the North Sea can be 100 miles or more. Once generated, a wave travels inexorably shorewards, and even with an interruption in the speed of the wind, the wave movement continues unabated. Wind acceleration itself, very characteristic of Wick Bay, will tend to make the waves bigger and generate some smaller intermediate waves.

N K Horrocks, in *Physical Geography and Climatology;* London, Longmans (1964) has notes about wave delivery on to obstacles. He shows that:

1 The direct impact of a large mass of water (perhaps hundreds of tons) at speed in a short time will cause large *impulsive* forces. These would tend to dislodge basic structures or parts of them. The forces involved could be quite considerable, especially when delivered in a short period of time. Thus, a mass of say 100 tonnes static weight, delivered at a velocity of 5 metres per second over a period of 2 seconds would strike a resistant object at a force of 25 tonnes of material at static weight. A more abrupt impact lasting, say, 1 second, becomes a static weight of 50 tonnes.

2 Rock fragments carried in the water at high speeds can do much damage. Their impact will be smaller than that of great volumes of water, but at the limited area of contact the destructive force generated can be very considerable. The masonry surface of a breakwater can by this means become badly chipped and eroded. Larger pieces would break way from the edges of exposed masonry.

3 Trapped air in passages in masonry (and rock) becomes alternatively compressed and expanded, causing material bedded together to become loosened, thus exaggerating the other effects. As we have seen earlier in this book, the geos that are so significant a feature of these coasts, are very largely caused by such 'explosions' when air is trapped in joints, compressed and released.

It is arguable that much of this kind of knowledge was available at the time of the Stevenson contract. G B Venturi, who experimented on the velocity of fluids in ducts constricted at a particular point, did much of his work in the later years of the eighteenth century. Of course, the movement of water up an estuary is not constricted in the same way as it would be if flowing in a pipe, but if the rock walls of the estuary are of a considerable height (which is true of Wick Bay) some similar kind of construction may be operative. The mathematics usually employed in theoretical calculations in such matters are those of Daniel Bernoulli, a Dutch scientist also working in the later eighteenth century. Regular measurement of rates of flow in ducts is made by use of the *flow meter* or *Venturimeter*.

Schemes of the kind undertaken during the nineteenth century in Wick Bay would nowadays be the subject of stringent and exhaustive tests with scale models. Nothing of this kind was attempted at Wick. When, during the Second World War the problem arose of closing the channels between the south islands of Orkney, to exclude the possibility of U-boat entry through these channels, even though time was very short, extensive measurements on models at Manchester

University and on site were made. Here, the chief problem was that of blocking off reversing tidal flows (four times a day), running in some of the channels at a rate of as much as 12 and 13 knots.

(The substance of most of these notes was contributed by Colin Salsbury.)

CHAPTER 17

WICK ON THE LINE

A FUGITIVE reference in the *John O'Groat Journal* in August, 1883 raises the interesting suggestion that soon fish may be taken from Wick in refrigerator railway cars. Such a possibility was now fairly commonplace, for Wick was on the railway line and refrigeration was now a routine, through all the way to London if need be. The story of Wick's railway connection is, however, relevant to, but quite detached from the big issues of major harbour extension and Wick's survival as a major fishing port. The very possibility of the place becoming connected up had more to do with the eccentric enthusiasm of the third Duke of Sutherland for railway trains, than any overt desire of the Wick fish-curers, business men and citizens to have a railway.

There was never any passionately cherished objective among railway developers to connect the bottom of Britain with the top: no Wick or bust project ever animated the minds of railway investors. In fact, the whole of the Scottish railway system came along in bits and pieces, newly created small companies, sometimes with the interest and support of the company that had reached its most recent northerly terminus, risking whatever modest capital they could command to venture further north still. All Scottish terrain was, from the point of view of the railway engineers, difficult, and especially so in the area north of Inverness.

Railways have never lacked for historians, though most railway 'histories' are richer in exciting facts about gauge, length of track, locomotives and rolling-stock, liveries and regalia – the kind of information that fascinates railway 'buffs' – than the economic and other factors that brought them into existence. It is possible that, had railways in Scotland always waited on the emergence of clear and compelling demand for the benefits the iron road could provide, many miles of the complex network through the Highlands would never have been constructed. There was little state involvement in railway building in Britain – as there had been for roads, especially in the Highlands, and virtually no interest as, for example, in France and Germany, in developing routes for purely strategic or defence purposes[1]. Many of the lines actually projected in the vague hope of profit, and many constructed in conditions of excessive competition, had a short life. The wonder is that a moderately coherent network at all was created. Absorption and amalgamation were constant features of railway evolution from the earliest days. The state's part in the process was limited to the granting of permission for ventures to go ahead, in the form of private Acts of Parliament which often absorbed inordinate amounts of financial resource before a single sod was cut.

'Difficult geography' was a particular limitation on rapid development of railways in Scotland, not merely the physical difficulty of crossing mountains, choosing and surveying routes along and out of tortuous river valleys, constructing almost countless numbers of bridges, viaducts and causeways, but also (once north of the industrial Midland Valley) of connecting potentially profitable isolated population and commercial localities. The prime industry of the north-east coast of Scotland, the fisheries, lent itself only very awkwardly to the planning of railway routes, and many of the smaller centres ever remained unconnected.

Another and not unimportant factor discouraging the development of convenient routes was the obstructive attitude of some landowners. A famous example was that of Lord and Lady Seafield when in 1845 Joseph Mitchell sought to build a railroad across the Seafield estates on Speyside,[2] though it must be added that eleven years later when the Nairn to Inverness line was started, the first sod was cut by the Countess of Seafield on 21 September, 1854, 'in the midst of great rejoicings'. The Earls of Grant and Seafield by this time, however, had learned something of the advantages to themselves of railway investment. Quaintly, however, a Mr Welsh of Milburn House, Inverness, opposed the extension of the line to Inverness Harbour as it 'would injure his policies; but his objections were overridden and the construction of the line proceeded.'[3]

Joseph Mitchell, whom we have already met in connection with Wick Harbour, a pupil in his earlier life of Thomas Telford and originally a road engineer, was one of the few thoroughly enthusiastic and imaginative of Scottish railway developers. He planned a line

---

1 The strategic value of the Sutherland and Caithness line during the First and Second World Wars was determined not by prevision but the Admiralty's belated decision to adopt Scapa Flow as the main base of the Grand Fleet.
2 H A Vallance: *The Highland Railway: The History of the Railways of The Scottish Highlands, Vol 2*; Newton Abbot, David and Charles (1985 – several earlier editions), pp 13 - 15.
3 Ibid, p 17.

from Perth to Inverness, joining the proposed Inverness to Nairn at Nairn and crossing the entire Cairngorms at high altitudes, but the Bill was thrown out by parliament largely on already obsolete advice that the gradients were too steep to allow for adhesion of train to track. Mitchell's line, with some variants, was not finally completed until 1861. By this time Inverness was already a railway centre, now connected up to Aberdeen, and a line north of Inverness had been completed to Invergordon, which was itself connected with Bonar Bridge in 1864.

A considerable railway industry grew up at Inverness, headquarters of what from 1865 was the Highland Railway, an amalgamation of four smaller companies, including the design and building of engines and rolling stock, so that further extension was always to the advantage of the town. Motivation for the extensions north must be sought rather in enthusiasm, 'railway madness' perhaps, especially on the contribution to the funds needed for the Sutherland Railway, running from the south side of the Kyle of Sutherland and Dornoch Firth at Bonar Bridge, over the Oykell and Shin rivers – later with a station at Culrain for the personal convenience of the Dowager Duchess of Sutherland, through difficult country to Lairg, back to the coast through Rogart and finishing up the coast at Golspie, the Duke's home village.

Other factors were hopes of good business perhaps from the fishing, getting fresh fish to London at high speed, a trade that had already become established through Aberdeen from the Moray coast, and for the movement of cattle on rail. Though at this stage getting fish from the Sutherland and Caithness coasts to the line was not much of a proposition, nor did the revolution in the cattle and sheep trades, which the northern line eventually brought about, occur until the line itself had persuaded cattlemen that transport of stock by rail car was sounder business than droving.

The Duke of Sutherland's Railway.

The next section of the line north was wholly the creation of the Duke of Sutherland himself. Disappointed that the Sutherland line so far had stopped short at Golspie instead of going on to Brora, where a small coal-mine was now in production, the Duke projected an extension from Golspie to Helmsdale.[1] Under the Act authorising this

1 Helmsdale was still at this time a significant herring *(continued at foot of next page)*

extension he obtained transfer of the intended six miles of the Sutherland Company's line from Golspie to Brora to his scheme and went on to complete, at his own expense and on his own initiative, construction all the way to Helmsdale – or just short of it, at a station called Gartymore. Vallance's account continues:

> An engine and some coaches were purchased for working the line, but since there was as yet no physical connection with the Sutherland Railway, at Golspie, the stock had to be placed on wagons and hauled along the road by a traction engine.
>
> The opening ceremony was performed on 1 November 1870 by Princess Christian, and for the next seven months a service of two trains a day in each direction was run. By that time the works were completed, and on 19th June, 1871 the railway was opened throughout, and the Highland Railway took over the working.
>
> The temporary terminus at Dunrobin became a private station serving the castle, at which trains called by request to pick up or set down passengers. In 1902 the buildings were reconstructed to the designs of the estate architect.[1]

The arrangement continues to this day, though most of the passengers now are visitors paying to see the grandeurs of Dunrobin Castle. The 'train-mad' Duke ran his line in his own way, until 1885 when working was transferred to the Highland Railway: even after that, for some years, the Duke enjoyed special privileges on the entire Highland Railway system, including the right to run his own train, drawn by *Dunrobin*, the Duke's own neat 0-4-4 engine, on the lines subject to agreement as to times and standard working practice. The third Duke's son who became Duke in 1895, shared his father's obsession, and had a larger and more efficient *Dunrobin* built to suit his purposes. A list of this Duke's journeys in 1904 includes visits (with and sometimes without private saloon and brake-van) to Inverness, Dornoch, Wick and Invergordon. Both Dukes liked driving, but usually the train was driven by a former Highland Railway driver, Alexander Rhind, who remained in his job until 1917.[2] Both Dukes, father and son, used the railway and their own engine, driver and

(continued from foot of previous page) port, developed indeed by the Dukes of Sutherland. It produced in 1874 5,940 barrels. There is no mention in any texts consulted of rail shipments of herrings out of Helmsdale, but it seems probable that could have been an intention.

1 Vallance, op cit. p 36.
2 D L G Hunter: *The Highland Railway in Retrospect*; Edinburgh, Moorfoot Publishing (1988). p 48.

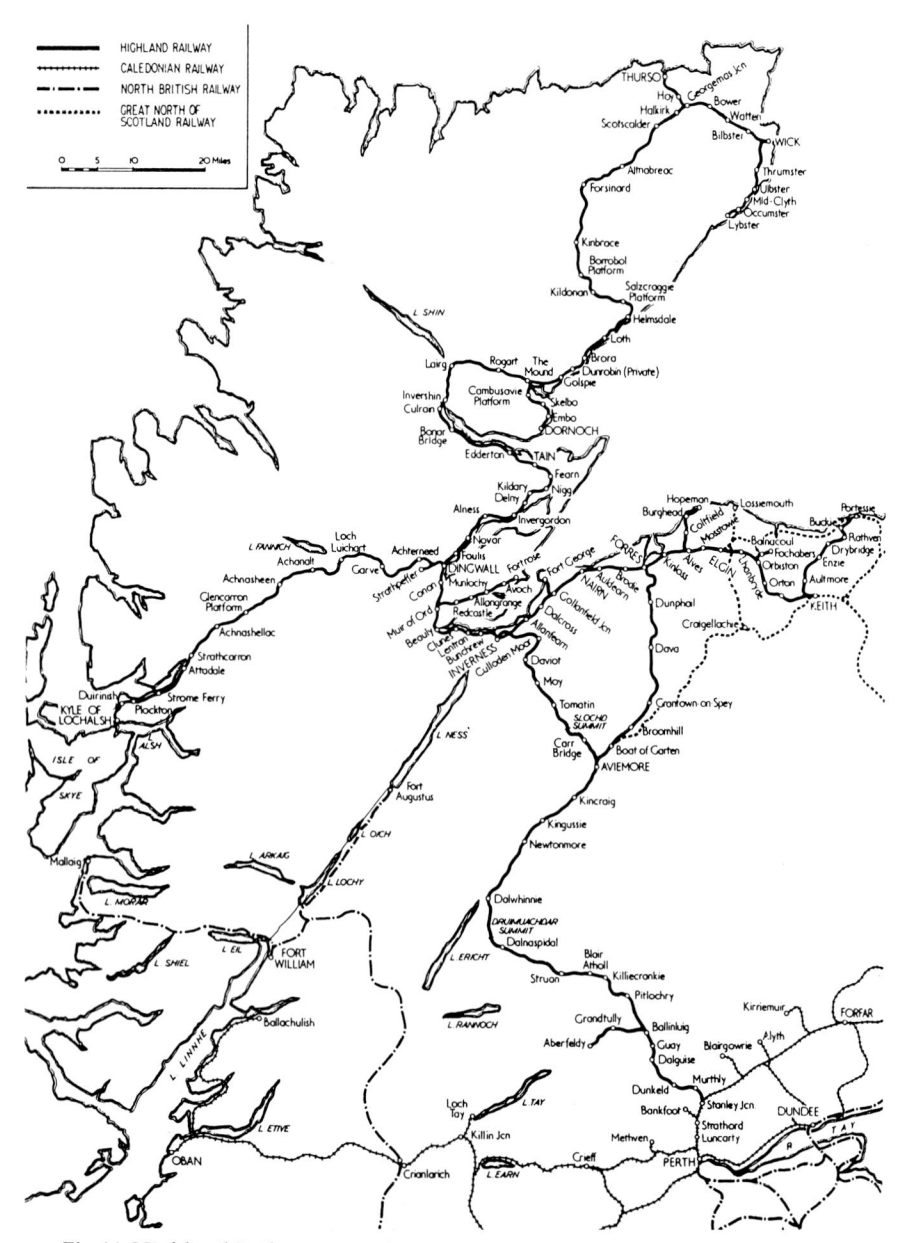

Fig 44 Highland Railway map. (From *The History of the Railways of the Scottish Highlands*, H.A. Vallance with kind permission of the author.

rolling-stock very much as well-off folk of the next generation used their Rolls and chauffeur. None of this private travelling hindered use of the Duke's line for public service trains up and down from Golspie, Brora and Helmsdale, the trains being advertised as a matter of routine in the public timetables.

The Duke, however, did not intend that the railway should stop at Helmsdale. The story of the transactions being conducted in the years before 1870 is told by Joseph Mitchell, involved up to the hilt in the projecting and planning that, somewhat belatedly, resulted in the creation of the Caithness Railway which finally connected up Wick. 'As the traffic on the railways opened in the Highlands,' says Mitchell,

> the noblemen and gentlemen interested in Sutherlandshire and Caithness were anxious that the benefit of rail communication should be extended northward through these counties, and in 1864 I was invited by the Duke of Sutherland and the heritors of Caithness to make a preliminary survey of a line through these counties to the towns of Wick and Thurso.

The Caithness Line – The Greatest Event.

Mitchell found the Duke a difficult customer to deal with. He gives the Duke a glowing character as a rich, benevolent and hospitable lord of 'thirteen hundred-thousand acres in England, with valuable mines, and the possessor of three palaces, Stafford House, Trentham and Dunrobin, besides five other territorial residences in England and Scotland,' with revenues of 'some £200,000, £142,000 of which most arise from the land.' Wealth and high-rank 'secure him with little effort the most distinguished society,' and among these he indulges his 'great fancy for mechanical engineering' and he 'cultivates the society of eminent engineers of that class,' of whom Mitchell himself was flattered to be counted.

However: 'Notwithstanding his immense possessions, he is rigidly economical, and has disturbing suspicions that his interests are not sufficiently guarded.' His Grace had let it be known that, for all his merits, he regarded Mitchell's estimates to be on the high side. On one occasion the Duke accused him of extravagance, and tried a dodge of paying him less than the proper rate. When it came to making the survey required for promotion of the necessary Bill through parliament, Mitchell jibbed at the terms offered, and a pair of English engineers was called in, Messrs Maclean (hardly an English name!)

and Stileman, Mr Maclean, at that time (1866) being no less than the President of the Institution of Civil Engineers.

The story becomes more complicated still, as a Mr Nettan Giles, the engineer usually favoured by Mr Brassey, 'the great contractor', whom it was intended should have the contract for building the Caithness line, was retained by Lord Caithness, independently of the Duke of Sutherland. Caithness was 'very anxious to promote any project which would bring railway communication to his county.' Giles was entertained (at Thurso Castle), 'and the people of Caithness displayed great enthusiasm for the railway up to the point of subscribing for the stock.'

Giles and Lord Caithness, now at odds with the Duke, got nowhere. The 'English engineers', Maclean and Stileman, did not do much better. First they surveyed the intended line between Wick and Thurso alone, in which the Duke was not very interested, and they and Lord Caithness got a Bill through parliament for the line between the two towns. It was, in a sense, a line from nowhere to nowhere, and 'the duke declined to have anything to do with this short line.'

In 1866 Maclean and Stileman surveyed the 'through line'. Mitchell continues:

> The Caithness people were rejoiced, as they were sure their favourite coast route, or some line better than mine [Joseph Mitchell's], would be selected. The local papers congratulated Caithness that they had gone to 'headquarters' [presumably the Institution of Civil Engineers itself] for engineers. The 'headquarters' spent three or four months in investigating the country, but were very reticent as to their proceedings. At last their report was presented, and a meeting of the railway shareholders and others was held at Wick on the 2nd October, 1866. 'They approved of the survey, and called for the co-operation and support of all the noblemen and gentlemen interested in Caithness and Orkney to support an undertaking so eminently calculated to promote the well-being of all classes.'
>
> At the same meeting 'the special support and co-operation of the Duke of Sutherland was earnestly asked.' But neither the duke nor the public responded to their solicitations and their Bill was consequently withdrawn.

Much of the disappointment of the local interest was almost certainly due to the fact that the proposed line, instead of following the Caithness coast north from Helmsdale struck off westward across country. Folk evidently believed that by some miracle the railway would be enabled, at modest cost, to either mount or pass through the Ord of Caithness, successfully climbed by Telford's road more than half a century before. Mitchell had already, in his preliminary survey, shown that this was not possible. He was fairly indignant that in addition to the promoters' 'unprofessional' behaviour in taking on the parliamentary survey, and wrote to the *Inverness Courier* to say that

> after three or four months of investigation, [they] were obliged absolutely to adopt the line I had selected and laid down. That the short deviations they made in Caithness had been surveyed by men and rejected; that their line did not communicate with the harbours of Wick and Scrabster, and so did not accommodate the traffic of Orkney and Shetland. That of the population of Orkney and Caithness amounting to 105,000, 79,7000 of these would suffer a detour for themselves and their traffic of nine miles in travelling south by their line; that as the rivers of Wick and Thurso were crossed at their mouth at the towns where they were wide, the waterways being 183 feet and 156 feet respectively, expensive bridges would be required, whereas by my line some miles up the country, small bridges with cheap approaches and waterways of 120 feet and 130 feet were only necessary. Hence, when they did not adopt my line, the extra railway making and bridges would cost an additional and unnecessary outlay of £45,000.

Brassey, he complained, put in a tender for the job way above that estimated by Mitchell. In the event, Brassey's tender was not accepted; Lord Caithness was forced to pay most of the bill of £4000 for the Maclean and Stileman survey, and the Duke refused to have any part of it 'although he was the means of engaging them.' 'So,' concludes Mitchell, 'the whole extension to Caithness stood in abeyance, and I concluded my letter by predicting that the route now being fixed, the Caithness Railway will at no distant period be made; but it will not likely be undertaken as a contractor's line.'

Work on the Sutherland and Caithness remained in abeyance until October, 1870. Mitchell concludes his account of the building of the Caithness section of the railway:

> The duke had extended his railway along the level coast to Helmsdale (17 miles); but he found the traffic of a sparse population, in a pastoral country which had been cleared,

wholly unremunerative, and the only hope of obtaining a return for the outlay for the railway works that had been made, was to extend the line through Sutherland and Caithness to Wick and Thurso. The duke got a subscription of £50,000 from the Highland Company, and other small contributions in Caithness and elsewhere, and resolved to extend the line to Wick and Thurso, as a feeder to his lines in Sutherlandshire.[1]

Thus Wick and Thurso got their railway partly as a result of the quirky generosity of the Duke of Sutherland and as a speculative 'feeder' extension of a line that could not expect to pay its way without them. Unenthusiastic reports on what was happening appeared in the *John O'Groat Journal* in July, 1874. Evidently deeming it time that the citizens of Caithness should know something about the Highland Railway, shortly to be opened up to them, a densely factual report of a meeting recently held in the Caledonian Hotel at Inverness, addressed by Mr Dougal, Manager of the Highland Railway Company, was taken from the *Inverness Courier* and printed in the *Journal*. This was packed with railway lore, telling how many miles of track the Highland Railway now commanded, the number of engines, trucks and carriages owned by the Company, the number of people employed, the wages bill, the coal and water capacity of typical engines, length of life of engines and their boilers.[2]

Up to this time, though the *Journal* had kept its readers informed of the progress of the railway north, there are few signs that the citizens of Wick were very much interested in railways and their affairs, or for that matter, in their own. Now they were imminently to be connected up with all places south. It was announced in July that the new railway was to be opened 'before the end of the month.' The Caithness Railway owed its existence chiefly to the Duke of Sutherland and the Highland Railway Company, 'who have been anxious for this important feeder to the system' to be completed. A brief history of the project was outlined. Work on the final stage had begun in 1872. The Duke of Sutherland had subscribed £60,000, and the Highland Railway Company another £50,000. With few exceptions, 'the Caithness proprietors and merchants rendered hardly any assistance.' Sir Tollemache Sinclair had subscribed £6,000 and had given fourteen miles of land near to Halkirk gratis.

1 Joseph Mitchell, op cit, Vol 2, pp 215-225. See also John Thomas & David Turnock: *North of Scotland*, Vol 15 of *A Regional History of the Railways of Great Britain;* Nairn, David St John Thomas (1989) pp 248-249.
2 *JOGJ*, 2 July, 1874.

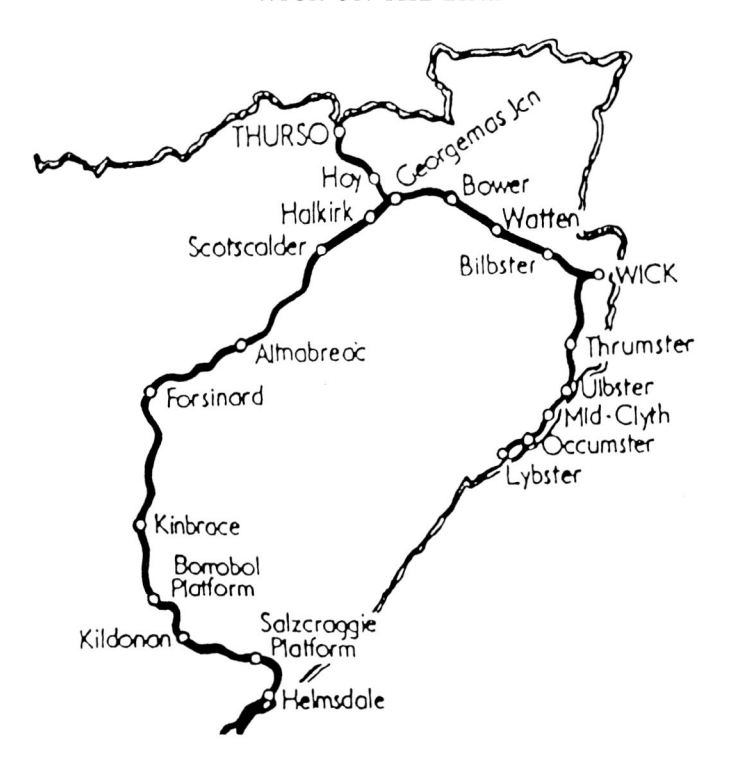

Fig 45 Caithness Line 1870 - 1874. Adopted from *The Highland Railway*, H.A. Vallance with kind permission of the author.

The apathy of Caithness people was caused, perhaps, by differences of opinion as to which route to adopt, though it was apparent that the 'most practicable and cheapest' was the one chosen. It was a pity that a more northerly line could not have been chosen, for as it is, places such as Lybster, where there were sometimes 200 boats at the fishing, Latheronwheel and Dunbeath were left out.

Readers of the *Journal* are introduced to a virtual mile-by-mile description of the route of the Caithness Railway from the point where it leaves the Sutherland 'march' between Forsinard and Altnabreac. Mostly the line had been cut though the moss, though in places there had to be 'heavy cutting through red gneiss, much harder than expected.' Most of the work on the Caithness section had been done by the contractor, John Scott of Helmsdale. The line 'cannot be called in any part picturesque,' says the *Journal* truly, with great stretches of open moorland along the route, the longest being from Forsinard to Scotscalder; 'the first signs of civilization to be seen after leaving Forsinard' was Brachow Cottage, some five or six miles to the east, 'the white walls of which were a welcome token of approaching homesteads and cultivation.'

Really hard put to for colourful detail, the writer attempts to pen sketch of the approaches to Wick as they might be experienced by a first-time visitor – for, of course, no common passenger had yet done the trip. The would-be traveller to Wick is conducted from Scotscalder across the Thurso river to Halkirk, planned by Sir John Sinclair, grandfather of the then present baronet [Sir Tollemache], across much of whose land the rail has just passed. Then by Braal Castle, residence of Mr Dunbar 'whose skill in the artificial propagation of salmon has done much to stock northern rivers.' On the north slopes of the village are held the Georgemas markets, and nearby is the Georgemas Hotel 'which we can honestly certify to be a wretched building, though kept by a very attractive landlady, whose cooking is good and whose charges are extremely moderate.' The lady provides a good tea, bed and breakfast and bill in the morning for 2s 6d. The Georgemas Roadside Station is a substantial building of the 'flat stone of the district,' which affords peculiar facilities for building. At the termini at Wick and Thurso the passenger platforms are roofed in, and ample accommodation is afforded for the railway officials and the public. Then follows another selection of tiresome technical facts such as the information that there is a 50ft girder bridge over the Sligard River at Altnabreac, that the track water-tanks are made of Caithness stone instead of iron, that the two girder bridge spans over the River Wick (at Sibster) are 'respectfully' (doubtless 'respectively') 80 feet and 50 feet, that at Wick there are three wrought-iron turntables, and an engine-shed capable of holding four of the Highland Company's largest locomotives.[1]

'A special loading bank for loading into truck fresh herrings for the Southern market,' had been constructed, and no doubt some Wick merchants in later years sought to profit from such a trade, especially when refrigeration cars were brought into service. But it is doubtful if prospects for such a trade were taken all that seriously, for at neither Wick nor Thurso was the railway continued to the docks. Such extensions in both places would have added significantly to the costs, though in neither case need there have been another bridging of the

1 *JOGJ*, 9 July, 1874.

river. At Thurso, intelligent planning would have carried on the line another two miles to Scrabster, to enable passengers for Orkney to transfer easily to the ferries. The station stands inconveniently distant from the Scrabster quays, connected today by means of a fairly haphazard bus service. Wick Station at Rosebank had little to offer the fish traders; carrying the railway over to Lower Pulteneytown would have meant taking the railway over the main road at the south end of the bridge. A station there and a line continuing to a fish dock at the Inner Harbour might have made good sense for the fortunes of Wick. However, little thought seems to have been given to this; and it may well have been that the Wick fish traders, sending the bulk of the catch over the North Sea, saw few advantages in switching a portion of their business to catering for the southern British markets.

An unscheduled and unannounced visit caused some interest on 13 July, 'when his Grace the Duke of Sutherland, as engineer-in-chief' arrived at the Wick station with his own engine and saloon carriage, which he had driven through from Dunrobin.' People were delighted with the 'unexpected call.' When the news got round the provost and some members of the council turned out to greet his Grace. 'We cannot say,' continued the *Journal* with undisguised malice,

> what the Duke thought of them, but they might well ensconce themselves behind the Duke's carriage and hide their diminished heads, for out of the whole council – Provost, Treasurer, Dean of Guild and all – they do not in the corporate or personal capacity hold a single £10 share of the railway among them, a circumstance, we believe, without parallel in the whole history of railways . . . They manage things better in France and they do the same in Thurso as regards the railway, and the Duke knows that. Here the people carp about a route, find fault with everything, but take all out of the Duke they can, while they button up their breeches pockets, saying in reality, 'The railway may go to Hong Kong for us,' while at the same time they all expect to benefit by it.

The opening of the Sutherland and Caithness Railway', declared the *Journal,* deserves to be inaugurated in no ordinary way, as being the greatest event in the history of Caithness or in the town of Wick.' The Duke, they thought, 'can afford to overlook the narrow-mindedness and the selfishness of those who did what little they could to oppose the scheme,' says the writer, in somewhat tortuous language. Unlike Wick, Thurso had laid on a 'festival' to celebrate the arrival of the railway, though it was a pity the Thurso folk had not consulted the Duke before making arrangements. He refused the honour of attendance himself, but accepted for the employees of the railway company. By making a small donation, based on the principle of 'a quarter % or 5 shillings for every £100 on their yearly drawings,' the proprietors of Caithness could between them 'gratify the noble Duke' with a fitting celebration, but somehow the *Journal* thought it unlikely that the Caithnessians would rise to the occasion.[1]

The opening of the Caithness and Sutherland Railway at Wick occurred on 27th July, 1874, 'in all reasonableness,' said the *John O'Groat Journal*, to 'be marked as a WHITE day in the annals of Caithness.' The *Journal* commented solemnly on the great blessing now conferred on the county, an event that had at last put Caithness 'in the position which every other county in Scotland has occupied for years,' a statement not wholly true. It continued:

> Our geographical position and our peculiar circumstances had combined to leave us behind the rest of the world, and to preclude the prospect of our overtaking the world in this particular. As a county, we may, in a general way, be described as poor; too truly we may be characterised as lacking in public spirit, and within all borders there are few men with a quickening spark of the faith which removes mountains. Yet here is the railway, and as certain as is that great fact, so certain is it that it will do much to wake us out of our sleepy tradition, to dispel our listlessness in business, to teach us punctuality and promptitude, to turn trade into new channels and new hands, and to quicken and reinvigorate us all.

The writer recalled the great benefits brought to the county 'since road making began,' during which the county rental had tripled. A similar benefit might be expected from the railway: not only would the trade of the towns be increased, but also 'the resources and wealth of the county may be expected to increase rapidly and largely now that the railway has come to us at last . . . Grateful acknowledgement of obligation to the princely Duke of Sutherland' had to be recorded, with the hope that his Grace's 'highest expectation' in terms of usefulness and 'remunerative' return might be realised. 'We hold,' intoned the editor, 'that the man who uses his wealth as the Duke of Sutherland does, in opening up the resources of important counties,

1 *JOGJ*, 16 July, 1874.

and quickening the lives of our people, is doing a far nobler and more truly philanthropic work than the style of munificence exemplified by the most charitable of Peabodys.'[1]

Every effort had been made by the contractors, Scott and Partners, to have the project finished in time for the predicted opening date, and latterly 'Mr Scott had men working day and night to accomplish this end.' Colonel Rich RE, the Board of Trade Inspector of Railways, had made his inspection over the past week-end, and having 'made examination of the bridges and other works, the gallant Colonel was enabled to make a satisfactory report,' making the official opening of last Tuesday, 27 July, possible.

Wick celebrated the arrival of the railway in the town in low key, and the *Journal* took the opportunity for some more jabs at the patent parsimony and lack of enthusiasm of the city fathers for such a signal event:

> An event of such great importance to the county might naturally be expected to evoke the enthusiasm of the authorities, and call forth some demonstration corresponding to that made on the occasion of laying the foundation stone of the breakwater. With this object in view the Town Council of Wick held a special meeting on Saturday, at which it was unanimously resolved that they should demonstrate to the extent of ordering the officer to ring the town bell at intervals throughout the day, and to recommend the merchants to give a half-holiday to their shopmen. It is rumoured that the members of the Council subscribed twopence each to pay the bellringer, but this was not done at the meeting, and so we cannot vouch for the truth of the story. The railway, thus, so far as Wick was concerned, opened without any ceremony. We were glad, however, to observe that on the opening day large numbers availed themselves of the facilities afforded for having a run on the line.

The first train out of Wick station ran at 5am, 'without, by the way, even a cheer to send it on its way.' It carried 70 to 80 passengers, and even larger numbers travelled on the three later trains out of the station; altogether 295 tickets were sold that day. Incoming trains also had 'a good many passengers.' People flocked on to platforms to

---

[1] The Peabody Trust, a philanthropic housing body, was at this time erecting in London and other towns, tenement block type accommodation for artisans. The comparison expressed here by the *John O'Groat Journal* seems rather gratuitous.

witness the arrival and departure of trains, and 'the business of the day was completed without accident.'

The first goods train despatched from Wick, 'appropriately enough, consisted of barrel staves, boat oars, and buoys,' doubtless for other fishing stations down the line. Altogether now, Caithness had 66½ miles of railway from the 'march' to Wick and including the line to Thurso.[1]

And for the time being, Wick station and the Highland Railway's services passed out of the news. There was complaint in the same issue of the *Journal* about the unwillingness of the Post Office to make full and speedy use of the town's new transport facilities for the mail, leaving the town no better off than it had been before. In such a manner did Wick, the once premier herring port become fully connected up with the outside world; though not with absolute assurance that the trains would always get through. The Caithness weather would never allow such assurance, as demonstrated by a report of 31 January, 1885, when 'rail traffic became completely disorganised'. A train from Wick that should have arrived in Inverness at 8 o'clock on Sunday, 25 January, did not arrive until 10 o'clock the next morning. This was a rather good run compared with some in later years, when Wick trains had to spend whole nights and days snowed up on the most northerly line in the kingdom.[2]

For this was by no means the last occasion when the trains to Wick and back became snowed up. No railway lines in Britain were more subject to snow hazards than those through Caithness. Thomas and Turnock describe some of the measures adopted to cope with the problems of snow drift:

> Snow was always a hazard in the winter and it was normal practice to place telegraph poles in sheltered positions and to carry signal wires on high posts. Snow fences were erected at vulnerable points. Sometimes these palisades of old sleepers would be erected two or three rows deep. and on the Caithness-Sutherland border a special 'blower' was installed. Close-boarded fences were erected on both sides of the track close to the rails. The inner edges of the blowers almost touched the ground, but the outer edges were raised some 8-10 feet (2.4-3m). These artificial troughs deflected the wind currents away

1 *JOGJ*, 31 July, 1874.
2 *JOGJ*, 31 January, 1885.

from the railway so that the snow was deposited away from the track.[1]

The Wick and Thurso line brought the two towns closer together, if not in sentiment at least in business. Two trains a day each way became the norm for weekdays, one each way a 'mixed' train, that is a train comprising passenger coaches and goods vehicles, presenting a technical problem in earlier years since trucks did not have all-through braking, so that it was not possible to run the trains at high speed. 'On sale days the afternoon passenger trains were permitted to attach not more than three trucks of livestock.' Times for the journey were about an hour and ten minutes. It took seven hours or more from Wick to Inverness in the early days and a through journey to Glasgow could take nearly thirteen hours. Even so, these were marvellous improvements on earlier journey times.

According to Thomas and Turnock 'the railway made a great contribution to the local economy,' although the evidence they quote is not very impressive. They recall, for instance, a comment by an earlier railway historian, W M Acworth, that it was felt in Wick and Thurso that before the coming of the railway 'it was never worth while catching the herrings at all until they were in good enough condition for curing,' and that now the railway had provided 'other means of disposal.'[2] No figures are available to illustrate this proposition. Fresh herrings were no doubt shipped south by rail from Wick in refrigerated cars, but it never amounted to a considerable trade. More likely was the sending south of fresh white fish, especially from Thurso. What Mr Acworth does not mention is the rise of cattle transportation as a business of the Highland Railway.

In addition to the lack of rail connection to the dock areas of both Wick and Thurso (explained no doubt by the costs of bridging and viaducting that would have been necessary – though not of the river), there are one or two other oddities in the siting of Wick and Thurso area railway amenities. These include the location of the junction at Georgemas instead of at Halkirk, and the failure to take the line through Halkirk itself. The Georgemas Junction site, in completely open country, was presumably chosen because of the nearness of the main road from Wick to Thurso. A station was placed on the line to the east of Halkirk, some distance from the town, and a 'local' station was also placed on the main Wick to Thurso road, both too far from

1 Thomas and Turnock, op cit, pp 253-254.
2 Ibid, p 254.

the village for convenience. Was Sir Tollemache Sinclair's grant of land conditional upon the railway not coming into the village and passing Braal Castle?

One effect of the transfer in 1924 of the Highland Railway to the London Midland and Scottish, was an attempt to extend the use of the northern railway to the introduction of weekend excursions, a very popular activity on the railways during the nineteen-thirties. Church folk, as might have been expected, strongly disapproved. In their petition, circulated through the area, the 'undersigned residents of the Northern Counties' respectfully appeal for discontinuance of any such trips 'either by Rail, Steamer, or Motor into the Highlands on the Sabbath Day,' which, the petitioners wished to have kept quiet 'against any encroachments on its sacred hours.' They objected 'against a policy which seeks to substitute the Continental Sunday for the Scottish Sabbath.'

The intensity of Sabbatarian sentiment in this part of Scotland was not, however, as great as that in western Scotland, where for many years – well after the Second World War – access of trains and boats was restricted, and cars were quite unable to obtain petrol on Sundays.

Perhaps the bravest moments in the history of the Caithness Line were those during both World Wars, when daily, 'Jellicoe's Express' ran to and from Thurso, carrying service-men, especially sailors, to their ships and stations in Scapa Flow, or more joyfully, home on leave. The daily 'Jellicoe Special' was not introduced until February, 1917, with the object of reducing the 'great disorganisation on the Highland Railway' that had been caused during the previous two years on account of the 'urgent transportation of Naval personnel to the Grand Fleet at Scapa Flow from Portsmouth', accomplished up to that time by *ad hoc* timetabling. To begin with the new through service, connecting Thurso with London and, by means of coaches attached and detached at Crewe, with Portsmouth, was called 'The Misery' for fairly obvious reasons.[1] It became the 'Jellicoe' in reference to the Admiral Lord John Jellicoe, Commander for much of the war of the Grand Fleet. The story, however, belongs to the two wars and will be told more fully in that context. (See below p 636-638).

1 *The Northern Times*, 2 April, 1982.

The Wick and Lybster

Wick never became the railway centre of the high north. It might have done so had the dice fallen differently. Unlikely though it now seems, between 1890 and 1893 the Highland Railway Company 'seriously considered the possibility of constructing a branch line between Wick and Gills Bay on the Pentland Firth. This was to cater for the considerable trade with Orkney, most of which was shipped in vessels which had called at Wick but recently had diverted to a large extent to Scrabster because of congestion in Wick harbour.'[1]

Yet another line to the north was considered in 1897 under the terms of the Light Railways Act of 1896, from Forsinard, the most westerly point reached by the Caithness Railway, and Portskerra in Melvich Bay on the north coast and, according to Iain Sutherland, this line was more favoured by the Secretary of State than the application he had received in March, 1896, for a line from Wick to Lybster, down the coast of Caithness. As we have seen, the influential essayist, Archibald Young, believed there was a herring potential at Melvich and Kyle of Tongue. The Duke of Sutherland (the Fourth) was interested in this project and powers were actually obtained but construction was never started. Wick and, of course, Thurso, would have been affected by the western venture, but neither would have had any direct connection with it.

Wick's second railway, the Wick and Lybster, was opened on 1 July, 1903; its last train ran on April Fool's Day, 1944. It was one of the many lines up and down the country, promoted under the provisions of the Light Railways Act of 1896, a measure intended to lighten the cost of establishing and running railways between localities where there was the likelihood of profitable traffic but not sufficient to warrant the expenditure of the time and money usually required under the Railway Acts, including the customary private Act of Parliament to authorise the project under consideration. What was required here was the submission of a properly supported application to the Light Railway Commissioners who, if they approved, would issue an Order 'permitting the new company to invite public subscription for shares' and to undertake construction. Some

---

1 Thomas and Turnock, op cit. p 262. The *John O'Groat Journal* commented regretfully on this failure: 'It would have opened up a poor and congested district, with excellent prospects of developing fine fishing grounds which are known to exist. But for the unsuccessful attempts made it may be seen that the really poor and necessitous districts do not stand the same chance as those districts which are wealthy enough to put money themselves.' (*JOGJ*, 18 October, 1901).

applications under the Light Railways Act envisaged the use of narrow gauge tracks, electric traction and sometimes passage through streets. There were tight restrictions on the speeds at which trains could travel, maximum 25 miles per hour and 10mph round curves. The Wick and Lybster was to be constructed with standard gauge track and ridden by 'light' engines and rolling stock, that is, weight on any one axle could not exceed 12 tons.

Just as the Highland Railway north of Golspie may never have been built had it not been for the Duke of Sutherland, so the Wick and Lybster depended for its genesis on another duke, the 6th of Portland, who had purchased the Lybster estate in 1883. As we have seen,

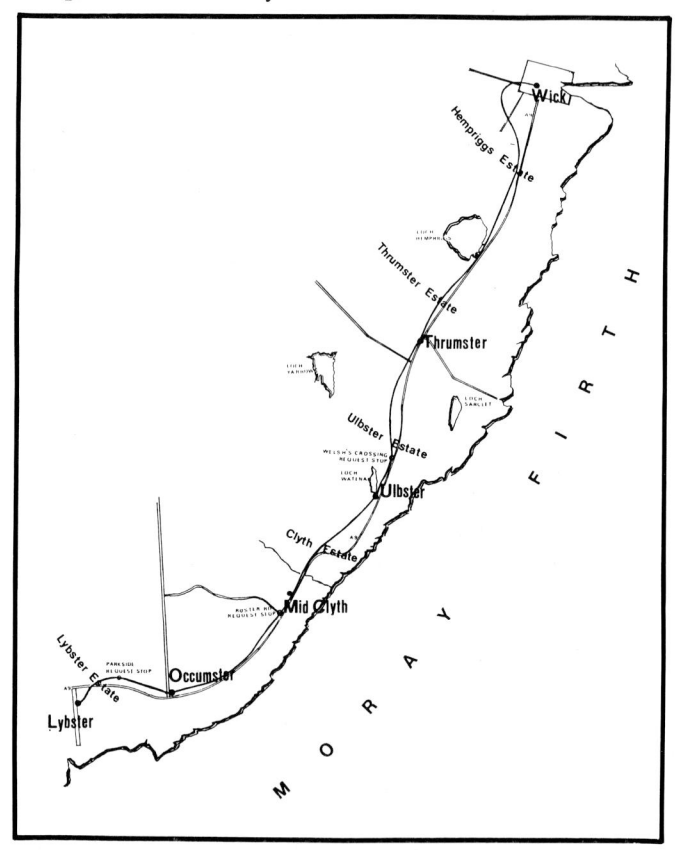

Fig 46 From *The Wick and Lybster Light Railway*, Iain Sutherland, with kind permission of the author.

Lybster had earlier enjoyed a fairly long history as a centre of the herring industry; in 1856 it attracted 292 boats and produced 26,572 crans of herring (compared with Wick's 88,284 for that year). By 1873 Lybster produced 18,400 and in 1874, 12,210 crans, and when the Duke of Portland bought the place, as Iain Sutherland explains, 'fortunes at the fishing in Lybster were very mixed indeed, mainly because of the poor state into which the harbour had fallen as a result of the failure of the previous proprietors to keep it maintained.' Lybster, of course, was being affected as elswhere by the increasing size of boats, its harbour facilities no longer providing adequate accommodation for the larger craft; and also by the capricious movements of the shoals. Between 1883 and 1888 the number of boats fell from 138 to 68; and the parish of Latheron (the largest parish in area of Caithness), to which Lybster belonged was already falling in population, from 7,400 in 1871 to 5,875 in 1991.[1]

Dukes like the Sutherlands and Portlands, however benevolently disposed, were not the kinds of capitalists to cherish wasting assets (both families had, indeed, made much of their money from their prosperous coal mines in the English midlands). Portland had no intention of letting Lybster go to the dogs and set up a programme of reconstruction of the Lybster harbour 'which was to cost him £18,000', or about £1.75 million in today's money. Part of his plan was almost certainly to get the fish coming into his improved harbour off to market as soon as they could be got away, and although unenthusiastic when the idea of a railway from Lybster came up, soon after the Act of 1896, he became one of the main supporters of the project some time after the Caithness County Council, quick off the mark, submitted to the Commissioners in March, 1896 an application to run a light railway from Lybster to Wick.

Iain Sutherland tells how this support came about:
> The application was supported on 5th March by Latheron Parish Council, on 14th March by Lybster Fishermen's Association and by Wick and Pulteneytown Chamber of Commerce on 11 August. The Secretary of State was not all that convinced and several letters passed back and forth about the financial backing, in spite of the fact that the County Council were prepared to buy one fifth of the share capital of £75,000. Approaches were made to the landed proprietors in the county and eventually the Duke of Portland, the Stocks family of

---

1 John S Smith: *Third Statistical Account*, op cit. p xi.

Latheronwheel and the Sinclairs of Dunbeath Castle agreed to support the scheme. Without them the line would never have obtained approval and it turned out that the Lybster line received the highest financial support from the landed proprietors of all light railways built in the country. However it was Portland's conversion to the idea that was of crucial importance, as he not only had the wealth to ensure solid investment, he had the social and political pull at Westminster to ensure that too much bureaucracy would not get in the way.[1]

The complicated story of the whole process of forming the company, calling in the funds, obtaining grants from the Board of Trade, and the actual building of the Wick and Lybster Railway is told in Iain Sutherland's well-illustrated *The Wick and Lybster Light Railway*, and it would be superfluous to attempt here to repeat that story. There were many discouragements during the lead up to the formation of the Wick and Lybster Light Railway Company, not least the difficulty of getting together the funds necessary before building could start. Take-up of the issue of the 50,000 £1 shares went rather slowly but together with the £25,000 grant (an additional £5000 having been squeezed out of the government to top up the usual £20,000 for such promotions), sufficient funds were available for construction to start in the summer of 1902. The larger shareholders included the Duke of Sutherland (15,000, later donated to the company), Caithness County Council (15,000), Wick Burgh Council (1500), Sinclair of Dunbeath (2000), Usher of Norton (1000), Pulteney Police Commissioners (1000 – this authority was shortly to go out of existence), and Stocks of Downham (landowners in Latheronwheel). Considerable numbers of local folk, merchants, teachers, farmers and a minister subscribed sums ranging from £100 to £5. Among the subscribers was William Nicolson, Provost of Wick, who took 100 shares. This involvement of Wickers in the Lybster is in marked contrast to their attitude thirty years before when the Caithness line to Wick was being promoted by the Highland Railway.

Other difficulties included rather fraught relations with the Highland Railway. It was obvious that the Wick and Lybster only made sense at all provided there was effective connection with the larger company's line. Traffic from Lybster, instead of being able to go directly south as at one time had been vaguely hoped, had to come

---

1 Iain Sutherland: *The Wick and Lybster Light Railway*; Wick, Iain Sutherland (undated), p 10. Much of the information in this section is derived from Mr Sutherland's text.

north to Wick, so that fish, for instance, going south, had an even longer journey (and transhipment) than fish cars from Wick itself. The Highland had monopoly control of routing, command of necessary expertise in railway running and management and availability of equipment, rolling stock etc. They drove a hard bargain with the Lybster on all these matters, requiring written undertakings that the Lybster Directors would 'personally guarantee' that the agreed £63,000 would be paid for their services in constructing and equipping the new line. Before the Working Agreement could be put into effect, there were tough negotiations with some of the landowners over whose land the railway had to run, of which those with Duff-Dunbar of Hempriggs proved the toughest. There were altogether five large estates between Wick and Lybster with whose owners agreements had to be reached.

It is, therefore, not difficult to understand why it took such a long time from the original application to the start of work in 1902. What, in retrospect, seems quite astonishing is that the project went ahead at all. The needs of Lybster and the localities between it and Wick, for rapid transport to Wick, were not, on the face of it, overwhelming even if improvements were highly desirable. Before the railway was put in, goods not transported by sea came to and from Wick in carts, taking several hours for the $13\frac{1}{2}$ mile journey, while passengers travelling by coach could take up to three hours. What, however, from hindsight seems strangest of all, is that here, as in many other places, there was as yet little awareness that a road-transport revolution was on the way. The car and motor-truck were already having an impact in the cities; but the notion that in less than twenty years road vehicles and improved roads to carry them would drastically change transport conditions does not seem to have so far affected the thinking either of ordinary folk or of transport planners. The many approvals of light railway projects are evidence of this. In the event, few of the light rail projects actually completed, including the Wick and Lybster, soon went into profit, and very many failed completely before the 1930s were out. At the end of his book (p 57), Iain Sutherland lists nostalgically some of these failures in Scotland and England, omitting what, to the present author, was the most romantic and saddest of all, the Leek and Manifold Light Railway which died in 1934.

If prospects for the Wick and Lybster depended to any extent on the Lybster fishing, they were to be disappointed. Lybster was already on the decline, and during the early years of the new railway, was visibly dropping out of the league. Apart from the 'bumper' year of 1908

Lybster catches progressively tumbled, between 1907 and 1911 quite drastically. Dunbeath disappeared from the picture altogether. By the same token, the population of Latheron parish fell sharply between 1901 and 1911, and has continued to fall since.[1]

Sutherland describes and discusses the creation, opening and fortunes – such as they were, of the Wick and Lybster until its demise on 1 April, 1944, at which time the railway, like all others in Britain, was being run under wartime regulations by the British Transport Commission. He quotes in its entirety the *John O'Groat's* 'detailed report of the proceedings' when the line was opened in July 1903, similar in style and content to its reports on the opening in 1874 of the Caithness line, the countryside through which it passes, the stations and station architecture of what, to train buffs of today, would have seemed a line to Paradise.

Iain Sutherland also draws attention to one curious consequence of the existence of the Wick and Lybster that neither duke nor directors envisaged:

> Above all, the event which was to put more character on the journey [from Wick to Lybster and back] than ever it had before, was on 14 December, 1920 when Wick voted to close all its licensed premises from May 1921. The decision meant that Wickers in need of refreshment after a hard week at sea or in the curing yards, could no longer obtain the beverages necessary in the town, nor of course could anybody else, which included hundreds of visiting fishermen, and the alternative was to visit Thurso or Lybster. Lybster was nearer, and special trains were run on Saturdays to cope with demand. Hundreds of thousands of pounds must have been spent over the years as the Wick shebeening industry, brilliantly organised as it was, simply could not cope with the demand. In Lybster, the travellers spread themselves among the Portland Arms, the Commercial, and above all the Bayview, and the hospitality of its famous proprietor, Mrs Maggie Donn, a very shrewd and capable businesswoman. It was of course the return journeys from these establishments, all of which stopped selling drink

---

1 The actual figures for Lybster are: 1907, 907 crans; 1908, 1701 crans; 1909, 832; 1910, 653; 1911, 590 crans. The Dunbeath catch in 1907 was 61 crans; 1908, 20; 1909, 30 crans. For the following years no figures are recorded (*Statistics of the Herring Season 1911; Herring Circular Supplement to the John O'Groat Journal*). The population of Latheron parish (which includes Lybster and Dunbeath) declined from 5,223 in 1901 to 4,514 in 1916 and to 1903 in 1981 (John S. Thomas *Third Statistical Account,* op cit p xi).

WICK ON THE LINE

over the bar at 9pm, which were the really interesting ones.[1]

In spite of this weekly lucrative windfall, the Wick and Lybster was a flop. Lybster did not recover as a herring port, and the population of the parish continued to decline. The last scheduled train ran on the line on Saturday, 1 April, 1944, but in fact official closure did not come until after a supposed official review. The Rt Hon Tom Johnston MP (Caithness and Sutherland) and Sir Archibald Sinclair MP (Orkney and Shetland) were among those who sought to persuade the wartime Central Transport Committee to reconsider. The MP's letters to the then minister responsible for railways, Lord Ted Leathers, elicited the response that 'the closing of the line is only a war-time expedient and does not prejudice the post-war position.' His Lordship assured Mr Johnston that 'at the end of the war it will be open to bodies such as the Scottish Council on Industry or the County Council to make any representations as they wish. We will then have had the advantage of seeing how road transport deals with the traffic.'[2] Needless to say, the road hauliers had no difficulty in showing how unnecessary was the Wick to Lybster Railway.

It is, perhaps, a pity that the inevitable closure did not come a few years later, by which time the railway preservation movement would have cottoned on to the possibilities of amateur running of a unique railway along the Caithness coast. Wick would doubtless have been provided with an irresistible tourist attraction. All that can now been seen of the Wick and Lybster is some of the shallow cuttings by the side of the A9 and the remains of the stations at such places as Thrumster, Occumster and Lybster itself, now country cottages. Wick town has no visible memorial at all to this last expression of railway madness in the north of Scotland, not even a plaque on the station wall. *O tempora! O mores!*

---

1 Iain Sutherland, *The Wick and Lybster Railway,* op cit. pp 58-59.
2 Ibid, p 64.

CHAPTER 18

A TALE OF TWO CITIES

WICK and Pulteneytown existed side by side in indeterminate and uneasy relationship for nearly a century, agreeing on little that they were not forced to agree about, sharing only what conditions compelled them to share, enjoying one another's company with somewhat sour relish. They faced one another across the Wick river with the same sort of love in their hearts as Manchester looking across the Irwell towards Salford, Newcastle facing Gateshead across the Tyne and Buda viewing Pesth across the Danube. Two things connected them, the Wick Bridge, the first made by Thomas Telford and its replacement put there in 1873 – supplemented in later years by the 'service' bridge downstream, and a common fishy source of livelihood.

Pulteneytown owed nothing to Wick for its birth and being. As we have seen, it arose from a treaty between the British Fisheries Society and the Dunbar estates. Its modern harbour on the south side of the river was decided on and built without let, hindrance or approval from the ancient royal burgh opposite, and precious little consultation. Its houses were new, its streets planned and straight and for nearly forty years it was governed autocratically by the Society. Eventually it became self-governing under an *ad hoc* 'Improvement Commission' on which the Society was represented, achieving its ultimate status as a 'Police Burgh' under the terms of the Burgh Police Act (Scotland) of 1892 which, like the earlier Police Act of 1862, covered a wide range of matters including sanitary and building affairs. It took on the style and paraphernalia of a traditional burgh, with provost, bailies and dean of guild.

Even so, Pulteneytown, though considerably larger than its neighbour (with a population of 9,476) in 1901 as compared with Wick's 2,962), was often identified with Wick in official descriptions and reports. The total population of 'Wick' as given in the census until 1911 included the 10,000 or more of Pulteneytown citizens.[1] And the

---

1 The population of 'Wick' in 1851 was given as 11,851, that of 'Wick Burgh' as a distinct community was 1,514, which indicates a population of 10,137 for Pulteneytown, Louisburgh and Broadhaven, all outside the 'Burgh'.

unofficial overlap was considerable; until Pulteneytown was formally recognised in the 1860s as an independent parish, church administration ranged over both sides of the river. Provost Rhind, as already noticed, was for years the Fisheries Society's Agent in Pulteneytown. The *John O'Groat Journal* liked to regard itself as a Pulteneytown institution (its offices, were indeed – and still are – the Old Society's offices at the south end of the bridge, just in Pulteneytown), but was generally thought of as Wick's newspaper. The famous 'Wick Riots' occurred mostly in Pulteneytown.

POLICE

In some respects Pulteneytown was, for much of its life, better governed than Wick burgh. Having the larger population (and the larger itinerant population in the summer) it was liable to endure the greater amount of disorderly behaviour, and in fact, the Fisheries Society installed its own 'police force' during the 1840s.

Wick, on the other hand, had no police force until the 1860s, and every time the subject was brought up in council there was a majority against establishing one. Not that such a force was not needed. There are frequent reports of rough houses, assaults, 'wanton outrages' disgracing the streets of both communities. The old jurisdiction of the kirk could now only be lamely exercised. The *Groat* complains in 1839 of 'the most revolting language . . . a braving of order and decency, which, in any town, with a force such as we have referred to, would not have been suffered for an instant. We will not allude to the danger to which it is liable from want of a force of this kind,' continued the *Journal*, doing just that:

> The numerous instances of petty theft and other outrages of a similar description which we have had to record in the columns of this paper must have disabused those who think that property runs no risk in this quarter, and that, as in the good old times, the shutting of the half-door, or turning the key in the shop door is still sufficient safeguard. The desecration of the Sabbath, from the streets, harbours and other places in this town and Pulteneytown being infested by hordes of wandering vagrant children, bent on mischief of all kinds, is an evil of the first magnitude, and for which the only remedy is a good police . . . . . We understand that regular and hard contested battles, betwixt the Wick and Pulteneytown boys, are of everyday

occurrence, and that the missiles used on these occasions are stones. Numerous accidents have happened, sundry broken heads and serious contusions have been the consequence, but we suppose those who feel opposed to the introduction of a police, wait to be convinced of its necessity by some *bona fide* murders, or are determined not to *see* the evil until one of their own eyes is knocked out; and if some remedy be not applied, we suppose the houses will next be the subject of attack.

Not only was there little control of dangerous and destructive behaviour, there was also no recognised means of keeping order when groups of people necessarily came together:

A scene occurred on Saturday evening last, on the arrival of the steamer, which beggared all description, and which, of itself, would fully warrant the organization of a police. The running, jostling, pushing and confusion was dreadful; and the wonder is, that lives were not lost. What idea the passengers by that vessel [this would have been the *Sovereign*] who have never been here before must have formed of the place and its inhabitants, we are at a loss to conceive. Carters, porters and, carriers blocked up the harbour stairs, and crowds of gaping ill-bred louts, with a sprinkling of females and children, made the progress of the passengers next to impossible. There was a scrambling for baggage, a pulling of trunks, and a hauling of carpet-bags such as were never [before?] witnessed. The only value which property seemed to possess in the would-be porters' eyes, desirous of securing it, was the pittance they expected to get for carrying it off, and the conflict for a precedence, in this respect was terrific.[1]

Stone throwing seems to have been a particularly prevalent habit of the youth in the two towns. Another report tells of the 'idle vagabonds' who threw stones, cutting and injuring people. To

such a pitch is the abominable habit of throwing stones carried in Pulteneytown, that it is actually dangerous to sit at, or open, the windows or doors. We ourselves have been witness to the demolition of entire windows by systematic attacks of the kind, and each day we have complaints of parents and others, whose children, servants etc., have suffered from practices which would never for a moment have been

1 *JOGJ*, 28 June, 1839.

tolerated in a well-regulated town possessing a police. It is clear that magistrates cannot act as justices and as policemen. The result of all this will be, that if the inhabitants continue the opposition to the introduction of a Police force, much and serious robberies will follow, and the place will gain such a reputation, as will prevent any respectable strangers from visiting it, or its inhabitants living with any degree of comfort or security.[1]

Following the Society's first measure of devolution of town government to the citizens, the elected Pulteneytown Improvement Commission was 'given authority to impose rates on the settlers, in return for which the Commission provided such amenities such as street lighting and cleaning, drains and a police force.'[2] The citizens of Wick, at least those enfranchised under the 1832 Act, obdurately refused to entertain the idea of their own police force. At a public meeting held in the Town Hall in April, 1840, with Provost Bruce in the chair, 102 voted for 'rejection of the Act' against 33 in favour, a majority of 69 against the introduction of a police force.[3] The Act in question was that of 1832 – invoked four years later by the Pulteneytown Commission, which would have allowed elected Wick magistrates to introduce a 'police commission' which would have had powers to raise rates for lighting, cleansing, water supply, drainage etc. Once again the men of Wick had indicated their reluctance to spend money, or rather to pay rates to allow for such spending.

During the 1850s moves were afoot to establish a proper police force in the county of Caithness as a whole. Following an Act of 1857 a government inspector was appointed to visit each Scottish county to report on the state and efficiency of policing in the county. The Inspector of Constabulary for Scotland, Mr John Kinloch set out on his rounds and arrived in Caithness in 1859. He found that the county with a population of 35, 209 and an acreage of 455,708, had a police force of eleven men, including a Chief Constable and an officer in charge of the Thurso district. Wick at this time was allowing itself to be serviced by the county force, the burgh council 'not blind to the fact that their Town officer could never be construed as an efficient police force.' The affair of 1847 had demonstrated how fragile was their power. On the other hand, Pulteneytown, newly independent,

1 *JOGJ*, 8 January, 1841.
2 Dunlop: *Fisheries* op cit. p 191.
3 *JOGJ*, April, 1840.

had no wish to unite with the county and ran its own 'force.'[1]

The War of the Orange.

What probably more than anything else persuaded the burghers of Wick to take a more positive line in the matter of a police force, and incidentally promoted a spirit (not a strong one) of co-operation with Pulteneytown, was the incident usually known as the 'War of the Orange' of 1859. This curious episode, christened and chronicled by Iain Sutherland and referred to by R.L.S., though he mentions an apple, was above all a manifestation of the tensions that quite inevitably blew up over the years between the inhabitants of Wick and Pulteneytown and the greatly more numerous temporary immigrants who crowded into the towns during the fishing season. Very many of these people were from the west of Scotland and islands, Gaelic in speech and manners, and not readily assimilated into the ways of life of 'native' Wickers and Pulteneytowners, bearing in mind that a majority of the settled inhabitants were themselves very largely second-generation immigrants themselves, mainly from the east of Scotland and almost wholly English speaking and 'lowlander' in outlook.

Generally speaking, it is astonishing that in most years the two very distinctive groups, regular inhabitants and immigrants, got on reasonably well together. The immigrants represented, of course, considerable profit to the Wickers, as workers, lodgers, drinkers and churchmen. Wick as we have seen had ample accommodation for both drinking and the solemnities of the Sabbath; to the disgruntlement of the temperance campaigners, Wick had a record number of pubs, and even before the Disruption of 1843, one of the conditions of appointment of the minister of the parish kirk was that he should be a fluent speaker of Gaelic. After the Disruption the Free Church prevailed in Wick for many years, so that those islanders and Highlanders who came to the town and who had themselves adopted Free Church allegiance, were well catered for. It is also true to say that although the Highlandmen (and women) had been coming to Wick in great numbers for many years, and although they were distinctive in attitude, dress and speech from their hosts, they had no record of trouble-making. They generally came and went in good humour,

[1] See David Conner: *CAITHNESS-SHIRE including Wick; Thurso and Pulteneytown;* unpublished paper (Highland Region Police Archives).

A TALE OF TWO CITIES

thankful to have earned a little money to see them through the winter.

As in most of his stories of Wick, Iain Sutherland conjures up a graphic picture of what happened. The 'Orange Riots' began on 27 August, 1859 and ended on Wednesday, 14 September, when the authorities officially concluded that the troubles were ended and stood down the special police. As David Conner puts it, the name of the episode 'has nothing to do with King Billy or any Order, but simply refers to the *fruit*,' the golden orbed product of Mediterranean plantations. Iain Sutherland sets the scene on the early evening of Saturday, 27 August, when

> the shops were all open as usual and the market trade[rs], Cheap Johns and Irish ragmen were doing their usual trade in the Market Place with the crowds all around listening to their sale patter, and, since the majority spoke no English, probably not understanding a word of it. Then, at about seven o'clock a boy from Lewis, or the Lews as it was then known, bought an orange at one of the stalls and crossed the road with it to the bottom of Tolbooth Lane. There he either tripped or stumbled and let it fall on the road where it rolled to the feet of a boy from Pulteneytown. He picked it up, and being bigger than the owner, refused to give it back. The smaller boy immediately attacked him, and they started fighting, but he was no match for his larger opponent who soon got the better of him. The Highland boy called in Gaelic to two men he knew, to help him; they joined in and returned the orange to its rightful owner. However, one of the men was slightly drunk and he hit the Pulteneytown boy, whereupon, as if at a signal, fighting exploded right across the Market Place. In a couple of minutes all the stalls were wrecked and the debris used as weapons as about 300 people fought in the square, where the numbers of local people were about the same as the Highland men and the sides were evenly matched. The noise attracted everybody in the vicinity and before long the police patrol arrived. Such was the respect for the law then that the fighting quietened down and the two policemen were allowed into the centre of the crowd. A few enquiries soon established the cause of the trouble, and they arrested the man who had assaulted the Pulteneytown boy and attempted to march him to the Police Station in Victoria Place. His friends, outraged by this apparent injustice, attempted to rescue him and fighting broke out again

as the locals came to aid the police, who with this protection, succeeded in getting their prisoner to the Police Station which was about 200 yards away.

They were unable to get in by the normal route as the crowd was so large that they brought him into the Court House which connects with the Police Station. The Court House was immediately besieged by the ever growing crowd of Highlandmen, among whom was a group of about 40 who were yelling in Gaelic and threatening violence unless the prisoner was released immediately. One individual was particularly menacing, and the police, under command of the Messenger at Arms, who happened to be in the Court House when they arrived with the prisoner, made a rush into the crowd to apprehend him before he provoked the crowd into action. They seized the offender but at once the crowd tried to release him and a tug of war developed, during which all the man's clothes were torn off. However, Mr Mackay, the Messenger at Arms and the police eventually managed to beat off the rescuers and get him into the Court House. This brought the crowd to a new pitch of anger and they began to threaten to demolish the building unless the prisoners were released. About half an hour had now passed since the trouble began and the situation must have looked extremely dangerous; but the Messenger at Arms kept his head although the Court House and Police Station were in a state of siege. He managed to send a message to the Chief Constable of the County Police force, under whose jurisdiction the town of Wick came at that time, since Pulteneytown had its own force which was not yet involved, and he succeeded in mustering some special constables in the police station yard by ten to eight. Meantime the crowd had grown to such an extent that the streets had become impassable but fortunately for the officials in the Police Station the vast majority had come along out of curiosity to see what had caused the trouble, and only about 100, of the estimated 2,500 present, were threatening violence. The Chief Constable sent a message to the cutter *Princess Royal*, a fishery protection vessel which was lying in Reiss Bay, asking for assistance, and just as the courier departed for Ackergill, stones began to fly. It has never been established who actually started throwing the stones but eyewitnesses were certain that stones were travelling both into and out of the Jail yard. Some minor cuts were sustained on both sides and 30 windows in the Town Hall were broken. This was the signal for a spread of violence and the Highlandmen, armed with the remains of the booths in Market Square began to assault the Jail yard and also attacked passers by. Several were hurt but seem to have been saved from serious injury by the sheer weight of numbers in the street which prevented the attackers from cornering their victims and allowed them to escape into the crowd which was still, to the great extent, more curious than anything else.

The siege of the Police Station and Town Hall went on but no haranguing of the crowd in English or Gaelic could persuade them to desist. The Chief Constable formed up the special constables and marched them out in front of the crowd; this seemed to calm them somewhat. It was now getting dark and the authorities were apprehensive that the 1500 or so people attending Saturday evening prayer meetings would now be disposed to join the crowd as soon as the meetings dispersed. They actually went straight home and the minister who had been leading prayers in the Free Church, the Rev Mackay of Tongue, came over to the Court House to see what he could do to disperse the crowd. He did his best with no result. The Chief Constable then formed his police, regulars and specials, into a riot squad which sallied into the crowd and drove the majority over the bridge from Bridge Street. A remnant of some forty of the rioters regrouped below Rosebank and surged back on to the bridge. Behind them the Pulteneytown Police led by Captain Tudor came down the hill towards the bridge, but they did not cross the river. Another group was forming in High Street, and there was the danger of a renewed attack, this time from both ends of Bridge Street, on Town Hall and Police Station. A determined force of police pressed the rioters back on either side of them and although there were casualties on both sides, the Highlandmen were driven back and the groups gathered in High Street and the lanes on the north of the town desisted and mostly went home. Vigilantes were recruited by the Town Hall officials to patrol the Wick streets and although there were some sporadic scraps 'with trouble spreading as far as Broadhaven, 2 miles away, where an inn was wrecked in a brawl which broke out when the news from Wick reached it,' all was quiet by midnight. The town was patrolled by men from the *Princess Royal*. The Pulteney Police 'returned to their headquarters on Bank Row and went on their normal night patrol as did the County Police. The trouble seemed to have passed.'

It was an illusion. Sunday was quiet and 'the churches were filled to capacity as usual.' On Monday morning, however, groups of men began to congregate in Bridge Street and High Street, waiting for the trial of the arrested men, which began at 9 o'clock. The numbers increased and apprehension was rising; various people including Chief Constable Mitchell, Captain Tudor, the Provost and the Rev Charles Thomson all spoke to the multitude asking them to disperse, with no result. As a gesture of conciliation, the magistrates released the two men on bail, but the crowd continued to grow, and some fighting began. At noon, apparently fortuitously, the retired soldiers of the town who were beginning their annual week's drill, formed up on the bridge, and at the sight of the uniforms the crowd began to melt and by two o'clock Bridge Street had returned to normal. Patrols continued including the men from the fishery protection vessel, *Princess Royal*.

Ominously, however, few boats were made ready for sea and the quays of Pulteneytown were strangely quiet. Crowds began to assemble in Pulteneytown where the writ of the county police did not run, and the Pulteneytown Commissioners did not see fit to order their police to disperse the crowds on the 'Wait'. The great majority of Pulteneytowners and the Highlanders did not leave their houses, but groups still lingered in the streets and there was great fear abroad. Specials were enrolled in Pulteneytown. During the whole week tension remained, and later in the week Sheriff Russell wired to Edinburgh for assistance. This could only mean bringing in the soldiers.

Some fishers went to sea on Thursday, and some work commenced on the quays, but there was no general feeling that the trouble was finished. News came that 100 soldiers would arrive from Edinburgh on Saturday morning; in fact, the authorities in Edinburgh had anticipated the request, and a contingent of the West Yorkshire Militia embarked on Friday and arrived aboard the *Prince Consort* on Saturday morning, a very quick passage. With the soldiers came Sheriff Fordyce, Russell's superior, who immediately on disembarkation called a council of war which met in the Pulteneytown Academy, from which the press, the representatives of the *Groat* and *Northern Ensign* were excluded. A flying squad was formed with the intention of swooping into upper Pulteneytown to bring in a Highlandman whom all believed was inciting to violence and had already 'committed a serious assault'. They could not find the man and came back empty-handed.

With the idea of not provoking reaction, troops, reservists, specials and police were kept as much as possible out of sight, and Fordyce set up headquarters 'in one of the hotels,' which was almost certainly the 'Caledonian'. It was now Saturday evening, 3 September. Patrols reported to headquarters every half-hour on the state of affairs, and in Wick itself things were fairly quiet, with just a few incidents, 'a fight among four men, a Highlander knocked out with a candlestick, but nothing more serious than a usual Saturday night.'

The real trouble centre was Pulteneytown, where sullen groups of Highlanders had been lurking all the week. Just before Sheriff Fordyce made his intended decision to let all his forces stand down, at ten o'clock,

> a messenger burst in with the ghastly news that four men had been stabbed in Pulteneytown. The Sheriff immediately formed a posse of specials who had been kept in the vicinity and they rushed over the bridge to investigate the trouble. But the news had spread very rapidly and mobs were already out, forming to attack each other to the extent that Fordyce and his party were unable to make their way to Pulteneytown as they were assailed by missiles by both sides. The pre-arranged signals were made and the troops were on the streets in five minutes. At the same time the naval ships in the bay had observed them and 60 bluejackets were sent ashore form the *Jackal* and *Princess Royal*. The organisation was good, for Sheriff Fordyce took command of the army and Sheriff Russell was on the quay when the bluejackets arrived to take command of them. The naval and military forces set about clearing the streets of the towns, which they did in about two hours. The police discovered when they got to Breadalbane Terrace, where the first stabbings had been reported that 11 men had been stabbed in the space of about ten minutes, in what was an obviously organised attack in the vicinity of Breadalbane Terrace, Argyle Square and Dunbar Street, all of which were popular lodging areas with Highland people.

The trouble had begun, about nine o'clock when some local Pulteney lads began a bombardment with stones of Highland boats in the harbour. The Pulteney police stopped this, but the young hotheads whose tempers were high, re-assembled in groups in Macarthur Street. Foiled by the police and Highlandmen in their original enterprise, they ran along Breadalbane Terrace looking for easier targets.

There the noise had brought people to the doors to see what was going on, and they were made victims of cowardly attacks as the gangs ran along the streets, stabbing indiscriminately as they went. As events turned out none of these who had been stabbed had in any way been involved in the previous trouble and were attacked just because they had been speaking Gaelic. Injuries were serious, most inflicted to the head and throat, but by some miracle, no-one died.

This was, in fact, really the end of the 'Orange Riots'. Police and soldiers rapidly cleared the streets on that Saturday night, and many of the local folk 'were so ashamed and horrified by the cowardly nature of the attacks that they put down their weapons and carried the injured into their homes to attend to their wounds. Women seem to have taken the initiative in this and the town's three doctors, Smith, Ellison and Banks were quickly on the scene.'[1]

For the following week patrols were maintained, and rewards were offered for information leading to the arrest of the stabbers. One young man, Alexander Reid of Ulbster was arrested and later tried, but mostly the trouble was just allowed to subside. Many Highland people cut short their stay for this year and, fishing still unfinished, went off home. The animosity between Highlanders and locals died down and there was no hint of it the following year. The two newspapers *Northern Ensign* and *John O'Groat Journal* continued for some time an argument between them, the *Ensign* taking the tolerant view, pointing out that there had never before been serious trouble, the *Groat* taking the line that greater severity in the handling of the visitors had long been called for.

Whatever else may be said about the 'War of the Orange', it demonstrated the need for greater co-ordination, and better training for the local police, and above all that the problems of Wick were the problems of Pulteneytown and vice-versa. It was, however, many years before this message was effectively picked up, by which time policing had become largely a county matter anyway.

---

[1] This and all the other quotations on this subject are taken from Iain Sutherland: *The War of the Orange, or the true story of Cogadh Mor Inbhir Uige;* paper published by the Wick Society (no date).

Wick Policing Under the Act of 1862

Mr Kinloch, H M Inspector of Scottish Constabulary commented on the events of 1859 in his report of 1860, reserving most of his obloquy for the Pulteneytown force which, unlike that of Wick, was independent of the county. He complained:

> On this occasion the Police of Pulteneytown [two Constables, who receive 11s 6d, per week or £30 a year, with cap coat and belt, a constable appointed by the resident officer (Captain Tudor) of the British Fisheries Society for the Harbour, with no superintendent or head of force], were utterly inefficient. They were directed by the Sheriff of the County to act under his orders and those of the Chief Constable (a direction however which was not complied with without demur on the part of the officer of the British Fisheries Society); but as they were neither men of intelligence, nor instructed in the duties of Police Constables, nor under proper discipline, they were found to be of no use on the occasion; and one of them was so drunk, that the Sheriff required the Pulteneytown Commissioners to dismiss him.
>
> Their inefficiency on this occasion is just what I expected would be the case if any emergency were to arise; and it proves the correctness of my last report, that 'the present force is utterly inefficient'.

He had nothing adverse to say about the county police and the Wick force, but complained that the town had no proper police station and lockup. He took a poor view of the practice by which prisoners arrested had to be accommodated in a part of the County Buildings.[1] Contrary to Kinloch's recommendations the Pulteneytown Commissioners were unwilling to throw in their lot with the county for the purposes of policing, no doubt, as David Conner suggests, being reinforced in their faith in independent policing by the terms of the General Police and Improvement (Scotland) Act of 1862, which encouraged burghs that had not already done so to take up policing powers.

Wick, up to this time participating in county policing, also took up the options offered. At a meeting of the Wick Burgh Council in December of 1862, it was decided to petition the county Sheriff to

---

1 David Conner, op cit. Though Iain Sutherland refers frequently to the 'Police Station' in his *War of the Orange*, it seems likely that the point in question was the Town Hall, and this would explain why Sheriff Fordyce set up his headquarters in the 'Caledonian'.

'extend the royalty of Wick [that is, the burgh boundaries] to include Louisburgh, Coach Road, Craigston and all properties lying within the Parliamentary boundary as far out as Scalesburn' and other small localities, and especially to set up a 'police establishment.' If the county did not 'object to the secession' it would, thought the *John O'Groat Journal*, 'all be plain sailing. But,' the columnist added sententiously, 'it would be a ticklish business if once again consideration of union came up.' This was, of course, a reference to the constantly rumbling notion on both sides of the river that it would make good sense for the two towns to join up, not just for policing but for other civic purposes.[1]

The County Sheriff agreed to the Wick proposal and Wick appointed its first Police Committee which sat for the first time on 25 May, 1863. As David Conner makes clear, however, the term 'police' in the context of the 1862 Act (and others), meant 'government' rather than just police work. The Police Committee was likely to find itself deliberating over various matters having to do with public order and decency, street cleaning, scavenging, reporting nuisances and dangers, matters which we have seen in the past handled by the 'Town Officer' in Wick.

The actual police function was carried out by the 'Superintendent' who earned the princely salary of £42 a year, John Swanson from Upper Ackergill who had done similar service before in Thurso; and his two 'constables' consisted of the Town or Burgh officer, 'given Police status and carrying out many Council and Police functions during the day shift; and one Constable – regarded even by the Council – as the Town Night Watchman.' Attention was given again by the Committee to the need for a proper lock-up; and in due course they reported that they could find no building in the town suitable for the purpose, 'and they recommended that in the meantime the south end of the Piazza of the Town Buildings should be fitted up as a temporary Lockup.' They were told by the Police Commissioners to 'get on with it'. A few astonishing days after the decision the job was done and the Committee was considering the accounts for the alterations: 'a grand total of £9 2s 10½d'.

Conner tells several stories illustrating the frugality and parsimony and consequent sketchy policing enjoyed by Wick Burgh in the coming years. Swanson had instructions from time to time on his other duties, including keeping a check on the scavengers and

---

1 *JOGJ*, 18 December, 1862.

reporting to the Council on 'all lanes and buildings in a dangerous condition'. On one occasion he was to obtain estimates for uniforms for the force, including coat, trousers and cap, but purchase in June was delayed because if the new clothes were worn now, they might be worn out when the winter came, thereby causing some expense. It was decided to recruit a new man to serve for the eight weeks of the fishing season, 'wages not to exceed fifteen shillings a week and the uniform already on hand to be used'. The final new clothing bill came to £7 7s 3d.

David Conner's last excerpt from the exceedingly confused minutes of the Police Committee is from June 1866 when

> the Commissioners had a lot on their plate. Following a letter on the subject of nuisances from the board of Supervision, the Police Commissioners appointed a Committee to accompany the Superintendent to tour the whole town 'for the discovery and removal of nuisances and disinfecting such places,' and also told them to enquire as to overcrowded houses within the Burgh. Doss-houses and hovels were, of course, havens of filth and disease and, not before time, the Victorians were trying to do something about it. It would not be easy, it would definitely not be pleasant for the Councillors – and it would mean more duties for the Police.

All this was prognosticated by the *Groat*. Short of political union, there were advantages of co-operation between the police in the whole area of Wick Burgh. Cleaning, lighting etc. 'coming out of a police assessment,' would be improved. The jurisdiction of Wick magistrates would be extended to those places 'without the royalty that are nests of vagrancy and crime'. But, knowing the niggardliness of Wickers when it came to public expenditure, the *Groat* added that 'the tenants will not relish the necessity of paying for a police assessment.' The change went ahead, but it is clear there was no relish for the assessment.

As for union with Pulteneytown:

> We said before that the secession from the county would be of little value to the community if there was to be a continuance of this divided jurisdiction, and we hope that now, when the first step has been taken, there will be no time lost in obtaining that which must ultimately, in the nature of things, be the final consummation – the issue of Wick and Pulteneytown under one jurisdiction. No sensible community would suffer such a state

of things to continue. . . . There was a committee appointed at one of the meetings to the Council to confer with the Pulteneytown Commission regarding a union. That committee did nothing – disobeyed its instructions, and quietly became defunct. Are the magistrates of Wick afraid of being swamped by the Pulteneytown side were there to be a union? Are they jealous of their little honours and dignities, and would they rather preserve them than further the interests of a larger community? Union is strength everywhere but in Wick, where discussion and sham dignity is the order of the day.[1]

But Wickers and Pulteneytowners did allow the state of things to continue for another forty years. It may be doubted whether Wick burgh was chiefly to blame for the postponement of the issue of union. At this stage the British Fisheries Society was still very much in charge of things on the other side, and the Directors, meeting usually in London, had no special interest in getting their affairs enlarged to include those of Wick burgh. The Society faced on its own and went through the tribulations of the harbour extension programme which began in 1863, and did not come to an end until 1884; and the Society did not finally and definitively pull out of Pulteneytown affairs until 1893. Town government was now completely in the hands of the 'Improvement Commission', whose status did not conform to the style or traditions of most urban local authorities in Scotland. In the future negotiations on union, Pulteneytown is usually described as a 'Police Burgh', in reference not to an anomalous authoritarian police regime but to the status and power it enjoyed under provisions of the Burgh Police (Scotland) Act of 1892, the term 'police' referring to civil responsibilities as well as law and order.[2]

It must be said, in the light of revelations made at the Enquiry called in August, 1902, to examine the application of Wick and Pulteneytown to combine to form one royal burgh, that police provision for the Harbour at any time had been modest indeed. In answer to questions from one of the Commissioners hearing the application, Mr D W Georgeson, Solicitor, representing the Harbour Trustees at the Enquiry said: 'The British Fisheries Society always kept a policeman for the harbour and paid for him.' The harbour, of course, was the place where most trouble might be expected. When after 1889 the assessment of the harbour fell to the County Council,

1 *JOGJ*, 18 December, 1862.
2 A brief account of this legislation may be found in Smout: *A Century of the Scottish People*, p 41. Lindsay of the Act of 1862 was Provost of Leith.

this amounted to 4d in the pound, and this resource enabled them to pay for the services of one policeman for Pulteneytown *and* the harbour. In the year 1901, the harbour paid £73 in police rates.[1]

SCHOOLS AND DRAINS.

By 1890 there were three – more correctly, five – public authorities handling the affairs of 'Wick', the Burgh Council of Wick, the council of the 'Police Burgh' of Pulteneytown, the Harbour Board and, for full measure, two School Boards, that for Wick and Pulteney burghs and the Landward School Board which dealt with schools outside the burgh in the rest of Wick Parish including Janetstown, Bilbster, Staxigoe, Stirkoke, and two small schools in Louisburgh; in fact, there was a third School Board, set up after the others for Keiss, but that dealt with territory in the Canisbay Parish as well as the Keiss area of Wick.

School Boards were an outcome of Young's Education Act of 1872. In no area of social reform did Scottish legislation more mechanically follow the English pattern than in education, though perhaps it might be better put to say that Scotland always had to wait for its reforms until after Parliament had tackled the big issues in English affairs. Even in the matter of public enquiry into social issues, Scotland seemed committed to following the British example, though in the field of education, for all its inadequacies, the Scottish system was considerably better than that of England. During the 1860s England had its Royal Commission on Elementary Education (appointed in 1859, reported 1861), and no fewer than two Commissions on other sectors of English education – not matched in Scotland, the Clarendon Commission on Public Schools in 1864, and the Taunton Commission on Endowed Schools of 1868. Acts of Parliament followed immediately after each of these two Commissions, the Public Schools Act of 1868 and the Endowed ('Grammar') Schools Act of 1869. Elementary education had to wait behind these two and was radically altered in its provision and scope by the Forster Elementary Education Act of 1870. Its chief provision was for the creation of schools where sufficient elementary schooling did not already exist, that is, very largely in the towns where the main – and inadequate – providers of elementary education so far had been the religious denominations. To provide and administer the new schools an

1 *JOGJ*, 1 August, 1902.

entirely new type of local authority was created, School Boards, elected by all local ratepayers, including women. The School Boards were enabled to levy a local rate for the maintenance of schools, the first time any such funds had been made available for the purpose. The Boards' effects upon popular education in England during the next thirty years was radical; the great anomaly of the system thus created was that 'secondary education' did not become eligible for rate aid, the grammar schools remaining wholly dependent on fees and endowments until 1902.

Scottish education had a completely different background. 'Grammar schools' of the English type, as a distinctive form of secondary education, had never flourished in Scotland;[1] the parish school, whether confining itself to elementary provision or carrying on to higher studies, catered for all, obtaining its funds as we have seen, from a variety of sources but essentially from the parish and some fees. Scotland had its Argyll Commission, reporting in 1867, discovering that one child in five of school age in Scotland was not receiving education. The Education Act of 1872 was modelled on Forster's English Act, to the extent that School Boards were set up; but their scope was different from that of the English. They, in effect, took over most of the existing parish schools, establishing new 'board' schools as in England where required. In England the existing denominational schools were left to the denominations, obtaining their state grant directly from Whitehall; Board Schools became the norm in English towns and cities. Scots were spared one educationally deleterious reform, introduced before the Elementary Education Act but applying to all English elementary schools until 1893, the appalling 'payment by results' by which all school pupils were examined each year by the inspectors in the 'three Rs', the school's grant being determined on the number of passes in this annual ordeal. 'Examination', as we have seen, existed in Scottish schools, but it was not the traumatic affair of the 'Inspectors' Examination in English schools. One other difference between the Acts of 1870 in England and 1872 in Scotland was that Young's Act imposed compulsory attendance on all children between five and thirteen, though there were numerous exemptions and 'half-time' provisions available for elevens to thirteens. English School Boards were empowered by Lord Sandon's Act in 1876 to introduce with due notice compulsory

---

[1] The 'grammar' in question (as is sometimes mistakenly supposed), had nothing to do with the vernacular. Latin and sometimes a little Greek were the staples of the curriculum.

requirements in their own area, but general compulsion did not come until 1880 with A J Mundella's Act.

The meetings of the Wick area School Boards were faithfully reported regularly in the *Groat*, but there was seldom much to say that aroused any excitement. The Act of 1872 saw the transfer to the Wick School Board of all the schools in the burgh whatever their origins, parish, General Assembly or Scottish Society for the Propagation of Christian Knowledge, comprising then the Wick Parish School on the Kirkhill, built in 1869, the Wick Ragged Schools, one in Wick burgh and the other in Pulteneytown, the Wick Free Church Schools, one in each burgh, and the Pulteneytown Academy, built in 1839 by the British Fisheries Society.

The new Boards found the amount and quality of education in the burgh patchy. The Free Church School in Stafford Lane (at the top end of Bridge Street) was evidently no great ornament either to education or to the Free Church congregation, for it was criticised as early as 1867 as 'certainly the most shameful for the greatest congregation in the North of Scotland to leave the young packed and nearly suffocated for want of room and air.' It consisted of an upper room below which was a store. The building has only recently been demolished. It had an average attendance of 180, considerably more than the parish school with an average of 140. The largest school in the district and probably the most progressive was the Pulteneytown Academy, with an average of 300 boys and girls in attendance. One of the duties of the school boards was to set up new schools and enlarge existing schools where needed. A new school was built in Girnigoe Street, Wick, and the Pulteneytown Academy and the Free Church School in Pulteneytown (on the corner of Macrae and Kinnaird Streets) were extended.[1]

In passing, it may be mentioned that the most surprising thing about the Scottish school boards, certainly that of Wick and Pulteneytown, as compared with the English, was the relative ease if not harmony with which the denominational religious controversies were bridged. Though Wick had been an intensely embattled area at the time of the Disruption in 1843, there is little evidence of concern or trouble in the schools about the differences of religious background of the children's families. Until 1902 the English 'Church Schools' remained quite separate from the Board Schools, and during the early

1 Omand, *The Caithness Book,* op cit, (R B McCallum: 'A Century of Education in Caithness.') pp 165-168.

years of the present century the 'religious question' bedevilled much educational discussion.

As compared with other areas of concern, in education at least, the two burghs had learned to work together, but not the burghs as such, for the School Board was quite independent of the burghs. The Boards had their own powers of rating and were elected on a ratepayer suffrage. The only 'educational' argument that arose when civic union came on the agenda was about the revenue that the Landward School Board expected to lose, as a result of the harbour area, until this time assessed for the Landward Board, now becoming assessed for the Wick Board.

There was nothing like this degree of harmony in the matters of water and drains. Generally speaking, the two burghs being geographically quite separate from one another, had made their own arrangements for water supply and sewerage. For some citizens on either side of the divide the notion of sharing these services was unfamiliar, and if the little story told in the *Groat* in December, 1901, at the height of a row between the two on such matters, be in any ways true, there was a water divide to be leapt:

> The comparative virtue of Wick and Pulteneytown water appears to be a matter of taste after all. One of the eminent men of Bridge Street met a worthy old woman coming across the bridge carrying a pail. 'Id's Poltney water,' she said, 'ye ken I'm living over in Wick now, but I always gae tae Poltney for water.' 'But haven't you the Wick water near you?' 'Deed, hev I, just at the door, but I wadna drink a drop o't. I win brocht up on Poltney water, and I'll no risk takin' anything else.' Listen to that, ye of little faith.[1]

It may be said that drains it was that brought Wick and Pulteneytown together. In February 1902 appeared a headline 'Amalgamation Again'. The topic had, needless to say, appeared from time to time since its mention in 1862, forty years before, when the *Groat* had confidently predicted that Wick and Pulteneytown would come under one jurisdiction. The time that it would take for the two communities to come to their senses had been seriously underestimated.[2]

A quarrel had arisen in September, 1901 about the drains of Pulteneytown. What appears to have happened was that in 1883 the

1 *JOGJ*, 6 December, 1901.
2 *JOGJ*, 14 February, 1902.

Local Government Board had authorised the passage of a Wick burgh drain through the East Banks area of Pulteneytown, a decision which rankled with the Pulteneytown people from the start, a 'preposterous decision' as the *John O'Groat Journal* describes it. Wick sought to drain its new cemetery in the East Banks area, constructing a new sewer for the purpose. This sewer had to run through Pulteneytown to the river. Up to this time, the two communities had developed their water supplies and sewerage systems independently of one another; here there was unavoidable overlap. Pulteney demanded payment for construction and consequent part use of the Pulteneytown drain. Wick was unwilling to pay the sum being asked.

UNION

Bitter words and recriminations began to pass between the councils, the sharpest being those of Councillor J Macadie, an influential man on the Pulteneytown Council, with an abiding animus against Wick. He accused Wick of high-handedness and bullying tactics, but when the *John O'Groat Journal* attempted to get accurate information about the dispute, it ran into difficulty. The relevant records, documents and letters on both sides, were all kept in a law firm's office in Bridge Street; this was because the two town clerks were members of this same firm, and for their own conveniences had permission to keep with them papers on which they were working on behalf of their civic employers. Now that they were formally in dispute, the two clerks no longer chatted across the table about matters, but rather exchanged letters across the same table. To have a civilised exchange between them over the office table would be 'reasonable', said the *Journal*, but the one did not personally communicate with the other.

When the reporters asked to see the 'books', at least those of Pulteneytown, they were told that they had been removed, and that the *Journal* 'representative' had no right to ask where the books were kept. When he queried as to how he could find out what he needed to know in the public interest, he was rudely told that he 'could get the information in the way that [he] got the information for the previous week's article', a clear 'piece of impudence' on the part of the clerks. 'When he read of letters passing between the Town Council of Wick and the Town Council of Pulteneytown, and when we have the Pulteney Council acting in private so that the agent of Wick may not

1 *JOGJ*, 14 February, 1902.

know what the Pulteney case is, how apparent to the ratepayers this farce becomes.' On a further attempt by the reporter to get 'copy' from the Pulteneytown clerk, the latter 'got very indignant. He called it a personal matter. Several councillors got indignant and called it other names.'

Charged with all the rancour and animosity that only such local disputes can generate, the threat emerged that the two councils, in the persons of their two clerks, were considering going to litigation, the business of both to be conducted by their own same law firm. Wick had evidently offered £150 to settle the drains dispute; Pulteney had demanded £250.[1] Neither side would accept arbitration.

Role of the John O'Groat Journal.

Professing strong sympathy with the Pulteneytowners, the *Journal* nevertheless saw only one solution to this kind of wasteful and time consuming argy-bargy, and that was amalgamation, brought up again and again and often by those 'who should have nothing to do with it,' in this case presumably the Provost of Wick, Mr Nicolson who was, doubtless, trying on the Wick side to force things along in a manner calculated to coerce the Pulteneytowners into agreement. It emerged as the row went on, however, that Provost Jamieson of Pulteneytown and several of the councillors, were beginning, treacherously in the view of some others, to harbour a favourable view of union.

It would not be especially interesting or enlightening to follow through the detail of the drains dispute, which disappeared from the agenda as more serious matters took up the attention of councillors on both sides; but one rather long comment by the *Journal* on the burgeoning quarrel is worth quoting, revealing as it does something of the petty tactics of Wick Council in seeking to get the amalgamation issue once more to the fore, and perhaps something of the quality of the *Journal's* professed adherence to the Pulteneytown cause:

> Seeing the circumstances in which Wick is placed in regard to the drainage of East Banks, one would actually think that as Pulteneytown is putting a drain down it would be a great saving to Wick if they could arrange to get the use of that drain for the district at anything like a fair and proportionate payment of the cost. What this share of the cost would amount

1 *JOGJ*, 4 October, 1901. See also JOGJ, 29 September, 1901, & 11 October, 1901.

to could easily be determined by comparing the extent that Pulteneytown was to drain into this main drain. But instead of this, what did Wick do? First they advertised for offers to construct a drain for themselves, but to be considered with and running into the Pulteneytown drain. There were offers sent to them, but they took good care not to accept any of them. Then they began writing us, time after time, saying that they were to begin immediately, that they were to commence 'forthwith', and so on, to construct the drain, but all the time they were doing nothing. Then after a time the most comical performance of the whole was gone through. A spring-cart was sent up with 3 drain pipes and two old men and a pick and a shovel, and they (the men) began to dig a hole in the road, but after working for two or three hours and no one interfering with them, they filled up the hole again. Of course, the whole thing was a sham, and to this day the Wick Council do not wish to hear a word about it. Such manoeuvring was scarcely becoming the dignity of a Royal Burgh.[1]

In the light of what happened subsequently it can hardly be doubted that Wick was playing a not very subtle game, anxious to play on the nerves of Pulteneytowners who were, in any case, expecting to be charged much higher rates to pay for Pulteney's water and drainage projects and who, if the *Groat* is to be believed, were pretty dissatisfied with their council, anyway. Whilst ostensibly on the side of Pulteneytown, the paper declared, 'our interests lie in Pulteneytown, and we have always believed that it would be to the advantage of Pulteneytown to amalgamate with Wick.' Pulteney, it was sad to say, 'always seems to get the worst of a deal with Wick. They are so peculiarly situated. As Provost Jamieson says, the position is anomalous. But he doesn't point out that the principal anomaly is that Pulteneytown is too much dependent on advice from Wick.' This really was the time for Wick to make an offer, 'so that the rates of Pulteneytown may be reduced.'

If the Wick Council was being devious, no less so was the *John O'Groat Journal*. Seeming – or trying to seem – not over anxious for union between the two communities, the paper played on the fears of the Pulteneytowners that almost certainly they would have to pay much higher rates if they could not come to an arrangement with Wick, and placed in its correspondence columns numerous letters in

---

1 *JOGJ*, 18 October, 1901.

favour of union. Perhaps the most interesting of these was a letter from a correspondent signing himself R J G Millar, who wrote from Dundee to say that while Provost Jamieson's 'proposals as to rating won't stand up', and while the 'people of Pulteneytown are likely to be opposed, for they have always been suspicious of Wick, and not without reason,' there would be many advantages to both communities in union.[1] Millar, of course, was well known in Wick and at the *Groat*. He had been Editor from 1889 to 1900, after which he had gone to take up the editorship of the *Dundee Advertiser*. Some years later Millar came back to the new Wick and to the *John O'Groat Journal* where he remained as Editor-Manager until 1946, retiring at 80.

The details of the proposals referred to had been published in an article of the *Groat* in December, 1901, formally reporting a meeting of the Wick Town Council, held on 17 December. The main speaker was Provost Nicolson, moving that 'an application be presented to the Sheriff under the Burgh Police Act, 1892, to revise, alter and extend the boundaries of the burgh so far as to include the districts of West Banks, Janetstown, Langley Park and the Wick and Pulteney harbours.'[2]

It was a cunning move on the part of Wick Council. If successful, Pulteneytown would be hemmed in by portions of burgh on its west side, and it is evident from Provost Nicolson's speech that the Wickers had every intention of discomforting the Pulteneytownians. There would be benefits for all affected in terms of 'the good drainage, lighting and cleansing of those districts' if they were included in the burgh. The crucial item on the list was 'Wick and Pulteneytown harbours'. Not only would there be benefit for the burgh of harbour fees; the rating regime would be in Wick's favour, for since 1893, when the British Fisheries Society pulled out, the harbour assessment for rates had fallen to county. Mr Nicolson got warm on this subject, leaving no doubt that it was the revenue and rating assessments from the area of the harbour that the Wick Burgh Council most coveted:

> The subject of the harbour, was, perhaps, more open to

---

1 *JOGJ*, 21 February, 1902. Provost Jamieson's 'proposals' were not in fact his own. As we shall see, they had emanated from the Wick Council. It is interesting to mention that R J G Millar had a namesake, who in the 1930s also ran a tight ship as Secretary of the National Council of Labour Colleges, a left-wing correspondence college sponsored by the TUC. It is doubtful if the two R J Gs had political sympathies in common, for the Wick editor was a very respectable Liberal, while the NCLC Secretary was an ardent Marxist, but also a good journalist.

2 *JOGJ*, 20 December, 1901.

criticism. The fact of it being the Wick and Pulteneytown Harbour would, or should, preclude any other community or Council from endeavouring to obtain the right to assess it. It was in the burgh of Wick, and was also included in the Bay of Wick. All along there had been an income from Wick towards the maintenance of the harbour. There was also a large income from the county. It might be said that at present this was a one-side arrangement. Whose fault was it? It should have been included many years ago as part of the united burghs had it not been for the objections of those who neglected to include it under the scheme of burgh extension. By their action a considerable sum of money had been lost to the ratepayers of the Parliamentary burgh. When the County Council came into existence [1889] they found the harbour outside their jurisdiction; they found it as a derelict; they put a crew on it, and had been assessing it ever since, and this for the simple reason that the Councils within the parliamentary burgh could not unite and have the assessments imposed by those who were best entitled to have them. While the assessments had remained stationary in Wick they had increased considerably in Pulteney, and the latter still had to supply water and drainage.[1]

Neither provost nor other speakers had much regard for the defunct British Fisheries Society, taking the opportunity when they could of ungratefully kicking the corpse. However, they clearly regarded the Pulteneytown corporation as mainly responsible for the mess they were now all in:

It would be very nice for Pulteney to have their assessments kept low by making Wick and the county share in paying towards the revenue of the harbour. He (the provost) thought that Pulteney should have taken up their minds more with the roads leading from the harbour. Pulteney was not quite the hub of creation – (laughter) – where everything centred, and where goods were landed and distributed throughout the adjoining districts. (Hear, hear). The peculiar thing was that when landed at Pulteney the goods could not reach the county without crossing over Wick roads. If it were their province good reasons could be given to show the British Fisheries Society was not an unmixed blessing. It would have been a good thing if the Society had let Pulteney alone, and if Sir William Pulteney had

1 *JOGJ*, 20 December, 1901.

remained in the south of England instead of coming to the north of Scotland. (Hear, hear). The savings of two generations were expended by the Society on the harbour, and expended to little purpose, thus saddling the place with a debt from which they could not recover for many a day. For Wick to sit idly by and see Pulteney making an application to have the harbour assessed by them was out of the question. If the case for Wick went to proof it would be seen that there are two sides to every question. They were not to allow their property – for they were as entitled to it as Pulteney (hear, hear) – to be interfered with in this fashion. Let us put our arguments in shape, the Provost continued, for we have a good case, and I believe that the prayer of our petition will be granted.[1]

Bailie Rae seconded the Provost's motion. On the face of it, neither Nicolson nor Rae was speaking about union. The object, according to Mr Rae was to get Pulteneytown to join hands with Wick in presenting claims to the county for control of the harbour. If they worked together 'the Sheriff would have no hesitation in granting the prayer of petition.' But that union was at the top of his mind was obvious from his next remark:

> The last time that Wick and Pulteneytown faced the question of amalgamation was in 1888. One of the principal objections raised by Pulteney was the difference of rates in the two towns. The rate in Wick was 3s 6d, while that of Pulteneytown was 1s 5d. Matters had changed very much since then. Wick had gone in for a drainage scheme, and although the rates had increased by 2d they had reduced their debt considerably. Setting aside the amount paid by Wick for their drainage scheme the rates of both towns were about level, with this advantage to Wick, that it had an excellent water supply, whereas Pulteney had the drainage and water questions yet to face.[2]

During all the transactions of the coming months, the *Groat* maintained its coy attitude to all the issues involved, continuing to profess 'impartiality', apparently favouring the interests of Pulteneytown in any arguments arising but making no secret of its earnest wish that a marriage could be arranged. For, as the *Groat* had declared forty years before, union was inevitable. It is very possible

---

1 *JOGJ*, 20 December, 1901. It is not quite clear which of the burghs moved first. Pulteney's proposals (see infra) were published first – by a week.
2 Ibid.

that the paper's systematic reporting of developments and its frequent moralising on the issue had an influence on the minds of voters in both communities when the matter was brought to the test of the ballot. It may be added, the *Northern Ensign* took a similar stance.

The Banns are Published.

There could be little doubt as to what Wick would be at. While not overtly proposing marriage, in seeking to persuade Pulteney to come along with Wick in getting the harbour assessment detached from the county, it was seeking something like firm betrothal, making it impossible for Pulteneytown ever again to break away.

In the meantime the Pulteney Council, perhaps not fully aware of what was going on, was playing very hard to get. At their meeting on 9 December, 1901, Provost Jamieson, revealed to the councillors that Pulteney had themselves made an application to the Sheriff to have the 'boundaries of this burgh extended, so as to include the district under the jurisdiction of the Wick and Harbour Trust,' and that the Harbour Trustees were to be asked to be 'consenting parties to the application.' He argued that the harbour had, in fact, no physical connection with the county, and not much with Wick. Under the provisions of the Local Government Act of 1889 'the harbour of Wick fell to be assessed by the County Council, and still continues to be.' Though a road tax of 11d in the pound was levied on the harbour, amounting to £200 per year, it nevertheless fell to Pulteneytown to maintain the harbour road, an insupportable injustice. 'We find,' said Mr Jamieson, 'all other harbours in the North of Scotland, such as Fraserburgh, Peterhead, Inverness, Stromness, Kirkwall, Lerwick, are all forming part of and are rated by their different burghs, and I fail to see any reason why Pulteney harbour should not be in the same position. (Applause).'[1]

Shrewdly, Mr Jamieson made no mention of Pulteney's differences with Wick on this and other matters, though J Macadie spoke with much less nicety; he believed that 'neither the County Council nor the Town Council of Wick have any moral right to assess the harbour than they have to lay on rates on the streets and houses of Pulteneytown.' The county, he said, had no more right to take rate revenue from the harbour than Pulteney had to 'charge rates for Spittal'. He went on:

1 *JOGJ*, 13 December, 1901.

The harbour is situated as near the heart of Pulteneytown as it is almost possible for a sea-coast harbour to be in connection with any town. There are eight of the streets of Pulteneytown leading to and terminated at the harbour. The harbour is the heart and life of Pulteneytown. The prosperity or otherwise of the harbour. Pulteneytown came into existence along with the harbour, and if the harbour were taken away it would become a dead, deserted place. The county, of course, will contend that they, as it were, have possession; that they have usurped the rates now for so many years, and that, because they have done so, they are justified in continuing their robbery. On the other hand, the Town Council of Wick have not even that same immoral claim to go upon, but if they do enter the field, it will be but a fresh start in the way of trying to rob their neighbours. In the face of all this it is surely high time that Pulteneytown as a burgh was arousing itself to the importance and claims of its position, and set about readjusting and recovering the various encroachments that have from time to time been made upon her. (Applause).[1]

There were undoubtedly grounds for Mr Macadie's suspicions about what was going on behind the Pulteney Council's back. The cat was finally let out of the bag two months later. Under the heading,

THE AMALGAMATION QUESTION AGAIN TO THE FRONT A PROPOSAL BY WICK,

a wedding contract was all but announced. The *Journal* reported a meeting of the Pulteneytown Council, held on Monday, 10th February, 1902, at which 'several items of business of more or less importance were first disposed of and the interesting but

VEXED QUESTION OF AMALGAMATION

with the Royal Burgh of Wick came up for discussion.'

It is evident from what follows that however little or much of his fellow councillors knew about it, Provost Jamieson had been fixing things with the importunate Wick Council. Having seen that each councillor was supplied with a copy of 'the minute of the Wick Town Council' of a discussion held on 7 February, attended by himself and Councillor Harper of Pulteneytown, the Provost 'delivered his

1 *JOGJ*, 13 December, 1901.

statement in a calm and judicial way.'[1]

The minute amounted to a complete outline of a proposed treaty of union and burgh extension, 'to include the Burgh of Pulteneytown, and the Wick and Pulteney Harbours, and also the district of West Banks, Janetstown, and Langley Park.' Gone was all reference to both Wick's and Pulteneytown's separate approaches to the Sheriff for boundary adjustments. The main terms were for

1 Representation as between the two burghs in the proportion of 3 to 5.

2 Division of the new burgh into 5 wards, three south and 2 north of the river.

3 Both councils to resign and a new council to be elected, 9 councillors on the south side and 6 for the north.

4 The 'common good' [the quaint term for a small reserve fund] and other heritable properties to be the joint property of the new burgh.

5 The expense of heating, lighting, policing, public health, roads and light railways assessments [this, of course, referred to the Wick and Lybster in which both councils had a stake] to be equally borne.

6 North and south of the river to be separate drainage districts.

7 Subject to various provisos, Pulteneytown to share the present water system and share the cost, but in general 'the extended burgh to share the whole Wick water system; extension to be done by the extended burgh; management to be equal to all.'

8 Questions 'arising with reference to water supply, including distributing pipes and the incidence of taxation, to be submitted to the present auditor of the burgh' who would consult with the water engineer of Edinburgh or Glasgow.

9 'Negotiations for the extension to be done jointly, and the Harbour Trust to be asked to co-operate; and the expense of the necessary proceedings to be borne equally by the three bodies.'

10 Any legal questions arising to be referred to Mr John F McLennan, Advocate, Edinburgh.

The Provost added the explanation that conference between himself and Councillor Harper of Pulteneytown, Mr Geddes, Chairman of the

1 *JOGJ*, 14 February, 1902.

Harbour Trust, Provost Nicolson and Bailie Rae of Wick was going on. 'They had agreed, believing that *amalgamation would be for the best interests of Pulteney, as the present position with two Councils and two sets of officials was an anomalous one* [present author's italics] . . . They [Mr Harper and himself] felt gratified at the downright honesty and fairness of the proposals which the Wick Council had made.'

Provost Jamieson added some interesting further details. The 'common good' referred to amounted to £110, and this 'and various other Wick interests were to be divided with Pulteney.' As for the assessable rentals, the total for Wick was £9545, and that for Pulteney £13,600. Wick 'lifted an assessment' (that is, took in a rate) of £970, and Pulteneytown of £1821. The joining of the burghs would mean a uniform rate of 2s 4¾d in the £, a reduction of 4½d for Pulteney and an increase in Wick of 3¾d.

The 'water question' was complicated because Pulteney had on hand a project to bring water from the Loch of Yarrows, some miles south of the town, 'but it was not possible yet to say what would be the benefit for Pulteney without having the advice of a competent engineer.' As to savings on officials' salaries etc, this might be about £150, though 'Provost Jamieson gave no indication of how the officials and their salaries were to be arranged.' This was a rather unfortunate matter in the upshot for one of the two town clerks likely to be affected, latched on to it. The question of the harbour 'would have been a troublesome one, while Wick was a disturbing element, but now Wick was to join hands with them, not only in getting the harbour into the town, but also in the larger question of amalgamation. Altogether they were convinced that *if proposals of the Wick Town Council could be carried out there would be an immense financial gain to Wick and Pulteneytown'* [author's italics].[1]

Councillor J Macadie, whose disapproval could be counted on, 'rose and proceeded to make a statement in reply.' Other councillors sought to speak at the same time. They were ruled out of order, but 'after some slight discussion, Mr Macadie was allowed to proceed.' Macadie, a known very vocal opponent of union, let fly a diatribe against the whole project, brought up the 'attempts of Wick to take possession of the East Banks drain', and went on to accuse Wick of every kind of deceit and chicanery in the book, 'scheming and wire-pulling' as the *Groat* put it. Wick was now seeking amalgamation only because they had 'no hope of securing the harbour for

1 *JOGJ*, 14 February, 1902.

themselves.' It was not their harbour anyway; 'as everyone knew it was the Harbour of Pulteneytown, and was so designated in every Act of Parliament relating to it.' The document put before them by the Provost, 'for cool calculation, presumption, and assertiveness . . . was the best he had ever come across. The whole thing was cut and dry for them, and, as the spider said to the fly, they had only to "walk into the parlour" and be done for. (Laughter)!'

This is as good a sample as any of the kind of verbal fisticuffs and expressions of bad blood between the councils of the two communities, now being drained away. Councillor Macadie's campaign of complaint and sometimes abuse continued, but it was all sound and fury. The die was really cast and although it was not all sweetness and light from here on, all that was left to be done to bind Wick and Pulteneytown together was the hard slog of negotiation and settlement of detail, involving both councils in numerous meetings, individual and joint.

The biggest single issue of discussion was the water problem. Pulteneytown had been going through a 'dearth of water' recently, according to Councillor Harper; various exchanges at the end of the critical February meeting, called to discuss – rather to present the *fait accompli* of union – brought Councillor Macadie to his feet again, recriminating some of his colleagues on the council for their delinquencies in getting Pulteneytown well watered. The report ends:

> Councillor Tait could not reconcile Councillor Macadie's statements at the table with some he had made during the storm, Mr Tait stating that he had seen Mr Macadie in great wrath over the water supply.
>
> Councillor Macadie thought that Councillor Tait must be dreaming.
>
> Councillor Tait said Mr Macadie was prepared to deny anything.
>
> Councillor Macadie retaliated that Mr Tait was prepared to say anything.
>
> With this small passage-at-arms the meeting closed smilingly.[1]

The *Journal* forthwith published a leader which was, to all intents and purposes, a manifesto for union. Since it probably had some effect on attitudes of one side of the river to those of the other, bringing

---

1 *JOGJ*, 14 February, 1902.

them together, if not cementing the betrothal, it is quoted in full:

> Some Pulteney councillors have been persistently acting in a way that is not calculated to bring the ratepayers of Pulteney round to have confidence in the scheme proposed. The *John O'Groat Journal* wants amalgamation on the very best terms that can be got. It is not wise to pick holes in the Wick scheme, but to agree positively for Pulteneytown's interests. It looks worse still for the Provost of Pulteneytown to try to pick holes in the finances of his own burgh. That looks like what is popularly known as trying to sell a hen on a wet day.
>
> There has been criticism of the *John O'Groat Journal* for objecting to the proposals because they came from Wick. This is not exactly true. What we say on the point [as to whether the terms are fair or not] is that the comparatively small population of Wick have fifteen able representatives of their own who will carefully see that Wick's interests will not suffer. The twelve Pulteney Councillors ought surely to be doing the same thing for Pulteney. Let the Pulteney councillors combine and try to take advantage of Wick if they can . . . . Ratepayers should continue to express themselves as strongly as possible, not against amalgamation but with determination to get the best terms possible.[1]

There was sufficient agreement in the air early in March for the two town councils to hold a joint meeting in Wick Town Hall, where two disgruntled Pulteney councillors (one of course being the irascible John Macadie) voiced their protests at their colleagues' apparent acceptance of the Wick terms for amalgamation without any discussion with the ratepayers. For all that, the joint meeting passed a resolution 'tentatively to adopt the Wick proposals, for the two councils jointly to meet the Harbour Trust.'[1] Notwithstanding this commitment, at the next meeting of the Pulteney Council, which Provost Jamieson was invited to speak, Councillor Macadie complained that things were being rushed.

Rushed or not it was decided forthwith to hold a ballot of ratepayers on the principle of amalgamation, and the date set was 17 March, a mere few days ahead. The *Groat* made a pious declaration that it was 'unwilling to join in the discussion', having so far virtually promoted it, and a few sentences later 'very very mildly' suggested

1 *JOGJ*, 3 March, 1902.

that 'the representation was not fair to Pulteney,' but that they had not seen any attempt on the part of the Pulteney Council to improve on Wick's proposals. It is fairly evident that the *Groat* though strongly in favour of the union, wished to preserve an appearance of impartiality, or, for that matter, generous partiality for the underdogs in all these doings, the interests of the Pulteneytowners.[1]

The Burgh Amalgamation Plebiscite, as it was grandly called, was held as arranged on 17 March. Of the roll of 1048 entitled to vote 803 did so, and the result was a 'decided majority in favour of amalgamation', 486 against 206, with 11 spoilt papers. Immediately a joint committee of the two councils was appointed to draft the Provisional Order that would have to be submitted to the Local Government Board. 'Although a good deal that has been done up till now,' stated the *Groat*,[2] seeking to maintain its paper-thin claim to impartiality, 'might very well be called in question, not being done in the usual way of public business, it is hardly worthwhile to carp over it when it has been so clearly shown that the general desire of the ratepayers is towards amalgamation.' And thus the citizens of Wick and Pulteneytown opted to become one.

E Pluribus Unum

There was no drama and little excitement in the rest of the two towns' progress to unity. This was dictated by the Private Legislation Procedure (Scotland) Act, of 1899. Like the Light Railways Act of 1896, this made the process of 'private legislation' easier than it had been when individual Acts of Parliament were required for alterations to burgh and county boundaries, etc. By it, a petition had to be made to the Secretary for Scotland for a Provisional Order, specifying in explicit detail all the changes intended, alteration to boundaries, incorporation of the new royal burgh, transfers of property, provision for water supply and drainage, valuation and voters' rolls, rating and representation and many other adjustments that had to be made when the 'Extension, Amalgamation and Incorporation' of the new burgh came into force. Drafting the Order on this occasion was the work of the two town clerks, Hector Sutherland of Wick and G A O Green of Pulteneytown, D W Georgeson, Solicitor to the Harbour Board and a

1 *JOGJ*, 21 March, 1902.
2 *JOGJ*, 14 March, 1902.

representative of Parliamentary Agents, A and W Beveridge of Westminster. Between them they drafted for publication in local newspapers an appropriate 'Public Notice'.

> NOTICE IS HEREBY GIVEN that application is intended to be made to the Secretary for Scotland by Petition under the provisions of the Private Legislation Procedure (Scotland) Act, 1899 for a Provisional Order promoted by the Provost, Magistrates, and the Councillors of the Royal Burgh of Wick, by the Provost, Magistrates and Councillors of the Burgh of Pulteneytown, and by the Wick and Pulteney Harbours Trustees incorporated by Act of Parliament, or by one or more of those bodies, for the following or some of the following objects, powers and purposes, that is to say:-

Then followed the draft, a long and tedious document of 34 clauses, rehearsing all the issues that had to be covered, from the actual amalgamation of the two burghs down to provision for payment of costs of the Order. It was published two weeks running in the *Groat*[1] and the *Northern Ensign* and by various other agencies, with the object of enabling those who wished to make representations, or in any way to oppose the Order, to give notice that they wished to do so. Clause 33 announced that 'The Petition for the Order and printed copies thereof and of the draft order will be lodged at the office of the Secretary for Scotland, Whitehall, London, on the 17th day of April next, and on the same day a printed copy of the draft Order will be deposited in the office of the Clerk of the House of Commons.'

Clause 31, near the end of the draft, gives a modest idea of the complications involved, the need to clean the slate of many of the conditions that had governed the life of the old burghs, imposed on them by previous legislation, in preparation for the new welter of such conditions that would determine life in the new burgh. The petition was to seek permission:

> To alter, amend and extend or repeal all or some of the provisions of the following Acts and Orders, that is to say, the Burgh Police (Scotland) Act, and the Town Councils (Scotland) Act, 1900, the Road and Bridges (Scotland) Act, 1878, the Local Government (Scotland) Act, 1889, the Local Government (Scotland) Acts, the Public Health (Scotland) Act, 1897, and all or any Acts explaining or amending any of those Acts, the

1 *JOGJ*, 21 March, 1902.

Caithness Roads Act, 1860, the Pulteney Harbour Act, 1879, and the Wick and Pulteney Harbours Order, 1883, the Wick and Pulteney Harbours Act, 1899, the Education (Scotland) Acts, 1872 to 1897, the Education (Scotland) Act, 1901, the Tramways Act, 1870, the Electric Lighting Acts, 1882 to 1890, and any Acts amending or extending those Acts, the Highland Railway Act, 1865, the Sutherland and Caithness Railway Act, 1871, and the Wick and Lybster Light Railway Order, 1899, and all other Acts and Orders relating to the existing Burgh of Wick or the existing Burgh of Pulteneytown or to the other districts annexed, and to the said Railway Companies.

Amalgamating the two burghs was obviously no simple matter. The Petition was to be considered and evidence heard by a Commission convened in Edinburgh under the provisions of the Act and headed by D Brynmor Jones MP, and including Sir Walter Thorburn MP, C E H Hobhouse MP, and A K Loyd MP. It was presented by C J Guthrie KC, John F MacLenan, Advocate of Edinburgh, Messrs Melville and Lindsay WS and Mr Georgeson, the Wick Solicitor. Objecting to the Order were the Caithness County Council, and Mr Green, the Town Clerk of Pulteneytown, who was dissatisfied with the arrangements for compensation of staff losing their appointments, himself probably among them. Landward School Board had entered a petition of protest (apprehensive that it would lose its harbour area assessment to the Wick Board) but withdrew it before the enquiry started. The enquiry lasted two days.

Much of the evidence consisted of details of the curious and separate histories of the two main communities affected, the present state of affairs in the two towns, valuations of property, the constitution of the Harbour Board and its revenue, and a variety of 'anomalies' which it was hoped confirmation of the Order would put right. Objection by the County Council, obviously less than happy at losing a considerable amount of rateable value, was not very coherent. Their first argument was 'that Wick was not a prosperous place,' though what this had to do with their case was not very clear. This resulted in exchanges that enabled the Wick solicitor to show that the fishing catch for the present season was the 'largest quantity on record,' larger even than that of Peterhead and Fraserburgh, a specious claim indeed, for the fishing season had only just begun.[1]

1 The *Herring Circular* published cumulated figures each week during the season. At this stage the total would be quite low.

Mr Georgeson, the Wick solicitor thought it possible that Wick even bettered Shetland.

Nobody seems to have come with genuine figures, which was just as well, since the seasonal totals for the previous year were wildly different from those hinted at: Shetland produced 320,453 crans in 1901, Peterhead 61,431, Fraserburgh 112,418 while Wick only managed 49,073. It is true, however, that from 1902 onwards Wick ran once more into big totals, but topping Peterhead only in 1902 and never again reaching totals anything like those of all the rivals. It is evident, nevertheless, that the Commissioners could see no good reason why, of all the major fishing ports, Wick should be the one that did not have direct control of its own harbour.

The county tried defending the view that while Wick, on its own, might be able to cope, its connection with the small fishing harbours of the Caithness coast, all doing less well than at one time, county support was needed throughout the area. There was much niggling cross-examination of the county's argument, but in the end the Chairman, Mr Brynmor Jones, forced Johnston KC, the county's Counsel, to admit that their 'main line of objection' was 'the loss of rateable area,' notably the harbour, Janetstown and the other areas that would be incorporated in the burgh. Jones persuaded the county people that, subject to the devising of a suitable formula for compensation, the county's claim on the harbour should be dropped. As to Janetstown, West Banks etc, it could be more disadvantageous to the inhabitants of those places to remain cut off from burgh facilities than if they were incorporated. Brynmor Jones brought the enquiry to a close with the statement that the Commissioners:

> were prepared to hold the preamble of the Order [the summary of changes proposed with which the draft Order began] proved conditionally on the insertion of a clause adequately protecting the interests of the county of Caithness in respect of any financial adjustment which was necessary.

The Commissioners 'proceeded to adjust the [relevant] clauses in detail.' They also adjusted Clause 24 as drafted, which would have allowed the payment of compensation to officials who might become redundant to 'such arrangements as they think fit, 'that is, to discretion. Mr G A O Green, Town Clerk of Pulteneytown, was the most senior officer likely to be affected by this one-sided proviso, and he had threatened to take the new burgh council to court if need be. The Commissioners' amendment to this clause 'provided for compensation of the official, and any additional emoluments he might have.' In any future dispute, the issue was to be 'referred to an arbiter appointed by the Secretary for Scotland, whose decision would be final.'[1]

Thus, 'subject to the modifications referred to, and with some other slight alterations, the Order was passed.' A Bill confirming the Order still had to go through parliament, but this was a formality, for such Orders, having been thoroughly vetted by one of its own committees, now went through 'on the nod'. Wick still had to wait until November for the completion of the parliamentary process, when it was announced 'The Wick Burgh Extension has reached its third reading in the House of Lords and has passed into law.'[2] The new enlarged Wick was now in being.

Exactly what had happened was that the Royal Burgh of Wick had become, at a stroke (or rather, many a stroke) a larger, richer municipality. From a population of 2,774 in 1901, it officially quadrupled to something over 10,000 (the entire population of the parish in 1901, which of course included Pulteneytown, was 12,250).[3] It was to have a new Council, slimmed to fifteen overall. The first election for the new Council was held three days before Christmas in late 1902.[2] Most of the fifteen elected had been members of one or other of the former burgh councils. Under the heading 'The New Town Council', the *Groat* wished the new councillors well, commenting:

> A fair selection has been made. It is satisfying to notice that all the candidates with the longest experience in public business have been returned .... In the past history of the town's public works, the objectionable and disturbing element has been the formation of cliques, and the amount of wire-pulling done to find salaries and jobs for officials, the Councillors and their friends. The burghs and the ratepayers seemed to exist for that

---

1 *JOGJ*, 1 August, 1902. All the above references to the Enquiry have been taken from this report.
2 *JOGJ*, 26 December, 1902.
3 John S Smith: *Third Statistical Account*, op cit. p xi. It may be noted by those more familiar with the English system before 1974, that royal burghs in Scotland had something comparable to the status of English 'county boroughs' under the terms of the 1888 County Councils Act, that is, they were all-purpose authorities, not answerable (as is not the case today) to the county authority for anything. Thus Wick-Pulteneytown, henceforth simply the Royal Burgh of Wick Burgh, assessed and collected its own rates and other dues, and the Caithness County had no preceptual claim on it. There is no doubt that the prospect of their inclusion in a 'royal' burgh had something to do with the Pulteneytown majority favouring union.

purpose. We have always done our best to raise public feeling against it, and not without effect. It has been gradually disappearing, and the result of the poll on Monday, we believe it has, for the meantime at all events, been completely stamped out.

No doubt in the course of a year or two, when public watchfulness relaxes, a clique may grow up, but as to the new Council now starting on their career, we think the ratepayers can congratulate themselves on having a representative body, who will act harmoniously together, and who will be more often open to the influence of public opinion than any Council that has previously existed.[1]

Fig 47 The combined burgh – Nos 1 & 2 Wards across the River (O.S. 1906).

1 *JOGJ*, 26 December, 1902.

CHAPTER 19

WARS AND RUMOURS OF WAR: 1

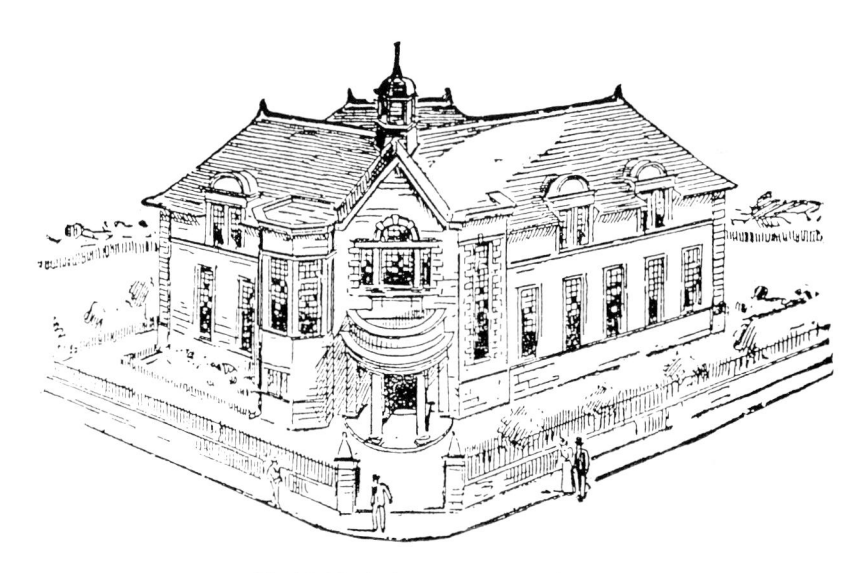

Fig 48 Wick Carnegie Free Library.

AT ONE time the illusion used to be fostered that the reign of Queen Victoria was a long time of piping peace. It is true that no nineteenth century conflict after the Napoleonic Wars impinged upon the shores of Britain, but wars of many kinds raged at one time or another in all the continents, advancing the 'science of warfare' far beyond the skills, techniques and armaments with which Napoleon was defeated. Though not involved in any European war during the whole glorious reign, except for the Crimean (1854-1856), and although she had no conscript army, no country was more embattled and more experienced in warfare on land and sea than Britain.

Fin de Siècle

The later years of Victoria's reign found Britain at war in Egypt, South Africa (several times), Afghanistan, all consequent upon the advance of British 'imperialism', the conquest of far lands to bring them under British rule and commercial influence or, as Kipling put it, to pacify 'lesser breeds without the law'. Britain's mainly 'successful' wars were always a long way off and the country avoided completely the kind of total national commitment that so characterised the wars of France and Germany and, for that matter, the violent civil war between the North and South in the United States. The gunfire of battle was not heard in Britain; her army and navy were mostly out of sight and so it was not difficult to maintain the illusion of prosperous peace.

The Queen had been made 'Empress of India' by Disraeli in 1877. In the 'Jubilee Years', 1887 and 1897, was celebrated the whole imperial triumph of her rule. In no community were these events observed more loyally than in Wick. The display for the 'Diamond Jubilee' was described by the *Northern Ensign* of 29 June, 1897:

> Here as everywhere else the weather was favourable for the gala-day proceedings. There was a holiday in the town and all through the county. Extensive preparations had been made for giving shape to the loyal sentiments which animated the whole population by a profuse display of bunting, and every quarter of the town presented a gay appearance. It is impossible to give minute details of the decorations. They were on an extensive scale, and the general effect was striking. Bridge Street was spanned with flags from the Station Hotel to the Commercial Bank and from the Caledonian Hotel to the Union Bank. The *Ensign* Office[1] and Stafford Place presented a fine display. Provost Nicolson's business premises in High Street and also Kirk House, his residence, were brilliantly decorated; and flags were waved at the home of Sheriff Mackenzie, and most of the houses in Miller Street hoisted a signal of loyalty. At Messrs M'Ewen's warehouse the motto 'Long Live our Glorious Queen' was shown in beautiful letters of raised gold, and the crown surmounting on a background of pink and blue draping, fringe and tassels, showed with fine effect, and was without

---

[1] The *Ensign* Office was in High Street, opposite the 'Cross'. When in 1922 the *Ensign* closed down, the premises were taken over by the 'Ensign' newspaper shop and store. The sign is still visible.

doubt a work of highly finished art. Inside the square one hundred flags were artistically displayed, forty of which floated from the large steam crane. The Established Church Manse had also a display of bunting, as also had ex-Provost Paterson-Smith; and among others who similarly testified to their loyalty were Councillor Mackay, Louisburgh, ex-Bailie Bruce, etc etc.

The town had a holiday; there was a Schoolchildren's Picnic and Games and a Public Banquet in Wick Town Hall (no details are vouchsafed as to how Pulteney celebrated). A United Religious Service was held in the Wick Old Parish Church, with a long sermon preached by Mr Clark, the Minister of the Church. A poem of praise was published that would have done credit to William McGonagal:

>   Our noble Queen
>   Seventy-eight years seen,
>   And has reigned sixty years
>   Without a stain –
>   A great gain –
>   The longest reign that appears.
>   Wick now rejoice,
>   In this choice,
>   And all are loyal and gay,
>   And homage render
>   Here we tender
>   And will ever pay.
>   This jubilee year,
>   Relief, gladness near;
>   Army, Navy
>   Give saluting rounds;
>   Crowned heads appear,
>   To Britain cheer –
>   It does excel all bounds.

Lest one part of the message be forgot, several of the traders put in elaborate advertisements, none more purposefully than McEwens, the town's main furniture dealers:

>   ADVERTISEMENT
>   IF YOU FORGET
>   Jubilee Day it will not be the
>   fault of
>   McEwen and Son
>   Grand Show of Furniture

In its issue of 25 May, a month before the Jubilee, the *Ensign* reminded its readers briefly that there was a 'War in the East', a war between Greece and Turkey. This was just one of the many wars in the Balkans that were fought during the nineteenth century, beginning with the liberation of Greece from Turkey in 1829 and continuing through to 1913, when Bulgaria, itself only recently freed from Turkey, fought Serbia, Montenegro and Greece in what Bernard Shaw characterised in 'Arms and the Man' as the 'Chocolate Soldier War'. Some of these wars were virtually tribal; others involved the 'Powers', for instance the war between Turkey and Russia in 1877 and 1878. In 1908 Austria annexed Bosnia to the great annoyance of Turkey. Italy fought Turkey in 1912 and annexed Tripoli.

Many of these conflicts were mentioned, sometimes fully reported in the *Northern Ensign* and more fully still in the *John O'Groat Journal*, but it is hardly surprising if these reports did not awaken passionate interest and concern among the readers of these journals. The events referred to remained far away, the affairs were complicated and Wick had other fish to catch. In general it is true to say that the *Journal's* international coverage was wider and better informed than that of the *Ensign*, which was probably the better, soberer and more reliable 'local' paper of the two.

It would, however, be a mistake to suggest that the people of Wick, northern Scotland, indeed and Britain as a whole were not alive to what was going on internationally. Affairs in the Empire and in particular South Africa gained increasing attention from the journals, as for example, the discreditable Jameson 'Raid' into the 'independent' Transvaal of 1896. A curious subsequent report in the *Ensign* raised the case of President Kruger's provocative sentence of death on leaders of a 'Reform' group in the Transvaal, including the brother of Cecil Rhodes, which prompted an angry but formal request from the belligerent British Colonial Secretary, Joseph Chamberlain, to Kruger, virtually ordering him to commute the sentences.[1] Increasingly too, both *Ensign* and *Journal* gave attention to the Irish question; two Irish Home Rule Bills having been defeated in the House of Commons, mainly by the votes of the 'Liberal Unionists' led by Chamberlain, and another one threatened.

This was not the kind of newspaper fare to provide for an indifferent and uninstructed readership. From 1900 onwards there was frequent reference to the apparent rising menace of German

1 *Northern Ensign*, 5 May, 1896.

imperialism. That unsettlement, if not war, was in the northern air is evident from the increasing references to the Caithness Volunteer Artillery, now consisting of over a hundred men, parading and attending camp regularly in the Wick area. They maintained a battery on the North Head. Though not exactly a prime expression of militarism, there were nevertheless, military undertones in the Boys' Brigade, founded in Glasgow in 1883 by the Caithnessian, William Smith, and taken up in Wick in 1887. Such undertones were stronger still in the formation of the Boy Scouts after the Boer War. Among the first groups to be 'mobilised' in Wick in 1914 were the Boys Scouts, who undertook observation and guard patrols at the beginning of the war. In 1906 Lord Haldane, Minister of War in Asquith's government, reformed the standing army, and created the Territorial 'week-end' soldier army, and by 1914, Wick had a sizeable Territorial company. They were among the first to go to Flanders.

Still, there was nothing yet that remotely resembled 'war fever', and Wickers remained chiefly concerned about their own affairs. At the Commission called in July, 1902 to decide about the application of Wick and Pulteneytown to amalgamate, the main case for the two towns was represented to the Commission by Mr C J Guthrie KC. A few months before, Mr Guthrie had been QC, a legal distinction worn by lawyers for so long that most had forgotten that it was ever otherwise.

Queen Victoria died on Wednesday, 22 January, 1902, and the commemorative black column markings appeared in the *John O'Groat Journal* on the following Friday, 24 January. The Great Queen was much less lavishly mourned in the *Groat* than the almost unknown William IV, whose death in May, 1837 had brought her to the throne, but William happened to be the first royal personage to engage the *Groat's* attention and so was entitled to a spread. Alongside the black-lined announcement was another saying that King Edward VII had been proclaimed by Provost Nicolson in 'the far north burgh of Wick,' and also by the Provost of Pulteneytown in Argyle Square. The Queen was dead: Long Live the King. Special meetings of the town councils were called to honour the two contingent events. Provost Nicolson, in his address to the Wick Burgh Council, employed every cliché in the book. The Queen had 'ruled wisely over the destinies of this great empire,' she had been left a widow by 'Albert the Good' many years ago, but she had continued to govern her 'great and ever increasing Empire with wisdom.' During the reign Britain had achieved an 'abundance of wealth and honour ... unparalleled advance in science, arts and commerce has,' declared Mr Nicolson, 'followed the British Flag which is the emblem of freedom and equal rights for all, race and colour being no distinction in our Empire, over which the sun never sets and which for splendour and pomp surpasses all others.'[1]

THE BOER WAR.

Other matters were engaging the newspaper's prime attention at this time, notably the amalgamation of Wick and Pulteneytown, but war in the British Empire was also reported. This was the second 'Boer' War, begun in the last months of the century just ended, and now continuing into its third and longest phase, the guerrilla war, which began in September, 1900. As part of its regular policy the *Journal* had kept its readers informed about affairs in South Africa, and had celebrated such events as the relief of Ladysmith, Mafeking and the occupation in June, 1900, of the Boer capital, Pretoria. The paper's sentiments were unexceptionally loyal and imperialist.

In February, 1901, interest quickened, as a group of nine volunteers from Wick, with three from Watten, one from Thurso and two from Halkirk, joined a detachment of the Seaforth Highlanders. Their mustering at Golspie and sailing for South Africa a fortnight later were reported with good wishes for the young warriors, and during the coming months the paper published a series of articles entitled 'South Africa with the Seaforth Highlanders'. Several of these pieces were contributed by 'A Wick Volunteer', unnamed, but probably known well enough to contemporaries. It was knockabout stuff telling readers little about the war but filling them in about the volunteers' adventures; how, for instance, they had trekked to the Basuto border, dug ditches for defence – finding on one occasion a 'Nigger's skull', visited Bloemfontein (now in British hands), how on one special occasion the volunteers had escorted to detention a party of prisoners of war and other 'undesirables' (these were the days of the South African 'Concentration Camps', thus providing for Hitler later in the century, a model for which he always gave the British credit).

Scottish regiments, notably the Black Watch, Argylls, Seaforths (to which the Caithness Volunteers belonged) and the Highland Light Infantry, played a significant part in the campaigning that eventually turned the tide against the Boers, and it was a Scottish adventurer,

1 *JOGJ*, 25 January, 1901.

WARS AND RUMOURS OF WAR: 1

Lord Lovat, who organised the famous 'Scouts' (from among the ghillies and stalkers of his own Beaufort estate) who explored the almost unknown terrain of the *veldt* and thus ultimately enabled the British to cope with the Boer *commandos*. In May, 1901, the *Journal* published a letter from one of Lovat's Scouts entitled, 'Chasing the Boers'. The fullest report to appear in the *Journal* at this time was that of the exciting campaign of September, 1901, during which Colonel Harry Scobell and his column ran to earth the notorious Commandant Lotter with his 130 commandos in a gorge north of the Orange River. It was a truly *Boys' Own Paper* affair in which the commandos were caught sleeping, penned in the gorge, surrounded and annihilated as a force, 13 dead, 46 wounded and 61 prisoners, including Lotter himself. Lotter was later executed along with seven other 'rebels', on the orders of Kitchener. The *John O'Groat Journal* tells in this report of no less than 681 Boers killed, wounded and captured in the action of which the Scobell raid was a part.[1]

The nine Wick volunteers did not themselves see a great deal of action, the only significant occasion being reported in a piece 'By one of the Nine' in February. This was 'an encounter with the Boers' on a *kopje* near to Jamestown, where they defended themselves with 'no maxim nor big gun', a reminder that by this date machine guns were already an important weapon in battlefield armament, the underestimation of which had much to do with the hugeness of Allied casualties in the 'Great War' of 1914-1918. No Wick men were lost in South Africa, and the nine returned home on the *SS Ulstermore* which docked at Southampton at the end of May, 1902. There was to be a welcome-home for the volunteers when they got back to Wick, but in the event the celebrations on their arrival 'were not of a very demonstrative nature'.[2] It is evident that the Boer War stirred no great patriotic feeling in Wick; indeed, there was by 1902, in the country as a whole, a very considerable mix of sentiments about this colonial war, raised later in British mythology to a status of importance not accorded to it in other European countries. The undisguised sympathy of the German Kaiser for the Boers, nevertheless became an ingredient of the hatred that twelve years after the end of the Boer conflict persuaded Britain to come in against Germany. The Peace of Vereeniging was signed, 31 May, 1902.

---

1 *JOGJ*, 13 September, 1901. See also: Thomas Packenham: *The Boer War*; London, Futura Publications (1982), pp 527-528.
2 *JOGJ*, 30 May, 1902, and 6 June, 1902.

Interlude for Fishing

During the early years of the twentieth century, Wick's fortunes as a herring fishery town revived somewhat, as we have seen. In 1910 its fishermen achieved their highest catch ever, though leaving them well behind Shetland, Peterhead and Fraserburgh, while exports of barrelled herring to Germany and Russia thrived. The nature of the fishing was undergoing a massive change: to catch 143,597 crans in 1855 – a year of very high production, took 952 boats, bringing in an average of 151 crans per boat; to catch 130,591 crans in 1905 had taken 300 boats at an average of 435 crans, and the great catch of 1910 (164,507 crans) took 290 boats at an average per boat of 567 during the season. Boats were now much larger than at one time, fishing gear more sophisticated and now steam was coming in.

It would, however, be a mistake to imagine that the steam drifter had completely taken over. Pictures of Wick in years before the Great War still show large numbers of sail boats, mostly half-decked and undecked 'Fifies' and 'Zulus', but steam drifters had greatly altered the pattern of the fishing, extending the range far into the open sea, extending the season, and, of course, bring home much larger catches – when the fishing was good. There are, regrettably, no figures available to demonstrate the extent of the change-over to steam in the years before the war, and after the war the picture had changed again, this time in favour of smaller boats powered by internal combustion engines, often auxiliary to sail.

Though it never established itself as a main centre of steam fishing, from time to time Wick made the claim to have 'invented' the steam drifter, never more strenuously than in April, 1914, when an article taken from *Chamber's Magazine* told how this came about. A certain Randall of Wick was said to have invented a portable propelling screw which could be mounted on a Fifie, but which failed on experiment because the miniature boiler was unable to generate sufficient steam for any length of journey. There was, claimed the writer, considerable official interest in the experiments (the support of Professor Huxley is even mentioned), but the trials were soon abandoned on account of hostility from the regular fishermen and the expected very high cost of mechanisation. The writer, a certain Walter Duff, made a comparison between this episode and the resistance of the hand-loom weavers to the introduction of the power-loom. This was in 1888.

Some time later 'a Mr Stewart', a native of Wick, returned to the

town:
> While sitting on South Head one day in July in the year 1898, watching the sails lying helplessly flapping against the masts, he determined there and then to order a boat to be built and steam to be applied to it as motive power. The order was at once given to a firm in Lowestoft, where the new venture was speedily inaugurated; and by June, 1899, the new steam drifter, the *Peep of Day*, was ready for sea, and put under the command of Robert Cook, who was one of the best and most practical fishermen belonging to Wick. The splendid success of this vessel led to the building of others, and infused such enthusiasm into the fishermen along the coast of Scotland, even among those who ridiculed the idea of steam. Such was the demand for the new type of vessel that for several years thereafter, every boat builder's yard on the west coast was busy turning out steam drifters with the greatest expedition to cope with the urgent demands of the fishermen.[1]

Claims of Wick were contested by Thurso, where, it was said, the *Alpha* was built and put to sea some time before the *Peep of Day*, and for Leith where the *Water Witch* was built. But be all this as it may, Wick was, as always, handicapped for significant development by the inadequacy of its harbours, especially as to the depth required for the deeper draught drifters.[2]

That something rather unusual was going on is confirmed by a curious article in the *Northern Ensign* in July 1896. This tells of 'New Steam Liners for Wick'. The term 'liner' may be taken to signify a vessel adapted to 'line' rather than 'net' fishing, something of a departure for Wick in any case. The fact that two boats were now being launched, meant that they were 'in all probability the first of a fleet of steam liners for Wick is too important a development of the town's staple industry to remain unchronicled or even to be allowed to pass by with an ordinary notice.' The writer comments that 'while the size of the [fishing] fleet has been greatly reduced, the individual vessels have become very much larger and more seaworthy, and accordingly there have sprung up many inventions whereby about the same number of men can still manage the larger boat, the heavier rig and the heavier fishing material.'

As compared with the 'best equipped boat at present hailing from

1 *JOGJ*, 17 April, 1914.
2 *JOGJ*, 14 April, 1914.

Wick,' the 'steel steam liners launched on Friday [10 July, 1896] on the Clyde for the Caithness Steam Line Fishing Company is rather a far cry.' The boats were being produced by the Govan shipbuilders, Mackie and Thomson. They were about 100 feet long, nearly 20 feet extreme breadth and with hulls $9\frac{1}{2}$ feet deep, of 135 tons gross. They were driven by an engine with an indicated horse-power of 250, operating a single four-bladed propeller, and their sails were reported to spread about 600 yards on their two masts.[1] There was accommodation for a crew of nine. Coal was stored in side bunkers. Forward of the engines and boilers was a compartmented 'fish-room', where 'the fish when caught will be packed away on shelves in ice, and thus kept in good condition until the boat reaches port.' There was an insulated compartment for the purpose of storing ice. The two vessels were christened on launching *Fleetwing* and *Redwing*.

There is little later information about these 'liners' in service from Wick, and it seems doubtful if they came into general use, at least for the herring fishery. They were naturally very much more expensive to build than the conventional boats and, in any case, as George Manson, the Wick owner of these innovatory craft explained to the company assembled to watch the launch of the first vessel at Govan, 'they were intended more especially for the deep sea line fishing, probably from Orkney southwards, but the crew who were going into the *Fleetwing*, wished to try nets at least as an experiment.' Mr Thomson for the ship builders said 'he had got the order in Wick, and he meant to go to Wick for more.'[2]

The subsequent silence of both *Ensign* and *Groat* about *Fleetwing* and *Redwing*, suggest that the experiment with nets did not succeed. In anticipation of the likelihood that this might be so, and perhaps that the Wick harbour would not, in any case, be suitable for a fleet of such vessels, it was announced that although the two liners would be commanded by Wick skippers and although 'acknowledging Wick as their port,' they would 'go to any place that may be considered convenient, either to land fish or for other purposes.' Wick again was losing out, for its harbour facilities were, as always, not adequate. Ever hopeful, in April 1914 the Harbour Trustees lodged with the Scottish Office a Draft Order under the provisions allowing such a submission of the Wick and Pulteney Harbours Order Conformation

---

1 This seems an improbable figure. '600' yards would signify '600 square yards', an area 60 x 10 yards or 30 x 20 yards, an enormous spread of canvas.
2 *Northern Ensign* 14 July, 1896.

THE NEW STEAM LINERS FOR WICK.
DESCRIPTION AND SKETCH.
(Written and Drawn specially for the Northern Ensign.)

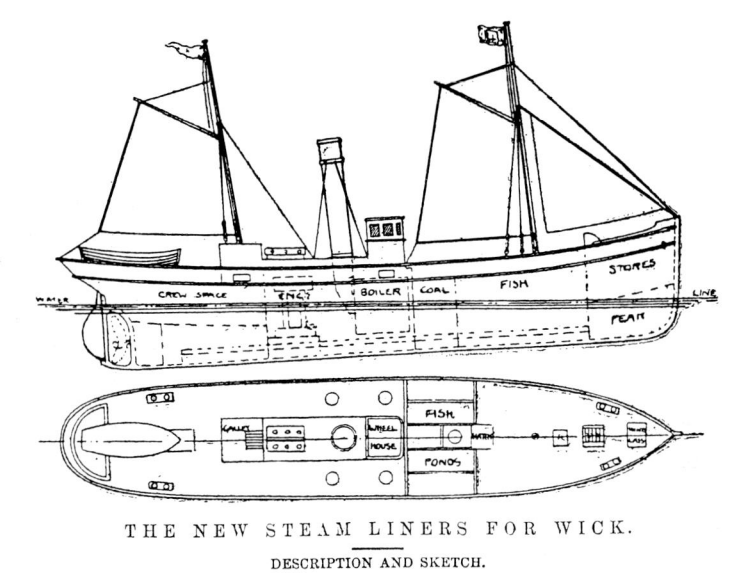

Fig 49 The new steam liners.

Act of 1903. This envisaged the deepening of Wick Water and the construction of a new 'retaining wall' 400 feet long on the north shore, the demolition of the swing service bridge and the building of a new, six-span bridge in its place. To finance this development the Burgh of Wick was willing to put up its share, but most of the money was to come from a £250,000 government loan.[1] Some months later, it was learned that 'various Aberdeen interests' and the 'Orkney and Shetland Steam Navigation Company' had filed objections to the development, and pessimism once more set in about prospects for the improvement of Wick Harbour. This was in June, 1914.

THE 'GREAT WAR' TO END WAR.

A much more momentous issue soon blotted out all hope of the plan. This was the dreaded but not unexpected event that lay behind the *Groat's* triple headline of 7 August, 1914:

1 *JOGJ*, 12 June, 1914.

THE GREAT EUROPEAN WAR

FATEFUL DAYS IN THE WORLD'S HISTORY
BRITISH CALMNESS & CONFIDENCE

The die was cast for the toughest and most devastating experience for Britain since the French Wars of a century before. Those wars may be said to have put Wick on the map for, as we have shown, Wick's fishing industry – or rather that of Pulteneytown – was a direct outcome of measures taken in the context of the wars to improve fishing boat harbourage in the entrance to the Wick river.[1] The new war, with Germany as the deadly enemy, once, in the character of Prussia, a chief ally against Napoleon, and France now the cherished ally of Britain, clasped to the country's breast by the *Entente Cordiale* of 1904. It is not too much to argue that the war of 1914-1918 changed the orientation of Wick's affairs as drastically as the earlier war, with the people of Wick themselves far more directly and personally involved in the fighting.

Wick Goes to War.

No-one in Wick could complain that they had not been warned about what was coming. For months, indeed, in a sense, for years the *Groat* – and to a less extent the *Northern Ensign*, had been filling in the background on tensions in Europe. The first specific mention of the war that was about to engulf all the European powers came in July, 1914 under the headline, 'European War Cloud', telling of the 'Grave Position in the Balkans', and the declaration of war by Austria on Servia – more commonly today known as Serbia. The whole fateful sequence, the murder of Archduke Ferdinand on 28 June by Gavril Princep, threat and finally a declaration of war by Austria, mobilisation in Russia, mobilisation in France and the attack on both by Germany, followed by the declaration of war by Britain on 4

---

1 The point is made by J D Mackie in his *A History of Scotland;* London, Penguin Books (Second Edition, 1978) p 295: 'Meanwhile, a traditional industry took a new lease of life. The fisheries, in spite of some government help given after 1727, had made little progress, but in 1786, the British Fisheries Society set up their "stations" – at Ullapool, Tobermory and Lochbay (Skye) – and next year established Pulteneytown near Wick; the long-continued war with France compelled Britain to look to herself for food supplies and, before long, Scottish fishing was in a thriving way.' Mackie's Pulteneytown date is, however, quite wrong.

August, 1914, all were reported in the *Groat*. The paper's first issue declared: 'The Great European War anticipated in our last week's issue has now become a matter of stern and dreadful reality, and the consequences must be stupendous in the history of the world.' For once the hyperbole was justified. Before the final war issue was published on 15 November, 1918, the *John O'Groat Journal* printed hundreds of thousands of words, some of them eloquent, on the most fearful cataclysm to engulf Wick during its whole existence, so far.

Throughout the war the *Groat* kept the story of the war going, subject of course to the wartime restrictions – especially those of the Defence of the Realm Act ('DORA') and censorship. So comprehensive was the *Groat's* coverage of the main developments of the entire war, that it would be possible no doubt to write a 'History of the First World War', of sorts, merely by using the *John O'Groat Journal* as source, though much allowance would have to be made for the inevitable euphoria about British 'successes' (even a few yards' advance on the Somme was apt to be described as a 'victory'), unstoppable 'advance' of the Allies in every direction and the bursts of a ferocious patriotism that surge through some of the columns. The Editor during these years was the indefatigable, fiercely patriotic R J G Millar.

To attempt such a task would be quite supererogatory, for more histories of the 'Great War', with vastly more reliable sources, have been written than of most other events in human history. The *Groat's* weekly eight pages could indeed be said to have become for the duration of a veritable chronicle of war, but its chief interest for us is the glimpses it affords of life in the one-time 'herring capital' of the north, and of Wick's own part in the war. Local and more pedestrian news continued to be printed, but they took second place to the war news, especially those about 'our men at the front'.

The first report of Wick's response went under the heading and sub-headings

STIRRING SCENES AT WICK

ROYAL NAVAL RESERVE CALLED OUT

MEN TO A GREAT SEND OFF

Wick's chief offering to the war was men. During the war many hundreds of men and some women left Wick to serve in the navy and

WICK OF THE NORTH

MAP OF CENTRAL EURO

WARS AND RUMOURS OF WAR: 1

Showing whole field of Military and Naval Operations with Boundaries, Rivers, Principal Towns, &c., clearly defined.

army. The first to go were the men of the Wick and District Naval Reserve, including some 380 men from Sutherland and Caithness. They were called out on Sunday, 2 August, two days before the declaration of war, motor cars being sent to John O'Groats and Helmsdale with the Notices that the Reservists should report at Wick Custom House at 10 o'clock on Monday morning. 'The Shore Road presented an animated appearance at that hour. It was crowded with men, women and children, and traffic for the time being was practically stopped. Large numbers of the Reservists in Uniform passed into the Custom House and received their service cards. The police attended and kept the crowd in good order.' As most of the reservists were fishermen, John Miller, President of the Caithness Fishermen's Association 'addressed a few words to the large crowd', inviting them to be at the Station at 4 o'clock in the afternoon, 'to hearten the brave fellows who were going off to do their duty to their king and country.'

Comparison was made between the departure of the 'Volunteers' of January, 1900, but with these 'Reservemen it was different.' The affecting description continues:

> Here were many married men with numerous family ties. It was difficult for the crowd to work themselves into the belief that they should be glad at the sudden domestic severance that was taking place before them. The sight, which was repeated over and over again, of a weeping mother holding up a little one for daddy to kiss, was touching in the extreme. The jolliest part of the crowd was the Reservists. They were in great spirits. Moving among the crowd they took their farewells of their friends in the cheeriest manner possible. The band played *Rule Britannia* as the men took their seats, and just when the train was moving off they struck up the familiar strains of *Will ye no' come back again*.[1]

This was the kind of scene, repeated and repeated for the coming weeks. It was, indeed, repeated the following day (4 August) when another 30 men from outlying districts were sent off. The Wick Territorials and the Wick Volunteer Artillery were embodied forthwith and despatched leaving, as the *Groat* reported, a 'scarcity of labour on farms.' A celebrated *Groat* picture of 6 August shows the platforms of Wick Railway Station crowded as the first batch of Territorials entrain on 'mobilisation for the Great War.'

1 *JOGJ*, 7 August, 1914.

In spite of all the illustration, description, recollection and tradition still available to us, it is almost impossible now to recapture in imagination much of the pathos mixed with patriotic fervour which accompanied these departures, knowing as we do the fearful sequel. Few of those milling along that August platform, 1914, could have been realistically sensible of the terrors, agonies and family distresses ahead. Nor was there much awareness of the hideous brutalities of twentieth century trench warfare. Moved less by prophetic insight perhaps than by tragic hindsight, Thomas Hardy asked in 'Song of the Soldiers', dateline 5 September, 1914:

> What of the faith and fire within us
> Men who march away
> Ere the barn-cocks say
> Night is growing gray,
> Leaving all that here can win us;
> What of the faith and fire within us
> Men who march away?

In reply the soldiers sing:

> In our heart of hearts believing
> Victory crowns the just,
> And that braggarts must
> Surely bite the dust,
> Press we to the field ungrieving,
> In our heart of hearts believing
> Victory crowns the just.

It may have been so. Much patriotic euphoria was released at the beginning of the 1914-1918 war. The Wickers who marched away in 1914 may have been ungrieving, and perhaps felt some noble sentiments about saving the nation and toppling the tyrant. Whether William Watson's sonnet, 'Troubler of the World', addressed to the Kaiser, and printed by the *Groat* on 14 August reached any nearer to the real feelings of the departing warriors may be doubted:

> At last we know you, War-Lord. You that flung
>   The gauntlet down, fling down the mask you wore.
>   Publish your heart, and let its pent hate pour,
> That you had God for ever on your tongue.
> We are old in war, and if in guile we are young,
>   Young also is the spirit that evermore
>   Burns in our bosom ev'n as heretofore,
> Nor are these thews unbraced, these nerves unstrung.

> We do not with God's name make wanton play;
> We are not on such easy terms with Heaven;
> But in Earth's hearing we can verily say,
>   'Our hands are pure; for peace, for peace we have
>   striven;'
> And not by Earth shall he soon be forgiven
> Who lit the fire accurst that flames today.

As we have noted before, the *John O'Groat Journal* had a penchant for bad verse, and during the war many dreadful lines were published which – perhaps like the Watson sonnet – would be better left in obscurity. Nevertheless, it conveys some idea of rhetoric evoked by the events of that time.

Enlistment for the first two years of the war was 'voluntary', but it was not long before the *Journal* joined in the flamboyant recruiting drive that drew to the colours the hundreds of thousands of young men which this unprecedented kind of warfare soon demanded. Kitchener's famous finger was soon pointing at the young men of Wick and on 14 August appeared the first of the strident calls for men. Early in September appeared

WICK'S CALL TO ARMS

PROVOST HARPER'S APPEAL TO THE
YOUNG MEN OF THE TOWN

The Provost's appeal was pronounced at a meeting of the Wick Town Council on Monday, 31 August, and in the inflated language now becoming the vogue, he adjured the young men of Wick to join up. 'Gentlemen', he began:

> Since we last met our nation has been thrust into the greatest war known in the history of the world. National honour, truth and righteousness alike demand that we should unsheath the sword and the nation has determined that the sword shall not return to its scabbard until an end has been made to German tyranny in Europe and the world.
>
> We may be weak in numbers on the field, but we are strong in our trust in the Lord of Battles, who will see that the cause of honour, truth and justice will in the end prevail.

During the coming weeks banner statements were published across the columns of page 7 of the *Groat*, financed by business interests in the town, consisting of brave quotations from words of the great and the good, mostly concerned with joining the forces for example:

TO THE PUBLIC – WHAT IS NEEDED

It is a holy thing to see a nation saved by its youth.
(Lord Beaconsfield)*

A TIME OF HEART SEARCHING.

I SHALL WANT MORE MEN – Lord Kitchener.

* Beaconsfield was the ennobled Benjamin Disraeli.

Another and quite mean side to the recruiting business did not take long to appear:

> The girls of Pulteney have entered heartily into the business of enlistment. In the intervals of knitting socks for our heroes in the field, they have made a number of nice petticoats which they have generously sent for post to a number of young men who have exercised the grace of self-denial, and elected to stay at home. In some cases they have followed the example of the Chancellor of the Exchequer and made a raid on the hen-roosts, with the result that many of these young gentlemen have got quite a number of white feathers. Whether they have worn them as buttonholes or not, history sayeth not.

A recruiting office was opened in the Old Post Office Building in Bridge Street. In charge of recruiting in the northern counties was Colonel J H Henderson, laird of Bilbster, formerly of the Seaforth Highlanders. Recruiting was doing well, said the *Groat* early in September: 126 had joined 'Kitchener's Army', and 63 the Territorials, since the beginning of the war.[1]

Appeals of other kinds began to be made. 'Ladies get to work on Red Cross activities' – 'Queen Alexandra issues a moving appeal on behalf of wives and families of soldiers and sailors' – Lady Lovat of Beaufort Castle asks for 'comforts' – shirts, cholera belts, mufflers etc to be sent to Beauly. The Duke of Sutherland appeals to fellow gentry to lend their houses for hospital purposes, and himself offers

1 *JOGJ*, 11 September, 1914.

Dunrobin Castle to the Admiralty as a naval hospital. The Admiralty accepts the offer and has the Castle converted as a 'central surgical base for the North Sea Fleet.'[1] The Duke makes available his yacht *Catania* for ferrying wounded to the hospital.

Life in Wick itself underwent a transformation. The magistrates immediately decided that from now on the public houses should close at 8.00 pm, a drastic enough imposition. Within a year prosecutions were being brought against people who sold drink to servicemen, though in one case the Sheriff confessed that he had great difficulty in understanding a regulation (under the provisions of DORA) which made such a prosecution necessary. The delinquent was accused of supplying a sailor with whisky 'to make him drunk and less capable of performing his duty.'[2] The two picture houses, one in Wick and one in Pulteneytown (both buildings still exist but not as cinemas), were obliged to close for the first month of the war, and then were allowed to open three nights a week.

But much the most serious of changes in Wick was the virtual cessation of the fish trade. Line fishing declined to nothing almost immediately on account of men enlisting. The herring fishing continued in August and produced a healthy catch of 113,538 crans (as compared with 104,667 in 1913), but it was known to be touch and go as to whether or not this year's fish could be sold and what might be allowed in the next season.[3] On the arrival in Aberdeen harbour of 15 trawlers and seven 'liners' on Monday morning, 10 August, an Admiralty notice was posted at the fish market to say: 'Please circulate widely the Admiralty order that no fishing vessels to go on until further notice.'[4] In this war the North Sea was to become a main theatre of operations, with increasing numbers of German craft afloat in its waters – at least until the Battle of Jutland in May, 1916, penned them in; extensive minefields, both German and Allied mines, were sown in the seaways, and the sea became infested with U-boats. Scapa Flow was now the home of the British Grand Fleet and the waters off Wick lay right across its approaches. Numbers of Wick ships, trawlers, drifters and other boats were commandeered for service in the Royal Navy. Wick's main source of livelihood had to all intents and purposes been cut off.

1 *JOGJ*, 11 September, 1914.
2 *JOGJ*, 10 September, 1915.
3 *JOGJ*, 4 September.
4 *JOGJ*, 14 August, 1914.

As for the main markets for barrelled herring, Stettin, Hamburg, Königsburg, they were all in enemy territory, while one of the earliest reports of the war told how the port of Libau in Russia (in the post-war world, Lithuania), 'a well known herring trade centre', was bombarded and mined by the Germans.[1]

Thus, in addition to patriotism, the need for a job helped to boost recruitment in the east coast fishery ports, and in particular recruitment to the Royal Navy. Commenting on 'Wick in war time', the *Groat* reflected in October, 1914, on the numbers of naval reservists, Territorials and Kitchener recruits who had already 'gone forth to fight' or were preparing to 'fight the battle of the Empire'. 'Conditions have changed at home after three months of continual conflict in Europe,' observed the writer, adding that had 'conditions been normal the Yarmouth fishing would have just reached its climax.' A few coopers were still at work here and there, but no longer were workers attending union meetings, 'if union meetings are being held'.[2] The Wick fishing trade was 'more severely affected than any other trade in the country' according to the *Journal*; a mere 20,300 cwts of fish were landed in 1915.[3]

In the meantime the real business of the war was being reported in column after column – 'Battle on the Aisne', 'Continued French and Belgian Victories', 'Heavy German Losses', 'Destruction of Rheims Cathedral', '168,000 British Troops in France', 'Kitchener's Appeal – men between 19 and 30 who are physically fit, and old soldiers up to 42.', 'Three British Battleships Sunk in the North Sea – *Aboukir, Hogue* and *Cressy* torpedoed', 'Germans Retreat from Paris'. One of the first men of Wick reported 'Killed in Action' was George Snowling lost aboard the cruiser *Carmania*, sunk off the east coast of South America.[4] Killed on the Aisne about this time was Peter Doull of Argyle Square, Pulteneytown.[5]

In November, Lord Roberts, 'Free Burgess of Wick' and hero of many Empire wars, died. It was recalled that 19 years ago he had spent the autumn in Ackergill Tower.[6] Roberts had been drawn to Wick's attention just a month before when his 'fine address' to the

1 *JOGJ*, 7 August, 1914.
2 *JOGJ*, 6 November, 1914.
3 *JOGJ*, 31 Decembver, 1915.
4 *JOGJ*, 25 September, 1914. (Carmania was not sunk, only crippled; she was escorted to Gibraltar for repair).
5 Ibid.
6 *JOGJ*, 20 November, 1914.

boys of Eton College was presented as a page seven banner text:

> Great calls will be made on our courage and patience. Let each one of you, then, who for one reason or another, is not able to take up arms for your country, determine to fight as courageously and as doggedly at home.
>
> Show a cheerful countenance to the world, and never let others see you give way to despondency. Preach to all around you the 'Glorious right' of this war in which we had to take our part, or else for ever hide our heads in shame.
>
> Be careful to spread no rumour or gossip, and be kind, gentle, and unselfish to all. Cheer others on, and help them to bear hardships, privations and sorrow in the spirit of true patriotism.

Wick suffered no lack of injunction to do the right thing and to join up. The *Groat* however, like most other newspapers in the country, did not lack for patriotic correspondents writing to complain about 'slackers' and 'shirkers'. As late as March 1917 appeared the slogan, 'A man who will not help his country is helping the enemy.' It is probable that there were few dodgers of military service in Wick, where enthusiasm for the war – if the pages of the local press are anything to go by – remained strong throughout.

When early in 1916 conscription of all men between 18 and 41 was introduced by the Military Service Act, there could not have been many in Wick still awaiting call-up, though there were some. As everywhere else a burgh Military Tribunal was set up (with Colonel Henderson as military representative) to hear appeals for exemption, usually for family, sometimes business or professional reasons. Grounds of exemption were less clear-cut and reserved occupation criteria less sympathetic than in the Second World War. At a hearing in May, 1916 several cases were heard: one was that of a fishcurer, left to run the business on his own, another a bread-packer working for a firm supplying the Navy, and George Gunn, the chauffeur of Dr Banks, the town's medical officer of health, were all given temporary or conditional exemption.

WARS AND RUMOURS OF WAR: 1

One case that would hardly have made it in 1940 was that of a draper, Fred Shearer, who explained that 'his three establishments, one in Thurso and two in Wick, were working with their lowest possible staffs.' If the girl in charge at Thurso fell ill, he would have to leave Wick to attend to things. 'His foreman had not enlisted and he couldn't ask him to do so. He might manage even if the foreman were taken, but the business needed his personal attention.' Mr Shearer was given conditional exemption.[1]

As during the Boer War the *Journal* published from time to time letters from men serving, to convey some feeling of what it was like. A 'Wick Soldier in the Thick of it', Lance-Corporal Alexander Fraser late of the staff of the *John O'Groat Journal*, a reservist of the Scots Fusiliers, was called for service immediately war broke out, and went with the 6th Battalion of his regiment to the front. He was invalided home as the result of an attack of fever, and wrote:

> We disembarked at Calais, and were at once sent to the north of France, about 30 miles west of Paris, and from that we were marching, checking the Germans when and where we could. . . . . . The Germans were everywhere, thick as peas, you couldn't miss them. My regiment was just in one heavy engagement. Out of 1100 only 180 were left, I was fortunate to be among the 180. All the rest were either killed, wounded or missing. The day after the fight I was down with fever, contracted through lying out in the rain in trenches filled with water.[2]

The lance-corporal recovered and was soon back at the front. In July, the following year, he was killed by a shell in the trench.[3] Lt H S Stalker of Auckengill, serving in the Cheshire Regiment, wrote of his 'Experiences in the Trenches':

> For the last few weeks we have been in the firing line all the time, and it is very hot. How I am here I don't know, but God has been kind, and I have been spared while others have not. One day I was lying in my earth hole, being heavily shelled by high explosives, when down came a brute and burst in front of my trench. Nothing but blue flame shooting around me. Another came just at my side, and I knew no more – knocked unconscious. I came to again all right without scratch but was absolutely buried in earth. Some of the men were not so

1 *JOGJ*, 16 May, 1916.
2 *JOGJ*, 4 December, 1914.
3 *JOGJ*, 23 July, 1915.

fortunate. You will say that it was a marvellous escape. How I managed to be untouched is beyond me. Next day we had a great scrap – all rifle fire – and I have a nice little souvenir in my right shoulder in the form of a bullet furrow, just cutting the flesh. My coat and shirt were cut, which testifies how near a miss I had. But never be glum. I got it dressed, and was back in the thick of it before nightfall none the worse.

Scratches are nothing in this war. At present we are resting, and verily in need of it, for fourteen days or more without three hours of running sleep exhausts a man rather much, especially when the weather is not too good. Just imagine a waterproof sheet pegged down over the edge of a ditch about four feet deep, a little straw at the bottom – wet straw in all probability – and you have my home; your greatcoat wet, of course; boots, clothes, face and hair all clogged with mud of the Millhall variety, and there you have the infantry, officers and men complete. Add to that a dash of happy-go-luckiness, a large dose of cheeriness and joking, and the picture is complete.[1]

Private W H Christie of Huddart Street, Pulteneytown, was serving with the 1st Gordons; he wrote:

I wondered what it would be like to be under fire, but for the present I can honestly say that I am quite indifferent. It might be different if we were under hot shelling for a few hours. I had my first wash for days. I enjoyed it, even although it was in a 'bully' beef tin, with which I had caught some rain water as it fell.[2]

Casualties were now mounting sharply. In November, 1915, the *Groat* started publishing its 'Full List of Fallen Heroes', running to four columns for Caithness and Sutherland, and later more. Of these some forty of the deaths, most of them 'killed in action' were men from Wick. The same issue gave totals for all British forces:

Killed	119,923
Wounded	338,758
Missing	69,546[3]

Many more were yet to be lost in this titanic struggle. The last issue of the year gave a review of the entire war so far, with comments on

1 *JOGJ*, 20 November, 1914.
2 *JOGJ*, 23 July, 1915.
3 *JOGJ*, 31 December, 1915.

the 'Western Front', 'Royalty and the War,' 'The Pirates' 'The Dardanelles,' 'Ineffective Frightfulness' – with some emphasis on the sinking of the *Lusitania* (7 May, 1915), Home affairs.[1] There was much worse to come.

The *John O'Groat Journal* was not, even in these times, above a little spoofing (but was it spoof, to have a head so full of horrors?):

THE TERRIBLE NIGHT
Thrilling Experience of a Caithness Territorial

I was going my round of the trenches seeing that my sentries were all awake and keeping an eye on the darkness, which did not even permit of a view of the few shell-scarred posts we dignified with the name of barbed wire. We were in what is known as a 'dead-end'; that is, there was a break in the trenches and the nearest troops on our right were a hundred yards away.

Every few minutes the monotonous call of the sentries came and went – 'All's clear on the left, pass it along,' growing louder and louder, though never much more than a whisper, till it came to the end of the line, when back went the word, 'All's well on the right, pass it along,' growing fainter and dying away in the distance.

Then along came the word that was the beginning of this, the most stirring episode, and which turned the night into what was for me 'la nuit horrible.' 'Corporal Jones wanted at headquarters, pass the word along.' Wondering what was up, I passed back the word 'Corporal Jones coming,' and made my way to Company headquarters, there to discover the 'skipper' (Coy. Commander) was nervous about the exceeding quietness, and wanted me – me! – to go and find out what the Huns were up to.

Orders are orders, so taking my rifle, with bayonet fixed, and slinging two bandoliers over my shoulders, I climbed up on to the parapet, bending almost double, and started my journey through that eerie, inky darkness that you could almost feel.

Before I had reached our own barbed wire I had trod on half-a-dozen jam tins, making, as I thought, a noise like thunder, and a cold sweat broke out all over me. But no, I wasn't afraid;

1 *JOGJ*, 31 December, 1915.

not I. On I went, straight to where I knew the Huns to be, when flop, splash, down I went in a shell hole, up to the neck in water. In vain I tried to scramble out; the mud held my legs and the water was as cold as death, and then, despairing, I cried for help. That did it. Immediately 'No Man's Land' was a blaze of light, THOUSANDS of star-shells soared into the air and burst above my head, which I didn't lower lest I filled my lungs with with water and drowned. Then the rifles began to speak, 'Zip, zip, zip' came the bullets. I FELT them all. Though none struck me, each one seemed closer. My hair was now on end and being shorn bit by bit by the bullets which grazed my head. Now our boys started, and soon quietened the Germans, but their artillery began to speak, and shells and shrapnel rained around me.

I gave myself up for lost. I closed my eyes when 'Fiz-z-z-z' bang! I could only escape by ducking. I ducked. Then I came up gasping and spitting out mouthfuls of water. I opened by eyes, and – what did I behold? My sister with a basin which she had been banging and a jug of water which she was engaged in emptying over my head to waken me – I was in my own bed at home! My first day back from the front was bright and sunny and 'la nuit horrible' a dream, ALL a dream.

The Sword of the North.

Distressing stories of life – and death – were printed frequently during the first two years of the war. Yet one other may be quoted. Pte Donald Dallas of Lower Duke Street, Wick, wrote:

> I had a bit of bad luck the other day. Our trench was knocked over on top of me, and I got my back and arms hurt a bit. All the same, I consider myself lucky that I am alive to tell the tale. We had a very lively time of it at Neuve Chapelle [this is March, 1915]. We took a lot of trenches from the Germans, and gave them one of the biggest defeats they have suffered since the war began. The unfortunate side of it is that we lost a lot of men ourselves. When we attacked them and got into their trenches the sight that met us was horrible beyond description. The German dead were lying three and four deep. We also took a lot of prisoners. They were only too glad to surrender to us as they got an awful cutting-up. Our Battalion is out of the

WARS AND RUMOURS OF WAR: 1

trenches again for a few days' rest, which they well deserved. I expect, however, they will soon be amongst them again. I myself am likely to be sent down to the base. (1st Seaforth Highlanders).

Most of the soldiers' letters home display a cheerful fatalism in the telling of their story, reflecting perhaps something of the fortitude that enabled them to withstand the totally unaccustomed terrors and horrors of the Western Front. Often too they give evidence of sympathetic understanding on their part of the predicament of their opposite numbers in the German trenches. Certainly in these early years there is nothing about the hated 'Hun' and his atrocities. Hate plays little part in the state of mind of the soldiers from Wick or, for that matter, most other places. Pride in regiment is often revealed and a tolerance of the arrogances of officers and other senior ranks that would not have satisfied the next generation of soldiers.

Something of the condescension and indeed insufferable snobbery of some officers of the time is to be found in the strange and lavish compilation, *The Sword of the North,* of Dugald MacEchern, Minister of Bower, former Lieutenant of the 5th Seaforth Highlanders. It consists of nearly 700 pages, beautifully produced, with many photographs and published evidently at MacEchern's own expense, probably with subscription aid from some of the families of fellow officers who enjoyed his flatteries. The writer prefaces his book with the information that he first intended it 'to be a personal and local record, but later widened its scope as to give a view of the general effort made by the Northern Highlands in the Great War.' It is hardly that. Rather it is full of detail, boring to those not connected, about the regiments and other service branches with which he came in touch mainly after 1917. It tells little of the action on the Western Front or elsewhere, and really not very much about the more interesting sides of personalities encountered, except when MacEchern has a citation for bravery to quote, or the memoir of an officer.

If Dugald MacEchern's emphasis is to be accepted, it would seem that the war was won by officers and sergeants, mostly pictured as immaculately uniformed, 'straight of eye, steady and aglow'. An abundance of posed regimental groups, smartly turned out (as no doubt out of battle they were) far more often of officers and sergeants, than of lowly rankers, appear in MacEchern's neat and beautifully ordered pages. When he deigns to mention privates and gunners, he calls them, officer fashion, by their surnames, but adorns the higher ranks with their forenames or initials. In the writer's rather ornate prose there are few hints of the grime, misery and nastiness of the war which the Highlanders endured, and which took away the lives of 307 men of Wick, out of the 900 or more who were lost from Caithness (MacEchern's list included 227 names, falling short of the names listed on the Wick War Memorial by 80). The nearest thing to a battle scene is a photograph entitled 'In the Trenches,' showing three officers in gum boots, standing in studied nonchalance almost knee-deep in water. They could, just as well have been standing knee-deep in the Thurso river, angling for salmon.

The book contains a battalion by battalion sketch of those regiments into which the Caithnessmen mostly were enrolled, eleven battalions of the Queen's Own Cameron Highlanders and thirteen of the Seaforth Highlanders. Many of these groups were incorporated into the 51st Highland Divison, which saw action on many critical parts of the Western Front, including Cambrai, Loos, the Somme and Festubert. The 51st Highland Division, of course, had a considerable part to play in North Africa in a later war. The character of MacEchern's deathless prose may be sampled from his introduction to

> The 51st Division (The Highland Territorials)
>
> The Invincible Fifty-First Division has placed a crown of imperishable fame on the brow of old Scotland. The Highland Territorial Division came upon the German hordes like the wrath of God, moving like lightning to whatever section of the Western Front was hardest pressed, striking, paralysing, and withering the proudest armies of the enemy. Well did the kilted Scotsman know that even among the mountains and the glens, or upon the moors of Scotland, or on the rocky shores of the Atlantic, life would be intolerable unless he were free as his fathers had been free: he had either to slay or fall a prey to the 'blonde beast' of brute force and lust: his struggle was with the Godlessness of a cold and cruel Materialism, which was the negation of the ideal and the spiritual; his struggle was with Germany's false philosophy, incarnate in her soldiers: with this 'abomination of desolation' it must be a wrestle to the death.

With such rhetoric the worthy Reverend Dugald probably regaled his congregations in Bower. Perhaps the most touching and worthwhile part of Mr MacEchern's grandiose and inflated composition is the hundred and fifty pages he devotes to 'Memories of the Boys of Bower and their Kinsmen in the Great War.' This section is well researched and amply illustrated by snapshot and studio portraits of the many men – and a few women – who played their part. Many of the named cheerful faces are underlined with the message: 'Killed in Action'. 'Died of Wounds', 'Lost at Sea'.

'A thousand Iliads could not exhaust the battle story of the Seaforth Highlanders, in whose battalions were enlisted for the World War 49,750 soldiers – over 50,000 if we include the Dominion Seaforths.' Thus MacEchern introduced his own regiment. Of the Fifth Battalion, into which very many of the Wick men were enrolled, he writes:

> The shores of the North Sea and the Atlantic, with the mountains of Sutherland and the moors of Caithness, bred these great fighting men. . . Thurso, Wick, Helmsdale, Brora, Golspie, and Dornoch – from these to Point of Stoer and Cape Wrath lies the territory inhabited in the first centuries, A.D. by Lugi, Smertae, Cornavii, and Caireni – that race whose name is Cruithnich, from Celtic Cruithne and Prydyn – Pretannoi and Britanni – is now born by the modern Britons. The descendants of these Cruitens, and of those lion-hearted, iron-handed young soldiers of Cataobh and Catness – Sutherland and Caithness – who in the World War have so powerfully wielded the Sword of the North.

The battalion had a death roll of 872 men and 40 officers. MacEchern quotes Kitchener who, 'inspecting the Battalion, has said to Colonel Davidson, "Well, Colonel, you command the finest body of men I have ever seen."' Such compliments from commanders like Kitchener were routine and are well enough until one recollects that such fine bodies, like cattle in the pens of Chicago, are being lined up for slaughter. MacEchern lists the forty officers killed, but not the rankers, and among the pictures the lowest rank portrayed is that taken by a Wick photographer of a Lance-Corporal, a sadly sick looking man named William Stephens, who served with the Black Watch in the Boer War and was 'severely wounded in France at Cambrai, 1917'.

What is without any doubt the most graphic and telling piece in the whole book is the quoted

Last Leaves from

The Journal of a Highlander Officer

Captain GEORGE ANGUS SUTHERLAND. M.C., BRORA
5th Battalion The Seaforth Highlanders, killed in battle.

Fig 51 Captain G. A. Sutherland. From *The Sword of the North*.

Sutherland was clearly no snob. A few excerpts from this vivid laconic record, illustrating something of what the Wick men went through, deserve repetition:

1917. January 16th. Left Brora for France. *17th.* Spent day with Alex. and Louie in Edinburgh. *18th.* Crossed to Calais; to Etaples. *19th.* in Tents. Ready to go to 5th Seaf. Hrs at front. *22nd and 23rd.* Entrenching Bn. Posted to command B Coy. 300 strong – 11 Officers. *24th* Had 8 shells fired at us: first time under shell-fire. *24th.* Anti-aircraft gun shell dropped beside me at the Camp. *29th.* R.E. Officer hit at V [Vlamertinghe?]: lost his leg: died.

. . . .

April 2nd. One man killed, 7 wounded, today in my Coy. *3rd.* Was out at Belgian Chapel, and took parts of Pte. N.'s body to cemetery: impressive service there at 11.15 p.m. *9th.* Great news from Arras – 10,000 prisoners, 40 guns: 51st Highland Division was in it. *12th.* At Pop. [Poperinghe?] with Hewlett, who was all thro' Gallipoli with 1st lot of Anzacs (wounded and killed later). *20th* To-day am put in charge of all men in camp and also officers. *21st.* In charge of all – 500 men – in camp. *24th.* 2000 prisoners. Boche shelling close in front of the camp. *25th.* Lt. Hewlett and Lt. Chippens killed. *26th.* Great air activity: 26 aeroplanes above us all day. *27th.* 40 Boche 'planes taken down; 2 British missing. *30th.* Boche shelling about camp continuously: 3 officers wounded to-day.

. . . .

June 7th. Start of Battle [This was the Battle of Messines Ridge, described by Liddell Hart as 'A Siege-War Masterpiece'[1]] Bombardment started at 3 p.m.: and never heard such a fearful affair. Got up at 2 p.m. Successful day. Big progress as regards ground, guns, prisoners. Saw about 100 prisoners in all. *8th.* 7000 prisoners captured. All rlys. taken and 3 miles advance. *9th.* Went over No Man's Land and 600 yds. Behind Boche front line – all huge shell-holes full of equipment, and dead here and there. *12th.* Poor Lieut. Morrice of the 5th killed up at the ridge in front of St. Eloi. *15th.* Today at 4 p.m. the obs. balloon close to us either burst or was hit by shrapnel or 'plane; terrific report. I

---

1 B H Liddell Hart: *History of the First World War;* London, Pan Books (1972) p322.

saw the balloon in flames and the two observers on fire. The two men fell thro' the roof of a house and were burned to death. At siding to-day killed 4 Men and 1 Officer, and wounded 19 Men. *18th.* Lt. Jones wounded at H. Corner to-day. *23rd.* Hun 'plane took 3 down in flames beside us: 10 parachutes were in the air at once. *28th.* Took down 5 Obs. balloons to-day. Saw 2 on fire.

. . . .

Septr. 2nd. Went up line, coming under heavy shell and machine-gun fire. *3rd.* In posts – 8 men – close up to the Boche near Pheasant Farm. Went out on patrol and went through White House alone. *4th.* Our posts crumped by Boche but no damage. Firing nightly on parties of the enemy. Tonight our reliefs were spotted by enemy, and we lost 4 killed and wounded. Went out and tried to get in Somerville. For 4 hours kept under machine-gun fire. *5th.* At Canal Bank: saw 2 planes, locked in one another, came down. Another came down in flames. *7th.* Hun 'planes bombed us whilst shooting: killed R.S.M. and 20 Gordons within 200 yds of us. *17th.* In these I lost my revolver, telescope, etc; and Bartleman was killed near me. *20th.* Called up line and arrived at Caen trench, where we viewed terrific battle going on. *21st.* Called to help 4th Gordons who were hard pressed, and got into Pheasant Trench. Dug ourselves in at Pheasant Trench. *22nd.* Went over battlefield; terrible sights: many prisoners, chiefly wounded. Terrible bombardment on us. Lost 11 killed, 32 wounded in our Company in two hours. 3 Officers. First Caen Trench, then Comedy Farm, and then Pheasant Trench in one night! *23rd.* Sent up post Pheasant Farm to hold line. Guide no use, and we manned wrong posts. Boche in a circle all round us here. *24th.* Shelled bombed, sniped, continuously in our small posts. *25th.* Sent up to fill gap in line, which I did at 8 in morning after being out new Cemetery all night. Snipers everywhere. *26th.* Terrible time but punished Boche. Attacked snipers. Worst time I ever had in trenches. *27th.* Back at Siege Camp: Bombed and also shelled. Out at 0, and then Poperinge on horseback. *29th.* Left this part of the line and everyone glad. Got praise from Army and Corps Commanders on our work up here during past two months.

Captain Sutherland and his company were in the line of the 51st

Division at the time of the great German offensive of March, 1918, in the area of Bapaume, south of Arras. His Journal continues:

> *March 21st.* Boche offensive opened early in the morning. 51st Div. covered themselves with glory holding Boche up. *22nd.* Boche advancing: Hun aeroplanes bombed Frevant. Wounded coming in fast all day. Divisions of hundreds of busses passing through all day continously. Wounded coming down. *25th.* Frevent Hosp. full of all kinds of wounded. Boche aeroplanes bombed heavily all around last night. . . . Great reputation of the 51st Div. Enemy papers singing their praises. On march to Frevent. King on the route and inspected some of our Brigade. Interviewed the Brigadier. *30th.* At F. Have lost 7 officers killed and 400 men. . .

Activity on this front during March, April and May was fast and furious . . .

> [*April*] *25th.* Gen. Having said that if 51st Div. had not fought so well Bethune, H - - [Hazebrouck?] and Lille would have fallen. The Boche used already 120 Divs. against my front. Britain had 62 Divisions in all. They lost 500,000 men. They had 200 Divisions: if we held them, we had won. . .

Sutherland tells casually of winning a distinction:

> *May 2nd.* Are now holding up the Boche. *3rd.* Many new Officers joined us – Lundie, Dues, Stewart and 5 Singapore Scottish. *7th.* Neuville St Vaast a heap of ruins and dust. *14th.* At Lewis Gun class. Am only representative of 51st Div. The Division has a tremendous reputation with everyone. Left G.G.Q.L.G. School. Joined the Battn. *22nd.* On working party on C. road; finished by leading out 550 yards into No Man's Land. *24th.* Left to hold line in front of Bailleul opposite Arras on to Vimy Ridge, A Coy, holding it with 2 platoons on a 600 yards front.
> *25th,* Saturday. Got the M.C. Hard day, and shelled continuously with all kinds of missiles. At 9.30 put two wiring parties to work round sap: then got party to fill up Boche trench. Went with a corporal 50 yards up trench. Met a big block and eyed three Huns, and returned. Took a Lewis gun out 500 yards in No Man's Land and fought with a Boche machine gun . . .[1]

---

1 Dugald MacEchern: *The Sword of the North: Highland Memories of the Great War;* Inverness, Robert Carruthers (1923); pp 377-397.

On 26th June, Captain Sutherland had his medal pinned on him by General Horne. In July he made his first move to join the newly created Royal Air Force. After a day in the air, and a visit to the Canadians, he rejoined his unit. Lieutenant MacEchern closes the record:

> A few days later Capt. G A Sutherland, whose journal ends here, was killed – revolver in hand, at the head of his men – in the historic second Battle of the Marne, July 21-28th, near Rheims, where the 51st and 67 Divisions helped the French to finally turn back the Germans, as the 15th and 34th Divisions did near Soissons.

MacEchern mentions – and includes a photograph – of General Baron Horne, but really says little about him, apart from describing him as 'Britain's greatest Artillery Officer in modern times.' Horne was a commander of considerable distinction. He 'showed,' says MacEchern, 'a Napoleon-like genius in the use of artillery, ending the stale-mate, and making a war of movement possible.'

Be that as it may, General Baron Horne, whose home was Stirkoke House near Wick, was credited as 'inventor of the famous "creeping barrage"' that played, above all, a significant but now controversial role in the Battle of the Somme in 1916, where this unconventional use of heavy artillery was first applied on that scale. Commenting on this at the time of his funeral in August 1929, the *John O'Groat Journal* commented that Horne (1861-1929) was 'one of the few artillery officers who rose to eminence. The distinguished Caithnessian has been described as the actual brains of the Battle of the Somme.'[1] Horne was much favoured by General Haig (later Field Marshal Earl Haig), whose fame (or notoriety) rests much upon the Somme. The 'creeping barrage' was in principle an artillery bombardment of enemy lines lifting forward from time to time to allow infantry to advance behind the barrage and so take the dazed enemy by surprise; the trouble at the Somme was that the barrage did not creep fast enough to allow such advance, and when the infantry came behind the ground was all churned up, made all the more difficult to cross by the rain, which was one of the most vexatious hazards of the Somme. In addition, by the time the soldiers arrived, the enemy had had ample warning of their coming. If it was Horne's 'invention', it did not make a very effective contribution to ultimate victory, and as for 'ending the stale-

---

1 *JOGJ*, 25 December, 1929

mate', it is evident that Lieutenant MacEchern had no great understanding of the matter.

General Horne had commands in four of the great battles of the war, Loos, 15 September, 1915, the Somme, June 1916, Arras, April 1917, and the Lys, 1918, when he was Commander of the 1st British Army. Liddell Hart has no great opinion of Horne's capabilities (for that matter, he had a poor opinion of Haig and some others belonging to the 'old school'). At Loos, Horne was in charge of the 2nd Division. Hart tells how in that engagement it was intended to use gas. The officer in charge of the gas

> declined to assume the responsibility of turning on the cylinders. But when this was reported to divisional headquarters, Horne replied with an order that 'the programme must be carried out whatever the conditions . . . .' As a result of this obstinacy many of the infantry were poisoned by their own gas. Those who were able to advance were soon stopped, and slaughtered by the ungassed German machine-gunners. Nevertheless Horne ordered a fresh assault, which was only abandoned after his brigade commanders had protested against the 'useless loss of life.'[1]

Other members of the Caithness gentry served, with some considerable distinction, notably Lieutenant-Colonel Sir John Sinclair, baronet of Dunbeath DSO, and three times mentioned in dispatches. General Horne's brother, E W Horne of Thuster, was Colonel of the 3rd Battalion, Seaforth Highlanders, at the time of its mustering, and later became commander of a battalion in an English regiment. The Duke of Portland was photographed and shown in MacEchern's book as Honorary Colonel of the 5th Battalion, Seaforth Highlanders.

The Navy in the North.

The naval war gains only slight mention in *Sword of the North*. MacEchern refers to 'Naval Officers with whom I came in contact,' including Captains Wells RN and Meredith RN, successively Senior Naval Officers at Thurso who, on account of their posting 'had also the whole personnel of the Grand Fleet through their hands.' He also met Captain Egerton RN, Chief Naval Officer in the patrol of the North and East Coasts of Sutherland and Caithness, and for one spell

---

1 Liddell Hart, op cit. p 199.

MacEchern was billeted in the House of the Northern Gate on Dunnet Head, 'one of the castles of Rear-Admiral Sir Edwyn Alexander-Sinclair KBE.' of Freswick. While here he 'had the honour of sending a signal to Admiral Jellicoe at Scapa Flow, intimating the presence of a German submarine, which was evidently one of a flotilla that was approaching from the west.' This was doubtless the submarine flotilla that early in 1917 began ravaging the shipping off the Caithness coast, sinking some twenty ships between Peterhead and Shetland during the next few days after the sighting from Dunnet Head.

In his admirable *This Great Harbour Scapa Flow*, W S Hewison tells the curious story of how the British Atlantic Fleet came to be based in Scapa Flow, the great inland sea between Mainland and the southern islands of Orkney. Since the days of the Vikings this wide and deep anchorage had been little used. There was some concern about it, not so much as harbour for British ships, as about the danger of its being occupied by Napoleon; and during the last phase of the war with France a 24-pounder battery was installed on South Walls, the southern 'island' extension of Hoy, and two Martello towers (still standing) were erected. The Admiralty's Maritime Surveyor, Graeme Spence, made a 'Proposal' to be considered by their Lordships of the Admiralty 'for Establishing a Temporary Rendezvous for Line of Battle Ships in a National Roadstead called Scapa Flow formed by the South Isles of Orkney.' Nothing came of Spence's ideas until a hundred years later.

The Germany of Bismarck and Kaiser Wilhelm II created a new alignment of powers in Europe; not only had France a permanent hostile neighbour along its frontier; Britain, the world's most powerful maritime nation, also found itself confronted, not by armies and fortifications, but by a newly constructed technologically advanced navy based at Kiel, Jade Bay and Heligoland (only recently traded to Germany by its former owner, Great Britain herself). Britain's own navy was rapidly modernised with bigger ships and more powerful guns. Its most menacing creation was HMS *Dreadnought*, launched in 1906, and the first of a new generation of capital ships with twelve and thirteen-inch guns. There was too, a new race of other big ships, battlecruisers, light cruisers and 'destroyers'. This mighty force needed to be based on the North Sea coast ready for rapid mobilisation, if required, against its threatening opponent on the opposite coast. Navy ships were based mainly at Harwich at the south end of the North Sea, the Firth of Forth, near Rosyth and

Inverkeithing, and the Cromarty Firth, with Invergordon as its technical base. There was felt to be the need for a satisfactory, deep-water and more spacious northern base. In an article in the *Naval Annual* of 1907, entitled 'Strategical Features of the North Sea,' the writer suggested that 'probably a good anchorage could be found somewhere in the vicinity of Wick.' Both Peterhead and Rosyth he considered to be too far south. He was clearly not *au fait* with the conditions and history of Wick Bay.

The July naval manoeuvres of 1908 in the north North Sea included a mock attack on the Caithness coast during which Wick was reported 'captured' by the invading force. From the summer of 1909, Scapa Flow came increasingly into use as a scene for such activities and other naval visits, but the final decision to adopt the Flow as the Navy's main base did not come until a few months before war actually broke out in 1914, the proposal now being strongly backed by the service chiefs but resisted until late in the day by the Admiralty itself. The advantages of the Flow, as Hewison lists them, included 'several navigable entrances and the protection afforded by its tides, skerries and climate;' its disadvantages were that 'it was not on the British mainland. It had no rail access for stores, nor could have, although an extension of the Highland Railway to Gills Bay near John O'Groats was actively considered for a time.' Almost certainly the biggest objection was the expense, for the creation of a naval base here would require many expensive installations, and also the establishment on the islands of strong coastal gunnery stations, an expense declined by the War Office though willing to let the Admiralty set up its own defences.

'Improvement works' at Scapa were included in the Naval Estimates for 1913-1914. On 1 August, 1914, Vice-Admiral Sir John Jellicoe arrived by train in Wick to board the cruiser HMS *Boadicea* which would take him to Scapa Flow, where he would take over as C in C of the Home Fleet from Admiral Sir George Callaghan, who had been in charge of developments so far. In some later comments Jellicoe claimed that 'the greatest anxiety confronting me was the defenceless nature of the base at Scapa, which was open to submarine and destroyer attacks.'[1]

The die was cast and the ships were in. Scapa Flow became the

---

1 W S Hewison: *This Great Harbour Scapa Flow;* Kirkwall, The Orkney Press (1985), p 65. Much of the information on the topic of Scapa Flow used so far is derived from this informative text.

WICK OF THE NORTH

home of what was now to be called the 'Grand Fleet', and so began the saga of naval occupation of 'This Great Harbour Scapa Flow'. It began with the First World War and ended shortly after the Second finished. The occupation transformed the whole economy of Orkney, and during the Second rather drastically altered the geography of the south islands by the construction of the 'Churchill Barriers'. Churchill was First Lord of the Admiralty when the occupation began, and again in 1940 when the barriers were constructed.

There is little doubt that the development of Scapa as a main naval base had quite an effect on the strategic status of Caithness and on its economy, for all main overland transit to the Flow was via the Highland Railway, though it was Thurso and Scrabster rather than Wick which handled most of the traffic. The precise impact of the development on Caithness, and Wick in particular, is difficult to trace, since there was a virtual blackout during both wars on all news of military and naval matters and movements in the area. Civilian access to and egress from the area was controlled by a pass system. Troop and supply trains shuttled regularly between Inverness and Thurso, the main service becoming known as 'Jellicoe's Express'.

Jellicoe's Express

This famous service, referred to in 'Wick on the Line' (p 538), was probably the most profitable – to the company – ever running over the Caithness line, perhaps the entire Highland Railway. The adoption of Scapa Flow as the main base of the British Grand Fleet entailed the frequent and rapid movement of service personnel to and from Orkney, via Scrabster. During the First World War the majority travelling were naval men, but in the Second, large numbers of Army and Royal Airforce people too were brought in and away from what, for many, was a much detested northern posting.[1]

Before the introduction of the 'Jellicoe', many trains including 'specials' and many changes en route were among the discomforts suffered by those assigned to ships, batteries and air-stations in the north. The 'Jellicoe', first called the 'Misery', ran daily both ways.

1 The Orkney posting is celebrated in the famous verses of the probably mythical Captain Hamish Blair (of the First War):
This bloody town's a bloody cuss –
No bloody trains, no bloody bus,
And no one cares for bloody us –
In bloody Orkney.
And so on, for eight verses.

WARS AND RUMOURS OF WAR: 1

South of Crewe it ran in two (sometimes three) parts, the main section to and from Euston, the rest mainly to and from Portsmouth. The description which follows comes from the Second World War, but conditions must have been much the same in 1917 and 1918. 'The train,' says Alex Cowie, reminiscing from 1939-45,

had double locomotives and towed an incredible number of coaches. It was intended primarily for the conveyance of all Service personnel, Merchant seamen and a limited number of categories of civilian personnel who were in Service employment. A services-issued pass was essential for admission on board.

It represented the longest, fastest train journey in the British Isles, from one end to the other . . . .

Every week-day in the Second World War it left Thurso about 5pm with a first stop at Helmsdale to take on water. Local women manned the tea-bar on the platform to supply thirsty sailors, soldiers and airmen, but there never seemed to be enough in the urns to go around the hundreds who clamoured for more.

A permanent-way man went round with his long-handled hammer tapping the wheels, and after a five to ten minute stop the train was off again – for its next halt at Inverness goods yard at Millburn, where the water tanks and coal tender was topped up.

On board the train itself, every available space was taken, with five passengers on each side of the compartment. If you could not get a seat, the alternative was to crouch down on a kit-bag or suitable case in the corridor, or stand there to the constant interruption of people coming and going to the toilets.

Frequent checks were carried out on board the train by military policemen [the 'Red Caps', the most hated race of both wars] to detect personnel who might have thoughts of deserting, or taking French leave. Occasional fights, impromptu concerts, and drunks were the normal feature of the journey, especially in its early stages.

No one was allowed to leave the train at Inverness. A quarter of an hour delay and it was off again for its next water stop at Aviemore. Passengers for the Inverness/Aberdeen area would leave the train there, and then the long line of coaches with its two powerful locomotives was off over Drumochter to Perth.[1]

The main difference between the journey north and the journey south was, understandably enough 'that southwards nearly everyone was in high spirits at the thought of leave, while on the north run there was a feeling of despondency that a leave was over.' A variation on this theme was told by an Orkneyman (and doubtless could have been just as lively a recollection of a Wicker): 'I almost had the train to myself. When I put my head out of the window at Rogart on the way north for leave, to look for the southward Jellicoe on the other line, there were hundreds of heads looking out, and calling out to one another, "Look at that crazy bugger, going north on leave!"'

Another story told of this famous train. Whether or not the 'Jellicoe' deserved its description, the 'war-time train that ran faster and farther than any today,' it was once nearly wrecked at speed on one of its runs north. The story was told by an old railway man, George Seaton, whose uncle, James Seaton, was stationmaster at Golspie during the First World War:

> He was meticulous in being there [on Golspie Station] when the Jellicoe went past. He always went out to the Kirton end of his platform beside the catcher – the device for picking up mails.
>
> On this particular day, he heard a strong whizz go past his head as the locomotive approached, and this turned out to be one of its wheels which had flown off.
>
> It passed right close to his head, travelled 150 yards up the platform, smashed right through his garden fence and came to rest in his garden.
>
> Mr Seaton was greatly surprised and alarmed by this occurrence. He telegraphed ahead to the Dunrobin Gates, to try to get them to stop the train, but it had already gone through. So he phoned Brora and had the train stopped.
>
> When driver Tom Grant saw what had happened he could not believe that such a thing could occur to a new locomotive. He just refused to take the train any further, and I presume that the passengers were picked up by a relief train from Wick or Thurso.[2]
>
> Two special locomotives were built 'to pilot trains on their north and south journeys. The were the *Snaigow* and *Dura*, built by R and W Hawthorne, Leslie and Co. Ltd.

1 *The Northern Times*, 2 April, 1982.
2 Ibid.

WARS AND RUMOURS OF WAR: 1

The Navy in the North Sea

Wick's boat building and repair facilities were put at the disposal of the navy for the repair of minesweepers and patrol boats. Some harbour improvements were, in fact, put in train almost at the beginning of the war, though it is doubtful if they were in any way an outcome of discussions with the Admiralty. A meeting of the Harbour Trust in September, 1914, approved the 'widening of the North Pier towards Martha Terrace' by the insertion at this corner of the old harbour of 'ferro-concrete piles with spending beach below.' The purpose was to 'lessen motion in the river harbour,' the very tidal 'river basin' produced behind the north and south 'river piers' erected during the last and limited phase of harbour development in the later years of the nineteenth century. This harbour was of little use except for smaller boats, but was subject to an exaggerated difference between low and high tide. The improvement was quite modest, amounting to a total cost of £5000.[1]

The whole harbour's value for naval purposes was limited by its traditional handicaps, small area and vulnerability to bad weather. War or no war, storms continued to blow at what times and with what ferocity they listed, as in December, 1915, when 'a storm of wind and rain of great violence, and probably unprecedented in point of duration,' blew up one Tuesday night and 'continued to rage with scarcely any abatement all night' and all the following day. 'As we go to press [Thursday night],' said the *Journal*,

> the gale is still raging. At times the wind, which was from a southerly direction, attained the force of a hurricane, and a very heavy sea ran along the Caithness coast. Wick Bay presented an impressive spectacle. Not within living memory, it was stated, has the sea raged more fiercely within the two heads of the bay. The great waves dashed with tremendous force over the piers and against the rocks on the north side, sending the spray in blinding sheaves far upon the land. The whole bay was one boiling scene of whitened and angry water, lashed to fury by the prolonged violence of the gale . . . . .'[2]

The writer clearly intended to emulate the same colourful prose style set by so many of his predecessors when wrestling with the familiar topic. As we know, such an event as a fierce storm, far from infrequently rendered Wick Bay an unsuitable place for anchoring

1 *JOGJ*, 25 September, 1914.
2 *JOGJ*, 24 December, 1915.

deep-keel vessels of any kind. Weather can rage in Scapa Flow, but the coast of mainland, the Hills of Hoy and the uplift of South Ronaldsay protect the basin from the worst effects of storms from all directions. Scapa Flow sea-sickness was a common affliction of sailors.

Nevertheless, there were occasions when Wick came in useful. A few days after the war started a party of seventy English and American tourists, escaping from Germany via Norway, were brought into Wick Bay by the *Pollux* of Bergen. They stayed overnight in the town and were taken out the next morning by train.[1] Early in the war Prince Albert, Duke of York (later to be King George VI), serving aboard HMS *Collingwood*, came to Scapa. His health was not good. It was suspected that he was suffering from appendicitis and he was transferred to the *Rohilla*, a hospital ship, lying at the time in Wick Bay. 'Intelligence reports indicated that the German fleet might be putting to sea at this time, so *Rohilla* with Prince Albert aboard still under observation was sent to Scapa with a destroyer escort, to take patients from the sick bays of the fighting ships in the event of their going into battle.'[2]

Action off the British North Sea coasts was considered to be all too likely during these early months of the war. A Scottish collier was fired on at Sunderland and two members of the crew wounded. Various attempts were made by the German High Seas Fleet to take control of the North Sea, culminating in an action north of Heligoland at the end of August, 1914, won by Admiral David Beatty, commander of the British Battlecruiser Fleet, when three German light cruisers were sunk with the loss of 1000 officers and men, at the cost of one British light cruiser and less than 50 casualties. This and later action off the Dogger Bank persuaded the German Admiralty not to send their ships out of their bases until they were reasonably certain of superiority in number of ships and fire-power as against the resources mobilised by the British fleet. Nevertheless, early in November, 1914, a German battle group bombarded the fishing port of Yarmouth, and in December, a flotilla of German battlecruisers bombarded Hartlepool, Whitby and Scarborough on the north-east coast of England, killing 122 civilians and wounding 433. It was clear from all this that all the fishing towns along the English and Scottish coasts were dangerously vulnerable to German attack, and there was, in consequence, little hope of extending periods of successful fishing.

1 *JOGJ*, 14 August, 1914.
2 Hewison, op cit. p 87.

WARS AND RUMOURS OF WAR: 1

As a result of the Yarmouth incident, Beatty's battlecruiser fleet was moved from the Cromarty Firth, with its service base of Invergordon, down to Rosyth in the Firth of Forth. Wick and all the other ports were never seriously attacked, but all were constantly aware that they were only a few hours away from the ravages that might be inflicted by whatever freely moving German ships there might be around (there was also constant fear that the Zeppelins might come); fortunately the watch by Beatty and the other commanders ensured that the coasts of north-east Scotland were never attacked.

Had the town known what was going on, Wick's most fearful hours during the whole war must have been those from 2.15 on the afternoon of 31 May, 1916, to 3am the next morning. Between these hours the British Grand Fleet and the German High Seas Fleet encountered in a mighty but inconclusive battle near the Jutland Bank, 250 miles ESE of Wick Bay, in which 6,097 officers and men of the British force lost their lives, the Germans 2,551. The British lost 14 ships, of which 3 were battlecruisers and 3 armoured cruisers; the Germans lost 11, of which 4 were light cruisers. After Jutland the High Seas Fleet made only two sorties out of its Jade anchorage at Wilhelmshaven, both abortive, leaving the 'German Ocean' in British control for the rest of the war, except for the German minefields still littering its waters, and U Boats. A controversy has been raised many times since the war as to who won the Battle of Jutland, Admirals Jellicoe and Beatty, or Scheer and Hipper. It is a profitless argument, since neither fleet had any significant contribution left to make towards resolution of the main conflict. At least the seaports of the east of Britain were left unmolested from now on.[1]

This was by no means the end of war in the North Sea. The menace was continued by the increasing use of German U-boats. The first ship to be lost off the Caithness coast was the *Sunbeam* of Chester. She was a three-masted top-sail schooner, carrying coal for Westray, Orkney. She was intercepted on 4 July, 1915, by a U-boat which gave her crew five minutes to abandon ship before she was sunk by gunfire from the submarine. They were picked up by an Admiralty trawler

---

1 Geoffrey Bennett: *Naval Battles of the First World War*; London, Pan Books, (1974), Chaps 9-12, pp 155-243. These chapters contain a fairly full account of Jutland and its immediate consequences. Bennett also shows that whichever navy won, technically speaking, effectively the North Sea mission of the German High Seas Fleet was now virtually completely blocked, Admirals Scheer and Hipper planned and actually launched attacks on Sunderland and Yarmouth a few days before the end of the war. Both were completely against orders of the *Admiralstab*, and were aborted within hours.

and landed at Wick. Captain Moodie later got his revenge as a member of the crew of a 'Q' ship (disguised merchantman) which sank another German submarine.

This first bout of indiscriminate sinkings of allied and neutral ships which were deemed to be carrying war supplies to Britain, ended rather suddenly after six months, on orders from the Kaiser, concerned about the effect that the policy was having on the attitudes of neutral countries which, at this stage, included the United States. In 1917, however, the submarine campaign was resumed, this time also in the wide Atlantic, an effect of which was indeed to bring in the United States.

In the first half of 1917 the Germans launched a submarine offensive against shipping off the north-east coast of Scotland. Eleven ships were sunk between Wick and Tod Head by torpedo or mine, but there may have been others, for information about sinkings are 'extremely sparse' on account of censorship at the time.

Mines also, both German and our own, did a considerable amount of damage. Fairly typical is the case of the Admiralty minesweeping trawler, HM *Pitstruan*, sunk in 1917, near to Wick:

> She had been escorting a trawler about two miles south-east of Noss Head when two floating mines were sighted. All hands were mustered on deck and ordered to wear lifejackets with a lookout posted on the bows. Shortly afterwards the trawler exploded a moored mine and sank immediately. The drifter *Lapwing* picked up two of the survivors, her commander and a trimmer, who were both suffering from shock and burns and landed them at Wick.[1]

German mines were responsible for one of the most shocking events of the war, shocking that is to government, the drowning of Field Marshal Kitchener, Secretary of State for War until this time, together with almost the entire crew of the cruiser *Hampshire*, wrecked off Marwick Head, Orkney. Kitchener was on his way to Archangel, to discuss military matters with the Russian government, two days after the Battle of Jutland, 2 June, 1915. Both these events were noticed in the same issue of the *John O'Groat Journal*, though needless to say, no great amount of detail was given.[2]

---

1 Ferguson, *Shipwrecks* op cit. p 97.
2 Hewison, op cit. pp 102-110. Also *JOGJ*, 9 June, 1916.

WARS AND RUMOURS OF WAR: 1

The Groat and the War.

It is possible through the pages of the *John O'Groat Journal* from August, 1914 to the last 'war issue' of 15 November, 1916, a few days after the Armistice of 11 November, 1918, to track not only the whole programme of the conflict in Europe and elsewhere, the triumphs, reverses and disasters, Allied changes of fortune, but also the shifts of mood and feeling, and despite reporting restrictions, quite a lot about the physical conditions of life in this still very isolated community in north Britain.

As to the general record, 1916 was a year of continuing difficulty for Britain. Jutland was not the triumph it was meant to be. Although it discouraged the German High Seas Fleet from further incursions into the North Sea, except for the two absurd and aborted sorties during the last few days of the war, it did not succeed in clearing the Germans out of the area. Submarine warfare intensified, not only in the North Sea, but also in the Atlantic where, until in 1917 the system of convoys, shepherded by destroyers and frigates of the Royal Navy was introduced, British shipping losses began to exceed our capability for new building; food and war material supplies from the Empire and from the USA began to run dangerously low. It was the declaration, above all, of the unlimited submarine warfare directed against all ships likely to be carrying such material, whether British or not, that persuaded President Woodrow Wilson to declare war against Germany on 6 April, 1917. Eventually the Americans insisted on mining areas of the North Sea even more thickly than before, laying some seventy thousand mines of their own. The programme was completed only days before the 1918 Armistice, and clearance had to be started almost right away. The purpose now, of course, was to ensure that no ships could get through to Germany, a blockade which brought Germany near to starvation in the later months of the war.

If not a year of total disaster, 1916 was not a year of high success for the Allies either. The Somme offensive, the 'first great action by a British army of continental size,' as A J P Taylor puts it, which lasted from 1 July, 1916 to mid-September, gained a sizeable acreage of mud in which to dig more trenches where Germans had recently had theirs, and it cost phenomenal losses: British, 420,000 killed, wounded and missing; French 194,000 and German (against both Allied armies) 465,000. Slaughter in warfare had never before reached such a scale. Wick, like many other towns in Britain, lost many of its best people in this struggle, and more in the 1917 battles at Arras, Ypres in Belgium, and during the German offensive of March, 1918.

Jutland was fought to a less than decisive result. In September, 1916, a great Zeppelin raid (though trivial by the standards of the air raids of the next war), created considerable dismay, even hysteria. At Easter in 1916 an Irish rebellion broke out in Dublin, suppressed ruthlessly by the British; it became a subject for the rest of the war of much bitterness, recrimination and charges of 'treachery' elsewhere in Britain. The *Groat*, while keeping readers informed about what was happening, for the rest of the war took a very condemnatory attitude towards the Irish.

In their turn, the events that marked the changes in Allied fortune were fully reported by the *Groat*: the American declaration of war (6 April, 1917); the Battle of Cambrai (30 November, 1917); collapse of the Italian Front (2 November, 1917); the 'February' Revolution in Russia, though curiously there is little mention of the Bolshevik (October) Revolution until some time after the event; the Peace of Brest-Litovsk (25 January, 1918); Russia Out of the War – Betrayal of the Allies (15 February, 1918); the Great German Offensive – 'Homeric Valor of the Seaforths' (29 March, 1918), Big Allied Offensive – drive from the Marne (26 July, 1918); 'Germany Whining for Peace' (18 October, 1918), 'Germany's Crafty Reply to President Wilson' (25 October, 1918).

There was time and space in the paper for events nearer home. 'Votes for Women' (22 February, 1918); the Scottish Education Bill (28 June, 1918) – both these measures had an effect on Wick in the postwar period. A quaint piece of domestic journalism in January, 1918, was a curious reference back to the Stevenson Breakwater, when it was recalled that Lady Caithness performed the 'ceremonial laying of the foundation' block of that doomed enterprise, on 8 October, 1863, when the 'tailors, shoemakers, coopers all had their flags.'

The Reverend Charles Thomson (Free Church Minister), it was recalled, declared the works commenced. The recollection continues:

> Then amid cheers of thousands of people, the playing of bands, the skirling of pipes, and the beating of drums, began the works which were to cost many thousand of pounds – all in vain, and ultimately to lie wrecked and ruined at the bottom of what the disappointed and somewhat spiteful RLS called 'the baldest of God's bays'. Slowly did the long procession wind its way back into town, each trade to its own hall to hang up the banners and prepare for the evening's festivities.

As the darkness came on the younger tradesmen formed a torchlight procession, marching to popular band tunes along the principal streets of Wick and Pulteney, ultimately breaking up at Kirkhill, where the torches were to burn out.[1]

What prompted this bright reminiscence at this time is not clear, but it served as a reminder that herrings and harbour-making had once been Wick's main pre-occupation. The Earl and Countess of Caithness's curious progress to the scene was recalled. They were taken out in the bay in the 'Captain's gig', then 'set down at a prepared landing-place near to the crane from which hung the ponderous foundation stone.'

Such lighthearted reminiscence was set in the context of increasingly optimistic news about the end of the war. Pages of the paper continued to be filled with 'obituaries' of service-men killed on the fronts, usually accompanied by snap-shots of the dead soldiers, supplied by the family. The troop and hospital trains rolled up and down the country, taking more and more men to the mincing machine, and bringing blinded and crippled and shell-shocked casualties back. But by the end of 1917, the tone of news from the front was increasingly hopeful. A 'survey' in the last issue of the year of the events of 1917, included a frank appraisal of the present state of affairs, with gloomy comment on the 'Russian Collapse' and 'Italian Reverses', but the main items of the list were about 'successes', the straightening of the whole Western Front at the expense of the Germans, the 'Capture of Jerusalem', advances in East Africa and Mesopotamia, the Zebrugge Raid. The biggest and most overwhelming item of all was the 'Entry of America' with the promise of three-million men soon swooping into France. The 'Irish Problem' continued to dismay the editors, free and liberal with their charges against the Irish of 'bad-faith' and 'treachery', while the 'Food Question' continued to be very worrying.

Wick, nevertheless, could hardly have been a jolly place. Its hopes for the future were none too rosy. The herring fishery disappeared almost entirely from the news and, indeed, from the Wick economy. In September, 1916, the *Groat* reported that catches, such as they were, were down to 'single crans'; five boats it said, had on Wednesday of that week brought in 9 crans.[2] The following month it said 'no herring

1 *JOGJ*, 11 January, 1918.
2 *JOGJ*, 8 September, 1916. Wick's catches and sales of herring remained low for the whole of the war. Some other main centres were not so *(continued on foot of next page)*

fishing at Wick this year' [meaning presumably no great access of boats coming to Wick] though there were plenty of herring on the quays, brought here for packing and re-exportation.[1]

The main means of livelihood for many, perhaps most families in Wick, must have been service pay and allowances, anything but princely but probably more regular and reliable than the fluctuating income from herring sales. That such pay and allowances were hardly princely may be supposed. In 1915, a soldier on enlistment was paid 7 shillings a week, from which most soldiers probably paid an 'allotment' to their families or dependants, compulsory in the case of married men. Including allotment, families were paid at rates depending on the size of the family, viz:

	Allotment	Supplementary Allowance	Total
Wife	3/6	9/-	12/6
Wife & 4 children	3/6	21/6	25/-[2]

It was not lavish but it was regular. And of course, there were incremental increases for length of service (and higher allotment), and for promotion. Many of the soldiers of Wick landed up as sergeants and some as sergeant-majors. However, by the end of the war, many of the wives were on widows' pensions.

Little other industry moved to Wick during these war years; although there was a certain amount of spin-off benefit to Wick as the result of the Navy's presence in Scapa Flow, there is little doubt that during the war years, the main income of the citizens of Wick came from service pay and allowances.

If advertisements are anything to go by, business in the shops was reasonably brisk. The drapers advertised enthusiastically and the patent medicine market was as vigorous as ever; Doan's Backache Pills were recommended week by week, the advertisement set as ordinary letter-press and accompanied by a sketch of a man or

---

(continued from foot of previous page) restricted. In the same report it was shown that the week's total catch at Peterhead was 7,400 crans, and for the season 71,400. Fraserburgh took in 90,000 crans, while Shetland produced 118,000 crans. The week of this report was considered 'a week of good catches,' at Wick. On the Tuesday 4½ crans had been 'brought in by local boats,' while another 5½ crans had come from Lybster by train. The prices obtained were good, from 51 shillings and 6d to 76 shillings per cran. Wick, of course, was too near to Scapa Flow for free open fishing to be allowed. In any case, many of the Wick fishermen were away in the RN Reserve. The figures for the other herring centres were doubtless boosted in 1916 by the virtual cessation of German raiding, as the result of the Jutland battle.
1 *JOGJ*, 6 October, 1916.
2 *JOGJ*, 22 October, 1915.

woman in back-bending agony, Carter's Little Liver Pills and Beechams. One intriguing frequent advertisement was directed to Wick's soldiers:

KILL THAT INSECT, TOMMY.

Harrison's Pomade.
Send to your pals.

When you haven't time to wash there's a
big chance you'll have companions.

Tins of Comfort! 4d and 9d.

A little Harrison's Pomade kills
EVERY INSECT on hair and body.

At long last came the headline of 15 November, 1918:

VICTORY – PEACE

'There were' said the *Groat*, 'deepest feelings of satisfaction in Wick.' The town was beflagged and the town bell and church bells were rung. Celebrations were, however, 'of a modified character for the thought of sympathy with the many who have lost near and dear ones in the struggle.' A thanksgiving service was held in the Parish Church.

As a reminder of the ordeal just ended, the death of Private John W Sutherland, a linotype operator of the *Groat*, was reported. He was killed in action on 28 September, 1918. From the *Groat* there had gone altogether fourteen men, of whom four had been killed and two wounded. It was reported, too, that Corporal John Bain (of the Royal Scots) had died in hospital at Rouen and Staff Sergeant Saddler J Johnston had died in a casualty clearing station, both from influenza. The war had ended amid a scourge of Spanish 'flu, which took away many servicemen and civilians alike. Sergeant George Mackenzie of Pulteneytown died in a hospital in Edinburgh. The melancholy tale of casualty reports, mainly on those still 'missing', and hospital cases continued for some time.

The most dramatic immediate sequel in the north of Britain came in June, 1919 when, hours before the expected signing of the Peace

Treaty at Versailles, seventy ships of the interned Germany Navy were scuttled in Scapa Flow, frustrating the intentions of the Allied peace-makers for that Navy, and providing lucrative salvage work for the Orcadians for some years ahead.

Even before that there had been new kinds of excitements. An immediate domestic consequence of the end of the war was the onset of a general election, as again happened in 1945. During the last two years of the war Lloyd George had headed a Coalition government including Liberals of his own party and Conservatives who had thrown in their lot with the government in the interests of the 'war effort'. Many tensions and disagreements had developed between members of the parties during the period, but these had been mostly suppressed in the interests of Coalition unity while the war was being fought.

Though unable to postpone an election, made all the more necessary by drastic changes in the size and composition of the electorate by the Representation of the People Act of 1918, Lloyd George sought to maintain as much inter-party unity as was feasible (or at least sufficient support for himself), in the hope of coping successfully with what everyone knew were going to be the difficult post-war conditions. In addition to the vast issues of demobilisation of Britain's largest civilian army ever and industrial reorganisation from a war time economy, there were the looming problems of Ireland and India. As the result of agreements between the parties – or rather factions of the parties, he led 'Coalition' minded Liberals and Conservatives into the election, called immediately after the Armistice of 11 November.

The MP for Caithness (including Wick) during the war had been R L Harmsworth, a brother of Alfred Harmsworth, first Lord Northcliffe, founder of the vastly influential *Daily Mail* and owner of *The Times*, minister of propaganda in Lloyd George's government. Harmsworth had been a strenuous recruiter under the Kitchener and Derby schemes in Caithness, and maintained during the war a somewhat strident campaign in the area for the sorts of things that Northcliffe stood for, especially harsh peace terms for Germany and trial – if not hanging – of the Kaiser.

The Harmsworth interest seems to have outraged some of his constituents in the later months of the war by propagating the charge that Caithness and Sutherland, like many other places, had provided cover and comfort during the war for 'spies of every nationality, including our own, in the pay of Germany'. German money, he is supposed to have said, 'has flowed out like water' during the war, and 'has percolated even into those northern regions . . . . .' The *Groat* believed that this 'vile insult' had come from R L Harmsworth himself, though how much evidence there was to back up the charge seems to have been a less important consideration than the fact that the *Northern Ensign*, the *Groat's* local rival (and supposedly at this time more Liberal in outlook than the *Groat* itself) had been bought up by R L Harmsworth, brother of the most powerful newspaper tycoon ever.[1]

'It behoves every elector in view of the coming fight [the General Election] to look circumspectly around with the question in his heart – Who are for the Kaiser?' On the strength of the charge a correspondent to the *Groat* had reported that the Caithness Liberal Association had asked Harmsworth to 'get out'.[2]

Harmsworth had no such intention. He stood as Coalition candidate for Caithness in the General Election held on 13 December, 1918. He was opposed by a Mr F J Robertson, standing as a non-Coalition Conservative. The result was quite a time coming through, for on this occasion, for the first time, the soldiers were allowed to vote, and time had to be allowed for the distant ballot boxes to come in. Harmsworth won easily, with a majority of 2733 in a poll of 10,805 electors, and so was one of the supporters of the shaky and ultimately much discredited government that took Britain into the turbulent world of peace.[3]

During the immediate post-war years, Wick and the localities around set up war memorials of variable standards of dignity. Lybster and Swiney's memorial listed 53 dead; that of Bower, 52; Staxigoe and Papigoe contains the names of 16 fallen, while Wick listed 297 names on the bronze tablets behind the monument, with 10 further to be added. The ten now have their own little tablet to themselves.

---

1 *JOGJ*, 11 October, 1918.
2 *JOGJ*, 6 September, 1918.
3 *JOGJ*, 3 January, 1919.
Note: During the preparation of this book Mr Ally Budge has been preparing a study of the First World War, to be published shortly.

CHAPTER 20

WARS AND RUMOURS OF WAR: II

VICTORY and Peace brought home in a short time the hundreds of men of Caithness and Wick, from France, the Middle East and some from Africa, seeking as earnestly as they might to get back to 'normal'. Normal for Wick was sailing out in small boats to bring in a great catch of herring. With astonishing celerity this was accomplished. In 1919 fishermen produced a catch of almost 100,000 crans, and although 1921 and 1922 were 'bad years', between 1919 and 1929 the Wick catch was above (in 1924 an 1926, well above) the 100,000 level.[1]

The market value of the 1919 catch was over £100,000. As yet the old customers of Germany and Russia were in no state to buy large quantities of Scottish herring; but in the following year, with a somewhat smaller catch and the customers returning, Wick fish exporters made a near quarter of a million pounds from the herring sales. Revenue was down during the next three years, in 1921 and 1922 largely on account of poor catches, but also reflecting the conditions of 'post-war depression' that hit many European countries from 1921 onwards. Depression still prevailed in 1923, for although the Wick herring catch nearly doubled on that of 1922, the 98,000 crans of herring were disposed of at little more than last year's figure. Then, in 1924 boom times began again, with more boats, large catches

1		Boats	Catch in crans	Market Value
	1919	185	99,954	£103.143
	1920	296	92,156	£232,728
	1922	180	54,925	£72,804
	1924	246	137,958	£215,668
	1925	340	119,554	£242,883
	1927	280	102,165	£179,122
	1929	260	103,240	£185,529
	1931	189	30,478	£62,974
	1932	289	76,298	£115,629
	1933	303	47,861	£88,222
	1934	211	42,314	£43,444
	1935	166	53,598	£63,958

(*JOGJ*, 6 September, 1935).

and good prices. Although Wick never again reached the sort of prosperity to which it had become accustomed in the good years of the nineteenth century, with no ideas above its station as a herring port, the town was doing reasonably well until the onset of the 'Great Crash' of 1929. From this time onwards not only did catches begin to fall off, not of course so much on account of the slump as of the movement away from Wick of the herring shoals; more importantly, revenue from the trade went into decline, relieved slightly in one or two 'good' years. As in many other places there was unemployment, but Wick – and Caithness generally – tended to 'export' this problem further south, for the steady decline in population of burgh and parish continued.[1]

The *Statistical Account* refers to a 'loss by migration' for the county between 1931 and 1951 of 18.6 per cent, a high figure for a short period. On the subject of the fishing, the *Account* comments: 'Until the beginning of the Second World War, the herring season was still important, but the glory had departed from what had been a great industry.' While the herring declined, white fishing, it should be mentioned, had been building up in the 'Wick district' (which included the whole length of the northern Caithness coast), so that by 1954 'the total landing of herring and white fish accounted for 119,315 cwts worth £341,791.'[2] Later returns show that herring catches had now become negligible, while the 'Wick district' now included Scrabster which 'has forged ahead as a white fishing station,' out-rivalling Wick port. The fishing of crab, lobster and other shell-fish became moderately important, especially as demand for the output from metropolitan hotels and the like increased and small, petrol and diesel powered boats became available for the daily collection of catches from creels at the marked sites.

It may be said that the two World Wars between them quite drastically changed the condition and status of Wick as a fishing port, forcing the town to look inland for its livelihood. As the herring disappeared, nostalgia for the great days of the fishery began to set in, and in 1927 was introduced the touching but increasingly anachronistic 'Herring Festival', the main feature of which was the selection and crowning of a 'Herring Queen'. It became an annual

1		1921	1931	1951
	Wick Parish	11,322	10,383	9,530
	Wick Burgh	9,086	8,115	7,548

(John S Smith: *Third Statistical* Account, op cit p xi)

2 John S Smith: *Third Statistical Account*, op cit. p 23.

feature in the life of the town, intended 'to be of entertainment to the public, help to advertise the town, and assist local charities.' The first Herring Queen was a very mature-looking senior pupil from Wick High School, Reta Shearer, the daughter of a Wick fisherman. Attended by classmates, she stepped ashore at the harbour, on the 'memorable summer day' of 17 July, from the decorated *Drift Fisher*.

'Unfortunately,' said the *Groat*, 'this new venture coincided with the most disastrous fishing in the history of the town, and took place midway into the season, when the people were in the shadow of the depression. It seemed a most inopportune time for celebrations, but, undaunted, the organisers went on – to success. In the face of adversity Wick rose bravely to the occasion, while those who understood looked on and wondered.' Hundreds of people turned up from all over the county, including a train load of 700 from Thurso, and a steam-load of visitors from far Aberdeen. A prize for 'original turnout' was won by Mr C Shanlin, of Mackay's Hotel, with a whale-sized model of a herring mounted on a car, not a wholly fitting representative of a dying trade. The proximate object of the festival was achieved, a 'nett profit of £118,' distributed between the Riverside and Town Improvements Committee, the Royal National Lifeboat Institution and the Wick Pipe Band.[1]

WICK ON THE WAGON

A continuing cause of depression in the minds of some citizens of the burgh was its almost unique status in Scotland, in Britain indeed, as a 'dry' town. As Iain Sutherland tells:

> For a quarter of a century, between 28th May, 1922 and 28th May, 1947 there were no public houses or licensed grocers in Wick open for the sale of alcohol to the public. They had been closed as the result of an election which had been led on 10th December, 1920, under the terms of the Temperance (Scotland) Act of 1913, and were to remain closed for these 25 years in spite of four attempts to have the decision reversed during that period.[2]

It is fairly well known that Scottish attitudes to drink have been

---

[1] *JOGJ*, 25 December, 1937 – see *Times Gone By; a compilation of John O'Groat Journal Christmas numbers;* October, 1991.
[2] Iain Sutherland: *Vote No-Licence: The true story of why Wick closed its licensed premises for 25 years;* published Iain Sutherland, Wick (no date).

curiously ambivalent. As we have seen, substantial increases in the consumption of alcohol, especially in the form of whisky were accompanied by a strong surge of support for temperance and ultimately total abstinence, both tendencies well marked in Wick. Excessive drinking, especially at the height of the fishing season, was in the 1840s matched by a striking rise in the strength of the total abstinence movement. To what extent this movement resulted in greater temperance among the working classes, and above all among the fishermen and coopers of Wick, cannot be gauged; but there can be no doubt that enthusiasm for restriction here, if not total prohibition of the use of alcohol, continued into the present century. In Scotland generally, the rate of consumption of whisky declined markedly between 1840 and 1910, a decline attributed by Smout much more to the imposition of excise duty on drink in the early years of this century than to the effects of temperance and 'TT' propaganda over the years. A Licensing Act providing for compensated limitation of public houses in localities was passed by the House of Commons but rejected by the Lords, but in his budget of 1909, the Chancellor of the Exchequer, David Lloyd George who had himself an animus against drink, placed heavier taxes on liquor. A Temperance Act of 1913, which but for the vote against by a dozen or so MPs might have turned the whole of Britain to Prohibition (with doubtless the dire consequences that followed such an Act by the USA some years later) was followed by the Temperance (Scotland) Act, which allowed localities to hold a poll on the matter of a veto against drink. The request for such a poll must be backed by at least 10 per cent of the electorate; for the poll to have validity at least 35 per cent of those on the roll must vote, and to ensure local prohibition at least 55 per cent of those voting had to be in favour of the no-licence resolution. No polls were held until 1920, and of the 584 polls then held, some 40 areas voted for either total prohibition or limitation. Most of these localities were either small towns or middle-class residential areas of larger towns; among the burghs voting for prohibition in the north were Stromness in Orkney, Lerwick in Shetland and Wick in Caithness.[1]

Wick persisted with its prohibition through thick and thin during the inter-war years and the entire second war itself. Considerable restriction on the drink trade was introduced during 1914-1918. Successively as Minister for Munitions, Secretary of State for War and

1 T C Smout: *A Century of the Scottish People*, op cit. pp 146-147.

then, as in December, 1916, as Prime Minister Lloyd George favoured a strong line against what he regarded as heavy drinking and the liquor traffic, though refused to go as far as the 'temperance advocates' who sought virtual prohibition; among the measures adopted were severe curtailment of drinking hours, closure of public houses at 10 o'clock; the 'afternoon gap (still with us – though not compulsory) was imposed – a lasting memorial of the Great War,'[1] and the 'nationalisation' of the liquor trade in Carlisle, abolished in 1980.

As we have seen, one effect of DORA in the whole area of the north of Scotland, a restricted area, was attempts at tight control of the sale of liquor, considered to be deleterious to the morale of the many servicemen in the north. This took the form of a ban by the national Liquor Control Board on the sale of spirits in the area, though the sale of wines and beers was still allowed. Shortage of supplies made this ban easier to enforce than it would have otherwise been at the end of the war. Wick temperance campaigners renewed their attacks on the drink trade, and a concerted programme of meetings of temperance advocates and weekly temperance services in the Breadalbane Hall on Sunday nights, led by ministers from the Baptist Chruch and the Central Church in Dempster Street, was inaugurated. The aim was to persuade the citizens of Wick to take action under the provisions of the 1913 Act, and accordingly to insist on a referendum during the following year, when the Act would come into effect. Perversely, at the very time when 'total abstinence' was virtually in their grasp, the Wick Total Abstinence Society, which had many years of campaigning behind it, pulled out of the movement, deciding on the 12th March, 1920 to wind up its affairs. £30 of their bank balance of over £200 was donated to the present campaign, led by the Wick and Pulteneytown Temperance Society, another £150 of it going to the War Memorial Appeal.[2]

Mr Sutherland draws attention to the part played by the women of Wick in all this. A 'formidable Sisterhood' as he terms it, based on the Bridge Street Church, was formed with the object of having all licensed premises closed. The women were in a much stronger

---

1 A J P Taylor: *English History:* 1914-1945; Oxford, The Clarendon Press, (1965), p 37.

2 Not the least of the ironies in this matter is that 'Temperance' does not signify, nor was originally intended to signify, 'total abstinence'. The term 'temperance' by this date, however, had come to imply total abstinence and even 'prohibition'. One of the town's leading hotels, Mackay's, still has the label, 'Temperance Hotel' showing through later legends on its north wall.

position than ever before. Not only was there a shift in the balance of the sexes as the result of the war; also the Representation of the People's Act of 1918 had, for the first time enfranchised women – not all of them, but those of 30 or over; parity with men at 21 was not established until 1928.

Sutherland's account of the whole prohibition episode in Wick is detailed and entertaining, and there is little need here to do more than mention the main phases of the movement's success and its eventual, and quite inevitable collapse. The chief matter for surprise is the length of time the ban endured. Once it was accepted that this unusual exercise in democracy was approved and legitimate, enthusiastic campaigning began in earnest. A Wick Citizens' No-Licence Union was formed in April, 1920, under the leadership of the Rev W H Millard, Minister of the Baptist Church, bringing in several organisations in favour of 'No-Licence' including the Wick Salvation Army group led, appropriately enough, by Captain Dry. This was a response to the formation of a local group affiliated to the national Anti-Prohibition Association and the Licence Holders (Local Veto) Defence Association in anticipation of the coming into force of the Act on 1st June. For it should be remembered that the whole drink trade of Scotland was, or believed itself to be, under threat. At the regular session of the Licensing Court of the local magistrates all the applications of the licensees of Wick, 6 hotels, 11 licensed grocers and 12 public houses, 29 in all, were renewed with little argument. It is evident that the burgh 'establishment', the burgesses, council and business-men were all against No-Licence.

Speakers were invited in from various parts of the prohibitionist movement including the Rev James Bar of Govan, a formidable campaigner and speaker 'who had been conducting a war on alcohol in its very heartland, the Glasgow slums, for 30 years.' There were speakers from far-away British Columbia where Prohibition had recently been brought in. A big crowd-drawer was the Rev Poole, an enthusiastic American campaigner who spoke in the Wick Rifle Hall in a 'new and rather theatrical style, in contrast with the heavy, hell-fire and brimstone style of the local activists.'

The date set for the referendum was 14 December, the same as that for the regular local council election. By that time 'both sides had worked themselves into a frenzy, and were making tremendous efforts to attract public support.' It was now known that of the 398 localities in Scotland which had already had a vote under the

Temperance Act, 348 had voted for 'No Change' and 26 only for 'No-Licence'. There must have been quite a number where the condition that 55 per cent majority in favour was not fulfilled, as in Watten, next to Wick, where only 86 from a voting electorate of 348 voted 'No-Licence' (25 per cent).

The day before the election, supporters of both ideas plastered the town with posters; the 'post office was nearly swamped with leaflets and several letter deliveries had to be made to clear the extra mail created in the system.' On the day, there was a procession, led by the band of the Boys' Brigade, of more than a hundred 'bairns' carrying umbrellas bearing the legend:

VOTE NO LICENCE. AS I HAVE NO VOTE
WILL YOU VOTE NO LICENCE FOR ME?

There must have been some of these Band of Hopers, as yet with no experience or understanding of liquor, who in later years abandoned their childish pledge. The Licence Holders' Defence Association made a big mistake of reducing the price of drink for voting day, thus immobilising susceptible voters.

'There has never been a day like it in Wick's electoral history,' says Iain Sutherland. There were meetings in 'packed halls'. The Wick voters, unlike their neighbours, were determined to abolish drink and made handsomely sure of the 'No-Licence' vote by turning out in droves, representing 77 per cent of all on the roll, the biggest turnout for any purpose ever. The result was 'No Change', 851; 'Limitation', 29; 'No-Licence', 1438, 62 per cent of the 2320 voting, from an electorate of 3013.

In the camp was great happiness, celebrated by an immediate Meeting of Rejoicing in the Breadalbane Hall, which lasted for three hours filled with prayers, hymn singing and sermons. Telegrams came from various places as far away as Stornoway (a great stronghold of 'Wee Frees'), Glasgow and Dunfermline. From nearer at hand came telegrams from Inverness, Lybster and Thurso. Doubtless during the coming years, there were those in Lybster and Watten who congratulated themselves that they had, after all, been spared, for they did excellent week-end business as the trains brought in the thirsty men of Wick.

The great day of drouth had to be postponed as the licensed victuallers put in legal objections to the poll and its result on the grounds of 'irregularities in the polling booths', and action was raised against the Town Council, naming Alexander Bruce as Town Clerk and Bailie David Davidson, Presiding Officer at the polls who, as it happened, was a manufacturer of soft drinks. Though it would have been much cheaper for the Council to give way and accept the poll result forthwith, they chose to defend the action, knowing of course that the business of the town would suffer and rate revenue would be affected. The matter had to be heard in the Edinburgh Court of Session and that process naturally took months.

Brewster sessions came round again and since no prohibition order was yet in place, the Court of Session granted 'Notes of Suspension' allowing the existing licences to stand, *pro tem*. There was great perturbation among the No-Licence majority and the actual meeting of the Wick Licensing Court of 12 April, 1921 was crowded with furious folk, one of whom sought to raise a petition to have the Provost removed from office. Licences were regranted to all the applicants, and the sale of spirits 'continued until such time as the ruling was given by the higher court.' The Court of Session ruling did not come until 2 December, 1921, and it was against the licence holders. 'The news was received jubilantly in Wick and there was another series of packed thanksgiving services, boosted by the great religious revival which was gathering momentum at that time.'

However, 'the prohibitionists were not yet out of the wood', for the licences of the Caithness Club and the Masons of Wick were falling due for renewal. In one of the other No-Licence communities, Kirkintilloch, the county sheriff had allowed clubs to retain their licences. So there was yet another appeal to the Court of Session. Meantime the Masonic Lodge withdrew its application but a licence was granted to the Caithness Club by the Sheriff of Caithness which, of course, had its rooms in Wick and was subject to the jurisdiction of the burgh. Mr Sutherland brings the saga to a period: 'On 17th March the great news came that the Court of Session dismissed the appeal by the licence-holders and finally the last object in the exhausting struggle had been removed. Licences were refused to grocers and public houses on 11 April and to the hotels on 25th April, all to take effect from 29th May, 1992.'

There was a decline in public drunkenness immediately and during the fishing season, though such scenes as were common in the old days had long ago disappeared anyway. The grocers merely lost the benefit of liquor sales, 'and the hotels had their usual non-drinking customers anyway.' The inn-keepers were considerable owners of fishing boats and could expect to keep going if the fishing was good, which this year was, however, poor (54,925 crans bringing in £72,804), less than a third of the income of 1920. Things picked up during the next few years so that, for the time being, resistance to prohibition died down.

In any case, various reliefs to the stress and difficulty of life without alcohol began to show themselves. It is doubtful if the doctors of Wick, as they did in America, began prescribing quantities of alcohol for medicinal purposes. The weekend excursions out of town have already been mentioned. Curiously it had remained legal to sell wholesale not less than 4 dozen bottles of beer at a time, and syndicates began making such purchases and arranging illegal drinking sessions in, for instance, curing yards in Lower Pulteney. As in America 'shebeens', that is, secret drinking premises soon came into existence in various parts of the town. Mr Sutherland tells of numbers of these, one just behind the Police Station and another two in High Street. He continues:

> The most daring of all operated in a restaurant whose regulars knew that when the fancy silver teapot was in use its contents had been brewed some considerable time previously. And not in India or China either. There were two mobile facilities, one a horse drawn van which signalled the availability of its special wares by having the whip struck vertically, and another who travelled on foot with his stock in his inside jacket pocket and the glass in a side pocket. This was dispensed at any handy, but secluded spot. There was an ingenious system whereby, during the food rationing period of the Second World War, poached salmon from Wick was sent daily to Thurso on the bus and whisky in payment came back the same way. There was another shebeen in Louisburgh and another in Staxigoe, although this was outside the range of all but the desperate.

As might be expected, illicit distilling returned to the Wick parish scene, after many years of relative law abidance in this classic and popular field of misdoing. Three skilled dodgers of the law became quite famous, and are still the subject of legend: Willag Thomson, his uncle James Thomson and his cousin, George Gunn, the 'Dhuloch' hero of the first war and holder of the Military Medal and the Croix de Guerre. Willag was given away to the Excise in 1939 and was brought to trial. 'The Customs Service issued them with warnings and frustration as the coolness of their quarry added insult to defeat. On one occasion they [the Excise men] left in their car accompanied on the pipes by Willag who was playing, *Will ye no come back again?'* The magistrates threw the book at him. Willag was fined £200, or 4 months, and the Dhuloch £25 for breaking bottles containing the evidence. Willag chose the 4 months, which he served in plus fours.

Many of the earnest evangels who had striven so hard by means of the No-Licence campaign to improve the morals of Wick must have been sadly dismayed at the new wickedness which prohibition had induced in the citizens. They stuck, however, to their guns and Wick remained dry through the twenties, thirties and most of the forties, including the period of the war from 1939 to 1945 which brought into the area many thirsty servicemen whose custom the Wick licensed (now 'unlicensed') victuallers would have been delighted to accept.

'Repeal' was the subject of a constant campaign during those years, sustained strongly by the former licensed hotels, retailers and inn-keepers and their numerous supporters. The inn-keepers, many of whom were part or whole fishing-boat owners, distressed by the increasingly poor herring catches from 1931 onwards (except for 1932), sought to attribute this decline to the lack of drink in the town. 'WHY HAVE WE NO FISHING FLEET? they asked in the raucous 'Repeal' pamphlet of 1937, and immediately explained why:

> The answer is simple. In 1919 Wick had a fishing fleet of nearly 100 vessels, owned by Wick business men and manned by Wick fishermen. Who were these owners? Seventy-five per cent were publicans, natives of the town, respectable citizens whose names are readily remembered. Whether the Prohibitionist Party admit it or not, every vote cast for 'No Licence' is a vote cast for 'NO FISHING,' as well as depression, poverty and suffering. The Prohibition Party tell us they are out to improve the town. When are they going to begin? They have had control for 15 years. What have they done? Nothing, absolutely nothing! The Prohibition Party is composed mostly of ministers, who declare Wick must be 'dry', and be an example to the rest of the world. In other words, poor old Wick is the mouse 'Pussyfoot' is to play with for the benefit of the world.[1] If being 'dry' is such a wonderful help to prosperity, why are not other towns following our example? Because they know it is all humbug and untrue. Are ministers themselves

1 'Pussyfoot' was 'the famous W E "Pussyfoot" Johnson, a skilful and humorous American opponent of intoxicating liquor.

sincere? What has any minister done to help the fishworkers of Wick? Last year – and in the previous years – the fishworkers of Wick were fighting for a shilling or two of an increase to their wages to cover the bare necessities of life and the increased cost of living. Did any of the ministers go to their aid? Certainly not.

In any case, as the same pamphlet asked: IS WICK REALLY 'DRY'?

Can anyone honestly say Wick has 'No-Licence'? It is all pure bluff. Wick, as every one knows, has four wholesale licences where you can buy four dozen bottles of beer quite legally. Six or eight men can club together, as they do at present, and purchase beer at any time. The law allows it. How can any one talk of Wick being 'Dry'?

We have a Distillery where one dozen bottles can be purchased. It is a well-known fact that drink is illegally sold in various ways. The Prohibition Party admit this. How then can they say Wick is 'dry'? The undisputed fact is – Wick is not, and never will be, legally dry.

The Americans abandoned prohibition in 1933 after it had assisted into existence a mighty empire of bootleggers and gangsters, famous for their outrageous deeds of savage violence and the corruption induced in many areas of public life. Most of the other localities of Scotland which had opted for prohibition soon had enough of it, but Wick stayed on. It was possible under the Temperance Act, under given conditions, to hold a referendum on 'Continuance' or 'Repeal' every three years. Wick had four such referenda between the wars with the following results:

	Continuance	Repeal	Majority
1923	1329	1002	327
1926	1429	876	548
1931	1405	1294	111
1937	1380	1296	84

Mr Sutherland concludes his account:

On 11 April 1939, Wick Burgh Licensing Court gave permission to the Station and Mackay's hotels to have a licence just in time for the huge numbers of servicemen who arrived at the three active aerodromes and numerous military camps in the county. Outside Wick the pubs and hotels were doing a roaring trade while the shebeeners were picking up the rest. The turnover was not lost on the town and on 10th December,

1946 another poll was held. There was very little excitement as the prohibitionists probably sensed that the time for change had come upon them. The vote was 1941 in favour of Repeal and 1500 for Continuance, a larger vote than put Wick dry in the first place. In May 1947 licences were granted again. So another chapter in the old town's history closed.[1]

Between the Wars.

If the splendid range of photographs of Wick between 1919 and 1939 is anything to go by, superficially the physical aspect of the place did not change greatly. Bridge Street and High Street as the main thoroughfares carried, as now, most of the traffic, but in 1919 there were still many horse-drawn vehicles, while in 1939 motor-cars and trucks had taken over. Shop and other business fronts changed, one of the most notable being the appearance of F W Woolworth's 3d and 6d Stores at the corner of High Street and Tolbooth Lane on the site of what had been the Commercial Bank and the old gaol before it. Street lighting had changed from gas to electricity, though there was not much of either, for it was still evidently felt that light from the shop fronts and windows made up for saving from public expenditure on such amenity.

Pictures of the harbour area look much the same, except that lined along the quays (or crowding at the entrance) are now steam drifters, though still there are brown-sailed 'Fifies' to be seen, even at the later date. The quays look much tidier than at one time, but the work of the gutters and the coopers is being carried in the same numbing conditions as heretofore. A Johnston picture of about 1935 shows the women gutting and sorting the fish 'at a rate of about 40 a minute' in Jock MacLeod's yards at the 'Camps'.

Perhaps the most noticeable difference between 1919 and 1939 is the change in dress. At the earlier date men were still to be seen in bowlers though the flat cap was obviously giving way to other headgear, rather wider than the style than had become fashionable in 1939; the professional folk, solicitors, bankers etc earlier wore the stock or hard collar while later on the soft shirt collar and looser tie is in favour. It is the women whose dress changed most. In 1939 long dresses and wide brimmed, hat-pinned hats are gone, giving place to close, sometimes cloche hats, sometimes none at all. Legs

1 Most of the detail of this episode is derived from Iain Sutherland's pamphlet, *Vote No-Licence*, q.v.

even appear in the picture and it was not unknown for the *Groat* to show a picture of bathing belles in one-piece suits, thighs and arms open to such suns as Wick and Thurso might afford. And at this time Wick had created for itself an open-air seaside pool on the Trinkie Rocks where, when weather permitted, it had become the fashion to resort. Gone completely from the advertisements were the tightly constricted corsetted wasp waists of old time, though the corset was not yet completely abolished. Children too were less covered in with clothes: a picture of the Boy Scouts out on parade in Argyle Square at the lifeboat procession in 1919 shows them in what would now be regarded as very antique garb, while the people watching all look as though they belonged to an ancient past.

Life in the town was considerably improved from the days when the citizens still used their street for the deposit of their waste. Streets cleaner, frontages less dilapidated and lighting generally either in transition or electrified. During the 1920s the Wick Town Council had gone to much trouble to provide itself with its own electricity power station. So considerable the demand for the new, cleaner and more effective source of power and light that, no sooner had the first power station been built than it had to be considerably enlarged. The power station itself, on the Lower Pulteney quay, has now gone, though the area left has an air of disuse and desiccation. The power station's enormous 125 foot chimney stands still, rising truly like the 'stalk' that it would at one time have been called, no ornament to the harbourside landscape.

Schools and school-buildings underwent considerable improvement and extension during the years after the war. The Scottish Education Act of 1918 followed rather different lines from the English (Fisher) Act of the same year, though motivated by the same spate of good resolutions in which the war was ending. By it local school boards were abolished and *ad hoc* county education authorities were created, elected on a common franchise but independently of the county councils themselves. Wick as a royal burgh had its own independently elected 'Divisional' authority, first elected in 1922 with no great surge of popular interest; its six elected members were chosen from 8 candidates only. In most constituencies there was no contest. The *Northern Ensign* soberly observed: 'this is surely indicative of indifference.'[1]

Wick had already provided itself with a fine new High School in

---

1 *Northern Ensign*, 5 April, 1922.

West Banks, opened on 13 August, 1909. In 1917 the Burgh School Board had responsibility for five schools: the High School with 436 pupils, the Academy with 534 (now removed from its original site on Sinclair Terrace to Seaforth Avenue), the South Public School on Macrae Street (556), the North Public in Louisburgh (284) and West Banks School (230).[1] A new North School was built off Henrietta Street and opened on 24 August, 1937. Still a neat-looking school (though now designated Primary only), it was described as 'a handsome, double-storey building, beautifully designed, with modern requirements greatly in advance of the other schools of Wick.'[2] By this date the 'Division' had been dissolved and Wick, for educational purposes, came under the Caithness County Council in 1929, like all counties now a full education authority.

One other public amenity greatly improved and developed during these years was the Carnegie Public Library, described by the *Groat* as 'an up-to-date northern institution'. The library, known from the beginning as the Carnegie Free Library resulted from a grant by the Carnegie Trust in 1897, a few years before the amalgamation of Wick and Pulteneytown. It was built on the corner of Cliff Road and Sinclair Terrace and completed the following year very much as it was designed. It was the subject of an article in the *Groat* in 1927 cast in typical fulsome style and beginning: 'A library well stocked with a good and varied supply of books is an institution highly prized by the reading public. When to this is added good service and courtesy and attention to those who visit the Library then there is an approach to an ideal state of things. This state of affairs is attained in Wick Carnegie Library.'[2]

The tenor of life in Wick during the inter-war years was interrupted from time to time by the usual catalogue of calamities, celebrations and achievements that punctuate the record of most communities. In October, 1923 Field Marshal Lord Horne unveiled the Wick War Memorial; a memorial was unveiled to Dr Alexander, the first and prestigious medical officer of health of Caithness County; trains got stuck in the snow and in June 1931 much of Wick went under water as

---

1 See *Times Gone By*, 25 December, 1937.
2 Ibid, 25 December, 1926; and *Northern Ensign*, 4 April, 1897.

Note: many of the events mentioned in this section are either pictured or recorded (or both) in *Times Gone By*, (1991); *Times Gone By* (1993); *Postcards from Caithness*, (1992); *and Vintage Wick: A Photographic History of the Royal Burgh of Wick and its People; Quatercentenary, 1589-1989*; all compiled by Clive Richards and published by North of Scotland Newspapers, Wick.

the Wick River overflowed its banks after an especially wet season. In 1936 the old 'Service Bridge', originally constructed to allow the passage of traffic while the Telford Bridge was replaced in 1877, was dismantled to make room for a new Wick Harbour Bridge. Fires destroyed George Davidson's shop in High Street, and McEwen's furniture yard in George Street in 1937. Though hardly at the centre of things, many of Wick's tradesmen came out in the General Strike in 1926. A new Post Office was built in Market Square and in 1937 the town took a day off to mark the end of the short reign of Edward VIII and the arrival of George VI.

THE SECOND 'GREAT WAR' – 1939-1945.

Though perhaps not quite so well informed by the *John O'Groat Journal* about international affairs before 1939 as before 1914, the people of Wick once again could not complain that they were left unaware of what had been going on during the last twenty years. In any case, these were the years when the 'wireless' came into common use; indeed, it was his manipulation of the 'wireless' that, above all, enabled Adolf Hitler to gain such a command over the minds of the German people, playing on their shame of defeat from 1919.

As in the first war, Caithness was subject to restriction and 'blackout' of news from the moment the new war between Britain and Germany broke out, 3rd September, 1939, but war-time restrictions this time were more severe. 'Censorship', according to Norman Glass, was summed up in the expression 'Thou shalt not':

> Thou shalt not mention a ship, a 'plane, or an army lorry, or anything that happened to them; thou shalt not comment on the weather or give the whereabouts of the boys from home, nor give particulars of Service men met or entertained; neither any clue whatsoever likely to be of value to the enemy. Dare not say that a bomb or mine exploded in your district. 'Thou shalt not' made letter-writing a confined and trying affair.

A particularly onerous restriction was the censorship of all civilian mail, even between localities in Caithness itself. All mail went to Inverness for scrutiny – 'even medicine posted by a chemist'; a letter from Wick to Thurso could take five days or more. Perhaps all this was understandable; but less forgivable was the incredible meanness by which the military authorities prevented friends and relatives from seeing off men of the 5th Seaforth Highlanders on the day after the

WAR AND RUMOURS OF WAR: II

outbreak, 4 September, as they entrained at Thurso Station. The Wick Company went off by bus from the Drill Hall in Dempster Street, the buses passing along streets lined with people, giving the men a good send-off. How different from the surging crowds that gathered on Wick and Thurso stations in 1914.

Other things were quite different too. For all its nearness to the maritime action of the first war, Wick never heard the guns from 1914 to 1918 (except rumbles from Scapa Flow); from October, 1939, Wick and the north of Caithness were in the war zone itself, in fact for several months, the only part of Britain that was directly under attack. The county's proximity to Scapa Flow was the reason for this immediate vulnerability, for Hitler's navy and airforce were disposed to attempt, if not a knockout at once, at least a highly significant couple of symbolic attacks in the Flow, on the assumption that the British were by no means yet ready for an attack. And they were not.

On the night of 13/14 October, the German U-47 under its Commander Günther Prien made a daring entry into the Flow near to midnight through the Kirk Sound, one of the eastern passages from the North Sea into Scapa and attacked the battleship, HMS *Royal Oak*, only recently come to anchor in Scapa Bay. U-47 fired its torpedoes and sent *Royal Oak* with 833 officers and men of the entire ship's company of 1400 to the bottom. Among British commentators, the most outrageous aspect of the episode was the ease with which the U-Boat was allowed to escape, through the same unguarded passage. This was a very palpable hit, winning for Prien the first naval Iron Cross of the war.

Three days later came another attack, highly symbolic too if less destructive of life. Norman Glass continues his story:

> There were five sharp bomb attacks . . . Fourteen 'planes were engaged in two attacks on October 17, 1939, and the *Iron Duke*, a depot and training ship, was damaged. Two enemy bombers were shot down . . . . The weather was fine on that October day, and it was an awe-inspiring spectacle as, amid thunderous droning of planes, the guns of ships and shore batteries rattled up hundreds of rounds and produced curtains of bursts in the sunny and almost cloudless sky.

Glass, for all the detail of his account, misses entirely the significance of these first attacks. He fails to mention at all the sinking of the *Royal Oak*, remembered by many people still alive as a fearful traumatic event, and commemorated annually by a wreath-laying ceremony above the 'war-grave' in the Flow of 833 seamen. On a smooth day oil seepage from the *Oak* may still be seen lining across Scapa Bay. The *Royal Oak's* bell hangs in a place of honour in Kirkwall Cathedral.

The *Iron Duke,* it must be said, was something more than a mere 'depot and training ship'. The great battleship had in fact, been Jellicoe's flagship at Jutland, a well-scarred old veteran. She was in October, 1939 moored off Lyness in the Flow. What exactly was to be her use is not quite certain, but she was still the flagship and the senior of all the ships then in Scapa Flow. She was a deliberately marked target of the *Luftwaffe.* On the 17th, four bombs were dropped around her, and she was holed and began to sink. On board she had numbers of the survivors of the *Royal Oak.* She was beached off Lyness and served for the rest of the war as a base headquarters.[1]

Thus, in the first few days, Hitler had accomplished two dramatic and well publicised – in Germany – acts of revenge. The war had begun in the north, literally 'with a vengeance'. There was a strategic benefit to Germany too. The Flow was immediately, though temporarily, evacuated.

A significant difference between 1914-1918 and 1939-1945 as far as Wick and Caithness are concerned, is the existence of a near contemporary record of main events in the second war, *Caithness and the War, 1939-1945,* written and compiled by Norman Glass – already quoted, a reporter at the time of the *John O'Groat Journal.* Most of Mr Glass's stories, however, could not be told at the time on account of the news blackout, and most were written from recollections as soon as the war ended. As compared with Dugal MacEchern's pretentious *Sword of the North,* Glass's book, recently re-published, is an excellent and sometimes moving composition, concluding with a full and detailed record of all those 'killed or died on service'.[2]

War Comes to Wick.

However 'phoney' the war might have seemed to those further south during the early months, Orkney and Caithness had sharp notice that Hitler meant business. Wick had its first air raid warning

---

1 Hewison, op cit: pp 255-263.
2 N M Glass: *Caithness and the War, 1939-1945;* Wick, North of Scotland Newspapers (re-issue 1994). To repeat here all of Glass's story would be gratuitous, as the book is readily available; but it is the main source of such comments as are made in this book about the Second World War.

on 17 October. Planes had been seen at great height over Caithness, and this first time round there was alarm in the town:

> Few people in the streets were carrying gas masks when the alarm warning came and many hurried home for the protecting facepiece. Police patrolled the streets in steel helmets and with gasmasks at the alert position. The police cars, too, were busy careering through the streets and ringing bells as a warning of danger. Excitement was everywhere – everyone believed the war had come to the county. Forty minutes elapsed before the 'All Clear' signal was given.

This was by no means Wick's last encounter with the *Luftwaffe*. The next was a by-product of the fourth attack by the *Luftwaffe* on Orkney, when on 8 April, 1940, there was an air battle between the German planes and British Hurricanes over Stroma. A Heinkel damaged over Orkney was pursued by Hurricanes and descended. Rather than ditch in the sea the pilot chose to land on Wick aerodrome; two men were killed and two became prisoners, Wick's first 'capture' of the war.

There was another heavy raid on Orkney two days later, with sixty bombers, seven of which were lost in the battle and others damaged. These, as Glass puts it, 'hirpled home in a crippled state.' The alarms were sounded in Thurso and Wick, 'and the sounds of gunfire and explosions were heard and the sky was lit up with the shellfire and the groping fingers of searchlights.' There was perturbation in Wick. 'ARP personnel promptly manned all posts, but happily their services were not needed. Danger threatened, however, and the townspeople were made aware of this because of the great activity over Wick – flights of Hudsons flying around continuously.' People 'flocked to the sea-fronts (foolishly it might have been) to gaze upon the distant scene.' Gunfire was often heard as was 'the crash of explosives, some of them sounding uncomfortably near.'

Wick itself was bombed. This occurred on 1 July, 1940 when an enemy plane 'released two bombs in the vicinity of the harbour. Fifteen citizens lost their lives and 22 sustained injuries. The dead comprised seven children, five men, and three women.' Serious damage done to houses and shops in Bank Row, providing the opportunity for the taking of what became, for the record, two of the most famous war pictures ever taken in Wick, the ruined houses and shops in that street. This attack is believed to have been the first daylight attack on mainland Britain of the war.

Glass's story deserves quoting:

German 'planes were far from Wick thoughts that Monday afternoon (the time would be about 4.40) when there was an alarming explosion that could be heard for miles around. The bombs fell within yards of each other on a hard road surface in Bank Row. The craters made were neither wide nor deep and the surface gave great play to the blast. The bombs falling and exploding simultaneously gave the effect of one crash – the loudest the townspeople had ever heard. A pall of black smoke rising skywards marked the spot.

The plane came in low from a westerly direction flying seawards and was seen by many – indeed it was fired at by an alert gunner at a South head battery as it passed over the bay on its homeward way.

There was an unforgettable scene. Buildings in Bank Row, comprising four shops and four dwellings, were shattered completely and property in Rose Street also suffered badly. Dead and injured lay among the debris, and those able to struggle clear staggered away dazed. Window panes were wrenched from their sockets over a wide area. A peaceful scene was in a moment replaced by ruin, wreckage, dust, tears, blood, excitement.

Wick's Civil Defence services (particularly rescue, first-aid and ambulance parties) responded quickly that afternoon and undertook much helpful work. The large number of casualties imposed heavy additional work upon the regular staff of the Bignold Hospital, but with the aid of medical practitioners (one came 20 miles to help) and a number of ladies (formerly trained nurses) who volunteered for service, the injured received due attention.

Yet another attack was made on the town on 20 October, 1940, much heavier but causing far less loss of life. The attack, made by three Heinkels, was meant for the aerodrome and more than 20 high explosives 'were dropped on the north side of the town'. Although the explosions 'shook the town' quite a number of the bombs actually failed to explode. A bungalow in Hill Avenue on the north edge of town received a direct hit, and adjacent bungalows and houses were seriously damaged, also house property in Rosebery Terrace, Henrietta and George Street.'

Bailie Duncan Sinclair 'stepped off a train that evening to find his home in Rosebery Terrace wrecked. "Nothing but the stairs standing," was how he put it, "but the old grandfather clock was still ticking in the lobby although its hands were blown away."' The Bignold Hospital, then the town's hospital, 'was within a hundred yards of some of the explosions and its windows were shattered, doors torn from hinges, and plaster stripped from the walls and ceiling by blast.' The nurses and doctors 'gamely continued an uninterrupted service for casualties.' Patients were later evacuated to a new school at Lybster which was adapted as a hospital for the rest of the war.

Perhaps the most touching sequel to this raid was the story told by George Cameron, a boy of 14 who lived with his family in the Hill Avenue bungalow destroyed in the raid. His brother, sister and another woman in the house were killed; he and his mother were badly injured. George spent the next three months in hospital and some time later responded to a teacher's invitation to write about 'The Greatest Experience of My Life' with a graphic and intensely felt account of his ordeal, both the shock of the bombing and his painful recovery in hospital. Norman Glass reproduces the whole essay but three particularly moving paragraphs are repeated here to illustrate the vividness of George's reconstruction of events:

> Suddenly there was a terrific flash, accompanied by a dreadful explosion. My brain seemed to snap and everything became a blank for a brief moment. I had then a terrible sensation. It seemed as if an electric current had been put into my body. My skin began to tingle while my chest and throat gradually began to tighten - tighten. I could feel myself being thrown in the air. Several times I felt searing pains in my legs as if a naked knife had been thrust into them. Suddenly everything became black and faded away.
>
> When I regained consciousness my eyes were clamped shut and it seemed they would never open. My face was wet with blood while my hair was plastered down on my head with a mixture of lime and blood. All the power had gone out of my body and it was only by a determined effort that I moved my arm across the ground to find that I was lying on a heap of stoney rubble. The air around me was filthy with gas fumes.

George and his mother were taken to hospital:

> When we reached hospital, it was then I began to shiver. I shivered and shook uncontrollably. I realised I was hurt, terribly hurt. My clothes were hanging in tatters on my battered body .... A little while after I felt a needle prick in my arm and

everything faded away. It was not until two days later that I saw daylight again. My neck was horribly stiff and my face – well, it was unrecognisable. My arms and face, not to speak of my legs, had been badly burned and a purple liquid had been painted on them. This liquid had become solid, so you can imagine what I was like. The next three days were simply awful. Every morning my legs had to be dressed. The dressings had to be pulled off my wounds, but as I was somewhat dazed I did not feel that much.

There were other occasions when Wick and district attracted the attentions of *Luftwaffe* pilots, as for example when on 4 June, 1941, a raider 'attacked with bombs and machine guns. It sprayed the streets before and after attacking the 'drome, where a hangar was set on fire.' At other times a seine-net fishing boat off the Wick coast was attacked with machine-gun fire, as were lighthouses here and in the Pentland Firth. The German airmen were, however, chiefly interested in the military objectives, such as the airfield and radio installations at Reiss. 'Luckily for Wick,' says Mr Glass, 'it did not experience indiscriminate bombing otherwise the town would have been a shambles.' He moralises on the issue: 'But while we give the *Luftwaffe* credit for sparing the town, the attacks on fishing craft and lighthouses are unforgivable. For longer than the living can recall the lighthouse has been the friend to men of all nations. Its striking whiteness is symbolical of its untainted record of service.'

By comparison with Wick, Thurso, through which thousands of servicemen were continually passing on their way to and from Orkney, had only one bomb, dropped on the town's refuse tip outside the burgh boundary, where it left a deep crater.

Wings Over Wick.

Wick's chief embattlement was its airfield, on what was once the Hill of Wick, a mile north of the town, and now its airport. It was partially completed before the war started. The airfield incorporated the new North School of Wick, only recently completed at a cost of £20,000, and used it as headquarters. It later took over the Bignold Hospital when that hospital had been repaired after being damaged by the bomb raid on 26 October, 1940, and used it as a casualty centre.

Another airfield was constructed at Skitten in 1940 and still another at Castletown. Various other 'war-time stations appeared – at

Tannach, Ulbster, Warth Hill, Noss' etc, all mainly to do with radio and, in later stages, radar. Perhaps the most interesting of the 'RAF' establishments was that at Thrumster on the Redmire moss, in fact, a dummy airfield, intended to attract and divert German airmen from more important sites. Some anti-aircraft batteries were located in the area, and certainly the *Luftwaffe* made some raids on the dummy airfield, two in March, 1941, when bombs were dropped and houses in the district were machine-gunned, though there is some doubt as to whether or not the real target was the dummy airfield - possibly Ulbster radio installations were in the bombers' sights. There was another raid in May, 1941 and 'during the next two months Thrumster had further unpleasant visits from units of the *Luftwaffe*, and bombs exploding there were always heard very distinctly in Wick.' It is to be hoped that the attacks were genuinely on the 'decoy 'drome', for Glass reckons that with its dummy planes it cost 'a bit of expense'. One cherished story in Wick is that at least one German pilot knew about the fake and was not deceived and accordingly dropped on it a wooden bomb; the story ought to be true though probably is not.

Glass describes the general circumstances of the RAF presence at Wick:

> The [Wick] station was under Coastal Command. The 'planes undertook much reconnaissance work (particularly photographic), played an important part in conquering the U-boat campaign, the bombing of targets in Norway and enemy shipping off the Norwegian coast and U-boat dispositions in the fjords. Many of the operational flights were successfully peformed, not always without loss and sometimes at heavy cost.

Among the Squadrons that at one stage or another were stationed at Wick (and sometimes overlapping) were 269, 48 and 608, and 220. Wick folk became very accustomed to seeing many different kinds of aircraft in the air above the town – beside Heinkels – including Hurricanes, Spitfires, Lockheed Hudsons, Whitley and Wellington bombers, Hampdens, Bristol Beaufighters, Warwicks, Liberators, Mosquitos and, in the later stages, Fortresses, in fact, most of the types flown by the British and later the Americans during the war. The airfield was fortified against attack, the defences being manned by a detachment of the RAF Regiment, while many inside and some field duties were performed by 'a great number of women'.

The expression *Wings over Wick* is quoted from a remarkable compilation recently published in Wick, telling the stories of a number of RAF people about their stay in the area at various times during the war. These were collected by children of the Hillhead Primary School, as part of an environmental studies project. They wrote to many men and women who had been stationed at Wick. The school, of course, had been part of the station. The 'memories' are immensely varied as to experience, as flyers, observers, gunners, riggers, armourers, cookhouse personnel, plotters, drivers and typists. They tell of actual sorties and other events, life on the base at Wick and Skitten, connections with and impressions of the town and encounters with the people of Wick. The book gives an insight into the feelings and attitudes of people involved that no ordinary 'history' could convey, and the variety and colour cannot possibly be represented here. A few examples must suffice.[1]

The first listed contributor, a former Wing Commander of the 269 Squadron tells of his arrival at Wick as a young Pilot Officer at the age of 21, a 'shattering experience for someone who had been brought up in the south of England. I was entering a strange, bleak land and I began to wonder what my destination would be like.' His first night was spent comfortably in the Station Hotel (now no longer a hotel). 'The buildings were solidly built but rather drab and the shape of the few trees I saw gave warning that the prevailing wind could be very strong indeed. There were two cinemas, a Woolworths and a number of small shops. The only other major hotel was Mackays which had been taken over as a officers' mess for a fighter squadron [this is doubtless how Mackay's was able to get its special licence to sell spirits!]'. The Wing Commander tells of his many flights from Wick in all kinds of weathers mainly on reconnaissance,

> but not all flights were against the enemy. We did a lot of practice bombing and firing of guns and had to air-test our aircraft after major service. Another flight which comes to mind was a mercy mission – a train had been marooned in deep snow near Forsinard or Frozenhard as we nicknamed it. The emergency rations had been consumed by the passengers and the situation was serious. We used an old Avro Tutor open cockpit aircraft to drop food to them. The dual control column in the rear cockpit was removed and I sat there with a sack of food on my lap. At the appropriate moment I threw the sack

---

1 *Wings Over Wick, 1939-1945: A collection of memories of RAF Wick:* Primary 7, Hillhead Primary School (1989).

over the side hoping it would not hit the tail plane.

The Wing Commander met his wife in Wick, as did quite a lot of other servicemen. Among the pleasures afforded by Wick were the films at the 'Breadalbane' (the 'Breadline') and the 'Pavilion' in High Street. Many profess never to have heard of the place before they came here. 'An aircrew man who came in 1943 wrote: "It even had a Woolworths," I was told. After Tiree it was civilisation. Not only Woolworths but a library, a hospital and a cinema. Most of all for me there was a railway station and a harbour with the latter walking distance from the airfield.' (It is interesting that so many mentioned Wick's possession of a Woolworth's as an indication of its being a 'civilised place'). A common complaint was the lack of pubs in Wick, but one relief was that the airfield had a good NAAFI. Universally the servicemen found that 'the people in Wick were kind, and we integrated well.'

One specially interesting story is that of the Heinkel that pancaked on to Wick airfield on 8 April, 1940. It is told first of all from the point of view of Sgt Jim Hallowes, a Hurricane pilot who was credited with the capture, having chased and fired on two Heinkels flying across his path from Orkney. They disappeared into rain clouds, and as Hallowes came out of the cloud to land at Wick he saw one of the two Heinkels following him down 'on to the flarepath but it was so badly damaged it made a forced landing.' The story, as told by Peter Townsend in *Duel of Eagles*, declares that the German pilot, one of the two out of the crew of four who survived, claimed he had been shot down by a Spitfire, a case of what Townsend had identified as 'Spitfire Snobbery', a dislike that some German pilots are supposed to have developed of being thought to have been shot down by anything less formidable than a Spitfire. There were other stories of this event.

A young WAAF who was billeted in 'what used to be married quarters' tells of her gay life in Wick:

> The hot water system was a back boiler in the downstairs of the house where the [aircraft] plotters lived, so we had no control over the hot water, even though we did have a bathroom. However, we did have weird Heath-Robinson contraptions (no doubt highly dangerous) to heat water, baked beans or anything we could lay our hands on. These were the elements from electric fires, laid uppermost in a roasting tin and fixed into the light sockets. As all the light sockets were used in this way for a pan of water for washing or frying eggs

collected from the Hen-wifey who lived on a croft at Staxigoe, the lighting in our flat was done by candles. It was so cold in Wick in winter we very rarely washed all over and we went to bed with more clothes than we worked in. The weight of the army blankets topped by a greatcoat on top meant you were so weighed down in bed you could hardly move.

With Wick being a dry town, it gave us an impetus for a lot of expeditions to the places outside the town – the excuse being for a drink. We could have drink if we went to the Rosebank overlooking the park for a meal. But most of the fun was making up a party and all piling into one small car owned by one of the pilots to go to Lybster. The car was so overloaded that I can remember the local policeman passing us on his bike. I can also remember sitting on the dicky seat at the back holding up the lid, then someone let go of the lid and it crashed down and knocked me out, and they all carried me into the Portland Arms at Lybster. The dances in the villages were great fun, and there were always events like the best male ankles, when a lot of men stood on the stage rolling up their trousers, a blanket was held in front and great deliberations went on choosing the best ankles.

We also went to dances at the Rifle Hall and on a Wednesday at the Breadalbane picture house when they used to take out the cinema seats for the dance, so you danced up the hill one way and down the hill the next.

'I have only amusing memories of Wick despite the terrible weather. My [other] wartime service was in the Far East and I have never been back to Wick,' wrote J W Hazeldine of Sedgley, West Midlands.

The Tread of Tackety Boots.

It is with these words that Norman Glass introduces his comments on the army in Caithness during 1939-1945. 'There were,' he says, 'soldiers from every corner of the globe' from Dunkirk onwards. 'Sodgers, sodgers, sodgers everywhere.' The majority were soldiers of the Highland Regiments, Camerons, Seaforths, Black Watch, HLI, Lovat Scouts and 'dozens of others as well,' Royal Engineers, Artillery, Pioneers, Royal Army Service Corps, Royal Army Medical Corps, Ayrshire Yeomanry. Complete units of Polish forces, too.

They occupied all available buildings, built camps in rural areas, and they 'mixed freely with the natives'. The Seamen's Mission, the Salvation Army and many other voluntary groups set up canteens and recreation centres. Since RAF were allowed to bring their wives into the area, the army had to be allowed the same privilege, and hundreds of wives helped to swell the population of Wick from its normal 7,500 to something like 20,000 which, if nothing else, served to boost the local economy on a grand scale. 'Happily, the available rations sufficed for all,' says Glass, but if stories are to be believed, as in Orkney, local farmers did excellent business rearing chickens and supplying the visitors and lodgers with eggs and other produce well in excess of the allowances elsewhere in Britain. In a sense, Caithness and Orkney, 'never had it so good,' and the end of the war was not so great a blessing locally as perhaps it might have been. Many are the stories too of hospitality and good fellowship generated in the area.

Naval men contributed to the throng. 'Minesweepers occasionally put in as also did Tank Landing Craft,' and occasionally a few foreign sailors put in an appearance. Glass continues:

> But the Navy was still the popular service in the Far North. A visit to the picture-house was convincing on this point whenever a march-past was depicted. The Army got a cheer, the Airforce got a cheer, but the Navy – well, you have heard of the Hampden roar! 'The sea' is still in the blood of the Northman and the young ever yearn to follow 'out where the crested billows foam, out where the fresh winds blow.'

Perhaps the most surprising addition to the population of Caithness was the arrival in the last year of the war of 1600 German prisoners of war, housed in an internment camp at Watten. The prisoners were put to work on farms, denuded of labour by the call-up, and although officially they were not allowed to 'fraternise' they got on well with the locals. Some were employed on the aerodromes and towards the end it was no uncommon occurrence to meet unguarded prisoners on the streets of Wick. 'Though maybe at heart unwilling guests, the German prisoners generally were docile in captivity.' They doubtless knew what they were missing.

Most of the more permanent British service residents manned the many batteries, especially those protecting service installations and mounted on the coasts, as for instance on Noss Head, North and South Wick Heads and other prominences. Whatever similarities there may have been between preparations to combat the enemy in this part of the world, there was one great difference: in the first war coastal counter-action was directed against attack from the sea; in the second the main apprehension was of attack from the air, so that many of the batteries, artillery and search-light, were for anti-aircraft purposes.

In the early years of the war there was also expectation that at some stage the Germans would invade, and some parts of the Caithness coast were regarded as likely places for landings. That there was some such intention was confirmed at the end of the war when German documents and maps were captured and examined, but it now seems improbable that such intention was a high priority, for Caithness itself offered no strategic advantages to an invasion force whose chief object would have been to strike at the heavily populated industrial heart of Britain, even that of central Scotland – and a long way from it. However that may be, in addition to gun batteries, parts of the Caithness coast, mainly north of Wick were prepared for resistance to forces landing from the sea. The links between Reiss and Keiss in Sinclair's Bay were thought to be the most likely place for such landings, and along great lengths of the shore-line were constructed huge sets of anti-tank concrete blocks, many of which are still there. Similar lines of anti-tank defences were set up in Freswick Bay too. A huge mileage of barbed wire was also thrown along the coasts and round the Wick burgh boundaries; and in places were erected small block-houses and look-outs. Such a pair is still to be seen along the beach on the north side of Keiss harbour, between the remnants of ancient brochs and the later Keiss Castle. All represent aspects of the response of people in the north to the danger of invasion by their enemies, the 1939-1945 pill boxes no less than the earlier structures. A good case could be made for preserving one or two to allow posterity to catch a glimpse of twentieth century coastal defence, but such as remain are rapidly crumbling.

Several stretches of the coast, too, were heavily mined. Glass describes the section in Sinclair Bay which, he says:

> was heavily mined by the Royal Engineers in the early months of 1941 [as an earnest, it might be said, of Churchill's stern warning to the enemy that we should 'fight them on the beaches'] – indeed the sands here were said to constitute the largest minefield in the United Kingdom. Between Keiss and Ackergill there was a continuous belt three and a half miles long and about 50 yards wide. These mines were originally laid in three rows and 20 feet apart. They were of the large anti-

personnel variety known as beach-mines, containing a heavy weight of explosive, and had been buried with the lid about six inches below ground level.

Not the least of post-war problems in the area was the removal of the mines, many of which had been shifted inland and swept into the sand of the dunes by the violence of the sea. When Glass wrote in 1946, clearance work had been going on for eighteen months and 'although more than 2000 mines have been located and destroyed the whole area is not yet regarded as "safe".'

One other post-war clearance job was the demolition of anti-invasion installations in the Wick harbour area itself. The earlier history of the Wick harbour had included long periods of intense and expensive construction, some of which installations as we know were catastrophically demolished by the elements. One of the early jobs of the war had been the creation by Royal Engineers of elaborate means for demolishing harbour walls and piers by explosive if and when the invaders came, seeking to 'come in through the front door, so to speak:'

> Batteries (including searchlights) were stationed on the headlands surrounding the bay, and flame-throwers were installed at the harbour entrance – not at small expense, it was said. The harbour quays were mined, ready for destruction, and road blocks were erected on all streets leading from the harbour and the bridges. Reinforced blockhouses were constructed at vantage points overlooking the bay and along the roadsides . . . The old steam-drifters *Lottie* and *Isabella Ferguson* were held in readiness for many months at the entrances to the old and new harbours, to be sunk there and so block the channels in the event of an attack. Troops were trained for this protective manoeuvre – and then sent abroad!

German prisoners, among others, were in 1946 put to the work of demolition of all these installations meant to discourage them from coming here in the first place. One other precaution against the successful landing of German troops in Caithness was the placing of poles in all the fields around the town thought to be useable as landing grounds for planes and gliders. These also, had to be removed. As in many other areas of Britain, all road signs were removed, though it is doubtful that this measure would have had much effect in discouraging the invaders from going where they willed.

Sea mines, British and German, as once before, littered the North Sea. Sometimes these floated free, and during 1941 a naval demolition squad was kept busy answering calls about beached mines 'all the way from Helmsdale to Duncansby Head'. The mines were usually killed by controlled explosion, *in situ*, but this sometimes meant a noisy time for seaside inhabitants, and the loss of their windows. Keiss and Papigoe are said to have suffered quite a bit. One night, 15/16 March, 1941, inhabitants of houses at the seaward end of Keiss were called from their beds at eleven o'clock so that some particularly dangerously located mine could be exploded.

'Several mines floated into Wick Bay,' says Glass. One such 'unwelcome visitor' came floating in 'during a high sea on a bitterly cold Saturday afternoon in November, 1941.' People watched it
> on its passage around the rocky coast towards the harbour where it almost came into heavy contact with the seaward end of the south pier. The sea clutched it away again and guided it on to the beach at Shaltigoe. There it was hurled to and fro by advancing and receding waves. It rolled on its horns – and nothing happened. Watchers believed it to be a 'dud'. Everyone had not taken police advice to get to the rear portions of the houses along the sea-front.
>
> The mine rolled again and the 'dud' exploded with a terrific bang that shook the town. Houses vibrated and slates from the roof-tops clattered to the ground in Smith Terrace and Bexley Terrace. Windows went west on a wholesale scale and the roadways became a mass of broken glass. Other streets in the vicinity did not escape unscathed. The explosion flung showers of stones from the sea-shore on to the streets above the brae. The electricity power station suffered severely, and about 150 houses were damaged.

Luckily no-one was injured. More than a thousand window panes had to be replaced, and on the Saturday evening a fierce blaze broke out in the Co-op bake-house, and 'despite the all-night efforts of three fire brigades against a conflagration whipped by a semi-hurricane wind the bakery, a store house and club premises were wholly destroyed. The damage amounted to several thousand pounds.'

Another calamity during 1941 was the burning down of the administrative block of the Town and County Hospital. A Whitley bomber preparing to land, circled the town several times and on a turn one of its wings touched the main hospital building and the plane came down on top of it. The block caught fire immediately and was gutted. The six members of the crew of the bomber were lost, and two maids in an attic bedroom of the block also died in the blaze. Patients from adjoining wards were all evacuated, but the fire remained confined to the administrative block.

Mercifully, the two major fires that lit up Wick during 1941 did not attract the attention of enemy flyers. 'What havoc would have ensued had one or two hostile aircraft dropped bombs among the dense crowds of sight-seers who watched the proceedings. Truly, Wick had a guardian angel on these nights.'

The summer crisis of 1940 led to the formation of the LDV, the Local Defence Volunteers, and by July, 1940 they had assembled a full battalion of 1540 men, many of them veterans from the trenches of the earlier war, Wick recruiting strongly. As the local 'Home Guard' Company (as they were re-named), these home defence soldiers took their role very seriously, meeting for training twice a week and undertaking periodic week-end exercises. In November, 1942, the town was 'invaded' by regular troops after it had been 'blitzed' (by Wellingtons). The invaders broke through the defences but were accused by the Home Guard of cheating by using 'dead men'.

The Home Guard was stood down in December, 1944, after the opening of the Second Front had quite eliminated the danger of invasion. 700 Home Guardsmen paraded to the Old Parish Church. In 1943, No 3 Platoon of the Wick Coy entered the Macworth Praed challenge trophy competition in which some 1600 teams took part, 25, including Wick, qualifying for the grand final which the Wick platoon went on to win with a score of 983 out of 1000 points. They repeated the triumph in the following year with the slightly lower score of 976. The Germans might have congratulated themselves that they did not often have to face marksmen of the calibre of the No 3 Platoon, A Company, the Wick Battalion of the Home Guard.

As for the Wick response to the general call-up, it was as enthusiastic as in the first war, with some of the veterans themselves enrolling as well as the conscripted young men between 18 and 40. Most of the men, as before, joined the 5th Seaforths and the Camerons, and saw service in France, North Africa and Italy and again in France as members of the 51st Highland Division, carrying with them an enviable prestige from the Division's 1914-1918 campaigns. This time the 51st had the honour of being the last away from Dunkirk, having fought the gallant rearguard that enabled 330,000 of the defeated British forces to return to Britain.

When in 1944 the Division returned to France they were fêted by the citizens of St Valéry-en-Caux where they had held up the Germans. The Division marched triumphantly through the liberated little town. After Dunkirk the 51st had re-trained and taken the long trip round the Cape to play a distinguished part in the Battle of El Alamein in October, 1942. They continued with Montgomery through North Africa, into Sicily and on to Italy. They took part in the D-Day landings, and were among the first British troops to enter Germany and to cross the Rhine.

Another unit that had a largely Wick identity was the 140th LAA (Light Anti-Aircraft) Battery, which in April, 1942, together with two other batteries formed the 40th LAA Regiment. Such batteries and regiments were a relative rarity in the first war, but in the second, aircraft of every kind represented a main arm. Anti-aircraft artillery had accordingly been developed to a high stage of sophistication. The first group formed in Caithness, 301 Troop, had their headquarters in the Rifle Hall in Wick. Their first stint of duty was across the Pentland Firth as part of the Orkney Defence, many of the men being based on Flotta very near to the main action over Lyness during the early months. Then they went out to provide AA protection for their fellow Caithnessians of the 51st Division on their way round to Egypt and left the Division to return home after the successful landing on Sicily. Again with their fellows they went across to France on D-Day, and campaigned through to the crossing of the German frontier. They were disbanded at the end of March, 1945, there being few German aircraft left to shoot down. Altogether some 71 army service people were killed and are commemorated on the Wick War Memorial. There is a line of graves of servicemen along the south wall of Wick Cemetery, a large number of them being RAF and naval men the majority of them not local, 22 of them 'unknown'.

As before, the Navy took in a lot of Wick men. They undertook service in almost every kind of vessel and between them must have visited every scene of activity in which the Royal Navy was involved. Forty-one seamen and naval ancillaries are named on the Wick memorial as having been killed or died, more than a third of all the Wick men lost. It must have been one of the largest proportions of seamen lost from any community in Britain.

Quite a large number of women from Wick served in uniform during this war, a much more socially accepted form of service than in the earlier war. Most were in the ATS, but several did distinguished work in the nursing service; but the really significant contribution of the women of Wick was made in the canteens, cookhouses, and in their own homes, providing lodging and hospitality to servicemen and many of their wives in every quarter of Wick, burgh and parish.

The 'Jellicoe Express' ran throughout the Second World War bringing up and taking away even more troops than during the First. It gets little honourable mention in the records, but at least one good story is told of it. The train was now pulled by two Hiker-Class locomotives:

> These great gleaming engines were kept in the loco sheds at Wick and were driven up to Thurso through Georgemas each day to hitch on to the coach loads of troops and Navy men waiting to go on leave, or posting through London.
>
> In the early part of the war – January, 1941 – the north suffered one of the worst blizzards in living memory, with one snow block after another on the line between Helmsdale and Georgemas.
>
> George Seaton [nephew of James, the former stationmaster of Golspie who nearly had his head taken off by a flying wheel of the 'Jellicoe'], recalls that Donald Grant, the permanent way inspector, was hard-pressed to find a way through to get the trains running again. Eventually he ordered – 'Send for Barney Taylor and twa Hikers!'
>
> Apart from the powerful Hikers, Barney Taylor from Wick was a legendary driver who, despite his diminutive size, was a giant on the footplate.
>
> Barney Taylor hitched his pilot engine to another and they went out from Wick with a massive snow plough and charged the deep drifts between Scotscalder and Altnabreac. Every window in the two locomotives was smashed, and even the pedestrian plates on the footbridge at Georgemas were dislodged by the speed of the steam battering ram.
>
> But Barney was able to telegraph back from Forsinard that he had broken through the snow blocks to allow the Jellicoe express to run.
>
> Donald Grant, the inspector, was so pleased that he treated the four footplate men to a dram in the Forsinard Hotel, George Seaton recalled.[1]

---

1 *The Northern Times*, 2 April, 1982. This is almost certainly the same blizzard during which Wing Commander Wheatley Smith did an unorthodox job of flying out food to the beleagured train, full no doubt of servicemen in a veritable passion of disgust.

Barney Taylor, the legendary engine-driver of Wick, is still spoken of. His son, Alistair Taylor, is manager of the Claymore Creamery, Wick.

The war came to an end in two instalments: 8 May when Victory in Europe was declared, and 14 August when Japan capitulated. On both occasions there was bell ringing and thanksgiving services. The most joyous of the victory celebrations was the lighting-up in the shops and streets after so many years of drear and darkness. Bonfires were lit in the streets of Wick: 'fireworks cracked all over the town, and bursting rockets sparkled in the misty air; there were sounds of music, song and laughter – merry-makers sang, they cheered and they danced; flags reappeared, and all was gay. Once again,' says Glass grandly, 'the beacon lights of Freedom gleamed brightly.'

WICK AND THE BOMB – *The War to End Wick!*

'The best that victory can give us is to banish from the earth the threat of war and the causes of war; to preserve mankind from fear and want, oppression and tyranny.' So declared Norman Glass at the end of his *Caithness and the War*. He had brought his account of the war in the east to an end with some comments on what was, on any showing, the most drastic and most brutally effective ending to any war, ever:

> Japan's homeland was seriously threatened and her surrender was hastened by the entry of Russia into the war against her and by the use of a new and fearful weapon of annihilation, the atomic bomb. The first fell on Hiroshima, a military stronghold, and was reckoned to have destroyed two-thirds of the city with an awful thoroughness. A Tokio broadcast said that it literally 'seared to death all living things, human and animal, in Hiroshima. Those outdoors were burned to death and those indoors were killed by the indescribable pressure and heat.' The second bomb fell on Nagasaki and again caused widespread devastation.
>
> The use of such an inhuman weapon was questioned even by our own people, and in the House of Commons Winston Churchill made it clear that the use of the atomic bomb was fully justified. It saved, he estimated, a million and a quarter Anglo-American lives.
>
> Sixty hours after the fall of the first atomic bomb Japan,

fearful of a continuance of the war she had so brutally and exultantly embarked upon and pressed to the limit of her might, offered to surrender.[1]

Though a number of Caithness men had served in the Far East, the war with Japan meant far less to Caithness than the war with Germany. There was rejoicing on 14 August, and, as in most other places, concern and questioning about the method used to bring about the Japanese surrender. During the coming years, especially when the 'Cold War' broke out and the hydrogen bomb was developed, these fears were enhanced, but no-one in Wick could have dreamed at the time that Wick itself was at one stage under consideration in Whitehall for hydrogen treatment.

Wet Wick.

The whole matter remained secret until a few intimations of what had been going on were revealed in 1985. Under the 'thirty-year rule', papers dealing with the Royal Australian Commission's hearings in London in the 1950s, were released. The revelation as to Wick was 'that the area was mooted as a potential test site.' Challenged on the matter, Mrs Thatcher 'said that the proposed test would have involved a trigger device in connection with nuclear weapon development – and not an atomic bomb.' She insisted 'emphatically' that there was no intention of letting off a nuclear explosion in Caithness.[2]

This however, was not the general interpretation of the paper referring to Wick. 'It is understood,' says the *John O'Groat Journal*,

> that the proposed tests at Wick would have been for nuclear airbursts – explosions which occur too high in the atmosphere for the fireball to make contact with the ground – while the Australian tests consisted of mainly ground-bursts which created large craters.
>
> Experts have stated that as well as the obvious direct danger [to] human life of a nuclear blast near Wick, effects would include the radioactive contamination of pastures, animals grazing and subsequently their milk and meat in addition to the crops, forest, fish and wildlife.

1 N M Glass, op cit: p 59.
2 *JOGJ*, 22 March, 1985.

The Ministry of Defence confessed that a paper had been prepared 'which was a proposal to carry out an experiment which would have involved the release of short-lived radioactive material called polonium, which has a half-life of 138 days.' It was thus evident that Mrs Thatcher's briefing, to say the least, had been inadequate and misleading, and in any case, that understanding of the effects of nuclear 'fall-out' was so defective at the time, that it was possible for authorities to envisage a nuclear 'experiment' charged with lethal implications of the kind that were much later confirmed by the 'Three-Mile Island' and Chernobyl disasters and, indeed, by the twelve British tests actually carried out in Australia's 'Emu Field' in 1956 instead of those proposed for Wick.

According to the Ministry of Defence statement, 'near Wick was not considered as a suitable location and this proposal was not proceeded with.' Also quoted in the *Courier* was the contemporary opinion of Dr W G Marley of the Harwell Atomic Research Centre that 'the wet conditions [in the Wick area] would have made it difficult to keep the sophisticated electronic monitoring equipment used in the tests in working order.'[1]

'New secret documents' released a few days later 'provided much more damning evidence than was suggested by the Prime Minister Margaret Thatcher and Government officials last week when they said the explosions would produce no nuclear fall-out and only a relatively small conventional blast.' The minutes and correspondence resulting immediately from the proposal

> show that contaminated debris could have spread up to 50 miles to sea and 20 miles inland and resulted in craters in the county being fenced off to keep out intruders.
>
> They also show that government scientists decided that it would be impossible to find all the debris; that ships at sea would be at danger; and that an enclosed site would have been necessary 'to guard against souvenir hunters picking up bits of material.'
>
> In one of the documents dated January 5, 1954, Lord Penney, the nuclear scientist and so-called 'father' of the A-bomb outlined some of the problems they would face if Wick was chosen.

---

1 *Caithness Courier*, 27 March, 1985.

'The weather was not reliable – in fact, poor. Contaminated debris is a problem – it is quite impossible to find it all, so that there will be at least 100 milli-curies left in a quarter-mile circle around each shot.

'The hazards of down-wind contamination are probably quite acceptable, but it will be difficult to give the local authorities an honest assurance that they are zero. We can do nothing about shipping outside the three-mile limit,' he wrote to Sir John Cockcroft, a leading scientist at Harwell research establishment.[1]

Boffin's Burble or Politician's Proposal.

The reaction of many people to the revelations when they were made in 1985 was one of incredulity that such a proposal could ever have been seriously entertained. Robert Maclennan, the Liberal Democrat MP for Caithness and Sutherland, commented:

> This sounds like a boffin's burble not a politician's proposal, dreamed up thirty years ago by some scientist wholly out of touch with reality and is of historical interest only. If it had surfaced as a proposal it would have been vetoed at once by any Minister who clapped eyes on it.

Maclennan may have been right about this, but that the proposal was taken seriously is evidenced by the comments and revealed attitudes of such recognisable scientists as Penney and Cockcroft. It is difficult to imagine any serious-minded politician taking up the idea, but Mr Maclennan might be regarded by some as more generously disposed towards the politicians of thirty years before than might be warranted, full, as some of them were at the time, of the desperate dangers of 'Communist Imperialism' and of the supreme efficacy of the 'nuclear deterrent'. In 1954 the Campaign for Nuclear Disarmament had not done its work in impressing people generally with the hideous implications of atomic warfare. Even today many people are convinced that 'Trident' is the essential means of maintaining 'peace'.

Among the reactions, especially of local people, was a sense of outrage that they 'had not been consulted'. Consultations with locals would have been far from the minds of proposers for what,

---

1 *JOGJ*, 27 March, 1985.

conceivably, might have been an 'experiment' that obliterated a whole northern community, and it is hardly surprising to learn that former provosts and ministers of Wick were utterly outraged that 'such an explosion without consultation with local people and authorities' could be even thought of.

One aspect of the local reaction is illustrated by a letter from Frances McKie of Orkney, a local politician favouring the Scottish Nationalist view of things, who wrote in strong terms to the *Caithness Courier* about how the 'news that the government was asked to consider allowing scientists to test a nuclear bomb over Wick.' Mrs McKie, like many other people, was exercised about the plans under discussion at the time for 'the re-processing of atomic waste' from nuclear power stations at Dounreay. Also very much in people's minds was the question of storing in the locality 'intermediate nuclear waste' (a problem still not solved). Were the government at that time, as perhaps in 1954, looking for 'an expendable area for yet more "experiments"?'

For all the ambiguity of the *Courier's* editorial reaction to this very understandable expression of feeling,[1] there was legitimate concern that *then and now* the government cared little about local feeling and opinion of such matters, that indeed, the north of Scotland, being 'far away' was 'expendable'. 'This is further proof,' said W G Mowat, a former provost of Wick and now chairman of Wick Community Council, that people in remote areas in Britain are regarded as second-class citizens.' On the revelation in 1985 of the proposal in 1954 for the 'bombing of Wick', there was retrospective resentment – and who is to say that it has dissipated? – that, except when the patriotic loyalty of citizens of 'remote' communities like Wick was necessary for national survival as in 1914-1918 and in 1939-1945, their opinions and feeling count for little.

And in passing, the fact that the nuclear 'experiments' thought of as possible for Wick (and for Shipsea and Donna Nook then in Yorkshire, now Humberside), we may reflect that the aboriginal inhabitants (or any other inhabitants) of 'Emu Field' in Australia, ultimately chosen as the site for the experiments were not in any way consulted either.

Had sanity – so far as Wick was concerned – not prevailed in 1954-1955, it is possible that this chronologically suitable moment to bring

1 *Caithness Courier*, 27 March, 1985.

the present study of the history of Wick to a halt, might have marked the entire and definitive end of history for Wick. As it is, there will soon be more to tell about the life and prospects of this vigorous community.

ADDENDUM

War Record of the 1/5th (Sutherland and Caithness) Battalion, Seaforth Highlanders TF

This Battalion absorbed large numbers of the Wick volunteers in both wars. Their record during the First World War reads:

1914 Mobilisation at Golspie on 4 August. Constructed defences on North Sutor at entrance to Cromarty Firth naval base.

1914-15 Trained at Bedford with Highland Territorial Division. One of the battalions in the Seaforth and Cameronian Infantry Brigade.

1915 Moved to France, 1 May. Took over from 1/6th Seaforths in trenches at Richebourg St Vaast.

1915 First major action along with 153 and 154 Brigades against Germans at Festubert – first time 'over the top.'

1915-1917 Held sections of line at Laventie, Albert and Arras.

1916 At beginning of Somme offensive, held Vimy Ridge; then to High Wood and Mammetz.

Took over opposite Beaumont Hamel – suffered 300 casualties

1917 Took part in the offensive at Arras, lost 300 casualties.

Took part with Highland Division in Third Battle of Ypres. Took many prisoners.

Battle of Cambrai in November. L.Cpl R MacBeath won VC.

1918 Held ground against the German offensive of March 1918 on Bapaume-Cambrai Road, 377 casualties. Returned to line in April, losing 200 casualties.

With 51 Highland Division to support French army at Epernay. Very heavy casualties as they helped turn the tide of German advance on the Marne.

Took part in recapture of Rouex on River Scarpe, August.

Moved back to Cambrai area in October. 'the 51st Highland Division advanced on 12-13 October and, although it took its objectives, it suffered heavy casualties. The 1/5th Seaforths were again in the line for the attack on Thun St Martin, their last battle of the war. The final 16 days fighting had cost the battalion over 400 casualties.'

Thus, the 1/5th spent most of the 1914-1918 war in and out of the front line on the western front, often as a component of the 51st Highland Division. Some men served in other battalions, including 1/6th Seaforths and 1/4th Queen's Own Cameron Highlanders.

5th (Caithness and Sutherland) Battalion Seaforth Highlanders T A, 1939-1945

1939 Mobilised at Golspie, 3 September. Formed part of 9th (Highland) Division, 'the duplicate division of the 51st formed when the Territorial Army was doubled in 1939.'

When 51st Division reformed after Dunkirk, 5th Seaforth formed part of 152 Highland Infantry Brigade, together with 2 Seaforth and 5th Camerons.

(Wick men were serving in the 4th (Ross-shire) Seaforth Battalion in France, taking part in the action at St Valéry-en-Caux in June, 1940, which caused the delay in the German advance thus enabling the bulk of the British force to be evacuated from Dunkirk. The majority of the soldiers of the Division were forced to surrender and thus spent the rest of the war in captivity.)

1942 Landed in Egypt, August 1942; six weeks intensive training with 51st Highland Division in readiness for the British offensive at El Alamein, which began on 23 October, 1942. 5th Seaforth the right assault battalion of the 152 Brigade which broke through Rommel's defences, together with 5th Camerons. Battalion suffered 177 casualties.

1943 Took part in the attack on German positions at Coradino; reached Tripoli and took part in victory parade there on 4th February, where salute taken by Prime Minister, Winston Churchill.

On to Mareth with 51st Division in February, 1943. Manned the tank ditch during efforts to break through Mareth line which was eventually outflanked by the 50th Division.

5th Seaforth formed right assault battalion (with 5th Camerons on their left) during forcing of the Djebel Roumana Ridge (Tunis). Took their objective but heavy losses. 5th Seaforth took 472 casualties during North African campaign.

Trained in Algeria for invasion of Sicily, and joined in this campaign in July, 1943. 'The 5th Seaforth had some hard fighting in the Plain of Catania, and in the 152 Brigade attack on 31st July-1st August, 1943 to capture the Sferro Hills.' 132 casualties during Sicily campaign.

1943-1944 51st Highland Division including the 5th Seaforths brought back to Britain to prepare for Normandy landings; 5th Seaforth billeted in Hertfordshire and Essex.

5th Seaforths landed Coursuelles in Normandy between 7-9th June.

Took part in breakout from Caen 7-8th August.

2nd September, 1944 5th Seaforths and 5th Camerons took part in the 51st Highland Division's recapture of St Valéry, and were first to enter the town in triumph. Took part in the attack on Le Havre.

October, 1944 5th Seaforths advanced through France, Belgium and Holland, taking part in action on R Maas, in November.

1945 Took part in 51st Highland Division's attack on Siegfried Line in February, 1945.

As one of the assault battalions 5th Seaforths crossed the Rhine, 24 March, 1945. Later established and maintained bridgehead over R. Astrang, though which passed armour for final advance into Germany.

5th Seaforths took part in victory parade at Bremerhaven, 12 May, 1945. During coming months billeted near Cuxhaven in Germany, carrying out 'dock duties' and being responsible for internal security.'

1945-1946 guarded SS concentration camp at Sandbostel.

The 5th Seaforths were disbanded, 3 September, 1946.

FORT GEORGE

As soldiers of the Seaforths and Camerons, many men in Wick saw the inside of Fort George, 'the most considerable fortress and best situated in Britain,' on the south shore of the Moray Firth, seven miles from Inverness. This was built as a measure of internal defence after the '45, though never needed as such. It is an enormous fortress, still maintained. It now houses as barracks two battalions of the Queen's Own Regiment, formed by an amalgamation of the two prestigious Highland regiments, the Seaforth Highlanders and the Queen's Own Cameron Highlanders in February, 1961. The Seaforth Highlanders (78th Regiment) were formed by Kenneth Mackenzie, Earl of Seaforth, in 1778. The Cameronian Volunteers (79th Regiment), were raised by Alan Cameron, Laird of Erracht, in 1793. Both regiments, recruiting from the northern counties, saw world-wide service during the nineteenth century. The 'Volunteer' and 'Territorial' Battalions of the north, formed between 1881 and 1914 (both are referred to in the text). The Volunteers were integral to the local regiments, but reserved until 1914 for home defence purposes and were not liable to be called for overseas service. Under the Haldane reforms of 1908 the Volunteers were re-designated the Territorial Force (TF), and were allocated a reserve field role, if required, on the continent of Europe. They took up this role when mobilised in September, 1914.

WAR AND RUMOURS OF WAR: II

All details in this Addendum are derived from: Lieutenant Colonel Angus Fairrie: *'Cuidich 'n Righ': A History of the Queen's Own Highlanders (Seaforth and Camerons);* published by H Q, Queen's Own Highlanders, (1983).
and Ian MacIvor: *Fort George;* Edinburgh, HMSO, Historical Scotland (1988).

Note: Since this chapter and *Addendum* were written, the *Queen's Own* have undergone yet another reorganisation, having now been combined with another famous regiment, the *Gordon Highlanders.*

Fig 52 Wick's War Memorial.

CHAPTER 21

SOME PEOPLE AND PLACES.

AS a small town in the very north of the kingdom, Wick has not been a favoured resort of the great and the famous. It has had its notables and, as we have seen, has been a place of some interest to some nobles of the past. None, however, ever came to rest here, if we except Earl George II of Caithness, the dust of whose heart was unceremoniously cast to the wind by the raiding Earl of Sutherland; Wick was never a seat of the mighty. There is a 'Baron Wieck' in the person of the Earl of Breadalbane, but apart from his retention of this quaintly spelled title, he has no connection with the present town of Wick.

The fact that earls, bishops and other aristocrats have never made much of Wick is reflected in the fact that there are no great houses in the town. A few decent if not exactly elegant town houses were built in Wick (or rather Pulteneytown) in the last century by several of her more prosperous merchants, fish-curers and provosts; but notable houses, of the kind that abound in and around many small Scottish towns, are to be found only in isolated localities in the parish and beyond, sometimes quite a distance from Wick. Several of these were built or started in the eighteenth century and extended and elaborated during the nineteenth when a few families hit prosperity, partly as a result of improved farming and partly through connections with the trading activities of Wick itself. A few ancient castellated sites were modernised and built up too, as for instance Ackergill, Keiss, Freswick and as far afield as Barrogill, better known today as Mey. The tightly-knit families that inhabited these oases of privilege, often Sinclairs or Dunbars of some connection, tended to look to Wick (and to a lesser extent to Thurso) for their supplies and services; and as we have shown in earlier pages, three families – more correctly, perhaps, four, have had a considerable inter-relationship with and influence upon the development of Wick during the last two hundred years.

The chief of these was the Sinclairs of Ulbster, from the early eighteenth century through to the present day in the person of Lord Thurso. Accordingly, even Thurso Castle comes in some sense into the ambit of Wick, though the family's later connections were close with

SOME PEOPLE AND PLACES.

Thurso burgh. Nearer to Wick and at times closely involved in its affairs have been the Dunbars of Hempriggs, whose houses, Hempriggs itself, three miles south of Wick and Ackergill Tower, two miles north, must appear in any guide-book to Wick. The two other families with organic connections have been those of the Dukes of Sutherland and Portland, the one based at Dunrobin in Sutherland and the other at Berriedale, whose doings one way or another affected the affairs of Wick quite considerably. Stirkoke House, the home since the mid-nineteenth century of the Hornes, also comes into our picture.

SOME PEOPLE

Like all other towns, Wick has its roll of honour. In the days of the old Royal Burgh, the town council used its powers from time to time of awarding 'Freedom of the Burgh' to such of its citizens – usually retired civic leaders, and to such gentry and national figures as it saw fit – or had the opportunity to honour. Among them we have mentioned William Wilberforce, and Lord Chancellor Brougham, awarded the freedom *in absentia* and with the request that on the day of the award they wear the 'ticket' confirming the honour in the bands of their toppers. During the century there were others, and indeed, awards have been made during the present century when the Burgh, for all its royal status, merged its identity with that of the 'District' of Caithness, the former county of that name – though it must be admitted that 'Freeman Burgess of the District of Caithness' has not quite the ring of 'Freeman Burgess of the Royal Burgh of Wick'.

Visitors.

The names of several notable folk who did Wick the honour of visiting it during the years between 1850 and 1923 are recorded on a masonry plaque set in the Rosemount wall of Station Road. There are a number of 'royals'. HRHs Albert Edward and Alexandra (from 1902 King and Queen of Britain), paid a rapid visit in 1876, crossing Wick's new river bridge on 6 October, 1876, some months before the official opening in May, 1877. HRH Prince Alfred, Duke of Edinburgh came in 1882 and was made a Freeman Burgess of the town; he died in 1900. HRHs Edward, Prince of Wales, later though briefly King Edward VIII in 1936, and also Albert, Duke of York, and later King George VI passed through the town, George on the occasion of his illness aboard HMS *Collingwood* in 1915 when he was taken on to the *Rohilla* hospital ship at Wick.

A former President of the United States of America, Ulysses S Grant, celebrated commander of the victorious Northern forces and President from 1868 to 1876, came along, and no less than three premiers of Britain, W E Gladstone, Lord Rosebery and David Lloyd George put in an appearance, though it is not clear whether the visits were during or after their terms of office. Two former Chancellors of the Exchequer, Sir Robert Lowe (later Lord Sherbrook) and Sir William Harcourt came to town. Other political eminences included Sir Oliver Mowat, a premier of Canada with Caithness connections and Viscount Haldane, Secretary of State for War, 1906 to 1914, the minister responsible for forming the Territorial Army in whose ranks so many of the young men of Wick fought and died between 1914 and 1918.

The visit of President Grant in 1876 was part of a tour of Grant country where he believed he had ancestors. Shepherded by the Duke of Sutherland and various other local notables, including William Dunbar, he continued north beyond Inverness, visiting Dunrobin, the Duke's Castle, and Dornoch before going further still. His ride to Thurso was accomplished aboard the Duke's own railway saloon drawn by the Duke's own railway engine, *Dunrobin*, doubtless driven for some of the eighty miles by the Duke himself, for as we know the Duke prided himself on this skill and enjoyed free running rights for his train on the Highland system. The Thurso station

> was lined by the Artillery and Rifle Volunteers, who had assembled to honour the occasion; and on the General's alighting he was welcomed with the general salute. Thereafter the party proceeded in carriages to Thurso Castle, escorted by the volunteers on each side, as a guard of honour, while the bands of the Artillery and Rifle Corps preceded and played alternately on the way. A display of bunting was made on some houses on the route, and Thurso Castle was decorated with the Stars and Stripes, while 'Welcome' showed conspicuously on a banner. A salute of seven guns was fired while the procession was nearing the Castle, on arriving at which the party alighted and entered, while a collation of cake and wine was partaken of.[1]

The civic dignitaries of Thurso were in attendance at the castle, where the host was Sir Tollemache Sinclair, great-grandfather of the

1 *JOGJ*, 13 September, 1877.

present Lord Thurso, grandson of 'Agricultural' Sir John Sinclair of Ulbster.

The party then paid a ritual visit to the house of the Sinclair Earls of Caithness, Barrogill, now known as the Castle of Mey and today a royal residence, John O'Groats House and on to Wick. Here Grant was met by the Provost and Magistrates in the Town Hall, where he was presented with a burgess ticket as a Freeman of the Royal Burgh, the Provost, William Rae, addressed the President:

> On the roll of our burgesses we have a number of names of distinction – men of various walks of life – chiefly statesmen. A former provost of Wick, the celebrated Sir John Sinclair of Ulbster, when getting his portrait painted which now adorns the walls of this hall, was so proud of a letter he had received from General Washington, that he selected to be painted in his hand, and those who have seen General Washington's handwriting can have no difficulty in seeing how the artist imitated the writing – (applause) – so that every time we meet in this hall, your country and one of the most distinguished of her citizens is brought before us. (Applause).[1] You are, sir, the first American citizen we have had the honour of adding to our burgess roll. We admire and honour you as one of the greatest men of our time, having immortalised yourself in your victories in the battle field on behalf of freedom. (Applause). The American nation twice elected you as President of that great country you have had the honour of being the first President of a wholly free people – (Applause) – and that with the approbation of all intelligent men in the world. We are proud of you speaking our language, and as descended from our own Scotland. You come as one whose name, so long as the English language is spoken, will be handed down with admiration and gratitude to posterity. The good feeling and happy relations which presently exist between the two countries is very much to be attributed to the influence exercised by your presence, a feeling, we hope, that will ever continue – (Applause) – as the people of both countries speak the same language they will unite in spreading civilisation, freedom and Christianity throughout the world. We pray that under All Ruling Providence you will long be spared and be led in the paths of

---

1 The portrait still hangs in the Town Hall. It was painted by one of America's greatest artists, Benjamin West.

virtue and freedom. I have the honour of presenting you with the freedom of the royal burgh of Wick.[1]

Neither Provost Rae – nor any other Provost of the Royal Burgh ever had a braver occasion for letting loose so much rich civic rhetoric. The President replied in slightly less inflated terms. Among his beliefs was that in the wake of this war and the later years of his own presidency, 'all questions and difficulties' between the two countries' had been amicably settled. 'I think,' said this most eminent master of the arts of war and one of America's most earnest promoters of international peace, 'that now we will get along together in harmony, and with the influence of the English speaking people, aid each other more and more in spreading civilisation, and in destroying war, and the causes of war, throughout the world.' He considered that these grand objectives could 'only be accomplished in no other manner by no other people,' that is, the English speaking peoples of the United States and Britain. Certainly in these times people in both countries believed they had a mission in the world of fostering in the rest of the world the sorts of peace and economic prosperity which they were triumphantly enjoying. And as we have seen in many a ripe quotation from the *Groat*, the sort of chord being sounded by their distinguished visitor often reverberated in Wick. A hundred and twenty years later, with some of the world's most vicious and destructive wars ever lying between, we need not doubt the sincerity of the speakers on this occasion; it was not, as we know, to be so.

On his arrival in Glasgow the President was moved to write a gracious letter of thanks to the Provost of Wick:

> Dear Sir, – Please accept my thanks for your remembrance of my request for a copy of the address with which you presented to me the freedom of Wick.
>
> It came duly to hand on Sunday morning, the 9th instant, while I was in Inverness spending the day.
>
> Your kinds words will be preserved by me as a remembrance of a most pleasant visit to the north of Scotland.
>
> With high regards for yourself, the town authorities, and the people of Wick, I am, with great respect, your obedient servant.
>
> U S Grant

The Provost of Wick.[2]

1 *JOGJ*, 13 September, 1877. An American account of the event was composed by John Russell Young in his *Round the World with General Grant, 1876, 1877, 1888*; New York, Subscription Book Department, The American News Company, Vol I, pp 81-83.
2 *JOGJ*, 20 September, 1877.

SOME PEOPLE AND PLACES.

Among the military chiefs who visited Wick were Field Marshal Lord Wolseley who, before he gained his Field Marshal's baton, led the expedition up the Nile in 1885 that was intended to rescue General Gordon in Khartoum, unhappily too late. There was Field Marshal Earl Roberts, the Boer War General who came to stay for a while in Ackergill Tower and who joined in the vociferous recruiting drive in Caithness during the early months of the First World War. Wick, as we saw, was not a great deal of use to the Royal Navy – except as a source of enthusiastic naval volunteers, but on their travels north to Scapa, Wick received Admiral Sir John Fisher (later Lord Fisher), First Lord of the Admiralty, and Sir John Jellicoe, (later Lord Jellicoe of Scapa), Commander during the early years of the war of the Grand Fleet in Scapa Flow and senior British admiral at Jutland.

Among the notable civilians who visited Wick – and in some cases left their mark on the place, were Hugh Miller, friend of Robert Dick of Thurso and pioneer worker and writer on the Old Red Sandstone, which underlies most of Wick and Caithness, and an admirer of Miller's work, Roderick (Sir Roderick from 1846) Impey Murchison, another distinguished Scottish geologist. Murchison was first Secretary and from 1843, President of the Royal Geological Society. His first visit to Wick occurred during his Highland tour of 1855 in the company of Professor Nichol, when he came to see 'the wonderful cliffs of Caithness; the granite and conglomerate of the Ord; Brora with its moraines etc,.[1] He was here again in the company of Benjamin Peach, Wick's own geologist and member of the Geological Survey. In 1860 Murchison was in Caithness with Professor Archibald Geikie, perhaps the most distinguished Scottish geologist of them all. Murchison is honoured in Wick by the naming after him of a street in Pulteneytown.

Another famous scientist, whom we have had occasion to mention, Professor Thomas Henry Huxley, the great and

---

[1] *JOGJ*, 25 September, 1884. The account tells how Murchison and Peach, 'hammer in hand', went fossicking around the Thurso quarries, 'gathering some of the fossils so characteristic of the rocks there'. It tells, too, of a conversation they had with Robert Dick in his baker's shop, and getting from Dick 'a sketch of the distribution of the rocks, which he graphically depicted with flour on one of his own baking boards. The conference between Mr Dick and Sir Roderick lasted so long that Mr Peach fell asleep, and had a good nap while they talked together.' Dick wrote and had published in the *Groat* some time after the visit one of those poems of the kind for which the paper had such a taste:

> *Hammers an' chisels an' 'a',*
> *Chisels an' fossils an' a',*
> *Sir Rory's the boy, o' the right sort stuff,*
> *Hurray for the hammers sae braw.*

famous palaeontologist, also came to Wick, probably in connection with his work on the fisheries of Scotland. He was in 1881 appointed Inspector of Salmon Fisheries in Scotland and he also became known as one of the national experts on herring. His visit to Wick could have been on both accounts. His associations with northern Scotland went beyond these connections for he was in 1874 elected Lord Rector of Aberdeen University, a most surprising achievement, for Huxley was now universally known as a champion of natural selection, a doctrine not much favoured by the University or the Scottish religious establishment generally.

Other visitors of less than firm devotion to the principles of the Presbyterian faith were Thomas Carlyle, a Scot from the ancient proving grounds of Covenanting; and Joseph Hume, the 'Philosophic Radical' MP from Montrose who died in 1855. Though no philosophic radical, the last visitor listed was also no chief supporter of the Scottish religion, the Right Reverend Randall C Davidson, Archbishop of Canterbury from 1908 to 1928. Episcopalian bishops were not regular visitors to Wick at one time.

One genuine radical who came here, the subject of several articles and many letters in the *John O'Groat Journal* during the 1880s, was Henry George, the American agrarian reformer – 'Single Tax George' – whose *Progress and Poverty*, published in 1879, attracted much interest and enthusiasm in many parts of Britain, especially in northern Scotland at the time of the Napier Royal Commission on the Crofters and Cottars of 1883-1884.[1] John Bright also came to Wick, but some time after the Repeal of the Corn Laws in 1846, an event which, as we have seen, caused some rejoicing in the burgh.

Sir Ernest Shackleton, the Antarctic explorer, paid a visit, as did

---

1 This Royal Commission investigated most of the districts of Scotland, including Caithness. It came along too late in the day to do much to remedy the damage to crofting and crofting communities by clearances, and in fact its recommendations were regarded by Gladstone as inadequate in any case, providing for protection for larger crofters but leaving 'cottars exposed to the risk of eviction as before, on the grounds that the area (the western Highlands) was already hopelessly congested.' Gladstone ignored the commission's findings, and had passed the Crofters' Holding Act which 'destroyed the very basis of landlord rights as understood everywhere else in Great Britain by establishing an independent body to fix rents; and it provided for the crofters to hand on their holdings to their children by inheritance.' The Act did little to 'encourage the reallocation to crofters of land previously cleared and now under sheep and deer.' (See Smout: *A Century of the Scottish People, 1830-1950*; op cit, pp 72-74). The Commission did not, apparently, investigate and report on Caithness, for Caithness, and Wick parish in particular, had fewer crofters than in most other parts of Scotland, but the Act applied here all the same; there were, of course, many in the area who could have benefited from 'reallocation'.

SOME PEOPLE AND PLACES.

Andrew Carnegie, whose benefaction to Wick, the public library, is one of the more distinctive buildings in a town not rich in architectural treasures. Among the writers who visited Wick and whose books doubtless formed part of the stock of the Wick Library was George Borrow, better remembered for his *Bible in Spain and Wild Wales* than any record of his visits to Scotland. Another inveterate wanderer to visit the town was Sir H Rider Haggard, author of *King Solomon's Mines, Alan Quatermain* and *She*.

But Wick's most prestigious literary visitor, the one who stayed longest and whom the town used to love to hate, was Robert Louis Stevenson. We have already sampled his experiences and opinions of Wick, and Wickers cannot be blamed for not greatly admiring his comments on the place. A Wick journalist of 1924, John Farquhar, took up an unwarrantable attitude of condescension to Stevenson. 'It has been asserted,' said Farquhar, in an appreciation in the *Groat*, 'that in his later years he departed from the sound religious doctrine of his youth, and that this was a dual personality, not altogether averse to questionable pleasure.'[1]

A more perceptive and informative view of Stevenson is contained in a *John O'Groat* article of December, 1933. It tells of Stevenson's acquaintances while in Wick when the Stevenson breakwater was being built:

> On Stevenson's arrival at Wick, Sheriff Russel and his wife, old friends of his parents, threw open their hospitable doors to the young stranger. It was from their seat in his namesake's church near Argyle Square that the writer first saw 'velvet coat' to be followed later by long talks as they sailed in from the new breakwater to the north quay of the old harbour in the contractor's schooner, *Mary Campbell*, to her berthing place. She was the first and the last vessel to be moored at the ruined harbour. Even at this early date the young engineer showed a strong desire to make the acquaintance of all sorts and conditions of men, especially the local tinkers. A favourite camping place of the wandering tribes was under the sheltering walls of Captain Tudor's stable on the road that led out to the South Cove, where they squatted among the boulders. It was also the road that led to their newly-found friend's drafting office. Here the Clan M'Phee, under the chieftainship of old

---

[1] See *Times Gone By*, op cit, (*JOG*), 25 December, 1924).

Willie with his wife Peggy, would sit for hours drinking raw whisky out of an old tin can, while their visitor sat spellbound listening to the weird tales they told of early wandering and savage fighting in the days of the Caithness markets, which stood for days and were the scene of many a fierce family feud.[1]

We have already repeated the story of Stevenson's adventure of going down in the diving suit on the breakwater, and of Bob Bain's misfortune as a block of stone came to rest on his foot. Stevenson became a personal friend of Bain's, as with the other divers on the job, all local Wick men. Walter Cormack ('Old Boy' of many contributions to the *Groat*), goes on to tell how Stevenson and the divers, who

> could only work below in fine weather, had many holidays, and with them Stevenson wandered around the countryside, entering the humblest of thatch-covered hovels and enjoying 'pot luck' with their poacher occupants, listening eagerly the while to their tales of midnight adventures with gamekeepers on some dreary Caithness moor far from the haunts of men. Amid such scenes his heart overflowed with pleasure; and every day added to his dislike of the family profession which his father had selected for him.
>
> Among the houses he visited in Wick was 'Kirkhill,' Provost Louttit's Montpelier, Dr Sinclair, Mount Hoolie, Bailie Bruce's; and in Pulteneytown that of Captain Tudor, RN, Mr Peter Reid's, Mr Macdonells, and Sheriff Russel's. The sons of the latter were his two chief companions.

Cormack derives much of his information about this informal side of Robert Louis Stevenson's stay in Wick from Stevenson's letters to his mother. There is little doubt that he gained much more pleasure from his visits to and acquaintance with the local down-and-outs than the engineers and masons on the building site. His contact with the 'clan McPhee' is thoroughly typical.

The MacPhees

And here comes into view one of the most curious and, in some respects the most sad and pathetic community of folk who ever inhabited the area. Sometimes presented as 'the clan MacPhee' and sometimes as the 'M'Fees', they appear seldom in the Wick story, not

---

1 *Times Gone By* op cit (*JOGJ*, 25 December, 1933, p6).

SOME PEOPLE AND PLACES.

because of absence from the scene nor yet because no-one knew about them. They were featured in two depressing photographs in *Caithness, 1925*, a nostalgic collection of pictures made by Herbert Sinclair, a journalist in London, long time exiled from his native Caithness. One shows a family group of 'two or three tinklers breaking "metal" [stones for road-making by the roadside]' There are two barefoot young children with their father, who carries another child as he strokes with his other hand his 'shaltie' standing by the side of a canvas humpy [popularised by the Greenham Common women as a 'bender'], while two other men sit on the ground to do the stone-breaking – though not very energetically. The other picture shows three children – sitting at the mouth of the humpy in what must be considerable cold and discomfort.

A rich account of the 'Caithness Tinklers' appears in the *Caithness Courier* early in January, 1993, and a strange story it is. The writer is Alice Calder, a retired teacher, who evidently encountered some of the deprived youngsters in school, for although the tinklers had been around for a very long time, the children had only recently been garnered into school. The origin of these people is, in the words of Alice Calder, 'very obscure'. Thought by some to be descendants of the aboriginal inhabitants of northern Scotland, the builders of the cairns and tombs of Caithness, by others that they are rather descendants of 'outcasts of the clans of Scotland, the Macallisters of Sutherland, the Macneils of Ross, the Whites of Aberdeen, the McPhees of Caithness.' Their ingrained disinclination for work may, she suggests, have been induced by some primeval 'feeling of superiority, owing no allegiance. They certainly have over the generations kept to themselves, intermarrying (according to their own rite) and in-breeding, variations occurring possibly on account of throwbacks to remote ancestors.'[1]

---

1 It is a controversy that can never be settled. The 'tinklers' of Caithness are not wholly unique, and probably have something in common with the 'tinkers' who at one time wandered round other parts of Britain. The name is said to relate to their supposed skills in making and repairing pots and pans. In the east country and west midlands of England groups of such people were often met on the road. They usually travelled with a cart, covered with a hooped canvas hood. Round the cart was sometimes a display of buckets, pans etc, mostly acquired wholesale on the tinkers' travels through the Staffordshire 'Black Country,' well known for tinkers and Romanies. They were always distinctively different from the gypsies in habits, dress, speech and mode of life. Gypsies used to travel in horse-drawn brightly coloured vans. Another name for the tinkers was 'nailers', probably on account of their concern in hardware. They were by no means so depressed as a race as the Caithness tinklers, but their women, children and animals, usually had a bedraggled, ill-kept look. A common notion was that they came from Ireland, where the tinkers still sometimes roam.

The tinklers were generally of relatively poor physique, but with skins 'weathered by the wind and sun to a dark tan.' Unlike the gypsies or 'Romanies' they had no distinctive language and no robust folk traditions, though they had a curious passion for piping, playing on their homemade and not very efficient pipes. The sound these pipes produced 'only vaguely resembled the true sound of the drones'. They maintained an obstinate unwillingness to live among others (would others have tolerated them?), to live by poaching, cadging, selling and exchanging items of small value, safety pins, buttons, elastic, pegs made from the hedge and, in some families, ill-made 'tin-ware', buckets etc, quite incapable of holding liquids.

They tended continually to be on the move, sometimes carrying their few and tatty belongings on a small cart, pulled perhaps by a shaltie. Most families had a lurcher, experienced in the art of driving out rabbits, to be clubbed by the men and skinned immediately for the pot or sometimes sold to folk willing to pay a few pence for them. They lived where they could find shelter, sometimes in rough and ready 'houses' built of stones assembled in disused quarries, and sometimes in caves along the seashore. It was evidently in the exceedingly draughty caves at the Cove on the South Head of Wick that Stevenson encountered the tinklers and noted their inordinate taste for whisky, mostly home distilled.

Such a feckless, ill-organised and, on the face of it, depressing and gloomy life-style, possible without much interest or interference on the part of the respectable folk of town and village, became increasingly difficult to maintain in the present century. Social and above all educational legislation began to have its impact on all kinds of 'outsiders', and the tinklers' families found it impossible, even had they so wished, to keep their children away from school. Alice Calder gives a touching picture of the children at school, how though quite intelligent, obedient and even compliant, they were 'sadly restricted by their parents up to the standards of hygiene increasingly expected of school children, with smelly clothes and the unwashed condition often doubtless keeping them apart from other children.' Mrs Calder tells how, if the teacher said the hair was too long, the boys would come the next day pretty well cropped to the skull except for a 'dossan' of longer hair at the ear lobe. If lice were mentioned – and these were the days of the regular visitation of the 'bug-hunter', the school nurse, in an attempt to get rid of the infestation children would arrive at school with the head soaked in paraffin. 'What,' says Alice,

SOME PEOPLE AND PLACES.

'might have happened if a spark had jumped from the open fire does not bear contemplation.'

Another thing that disrupted – and in the long run tended to improve the tinklers' way of life – was war. The tinklers' men were just as eligible for call-up as all other men and, as Alice Calder puts it:

> They were called up, along with the rest of the eligible men and women, to serve in the armed forces and for the first time in their lives mixed with other people on an equal footing. Their army training introduced them to a daily routine; they slept in beds [their customary bedding was heather on moss laid on the floor or in convenient corners in the caves or other hide-outs in which they lived], and they washed. They were given equipment, clothes and regular meals.

In the First World War they were mostly kept together, as were the men from most localities wherever possible. Accordingly, the Caithness tinklers found themselves in the 5th Seaforths. Some other Caithness recruits encountering a contingent of the tinklers when they arrived for training at Ripon in Yorkshire, spoke of them as 'a pitiful group'. They were

> suffering a considerable culture shock. They had never been away from their homes, not even to the local school. They could neither read nor write. They were confused. Their misery was compounded by the fact that they were joining a society that had in the past seen them as outcasts, and they did not know how they were going to be treated by their 'comrades.'
>
> Dishevelled in appearance, and obviously apprehensive, they were taken to the dining hall and given a meal – but, of course, they had never used knives and forks. They made a brave effort with the meat and potatoes, but were beaten by the peas.
>
> After several attempts to balance them on their knives and watching them cascade on to the floor, one of their number took a furtive look around the hall, grabbed the peas in his hands and soon made an end of his dinner. The others seeing his success, followed suit.
>
> Their lack of academic skill and their poor physical condition limited their choice of options after the initial training period, and they were mainly channelled into kitchen work, walking round the camp, picking up rubbish. They took badly to army discipline, and the curtailing of their freedom left them despondent and listless. But they did find one source of great pleasure, and that was listening to the regimental pipe band.

The music of the pipes is in their blood.

At home, every evening the skirl of the pipes could be heard coming from their community. Their inability to read music was no handicap to them, and the resulting tune could be a mixture of march, reel and pibroch. Their pipes were as unorthodox as the tunes and produced noises that only vaguely resembled the true sound of the drones. On one occasion a young tinkler was making even stranger than usual noises and he was asked what sort of reed he had. It was a dandelion stalk bitten flat at one end.

Given the chance to learn the theory of piping and to read music, many tinklers became first-class pipers. One man given this opportunity [this evidently in times before twentieth century army call-ups] in the army had become the Regimental Pipe Major [presumably of the Seaforths] and played to Queen Victoria at Balmoral.

Some tinklers must have made good soldiers in the ordinary way. A photograph of Andrew McPhee's family in a group some time after the First World War shows Andrew, father of the family, with a crutch, having lost his leg in the war. Whether or not they made good soldiers the tinklers are said to have loved fighting among themselves, an exercise in which they were apt to indulge themselves at county gatherings such as the Fergusmas, Marymas and other fairs still flourishing in Caithness. They usually went there to do some trading, the women selling whatever knick-knacks they had available, the men selling such horses and shalties as they could get hold of. Mrs Calder tells of one encounter at a Marymas Fair at Dunnet:

> What started off as a social event usually ended in a grand fight, for as soon as the day came to a close, they made their way to the back door of the nearest hotel and drank themselves into a state of murderous aggression, turning on each other as soon as the money was spent.
>
> For nearly a week afterwards black eyes and cut faces were reminders of the great day. The local constabulary – in most cases the lone village bobby – broke up the fight by charging in the melee swinging his truncheon to right and left with all the force he could muster and regardless of whom he hit or where.
>
> How the families managed to get home afterwards was a matter of conjecture, as the horses were often too weak and the tinklers too drunk, to walk.

For some unaccountable reason, Mrs Calder's follow-up article was never published, but the author has had the pleasure of seeing it. This is also very entertaining, telling especially of the almost legendary couple, Leezie and George (or Geordie) McPhee who were, like most couples in the old days, married by custom 'in front of a gathering from both sides.' Usually at this stage, 'too drunk to know what was going on anyway, they took their vows by biting into the centre of a flour bannock.' This couple, like many others, seem to have lived faithfully together, 'if not in harmony, at least with [a] strong sense of loyalty to one another.'

The picture of Leezie that Mrs Calder presents is as memorable as that of Keat's 'Meg Merrilies':

> Old Meg she was a Gypsy
> And liv'd upon the Moors:
> Her bed it was the brown heath turf,
> And her house was out of doors.

Meg was a loner, but not Leezie. The tinklers, unlike gypsies, had no king and queen, 'but,' says Alice Calder,

> if ever the Caithness tinklers had an unofficial queen, then Leezie was she. She was the grandmother to almost all the Caithness tinklers, and she was known to everybody throughout the county. She was small, being only about five foot tall, and her skin was like hide, brown and coarsened by the wind and sun. She smoked an old brown-stained clay pipe, broken down to about half an inch of the bowl. On her head, which seemed too big for her body, she wore a man's old cloth cap, and on one occasion was seen wearing a pair of red and white striped football socks inside a pair of enormous tackety boots.
>
> She would climb the stone stairs into my grandmother's kitchen, unheralded except for the sound of wheezing and the smell of tobacco. She smoked black twist, boget roll, or, when that was finished, dried moss or tea-leaves. She would be given a bowl of tea, and perhaps an egg if the hens were laying well. She would drink her tea, stay a little while and then wheeze her way back down the stairs, thanking everyone kindly until she reached the door and leaving the smell of smoke lingering behind her.
>
> Leezie was attributed with having the 'Evil Eye', and the local people were cautious in their dealing with her. Fortunately, her demands were modest and could be met

without great difficulty – an egg, a 'droppie oatmeal' or tea was what she usually requested.

She did not, as her benefactors knew, always take this food home with her for her next meal, but instead used it to barter to buy drink, or for money so that she could buy a drink. She was an old profligate and would have liked, if the money had been available, to spend her days in a constant alcoholic haze. As it was, she did her best ......

Her perception of the world around her, and of her husband Geordie, mellowed in direct proportions to her consumption of alcohol, and she could be seen, on occasions, throwing her arms around his neck and declaring him her 'darling long, lost one'. Why 'long lost' no-one was able to understand as they had been together for fifty years and had never been apart in that time.

Leezie's 'evil eye' reputation was hardly well earned. Country folk, of course, were in earlier times apt to attribute evil intention especially to old women; the age of witch-hunting and burning is not far behind us. Leezie is said, on one occasion to have asked at a house for a bone to make soup, having doubtless seen it through the window. She was refused. On her way out she called in disgust, 'there will be plenty of bones in this house before night.' As it happened, on that very day, someone in the family at the house met with a fatal accident. This event probably startled Leezie as much as those who heard her supposed malediction. The incident probably 'gave Leezie confidence to try out her skill in this field on other occasions.'

Towards the end of the flagstone working at Burkle Hill, Leezie moved into a house on the edge of the quarry and day by day the excavations moved nearer the door. After threats, curses and profanity had done nothing to keep the quarrymen back, she remembered her 'Evil Eye'. Every morning and evening, in full view of the men, she danced seven times round a tuft of grass, chanting and yelling, her boots kicking to the sky. She did this for some time but to no effect. Superstitious and frightened of her as the quarrymen were, they were more afraid of their bosses. And the house came down.

Leezie's reputation seems to have been quite independent of that of her husband, Geordie, whose stocky figure appears in the MacPhee family photograph just mentioned. He died long before Leezie, who herself died 'well over the age of ninety.' When, after the wind had blown the roof off her house, she was taken to the parish 'poorhouse' at Rangag, 'a grey stone building enclosed by a high wall, bleak beyond words, and probably responsible for the speedy demise of many a poor soul.' Leezie did not stay to live the short rest of her life with the family. Her cherished memory of the poorhouse was of the vast number of chamberpots in the place, 'a room full of them.' They 'gave her "physic every Friday – and she had never taken physic in her life before."'

Some Notable Locals.

Few Caithnessians in any age could ever have lived lives of greater deprivation than that of the Caithness tinklers. That they survived for such a long time in such rootless conditions says something about their hardihood and possibly even content. 'By the sweat of thy face,' said the Lord to Adam as he shooed him out of the Garden, 'shalt thou eat bread.' Caithness is no Garden of Eden; a less benign habitation for men who have rejected the Lord's dictum can hardly be imagined, but sweat of the body and striving of the spirit, seem to have played little part in the Caithness tinklers' undoubted will to survive.

Striving and sweat, however, have been the lot of all the rest of Wickers, memorable and less memorable. Memorials have been erected to a few of the strivers. That to James Bremner on the high cliffs of South Head has been noticed. Bremner is, without doubt, the greatest of its native sons to have made their mark in the wider world, though even Bremner, businessman, boat builder, rescuer of lost ships, mason and harbour designer, burgh councillor and civic hero, was not actually born in Wick parish. Professionally he never stayed for long away from the burgh.

Two other local men, statues of whom have been raised on plinths to survey the town from the south bank of the Wick river, were John Alexander MD, Caithness County's first Medical Officer of Health, and James T Calder, 'Historian of Caithness,' whose writings have formed the background to the earlier stages of this present work. Neither of these two was a native of Wick; in fact, few of Wick's notables were Wickers in origin, though Wick seems to have attracted a great deal of service and loyalty from people such as Alexander and Calder.

Dr John Alexander was born in Watten in 1838. Originally intending to become a teacher, he attended Moray House in

Edinburgh, but his inclinations shifted towards medicine; he took the college medical course and later took an MD at Durham University. He was admitted also to LRCP of Glasgow and took a diploma in Public Health. He practised briefly in the north of England but in 1868 came back to Wick, where in partnership with his brother, Alexander, he 'conducted an extensive general practice'.

Soon after the creation of Caithness County Council under the 1889 County Councils Act he was taken on as County Medical Officer of Health. Though both burghs, as such were outside the county administration, Alexander's duties came to include Wick and Thurso. He lived in Wick and for several years was a member of the Wick Burgh Council. He was an active member of the town's Carnegie Library Committee.

Dr Alexander was 'not unduly severe in enforcing the requirements of the new Public Health Acts,' but by persuasion and support he saw through considerable improvements in rural housing, water supply and sewerage. He died early in December, 1901, and his funeral was held at the Free Church of Watten, while a service was held in the Wick Town Hall, attended by representatives from the County Council, Wick and Pulteney town councils, and other public bodies. Though not a rich man, he left £300 towards the running of the Wick Cottage Hospital, in memory of his brother Alexander.[1]

James Traill Calder came from Stanergill near to Castletown, where he was born in 1794. His father was a farmer and innkeeper in Castletown after some years as gardener to another Caithness notable, James Traill of Rattar, originator of the 'pavement trade', that is, the export of dressed flagstones for laying pavements, from the Castlehill Quarry, Castletown, at one time a prime industry in Caithness. Calder took a much interrupted course in arts at the University of Edinburgh and spent most of his working life as master of the Canisbay parochial school. He was a frequent contributor to the *Groat* from its earliest days, especially to its verse columns, publishing a collection entitled *Poems from John O'Groats* in 1856. His chief work was his *Sketch of the Civil and traditional History of Caithness from the Tenth Century*, first published in 1861, with a second edition in 1863. He died in Shapinsay, Orkney, on a visit to his brother's house at Elwick, and is buried in the old kirkyard of Shapinsay alongside his brother, Marcus, who died in 1881. A monument was raised to the brothers in Shapinsay; a granite obelisk stands in Canisbay churchyard with the

1 *JOGJ*, 6 and 13 December, 1901.

SOME PEOPLE AND PLACES.

inscription:
> Erected by a few Caithnessmen to the memory of JAMES TRAILL CALDER Schoolmaster, of Canisbay, the Poet of JOHN O'GROATS and the Historian of Caithness, who died 15th January, 1864, aged 69 years. 'Vir Integer Vitae.' John iii, 16; Matthew xi, 28, 29, 30.

One of the distinguished geologists already mentioned, Dr B N Peach, was near native. Though born in Cornwall, he lived in Wick during his youth, and was one of the bright pupils of the Pulteneytown Academy. He was brought here by his father, C W Peach, who came to fill the post of Comptroller of Customs at Wick. He attended the Royal School of Mines in London and was taken on as a member of the Geological Survey at the age of 20. Much of his survey work he did in the company of Dr John Horne, a Scot from Stirlingshire. Between them they investigated Shetland, directing much of their attention to the effects of the ice ages on northern Britain and the North Sea; they published in 1881 *The Glaciation of Caithness*. Their later and highly authoritative work was on the complex geology of north-west Scotland, their final work, published in 1930 after their deaths being *Chapters on the Geology of Scotland*.

Another innovative character who had close associations with Wick and was also a near native, was Alexander Bain, born at Houstry on Backlass Hill, Watten, in 1810. He attended the small village school on Backlass Hill but proved no great scholar. He had a fascination for clocks, an unusual interest for someone born into an area where few clocks were to be seen and none to be heard chiming in church towers. 'His father,' however, 'took note of his aptitude for clocks and arranged an apprenticeship for him with John Sellar, watchmaker, Stafford Place, Wick.'

His introduction to electricity took the form of an article on 'the strange new source of power as it was then called,' and attendance at a lecture on 'heat, sound and electricity' given in the Masonic Hall, Thurso, to which he had walked the 21 miles from Wick. This was in 1830. In order to learn more about electricity he broke his apprenticeship (costing his father £40, which later he paid back) and went off to Edinburgh, and in 1837 on to London where he attended lectures at the Polytechnic Institution, Regent Street.

All the while he was working on his own making a clock worked by electricity, and an electric telegraph that could print out the message at the receiver's end. During the coming years he further developed both mechanisms, but fell foul of Charles Wheatstone who, together with W F Cooke, was working on telegraph machines. Wheatstone is said to have sought to buy Bain's models, for which he offered the paltry sum of £5, having promised £150. There was a war of claims and patents. Bain gained the interest and support of John Finlayson, Actuary of the National Debt Office and a native of Thurso, who helped to ensure that Bain succeeded in his claims against Wheatstone, who is said to have sought to present Bain's inventions as his own. In 1843 Finlayson wrote a book entitled *An Account of Some Remarkable Applications of the Electric Fluid to the Useful Arts, by Alexander Bain; with a vindication of his claim to be the First Inventor of the Electric-Magnet Printing Telegraph, and also of the Electric Magnetic Clock.* If one discounts Wheatstone's claims, it is no exaggeration to describe Alexander Bain as the originator of the 'Fax' machine.

The controversies with Wheatstone continued, especially in connection with Wheatstone's attempt to form an Electric Telegraph Company which, among other things, proposed to make Bain's clocks and telegraph machines without recognition of Bain. Finlayson again came to the rescue, presenting Bain's case to the House of Lords Committee considering Wheatstone's application; Bain's patents were to be recognised. He was to receive £7,500 for some of the patents, and a further £2,500 for any others used. Wheatstone objected to the terms and withdrew from the enterprise, while Alexander Bain became Scottish Manager of the Electric Telegraph Company. One of his company's most spectacular achievements was the construction of a line between Glasgow and Edinburgh which enabled the public clocks in the two railway stations to be synchronised with one another. 'This was the first time an electric clock had been operated by a telegraph line and by this means Bain realised one of his dreams of having a central clock operating several clocks in different places. This method was later used to transmit Greenwich mean time throughout the country.'

There were later controversies and lawsuits when Bain sought to develop some of his inventions in America, where competition in the field of electrical devices was even more fierce than in Britain. Bain gained little success in America, and when he came back here he found that control of the Electric Telegraph Company had been taken over by the government.

Bain was unable to obtain any form of employment in what had been his own company, and there is evidence 'that there was a plot against Bain' in the form of a letter from the then present manager of the Telegraph Company, a man named Scudamore, to an old

SOME PEOPLE AND PLACES.

electrician friend of his in Glasgow, John Stephen, formerly of Bower, Caithness, warning Stephen not to try to help Bain. What lay behind this is not revealed, but it doubtless had something to do with Bain's earlier quarrel with Wheatstone, and the fact that Bain was still something of a 'country lad', without the resources to defend himself. The intervention of Sir William Thomson, later Lord Kelvin, secured for Bain a small civil list pension of £80 a year, and the Royal Society, no less, gave him a grant of £150 'for his pioneer work in electricity'.

A few years later, at the age of 66, in 1876, Bain suffered a severe brain haemorrhage, and Thompson, who evidently thought very well of Bain arranged for him to be admitted to a Home for Incurables in Kirkintilloch, where he died in January, 1877. A granite memorial erected to him by fellow Glasgow electricians, was inscribed:

Alexander Bain, Electrician and Telegraph Engineer, distinguished for many inventions of the greatest value to electric telegraphy.
Born in the parish of Watten, Caithness-shire, 1810, he died, 2nd January, 1877. Interred here.
On the 10th April, 1959, the Town Council of the Burgh of Kirkintilloch, noted the importance of the inventions of Alexander Bain, who died at Broomhill Home, Kirkintilloch, particularly the electric-magnet clock and resolved that this inscription be placed thereon and that this tombstone be maintained in perpetuity at public expense. He thought above himself and also helped to secure a greater and better world.

A plaque was raised to Bain in Hanover Street, Edinburgh on the place of his workshop recording him as inventor of the 'Electric Clock and Telegraph Inventor.' At Watten, Bain's birthplace, the parish has placed a dignified memorial on the side of the main road through the village. A small plaque on a building of the Caithness District Council, once the home of the *Northern Ensign*, carries the message:

INVENTOR
OF THE ELECTRIC CLOCK AND THE
ELECTRIC PRINTING TELEGRAPH

ALEXANDER BAIN

WAS BORN IN WATTEN, CAITHNESS, IN 1810.
PART OF HIS APPRENTICESHIP AS A CLOCKMAKER
WAS SERVED WITH JOHN SELLAR, WATCHMAKER,
IN THIS BUILDING, 1829-1830.

In his tribute to Alexander Bain, published in 1990 in the *John O'Groat Journal*, Robert Gunn, comments:
> It is clear that there was a plot against Bain. He was such a genius that people in authority did not want to know him as he might show up their methods.[1]

There seems little doubt that Wheatstone, who was already a member of the science establishment in London when Bain appeared on the scene, and already had inventions to his credit, was piqued by the intrusion into his field of an unknown country boy from heaven knows where with ideas in advance of his own. Established authorities and academics sometimes react ungenerously towards those they regard as undoctrinated upstarts. Charles Wheatstone gained fame and honour, eventually receiving a knighthood for his work. Alexander Bain's achievements were those of a gifted, self-taught practitioner, of the kind that contributed so much to the British industrial revolution. He had published two books, *A Short History of the Electric Clock* which appeared in 1852, and *A Treatise on Numerous Applications Electrical Science to the Useful Arts*, published in 1870. He died a poor man, though not without a measure of public recognition.

Preachers and Soldiers.

Wick has had its quota of interesting and eccentric ministers and schoolmasters, some of them earnest contributors to the records and lore of the place. None has been more influential in an individual way than the Reverend Charles Thomson and the Rev Donald Beaton, both of whom have appeared elsewhere in our story. It was Thomson who, immediately on his arrival in 1840, was called on to compile perhaps the most informative of all contemporary accounts of Wick in the nineteenth century, the *New Statistical Account* of that year, and who three years later led his entire congregation of perhaps 1500 souls out of the Wick parish church, up to that time faithful to the tenets of the Established Presbyterian Church of Scotland, to form Wick's first congregation of the Free Church, for some years without its own church building. Thomson lived until 1871, still a force in the life, religion, and public affairs of the town; 'he is said to have had uncommon force of character, with great generosity of nature.' The remains of Charles Thomson lie in the Kirkyard of the Old Parish

---

1 *JOGJ*, 7, 14 and 21 December, 1990.

Church of Wick, to which Thomson was called in 1840 and left precipitately in 1843 at the time of the Disruption. His graveside neighbour is the Rev William Lillie, who succeeded him in the vacant Parish Church pulpit, and who laboured to recruit a new orthodox congregation.

A later successor of Thomson in the pulpit of the Free Church, was the Rev Donald Beaton, a formidable scholar who, in addition to regular pastoral duties was, for three years a member of the Caithness Education Authority and a keen promoter of the Rural Libraries scheme. He wrote frequently in the *John O'Groat Journal*, especially on his travels which included his visits to Canada as 'deputy to the Free Presbyterian Churches' in that country. For some years he was editor of the *Free Presbyterian Magazine* and also edited Angus Mackay's *History of the Province of Cat*. His most important and highly informative work (quoted a number of times earlier in this book) was *The Ecclesiastical History of Caithness*. Whatever this province may lack in the way of pre-Reformation historical records, there has been generous compensation in later times in the work of Beaton and other humane writers on ecclesiastical themes.

Yet another pastor of high reputation has figured often in this work. Born in 1861 in Louisburgh, John Horne had his schooling in the Wick Parish School and started work in the compositor's room of the *Northern Ensign*. He went on to study theology at Spurgeon's College, London, following this with three periods of ministry, one at Ayr, another in Springburn, Glasgow, and after an illness, another in Kirkintilloch. At the age of forty-eight, he gave up the ministry and ran a footwear business in Ayr. After the *Ensign*, none of his working life was spent in Wick, but he kept closely and sentimentally in touch with his native town, writing stories, essays, historical anecdotes and poems, many published in the *Groat*. It was his initiative that resulted in the raising of the monument to the battle on Altimarlach Hill.

He was responsible for two other monuments in the town – which does not abound in 'storied urn or animated bust' (though there are a few draped urns in the kirkyard). These are the statue of Dr John Alexander, Caithness's first Medical Officer of Health which stands on the south bank of the river near the Station, and the strange, little regarded and remarkably ugly tower which, in its present form would do credit as the stack of a herring smoke-house. It is nonetheless unique and interesting. John Horne was nothing if not a local patriot. A plaque on the upper part of the tower on its western face announces that the monument's purpose is

> TO PERPETUATE THE PATRIOTISM
> OF THOSE
> NATIVES OF CAITHNESS
> WHO
> SERVED THEIR COUNTRY
> ON
> LAND AND SEA.

It explains, too, that 'many of the names [have been] rescued from forgetfulness, preserving for posterity in this memorial tower.' Solemnly and sententiously, the announcement concludes:

> Their names are
> here. Their
> Deeds are in the history
> of the
> world.

The 'deeds' are recorded on plaques on other faces of the tower; on the north side are listed great land battles from Waterloo to Balaclava and Sevastopol, and below this a list of actions at sea in which the British Navy triumphed, including all of Nelson's victories and ending dubiously with 'China.'[1] Facing the river is yet another list of land battles, including Corunna, Gabon, Kandahar, Chitral, Egypt, Afghanistan, Zululand and South Africa. The lists were doubtless dictated by Horne's discovery of names of Caithness men who had taken part in these now, mostly long-forgotten actions. They represent, as does the tower itself, an expression of the still triumphal imperialism that dominated so much of British political feeling in the years before the First World War, and which we have noticed in the pages of the *Groat*. A fair guess may be hazarded that most of the people contemplating these curious lists of 'deeds in the history of the world' have difficulty in identifying some of the events. There is something rather sad and pathetic about this dilapidated monument to faded glories of the British Empire.

John Horne was an enthusiastic member of the Glasgow-Caithness

---

1 This must refer to the less than reputable 'Opium War' as it is sometimes called, of 1839-1842, in which the British Navy bombarded Canton in response to the confiscation of a quantity of opium in that port owned by British merchants. Among the actions during this episode was the occupation by the British of Hong Kong. Under the Treaty of Nanking of 1842, the island was ceded to Britain. In 1898 this cession was converted to a 99-year lease, the lease that is to due to run out in 1997.

SOME PEOPLE AND PLACES.

Society which served so well to keep him in touch. He died 10 November, 1934, and lies under a sun-dial monument in the Wick Parish cemetery. His birthplace in Louisburgh Street is marked by a plaque above the front door. Recently a miscellany entitled *John Horne: His Life and Works*, edited by George Cameron has been published by North of Scotland Newspapers.

In passing, it may be mentioned that the Proudfoot Rocks above which the North Head Tower stands were the scene of the wreck of the *St Nicholas*, a passenger-cargo coaster trying to make Wick Bay in foggy weather on 17 June, 1914. She was on her way from Scrabster and was calling at Wick to take a cargo of herring for Leith. The ship went hard aground on the rocks and the crew were able to get ashore safely. Attempts to get her off were abandoned when war broke out and she slipped off into eighty-feet of water in the bay. Some of her iron hull still lies off Proudfoot, and recent attempts have been made to raise the remnants of the propeller, two blades of which are sometimes visible at low tide.[1]

Though as we have seen Wick and district have had many military encounters, they cherish the memory of few soldier heroes. The most heroic of all, those who did not return from both of the World Wars are named on the monuments of Wick, Staxigoe, Papigoe, Noss, Bilbster and Stirkoke. The most famous of Wick's warriors in recent times was Baron Horne of Stirkoke. He was the son of a professional soldier, Major James Horne, born in 1861 and died 14 August, 1929. Horne was, according to the account of his funeral, 'a most popular personality and familiar figure in the life of the community.' He died from heart failure while out shooting, a more merciful and quieter death than he might have endured a dozen years earlier. In a flurry of journalistic rhetoric, the *John O'Groat Journal* commented:

> He was one of Britain's soldiers whose physical and mental strength were taxed to the utmost with the cares of leadership during the disastrous days when the world was a whirlpool of maddened emotions, and our backs were to the wall. With his aid we won the war, and the King and country honoured him for his brilliant abilities and self-sacrificing service – but he himself suffered from the strain of the strenuous and prolonged struggle, and his death was as much the effect of the fighting as if he had been killed on the battlefield.

[1] Ferguson, *Shipwrecks of North East Scotland* op cit, pp 93-95; and also *JOGJ*, 18 June, 1993.

At the age of 69 he was not far short of the three-score years and ten allotted in the Burial Service to the age of a man, which is more than can be said for the young men whose names were listed on the Wick memorial, whom Lord Horne honoured by unveiling in 1923. Age, indeed, did not weary them nor the years condemn. There were tributes from far and wide to Lord Horne, and the *Groat* published a sonnet that is best left in obscurity. 'The scenes at his funeral were unprecedented in Wick.' Over the weekend the body lay in state at Stirkoke House; on the Monday morning there was a service outside the House and the coffin 'was conveyed to Wick on a farm wagon, without ostentation and with no military honours.' The streets were lined 'in dense throngs on the route to the cemetery as the cortege passed, and the remains of Caithness's most famous old soldier were conveyed to their last resting place among his kindred in the most beautiful burial ground.'

Often mentioned as a Wick connection is Sir William A Smith, founder of the Boys' Brigade in 1883. In fact, the movement was founded by Smith in Glasgow as a measure for introducing recreation, purpose and discipline into the lives of the masses of young boys then roaming the streets of the great city. It caught on and was soon introduced to Thurso and Wick in the very north of the country, but Smith's main connection in Caithness is with Thurso rather than Wick, and he does not really come into our story. Wick's three companies were founded in 1887, though it seems that the first flush of enthusiasm soon waned and by 1896 'the movement was in danger of dying out'. A reorganisation brought it back to life and its band of buglers led or enlivened many a Wick procession in the years to come.

All of the notable folk so far mentioned are featured, often with photographs, in the two volumes of *Times Gone By*, the one of 1991 and the other of 1993, published by North of Scotland Newspapers, both a veritable gold mine of information about people and places at the turn of the nineteenth and the earlier years of this century. Many others appear in the pages of these lavish collections of 'Christmas Numbers'. A few outstanding women of Wick and district are mentioned, but the operative word is 'few'. Among these are the severe-looking Mrs Gunn, graduate of St Andrews and 'for over 25 years a teacher of various schools in Caithness.' Others mentioned are Mrs P A Robertson, 'talented authoress of *Until the Dawn, and Other Poems*' and Mrs Margaret Robertson, an enthusiastic worker for social improvement and an energetic member of the first Caithness Education Authority. Perhaps the most interesting of all the women

SOME PEOPLE AND PLACES.

whose contributions to Wick are featured, is Miss Adelaide Henderson, last survivor of the Henderson family of Bilbster, who on her death in October, 1927, willed her handsome home on Rosebank to the Wick and Pulteneytown Nursing Association together with £15,000 for the building of a Nursing Home on the site. This is now the location of the Caithness General Hospital, crowned by the most hideous black eyesore in the whole of Wick.

SOME PEOPLE'S HOUSES.

Wick has few distinctive houses. Some well-built, crow-stepped residences are to be seen at each end of the town, and along Miller Avenue and Thurso Road. These were mostly the dwellings of the richer fish salesmen, curers, manufacturers and professional people of the town, and are decent and substantial. Among them were Dr Leask's house near the parish church, and Bignold House, further along. Some have been converted to modest hotels, while Bignold House spent some years as Wick's main hospital. One handsome house was Rosebank, left in her will by the last surviving Henderson of Bilbster, Miss Adelaide Florence, to the Wick and Pulteneytown District Nursing Association and converted in 1931 into the Henderson Memorial Nursing Home. This dominated the hill overlooking the town above the south end of the bridge, but has now been demolished and replaced by a highly efficient but less than architecturally edifying District Hospital.

Wick's town too has little in the way of impressive civic buildings. The Town Hall with police headquarters and courts alongside and below, built in 1828 is typical of its time, gloomy and undistinguished. Its pepperpot turret houses the town clock with its modest bell that sprinkles the hours across the town, unnoticed during the day but audible almost everywhere during the hours of darkness. There can be few towns in Britain where the nights are quieter. Pulteneytown, much larger and probably much richer than Wick Burgh during last century, has a few rather more striking buildings, the Assembly Rooms along Sinclair Terrace, formerly the Pulteneytown Academy, the Wick High School built about 1910 on West Banks Avenue and the near-Edwardian Carnegie Library on the main road corner of Sinclair Terrace. The Rhind Institution on West Banks Avenue is now the Wick Education Office.

The shopping streets, Bridge and High Streets, have little grace or grandeur about them, and are all the less interesting than they once were now that so much of the town's grocery and general stores shopping has shifted to the supermarket sites of Presto on Macleay Lane and the Co-op along Thurso Road. At one time both Bridge and High Streets had perhaps more character than today, with their mixture of grocery shops, ironmongers', drapers', boot and bakers' shops. No *grands magasins* along the street, but two hotels, the Caledonian and the Station, both now converted to other uses.

The Hotels of Wick.

In 1900 the 'Caledonian', where many of the town's functions, dinners and entertainments were held, had the reputation of being the 'premier hotel in Wick.' In those days of Wick's herring prosperity, the town needed to provide accommodation for travellers of all kinds, merchants, fish-buyers, salesmen, officials and ministers in transit, mostly coming and going by coach and train. The Station Hotel, opened in 1881 some time after the arrival of the railway in 1874, the 'Caledonian' and later the 'Commercial Hotel' – now 'Mackay's' – competed for the considerable trade, though all the hotels were handicapped to some extent during the inter-war years by the restrictions on licensing. This was the time, too, when more and more of the travellers and visitors came in their own vehicles, with the ultimate result that there was less and less demand in the town for high-grade accommodation – there never was much demand for the five-star level in Wick, and travellers, if they required such amenity were willing and able to suit themselves afield, in Dunbeath, Lybster and even Watten, where the liquor still ran. Wick never enjoyed a great tourist trade.

An issue of the *John O'Groat Journal* at the turn of the century reminisces about Wick as a stopping place for travellers and the accommodation available to them. Thus, a voyager of 1677, Thomas Kirk, on his way to Orkney 'was compelled to tarry a day or so in the ancient burgh of Wick.' All he could find was 'a miserable poor change house.' This was apparently in the old Market Place, enlarged and improved by the town council in 1871. The old 'change house' was still there but in a dilapidated condition. Too late the council learned that 'quietly' and 'expeditiously' the contractors set about demolishing it; they called in the photographer, Alex Johnston, to get a picture of the place, noted in the annals as the site of the workshop of John Swanson, 'of political and Chartist fame,' but there was

SOME PEOPLE AND PLACES.

nothing left to photograph. The 'Old Inn' of the Market Place was replaced by the 'New Inn' at this time, 'where the Crown Inn now stands.' Of course, inns for the dispensation of ale and whisky, were for much of the nineteenth century, more important to Wick's trade and prosperity than smart hotels. At one stage there were over fifty inns in Wick and Pulteneytown.

The 'Wellington Hotel' towards the north end of Bridge Street was the scene of occasional exciting events, such as the time when, 'one fine summer evening, as the people gathered round the corners to chat and discuss the latest news, a horseman – "bloody with spurring and fiery red with haste" – was seen to dash down the Cliff and fly down Bridge Street at a gallop.' He stopped at the 'Wellington', 'threw the reins to an attendant, leapt to the ground and hurriedly passed to the polling booth to record his vote in the county election.' The fiery traveller was Captain Davidson of Tulloch who had votes in Inverness, Ross-shire and Caithness. He accomplished his votes in Inverness and Ross-shire without much difficulty; he then discovered that the poll at Wick was the next day, a ride of more than a hundred miles away. 'The groom brought forth the gallant steed, and the gallant horseman flew on his way to the Royal Burgh of Wick.' The ride, which the Captain completed before the closing of the poll, took a second and a third horse. The legend – untrue – grew up that Captain Davidson was the man 'that *killed* three horses in riding from Inverness to Wick.' The Captain is said to have lived to a ripe old age, and was married three times. His ride, at least as dramatic as that of John Gilpin, never made the headlines nor the ballad anthologies.

The 'Wellington' was gradually supplanted by the 'Caledonian', and it was here until 1874 that the stage coach carrying the mail as it passed to or from Thurso used to stop, the Post Office having removed from Shore Lane to Bridge Street. The *Groat* writer sets the scene:

> The arrival and departure of the coach was an event of no ordinary importance. It eclipsed even the arrival of the present-day railway train. Both sides of the street were lined with spectators, and as the guard and driver, both arrayed in red coats, descended from the coach the admiring throng made way for them as well-known, respected and responsible representatives of Her Majesty's mails. The driver usually entered the hotel to deliver his way bill, and retail the latest news from the south. The guard's first visit was to the Post

Office, to see the safe delivery of the mail bags. And then, what an exciting time it was for the numerous spectators when the fresh horses were being yoked! The driver had mounted his 'box'; the 'Wheelers' were prancing and rearing while the leaders were straining upon the start, but held in check by the 'strappers.' Then the guard got up, and shouting to the driver, 'All right, Tom,' away went the four fresh horses at a trot or gallop.

The 'Caledonian' itself had to give way to the 'Station' as 'premier hotel,' but the 'Caley' remained in business for many years yet, serving especially as the 'farmers' house' on market days. In the 1930s the 'Station' was advertising itself as *'The Centre* of all Leading Public and Social Functions of the County.' It boasted '50 handsomely appointed bedrooms with hot and cold running water' and as the 'booking Centre for Highland Airways and the Orkneys.' Mrs Taylor and Miss Mackay were a little more modest in their claims for the 'Commercial Hotel,' which they described as 'the Principal Hotel in Town.' This was also advertised as a 'Temperance Hotel.' During the Second World War it became an RAF officers' mess and so gained the advantage of a licence; in post-war years, as 'Mackay's Hotel' and 'Ebenezer's Bar,' still and now unquestionably 'the principal hotel in Wick', under the proprietorship of Donald Lamont, took pride in advertising itself as 'Fully Licensed'. The newest of Wick's hotels is the 'Mercury' on Riverside, motel rather than hotel to suit the times; while along Francis Street the 'Queen's' still does modest business.

Two other buildings of popular entertainment were the 'Pavilion' and 'Breadalbane' cinemas. The 'Pavilion,' altered and newly decorated in 1930 advised its patrons that the 'New Pavilion' now had the '"Talkie" Apparatus,' and was ready 'to cater for your every want in entertainment in the most up-to-date manner.' Admission (including tax), cost 6d, 1s and 1s 6d (reserved, 2s), to two nightly performances, 6 and 8.30 pm. Today the 'Pavilion' premises house a nightclub. The Pulteneytowners had their 'Breadalbane', not quite so lavish but catering bravely for all tastes. As we have mentioned, it was converted during the war into a dance-hall, with a floor that of necessity sloped up and down. In recent years, this former cinema suffered a serious fire, but is now again in business as the Wick Dounreay Club. Wick today has no cinema, but the *John O'Groat Journal* most weeks carries a lavish advertisement for entertainments at the Eden Court Theatre of Inverness, more than a hundred miles away.

Wick was and is very much a working-class town. Louisburgh and Pulteneytown were expressly built to house workers. Had Telford's ideas for the design of the houses and terraces of Pulteneytown been carried into effect, it is possible that the town might have possessed more grace and charm than it does today. The concept of Argyle Square was quite imaginative, and lined as it is today with sycamores (Caithness's ubiquitous deciduous tree) and a riot of daffodils, it is not on a good spring day unattractive. The general aspect of housing in the area is drab and uninteresting. Gardens and cultivated seclusion are commoner in the rather more affluent areas of Janetstown, Langley Park and East Banks, but Wickers could never boast that, although much of their town was at one time the outcome of planned community development they live, accordingly, in a garden city.

Mansion Houses.

The *Times Gone By* compilations include pictures and comments on numerous 'Caithness Mansion Houses,' a few of which, and their one-time lordly or lairdly inhabitants, have had significant connection with Wick. They represent a feature which, say the editors, 'we have found much appreciated'. Whether loved and admired or not, there is no doubt that people generally are interested in, sometimes inordinately curious, about the doings of their gentry and like to know about them and visit their dwellings and establishments when allowed.

There are along the eastern coast from Dunrobin northwards a number of great houses, usually developments of or standing on the sites of old castles. The history of most of them could be shown to have some bearing on the story of Wick: Dunrobin was, and is, the home of the rich and powerful Sutherland family, whose activities have arguably had as much, if not more, to do with the fortunes of Wick than the earls of Caithness themselves.

Sutherlands of Duffus took over the De Cheyne stronghold of Berriedale, standing on the precipitous cliffs of the Berriedale Gorge. It passed to the earls of Caithness but little of it now exists. Dunbeath has a much modified castle that has since the fifteenth century housed Sutherlands, Chrichtons, Inneses and Sinclairs whose direct impact on Wick has been less definable. It was occupied by Montrose in 1650 on his way to Carbisdale; and during the nineteenth century overlooked the modest development of Dunbeath Harbour to enable the community of the village to share in the herring bonanza. Refugees from the Sutherland clearance found or made homes in the Dunbeath Strath. The coast's most considerable writer, Neil Gunn, was a native of Dunbeath, the 'Dunster' of *Silver Darlings*, the most vivid and evocative of all accounts of the Caithness fishing.

Houses of Portlands, Dunbars and Hornes.

Above Berriedale – the nominal patrimony of the heirs of the Caithness earls, usually known as Lords Berriedale – is the white nineteenth century mansion of Langwell House, which became the summer residence of the Portland family, coal-owners whose Midlands home was in the 'Dukeries' of Nottinghamshire. Without doubt it was the presence of Portlands as landowners on this coast that explains the location of 'Nottingham Mains' just below Lybster, which owed its short-lived status as a railway terminal to the same Portlands. The most prestigious hotel in the area also bears the Portlands' name.

Near to Wick itself is Hempriggs House, now a private nursing home but for more than a century one of the homes of Dunbar of Hempriggs. This is one of the two families of Dunbars who became established in this part of Caithness, the other being the Dunbars of Northfield and Bowermadden. There is not much to say about the Northfield family, who sprang from John Dunbar of Hempriggs and Latheronwheel. He in fact succeeded to Sir William's Nova Scotia baronetcy and was styled Sir Robert Dunbar of Northfield. His chief claim to fame was his flamboyant visit to Wick Market Place in 1715 to raise a cheer and drink a bumper for James, the Old Pretender. This line of Dunbars soon ran out.

The Dunbars were an offshoot of the earls of Murray, arriving in Caithness in the sixteenth century where they acquired by marriage and purchases considerable estates. William Dunbar became a 'portioner' of Hempriggs in 1577, and purchased the estate of Telstane south of Wick which he renamed Hempriggs, site of the present Hempriggs House. In 1691 he extended his holdings to include Old Wick, which was the origin of the tenure of the south bank area of Wick, the subject of treaty between the Dunbars and the British Fisheries Society in the early years of the nineteenth century, and which became the new town of Pulteney. In 1699 William acquired the

SOME PEOPLE AND PLACES.

Ackergill estates which had formerly been the barony of the Keiths, Earls Marischal, further areas of Wick, Papigoe and South and North Killimster from the Earl of Sutherland. During the short reign of Glenorchy as Earl of Caithness, Sir William (as he now was, having been made Baronet of Nova Scotia), Sheriff and Justiciar of the county. It was a rapid rise to power and influence, and for the next century and a half the Dunbars had a virtual stranglehold on Wick, and they made a strong claim to the 'hereditary' provostship of the Burgh which, as we have seen, was eventually shaken off by the Sinclairs of Ulbster, the other main landowners of the locality.

Sir William died in 1701 and his widow married a son of Lord Duffus, thus acquiring this title for the family. In his own right, James, successor of Sir William, became baronet with the Hempriggs title, and his son, Sir William, was succeeded by Sir Benjamin Dunbar of Hempriggs whom we have met in various encounters, especially the feuing of the south bank of the Wick river to the Fisheries Society and the enclosure controversy of the Hill of Wick. The somewhat mysterious Duffus title fell into abeyance when Sir Benjamin died in 1843, to be followed by his son, Sir George. We meet George in connection with our visit to Ackergill Tower, where the Duffus Dunbars now lived. The family, it may be added, though rich and influential, was one of no great distinction, though Sir Benjamin played a considerable part in the raising and arming of the Caithness Fencibles during the French wars.

There is little to say about Hempriggs House. It is a pleasant, two-storeyed house with a wide embayment at the front, and surrounded by a considerable plantation of trees. It has not been occupied by Dunbars for a long time. When pictured in the second *Times Gone By* (*JOGJ*, 25 December, 1924), it was the residence of Mrs Sinclair Wemyss of Southdun. More recently it has been set up as a nursing home.

Also within the parish of Wick is Stirkoke House, the home from the mid-nineteenth century of the Hornes of Stirkoke. The house is reputed to have been built by one of the most celebrated Scottish architects of his day, David Bryce, creator and improver of many of the 'Scottish baronial' residences of the North of Scotland; his style was a response to the demand in various parts of Scotland for 'castles' to suit the tastes of industrial gentry and *nouveaux riches* in the aftermath of the early nineteenth century industrial revolution. Stirkoke could be reckoned a good example of the style, tall, four or five-storeyed, steep crow-stepped gables, turreted, compact confections, with interiors designed for good living, plenty of stairs for plenty of servants to mount and descend, ample kitchens and outhouses. It is nevertheless described by John Gifford in his *Buildings of Scotland* as 'built in the manner of David Bryce', (1858-1859). Stirkoke's first owner was Major James Horne whose son, General The Lord Horne of Stirkoke, we have discussed earlier.

It should rather be said, 'was a good example', for on the night of Sunday, 19 June, 1994, the entire pile was gutted. The house had been empty for some years, and was in a poor state of repair. It was occupied from the date of Lord Horne's death in 1929 to 1957 by Horne's daughter Kate and her husband, Colonel Henry Hildreth. It seems very unlikely that the house will ever be restored; the Wick area has probably lost for ever at least one of its 'noble mansions.' Today the ruin stands lonely and hidden in a deep, fast-growing brush of elder, bramble and Japanese wineberry – probably an escape from the more exotic Stirkoke garden of years ago, almost impenetrable, buried in the depths of a gloomy sycamore wood. Robert Louis Stevenson, aboard the night-mail from Wick to Helmsdale in 1868, speaks of a 'stunted plantation at Stirkoke', clearly at a time when the sycamores had not grown up; they are tall, rank and lichen festooned today.

David Bryce did impressive work too on what is the most interesting and striking of all the great mansions near Wick, the Ackergill Tower. This castle has been mentioned often in the text of this book and, since its construction in 1476, has been the scene of many exciting and sometimes bloody events, though unlike Girnigoe, its neighbour two miles east along the coast, it was never subjected to prolonged siege. During the years of its occupation by the Keiths, Earls Marischal, it was nevertheless the focus of continual quarrels between the Keiths, Gunns and Sinclairs, all competing with one another for power and influence in this fertile area.

The Tower, in fact, controls access from the sea at the south end of the immense Sinclair Bay. It was this access that determined Cromwell in 1651 to garrison the Tower with troops after the defeat of Montrose's army at Carbisdale; Montrose had invaded Caithness from Orkney, and Cromwell had no intention of allowing a repeat performance from Orkney, Denmark or anywhere else. Ackergill village, a little to the east of the Tower, was developed to some extent during last century as a herring station. In 1876, after a serious disaster at sea just off the Ackergill shore, a lifeboat station was established here. Ackergill was generally regarded by seamen as a better place of refuge in bad weather than Wick Bay, but its use for such a purpose was limited by the dangers of getting through the turbulent waters off Noss Head. The lifeboat was withdrawn in 1932, since the station had never been really effective, the Wick lifeboat generally getting to the scene of the incident before the boat from Ackergill on account of its difficulties of getting out to sea beyond Noss Head.

Unlike Girnigoe, Ackergill is in easy command of a large area of open hinterland, most of it in use for farming. The Ackergill Mains farm just inland from the Tower is, and has long been, a very productive unit. As we have seen, it was mainly from farming revenue in this large area that the Dunbars gained their wealth. The Dunbars were effective 'improving' farmers and landowners. Sir George Duff-Dunbar determined in 1850 that his residence should be improved to match the style of living to which he aspired – and doubtless to vie with the other mansions going up in Caithness, and it was on this account that Bryce was called in to remodel the building and to add offices, stables and servants' accommodation to suit the style. Generally speaking, however, the Tower retained its classic Scottish tower profile, and it may be viewed today both from the land side and the sea as one of the more striking Scottish tower castles.

The Duff-Dunbars remained at Ackergill for many more years after Sir George, and the names of various members of the family may be frequently seen in the records of Wick as being involved in public and charitable affairs. For some years Mrs Kenneth Duff-Dunbar was an influential member of the Management Committee of Rosebank Nursing Home that in due course has become the Caithness General Hospital. But the time has long gone when individual families, however affluent can – or even wish – to live in and maintain establishments on the scale of Ackergill. Servants are no longer obtainable in the numbers or on the sorts of wages that Victorian and Edwardian conditions allowed; nor do the gentry now need stables full of horses for the mere convenience of getting about.

Accordingly, Ackergill Tower was abandoned as a family residence, and the building, especially its outhouses, was let go into dilapidation. The Tower was, however, bought in 1987 by a business consortium with plans to make the most of this unique complex in terms of the high living modes of the later twentieth century. The building was 'sensitively renovated to a luxurious standard without losing any of its true mediaeval and Victorian charisma.'

It is now in regular and profitable use as an international residential and conference centre. Its seventeen bedrooms ('9 doubles, 6 twins, 2 singles') are available for individual guests, but the commonest use of the Tower, with its splendid dining room, drawing room and conference facilities, is for party bookings from firms, associations and organisations for conferences and get-togethers. Visitors are encouraged to make use of the excellent sporting facilities in the area, for fishing, shooting and golf. Every comfort short of out-and-out luxury is catered for. An extremely high standard of cuisine is one of the main aims of the enterprise, with an emphasis on locally produced food such as salmon, smoked in the Tower's own smoke house, lobster, crab, Caithness beef and North Ronaldsay seaweed-fed lamb. There is a deep rock cellar charged with high quality vintages and speciality malt whiskies. Banquets with all the classical trimmings of fine napery, Highland dance displays and piping, are included in the programme of those groups who wish it.

The management speaks of visitors from 'Germany, Holland, Belgium, France, all corners of Scandinavia, the USA, Japan, Peru and Mexico,' and there are doubtless those from England and from Scotland itself. They come mainly via Wick Airport, two miles away – built on what was once prime Dunbar farm land, and are ferried to the Tower by the company's own transport. Recently some of the more distant out-houses have been refurbished, including the large building that was once the family's coach house. This has been converted into a small 'opera house' where concerts are now given from time to time. The first opera actually to be performed here on the small stage was Mozart's 'Bastien et Bastienne,' as part of the Wick autumn festival of 1994, a high success. The aim, if not perhaps to create here on the most northerly shores of Britain the Glyndebourne of the north, at least serves as a unique centre for high-class music and drama. Nothing like this could ever have been imagined in the minds of the rough and often brutal lords who once reigned from this tower keep.

The earls of Caithness never had possession of Ackergill, though one at least, the Sinclair who toppled Glenorchy from the earlship in 1701, lived in a neighbouring keep, that of Keiss, further north on the shores of Sinclair's Bay.

Keiss Castle beyond Keiss village, inland from the old and much ruined tower perched on the rocks, and due one day for a spectacular collapse into the sea, is described by Gifford as 'solid baronial', and as seen today is wholly the work of Bryce. It incorporates the remnants of a Georgian farmhouse built perhaps in 1760, but from the distance has the aspect of a free-standing Gibbs' dentifrice castle, or in more contemporary terms, Disneyland. To remain good-looking and its roofs water-tight, its face needs constant re-whitening and its tiling regular attention; demanding requirements in this battering climate. Gifford comments on its two 'flat candle-snuffered bartizans at the crow-stepped west gable.'[1] Entrance is through a round-arched moulding knotted at each end. The south-west corner of the house in which the door is set is rounded, but squared above to accommodate a square battlemented tower.

The Castle today is American-owned, but since it came into the possession of Sir John Sinclair of Ulbster in the early nineteenth century, it has passed through the hands of no less than eight owners. Sir John sold it to John Macleay, a provost of the town in later succession. Yet another Macleay inherited the house in 1823, and in 1866, the Duke of Portland, seeking to consolidate his tenure of Caithness territories bought it though did not live in it. After four more owners before the Second World War, it came into the possession of Mr Albert Fullerton Millar, and is now held and maintained in excellent condition by the American side of his family.

One other house should perhaps be mentioned, the Freswick Tower in the south corner of Freswick Bay. This is a tower house of no great distinction and with little historical significance. It was probably built for William Sinclair of Freswick in about 1760, probably on the site of an existing farm. Near to are the Freswick Links, the site of recent extensive excavations of the Viking settlement that was established on the bay; and a mile or so southward, around the Ness Head are the fragmentary remains of the Buchollie Castle, sometimes in the past called Freswick Castle. This is generally reckoned to be the site of Lambaborg, Svein Asleifarson's sea-girt stronghold. It was for two centuries the possession of the Mowats, a somewhat shadowy family that owned the lands of Freswick, granted to them by Robert the Bruce.

1 'Bartizan' (or 'bartisan') is the name given to the corner towers springing out from the upper wall or corners of Scottish baronial style castles. Usually they are supported by an inverted conical masonry base, worked back into the main structure; this is evidently the 'snuffering,' so-called on account of its supposed resemblance to the inverted cone of a candle-snuffer. The Keiss bartizans are supported on three recessed rolls rather than a plain inverted cone. This feature is much associated with the style of David Bryce.

Royal Residence.

The earls of Caithness, as we have said, maintained no 'seat' in the Wick area, other than the Sinclair and Girnigoe Castles, which they still own but abandoned to ruin many years ago. As the result of the failure of two lines of direct descent, the successsion came into the line of the Sinclairs of Mey, following an appeal by the claimant, Sir John Sinclair of Mey to the House of Lords which was concluded in 1790. Since that time there has been a succession of some nine earls, four of whom lived at Barrogill Castle, or as it is known today, the Castle of Mey. This in many ways is the most intriguing castelar dwelling of all on the castellated Caithness coast. It is in Canisbay parish, quite a long way from Wick but for various reasons often associated with the burgh.

The chief eighteenth century association, of course, was that maintained by the Sinclairs of Mey when the merchants of this burgh and those of Thurso, as revealed in *The Mey Letters*, derived some of their best businesses from supplying the luxuries, rich cloths, foodstuffs and wines which these Sinclairs required for keeping up the style. Lucrative it may have been at times, though the profligate spending of Mey Sinclairs meant that they eventually landed in deep debt, and among their debtors were these same Wick merchants. One of the indebted Sinclairs, as we know, died in Kirkwall prison.

The castle faces almost due north giving a splendid view in good weather across the Pentland Firth, and through the Hoxa Sound into Scapa Flow can be seen in good weather a pin-point of light from the waste-gas flame of the Flotta refinery. Its building was probably begun in 1567 by Earl George II, one of the two 'wicked earls', some time before the building of Girnigoe began. This was the earl who headed the jury that acquitted Bothwell of the murder of Darnley, and in consequence was made 'Justiciar' of Caithness and Sutherland by a Queen, grateful for the service thus performed. It was, too, his remains that were desecrated in Wick by the Earl of Sutherland in 1588.

When it became available, the earls moved to Castle Sinclair, the improved accommodation built on to Girnigoe by Earl George III, and various Sinclair relatives occupied Barrogill. The rather flowery *Romance of Barrogill Castle* of Christina Keith (no longer in print) brings to Barrogill the coiner, Arthur Smith, normally given accommodation by historians in a 'retired apartment of Castle Sinclair.' Earl George IV, in debt to almost every businessman in Caithness, was forced to

SOME PEOPLE AND PLACES.

live abroad and for a time all the Sinclairs' castles were at the disposal of the crown.

The earls thus did not live in Barrogill for much of the seventeenth and even the eighteenth centuries. Lord Glenorchy, who highjacked the title of Earl of Caithness after Altimarlach in the years after 1680, is said to have moved into Barrogill, but the earls as such did not return to this less than grand castle until the line, broken twice during the eighteenth century, reverted as late as 1793 to Sir John Sinclair of Mey, whose home was Barrogill Castle itself. It was not a straightforward succession, the whole issue having eventually to be decided by the House of Lords. From then on Barrogill Castle was the home of the earls of Caithness and so remained for the nineteenth century, quite commonly now being called 'The Castle of Mey'.

The most notable of the Caithness earls of this century was James, 14th Earl (1855-1881), who took his role as a senior earl of the north country very seriously and put in hand various improvements to the rather awkwardly shaped and not quite comfortable castle. James had considerable scientific interests and gained Fellowship of the Royal Society for his work on steam, for, like his contemporary at Dunrobin, he was interested in steam locomotion. Unlike the third Duke of Sutherland he was all for steam on the road rather than on rail, and is credited as the inventor of a steam carriage which, in about 1870, he drove himself all the way from London to Barrogill. He was accompanied by Lady Caithness on the last phase of the journey, from Inverness to the Castle. 'It is recorded that his lordship encountered no difficulty on the road; the steep and somewhat dangerous passes at the Ord, Berriedale, Dunbeath etc. being surmounted with ease.' The machine was, according to a print 'kindly furnished by Pastor Horne' to the *John O'Groat Journal,* constructed as follows:

> The water tank, of about 170 gallons capacity, formed the bottom of the carriage, extending to the rear of the boiler, into which the water was conveyed by means of a small force-pump worked by the engine. There were two cylinders, one on each side, six inches diameter, and seven inches stroke. These, and all that was necessary to apply the power to the axle, were arranged in a small space between the tank and boiler. The coal, 1 cwt of which was sufficient for twenty miles on an ordinary road, was held in a box or tender in front of the stoker. The speed attained was, on the average, about eight miles an hour, though a higher rate of speed could be run for distances on

level roads.

Christina Keith tells of the people who in those days lived at Barrogill, including the 14th Earl himself, his first wife Louisa and his second wife, an exotic Spaniard, Maria, Duchess of Pomar (a papal creation). Keith presents a scenario in which all the glittering folk who could at that time be assembled to celebrate the coming of age of Earl James's heir, George Phillip, Lord Berriedale (the title by which the eldest Caithness son was known), when after much eating and drinking the young lord was toasted in 'goblets with the old gold brandy' from the celebrated Mey cellar; within eight years of his succeeding to the title of Earl in 1881 he was dead, and since he was unmarried and childless, the line was broken again. James, 16th Earl, was a fairly remote relation, being a descendant of Robert Sinclair of Durran (a locality near to Mey), and younger son of Sir John Sinclair, first Baronet of Mey.

The title remained in abeyance for a year until, once again, the House of Lords was called on to rule on succession in the house of Caithness. James, 16th Earl, who succeeded in 1890 at the age of sixty-two, held the title for only two years before he was succeeded by his son John Sutherland, also a solicitor, who died in 1914. The 18th Earl was John's brother, who assumed the surname McLeod and arms of Buchan in 1911. He was followed by James, usually known as 'James Roderick', a nephew who derived his claim from the fact that his father, Charles, was the third son of James, 16th Earl. From 1957 to 1965, James Roderick, 19th Earl, was factor at Balmoral. It may be mentioned, too, that James Roderick Sinclair, had behind him a distinguished record as a soldier, serving in the Gordon Highlanders in which he reached the rank of Brigadier.

So much for continuity of succession. Some of the later generations of Caithness earls have not shared close consanguinity and the constant switching of the line seems to have been possible only because there were so many related, however distantly, Sinclair families from which to select an heir. One consequence of the switching was desertion by the earls of Caithness of the Castle of Mey as ancestral home, and in due course of Caithness altogether, a very different state of affairs from that of the earls and dukes of Sutherland who have remained faithful to Dunrobin. On the death of the 15th Earl, George, in 1889, the Dowager Countess, Maria, decided that Mey had to be cleared and the furniture, plate, china, glass and kitchenware and even the portraits were to be sold. It was a sad place.

SOME PEOPLE AND PLACES.

As Christina Keith puts it: 'No babies were ever born in Barrogill Castle, never a bride went out through its great door.' The Duchess Maria had no wish to keep it going. She herself died in 1895.

Already in need of considerable repair, the castle was lived in for some years by Mr Heathcote Sinclair who was a friend of the 15th Earl from university days at Trinity, Cambridge. He had added the 'Sinclair' to his name to bring himself, so to speak, 'into succession'. When he died, occupation was continued by his widow, who remarried and, as Mrs Gerold, sold the building in 1928 to Captain Imbert-Terry and his wife. The lavish *John O'Groat Journal* publication of 1990, *The Queen Mother and Family at Home in Caithness*, pictures life in the castle as a gloomy business: 'There were no bathrooms. The Imbert-Terrys lived in only a few of its 30 rooms. They bathed in a Victorian hip-bath, their illumination came from oil lamps and candles and their heat came from peat fires in the massive open grates.'[1]

Mrs Imbert-Terry died in 1949 and the Captain decided to sell Barrogill before the Queen Mother, as she now had become, started 'to find a retreat far away from the pageant of Royal life in London.' Her husband, King George VI, had died on 6 February, 1952. In her early fifties, the former Lady Elizabeth Bowes-Lyon of Glamis, a Scot herself with strong feelings for her native land, now decided to look round the north, and to stay with her friends, Commander and Lady Vyner, who lived in the starkly white House of the Northern Gate on the high moors of Dunnet Head. It is difficult to imagine a spot more bleakly isolated and distant from the hurly-burly of London. She flew to Wick Airport, was met by the Vyners, and spent some time during the coming weeks looking around. It was on a drive along the north coast that she spotted the tower of Barrogill above the trees, asked about it and within a short while announced that she intended to buy it and to make it into her Scottish home.

The story of how the Queen Mother came to Barrogill Castle, from now on to be known as Castle of Mey, is told and illustrated in the *Groat* publication in some detail and needs no repetition here. Suffice to say, that Her Majesty spent generously on the refurbishment of the castle. This included re-wiring the castle and the upgrading of the electricity supply. Additional building was done, including

---

1 Author's Note: I am now led by better authority to understand that this is a romantised view and that the Imbert-Terrys installed modern plumbing, bathrooms and even electric light.

accommodation for the resident housekeeper and the Butler's Pantry. There were, too, renovations of the crenelations of the bartisan turrets. The walled garden and the shrubbery and east garden developed by the 14th Earl were brought back to fine condition and the fifty-acre 'policies' tidied and cleared. Since most of the house's old fittings, furniture and treasures were long gone, the Queen Mother sought to recover what she could, including some of the portraits, and to re-appoint and refurnish the rooms to her own taste. At the same time she wished the place to remain faithful to the style and tradition of the Sinclair inheritance of Barrogill, so although there was considerable alteration and re-fitting, the structure was kept intact – and remains convincingly 'Scottish baronial'. The interior, however, has light, warmth, colour and comfort that would have astounded the tough old Sinclair earls who built the place, with defence against other warlords of the area more in mind than charm, contentment and high living.

Today the Castle of Mey is an unpretentious house of unusual aspect, bearing few of the marks and symbols of Royal occupation, except for the Queen Mother's Standard which flies over the building when Her Majesty is in residence. The state rooms are modest, tastefully but substantially furnished and the walls adorned by a few portraits and a number of intriguing watercolours mostly of local scenes, some by members of the Queen Mother's own family. Two fine tapestries, one from eighteenth century Flanders and the other a recent one – that took three years to make –, depicting the Royal Standard and the flowers and plants of Mey in excellent natural colours, hang in the drawing room and the dining room respectively. At the entrance hang the portraits of the 12th, 13th and James, the 14th Earl and his second wife, Maria, Duchess of Pomar, and in various corners of the rooms are preserved a few of the treasures of Caithness, including the 'Vinegar Bible' in which is recorded the pedigree of the Caithness earls 'and the great silver bowl with Canisbay and Barrogill and the Mains of Mey etched on it, that stood before Lord Berriedale on that last gaudy night' of his coming-of-age party. There are too some of the Queen Mother's own souvenirs. Perhaps the most impressive of these is the hand-crafted maple casket containing the scroll which records the award at Wick to the Queen Mother, on the occasion of her ninetieth birthday, of the Freedom of The District of Caithness.

This, it should be added, is in a sense a doubling of the honour. In August, 1956, some years before the absorption of the town into the

SOME PEOPLE AND PLACES.

District of Caithness, the Royal Burgh of Wick, decided on what, for the Council of that tradition-bound municipality must have been an exceedingly bold innovation: they would create their first woman Freeman ever, and who more fitting to receive the honour, than their new and now familiar royal neighbour? In any case, the burgh has already broken with precedent (and prejudice) in taking as its Provost, the worthy Miss Bessie Leith. The old graveyard on Kirkhill must have been in turmoil as the old burghers, dreaming of the 'leet' which once simplified all their electoral problems into that of making a cut-and-dried list, revolved in their tombs.

'This day we feel so proud,' declared Provost Leith, 'to carry the illustrious name of Your Majesty on our Burgess Roll – the very first lady and the very first Royal lady whose name will adorn it.'[1] The burgh made a gift to the Queen Mother of a writing desk of Honduras mahogany with a Serpentine front and a chair to go with it. This now stands in the window embrasure of the Queen Mother's study. The Provost marked the occasion by quoting in her speech some verses in the style of McGonagal. As we have seen before, Wick poets were apt to produce such verse on great occasions.[2]

---

[1] The Queen was reminded that she was not the first 'royal' to be so honoured. HRH, the Duke of Edinburgh, who visited in 1882, was enrolled as a Freeman Burgess. 'The Duke of Edinburgh, said Provost Leith on this occasion, 'is a name with which Your Majesty is no doubt familiar.'

[2] For those who would like to know more, the verses are quoted on the next page. The sources used for this section of the chapter have varied, and have included Clive Richards' celebratory compilation of 1990, *The Queen Mother and Family at Home in Caithness*, published by North of Scotland Newspapers; Christina Keith's, *The Romance of Barrogill Castle*, published by Pillans and Wilson Ltd, Edinburgh (no date – out of print, the two *Times Gone By* collections published by North of Scotland Newspapers; various excerpts from the *John O'Groat Journal* itself; and especially conversations with Mrs A Bannister of Ackergill, Mrs Webster at Castle of Mey, Mrs Dunnet of Keiss Castle, Clive Richards himself and numerous other people in Wick. All these contributions are included with grateful thanks from the author in the *Acknowledgements* list at the beginning of this book.

The author wishes to record special thanks to Her Majesty Queen Elizabeth the Queen Mother in allowing him to visit the house and garden of Mey. Many others have written more informatively of Mey, but the appreciative comments in this book would not have been possible without the impressions gathered on an enjoyable visit to the castle.

The verses:

Caithness Makes Her Curtsey

We're proud today,
For the beloved Queen Mother comes here to stay,
Not alone a Royal smile passing this way –
But coming to rest in her Castle of Mey.

So there shall be
A hundred thousand welcomes o'er land and sea.
The greeting of the Celts, its ancient heraldry,
For a Queen who has served right loyally.

Lest any dare,
To say this land is bleak or bare –
Pray have a care, yea have a care.
For the eyes of a Queen have rested there –
And behold the land is forever fair.

CHAPTER 22

WICK TODAY

WICK today is a miracle – a miracle of survival. Bearing in mind the express reason for Wick's arising as a moderate sized town on a craggy coast in the very north of mainland Scotland, Wick as we know it has no significant licence for existence other than the marvellous invasion of the North Sea by the multitudinous herring two hundred years ago, or at least the discovery at that time of the ease with which large quantities could be caught in this area, processed and sold.

The settlement's history as Royal Burgh, county town and locale of the earls of Caithness is almost irrelevant to its one-time status as 'herring capital of Europe'. Caithness had to be governed from somewhere, and Thurso could have done just as well, nearly did. Herring made it and herring kept it going until the fateful 1950s when, quite suddenly (though not unexpectedly), *Clupea harengus* departed. Wick of the North might veritably at that time have collapsed and died; but it did not.

There has been decline: a recorded population of 9,530 in 1951 dropped to 8,754 in 1991, a fall of 9 per cent over the forty-year period; but it may be noted that in each of the three censuses between, the number of people shown as living in Wick was actually higher than the figure for 1951 by more than 300.[1]

How Wick became adapted to a new life could be the subject of a whole new treatise, a study in civic and sociological transformation, different from but at least as interesting as, say, the rise of a new Scottish town such as Cumbernauld over much the same period, between the 1950s and 1990s. This would set, however, a new and supererogatory task for both writer and reader of what set out to be as straightforward a 'history' of the town as could be told, complicated and involuted as some sequences of the history have proved to be. Instead, what has been added is a tail-piece that concludes the tale by illustrating rather than analysing and dissecting 'what happened next,' surprising and unexpected though many of the changes have been since the herring went.

1 The figures are: 1961, 9,834; 1971, 9,889; 1981, 9,831.

Accordingly we shall take a view of some typical though by no means all of the developments that have made Wick as we know it today, economic, constitutional, scenic and social. For Wick in all these aspects is not the place it was and, perhaps, not much like the place it may be becoming. Many of the changes that have been accomplished in this very northern Scottish burgh are the same that have swept through the whole country since the Second World War, standards and ways of living, family and group relationships, expectations and education, recreation and entertainment, mobility. Wick has not lagged behind the rest of the country in these matters nor on the other hand advanced beyond it. It has kept up, but in order to do so, it has had to adopt new ways of earning a living, new sorts of employment and new patterns of administrative and social expenditure. We take a selective look at some of the more obvious aspects of change, beginning with what was once the industrial heart of the town, the harbour, the fishing and its ancillary activities.

WICK HARBOUR TODAY.

The most egregiously obvious difference between Wick Harbour today and any picture of the nineteenth century is the lack of boats in nowadays, not just sailing boats but all kinds of vessels. A few trawlers, a few drifters, a ship perhaps on the slips of the boatyard or another one high and dry on the Harbour Quay being careened or even painted. A crab boat or two and a few others including a number of pleasure craft are sometimes to be seen. The *Pentland Venture* comes in for clean-up and safe harbourage during the winter, waiting for next season's twice or thrice daily passage both ways between John O'Groats and Burwick in South Ronaldsay.

Harbour dues are a mere fraction of what they once were, not just on account of the drastic fall-off in fishing, but also the dues collectable on account of more general shipping activities. Wick still serves – very modestly – as a port for goods: with sporadic imports of gas, oil, fertilisers and agricultural lime, small unit steel goods, coal and road salt; and exports in steel, processed calor gas, a few locally manufactured goods, peat and barley. Dues collected in 1993 amounted to some £24,280, made up from general shipping, £9,981, imports, £12,520 and exports a mere £2,779. Such figures fluctuate from year to year, but only within a narrow compass. Imports in 1992, for instance netted £9,141 in dues, but up to the beginning of November of 1994 rose to £20,917. This almost certainly reflects a higher, but far from spectacular rise in economic activity in 1994 as recession fades. Some small revenue is earned most years from ship repairs as the ship repair facilities are owned by the Harbour Trust. In 1992 £714 was collected in dues from yachts in harbour; this was down to £440 the following year.

The Harbour Trust's most consistent source of income, as it always was, comes from fish landings, small though these are as compared with figures of earlier in the century and the nineteenth century. For instance, recent fish landing revenues have been running as follows:

Years 1992 and 1993 to 31 October, at rates of 3p in the £, mart value for White Fish (1); 2p for Shell Fish (2); and 1½p White Fish consigned (not landed for mart but consigned to customer immediately,) (3):

	1992	1993	1992	1993	1992	1993
	Total		Strangers		Locals	
	£	£	£	£	£	£
(1)	24,164	12,820	3,839	638	20,325	12,182
(2)	26,798	24,127	26,340	23,845	458	282
(3)	25,131	33,074	19,667	24,092	5,464	8,982[1]

As always with fish landings, there is considerable variability from year to year. Very noticeably shell fish landings from moderate sized boats are now almost as important as the white fish landings; and not surprisingly at all, there is no mention of herring.

Wick is now the headquarters of the 'Wick Fishery District', an area stretching down the coast to Helmsdale and north and west to John O'Groats and Portskerra, but this signifies little in terms of Wick town's status and importance as a fishery centre itself. A recent set of figures for landings in the area shows a total area landing of 10,756 tonnes of fish, demersal, pelagic and shellfish, valued at £13,549,800. Of this total, Wick itself accounted for 3,261 tonnes with a total value of £3,852,700, as compared with 7,395 tonnes landed at Scrabster, with a value of £9,564,900. Across Scotland as a whole some £250,000,000 worth of fish of all kinds was landed, a total of 442,000 tons; the main species being cod, haddock, mackerel and herring (84,000 tonnes); but it is evident that Wick, in its own area has only very modest standing now as a fishing centre.[2]

Scrabster has long overhauled Wick and has had more money spent

1 Figures derived from Harbour Trust returns, 1992, 1993.
2 *Caithness Courier*, 9 February, 1994.

on its harbours and is the main base in the area for trawlers. Most of the boats fishing from Wick for all types of fish are 'strangers', that is, they come from Orkney, Oban, Ballantrae and other fish ports. With the restrictions on sea-fishing now being enforced by the EEC it seems very unlikely that there could ever be much recovery of Wick as a fishing station, and there are few prospects of its developing much further as a general trading port. A few new uses are being attempted, the most significant of which are those connected with the landing at Wick of pipes and 'towheads' connected with the Rockwater development at Wester.

But such activities require sound and adaptable quayside facilities. Wick harbour is still very vulnerable to the weather, and still needs large sums of money for its maintenance and repair. Especially subject to the traditional ravages of the seas are the River Basin Piers which enclose the least active area of the port as a whole, the River Basin. All, however, is not lost. The year 1994 began for the Harbour Trust with the news that the Scottish Office had agreed to provide 95 per cent of the funds required to finance the Trust's scheme for refurbishment of some of the harbour installations, the North Quay, the slip-way, the old timber wharf and some 'upgrading' of the fish mart, a mere shadow of its former self.[1] On the other hand, the Highland Regional Council refused help towards the specific project of repairing the 'crumbling' North and South piers of the harbour, which the Trust has reported 'will collapse, eventually threatening the road which bounds the harbour'. The Regional Council's road and transport committee commented that there was no money to help the Trust, but that 'if the collapse of the piers threatened the road, it would become a matter for the coastal protection budget.'[2] Major improvement and re-development of the quayside area itself in Lower Pulteneytown is envisaged both by the Caithness and Sutherland Enterprise Board and the 'Wick Project' now being promoted by the town.

Lifeboats, Coastguards and Rescue.

Though rather a shadow of its former self, Wick Harbour is still the home of a prestigious lifeboat. Until very recently the boat was housed as it had been for many years in the stilted boat-house near

---

1 *Caithness Courier,* 12 January, 1994.
2 *JOGJ,* 4 February, 1994. See also *Caithness Courier,* 16 March, 1994, and *JOGJ,* 4 February, 1994. The story, however, continues.

the Memi Steps down the cliff below Pulteney House. Now, like many of the new generation lifeboats, it remains afloat, mostly in the Outer Harbour, ready to put to sea on the instant. It is named the *Norman Salvesen*, one of three lifeboats provided from the bequest of Mary Salvesen, wife of the transport magnate, and each costing about half-a-million pounds, immensely powerful with two 425 hp engines, with a top speed of eighteen knots, twice that of its predecessor, the *Princess Marina*, which at £72,000 had been thought of as fantastically expensive and which put in 18 years' service, was called out 71 times and saved 31 lives. The *Princess Marina's* predecessor had been the *City of Edinburgh* which served throughout the Second World War, and which is believed to have been called out nearly fifty times, rescuing 79 people.

This kind of record has been kept up by the *Norman Salvesen*. Between August 1988 and February, 1993 she was called out 50 times and saved 28 lives. Her calls came in a different manner from those for which the earlier Wick lifeboats were launched, information coming now from a coastguard service which has been radically reconstructed from the days when Wick had its own 'look-out' Coastguard Station on South Head. With the massive changes in meteorological technique and radio communication that have occurred during the last twenty years, visual observation has now been phased out, and the Wick Station with it. Though the change-over did not occur overnight, Wick, so to speak, 'went out of the circuit' in the years 1982 and 1983. There are in the 'Pentland' area five lifeboats, Wick, Thurso, Longhope, Stromness and Kirkwall. All in the final instance are called out from Kirkwall Coastguard station, to which information about emergencies at sea in the entire area is networked. Whereas at one time the lifeboat-men were called by maroon, whose boom told everyone in the locality that there was an incident. Now they are called by 'pagers' or 'bleepers' in their own homes and at their places of work.

There is a Coastguard office in Wick whose officer is responsible for a variety of duties, including the training of auxiliaries, communication with the coastguard stations and helicopter services. He turns out during off-shore emergencies and may have to fire rockets and flares for signalling and illumination of the scene. Also he may be involved in cliff rescues of people and animals. A call-out for sheep stranded on rock ledges is not uncommon.[1]

1 Information supplied by John Livitt of Kirkwall Coastguard Station and Sandy Taylor of the Wick Office.

Whatever the state of technology, the sea makes no concessions. Storms as bad as that of 19 August, 1847 still happen, and those who man the lifeboats still serve in great peril, as the story of the Longhope Lifeboat of 1968 demonstrated. In March 1991 The *Norman Salvesen* of Wick came to the rescue of the P&O ferry, *St Rognvald*, which plies between Shetland and Aberdeen, the circumstances as dangerous as any encountered in the nineteenth century. The *St Rognvald* was struck by a Force 9 ESE gale as she came southward round Duncansby Head, shortly after midnight. She lost compass and steering and was in danger of drifting on to the Duncansby rocks. The *Norman Salvesen* was called out:

> Conditions in Wick Bay were atrocious, with confused, breaking seas up to 18 feet high. The Coastguard were also called out, to light Wick Bay using paraffin paraflares and by the light of these Coxswain Walter McPhee waited for a lull between the heavy seas, as they smashed on to the lifeboat slipway. Choosing the moment very carefully, he then gave the order to 'launch', the retaining pin was knocked out and at 12.27 am, the *Norman Salvesen* slid down the slipway and headed into the white, churning seas. Using the lifeboat's radar, they cleared Wick Bay safely and the course was set for the stricken ferry, which had 19 people on board. As Coxswain McPhee headed towards the casualty, the lifeboat was struck by an exceptionally heavy sea on her starboard quarter and broached to, but was quickly brought back on course again and full speed was resumed; the lifeboat reached the ferry at 1.11am.
>
> She was rolling heavily and shipping huge seas, with spray flying clean over her. The crew could be seen gathered on the afterdeck. In seas up to 35 feet the ferry was found to be making about 12 knots, but she was circling to port, with her steering being out of action. In the appalling conditions, with torrential rain, the visibility was only about 1 mile. A helicopter had also been called out and, by the light of the flares fired off by the lifeboat men, she began to take some of the crew off the ferry. The Pilot had considerable difficulty in the conditions, the situation being made even worse by the constantly changing course of the ferry. By 2.07am, 4 men had been airlifted off the ferry, but by then the helicopter had broken off all her 'airlines' and so she headed off for Lossiemouth, to pick up some more.

As the ferry continued to circle, she drew closer and closer to the shore and at 2.40am, Coxswain McPhee informed the ferry's Chief Officer, who was then in command, as the ship's Master had been injured, that, at times, the ferry was less than half-a-mile from the shore and he suggested that preparations should be made to drop anchor. However, just before this became necessary, the ferry's engineers succeeded in rigging up an emergency steering gear and, guided by the lifeboat, the ferry moved slowly away from the coast, Coxswain McPhee constantly giving helm orders by radio to the crew of the ferry. The helicopter returned at 2.55 am. and lifted off another 10 non-essential members of the crew, the last man being taken off at 3.40 am., by which time the ferry was just over 6 miles from Duncansby Head and 2½ miles off shore.

Coxswain McPhee continued to give help in guiding the ferry and, at 5.00am, the helicopter put a relief master on board the *St Rognvald*, who requested that the lifeboat remain with the ferry and guide her to a safe anchorage. As the wind began to ease, an emergency compass was rigged on board the ferry and Coxswain McPhee radioed a course for Noss Head, the tug *Einer* arriving on the scene at 6.15 am. She too escorted the ferry as Coxswain McPhee continued to pass course-headings to the ferry's crew by radio and, slowly, they made for Sinclair Bay, where the ferry was safely anchored at 7.30 am. The lifeboat remained with the ferry until 8.17 am. For his outstanding leadership, expert seamanship and great courage, Coxswain Walter McPhee was awarded the RNLI's Thanks on Vellum for this excellent service, the other 8 members of the crew each receiving Vellum Service Certificates.[1]

Since the RNLI took over the Wick Lifeboat Station, its lifeboats have been launched on service 319 times and saved a total of 346 lives. It is a splendid record of service in seas that are all too often violent beyond most people's imagining.

NEW INDUSTRIES IN WICK.

It is very evident that, fishing apart, Wick Harbour offered little prospect in the 1950s of enabling Wick to survive as an economic

---

[1] This and most of the information in this section from Jeff Morris: *History of the Wick and Ackergill Lifeboats*, op cit.

entity. The survival has been accomplished by means of co-incident land-based enterprise in the area, some of it fortuitous, some very deliberate. The most significant development had little to do with native resources, trends and enterprise in Caithness itself, and can truly be described as fortuitous, except for the canvassing and lobbying in Parliament of the county's Tory MP from 1950 to 1964, Sir David Robertson. He had replaced E L Gandar-Dower, flyer and commercial airline developer in northern Scotland, National Unionist, who held Caithness and Sutherland following the departure of Sir Archibald Sinclair in 1945. The development in question was that of the Dounreay Experimental Reactor establishment, some miles west of Thurso, and now much the best known – or, depending on point of view, notorious – nationally and internationally of all industrial enterprises in Caithness.

Dounreay.

This is not the place to attempt a account of the unique Dounreay experience, a task already accomplished by the ubiquitous Iain Sutherland in his inimitably idiosyncratic style. It is a story that has deserved the telling, representing perhaps the oddest, most unpredicted episode in Caithness's whole history. There can be little doubt that it was the very northerliness of Britain's most northern mainland county, a terrain remote from the populated centres of Britain, that brought the establishment here to begin with.

Its connection with Wick is much less close, geographically and economically than with Thurso, whose rise of population between 1951 and 1961, from 4,210 to 8,922, a dramatic doubling in ten years, is almost wholly accounted for by the Dounreay establishment. The rise continued during the next ten years, though not at the same rate, from 8,922 to 10,028. As the population of the area increased even beyond the expectation of the United Kingdom Atomic Energy Authority (UKAEA), it was decided that housing for newcomers, who were arriving in droves, mainly from the south of Scotland and the north of England, should from now on be more dispersed; Halkirk and Castletown were chosen. Houses were built in Halkirk but very few in Castletown. Halkirk showed no increase until after 1971, when its population rose from 1,420 to 1971 to 1,903 in 1981, a manifest result of a deliberate housing policy. In the meantime, the rapid expansion of the plant at Dounreay and its complex ancillaries had virtually mopped up most pools of unemployment that had existed in the area. By August, 1957 Thurso reached its lowest rate of unemployment ever of 20 men and 11 women registered unemployed, while the figures for Wick was 20 men and 45 women.'[1]

Wick, it is clear, was responding to the call for labour at Dounreay, from the lowest labouring grades to levels of highest skills, as readily and rapidly as Thurso and other localities nearer to the plant. However, Wick and Thurso's industrial history had so far been such that they had few reserves of technically skilled and qualified workers. So that the Dounreay establishment's very considerable needs in this respect had to be filled by immigrants. Mr Sutherland reproduces in his book an advertisement from 1956 in which the UKAEA calls for workers at all levels, from labourers and laundry hands (male) to electricians, welders, turners, fitters and instrument mechanics. There was still shortfall, and with the encouragement of the Authority, the Caithness County Council was persuaded in 1957 that it must now set up a technical college in the area for the training of workers as welders, fitters and the like. Hence was opened and equipped the Thurso Technical College which began a process locally of training young people in the whole area in a considerable range of industrial skills. While the main concern in the earlier stages of development of vocational education in Caithness was training for skills for the purposes of the UKAEA, the spin-off benefit for other industrial and commercial enterprises in Caithness was considerable. For the purposes of such benefit, Wick, of course, has had to rely almost completely on the facilities offered by the Thurso College, for the education authority, then the Caithness County Council, never felt that demand in the Wick area justified expenditure on a Wick College of Further Education. Such demand may in due course have developed as Wick changed its working patterns, at least for lower grade skills, but long before this the Thurso College had established an unbeatable hegemony in the provision of vocational education in the area. So for practical purposes, through all the stages of post-war industrial development, Wick has remained dependent on Thurso for such a service and, among other amenities, the services of the Highland Bus Company in fetching people from Wick to College

---

[1] Iain Sutherland: *Dounreay: An Experimental Reactor Establishment;* Wick, published by Iain Sutherland; 1990; p 77. Unless otherwise indicated all data on the subject of Dounreay is derived from Mr Sutherland's book. Regrettably, though the book is full of interesting information and illustration, there is neither bibliography nor index. Mr Sutherland himself worked for twenty-eight years at the establishment.

and back and, for those who do not use their own transport, workers from Wick at the establishment. Fortunately good straight roads run between the localities.

One interesting effect of the activities of the Dounreay Establishment and the College has been the creation in the whole area of northern Caithness of pools of skilled labour, available to be absorbed into new developments besides that of the UKAEA, such as Norfrost at Castletown, Rockwater at Wester and numerous other businesses that have come along during the last forty years. And since Wick, Thurso, Castletown etc have become very dependent on motor transport of every kind, and have during these years, like most other parts of Britain, shared in the expansion of electrical services and equipment, household and commercial, northern Caithness has been enabled to provide itself with some of the basic training required for the installation and development of such contributions to the standard of living. For the higher levels of training, however, Wick and Thurso have continued to send people to Inverness and Aberdeen, and this is unlikely to change.

Since its inception, the Dounreay establishment has gone through several transformations. It started as a 'conventional' atomic energy reactor plant, ostensibly designed for the generation of electricity; then it became a prime centre for experimentation in and possible development of the 'Fast Breeder Reactor,' originally 'Prototype Fast Reactor,' (PFR in the acronymic jargon of the trade), in which plutonium rather than uranium is used. For a time the plant went in for re-processing of spent plutonium fuel rods, but this eventually went to Windscale – now Sellafield. Serious doubts about fast-breeder techniques set in during the 1980s partly as the result of the disasters at Three-Mile Island and Chernobyl, and the partially consequent collapse of potential markets for fast-breeder processes and equipment. Work on every front at Dounreay has been down-graded, with drastic effects on employment levels in the area.

From about November, 1993 issues of the *Groat* and *Caithness Courier* have been swamped with reports of cut-down at Dounreay. PFR at Dounreay was finally killed off on 31 March, 1994, with a consequent unhappy message for Dounreay workers on April Fool's Day.[1] In March 1987 2,300 people worked at Dounreay. By January 1994 the workforce had fallen to 1,474; with the closure of PFR it went down further, and by the end of the year it is believed that the

1 *JOGJ*, 1 April, 1994.

Dounreay workforce will number no more than 1000.[1]

In the meantime, NIREX, the nuclear industry's body concerned with the disposal of nuclear waste materials, yet another area of increasing concern about the safety and viability of industrial nuclear processes, had been seeking to get Dounreay adopted as a significant nuclear waste depository, though only as a 'fallback' location in case their preferred site, Sellafield, was refused them. There was, indeed, much discussion over several years about sites for deposit of various grades of waste, including localities in the Midlands and South of England, all eventually dismissed by the government on account of fears of heavy anti-government vote at the next election in the constituencies affected. Once more the north of Scotland seemed to be favoured, on account of its remoteness. There were, needless to say, many apparent technical objections to Dounreay for the purpose, a main one being the fissured and jointed nature of the rock on which Caithness stands. In the end Sellafield was chosen, creating more worries for employment here.[2]

There was, too, the contretemps of the American decision in 1993 to call in all 'HEU,' 'Highly Enriched Uranium', regarded by the American government as a dangerous commodity in the hands of all but the USA itself, on account of its usefulness as bomb-making material. Dounreay had a certain amount of this for research purposes, probably had been producing it secretly for Aldermaston over the years. This is not to go on either.[3] Nor, it was decided in late 1993 and in spite of protests from the Tourist Board and Caithness and Sutherland Enterprise, was Dounreay's quite famous 'exhibition centre' to continue.[4] Here many thousands of people visiting the county had been taught during the 33 years of the centre's existence about the great benefits to society of atomic energy.

Thus, for many reasons, political and strategic, the credit and the industrial benefits to north Caithness of the United Kingdom's atomic energy plant are now being dissipated. It is unlikely however, that the Dounreay establishment will be closed down in any hurry, if for no other reason than the probable cost of 'clean-up' of the site, assessed in one report as astronomical. 'The cost to the taxpayer of returning the nuclear complex at Dounreay to a greenfield site,' commented the

1 *JOGJ*, 28 January, 1994.
2 *JOGJ*, 24 December, 1993.
3 *JOGJ*, 5 November, 1993.
4 *JOGJ*, 26 November, 1993.

Groat recently, 'has been put at £3 billion at today's prices.'[1] Thus, though Dounreay has had remarkable effects on the industrial and employment scene in Caithness and especially in Thurso and Wick, future prosperity in the area can clearly not rely on developing prospects in the nuclear industry, civilian or military.

The military aspects of the industry have always been less emphasised in Caithness than the civilian, but one development should be mentioned that may have a somewhat longer life than other elements of the Dounreay complex. This is the location at Dounreay of the 'Vulcan facility' of Rolls Royce, a 'fusion,' as a press advertisement in the *Caithness Courier* puts it, 'of local skills and a belief that confidence in the future and matching investment could sustain employment levels.'[2] Vulcan was established some years ago as a supply facility for 'submarine main coolant facilities,' that is, for the nuclear-powered engines of 'Trident' submarines. Though not strictly nuclear technology but essentially an aspect of the unmatched engine-building competence of Rolls Royce, and as such representing a welcome addition to Caithness's demand for high-tech skills. It does not seem very probable that this can survive indefinitely as a basic programme here, especially if at some stage 'Trident' itself is abolished.

The permanent rescue of Wick from the predicament in which it found itself when the herring ran out, in so far as the town has depended on a major development of the nuclear industry, does not now look as certain as it seemed a few years ago. Unemployment levels in Wick and Thurso vary from month to month, but are generally running at between 10 and 12 per cent, and thus considerably higher than they have been during the UKAEA 'boom.'[3] It is just as well that other and more benign industrial enterprises have come along to fill the gap that at one time threatened the economic survival of Wick.

---

1 *JOGJ*, 15 July, 1994.
2 *Caithness Courier*, 9 March, 1994.
3 *JOGJ*, 14 October, 1994. It may be added that both the *John O'Groat Journal* and the *Caithness Courier* are constantly reporting on affairs at Dounreay. Changes in the picture are occurring all the time. Three articles of special interest in the saga so far have been those by Colin Punler, *JOGJ*, 1 April, 1994, dealing with the political background of the whole Dounreay development; *JOGJ*, 5 November, 1993, discussing the 'HEU' issue; and *Caithness Courier*, 30 March, 1994, entitled 'Slow Death of the Fast Reactor,' commenting on the closing down of the Dounreay 'PFR' facility, which Punler regards as a mistaken exercise in 'short-term economics.'

Caithness Glass

It would be difficult to find a more benign sort of enterprise than Caithness Glass, one of the very earliest of the local endeavours to create in Wick some industrial alternatives to the dying herring trade. It was founded, appropriately enough, mainly as the result of the initiative of Robin Sinclair, now Lord Thurso, great-great-great-grandson of the virtual founder of the Wick herring industry. At a time when Wick had 800 names on its unemployment register, Sinclair was looking for an enterprise 'that would convert cheap raw materials into a relatively expensive product by means of artistry and skill.' Artistic glass production seemed ideal. Though he knew little about glass-making to start with, he immersed himself in literature on the subject, and like his ancestor he made considerable use of his official connections and acquaintance with people in high places, to gain backing for the enterprise from the then Scottish Council (Development and Industry). He recruited 'someone with the necessary artistic skill and experience, Dohmnall O'Broin,' a postgraduate student from the Edinburgh College of Art, then experimenting in ornamental glassware. Sinclair then set about the building and equipping of a factory.

The site chosen was at Harrowhill above Bignold Park in Pulteneytown. Subject to an indemnity amounting to £50,000, in case the capital could not be raised, Sinclair arranged with Scottish Industrial Estates of Glasgow to build the factory. The capital was raised, was in fact over-subscribed by the public when the residue of £30,000 worth of shares was put on the market after the directors had taken 20,000 of the £1 shares, a sure indication of local public support for the venture.

The factory was built and equipped in record time, and a team of eight glass-blowers, straight from school, was trained at Foley College, Stourbridge, Worcestershire, a famous centre of glass-making. Glass was first melted in August 1960 and the factory was officially opened in October of that year. The early years were difficult, even though the firm's products, 'characterised by their strong dark colours and clean lines, were well received.' In 1962 the factory took on a well-known maker of decorative glass paperweights, Paul Ysart, but difficulties continued with three general managers coming and leaving in quick succession. In 1964, the factory was kept afloat by means of a personal cheque presented by one of the directors, Bill Tawse, to enable the wages of the staff to be paid; but still the company was struggling. The Highland and Islands Development Board was approached for aid early in 1966, but this body turned down the request for help when it decided that 'Caithness Glass was beyond redemption'.

Nevertheless, led by Robin Sinclair, the directors made a manful effort to keep things going, brought in as Chairman of the Board, George Mackie, MP at this time for Caithness and Sutherland, and new capital was found. Losses continued to mount, reaching the high level of £150,000, but by strenuous effort the firm increased its sales effort and by 1967 it had turned the corner. A main element of the turn-round was the shifting of Paul Ysart from supervisory duties to the specialised making of *millefiori* paperweights, which were to become one of the company's most popular and lucrative lines. Millefiori work became even more important in 1969 and 1970 when, under the supervision of a young graduate from the Edinburgh College of Art, Caithness Glass began marketing abstract paper weights and distinctive jewellery featuring miraculously tiny *millefiori*. At about the same time an engraving department was started, its most famous product now being the engraved Caithness bowl awarded annually to the BBC's 'Mastermind'.

Over the years there have been other injections of capital. The Highland Board changed its mind about Caithness Glass after the successful opening of a sales shop at Inverewe Gardens in 1967, becoming in 1975 the company's largest shareholder; in fact, the company achieved its first small profit in 1968 when also it was granted a Royal Warrant by Queen Elizabeth, the Queen Mother. In the following year another factory was opened at Oban. Since then, in 1992, this factory was replaced by a new one. In 1979 was opened by the Prince of Wales, a large factory, showroom and restaurant on the northern ring-road area of Perth.

1975 was a notable year, when 'the long-suffering shareholders were paid a dividend for the first time. Ups and downs have continued. Expensive glassware manufacture is by its very nature a luxury goods trade, and accordingly it tends to thrive during periods of industrial prosperity, its sales dropping during periods of recession. The economic balance of the enterprise may in every sense be said to be 'consumer led'.

1980 was a bad year; sales fell off and costs rose. There were heavy redundancies, but the Highland Board came to the rescue, and again things began to improve. Lord Thurso retired in 1984, 'in the knowledge that the candle he had lit and which had flickered alarmingly at several moments, was now burning with a steady flame.' Fortunes of the company have continued variable, 1985 being a 'successful' year, the next few years building up to 1988 and 1989, 'record years for the company, after which recession hit once again'.

During 1986 the factory at Perth had a visit from the Queen and the Duke of Edinburgh, and the Harrowhill factory was visited by the Queen Mother on the occasion of its 'Silver Jubilee'. In the following year, now a well-established concern in the field of ornamental glass, Caithness Glass spread its influence further afield still, buying up the Waterford Glass Company's former Wedgwood Crystal factory at Kings Lynn and re-opening the manufacture of crystal there.

At Wick itself the company took up residence in a splendid new factory on the town's industrial estate, alongside the A9 main road, a very strategic site for attracting in visitors to see the whole glass-making process from melt to finish from a purpose built two-level gallery. The sight of a dozen or two glass-blowers shaping and handling the elegant products of this enterprising firm is now easily the most visited tourist attraction in a town which has lacked many such excuses for halting on the way to John O'Groats. The upper gallery leads into a spacious showroom and shop where an exciting range of 'seconds,' vases, goblets, tumblers and the astonishing *millefiori* weights and jewellery – to the inexperienced eye totally indistinguishable from 'firsts,' – may be viewed. For those with any loose currency about them, it is almost impossible to escape buying an elegant piece, thought of which had never entered their heads before they pulled up in the car-park or disembarked from Dunnet's coach.

Now Caithness Glass is one of the largest and certainly the best known of businesses in the town. It has a workforce that fluctuates with the state of business, running at present at about 100, many of the workers being young people. Since 1993 the firm has been owned by the management and employees themselves. It is a model of self-help in a town that has never lacked for improvers and self-helpers.[1]

Grampian Records.

A near neighbour of Caithness Glass on the Industrial Estate is a similiar example of local initiative and enterprise paying off. Grampian Records really started in 1954 when James Johnston began

---

[1] Most of the information used in this account is derived from a company document and from discussion with Mrs Ray Richards, and some from Lord Thurso himself.

recording live band music, which came to involve him in trips round Scotland to pick up the music of bands in Glasgow and elsewhere. The group established themselves in a small premises on Bank Row where they set up a recording studio. This was still in the days of large reel-to-reel magnetic-tape recording systems.

Audio-cassette recording was coming in and the group moved on to the Industrial Estate in 1974. They had, as they explain in their publicity, 'graduated to cassette duplication as a response to the poor quality they found among the existing UK product.' From here on, using the latest research and 'recognising the Gauss standard in engineering as one they should aim at,' they developed a technique of duplicating recordings. This is not a simple process of copying the original as in amateur recording, but usually involves 'slight changes in emphasis' in the body of the sound, to ensure high fidelity of reproduction. The processes they use have been evolved very largely by themselves; again, as they put it in their explanatory literature, they 'utilise all their experiences from the studio days to deliver a clean sound that will always mirror the master.' Part of the technique is to maintain very high standards of 'duplication hygiene,' which includes 'clean heads (for every new reel), a clean tape path, in fact, a clean factory are all essential and always assured through regular maintenance.'

There is little doubt that the firm lives up to its claims. Its output and sales match its claims handsomely. Output capacity runs to $2\frac{1}{2}$ million cassette units per month. 'With the cassettes recorded,' they say, 'printed, sealed and boxed, our daily transport operation regularly delivers orders of 250,000 units to London overnight.' There is a staff of some 90 workers, a large proportion of them women, and the factory runs for 24 hours a day on a three-shift basis, 7 days a week for half the year, and two shifts for the rest. Grampian includes among its customers the Readers' Digest Association, Sony Music (UK and Holland), Telstar Records, EMI, Virgin and several other well known companies in the music business.[1] The firm uses its 'remote' location from the rest of the trade as a proud selling point.

As evidence of Grampian Records' success, it was reported early in 1994 that the firm was undertaking a £500,000 extension on its present site. Floor space of the factory was, in consequence to be doubled from 1,500 square feet to 3,000. The new building is being financed by

---

1 Information derived from the publicity brochure, *Grampian Records*, and discussion with Mr John Hunter, General Manager of Grampian.

Caithness and Sutherland Enterprise (CASE) which will probably also help with the installation of new machinery. The extension is then being leased to the company in the same way as the previously existing premises. It is expected that the workforce will rise in due course to about 120.[1]

Norfrost, the Environmentally Friendly Freezer Firm.

Other enterprises have become established on the Wick Industrial Estate, including Osprey Engineering, a firm which specialises in underwater television equipment and systems; they also do work on sonar. Ministry of Defence contracts fill a large part of Osprey's order books. Having in 1992 joined the Simrad Group, in January 1995 the name Osprey is being dropped; for the future the name will be Simrad, Wick. The firm employs about 60 people. There are a number of small firms, which between them provide employment to technicians and operatives from Wick and outside.

By a similar token, not all the industrial development that has steered Wick out of the doldrums that threatened to engulf it in the 1950s is to be found on the burgh's Industrial Estate. Two firms that have become established well outside the burgh in particular have had a significant impact on employment patterns in Wick and the immediate area around it. These are Norfrost Ltd of Castletown and Rockwater Engineering at Wester, north of Wick.

Norfrost in many ways has been the most spectacular success of all. It began as a 'small electrical appliances shop situated in the main street of the village of Castletown.' In 1972 the owner and manager, Alex Grant and his wife, Pat, had the idea of patenting and manufacturing a small, compact freezer unit which Alex had designed, for sale on a larger market. That such a move was possible was confirmed by a visit the Grants made to a successful domestic freezer plant in Devon, not quite as far away from London and the south-east of England where a substantial market lay, as Castletown in Caithness, 700 miles away. Any commodity manufactured here would have to be economical of materials, easily packed and bulk transportable, and, above all, impressively efficient. A freezer put on the market from Castletown would have to advertise itself.

The Grants made a brave decision to go ahead with what, to most people would have seemed a leap into the blue; with no

1 *JOGJ*, 14 January, 1994.

resources other than income from the retail business in Castletown, they spent £1,200 on buying a lot of disused RAF huts at Murrayfield. Nearly all the advice they received was against such a foolhardy enterprise, but they set about it nevertheless. 'The prototype was replicated,' says a version of the 'Norfrost Success Story', and 'production started using second-hand metal-forming machinery and other tools.'

The early days were difficult with shortage of resources, experience and even skills, but the business forged on, the Grants learning lessons, as they now put it, 'to form the bedrock upon which Norfrost still stands. Two other factors had to be added to the engineering skills of Norfrost in order for the company to be a success. The first had to be the ability to buy right! This meant persuading suppliers to sell them raw materials and components at high-volume prices. The other ingredient had to be selling the freezers.'

The story of this extraordinary firm's boot-straps operation is quite special. It rose from very modest beginnings to become 'the world's largest small chest freezer manufacturer,' making some 8000 units a week, supplying half of all chest freezers used in UK, sending two thirds of its output abroad to 90 different countries. Norfrost brings in each week 2000 tons or more of sheet steel, 3m metres steel tubing, great quantities of plastic for shaping on site and thousands of small components. It should be mentioned, too, that Norfrost has from the start generated its own electric power, 'as the factory cannot afford any down-time due to electricity failure'.

The factory is highly automated and has at its heart a programme of 'continuous research and development.' Of special concern in this department in recent years has been Norfrost's response to the environmental alarm caused by the discovery that chlorofluorocarbons (CFCs), until recently the main gases used in freezer units, are destructive of the ozone layer. A substantial proportion of Norfrost output is already free of CFCs. It is expected that in consequence of the development programme already under way, with an investment of £500,000 involved, to modify the firm's operation, that in a few years the entire output will be CFC-free.[1]

Another interesting element of the development programme has been 'an engineering evaluation into a modern version of an electric motor originated by the acclaimed Caithness-born genius, Alexander Bain (1810-1877) who lived in the nearby village of Watten.' Bain's

1 *JOGJ*, 14 January, 1994.

original 'Switched Reluctance Motor' is exhibited in the Thurso Museum. 'Norfrost's work on this remarkable motor may feature in the expansion plans,' says the columnist of 'The Norfrost Success Story'.[1]

The expansion plans referred to are already going ahead. The present workforce of over 300 people, according to the *Groat*, is expected to rise by another 120 during the next three years. Mrs Grant, says the paper, 'predicted that the workforce would increase to 435 with new jobs in production, transport and middle management and administration.' Output will 'jump from 8000 to 20,000 a week.' Efficient transport is obviously an essential ingredient of such a firm. Much of this is performed by Norfrost Haulage, a subsidiary but separate part of the organisation, with a fleet of some 25 Scania drivers who, between them notch up 'around three million miles every year with a wide range of cargoes.' The trucks will load several hundred units on the outward journey and return with cargoes of raw materials and other 'back-cargoes' which may include 'livestock and local farm produce'. Units are carried to all convenient ports for despatch to overseas customers, and Norfrost Haulage trucks now make frequent journeys across Europe. The firm has a large maintenance department and there are depots in Perth, Leyland in Lancashire, and Leicester, manned by 40 staff.

The firm represents a quite remarkable development in a locality which, ostensibly lacked traditional resources and skills. There is little doubt that as Dounreay has shed skilled labour, an appreciable quantity of this has been absorbed by Norfrost; but the Dounreay supply of ready-trained engineers with some of the skills required at Norfrost is not inexhaustible. Like several other firms in the area, assisted by training developments at the Thurso College, Norfrost has its own apprentice-training scheme, with something like 14 or 15 young people being taken on each year. Other kinds of training are, of course, essential to the wellbeing of a firm that depends heavily on high-tech, and this is being attended to also.

Perhaps the most remarkable aspect of this whole achievement – the firm is still privately owned and self-financing – has been the energy, innovativeness and sheer flair of the Grants themselves, and without making invidious distinction between the two, the phenomenal drive and colourful personality of Pat Grant, Business Woman of the Year in

---

[1] *Icing on the Cake; 21st Anniversary Supplement:* a highly informative 'celebration of Norfrost in words and pictures,' published by *JOGJ*, 1994. Much information in this section is derived from it.

1986 and OBE in 1988.

Rockwater

There can be little doubt that, Dounreay apart, nothing quite so high tech as Rockwater has yet hit north Caithness. Over the years Wick has harboured a certain sense of disappointment that it has captured little attention from the oil interests that now dominate affairs in the upper North Sea, especially as Beatrice platforms on every clear day are very visible from the Heads of Wick. The disappointment is tempered by a certain pride that Rockwater has come to lodge in the vicinity and that to a modest extent Wick Harbour offers some benefits to this unusual and enterprising firm.

The interest of Rockwater in this part of the Caithness coast arose from a connection that the former Kestrel Marine Engineering firm had with the harbour, and it was while Kestrel Marine was developing the harbour base at Wick for the potential supply/service activities which they had hoped to capture from the Northern oilfields that Conoco approached Kestrel to consider the fabrication of a pipeline bundle for the Murchison Field. In a joint venture with the Dutch company Smit, very much involved in subsea technology, the attention of Smit-Kestrel was drawn to the possibilities of Sinclair's Bay, just north of Wick, for the landward assembly and launching of pipeline bundles for offshore installation, a new, adventurous and innovatory technique. The running of multiple pipelines within a single 'carrier pipe' is necessary to save duplication and sea-floor pipeline congestion. Such bundles may be up to 6.6 kilometres long, and their fabrication on land before their towing out and positioning offshore involves intricate, sophisticated and constantly developing techniques. The Wester site lies towards the south end of Sinclair's Bay and has become the location of a unique and complex fabrication process.

This takes place in an enormous 'Fabshop' close by the sea-shore at the mouth of the Wester River, a short flow from the Loch of Wester fed by the Lyth Burn. The site extends back for 6.6 kilometres inland over the Moss of Wester, and incorporates a light-rail line, on which travel bogies which carry the outer protective steel pipes or 'carriers', as much as 28.25 inches in diameter, inside which are threaded and secured the actual 'bundles' of flow and control pipelines of the system. The interior flow and other pipes are supplied in lengths of 12 metres and are welded together to form 'Through Flow Lines'. The insides are cleaned and sometimes coated with corrosion-proof paint thrust along in 'slugs' between a pair of 'pigs' by means of compressed air. The welds are inspected by radiographic techniques before the interior pipes are fixed in polyurethane spacers inside the carrier pipe, and are finally hydrostatically tested. As the string is being assembled it is pulled out landward on bogies which carry it back along the straight track, where it remains until launching.

The location was chosen precisely because Sinclair's Bay shelves out to sea on a very shallow gradient, while behind the bay the land is fairly flat, allowing for the construction of a straight track without humps. A chief difficulty experienced until recently along the track was the lowness and narrowness of the bridge that straddled the site and the A9 between Wick and John O'Groats, making passage impossible for the wider-diameter assemblies contemplated. Impossible, too, was the accommodation on the track of the huge towheads now being used, a problem now eased by the recent construction of a lift-bridge. Towards this Caithness and Sutherland Enterprise and the Highland Regional Council contributed in the region of £300,000 each, the balance being supplied by Rockwater itself.[1] Near the shore is the remnant of an ancient monument in the form of a broch which has, however, been bypassed by skilful alignment of the track.

Before the launch, attached to each end of the string is a 'towhead', a fairly complicated structure which arrives on the site already fully fabricated, and which serves both to facilitate the towing operation when the string is taken out to sea, that at the front taking the stress of the pull and that at the rear serving to maintain a proper tension on the string so that it does not flex unduly. When the platform site has been reached the towheads enable the whole assembly to be flexibly connected with the platform delivery pipe systems themselves. Towing to the site is accomplished by means of a powerful tug, connected to the string by means of high-tension steel cable, aided as necessary by means of another tug or tugs. The process is known as 'Controlled-Depth Tow Method' (CDTM). The bundle is towed to site at a controlled depth in the water, the control being effected by lengths of heavy chain sufficient to keep the string at a regulated depth, thus avoiding stresses caused by waves and allowing surface

1 *Highland Focus* (the Development Department Bulletin of the Highland Regional Council), Vol 4, No 2, Autumn 1994. Without the lift-bridge the contract would have gone to Norway.

craft to proceed across the line of tow without hindrance.

Launching can only take place when the weather conditions are sufficiently calm for the long and carefully monitored operation. As the string reaches the beach at Wester the burden of each length of pipe is taken up by 'grillages' which relieve the bogies of their load, these being shunted off track. Once launched the bundle may be towed for distances as far away as one thousand kilometres, if required, to installations only a short way south of the Arctic circle. Arrived at the site and the 'bundles' connected up and systems tested, the annulus or interior of the carrier is flooded and for its life in service, the system lies on the sea-bed which has been previously cleared of possible obstructions. The wellbeing of the system is maintained by the aid of highly sensitive computer-controlled monitoring and undersea inspection devices and, if necessary, repairs and maintenance can be conducted by divers or by operating 'Remote Operated Vehicles' or 'ROVs' from a 'ship-work' vessel.

The pipes and towheads required for the sophisticated processes undertaken at Wester, Caithness, of necessity have to be made in plants far to the south. Transport to the site is, therefore, itself a considerable task. The 27m-long carrier pipes are brought north on long transporters which have to negotiate some extremely difficult bends and curves en route, for instance at Navidale and the Ord and in the main streets of Wick itself. Wick Bridge Street joins High Street at a quite narrow T-junction, which the transporters are unable to get round without a rather complicated manoeuvre. The 'carousel' as it is called, has two tractors, one at the front which operates in much the same way as the tractor of an articulated truck. The rest of the vehicle cannot, however, get round the right-angled corner without the aid of a rear tractor, which is put in power and is driven independently of the front tractor while the towing tractor is manoeuvred to the off-side kerb, the rear tractor is put in power to push the rear of the load on to the near-side of Bridge Street, thus crooking or 'jack-knifing' the entire vehicle so that it can get round the corner without chopping off the corner shop. This exercise provides the citizens of Wick with a fairly frequent free entertainment; no failures have so far been recorded.

The towheads are a different problem. When completed they are extremely heavy – the figure of 180 tonnes is mentioned for a towhead assembly being towed ashore in Wick Harbour from aboard a low-loading barge, *Last Drager*, in a recent report in the *Caithness Courier*. As the report and picture indicate, it was a difficult operation in which 'the old dry dock of Scalesburn was pressed into service to make the manoeuvre possible.'[1] Reports appear from time to time of other equipment for the firm arriving at the harbour, for instance buoyancy tanks for towheads.[2] The actual handling work on the towhead was undertaken by a Glasgow firm specialising in heavy lift contracts. All this is in connection with a very large contract being undertaken by Rockwater for the Conoco Heidrun field. Towheads for another contract, that of BP Cyrus, are being constructed at Highland Fabricators, Nigg, on the Cromarty Firth.

Subject to good weather, Sinclair's Bay is an ideal site for CDTM. The Caithness Rockwater unit that has pioneered this method of pipeline construction, earlier part of Smit-Kestrel, is now owned by Brown and Root, a wholly American company. Wick, as such, may well in due course be brought more into the picture since, subject to considerable repairs to the fabric of the harbour, it is evident that Rockwater has an interest in utilising the facilities that it offers even in its present condition; it would be happier still with harbour improvements.

Rockwater in Caithness, of course, is a unit of Rockwater UK, based in Aberdeen, itself one of seven subsidiaries of the main company in different parts of the world. Its nearest neighbour, with which it cooperates as necessary, is Rockwater A/S of Tastagen, Stavanger. Between them these companies undertake many different sorts of undersea oil field installation projects, for example, drilling support, extended well-testing, tensioning leg platforms, monopod platform developments, all at a high level of technical innovation. The firm boasts in its publicity – *ANY DEPTH, ANY ENVIRONMENT, ANY FIELD.*

The Wester Site operation is by no means the least important of the sub-sea activities of this worldwide enterprise, but it is by far the most exotic of the post-war industrial developments in this locality. Contracts tend to be episodic, and accordingly the district work force fluctuates according to the projects in hand, between 50 and 100. Among the work completed since 1979 have been projects for all the

1 *Caithness Courier,* 13 March, 1994.
2 *Caithness Courier,* 16 April, 1994.
The rest of the information on this section has been derived from a Rockwater Video on the subject of 'CDTM', the Rockwater trade brochure, *The Total Service in Offshore Contracting,* a background brief entitled *Wester Site Construction Facility,* and a very instructive conversation with Mr William Watt, Construction Site Manager, Rockwater, Wester Site, Caithness. Mr Watt has also kindly vetted the piece to ensure its technical correctness.

main oil companies operating in the North Sea. Prospects must now include work on the projected development in the new field to Fair Isle.

Two kinds of Nourishing Liquor.

Two establishments well known in Wick deserve a mention in these annals; neither has contributed much to the post-war developments of Wick, though arguably have had a lot to do with the content of its state of mind. They are the Claymore Creamery and the Pulteney Distillery, both producers of nourishing liquids that have never yet lacked for a sale and appreciative buyers. The Creamery is housed in a self-contained dairy behind the Wick Railway Station. Until recently its tankers have collected most of the milk produced in this area of Caithness, but the pattern of collection has changed greatly since the creamery was set up in 1946 by the newly created Milk Marketing Board – now, but very recently, defunct. At that time there were no less than 140 producers from whom the milk was hauled, at that time in churns. By 1965 the number had been reduced to 79 and by the present year, it had dropped to 12, though the 12 between them produce more milk than the original 140. The daily throughput of liquid milk through the creamery is 3,000 gallons.

Up to now Claymore has processed most of the milk drunk in Wick, has been in the habit of supplying milk as far away as Tongue, and is even known to send processed milk to Skye. One other milk purveyor operates in the area, the Ronaldsons of Westerseat, though this may well soon change under the new conditions of 'freedom' awarded to farmers to sell to whom they wish. Instead of the Marketing Board we have the 'Milk Marque', whose first effect was to raise the price of retailed milk.[1]

Stoddart's Pulteney Distillery has appeared before in our story. It is a small establishment as distilleries go, in Huddart Street, and like the Creamery employs only a few, perhaps a dozen workers. It has existed since 1826 and has sustained during its existence many a flagging spirit. As we have earlier mentioned, Professor McDowall says of its product, 'Old Pulteney': 'It is a whisky of considerable distinction having a succession of flavours and not noticeably peaty; indeed, one is tempted to think that a good whisky could be made without peat at all. The distillery was closed down between 1926 and

1 Discussion with Creamery's General Manager, Alistair Taylor.

1951, coinciding fairly closely with the years of alcohol drought in Wick, from 1921 to 1947. For Old Pulteney then, as now, was 'only available locally'. It is, he says 'a pity that there is not more of it in the south, but it must be remembered that the Scots do not export all their best products.' When it came it is little wonder that prohibition strangled Old Pulteney's restricted market.

McDowall regards Old Pulteney as a necessary means to warm up the 'bare county' of Caithness and 'this grim, windswept fishing town on the North Sea.' During prohibition no doubt many Wickers and Pulteneytowners felt the draught. Mercifully Old Pulteney came back to resume its central heating role in Wick. The re-born distillery was bought up by Hiram Walker, originally a Canadian concern, which has acquired over the years several important Scottish distilleries, and is assiduous in maintaining their reputation. Pulteney is used in the blending of 'Old Smuggler' and 'Ballantine's'.[1]

TRANSPORT

One of Wick's perennial economic handicaps has been its great distance from almost every place else with which it could do business. We have seen how in mediaeval times and as late as the eighteenth century the town was cut off from southerly centres of government and trade. Matters began to improve in the nineteenth century when new road systems spread north and most notably Thomas Telford's trunk road along the east coast at last rendered Wick accessible to wheeled transport. Communication by boat was and remained difficult on account of the town's fractious seas and capricious weather, and inadequacies of harbourage in Wick Bay. Steam shipping made access to Wick easier for travellers and businessmen, but as we have seen, the *Sovereign* and its successors were not always able to land or board passengers safely at Wick.

We have seen, too, something of the difficulties and dangers of land travel even along the improved roads, how coaches were liable to be overturned in evil weather or buried in snow. How great excitement was generated by the epic horseback ride of Davidson of Tulloch from Inverness to Wick in a day, and by Lord Caithness driving his steam-carriage from London to Mey through Wick. Even when the railway came, the story has often been one of trains disappearing in

1 R J S McDowall: *The Whiskies of Scotland*, London, John Murray.

snow-drifts; and by comparison with other schedules in 'Bradshaw,' the ride from Inverness to Wick and Thurso was always a long one.

Though improved from the nineteenth century, personal travel and goods haulage to and from Wick remained difficult until the age of the motor vehicle, and even so improvements were not spectacular until after the Second World War. Post-war Wick has, however, now become connected in ways utterly unimaginable in earlier times, with much better roads, speedier cars and powerful trucks. Articulated tractors and trailers bear their thirty-four tonne loads to and from Wick with impressive celerity, negotiating with ease the hills and hairpins of the Ord and Navidale. Nevertheless, the cost of transport has always been critical in economic decisions in north Caithness, and has greatly influenced the nature of the industrial development that has occurred here since 1945. Practically all the industries that have succeeded involve the manufacture of high value goods from non-bulky lower-value materials.

Wick has quite as high a level of car ownership as anywhere else in Britain, and the locality is served, west, south and north with a network of bus lines, the services mainly of the Highland Bus Company and Dunnets and a number of minor operators. The railway, though still fortunately with us, carries very little freight and provides only a modest under-used passenger service, three 'Sprinters' a day each way in winter and four in the summer, all subject to severe competition from long-distance bus services. A frequent issue of gloomy discussion in Wick today is whether or not the rail service will survive at all, especially now that 'privatisation' is upon it. While road mileage between Wick and Inverness has been handsomely cut by the building of the Dornoch Bridge, the prospect of a rail bridge across the Firth to match it, proposed often enough, now seems a forlorn hope. The most go-ahead development in Wick transport today is undoubtedly that centred on Wick Airport.

Wick Airport and Services.

Air services at Wick were started in the 1930s by Captain E E Fresson OBE, who first came to the locality to survey land for possible use as an airfield. He identified two sites as being suitable, Barnyards south-west of the town and Hillhead Farm to the north. Hillhead was chosen, walls, hedges and ditches were cleared and the site was licenced as a landing ground. Fresson's airline, Highland Airways

Ltd, was incorporated in April, 1933 and the first scheduled flight from Longman Field, Inverness, to Kirkwall (Wideford Brae) was made on 8 May, a month later. There was a short stop at Wick, the first landing here. It is believed that the flight was in fact the first scheduled flight anywhere in the United Kingdom. From Inverness to Wick took 50 minutes; Fresson spent 15 minutes at Wick and went on to complete the flight to Wideford in a total time of an hour and fifteen minutes flying.

By the end of May of that year Highland Airways had carried 143 passengers between Inverness and Kirkwall. In his autobiography Captain Fresson tells of the enthusiasm and excitement generated in the north of Scotland by these pioneering efforts. Longman Airfield at Inverness was opened by the Duke and Duchess of Sutherland on 17 June, 1933, which Highland Airways made the occasion of a monster Air Display which was attended by 20,000 people, who at the beginning of the proceedings attempted to invade the airfield without paying. 'Quickly I gathered all the police I could,' says Fresson, 'and marched them across the aerodrome to the end of the road situated alongside the airport. We closed arms and marched forward, holding the barbed wire barrier in front of us, the police at the same time shouting to the crowd to get back. Gradually they retreated and at last we got them behind the houses on Longman Road. We then admitted them after payment of an admission fee.'

No such scenes were enacted at Wick. Fresson's next mention of Wick refers to the scheduled flight of 3 July: 'We ran into the fog at Wick and scuttled across the Firth under it.' This would not be the last time that Wick airfield became fog-bound. Worse was to come. 'Swirling mist,' enveloped the plane as it approached the top of the hill at Wideford. The pilot

> turned at right angles to the North to slip down the hill towards the sea. 'We got under it again and had another try to reach Wideford. As I reached our airfield, I started to run into swirling mists again and as there was a nice field in front and uphill, I put the plane down just over the stone dyke. There was a terrific bump and the plane quickly came to rest. What a sight presented itself when we got out of the aircraft. The two motors were hanging down as if they were falling out of the wings, and the undercarriage was twisted and bent. We went back along the line of the landing to find out what had happened, and discovered that there was a shallow pit which was completely

overgrown with high grass. The landing wheels had struck it about six inches below the sharp edge and the force of impact must have been terrific at the speed we were travelling. No wonder the plane was bent, and what frightful luck, for there was not another rough place in the whole field and had I been five yards right or left or three feet higher, I should have missed that lone hole.

Captain Fresson, 'overcome with despair', was comforted by his passengers, who seem to have been less put out than the pilot himself. Such were the hazards of early commercial flying in the north of Scotland. Fresson also had his development problems. Having invested in a couple of de Havilland 'Dragon Rapide' planes, his company had plans to establish a regular line between Aberdeen and Orkney, only to find that E L Gandar Dower had bought the airfield site that was to become Dyce Airport, Aberdeen, and was busy setting up a service of his own to the northern islands. Fresson was aware that at this stage 'there was no room for two services in competition on the Orkney run.' He gives a graphic account of how he visited Gandar Dower in the 'Caledonian Hotel,' Aberdeen, and made a compact with him that Highland Airways would concentrate on the routes from Aberdeen to the north, while Gandar Dower's Aberdeen Airways worked his planes west and south. The compact was broken shortly after by Gandar Dower, and 'from that date a war of attrition began that was to last until 1939,' when a Licensing Court 'robbed us of our Aberdeen services.'[1]

However, after a successful twelve months of operation, Highland Airways were awarded a Royal Mail contract by the Postmaster General, and the first mail-carrying flight from Inverness to Kirkwall was on 22 May, 1934. On 1st December, the same year Fresson began carrying mail at normal surface postal rates from Inverness to Wick. During the rest of the 1930s there was strenuous rivalry between Fresson and Gandar Dower, with various attempts at establishing regular routes between Aberdeen and different localities in Orkney including Longhope, Cumminess and Stromness, none of them really viable. Both companies, that of Fresson and of Gandar Dower, changed their names and status during the period, that of Gandar Dower from Aberdeen becoming Allied Airways in 1936, while Fresson's company was bought up by British Airways in 1937 and

[1] E E Fresson: *Air Road to the Isles: The Memoirs of Captain E E Fresson, OBE*; David Rendell (1963), pp 103-105.

renamed Scottish Airways. Neither company was very kind to the other, mostly refusing to allow the other to use its own airfields; Gandar Dower, for instance, was the prime mover in developing Dyce at Aberdeen; Fresson was obliged to operate from Kintore.

Perhaps the most interesting development to affect Wick before 1938 was the controversy about whether or not Thurso should create a municipal aerodrome. The prospects for such a development were considered good by both competitors, but the Thurso Town Council despite its 'large summer tourist trade,' havered on the question. The Air Ministry sent up surveyors who favoured the site of Dixonfield Farm, owned by Sir Archibald Sinclair, then Secretary of State for Scotland – later Secretary of State for Air. The move locally was led by James Wilson, a Thurso businessman. The story is told in *Rivals in the North*,[1] of how plans for a Thurso airport collapsed. In the words of Captain Fresson, 'Nothing further happened and Thurso probably lost for all time the chance of holding her position in air transport in the extreme north. Had Dixonfield been constructed, more than likely the Air Ministry would have developed it further during the war, just as they developed Scottish Airways airfield at Wick, and today they would have had a modern airport!'

For a time Wick Town Council became alarmed; according to Fresson, 'for some unknown reason they got it into their heads that we were going to cut Wick off with their airmail service and so commenced writing to Ministers, Postmaster General and licensing authorities to continue to bring pressure on Scottish Airways to continue the airmail service!' Though not over enamoured of the idea of one of the alternatives to Dixonfield, Claredon, being used at the time by Gandar Dower, as he thought it too small for general purposes, Fresson agreed to the idea of using Claredon for light mail deliveries, as it might 'encourage the Thurso Town Council to provide a Municipal Airfield at Dixonfield Farm.' His main reason for wanting a proper airfield at Thurso was 'on account of the weather. Frequently it was extremely difficult and even risky trying to land at Wick. Situated bang on the north-east coast, the town was subject to sea mists and low cloud which frequently settled over the area, whereas Thurso did not suffer so acutely from that type of weather.' However, Dixonfield was not to be and Wick remained the only properly licensed airfield in the north. Fresson expressed himself, too, as grateful to Wick on a different count: 'With the exception of Inverness

---

1 Peter Clegg: *Rivals in the North;* publisher not identified (1988), pp 131-132.

Town Council, the Wick City Fathers were the only public body to give us any help in those difficult days.' The fog still rolls in at Wick.

Wick did not retain control of the small airfield so far used by Fresson. Ostensibly to 'serve the increasing number of passengers and freight being carried,' but doubtless in anticipation of possible war, the Secretary of State for Air bought from the Hempriggs Estate an area of 277.36 acres comprising the farms of Westerseat, Lochshell and the farm of Clayquoys on which to construct an aerodrome. No runway was constructed at this time, the planes landing on a grass strip.

Construction of the aerodrome went on apace, and on 15 September, 1939, a few days after the start of the Second World War, the Wick RAF Station was formed on this aerodrome site. This speeded up construction work and by the end of September sufficient equipment and stores were on site to accommodate 803 Squadron, and in October 269 Squadron of Avro-Ansons moved to Wick from Montrose. Their task was anti-submarine and convoy patrol work. As there was still no hard runway, the grass airstrip became a quagmire and there was a rush to lay down tarmac. Flying in and out of the mud continued while construction was going on.

The Wick RAF Station became the major airfield north of Inverness. It eventually had three 150 foot wide runways, the longest 6,000 feet in length, capable fo taking the largest craft then flying. A range of RAF buildings was constructed. Until more permanent structures were available, aircraft were serviced in three Bessanau hangars consisting of a wooden frame covered with canvas. These were eventually replaced by four massive 'CI' hangars, two of which still survive and are still in use on the Wick Airport. Aircraft from Wick undertook some of the earliest action of RAF planes over Scapa Flow, and as we have seen, the Wick and other RAF airfields in the area accommodated a great variety of planes on many different kinds of service during the war. Although initially ordered to cease operating his air service, in no time Fresson found himself in the 'Gilbertian situation' of running 'a spate of Charter flights' over the route and shortly after that Scottish Airways were ordered 'to resume the Orkney service as soon as possible.' Though not necessarily doing much flying himself, Fresson found himself, in October, 1940, instructed to 'take charge of the air communications for the North of Scotland on behalf of the Air Ministry,' a responsibility continued throughout the rest of the war. There were, needless to say, some hairy moments for the civilian pilots who flew the service.

At the end of the war the airfield quickly reverted to civil use. Gandar Dower was elected, by a margin of six votes, MP for Caithness and Sutherland in July, 1945. British European Airways came into existence in January, 1946, and took over responsibility for all domestic scheduled air services in Britain. In February, 1947, BEA assumed full control of Fresson's scheduled services and in April did the same with Gandar Dower's routes. Traffic into and out of Wick remained 'marginal' for many years, and in 1983, owing to continuing losses, BEA withdrew its services in the area, its place being taken by Air Ecosse, which itself went out of business in 1990. Up to this time, although it had more than fifty years of experience behind it, Wick Airport and the services using it cannot be said to have been a huge success. Wick, unlike Sumburgh, had no share in the boost to traffic that came with the opening up of the North Sea oilfields.

Prospects, however, were improving. In 1985, the airport had been acquired and was subsequently run as a wholly owned subsidiary of the Civil Aviation Authority, incorporated in March, 1986 as a private limited company. Wick is one of nine such airports, ranging from Islay to Sumburgh and including Inverness. Since most of these airports are committed to providing 'remote communities with vital social, business and welfare links,' the Authority is subsidised by the Scottish Office, to the extent of £4½m during the operational year 1991-1992 (to 31 March) and £6m in 1993-94. This against a turnover of £15m and a profit, after taxation of £1,533,000 for 1993-94.

Air Ecosse went bankrupt in 1990, and British Airways again ran the Wick-Aberdeen service until in 1992, another company, Gill Air, took over. This Company had been building up since 1969 a substantial domestic air service based in Newcastle. Gill Air now operates the main service from Wick to Aberdeen, and from there on to various destinations in the United Kingdom, including Newcastle, Manchester, Belfast, London and Guernsey. The work-horse of the Gill Air fleet is the Short 330, a sturdy aircraft that may not perhaps win any prizes for elegance but is extremely reliable. In addition to considerable streamlining of the Gill Air services, there have been changes in management structure. The Wick unit, supervised by a Manager/Engineer, Andrew Duncan, is self-contained, consisting of a well-trained stable team, trained locally and no longer subject to frequent changes of duty.

In the meantime, Loganair, a Scottish based company had been developing routes especially to the western and northern islands of Scotland. Until recently Loganair operated from Wick a considerable number of Islander aircraft, small eight-seater planes, buoyant and very convenient for the short-run schedules between, for instance, the individual Orkney Islands; but in 1995, flight policy has changed as Loganair has been integrated with British Airways to the extent that all services are now advertised as those of British Airways, but operated under concession by Loganair, whose management structure, though intact, is now that of a subsidiary company under the British Airways umbrella. Most services between Wick and Kirkwall now involve the use of Short 360 machines, with a considerably larger capacity than the little planes that used to flip across the Pentland Firth.

Wick Airport itself has recently undergone a major re-development costing £1.2m. This has included the complete refitting and extension of the terminal building, a new control tower, administrative buildings, motor-transport accommodation and a fire-station which, with appliances alone cost £500,000. This expensive reconstruction had been partly a response to improved prospects and greater diversification of business, and faith in the development potential of air passenger and freight traffic to and from Wick. The decision of the Highlands and Islands Airports Board to go ahead with the scheme was, according to a former Chairman of HIAL, Robert Crawford CBE, partly prompted by awareness that Wick airport, unlike the company's six island airports, is faced with 'strong competition from road and rail'.[1]

Among the sorts of traffic which the Company now seeks to attract are more business travellers as new business develops in the locality, an increase in tourist use of the airport, and freight in the form of light spares and supplies for local industries. Chartered flights especially to and from Scandinavia are on the increase. Modest club flying services are now based on Wick and from 1991 're-fuelling facilites during airport hours has broadened the services available to local operators and the wider aviation community.' These facilities, among other things, have meant the arrival on the airport from time to time of helicopters, operated from elsewhere and mainly concerned with ferrying personnel to and from oil-rigs in the West Shetland Basin. Expectations are high, but it was reported in July, 1994 that 'passenger traffic and aircraft movements fell dramatically in the

1 *Caithness Courier*, 27 October, 1993.

financial year, 1993-1994.' 33,388 people used the airport, a drop of 16 per cent on the previous year, but there was a 4 per cent increase in the amount of freight handled.[1]

A recent alteration to the geography of the airport has been the closure, under an order from the Secretary of State for Scotland, of the unclassified road that used to cross the runway at its eastern end, cutting off that route to Staxigoe and Noss. This has been greatly objected to, but clearly there is not much to be said for a 'level crossing' on an aircraft runway on which increased aircraft movement is expected. The Airport is now managed by Angela Donaldson who was appointed in April 1992 and who looks forward to a considerable increase in the importance of the airport to the life of Wick and Caithness generally.

PROMOTIONAL AND DEVELOPMENT AGENCIES

It would be a mistake to assume that Wick's impressive adaptation to its new circumstances was wholly a matter of individual enterprise. The new concerns that have brought Wick a new prosperity – however patchy this may sometimes seem – have as often as not been assisted by one or more of the development agencies that now function in Caithness, creating a picture not wholly dissimilar to the conditions which prevailed when Wick was planted on the herring map at the beginning of last century. Then Sir John Sinclair and others concerned with the development of Pulteneytown were amply assisted by the British Fisheries Society, the network created by the Commissioners for Highland Roads and Bridges and contributions from local landowners, of whom Sir John himself was among the more generous. The main bodies involved in recent times have been the one-time Scottish Council (Development and Industry), in the case of Caithness Glass, Caithness County Council (before its demise in 1975), the Highland Regional Council since that time, and most recently the Caithness and Sutherland Enterprise Board. The area has also in recent years been benefiting from EEC development grants, as plaques at the entrances to the Wick Industrial Estate announce.

We saw how the present representative of the Sinclair of Ulbster

---

1 *Caithness Courier*, 27 July, 1994.
Much of the detail of this section is derived from Annual Reports of Highlands and Islands Airports Ltd, 1991-92, 1992-93, 1993-94, and from discussion with Angela Donaldson, Manager of Wick Airport. A brief history is also exhibited in the Airport Lounge.

dynasty took a bold initiative in setting up Caithness Glass. When able and ready the firm moved on to the town's Industrial Estate, sometimes called the 'Airport Industrial Estate' on account of the fact that the main acreage of this extensive area was bought from the Defence Department in the 1960s by the County Council. The initiative was taken by Fred Levens, the then Industrial Development Officer of the Council. Included in the purchase were the large Canadian hangar buildings which are now among the facilities available for leasing to tenants. They remain in the compound of the airport and one is used as workshop and hangar by Gill Air. The other is partly used as garage and workshop by the Highland Bus and Coach Company. Both remain the largest buildings on the Wick horizon.

From 1975 onwards the policy initiated by the Caithness County Council was continued by the Highland Development Council, to which ownership of the estate now reverted. In the 1980s a substantial programme of 'land renewal' and clearance of 'industrial dereliction' on the site was undertaken, making use of funds provided by the Scottish Office. Conditions of letting include decent maintenance of the area rented by the tenant. Today the Estate has an adequate system of roads and service amenities and, as we have seen, several fairly large concerns are now located there. It is believed that upwards of 250 people are employed on the estate, the largest single employer being Grampian Records which expects in due course to take on more workers.

The Highland Regional Council is one of the very largest umbrella local government units in Britain, with a total area of 9,800 square miles, stretching from Durness and John O'Groats in the north, to Ballachulish and Dalwhinnie in the south, a distance by road of well over 200 miles of difficult and mountainous terrain. From Wick to the Highland capital of Inverness is 110 miles. The distances by rail, are, if anything longer, on account of the inland loop that takes the railway to Lairg. The area has a population of 206,000 which gives a density for the area of 21 per square mile, one of the very lowest in the country, and rurally much less, bearing in mind that the majority of the people live in towns which include Inverness, Fort William, Nairn, Grantown and Thurso and Wick. To complete the picture the Highland Regional Council maintains 4,600 miles of road, 1,720 bridges, operates 450 of its own vehicles and 2,050 items of mobile plant. The region claims to have a staff of 10,000, many of whom –

especially senior staff – must cover vast mileages doing their jobs.

It is this area, which, under the recent Local Government Act (Scotland), is to take over direct responsibility for 85 per cent of all local authority services in the Highlands. This development will probably make little difference to the management and funding of the Wick Industrial Estate, which is one only of 36 already administered by the Highland Council, making a base for 2,300 jobs.[1]

The Caithness and Sutherland Enterprise Board (CASE)

The public body today most concerned with industrial and social development is the Caithness and Sutherland Enterprise Board, one of a network of ten such bodies in north and west Scotland constituting Highlands and Islands Enterprise (HIE), covering 'a vast and diverse area with many distinct communities,' stretching from Shetland to Argyll and affecting the lives of '370,000 individuals with skills and potential of their own and more than 3,000 voluntary and community groups.' Each has its own board, a 'quango' of up to a dozen local representatives of various interests in the area. The boards are funded by the Scottish Office. They operate through a salaried Chief Executive and their 'strategic theme' is to advise locally on 'the environmental, scenic and cultural heritage, and the advantage this gives to the area, its products and services in competitive markets.' They take an annual overview of development, employment and economic prospects of the area, publish statistics on these matters, give advice and assist in promoting training facilities, and where, after assessment the board considers it appropriate provide financial and logistic support for new and expanding individual enterprises, a process the Caithness Board describes as 'our primary catalyst.' During 1993 the Board supported some 135 cases 'throughout Caithness and Sutherland from Lochinver to Lybster and from Durness to Dornoch.' Even fishing gets support, though mostly in these days further west than Wick. As we have mentioned, several businesses in the Wick area have gained CASE support, notably Grampian Records, Rockwater and Caithness Glass. Total operational expenditure, mainly in the form of investment, initial and training grants in the year up to 31 March, 1994 ran to some £5,420,000, an increase of more than £1m on the previous year.

1 *Highland Regional Council, 1974-1994* (Fact Sheet) published by Highland News Group, Dingwall (1994).

As successive issues of the *Caithness Courier* and the *John O'Groat Journal* constantly reiterate, a prime problem and worry in the whole area is the effect of the rundown of Dounreay. So far, CASE claims that this rundown, 'which is now well over half complete, has not yet resulted in the economic decline many predicted. On the contrary, the loss of jobs at Dounreay has been compensated by new jobs elsewhere in the county. Unemployment remains close to the national average.'[1]

Indeed, satisfaction with what has been achieved so far by CASE is not restricted to the Board's opinion of itself. According to a mid-summer report in the *Groat*, 'Caithness had recorded the highest economic growth rate of the eight Highland districts, showing an increase of 1.8 per cent.' As compared with Sutherland, Caithness was well ahead, but 'of the 56 districts [of Scotland], Caithness showed the 17th highest increase in output, as measured by gross domestic product. The total estimated production for Caithness was £215.8 million, third highest in the Highlands, but only ranking 43rd out of the 56 Scottish districts.'[2] On the other hand, 'four out of five businesses in Caithness are concerned about the whereabouts of the £9 million aid package for the Dounreay rundown,' and 'a startling 95 per cent of businesses either don't believe or don't know if the figures about the number of jobs which CASE claims to have supported are true.'[3]

It is not here our concern to advance or refute the claims of the Caithness and Sutherland Enterprise Board to have put Caithness and, with it, Wick, on the way to a new prosperity. There can be little doubt that both population and employment rates in the area fell between the two censuses, 1981 and 1991, and also that the age distribution of the locality has also changed, an increase in the number of residents between 20 and 64 (the so-called 'economically active' proportion of the population), a small increase in the over 65s, 'while the population of those aged 19 or under has experienced a substantial fall.' The indications are that, with the help of CASE, the area has been able to hold its own in economic terms, but that the unemployment rate (11.8 per cent for the Caithness and Sutherland area as a whole) is rather high as compared with the HIE area generally and Scotland as a whole.[4] The future, however, holds no

1 *Annual Report*, 1993-1994, CASE.
2 *JOGJ*, 6 July, 1994.
3 *JOGJ*, 18 June, 1994.
4 *Caithness and Sutherland Update;* Highland and Islands Enterprise, Network Economic Information, May 1994.

certain promises of high employment and high prosperity for Caithness. CASE is assisting the area to keep its head above water, and by its own efforts and helping to funnel in EEC aid, is probably justified in believing, as the ex-chairman, Don Clarkson, puts it, that CASE is 'on course to achieve our mission of "prosperous and self-sustaining business and social communities in Caithness and Sutherland by the year 2000".'[1] There are, nevertheless, many straws in the wind suggesting that this is going to remain uphill work, and that whatever levels of ingenuity and enterprise have so far been exercised to keep Caithness – and Wick in particular – going well to maintain these levels, will have to keep on running fast, like the Red Queen, to keep in the same place, and faster still if there is to be advance in the future.

THE BODY AND SOUL OF WICK.

To comment only on the basic economic and political transformations with which we have so far been concerned in this sketch of Wick today, would be to leave out of account other critical influences that have helped to convert the town from the drab, rather gloomy, fishy place it once was into a brighter, cleaner, healthier and perhaps livelier locality. Other aspects of modern Wick deserving our attention before we end our story of this most northerly royal Scottish burgh, include its health, educational and recreational facilities; nor can we leave the story without a word or two about the churches today, at one time so important a part of people's lives here.

Health and Welfare.

It can hardly be said that in old Wick that provision for the sick was exemplary. Symptomatic of Wick and Pulteneytown's apparent lack of interest in the well-being of the body beautiful of its citizens is the almost complete lack of reference in the many pages of *Times Gone By,* both issues, to doctors, nurses and hospitals. One notable exception is a portrait of Dr Eric Sinclair, whose 'stately form' was well-known and who was 'the town's leading physician and surgeon'. He lived in Montpelier House and 'made all his visits from his carriage, a roomy Brougham drawn by two grey, richly-caparisoned horses.' This would be during the middle years of last century. Dr Sinclair's 'presence in a sick room brought with it a ray of comforting confidence.' Among

1 *Annual Report,* CASE, 1993-1994, p2.

those who were comforted by his presence were the Earl James and Countess of Caithness with whom he was 'a great friend' and 'they resided with him while visiting Wick.' There is no representation of his house, which was evidently a fine one. The house near the parish church of Dr James Leask of a later generation also is shown – or at least its position is indicated in the Bishop engraving printed in the *Groat* of 19 March, 1847 (See Chapter 12 p. 305) is shown. Yet one other reference to medical affairs occurs in *Times Gone By*, in the form of 'Wick's new health clinic' of the 1930s, actually a child welfare clinic, in fact, the reconstructed Pulteneytown 'lock-up' of seventy years before, standing on the 'upper end of James Bremner's shipbuilding yard'. It was no doubt difficult to attract doctors here.

It is probably unfair to judge the town's attitude to health and welfare by the lack of reference to such matters in the hundreds of pages of these compilations, but by contrast there are dozens of pictures of ministers, policemen and soldiers. It is evident that until Dr Alexander was appointed Medical Officer of Health to the county in the 1880s, Wick enjoyed only rudimentary medical services, and it is fairly probable that the town's few doctors saw less of poor patients than those who could pay well. That the poor were visited and treated when absolutely necessary is confirmed by the assiduous records of the doctor who dealt with cholera victims of 1849 and which we have examined. There is reference in the description of 1847 to a 'cholera hospital' in Pulteneytown, but no information. If Dr Sinclair is anything to go by, the doctors that came believed in maintaining a grand style.

The first significant hospital foundation in Wick came late in the day, when Arthur Bignold, MP for the Northern Burghs, in 1903 gave a house on the main road opposite the corner of Hill Avenue and George Street which, added to and improved, continued in use as a hospital until 1986. The building has since been converted into residential flats, the compound now being known as Bignold Court. This was not the only gift of this philanthropic MP to the town, as we shall see. As already told, the patients of Bignold Hospital were transferred to Lybster after the Wick buildings had been bomb-damaged (p 669). When repaired the Bignold was taken over by the RAF for the duration, and it resumed its pre-war status and functions in 1947. A brief account of it during its exile was published in 1946, based on a survey conducted in 1942-1943:

> This cottage hospital is a stone building, with an extension,

on a restricted site unsuitable for further additions. It has 28 beds, in two wards of 10 beds each, two rooms of 3 beds each, and two single rooms; small operating theatre with anaesthetic and sterilising rooms; fixed and portable X-ray units; kitchen fair size; small mortuary. It has all mains services; partial central heating, and open fires; no laundry.

This account, part of an official survey of Scottish Hospitals, is followed by recommendations that the Bignold be replaced by 'a new cottage hospital, associated with and on the site of the Henderson Memorial Nursing Home,' and when so replaced, Bignold 'should then be used for the care of the chronic sick and for advanced cases of pulmonary tuberculosis.' The two hospitals, Bignold and Henderson 'should be staffed by a common nursing staff, and it would be desirable to aim at common ownership and administration for the two hospitals and the Henderson Memorial Nursing Home.'[1]

The other hospital, the 'Town and County,' on the south edge of the town (Hospital Road) was in fact the district's 'fever' or infectious diseases hospital, 'an old hospital built in separate blocks, all but one of stone. Its administration block with nurses' accommodation was largely destroyed by fire in 1941.' Thus it was described in the survey published in 1946. The fire was caused, as we know, by a plane crash. It had 28 beds, 18 for infectious disease patients and 10 for those with pulmonary tuberculosis. Recommendations were that the hospital should continue to serve for the time being its present purpose, reserving its tuberculosis accommodation 'for advanced cases along with other chronic sick in the present Bignold Hospital.' In the long term, infectious diseases should be treated in an infectious disease wing of the proposed 'new cottage hospital in Wick'.[2] The 'Town and County,' it may be added, was a Caithness County and Wick Burgh jointly maintained local authority hospital.

A few early records of Bignold Hospital survive including the Visitors' Book from 1903, which refers chiefly to notable folk who 'visited' in these days, supporters, contributors to hospital funds and hospital committee members and trustees who wished to assure themselves that things were going well – for it must be remembered that in those days Bignold, like many other hospitals, was 'voluntary', maintained by bequest, subscription, public collection and 'flag days'. Among visitors listed in the early days were Lady Duff Dunbar of

---

1 *Scottish Hospitals Survey*, 1946, Caithness County; paras 138-140.
2 Ibid, paras 133-135.

Ackergill, Sir John Sinclair of Barrock, the Duchess of Portland, Arthur and Mrs Bignold and E W Horne of Stirkoke, who, on a visit in August, 1904 'found everything in excellent order.' Sir Archibald Sinclair MP visited in 1933.[1]

Wick stumbled on with its two modest hospitals until 1928, when Miss Adelaide Florence Henderson, the last surviving Henderson of Bilbster, left the house and grounds of Rosebank House, on the south bank of the Wick river just beyond the bridge, together with a legacy of £1,500 'for the purpose of establishing, equipping and partially endowing a Nursing Home in Wick to be known as the "Henderson Memorial Nursing Home" in memory of her sisters and herself.'[2] It was on this site that all major hospital development from now on was to be located, and where the Caithness General Hospital now stands.

The first meeting of the *ad hoc* committee, assembled to set up the hospital, was on 13 March, 1928 in the Carnegie Library on the opposite side of the road. It was more than three years before the Henderson Nursing Home was opened, the interval being filled by a long and tedious sequence of 'Rosebank Committee' meetings concerned with terms of the bequest, the agreement between the representatives of the donor Board of Trustees, which included Provost Duchart, a Bailie of the Burgh and the Town Clerk and three representatives of the Wick and District Nursing Association, and, of course, the actual business of conversion of the house and extra building, the appointment of staff and the letting of a substantial part of the grounds to the Tennis and Cricket Clubs and the Playing Fields Association of Wick. It was decided that the new nursing home must include a maternity department, and 'boarding fees' for patients were agreed under a county scheme at between 5 shillings and 6 shillings per day.[3] The land let to the Playing Fields Association had to be properly fenced in with cast-iron railings and a gate, similar to those of Rosebank House itself, and since such railing could not now be purchased on the market, the Wick Foundry further along Francis Street, undertook to make the required fencing and gate. Ironically, it is now only the Wick-made replicas of the handsome iron fencing that once enclosed Rosebank House and Garden that survive.

A Wick lady, Miss Agnes Begg, who had seen wartime nursing service in Egypt, was appointed as Matron in May, 1931. Opening

1 Wick Bignold Hospital Visitors' Book, 1903-1933.
2 *Times Gone By*, Vol. I, 26 December, 1927, p3.
3 Henderson Nursing Home Minute Book (Caithness General Hospital Library), 1928-1933.

took place on 13 August, 1931,[1] and the first child born in the maternity unit came a month later, 11 September. During the coming years the 'Henderson Nursing Home' (the name 'Hospital' did not come into use during this phase) served Wick as well as might be for the best part of the next twenty years.

The 1946 Survey describes the Henderson as a 'small maternity hospital' run 'in conjunction with the District Nursing Association; it takes chiefly private cases and excludes unmarried mothers.'[2]

As the Survey indicates, the Henderson provided a fee-paying service, and the management committee soon ran up against the problem of dealing with those who were too poor to pay. One of the doctors made a request that they should be treated free, but the committee argued that 'considering the very small charge, it would be impossible to create a precedent by lowering [it] for any case.' Eventually, doubtless, some arrangement had to be reached about free treatment as in many other places, but just how different a world was the voluntary hospital system from the – comparatively – well-provided National Health Service hospitals of today, is illustrated by an entry in the minutes for March, 1932 which refers to an earnest discussion in the committee about the cost of medicines and the expense of installing a 'Violet Ray' machine – the issue to be postponed until it could be considered 'in the light of a year's expense'. In the same minute, the Matron is given permission to 'keep hens and chickens' in the yard of her lodging for her own use. As for the unmarried mothers, the committee came to the weighty decision that they would only admit unmarried mothers to the maternity unit 'when passed in by a doctor'. If by 1942 – the year of the survey – unmarried mothers were not being admitted, this represents a hardening of attitude from the minutes of 1932. Also, it appears from the survey that by 1942 the Henderson was effectually a maternity hospital only. The numbers of patients admitted to the nursing home in the early years is indicated by monthly figures, very small to begin with, thus:

1 Ibid, entry for 17 September, 1931.
2 *Survey*, op cit. paras 141-142.

	Admitted	Births	Deaths	Number in Home on date recorded
October, 1932	4	2	1	3
November 1932	3	3	1	1
December 1932	6	5		1
May, 1933	7	3		5[1]

According to the figures given in the Survey of 1946, the Henderson does not seem to have advanced greatly during the decade. It is reported as having only 8 beds in 1942, 4 in one ward, 2 in another and two single-bed rooms; there was a nursery and bottle room, a labour room, no laundry and 'inadequate nurses' accommodation'. 'The work of this well-equipped little hospital has increased rapidly and its accommodation is over-taxed.'[2]

Wick Health services weathered the storm of the war in their own way, taking the Bignold out of town. The North School was converted into an RAF hospital. But as in education, the war seems to have focused some hard thinking about public health and about the haphazard sort of hospital provision to be found all over Britain. The Survey of 1946 – compiled during the war – is evidence of this, but thinking, more radical still, overtook the system with the passage in 1947 by the Labour Government of the Act that brought in a comprehensive National Health Service.

Things began to move in a quite different way from custom. In June, 1958, a new Caithness Board of Management to administer the hospitals of the county was appointed, with Provost Harper of Wick in the chair. At its first meeting House Committees were appointed for each of the county hospitals: the Dunbar Hospital in Thurso, Bignold Hospital in Wick, Henderson Memorial Home, Wick, Town and County Infections Diseases Hospital, Wick. There is reference also to Forse Auxiliary Hospital, Latheron, today a private residential home for old people.

Copious and detailed hand-written minutes exist for the activities of the Caithness Hospital Board in the years between 18 June, 1948 and 5 October, and it is clear from these that much development was set in motion at this time. The most significant reference of all is that

1 Henderson Memorial Nursing Home Minute Book, 13 March, 1928 to 15 May, 1933 (Caithness General Hospital Library).
2 *Survey*, op cit, paras 141-143. Also notes supplied by Fiona Watson, Archivist, Grampian Health Board.

in the minute for 21 June, 1950, approving the 'Findings of the Special Sub-Committee set up to Enquire into Future Hospitalisation Requirements in Caithness.' The main findings are that:

1 The Dunbar Hospital of Thurso to be retained and extended.

2 'A complete new hospital for Wick to be built, to comprise separate surgicial, medical, maternity, infectious diseases, T.B. units and laundry, as a single administrative unit. This would make for considerable economy in overhead expenses, and be more efficient from the administrative point of view.'

3 Preferably the new hospital was to be on the Henderson Home site of Rosebank, with the original Rosebank House to be used as a nurses' home. Bignold was to be used for 'the chronic sick,' with some of its physiotherapy facilities retained. The immediate priorities were the 'hospitalisation of "Tuberculous cases"' (there were 41 known cases of tuberculosis in the county) and 'of equal priority is the hospitalisation of Maternity cases in the east end of the County.' (In the years since, tuberculosis has almost disappeared from the record.)

4 Taking into account the existing beds at the Dunbar Hospital in Thurso, the county should have a generous increase in beds for all purposes, mostly in Wick, including 25 for tuberculous patients, 15 for infectious diseases, 24 surgical beds with 4 extra for 'special surgical cases such as Ear, Nose and Throat cases,' 10 medical beds, 24 maternity beds (16 for Henderson Memorial Home, Wick, and 8 for Dunbar), 3 cubicle beds 'for special diseases such as Skin Disease, Venereal Diseases etc, 50 beds for the chronic sick.' The proposals were made on 2 June, 1950 and accepted a few days later by the Board of Management. Building was to go in phases, bringing on to the Rosebank site most of the units.[1]

The intended development proceeded during the coming years, under the aegis of the North East Regional Hospital Board, constituted in 1955, but more slowly than envisaged in the heady years of the late 1950s. The first building programme on the Rosebank site was completed in 1966, and gradually, with the completion of the second phase in 1983, the pulling together of most of the various units on this site was accomplished. For some years the hospital was known as 'Caithness Central', but under its present management it has become 'Caithness General Hospital'.

The present Caithness General Hospital on the Rosebank site, Phase

1 *Special Sub-Committee Report,* 21 June, 1950.

II was begun in 1983, the Henderson Home being demolished to make room for the vastly extended accommodation now being erected. During this phase all maternity work was transferred to the Dunbar Hospital, Thurso, moving back to Wick in 1986 when the main block was completed. Incorporated into the hospitals are wings named after two pioneers of hospital services in Wick, Bignold and Henderson, and two others, Rosebank and Queen Elizabeth Wing: the Queen Mother having maintained considerable interest in developing at Rosebank, opened the new buildings at the end of each constructional phase. This was the second time she had pulled the cord for Wick hospital; she had in fact opened the first phase blocks in 1974.

The Bignold was closed in 1986 and the building sold. The Town and County was retained for quite a time, changing from its infectious diseases role to that of accommodating elderly and long-stay patients. A very defective building, the old Town and County was demolished and put in its place was a quite handsome single-story building, renamed in honour of a nationally known pioneer in the field of geriatric medicine, Dr Timbury, and for some years it retained the title 'Timbury' but has now reverted to the old familiar name, 'Town and County'. It houses some twenty-four patients.

There have, of course, been considerable changes in management since 1986. Under the new structures introduced into the Health Service by the present government, the former Northern Regional Health Board has given place to the Highland Health Board, under which the Caithness and Sutherland NHS Trust is a self-contained and self-managing unit. The Trust has some five hospitals in its care, Caithness General, Thurso Dunbar, Helmsdale, Lawson Hospital, Golspie, and Inverness Community Hospital. Caithness General maintains a high level of general service, including general surgery, medical, orthopaedic, maternity and geriatric services and a full accident and emergency facility. Specialised and intensive care cases are mostly sent to larger hospitals such as that of Inverness within the Trust area, and sometimes to hospitals in other trust areas such as Aberdeen Royal Infirmary, Forresterhill, Aberdeen. The hospitals can call on adequate ambulance services from the Highland Ambulance Trust, and when necessary helicopter service can also be called upon.

The actual pattern of management is illustrated in the first Annual Report of the Trust, issued in August, 1994. This presents a comprehensive account of development since the Trust was set up, but though informative on general issues such as 'Leadership', 'Patient Focus', 'Learning', 'Personal Development' and training of staff, and on 'Effectiveness and Efficiency', it provides no breakdown of local services in Wick, Thurso and the other hospital centres. There is a strong emphasis on awareness 'of the need to be cost conscious,' so that 'everyone within the Trust is committed to avoiding waste.' The Trust's total income for the year from April 1993, to March 1994, was £14,072,000, mainly derived through a contract with the Highland Health Board, and it is evident that during its first year of operation the Trust remained comfortably within its budget. The Report has much in common with the sort of report presented to shareholders of a large company, with half its pages, 17 to 32, devoted to financial details. This, of course, fully reflects the emphasis and spirit of recent reforms. The general feeling within the Wick hospital seems to be one of considerable satisfaction with the changes that have occurred. Within the general ambit of the Trust's management structure, the local hospitals have so far enjoyed a fair measure of 'autonomy,' more they claim than in the earlier dispensations of the NHS. Long may it remain so. Town and district have been provided with a fine medical service, far in advance in quality and availability, of provision at any earlier stage in the history of the locality.[1]

The Wick hospital, standing on one of the few distinctive eminences of the town, the Rosebank, is easily Wick's most prominent building. It is commendably accessible and the main extended block, bent half way along to accommodate to the Rosebank corner, though functional and convenient inside, has a commonplace flat-faced front elevation that does nothing to add to the architectural beauty of Wick. The piling on top of its roof of a high profile black (it is said to be 'blue' which makes it no better) box, a housing for central heating ducts and tanks, converts it into a veritable 'carbuncle'. From almost any angle below it, what could have been Wick's most distinguished building is egregiously ugly. NHS Trust officers and planning officers decisively reject any responsibility for approving the design, and usually suggest that the architects, free from planning constraints, were solely to blame for turning Wick's hospital into the town's most eminent eyesore. Nor does the indiscreet concrete smoke 'stalk' (as such erections used to be called) do anything to enhance the unfortunate view from the town.

1 Most of the information in this section derived from the first *Annual Report and Financial Statements*, of the year ending 31 March, 1994, and from discussion with Mr J E Bogle, Contracts Manager, Caithness General Hospital. The views on the architecture of the hospital expressed in the last paragraphs are entirely those of the author.

Education in Wick.

Before 1918, when management of education shifted to the county, Wick had evolved an educational pattern that was not vastly different from that which operates today. The smaller and ill-housed schools of the old regime were closed, and new and much better accommodation has been provided. Primary education is today provided in four schools, North near the airfield, South near the southern boundary of the town on Roxburgh Road, Pulteneytown Academy Primary on Seaforth Avenue, and Hillhead along Willowbank on the way to Papigoe. Secondary education is centred on the Wick High School, a large school on West Banks. Scottish education, unlike that of England, never needed to be 'comprehensivised', to use the unlovely appropriate word, since in broad terms the whole system was 'comprehensive' in origin, and except in certain localities in the cities and south, invidious modes of 'selection', 'eleven plus' and even de-segregation (as between boys and girls) were less used than in England, though there was a time when some Scottish authorities were 'copying' the English in creating that educational anomaly the 'secondary-modern school'. When 'secondary' was separated from 'primary', all-age schools disappeared from the 1920s onwards; in many localities, as in Wick, transfer to the 'grammar' school, the 'high school' or to the 'academy' (a term much less in use in England) was automatic. And the term 'grammar' here had no class connotation as in England.

School boards gave place to the county, and Caithness County lost its educational responsibilities to the Highland Council in 1975. The Caithness schools are directly administered by a Caithness Divisional Executive, whose offices are in Rhind House, West Banks Avenue. There seems little likelihood that local autonomy in school government will return, except in so far as Scots again copy the English 'opt out' system and choose 'direct grant status'. That has not so far happened in any of the Wick schools. There was a total school population of 1,860 in August, 1994, almost equally divided between primary and secondary.[1]

A main aim in staffing the schools is that of maintaining stability of quality. This is more difficult than in more densely populated localities further south, since there is only ever a small 'surplus' of teachers in the area, if any surplus at all, partly owing to the problem

---

1 Information derived from discussion with the Divisional Education Officer for Caithness, Mr John H Edgar, of Rhind House.

of recruiting teachers from elsewhere in so northerly a community. There is an almost perennial shortage of secondary school teachers. The Division maintains a 'supply' list and has a policy sharing this out fairly between the schools of the area, giving a priority of placing to new graduates to enable them to gain experience. The chief sources of new teachers are North College, Aberdeen and the University itself.

Vocational further education for Wick is almost wholly supplied by the Thurso College, while community education of the conventional kind is provided usually in the schools during evenings, and is administered by a Community Education Organiser in Brora, Sutherland. There is a small adult training centre on the Industrial Estate, funded by the Highland Council, for people who are handicapped.

Recreation and Sport

For all its apparent drabness, Wick was never a place to give way to misery and gloom. The Rev William Sutherland in his *Wick 1794* tells how the folk made the most of weddings and funerals, had a great love of finery, 'good English cloth, muslin gowns, white stockings, silk ribbands etc.', which they wore whenever there was an opportunity, how they were 'extravagantly fond of dancing', and 'whatever the kirk thought about it, almost every town and village kept a day' in honour of the tutelar saint of the place,' and 'devoted it to mirth and jollity,' especially at Christmas and New Year. The various '–mass' fairs surviving from old times were well attended by ordinary folk as well as the farmers doing business. As for the spiritual recreation, Wickers developed an inordinate taste for *usquebaugh* and patronised many public houses.

Though many aspects of the church life of the town may seem to us dour and tedious, people really quite enjoyed it, not least on account of the fierce sermons that some of their pastors aimed at them. Such social amenity as the town possessed during most of the nineteenth century was provided in church rooms and the Temperance Hall.

Things have changed a lot from those times, and folk these days have much more leisure in which to have fun, and expect from their local authorities sophisticated recreational facilities that would have made the city fathers of a hundred years or more ago curl up with outrage. Even before habits of public spending on leisure amenities set in, clubs and sports teams, some of which still flourish though others have been superseded or given way to entertainment on the pool table or watching telly.

A full account of all the endeavours and enterprises that have enlivened Wickers over the years would take us far from our present brief, 'Wick Today,' but several of them deserve special mention. We have mentioned the founding of the Boys Brigade in Wick, a short while after William (later Sir) Smith founded the organisation in 1883, the Wick troop being formed four years later in 1887. This body had many side effects on the life of Wick, none more cherished than the Boys' Brigade Band, formed in the early years of this century but now defunct, 'one of the casualties of "progress"' as the indefatigable Mr Wicker (Noel Donaldson) puts it.[1] From the ranks of the Brigade came many recruits for the forces in the two wars, now long deceased, and the still powerful blowing in the Royal British Legion Pipe Band of Wick, which celebrated its seventy-fifth anniversary in 1994.

The story of this distinguished band began in 1919, when a group calling themselves 'The Wick Comrades of the Great War Pipe Band', came together to continue some of the musical traditions Wick pipers had shared in the making with the Seaforths. Its fortunes have varied over the years, almost disappearing altogether in the late 1920s, but now enjoying a wave of high popularity. One past Pipe-Major, Dada Davidson, when asked about it, explained the band's continued existence and popularity, 'Wur pipe band daft'.[2]

Another pipe band regrettably no longer seen or heard was that of the Wick Girls who marched and piped in the years following the Second World War. Girl Guides and Boy Scouts still flourish in Wick, though little is heard of their musical propensities. They still march on the town's occasions, the Gala, usually held in July and at Armistice time, but the military theme is less popular than it once was in Wick. Nor, if a report in the *Groat* in July, 1994 is to be believed, do Wickers respond with their old enthusiasm on the Gala occasion itself. At the 1994 Gala – successor to the one-time Fisher Queen parade – 'youngsters' were accused of pocketing coins 'coins which missed the floats and landed on the street,' an unthinkable misdemeanour in the old days. Nevertheless, the Gala Committee was able to report a near record collection of £6,400 during the Gala Week festivities, for distribution to a number of charities which in 1994 included Rwanda.

1 *JOGJ*, 21 January, 1994
2 *JOGJ*, 8 July, 1994.

The biggest turnout of pipe bands in Wick, indeed, of Wick townsfolk, was the occasion of the Quatercentenary, the 400th Anniversary of the Royal Burgh of Wick in September, 1989, when they harked back to the time when 'King James VI granted Wick its Royal Charter, giving it Royal Burgh status and opening of the doors of commerce for easier trade.' Since the Royal Burgh of Wick no longer exists as a political entity, it fell to a sub-committee to organise the celebrations which lasted for a week and included a special exhibition at the Town Hall of the Charter, now 'frail but in a fairly good condition', there were parades, sports tournaments, this year's County Show on the river meadows, dancing displays and the attendance of the Queen Mother at several functions. *Clupea harengus*, now absent from the scene but arguably the very makers of Wick, was honoured in Iain Sutherland's *By the Cran*, a colourful review at the Assembly Rooms of 'the town's herring heyday', but otherwise not much remembered. Led by the Wick British Legion Pipe Band, 'one of the most spectacular events of quatercentenary year' was the parade of 150 massed pipers and drummers from many places north and a contingent from Edinburgh. There were special quatercentenary services in several churches of the area, and Brownies, Guides, Scouts and Boys' Brigade paraded as never was. A team of Aberdeen Football Club 'select' came to Harmsworth Park and defeated the Caithness team 6-1. Celebrations ended with ball and mighty bonfire and firework display on the meadows, to which the procession was conducted by the pipers.[1]

Wick people are well provided with open spaces in which to disport themselves in a routine way, including the river banks, the riverside meadows just above the bridge, Harmsworth and Bignold Parks. Both riverside banks have been generously planted with daffodils so that spring is now brought in for Wickers by as brave a 'show' as gladdened the heart of Wordsworth, and there are coast paths north and south that can take them out of the town within ten minutes' walk; the path over South Head leads within a short way (including a stretch of cul-de-sac roadway) to the rugged cliffs of the 'Old Man' and beyond. Harmsworth and Bignold Parks are both gifts to the town of former MPs for the area. Arthur Bignold bought and made over the land beyond Northcote Street to be 'utilized as a public

---

1 The *Groat* published on the occasion a *Quatercentenary Review, Celebration of Wick's 400th Anniversary as a Royal Burgh*. It contained very little information about the granting of the Charter by King James in 1589.

park and recreation ground for the inhabitants of Wick and Pulteneytown' in 1903.[1]

Beyond Bignold is Harmsworth, gifted some years later. Both parks are used for organised sport, but a portion of Harmsworth is enclosed as the town football ground, now equipped with floodlighting, a very desirable amenity in an area subject to long, dark winter afternoons. Here the town's main football team, Wick Academy, play their home league fixtures. 'Wick Academy' like 'Thurso Academicals' (and the still better-known 'Hamilton Academicals') have a manifest origin in school sport, but have long lost these associations. It is believed that the first appearance of the team was a school group formed by John Davidson MA, a teacher at the then Pulteneytown Academy, and which played its first match in 1905 against the Thurso Miller Institute team.[2] School sport took a different turn with the opening of the Wick High School in 1911, but the Wick football team stuck to its original title, and today, any reference in Wick to 'the Academy' is likely to mean the footballers. Their fortunes have varied greatly over the years, sometimes – especially before the last war – heading their league. In recent years they have not fared so well, but they command impressive local support. Their chief problem is that they have traditionally had to play many of their matches away, since other teams have felt it more convenient for Wick, if they want a match, to travel south rather than for them to come so far north. On the other hand, the Academy team in fact claims to have been the first Scottish football team to have travelled by air to a match, when in May, 1934, they were flown by Highland Airways to Kirkwall where they 'played a friendly match with an Orkney Select'. It is not recorded that they won.[3]

Soccer is easily the most popular single sport in Caithness, with five other teams registered as paid-up members with the Caithness District Sports Council from Wick alone, and another seventeen football clubs in the District as a whole. Known to exist though not at present registered as fee-paying members are another eighteen clubs. The Council, on which are represented most sporting groups in the county, is based in Wick and includes – or has included – from Wick, athletics, cricket (a sport which has a surprising following in the county with a County Association and no less than three clubs in

1 Deed of Gift, registered at Edinburgh 'on the fourth day of May one thousand nine hundred and three.' General register of Sassines.
2 *Times Gone By*, op cit, 1930, p 19.
3 Ibid, 1934, p 30.

Wick, of which only one, the Osprey Club is at present registered), cycling (including the Wick Wheelers), golf, tennis, and a wide range of indoor sports, including badminton, archery, boxing, fencing, squash, keep fit, bowling and above all small-bore shooting, for which the area has quite a reputation. Swimming is popular in Wick and Thurso where there are up-to-date swimming pools. The Wick Pool in the new Sports Centre on Martha Terrace is one of the early achievements of the 'Wick Project', the quite impressive programme for improving and brightening up Wick which is now in progress. The Pool had core funding from the Caithness District Council and additional costs were met by an input from the Highland Regional Council and the Scottish Tourist Board. Other and less popular sporting activities are listed for Wick and district, such as board and canoe surfing and pony trekking.

Benefits of membership of the Sports Council include the possibility of gaining 'facility/minor capital grants' (which may include 'starter' and 'booster' grants) and equipment grants 'to assist with the purchase of non-structural assets and equipment that clubs would be expected to provide for its members.' In recent years the Sports Council has disposed of equipment and other grant funds to the sum of £5,000 a year or more in the Caithness area.

'Beatrice Awards' for various club purposes may be obtained according to certain conditions, to assist clubs mainly with transport and subsistence costs, to enable them to accept fixtures away from the area, attendance at 'sporting events which are of a standard that cannot reasonably be obtained in Caithness,' and the like. This award scheme was evolved between the Caithness Sports Council and the Trustees of the Beatrice Oilfield Trust Fund (Caithness), but there are indications that this fund is soon likely to dry up and the Council is looking for new supporters and sponsors for the kind of aid that Beatrice provides.

The Council, at present headed by Mr N C Scott, and general sports business, are conducted from the Leisure and Recreation Office at Market Square, Wick under the direction of Mr Iain Robertson. The Council, too, has at its disposal for letting a number of facilities in or near Wick, such as the Rosebank Playing Fields, the Wick Swimming Pool and the Trinkies Pool, an open-air facility on the rocks beyond South Head, and the Wick Assembly Rooms, the one-time Pulteneytown Academy on Sinclair Terrace. Tennis, trampolining, open-air bowling and putting are the main activities of the Rosebank the Rosebank Playing Fields, first leased for the purpose in part of the grounds of the Henderson Home – now the General Hospital, in the 1930s and still in use. It may well be said that Wick enjoys a vigorous and generously fostered sporting life. As in other branches of present District Council activities, there is some apprehension of what are likely to be the effects of the new local government arrangements for the area.[1]

The Churches in Wick Today.

It is difficult to say much about the state of organised religion in the town today. As we have amply seen, a hundred years ago and more, the churches of Wick represented a significant element not only in the religious outlook and convictions of the people, but played quite a vigorous part in the civic life of both burghs, Wick and Pulteneytown. Ministers, orthodox and Free Church, were regularly consulted and had much to say on matters of general concern, as witnessed by their frequent and lengthy letters in the *Groat*. While not strictly a direct effect of ecclesiastical concern, there can be little doubt that high levels of evangelical fervour had much to do with the temperance campaign that kept Wick 'dry' for twenty-five years. Most clubs and youth activities, including Boys' Brigade, Scouts and Guides, were connected with the churches, as were many of the social and recreational groups that flourished in the town. It is true, also, that the church women's organisations had much to do with maintaining prohibition in the town for so many years, especially as women in the main were excluded from the public houses and were unable to share in what pleasures they might have afforded.

Most of this has changed. There can be no more melancholy sight to a loyal church member than boarded-up churches, and church buildings converted into shops, garages and the like, of which there are now a number in Wick and Pulteneytown. The two main churches of Wick, the Old Parish Church and the Bridge Street Church, at one time the focal centre of Free Church thinking, now work closely together, and their mission is strongly biased towards the 'social' and the 'communal' rather than the expressly spiritual, doctrinal, sectarian and, to coin a phrase, 'affilial' allegiance of each of them to two

---

[1] Information derived from a variety of sources including discussion and correspondence with Miss Fiona Smith of the Leisure and Recreation Department of Caithness District Council, Mr N C Scott, Chairman of the Council, and current explanatory documents giving details of the grant and aid schemes of the Council, member clubs and other aspects of the work of the Council.

different Assemblies in the fervent years after the Disruption and establishment of the Free Church Assembly, once the very breath of their being.

Religion still plays a formal and for many people, a satisfying and comforting part in their lives, and is none the worse for being more community oriented. And although it would be an exaggeration to say that church marriage and burial signify a residual firm faith, the churches are still much favoured for those purposes. The Old Parish Church has recently undergone a thorough-going reconstruction, converting the upper part of its ample space into a far more comfortable and colourful place of worship than it ever was before, and the new ceiled-in lower storey to an assembly hall, where functions of all kinds may be held, secular as well as religious, and an attractive suite of meeting rooms, so that at any one time, a whole variety of activities may be going on. The Bridge Street Church, now unambiguously affiliated to the Church of Scotland, still attracts a rather different kind of congregation from the Parish Church, numbering among its faithful rather more of the 'substantial' citizens of the town, the businessmen, shopkeepers and professional people who keep the place going. Such were the veritable leaders in 1843 – now virtually forgotten – of the Disruption, dissatisfied with the stand-offishness and patronising ways of the heritor class. Union between the two churches does not now seem far away.

In Pulteneytown the same sort of easy-going spirit tends to govern the outlook and habits of the congregation of Pulteneytown and Thrumster Church, itself reconstructed to new standards of comfort and cheerfulness and provided with a New Hall in which social activity thrives. A very strong and busy feature of the Pulteney and Thrumster Church is its Women's Guild, which maintains a lively programme of functions including fund-raising social and 'congregational social' events, all relying on high levels of social participation and fellowship. It is possible that fiercely partisan ministers such as Charles Thomson, who led the 1,500 strong congregation of the Old Parish Church out into the wilderness, as it must have seemed to many, of Free Church life, would have found much present practice not austere and godly enough for the salvation of the flock. The churches of today have shared unashamedly in the blessings of affluence. Evangelicals are still around to remind the faithful of the evils of Mammon, but they are not the same breed as the evangelicals of old. Their impact is more sporadic and their religion tinged with an authoritarianism that makes for emotional disturbance and disruption of the ways of steady and still numerous church-goers.[1]

PROJECT WICK

That the people of Wick today enjoy greater content than their forebears in Edwardian and Victorian days may be doubted, but that most of them are better off, more comfortably housed, breathe cleaner air, walk in cleaner streets, that their general health is better, are better fed, educated, policed and serviced can hardly be denied. That the town has its black spots and that there are among Wickers those less fortunately circumstanced than the majority is also true. Official help for the distressed and the drop-outs is rather more readily available than it once was, and neighbours are still more often kind than unkind.

There are those who would claim that one effect of the improvements of the post-war years has been to make the town a duller place than it once was, and the pictures in both issues of *Times Gone By* tend to support such a view, certainly along the main streets, Bridge and High Streets. Shopping in Wick is perhaps much less fun than it was when there were half-a-dozen bakers' and butchers' shops, Liptons, the Co-op and Templetons for groceries, greengrocery, drapers and clothiers lining the streets; Saturday mornings must have been quite a bustle when much of the regular shopping was done, with housewives and laden husbands carrying home the week's provender, or lining up to catch the midday bus. Not all have gone even now, but most of the town's shopping for grocery, greengrocery and meat is now done in the Presto supermarket on Macleay Lane, and the Co-op store on Thurso Road. Both of these concerns were on the main streets, Templeton's (Presto's predecessors) where Boots' is now and the Co-op also in High Street and Upper Pulteneytown. Now the shoppers are there in droves all the week, and carry away their goods in plastic bags as far as the car park outside. Both moved away from the main streets in the mid 1980s, and it is probably true to say that no single commercial event in Wick did more to alter the habits of ordinary folk in their use of the town. The Co-op and Presto have nothing in their windows for people to look at – there are no windows

---

1 Information from observation, casual discussion and an interview with the Rev Alistair Roy, Minister of the Bridge Street Church. The views expressed are entirely those of the present author.

round much of the building, while main street shops, like such shops everywhere else, have plastic fascias in place of the one-time carefully painted signs above windows and doors.

Such matters when thought about tend to bring on attacks of nostalgia, in which the old times seem much better than they were. Wick, as we have seen, changed in constitution perhaps more than many other places after its herrings went, and for many years its aspect of drabness was a common subject of comment. A significant recent report on Wick comments: 'Wick became a boom town because of the herring fishing but has declined since the herring moved away. Since the Second World War there have been occasional periods of prosperity but the general trend has been one of a slow decline in economic activity and population.'[1] The *Study* recounts some of the issues which have been discussed in this chapter on the economic rehabilitation of Wick, and concludes that 'as far as the basic factors of the Wick economy are concerned, the prospects are for a slow decline.'[2] In its conclusions section the Study further states: 'Wick is a depressed economy and this is illustrated by the physical appearance of the town.'[3]

The *Study* is the work of consultants called in by several bodies concerned with the well-being of Wick, the Highland Regional Council (HRC), Highland and Islands Enterprise (HIE), Caithness District Council (CDC), Scottish Homes (SH), Caithness and Sutherland Enterprise Board (CASE) and Wick Harbour Trust (WHT), to investigate 'a strategy for redevelopment,' and 'with the recent formation of an ad-hoc Committee to investigate the prospect of establishing a major project to revitalise the Pulteneytown and town centre parts of Wick.' This is no place to examine in any detail, much less criticise, the contents of Mackays' Report or the work of 'Project Wick,' the constituted ad-hoc body which has now been in existence for two years and which is already able to show some benefits from its operations. The body is financed from various sources including HIE, CASE and CDC, and wherever project objectives impinge on the objectives of other agencies, such as Historic Scotland (HS) appeals are made for assistance from them. It is, too, envisaged that there will be private sector input, especially where redevelopment benefits particular concerns.

1 *Lower Pulteney and Central Wick Development Study,* Mackay Consultants, July 1991, para 3.1.
2 Ibid, 3.12.
3 Ibid, para 11.1

The Harbour Trust, though as we have seen, not very affluent, was enjoined to 'explore the possibilities of EC funding for appropriate projects.' Such appropriate projects we have already mentioned, such as slipway, boat repair and dry-dock facilities, leisure and recreational uses, oil-related activity. The section of the *Study* dealing with the harbour (Section 6) makes rather depressing reading, since the prospects of development in each of the areas considered are thought to be none too promising. As for fishing itself, 'Wick has experienced a decline in the last ten years [1980-1990]' in common with many other fishing ports; and as we have already shown in this chapter, the prospects for general shipping and trade are fatally limited by inadequate deep-water harbourage facilities, especially when compared with Scrabster, which is at present attracting considerable funds for development.

One aspect of development in the harbour area the *Study* considers hopeful is closely related to the 'Project's' initial prime concern, the rehabilitation of Lower Pulteneytown. The *Study* envisages very little improvement in the use of the harbour as a yacht marina (in 1990 the number of such craft using the harbour was 106, of which only 35 came from foreign countries across the North Sea), partly because of 'inadequate moorings and the lack of pontoons,' but also on account of the fact that yachtsmen usually only put in on the way elsewhere (mostly Orkney and Shetland). The installation of pontoons at relatively low cost in the inner basin would improve things, the consultants believed.

There is, they consider, considerable potential, however, in some fairly drastic re-development of the landward area of the harbour. 'In most towns the size of Wick with an active fisheries harbour,' they say, 'the harbour area is usually a magnet to tourists and a focal point within the town. This is not the case with Wick. This is largely due to the geography of the town and the unattractive appearance and industrial atmosphere of Lower Pulteney.'[1] It would be no exaggeration to say that many visitors to Wick, especially the short-term and those in transit, are quite unaware of this interesting area, even in its present depressed state.

Among the proposals to increase the number of visitors to the area and to persaude them to stay longer were:

1 Relocation of haulage firms on the harbour front. The fact that along Martha Terrace and Harbour Quay there are several disused

1 Mackay *Study*, op cit. para 6.49.

roomy buildings has encouraged, among other activities, the garaging and servicing here of heavy trucks. The Stevens company is the largest and most wide-ranging of these concerns. Their articulated vehicles do much trunk service up and down the A9 and down to England, though to get on to the A9 they have an awkward manoeuvre at the Bridge corner, or through the narrow side streets of Pulteneytown. Persuading this successful company to move elsewhere, preferably perhaps, the Industrial Estate, would have its problems, and even then there is the T-junction on to High Street to negotiate.

2 Provision of car and coach parking in Lower Pulteneytown and at the harbour front. This, too, presents problems. At present no great numbers of visitors seek such parking.

3 Provision of a riverside/harbour walkway. This is one item of the Project that has already been accomplished, a neat metal rail fence and stone walkway having been constructed along the south riverside between the two bridges. This, at least, is an earnest that improvement in the area is possible. There is a suggestion, too, of a pedestrian bridge across the river (perhaps on the model of Inverness walk bridges) between the two road bridges.

4 Refurbishment of harbour front properties and utilisation for flats, appropriate retail outlets and self-catering flat accommodation. The fact that few people come here at all now should be no discouragement; more would come if the place were not so dilapidated anyway. Something as adventurous and extensive as recent riverside development in places such as Bristol or Liverpool is not conceivable here, but the whole riverside area of Lower Pulteneytown could with imaginative and thoughtful planning and encouragement attract businesses, especially retail and customer-oriented concerns, turn this into a locality that draws in tourists and visitors by its own charm and reputation.

5 Better promotion and signposting for the Heritage Centre. This excellent amenity on Bank Row – behind the dilapidation – has a potential that is probably far from being fully realised. The Centre is full of interest on many aspects of the town's life and evolution, but is apt to give an impression of clutter as it fills up with more and more unique artefacts, and it is, in any case, open less than half the year. It is now well sign-posted.

6 Provision of pontoons in the harbour.[1]

1 Mackay *Study*, op cit. Section 6.50.

Though not discussed in this precise context, the *Study* recommends that the town should adopt a 'flagship project'. This it has done and constructed a fine new swimming pool and recreation centre in Lower Pulteneytown, just as the consultants suggest. Beside it on the riverside is also the town's equally well conceived Medical Centre.

It would not do at the end of a long history of Wick, to go into more detail about this comprehensive, realistic, well-considered study of a town, as the consultants put it, urgently in need of 'revitalising, economically and physically'. The *Study* is handsomely worth reading for its own sake by members of the business community of north-east Caithness, the town, district and regional planners, and not least by the folk themselves who have to live in Wick and who have not always been consulted about what environment is being created for them. The Lower Pulteneytown suggestions quoted are a mere sample of the hundred or two discussion points and positive suggestions both for Pulteneytown and the High Street and Central area of the town.

There is in the *Study* no reticence about the 'negative features' of Wick that have to be overcome, including for example, traffic congestion in the town centre, 'vacant and dilapidated premises on the north end of Bridge Street' and, of course, in Lower Pulteneytown, lack of 'due attention' by business concerns in the past to 'important architectural fabric and features of the town centre' – and elsewhere, retailers' lack of cash flow to undertake costly renovations. The *Study* regrets the tendency of the town to postpone improvement and development recommended in the past, especially in the case of the SDA initiative for Lower Pulteneytown of 1988 while boom was still going, until times when people are all too aware of recession.

The main implication of the *Study* is that by means of the sorts of help now available, imagination and the kind of boot-straps activity that rescued Wick in the 1950s, Wick town could become a much livelier, more attractive and stimulating place than its present image projects. As for Lower Pulteneytown, the *Study* does not go on to suggest that this sadly run-down quarter could become Wick's chief asset, bringing people in to shop, admire, relax and wonder that such a complex ever came into existence, but that is by no means beyond the bounds of possibility. The very fact that Pulteneytown was one of the most positively imagined and planned 'new towns' in the whole British Isles in the early nineteenth century could itself become a matter for wisespread curiosity and even perhaps admiration.

One aspect of the town beyond the consultants' brief is that Wick is not just the old county town; it is an access point to some of the most interesting archaeology of Scotland, not just a few individual items, but a whole catalogue of pre-historic and historic remains, and although it is not now greatly in favour, the harbour area is itself a splendidly unique, almost self-explanatory piece of 'industrial archaeology'. Within a short distance of the town are the monstrous and magnificent castles of Girnigoe and Sinclair, at least as full of Scottish history as, say, Urquhart and Dunnottar; Ackergill now becoming known to people interested in the arts; Keiss harbour and castles, Wick's own though not much advertised 'Auldwick'. There are also, in the area, some of the most dramatic coast walks in the kingdom. Not far away to the south are some examples of the finest cairns and other ancient monuments, which almost everyone in Wick knows about. Wickers, an easy-going phlegmatic race, take very much for granted and do not enthuse about the many interesting, even exciting features of their unusual environment. Orkney shares with Caithness a wealth of antique remains and sites of interest. The Orcadians and Kirkwall in particular seek enthusiastically to promote the attractions of their locality, and are rewarded annually by a large influx of visitors. Caithnessians by contrast and the citizens of the ancient Royal Burgh don't do much to fetch in the tourists. Wick has a lot to offer and the Heritage Centre does something to uncover to the world its curious and unique aspects; but the Burgh has much more to offer than it has so far realised.

A future version of our opening conversation might go thus:

Wick! Here we are at last.

Yes, I've heard that there are a lot of interesting things here.

OK. Here's a handy car park.

Let's have a break.

Jolly good. There's a lot to see!

POST SCRIPTUM – POST MORTEM?

FOR nearly four centuries Wick enjoyed the distinctive status of Royal Burgh, which meant that the town had the privilege of governing itself, *mutatis mutandis*, through its days of testing, tribulation and triumph. When in 1989 the Royal Burgh celebrated the Quater-Centenary of its 'erection', it had already suffered some attenuation of its regal and constitutional status. Under the new local government arrangements of 1975 Wick, merged into Caithness *District*, itself the downgraded former Caithness *County*, of which Wick was the 'county town'.

The latest Local Government Act is inflicting on the Royal Burgh and the District of Caithness a put-down which the old city fathers would undoubtedly have regarded as high humiliation. 'Royal Burgh' it may proudly announce itself to incomers on the signs at the burgh's old borders, but the term has now no strict constitutional meaning at all. Wick is little more than a mere constituency in the local government electoral area of the Highland Regional Council, shortly to become the 'Highland Council', a huge, amorphous territory stretching from east coast to west coast, taking in Wick and Thurso at its north end, and Fort William at the south. Under the new dispensation neither Wick nor Caithness will have any self-governing functions. They do not even have the authority to put up notices declaring the ancient royal glories.

The town used to boast – still does – under its ancient town arms, that WICK WORKS WEIL. Some years before its virtual extinction, the Royal Burgh, 'having used Ensigns Armorial anterior to the year 1672', belatedly petitioned the Lord Lyon King of Arms to have the town arms 'matriculated in the Public Register of All Arms and Bearings in Scotland', fortunately ensuring its right to sport the achievement on all suitable occasions. The application was granted in the following terms:

> The Lord Lyon King of Arms by Interlocutor of date 3rd June 1954 Granted Warrant to the Lyon Clerk to matriculate in the Public Register in the name of the said Burgh the following Ensigns Armorial, videlicet:
>
> Azure, a chevron round embattled on the upper edge and ensigned of a cross patee at the apex close fitched Argent, between two lymphads Or sails of the second, flagged Gules, in chief, and in a base upon the sea barry wavy Argent and Vert

POST SCRIPTUM – POST MORTEM?

an ancient boat of the third, and there two naked men proper handling oars in action Sable, and a Bishop erect attired of the second, mitred of the third, holding in his sinister a book of the last his dexter hand raised in act of blessing, and in the base of the shield a crozier-head also of the third; Above the Shield which is ensigned of the burghal coronet is placed in an Escrol this motto "NISI DOMINUS FRUSTRA", and below the shield is placed a Compartment suitable to a Burgh-Royal, its turrets having string courses engrailed and thereon this Motto "WICK WORKS WEIL."

Matriculated the Twenty-First day of July 1954.

Extracted furth of the 21st page of the Fortieth Volume of the Public Register of All Arms and Bearings in Scotland this Twenty-First day of July 1954.

N A B Lawson.
for Clerk Keeper of the Records.

It is just as well the old Royal Burgh Councillors took the step of getting the town arms 'matriculated', for there is no body today competent to make such an application. For all its 'working weil' (and there is little doubt that it did!), when the crunch came in 1994, Wick was quite unable like all its neighbours to get any release from the compulsions that were driving into the shadows all its ancient claims to 'independence'.

It is very doubtful now whether or not a convincing campaign for the return of the antique burgh privileges and powers could be mounted, and even it it could there are many good reasons why integration with at least a 'county' authority should remain. Recreation of a Caithness County was the main burden of representations made to the Scottish Secretary, the Rt Hon Ian Lang, MP when, in the wake of the local government tax reforms ('Council Tax'), the Scottish Office announced plans for some drastic reorganisation of Scottish local government. The plans for the north of Scotland involved the creation of a 'single-tier', all purpose Highland Council based in Inverness, the area and centre of the existing Highland Regional Council, which would abolish the existing 'Districts' of Caithness, Sutherland and Ross and Cromarty.

Furious campaigns built up in all parts of the Region to get the plan dropped, none more constructive and vociferous than that mounted in Caithness. This was led by Councillor John Young, Convener of the

Caithness District Council, and the Depute Chief Executive, Brian Whitelaw. Many local bodies including the District Council itself, trades and community councils, churches, chambers of commerce, Rotary and other clubs participated in the campaign, collecting between them 6000 signatures to a petition to the Scottish Office demonstrating 'public support for a Caithness Council and public abhorrence of a Pan Highland Council'.

The Save Caithness Campaign was reported on extensively in such Scottish papers as the *Press and Journal,* and the *Scotsman,* and was the subject of vigorous exchanges of views in the *John O'Groat Journal* and the *Caithness Courier.* The case for a 'wider view of council reform' was put in some detail in an article by Roy Godfrey, a Caithness District Councillor who, in general, favoured the Scottish Office plan, published in the *Groat* on 27 November, 1992, it focused on the benefits and economies of regional planning and provision for technical services. A thorough-going summary of the whole argument in favour of the creation of an 'all purpose Caithness authority' appeared in the *Groat* on 22 January, 1993. A feeling grew up locally that this case was unanswerable.

It did not prove so. Right from the start, the Secretary of State warned that 'there could be no going back on radical reform plans', including those for the Highland area; and by the time Ian Lang was succeeded as Secretary of State by the Rt Hon Michael Forsyth, MP, in the summer of 1995 the new arrangements were already *fait accompli'*.

One district councillor described the process, so far as Wick was concerned, picturesquely enough, as democracy going 'down the tubes,' while Brian Whitelaw, just as aptly, called it 'centralisation of centralisation'. In another statement he declared: 'If we lose this battle all the services currently controlled by Caithness people will be controlled from Inverness.' As this history shows, no earlier Scottish regime under which Wick has lived, even in the wildest days of the earls, has been as distantly placed as this.

There is some hope that the new Highland Council, when it comes formally into existence in 1996, will devolute some of its powers that have special relevance to particular localities and functions. Councillor Godfrey, however, has his reservations: 'Central government thinking seems to lean favourably towards the formation of "enablers" and quangos, or to take more power to the centre, ie, quasi or partial privatisation. No doubt this is the Government's response to the dafter antics of some councils south of the Highlands, but nonetheless we inevitably get swept along with unwanted legislation aimed at others.'

It cannot be argued away that the new local government constitution for the area represents in principle a significant departure from systematic ideas about local democracy. Whatever local boards or 'quangos' get appointed by a centralised council that cannot cope without their help, they will usually have no direct mandate from the inhabitants of the localities to legislate or recommend legislation on local issues as used to be the case. Is the wheel coming full circle, when the fiat of an authority as distant as the Viking Earl of Orkney in Kirkwall, will once again govern affairs in the ancient town of Wick? Perhaps the traditional mottoes of the town arms should be slightly modified to read: WICK WORKS WEIL – NISI CONCILIUM LOCA MONTORUM FRUSTRA.

BIBLIOGRAPHY
MAIN TEXTS

BEATON (Rev) D.: *The Parish Registers of Canisbay*, 1652-1666; Edinburgh (1914).

BEATON (Rev) D.: *Ecclesiastical History of Caithness and Annals of Caithness Parishes*; Free Presbyterian Church, Wick, Wm Rae (1909).

CALDER, J.T.: *Civil and Traditional History of Caithness*; Murray, Wick (reprint 1887).

CAMERON, George: *John Horne, His Life and Work*; North of Scotland Newspapers, Wick (1993).

CAMPBELL, R. H.: *Scotland Since 1707: The Rise of an Industrial Society*; Edinburgh, Donald (1985).

CLEGG, Peter: *Rivals in the North*; (1988) – An Account of the Rivalry between Fresson and Gandar Dower in the 1930s – no publisher given.

CRAVEN, (Rev) J.B.: *A History of the Episcopal Church in the Diocese of Caithness*; Kirkwall, Peace (1908).

CRAVEN, (Rev) J.B.: *Journal of the Episcopal Visitations of the Right Rev. Robert Forbes*; Kirkwall, 1886.

CRAWFORD, Barbara: *Scandinavian Scotland*; Leicester University Press (1987).

DONALDSON, John F.: *The Mey Letters*; Sydney, Australia, Donaldson (1984).

DONALDSON, John F.: *Caithness in the Eighteenth Century*; Moray, Edinburgh (1938).

DUNLOP, J.: *The British Fisheries Society, 1786-1892*; Edinburgh, John Donald (1978).

FERGUSON, David M.: *Shipwrecks of Orkney, Shetland and Pentland Firth*; Newton Abbey, David and Charles (1988).

FERGUSON, David M.: *Shipwrecks of the North of Scotland*; 1444-1990; Edinburgh, The Mercat Press (1991).

FAIRRIE, Lt Col Angus: *Cuidich 'N Righ: History of the Queen's Own Highlanders (Seaforths and Camerons)*.

FRESSON, E.E.: *A Road to the Isles: The Memoirs of Captain E.E. Fresson, OBE*; David Rendall (1963).

GIBSON, W.H.: *Stronsay – The Herring Fishing, Vol I*.

GIFFORD, John: *The Buildings of Scotland*; Penguin Books (1989).

GLASS, Norman: *Caithness and the War, 1939-1945*; Wick, North of Scotland Newspapers (1994).

GRANT, I.F.: *The Social and Economic Development of Scotland Before 1603*; Oliver and Boyd (1930).

GRAY, Malcolm: *The Fisheries of Scotland, 1790-1914*; University of Aberdeen Press (1978).

GUNN, Neil: *Whisky and Scotland*; London, John Murray (1967).

HART, F.R. Pick, J.B.: *Neil M. Gunn: A Highland Life*; London, John Murray (1981).

HENDERSON, John: *Caithness Families*; Edinburgh, David Douglas (1884).

HEWISON, W.S.: *This Great Harbour Scapa Flow*; Kirkwall, Orkney Press (1985).

HORNE, John: *Ye Towne of Wick in ye Olden Tyme*: Wick, Rae (1895).

HOSSACK, B.H.: *Kirkwall in the Orkneys*; (Re-issued Kirkwall Press, 1986).

HUNTER, D.L.G.: *The Highland Railway in Retrospect*; Edinburgh, Moorfoot Publications (1988).

LYNCH, Michael: *Scotland: A New History*; London, Pimlico (1992).

MACECHERN, Dugald: *The Sword of the North: Highland Memories of the Great War*; Inverness, Robert Carruthers (1923).

MACFARLANE, W: *Geographical Collections Relating to Scotland, Vol 3*; Edinburgh (1906-1908).

MACKINTOSH, Charles: *Curious Incidents from the Ancient Records of Kirkwall*; Kirkwall, Orkney Press (1897).

MACKAY, (Rev) Angus: *History of the Province of Cat, Caithness and Sutherland from the Earliest Times to 1615*; Wick, Peter Reid (1914).

BIBLIOGRAPHY

MACKIE, I.D.: *A History of Scotland*; London, Penguin Books (2nd Edition - 1978).

MACLEAN, Fitzroy: *A Concise History of Scotland*; London, Thames and Hodson (reprinted 1983).

MILLER, James: *Portrait of Caithness and Sutherland*; London, Robert Hale (1985).

MITCHELL, Joseph: *Reminiscences of My Life in the Highlands: Notices of the Changes in the country during the present Century – with a narrative of the Works of the Caledonian Canal, and the Highland Roads, Bridges and Harbours*; Chilworth and London, Unwin Brother (1883).

MITCHISON, Rosalind: *Agricultural Sir John: The Life of Sir John Sinclair of Ulbster*; London, Bles (1962).

NICHOLSON, K.: *Scotland: The Later Middle Ages*; Edinburgh (1974).

OMAND, Donald (Ed): *The Caithness Book*; Wick, North of Scotland Newspapers (1989).

PALSSON, Hermann S.: Edwards Paul: *The Orkneyinga Saga*; London, Hogarth Press (1978).

PENNANT, Thomas: *Tour of Scotland in 1769*; London, 1771.

PREBBLE, John: *The Highland Clearances*; London, Penguin Books (1969).

PRYDE, G.S.: *The Burghs of Scotland*; London, 1965.

SAGE, Donald: *Memorabilia Domestica*; Wick (1899).

ST. CLAIR, Roland: *The Saint Clairs of the Isles*; Auckland (New Zealand) (1898).

SINCLAIR, Herbert: *Over the Ord and Caithness Your Home*; North of Scotland Newspapers (1994).

SINCLAIR, Sir John: *Essays on Miscellaneous Subjects*; London, T. Cadwell Jnr & W. Davies in the Strand (1802).

SMITH, John E.: *The Third Statistical Account of Scotland: The County of Caithness*; Edinburgh, Scottish Academic Press (1988).

SMOUT, T.C.: *A History of the Scottish People, 1560-1830*; London, Collins (Fontana Press 7th Impression - 1987).

SMOUT, T.C.: *A Century of the Scottish People, 1830-1950*; London, Collins (Fontana Press - 3rd Impression – 1990).

SUTHERLAND, Iain: *Wick Harbour and the Herring Fishing*; Wick (1984).

SUTHERLAND, Iain: *From Herring to Seine Net Fishing on the East Coast of Caithness*; Wick (1985).

SUTHERLAND, Iain: *The Wick and Lybster Light Railway*; Wick (1987).

SUTHERLAND, Iain: *Dounreay: An Experimental Reactor Establishment*; Wick (1990).

THOMAS, John: TURNOCK, David: *North of Scotland: Vol 5 Of a Regional History of the Railways of Great Britain*; Nairn, David and St John Thomas (1989).

THOMSON, Wm: *History of Orkney*; Edinburgh, The Mercat Press (1987).

TORFAEUS, Thermodus: *The Ancient History of Orkney, Caithness and the North* (translated by the Rev. Alexander Pope); Wick, 1866.

VALLANCE, H.A.: *The History of the Railways of The Scottish Highlands, Vol. 2*; Newton Abbot, David and Charles (1985).

OTHER BOOKS CONSULTED

BAIN, Robert: *The Clans and Tartans of Scotland*; London, Collins (1956).

BENNETT, Geoffrey: *Naval Battles of the First World War*; London, Pan Books (1974).

CANNON, John and Griffiths, Ralph: *The Oxford Illustrated History of the British Monarchy*; London, Guild Publishing (1988).

HUXLEY, Leonard: *Letters of Thomas Henry Huxley*; London, Macmillan (1909).

McDOWALL, R.J.S.: *The Whiskies of Scotland*; London; John Murray (1967).

PACKENHAM, Thomas: *The Boer War*; London, Futura Publications (1982).

PREBBLE, John: *Mutiny*; Penguin Books (1977).

SMITH, Adam: *The Wealth of Nations;* London, Everyman Edition, 2 Vols (1933).
TAYLOR, A.J.P.: *English History, 1914-1945;* Oxford, Vol XS of the Oxford History of England at the Clarendon Press (1965).
TREVELYAN, G.M.: *History of England;* London, Longmans Green & Co (1945).
WATSON, J. Steven: *The Reign of George III, 1760-1815;* Vol II of the Oxford History of England, at the Claredon Press (1960).

PAMPHLETS, PAPERS, ARTICLES, REPORTS ETC.

BREMNER, J.: *Account of the town and harbour of Pulteneytown; Proceedings of the Institution of Civil Engineers (1844).*
BUCHAN, J.: *Bygone Buchan;* Peterhead.
CLAN HERITAGE BOOKS: Alan McKie: *Clan Keith;* 1986 Jedburgh Cascade Publishing Coy; Alan McKie: *Clan Mackay;* 1983 Jedburgh Cascade Publishing Coy; Alan McKie: *Clan Sinclair;* 1836 Jedburgh Cascade Publishing Coy; Alan McKie, *Clan Sutherland;* 1986 Jedburgh Cascade Publishing Coy.
CONNER, David: *Caithnessshire including Wick, Thurso and Pulteneytown;* Unpublished paper on Policing in Caithness; Highland Constabulary Archive, Inverness.
CRAWFORD, Barbara: *The Earls of Caithness and Their Relations with Norway and Scotland, 1158-1470;* unpublished PhD Thesis, University of St. Andrews (1971).
CRAWFORD, Iain: *War or Peace – Viking Colonisation in Northern and Western Isles of Scotland;* Report of 8th Viking Congress, Orkney (1977).
DUNLOP, Jean: *Pulteneytown and Planned Villages in Caithness: in a Cultural Crossroads;* Scottish Society for Northern Studies; Edinburgh, Edina Press (Ed. John Baldwin - 1982).
GOSTWICK, Martin: *The Legend of Hugh Miller;* Cromarty Courthouse (1993).
GUNN, Robert P.: *Svein Asleifson: A Northern Pirate;* Latheronwheel, Caithness, Whittle Publishing (1990).
GUNN, Robert P.: *Tales from Braemore;* Latheronwheel, Caithness, Whittle Publishing (1991).
HALLEWELL, Richard: *Scotland's Sailing Fishermen: The History of the Herring Boom;* Strathummel, Perthshire, Hallewell Publications (1991).
HAMILTON, W.: HM Prison at Peterhead; *Transactions of the Buchan Field Club,* Vol 18, Pt 4.
KEITH, Christine: *The Romance of Barrogill Castle;* Edinburgh, Pillans and Wilson Ltd.
McIVOR, Ian: *Fort George* (Historical Scotland, HMSO (1988).
MACKAYS (Consultants): *Lower Pulteney and Central Wick Development Study;* Wick (1991).
MATHESON, Andrew: *The British Looking Glass;* Laidhay Preservation Trust, Latheronwheel, Whittles Publishing Services (1993).
MORRIS, Jeff: *Wick and Ackergill Lifeboats;* Lifeboat Enthusiasts Society, Coventry (1993).
MOWAT, John: *James Bremner: Wreck Raiser;* Wick, J.S. Duncan (no date).
OMAND, Donald: *The Making of the Caithness Landscape;* from John E. Baldwin, (Ed), Caithness; *A Cultural Crossroads;* Edinburgh, Edina Press (1982).
SIMPSON, A. T. Stevenson: *Historic Wick; Scottish Burgh Survey (1893).*
Memorandum for Sir A. Sinclair, Bart, MP: *Chronicle of the Harbour (of Wick) and its Finances;* Report submitted to Sir Archibald Sinclair, February (1929).
SINCLAIR, Archie: *Strange Tales of the Causeymire;* Wick (1988).
SMOUT, T.C.: *The Landowner and the Planned Village in Scotland (1730-1830);* (in N.T. Philipson and R. Mitchison (Ed), *Scotland in the Age of Improvement).*
STEVENSON, R.L.: *Night Outside the Wick Mail;* unpublished letter to his cousin (1868).
SUTHERLAND, Iain: *The War of the Orange, or the true story of Cogadh Mor Inbhir;* published by the Wick Society (undated).

BIBLIOGRAPHY

SUTHERLAND, Iain: *Vote No-Licence:* The True Story of why Wick closed its licensed premises for 25 years (undated).

SUTHERLAND, (Rev) W.A.: *Wick 1794:* A reprint from the First Statistical Account of Scotland (drawn up from the Communications of the Ministers of the different parishes, by Sir John Sinclair, Bart; Edinburgh: William Creech, 1794); Thurso, the Pentland Press.

THOMSON, (Rev) Charles: *Parish of Wick* (Presbytery of Caithness Synod of Caithness and Sutherland), October, 1840, from The New Statistical Account of Scotland by the Ministers of the Respective Parishes, under the Superintendence of the Society for the Benefit of the Sons and Daughters of the Clergy; Vol XV; Sutherland, Caithness, Orkney, Shetland. Published by William Blackwood, Edinburgh and London (MDCCCXLV).

WATERS, Falconer: *Thurso Then and Now;* Thurso, John Humphries at Caithness Books (reprinted - 1991).

Wick Old Parish Church: QuaterCentenary 1567-1967; (1967) The Bazaar: Local Literary Magazine and Official Programme of the Wick Parish Church Bazaar, 6 and 7 September, 1906.

WILSON, George Washington: *Caithness and Sutherland;* Aberdeen Dalesman Books (1988).

ORIGINAL DOCUMENTS

RECORD BOOKS of the Royal Burgh of Wick, 1660 onwards.
(The second volume – 1715-1714 is missing)

INFORMATION for Sir Benjamin Dunbar of Hempriggs and others Against the Reverend William Sutherland and his Cautioners, dated 21 June, 1808 (Dispute as to the responsibilities of Mr Sutherland in the matter of the new parish church, taken to Court of Session, Edinburgh).

PROOF, led in 1818 and also in 1830, 1831 in Process of Division of Commonty of the Hill of Wick, and Report by James Gregg, Esq., Commissioner of the Court, dated 30 May, 1831.

MINUTES and other Records of the Bignold Hospital, the Henderson Memorial Nursing Home, and the Caithness General Hospital – various dates. See text for details (Chapter 22).

NEWSPAPERS

The *John O'Groat Journal* – dates from February, 1836 to present day.

The *Caithness Courier* – various dates.

The *Northern Ensign* – various dates.

John O'Groat Supplements and Special Publications.

Times Gone By – A compilation of the *John O'Groat Journal* Christmas Numbers, Vol I, October, 1991.

Times Gone By – Vol II, October, 1993.

John O'Groat Journal, Special Supplement to celebrate the 150th Anniversary, 1836-1986.

Vintage Caithness, Special Supplement to celebrate the work of the Wick Society, and three generations of the photography of the Johnston family.

Quatercentenary Review – Special Supplement to celebrate Wick's 400th Anniversary as a Royal Burgh.

Icing on the Cake, Special Supplement to celebrate the 21st anniversary of the founding of Norfrost – 1972-1993.

Various issues of the *Caithness Explorer* – published annually.

Vintage Wick – A Photographic History of the Royal Burgh of Wick and its People, 1589-1989.

Postcards from Caithness (1992).

Most of these Special Supplements were produced and designed by Clive Richards, as was *The Queen Mother and Family – At Home in Caithness*, published by *North of Scotland Newspapers (1990)*.

LITERARY BACKGROUND

ALEXANDER, William: *Johnny Gibb of Gushetneuk in the Parish of Pyketillim – with Glimpses of the Parish Politics about A.D. 1843*; Edinburgh, David Douglas (1881).

BUCHAN, John: *Witchwood*; Edinburgh, Canongate Classics.

ELPHINSTONE, Margaret: *Islanders*; Edinburgh, Polygon (1994).

GELDER, Kenneth: *Robert Louis Stevenson's Scottish Stories and Essays*; Edinburgh, University Press (1989).

GUNN, James: *The Battle of Sommerdale*; London, Nelson (1909).

GUNN, Neil, M.: *The Silver Darlings*; London, Faber and Faber (1941).

GUNN, Neil M.: *The Atom of Delight*; Edinburgh, Polygon (1986).

A variety of official, trade and other publications, annual reports etc, were consulted, especially for Chapter 22. These are all identified in relevant text and footnotes.

INDEX

ABBOT, Charles (Speaker of House of Commons), 219.
Aberdeen: Dyce Airport, 762ff; fishing at, 499; railway reaches, 541; University of, 189, 220, 235, 497-498; Earl of, 376-377.
Ackergill: Tower of, 10, 12, 49 ('Arrow incident) 73, 74, 75; (the 'Beauty of Braemore), 121, 259, 322, 460, 461, 692, 697, 723, 724-726; proposed harbour development, 477-478; lifeboat, 488-491.
Acts of Parliament: Fishing bounty system, 276; Fishery Act (British), 283-284; Fisheries Society 1808, 316; 1844 Act, 452-453, 464, 474, 479; 1857 Act, 505; (Amendment) 1879, 520; Reform Act 1832, 338; Abrogation of Superiority, 326; Scottish Poor Law (1845), 343; Forbes-Mackenzie – liquour trade (1853), 359; Methylated Spirits Act, 359; Education Acts, 577; 1864 Public Schools Act, 577; 1860 Endowed Schools Act, 577; 1870 Elementary Education (England) 396, 577; 1902 Balfour Act, 579-580; 1872 Young Education Act (Scotland) 396; 1876 Sandon's Act, 578-589; 1880 Mundella's Act; 1918 Education Act, 579; Police Acts (Scotland) (1857) 565; (and General Improvement) (1862), 565, 572; Local Government Act (1889) (1892) 576, 582; Fisheries Act (1889), 500; Light Railways Act (1896) 555, 593, 595; Harbour of Refuge and Peterhead Prison Act (1884), 523-524; Private Legislation Procedure Act (1899), 594; List of Acts, application of which was to be modified at union of Wick and Pulteneytown, 594-595; Temperance Act - Scotland (1913), 653; Crofters Holding Act (1889), 698.
ACWORTH, William (Highland Railway Traffic), 553.
Altnabreac (Highland Railway), 547, 548.
ALEXANDER, Dr John (Medical Officer of Health) 663, 707-708, 713.
ANDERSON, Andy (lifeboats), 484 ff.
ANDERSON, John (Herring fishery pioneer), 136, 280.
ANDERSON, John (teacher), 396.
ANDERSONE, James (Merchant), 179-180.
ANNE, Queen (1702-1714), 154.
Anstruther, 450.
Ardvreck (Castle), 97.
ANGUS, Earls of, 43.
ARGYLE, Duke of, 204.
Arminianism, 260.
AUD the Deep-minded, 19.
Aukengill, 12.
BAILLIE, Alexander (Dornoch), 168.
BAIN, Alexander (fisher drowned), 487.
BAIN, Alexander (Electrical Inventor), 707-712, 753-753.
BAIN, (Bayne), Eaneas (minister), 120, 121-122, 176, 185.
BAKEWELL, Robert (cattle breeder), 204.
BANKS, (Sir) Joseph (scientist), 202, 204.
Battles (in sequence of mention in text): Skitten, 9, 16, 21, 22; Standards 40 (and N.); Largs, 24; Wick* 42 (and N₁); Flodden, 46, 57; Bosworth, 46; Halidon Hill, 51; Clyne, 87; Harlaw, 90; Carbisdale*, 97; Dunbar, 97; Dalnaspidal, 98; Altimarlach*, 101-111, 263-264; Sheriffmuir, 127; Trafalgar, 217-219.
BEATON, (Rev.) Donald, 236ff, 255, 367ff, 713.
BERRIEDALE, 12, 52, 71, 281, 721-722; John, Master of, 96; Lord Berriedale, 129.
BEATTY (Admiral) David, 640, 641.
BIGNOLD (Sir) Arthur, 772ff; Mrs Bignold, 714; House/hospital, 717.
Bishops, 65, 68; Adam -. B. of Halkirk, 65-66; Gilbert - B. of Dornoch, 66; Stewart-B. of Caithness, 67, 236; Murder of Bishops, 119, 422-423; Rule of B.'s, 248-254; Restoration of, 252-253; (The) Bishops Wars (1639-1640), 95, 250-257.
Black Saturday (19 October, 1848), 457-466 (see Wick).
Board of Agriculture, 133, 202ff, 205, 208.
Board of Trade, 481, 482, 520.
B of T Medal, 487.
BOTHWELL, Earl of 52, 728.
BURROW, George, 699.
Boy Scouts (See Wick), 603.
Boys' Brigade, 608.
Bounty System, 288.
BRAWL, Olvir, 26-27.
BREADALBANE, Earl of, 124, 127, 146, 156, 190.
Breadalbane Terrace, 298, 673.

803

Scool 'Brothers' 301

BREMNER, David, 306.
BREMNER, James, 14, 135, 176, 281, 301, 317, 419, 426, 456-457, 470, 472-473, 482, 514, 527. Great Britain – Biography, 318-323; lifeboat – The 'Great Britain' affair, 446-447; Bremner's lifeboat, 484-486.
BRIGHT, John, 698.
British Fisheries Board, 450, 460.
British Fisheries Society, 13, 15, 135, 178, 204, 209, 210, 213, 217, 218, 220, 279, 283, 284, 287, 295-304, 299, 307, 314, 316, 318, 327, 334-335, 367, 380, 387, 420, 449ff, 474-475, 484ff, 482, 519-520, 527-528, 562, 573, 576, 584, 585-586, 722, 767.
British Wool Society, 133, 172, 204.
Broadhaven, 13, 213, 281, 313, 457, 460.
BRODIE, David, 207, 281, 302.
BRUCE, Robert (King of Scotland – 1306-1329), 24, 44, 72, 164.
Brora, 541-542.
BROUGHAM, (Lord) Henry, 391, 413 (and N.), 693.
BRUNEL, I. K., 446-448.
BRYCE, David (architect), 130, 723ff.
BOCHOLIE (Castle – Lambaborg) 12, 25, 29-31, 727.
Buchan Field Club, 523.
Buekel (Bueaukler), William, 274-275, 421.
Burghead, 10, 23.
Burghs (constitution and status), 84-86, 144.
BURKE, Edmund, 171.
BURN, George, 298ff.
BUTE, (Marquis of), 373.
Caithness: Early days, 3, 18, 24ff, 38; 18th century onwards, 98, 122, 197-200, 216-223; Protestantism in, 249-250; Caithness Presbytery, 250, 256, 264, 378, 385-386; Fisheries etc, 287ff, 422-423; 453-455; Caithness County Council, 576, 585, 595-596, 708, 743, 767ff.
Caithness Glass, 747-749, 767, 768, 769.
Caithness and Sutherland Enterprise Board (CASE), 745, 767ff, 769-711.
Caithness Volunteers, 603.
CALDER, Alice, 701-707.
CALDER, J. T., 16, 21, 47, 49-50, 52, 54, 55, 56, 73 (and N₁) 75-76, 77, 86, 90, 95-96, 97, 99, 101-111, 127 (N.), 129 (N₁), 146 (N₁), 148, 149, 150, 180, 190, 193, 221, 370, 391-394, 406, 407, 707, 708-709.
CALDER, (Bailie) R, 141.
CALDER (Dean of Guild), William, 156.
CALDWELL (Rev). Robert (daughter Maria M. P. Reid), 406.
Caledonian Canal, 215, 220.
Caledonian Hotel (see Wick Hotels), 306.
CALLAGHAN, (Admiral Sir) George, 635.
CALLUM, William (Hangman), 180-181.
CAMPBELL, John (of Loudon), 128.
CAMPBELL, R.H. (Historian), 283, 284.
CAMERON, George (Author), 715.
Camps (The –), 98, 125.
Canisbay, 98, 118.
CARLYLE, Thomas, 698.
CARNEGIE, Andrew, 699.
Castletown, 12, 742.
Causewaymire ('Causeymire'), 221.
CHALMERS (Rev. Dr.) Thomas, 246, 372-374, 377.
CHARLES, T. (King 1625 - 1647), 68, 80, 86, 95-96, 257.
CHARLES II (King 1660 - 1685), 97, 100, 101, 257, 253.
CHARLES, Edward ('Bonny Prince Charlie'), 127.
Chartism, 414, 417, 424, 435.
Chernobyl, 744.
Cholera, 311, 349-357, 404-405.
Christian Knowledge Society, 250.
Church of England, 253.
Civil Aviation Authority, 765.
Civil War (1642-1646), 96.
Clan Systems and Tenures, 64, 68.
Claymore Creamery, 758.
Clearances (The), 76ff, 78-79; In Caithness, 130, 196, 204, 206, 221-2, 317.
Clyth, 12, 76, 213, 231. 281
Coastguards, 739-740.
COGHILL, W (gaoler), 332-334.
Commissioners for Highland Roads and Bridges, 767.
Communications, 325-326.
Continental System (1802-1815), 217.
CONNER, D. (Police), 563ff.
Convention of Royal Burghs, 89, 118 (and

INDEX

N₁), 127, 146-147, 148, 155, 156, 158, 164, 165, 167, 171, 178, 189, 190, 328.
CORMACK, Alexander, 156.
Corn Laws, 417, 418, 419, 427, 698.
Court of Session (Edinburgh), 158, 162, 192, 329-330, 372.
Covenant (The National), 95, 243, 250-257.
CRAVEN, (Rev.) J. B., 240, 254.
CRAWFORD, James (Evidence to Washington Enquiry), 466-467.
CRAWFORD, Barbara, 21, 34.
CROMARTY, (Earl of), 127-128, 523.
CROMWELL, Oliver, 97, 252, 724.
Crusades (The), 66.
CUMBERLAND, Duke of, 232.
DAVID, I (King of Scotland, 1124-1153), 23, 31, 42, 65, 84.
DAVID, II (King of Scotland – 1329-1371), 51.
DAVIDSON, David (Evidence to Washington Enquiry), 471.
DAVIDSON (Of Tulloch – ride to Wick), 719.
DAVIDSON, Randall (Archbishop of Canterbury), 698.
DE CHEYNE, Reginald, 63, 69, 72, 77, 86, 90, 91, 721.
DEMPSTER, of Dunnichen, 202, 204.
Depression – post war (1920-1921), 650; (1929), 657.
DICK, Robert, 352, 697.
DINGWALL, Royal Burgh of, 118, 165, 232.
Dirlot (Dilred), 77, 229, 230.
Dissent and Succession, 242-248; Antiburghers, 243-245; Patronage Act, 244; Erskine, Ebenezer, 246; Moderates, 246, 371ff; Disruption, 246-248, 369-338; Veto Act, 82, 566, 579.
DONALDSON, Angela (manager of Airport), 765-767.
DONALDSON, J, 135, 141, 142, 175-176.
Dornoch, (Royal Burgh of), 165, 229; Cathedral 66; Presbytery, 232; Highland Railway-branch, 540, 542, 694.
DOUGAL, (Manager Highland Railway), 546.
DOULL, Alexander, 148, 157.
DOULL, James, 157.
DOULL, Thomas, 159.

Dounreay, (UKAEA), 11, 495, 742-746; Vulcan 'facility', 746, 770.
DOW, Patrick, 91.
DUDOCH, (Saint), Church of, 119, 238.
DUNBAR, (of Hempriggs), 101, 130, 134, 146, 150, 341, 387, 520, 562-722; Sir William, 121, 124, 127, 157, 162-163; Robert, 127, 239, 723; Sir Benjamin, (later Lord Duffus), 138, 140, 190-192, 201-202, 213, 256-257, 284, 294, 296, 299, 313, 371, 427, 723; (Rev.) James, 253; Patrick of Northfield, 130, 131, 134; and Bowermadden, 722; Sir George, 73 (N₁), 378, 723; Duff-Dunbars, 725.
DUNBAR, Alex D. (Schoolmaster), 386.
Dunbar Tomb, 254-255.
Dunbeath, 12, 281, 282, 289, 311-312, 461, 721.
DUCHART (Provost), 774-776.
DUNDAS, Sir T. (of Orkney), 166; Henry, Lord Melville, 82, 202, 206.
Dundee, 220.
Duncansby, 20, 25, 29, 57, 96.
DUNLOP, Jean (Munro), 214 (N₁), 281 (N.), 313, 322, 450ff, 480, 484, 509-510, 519-520.
Dunnet Head, 3; Church, 379, 385.
DUNNING, John, 169.
Dunrobin (Castle), 53, 79, 122, 128, 541-542; 694, 721; 'Dunrobin' (Railway engine), 541-542.
Dutch, Herring Fishery, 217, 220, 225, 284-286.
EDEN, (Captain) Henry, 465, 471, 479-480.
Editors (of 'John O'Groat Journal'), Kennedy, Benjamin, 407-411; Anderson, James, 410; Millar, R.J.G., 411, 548, 584; McArdle, Bette, 411.
Edinburgh, 208, 297, 373; –Caithness Society, 389ff.
Education (in Scotland), 577ff; Department (Scottish), 396. 384
ELIZABETH, (Queen Mother), 731ff.
Engineers (see individual names): ABERNETHY, 541; BARRON, James, 524; COODE, Sir John, 521-522; GIBB, 475; HAWKSHAW, 509, 511; LESLIE, 509; MITCHELL, James, 476-477, 514-575, 528-529, 539-540; NICOL, R. Gordon, 515ff; Study of Stevenson's Breakwater, 516-519; Later Proposals,

805

529ff; RENDELL, A.M., 516, 523-526; SCOTT RUSSELL, J., 509; Railway Projects: NETTAN, Giles; McLEAN, Stileman, 543-544; BRASSEY, Wm., 545; SCOTT, J., 547, 551.
Episcopals and Episcopal Church of Scotland, 13, 248-254, 369.
ERIC, Bloodaxe (King of Denmark) 21.
ERLEND, Haraldsson, 31, 32, 34.
EVANS, Sir Frederick (Convict Committee Chairman), 522ff.
EWING, Janet, 128.
Fairs & Markets, 228, 383-384, 704-705.
Farming, 138-139, 141.
Fencibles, 82.
FINLAYSON, John, 710, 712.
'Fifies', 465.
Fisheries (Scottish), 289-292, 293, 465, 495.
Fishery, 289, 299.
FORBES, Bishop, 124-125, 185 (N.), 239-240.
Forse, 461.
FERGUSON, Adam (of Kilkerran), 161.
FORDYCE, Sheriff, 570.
Forsinard, 547-548.
Fort George, 691.
FOX, Charles James, 165, 166, 167 (Notes), 170, 171.
FRAKKOK, 25-27.
Fraserburgh, 422, 450, 464, 495, 499, 502, 503, 525, 587, 596.
FREDERICK, 'The Great', 74.
Free Church of Scotland, 374-375, 566.
FRESKIN of Moravia, 50, 69.
Freswick, 12, 32, 34, 692, 727.
FRESSON, Reg. (Air pioneer), 760ff.
Gairloch, 288.
GANDAR, Dower E.L. (Air pioneer, MP), 742, 762ff.
Geology (of Wick district), 4-9, 352-353.
GEIKIE, Sir Archibald, 697.
General Assembly (Church of Scotland), 68, 95, 205, 244-248, 257, 253, 259, 262, 366, 371ff.
GEORGE II (King of Britain), 326.
GEORGE III (King of Britain), 165, 169, 170.
GEORGE VI (King of Britain), formerly Albert, Duke of York, 640, 694.
GEORGE, Henry (Writer), 698.
GEORGE, D. Lloyd, 648, 653-654, 694.

Georgemas, 383-384, 548.
GEORGESON, D. (Solicitor), 576.
Germany: Herring Imports, 499, 526-7; France-Prussian War (1870), 527; The Germany Menace (1914-1918), 620ff, 650; Second World War (1939-1945), 664-682.
GIFFORD, John (Writer), 724, 726.
GLADSTONE, W. E., 694, 698.
Glasgow, 308, 696.
GLASS, Norman (Writer), 664ff.
Glencoe (Massacre of), 108.
GLENORCHY, Lord, 96, 99-111; as Earl Breadalbane, 108, 126, 132, 326, 726, 709.
GIRNIGOE (and Sinclair) Castle, 48, 53, 54, 55-56, 57, 59, 70, 77, 87, 91, 119, 122, 132, 724.
GORDON, John (Fishery harbour), 499.
GOWER, Viscount (2nd Duke of Sutherland), 72, 326-328, 330, 335.
Grand Fleet, 16.
Godings, Ship, 43.
Golspie, 541-543.
GORDON, John (of Tain), 166.
GRAHAM, (Rev.) Andrew, Vicar of Wick, 67.
Grampian Records, 749-757, 768.
GRANT, (General) Ulysses S., 694-695.
GRANT, Alex & Pat (Norfrost), 751-753.
GRANT, I.F., (Historian), 145, 146-147.
GRAY, Malcolm (Historian), 274, 283, 287ff, 295, 308-309, 311, 313, 344, 499-500.
'Great Britain' (The), 319-320, 446-449.
GREEN, G.A.O. (Civil Clerk), 593, 595, 596.
GRIMSON, Margad, 29, 30.
GUNN, (Rev.) J., 372.
GUNN, The Clan, 63, 74-79; The Battle of Tanach, 80.
GUNN, Neil (Writer), 79, 282, 289-291, 311-312, 256 (and N₁).
GUTHRIE, G.J., 603.
HAKON, IV. (King of Norway), 44.
HAKON, Paulsson (Earl of Orkney), 23, 24.
HAKONSSON, Hakon (Earl of Orkney), 24.
Halberry, 12, 76.
HALDANE, Lord (Minister of War,

INDEX

HENDERSON NURSING HOME 773

1908), 603, 694.
Halkirk, 11, 12, 57, 65, 207, 208, 495, 548, 550, 742.
Hallawell (Rev.) Wm., 280.
HARALD, Maddadarson, 23, 24, 26, 31, 39, 40, 41, 67.
HARALD, Unge (the Young), 40, 41.
Harbour(s) of Refuge, 521ff, 565, 580.
HARCOURT, Sir Wm., 694.
HARMSWORTH, L. M. (M.P.), 648-649.
HARPER, Councillor, 588, 590, 591.
HART, H. Liddell (Historian), 633.
Hebrides, 23, 28, 29.
Helmsdale, 15, 27, 70, 71, 77, 78, 281, 450, 461, 541, 543.
Hempriggs (House and Estate), 12, 136, 722-723.
HENDERSON, James, 307, 352. (306) 214, 300
HENDERSON, (Colonel) J.A., 617.
HENRY VII (King of England 1485-1509) 46 (N).
HENRY VIII (King of England 1509-1547), 46(N).
Heritors, 255-258, 260ff.
Herring Fishery (Scottish), 136, 178, 217ff, 273-286, 287, 288-289, 368, 449-456, 499, 500, 526 (statistics), 527, 596 (statistics).
Herring (*Clupea Harengus*), 11, 273, 314, 308-313, 420-422, 496-498, 501-502.
HEWISON, W.S. (Historian), 635-636.
Highland Airways, 720.
Highland Bus Coy, 743-744.
Highland (51st) Division, 688-691.
Highland Railway, 25, 72, 672.
Highland Regional Council, 738-767ff.
Hill of Wick, 190-193, 371.
HISLOP, Alexander, 372, 374, 376, 390-393.
HORNE, (General Baron), 682-633, 663, 715-716.
HORNE (Rev.), John (Writer), 105, 131-132, 141, 180-181, 183, 185, 262, 263, 332-338, 386, 713-715.
HORNE, Jas (Bailie), 178, 189, 262.
Hospitals (Wick area): Cholera hospital, 307; Bignold hospital, 69, 771, 772-773, 777-778; Town & County hospital, 178-679, 773ff; Henderson Memorial Nursing Home, 717, 735, 773ff; Caithness General, 776-779; Impact of NHS on Wick, 773ff.

HOSSACK, B. H. (Historian), 131 (N.).
HOTELS, (Wick): Caledonian, 306, 349, 719; Commercial, 306; (later Mackay's), 363, 718, 719, 654, 660 (N.), 730; Station, 672, 718; Wellington, 306, 719; 'Old Inn' 'New Inn', 718, 719; Mercury, 720; Queen's, 726.
HUME, Joseph (MP), 698.
HUXLEY, T.H. (Professor), 498-499, 606, 697-698.
Improvement, 195-226.
Invergordon, 542.
Inverness Airfield, 540, 552, 587.
Inverugie, 72.
JACK, (Rev.) Dr., 269.
JAMES II (King of Scotland 1437-1460), 45, 72.
JAMES III (King of Scotland, 1410-1488), 46, 145.
JAMES IV (King of Scotland, 1488-1513), 14, 50.
JAMES V (King of Scotland, 1513-1452), 52, 73, 144.
JAMES VI and I (King of Scotland 1567, King of Britain 1605-1625), 38, 48, 53, 54, 58-59, 86, 87, 146, 148, 244, 249, 250, 257.
JAMES VII and II (King of Britain 1685-1688), 107, 168, 169 (N₁), 244, 253.
JAMES 'The Old Pretender – III' 74, 154.
JAMIESON, Provost of Pulteneytown, 582, 583, 587, 590.
'Jellicoe's Express', 554, 636, 638.
John O'Groat Journal, 397, 401-441, 478-479, 501-502 (N₁), 562 (N₁), 546ff, 582ff, 592, 600.
John O'Groats, 2, 3, 14, 15, 98.
JOHN, Earl of Caithness, 50.
JONES, Brynmor (Commissioner), 595.
Keiss, 10, 11, 16, 54, 60, 119, 121, 124, 135, 213, 281, 282, 318, 386, 396, 457, 676, 692, 726-727.
KEITH(S), Earls Marischal, 49, 72-74, 121, 723, 724.
KEITH, Christina (Writer), 728ff.
KENNEDY, Captain (Antiquaries Writer), 87.
KENNEDY, Robert, 48 (N₁), 422.
KENNEDY, Benjamin (Founding Editor of *John O'Groat Journal*), 358-359, 407-411, 419, 426.
Kildonan, 78, 80, 81, 229, 257.

807

Kilchurn (Castle),
Killimster, 12, 119, 239,
KINLOCK (HM Inspector of Constabulary), 565, 573-574.
KIRK, John (Merchant), 372, 395.
Kirkwall, 131, 165, 116, 587.
KITCHENER, (Lord, Minister of War), 617, 627, 642.
KNOX, John, 230, 248, 250.
KOLBEIN, Hruga ('Cubbie Roo'), 35(N1), 42.
LAING, Robert (of Kirkwall) MP, 166.
LAING, Samuel (scholar), 480.
Laisser-faire (doctrine of), 71.
LAMONT, Donald, 720.
Land Tenure (system in Scotland), 64.
Latheron, 12, 54, 71, 213, 249, 281, 495, 557.
Latheronwheel, 130, 281, 461.
LESLIE, Alexander (Commonwealth General) 95, 97.
Lerwick, 587.
Lewis (island of), 461, 499-500.
Lifeboats (Wick and Ackergill): Bremner's, 470, 474-475, 483-491; RNLI, 485, *Thomas Dougal* (1839), 485-487; *Greathead* (1848), 485; *Princess Marina*, 738-741; *City of Edinburgh*, 739; *Norman Salvesen*, 739-741.
LIFOLF, (Viking Warrior), 41.
LJOT, (Viking Warrior), 21.
LOCH, James – MP, 71, 81(N1), 310, 380.
Lochbay (Skye), 283.
Lochinver, 283.
Lossiemouth, 319.
Louisburgh, 13, 140, 386, 577.
LOWE, Robert (later Lord), 694.
Loyalty, (Declarations of), 168ff.
LYNCH, Michael (Historian), 145-146, 230, 243-247, 287(N.), 371, 373, 374.
Lybster, 12, 281, 456, 457, 461, 555-561, 557(N1), 570.
MACADIE, John (Councillor), 581, 587, 588, 590, 591, 592.
MACAULAY, T.B. (Lord), 198.
MACBETH, 21, 22(N1), 23.
MACECHERN, (Rev and Captain Dugald), 624-633.
MACFARLANE (Geographical Collections), 118.
MACGILLIVRAY, (Rev) Duncan, 232-233.
MACIVER, Finlay (Piper), 106-107.
MACKAY(S), 79-83; Lord Reay, 80, 98; Ronald M., 91-94; Hon. Alexander, 158; Benjamin M. (Schoolmaster), 389ff; William T. (gaoler), 522.
Mackay's Hotel (see Hotels).
MACKENZIE, Dr (Inventor of innoculation), 124.
MACKINTOSH, Charles (of Kirkwall), 166.
MACLEAY, William (Banker, Bailie, Provost), 234, 235, 302, 306, 331.
MACLENNAN, Robert M.P., 685.
McLEOD, (of Assynt), 97.
MACPHEES (The), 699, 700-707.
McPHEE, Walter (Coxswain), 741.
MADDAD (Earl – of Atholl), 26, 27.
MAGNUS, Erlingsson (King of Norway), 40.
MALCOLM III (King of Scotland – 1058-1093), 23.
MALCOLM IV (King of Scotland – 1153-155), 31.
MALISE IV (Earl of Orkney – 1336-1353) 43, 44.
MAR, (Earl of), 90.
Marischal College (Aberdeen), 220, 235.
MARY, Queen of Scots (1542-1557), 53, 54, 68, 249, 266, 728.
MARY II (Stewart – Queen with William III 1689-1494), 251.
MATHESON, A, 204.
May, Isle of, 31.
MEDLEY, Capt. E., 457.
Mey, Castle of, 141, 692, 728-733.
Mey Letters (The), 142, 175.
MIDDLETON (General), 96, 98.
MILLER, Alexander (Fishing pioneer), 136.
MILLER, Alexander (Merchant), 162.
MILLER, Hugh (Geologist), 352-3, 374-5, 697.
MILLER, J. (Merchant), 61(N1), 65.
MILLER, James (Bailie), 158, 162.
MITCHELL (Rev) D., 337, 364, 381, 382.
MITCHELL, John M. (Engineer), 496, 589ff.
MITCHELL, (Chief Constable), 568ff.
MITCHISON, Rosalind (Historian), 126, 134, 149, 155(N1), 157, 158, 160, 161,

808

INDEX

163, 164, 168, 201(N₁), 205, 208-209.
MONCK (General) George, 98, 252.
MUNRO, Donald, 237.
MONTROSE, (Marquis of), 95, 96, 97, 100, 250-257, 721, 722, 724.
MOSS, Jeff (Writer), 483-491.
Mount Hooley (Wick), 240-241.
MOWAT, Sir Oliver (Canadian Premier), 694.
MUIR, (Traveller), 242.
MUNRO, Andrew, 100.
MUNRO, Duncan (of Dingwall), 168.
MUNRO, (Artist), 258-259, 305-307.
MURCHISON, Roderick (Sir – geologist), 697.
New Lanark, 297.
New Towns, 297-298.
NICHOL, Professor, 697.
NICOL, Gordon (See Engineers).
NICOLSON, Provost of Wick, 582, 584-585, 603-604.
Norfrost (Manufacturers), 744, 751-753.
North Head Tower, 715.
NORTH, (Lord - Premier), 171.
Northern Burghs (see Convention of).
Northern Ensign, 319, 411, 602, 602, 607, 649.
Northern Star, 411-413.
Noss Head, 48.
OLAF THE WHITE, 19.
OLAF, Hroaldson, 25.
'Old Pretender' (See James the).
OLIPHANT(S), (The), 57, 63, 86, 91, 92, 121.
OLIPHANT, (Rev. – Minister of Wick), 118ff, 241-242, 255, 260.
OMAND, Donald, 9, 67, 94(N₁).
Ord (The), 15, 52.
Orkney, 14, 19, 21, 41ff, 52, 58-59, 132, 243(N.), 461, 502, 545, 606, 635-636, 642, 665ff; Airfield, 761ff; Orkneymen, 97, 98.
OVERTON, Colonel, 97.
PAUL, Hakonsson (Co-Earl of Orkney), 26.
Pauperism, 180.
PALMERSTON, Lord (Premier), 410.
Papigoe, 7, 12, 13, 451, 459.
Pathetic Fallacy, 90(N₁).
Patronage, 232ff, 369ff.
PEACH, Benjamin (Geologist), 697, 709.

PEEL, Sir Robert (Premier), 417, 429.
PENNANT, Thomas (Writer), 104, 121(N.), 124, 176, 227.
Penny Post, 417.
Peterhead, 72, 220, 309, 450, 460, 464, 475, 499, 502-503, 523ff, 525, 587, 596.
PHIN, (Rev(s) – Minister of Wick, 233, 234, 323, 364, 376, 380, 395, 424-425.
PITT, Wm. (the younger) – Premier, 172, 202.
Place Names – (and land tenure), 64 (and N₁).
Plockton, 282.
Ploughs, 200.
Police Acts (1857), 565; (1862), 573; (1892), 562-563.
PONT, (Rev), Timothy (map-maker), 48(N₁), 87.
PONT, (Rev), R., 236.
Popery, 67, 199, 235ff, 249ff, 268-269, 383.
Poor Law, 266, 466.
PORTLAND, (Duke of), 556-559, 722.
POTTINGER, M., 98(N₁).
PREBBLE, John, 71, 79, 81.
Public Works Loans Commissioners, 482, 505, 575, 579, 521, 524, 528.
Pulteney, Sir William, 13, 202, 210, 211, 218, 219, 220, 223, 296, 297.
Pulteneytown: 13, 15, 214(N₁), 220, 269, 281(N.), 283-284, 294-304; Rise and population, 294-304, 301-304, 390, 313, 316, 562-3 (and N. 562); Religion in, 364, 379-383; Academy, 38, 386, 387, 390, 519, 717; Disturbances in, 429ff, 450ff; Harbour, 473-479, 505, 520, 565, 524ff, 531; Police Commissioners, 558, 565ff; Movement towards Union, 583ff.
RAE, William, (Bailie, Provost), 524, 586, 695, 696.
RAGNHILD, 21.
Railway, The Highland, 445, 538-561, 534-540, 540-541, 541-543; 545ff, 546-552, 554, 555, 636-639, 681-682; Wick and Lybster, 555, 556-559, 635, 636.
Rebellion, the 1715: 127, 227.
The '45', Rebellion (1745-1745), 127, 150, 154, 227.
Reform Act, 402.
Reformation (Scotland), 67, 144, 229-230, 242-243, 384.
REID, Peter (founder of the *Groat*), 307, 358-359, 403-407.

809

REISS, 12, 676.
RENNIE, John (Engineer), 14, 135, 178, 197, 198, 205, 210ff, 214, 220, 295.
'Restoration', The (1660), 118, 153, 252-253.
RHIND, Alexander (engine driver), 542.
RHIND, Josiah (Provost, Fisheries Society Officer), 307, 432-433, 466, 471, 478.
RIDDOCH, John (of Kirkwall), 165.
Roads and Bridges, 198, 212-213, 215, 221-223.
ROBERT II (King of Scotland 1371-1390), 45.
ROBERT III (King of Scotland 1390-1406), 50, 86.
ROBERTS, Earl, 697.
ROBERTSON, Sir D., 742.
Rockwater Company, 744, 757, 754-758, 759.
ROGNVALD, Earl of More, 19.
ROGNVALD, Earl of Orkney, 23, 24, 26, 28, 30-33, 39, 41.
Roman Catholics, 253.
Rohilly, Sir Samuel, 198-199.
ROSEBERY, Earl of, 480.
ROSS, C.R. (Colonel – MP), 168.
ROSS, D. (of Tain), 161, 166, 168.
Royal Airforce, 632, 636.
Royal Commissions (and Parliamentary Committees) on British Fisheries, (1785), 218, 287; British Herring Fisheries (1798), 218, 287; Jurisdiction in Wick (1825-8), 331ff; Inspection of Wick Bay (1858), 498; Exciseable Liquors (1859), 359, 529; Argyll Commission (1876), 396; Dalhousie Commission on Trawling (1885), 500; Select Committee on Harbour Accommodation, (1866), 521; R.C. on Harbour Accommodation, (1883), 521; Select Committee on Harbour Accommodation (1883), 521; Committee on Convict Labour, 522ff; Committee on Harbour Proposals, (1859-1861), 524-525; Elementary Education (England) (1868), Newcastle, 577; Public Schools – England (Clarendon), 577; Endowed Schools – England (Taunton), 577; R.C. on Crofting and Crofters, (1883-1884), 698.
Royal Occasions in Wick: Death of William IV, 1837, 416-417; Accession of Queen Victoria 1837, 424, 603; Marriage of Queen Victoria 1837, 424, 603; Marriage of Queen Victoria, 1839; 425-426; Birth of Prince of Wales, 1841, 426; Attempt at Assassination of Queen Victoria, 426; Death of Duke of Sussex, 427; Jubilees of Queen Victoria, 1887, 1897, 600-601; Visits to Wick of Prince and Princess of Wales 1876, 693; Duke of Edinburgh 1882; 693; Edward Prince of Wales, 693; Albert Duke of York, 693 (see also, Elizabeth, Queen Mother).
Royal Society of Edinburgh, 215.
RUSSEL, 699.
RUSSELL, John (Clerk to B Council), 159, 478.
RUSSELL, Sheriff, 570.
St. Fergus (Parish Church of), 21, 73, 68 (and N.), 140, 240.
St. Joachim (R.C. Church of), 13.
St. Magnus (Cathedral of), 33.
St. Mary (Chapel of – 'Marykirk'), 241.
St. Ninian, 240 (and N₁).
St. Tears (Chapel of), 77, 239-240.
SAGE, (Rev.) Alexander, 229, 230, 232.
SAGE, (Rev.), Donald, 81, 228ff, 256.
SAGE, (Rev.), Eneas, 229, 231-232.
Salmon (Fishery and Processing), 123.
SALSBURY, Colin (Engineer), 515(N₁), 534-537.
SALTON, C. (Secretary to BFS), 301-303, 314.
Salt Duty, 136, 138.
Sarclet, 12, 207-208, 211, 291, 296, 451, 453.
'Scaffies', 292, 465.
Scapa Flow, 16, 634-636, 665ff.
Scottish Council (Development and Industry), 747, 767-768, 769.
Scottish Office, 523, 608, 738, 768.
Scotscalder (station), 548.
Scrabster, 14, 209, 422, 545, 549, 636, 737-738.
Sea-ware (Seaweed), 135 (and N₁).
SEAFIELD, Lord and Lady, 539.
Seaforth Highlanders, 664-165.
Seal-catching, 123, 124.
Secretary (of State) for Scotland, 593.
SELKIRK – Lord S's emigration scheme, 7.

INDEX

SELLAR, Patrick (Sutherland Estates factor), 77, 77-78, 81, 83, 230.
SHACKLETON, Sir Ernest, 198.
SHELBOURNE, Lord, 171.
SHEFFIELD, Lord (improver), 202, 204.
Shetland, 98, 500, 502, 587, 606.
Ships – mentioned in text: *Anne Elizabeth* (1848); *Colin Finlayson*, 464; *Collingwood*, 640; *Huntress* (1859); 487; *Janet* (of Puttganden, 473; *Maria* (1860), 488; *Mary Campbell*, 699; *Pittstruan* (1917), 642; *Pollux* (of Bergen), 640; *Rohilla*, 640; *St Nicholas* (1914), 715; *Sovereign* (ferry); 495; *Vronia Santina*, 486-487.
SIGURD – The Mighty, 20, 22.
SIGURD, 'Mite', 41.
SIMRAD ENGINEERING, (formerly Osprey Engineering) 757.
SINCLAIR, Sir Archibald, 515, 516 (N₃), 534, 561, 762, 763, 774.
SINCLAIR, (Rear Admiral) Sir Edwyn Alexander KBE, 634.
SINCLAIR, Earls of Orkney and Caithness: Early Sinclairs, 10, 38ff, 63; Eighteenth Century, 127; Henry, First Earl, 43, 44; The 'Disputed Succession', 42-43; Succession of Earls of Orkney and Caithness, 43, 44; William, first independent Earl of Caithness, 48; The Feud with Earls of Sutherland, 48, 54ff; William, Earl of Orkney, 46, 91; Earl George II (the 'wicked Earl' – 1529-1582), 52; Earl George III (another 'Wicked Earl' – 1582-1643), 53ff, 61, 68, 69, 132, 144-146; Earl George IV (1643-1676), 68, 86-87, 95, 96, 99, 100, 126, 151; Earl George V, (1676-1688), 101-111; (The Glenorchy interlude V – 1688-1698), 95, 101ff; Earl John (1698-1705), 127; Earl Alexander, 127-129; Earl Alexander, 155; Later and 19th century succession, 544, 575, 728ff.
SINCLAIR, incidents and affairs: Burial of George II's heart, 53; Sinclair 'Aisle', Wick, 61, 98, 119, 254; Believed to be Catholic, 68; The siege of Kirkwall (George III), 58-59; Castles Girnigoe and Sinclair, 107; 14th Earl's Steam-car, 759; Maria, Duchess of Pomar, 730-731.
SINCLAIR, 'Cadets', 57-61.
SINCLAIRS of Mey, 68, 130ff; Sir William of Mey, 68; Sir James of Mey, 121, 129, 131 (N₁); Sir James of Murkle, 101, 108; Col. George, 109-110.
SINCLAIR J, of Barrock, 121.
SINCLAIR C of Bilbster, 121.
SINCLAIR of Freswick, 124, 130.
SINCLAIR, Sir William S. of Dunbeath, 124, 254.
SINCLAIR R. of Brabster Doran, 127.
SINCLAIR of Rattar, 128.
SINCLAIR, of Bray, 128.
SINCLAIR Wm. of Berriedale, 97, 129.
SINCLAIR of Assery, 156, 157.
SINCLAIR, Robert Manson, 159.
SINCLAIR, Sir John (Lt. Col.) – baronet of Dunbeath.
SINCLAIR D of Oldrig, 121.
SINCLAIR, John (Rev.) of Bruan, 371.
SINCLAIR, David S. (Customar), 176, 181.
SINCLAIR, Dr., 306, 773-774.
SINCLAIR (Rev.), John (of Bruan), 371.
SINCLAIR(S) of Ulbster, 72, 146-147, 154, 157; 1st John of Ulbster, 121, 125, 126 (N₁ and ₂), 127; Patrick of Ulbster, 132; John of Brims and Ulbster, 132; Succession, 132-133; George of Ulbster, 125, 127, 158, 164, 201; James of Harpsdale (uncle to Sir John), 133, 150, 157, 159-160, 161, 163, 185-188; The 'heritable' provostship of Wick, 150; Sir John Sinclair of Ulbster (1760), 18, 135, 134, 139, 160, 161; Parliamentary candidate, 164, 165; Member of Parliament for Caithness, 167; Member of Parliament for Lostwithiel, 168; Provost of Wick, 167, 168, 171, 172, 177-178, 190, 200ff, 256, 284-286; (Proposals for herring fishery), 287, 296, 299, 314, 320, 326, 337-338, 414, 420, 694, 695; Sir George (son of Sir John), 326, 341, 376, 377, 386, 417.
SINCLAIR, Thomas, ballivus (bailie) of Wick, 44.
SINCLAIR, Thomas (Historian), 98, 133, 149, 150, 190.
ST CLAIR, Roland, 52, 58, 86 (N₁).
SINCLAIR, Sir Tollemache, 579, 546, 548, 694-695.
Sinclair's Bay, 74, 754, 758.
Skitten, 9, 16, 21, 22, 670-671.
SKULI, (Viking Warrior), 21.
SMILES, Samuel (Writer), 197, 198,

215(N₁), 220, 223.
SMITH, Adam (author of *Wealth of Nations*) 170, 171, 195, 206, 235, 420.
SMITH, Arthur (Coiner), 57-58, 728.
SMITH, Sir William (founder of Boys Brigade), 316, 716, 782.
SMOUT, T.E. (Historian), 308, 325, 327, 359, 653.
South Africa, 602-603, 604-605.
South Head, 14.
South Ronaldsay, 15.
Society for the Diffusion of Useful Knowledge, 391.
Society for the Propagation of Christian Knowledge (SPCK), 386.
Society for the Propagation of the Gospel (SPG), 262.
Statistical Account of Scotland, 1st Account (Wick) (1794), 77, 134, 148, 204, 205, 212, 214, 281(N₁), 282-283, 420; 2nd Account (Wick) (1840), 238, 323-353, 363-369, 398; 3rd Account (Wick) (1983), 494,.
Staxigoe, 7, 12, 13, 135, 141, 143, 213, 280-281 (and N₁), 282, 313, 396, 451, 461.
STEVENSON, Robert Louis, 14, 485, 512, 514, 566, 699-700.
STEVENSON, Thomas (Engineer), 14, 472, 475, 482, 483, 533ff.
STEWART, Col. Robert, 71, 79.
STEWART, Patrick (Earl of Orkney), 59(N₁).
STEWART, Walter (Earl of Athol), 45.
STRATHNAVER, 71, 79.
STRACHAN, ~~Colonel, 97,~~ GENERAL 98
Stirkoke, 12, 101, 131-132, 387, 396, 577, 716, 723-224.
Stonehaven, 461.
Stornoway, 308, 499.
STOW, David (Educationalist), 392.
Stromness, 587.
STURLUSON, Snoors (Writer), 19.
'Superiority', 72, 89(N₁), 125, 126, 146, 153, 154, 326-327.
SUTHERLAND, 10, 18, 215.
SUTHERLAND (Earls and Dukes of): Early Sutherlands, 10, 50, 57, 73, 86; Sutherland Family and Clan, 63, 69-72; The Feud, 15, 48, 52, 54, 86; Suspected of Catholicism, 68, 204; Sutherland of Berriedale, 52; Seton-Gordons, 69; Countess Elizabeth, 70; Staffords – Leveson Gower (Duke of Sutherland), 70-71, 80, 232, 282, 326-327, 356, 380-381; 721-722; The Clearances, 71ff; 2nd Duke (Chairman BFS), 486; 3rd Duke (Railway developer), 538-561; 4th Duke (Railway enthusiast), 555-556.
SUTHERLAND, (Lt.) George Angus, 627-632.
SUTHERLAND, Hector (Clerk of Wick), 593-594.
SUTHERLAND, Iain, 276, 280-281, 284, 292-293, 311, 316, 318, 392-393, 355(N₁), 496-498, 555-561, 566ff, 653ff, 743ff.
SUTHERLAND, James (Bailie), 173.
SUTHERLAND, John (of Wester), 162, 163.
SUTHERLAND, John (Merchant), 176.
SUTHERLAND, John S. (BFS Agent), 459, 466, 469.
SUTHERLAND (Rev.) William, 7(N₁), 134-143, 147-148, 179, 189, 196, 202, 227-228, 233, 234, 236, 255-257, 277, 279, 280, 282, 283, 325-353, 354, 385, 386.
SVEIN, Asleifarson, 23ff, 33.
SVEIN, Hroaldsson, 28, 30, 31.
SVERRE, (King of Norway), 40, 42.
SWANSON, John (Police Superintendent), 574-575.
SWANSON, John (Reported Chartist), 718-719.
Tain, 165, 168.
TAIT, Councillor, 591.
TAYLOR, A.J.P. (Historian), 643, 654.
TAYLOR, Barry (Engine-driver), 681-682.
TAYLOR, Peter (Harbour-master), 469-471.
TELFORD, Thomas, 14, 15, 135, 178, 185(N₁), 197ff, 210ff, 284, 285, 294-304, 529, 545, 759.
Temperance Hall, 240, 360, 361, 434.
Temperance Movement, 357-363, 369, 652-661.
Thirty-years War (1618-1648), 95.
THOMAS, Turnock, 552-553.
THOMSON (Rev.) Charles, 238-239, 309, 322, 323-353, 354ff, 364-365, 384ff, 398, 570, 644, 712-713.
THOMSON, William, 43.
THOMPSON, Sir Wm (Lord Kelvin), 711.
Three-Mile Island, 744.
THORSTEIN, The Red, 19.

INDEX

Thrumster, 11, 16, 288(N₁), 242, 396, 671.
Thurso, 3, 10, 11, 42, 66, 86, 96, 100, 133, 142, 145, 161, 134, 206, 208-209, 329-330, 390, 495, 548-549, 550, 636, 674-675, 692, 694, 742, 743, 763-764, 773ff, 692, 747ff.
Thuster (Viscount), 121.
Tobermory, 220, 283.
Tongue, 461.
TORFAEUS, T. (Danish historian), 20(N₁), 21.
Torridon, 283.
Trades in Wick (see Wick),
TRAILL, James (of Rattar), 320, 329, 406, 522, 708.
Trentham, 70.
TREVELYAN, G.M., (Historian), 253-254.
TUDOR (Capt.) John (Harbour master), 486, 487, 488, 570, 572, 699.
Ulbster, 12, 133, 396.
Ullapool, 213, 283.
Union (of England and Scotland – 1707), 69, 165, 244, 287(N₁), 369-370.
VALLANCE, H.A., 539ff.
VANSITTART (Baron Bexley), 219.
VICTORIA (Queen), 424-425, 425-426, 427, 599-603, 600-601, 603-604.
Vikings, 3, 4, 7, 11, 18ff, 19, 21.
WARDLAW, Andrew, 86.
War in Wick: Boer War (1899-1902), 604-605; First World War (1914-1918), 609-649; Wick in War, 610-623; Call-up and recruitment of volunteers, 611-612, 616-620; Conscription/Exemptions, 620, 620-621; Reports from the Front, 621-625; Casualties, 602, 629, 642-643; Naval activity in North Sea, 633-636, 640; Battle of Jutland, 641; U-boat activities, 641-642; Peace, 645-648; War Memorial(s), 663-664; Second World War (1939-1945), 665-682; Attacks on the North, 665-666; Attacks on Wick, 666-670; Coastal and harbour defences, 676-679; Casualties, 649; RAF and Army in Wick, 670-681; Wick Home Guard, 679-680.
Other Wars – Seven Years' War (1756-1763), 82, 170; War of American Independence (1773-1783), 169-170; and Napoleonic Wars (1792-1815), 82, 143, 196, 283, 418; Turkish-Egyptian War (Battle of St. Jean D'Acre) (1839-1840), 409-410; Crimean War (1853-1856), 600; Afghanistan (1879-1880), 600; Franco-Prussian War (1870-1871), 600; American Civil War (1861-1865), 600.
WASHINGTON (President) George, 695.
WASHINGTON (Capt. later Admiral) John, 457ff, 465; Enquiry into 'Black Saturday', 468-474, 475-478, 483, 505, 514.
Watten, 11, 118, 496, 708.
Wave Energy Amplification, 534-537.
West Indies, 217, 248, 417.
Whaligoe, 213-214, 281.
WHEATSTONE (Sir) Charles, 710-712.
Whisky, 97, 354-357, 463-464, 653, 758-759.
WICK: General history, location, 2-57; Auldwick (Castle), 35, 48, 50, 69, 89-95; Wick Airfield Airport, 670-674, 761ff, 765-767; Air Lines, 761-766; Post-war development, 765-7; Wick and the Bomb, 682-687; Bridges in Wick, 240, 521, 525, 531-532, 664; Hon. Burgesses of Wick: W. Wilberforce, 693; Lord Brougham, 693; Duke of Edinburgh (1882), 693; General Grant, 695-696; Queen Elizabeth (Queen Mother), 737-738; Wick Chamber of Commerce, 55; Wick Charter (The), 155-168, 179; Wick Cinemas, 720-721; Wick Cleansing and road improvement, 183-188, 338-339, 661-662; Education in Wick, 384-397; School Boards, 577-588; Effects of Education, 662-663; Acts of 1918, 780-781; Public Library, 663, 717; (Herring) Fishery, 277-284; 287-293; 309, 343-344; 420-422; 449-453; 463, 500 (N₁), 501-504, 509, 535; Harbour, 7, 136, 175-178, 209, 210ff, 283, 284, 292-293, 295ff, 313-318, 319, 445-446, 452ff, 456ff; (Black Saturday), 476-477, 504-537, 570ff, 587; (Harbour Trust), 520, 522, 524ff; (1915), 533ff, 585ff, 592, 608-609, 639-640, 644-645, 736-738; Health and Welfare, 771-779; Houses in Wick, 692, 722-732; Industrial Estate, 767-769, 781, 789; Law and Order, 179-183, 329-330, 330-337; 341-343, 409, 417-419, 427-436; (the Wick Riots – 1847); 563-577, 566-573 'War of the Orange'; Population, 323-326, 494-495; 562-563 (N₁ p562), 597, 657, 735; Post Office, 719-720; Post-war conditions, 650-656; Prohibition in, 560-561; 652-661; Project Wick, 789-793;

813

Quatercentenary, 663ff; Railway Wick, 583-561, 672-673; Opening of, 549-552; Wick to Lybster, 555-561 (see also 'Railway').

Religion in, 118, 254ff; Parish and Parish Church, 120, 261ff; Kirk Session, 241-242; Kirk Records, 261ff, 363-364; Jurisdiction, 264-270; Churchyard, 263-263; The 'Old Kirk', 255-257; The 'New Kirk', 258ff; Other Churches and Congregations, 364-369; Catholic, 307, 366; Baptist, 259, 365; Salvation Army, 259; Independents, 365; Free Church, 306, 377-378, 786; Congregational, 365-366; Methodist, 366; Morisonianism, 367-368; Evangelicals, 367-369; The Disruption in Wick (1843) 375-383; Wick Today, 781, 786-787 (see also Pulteneytown).

Ministers of Wick: MERCHISTON, 68, 233, 234, 249-254; PHILP, 249; PRUNTOCH, 249; INNES, 250, 260; ANNAND, 250; FORBES, 257; GEDDES W., 251-253; KEITH, 259-260, 385; OLIPHANT, 260-261; FERME, 260; DUNBAR OF OLRIG, 260; SUTHERLAND (see Sutherland); SCOBIE, 260; THOMSON, 364ff.

Royal Burgh, 84-115; Charter, 111-113; Wick in the 18th century, 118-143, 119-121; Sutherland's Study of (Statistical Survey, 1794), 134-143; Industries and Trade, 94, 95, 139-140, 141ff, 152, 153, 176, 334-345, 767ff; Sett (government of W.), 144-174, 338-339, 416; Parliamentary representation, 164ff, 328-329; Union with Pulteneytown (1902), 562-598; Wick Burgh Arms, 794; 'The War of Independence' (from Superiority), 148, 155-168; Sport and Recreation, 781-786; Public Parks, playing fields etc., 783-784; Pipe bands, 782-783; Sports Council, 785-786; Town Hall, 336-337, 418, 436ff; (and other public buildings), 565, 568ff, 573, 708, 717; Water and Drainage, 580ff.

WILBERFORCE, William, 693.
WILLIAM I (King of Scotland, 1165-1214), 40, 41, 42.
WILLIAMSON, James (BFS Agent), 300.
WILKES, John, 162.
Windscale (Sellafield), 744, 745.
WOLSELEY, Lord, 697.
Women – notable W. of Wick, 710-717.

YOUNG, Archibald, 555.
YOUNG, D., 71, 77-78.
ZOLLVEREIN, 310 (and N₁).

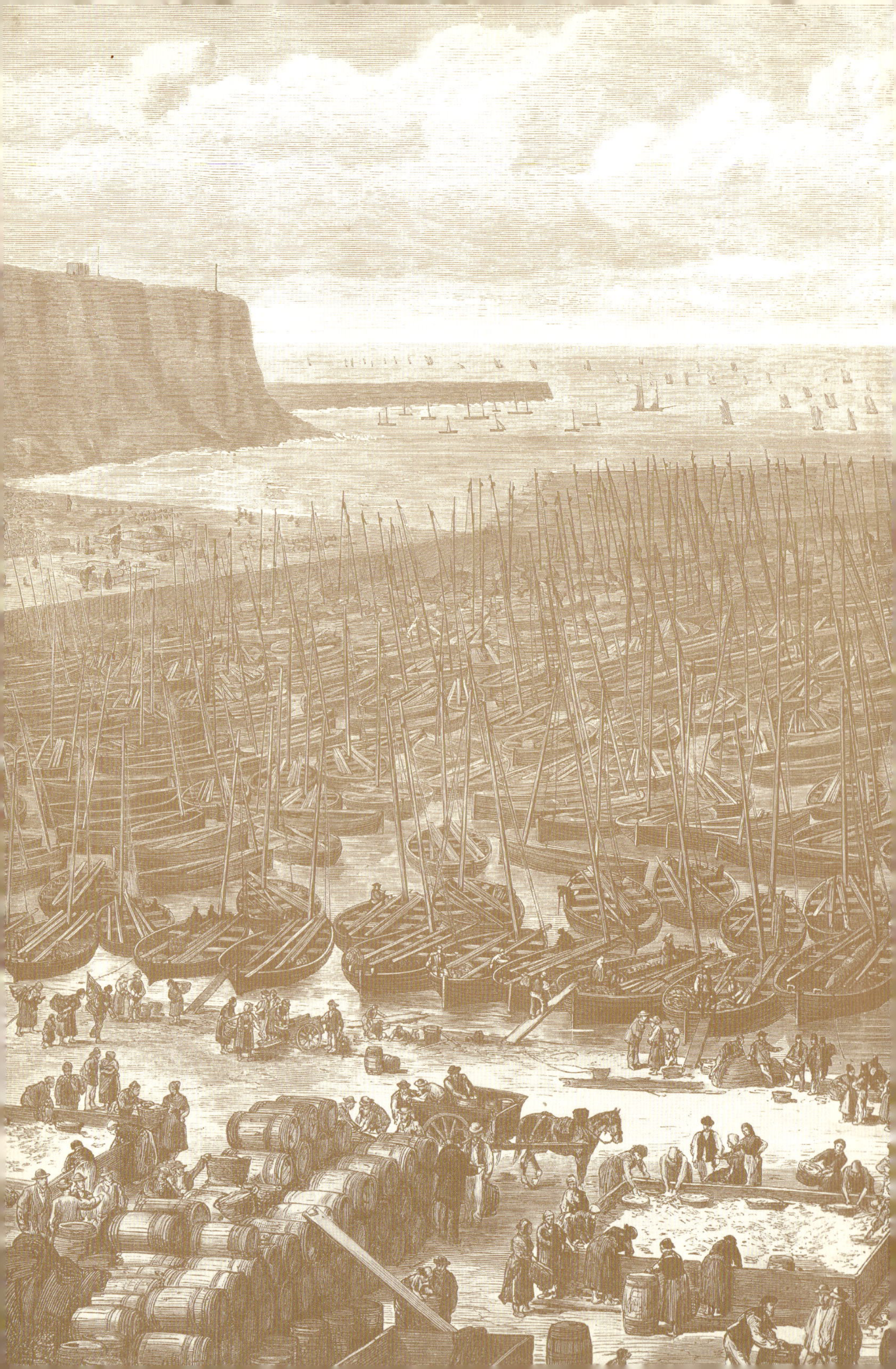